SPECIAL EDITION

USING
Lotus Notes
and Domino 6

Jeff Gunther

Randall Tamura

800 East 96th Street

Indianapolis, Indiana 46240

Contents at a Glance

SPECIAL EDITION USING LOTUS NOTES AND DOMINO 6

International Standard Book Number: 0-7897-2848-6

Library of Congress Catalog Card Number: 2002117341

Printed in the United States of America

First Printing: May 2003

06 05 04   4 3 2

Trademarks

All terms mentioned in this book that are known to be trademarks or service marks have been appropriately capitalized. Que Publishing cannot attest to the accuracy of this information. Use of a term in this book should not be regarded as affecting the validity of any trademark or service mark.

Warning and Disclaimer

Every effort has been made to make this book as complete and as accurate as possible, but no warranty or fitness is implied. The information provided is on an "as is" basis. The authors and the publisher shall have neither liability nor responsibility to any person or entity with respect to any loss or damages arising from the information contained in this book.

Bulk Sales

Que offers excellent discounts on this book when ordered in quantity for bulk purchases or special sales. For more information, please contact:

U.S. Corporate and Government Sales
1-800-382-3419
corpsales@pearsontechgroup.com

For sales outside of the U.S., please contact:

International Sales
international@pearsoned.com

Associate Publisher
Michael Stephens

Acquisitions Editor
Loretta Yates

Development Editor
Sean Dixon

Managing Editor
Charlotte Clapp

Project Editor
Matthew Purcell

Copy Editor
Krista Hansing

Indexer
Larry Sweazy

Proofreader
Jessica McCarty

Technical Editor
Philip Bocko

Team Coordinator
Cindy Teeters

Interior Designer
Anne Jones

Cover Designer
Anne Jones

Page Layout
Michelle Mitchell

Graphics
Tammy Graham
Laura Robbins

TABLE OF CONTENTS

III Introducing Domino Designer 6

ABOUT THE AUTHOR

Jeff Gunther is the General Manager and founder of Intalgent Technologies, an emerging provider of software products and solutions utilizing the Lotus Notes/Domino and Java 2 Enterprise Edition platforms. Jeff Gunther has been a part of the Internet industry since its early, "pre-Mosaic" days. Prior to starting Intalgent, Gunther was the Director of Internet/Groupware Development at Southern Illinois Healthcare. He managed software development teams responsible for user applications and mission-critical groupware infrastructure and applications. Additionally, he has professional experience in all aspects of the software lifecycle including specific software development expertise with Lotus Notes/Domino, Java/J2EE, DHTML, XML/XSLT, database design, and handheld devices.

Randall Tamura is a Principal Certified Lotus Professional and this is his sixth book covering Lotus Notes and Domino. He has lectured in Europe and throughout the United States on Lotus Notes and Domino. He is currently vice president of software for United Online, the leading value-priced Internet Service Provider in the United States. He previously held positions as founder and president of Graphware Corporation and general manager for engineering systems software development for IBM Corporation.

ABOUT THE CONTRIBUTING AUTHOR

Curt Westra develops and manages groupware and Web-based applications for Southern Illinois Healthcare, primarily within the Lotus Notes/Domino architecture. He also has experience in developing applications using Visual Basic, VBScript, DHTML, XML/XSLT, and most recently, Open Source tools such as MySQL and PHP. Westra spends most of his time creating workflow-oriented applications for implementation in Web and Notes environments, designing and managing intranet and Internet sites, and scheming to find a way to get high-speed Internet access in his home. Prior to discovering Internet/groupware development, Westra was a Research Scientist with Battelle. While working with Battelle clients to improve organizational systems and work processes, he coauthored handbooks, practical job guidance manuals, newsletters, user guides, and various reports.

DEDICATION

To my wife, Melissa, and our daughter, Emeline, who continue to remind me how sweet life is.

ACKNOWLEDGMENTS

As I learned during this project, the development of a book is never a product of one single person, but rather the collective efforts of many. So many people have contributed to this project, some whom I've never met. Nevertheless, your work and efforts are greatly appreciated.

I'd like to thank the previous authors, especially Randall Tamura, for a great foundation of knowledge that provided the basis for this book. In addition, I'd like to thank the very talented editors at Que. Loretta Yates, the acquisition editor, has always been very supportive and patient with me throughout the writing process. Sean Dixon, the development editor, always provided constructive feedback and detailed suggestions. I appreciate Phil Bocko, the technical editor, whose keen insight and valuable feedback greatly improved the book's accuracy.

I need to say a special thanks to Curt Westra for his contributions to the book. Curt is a good friend with a real talent for writing. Thank you to Allan Liska and Neil Salkind at Studio B for their recommendations that I should explore this project. Special thanks to my family for their continued love and support in whatever I do. I would be remiss if didn't thank Frank Sears at Southern Illinois Healthcare who gave me, a kid at the time, a wonderful environment to grow my software development skills.

Finally, I'd like to thank my wonderful wife, Melissa. It was only through her patience, unconditional love, and on-going support that I was able to tackle this project. I'm indebted to her for the late nights of editing and believing in me from the beginning. Melissa deserves as much credit as I for the existence of this book.

WE WANT TO HEAR FROM YOU!

As the reader of this book, *you* are our most important critic and commentator. We value your opinion and want to know what we're doing right, what we could do better, what areas you'd like to see us publish in, and any other words of wisdom you're willing to pass our way.

As an associate publisher for Sams, I welcome your comments. You can email or write me directly to let me know what you did or didn't like about this book—as well as what we can do to make our books better.

Please note that I cannot help you with technical problems related to the *topic* of this book. We do have a User Services group, however, where I will forward specific technical questions related to the book.

When you write, please be sure to include this book's title and author as well as your name, email address, and phone number. I will carefully review your comments and share them with the author and editors who worked on the book.

Email: feedback@quepublishing.com

Mail: Michael Stephens
            Sams Publishing
            800 East 96th Street
            Indianapolis, IN 46240 USA

For more information about this book or another Que title, visit our Web site at www.quepublishing.com. Type the ISBN (excluding hyphens) or the title of a book in the Search field to find the page you're looking for.

INTRODUCTION

ABOUT THIS BOOK

Lotus Notes and Domino is the most successful software product in the history of personal computing. Not unlike previous releases, Release 6 continues Lotus's proud tradition of continually evolving and improving this powerful and mature platform for group collaboration.

Whether you are simply using Lotus Notes and Domino for messaging and calendaring or are fully integrating it within your enterprise, you'll find a platform that can scale to address your needs while providing applications and capabilities that far surpass other collaboration systems.

WHO SHOULD READ THIS BOOK

This book is designed to provide you a comprehensive coverage of Lotus Notes and Domino. It's intended to give you detailed information about how to utilize the Lotus Notes and Domino platform to the fullest extent.

During the journey of exploring this amazing environment, you'll explore Release 6 from following three distinct perspectives:

- *Notes End-User*—Whether you're a new user to Notes or an experienced user who is upgrading from a previous release, this book provides detailed information about the new features of Release 6. You'll learn about the rich user interface that Notes and iNotes Web Access provides for electronic mail, contact management, calendaring/scheduling, and group collaboration.
- *Domino Application Developer*—From the developer perspective, this book explores the new and powerful features within Release 6 that make it fun to develop traditional Notes and Web-centric applications, while at the same time covering the basic fundamentals of building applications.
- *Domino Administrator*—From the administrator perspective, this book covers the basic questions and issues that might arise during installation, configuration, and administration of your Domino environment. In addition to the fundamental topics of Domino administration, this book covers more advanced topics about troubleshooting, security, and the upgrade process from previous releases.

Regardless of whether you're currently using Lotus Notes and Domino with your own computing environment, or determining whether the platform is the best fit for your organization, this book is for you. This book provides a comprehensive guide to an amazing platform that continues to evolve and improve group collaboration.

HOW THIS BOOK IS ORGANIZED

This book is divided and organized into nine parts with each part consisting of several chapters. Part I, "Presenting Notes and Domino Release 6," provides general information about Notes and Domino 6. It's designed to help you understand the various parts of the product and why you should consider it for your organization. Part II, "Using the Lotus Notes 6 Client," describes how to get started with Notes and how to use some of its more important features. Part III, "Introducing Domino Designer 6" and Part IV, "Using LotusScript, Java, and JavaScript," provide you with detailed information about creating applications using the Domino Designer development environment. Part V, "Developing Web Sites with Domino," is devoted to topics relating to the development of Web sites using Domino Designer's full-featured Web-centric development tools. Part VI, "Installing and Configuring the Domino Servers," provides you with some core guidance on installing the Domino server, including a chapter regarding the installation process on Linux. Part VII, "Administering the Domino Servers," covers the ongoing maintenance and administration of your Domino infrastructure. It covers topics such as adding and deleting users, handling electronic mail, and replication. Part VIII, "Advanced Domino Administration," covers specialty topics, including performance and capacity planning.

PART I—PRESENTING NOTES AND DOMINO RELEASE 6

Part I covers some basic concepts and fundamental information about Notes. Chapter 1, "Introducing Lotus Notes and Domino," describes Notes and Domino and gives you an overview of the platform's capabilities.

PART II—USING THE LOTUS NOTES 6 CLIENT

Part II provides you with information about using the Notes client. Whether you are simply a Notes user, developing custom applications for Notes, or administering a Domino infrastructure, you should read this section. Chapter 2, "Installing and Customizing the Notes Client," starts at the beginning, showing you how to install and customize the Notes client. Chapter 3, "Understanding the Notes User Interface," examines the rich user interface and the standard databases supplied by Lotus. Chapter 4, "Getting Started with Electronic Mail," covers the use of electronic mail and general applications. Electronic mail is now a critical part of business, and with Release 6, Lotus has enhanced the email interface so that it is even more user friendly and intuitive. Chapter 5, "Working with Text and Documents," shows you the key features of documents in Notes that are used within the context of all databases. Chapter 6, "Getting Started with Contact Management," illustrates how to manage your personal contacts. Chapter 7, "Getting Organized with the Calendaring and Scheduling Features," explains how to improve your productivity by creating and managing appointments and meetings. Chapter 8, "Using Mobile Features from Home or on the Road," covers the topics you need in order to set up replication and usage for your mobile or remote Notes environment. Chapter 9, "Using the Notes Client on the

Internet," highlights Web-centric features and capabilities that the Notes client provides. Chapter 10, "Using iNotes Web Access," covers how to use the highly interactive Web-based user interface for managing electronic mail and scheduling.

Part III—Introducing Domino Designer 6

Parts III, IV, and V are devoted to application development issues. Part III begins with Chapter 11, "Creating and Accessing Domino Databases," which is a description of Domino databases, an introduction to the Lotus templates, and the various methods of creating and using Domino databases. Chapter 12, "Exploring the Integrated Development Environment (IDE)," shows you how to manipulate the powerful development environment for creating custom applications. Chapter 13, "Designing Pages, Forms, and Subforms," and Chapter 14, "Developing Views and Folders," cover both the fundamental design elements and some of the new capabilities of these elements as well. Chapter 15, "Using Framesets, Outlines, and Navigators" and Chapter 16, "Using Shared Resources," complete the series of design element chapters, which show you how to integrate the design elements in both Web and Notes client environments. Chapter 17, "Access Control Lists (ACLs) and Database Security," gives you information on securing your databases. Chapter 18, "Working with Formulas, Functions, and Commands," completes Part III and covers important functions you need to know to develop Domino databases.

Part IV—Using LotusScript, Java, and JavaScript

In Part IV, you'll explore the programmatic capabilities of Notes and Domino. Chapter 19, "Using the IDE with LotusScript, Java, and JavaScript," begins Part IV by describing the development environment within the Domino Designer. Chapter 20, "Object-Oriented Programming and the Domino Object Model," provides you with the knowledge required to effectively use either LotusScript or Java. Chapter 21, "LotusScript Variables and Objects," is a tour of LotusScript, the scripting language for Notes and Domino. Chapter 21 covers both the fundamental language elements and the data types used within the language. Chapter 22, "LotusScript Subroutines, Functions, and Event Handlers," describes how to modularize your program and provides information on the built-in functions of LotusScript. In Chapter 23, "Creating and Using Java Applets and Agents," you learn about both the Java language and how to create applets and agents for Domino. Chapter 24, "The Session and Front-End Classes," Chapter 25, "Database, View, and Document Classes in LotusScript and Java," and Chapter 26, "Using Fields and Items in LotusScript and Java," describe the Domino Object Model classes. These chapters cover the model, using both LotusScript and Java examples to ease your learning experience. If you are familiar with one language, it should make it much easier to learn the other.

Part V—Developing Web Sites with Domino

Part V provides you with information about creating Web sites with Domino. Chapter 27, "Building a Web Site with Domino," describes some approaches you can use to building a Web site with Domino. Chapter 28, "Using Domino Designer's Web-Development

Features," illustrates some of Domino's new Web development capabilities. Chapter 29, "Domino and Enterprise Integration" provides a brief overview of the various products and tools for integrating Domino with other data sources, including coverage of the new database connection design element.

PART VI—INSTALLING AND CONFIGURING THE DOMINO SERVERS

Part VI covers the initial installation and configuration of your Domino server. Chapter 30, "The Domino Family of Servers," begins Part VI and discusses the different servers and their capabilities. Chapter 31, "Initial Planning and Installation," provides some background on which decisions you should consider before you actually install the software. You'll learn about certification, domains, and the initial setup of a server. Chapter 32, "Installation and Configuration of Domino on Linux," covers the steps to install and configure Domino under Linux. Chapter 33, "Upgrading from Domino 5 to 6," is an important chapter for anyone considering upgrading from a previous release of Domino. You'll find the information you need to make the upgrade here. Chapter 34, "Initial Configuration of Servers with the Domino Directories," discusses the Domino Directory. Key configuration parameters are described. Providing security for your Domino system is the topic of Chapter 35, "Domino Security Overview."

PART VII—ADMINISTERING THE DOMINO SERVERS

Whereas Part VI covers the initial installation and configuration of Domino, Part VII focuses more on the ongoing administration of your Domino system after you have installed, configured, and deployed it. Chapter 36, "Administering Users, Groups, and Certification," covers the main points you need to know about administering users and groups in Domino. You'll learn about adding and deleting users, creating groups, and more. Electronic mail is one of the most important applications of Domino today. Chapter 37, "Administering Electronic Mail," provides the keys to a successful implementation in your business. Chapter 38, "Replication and Its Administration," discusses replication, one of the core features of Domino. You'll learn when a database is a replica of another database, how to schedule replication, and some points regarding replication of mail databases. Chapter 39, "Administering Files and Databases," shows you some of the features that you can use to manage the databases in your system. Chapter 40, "Managing Your Domino Server Configuration," describes some advanced topics regarding the management of the Domino server document in the Domino Directory. Chapter 41, "Troubleshooting and Monitoring Domino," rounds out Part VII with important tips and hints to get you out of trouble and keep your system running smoothly.

PART VIII—ADVANCED DOMINO ADMINISTRATION

Part VIII discusses some advanced administration topics. Chapter 42, "Performance, Scalability, and Capacity Planning for Domino Servers," describes key points to consider when deciding what kind of server(s) you require for your network. Chapter 43, "Using the Enterprise Domino Server with a Large Domino Network," examines some of the unique features of this version of the Domino server and provides hints and tips for managing a large Domino network.

PART IX—APPENDIXES

The last part of the book, Part IX, provides some reference information that is useful during the development of Domino databases. Appendix A, "Notes/Domino Class Reference," provides a quick, easy-to-use reference for the Domino Object Model classes. The classes are organized by front-end and back-end, and are sorted in alphabetical order. Appendix B, "@Function and @Command Listings," contains a listing of the @Functions and @Commands available in Release 6. Each function or command that has changed or is new with Release 6 has been indicated for easy reference.

CONVENTIONS USED IN THIS BOOK

This book uses the following various stylistic and typographic conventions:

- Menu names are separated from menu options by a comma. For example, File, Open means "Select the File menu and choose the Open option."
- When you see a note in this book, it indicates information that might be helpful for you to avoid pitfalls or problems.
- Tips suggest an easier or alternative method of executing a procedure.
- Cautions warn you of potentially hazardous actions.

Presenting Notes and Domino Release 6

If you're new to Notes and Domino, you might be interested in the following brief descriptions of what the components of the platform are and what they do.

COMMON TERMS

Before we continue our discussion, it's helpful to define a common set of terms that are used by both the family of Notes clients and Domino server.

- **Database**—A database contains all documents and design elements within a single file. Typically, database file names end with an extension of .NSF.
- **Document**—Documents, the core of the Notes and Domino platform, are the storage containers that allow users to store text, images, file attachments, and other media-rich content in a Notes database.
- **Form**—Forms provide a template and a structure for users to create and edit documents within a Notes database. Different than a document, forms are a design element created by developers to allow users to manipulate documents.
- **Views**—Views display individual documents as separate rows within a gridlike structure. Each column of the grid can contain text, images, or formulas that perform data calculations.

FAMILY OF CLIENTS

Lotus provides three different and distinctive clients with Release 6. They include the following:

- **Notes Client**—The Notes client gives end users a collaborative environment for messaging, group calendaring and scheduling, and custom applications.
- **Domino Designer Client**—The Domino Designer client is a sophisticated tool that allows application developers to create applications that are hosted within a Domino server.
- **Domino Administrator Client**—The Domino Administrator client, including the new Web Administrator, allows system administrators to configure, monitor, and maintain the Domino infrastructure. Any component of Domino, including users, servers, and domains, can be administered from this tool.

NOTES CLIENT

The Notes client is probably the first component you'll use, so we'll start the discussion there. In Figure 1.1, you'll see an example of the Notes welcome page. A welcome page is also sometimes called a headline page. This feature of Notes 6 greets you when you first start the Notes client.

Figure 1.1
The Notes welcome page provides basic options.

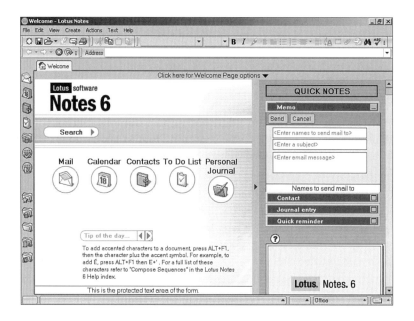

The welcome page is where you start your session, and it can be considered your base of operations. This page can be completely customized to include news, Web content, and other Lotus Notes databases. See Figure 1.2 for an example of the welcome page configured with email, your daily calendar, and the news of the day from Google.

Figure 1.2
A customized welcome page that provides email, a calendar, and news.

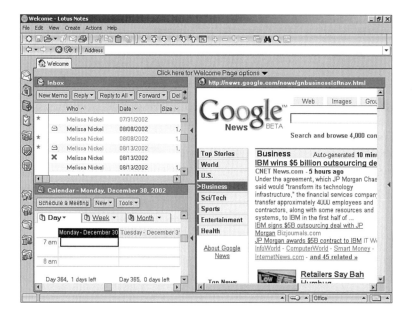

You can see by contrasting Figures 1.1 and 1.2 that the welcome page is very flexible. System administrators can customize the welcome page and roll out an organization-wide welcome page to provide context-sensitive information or important notifications.

DOMINO DESIGNER CLIENT

The Domino Designer client, shown in Figure 1.3, is the second type of Notes client. It has a different user interface and a different purpose from the regular Notes client. With Domino Designer, you can create your own Domino applications that can be used with Notes clients, Web browsers, or handheld devices.

Figure 1.3
Domino Designer contains a rich set of tools for application design and development.

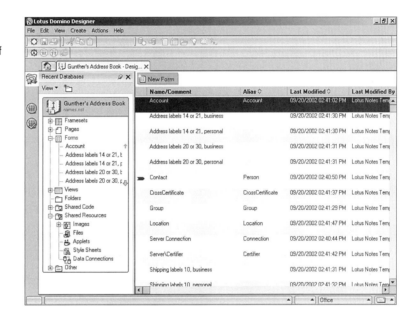

If you have designed applications with a previous release of Notes, you will recognize forms, views, folders, navigators, and subforms as a few of the familiar design elements. These elements were central to the design of Lotus Notes applications in earlier releases. All the design elements from these previous releases are still available with Release 6 of Domino, but there are several new design elements as well. The integration of database connectors, Cascading Style Sheets, and JavaScript libraries provide you with a rich set of features for Web development.

DOMINO ADMINISTRATOR CLIENT

In earlier releases, Domino administration was mainly achieved by editing documents in the Public Address Book. With the introduction of Release 5, Lotus enhanced the overall administration experience with an easy-to-use interface. Version 6 continues to polish the administration client with new features to administer your Domino infrastructure.

NOTE

Lotus renamed the Public Names and Address Book to the Domino Public Directory in Release 5.

Several generic kinds of tasks are involved with system administration, such as the following:

- Initial installation and configuration of the Domino software.
- Ongoing management of server hardware. Adding and changing communication connections, memory, disks, and connectivity parameters.
- Ongoing management of users. Adding, deleting, and changing user IDs.
- Ongoing management of databases. Making sure that access control lists (ACLs) are correct and that database security is maintained.
- Real-time monitoring of server status. Making sure that the various Domino services, such as Web serving, message routing, and database replication, are up and running.

Of course, if you are a system administrator, you know that there are many more parts of your job. For new Domino administrators, the learning curve to tame the administration client is relatively low. The user interface, as shown in Figure 1.4, is similar to other Windows applications and makes it easy to manage people, groups, and databases.

Figure 1.4
You can manage people and groups with a Windows Explorer–like interface.

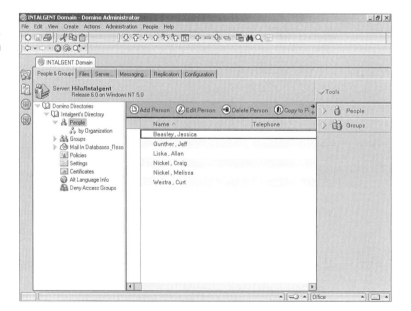

In addition to managing users, you can now access the Domino directories to manage databases, templates, and access control lists. You can even manage your Domino infrastructure via a Web browser using the new Web Administrator. Unlike previous releases of Domino, the new Web Administrator client with Release 6 has the full fidelity and capability of the traditional Microsoft Windows desktop client (see Figure 1.5).

Figure 1.5
The new Web Administrator client enables you to administer your environment via Internet Explorer or Netscape Navigator.

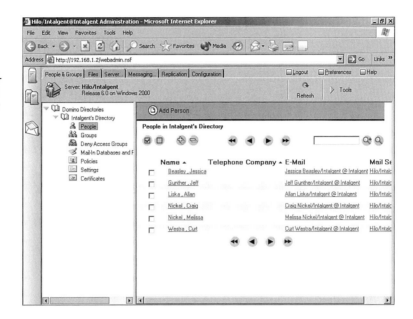

The Server section of the administration client enables you to see the real-time status of your servers and to monitor and review server statistics. You can see who is logged on, send broadcast messages, check the status of tasks, and perform a variety of other useful functions, as shown in Figure 1.6.

Figure 1.6
You can monitor your servers in real time from the administration client.

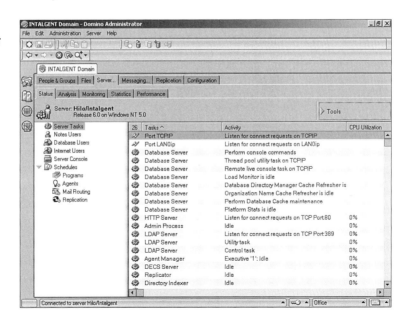

The Messaging and Replication tabs provide a variety of features that will be covered in depth in Chapters 37, "Administering Electronic Mail," and 38, "Replication and Its Administration."

The Configuration section grants easy access to the information for each server. The Server document consists of multiple tabs, making it easier to find specific settings. See Figure 1.7 for an example of just one aspect of the configuration.

Figure 1.7
All configuration information is centrally located and easily accessible.

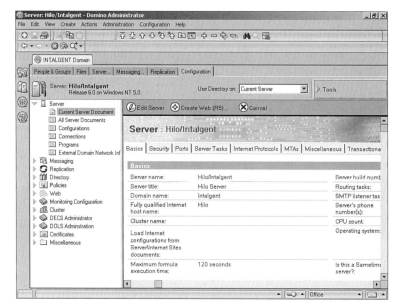

DOMINO SERVER

The heart and soul of the Notes and Domino platform is the Domino server. Domino is an integrated electronic messaging and application server.

Lotus provides the Domino server in three separate models depending on the needs of the organization:

- **Domino Messaging Server**—Provides messaging and collaboration capabilities, including electronic mail, calendaring, group scheduling, and task listing
- **Domino Enterprise Server**—Provides the same capabilities of the messaging server, plus a collaborative environment to deliver applications with features to integrate enterprise back-end systems, enterprise clustering support, and failover features to ensure maximum reliability

NOTE

> The Domino Enterprise Server under Release 6 replaces the Domino Application Server and Domino Advanced Enterprise Server that were available with Release 5.

1

- **Domino Utility Server**—With Release 6, Lotus has added a new Domino server to its offerings. Unlike the Domino Messaging and Domino Enterprise servers, the Domino Utility Server doesn't provide for mail or scheduling; instead, it is designed for organizations that need a Domino server only for applications. This offering allows organizations to run Domino applications without purchasing any client licenses.

To recap, Lotus Notes and Domino provide an operating system–neutral platform with tools for applications. The Notes client can be used with the Domino server, or the two parts can be used independently. Lotus ships several important applications, such as email, that are ready to use and provides templates for you to easily create many other applications as well. Notes and Domino provide a very rich set of tools for you to create custom applications that you can use internally or on the World Wide Web.

WHAT'S NEW IN NOTES AND DOMINO 6

In 1989, Lotus Notes was released to the market and offered a revolutionary way for teams to share knowledge and distribute information. Lotus's innovative software product provided organizations with a collaborative environment to share knowledge and applications across disperse teams in a time at which there were no standards, no off-the-shelf components, and simply no technology readily available to facilitate team collaboration.

Since those early days of Lotus Notes, the computing landscape has changed dramatically. With the inception of the Internet, many of the early, proprietary, and uniquely innovative concepts in Notes were being reproduced and became commonplace. The coupling of an industry-wide effort toward standards adoption with the growth of component-based architectures began to give Lotus Notes competition in an area that it previously dominated. The ease of use of Web-based applications and near-zero application administration made them very attractive over traditional client/server applications such as Lotus Notes. During the mid-1990s, many critics were forecasting that Lotus Notes was in serious danger of becoming obsolete, insignificant, or extinct with the advent of the Internet. However, as the computing environment changed, so did Notes.

With Release 4.5 in late 1996, Lotus continued its effort to evolve the product and introduced Web application capabilities into the existing Notes platform. With the introduction of the Notes server and the integration of Web functionality, Lotus renamed the Notes server to Domino. The separate names provided an identity to the client and server components in a Notes client/server architecture. In reality, Lotus built a brand for the Domino server and Notes clients. As it turned out, the pundits that predicted the demise of Notes have been proven wrong due to the power of the applications that Notes and Domino can provide.

1

With the introduction of Release 5.0, Lotus continued its commitment to Notes and Domino by extending its effort to integrate the Internet into its product line. All areas of the platform, from the Notes client to the Domino server, were influenced by the Web and the Internet. Release 5 introduced users to a new browser-centric user interface, while the server continued to support a variety of Internet protocol standards. The Domino Designer and Administrator clients were substantially improved and received their own product identities. By combining the strength of Domino's database architecture with the platform's Web-centric application development capabilities, Lotus has secured Domino's position as the leading collaboration platform.

In Notes 6, this transition continues. The Internet and the Web are central to the features and functions of Notes and Domino. Lotus continues to embrace an open architecture and standards-based components, to provide a powerful and dynamic product with many significant improvements. Release 6 continues Lotus's efforts to improve the product line with innovative features.

NOTE

> Lotus has always taken great care to ensure backward capability. In fact, Release 6's code base is a direct descendant of Release 1.0 from 1989. Parts of the architecture are still supported by Release 1.0 clients.

Lotus has worked diligently to keep Notes and Domino the messaging and collaboration leaders. Although many more competitors that provide collaboration solutions exist today than did 10 years ago, Lotus has continued to remain competitive by evolving Notes and Domino while remaining flexible regarding the needs of its customers and the marketplace. One of Notes and Domino's most attractive features is the capability to deliver freedom. Whether it's the freedom to implement Domino on a variety of operating systems or the capability to use the newest programming languages, choice is coveted by Lotus and its customers. Release 6 continues Lotus's tradition to innovate and demonstrate the value of the platform.

WHAT'S NEW IN THE NOTES CLIENT

With this new release, Lotus targeted improvements to the Notes client that enhanced the end-user experience with its messaging and collaboration capabilities. With Release 6, Lotus officially identified and announced the following design goals for the newest release of Notes client:

- Improve ease of use and productivity
- Strengthen replication and mobility features
- Enhance performance
- Streamline administration

Table 1.1 summarizes the new features of the Notes client and briefly discusses the practical benefit that each feature provides.

TABLE 1.1   NEW FEATURES AND BENEFITS FOR THE NOTES CLIENT

Feature	Real-World Benefit
Wizard enhancements	Many common tasks, such as the setup and connection of the Notes client, have been improved to increase user productivity.
Login dialog box	Users can quickly move between different user configurations and locations before launching the Notes client.
Welcome page	The new welcome page provides a central area for users to access many types of content and critical information within one unified interface.
Bookmark enhancements	Bookmarks have been dramatically improved. New bookmarks from desktop applications and local files can be linked from within the Notes client user interface. A Startup folder and History folder can include bookmarks from databases, Web content, or other applications. Bookmarks can be searched and used to perform multiple actions.
User interface improvements	Users can personalize many elements of the new interface. Toolbars can be completely customized. Dialog box and frameset properties can be modified and automatically saved for later use. Many common actions can be performed using drag-and-drop actions.
Replication	Replication, one of Notes and Domino's most attractive features, continues to improve. During replication, users can monitor the status and progress of replication. Users have flexibility with the order of how documents are streamed. Additionally, developers can control replication settings for custom applications.
Multiuser/roaming support	An exciting feature of Release 6 is the introduction of multiuser and roaming support. Users can securely move from one workstation to another and work from any location. Roaming enables users to have all pertinent data, such as the personal address book, user ID, and bookmarks, "follow" them from workstation to workstation.
Messaging	Improvements in messaging are apparent in the new release. In addition to a new user interface, the process of detaching files is now a background task. This feature enables users to continue working within their mail database.
Calendaring and scheduling	The process of creating and manipulating calendar entities has been streamlined. A new view gives easier access to appointments and calendar entities while showing any conflicts. Printing is improved with support for various layouts and formats.
Performance	From graphical rendering to network traffic and support for multitasking, the Notes clients continues to get faster. Improvements in response time and resource utilization are welcome changes.

1

WHAT'S NEW IN THE DOMINO DESIGNER

Domino Designer 6 continues Lotus's effort to build the best-of-breed rapid application-development environment. The integration of Internet technologies coupled with support for back-end connectivity enables developers to build and manage complex applications from within one open environment.

Lotus officially identified and announced the following design goals for the newest release of Domino Designer 6:

- **Database development**—Most of the changes in Designer 6 make it easier for developers to develop, from the subtle tweaking of the user interface to major additions such as the Data Connections resource type.

- **Content presentation**—Designer 6 includes many changes and additions that bring the creation and management of new presentation elements, such as layers and style sheets, into the IDE. These modifications are intended to make Designer a tool that Web designers—as well as Notes developers—can use.

- **Reusability**—When projects become large and complex, code reusability helps to streamline the development process. Designer 6 includes many changes that make it easier to reuse code.

- **Managing complex applications**—Designer 6 provides better support for managing large applications that span multiple databases and includes elements that usually are not in a Notes database.

Table 1.2 summarizes the new features of Domino Designer and briefly discusses the practical benefit that each feature provides.

TABLE 1.2   NEW FEATURES AND BENEFITS FOR DOMINO DESIGNER

Feature	Real-World Benefit
Database connections	Support for connections to relational databases is integrated within the database design and development environment.
Autocomplete code completion	The programmer's pane boosts developer productivity by providing type-ahead code completion for the Formula language, LotusScript, and JavaScript.
Java features	This is the first release to add much-needed support for a Java 2 software development environment. Designer and the server use JDK 1.3 and include support for many of the leading Java packages, including Swing, JavaMail, JMS, and Java2D. The replication of Java libraries contained with a database's design is a welcome feature.
JavaScript features	Support for JavaScript 1.4 has been added while enabling developers to manage errors by performing exception handling.

Feature	Real-World Benefit
LotusScript features	Improvements to LotusScript have increased the flexibility and functionality that developers have in developing applications. The introduction of XML and XSL classes, access to Rich Text fields, manipulation to change or add views, remote debugging of agents, and interoperability with Java agents continues the evolution of the programming language.
Formula language	Performance and functions of the Formula language is superior to previous releases due to a new formula engine. Formula looping and new formulas have been added.
User interface	The Designer user interface has been enhanced to help developers use and extend the integrated development environment (IDE). A new menu item called Tools enables developers to add and customize tools within the IDE. Any design element can be locked to prevent design conflicts between development teams. Designer also includes the capability to group design elements, to assist in the management of a database. The addition of custom folders enables a variety of content, from design elements to Web links, to be included within an application.
Design element enhancements	Many design elements have new features to improve the end user's experience with applications. Any form or page can include multiple embedded views. Views can have hide-when formulas that hide or display columns and also can include custom twisties for collapsible categories.
Extended XML support	XML capabilities have been expanded throughout Designer. All design objects and data can be exported in Domino XML (DXL) format, giving developers an easy way to manage a database's design. The addition of native LotusScript XML processing classes extends the integration capabilities of Domino. The classes include a DOM parser, a SAX parser, and an XSLT transformer.
HTML rendering and editing	HTML rendering and editing features have been enhanced. The color palette is consistent between the Notes client and the Web browser. Pages containing HTML content and graphics can be rendered within both the Notes client and a Web browser. The editing of HTML as plain text or rendered HTML improves productivity by enabling developers to toggle between code and display.
Style sheets	Cascading Style Sheets allow developers to improve productivity by utilizing a common design across multiple pages and HTML elements. Style sheets can now be included within the design of the database.
Web services	Web services can be created and hosted on Domino 6 using developers' existing skills of LotusScript and Java.

What's New in the Domino Server

The improvements to Domino Server 6 focus on two primary concepts: administration and performance. From adding support to hosting multiple organizations on a single Domino server to security enhancements, the Domino server continues to evolve and assist administrators in managing complex and diverse environments. Lotus officially identified and announced the following design goals for the Domino 6 Server:

- Improvement of the core messaging infrastructure
- Faster server performance and improved scalability
- Broadened directory support
- Better and simpler administration tools

Table 1.3 summarizes the new features of the Domino server and briefly discusses the practical benefit that each feature provides.

TABLE 1.3   New Features and Benefits for the Domino Server

Feature	Real-World Benefit
Replication	The new replication features reduce network traffic and assist mobile users' productivity. Replication streams documents from smallest to largest while exchanging documents in a single transaction.
Mail server enhancements	Release 6 introduces many new enhancements to Domino's messaging services. A new IMAP server and IMAP interface to the Domino object store improve how messages are stored in mail databases. Shared mail enhancements include support for multiple shared mail databases, garbage collection, and central configuration, all while easing administration and enhancing the reliability of the service.
Performance	The Domino server boasts a host of performance improvements. The formula engine for Domino was rewritten and improves formula evaluation two- to fourfold. The full-text processor results in faster full-text searches while allowing for in-place updates.
Policy management	In the effort to help the remote administration of Notes clients, improvements to policy management have been included. Features include control of user registration options, control over desktop configuration (including bookmarks), a welcome page, and archive settings.

Feature	Real-World Benefit
Console and logging improvements	Remote administration via the remote console has been enhanced to include event color coding and filtering, stop triggers, and background processing.
Web administration client	Web administration of Domino no longer means dealing with a less functional client. The Web client is amazingly similar to the full desktop administration client, with support for role-based permissions.
Monitoring	Domino's server reporting was improved with the introduction of the Tivoli Analyzer, historical graphing of statistics, and a new Database Monitor Usage form.
Virtual hosting	A new virtual hosting feature, called Multiple Hosted Organizations, enables organizations to host multiple server environments within a single server. Each shared server is seen as a standalone server to that organization's users.

Now that you know a bit about Release 6, let's move on to using it. We'll begin with the installation of the Notes client.

PART

II

USING THE LOTUS NOTES 6 CLIENT

Figure 2.1
The Installation
Wizard enables you to
add, remove, and
repair Lotus Notes 6.

Figure 2.2
Input your name and
your organization's
name.

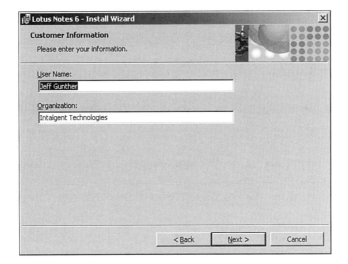

5. Choose your destination folders for program and data directories, as shown in Figure 2.3. To change either of the directories, click Change and locate the desired directory. Typically, you can accept the default directories. To make subsequent maintenance simpler, the program and data directories should remain separate. When you have finished specifying the directories, click Next.

Figure 2.3
The Program Destination Folder dialog box enables you to choose where the client programs are installed.

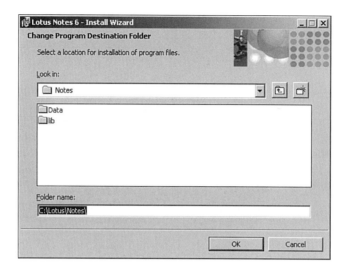

6. The final choice before copying the files is to decide which clients and features to install (see Figure 2.4). The following is a list of the available types:

Figure 2.4
The Custom Setup step of the Installation Wizard enables you to choose the type of client(s) and feature(s) to install.

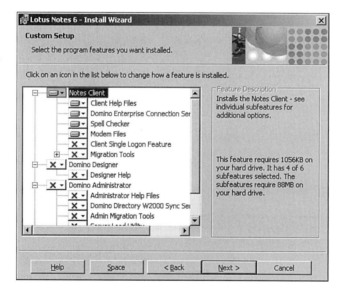

- **Notes Client**—Recommended for most end users.
- **Domino Designer**—Enables users to design Domino applications and databases.
- **Domino Administrator**—Enables remote administration of the Domino server.

    You can selectively include or exclude optional features. Figure 2.4 shows the top-level and sublevel components that can be selected for the workstation's installation. For an explanation of the feature's install state, click the Help button. After all the features have been selected and you are ready to start installing the files, click Next.

7. Click Finish to complete the first part of the installation and copying of files.

To begin the configuration phase of the Notes client, Domino Designer, or Domino Administrator installation, follow these steps:

1. Locate and launch the Notes client within your operating system. On Windows 95, 98, NT, 2000, and XP, you can do this by clicking the Start button, selecting Programs and Lotus Applications, and finally choosing the Lotus Notes client item.

2. The first time you run the Lotus Notes client, you're presented with the Lotus Notes Client Configuration Wizard, as demonstrated in Figure 2.5. Before you started, you gathered some information regarding how to access your server. You'll need this information through the next couple of steps. Click Next.

Figure 2.5
The Lotus Notes Client Configuration Wizard leads you through the configuration process.

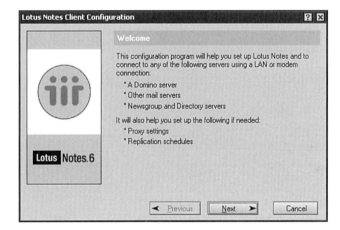

3. At the next step, you need to identify yourself (see Figure 2.6). Enter your full name as was used by your Domino administrator to register you within the Domino Directory.

Figure 2.6
The Lotus Notes Client Configuration Wizard asks for user information to establish a connection to the Domino server.

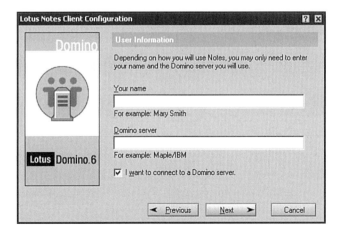

4. You are now asked for your Domino server's name. Enter a fully distinguished name, such as Coruscant/Republic/Galaxy.

5. Subsequently, you are asked whether you want to connect to a Domino server. Under most situations, you will be connecting to a Domino server. If you are connecting to a POP3 or IMAP server, uncheck the check box. Click Next.

6. Assuming that you have indicated that you will connect to a Domino server, the next step in the Configuration Wizard asks you how you want to connect to the server (see Figure 2.7).

Figure 2.7
You can connect to the Domino server either via a local area network or remotely via phone.

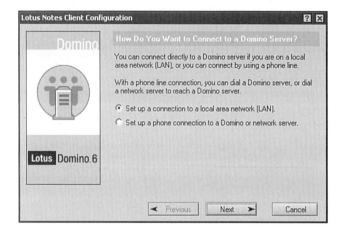

You can choose from two options:

- **Set Up a Connection to a Local Area Network (LAN)**—This is the most common option for office environments. Choose this option if you are connected to a local area network or if you have a modem but you will not be dialing directly into your Domino server. In this case, your Domino server might be attached to the Internet or accessible via a Virtual Private Network and you will access your Domino server via an Internet service provider (ISP).

- **Set Up a Phone Connection to a Domino or Network Server**—Use this if your Domino server has modems attached and you will dial via phone directly from a remote location to the Domino server. This is one possible option for laptop computers. This option is easy and relatively inexpensive to implement, but it can incur expensive phone charges.

Choose the appropriate option and click Next.

7. Depending on your network type and configuration, you might need to input specific network details on how to access your Domino server. Figure 2.8 demonstrates how to set up connectivity for a local TCP/IP server.

Figure 2.8
Depending on your network connectivity type, you might be requested to provide additional network details.

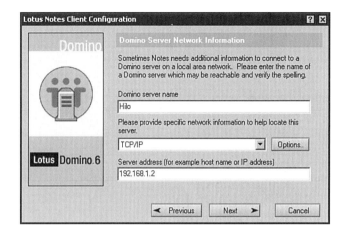

Choose the appropriate network connectivity options and click Next.

8. After the connection to the Domino server is made, you will be asked to input the password to your ID file (see Figure 2.9).

Figure 2.9
After a connection has been made to the Domino server, you're prompted to provide the password for your ID file.

9. Your network connectivity is now complete. As shown in Figure 2.10, you can optionally specify a variety of Internet details, including support for an Internet mail account, access to a newsgroup or directory server or a proxy server, and replication settings. To set an external POP3 or IMAP account, you must know your SMTP (outbound) server name, your POP or IMAP (inbound) server name, your account name, and your password. You can also set up or modify this feature after the Notes client is installed.

Choose the appropriate services and click Finish to complete the installation. The Notes installation process then creates several databases and configuration parameters on your workstation.

Congratulations—you have successfully installed the Notes client. Your workstation should now resemble Figure 2.11.

Now that the installation, setup, and configuration are complete, you're ready to begin using the client.

Figure 2.10
The Notes client natively supports a variety of Internet services.

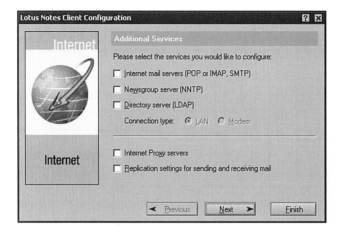

Figure 2.11
The Notes client's default Welcome page greets you after you complete the installation.

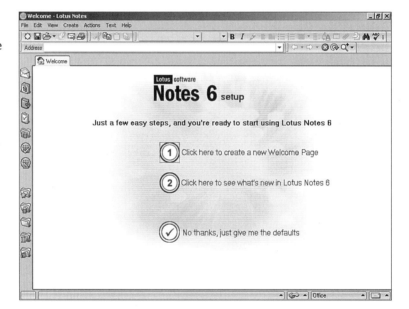

LOGGING ON TO THE NOTES CLIENT

Most networked applications, including Lotus Notes, require you to authenticate before you can access any network resources. Typically, when you log into an application, you're asked to supply a username and password. Using both pieces of information, your credentials are verified against the server. If your credentials are valid and accurate, you are granted access to any resources that you are authorized to use. From the surface, it appears that the Notes authentication mechanism operates similarly to its counterpart in other networked applications, but it's quite different.

In Notes, when you supply a password, your identity is authenticated against an ID file, not an authentication service on a central server. Your ID file, typically located on your workstation, contains all the information needed to verify your identity to the network.

By entering the correct password, you are granted access to network resources associated with that ID file. Most users have a single ID to authenticate them, but some users, such as administrators, can have several. Each ID file can have distinct rights associated with it, allowing access to use databases and other network resources. Later in the chapter, we'll explore the ID file in detail.

In Figure 2.12, you'll see the Notes Password dialog box. As a preventative measure, when you type each letter of your password into the dialog box, a random number of *X*s appears in the password field. This feature prevents someone from looking over your shoulder and guessing the number of characters in your password.

Figure 2.12
A random number of *X*s prevents casual observers from knowing how many characters are in your password.

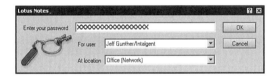

TIP

> All passwords in Notes are case sensitive, so if you have trouble logging on, check the Caps Lock key on your keyboard. If your password is not completely capitalized and the Caps Lock key is inadvertently left on, your capitalized password will not match your real password stored in the ID file.

You'll also notice that there is a key chain displayed to the left of the password field. Starting with the fifth character you type, the key chain changes color and continues to change with each subsequent character. You might be wondering what significance the changing key chain has to do with passwords. The answer, as you might imagine, has to do with security. For this particular security measure to be effective, you need to know what it's for and why it's important. The key chain as shown on the Password dialog box is designed to prevent spoofing. *Spoofing* is a technique that a potential hacker might use to fool you into giving your password. For example, a malicious application might be developed to look and behave like the standard Password dialog box to fool you into providing your password. You might type your password into the program, unaware that it is saving your password and sending it across the Internet.

How can Notes prevent this type of spoofing? Each time you type your password, Notes uses a special algorithm to compute the shape and colors of the key chain displayed to the user. After the first five characters and with each subsequent letter, the key chain changes with the same sequence of colors and shapes and concludes with the same specific key chain.

It would be nearly impossible for a malicious application to mimic the same symbols as you typed them. So, the next time you type your password, watch the key chain carefully. If you find that the symbols are not what you expect, you might be dealing with a spoofing program.

EXPLORING LOTUS NOTES

Most Notes users interact with a variety of databases and the Internet during an average day. The Notes user interface provides a structure for users to easily organize and manage information. With Release 6, Lotus introduced a toolbar across the top of the user interface. This toolbar enables users to customize their environment. The various parts of the Notes window and toolbar preferences are demonstrated in Figure 2.13.

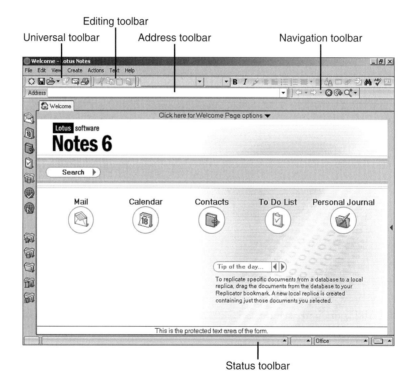

Figure 2.13
Many new features are present in the Notes window.

THE MENU BAR

Figure 2.13 demonstrates various components of the Notes user interface. The topmost line of the screen contains the Windows title bar. The contents of the title bar change, depending on your context. Directly underneath the title bar is the menu bar containing the Windows menu items. Many of the general-purpose commands can be executed from the menus. The menus are context sensitive and change depending on what you are viewing at the time. File, Edit, Create, and Actions are some of the most commonly used menus.

The following menu items are available while you are viewing your Welcome page (in other contexts, the menus are different):

- **File**—This menu item enables you to open and manipulate databases. It allows you to attach, import, and export files, and it also contains the Print, Security, and Tools menu items. Selecting the Document Properties menu item lets you find out about a document's attributes. The Preferences menu item enables you to set many preferences for the Notes environment, including status and toolbar preferences, user details, and administration preferences. The Tools menu item contains several useful tools that you will use in Notes, including a new Release 6 feature: Notes Smart Upgrade. From the File menu you can also access the Security preferences that enable you to lock the workstation, switch to another ID file, and retrieve and manipulate user certificates.

- **Edit**—The Edit menu contains the traditional Windows Cut, Copy, Paste, and Undo menu items. You can delete an object or find its properties. From this menu you can select or deselect all objects within a given context. You can search and replace text or check the spelling of your document. Finally, you can control links and unread marks from this menu.

- **View**—The View menu enables you to refresh the screen to obtain new information, show the horizontal scrollbar, and control document previewing.

- **Create**—The Create menu enables you to create mail messages and use certain database design elements, such as an agent, folder, or view within Domino Designer.

- **Actions**—The Actions menu is context sensitive. The actions allowed here depend on the database being viewed. Some typical actions are editing documents, forwarding mail, moving documents to folders, and doing other kinds of document manipulation.

- **Text**—The Text menu enables you to set the properties of any editable text, including paragraph alignment, control over the highlighter and permanent pen, and visual design of the text.

- **Help**—The Help menu enables you to get additional information about the Notes client, including resources provided by Lotus on the Internet. This menu item also gives you access to two special design elements normally contained in each database: the About document and the Using document. The About document provides a description of the database and identifies its purpose. The Using document details instructions on how to use the database. These design elements are included only if the designer created them during the development of the database.

THE NAVIGATION TOOLBAR

In Release 6, the navigation icons are located within the Navigation toolbar, as demonstrated in Figure 2.13. By default, the Navigation bar is located to the right of the Address toolbar. The navigation icons are as follows:

- **Go Back**—The Go Back navigation button works similarly to the Back button found within a Web browser. Just to the right of the Back button is a down arrow where you

2

can click to get a drop-down list of previous locations. The Go Back button can also be activated via the ALT+left arrow keystroke.

■ **Go Forward**—The Go Forward navigation button behaves like a Forward button in any Web browser. Just to the right of the Go Forward button is a down arrow where you can click to get a drop-down list of locations. The Go Forward button can be activated via the ALT+right arrow keystroke.

■ **Stop**—The Stop button works similarly to the Stop button found in a Web browser. It cancels the current operation. Note that some operations cannot be canceled in the middle and must complete before stopping automatically.

■ **Refresh**—The Refresh button works like a Refresh button in a Web browser. If you are a Notes user, this icon is similar to the action that appears in Views when new documents are available in a view.

■ **Search**—The Search button can be used to locate text within a Notes document, search for Notes databases, or explore common Web search engines for content containing certain text. You can also use the Search button to look for people within your Domino environment and on the Internet. As with the other navigation icons, a down arrow directly to the right of the icon provides a drop-down list of previous search options. Use this if you have a modem but you will not be dialing directly to your Domino server. You can also choose this option if you are dialing into an ISP. In this case, your Domino server must be attached to the Internet and you will access Domino via the ISP and the Internet.

THE ADDRESS TOOLBAR

The Address toolbar, as shown in Figure 2.13, is an element within the Notes toolbar that enables you to open any Web address of Notes databases. Similar to other toolbars, a drop-down arrow appears and enables you to navigate through previous URLs used within the field. In addition to standard Internet URLs, you can specify Notes URLs using the `Notes://` protocol. For example, you can open the Domino Directory with the Address toolbar by typing `Notes://SomeServer/names.nsf`.

You can also specify local databases on the workstation using the Notes protocol by leaving out the server name. For example, to open your local address book, type `Notes:///names.nsf` with the Address field. Lotus has also extended the use of the Notes protocol. In addition to the Notes client, Internet Explorer can process the protocol.

USING TOOLBARS

Toolbars contain buttons that can streamline your work and improve productivity. A toolbar contains a series of similar shortcuts to commonly used operations. Unlike in previous versions, these shortcuts are easier to manage and control in Release 6. You can easily enable or disable a set of icons by right-clicking the toolbar and selecting any or all toolbars. Each toolbar appears within the toolbar section, just under the Windows menu items. The buttons within these toolbars can perform operations that correspond to menu selections, or you can add a custom formula to be executed when the button is clicked. As with all icons on the toolbars, you can get a short description of the button by moving your mouse cursor over the button without clicking it.

Notes provides about 170 predefined shortcuts that are associated with common tasks and operations within Notes. Some of the buttons and toolbars operate only within a particular context. For example, under the Text toolbar, one button changes the currently selected text to bold. If you are not editing text and do not have text currently highlighted, this button is not enabled.

The buttons are categorized within several toolbars, including Editing, Table, Text Properties, Universal, and View. By default, the Universal set of icons is displayed. As its name implies, this set of buttons is available in all contexts. You can change the buttons that are displayed in the Universal set, or you can create your own toolbar. As demonstrated in Figure 2.14, each toolbar can be added or removed by right-clicking the toolbar and choosing the appropriate toolbar. Additionally, if you right-click on a particular toolbar, you can choose Hide This Toolbar to hide the toolbar from being displayed.

Figure 2.14
Each toolbar can be enabled or disabled by right-clicking the toolbar.

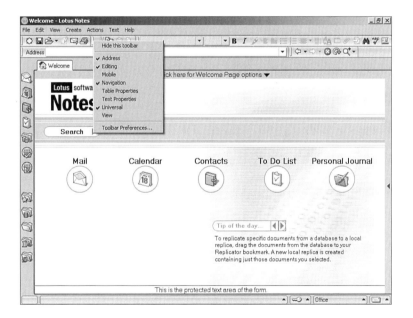

All of the other toolbars are context sensitive. In addition to the predefined buttons, you can define a formula macro that executes when you click a custom button. With this capability, you have the flexibility to control the entire environment of Notes within a single formula. Formulas enable you to manipulate text, send messages, and even create new databases.

CUSTOMIZING A TOOLBAR

You can customize the Universal toolbar of buttons, or you can create and customize your own toolbars. Many configuration settings of the toolbars and buttons can be managed under the Toolbar preferences. To customize a toolbar of buttons, follow these steps:

1. From the toolbar, right-click and select Toolbar Preferences.
2. Click Customize tab located on the left. Figure 2.15 shows the Toolbar Preferences dialog box.

Figure 2.15
The Toolbar Preferences dialog box enables you to create and manage toolbars and buttons.

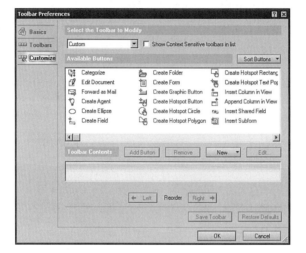

3. The buttons under the Toolbar Contents label comprise the current set of buttons contained in the selected toolbar. The current toolbar appears under the Select the Toolbar to Modify label and above the complete list of buttons. Initially, the drop-down box contains only the Universal set. If you want to create your own toolbar, proceed with the following step. Click Toolbars on the left of the dialog box to see the Toolbars tab (see Figure 2.16).

4. Click the New Toolbar button and provide a name for the new toolbar. When you have finished, click OK.

   Under the Toolbars tab within the Toolbar Preferences dialog box, you can also selectively choose what toolbars are visible. Additionally, the Show Context-Sensitive in List check box enables you expand the list of toolbars to control.

5. If you created your own toolbar, you'll see its name appear in the list of available toolbars. See Figure 2.15 for the following operations:

   • To add a button to the toolbar, click the Customize tab and scroll through the list of available icons until you find the one you want; then drag it to the toolbar. Drop the icon at the point where you would like it to appear. You can add a spacer or text to the toolbar by clicking the New button.

- To delete a button or any other toolbar element from the toolbar, select the item within the toolbar and click the Remove button.

- To reorder any element within the toolbar, click the item that you would like to move within the toolbar, drag it to the location where you would like it to appear, and drop it. You can also use the Left and Right buttons to perform the same function.

Figure 2.16
You can give a name to your new toolbar of buttons.

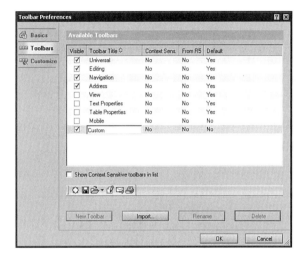

6. Under the Basics tab within the Toolbar Preferences dialog box, there are a few other options:

- You can restore all defaults to the toolbars by clicking the Restore All Defaults button.

- The Show Toolbars check box enables you to turn off the toolbars.

- The Show Context-Sensitive Toolbar check box gives you the option to display the context-sensitive toolbar of icons.

- The Show Pop-Up Description Text check box enables you turn off the display of the ToolTips for the buttons and toolbars.

- The Toolbar Appearance section enables you to change the size and display of your buttons. You can specify either Small or Large. The default display size is Small. Normally this is desirable because you can then use many more icons than if you specify Large. The Button Displays drop-down field enables you to choose the buttons display type. You can choose either Icon Only, Text Only, or Icon and Text.

TIP

If you work within a Domino environment that requires you to switch ID files regularly, you might want to consider adding the Switch User ID button to your Universal toolbar. With a single click, you can switch to another ID file.

2

EDITING A CUSTOM BUTTON

Occasionally you might find it useful to create your own button that performs a specific task that you cannot execute with a standard Notes menu command. Suppose, for example, that you would like to invoke a program from within Notes. We'll review how to launch the Windows Paint program within Microsoft Windows XP, but you can use any program. Also, you are not restricted to executing programs; you can use the Formula language to write any custom formula. See Chapter 18, "Working with Formulas, Functions, and Commands," for more details on the Formula language.

To create your own button to execute the Paint program, follow these steps:

1. From the toolbar, right-click the toolbar and select Toolbar Preferences to open the Toolbar Preferences dialog box.

2. Click the Customize tab on the left side of the dialog box. If you want to add your custom icon to a toolbar other than the Universal toolbar, select the appropriate toolbar from the drop-down list.

3. Click the New button and choose Button to display the Edit Toolbar Button dialog box (see Figure 2.17).

Figure 2.17
You can specify text or help text and attach your own formula to a custom button icon.

4. Click the Change Icon button to display the Insert Image Resource dialog box. This dialog box, shown in Figure 2.18, displays all of the image resources within the database. You can scroll through the icons list and select one of the predefined images, or you can add your own icon.

   After you've selected your button's icon, click OK.

5. Now that you've defined the attributes of the button, it's time to define the formula. Click the Commands and Functions button (see Figure 2.19).

Figure 2.18
The Insert Image Resource dialog enables you to select a predefined icon or add your own image.

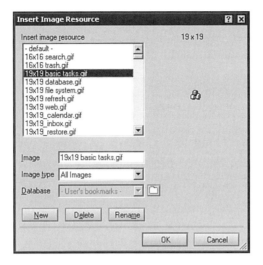

Figure 2.19
The Commands and Functions dialog box enables you to browse the exhaustive list of available commands and functions.

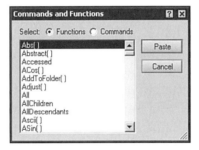

Select the Commands radio button, select Execute from the list of commands, and then click Paste.

NOTE

You might be wondering about the difference between @Commands and @Functions. In general, @Commands execute commands found within the standard menu inside the Notes client. For example, @Command([FileExit]) performs the menu command File, Exit. In contrast, @Functions are specialized formulas that perform calculations and return some type of value. For example, @Abs(someNumber) returns the absolute value of a number.

6. You now need to modify the formula to execute the Paint application. To try the Paint sample, enter the following formula:

```
@Command([Execute];"mspaint.exe ")
```

7. You should now enter a short description for your new custom icon in the Pop-Up Help Text field. The contents of this field are used to display a ToolTip for your new custom icon. Click OK after you have entered your description.

8. With the toolbar contents, you can move your custom icon to a desired location by dragging the icon from left to right.

9. Close the Toolbar Preferences dialog box by clicking OK.

You can test your new button by clicking it and making sure that it behaves as you expect.

THE STATUS BAR

The Status bar, located at the bottom of the Notes main window, gives you useful information about various aspects of your Notes session (see Figure 2.20). As with most areas within the Notes client, the Status bar is context sensitive. With Release 6, the Status bar has undergone a number of improvements, including the introduction of a preferences menu that enables you to change certain settings.

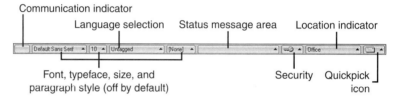

Figure 2.20
The Status bar enables you to view and change important information about your environment and session.

The Status bar is divided into eight sections:

- **Communication Indicator**—Displays a lightning bolt when Notes is accessing the network. If you are using Notes via a mobile connection, a modem with flashing lights appears.

- **Font Typeface Indicator**—Displays the current font typeface when you are editing a document. If you click this indicator, you can change the current typeface by selecting one of the available fonts in the pop-up list.

- **Font Size Indicator**—Works like the Font Typeface Indicator. You can view the current size and change it by clicking it and selecting from the list.

- **Paragraph Style Indicator**—Shows you the current style, if there is one, and enables you to change the style by clicking the indicator. As with the Font Typeface and Font Size indicators, this indicator is only available when you are editing a document.

- **Language Indicator**—Displays the language tag for current or selected text within a document. As with the Font Typeface and Font Size indicators, this indicator appears only when you are editing a document.

- **Status Message Area**—Displays system messages and provides a recent history of user and system actions.

- **Security Icon**—Visibly shows your access level for the currently selected database. If you click this icon, you get more detailed access level information.

- **Location Indicator**—Shows you the name of the current location document. If you click this indicator, you can see a complete list of all your locations and you can select a new location from the list or edit your current location document.

- **Quickpick Icon**—Enables you to perform common mail regarding your electronic mail and also indicates when you have new mail. If you click this icon, you can send and receive mail, open your mail database, scan for unread mail, and create a new email message.

Release 6 enables you to configure and completely manage your Status bar. The new Preferences menu enables you to selectively control what items appear within the Status bar, including an item's size and placement. To access the Status bar preferences, right-click the Status bar and choose Status Preferences. Figure 2.21 displays the Preferences dialog box.

Figure 2.21
The Status bar Preferences dialog box enables you to completely modify and control the Status bar.

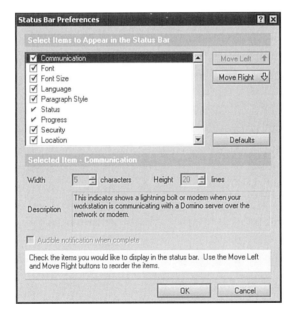

WINDOW TABS

Window tabs, located underneath the toolbars (see Figure 2.22), provide a mechanism to easily switch among various databases and documents. All windows occupy the same area within the Notes environment and can be toggled by simply clicking the appropriate tab. This maximizes the information you can see in each window while still enabling you to switch easily from one window to another.

TIP

As with previous version of Notes, you can open multiple windows with the Notes client. You do this when you open a database or document. From the Bookmark bar or a view, right-click the database and select Open in New Window. This opens a second window, complete with its own set of window tabs. You might want to use this feature to compare two different versions of the same database in two windows side by side, for example.

As demonstrated in Figure 2.22, the window currently being viewed has a tab with a white background, and any window that does not have focus has a light-gray background. When you view a document window with the default setup, the window tabs appear below the toolbars. To switch from one window to another, simply click the tab of the window you want to view.

Window tabs

Figure 2.22
The window tabs enable you to quickly switch from one window to another.

Bookmark folders

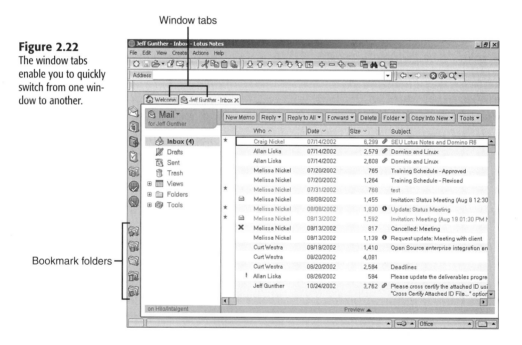

On the right side of each active tab is an *X*. This *X* can be used to close the window without actually viewing it.

BOOKMARKS

In Figure 2.22, a set of icons called bookmarks is displayed on the left side of the user interface. The bookmarks in Notes behave similarly to bookmarks in Web browsers. They are used to store the location of Web content, Notes databases and documents, or views that you use frequently to do your job.

When you initially start Notes, the top four bookmark icons are used for the four basic Notes operations: Mail, Calendar, Address Book, and To Do. Under these four you'll find the Replication icon, which is similar to the Replicator tab of older releases of Notes.

Under the Replicator icon are two optional icons. The first launches Domino Administrator, and the second launches Domino Designer. These icons appear only if these clients are installed and configured on your machine.

After a little space on the bar, you see up to six folders that you can use to store your bookmarks. The first four are standard: Favorite Bookmarks, Databases, More Bookmarks, and History. Underneath these are folders for Internet Explorer Links and Netscape Navigator Links. These last two folders appear only if you have the corresponding Web browser installed on your machine.

You can add bookmarks to the Bookmark bar or to the folders. Each folder can hold multiple bookmarks. A bookmark can be a link to a document, view, or folder within a Notes database. You can also link to Web pages or Web sites. Add a bookmark by clicking the item that you want to save and dragging it to the Bookmark tab where you would like the bookmark to appear.

As illustrated in Figure 2.23, when you click one of the folders, a window frame pops out from the left. This frame shows you the objects within the folder.

Figure 2.23
Bookmark folders can be permanently left open.

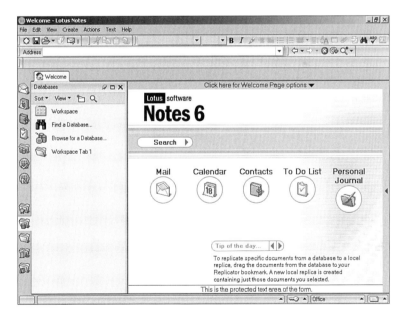

The bookmark frame can be sized by clicking and dragging its right edge. You can leave this area permanently open by clicking the pin icon.

NOTE

> If you are familiar with using the Workspace in Release 5, you'll be happy to know that Lotus has made some improvements for bookmarks. Any folder containing bookmarks can now be opened as a grid within Notes. This grid is similar to the workspace from the days of Release 4. With these improvements to bookmarks, you can get the best of bookmarks with the comfortable feel of the workspace.

ID FILES AND CHANGING YOUR PASSWORD

When you log into any type of networked application, you are required to provide a username and a password for authentication. The Notes client is no different; however, an extra element of security, the ID file, is utilized. This ID file is an essential component of Notes security and can be stored on a floppy disk or on your local workstation's hard drive.

In the most basic sense, security is based on one of two distinguishing characteristics: what you have or what you know. For example, a padlock can use a key (what you have) or a combination lock (what you know). When you log on to most computer systems, they are usually based on a password (what you know). If you work for a large company, you might have an authentication mechanism such as a card-key security system to let you into your building or parking lot. This card-key system is based on what you have.

The most secure systems, however, are based on a combination of what you have and what you know. For example, if you use an ATM card at your bank or the local grocery store, you must have the card, and you must also know your personal identification number (PIN). This system means that if someone has your card but does not know your PIN, the card is useless. The user must have something and know something.

The Notes ID file is a physical file that you must possess in conjunction with your user ID and password. In other words, even if someone knows your password, unless that person also has your ID file, he cannot log into the Domino server. This mechanism is much stronger than systems with only a user name and password. If you keep your ID on a floppy disk, for example, and store it locked away in your desk, no one can log on with your ID unless that person can also get the floppy from your desk.

The most common cause of security breaches, however, is the careless handling of passwords. One bank, for example, was rigorous about changing passwords daily. The bank thought that changing a password daily would surely foil anyone trying to electronically rob it. However, because the tellers forgot passwords that changed daily, they posted the passwords on the wall. Guess what? Of course, when they investigated how millions of dollars were stolen, it was traced back to this rather careless handling of the password itself.

The moral, of course, is not only to change your password, but also to be careful of how you handle the passwords themselves. Don't post them next to your computer, leave them where someone else can find them, or share them. These are common-sense rules, but sometimes you might violate them when you are in a hurry to get the job done.

Passwords

Passwords in Notes can be up to 63 characters long and can consist of letters, numbers, spaces, or other keyboard characters. The first character of your password must be an alphanumeric character. Additionally, passwords are case sensitive. The following passwords are *not* identical: HomeRun, homerun, and HOMERUN. They are considered different because of the capitalization. To make your password more secure, you can use the following techniques:

- Make your password at least eight characters long.
- Use a combination of upper- and lowercase.
- Use one or more numbers or special characters.
- Do not use your name, your birthday, your pet's name, or other common information about you.
- For the strongest passwords, use a random combination of letters and numbers, not regular words. Although this has the drawback that these passwords are easier to forget, the benefits outweigh the risk.

Changing Your Password

To change your password, follow these steps:

NOTE

> If you use the Windows NT/2000 client and you have specified that you want Single Password Logon, you must keep your passwords for Notes and Windows NT synchronized. If you change your Notes password, you need to change your Windows NT password to continue to use the Single Password Logon feature. Notes prompts you if you change one but not the other.

1. From the menu, select File, Security, User Security. You are prompted for your current password (see Figure 2.24). This first password prompt enables you to review information contained in your ID file.

Figure 2.24
You must first enter your old password before you can access the User Security dialog box.

2. After you type your current password, you see a dialog box similar to Figure 2.25.

Figure 2.25
The User Security box enables you to examine and change many aspects of user security, including your ID file.

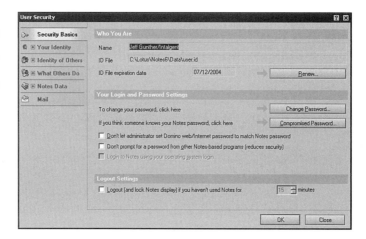

3. To change your password, click the Change Password button or press Alt+P. You are again prompted to enter your current password. After you type your password, you see the Change Password dialog box, as shown in Figure 2.26.

Figure 2.26
Your new password is case sensitive.

4. In the Change Password dialog box, enter your new password. Passwords are case sensitive. Mixed-case passwords, as well as passwords containing both letters and numbers, are the most secure but the easiest to forget. Your Domino system administrator will set up a minimum length for your new password.

5. When you have entered your password, you are required to type it again. This ensures that you have typed it correctly because you cannot see the characters as you are typing them. When you have finished, click OK on the Change Password dialog box to exit.

Before you move on to the next topic, let me briefly summarize the other items contained in the User Security dialog box. Besides giving you the capability to change your password, the Security Basics tab enables you to log out and lock Notes on your workstation. The Your Identity tab includes information about you and enables you to view and manipulate the certificates that are contained within your ID file. See Figure 2.27.

Figure 2.27
Certificates are authorizations that enable you to access servers.

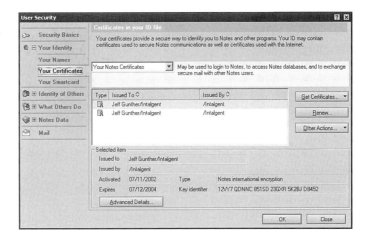

You must have a certificate to access a Domino server. When you are registered to a Domino environment, a certificate is issued and placed within your newly created user ID file. Normally, certificates are organized via a hierarchical organization that is defined by your system administrator. You can think of a certificate as an authorization key for access. If you do not have this authorization, you are not allowed to access your organization's servers.

You do not typically need to do much with certificates, but if your organization has a complex hierarchy or you deal with several domains or external companies, you might need to request certificates or cross-certificates (allowing cross-domain access). Certificates are covered in more detail in Chapter 35, "Domino Security Overview." You can access other ID management options in the Your Certificates tab in the User Security dialog box. In this tab, you can request a name change, obtain a new public key, and create a safe copy of your ID that can be used by an administrator of another domain to cross-certify your ID.

The Notes Data tab in the User Security dialog box can be used to create encryption keys (see Figure 2.28). These keys are stored in your ID file and can encrypt fields within documents. If a document is encrypted with a key, only users who have the key contained in their ID file can read the encrypted fields of the document. When you have created a key, you can mail the key to others. Note also that the designer of the form must enable encryption on fields to be encrypted; encryption on fields is not enabled by default.

Figure 2.28
Encryption keys
enable you to encrypt
fields within docu-
ments.

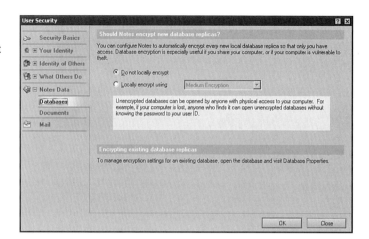

2

CHAPTER 3

UNDERSTANDING THE NOTES USER INTERFACE

In this chapter

THE WELCOME PAGE

Previous releases of Lotus Notes used a concept called the *workspace*. This workspace was a large area containing square button icons that represented databases. Although the workspace is still available, mainly to ease transition and training, Notes 6 has improved the Web browser-type user interface. Release 6 has merged the concepts of the traditional Notes workspace and bookmarks, now allowing any folder of bookmarks to be opened in a grid.

The workspace user interface will not be discussed much here because users upgrading from earlier releases are already familiar with it, and users new to Notes with Release 6 don't really need to learn it. However, understanding how to open bookmarks in a grid brings together the best of the workspace and bookmarks.

In Figure 3.1, you see the Basics Welcome Page, also sometimes called a headline page.

Figure 3.1
The Basics Welcome
Page, with Quick
Notes opened,
enables you to quickly
access common
applications.

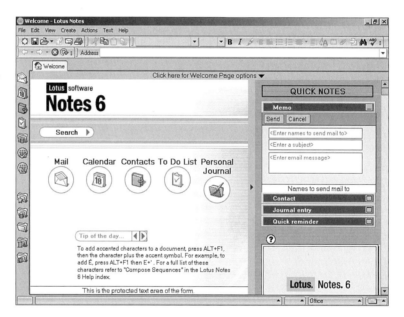

THE BASICS WELCOME PAGE

On the left side of the screen you see the four most common Notes applications: mail, calendar, address book, and To Do list. An overview of each of these topics is presented within this chapter, but each is covered in detail later in the book. Mail is covered in Chapter 4, "Getting Started with Electronic Mail." The calendar and the To Do list are covered in Chapter 7, "Getting Organized with the Calendaring and Scheduling Features." The address book is discussed in Chapter 6, "Getting Started with Contact Management."

On the right side of the screen you see a set of icons called Quick Notes. You can use Quick Notes, a window within the Basics Welcome Page, to create and send an email message, add a contact to your list of contacts, make a journal entry, or schedule reminders. To display the Quick Notes frame, simply click the arrow on the right-hand side of the Notes window.

CUSTOMIZING THE WELCOME PAGE

In the first two chapters, you saw several different welcome pages, but you haven't been shown how to modify or create your own. As with previous releases, you can choose a style from the built-in welcome styles, or you can create your own page style.

To modify your welcome page style, click the black arrow located underneath the toolbar named Click Here for Welcome Page Options (see Figure 3.2). A frame appears enabling you to configure the welcome page. If you choose Headlines with Lycos, for example, you will see a three-pane welcome page containing your mail, your calendar, and a Lycos news page.

Figure 3.2
You can show your mail, your calendar, and news on your welcome page.

Figure 3.2 demonstrates the Headlines with My Lycos welcome page containing useful information. However, what if you want different information? No problem. Follow the steps here to customize your welcome page:

1. Click the black arrow next to the words Click Here for Welcome Page Options.
2. Click the Create a New Welcome Page button to display the New Page Wizard.
3. Give your welcome page a name and click Next.
4. You'll be asked whether you want a welcome page with resizable regions using frames or a personal page using customizable rich text. Frames use only one content type per frame and provide the capability for you to resize the content within the Notes environment. In contrast, the personal page enables you to choose from a variety of layouts that

can include personal pictures, Web links, and a background graphic. For the following steps, you'll use frames; verify that the I Want Frames radio button is selected and click Next.

5. The next step in the wizard asks you to pick and choose the content to include within your welcome page (see Figure 3.3). Content can include your inbox, your calendar, your To Do list, a Web page, content from other Notes databases, and local files. Some content areas such as Notes databases, files from the local workstation, and Web pages can include multiple frames of each content type. Additionally, you can choose to include a preview pane. The preview pane lets you display a selected document from any of the Notes database-driven content types, including your inbox, calendar, and task list.

Figure 3.3
You can personalize the welcome page by selecting the content areas that are of interest to you.

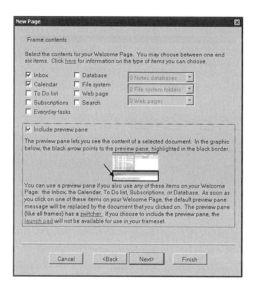

6. Choose the desired content areas and click Next.

7. After you select the content types, you'll be asked to select the desired frame layout. Depending on the number of content types that you selected, the frame layout might vary, but the dialog box that you see should be similar to Figure 3.4. If you find that the frame layout is too crowded, click Back and reduce the number of content types. After you choose your layout, click Next.

8. Each frame in the dialog box enables you to choose from your preselected content types. Content types can include content from internal Notes databases, extranet content provided by your organization's business partners, or your favorite Web site (see Figure 3.5).

Figure 3.4
Select your desired
frame layout.

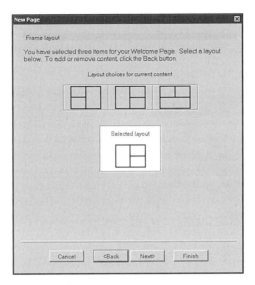

Figure 3.5
You can choose and
set properties for
each frame of your
welcome page.

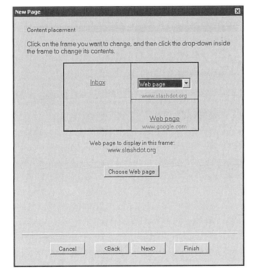

9. After you have finalized each frame's properties and location, click Next.

10. Your welcome page is almost complete. The final choice is to decide whether to include action buttons or the launch pad (see Figure 3.6). *Action buttons* are graphical shortcuts that appear at the top of each view within the inbox, calendar, and To Do list. The *launch pad*, a new feature of Release 6, provides an easy-to-use interface to launch a variety of commonly used Notes shortcuts.

11. Click Next to complete the wizard to finish your customized welcome page. Figure 3.7 demonstrates the result of customizing content from the both the Web and Notes.

After you create a custom welcome page, it appears in the list of welcome pages. You can have several different welcome pages; if you are working on several different projects, you can conveniently switch back and forth among the various different welcome pages you set up.

Figure 3.6
The final step in customizing your welcome page is to choose to display the new launchpad or action bar buttons.

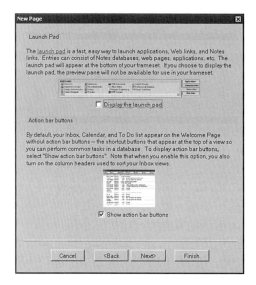

Figure 3.7
A welcome page can contain various types of content with an optional launch pad.

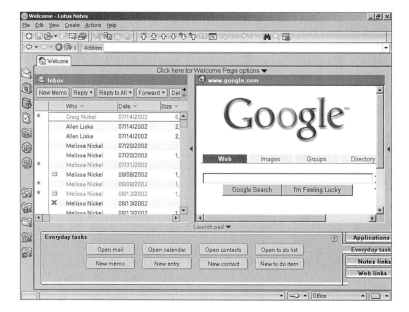

STANDARD DATABASES

During the average day, several databases are accessed with the Notes client. The following section describes four of these databases: your Personal Address Book, your email database, the public Domino Directory, and your personal Web navigator. Depending on your Domino environment, your system administrator might have customized your company's version of Notes and Domino to include company-specific databases.

We'll start by touring the Personal Address Book that enables you to store information about your personal contacts. Next, we'll review the email database that enables you to send and receive email. The public Domino Directory is typically stored on your Domino server and contains information about all the users and resources across your Domino environment. Finally, we'll review the personal Web navigator database that is used when you browse the World Wide Web.

YOUR PERSONAL ADDRESS BOOK DATABASE

Your Personal Address Book database (names.nsf) is used to store information about your personal contacts and information on how to access your Domino environment. Figure 3.8 shows the default view of the contacts in the address book. For quick reference, the letters to the left of the names provide rapid access to the user's first names.

Figure 3.8
The Contacts view lists all of the contacts within your address book.

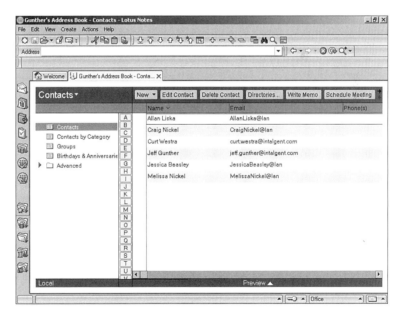

For each contact, you can fill in information such as name, company, address, phone numbers, and email addresses, as illustrated in Figure 3.9. You can create a new contact by clicking the New action button and selecting Contact from the Contacts view.

In addition to the standard name and address information, you can store attachments, documents, and comments with each contact. Click the Briefcase tab and attach any type of file by using the Attach button in the Editing toolbar. The Attach button has a paperclip as its icon. Additionally, you can add comments regarding the contact.

Under the Advanced tab, you can organize any contact into a group and assign categories to each contact. In Figure 3.10, you'll notice that each user can be assigned to multiple categories. Each category can be created and managed by you, the user.

Figure 3.9
You can store names, phone numbers, addresses, and comments for each contact.

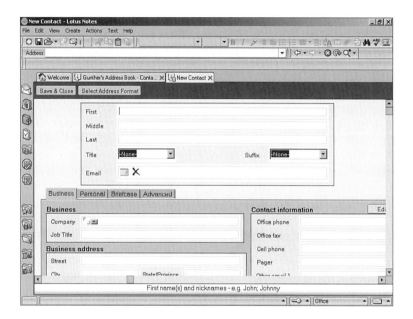

Figure 3.10
Contacts can be in more than one category.

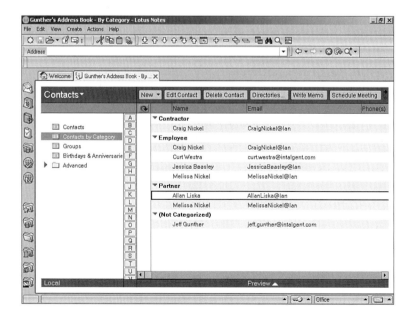

In addition to managing your contacts, the address book contains all the information needed to manage and control the connectivity settings for your workstation.

In Figure 3.11, you can see the Accounts view within the Personal Address Book. The Accounts view enables you to set up different accounts for email, newsgroups, and directory services on the Internet. You can use IMAP, POP, or SMTP for email; NNTP for newsgroups; and LDAP for directories. By configuring your accounts, you can access non-Domino servers from your Notes client. Adding an account document enables you to configure your Notes client to download your mail from another Internet service provider (ISP).

Figure 3.11
The Accounts view enables you to set up accounts for various Internet protocols.

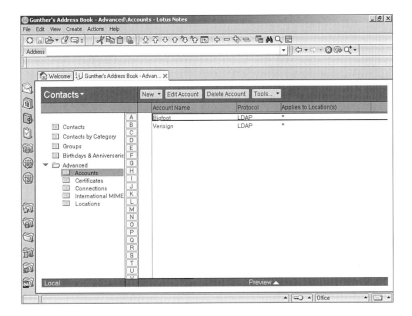

Server connection documents specify communication protocols such as TCP/IP, SPX/IPX, or Modem for a specific destination. A connection document is used when you try to connect from your local workstation to a Domino server. Notes selects the appropriate connection document, depending on your user ID's identity, the location you are connecting from, and the communication method protocol you are using. Connection documents can also be used to limit the users that can utilize the connection and the locations from which they can initiate the communication.

As shown in Figure 3.12, the location document can be configured depending on whether you have a mobile computer or a home office computer, or whether you access your office server remotely. You can configure settings such as the type of connection (Local Area Network, Notes Direct Dialup, Passthru Server, or Hunt Group). You can also indicate your preferences for Internet browser, replication, mail, and other parameters that might vary when you are in one location or another. Notice that in the lower-right corner of the status bar on the bottom of the window, you can change your current location. Figure 3.12

demonstrates the location document named Office. When you click it, a window pops up so that you can choose the location document you want to use.

Figure 3.12
The location docu-
ment specifies where
you are and how you
are connected.

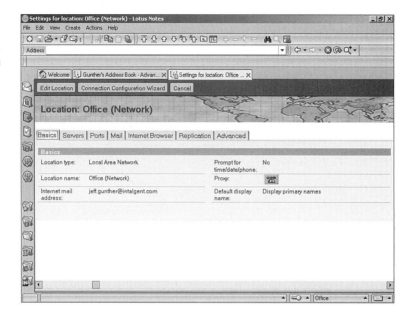

YOUR MAIL AND CALENDAR DATABASE

Since the creation of Notes, the mail database has been one of the most important databases on the desktop. Your mail database includes not only your electronic mail, but also your calendar, meeting manager, and To Do list. Keeping all of this information in a single database makes everything easily organized. Another important reason for keeping this information together is for *replication*. Domino's replication feature enables you to replicate this database to your laptop or another machine so that you can handle your email and calendar tasks offline. See Chapter 38, "Replication and Its Administration," for more information about replication.

You can display your calendar with a variety of views, including views for one day, two days, one week, two weeks, or one month (see Figure 3.13). Click the appropriate tab to view scheduled events in a particular Calendar view. The Day, Week, and Month views also allow you to filter the displayed events to only the work week. Figure 3.13 demonstrates how to choose between the various views for the Week. When you view either the weekly or monthly formats, you can also double-click a date's header line to zoom to see the contents of that day. If you double-click a particular calendar entry, you see a zoomed view of that entry.

You can set several kinds of user preferences in your mail and calendar database. To access the preference settings, follow these steps:

1. Open the database by clicking the calendar bookmark icon.

2. From the menu bar, select Actions, Tools, Preferences to open the Preferences dialog.

Figure 3.13
Scheduled events can be displayed using the Day, Week, Month, and Meetings views.

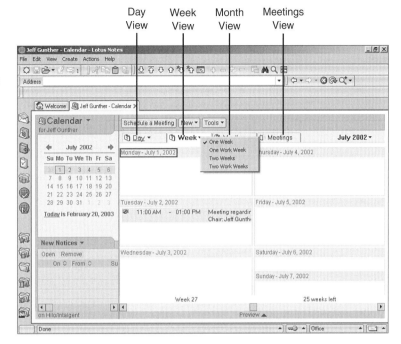

Day View   Week View   Month View   Meetings View

REVIEWING THE DOMINO DIRECTORY

Now let's review the Domino Directory. This section assumes that you set up your Notes client with a connection to a Domino server. If you set it up as a standalone client with no Domino server connection, your installation will not include a Domino Directory. For most users, however, the Domino Directory is available and contains information about other people and resources within your organization. Confusingly enough, this database is also named NAMES.NSF, but unlike your Personal Address Book, it is usually stored on the Domino server and accessed over the network.

To open the Domino Directory, follow these steps:

1. From the menu, select File, Database, Open, or click Ctrl+O.

2. You will see the Open Database dialog box (see Figure 3.14). In the Server field, click the drop-down box and select your organization's main Domino server from the list.

3. Scroll down the list of databases and find an entry for your company's name with the phrase Directory. The filename for this database is typically names.nsf. Figure 3.14 has Intalgent's Directory selected.

4. Click the Open button. Your screen should resemble Figure 3.15.

Figure 3.14
Open your company's address book, also called the Domino Directory.

Figure 3.15
The Domino Directory contains information about all the people and servers in your domain, and much more.

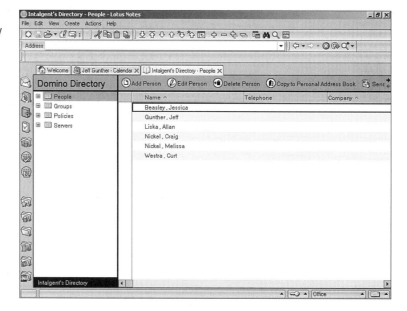

NOTE

> Beginning with Release 5, Lotus changed the name of the Domino Directory to become more consistent with the software industry. In Release 4, the Domino Directory was called the Public Names and Address Book. Typically, when you have lists of users, computers, and resources, this list is called a *directory*. Novell, for example, has Novell Directory Services (NDS), and Microsoft has something called an Active Directory.

The People section of the Domino Directory is probably the most useful section for end users. You can use this section as a sort of telephone book for other individuals within your company. The Groups section contains information that your administrator has set up to manage groupings by function (engineering, marketing, finance), by departments within these functions, by location, by managerial authority, or other criteria. Groups are also most useful for addressing electronic mail to a bunch of people at once.

A lot of information is contained under the Server section of the Domino Directory. This information is configured by the administrator and includes certificates (security authorizations), connections (how and when servers connect to each other), domains (logical groupings of servers and users), holidays (days you wish you had more of), and other parameters that administrators can tweak.

If you are a current administrator of a Notes/Domino system, the Domino Administrator provides a powerful user interface for managing your Domino environment. Read Parts VI, "Installing and Configuring the Domino Servers," and VII, "Administering the Domino Servers," for much more information about Domino servers.

THE PERSONAL WEB NAVIGATOR DATABASE

The Personal Web Navigator database (PERWEB.NSF) is stored locally and is used when you browse the Web via Notes. It is used as a page and resource cache, so when you access the same page multiple times, your response time is improved. Normally, if all you do is browse the Web, you don't really need to open the Personal Web Navigator database. The database does have a few useful features, however, if you want to do offline Web browsing, if you want to monitor Web sites, or if you want to control page caching.

The Personal Web Navigator database keeps recently accessed pages, and sometimes it is interesting to review the pages. See Figure 3.16.

Figure 3.16
The Personal Web Navigator database stores previously viewed pages.

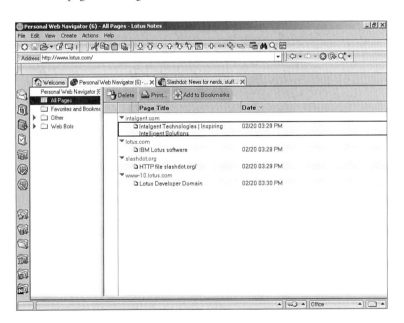

Some additional features in this database can make your Web browsing more productive. You can use Notes as your browser, or use Notes with Internet Explorer to get the benefits of the Personal Web Navigator. In the latter case, you must turn on the offline viewing feature manually. Here are some features of the Personal Web Navigator database:

- **Offline browsing**—Because the database caches pages, you can download Web pages for offline viewing. This is great for use on a disconnected laptop.
- **Page caching**—As mentioned, caching improves performance.
- **Web Ahead**—This is related to page caching. Web Ahead is an agent that runs in the background on the Notes client. It checks the links that are located on a particular page and downloads them so that you can read them later. You can indicate how many levels of pages you want the agent to retrieve. To use Web Ahead, click its name in the Navigator pane and double-click the instructions line that appears in the view.
- **Page Minder**—This is a scheduled background agent that runs on the Notes client. You can specify the frequency, from one hour to a day or a week. The agent checks Web pages that you specify to see whether they have changed. If they have, Page Minder notifies you via email. To use Page Minder, click its name in the Navigator pane and double-click the instructions line that appears in the view.

BOOKMARKS

Chapter 2, "Installing and Customizing the Notes Client," introduced the concept of bookmarks. In Release 6, Lotus continues to evolve the idea and implementation of bookmarks within the Notes client.

As we have briefly reviewed, Notes comes with several built-in folders and applications. Additionally, you can create your own folders to hold bookmarks, databases, documents, Web sites, and desktop applications. The folders that you create either can be at the top level on the Bookmark bar or can be embedded within other existing folders. After you create a folder, you can also change its icon, rename it, or delete it if you want to reorganize.

To create a bookmark folder, follow these steps:

1. Right-click any folder bookmark on the Bookmark bar located on the left side of the Notes interface.
2. Select New Folder. Figure 3.17 demonstrates what you should see when the Create Folder dialog box appears.
3. Give the folder a name in the Folder Name field, and navigate to the parent folder where you want your new folder to appear. If you want your new folder to appear on the Bookmark bar, highlight the top line, titled Folders.
4. Click OK.

Figure 3.17
You can create your
own bookmark
folders.

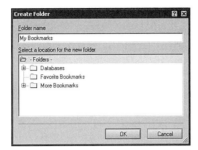

To remove a bookmark folder, simply right-click it and select Remove Folder. To rename the folder, right-click it and select Rename Folder. You can also drag and drop bookmarks from one folder to another folder.

In the Databases folder you will also find a special bookmark called Workspace. If you click this bookmark, Notes opens the familiar 4.*x* workspace.

As you can see in Figure 3.18, a bookmark folder called Workspace Tab 1 is automatically created. This can give you the false impression that bookmarks are somehow synchronized with the workspace. They are not synchronized. When you create new bookmarks, they are not automatically placed on your workspace; when you create new icons in your workspace, they also are not automatically placed in a related bookmark folder. The Workspace Tab 1 folder is created when you first set up your workstation, but after that you can customize its contents.

Figure 3.18
The Notes 4.*x* work-
space is still available.

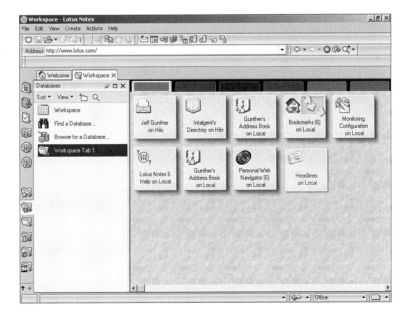

With Release 5, some users found themselves using the workspace instead of bookmarks. For some users, the workspace was just more comfortable; others found the bookmarks difficult to navigate and use. To integrate the best of bookmarks with the workspace, Lotus has added the capability to open any bookmark folder as a workspace. To open any folder as a workspace, right-click the folder and select Open as Workspace.

This new feature will most likely move even the most diehard workspace users to bookmarks. You can see in Figure 3.19 that the Replicate indictor for the workspace is now located in the lower-right corner of the database icon instead of the upper-right corner, as within the traditional workspace.

Figure 3.19
Any folder can be opened in a work-space.

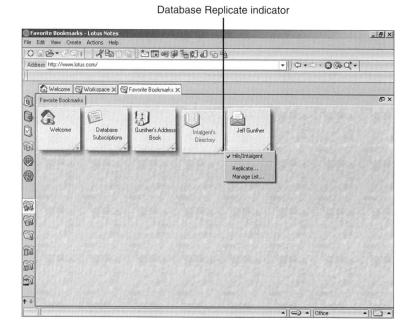
Database Replicate indicator

SUBSCRIPTIONS

Subscriptions enable you to monitor the contents of a Notes database and be notified when the content changes. Notifications of the changes are not sent via an active notification mechanism such as email, but rather by passive notification. All changes are stored within your Subscription results database and can be viewed whenever you like.

To begin creating a subscription, open the database to be monitored. From the menu bar, select Create, Subscription. Give the subscription a name, and then provide some parameters on what you want monitored.

Suppose that you want to know whenever a new employee joins your organization. In this case, assume that the addition of a person to the Domino Directory signifies the addition of a new employee. How can you set up a subscription to give you this information?

To set up a sample subscription to monitor for new or changed employees, follow these steps:

1. Open your organization's Domino Directory.
2. From the menu bar, select Create, Subscription. A new document appears similar to Figure 3.20.

Figure 3.20
You can add a sub-scription to monitor databases.

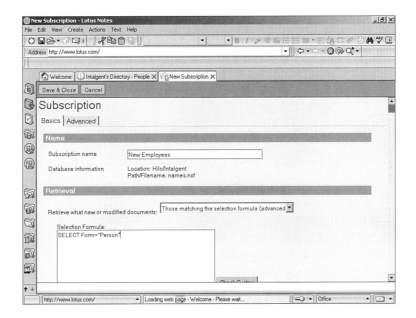

3. In the dialog box, enter **New Employees** as the subscription name.
4. Under Retrieval, choose Those Matching the Selection Formula (Advanced).
5. For the selection formula, enter **SELECT Form="Person"**.
6. Click the Save and Close action button.

That's it. You now have a subscription to tell you when new employees arrive. Actually, it tells you whenever any person's record changes. Now take a look at how you can monitor the results. Open your Favorite Bookmarks folder. Click Subscription Results. By clicking the Subscription Options hotspot in the upper-right corner of the screen, you can see a list of all your subscriptions, and you can selectively enable, disable, and edit your subscriptions.

CHANGING YOUR USER PREFERENCES

You can control and customize many preferences within Notes. Although some settings are stored within individual databases, such as the Mail database, global settings can be changed via the User Preferences dialog box. To change these preferences, follow this procedure:

1. From the menu bar, select File, Preferences, User Preferences to open the User Preferences dialog box (see Figure 3.21).

Figure 3.21
The User Preferences dialog box enables you to customize your workspace, international language settings, mail, and ports.

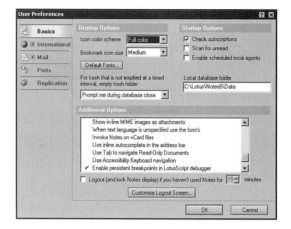

2. When the dialog box appears, you can change many options. The options are divided into five categories:

   - **Basics**—Enables you to change startup and display options, including the capability to lock your workstation (requiring a password to reactivate it). You can also set several options regarding the operation of your workspace.

   - **International**—Consists of three subtabs that enable you to change collating sequences, character sets, international dictionaries, units of measure, language dictionaries, and various calendar settings, from the start day of the week to pop-up calendar direction.

   - **Mail**—Consists of two subtabs that enable you to specify mail and news options such as message format, frequency of checking for new mail, inbox notification, the format of all outgoing Internet mail, and which local address books should be used for name lookup.

   - **Ports**—Enables or disables various communication protocols and includes the capability to configure each protocol's options. This tab also provides the capability to enable network compression and encrypt all network traffic between the Notes client and the Domino server.

   - **Replication**—All replication defaults can be configured, including the capability to restrict how much of each document Notes should replicate from the server. This includes the capability to specify whether the local replicas should be encrypted and what level of encryption to use.

3. After you have changed your options, click the OK button to close the User Preferences dialog box.

BASIC USER PREFERENCES

When you launch File, Preferences, User Preferences, the basic user preferences are shown as in Figure 3.21. This tab allows you to specify several startup options, including but not limited to those described in the following sections.

ICON COLOR SCHEME

Use the Icon Color Scheme setting to control the appearance of the buttons as well as the bookmark icons. Options include Full Color, Gray Color, System Color, and Pale Color.

BOOKMARK ICON SIZE

You can control the bookmark icon size. The settings are None, Small, Medium, and Large. When you change the setting, it does not take effect until you exit Notes and restart it.

DEFAULT FONTS

You can click the Default Fonts button to set the fonts that Notes uses by default. You change the settings for four fonts: Default Serif Font, Default Sans Serif Font, Default Monospace Font, and Default Multilingual Font. If you set fonts for your own use, you can change each of these to a font that you find appealing. If you design databases for others, be careful: The end user might or might not have the same fonts available that you do.

CHECK SUBSCRIPTIONS

If you enable the Check Subscriptions options, your subscription database is searched for the subscriptions you have created. In essence, you enable a background agent that will query each database subscription for new data. If you use subscriptions, you should enable this option.

SCAN FOR UNREAD

The Scan for Unread option enables you to have Notes scan your preferred databases for unread documents when you start Notes. You specify your preferred databases by issuing Edit, Unread Marks, Scan Preferred from the menus. If you select this option, it takes Notes longer to start up, depending on the size and number of your preferred databases.

ENABLE SCHEDULED LOCAL AGENTS

When you select Enable Scheduled Local Agents, the Agent Manager and Notes Web Retriever programs are started when you start the Notes client. Both of these programs are separate processes that run in the background while Notes is running. The Agent Manager manages when agents are initiated and run. The Web Retriever program manages retrieval of Web pages in the background while Notes runs.

LOCAL DATABASE FOLDER

The Local Database folder is the root directory for all your Notes databases. This directory is set when you install Notes, but you can change it in User Preferences. In addition to the databases, Notes relies on this directory for system information, icons, and so forth. You should not change this directory unless you make sure that Notes will still be capable of accessing its system information.

ADDITIONAL OPTIONS

Additional Options is a set of options that can be on or off. Each option controls an aspect of your environment. Some options deal with the display, others deal with user interface actions, and some deal with security.

MARK DOCUMENTS READ WHEN OPENED IN PREVIEW PANE

If you normally work in a three-pane view when handling your mail, you might want to set this option. Mark Documents Read means that the unread marker (the star) disappears from the Inbox folder if you view a document in the preview pane. If you want to use the preview pane in a true preview mode, you might want to leave this option off. The unread mark is turned off only if you open the document (or you turn off the mark manually via Edit, Unread Marks, Mark Selected Read).

MAKE INTERNET URLS (http://...) INTO HOTSPOTS

When you review documents, it is convenient to have all references to Web pages turned into hotspot links. If you turn on this option, you will easily be able to link to a Web page that is referenced in material you are reading. Without this option on, you would have to manually type the URL into your Web browser to access the page. Normally you should leave this option on unless you do a lot of work with Web addresses and you don't want them turned into links.

TEXTURED WORKSPACE

The textured workspace is a more visually appealing 3D look than the single-color workspace background, which appears flat. The workspace is available in the Databases folder, and the user interface is the same as in Release 4.*x* of Notes. To view the textured workspace, your display adapter must be set to handle at least 256 colors. By turning on this option, it is a little easier to see when a database is selected and the workspace looks more interesting. Normally you should leave this option on.

RIGHT DOUBLE-CLICK CLOSES WINDOW

The right double-click option to close a window has been a part of Notes for a long time. If you are accustomed to this feature (or even if you are not), you might want to enable it. This is a convenient feature of Notes that enables you to close a window by double-clicking with the right mouse button when the cursor is placed on or in the window. There is not too much danger in leaving this option on: Right double-clicking is not really used in too many other programs, so you are unlikely to do it by mistake.

ENABLE JAVA APPLETS

The Java programming lanquage can be used by Web page developers to enhance their Web pages and is triggered on Web pages via the <APPLET> tag. This option and several others control the operation of the Notes Web Navigator (the Web browser embedded within Notes). If you use the setting Notes with Internet Explorer in the location document in your personal directory database, you might also need to change some settings in Internet Explorer.

In addition to enabling Java applets within User Preferences, you must review and enable the Java Applet Security section within Security Preferences under the tab titled What Other Do, Using Applets. Under the Using Applets security section, you can allow Java programs to connect to other network resources.

Normally Notes does not allow Java programs to access your local resources such as files, but in the Execution Control List security option, you can enable file access.

Finally, if you will use Java agents on the server, you must review and enable the Run (Un)restricted LotusScript/Java Agents entry in the Domino directory (name and address book) for your company.

ENABLE JAVASCRIPT

The Enable JavaScript option enables JavaScript within the Notes browser. JavaScript is just one of the scripting languages that can be used to control browser functions. Several functions in Domino can generate JavaScript, so normally you should consider leaving this option enabled.

ENABLE JAVA ACCESS FROM JAVASCRIPT

Java and JavaScript are two distinct programming languages. Java is a compiled language and can operate in many contexts, including browser applets, Java Notes client agents, Domino server agents, and Domino server-side servlets. JavaScript generally runs only in Web browsers. By enabling this option, you allow JavaScript programs to invoke Java applets in the Notes Web browser.

ENABLE PLUG-INS IN NOTES BROWSER

Whereas Java programs are typically created by Web page designers and apply usually to a small number of Web pages, plug-ins are useful programs that augment the Web browser itself. Plug-ins are available to all Web pages viewed by the browser and support various enhancements such as video, multimedia, sound, and so forth. Plug-ins are triggered on a Web page with the <EMBED> tag.

If you use the Notes Web Navigator, you enable plug-ins by checking this option within the User Preferences dialog box.

ENABLE ACTIVEX IN NOTES BROWSER

ActiveX programs are similar to plug-ins. Plug-ins are a Netscape technology, whereas ActiveX controls were developed by Microsoft. The Notes browser supports both kinds of technology. You can enable ActiveX controls via this option.

ACCEPT COOKIES

Cookies in a Web browser are containers that can store information between browser sessions. This enables the browser and server to retain information. Normally, cookies provide convenience features, such as eliminating the need to constantly re-enter data to a Web site that you frequently visit. On the other hand, you might not want a Web site to be capable of storing and accessing information without your knowledge. You can enable or disable cookies with this option.

PROCESS PRINT REQUESTS AS A BACKGROUND TASK

With previous releases of Notes, all printing by Notes was handled within the foreground. Any foreground process in Notes locked the workstation until all processing was completed. This new feature option enables you to request all printing to be handled as a background process. Using a background process for an intensive process such as printing enables you to remain productive.

RETAIN VIEW COLUMN SORTING

One of the debates among Notes developers is whether the mail stored in the mail database should be sorted by most recent or most ancient first. Regardless, everyone can set their own preferences with the Retain View column-sorting setting. By enabling this option, you can sort your email with the most recent mail first; the next time you open the view, it will retain its previous sort setting. By default, this option is enabled.

MAKE NOTES THE DEFAULT WEB BROWSER ON MY SYSTEM

If you make Notes your default Web browser in Microsoft Windows, when you link to the Internet from other applications, such as word processors or other programs, Notes is launched automatically. If you now use Microsoft Internet Explorer or Netscape Navigator/Communicator, you might find that one of these browsers is installed as your default browser. Checking this option replaces that browser with the Notes Web browser.

USE WEB PALETTE

Because everyone browsing the Web might be using different browsers, operating systems, and hardware, the set of colors used by browsers could easily be chaotic. Lotus has its own color palette for use within Notes. In addition, it supports a platform-independent 256-color palette called the Web palette.

If you are developing for Notes only, you can use either palette. However, if your applications will be used on the Web, you should enable the Use Web Palette option. Using this option provides better graphics fidelity with Web browsers.

SHOW EXTENDED ACCELERATORS

Extended accelerators enable you to access tabs and bookmark icons in the Notes workspace via the keyboard. Normally, if you have a mouse, you can click these buttons, but if you want to access the buttons from the keyboard, you can do it via the extended accelerators. The accelerators work with or without the Show Extended Accelerators option checked, but if the option is turned on, you will see prompts on your screen.

To use the extended accelerators, hold down the Alt key and click either W or B. To access the window tabs, click the W key; to access the bookmarks, click the B key. If the Show Extended Accelerators option is on, you are then prompted with a number. Each number corresponds to a different button. Click the number that corresponds to the window or bookmark that you want to access.

ENABLE MIME SAVE WARNINGS

The Multipurpose Internet Mail Extensions (MIME) Internet standard specifies how electronic messages must be formatted to be exchanged between different messaging platforms. This feature enables Notes to notify you when a message cannot be encoded according to the MIME standard.

ENABLE UNICODE DISPLAY

Typically, the Enable Unicode Display option should be enabled. If this feature is disabled, Notes uses its own native-language fonts. If you get mail in Unicode format but don't have the fonts, Notes automatically displays the information using the available fonts, so there is no harm in leaving this option on. This option exists mainly to disable usage of Unicode fonts that are corrupted.

LAUNCH THE CORBA (DIIOP) SERVER ON PREVIEW IN WEB BROWSER

The Common Object Request Broker Architecture (CORBA) is the technology that Domino utilizes to enable other clients to implement remote procedure calls. Essentially, this is a sophisticated form of distributed computing that allows any type of client, including Web browsers, to communicate with the Domino server.

When you develop applications locally, however, you might not need the DIIOP service. With this option enabled, a portion of the server executes locally so that you can test a CORBA application without a Domino server. Typically, this option is used by advanced developers.

LOCK ID AFTER INACTIVITY

Notes enables you to lock your workstation if you have not had any keyboard or mouse activity within a specified amount of time. This feature protects your system in case you leave your desk. If the time expires, you need to re-enter your password before you can access the Domino server again. In addition, you can customize your logout screen by selecting an existing image resource or creating a new one.

INTERNATIONAL PREFERENCES

To change your international preferences, click the International tab within the User Preferences dialog box. The International Preferences tab is shown in Figure 3.22. In this dialog box, you can change the regional settings, set the collation order (which is used for sorting), choose units of measurement (imperial or metric) used, select the spell checker's dictionary, and specify character sets.

Figure 3.22
The International Preferences controls many settings including the Calendar view's starting day.

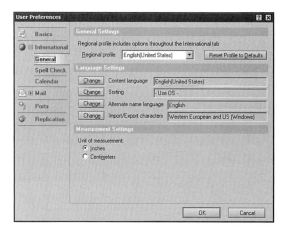

This dialog box also controls the starting day of the week and starting calendar view day. These are not strictly international options, so if you use Notes within the United States, do not ignore the International Preferences box.

MAIL PREFERENCES

Click the Mail tab within the User Preferences dialog box to access the Notes mail and news options, as shown in Figure 3.23.

You can choose an alternative mail editor, such as Microsoft Word or Lotus WordPro. The Local Address Books field enables you to indicate the filename for your Personal Address Book and local replica copies of other company address books (Domino Directories).

When sending mail, you can choose to keep copies of email that you send as well as automatically sign or encrypt email that you send. You can also choose to encrypt saved mail.

Figure 3.23
You can control which
editor to use for email
memo documents.

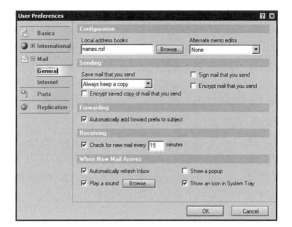

The Receiving options enable you to control how frequently your Notes mail client checks with the server to see whether there is new mail. You can also control whether you will be notified and whether you would like visible or audible notification. The second tab, titled Internet, under the Mail tab, enables you to control the Internet mail and news formats and to specify HTML or plain text.

PORTS PREFERENCES

The Ports preferences contain only advanced options. If you don't know the difference between TCP/IP and SPX, you typically do not need to worry about the options in this area. The only exception is if you need to enable your modem for remote access. In this case, you might need to enable one of your COM ports (see Figure 3.24).

Figure 3.24
You enable, disable,
and trace ports using
the Ports User
Preferences.

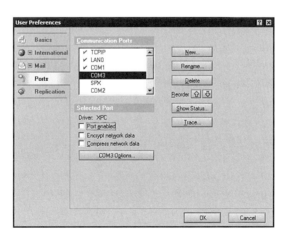

You can enable or disable any of your ports by highlighting the port in the list and selecting the Port Enabled check box. For each different port, you can also click the Options button to obtain specialized options for that port. You can reorder the ports so that they are searched in a different order, show the status of a port, and trace a port.

Tracing a port is an important diagnostic tool if you have communications problems. If you get a message indicating that Notes cannot access the server, open Ports User Preferences and click the Trace button. You will see a dialog box similar to Figure 3.25.

Figure 3.25
You can trace the connection to a server using the Trace Connections dialog box.

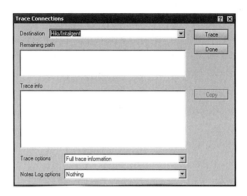

To trace the connection to a destination server, follow these steps:

1. Select the server from the Destination drop-down list.

2. Click Trace. You will see the trace in the window. This is usually very helpful information in diagnosing any connection problems with your ports.

REPLICATION PREFERENCES

The Replication preferences enable you to control the size of each document that is replicated between your local workstation and the Domino server. This tab also includes other database preferences that are used during the creation of a replica. You can see the Replication tab within the User Preferences dialog box in Figure 3.26.

Figure 3.26
Replication preferences enable you to control replication settings.

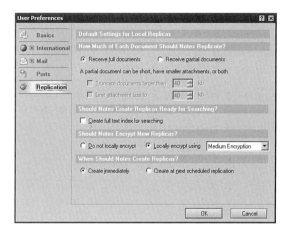

CHANGING YOUR SECURITY PREFERENCES

In addition to controlling your user preferences, you can modify your Notes workstation security options. To modify these preferences, follow this procedure:

1. From the menu, select File, Preferences, Security Preferences to open the User Security dialog box (see Figure 3.27). You'll be asked to authenticate first before accessing the dialog box.

Figure 3.27
The User Security dialog box enables you to customize your security preferences.

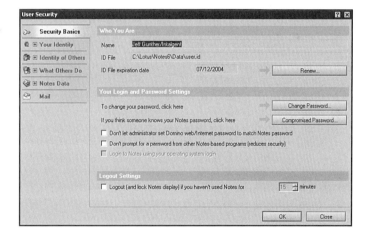

NOTE

Your system administrator might have created an Execution Control List for the entire organization and disabled your ability to modify it. If so, you will not be able to see or use the Workstation Security dialog box.

2. When the dialog box appears, you can change many options. The options are divided into six categories.

- **Security Basics**—Enables you to perform tasks relating to your user ID file, including renewing your ID file, changing your password, dealing with a compromised password, and setting the logout settings for your workstation.

- **Your Identity**—Enables you to perform several functions relating to your certificates, including importing and renewing certificates, creating new public keys, and requesting a name change.

- **Identity of Others**—Consists of two subtabs that enable you to view certificates for people and services and also view certificate authorities and their issued certificates.

- **What Others Do**—Enables or disables various levels of security, called the Execution Control List, for Notes code that can access the Notes/Domino environment, local workstation, and network resources. This tab also provides the access of applets and JavaScript to the local workstation and other resources.

- **Notes Data**—Manages all secret keys for document encryption. This tab includes the capability to create, import, and mail secret keys.

3. After you have changed your options, click the OK button to close the User Preferences dialog box.

The heart of the workstation's security is under the What Others Do tab within the security preferences (see Figure 3.28).

Figure 3.28
The User Security dialog box gives you fine-grained control over programs that execute on your workstation.

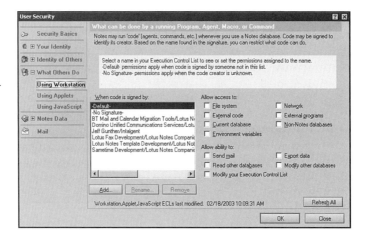

You can control the execution based on whether the program is signed or who has signed the document or mail message. Regular workstation security enables you to control the following:

- Access to the file system
- Access to the current database
- Access to environment variables
- Access to non-Notes databases
- Access to external code
- Access to external programs
- Capability to send mail
- Capability to read other databases
- Capability to modify other databases
- Capability to export data
- Access to modify the Execution Control List (ECL)

3

Java applets and JavaScript run within a Web browser on your workstation, but they are created by some unknown Web page designer. So, you are running someone else's program on your machine. For this reason, you typically do not want to allow Java applets to access your file system. It's recommended that you enable this option only for specific groups or individuals, not for default access.

Access to the Notes Java classes allows a Java applet to access data stored within a Notes database that might reside on your local machine. The same caution applies: You will be running someone else's Java program, and it can access data within your local databases. I recommend that you enable this option only for trusted groups or users.

NOTE

> Java applet security is controlled in three places. First, it is addressed in the User Preferences Advanced options. You must enable Java applets. Second, within the Execution Control List you can control whether Java applets can access your file system or the Notes Java classes. Third, within the current location document in the Advanced tab is a Java Applet Security tab. Review all these places if you suspect that Java security is giving you a problem. Finally, Java agents running on a Domino server are enabled in the Domino Directory.

The JavaScript security controls are shown in Figure 3.29.

Figure 3.29
JavaScript security
ECL controls reading,
writing, and URL open
access.

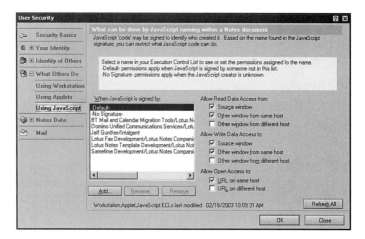

3

CHAPTER 4

GETTING STARTED WITH ELECTRONIC MAIL

In this chapter

OVERVIEW OF ELECTRONIC MAIL IN NOTES

The Lotus Notes electronic mail service follows a *store-and-forward* model. Simply stated, this means that an email is stored in a central repository on the Domino server until it can be routed to the recipient's mail database.

On a local area network, that usually means that the message is delivered instantaneously. On a dial-in or remote workstation, mail is stored in a local outgoing mailbox until a connection is established to a Domino server. The mail is then sent to the server and electronically routed. If a recipient's mail database is in another domain, the server routes the mail to that domain, and that other domain handles the task of delivering the message.

This routing process is similar to sending mail via snail mail (the post office). You address the letter and it gets picked up by the mail carrier, who takes it to a substation. From there, it is routed to the appropriate ZIP Code and handed to another carrier, who delivers it to the addressee. In the case of Notes mail, the Domino server's router service handles the delivery, using the Domino Directory to determine the correct location for an addressee's mail database.

To help you get oriented, we'll take a brief tour of the Notes mail application. This application can be accessed via the mail bookmark (usually the first bookmark). The default Inbox view of the mail database is shown in Figure 4.1.

Figure 4.1
The Inbox view is displayed when you first open your Notes R6 mail application.

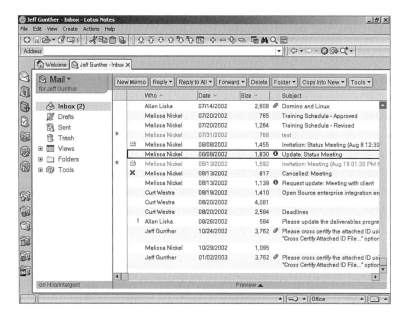

As with any Notes application, you can open a preview pane at the bottom of the screen to view the contents of the selected document without actually opening it. Open the preview pane by dragging or clicking the blue preview bar, located at the bottom of view, up toward the Action bar.

VIEWS IN THE MAIL APPLICATION

The left pane lists the different views and folders in the mail application. The views include the following:

- **Inbox**—This folder holds incoming mail until you decide what to do with it.
- **Drafts**—This view holds various types of mail documents that you have created and saved but have not yet sent.
- **Sent**—This view contains copies of messages you've sent.
- **Trash**—This folder holds documents that have been selected for deletion and provides a single location for checking on documents before they are irretrievably deleted.
- **Views**—The All Documents and Mail Thread views are located under the Views section. These views provide access to all messages within the databases. The Mail Thread view organizes documents so that reply documents are grouped with the memo documents to which they are responding. This makes it easier to follow threads when you have a complex exchange of documents discussing a topic.
- **Folders**—There are no folders when the database is first created. Personal folders are used to group documents that you want to refer to later.
- **Tools**—A few default tools are included with the mail application, including Archive, Rules, and Stationery. A Stationery view holds documents that have been saved as stationery templates. When you open a stationery document and edit and then send it, a copy of the stationery document is used; the original stationery document remains intact in the Stationery view.

SENDING A MESSAGE

Sending a basic email message is what most people think of when talking about email. In Notes, the basic email message uses the Memo form. If your mail application is set up correctly—that is, as a local application when you are working remotely, or on the Domino server when you are working on a network—you can create a memo from anywhere within Notes. Here are several ways you can start the process of creating a memo:

- Select Create Memo from the Quickpick icon on the Status bar (in the lower-right corner of the screen).
- Select Create, Mail, Memo from the menu bar. If you have the mail application open, the menu option is Create, Memo.
- Press Ctrl+M from anywhere within Notes.
- Click the New Memo button on the Action bar in the mail application.

After you initiate a memo, a form similar to the one in Figure 4.2 is displayed.

Figure 4.2
Use the basic Memo form to create a new email message.

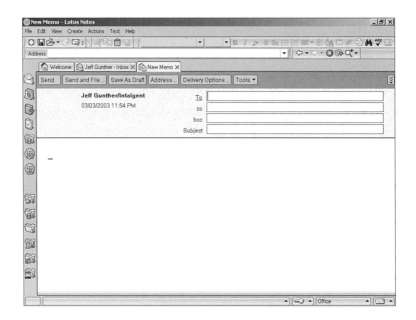

This basic form has only five fields. The first three fields are used to address the memo to one or more individuals or groups of individuals. These three fields are for the primary addressees, carbon copies, and blind carbon copies. The Subject field provides the subject of the memo, which appears in the listing of messages within the inbox. The Body field is a rich-text field that enables you to include any type of attachments, tables, section, and graphics.

ADDRESSING AN EMAIL MEMO

In each of the addressee fields, users' names must be entered in a way that Notes recognizes them. This is made simple through directory lookups. As you type, Notes looks up names in Domino directories or in your Personal Address Book, displaying the name as soon as it is recognized. Usually, all you have to do is type enough of a person's (or group's) name until Notes can recognize it as unique. Notes's type-ahead feature works for first names and last names or group names. The name you enter can be a common name or even a nickname, as long as the Domino server can resolve the name in the Domino Directory. For example, you could address a memo to Melissa; if your organization had only one Melissa, the name would be resolved by the server. You can also look up names in the Domino directories by clicking the Address button; this is a good way to ensure that you enter names correctly. If duplicate matches are found during the execution of the type-ahead lookup, you're prompted to choose the appropriate individual.

If you want to send a memo to someone who is not listed in any of the directories, you must enter an explicit address. For example, if Joe Schmoe were a user in another domain, you could address him as `joe.schmoe@somedomain.com`. The Domino server would attempt to deliver the message to the Internet domain, provided that appropriate connections are in place to allow mail routing.

COMPLETING YOUR MEMO

Complete the memo by entering a subject in the Subject field and entering the body of your memo in the rich-text field below the address portion of the Memo form. A completed memo is shown in Figure 4.3.

Figure 4.3
This completed email memo is ready to be sent.

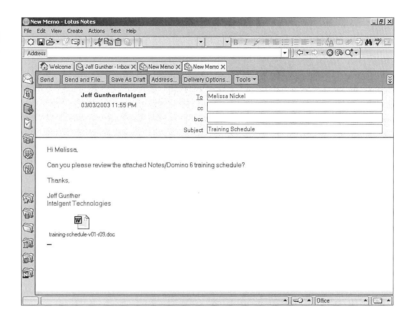

You attach files like the one shown in Figure 4.3 to email messages by choosing File, Attach and selecting the file to be attached. It could be any type of file, but in this case, it is a Microsoft Word document. New within Release 6, you can drag and drop a file from your workstation's hard drive to the completed memo.

SENDING THE MEMO

From the Action bar, you can click a button for any of the following three send options. The button you click determines, to some extent, what happens to your sent mail:

- **Send**—When you click Send, the memo is sent immediately. The memo is saved in your mail database unless you have elected not to save sent mail (an option under File, Preferences, User Preferences, and the Mail tab).

- **Send and File**—When you select this option, the memo is sent immediately. The Folders dialog box, as shown in Figure 4.4, is displayed that lets you select which folder the memo should be saved to. When saving to a folder, you might want to add a new folder if there isn't one that is appropriate. You can add a new folder from within the dialog box using the Create New Folder button.

Figure 4.4
Save outgoing mail in the folder of your choice.

■ **Save as Draft**—When you select this option, the memo is saved in the Drafts folder in your mail database. The memo is not sent. You can open the draft memo later, edit it, and send it by selecting either of the send options I've just described.

SPECIAL DELIVERY OPTIONS

Sometimes the default delivery options might not be enough for a particular situation. Many of the delivery options can be customized by clicking the Delivery Options button on the Action bar. You can then select options in the Delivery Options dialog box shown in Figure 4.5.

Figure 4.5
Set special delivery options for your out-going memos.

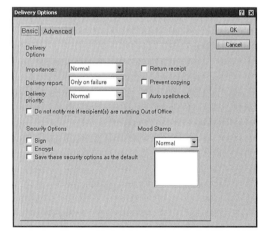

The Basic tab of the Delivery Options dialog box provides you with the following options:

■ **Importance**—You can set an importance marker to indicate whether a memo is of high, normal, or low importance. High-priority memos have a red exclamation point displayed beside them in the user's mail database. By default, all messages are of

Normal importance. The importance of a message does not affect the speed at which Domino delivers the message.

- **Delivery Report**—This option lets you select what type of notification you receive when your memo is successfully delivered to the recipient's mail file.

- **Delivery Priority**—High-priority mail is always delivered immediately. Normal-priority mail is delivered immediately within your own Domino named network, but if destined for a server in another named network, it is delivered on a schedule determined by the Domino administrator. Low-priority mail is delivered during off-peak hours—usually during the middle of the night, again at the discretion of the administrator.

- **Return Receipt**—If you select this option, Notes generates a memo to you at the moment the addressee opens your memo using a Notes client. That way, you know that the user not only received your memo but actually opened it to read it.

- **Do Not Notify Me if Recipient(s) Are Running Out of Office**—If you select this option, Notes refuses any messages that are received if a individual has the Out of Office feature running. This options prevents the Out of Office message from ever being sent to you.

- **Prevent Copying**—When you select this option, the recipient cannot copy the data in the memo electronically, nor can the recipient print it from a Notes client. This feature also prevents the recipient from forwarding the memo or replying with history.

- **Auto Spellcheck**—If you do not have spell checking turned on as a workstation preference, you can select it for this one document.

- **Sign**—If you select this option, Notes attaches your digital signature to the message. This digital signature provides proof that you, or at least someone using your Notes user ID, created the memo.

- **Encrypt**—If you elect to encrypt this memo, the only person who can read it is the person to whom it is addressed. The memo is encrypted during transit to prevent unauthorized reading.

- **Save These Security Options as the Default**—If you select this, all subsequent memos will have the same delivery options.

- **Mood stamp**—This displays an icon on your memo when it is opened by someone with Notes mail. Examples of icons include Personal, Confidential, Private, and Flame.

- **On the Advanced Delivery Options page, you can stamp the message with a Please Reply By date to indicate time sensitivity**—You also can define an expiration date for the memo and provide an alternative address to which replies should be sent—for example, you might want replies to be collected in a mail-in database. You also can define the display format for Internet messages on this page.

CAUTION

Most of the delivery options increase the size of the memo and the amount of processing needed. It's always a good idea to use the options judiciously and when necessary.

MANAGING YOUR MAIL MESSAGES

You can open your email in several ways. You can locate it on the Favorites bookmark page or on the Mail bookmark. You can follow a link from your Welcome page. From anywhere in Notes, you can click the Quickpick icon in the lower-right corner of the Status bar and select Open Mail.

When you open your mail, the Inbox view is displayed from your mail database that resides on the server. Locate a document that you want to read. Open the document by double-clicking it, or by selecting it and pressing Enter. An example of the inbox with a preview pane opened at the bottom of the screen is shown in Figure 4.6.

Figure 4.6
Open and read a document from the inbox in the Notes mail application.

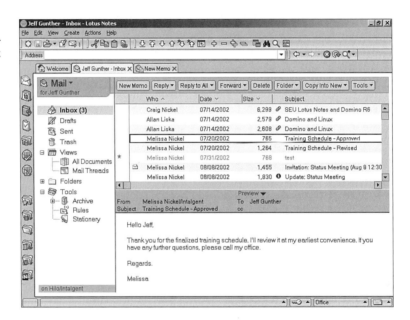

If a message document is open, you can close it by clicking the *X* beside the document name on the Window tab. You can also close the document by pressing the Esc key or by selecting File, Close (Ctrl+W). Notice in Figure 4.6 that some of the documents are preceded by an asterisk and are displayed in a different color. The asterisk indicates that the document is *unread*. An unread document is one that has not yet been opened. You can manipulate the list of unread documents by selecting a document and selecting Edit, Unread Marks. You can then mark a document as read or unread so that you can locate it later.

When you are reading documents in a view, it is easy to move from one document to the next. If a document is opened for reading, you can navigate to other documents as follows:

1. Press Enter to close the current document and open the next document in the view.

2. Press Backspace to see the previous document in the view.

3. Press Tab to view the next document that is marked as unread.

4. Press Shift+Tab to view the previous unread document.

5. Press up- and down-arrow buttons within the View toolbar to view Next, Previous, Next Unread (*), and Previous Unread (*) documents.

You would rightly expect any good email application to handle a couple of other basic email functions. When using Notes 6 email, it is easy to delete documents, and it is easy to reply and forward documents to others.

DELETING DOCUMENTS

To delete a document, press the Delete key while the document is selected in a view or is opened for reading. When you press Delete, the message is moved to the trash for removal. You can then easily change your mind by selecting the Trash folder and marking the documents that you want to keep by selecting them and clicking the Restore action button. Additionally, you can restore all the documents within the trash by clicking the Restore All action button. When you delete mail messages in Release 6, Notes places them in the Trash folder within your mail database. Messages in the Trash folder stay in your database for the time specified in your mail preferences or until you force removal.

You can also delete documents by dragging them to the Trash folder. You can then go to the Trash folder and select Empty Trash, as shown in Figure 4.7.

Figure 4.7
Use the Trash folder to work with documents that are due to be deleted.

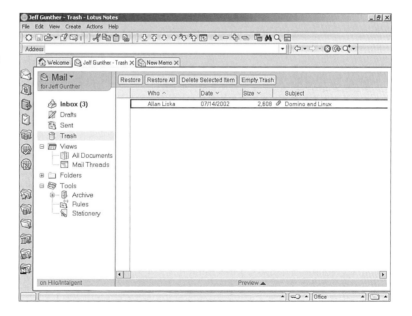

NOTE

You can also use the Empty Trash, Restore, Restore All, and Delete Selected Item action buttons to manage the documents in your Trash folder.

REPLYING TO A MESSAGE

To reply to a message, open the message for reading or select it in the Inbox view. You can reply to a message by selecting one of two action buttons: Reply or Reply to All. Both buttons provide the following four options:

- **Reply**—Creates a response without the original message text to the person who sent the original memo.

- **Reply with History**—Creates a reply that includes a response with the original message text.

- **Reply Without Attachments**—Creates a response with the original message text, but without any of the original file attachments. As a reference to other users, a comment is placed within the body of the reply that details that the attachment was removed.

- **Reply with Internet-Style History**—Creates a reply that includes a copy of the original memo formatted with your preferences of line length and a left margin character. By default, the > character is used on each line of the reply. This reply does not include any of the standard rich-text elements, including file attachments, images, and embedded OLE objects. You change the preferences for this action by selecting File, Preferences, User Preferences, Internet tab.

The primary difference between Reply and Reply to All is that the Reply to All action addresses the memo to everyone who was listed in the To or the cc field in the original message.

You learn how to tailor your message defaults in the next section.

SETTING UP MAIL PREFERENCES

You can define all your mail preferences in a Mail Preferences dialog box. To open this dialog box, click the Tools action button and select Preferences. You can also choose Actions, Tools, and Preferences. The first tab of the Preferences dialog box is shown in Figure 4.8.

Mail preferences consist of the following:

- **Basics**—Enables you to specify the owner of the mail database, choose whether you want an automatic spelling check of outgoing mail, delete preferences for Sent view, and set soft delete expiration time. The Suppress Delete Dialogs for Calendar and Scheduling Items check box curtails Notes from displaying caution messages each time you try to delete a Calendar item, such as a meeting invitation.

- **Letterhead**—Enables you to indicate the graphical letterhead to use when sending email. There are many styles to choose from. Any individual that receives your message via the Internet will not be able to see your personalized letterhead; this is available only to Notes users.

- **Signature**—Enables you to specify a signature in either text or HMTL format. If you choose the check box within the Option tab, this signature is automatically appended at the bottom of your outgoing email.

- **Colors**—Enables you to choose different background and text color combinations to help differentiate between senders.

Figure 4.8
Define spell-checking and owner options on the first page of the Preferences dialog box.

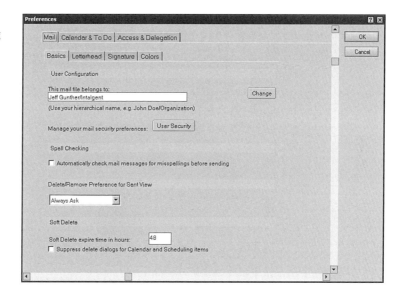

SETTING UP THE BASICS

By default, you are the owner of your own mailbox. However, in some instances you might want to reassign ownership to someone else by selecting that person's name from a Domino Directory using the button beside the field. For example, if a member of senior management wants someone to screen and respond to incoming messages, this feature provides a mechanism to securely reassign ownership.

Another option is to enable or disable automatic spell checking. If this field is enabled, all outgoing mail is checked for misspelled words before being sent.

The Basics tab also includes features regarding the removal and deletion of messages from your inbox. The preferences for Sent view can be changed to enable you to specify whether you are prompted to remove or delete messages from the Sent view. Also, you can define the expiration date for any soft deletions.

DEFINING A LETTERHEAD

You can select from one of the numerous letterheads that come with Notes 6, or you can design your own. The letterhead styles are stored as subforms within the mail databases.

Figure 4.9 shows some of the available letterhead templates that are available on the second tab of the Preferences dialog box.

Figure 4.9
Select a new letter-head from this list of predefined styles, or create your own.

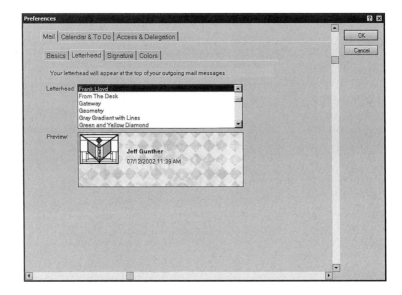

APPENDING A SIGNATURE TO YOUR MEMOS

You've probably seen email messages that have a quote, someone's business address, a bit of humor, or maybe even a copy of an actual signature at the bottom of the message. Well, you can do that, too!

On the Signature tab of the Preferences dialog box, you have the choice of typing a message of your own choosing or referencing an HTML or image file. The Signature tab of the Preferences dialog box is shown in Figure 4.10.

COLORS

The Colors tab enables you to selectively choose up to three color combinations to differentiate mail memos that you receive from individuals. In the Sender Names field, choose a full or partial name and choose a background and text color, as in Figure 4.11. For example, you might choose a black background and white text for messages that come from an important colleague. Using color distinction provides an easy way to manage your incoming messages.

Figure 4.10
Automatically append a signature or quote at the bottom of all your memos.

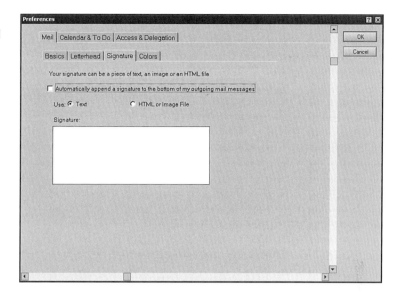

Figure 4.11
Choose a background and text color to provide distinction within your inbox.

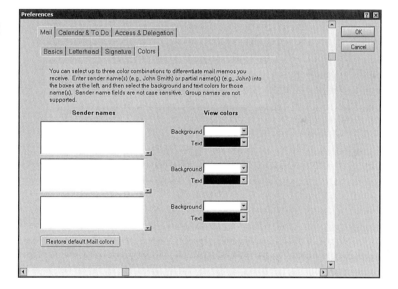

DELEGATING FUNCTIONS IN YOUR MAIL APPLICATION

The Delegation tab of the Preferences dialog box enables you to delegate authority to perform certain functions in your mail application, including mail and calendar delegations. For example, you might have an executive secretary who screens email for you. Before you ever see the mail, the junk mail has been weeded out, and misdirected messages have been forwarded to the appropriate person within your organization. You can delegate functions in your mail application using the page shown in Figure 4.12.

Figure 4.12
Give others the capability to access your mail for certain functions.

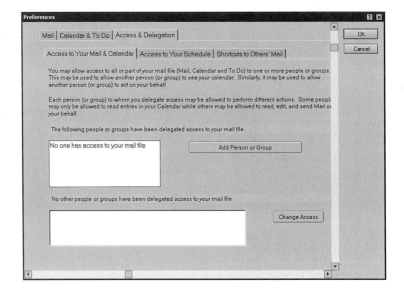

You will notice when you learn about Access Control Lists in Chapter 17, "Access Control Lists (ACLs) and Database Security," that the delegation options closely parallel application security options. You can give specific people or groups the capability to read your mail; read your mail and create new messages using your mail application (that is, under your signature); read, create, and edit messages; and read, create, edit, and delete messages.

When you finish selecting preferences, click OK. Your preferences take effect for all subsequent memos.

USING OTHER MESSAGING FORMS

Notes messaging involves considerably more than just electronic mail. See Chapter 7, "Getting Organized with the Calendaring and Scheduling Features," for details regarding the To Do form. Some of the special message forms are located under the Create, Special menu; others are directly under the Create menu.

CREATING LINK MESSAGES

Unlike an electronic mail message that is simply a snapshot of the document, a *link message* provides the recipient direct access to the most current document. If you want to refer a particular document to an individual, you can create a link message and mail it:

1. Open a document or select the document in a view. Make sure that the document is in a Domino application to which others (the recipient, in particular) have access.

2. Select Create, Special, Link Message.

3. Address the link message to one or more people.

4. Select any special delivery options.

5. Send the link message.

An example of a link message is shown in Figure 4.13.

Figure 4.13
Create and send a link to a document using the Link Message form.

When recipients receive a link message via their inbox, they can open the linked document by clicking the DocLink, which looks like a small document icon. You can handle links in a couple of other ways, even if you don't want to use the link message document. In any rich-text field, you can create a DocLink to a Notes document or a hyperlink to a Web page. To create a DocLink to a Notes document, follow these steps:

1. Open the document to which you want to create a link, or select the document in a view.

2. Select Edit, Copy as Link, and select the type of link you want to create. The link is copied onto the Clipboard.

3. Switch to the document where you want to place the link. Make sure that the document is in edit mode.

4. Position the cursor where you want the link placed. Verify that the cursor is in a rich-text field rather than a simple text field.

5. Select Edit, Paste (Ctrl+V).

The types of DocLinks you can create include the following:

- **Document link**
- **View link**—This takes whoever clicks on the link to a view rather than to a specific document. For example, if you want to provide a recipient with a link to a list of documents rather than a specific document, use a view link.
- **Database link**—This takes the user to the default view of a Domino application rather than to a specific view or document.
- **Anchor link**—This takes the user to a specific location within a document, including a specific location within the document that is currently open.

Links work when accessed with a Notes client or from a Web browser. If you want to create a link to a Web page, a couple of approaches will work, depending on your circumstances:

- You can open the Web page and copy the URL into memory. Then return to Notes, select Text, and select Create, Hotspot, Link Hotspot.
- You can create a Personal Web Navigator application on a Domino server and create a DocLink to a document in that application. In the Personal Web Navigator, Web pages are saved as Notes documents, so they can be read offline.

When you have created a link hotspot of any sort, you can use the Link Properties info box to modify the appearance of the link.

PHONE MESSAGES

Phone messages can be taken and routed with a simple form designed specifically for the purpose of tracking phone calls. The Phone Message form is shown in Figure 4.14.

Figure 4.14
Save paper by creating an email version of a phone message.

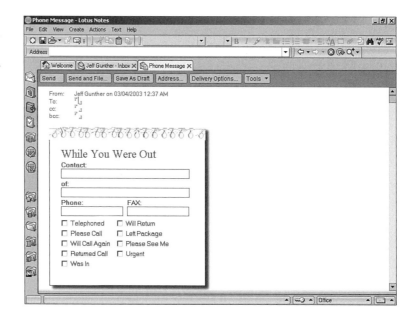

Not visible on the Phone Message form in Figure 4.13, but visible if you scroll down, is a rich-text field in which you can enter a detailed message. You can access this form by selecting Create, Special, Phone Message from the menu bar.

CREATING AND USING STATIONERY

In Notes terms, stationery is an email template that you can reuse. For example, in your office, you might get a reminder notice every two weeks that your time sheets must be turned in before you can get paid. The only thing that changes from one pay period to the next is the deadline for turning in time sheets.

This is an ideal application for stationery. To create stationery, do the following:

1. Switch to the Stationery view under the Tools folder on the left side of the screen.

2. Click the New action button and choose Stationery—Memo or Stationery—Personal.

3. Create a memo that you want to be able to reuse.

4. Click Save.

5. Enter a name for your stationery, as shown in Figure 4.15.

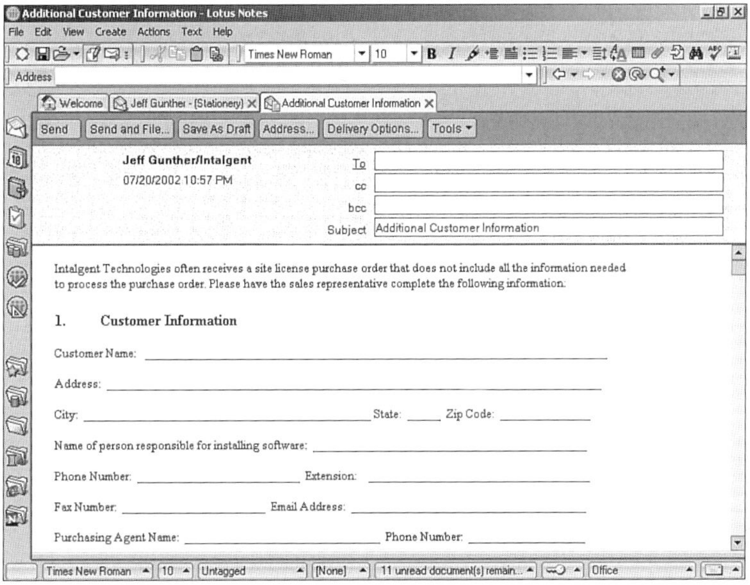

Figure 4.15
Create a memo and save it as Memo Stationery.

The stationery is saved in the Stationery folder under the Memo Stationery category. If you don't like any of the letterheads provided with Notes, you also have the option of creating your own personal stationery. From within the Stationery folder, click the New action button and select Stationery—Personal. The Personal Stationery template has two extra rich-text fields that can be used for inserting your own graphics and text, as shown in Figure 4.16.

Figure 4.16
Create personal stationery, which has two extra rich-text fields for inserting text and graphics of your choice.

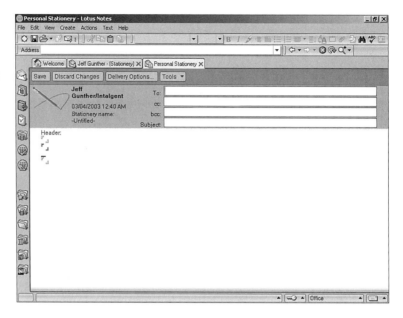

4

After you have created your stationery, you can use it at any time. To create a new memo using your stationery, follow these steps:

1. Open the Stationery folder under the Tools folder.

2. Click the New button and select New Memo, Using Stationery. A Selection dialog box is displayed. Alternatively, you can select Actions, Tools, New Memo, Using Stationery from the Inbox.

3. Select the stationery that you want to use in your new memo. A new memo is displayed using your stationery template.

4. Modify any information you want, and send the memo just like a normal memo.

ARCHIVING

You can set up archiving for the mail application just as you can with any other Notes application. Archiving copies documents to an archive database and deletes the documents from the original application.

Archiving can be manual or automatic, based on the criteria you define in your archiving profile. To set up an archiving profile, open the Inbox view, click the Tools action button, and choose Archive Settings. The Archive Settings dialog box is displayed, as shown in Figure 4.17.

Figure 4.17
The Archive Settings
dialog box enables
you to define how
documents are
archived.

The Archive Settings dialog box contains the following tabs:

- **Basics**—Enables you to choose how archiving will take place on this database and where the archive database resides (locally or on the server).
- **Settings**—Allows you to enable archiving for the database and create, edit, and delete archive criteria. By clicking the Add or Edits button, you can choose an archive database, choose a clean-up procedure, and control the document selection criteria.
- **Advanced**—Contains various settings that enable you to specify the database in which all logs are deposited, enable or disable documents that have responses, and schedule when archiving will take place.

USING MAIL TOOLS

If you check under the Actions menu, you'll find many special mail tools. Some are found directly under the Actions menu, while others are found under the Tools submenu. The options are simply various tools that you can use to make it easier to use your email. This section reviews these tools.

ADD RECIPIENTS

When you receive an email that is addressed to a group of users, you might want to add those users to your Personal Address Book or to a group calendar. For example, if you receive an email addressed to everyone within a team, you can easily add the team members to a single group in your address book. Simply open the email and choose Actions, Add Recipients to New Group in Address Book. The individuals are added to the address book, and a new group is created. All you have to do is name the group. For example, a team could be named Quality Assurance; then an mail to everyone on the quality assurance team would be sent by addressing your memo to Quality Assurance.

ADD SENDER TO ADDRESS BOOK

This is a corollary to adding recipients to the Personal Address Book. When you receive email from someone you want to add to your Personal Address Book, choose Actions, Tools,

Add Sender to Address Book. The person's name and email address are added to your address book automatically. You can later return to your address book to enter additional information about the individual.

OUT OF OFFICE

Wouldn't it be nice to take a vacation and not come back to the office to face dozens of unanswered email messages? You can set up an Out of Office agent that automatically informs people that you are not in the office. If people know that you are not answering your email, your mailbox will be a lot less full when you return.

To create an Out of Office profile, choose Actions, Tools, Out of Office. The dialog box is displayed in Figure 4.18.

Figure 4.18
Define a profile to automatically reply to email while you are out of the office.

The Out of Office profile lets you do any of the following:

- Enter the dates you will be out of the office
- Book busy time in your calendar during those dates
- Create a message that is sent to people the first time they email you while you are out of the office
- Create a special message for specific individuals
- Identify people who should not be sent your out-of-office message

The Out of Office profile does not take effect until you enable it. You can toggle between Enabled and Disabled by clicking on the Enable/Disable button. When the profile is enabled and you are out of the office, messages that come into your mailbox on your home server are answered automatically based on the parameters in your Out of Office profile.

SEND MEMO TO DATABASE MANAGER

This creates a new memo addressed to anyone who is listed as Manager in the Access Control List (ACL) for the currently open database. The To field is the only one filled in. You are responsible for filling in the body of the message.

Because you are the Manager for your own mail database, it wouldn't make much sense to use this option while you have your mail open. However, when you have another database open and are having access problems, you don't always know who to ask for help. This option ensures that your memo goes to the correct person.

SETTING UP RULES FOR HANDLING MAIL

Rules can be configured and set up to allow easier handling of incoming email. Rules are similar to macros that perform certain actions based on the rules that are defined and enabled. When you select the Rules view under the Tools folder, a list of all your current rules is displayed. You can change the order in which the rules are applied by moving them farther up or down the list so that they are applied before or after other rules. To create a new rule, select the Rules folder and click the New Rule action button to display the New Rule dialog box, shown in Figure 4.19.

Figure 4.19
Define rules for handling email messages on the New Rule screen.

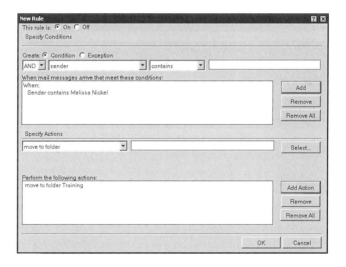

SPECIFYING CONDITIONS

You can build the conditions for a rule using the helper buttons on the New Rule screen. First, you must specify the part of an email message to examine. The choices include any of the following:

Sender

Subject

Body

Importance

Delivery Priority

To

CC

BCC

To or cc

Body or Subject

Internet Domain

Size (in Kbytes)

All Documents

Next, you have to specify whether you want to test the field to see if it contains or is a specified value. You then enter the value you are looking for and click Add to add the condition to the list of conditions.

Subsequent conditions enables you to specify whether the action uses AND logic or OR logic. You can delete a condition by highlighting that line and clicking the Remove button, or you can remove all conditions and start over from scratch.

SPECIFYING ACTIONS

You specify actions in a similar manner to how you specify conditions. You can specify a folder to which you want to move or copy the message, you can promote or demote the importance of the document, or you can have the message automatically deleted.

Before you click OK to save the rule, notice at the top of the New Rule page that you can click a button to enable or disable the rule.

USING OTHER SOFTWARE PACKAGES WITH NOTES

Although you are using Lotus Notes mail, you have the option to use alternative document editors, and you can access a Notes mail database using another mail program such as Microsoft Exchange. To use an alternative editor, select File, Preferences, User Preferences. Navigate to the Mail and News tab and select an alternative mail editor from a list of compatible word processors installed on your workstation.

To use Microsoft Exchange to access a Notes mail database, the Domino administrator must create a profile that lets you use Notes service providers for the Messaging Application Programming Interface (MAPI). This is done during setup of the Domino server.

After you are set up for MAPI mail, you can send mail as usual, selecting the profile for the Notes service provider. Addressing is done using the address book that you specified in your Notes service provider profile. You can use the Exchange interface to access the Notes mail database. You can actually use the Exchange commands to create, send, and read mail; you also can address mail using an Exchange address book, but it must be resolved using a Domino Directory. You also can use the Notes mail database to store your mail. You're able to do virtually anything that you can in Notes except verify the signature on encrypted data.

MAIL AND MESSAGING STANDARDS

Notes is a standards-based mail platform with a universal mail client. The Notes mail features previously described exist entirely within the Notes environment, but Lotus supports other mail clients and protocols, including the POP3/IMAP protocols described later in this chapter.

The Domino server includes support for the following:

- IMAP protocol support lets users with an IMAP client program such as Netscape Navigator client read Notes mail databases that are stored on a Domino server.
- LDAP V2 Protocol RFC 1777 is supported for searching for resources with an LDAP directory. A subset of LDAP object classes is supported for searching, including Person, Organizational Person, GroupOfNames, Organization, and OrganizationalUnit.
- MIME support is available for Internet mail. The mail router stores incoming Internet mail messages as attachments to ensure that message integrity is maintained. This functionality is optional. Appended messages are also stored as attachments.

USING POP3/IMAP INTERNET PROTOCOL MAIL

You have the option of using Internet mail as your default mail database. You can use Internet mail even if you are running the Notes client without a Domino server. You pick up your Internet mail from your ISP or from your own POP3/IMAP mail server, and you can share the same mail database with your Notes mail. Outgoing mail can go through an SMTP server or through the Domino server.

To set up POP3 or IMAP mail, you create or modify a location document in your Personal Address Book that defines the database in which incoming mail is stored. This database appears on the Replicator page and gathers mail from your ISP when you select Send and Receive Mail from the Replicator page or connect using a replication schedule. You can also collect your mail using a menu command. Outgoing mail is sent through SMTP if you are connected to the Internet when the mail is created. Otherwise, the outgoing mail is held in an outgoing mailbox (SMTP.BOX, based on the MAILBOX.NTF template) until you connect to the Internet again.

The Notes mail client supports Multipurpose Internet Mail Extensions (MIME) for both outgoing and incoming mail from the Internet. That means that you and Internet mail recipients will both see mail with full fidelity. Notes also supports Secure Multipurpose Internet Mail Extensions (S/MIME) for sending and receiving encrypted mail.

CHAPTER 5

WORKING WITH TEXT AND DOCUMENTS

In this chapter

UNDERSTANDING DOCUMENTS

Notes is a document-centric system. All data is stored in documents. When you create a new document, it is given a unique identity the instant you save it.

Part of the data stored in a document includes the name of the form that should be used to display and format the document the next time it is opened. The form might or might not be the same one that was used to guide you in creating the document. If the original form was designed with a field named Form (usually a hidden field), the form identified in that field will be used to display the document when it is next opened.

You can create documents using a variety of forms within Lotus Notes. An application designer can assign a number of data types to a field. Examples of data types include text, rich text, time, and numeric. The form usually also contains a variety of design elements, such as graphics, static text, buttons and hotspots, and hidden header fields that can contain vital data to determine how the document is processed. Every application has its own forms.

Forms include everything from email forms and simple discussion forms to complex work-flow forms that change dynamically as you enter data and route your completed document to others for approval or further action. There are hundreds of forms. Some come from standard Notes templates, and some are custom built.

ANATOMY OF A DOCUMENT

A form gives underlying structure to every document in a Domino database. By selecting the form used to display the document, you can change the appearance and the logic of how the document is rendered. In other words, the raw data is the important component. The form is used to format and present the data in the document. The information is organized into documents as a convenient way to package and deliver information to the person using the data.

An example of a discussion document is shown in Figure 5.1. Note that the document contains a variety of graphics and static text on the form. The text entered into editable fields is the data that has been entered into this form.

The data within a document can come from practically anywhere. It can be retrieved from an enterprise system running on a mainframe computer or an AS/400, for example. It can be downloaded from the Internet, or it can be picked up from another Domino database. It can be inherited from another document, and (of course) it can be entered directly into the form when you create a new document.

Graphical design
elements   Static text

Figure 5.1
A document is raw
data entered into and
displayed via a form.

Editable text (data)

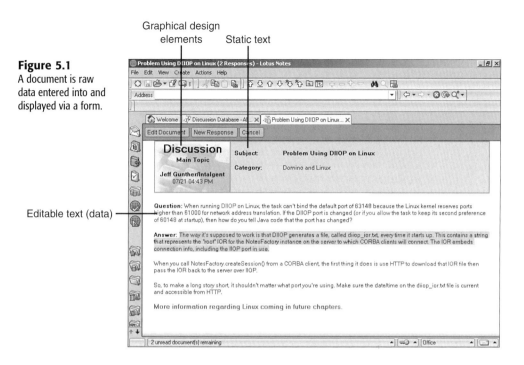

WORKING WITH TEXT

Virtually any data other than graphics that is stored in a Domino database can be considered "text" in one form or another. The designer of an application determines how information is displayed. The designer defines which form is used and selects the appearance and data type of all fields on the form. By defining the data type for each field, the application designer determines whether the text in a particular field will be formatted and stored as a date, a username, simple alphanumeric text, rich text, or even HTML. In this chapter, we are concerned mostly with plain text and rich text.

STATIC TEXT VERSUS DOCUMENT-SPECIFIC TEXT

When you look at a form before any data has been entered into it, you will see two things in addition to any design elements such as graphics and tables. You will see *static text*, which provides a context for users and guides them to the parts of the form where they need to enter data, and you will see *fields*, the predefined areas on the form where users can enter data. The static text is part of the form; any document created and displayed with the same form will have the same static text.

Data is input and displayed using the form. When you create a new document, some fields might already be filled in by inheriting data from a parent document or as the result of a formula. Other fields will be empty, awaiting your input.

With Notes, the location of input fields might not always be apparent. For some types of fields, you might see only a cursor to indicate where data should be entered. Other fields might be displayed as rectangular input areas, as bracketed fields (as with earlier versions of Notes), or as various selection-type fields, such as radio buttons, check boxes, or list boxes. The Calendar Entry form in Figure 5.2 illustrates various types of input fields that are available in Notes.

Figure 5.2
The appearance of the input field depends on how the form was designed.

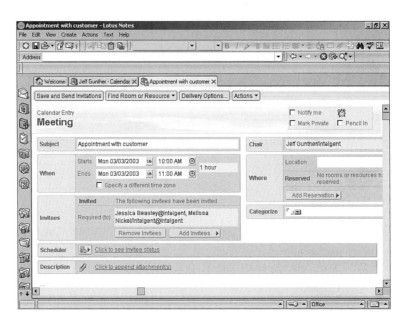

FIELD DATA TYPES

Most data can be displayed on the computer screen as text. When you input data, it is displayed on the screen as you type. But the type of data allowed in a field depends on how the field was defined by the application designer. The data types include the following:

- Text
- Date/time
- Number
- Dialog list
- Check box
- Radio button
- List box
- Combo box
- Rich text
- Authors

- Names
- Readers
- Passwords
- Formulas

With the exception of rich text, an end user has no control over how information is displayed. The application designer defines the layout and appearance of the information in a field.

NOTE

Some fields remain hidden from users, even though they might hold information such as that used in calculations or identifying information unique to a document. For example, reader or author fields and password fields are usually hidden. Other fields are hidden in certain circumstances. Some information might be hidden when a document is printed on the Web, for example, although it is not hidden when seen through Notes.

EDITING TEXT VERSUS VIEWING TEXT

When you view a document, the text cannot be edited unless you are in *edit mode*. Some text that is visible while editing or creating a document might be hidden when the document is being viewed, and vice versa. When you create a new document, it is automatically in edit mode. When you open a document that has previously been created and saved, it usually is in read mode. If you have document-editing privileges (defined in the Access Control List), you can put the document into edit mode by pressing Ctrl+E or by double-clicking anywhere in the document's whitespace. Another popular way to put the document in edit mode is to click Actions, Edit Document. An application developer might have added an Edit action button that can be clicked.

WORKING WITH RICH TEXT

Rich text is essentially a free-form field. You can add and delete text just as you can with a regular text field. However, you can also do any of the following with rich text:

- Format the text
- Change the font, size, and color of the text
- Format paragraphs
- Apply styles and add links
- Insert or embed graphics and objects, such as spreadsheets
- Create tables
- Attach files

5

In short, you can let your imagination loose and create the same sort of pages that you would with a word processor or page-layout program.

Three simple signals tell you when you are in a rich-text field:

- You can use all the options on the Text menu.
- If you've added the Font and Font Size items to the Status bar at the bottom of the Notes environment, the name and size of the font are displayed.
- You can right-click anywhere in the field to see a floating menu that offers Text Properties as the first option.

If you choose Text Properties from the floating menu, you see the Text Properties box. The first tab of the Text Properties box is shown in Figure 5.3.

Figure 5.3
The Text Properties box is used to define the appearance of text.

The following sections discuss the text-editing features available on the different pages in the Text Properties box.

WORKING WITH FONTS

5

In the Text Properties box, you can see that the default font for Lotus Notes is 10-point Default Sans Serif, which is designed for easy online reading. You can change to another font of another point size by scrolling through the font and size windows in the Text Properties box. Directly beneath the Size box is a control that lists the current font size. Clicking the down or up arrows next to the current size decreases or increases the font size a single step at a time. As with most word processors, when you change to a new font attribute, the attribute is effective from that point forward. However, if you have text selected, only the selected text is changed to the new attributes. You can change the font style to include a variety of attributes, as shown in Figure 5.3.

NOTE

Some of the common font attributes are available from the drop-down Text menu and from the floating menu (right-click). You can also select bold, italic, and underline attributes using keyboard shortcuts (for example, Ctrl+B to select bold, Ctrl+I to select italic, and Ctrl+U to select underline).

You can select a new color by clicking the color control. A panel is displayed so that you can select from up to 256 colors or create your own color using the color wheel button.

USING THE PERMANENT PEN

After you define unique font attributes on the Font tab of the Text Properties box, you can select Text, Permanent Pen, Set Permanent Pen Style to set a Permanent Pen style. The attributes that you currently have selected become your new Permanent Pen font.

The Permanent Pen enables you to type anywhere within a document in a unique font. For example, suppose you want to annotate a document, as shown in Figure 5.4, and then forward the document with your annotations. You want to make sure that your annotations are in a unique font, so you click the Permanent Pen from the Edit Document toolbar and begin typing. Everything that you type from then on will be in your Permanent Pen font—for example, red italics in a larger point size. Move the cursor to a new location, and you will still be in your Permanent Pen font. It is like picking up a red pen, for example, and editing a document.

Figure 5.4
The Permanent Pen displays your selected font wherever you start typing.

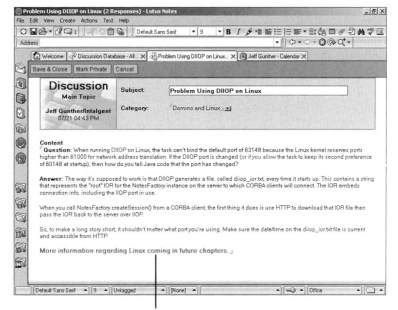

Text created using permanent pen

If a document is being routed to several members of a workgroup, each can use a unique Permanent Pen font so that everyone can see who inserted which text into the document.

NOTE

You can toggle the Permanent Pen by clicking the Permanent Pen button or by selecting Permanent Pen from the Text menu.

USING THE HIGHLIGHTER

Somewhat similar to the Permanent Pen is the Highlighter function. The Highlighter is not available from the Text Properties info box; it is available from the Text menu (select Text, Highlighter) only when a document is in edit mode. With the Highlighter activated, you can hold down the left mouse button and drag the cursor over text to highlight it in yellow, pink, or blue, just as you would when highlighting text using a highlighter pen. This is shown in Figure 5.5.

Figure 5.5
Use the Highlighter to mark text as you would with a high-lighter pen.

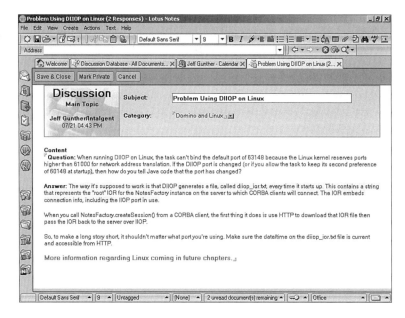

5

To highlight text, drag the Highlighter from left to right. To erase the highlights, drag from right to left.

PARAGRAPH FORMATTING

The Paragraph Alignment tab of the Text Properties box enables you to control paragraph formatting. This tab is shown in Figure 5.6.

On the first line, you can set the paragraph alignment to flush left, centered, flush right, or fully justified. You can also turn off justification. Normally, when you type using the Domino Editor, text wraps automatically to the width of the screen. This is true no matter what type of justification you set. Full justification wraps at 3 inches if you have your editing window set to 3 inches in size (by using the Minimize button in the top-right corner of the workspace), and it wraps at 7 inches if your screen has 7 inches of workspace.

With fully justified text, the Domino Editor pads word spacing so that both ends of the line to the edge of the editing window remain justified. When you turn off justification, there is no line wrapping until you get to the maximum line length.

Figure 5.6
The Paragraph Alignment tab of the Text Properties box is used to format paragraphs.

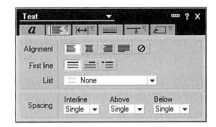

The second item on this controls the indentation of the first line of text in paragraphs. If the cursor is in a paragraph, or if any portion of the paragraph is selected, the indent rules are applied to that paragraph.

You can set your paragraphs so that they have no indent, so that they are indented to the first tab (.5 inches by default), or so that the paragraph has a hanging indent (that is, the first line hangs out to the left of the remainder of the paragraph). To change the indent, simply place the cursor in a paragraph and click the icon representing the type of indentation you want.

The next item is a drop-down field that is used to control the appearance of *lists*. Lists can include a variety of characters, such as numbered text, bulleted text with solid bullets, circles, solid squares, check boxes for To Do lists, and upper- or lowercase alpha characters. You can also turn off bullets by clicking the Bullet button.

You can also create a list, within a list, within a list, within a list. For example, you can start a numbered list and then click the Text Indent button to indent a line. A new numbering series is started on the indented line, or you can change the line to bullets. You can restart the previous numbering sequence by clicking the Text Outdent button.

The next paragraph setting on the Paragraph Alignment tab of the Text Properties box is used to set line and paragraph spacing. You can set interline spacing so that a paragraph is single spaced, spaced at 1 1/2 lines, or double spaced. You can also offset the paragraph from the one above it by 1, 1 1/2, or 2 lines. You can set a paragraph apart from the one following it by the same increments.

TIP

Interparagraph spacing is especially useful if you want to set off bulleted text from the main body of your typing. For example, you can have the regular paragraph spacing set to double spacing, but the bulleted text can be set off by 1 1/2 spaces from the text above and below. For certain international settings, you can also define the reading order of text—left to right or right to left.

PAGINATION

The Paragraph Margins tab of the Text Properties box is used to set pagination and tabs. With pagination, you can define whether a paragraph should start on a new page; whether it should be kept on a single page without breaking, if possible; and whether it should be kept on the same page as the next paragraph. Pagination relates to text only when it is printed because there are no pages in a scrolling document.

SETTING BORDERS

The Paragraph Border tab of the Text Properties box is also used to set paragraph borders. Borders enable you to customize the format and the look/feel of the paragraph. Many elements of a paragraph's border can be modified, including style and thickness, color, drop shadow, and spacing control.

SETTING TABS WITH THE RULER BAR

You can do more customizing of margins and tab settings using the Ruler bar. To display the Ruler bar, select View, Ruler, or click the Ruler button or press Ctrl+R.

The left side of the ruler represents the left margin. You can drag the top triangle to set the first line of a paragraph to a new location. You can drag the bottom triangle to set the location of all other lines in the paragraph. You can drag both the top and bottom triangles by dragging them from the small rectangle beneath the two triangles.

You can set tabs by clicking the ruler at the location where you want a tab. The tab setting applies to the paragraph where the cursor is located and any paragraphs that are at least partly selected.

You can remove tabs by clicking directly on them. You can move tabs by holding down the mouse button while pointing at the tab. Slide the tab to its new position, and then release the mouse button.

By default, there is a tab every half-inch, although they do not show on the Ruler bar. If you set any tabs, the default half-inch tabs begin to the right of the last tab that you set. When you click the Ruler bar using the left mouse button, a left tab is set at the spot. With a left tab, your typing is left-justified from the tab setting. If you click the ruler with the right mouse button, a floating menu appears from which you can select a left tab, a right tab, a centered tab, or a decimal tab. A right tab causes text to be right-justified from the tab setting. Text is centered with a center tab. With a decimal tab, text is justified on a decimal—for example, when you are typing a column of prices.

TIP

> You can also set margins using the Paragraph Margins tab of the Text Properties box. You can set absolute margins from the left edge of the page, such as 1" and 7". You can also set relative margins as a percentage of the page width. For example, the default left margin is 13% and the right margin is 100%.

HIDING PARAGRAPHS

As mentioned earlier, text is hidden under certain circumstances. Text can be hidden under any of the following conditions, using the Paragraph Hide When tab in the Text Properties box:

- **Hide from Notes R4.6 Clients or Later**—If you are using advanced functionality, such as embedded Java or programs that depend on newer LotusScript functions, you can hide that portion of your document. Or, you might have instructions for workarounds that are explicit to users of earlier versions of Notes. This function is commonly used to hide parts of the document from Notes clients when functionality is put in especially for Web clients.

- **Hide from Web Browsers**—You might have information that is intended for Notes users but not for people who access the same page using a Web browser. If you highlight the paragraph and click Web Browsers, the paragraph will not be visible when the document is viewed from the Web.

- **Hide from Mobile**—You might have information that is intended for Notes client users but not for people who access the same page using a mobile device such as a handheld or wireless device. If you highlight the paragraph and click Mobile, the paragraph will not be visible when the document is viewed from mobile devices.

- **Hide When Document Is Previewed for Reading**—You can adjust a Notes view so that you can preview documents without opening them. To make the preview more meaningful, you might want to hide unessential design elements so that the previewer can quickly have a meaningful idea about the content of your document.

- **Hide When Opened for Reading**—You can use this to hide text that is intended only as annotation or instructions while the document is being edited or created. If text is hidden when opened for reading, it is automatically hidden when printed as well.

- **Hide When Printed**—This option can be used to prevent information from being printed. For example, you might have information intended to be read only when a document is accessed online so that you can hide it when the document is printed.

- **Hide When Embedded**—This option can be used to prevent embedded information from being displayed.

- **Hide When Previewed for Editing**—You can do limited editing when accessing a document through the preview pane. Hiding text with this option is the way to limit what can be edited from the preview pane.

- **Hide When Opened for Editing**—With this option, you can have information that is visible to someone reading the document, but the information is hidden from anyone who is editing the document. For example, you might have a standard template in which only certain paragraphs are edited. The remainder of the template can be hidden to avoid confusion for the editors.

CAUTION

> As a document creator or editor, you cannot hide an entire field when the document is being edited. The first and last paragraphs in the field must remain unhidden. You can make these lines blank as a workaround if you want to hide the entire contents of a rich-text field.

5

- **Hide When Copied to the Clipboard**—This option enables you to be sure that somebody does not copy confidential text and paste it into another document in an unsecured database. If you check this and Hide When Printed, the only way data can be copied from the document is to do a screen print or gain Editor access to the document.

- **Hide Paragraph If Formula Is True**—You can create a formula that tests for the presence or absence of a certain value and hides the paragraph when the formula's criteria are met.

→ **See** Chapter 18, "Working with Formulas, Functions, and Commands," **p. 465** for details about formulas.

TIP

> You can hide text using the Text Properties box. Most of the hide-when options are displayed as simple check boxes.
>
> Place the cursor anywhere in the paragraph that you want to hide. Click the appropriate check box. The text will be hidden under the checked conditions the next time the document is opened after it has been saved. Hide-when is used extensively by designers to show certain parts of the form under certain conditions, but it is not likely to be used much by end users when working with documents.

USING TEXT STYLES

It has taken a lot of work to get this far. Imagine what it would be like if you had to go through every step in the Text Properties box for every paragraph in every document! It would hardly be worth it. Well, I have some good news for you. When you get a paragraph to work just the way you want it, you can save the text attributes as a style. The style can then be applied to other paragraphs within the same document. You even have the option of using the same style for other documents in the same Domino database or in other databases on the same workstation.

CREATING A TEXT STYLE

To create a new style, you first format a paragraph that has all the attributes you want in your style. You then highlight the paragraph and save it as a style. When saved, the style can be applied to other paragraphs. To save a new style, complete the following steps:

1. Select the text whose attributes you want to save as a style. All you have to do is place the cursor anywhere in the paragraph that you want to make into a style.

2. On the Style Tag tab of the Text Properties box, click Create Style.

   The Create Paragraph Style dialog box is displayed (see Figure 5.7).

Figure 5.7
Define your new style in the Create Paragraph Style dialog box.

3. Enter a name for your style.

4. Indicate whether you want to include the font in the named style (default), whether to make the style available to all documents in the Domino database, and whether to include the style in the Style Cycle key (see the next section, "Applying Styles to Text," for a discussion of the Cycle key).

5. When you are done, click OK to save the style.

APPLYING STYLES TO TEXT

After you select a paragraph, you can apply a named style to a paragraph in four ways:

- From the Text menu, select Apply Style and select the style that you want to apply.
- Click the Cycle button to cycle through any styles that have been assigned to the Text Style Cycle key, or press F11 to cycle through the styles.
- Select the style from the Style indicator near the left side of the Status bar, near the font and size indicators. Remember that this is available to you only if you chose to add this item to your Status bar.
- Select Text, Text Properties from the menu bar. Click the Paragraph Styles tab and choose a style from the Paragraph Styles listing.

If you decide later that you want to assign or remove a style from the Text Style Cycle key, follow these steps:

1. Open the Text Properties box.
2. Click the Assign to Keyboard button on the Style Tags page.
3. Select or deselect styles from the list.
4. Click OK to save your changes.

The Assign Style to Keyboard dialog box is shown in Figure 5.8.

5

Figure 5.8
Place a check beside styles that you want to assign to the Cycle key.

If you want to redefine a style, select a paragraph to which the style has been assigned. Edit the text attributes to what you want, and then click the Redefine Styles button. The new attributes are applied to all paragraphs defined with that style.

USING LINKS IN RICH-TEXT FIELDS

In a rich-text field, you can insert hypertext links to Web pages, Notes documents, Notes views, and Domino databases. You can also include anchor links to text within the same document.

Based on the link type, Notes deals with each link and its intended target. Whether the link is to a Web site, a Notes document, a view, or a database, the Notes client will send you to the appropriate destination.

Creating a link to a Notes document or to a Web page opened through the Personal Web Navigator involves the same basic process:

1. Go to the location to which you want to link.
2. Select Edit, Copy as Link, and select Anchor Link (not available for Web pages), Document Link, View Link, or Database Link.
3. Return to the Notes document where you want to place the link.
4. Select the text (or a graphic) that you want to turn into a link.
5. Select Create, Hotspot, Link Hotspot.
6. The Hotspot Resource Link box is displayed, as shown in Figure 5.9. You can modify the link appearance and properties.

To create a URL link to a Web page opened outside Notes (for example, a page opened in Internet Explorer), copy the URL for the page while in your Web browser. Return to Notes, highlight the text that you want as a hotspot, and select Create, Hotspot, Link Hotspot, as you did previously. Paste the URL into the Value field of the Hotspot inbox.

You can tailor a link using the Hotspot Resource Link info box, shown in Figure 5.9.

Figure 5.9
Set attributes for a
link in the Hotspot
Resource Link box.

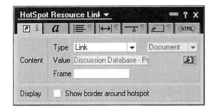

The link can be a Notes link, a URL link, or a named element link (that is, a page, a form, a frameset, or a view). The Value field holds the name of the link, whether it is a URL or a DocLink, a formula, or the name of a named element. The Frame field identifies in which frame the linked document or element should be displayed.

On the Hotspot Extra HTML tab of the Hotspot Resource Link box, you can define HTML tags to control the appearance and behavior of the link when it is viewed using a Web browser. The other pages enable you to define the text attributes of the linked text, just as you would define the attributes of any other text. To remove a link, put the document in edit mode and place the cursor on the link. Select Hotspot, Remove Hotspot.

WORKING WITH TABLES

If you are familiar with tables in version 4.x of Notes, you are in for a treat with tables here. Features include alignment of tables, collapsible and tabbed tables, gradient colors, drop shadows, backgrounds, and autoresizing of columns based on the text included in the cells. Figure 5.10 illustrates some of the features of tables.

Figure 5.10
Tables offer a rich
variety of graphical
features.

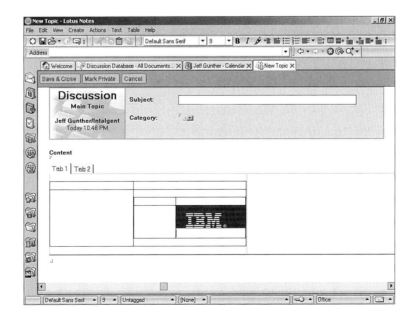

You can create a table in a rich-text field by clicking the Insert Table button within the Table toolbar, or by selecting Create, Table from the drop-down menu. Select the number of rows and columns for your table in the Create Table dialog box; you can also select the type of table. The following types of tables can be created:

- Basic table
- Tabbed table
- Table with collapsible sections
- Animated table
- Table within a table
- Programmable tables

After the table is created, you can add colors, change the width of columns, stack rows, insert graphics, embed other tables, and so forth.

TIP

> Info boxes are available for anything that you can assign attributes to in Notes. To open any Property info box, do one of the following: Select the item and click the Properties button within the Universal toolbar, right-click the item and select Properties from the floating menu, or select Properties from the menu for the selected item.

To modify the attributes of a table, you use the Table Properties box. Moving from tab to tab to complete the following tasks:

- Define the size of the table, the rows, and the cells within the table. Experiment with a variety of sizing options on the Table Layout tab.
- Define the borders of the cells. Borders can be colored; they can be made solid, ridged, or grooved; or they can be made selectively invisible by making the cell border the same color as the cell background. This is done on the Cell Borders tab.
- Define the color of cells, rows, or the entire table. You can add color gradients and a drop shadow. These are done on the Table/Cell Background tab.
- Define table borders similarly to the way you defined borders for individual cells. This is done on the Table Borders tab.
- Set absolute margins from the edges of the page, as you can with text, on the Table Margins tab.
- Set the row attributes, including height, and define whether rows are fixed or expandable (for example, Don't Wrap) and where in the row text is displayed on the Table Rows tab.
- On the Table Programming tab, define HTML tags for the entire table, for individual rows, or for cells to give you more control over how the table is displayed on the Web.

5

You have a lot of control over the table. For example, depending on the type of table you create, you can collapse the table, if you want. With a collapsible table, you can show a single row and have the next row appear when the user clicks the table. You can set the table so that it starts automatically, with a timer that is set in milliseconds. You can have the table cycle through each row once when the document is first loaded, or when the table is first clicked. With any of the cycle options, you can set a number of transition effects. You can also select Tabs or name the different rows and have them displayed based on the contents of a field.

TIP

Table attributes can be used in a number of ways. Just to get you thinking, here are a few of my ideas. You can create banner ads, a stock ticker, or a display of inspirational thoughts. You can create an effect such as an animated GIF, you can display credits, or you can display information that reinforces company policies.

WORKING WITH GRAPHICS IN RICH-TEXT FIELDS

You can insert graphics into rich-text fields, and you can then manipulate those graphics using the Picture Properties box. You can do the following to a picture:

- Change the size of the graphic
- Set the position of the graphic so that text wraps around it (float left) or so that it spans multiple lines of text
- Create alternative text for display through a Web browser, and define the alternative text as a caption

The technique for floating a picture is shown in Figure 5.11.

To work with a graphic, select Create, Picture. Or, you can import a graphic using File, Import. Click the picture and open the Picture Properties box by selecting Picture, Picture Properties from the menu bar.

TIP

You will get better results if you insert rather than import a picture. Importing can distort the color palette, giving you unpredictable results. If you will be using pictures on the Web, you might want to select Use Web Palette from the Advanced Options portion of the Notes Preferences dialog box (choose File, Preferences, User Preferences) to ensure that graphics are optimized for the Web.

Most of the options in the Picture Properties box are the same as text options, except for the Picture Info tab (refer to Figure 5.11). On this page, you have the following options:

- **Text Wrap**—You can set the position of a picture as left, right, or center using text alignment. But you can also align or wrap text. The alignment options include Top,

Center, Baseline, and Bottom, which describe the position of a single line of text beside the picture. If you choose Float Image Left or Float Image Right, the picture will be on the left or right side of the picture, with text wrapped around it. You can also place text to the side of the picture by selecting Span Lines.

- **Scaling**—Scaling is used to change the size and proportions of the picture. You can grab a corner of the picture and drag it, but you will get better results if you change the height and width by the same percentage.

- **Alternate Text**—You can type alternative text to appear when a graphic is loading in a browser and to appear as a caption with the picture. You cannot select Display Text as a caption until after the text has been typed and saved by clicking on a check mark that will be displayed beside it.

- **Caption**—You can add a caption to your picture.

- **Hotspots**—You can transform a graphic into a hotspot (a link or an action defined by a formula).

Figure 5.11
Float a picture to display text to the left or right of it.

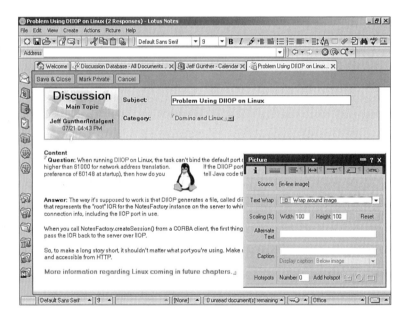

WORKING WITH ATTACHMENTS

You can attach files in the rich-text field of any document. When someone reads the document with an attached file, it might be possible to view the attachment (for more than 100 different file formats), launch the attachment if you have a local application capable of opening it, or copy the file to a local drive.

To create an attachment, follow these steps:

1. Place the cursor where you want the attachment to be located.
2. Select File, Attach.
3. Select the name of the file you want to attach.
4. Click the Create button.

The attachment is inserted. An icon represents the attachment. If you have the application that was used to create the file, the icon for the application is displayed. If you don't have the application on your system, a generic document icon represents the attachment.

TIP

> Beginning with Release 6, you can attach files to any document by simply dragging files from the workstation's operating system into a rich-text field. Similarly, you can detach files from a document by dragging them out of a document and into a folder on the hard drive.

WORKING WITH DOCUMENTS IN VIEWS

A Notes view is a list of documents that meet predefined selection criteria. For example, a view might contain all documents created using a form named Main Topic. You can create views that select documents based on unique values in any field except rich-text fields. In a typical view, you use the left pane to navigate to other views. You use an optional bottom pane for previewing documents. The remainder of the screen contains a list of documents that are available for reading, editing, printing, or performing other actions on, such as copying or deleting.

Documents may reside in a Domino database but don't necessarily have to. Documents can also be stored on the Internet as Web pages or documents that contain data that resides in various types of databases. Traditionally, however, documents are stored in a Domino database. For the sake of clarity, Figure 5.12 shows a typical view in a Domino database so that you can more easily understand the different elements.

Some views contain all documents in a database. But the strength of views is their capability to filter out documents, showing you only what you need. For example, suppose you have a database that you use to track sales. You probably have a view that displays active invoices. You have another view with orders sorted by salesperson. The documents in each view are from the same database, but they are selected because they contain specific criteria—an invoice form with a status of Active, and an order form that is categorized based on the Salesperson field.

The documents that you see in the view are those that meet the selection criteria and are in the database at the moment the view is opened. If a document is added to the database after the view is opened, you must refresh the view before you can see the new document.

5

To refresh a view, press F9 or select View, Refresh from the drop-down menu. The view is automatically refreshed if you close and reopen a view.

ELEMENTS OF A VIEW

The view has numerous elements that can guide a user, making the view more useful. Figure 5.12 shows a mail database and identifies some of these elements.

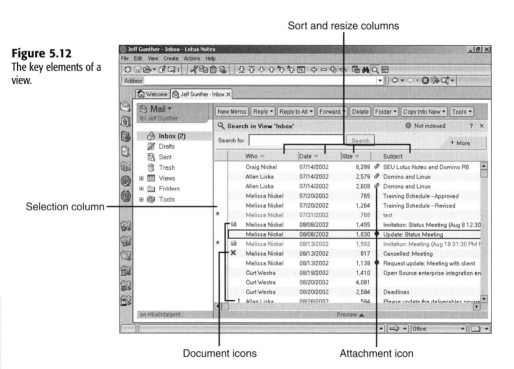

Figure 5.12
The key elements of a view.

USING UNREAD MARKS

The column to the left of the list of documents contains "unread" marks. These are displayed at the discretion of the application developer. Sometimes there is a star beside a document—and, in some instances, a different text color—to indicate that the document has not been opened for reading. The list of unread documents is maintained for each individual as part of the Notes desktop. The unread marks disappear when a document is opened.

TIP

> Unread marks are a real help in views that hold a large number of documents—for example, a view in a research database. You can toggle a document between read and unread by selecting Edit, Unread Marks and selecting the appropriate entry. I sometimes mark a document as unread so that I can find it more easily the next time I open the view.

DELETING DOCUMENTS FROM A VIEW

To delete a document from a view, select the document and press the Delete key. A deletion icon is displayed beside the document in the same column as the unread marks. If you change your mind, select the document and press the Delete key again to turn it off. The document is deleted when you exit the database or when you refresh the view.

CAUTION

> When a document has been deleted, it cannot be easily recovered. There are a couple ways to restore a document, though, depending on how Notes is used in your organization. If there is a copy of the document in a replica database, you can edit and save the document in the replica, and then replicate the document to the replica copy of the database that you normally access. You can also restore a backup copy of the database. However, you will lose any changes that were made in the database since the backup was made.

SELECTING DOCUMENTS FOR BATCH PROCESSES

In the same column as the unread marks, you can place a check mark to indicate that a document has been selected for a batch process, such as printing, copying, or deleting multiple documents.

To select a single document, click in the left column beside the document. To select multiple documents that are adjacent to each other in the view, click and hold down the left mouse button beside the first document in the list, and drag the mouse up or down the list. Release the left mouse button when you are done selecting documents.

You can deselect documents using the same process. Click the check mark to make it disappear. Hold down the left mouse button while pointing to a check mark, and drag the mouse up or down the column to deselect other documents. Release the mouse button when you are done.

After you have selected the documents you want, you can copy them, mark them for deletion, or print them as you would a single document.

WORKING WITH VIEW COLUMNS

Rows in a view represent documents (and in some view designs, a single document might span multiple rows). The *columns* display the values held in specific fields within a document, or they contain values computed based on the value in view column formulas. Each view column has a header at the top of the view, and some of these headers are dynamic. If a column header has a small triangle, the column can be resorted by clicking the header. For example, in the mail database, the default view shows unread incoming messages in the order that they are received. But you can click the first column header to display documents sorted by author. You can click the header for the second column to show the documents by date, with the most recent documents at the top. You can also change the width and order of some columns by clicking and dragging the edge of the column in the header. These changes will be saved and restored when the view is accessed again.

WHAT ARE DOCUMENT AND ATTACHMENT ICONS?

Many views use visual clues to tell you something about the contents of a document. A column can contain a small envelope icon, an exclamation point, or a handshake icon, for example. The envelope icons indicate that you, the owner of the mail database, sent the documents. The exclamation point indicates that the sender marked the document as high priority. The handshake represents a meeting invitation, and the string around a finger represents a reminder. The icon selection is based on the results of a formula provided by the view's designer.

The Attachment icon, which looks like a paper clip, is in another column in Figure 5.12. This indicates to users that the document contains an attached file. This visual clue helps them decide what they want to do with the document.

CATEGORIZED DOCUMENTS

In a categorized view, the first column of the view displays a category. When the category is expanded, you can see the documents within the category. Figure 5.13 illustrates a categorized view from the Discussion database used earlier. Some categories are expanded, and other categories are collapsed. Note that some individual documents have responses, and they can be expanded or collapsed as well to show or hide the responses.

Figure 5.13
A view showing documents contained in categories.

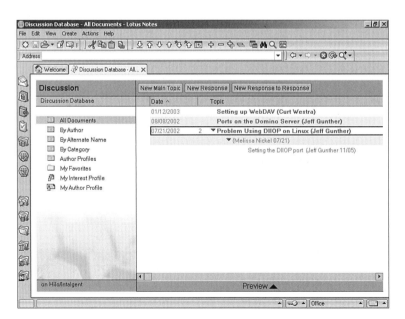

The small arrowhead to the left of the first sorted and categorized column in a row is commonly referred to as a *twistie*.

If the twistie points downward, the category is already expanded and you can see any documents (or other categories) contained within the category.

You can expand or collapse categories by clicking the twistie. You can also press the +, *, and - keys on the numeric keypad; or, you can select View, Expand/Collapse, and then select Expand Selected Level, Expand Selected and Children, or Collapse Selected Level. If a document has been categorized under multiple categories, it is listed in the view under each of its categories.

OPENING DOCUMENTS FOR READING OR EDITING

If you want to read one of the documents in the view, you can double-click it to open it for reading. Another option is to select the document and press the Enter key.

When the document is open for reading, you have a number of means to get to the next or previous document in the view:

- Press the Enter key to see the next document in the view.
- Press the Backspace key to see the previous document in the view.
- Click the Next Document or Previous Document buttons to see the next or previous documents in the view.
- Press Tab to see the next unread document in the view.
- Click the Next Unread or Previous Unread buttons to see the next or previous unread documents in the view.

You can open a document for editing only if you have Editor rights for that document. You can open the document in edit mode by pressing Ctrl+E (from the view or with the document open), or you can double-click the document when it is open in read mode. Another popular method of getting into edit mode is to choose the Actions, Edit Document menu item. Some documents are designed so that you can open them for editing by clicking an action edit button.

When you are done viewing or editing a document, you can close it by pressing the Esc key, or you can select File, Close (Ctrl+W from the keyboard). You can close any document from the taskbar by clicking the X beside the document name. If changes were made to the document, you are given the option of saving your changes before the document is closed. If you select Yes, the changes are saved. Closing the document returns you to the view from which you opened the document or to the location of the link from which you opened the document.

COPYING A DOCUMENT

To copy a document, highlight the document in a view. Select Edit, Copy, or press Ctrl+C. Then select Edit, Paste, or press Ctrl+V to paste a copy of the document.

You can paste a document into any view in any Domino database as long as you have document-creation privileges. However, the document is displayed only in views for which it matches the selection criteria.

CAUTION

> You can paste a document into another database. However, the data and the form are stored separately, and you might not have the right form for viewing the data in the new database.

PRINTING A DOCUMENT

The basics of printing a document are simple. With a view opened for reading, select File, Print, or click the Print button within the Universal toolbar (if you have added the Universal set to your toolbar). The document is sent to your default printer from the dialog box shown in Figure 5.14.

Figure 5.14
Select printing options for a view from the Print View dialog box.

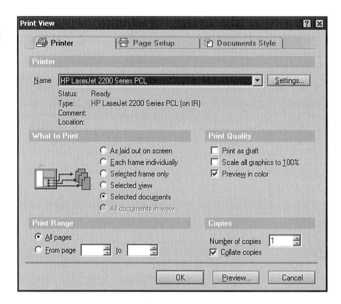

You have the option of printing the view, selected documents, or the screen as displayed. If you print the view, you get a list of all the documents in the view, not just those shown as selected on the screen.

If you print a document, you have the option of limiting printing to a range of pages. You can also select draft mode, scale graphics to 100%, and choose from a variety of page setup options.

When you are done selecting options, you can preview the printed document online by clicking the Preview button at the bottom of the Print dialog box. As you preview your print options, remember that most documents were designed for online display; they might not look good when printed. You have a couple options to improve the appearance of documents: using headers and footers and using alternate forms. You can preview the print job from the File menu with the Print Preview command.

CREATING HEADERS AND FOOTERS FOR PRINTING

You can tailor your document printing by creating headers and footers for a single document or for an entire database. If you have a header/footer setting for a single document, this setting overrides any settings you have for the database as a whole.

To create headers and footers for your printed documents, display the Document Properties box (display the Database Properties box if you want to apply headers and footers to the entire database). Click the Printer tab as shown in Figure 5.15.

Figure 5.15
Create a header and footer using the Printer tab in the Database Properties box.

To create a header, follow these steps:

1. With the Printer tab selected, position the cursor inside the header text field.
2. Select the Calendar icon to insert the system date (given the notation &D), the Clock icon to insert the current time (&T), the Page icon to insert the page number (&P), or the Title icon to insert the document title (&W). Or, type your own text to appear in the header.

   Whatever you insert is positioned on the left side of the header.
3. Click the Paragraph Indent icon to insert a vertical marker (¦). The vertical marker is used to separate the left, center, and right sides of the page.
4. Insert another item (page, text, date, time, or title). Anything placed immediately to the right of the first vertical bar is centered at the top of the page.
5. Click the Paragraph Indent icon again to insert another vertical marker.

6. Insert another item. Whatever you insert after the second vertical bar is right-justified at the top of the page.

7. Select the font for your header (footer).

8. Click the check box if you want the header/footer to appear on the first page of your print job.

Here is an example of a header:

`&D | &W | Chapter Five`

The header has the date on the left, the document title in the center, and the text `Chapter Five` on the right. If you want your entire header to be right-justified, you enter two vertical bars before entering a code or some text:

`||Knowledge Base.`

The process for creating a footer is the same. Click the Footer radio button and then create your footer.

USING AN ALTERNATIVE FORM FOR PRINTING

Another strategy for printing good-looking documents is to use a form that is formatted especially for printing. I won't teach you how to design that form in this chapter, but I will show you how to select an alternative form.

Go back and look at Figure 5.15. If you elect to print selected documents, the Documents Style tab is activated within the dialog box. Click the Documents Style tab to display the portion of the dialog box shown in Figure 5.16.

Figure 5.16
Select an alternate form for printing documents.

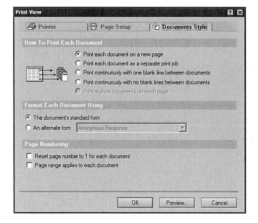

At the bottom of the Documents Style tab, click the Alternate Form radio button and select the name of the alternative form to be used. A list of all forms in the database is displayed for your selection.

CAUTION

The alternative form used for printing must have matching field names for any fields on the original form that are to be printed.

5

6

GETTING STARTED WITH CONTACT MANAGEMENT

In this chapter

SETTING UP YOUR PERSONAL ADDRESS BOOK

Since its inception, Lotus Notes was designed to operate within a networked environment. Although many organizations implement Notes as a communication tool, Notes can also be an indispensable tool for managing contacts both inside and outside the organization. Contact-management software can provide an integrated solution to create, manage, and stay in contact with individuals. Many Lotus business partners provide an assortment of contact applications that can be implemented within a Notes environment. However, before you evaluate a dedicated contact-management system, you should evaluate the software provided by a standard install of Notes and Domino.

The Personal Address Book is used to store your workstation's connections to the Domino environment. Additionally, it's used to manage the contact information of people you communicate with frequently, whether they are inside or outside your organization.

You can define the appearance and control some of the functionality of your Personal Address Book by configuring the preferences. The Personal Address Book Preferences is accessible from the Tools action button or the Actions, Tools, Preferences menu items, as shown in Figure 6.1.

Figure 6.1
The Personal Address Book Preferences is used to define your personal preferences for your address book.

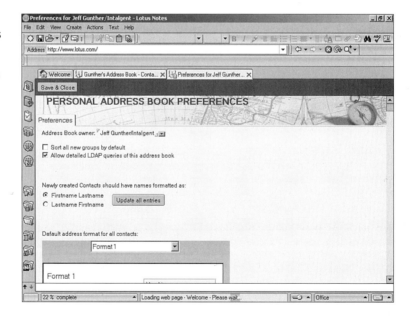

SELECTING AN ADDRESS BOOK OWNER

The first field in the Preferences profile refers to the address book's *owner*. The owner is the individual or group allowed to use the address book for name lookups when creating or sending messages. By default, you are the owner of the address book, although you can assign ownership to another individual.

When you click the helper button next to the Address Book Owner field, the Select Names dialog box is displayed. Within this dialog box, you can select an address book or directory for lookups and choose a user or group. The selected individual or group is inserted as the owner of the address book.

AUTOMATIC GROUP SORTING AND ALLOWING LDAP QUERIES

Two check boxes are available for selection in the Personal Address Book Preferences tab:

- Sort All New Groups by Default
- Allow Detailed LDAP Queries of This Address Book

SELECTING THE FORMAT OF ALL NEW NAMES

The Personal Address Book Preferences enables you to choose the format of an individual's name for all newly created contacts. If you decide that you don't like how the names are displayed within the Contact view, simply make your change and click the Update All Entries button to make the change globally in your personal address book.

SELECTING A DEFAULT ADDRESS FORMAT

You can choose from six default address formats to give your Contact form a format that meets your personal preference or locality. To select a different format, select the combo box and choose a different format. When you select a format, the area underneath the field is immediately displayed so that you can see whether you like it.

ADDING A CONTACT TO YOUR ADDRESS BOOK

When you want to add a new individual to your address book, you create a contact document in one of two ways:

- When you receive mail from someone, choose Actions, Tools, Add Sender to Address Book from the menu bar.
- Click the New action button and select Contact from any of the views in the Personal Address Book.

When you add a contact, the basic details about the individual are displayed on the Contact form. Add the person's name and email address, as illustrated in Figure 6.2.

6

TIP

> Many wizards are available for more involved fields. For example, when you click the helper button in the Email Address field, a Mail Address Assistant guides you as you enter the email address. In the Mail Address Assistant, you have a choice of the following types of addresses: fax, Internet mail, Lotus cc:Mail, Lotus Notes, other, or X.400 Mail. An assistant is displayed after you make your selection and click OK. The assistant helps you fill in any required information for that type of address.

Figure 6.2
Enter a person's name and email address to create a new contact document.

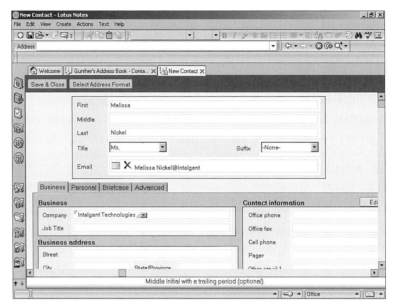

As you continue to add information to the contact, you encounter the following four tabs to capture information about the individual:

- **Business**—Enables you include the name of the person's company, job title, business address, and contact information. If you already have other contacts within your address book for the same organization, the helper button beside the Company field enables you to choose the company's name. If this is the first person, simply type the name of his company into the field. The Additional Business Information collapsible section provides an area to specify both the physical location/department, Web site address, and the names of his manager and assistant.

- **Personal**—Enables you to enter personal details about the individual, including home address, names of spouse and children, birthday/anniversary dates, and home contact numbers.

- **Briefcase**—Enables you to include attachments, documents, and pictures regarding the individual. If you read the previous chapter on working with text and documents, you know that you can do practically anything you want in this field. Want to add a picture of the contact? This is the place to do it. Want to attach a sound file with his voice? Place the cursor on the Comments page, select File, Attach, and locate the file that has his voice. See Chapter 5, "Working with Text and Documents," for details on using a rich-text field. A Comments field enables you to add comments about the individual that might serve as a reference for later use.

- **Advanced**—Contains more advanced options, for example, if you need to set up secure communications with the person you are creating a contact for. On this page, you add the person's full user name and the short name that you want to use to address her. The full username is the person's hierarchical Notes name, as in Melissa Nickel/Accounting/Hilo. You can add other names to the Full Name field, and you can then address email to the person using any of the variants in this field or in the Short Name field. Enter the person's email domain, which is the domain portion of the email address.

If you need to share encrypted mail with the person and you do not have access to the Domino Directory, paste in the contact's certified public key after she sends it to you, or enter the person's flat name key if the user does not use hierarchical names. When you have the correct key, you can decrypt documents this person sends to you.

You can also specify personal categories by which you can group your contacts; you can enter a phonetic name to assist you with locating the person using a name-picker dialog box if you have other contacts with similar names; and you can override the default first name/last name order for displaying this person's name.

ADDING A NEW CARD FROM NOTES MAIL

An individual can be added to your Personal Address Book from within Notes mail. Open a message from the person. Select Actions, Tools, Add Sender to Address Book to see the dialog box shown in Figure 6.3.

Figure 6.3
Add a person to your
Personal Address
Book from within
Notes mail.

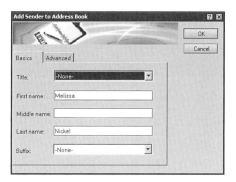

The person is added to your address book automatically. Later, you can open that person's contact document, put it in edit mode, and enter additional information about the person. But you can use that contact for addressing email immediately.

If you have privileges to create documents in the Domino Directory, you can also open the directory and create person entries that are accessible to everyone in your Notes network. Usually only Notes administrators have this privilege. Even though someone is listed in the Domino Directory, that person cannot access the Domino server using Notes without a valid Notes user ID.

6

CATEGORIZING YOUR CONTACTS

The primary purpose of any contact-management application is to ease the task of keeping in touch with people. The Personal Address Book provides two views that can be used to simplify the task of contacting someone listed within your address book. You can use the default Contacts view itself, or you can use the Contacts by Category view shown in Figure 6.4.

Figure 6.4
Use the Contacts by Category view to communicate easily with your contacts by category.

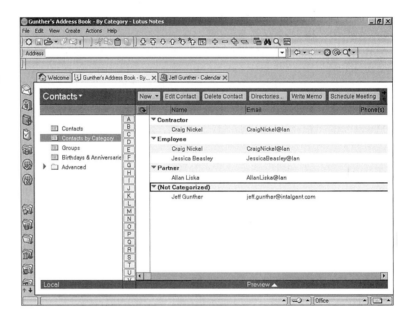

The only difference between the Contacts view and the Contacts by Category view is the way documents are sorted and categorized.

ADDING A CONTACT TO A CATEGORY

When you create a contact, you can categorize the individual by filling in the Categories field on the Advanced page.

You can also categorize multiple contacts at a single time by selecting the documents with the view and selecting the Tools action button and choosing Categorize. For example, in Figure 6.5, the Categorize dialog box is displayed after selecting individuals to categorize.

In the Categorize dialog box, you can assign a contact to an existing category by clicking the category so that a check mark appears next to it. Clicking it again turns the category off. You can also create a new category by typing the name of the category at the bottom of the dialog box and clicking the Add button. When you click OK to indicate that you are finished, the new category is created and the document is placed into that category.

Figure 6.5
Select an existing category or create a new one for one or more contacts.

A single contact can appear in more than one category. Contacts that are not assigned to any categories are listed under the generic Not Categorized heading in the Contacts by Category view. If you add people to your address book from an email memo, this is where you will find them listed. You can expand the Not Categorized category and assign them to an existing category so that they are easier to find next time.

SENDING A MESSAGE TO A CONTACT

Just as Notes improves communication productivity within an organization, each component with Notes provides its own unique set of productivity improvements that assist in making your job easier. The Personal Address Book is no different. For example, the process of authoring an email to an individual now allows you to select the recipients in one click.

To send an email message to a contact, follow these steps:

1. Highlight or select the name of the contact recipient in either the Contacts view or the Contacts by Category view.
2. Click the Write Memo action button within the view.

   An email is created in your default mail client. The memo is automatically addressed to the person(s) whose name(s) were selected.
3. Fill in the Subject and the body of the memo.
4. Send or Send and File the memo.

If you want to send the same message to multiple people, select multiple names within the view and click the Write Memo action button. All selected names are included in the To field of your memo.

TIP

If you want to keep track of all the times you contact a client, it will take a little bit of discipline because the process is not totally automatic. When you send a memo to one of your contacts, you can file a copy of the memo in the appropriate folder using the Send and File action button on the new memo. If you need a refresher on how to create folders, review Chapter 4, "Getting Started with Electronic Mail."

6

SCHEDULING A MEETING WITH A CONTACT

When you want to schedule a meeting with a contact, you can use the scheduling functions of the Notes mail client. The process is similar to what you did when sending a memo to the client. In this instance, though, you are using the calendaring and scheduling functions, which are described in detail in Chapter 7, "Getting Organized with the Calendaring and Scheduling Features." You get a quick taste of one of those features here.

To schedule a meeting, here is what you do:

1. Select the people within the view whom you want to invite to the meeting.

2. Click the Schedule Meeting action button located within the view's action buttons.

   The Calendar Entry form is displayed. The names you selected are listed in the Invite field. Selecting names and clicking the Schedule Meeting button is shown in Figure 6.6.

Figure 6.6
Select multiple people and then schedule a meeting that is automatically addressed.

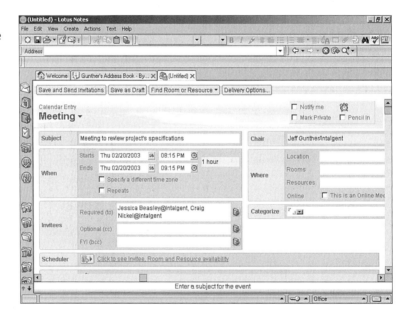

3. Fill out the Calendar Entry form, as described in Chapter 7. When you are scheduling a meeting with someone inside your organization, you can tell whether the person is available by looking up his or her free time (the dates and times he or she is available for meetings). You don't have this option when you are dealing with people outside your organization. In addition, you might not have locations set up for making room reservations for outside sites.

VISITING WEB PAGES

If any of the contacts in your Personal Address Book contain a Web page link, you can link directly to that person's Web page; you do not have to leave Notes. You can visit a Web page or a Notes document with equal ease. Notes automatically uses its built-in Web browser if a link leads to a document stored on the Internet.

When you use the Personal Address Book for contact management, visiting a person's Web page is a simple two-step process:

1. Highlight the name of the person whose Web page you want to visit within the Contacts view.

2. Click the Tools action button and select Visit Web Page.

   Setting up Web integration can involve a number of variables, but there are two essential steps for the integration to work within Notes using the Personal Address Book and the built-in Web browser:

   - You must enter a person's Web page URL on the contact document.

   - You must set the location document for your current location to use Notes with Internet Explorer as your Internet browser.

NOTE

> This assumes that you have Internet access and that you are connected to the Internet through either a network connection or a dial-up connection.

MAKING GROUP FUNCTIONS EASIER BY CREATING GROUPS

So far, we've covered how to work with individuals one person at a time using your Personal Address Book. When scheduling appointments, you learned how to select more than one person by placing a check mark next to their contact documents. What if you frequently work with groups of people?

Instead of selecting multiple contacts every time you want to deal with multiple people, you can create a group document and deal with the group as a single unit. When you address something to that group—for example, a mail memo or an invitation to a scheduled meeting—all you have to do is address the group. Each individual in the group automatically receives a copy of the same memo or invitation.

6

To create a group, follow these steps:

1. In the Personal Address Book, select the Groups view.

2. Click the New action button and select Group. Groups are defined using the form shown in Figure 6.7.

Figure 6.7
Use the Group form to define a group of users who can be addressed as a unit.

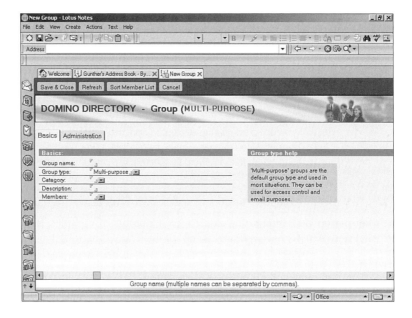

3. Provide a group name and a description of the group.

4. Make the group type Mail Only if you are creating a mailing list. Otherwise, select a group type such as Multipurpose, ACL, Servers, Deny Access, and so on.

5. Enter the names of the people to include in the group. The names can be selected from your list of contacts in your Personal Address Book by clicking the helper button beside the Members field. The Select Names dialog box is displayed, as shown in Figure 6.8.

Figure 6.8
Use the Select Names dialog box to choose the contacts you want to add to a group.

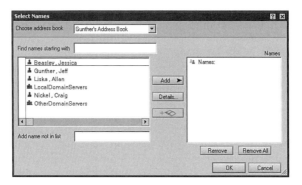

6. In the left panel, click to add a check mark beside the names you want to add to your group. Click Add to copy the names to the right panel. When the right panel contains all the names you want to add, click the OK button to add them to the group.

7. Click Save and Close when you are finished creating or editing the group. When a group has been added, you can create a mail memo to your group from anywhere in Notes. The keyboard combination Ctrl+M displays a new mail message form. Enter the name of the group—for example, **Demo**—in the To field. The message is sent to everyone you have added to your Demo group in your local Personal Address Book.

TIP

> You can also add names to a group from other directories, such as from the Domino Directory. Select the name of the directory from the Select Names dialog box, and add the names to your local group. When mail is sent, Notes expands the names in the group into valid email addresses.

USING THE DOMINO DIRECTORY

The Domino Directory can be used for contact management, but there are some distinct differences that govern what you, an end user, can do. The Domino Directory holds the names of people registered as Notes or Web users within your organization. For all intents and purposes, though, you cannot add people to the directory. The Domino Directory also contains the names of groups, but only the system administrator can add people and groups.

When you mail something to a group of users within the Domino Directory, the mail goes to all members of the group, just as it does with groups in your Personal Address Book. But other users in the organization have access to the same group record. The groups in the Domino Directory are for public use (meaning others in your Notes organization).

One of the primary purposes of the Domino Directory is to define to the router how to route documents to others within the organization and through gateways to people outside your organization. When you send a message or an invitation to a meeting for someone listed in your Personal Address Book, it gets routed using information stored in the Domino Directory. Without access to the Domino Directory, messages could not find a route to an Internet domain, for example.

You have some control over how much the Domino Directory gets used when you are addressing and sending mail. For example, in the location document for your current location, you can define whether type-ahead lookups work using only your local directory (the Personal Address Book) or the local directory and then the Domino Directory. Figure 6.9 shows the information that can be adjusted in the location document.

The important information for contact management includes the following:

- Recipient name type-ahead
- Recipient name lookup
- Mail addressing
- Send outgoing mail

Figure 6.9
Use the Mail tab in the location document to define how local and public directories are used.

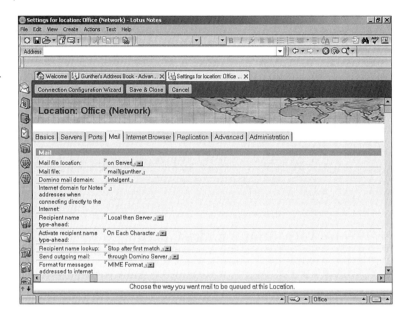

CHAPTER 7

GETTING ORGANIZED WITH THE CALENDARING AND SCHEDULING FEATURES

In this chapter

OVERVIEW OF SCHEDULING IN NOTES

In today's hectic business environment, time management is an important part of everyone's daily work. From keeping track of appointments, events, and anniversaries, to scheduling meetings with other people, organizations need an effective mechanism for team members to manage their time and resources.

In the past, Lotus introduced several applications that provided individuals with group scheduling features. Release 6.0 continues Lotus's effort to integrate and extend group scheduling with workflow and information databases.

With Notes, you can easily schedule a meeting by checking other people's schedules for free times and finding a room that is available when you want to meet. Notes sends and manages the delivery of the invitations to all the attendees and automatically reserves the room for you. The Calendaring and Scheduling features enable the mobile user to create appointments and meetings while disconnected from the network.

A default view of your calendar is displayed in Figure 7.1.

Figure 7.1
You can view appointments using the Calendar view.

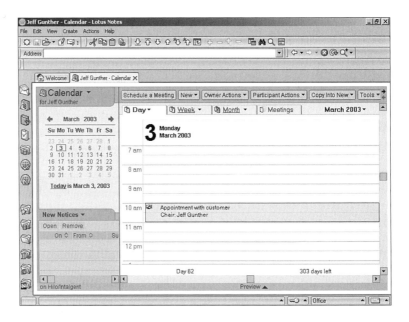

The elements of the calendar include the following:

- **Calendar view**—Enables you to view appointments and events using hourly, daily, weekly, biweekly, or monthly formats
- **Calendar Entry form**—Used to create personal appointments, meeting invitations, all-day events, reminders, and anniversaries

7

- **Meetings view**—Enables you to work with calendar entries as documents in a more traditional Notes view
- **Group calendars**—Enables you to view the calendars of multiple users

You manage your schedule by creating appointments, inviting others to meetings, and responding to invitations to meetings. If you invite other people to a meeting, Notes sends the invitation to the attendees, who, in turn, can choose to accept or decline the meeting. Notes can also automatically reserve a room and resources, such as a conference room, an overhead projector, or a laptop.

SETTING UP CALENDAR PREFERENCES

Before you start using the calendaring features of Notes, you should review the calendar preferences to define the details of how your calendar operates. The Preferences dialog box enables you to define default information that is used when you schedule meetings and events. Examples of optional settings in the calendar preferences include the following:

- Configure the colors used to display different types of entries within your calendar
- Define how your Calendar view is displayed
- Enable alarms for appointments, events, and anniversaries

To ease the task of configuring your preferences, all preferences for mail, the calendar, and the To Do list are defined within the same dialog box. You can access your calendar preferences two ways:

- Click the Tools action button on the Calendar view and select the Preferences item
- From the menu bar, select Actions, Tools, Preferences

Figure 7.2 shows the Calendar and To Do tab of the Preferences dialog box.

The subtabs of the Calendar and To Do tab include the following:

- **Basics**—The Defaults for New Calendar Entries section is used to define the default type of calendar entry, the default duration of a meeting or appointment, and how many years into the future an anniversary should be marked in your calendar. In the Personal Categories section, you can define the categories that are used to define the types of events that you add to your calendar or To Do list, such as a birthday category. Personal categories of events are selected from a drop-down list of event types that you define. Any change to this list affects only new entries.
- **Display**—On the Display tab, you can define the range of hours for a work day, the days to display within a work week, and the default time interval for individual calendar entries. Additionally, you can define whether calendar entries should be displayed in Mail views, and you can define the type of meeting notices that should be displayed in your inbox.

Figure 7.2
Complete the
Calendar and To Do
tab of the Preferences
dialog box before
using the scheduling
features.

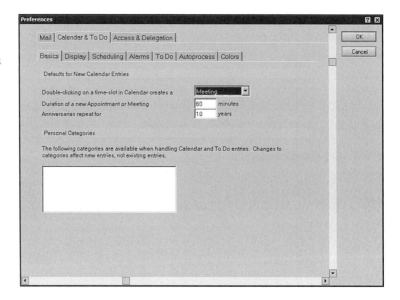

- **Scheduling**—On this tab, you define the times during which you are available for appointments and meetings. In other words, you define your work hours during the week so that others will know when you are available for meetings. If your available hours are different than your workstation's local time zone, you can define your work hours using a different time zone.

- **Alarms**—You can enable alarms for various types of calendar entries. Alarms can be enabled or disabled for each calendar entry type. If alarms are enabled and set for a particular entry, a visual notice is displayed on the screen at a set interval before or after the entry calendar event begins. You can also select a sound file to be played at the time of the alarm.

- **To Do**—The To Do tab enables you to define whether tasks that you or others have assigned to you should be displayed on your calendar. Additionally, you can allow Notes to manage and maintain the status and dates of each To Do item within your task list.

- **Autoprocess**—On the Autoprocess tab, you can determine how invitations are handled when they are sent to you. If you want meeting invitations processed automatically, you can elect to have either all invitations processed or only those from a set list of individuals. You can also have your meeting requests forwarded to another individual, for example, if someone is handling your duties for a period of time. Autoprocessing automatically adds meetings to your calendar if your free time allows it. Automatic Inbox Management provides the automated removal of meeting invitations from your inbox after you have responded to the invitation or notice.

- **Colors**—On the Colors tab, you can customize each type of calendar entry to distinguish them from one another. As shown in Figure 7.3, you can choose a color from the
standard Notes color palette or a color based on any RGB color combination.

Figure 7.3
Choose any color
using the color RGB
sliders or Eyedropper
color tool.

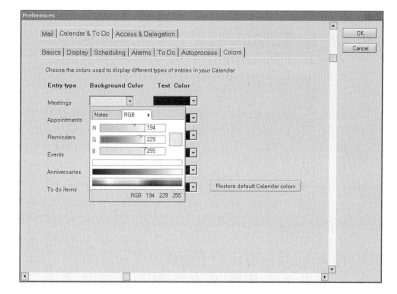

CALENDAR ACCESS AND DELEGATION

The top-level Access and Delegation tab enables you to control delegation and access to
your calendar. The Access to Your Mail and Calendar subtab lets you choose which users
can read, edit, and create calendar entries on your behalf, including controlling the forwarding of meeting notifications to other users.

You can choose to delegate calendar privileges to everyone, or you can restrict access to specific individuals or groups. If someone is granted read privileges to your calendar and To
Dos, that person can view such entries in your calendar. Someone with read, edit, create,
and delete privileges can not only view entries, but also modify and delete them or create
them on your behalf. An administrative assistant who needs to maintain a manager's schedule is a logical candidate for this type of delegation.

NOTE

> Users with reader or manager access to your calendar through the Preferences dialog
> box will not be able to read or edit your personal mail or any calendar entries that are
> marked Private.

7

The Access to Your Schedule tab, shown in Figure 7.4, enables you to control which individuals can view your schedule information and details. Additionally, you can specify what
information they can view.

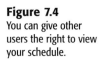

Figure 7.4
You can give other users the right to view your schedule.

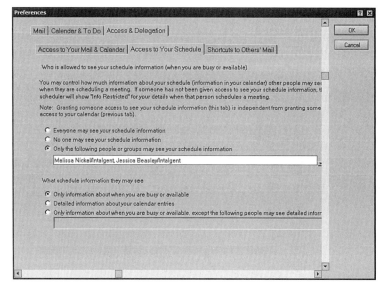

CREATING A CALENDAR ENTRY

After you have set your calendar preferences, you are ready to start creating your calendar entries. To create any type of entry, you can do one of the following:

- Open your mail database and choose Create, Calendar Entry. The default calendar entry type is displayed. If you click the arrow next to the default entry type, a pop-up box lets you choose the type of entry you want to create.

- Click the Calendar icon on the Bookmark bar located on the leftmost side of the Notes environment to open the calendar. Then click the New action button and select the type of entry you want to create, or click the Schedule a Meeting button.

- Choose Create, Mail, Calendar Entry from within any other Notes application. When the default Calendar Entry form is displayed, click the type of entry you want to create.

- Double-click on your calendar the day you want to create an appointment.

SCHEDULING AN APPOINTMENT

The Appointment form (a Calendar Entry form with Appointment selected as the entry type) is used to block off personal free time on your calendar. Figure 7.5 shows the Appointment form.

On the Appointment form, fill in the following information:

- **Subject**—Enter a brief description of the appointment. The description is visible when the document is displayed within the Calendar view.

■ **Start and end dates**—Enter the begin and end dates of the appointment. The default date is today's date. You can pick a date from a calendar by clicking the Calendar helper button. A pop-up calendar is displayed, as shown in Figure 7.6.

Figure 7.5
Fill in the Appointment form to create a new appointment on your calendar.

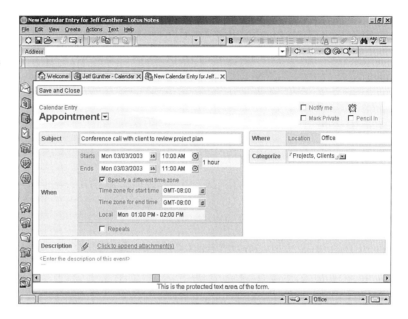

Figure 7.6
Select a date using the pop-up calendar.

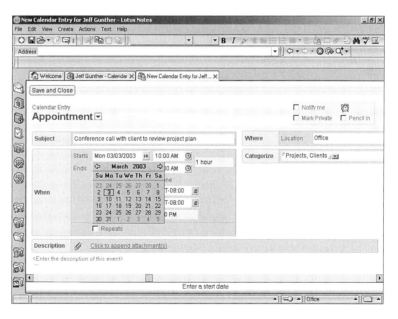

■ **Time**—Select a begin time and an end time for the appointment. If you type just a number, the time defaults to a.m. If you type **7 pm**, the system displays 7:00 p.m. You can also click the Clock helper button to display a slider bar. Slide the bar to the desired start time (or end time) for the appointment. The end time automatically is set to the default interval after the start time, but you can adjust the end time. The slider bar is shown in Figure 7.7.

Figure 7.7
Use the clock slider bar to set the begin or end times.

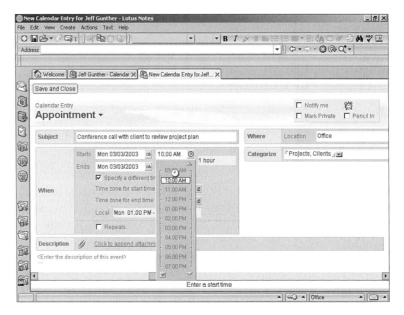

- **Time zone**—If the appointment is outside your own time zone, simply check the Specify a Different Time Zone option. Select an appropriate start and end time zone for the appointment. To choose a time zone, click the Globe helper button to display a list of possible time zones. The pop-up list is shown in Figure 7.8.

- **Repeats**—If you click the Repeats check box, a Repeat Options dialog box is displayed so that you can select rules for the repeating appointment. For example, you might have a meeting that repeats on the third Thursday of every month for the next two months, or every second day for two weeks. This is set up in the dialog box shown in Figure 7.9.

  When you save a repeating appointment, Notes automatically creates calendar entries for all occurrences of the appointment for the time period you specified. Later, if you need to move or delete a single occurrence of the appointment, Notes asks whether you want to apply the change to all the repeating appointments, update all future or all past occurrences, or change only a single occurrence.

- **Location**—Because the appointment is for you alone, you do not need to reserve a location, but you might want to enter the location of the appointment as a reminder to yourself.

Figure 7.8
Select a time zone using the Globe helper icon.

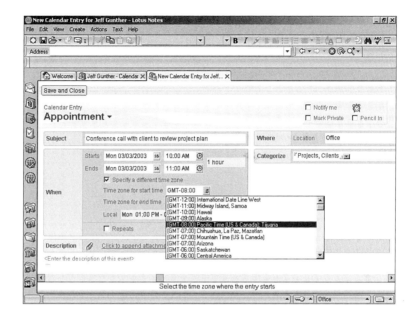

Figure 7.9
Define the repeat interval for repeating appointments.

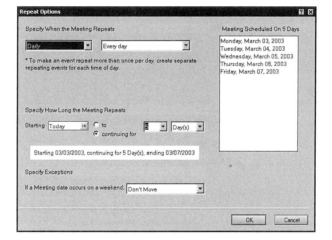

- **Pencil In**—Enable Pencil In to make the appointment without blocking off any free time. For example, you might want to pencil in a tentative appointment and then change it later. If the appointment is penciled in, you can still schedule another activity at the same time without creating a scheduling conflict.

- **Mark Private**—Check the Mark Private box if you do not want the appointment viewed by people to whom you have delegated read or edit access to your calendar. Others will still see that your free time has been blocked during the time of the appointment.

7

- **Alarm**—Click the Alarm Clock icon to enable alarms (visual and audio) for the appointment. The Alarm Notification Options dialog box is displayed so that you can set the alarm options. The dialog box is shown in Figure 7.10.

Figure 7.10
Select alarm options for your appointment.

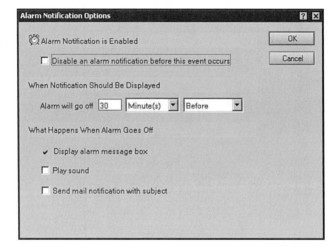

- **Categorize**—Categorize your appointment with categories such as Holiday or Travel. Select a category for your appointment from the Categorize list. You can add new categories to the drop-down list by entering them in the Categories field in your calendar preferences or by entering something in the New Keyword field of the Select Keywords dialog box that opens.
- **Description**—The Description field is a rich-text field, so you can enter details regarding the appointment, including file attachments.

INVITING OTHER PEOPLE TO A MEETING

Use the Meeting Calendar Entry form to create a meeting and invite people to it. The first page of the form is virtually identical to the Appointment form, but there are several meeting-specific features (see Figure 7.11).

Similar to the Appointment form, you enter a subject and a begin and end date and time for the meeting. You can set up the invitation for a repeating meeting and enter a description of the meeting location. In addition to specifying the meeting location, you can choose a room or resource to reserve. You can include the following information:

- **Invitees**—Enter the names of all the meeting's invitees, including those whose attendance is required, those who are optional attendees, and those who should receive an informational notification. As you type names, Notes does a lookup in your Personal Address Book or the Domino Directory, as it would if you were addressing an email. Click the helper button beside a field if you want to look up names in an address book, as shown in Figure 7.12.

Figure 7.11
Invite others to a
meeting using the
Meeting Calendar
Entry form.

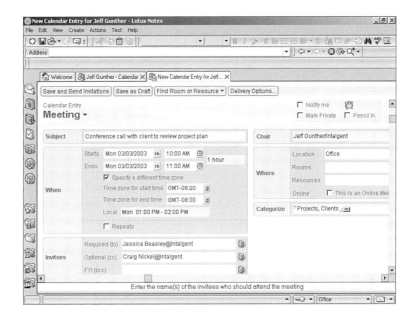

Figure 7.12
Selectively choose
your invitees from the
address book.

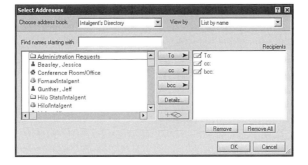

- **Rooms and resources**—Rooms and resources are defined by the Domino
  Administrator in the Domino Directory, and they are maintained in a separate view in
  the Domino Directory. You can do a lookup in the Domino Directory by clicking the
  helper button beside the Rooms and Resources fields.

- **Scheduler**—When you click the Scheduler helper button, a new area underneath the
  scheduler section appears, listing each user and suggested meeting times. You can have
  Notes look for the best times or use the Schedule Details view until you find a time
  when everyone is free. Figure 7.13 demonstrates the Schedule Details view.

  You can look at the free-time schedules for those who have to attend the meeting and
  then pick a time. The scheduler also includes information for invitees, rooms, and
  resources. Resources and rooms are defined in the Domino Directory. Examples of
  resources include items such as audiovisual equipment, refreshments, and even an outside instructor or facilitator for your meeting. It's up to your Domino Administrator
  how to define resources.

7

Figure 7.13
Click the Details radio button to view free time for invitees so that you can find a good meeting time.

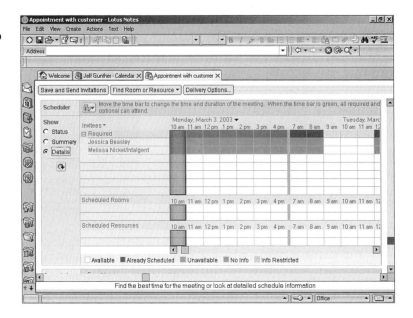

- **Delivery options**—Click the Delivery Options action button to define how your meeting invitation will be handled. You can tell the system that you don't want responses from invitees—for example, you might invite people to attend a free lunchtime seminar on the company's 401(k) plan. It's up to them if they want to attend; you don't need an RSVP. You can sign and encrypt the invitation. You can prevent people from proposing an alternative meeting time. You can also prevent them from delegating the meeting to someone on their staff. The dialog box for defining these options is shown in Figure 7.14.

Figure 7.14
Define how your invitation is handled by the system in the Delivery Options dialog box.

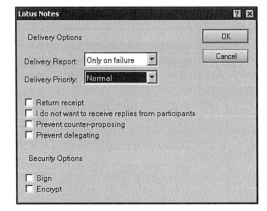

TRACKING A MEETING INVITATION

When you send out an invitation, the invitees who receive the invitation have different ways they can respond. They can accept or decline the invitation. They can choose someone else to attend the meeting in their stead. They can propose an alternative meeting time. This is all handled in the invitation itself. An invitation requesting a status meeting is shown in Figure 7.15.

Figure 7.15
You have several options when responding to a meeting invitation.

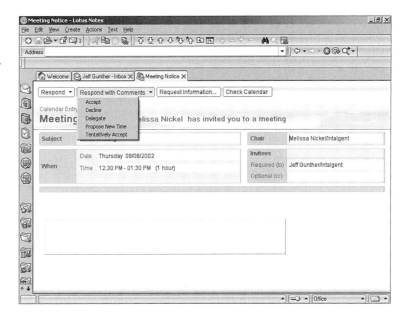

By clicking the Respond with Comments button, you have several options:

- **Accept**—If you want to accept the invitation with comments, a mail memo is displayed. The memo is addressed to the person who sent the original invitation.

- **Decline**—If you want to decline the invitation, a dialog box is displayed that gives you the option of staying updated if there is any further correspondence related to the invitation. Your message is sent automatically to the convener of the meeting.

- **Delegate**—If you choose to delegate the meeting to someone else, a dialog box is displayed in which you can specify the person you delegate. You also have the option of receiving any further correspondence regarding the invitation. Your message is sent automatically to the convener.

- **Propose New Time**—If you want to propose a new time, a dialog box is displayed in which the new time is proposed. This is sent automatically to the convener.

- **Tentatively Accept**—If you want to tentatively accept the invitation, a memo is addressed to the convener with a Comments field.

7

If you simply want to accept the invitation without comments, you can click the Respond button. If you change any information relating to the meeting, the information on your calendar is updated automatically.

If you need additional information about the meeting before deciding how to respond, you can send an email to the sender of the invitation by clicking the Request Information action button.

If you need to check your own calendar before deciding how to respond, you can click the Check Calendar button.

ACTIONS YOU CAN TAKE

If you sent the original invitation, you can also take various actions, such as changing or canceling a meeting, or sending additional information to attendees before the meeting. Open the saved invitation by double-clicking the entry in a Calendar view or locating the document among your saved email. Figure 7.16 shows a sample meeting invitation.

Figure 7.16
You have several actions you can take as the chair of meeting.

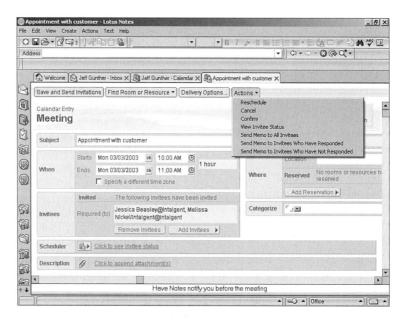

Click the Actions action button to display a drop-down list with the following options:

- **Reschedule**—If you have to reschedule the meeting, a dialog box is displayed that enables you to set a new date and time, check schedules, and add a written note to go along with the time change. When you save the Reschedule dialog box, a Memo form is displayed on which you can write a message. The memo is already addressed to all meeting participants, with a subject line referencing the rescheduled meeting. After it is submitted, invitees' calendars will be updated with the new time automatically when people acknowledge the new time. Figure 7.17 shows the Reschedule Options dialog box.

Figure 7.17
The Reschedule Options dialog box enables you to specify parameters for rescheduling a meeting.

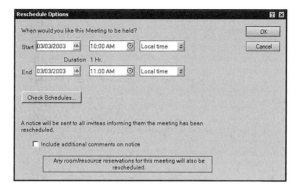

■ **Cancel**—When you cancel a meeting, a dialog box is displayed that enables you to select options to clean up calendar notices and resource reservations for the meeting, and to create a message to meeting participants.

■ **Confirm**—If you select Confirm, a confirmation is sent to all participants. You also have the option of including a message with the confirmation notice.

■ **View Invitee Status**—When you select View Invitee Status, a status box is displayed, as shown in Figure 7.18. You can scroll through a list of all invited participants, see whether their attendance is required or optional, and see whether they have accepted, declined, proposed a new time, and so forth. You can sort the Invitee Status list by clicking the arrow above the list of invitees. You can sort the list alphabetically by all invitees, who has accepted, who has declined, and who has not responded.

■ **Send Memo to All Invitees**— This option addresses a memo to all invitees, regardless of whether they have responded to the meeting invitation.

■ **Send Memo to Invitees Who Have Responded**—This option addresses a memo to all invitees that are participating in the meeting. You can use this to send a meeting agenda, background information, last-minute instructions, and so forth.

■ **Send Memo to Invitees Who Have Not Responded**—This option addresses a memo to all invitees who have not responded to the invitation. You can use this to send a reminder requesting that individuals respond to the invitation.

CREATING AN ANNIVERSARY ON YOUR CALENDAR

An anniversary is just what it says: a date to remember. This might be somebody's birthday, your first day on the job, or a wedding anniversary. Or, if you like, you can set once-a-month anniversaries, such as a meeting of your professional organization.

Ordinarily there is no set time of day for an anniversary, as there is with an appointment or a meeting. To create an anniversary, click the New action button in the Calendar and select Anniversary. Merely fill in the subject, the date, the location (if relevant), display options, and details into the form. These fields are all used exactly as they are on the Appointment form described earlier.

7

Figure 7.18
You can get a quick overview of the responses to your invitation.

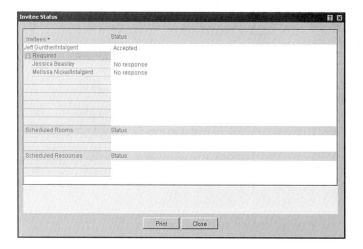

Anniversaries repeat on the same date each year. You can use the Calendar Preferences dialog box to define how many years you want your anniversaries to extend into the future.

In addition to setting up your own anniversaries, you can import anniversaries into the calendar. For example, you might want to import all the religious holidays for your religious affiliation, plus all the national and state holidays. You find the Import Holidays function under Tools on the Actions menu, or from the Tools button in the Calendar view. National holidays are included in a special view in the Domino Directory. If you want other holidays downloaded, you work with the Domino Administrator to put them into the Domino Directory for importing.

Creating a Calendar All-Day Event

An all-Day event entry on your calendar is another variation on the theme. An *event* is considered a one-day or multiple-day occurrence, such as a trade fair or a conference that you will be attending. You can even book your vacation as an event because it is a block of days during which you won't have any free time. A necessary characteristic of an All-Day event is a lack of free time.

You simply enter a subject, begin and end dates, a location, options, and a description. You can also set up repeat intervals if it is a recurring event.

Creating a Reminder

A *reminder* is yet another variation on the same theme. With a reminder, you have a begin date and time, but there is no end date or time. For example, you might want to set an alarm to remind you that you have to submit a status report every Monday morning, or that taxes are due anytime after January 31. If you really need someone to nag you to get the taxes done, you can even set the reminder for every day.

NOTE

A reminder document does not automatically contain an alarm.

MANAGING A TO DO LIST ON YOUR CALENDAR

You can manage your personal tasks or assign tasks to others using the To Do list feature of Notes. The To Do forms look very much like the other calendar forms, but they include a Priority field and a Status field to help you keep track of tasks until they have been completed. You can navigate to your To Do list by clicking the Check Mark icon within the Bookmark bar. Create a To Do item by clicking the New To Do Item action button, or by selecting To Do from the Create menu when you are in your Mail database.

Two To Do types exist. The first type is for a personal To Do list. The other type is similar to a meeting invitation. You can assign a task to one or more people and then track the response of the assignees as well as the status of the task. With both types of To Do lists, you can set alarms to remind you to keep after the task until it has been completed. Figure 7.19 shows a To Do form being assigned to other individuals.

Figure 7.19
Define a task and assign it to others using the To Do form.

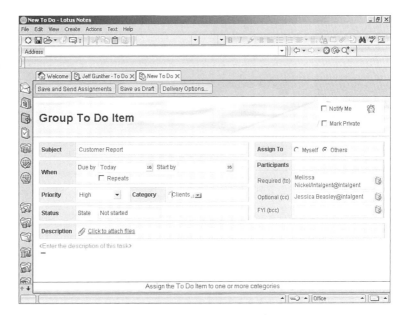

You can assign a start date, a due date, and priority. In the Participants area, you can assign the task to one or more individuals, entering their names into an address field just as you did with a meeting invitation.

7

You handle a task pretty similarly to the way you handle a meeting invitation. Invitees must respond by accepting or declining a task, or by proposing a new timeline for the task. You, as the task originator, can cancel the task, change the dates, or send additional information, just as you did with an invitation.

WORKING WITH THE CALENDAR VIEWS

Notes 6 has a number of different ways of looking at your calendar. You can look at your schedule using five main calendar selections: One Day, Two Days, One Week, One Work Week, Two Weeks, Two Work Weeks, One Month, and One Work Month. The Calendar views are similar to the interface of a notebook planner. Figure 7.20 shows the Calendar view using the One Week display.

Figure 7.20
The Calendar views enable you to see appointments using a standard calendar format.

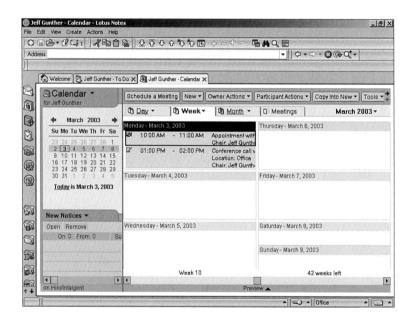

You can choose the view type you want to see by selecting it from the tabs underneath the view action bar (Day, Week, or Month). Each main type has a arrow that enables you to select views based on the main type. For example, you can select a two-week view by clicking the arrow on the Week tab and selecting Two Weeks.

The Calendar view enables you to easily change your schedule using drag-and-drop methods. If you want to move an appointment, simply click the entry in the Calendar view and drag it to the new day. Notes automatically moves the entry, checks for time conflicts, and sends reschedule notices to meeting attendees, if necessary.

You can also create new calendar entries in your calendar by double-clicking the day on which the new entry will be scheduled. Notes displays a new Calendar Entry form on which you can type the details of your new entry.

You can customize how the calendar prints using a variety of layouts. For example, you can set up the calendar so that it prints in a DayRunner Running Mate layout and hides private entries. Printing can be initiated using the Print button on the Universal toolbar or by selecting File, Print from the drop-down menu. As shown in Figure 7.21, the advanced calendar-printing features are found on the Calendar Style tab located in the Print Calendar dialog box.

Figure 7.21
The Calendar Style tab within the Print Calendar dialog box contains advanced printing and layout options.

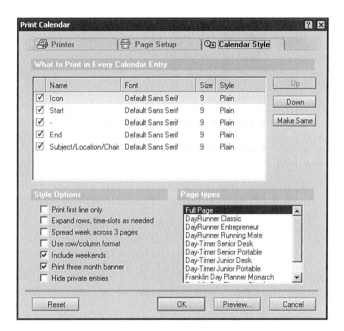

WORKING WITH MULTIPLE CALENDARS

A group calendar enables you to select any number of individuals from the Domino Directory and display their free time. You can define multiple group calendars for different project teams. You might have one calendar for in-house sales staff. When a new client enters your office, you can look at the group calendar and immediately see who is available. You could have another calendar for executives so that you can see who is available for a quick brainstorming session. A third calendar might list everyone in the company so that you can come up with a time for scheduling a staff meeting.

To set up a group calendar, select View and Create Group Calendars from the mail and calendar Navigation button (see Figure 7.22).

When the Group Calendar view is open, click the New Group Calendar action button to display the New Group Calendar dialog box, shown in Figure 7.23.

7

Figure 7.22
Select View and Create Group Calendars from the mail and calendar Navigation button.

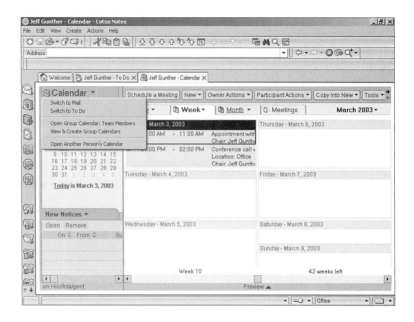

Figure 7.23
Name a new group calendar and list the people who should be included in the calendar.

Give the group calendar a title and enter the names of the people whose calendars you want included. You can select names from an address book by clicking the helper button beside the Members field.

After the group calendar is defined, you can open it from the Group Calendars view. Double-click the group calendar that you want to display, and you can see the free time for each of the people defined in the calendar (see Figure 7.24).

You can click the arrows next to the date display to pop up a calendar helper to select a date other than today. You can schedule meetings by double-clicking in a free time slot.

Figure 7.24
The group calendar displays free time for multiple users.

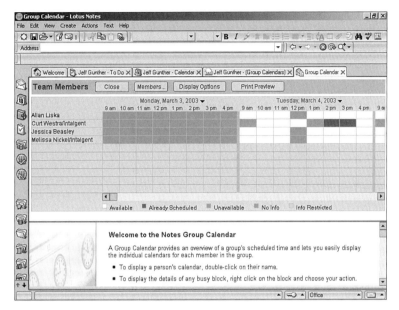

CALENDARING AND SCHEDULING WHILE TRAVELING

The calendaring and scheduling features can be used even when you are disconnected from the network. You can create new calendar entries, including invitations, while traveling. The invitations are stored in the outgoing mailbox and are routed to the attendees when you perform your normal mail replication. Your schedule also is updated in the Notes server Free Time database during replication.

One unique feature of Notes calendaring and scheduling is the capability of checking other people's free time while disconnected. You can create a replica of the Free Time database on your local computer that is used when displaying the Free Time dialog box. The information reflects the other user's free time at the time you last replicated with the server. Before accessing the free-time replication settings, you need to put your workstation in Island (Disconnected) mode. In the lower right, select the Island location via the Status bar, as shown in Figure 7.25.

→ **See** Chapter 2, "Installing and Customizing the Notes Client," **p. 27**, for more information about using and customizing the Status bar.

To access your local Free Time database's replication settings, click the Replicator icon on the Bookmark toolbar on the left side of the Notes screen. The Replication page includes a replication icon titled Local Free Time Info, as shown in Figure 7.26.

7

Figure 7.25
Select Island from the list of available locations from the Status bar.

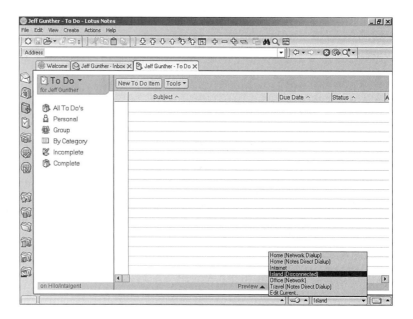

Figure 7.26
The Local Free Time Info icon is included in the Replication page.

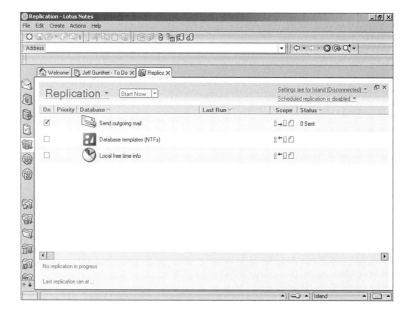

You can edit the free-time replication options to set which user's free time is reflected in your local Free Time database, the amount of free-time information that is stored, and how often the local free time is updated. Right-click the Local Free Time Info icon on the Replication page to select Options. The Local Free Time Settings dialog box is shown in Figure 7.27.

Figure 7.27
Select the users for
which you want to
replicate free time.

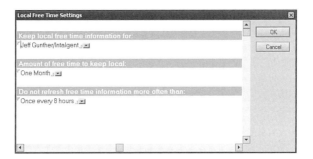

USING THE RESOURCE RESERVATIONS DATABASE

Lotus Notes automatically tracks rooms and resources using the Resource Reservations database. Resources that can be reserved include conference rooms, an overhead projector, or other equipment. The Domino Administrator creates this database on the server using the RESRC60.NTF Resource Reservations database template. This database is used to create site, room, and resource documents, and it can be used to directly enter a reservation without using the standard invitation process.

The administrator must then create a site profile, new rooms, and resources in the database. The room and resource documents include the time ranges when the room is available for reservations. Notes automatically creates a request for the administration process (adminp) to enter a resource document in the name and address book.

Notes uses resource categories when multiple resources are available. For instance, you might have three overhead projectors available. The person reserving a projector does not care which projector is used—only that one is available. Notes randomly reserves a projector out of all the projectors available to balance the resource usage.

Rooms and resources are normally reserved as part of creating a meeting invitation in your mail database. If you need to reserve a room or resource without creating a meeting, you can use the Resource Reservations database directly. Notes guides you through the reservation process, asking you to choose a resource type, and then requests more details about the reservation.

CALENDARING SERVER TASKS

Two server tasks support the calendaring and scheduling process. The first of these, the Schedule Manager, automatically creates the Free Time database (BUSYTIME.NSF) and updates the database as users create new calendar entries. When a user requests to view free time, the Schedule Manager references the Free Time database to populate the Free Time dialog box. The Free Time database is a special database that can be accessed only by the Schedule Manager task.

7

The second task, the Calendar Connector, is used when a server receives a free-time request for a person whose mail is located on another server. The Calendar Connector automatically communicates with the other server in real time to retrieve the free-time information and display it to the current user.

USING CALENDARING AND SCHEDULING IN OTHER NOTES DATABASES

All the calendaring features in your mail file are available to you while you're designing new Domino applications. You can create special calendar entry forms, check free time, and display your Notes documents using the Calendar views.

These features have many potential uses. For example, a customer service application could display customer orders by order date or ship date using the new Calendar view. Managers and production staff could easily see which orders needed to be shipped in the next day or week.

The date and time controls make any time-based application more user friendly. Your Notes users will no longer need to waste time figuring out which day of the week the 15th of next month falls on; they can simply click the date using the new calendar control.

CHAPTER **8**

USING MOBILE FEATURES FROM HOME OR ON THE ROAD

In this chapter

THE POWER OF MOBILITY

Notes provides members of a team a virtual space to collaborate on projects and share knowledge throughout an organization. The members of your team might all work in the same office and might be constantly connected to the same local area network, at least from 8:00 a.m. until 5:00 p.m. Then again, they might be scattered around the globe. Connections between team members might take place once a day or once a week. Users might be replicating at noon in Bangalore, India; at midnight in Paris; or at 8:00 a.m. in Boston.

Notes users might well say that they carry their office desk with them on their laptop computer. For example, imagine a busy sales representative, Melissa Nickel, who travels to visit several sales areas and occasionally visits a regional office. At the company headquarters in Virginia, she is connected to the local area network (LAN). She reads her Notes mail, which is stored on the Notes server, and works with several of the corporate databases on a daily basis.

We will follow her on one of her sales trips. On the morning before she is scheduled to leave, she updates a local replica copy of her mail database. She also updates a few other vital databases, such as her company's customer-tracking database, an online sales brochure, and a travel planner that lists good places to eat in the cities she will be visiting. If she made full replicas of all the databases she used in the office, her laptop computer would quickly run out of storage space, so she uses a replication formula that collects only those documents that might be relevant to her during her travels. Then she leaves with her most important parts of her desktop stored on her laptop computer.

The first hop of her journey is a long one to Los Angeles, where she has a connecting flight to New Zealand. She visits the Los Angeles office for a meeting before continuing. She connects to the office LAN and selects LA OFFICE as a location. She has already defined the parameters for that location. She doesn't have to define the protocol she is using. She doesn't have to tell the computer that her home/mail Notes server is in Virginia.

Soon, she heads to the airport. Just as she is going toward the departure gate, her mobile phone goes off with a text message. An urgent email is waiting for her. She connects her mobile telephone to the laptop and changes the location setting to MOBILE. She goes to the Replicator page and selects Send and Receive Mail. As soon as Notes is finished picking up her mail, Melissa puts her laptop in her briefcase and heads for the plane.

The call from the airport didn't dial directly to her home/mail server. Instead, the MOBILE location document in her Personal Address Book dialed the L.A. branch office. There, she had defined a passthru server that put her through to Virginia. Because her company uses the Passthru-Server feature, she was able to connect to her personal mail file directly. She used a local call even though her home server was in Virginia.

Soon, Melissa is airborne somewhere high above the Pacific Ocean. She opens her laptop and reads her email. She creates responses to mail when necessary. She selects Send and File as soon as she is done creating a memo. The outgoing mail is held in an outgoing mailbox right on her laptop computer, ready for transfer to the server the next time she connects. She sends another memo to coworker Jessica Beasley, who sent a spreadsheet that she will need in New Zealand. The spreadsheet was sent as an attachment in a message. She addresses a memo simply to Jessica, knowing that Notes will look up the correct address in her Personal Address Book.

The urgent message that Melissa picked up in L.A. mentions a new client who can see her for only 15 minutes at the airport because he is catching an outgoing flight. No problem. The client is in the Client Tracking database on her laptop. She opens the client's profile to brush up on his background. She examines her proposal and works on a presentation for her 15-minute meeting. When she meets the client, she will be able to launch the application from within the proposal in Notes.

She continues to read and respond to her email, takes time out for lunch, browses the latest updates to the Lotus Web pages (offline, of course), and then has a nap.

When she lands in New Zealand, she meets the client as soon as she gets off the plane. She shows him her proposal. He likes it. As soon as he boards his flight, she hooks up her laptop to a phone line in the airport and changes the location to Travel, another location that she has predefined. From the Replicator page, she selects Send Outgoing Mail. Notes dials an Internet account with a local number to an ISP set up through a location document. The proposal is routed through her home server in Virginia along with all the other mail in her outgoing mailbox. By the time she gathers her luggage and picks up a rental car, the proposal is sitting in the client's mail box. The result is another sale. The elapsed time: half an hour on the ground.

When she finally reaches her hotel, she hooks up her modem line to the hotel telephone and switches to a location named Hotel. She clicks Start from the Replicator page. Notes prompts her for the telephone number to call. She selects the phone number for the Internet provider, and the modem dials 9 before dialing out. By the time she sits down to dinner, she has current data on her laptop computer, an order from her newest client has already been sent to the fulfillment clerk, and she is ready to enjoy a stroll down Mount Maunganui beach.

Notes deserves a lot of the credit. It made Melissa's work effortless because of the mobile features.

SETTING UP A LAPTOP FOR MOBILE COMPUTING

You must do a few things before you can travel the world as easily as Melissa. First, you need Notes 6 and a valid Notes user ID. You need a Notes-compatible modem set up to use with your laptop. You must also have the phone numbers of the Domino servers that you want to contact or, alternatively, the phone number for an Internet provider and the IP address of the Domino server. You need an analog phone line to connect to, plus a phone cord, extra batteries, a power adapter, and so on.

8

Within Notes itself, five items need to be set up properly before you can take full advantage of Lotus Notes on the road:

- You need to set up and define ports.
- You need to set up and define locations.
- You need to make local replicas of databases.
- You need to set up and define replication schedules if you will be replicating on a scheduled basis.
- The Domino Administrator needs to set up passthru servers, if necessary, and you need to create server connection documents to identify the passthru server and any other servers you will be using.

Many of the mobile options can be initiated from the File, Mobile menu option. The options on this menu include the following:

- Choose Current Location displays a list of available locations from which you can select. The same list is available from the Locations section of the status bar, found near the bottom-right corner of the Notes window workspace.
- Edit Current Location displays the location record for the currently selected location. You can also edit the location record from the Locations section of the Status bar.
- Edit Current Time/Phone displays a dialog box so that you can enter specific dialing information for the current location, including the current time, the number to dial to get an outside line, and the country and area codes.
- Locations displays the Advanced Locations view in the Personal Address Book; from here, you can select location documents for editing or create new locations.
- Server Phone Numbers displays the Advanced Connections view in the Personal Address Book so that you can edit existing server connection records or create new records. The server connection documents hold the phone number to call a specific server.
- Call Server enables you to select a server from a list of those servers for which a connection document exists, and initiate the call so that you can directly access databases on the server (assuming that you are authorized to do so).
- Hang Up disconnects your modem from the server.

SETTING UP PORTS

Any discussion about Notes 6 as a mobile computing platform depends on your capability to establish communications between your workstation and the Domino server with which you are communicating. That means configuring either a network connection or a connection via a modem.

You can set up multiple ports. You can then choose which port to use for a specific location, depending on the type of connection that is available. Each port uses a specific communications protocol, which must match one of the protocols being used by the Domino server that you are communicating with.

COMMUNICATIONS PROTOCOLS

All connections between a Notes client and a Domino server are classified as either a network connection or a dial-in connection, regardless of whether the connection is made locally or from a mobile computer. Although we usually think of a network connection as being local, physical connections to a network, a network connection also includes a wide area network (WAN) with a link to the server through a bridge or router and a connection over the Internet via TCP/IP. Notes provides several communications drivers and protocols, including the following:

- NetBIOS is used to communicate over any network that uses NetBIOS.

- NetWare SPX is used to communicate over a Novell network using the native SPX protocol rather than NetBIOS. Beginning with Release 6, support for SPX from Unix platforms has been has been removed. However, it is still possible to manage servers running older releases of Domino from Release 6 servers.

- TCP/IP, the most common protocol, is used to communicate between client and server and between Notes servers across all supported Notes hardware platforms. Because of its cross-platform capabilities, TCP/IP is widely used. Of course, TCP/IP is also the protocol used on the Internet. This means that you can connect to a Notes server via the Internet through a local call to an ISP, no matter what your location is.

TIP

> Although one of the banner applications in Notes is the integrated browser, you do not need to use TCP/IP on your workstation to navigate on the Web. You can also have the Domino server handle all Web retrievals while you connect to the server over an internal network using a protocol other than TCP/IP. In such a setup, you can read Web pages while you are disconnected from the network. Browsing the Web while on the road is discussed in greater detail near the end of this chapter.

- XPC is built into every Notes client and server, and is used to communicate over dialup or null modem connections when no other communication drivers are available.

NOTE

> Beginning with Release 6, Lotus has stopped supporting the Banyan VINES and AppleTalk network protocols. The AppleTalk protocol was traditionally used to communicate with Macintosh clients. The Banyan VINES network protocol was used for communication over a Banyan VINES network.

8

DEFINING A NEW PORT

You can define more than one port. Each port that you define is associated with a particular communications protocol. Follow these steps to define a new port within the User Preferences dialog box:

1. Open the Lotus Notes client and select File, Preferences, User Preferences from the menu bar.

2. Click the Ports tab on the left of the dialog box. The User Preferences screen is shown in Figure 8.1.

Figure 8.1
Set up ports using the User Preferences dialog box.

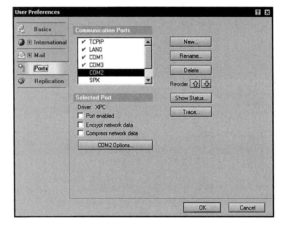

3. Click the New button to display a dialog box where you type the name of the new port (for instance, COM5).

4. Select the protocol and specify at which locations you will use this protocol.

   Each port name is associated with a single communications protocol. You can rename or delete a port, but you cannot change the protocol assigned to that port. If you want the port to have a different protocol, you must delete the port and then create a new port by the same name using the new protocol.

5. Click OK.

After you name the port, select a protocol, and identify locations where the port will be used, you can define additional optional information by clicking the Options button under the protocol name, as listed here:

- **TCP/IP**—You can define the duration of a connection-attempt timeout.

- **NetBIOS**—You can choose between automatic and manual setup. If you choose manual setup, you can specify the NetBIOS unit/LAN0 number.

- **IPX**—You can choose between automatic and advanced configuration for NetWare Services. The advanced configuration enables you to choose NetWare Directory and Bindery Services, NetWare Directory Services (NDS), or Bindery Services.

8

- **XPC**—For all COM ports, the default protocol is XPC, which depends on having a modem connected to the COM port (either internally or externally) or a null modem that connects one computer to another directly via a null modem cable.

SETTING UP A MODEM

Because we are talking about the mobile use of Notes, you need a modem and a phone connection to communicate with the Domino server. Setting up a modem is done when you select the XPC protocol. If you select XPC, you need to define the type of modem you are using before you can finish defining the port.

Because we created a new port named COM5, the User Preferences dialog box displays a button labeled COM5 Options. Click this button to display the Additional Setup dialog box, shown in Figure 8.2.

Figure 8.2
The Additional Setup dialog box is used to define modem communications for a COM port.

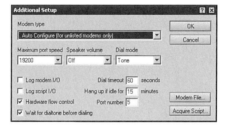

In this dialog box, you select a modem type from among the nearly 150 modem files that ship with Notes. If you cannot find a file that matches your modem, some generic modem files are available. If you cannot find your modem, you can select Auto Configure near the bottom of the list of modems, and Notes will select the file that most closely matches your particular modem. The modem files are placed in a Modems directory in Notes's default data directory upon installation, so if you have moved the modem files to another location, Notes might have a hard time locating the files.

After you select a modem type, you can select the following options for the modem:

- **Maximum Port Speed**—Select the first speed above the highest-rated speed for your modem. For example, if your modem is rated at a port speed of 14400, select 19200 as your maximum port speed so that your modem can then operate at its highest-rated speed. If you are having problems with a noisy phone line, try dropping back to the next lowest speed, and then continue to drop down incrementally (if necessary) until the noise disappears.

CAUTION

Some modems might not connect if the Notes speed is set too high. You might have to experiment if you are having trouble connecting with your modem.

8

- **Speaker Volume**—Set the speaker volume on your modem to Off, Low, Medium, or High.

- **Dial Mode**—The dial mode can be Tone or Pulse, depending on the type of phone system you have. Normally, this should be left on Tone.

- **Log Modem I/O**—If you select this option, modem-control strings and responses are recorded in the Miscellaneous Events view of your local Notes log database. Keep this selected only if you are troubleshooting suspected modem problems. Otherwise, leave it deselected; the logging adds a lot of extra information to the log files.

- **Log Script I/O**—If you select this, asynchronous script-file responses get recorded in the Miscellaneous Events view of your local Notes log database. Keep this selected only if you are troubleshooting suspected problems with a script file. Otherwise, keep it deselected because this also adds a lot of extra information to your Notes log.

- **Hardware Flow Control**—This controls the flow of data between your computer and the modem. Select this for most modems. Deselect this only if your modem doesn't support flow control or if you are using certain null modem connections or some types of add-in equipment, such as older versions of DigiBoard. If a modem doesn't support flow control, set the maximum speed for the computer and the modem to the same lower-speed settings, to reduce CRC errors.

- **Wait for Dial Tone Before Dialing**—This makes sure that you have a dial tone before the modem starts attempting to make a connection.

- **Dial Timeout**—This is used to tell the modem to pause for a set length of time before trying again if a connection cannot be made with the server. It keeps the modem from dialing constantly, and it gives the server a better chance of being available on the next try. You might want to increase the timeout to 120 or 180 seconds to minimize the number of retries.

- **Hang Up If Idle For**—This setting tells the modem to hang up if there is no activity on the phone line for a set length of time. If the phone line is idle for too long, the connection is broken and the modem hangs up the phone. This greatly reduces the cost of long-distance calls if you are away from the computer when your call is finished.

- **Port Number**—This is the COM port that is being used by the modem.

- **Modem File**—This button displays the modem text file for the selected modem. If you are familiar with modem drivers, you can edit and customize the modem file.

- **Acquire Script**—This button opens a box that lists available acquire scripts. An *acquire script* is a text file used to find a communication device, such as an ISDN modem, before the modem script is run. For example, you might need an acquire script to connect to one of the modems. The acquire script is stored in the modem directory and has a filename extension of .SCR. When you select an acquire script, it is permanently associated with that COM port. To disconnect from the script, edit the port, select the Acquire Script button again, and select NONE as the script that you want to associate with the port. If you need to create or edit a script file, you should refer to the Administrator's Guide that comes with Notes. The guide provides sample files and definitions of script file keywords and script command lines.

When you are done selecting advanced options, click OK to save your changes.

You should be aware of two other check boxes on the Ports tab of the User Preferences dialog box:

- **Encrypt Network Data**—If you select the Encrypt Network Data option, all communication through the port will be encrypted, regardless of whether it is implemented on the workstation end or on the Notes server end. If you elect to encrypt data through the port, the other end will also be forced to encrypt the data. This will slow the transmission of data slightly.
- **Compress Network Data**—If you select Compress Network Data, you can improve performance by compressing all network traffic between the workstation and Domino server.

USING LOCATION DOCUMENTS

The Personal Address Book that's created during the installation and setup of the Notes client contains the following default locations:

- Office (Network), which you use when you are directly connected to the Notes network in your office
- Home (Notes Direct Dialup), which uses a modem to dial into a Notes server
- Home (Network Dialup), which uses a modem to dial into a network
- Travel (Notes Direct Dialup), which enables you to define how to connect to the Notes server when you are on the road
- Island (Disconnected), which enables you to work as an isolated workstation with no connection to a Notes network

You can edit the definitions for each of the locations, and you can create additional location documents. For example, you might want to define a Hotel location document that automatically enters your phone card number when you dial.

A location document defines where to find your mail file, how to make a connection to your home server (the one that holds your mail file), and other specifications for the location.

WORKING WITH LOCATION DOCUMENTS

To view a location document, select Advanced, Locations in the Personal Address Book. Click an existing location document, or click the New action button and select Location to add a new location. You can also select File, Mobile, Locations to open the Locations view.

Each type of location from which you want to use Notes has its own location document, as shown in Figure 8.3. The document is divided into several tabs, including: basic details, server information, connectivity ports, configuration details of mail database, Internet browser integration, and replication settings. Dialup locations have a tab for phone settings. Two additional tabs provide access to advanced and administrative functions.

8

Figure 8.3
Name your location and define the type of connection on the first page of the location document.

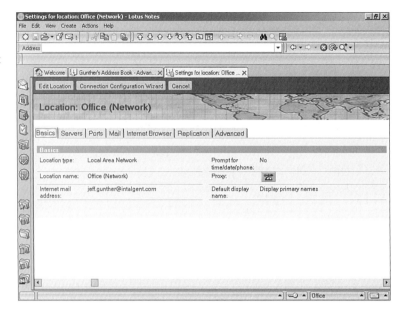

The tabs of the location document are described in the following sections:

BASICS

The information on the Basics page includes the name of the location document. Select the type of connection from among the following:

- Local Area Network (including an Internet connection to a Domino server)
- Notes Direct Dialup (modem connection to a Domino server)
- Network Dialup (modem connection to a network)
- Custom
- No Connection (Notes on a standalone workstation)

Depending on the type of location, you are prompted for other information. For example, with a dialup connection, you can elect to have Notes prompt you for the time, date, and phone number every time you connect. This might be necessary if you travel a lot and don't want a separate location document for each time zone. At a minimum, you must enter the name of the location; you also can enter an Internet address; whether to prompt for date, time, and phone number; and whether to display your primary name or alternate name from the Domino Directory.

SERVERS

You can define five different servers for a location:

- The home/mail server is the Notes server on which your mail database is stored.

- The passthru server is your default Notes passthru server, if you have one defined. The passthru server enables you to dial one Notes server and, from that single connection, get passed through to other Notes servers. This enables you to make a single phone call and replicate all your databases, even if they reside on different servers. Refer to "Verifying the Passthru Server in the Location Document," later in this chapter, for details.

- The catalog/domain search server is the server on which you want to perform domain-wide searches for information using the Search icon on the toolbar.

- The Domino Directory server is the server where Notes should look for the Domino Directory when doing name lookups.

- The catalog/domain search server is the server on which database catalog or domain searches are performed. Ask your administrator whether your organization has a dedicated server for this. If this is left blank, the home/mail server is used.

- The Domino Directory server is the server where Notes should look for the Domino Directory when addressing mail and doing name lookups. If it is left blank, the home/mail server is used for this.

- The Sametime server is the name of your Lotus Sametime server. A Sametime server allows you to instant message individuals and get real-time information about who's online within your organization.

PORTS

Select one or more ports for use at this location. You will see a list of all ports that you have set up and enabled. If a connection cannot be made from the first enabled port, Notes tries the next one until a successful connection is made.

MAIL

For each location, you can specify details about your mail. For Notes mail, you specify whether your mail database is located on the Domino server or on your workstation. If you have server-based mail selected, you must connect to the server either remotely or via a LAN to access your mail. If you have workstation-based mail selected, you can perform functions such as compose mail or forward documents without having to connect to the server. The difference between the two types of mail is that, with server-based mail, documents are immediately routed to the user's mail file on the Notes server. With workstation-based mail, documents are held locally in an outgoing mailbox (with the filename mail.box) and are transferred later, when a connection is made to the home server. Enter the path to your mail file from the Notes data directory into the Mail file field.

The location document's Mail tab is shown in Figure 8.4.

Figure 8.4
Enter mail informa-
tion on the Mail tab
of the Locations
dialog box.

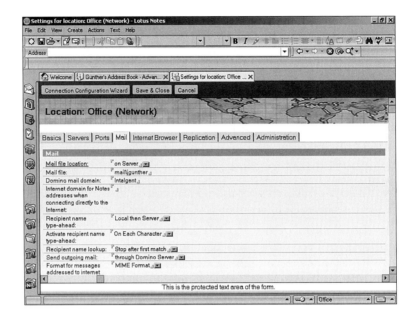

Other fields on the mail setup page include the following:

■ **Internet Domain for Notes Addresses When Connecting Directly to the
   Internet**—Specifies the Internet domain to use if you have Internet mail accounts
   enabled for the workstation.

■ **Recipient Name Type-Ahead**—Enables you to address mail memos using type-ahead,
   with Notes looking in either your Personal Address Book or the Domino Directory on
   your mail server to find a name and display it as soon as you type enough letters to
   uniquely identify the addressee. If the field is Disabled, the Notes client does not automatically suggest the names when addressing a new mail memo.

■ **Activate Recipient Name Type-Ahead**—The On Each Character option enables
   Notes to find a name from your address books with each letter that is entered into the
   memo. The On Delimiter choice instructs Notes to look for names only after you've
   completed typing the name.

■ **Recipient Name Lookup**—You can choose to stop looking up names when you come
   up with a match if you select Stop After First Match. Otherwise, Notes finds all the
   names that match the typed recipient name and requests that you select the correct
   name.

■ **Send Outgoing Mail**—With Notes mail, the mail goes through the Domino server,
   where it is routed to the Internet. If you are using an alternative form of mail, you can
   opt to send it directly to the Internet.

■ **Format for Messages Addressed to Internet Addresses**—You can specify Notes
   Rich Text Format or MIME for outgoing mail to the Internet.

8

- **Transfer Outgoing Mail If**—If you're using a dialup location document, the final field in the Mail tab of the location document has to do with mail routing. If you have set up a location with the mail file defined as local, you can have your workstation dial the server automatically when a certain number of outgoing messages are waiting. As soon as the minimum threshold is reached, your workstation automatically calls the home server and transfers outgoing mail.

INTERNET BROWSER

The Internet Browser section is used to define which browser you want to use from this location.

If you select Notes as your browser, you can define whether to retrieve Web pages from the local workstation (that is, directly from the Internet) or offline.

Otherwise, you have a choice of using Notes, Notes with Internet Explorer (IE), Internet Explorer by itself, Netscape, or another browser whose EXE file you can identify. For a fully integrated browser in the Notes client, you should select Notes with Internet Explorer. Notes uses the Notes browser interface but uses the IE engine and executables to retrieve pages, so you can move between Notes and the Web seamlessly.

> **NOTE**
>
> The Notes and Notes with Internet Explorer options enable you to view Web pages within the Lotus Notes client environment. The other choices launch an external application when trying to access a Web site.

REPLICATION

The process of replication is described in detail in Chapter 38, "Replication and Its Administration." Basically, it is the process of synchronizing databases that have a single, identical ID but that reside on different systems. Replication takes place between two servers or between a workstation and a server. However, no peer-to-peer replication takes place between workstations.

> **NOTE**
>
> Notes and Domino use the replica ID number to locate and replicate all replicas of a database. A database copy (created by choosing File, Database, New Copy) does not have the same ID number as its original database, and doesn't replicate.

The replication that is initiated from the location document is workstation-to-server replication. You can enable a schedule and then, when the scheduled replication time arrives, the workstation automatically connects to the server and replicates. The process takes place in the background so that you can continue working without interruption. When a process runs in the background, you can continue doing other work while replication is taking place.

8

The Replication section of the location document gives you the option of enabling or disabling a schedule.

You can set up a schedule that includes a range of times during which scheduled replication will take place, or you can set specific times for replication. Multiple times are separated by commas. If you define a range of times, you can also enter a repeat interval. A repeat interval of 360 minutes, for example, means that the workstation will dial the server 6 hours after the last successful replication completed.

Normally, you will want to set up scheduled replication only for time-sensitive databases. You can then select a repeat interval that is appropriate for your situation. Note that you can also set up the schedule so that it works only on specified days of the week. You might want to set up scheduled replication if you are working from home on certain days of the week and use manual replication when you are on the road away from your office or home, when your connection times to the Domino server are likely to be of shorter duration.

A check box also gives you the ability to enable high-priority replication with set intervals. Replication priority is set using the Replication Settings button in the Database Properties dialog box. If a database is defined as a high-priority database, it shows up on the Replicator page with a red exclamation mark beside it. You can save time on the road and replicate just high-priority databases by using a scheduled replication or by selecting Replicate High Priority Databases from the Start Now button on the Replicator page.

ADVANCED

The Advanced section has a number of fields used to refine how Notes works with data. The Advanced Basics page for a local area network connection is shown in Figure 8.5.

Figure 8.5
Define advanced location options by moving among subtabs on the Advanced page in the locations document.

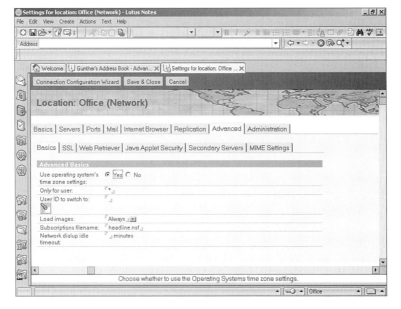

All location documents enable you to specify whether daylight saving time is observed at the location so that Notes can coordinate differences in time between the server and the mobile workstation.

If a workstation is being used by more than one user, you can specify which user or users are authorized to use a particular location document in the Only For User field. You can also specify which user ID should be used from the location. This is useful only if you have multiple user IDs or multiple users on the workstation.

You can specify whether to download images immediately when the document is first loaded. This feature can be useful if you're using a slow network connection.

You can specify the name of your Bookmarks file. The Bookmarks file determines which Domino applications are available from the Bookmark buttons. You can also specify which database to use for your subscriptions. Using these two databases, you can set up a workstation so that it can be customized for different users by switching between locations.

The last option on the Advanced Basics page lets you set the length of idle time after which a dialup connection should automatically disconnect.

The following are the other Advanced option tabs:

- **SSL**—You can determine whether your computer will accept SSL site certificates and expired SSL certificates. You can also define which SSL protocol version you want to use.

- **Web Retriever**—You can use this page to define options for the integrated Web browser, including the name of your Personal Web Browser database, how many concurrent retrievers you can have open (up to 25), what level of activity logging you want for your Web retriever, and how often to update the cached Web pages.

- **Java Applet Security**—Use this to define location-specific security settings for Java applets.

- **Secondary Servers**—If your location is a LAN connection, you can set up secondary servers. If you set up TCP/IP as the communications protocol, for example, you can use a secondary domain name server when the first server is not available. When TCP/IP is used as your communications protocol, the location is set up as a LAN connection.

- **MIME Settings**—You can define how MIME conversions are handled.

SETTING UP PASSTHRU SERVERS

Passthru servers provide a single point of contact for users who might want to contact multiple servers. Instead of calling each server separately to work with one or two databases, you can call a single passthru server, and it will forward-link you through itself and possibly through other intermediate passthru servers until you are in contact with the destination server.

Passthru servers provide a couple of advantages. First, the passthru server can act as a conduit for all requests to a number of servers in an organization. All the external communication comes through a communications hub server, which passes users through to the server they want to contact. The passthru server does not need to hold replica copies of the databases that users want to access. Instead, it must provide only the connection to the destination server. Second, the passthru server can handle multiple protocols, thus enabling connection from a variety of users. The destination servers need only a single protocol—one that can communicate with the passthru server—and the users need only a single protocol that can communicate with the passthru server. The server provides the connection between the different protocols. This simplifies setup by minimizing the number of multiple-protocol servers needed in the organization.

The mobile Notes user at the beginning of this chapter was able to call a local passthru server in Los Angeles. The server passed her through to her home server in Virginia. In this way, all the communication costs were incurred through the corporate WAN, which is a fixed cost to the corporation, rather than through a long-distance telephone call at much higher rates.

Setting up the passthru server is an administrative function and requires the correct documents in four locations:

> A passthru connection document must be created for each server in the Domino Directory.

> The passthru restrictions for each server document must be properly filled in. This is done in the server document itself, not in the passthru connection document.

> Users must verify that they have the correct information in a passthru server connection document in their Personal Address Book.

> The Default Passthru Server field in the location document must correctly identify the passthru server that will be used from that location.

The first two steps are for the system administrator. The second two steps are done on your local machine and are described in the next sections.

MOBILE USER PASSTHRU CONNECTION DOCUMENTS

Mobile users must set up a connection document for the passthru server in their Personal Address Books. To do this, open the Personal Address Book and add a passthru server connection document, shown in Figure 8.6, by clicking Advanced, Connections, and then choosing New, Server Connection.

Select Passthru Server as the connection type. Enter the name of the destination server and the name of the passthru server that will be used to connect to the destination server.

In the Advanced section of the connection document, you can specify which locations can use this passthru server connection. For example, suppose you have a laptop that you take to client sites and a docking station with a modem at home. You can define two location documents (such as Home and Client) to use the same passthru server. But if you are staying in a hotel in another city, it might be more economical to dial the destination server directly. You can restrict the use of this connection document so that it is valid only for certain locations.

Figure 8.6
Add a passthru server document in your Personal Address Book.

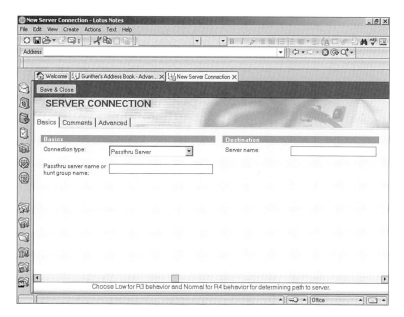

VERIFYING THE PASSTHRU SERVER IN THE LOCATION DOCUMENT

On each location document in the your Personal Address Book are four server fields, described earlier: They specify the home/mail server, the passthru server, the search server, and the Domino Directory server. You should verify that the correct server is named in the Passthru Server field and that the server name is spelled correctly. Use the fully distinguished name of the passthru server—for example, Coruscant/Republic/Galaxy.

Setting a passthru server makes the process of connecting as automated as possible. You select a replica of a database that is on the destination server, and then you replicate it. Assuming that you are hooked up to a telephone at some mobile site, Notes does everything without having to prompt you for information. Notes automatically calls the server. The passthru server authenticates your user ID. The passthru server then calls the destination server, authenticates with the server, and passes you through to your destination. Authentication takes place at every step of the way, so you cannot use the passthru server to gain unauthorized access to another Notes server.

SELECTING DATABASES FOR REPLICATION

The primary tool that gives you access to remote data is replication. As a mobile user, you should consider a couple of things: which databases you will need to have available locally and which documents within those databases you will need.

A corollary to those two considerations is the determination of when you should replicate. As a rule, you will want to make an initial replication before you leave. The initial replication is much quicker over the LAN, and you don't have to tie up the telephone lines as you would if you decided later to replicate from somewhere on the road. If you choose to perform the initial replication over the network, subsequent replication while on the road will only update documents that have changed since the last replication.

For a database to replicate, there must be at least two replica copies of the database: one on your workstation and one on the Domino server. You create the replica on your workstation by opening the server application and selecting File, Replication, New Replica. Make selections in the dialog box that is displayed to create the new replica on your local workstation.

TIP

You can open any folder of bookmarks as a workspace by right-clicking the folder and selecting Open as Workspace.

With a set of bookmarks opened as a workspace, you can switch from one replica to another by clicking the small arrow in the lower-right corner of the database icon and selecting the replica you want. Figure 8.7 demonstrates how to select a replica.

Figure 8.7
Select a replica database using the arrowhead in the lower-right corner when a folder of bookmark is open as grid.

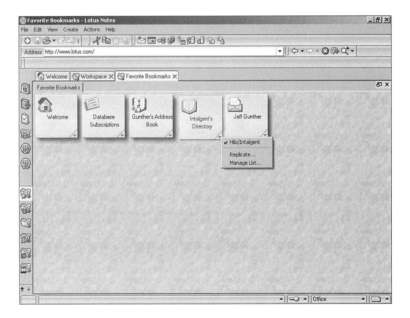

Whichever icon is on top is the currently selected version of the database. So, if the top icon is the server-based replica of the database, when you select it, Notes attempts to contact the server. If it is a local replica, Notes opens the replica that is on your workstation.

8

Notes determines which databases are replicas of each other by comparing each database's replica ID to see whether they are the same. The replica ID can be seen on the information page of the Database properties box, shown in Figure 8.8.

NOTE

> If a copy of a database is created using the operating system, the databases will have the same replica ID as the original.

Figure 8.8
Identical replica IDs mean that two databases are replicas of each other.

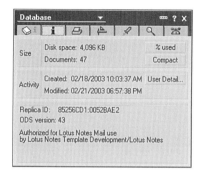

If the replica IDs are the same on two databases, they are replicas of each other, even though you might have renamed one of the databases. The databases might even contain a different subset of documents as the result of selective replication. You can also tell whether they are replicas by opening the folder of bookmark as a workspace. If a database's icons are not stacked on top of each other, they are not replicas. If they are stacked, they are replicas of each other.

INITIATING REPLICATION

To replicate a local database from a mobile location, the database must have a replica on the server you call or on another server that can be reached using a passthru server.

You can initiate a replication from a mobile workstation in these ways:

- With the application open, choose File, Replication, Replicate.
- Set up scheduled replication on the location document.
- Use the Replicator page to manually initiate replication. You can open the Replicator page by clicking the Replicator icon on the Bookmark bar. The icon illustrates a folder with two same databases.

The Replicator page, illustrated in Figure 8.9, consolidates all the replication options in a single location. This page holds entries for all the databases that you want to replicate. You can select specific databases for replication by clicking in the check box to indicate that those databases should be replicated during the next replication with the server. You can select replicas that are on different servers if you are using a passthru server for replication.

8

Figure 8.9
You can control replication from the Replicator page.

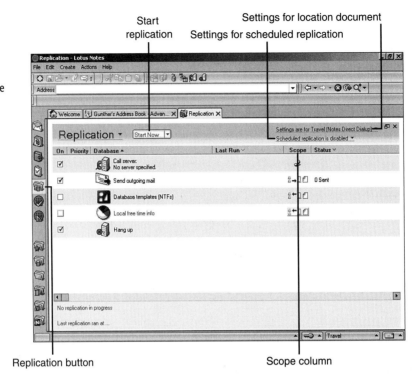

Start replication

Settings for location document

Settings for scheduled replication

Replication button

Scope column

Each row on the Replicator page has a check box beside it. If an item is checked, it will be replicated during the next replication session. If it is not checked, it will not replicate during the next replication session:

- If you check Call Server, Notes calls the selected server even if the replica is not on that server. You could specify a passthru server to call. Call Server is created only for replication through dialup connections. You can add this to your Replicator page by selecting Create, Call Entry from the menu. It can be paired with a Hang Up entry to complete the call when you are done replicating.

- If you check Send Outgoing Mail, Notes checks your store/forward mailbox and sends any outgoing mail messages at the same time it replicates.

- If you check Database Templates, template files are replicated.

- If you check any databases, those databases are replicated. Notes automatically puts databases on the Replicator page when the replica is first created. If you want to remove an icon from the Replicator page, you can select the icon and press the Delete key. If you want to put the icon back in the Replicator page, you can select File, Database, Open from the Replicator page or initiate replication from the File menu. You can set replication settings for an individual database by selecting File, Replication, Settings. This enables you to specify which documents get replicated before replication actually takes place.

■ If you check Hang Up, Notes hangs up as soon as the replication is completed. If the Hang Up icon is not checked, Notes remains in communication with the server after the replication is completed.

You can manually initiate replication from the Replicator page by selecting the Start Now action button. If you click the Replication button, as demonstrated in Figure 8.10, you can create a folder to arrange and organize all your icons for replication. For example, you might want to have a folder called Personal that contains all your replicas. When you choose the Create Folder menu item, the New Folder dialog box is displayed (see Figure 8.10).

Figure 8.10
Folders allow you to arrange and organize all your icons for replication.

To add databases to the folder, simply drag a row from the Replicator page to the folder. Figure 8.11 shows a replica of a mail database being added to a Personal replication folder. In this figure, the database template replication icon is being dragged and dropped into the Personal folder.

Figure 8.11
Replicas can be added to a folder by dragging and dropping.

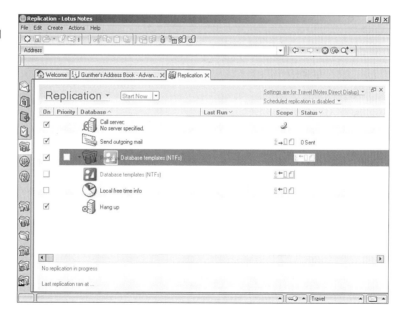

Finally, for each row on the Replicator page except the Hang Up row, you can click the button in the scope column to change settings for the action or database. For example, you could change a database's replication settings to send documents but not receive any new documents.

8

NOTE

Replication is discussed here in the context of the mobile user. However, in some instances a user might use replication over a local area network. For example, a designer might want to make design changes on a replica of a database rather than making modifications directly on a production database. When the design changes are completed, they can be replicated back to the production database.

REPLICATING OVER A DIALUP CONNECTION

You can connect over a modem in a couple of ways, depending on the type of work you will be doing. If you are always working with a particular subset of documents that you carry around with you on your laptop, you will want to connect to the server to replicate those documents, either on a regularly scheduled basis or on an as-needed basis. On the other hand, if you are looking up something in a large database that you do not need to access routinely, you can stay connected to the Notes server for a few minutes, open the database to find the information you want, and then disconnect from the server.

To replicate a single database, follow these steps:

1. Open the local replica of the database you want to replicate.
2. Choose File, Replication, Replicate, and then go to Step 3.

    or

    Locate the database icon on the Replicator page and make sure it is the only database with a check mark beside it. Then click the Start button to start background replication immediately.

3. Notes displays a dialog box that enables you to decide between background replication and replication with options for this one-time replication. Options include which server to replicate with, whether to send documents, whether to receive documents, and whether to receive whole documents, summary information plus 40KB of rich text, or summary information only.

4. Click OK to begin replication. The status bar will report the status of replication. When replication is completed, Notes disconnects from the server connection automatically if you have the Hang Up icon checked.

To replicate multiple databases, display the Replicator page, make sure that the databases you want to replicate are checked, and click the Start Now button. You can also edit the location document to enable automatic replication, as described earlier in this chapter.

You have a couple of options if you want to connect to a server so that you can work with databases online, or if you want to add new databases to your desktop while using a dialup connection:

- Open the database using File, Database, Open, and then select the name of the server. Notes displays the Open Database dialog box to verify that you want to make a dialup connection, and then it calls the server and opens the database. You will remain connected to the server when you are done working with the database, so remember to hang up (described later) when finished.

- Select File, Mobile, Call Server. A list of phone numbers that can be called to connect to the server is displayed. Select or type the number you want to call and click Auto-Dial. Notes calls the server. You can then work with any databases to which you have access on the server. When you are done, remember to hang up.

- Click the Call Server button on the replication toolbar. Everything else is the same as when calling the server from the drop-down menu.

To hang up when you are finished connecting to a server, select File, Mobile, Hang Up, or click the Hang Up button on the replication toolbar. Notes displays a list of COM ports. Select the port that is currently connected and click Hang Up.

USING MOBILE NOTES AFTER IT IS SET UP

So far, the focus of this chapter has been how to get set up as a mobile user. Now let's assume that everything is set up correctly and that you are ready to work on the road. There is no single correct way to work with Notes. How you manage your databases and your connections to the Notes server depends on the type of data you are using and the type of organization you are working with. The options described in the following sections are, therefore, just some of the ways you can work with Mobile Notes.

SELECTING A LOCATION

As a mobile user, you select a location to work from by selecting the appropriate location document. You can do this in either of two different places:

- Choose File, Mobile, Choose Current Location. Then select the location you want from a list.

- Click the Location button (located near the right side of the Status bar at the bottom of the Notes window) and select the current location from a list.

The location document contains relevant information for each location, such as what type of connection (if any) you have to the server, whether your outgoing mailbox is local or on your home server, and which databases should be replicated on what sort of schedule. You can edit the current location document so that replication and mail parameters suit your particular needs. After this is set up the way you want it, all you have to do is select the location; Notes takes care of everything else. Notes knows whether to dial the server directly or use a passthru server, which databases should be replicated, which phone numbers to dial, and so on—all based on the location document for that location.

CONNECTING OVER THE INTERNET

To connect to a Domino server over the Internet, you must have your server set up with a direct connection to the Internet, the server must be running TCP/IP, and it must have its own IP address.

If you already have an account with an Internet service provider (ISP) for browsing the Web, and if your Domino server is connected to the Internet using TCP/IP, you are all set—as long as you know your server's Internet IP address.

After everything is set up, follow these steps:

1. Establish either a direct or a dialup Internet connection. You can use either the Serial Line Internet Protocol (SLIP) or the Point-to-Point Protocol (PPP). This gives your workstation the equivalent of TCP/IP functionality.

2. After you have an Internet connection, start Notes and make sure that you are using a location document that uses a TCP/IP port—for example, the Internet location. You are then seen by the server as a node on the local Notes network, and you can open databases or replicate databases from the server, just as you would if you were in the office working over the local area network.

SENDING MAIL AS A MOBILE USER

To send mail, create a memo just as you would if you were directly connected to the office LAN. When you are disconnected as a mobile user, however, you are creating a memo using your local replica copy of your mail file. Notes can look up names for addressing in any address books that you have defined under File, Preferences, User Preferences, Mail. You must have a local replica of the address book or Domino Directory to do a lookup while disconnected.

Outgoing mail is placed into your outgoing mailbox. The mail is sent to the server's mailbox by the router when you replicate. This assumes that you have Send Outgoing Mail checked on the Replicator page. Otherwise, you can send mail without replicating other databases by clicking the Send and Receive Mail button on the Replicator page. You can also send and receive mail from the mail icon in the right corner of the Status bar at the bottom of the screen.

You can replicate your mail database with your mail database on your home server, just as with any other database.

DATABASE SECURITY FOR MOBILE NOTES

The one problem with using Notes on the road has always been the fact that a laptop computer can be lost or stolen. That means that databases on the laptop can also be stolen, and those databases might contain valuable information that you don't want to have fall into the wrong hands. Notes 6 provides two security features for databases that the mobile user should be aware of:

■ **Local enforcement of the Access Control List**—The Database Manager can elect to enforce a consistent Access Control List across all replicas of a database. With this feature turned on, replica databases on your laptop cannot be accessed unless the user has a valid ID (and a password that lets him use that ID).

■ **Encryption of local databases**—You can elect to encrypt local databases, thereby making the database unusable to anyone unless the person has the proper user ID and its associated passwords. This is set up by clicking the Encryption button on the first page of the Database properties box and selecting the options you want.

8

CHAPTER 9

USING THE NOTES CLIENT ON THE INTERNET

In this chapter

SETTING UP AND USING THE TCP/IP PROTOCOL

Lotus Notes has evolved quickly along with the Internet. Today, your data can be sitting on a computer practically anywhere in the world, and you can still access it over your local area network. You have to be using the TCP/IP protocol, and you need an Internet connection. The rest of the puzzle depends on how the data is stored. If the data is on a Domino server, you can gain access to the data using a Notes client. If the data is being served to the World Wide Web, you can use any Web browser to access it.

To set up TCP/IP, you need to have one of the following:

- A defined TCP/IP port
- A location document that has TCP/IP as its communication protocol
- A connection document that accesses a Domino server with access to the Internet
- A direct connection to the Internet through an ISP

DEFINING A TCP/IP PORT

To use TCP/IP, you have to define and set up a port. See the previous chapter, "Using Mobile Features from Home or on the Road," for an overview of setting up ports. Here, we look specifically at TCP/IP, the protocol used for communicating over the Internet. Before you can use TCP/IP, it must be configured to run with your operating system. The following information assumes that you have already set up TCP/IP to run with your operating system.

To set up a TCP/IP port, follow these steps:

1. Choose File, Preferences, User Preferences.
2. Click the Ports tab to display the Ports preferences.
3. Highlight TCP/IP in the Communications Ports list box.
4. As shown in Figure 9.1, click the Port Enabled check box to enable TCP/IP.

Figure 9.1
Enable the TCP/IP port in the User Preferences dialog box.

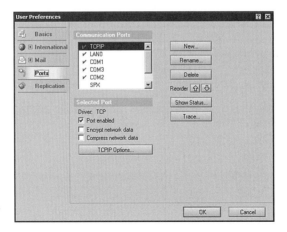

5. Click the TCP/IP Options button to select the timeout period before a reconnection is attempted. The TCP/IP Port Setup dialog box is shown in Figure 9.2.

Figure 9.2
Set the default time-out interval for your TCP/IP connection.

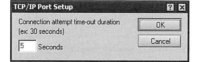

6. Click the Show Status button if you want to verify the driver that is being used for your TCP/IP port.

7. Click the Trace button if you want to trace the connection to a particular server. Enter the server name or TCP/IP address in the dialog box shown in Figure 9.3, and click Trace to view all the logged messages as your workstation attempts to reach the designated server.

TIP

You must have an active connection before you send a trace. You can also copy these messages and paste them into another application, or you can use the trace options and have them logged automatically to help you troubleshoot communication problems.

Figure 9.3
Trace TCP/IP connections to a server if you are having communication problems.

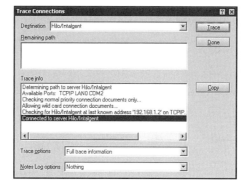

After the TCP/IP port is set up, click OK on the User Preferences dialog box to accept your changes. You can then make TCP/IP available from any location document.

SETTING UP AN INTERNET LOCATION DOCUMENT

You can easily switch to a TCP/IP location by defining a location document that uses your TCP/IP port for communications. When you want to use Notes using TCP/IP on the corporate LAN or on the Internet, switch to that location document, connect to the Internet, and you are up and running.

9

In the location document, you set up the capability to browse Web pages from within Notes. That means that you can view full-featured Web pages from within Notes while you are connected to the Internet. You can later review those pages offline from within a Notes database or share them as Notes documents with other users. Links to documents can lead to either a Notes document or a Web page.

Fields in the location document are used specifically to define your Internet setup. To ensure that you have set up Personal Web Navigator correctly, we'll begin there as we look at the location document. You can view location documents in your Personal Address Book either by choosing File, Mobile, Locations or by clicking the name of the current location on the Status bar in the lower-right corner of the screen and selecting Edit Current. The Internet Browser tab of the Notes 6 location document is shown in Figure 9.4.

Figure 9.4
Set up a Web browser on the location document so you can access the Internet directly from within Notes.

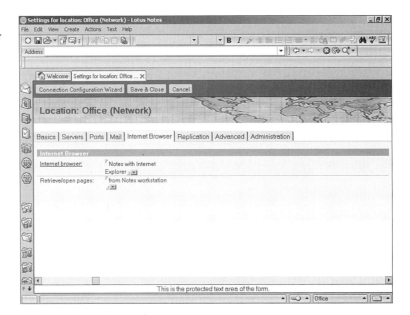

On the Internet Browser field under the Internet Browser tab, you have a choice of how to connect to the World Wide Web from within Notes. You can select one of the following:

- **Notes**—By using this option, you are electing to use the Personal Web Navigator to view Web pages directly using a built-in Notes browser. You can retrieve Web pages when offline using this built-in browser.

- **Notes with Internet Explorer**—Notes has the Internet Explorer browser built into it through a licensing agreement with Microsoft. Similar to the Notes option, this option lets you view Web pages without leaving the Notes user interface (see Figure 9.5). Although it has a different interface than the regular Internet Explorer, it is the same engine in the background. You can still use Notes with Internet Explorer to view pages that you have stored locally in your Personal Web Navigator application.

Figure 9.5
The Notes with Internet Explorer option uses the same rendering engine as the regular Internet Explorer.

- **Netscape Navigator**—If you select this option, Netscape Navigator is launched if it is not already running, and it is used to view any Web pages.

- **Microsoft Internet Explorer**—You can use the full version of Microsoft Internet Explorer rather than the built-in Internet Explorer. The full version of Microsoft Internet Explorer is launched to view any Web pages (see Figure 9.6).

Figure 9.6
The Microsoft Internet Explorer option launches Internet Explorer as an external application.

■ **Other**—If you have another browser that you prefer, such as Mozilla or Opera, you can search for the EXE file for that browser. Notes automatically launches it when you want to link to a Web page.

If you are using a proxy Web server rather than connecting directly through an Internet service provider (ISP) or over a corporate network, go back to the Basics tab and enter the proxy setup information in the Proxy field. This is found on the first tab of the location document. Click the propeller beanie to display the Proxy Server Configuration dialog box shown in Figure 9.7.

Figure 9.7
The Proxy Server Configuration dialog box is used to set up a proxy server for use with your integrated Web browser.

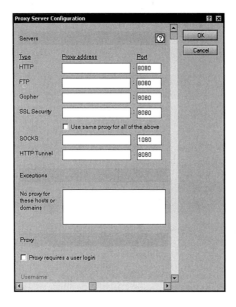

You can enter separate proxies for different application services, including FTP, Gopher, and SSL security, or you can use the same proxy for all Internet protocols. Separate proxies provide additional security by limiting what can be done through any one proxy.

You can enter a SOCKS proxy as well. This is a proxy server for IP hosts behind firewalls. In other words, it intercepts and reissues requests to an Internet provider when you use a dialup connection from your server. If you use a SOCKS proxy, it overrides an HTTP proxy, but it does not override an SSL Security proxy.

A proxy server provides an extra layer between you and the Internet. When you request a Web page by clicking a link or typing a URL, that request is intercepted and reissued by the proxy server. Because there is no direct connection between you and the Web, external users can't use a Web connection to piggyback into the corporate network to steal data. The proxy server is one form of firewall. The Domino server is not a proxy server. If you want to set up a firewall using a proxy server, refer to any of the popular books on firewalls.

WORKING WITH NOTES AND A TCP/IP CONNECTION

After you have a TCP/IP connection set up correctly, you have a choice of how to work:

■ You can open a database directly on the Domino server. The connection is the same as if you were working over a LAN. If you are using TCP/IP on your local network, in fact, the connection is virtually instantaneous and you don't need a connection document. However, if the connection is through the Internet via an ISP, the connection is apt to be somewhat slower if you are using a dialup connection.

■ You can create replicas on your workstation and replicate the databases that you use most frequently. See Chapter 8, "Using Mobile Features from Home or on the Road," and Chapter 38, "Replication and Its Administration," for details on replication.

The first time you open a new database, you might need to enter the name of the server on which it resides. After you have opened and bookmarked a database from a server, it will show up in the search list in the future.

LOOKING AT THE INTEGRATED NOTES CLIENT

Consider how you have used the Internet in the past. Usually, you had to start the Web browser and leave it running in the background. If you wanted to visit a Web page, you had to toggle to your browser. More recently, you clicked a hyperlink and your system toggled to the browser automatically.

With the integrated Lotus Notes client, you have the best of both worlds. You have the Personal Notes Navigator application, which enables you to store Web pages and work with them as Notes documents. But you also have an integrated Web browser. It is no longer necessary to have another browser running in the background.

THE BROWSER INTERFACE

The Notes browser interface is never farther away than the Navigation toolbar within your Notes workspace. Browser controls are always available, whether you are working with Notes documents or Internet Web pages. The controls are used whenever you access Notes documents or Web pages. The buttons within the Navigation toolbar are shown in Figure 9.8.

Figure 9.8
The browser controls are in the Navigation toolbar and are always available when you are in Notes.

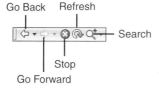

The browser controls, from left to right, are listed here:

- **Go Back**—The Go Back button works like the Back button on a Web browser. Simply, it takes you to the previously opened document or Window tab. You can navigate quickly to any Web document or Notes Window tab that you previously opened by clicking the arrow and then selecting the appropriate selection.

- **Go Forward**—The Go Forward button works like the Forward button on a Web browser. You can go to a Web document or Window tab by clicking the arrow to display a list of documents that are available.

- **Stop**—The Stop button stops a Web page or a Notes document from downloading. Clicking this control is the same as pressing Ctrl+Break in the Notes client.

- **Refresh**—The Refresh button causes the current page to be reloaded. On a Web page, you might want to do this to display the latest data rather than looking at a cached Web page. On a Notes document, clicking the Refresh control (or pressing F9) causes all fields to be recalculated. If you are displaying a view, any documents added to the view since you opened the page are displayed in the refreshed view.

- **Search**—The Search button is context sensitive. You can search the current Web page, search the current Notes document, or search the current Notes view. You can also select a Domino Domain search, or you can select a popular Internet search engine such as Lycos or Hotbot.

The Address bar, a complement to the Navigation bar, enables you to specify a URL to open. Type the URL and press Enter to retrieve the document or Web page. If a URL points to a Web page, the Web browser is used to retrieve the page. If the URL points to a Notes document, the Notes client is used to retrieve the document. In addition to the control buttons and Address bar, you can launch Web pages by clicking links within Notes documents and links on Web pages.

THE PERSONAL WEB NAVIGATOR

The Personal Web Navigator is a standard Notes application that stores Web pages as Notes documents. The documents can then be accessed using full-text searching. They can be shared with other users and can be read when you are offline. With the Personal Web Navigator database, each document listed in the All Pages view is actually a Web page stored as a Notes document. In addition to Web page storage, Notes can automatically refresh selected Web pages that are stored as Notes documents. Several agents are provided with the database that provide functions to the database, including scanning the Web for new or changed content, notifying you when a page has been modified, and preloading of pages multiple levels deep.

For example, if you have enough disk space available, you can have a Web site load links three pages deep. This can be particularly handy if you are getting ready to unplug your computer to take on the road with you and you want to browse a favorite Web site while on the airplane.

SETTING UP THE PERSONAL WEB NAVIGATOR

As you set up the Personal Notes Navigator, you'll have occasion to access the following screens:

- The location document in your Personal Address Book
- The Internet Options document in your Personal Web Navigator database
- The Properties box for your Personal Web Navigator database
- The User Preferences screen under File, Tools

OPENING THE PERSONAL WEB NAVIGATOR

To open a URL, type the complete URL of one of your favorite Web sites into the Address field within the Address toolbar. For example, type the following:

```
http://www.lotus.com/ldd
```

In addition to opening the Web site, Notes creates and opens the Personal Web Navigator database. To save a copy of the Web page as a Notes document for offline viewing, simply open the site within the Notes environment and select Actions, Keep Page from the menu bar. The Personal Web Navigator database is shown in Figure 9.9.

Figure 9.9
The Personal Web Navigator has a View pane, a Navigation pane, and a document preview screen, like any other Notes database.

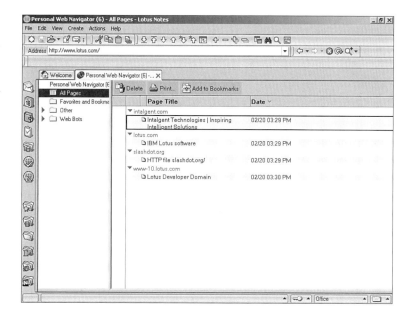

To access the Personal Web Navigator database directly, select File, Database, Open from the menu bar. The result is the Open Database dialog box, shown in Figure 9.10.

On your local workstation, you should find the Personal Web Navigator database. This database is added to the Notes environment during the installation of the client.

Figure 9.10
The Open Database dialog box enables you to open databases from within the Notes environment.

VIEWS AND FOLDERS IN THE PERSONAL WEB NAVIGATOR DATABASE

You can navigate through the Personal Web Navigator database just as you would with any other Notes database. Click a view or folder in the Navigation pane to display a list of documents (that is, Web pages) in that view or folder.

The views and folders available in the database include the following:

- **All Pages view**—This view contains all the Web pages that have been retrieved using the Notes Web browser interface.

- **Favorites and Bookmarks folder**—This folder holds links directly to Web pages rather than stored Web pages. If you click a link, you open the live Web page, not a Web page stored as a Notes document.

- **Other/Cookies view**—This view holds all your cookies. Cookies hold information about a Web site, such as the URL, and tell the site that you have visited before.

> **NOTE**
>
> In the early days of Internet development, cookie technology was designed to make browsing the Web a more personal experience. Many retailers use it to track your Web-based shopping cart or your account information, but many are using this technology for other, more sinister uses. Regardless of whether a site uses cookies, it's a good idea to thoroughly read and understand its user policies. You might be surprised by how organizations are using this information.

- **Other/File Archive view**—This view displays all Web pages that contain attachments.

- **Other/House Cleaning view**—This view displays Web pages sorted by size. You can choose which ones you want to delete or reduce to URLs.

- **Web Bots/Page Minder folder**—You can drag Web pages into this folder to be notified when they are updated. The Page Minder is set up on the Internet Options page, which can be accessed by selecting Actions, Internet Options from within the Personal Web Navigator.

- **Web Bots/Web Ahead folder**—You can drag Web pages into this folder to start an agent that will retrieve all linked pages, as defined in Internet Options, on the Web Ahead tab.

We return to many of these views and folders in the next section, which shows you how to customize your Personal Web Navigator.

CUSTOMIZING THE PERSONAL NOTES NAVIGATOR WITH THE INTERNET OPTIONS DOCUMENT

Now that you know your way around the Personal Notes Navigator screen, it is time to customize the document with your personal preferences. Your navigator is customized using the Internet Options document. You can display this document, shown in Figure 9.11, by choosing Actions, Internet Options in the Personal Web Navigator database.

Figure 9.11
The Internet Options document enables you to customize your Personal Web Navigator database.

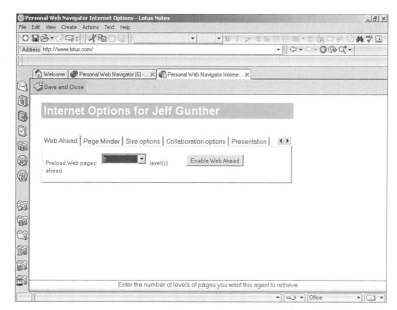

The Internet Options screen is divided into six tabbed pages with the following functions:

- **Web Ahead**—Notes preloads Web page links up to four layers deep if you activate this option. Enter the number of layers you want to preload, and then click the Enable Web Ahead button. To preload pages for a site, drag and drop the Web page into the Web Ahead folder. While you are reading the first page, Notes is busy in the background loading additional pages that are linked from that page. You can then access those linked pages more quickly, or you can read them offline at a later time.

  The Web Ahead feature runs an agent on your local workstation.

9

- **Page Minder**—If you enable Page Minder, Notes automatically searches Web pages that have been dragged and dropped into the Page Minder folder. If a page has changed on the Internet, you or the person you designate will be mailed a summary of the page or a copy of the full page, depending on the options you select. You can have the Page Minder run once an hour, once every four hours, once a day, or once a week.

- **Size Options**—You can specify that documents are automatically deleted or reduced to links if they have not been read in 15, 30, 60, or 90 days. You must enable Housekeeping for Notes to automatically delete documents or reduce them to links. You can also have Notes warn you when the Personal Web Navigator reaches 5, 10, 25, or 50MB in size. You can then go to the House Cleaning view and delete pages that you no longer want to save.

- **Collaboration Options**—You can specify a server and a shared Web Navigator database where Web pages and your personal ratings are sent when you select Actions, Share.

- **Presentation**—You can specify how the Personal Web Navigator displays rich text that is defined using different HTML tags, such as body text, address text, and anchor text (that is, links). You can also specify that you want to save rich text and HTML if you want to have access to the code used to create the page, or you can save pages as MIME only.

USER PREFERENCES

In the Additional Options list box, which you can find at the bottom of the Basics tab of the User Preferences dialog box (choose File, Preferences, User Preferences), are several options to check that control some aspects of the Personal Web Navigator when it is used with the Notes browser. You can check the following options to turn them on:

- Make Internet URLs (`http://...`) into Hotspots
- Enable Java Applets
- Enable JavaScript
- Enable Java Access from JavaScript
- Enable JavaScript Error Dialogs
- Enable Plug-ins in Notes Browser
- Enable ActiveX in Notes Browser
- Accept Cookies
- Make Notes the Default Web Browser on My System
- User Web Palette
- Enable MIME Save Warning

ADVANCED SETUP OPTIONS

The Advanced section of the location document provides further control over the Personal Web Navigator. You can access the current location document by selecting File, Mobile, Edit Current Location from the menu bar. You can also access the location document from within your Personal Address Book.

Five types of Internet parameters can be set up in the Advanced section of the location document:

- SSL Configuration
- Web Retriever Configuration
- Java Applet Security
- Secondary Servers
- Mime Settings

SSL CONFIGURATION   SSL is a Secure Socket Layer, a type of secure data transfer that is used on the Internet. By way of contrast, Notes has RSA security built in. RSA security uses a public key in the public address book and a private key (part of the Notes user or server ID) to solve mathematical algorithms to ensure that communications are authentic.

However, when navigating the Web, you'll encounter secure Web sites that require a certificate (such as a public key) from a Certificate Authority (CA) other than RSA to authenticate communications. The following options are available on the SSL tab:

- **Accept SSL Site Certificates**—Indicate whether you want to accept SSL site certificates.

- **Accept Expired SSL Certificates**—You can choose to accept expired SSL certificates, or you can decline certificates that have expired.

- **SSL Protocol Version**—You can select which version of SSL protocol you use, including V2.0 only, V3.0 handshake, V3.0 only, V3.0 with V2.0 handshake, or Negotiated. Negotiated is the default value.

WEB RETRIEVER CONFIGURATION   The Web Retriever Configuration section of the Advanced options in the location document enables you to tweak how the Personal Web Navigator is configured on your system. The Web Retriever retrieves Web pages so that you can view them with the Notes Web browser. The Web Retriever options are shown in Figure 9.12.

The fields that you can set include the following:

- **Web Navigator Database**—This field holds the name of the Web Navigator database. The default name is PERWEB.NSF, but you can change the name of this file at the OS level—or, you may have multiple Web Navigator databases for different purposes.

- **Concurrent Retrievers**—You can set up to 25 concurrent retrievers and then open multiple documents and select them in your Navigator. In other words, you can have up to 25 Web pages open at one time.

- **Retriever Log Level**—You can determine how Web Retriever events are recorded in your LOG.NSF file. Options include None, Terse, and Verbose. Select Terse (Less) or Verbose (More) to control the length of the message, or select None to send no message. LOG.NSF is created automatically during Notes setup. It provides a log for tracking the various communications that take place on the Notes workstation.

- **Update Cache**—When you open a Web page that is already stored in your Personal Web Navigator database, you can determine how often Notes refreshes the stored document from the Internet. Options include the following:

  - **Never**—Notes opens the locally stored version.

  - **Once Per Session**—Notes reloads pages only once during a session.

  - **Every Time**—Notes always downloads pages from the Web, even if they are already stored in the Personal Web Navigator database.

Figure 9.12
Set up your Web Retriever on the Advanced, Web Retriever page of the location document.

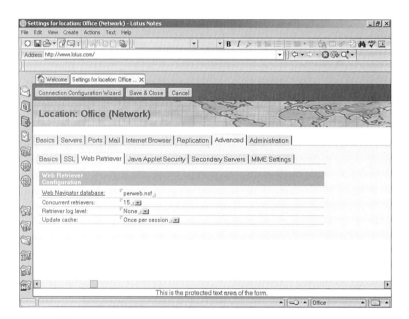

JAVA APPLET SECURITY   Since Notes 5, you can run Java applets using either the Web or the Notes client. Security for Java applets is set up on the Advanced page in the location document. Figure 9.13 shows the Java Applet Security tab.

The options on this tab include the following:

- **Trusted Hosts**—Enter the names of specific Java hosts that you trust, or use a wildcard to indicate that all hosts are trusted.

- **Network Access for Trusted Hosts**—You can disable Java, allow no Java access, allow access only to the originating host, allow access to any trusted host, or allow access to any host.

- **Network Access for Untrusted Hosts**—You can disable Java for untrusted hosts, allow no Java access, or allow access only for the originating host.

- **Trust HTTP Proxy**—You can choose to trust or not trust the HTTP proxy.

Figure 9.13
In the location document, define how Java applet security is handled.

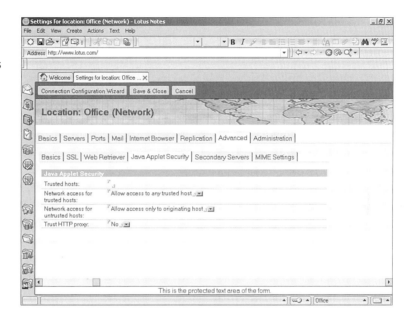

If you need help understanding hosts and proxies, talk to your network administrator or refer to almost any publication about TCP/IP.

SECONDARY SERVERS   Secondary servers are servers that Notes turns to when the primary home server is not available from the network. Defining a secondary server is not required, but it helps to ensure uninterrupted availability from the Internet:

- **Secondary TCP/IP Notes Name Server**—Enter the name of the Domino server that is to be contacted for Domino Directory information if your home server is not available on the TCP/IP network.

- **Secondary TCP/IP Hostname or Address**—Enter the fully qualified hostname or IP address to be contacted for address book information if your home server is not available on the TCP/IP network.

The Secondary NDS Notes name server and secondary NDS name server address fields are used for identifying a secondary Domino server on an IPX/SPX network; a secondary NetBIOS Notes name server field identifies a secondary NetBIOS Domino server. These types of network connection can be used for Internet access only if the Domino server provides the access. You open up Web pages as Notes documents from the Web Navigator database on the server.

MIME CONVERSION The Mime Conversion tab on the Advanced page of the location document is used to define how attachments are encoded. Attachments can be encoded as base64 (the default value) or Quoted-Printable. For outbound Macintosh attachment conversion, you can try AppleDouble (base64 only) or BinHex 4.0. Modify these settings only if you have a specific reason for doing so.

SUMMARY OF THE PERSONAL WEB NAVIGATOR SETUP

To use the Personal Web Navigator, you need to be connected to the Internet. This connection can be over a network or via a dialup connection. The connection also can be direct to the Internet, or it can be through an HTTP proxy server.

You need to set up your location to recognize the HTTP proxy server if that is how you are connecting, and you must define Notes or Notes with Internet Explorer as the Internet browser. You also must define Web retrieval as being from the Notes workstation instead of retrieving Web pages from the server. In effect, this says that you want to connect directly to the Internet instead of sharing a Web Navigator database with others in your organization.

In the location document, you also can configure advanced options, such as logging and handling SSL certificates, and Java options. Java applets must also be enabled in the additional options on the User Preferences page.

CHAPTER **10**

USING INOTES WEB ACCESS

In this chapter

AN OVERVIEW OF iNOTES

iNotes Web Access provides browser-based access to mail, the calendar, other personal information, and Domino services. Lotus Notes users can view their mail, calendar, To Do list, and contacts information from the iNotes Web Access client. When mail databases are set up properly on the Domino server, iNotes users need nothing installed on their computer except a compatible browser. It can be implemented to extend access to Domino messaging and collaboration tools for users who do not have access to a workstation with the Lotus Notes client; it can be utilized as a *thin* client for new users who have no need for the traditional desktop Notes client.

First introduced in the 5.0.8 release of Notes and Domino, iNotes Web Access is the successor to the Lotus WebMail client. WebMail is the first-generation Web client that relies heavily on Java applets to carry some of the Notes client functionality and look to the Internet. But let's face it: If you are a current or former user of WebMail, you know that it's limited functionality, performance, and user interface are lacking by today's standards.

By contrast, iNotes Web Access drops reliance on the slow Java applets and utilizes a completely new architecture based on XML, DOM level 2, and Dynamic HTML (DHTML). This approach makes possible a far more robust, feature-rich application with rather good performance.

To help you understand iNotes Web Access, we'll first briefly describe each of the main applications (welcome page, mail, the calendar, the To Do list, contacts, and the notebook). Then we'll take a tour of the iNotes "look and feel" and review the features and functions that are available throughout iNotes Web Access. When we've concluded the overview of the iNotes user interface, we'll take a detailed look at each of the applications and how to use them.

GETTING STARTED

iNotes Web Access works with Internet Explorer 5.01, Service Pack 1, or later. Although it displays well in a screen resolution of 800×600 pixels, iNotes Web Access works best at 1024×768 pixels. To print calendar entries, you'll need Adobe Acrobat Reader Version 4.0 or later.

Before you can use iNotes, your administrator will need to replace the design of your mail file using the iNotes Web Access (R6.0) template. This template supports Notes, iNotes Web Access, and WebMail clients.

To access iNotes, open your Web browser to the iNotes Web Access address provided by your administrator; log in with your username and password when prompted.

The first time you use iNotes Web Access, you are prompted to download the iNotes Control from IBM. This control is necessary for iNotes Web Access to work properly and help secure logouts, so be sure to choose Yes.

Let's start with an overview of the key functional areas of iNotes. The iNotes Web Access client consists of six main applications or sections:

- **Welcome page**—Similar to the Lotus Notes client, the welcome page is a customizable page that first appears when you open iNotes. You can tailor its layout to display any combination of your mail inbox, today's schedule, your To Do tasks, and even a favorite Web page or quick links. From this page you can open all the applications of the iNotes Web Access client.

- **Mail**—The iNotes Web Access mail application provides much of the functionality you have in the Lotus Notes client, including the capability to access your Notes mail folders, support for unlimited attachments, and spell checking.

- **Calendar**—You can manage your personal and group calendars, compose and accept or decline meeting invitations, and enjoy robust calendar-printing options similar to those in Lotus Notes.

- **To Do**—iNotes Web Access allows management of your To Do lists, supporting establishment of due dates and times and alarms.

- **Contacts**—Designed with similar functionality to the Notes-based personal name and address book, contacts enable you to manage all your personal contact information. You can synchronize contacts with your personal name and address book entries from Lotus Notes as well.

- **Notebook**—Similar to the journal in the Lotus Notes client, you can use the notebook to keep a journal or write notes for yourself. You can also synchronize your journal with the notebook from Lotus Notes.

In Figure 10.1, you see a typical welcome page in iNotes Web Access. All the iNotes applications, including the welcome page, have six main areas:

- **Content area**—Displays data for the open application

- **Date Navigation control**—A calendar and date picker available on the upper left of this and every application in iNotes Web Access

- **Task bar**—Tabs displayed near the top of every page for access to the welcome page, mail, the calendar, the To Do list, contacts, and the notebook, each with context-specific drop-down menus

- **Action bar**—A set of tools unique to the open application, located at the top of the content area, some with context-specific drop-down menus

- **Top menu**—Buttons displayed at the upper right of every page for Logout, Go Offline/Go Online, Preferences, and Help options

- **QuickSearch**—Enables you to perform keyword searches within the data displayed in the open application

Figure 10.1
The welcome page provides you with updated information and access to your applications when iNotes Web Access opens.

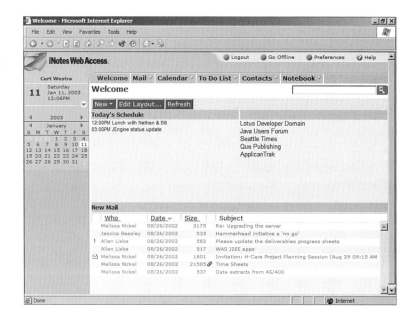

The content area is where context-specific data is displayed for each iNotes application— mail files, calendar entries, and so on.

DATE NAVIGATION CONTROL

The Date Navigation control, also called the date picker (shown in Figure 10.2), enables you to view dates for different months and years by simply clicking the Previous or Next arrow icons.

Figure 10.2
View dates quickly with a click of the mouse.

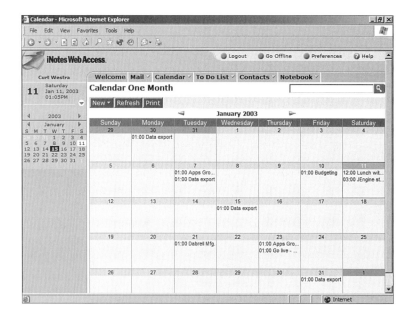

The date picker is available on all main pages within iNotes Web Access, but it is not shown by default in the mail and contacts applications. You can hide or show the date picker by clicking the Collapse/Expand arrow beneath the display of the current day, date, and time.

Within all applications other than the welcome page, you can immediately open the calendar by clicking a date in the date picker.

NOTE

> Whenever you need help understanding any part of the iNotes Web Access interface or its features, press the F1 key or click the Help icon at the top right of any given page or form. A context-sensitive help window opens to assist you.
>
> To see a table of contents for iNotes Help, click the Help icon when you are on the welcome page, or click the Help icon in any other view and then click the Contents button displayed in the Help window.

When the welcome page is displayed, and if it includes today's schedule, you can quickly view the schedule for a given day using the date picker. Simply select the date in the date picker, and that day's schedule loads in the content area.

TASK BAR

The task bar enables you to navigate quickly to all the applications housed in iNotes Web Access, including mail, the calendar, the To Do list, contacts, the notebook, and the welcome page. Clicking any given tab opens the default page for the related application.

A useful feature of the task bar is the drop-down menu. As you mouse over a tab, a menu of action items drops down and enables you to move directly into parts of the application or perform tasks with a single mouse click. Figure 10.3 shows the drop-down menu that appears when the mouse hovers over the Calendar tab.

ACTION BAR

Within each application or section of iNotes Web Access, an action bar with context-specific tools appears along the top of the content area. For example, within the mail application the action bar tools permit you to forward, delete, reply to, or move a selected or opened message (see Figure 10.4).

Similar to the task bar, some of the action bar tools include context-specific drop-down menus. No matter which application you're in, the New drop-down menu is always available. This menu enables you to create a new message, calendar entry, To Do item, contact, or notebook page from anywhere within iNotes Web Access. I've found that the action bars and drop-down menus make navigation within iNotes Web Access relatively easy, especially in comparison to what was available in Lotus WebMail.

Figure 10.3
The task bar's drop-down menus in iNotes let users move easily and quickly among tasks and applications with a click of the mouse.

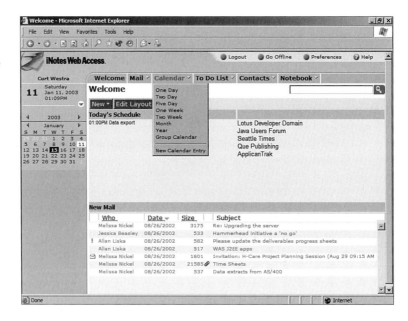

Figure 10.4
The action bar displays tools and drop-down menus specific to each application. Among the tools displayed on this mail page is the New drop-down menu, also available in every application.

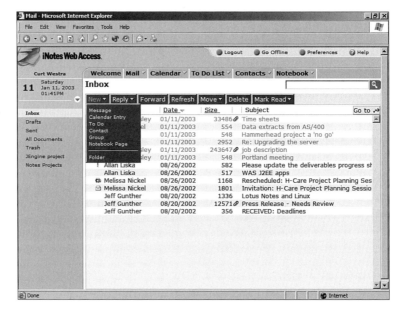

TOP MENU

The top menu is displayed at the top right of all the main pages of iNotes Web Access. It includes the following functions:

- **Chat**—If your company has implemented Sametime 2.0 or later, you have the capability to see who is online, create chat groups, and send instant messages to others. Refer to this chapter's section on using iNotes chat for more information.

- **Logout/Login**—If you access iNotes from a shared device, this feature enables you to close your iNotes session without allowing personal or sensitive information to be accessed by others. Refer to the logging out section of this chapter for details on how to exit iNotes securely.

- **Go Offline/Go Online**—Use this function to move offline or online within iNotes Web Access. When connected to the Domino server, going offline synchronizes data from your iNotes applications to your local device and enables you to work with all your updated applications. The same applies in reverse when you have been offline and want to connect back to the Domino server. This topic is covered in detail later in the "Working Offline" section.

- **Preferences**—Similar to the Lotus Notes client, you can change settings in the iNotes Web Access client to reflect your preferences for mail, the calendar, delegation, work hours, date and time, archiving, and more. This chapter addresses how to modify preferences within the sections covering each iNotes application. Other preferences not associated with one iNotes application are described in a later section.

- **Help**—Context-sensitive help is available any time by clicking the Help button or the question mark icon located in the upper right of any page, or by pressing the F1 key.

Now that you're familiar with the iNotes Web Access user interface, let's take a detailed look at each of the applications and how to use them.

THE WELCOME PAGE

As mentioned previously, the welcome page is a customizable page that first greets you when you open iNotes. The welcome page lets you see and instantly access your new mail, today's schedule, your To Do tasks, quick links, and a Web page—all in one place.

The value of the welcome page lies in the ability to customize it to display any combination of these elements; this way, you can see the information most important to you each time you open iNotes. Let's take a look at how.

CUSTOMIZING THE WELCOME PAGE

On the welcome page, the layout of the content area can be tailored to meet your needs or your organization's needs. For example, the Administrator can set the default layout to display your new mail, recent To Do items, and the company's Web page.

When you open iNotes Web Access the first time, you are given the option to create your own welcome page layout. If your Administrator permits it, you can customize the layout to display any combination of your new mail, today's schedule, To Do list, a Web page, or quick links.

To edit the welcome page layout, follow these steps:

1. On the welcome page, click the Edit Layout button. The Edit Welcome Page Layout form opens. Figure 10.5 displays an edited layout form.

Figure 10.5
You can personalize the iNotes Web Access Welcome Page by selecting the content areas that you want to see every time you open the iNotes Web Access client.

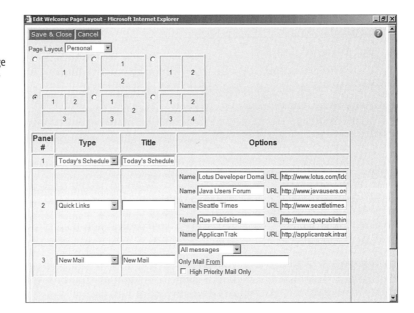

2. Select Personal from the Page Layout drop-down menu.

3. Select the number of panels and the panel arrangement you want for your welcome page by clicking a radio button.

4. For each panel, select the content type from the drop-down menu.

5. (Optional) For each panel, enter a title in the Title field.

6. If applicable, select an option for each panel in your welcome page. Each content type and the related options are shown in Table 10.1.

TABLE 10.1 CONTENT TYPES AND DISPLAY OPTIONS FOR THE WELCOME PAGE

Type	Option
New Mail	Select the last 10 messages or all messages. If you want to see mail from only certain people, enter the names in the Only Mail From field. Enter each person's name, followed by a comma. You can also click the word From in Only Mail From to select names from your Domino directory or contacts. To view only priority mail, select High Priority Mail Only.
Today's Schedule	None.

Type	Option
To Do List	None.
Web Page	Choose a Web page from the list, or select Other and enter the URL of your favorite Web page—for example, http://slashdot.org.
Quick Links	Make several URL links available on your welcome page by entering a name and Web address for each link. If your company has implemented Lotus QuickPlace, you can enter any QuickPlace URLs that you want to monitor from your welcome page.

7. Click the Save and Close button.

Now your browser displays your own customized welcome page. If at any time you decide to change your welcome page layout, just repeat these steps.

Using iNotes Mail

iNotes Web Access mail lets you create, send, reply, forward, and receive email messages. You can organize your mail into folders and send any number of attachments, such as files and pictures, with your mail. When you are not connected to the Internet, you can go offline and create, send, reply, and forward mail. iNotes Web Access stores all your outgoing messages and sends them when you go back online. Details about working offline are discussed in the "Working Offline" section later in this chapter.

Overview

To help you get oriented, we'll take a brief tour of the iNotes Web Access Mail application. The mail application can be accessed from anywhere in iNotes via the taskbar's mail button. The default Inbox view of the mail database is shown in Figure 10.6.

Your various mail folders are listed on the left, and the contents of the selected folder are displayed in the content area. As you'll see later, you can use folders to organize all your messages.

Along the top of the content area is the Mail action bar. This bar includes most of the tools you need to work with iNotes Web Access Mail. Using the Mail action bar, you can create new messages and reply to, forward, move, copy, delete, or mark as read or unread selected messages from the view or folder contents. In addition, you can refresh the displayed contents.

We'll talk about these features in more depth in the section on managing your mail in iNotes, but for now let's jump right in and look at sending a new mail message.

Figure 10.6
Incoming mail is listed
within the inbox.

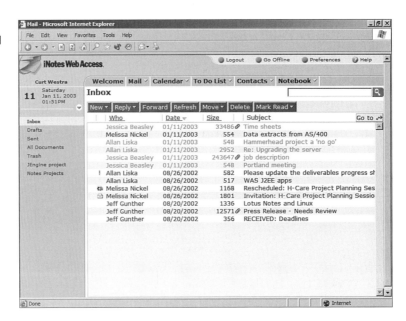

CREATING AND SENDING A MESSAGE

In iNotes Web Access, emails are referred to as messages. This contrasts with Lotus Notes, in which they are called memos. This distinction isn't important as far as you are concerned, but it's worth pointing out to Lotus Notes users who are accustomed to the term *memos*.

You can initiate the creation of a new mail message in one of three ways:

■ Point your mouse to the Mail taskbar button on any page within iNotes Web Access, and choose New Message from the drop-down menu.

■ Point your mouse to the New action bar button on any page within iNotes Web Access, and choose Message from the drop-down menu.

■ Point your mouse to the New button within the mail application and click.

A Message form opens in a new window, as shown in Figure 10.7. You can create and open several message windows at the same time and still view your inbox. This is a useful feature because you can refer back to an open folder or any underlying open messages without using the Back button in your browser, potentially losing any work you've already done in a new message.

The Message form includes six fields. The first three fields are used to address the message to one or more individuals or groups of individuals. These three fields are for the primary addressees, carbon copies, and blind carbon copies. The Subject field provides the subject of the memo, which appears in the listing of messages within the inbox. The Body field is a rich-text field that enables you to include formatted text, links, and images. Finally, there's an area for file attachments.

Figure 10.7
Create and edit mail messages using the Message form.

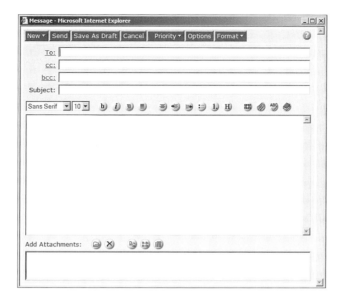

ADDRESSING A MESSAGE

In each of the addressee fields, you can enter Internet email addresses, names from your contacts, or user's names that are in your company's Domino directory. If you enter partial or full user's names and try to send the message, however, iNotes checks your contacts and the Domino directory for matching first names, last names, and group names. If a match cannot be found, it alerts you and gives you the option to cancel sending the message or to send it anyway.

If iNotes finds more than one match, you are prompted to select one of them or to skip that addressee before the message can be sent.

Whenever you're not sure that you're entering a name properly, you can check for the name in your contacts or Domino directory when entering the addressees, rather than waiting for iNotes to check when sending your message. There are two ways to do this:

- Type in the names and, when you're ready to confirm their accuracy, click the Check Name(s) icon that appears to the left. INotes then checks for the name in your contacts and Domino directory and alerts you if there are problems.
- Open your contacts or Domino directory and select the names directly.

To select addresses from your contacts or Domino directory, follow these steps:

1. Click either the To, cc, or bcc fields, depending on which of these fields you're filling out. The Select Addresses window opens, as shown in Figure 10.8.

Figure 10.8
You can select addresses directly from your contacts or your company's Domino directory.

10

2. Select whether to search your contacts or the Domino directory in the Search drop-down menu.

3. Search the displayed list of names by entering the name in the Find box and choosing Search, or by scrolling through the list.

4. Select the name or names that you want to enter in either the To, cc, or bcc fields by clicking them.

5. Click the To, cc, or bcc buttons to enter the selected names into the appropriate address field in the Message form.

6. Repeat steps 2–5 to populate the remaining addressee fields that you want to complete.

7. Choose Exit to return to the Message form. Note that the names you selected now appear in the appropriate address fields of the Message form.

Just as with mail in the Lotus Notes client, if you want to send a message to someone who is not listed in any of the directories, you must enter an explicit address. Our example of Joe Schmoe from Chapter 4, "Getting Started with Electronic Mail," also applies in iNotes: If Joe Schmoe were a user in another domain, you could address him as joe.schmoe@ somedomain.com. The Domino server would attempt to deliver the message to the Internet domain, provided that appropriate connections are in place to allow mail routing.

CREATING THE SUBJECT AND BODY

Enter a subject in the Subject field, and then enter the body of your message in the rich-text field below the Subject field. You could stop here and send your message, but if you want to dress up your message text a bit, insert an image, or attach any files, you have a few more tools at your disposal. By taking advantage of some of these tools, you can end up with a completed message similar to that shown in Figure 10.9.

These tools enable you to format and spell-check your message, insert images, create Web page links, and attach files. Let's look at message formatting first.

Figure 10.9
This completed message takes advantage of some of the powerful and easy-to-use tools available in iNotes Web Access.

FORMATTING THE TEXT

You'll notice that above the Body field is a row of drop-down lists and icons. The first drop-down list enables you to change the font type and size of text. The set of icons to the right of that enables you to format text using features such as bold, italics, underlining, text color, alignment, indenting, outdenting, unordered bullet lists, numbered lists, and headlines.

To change the format of any text, highlight the text and then click one of the formatting icons. Examples of some of the text-formatting options, such as bold and italics, are evident in the message shown in Figure 10.9.

INSERTING AN IMAGE

Inserting an image into the message can be useful when you want the recipient to see a photo or graphic immediately upon opening the sent message. iNotes Web Access enables you to insert JPEG or GIF images with the .jpg or .gif extensions, respectively, in their filenames.

If you want to load an image from your computer, follow these steps:

1. Click the Insert Image button above the message body, represented by the icon resembling a strip of film. A dialog box opens, as shown in Figure 10.10.

2. Choose Browse. Then find the file, select it, and choose Open. You can also drag and drop an image file from your desktop or folders.

3. If you change your mind and want to replace the image you selected with another one, choose Replace, find the file, select it, and choose Open. If you decide against inserting an image at all but have already selected one, just click the Delete Current Image icon next to Replace. Click Yes to confirm the deletion, close the dialog box, and skip Step 4.

Figure 10.10
You can insert an image into your message from your computer or from iNotes.

4. Simply choose the Next button to insert your image, and you're done.

Instead of inserting an image from your computer, you could select from one of the graphics available from the iNotes gallery. Be warned: This "gallery" doesn't include any great works of art and primarily consists of some colorful graphics that might be useful as headers or dividers in your message. To insert a graphic from within the Insert Image window, click the Select Image button, select a graphic from the options that appear, and then choose Next.

> **TIP**
>
> Appropriate use of inserted images can enhance your message and can save the recipient more effort and time than if he had to try to open it as an attachment instead. But not all your recipients' email programs will readily support display of inserted images sent by other mail clients such as iNotes—the Lotus Notes mail application is a good example. Images inserted within messages from iNotes and many other email programs are delivered in the Lotus Notes mail application as attachments. Furthermore, as a general rule you should limit your images to small and medium-size files to avoid excessively long message load times for your recipients. You also should consider whether inserting an image—large or small—helps get your ideas across to recipients or if it just gets in the way. The capability to insert images in emails is one of those features to which one of my favorite rules applies: Just because you *can* do something doesn't mean you *should* do it!

INSERTING A LINK

Sometimes you want to send somebody a message that includes a link to a Web site that might be of interest to that person. This is relatively easy to do if you know the Web address for the page: All you need to do is type or paste it in the message body, and it becomes a clickable link after the message is sent. Most, if not all, email programs recognize a Web link as long as you include the http:// at the start. For example, a valid Web link to type in a message would be http://www.webreference.com/.

Let's say you want to send a link, but instead of having the recipient see the link's Internet address, you want the recipient to see and click some other text, such as Check out this great Web site!. Or maybe you don't want to bother with typing out the http:// portion, but you know the rest of the site's Internet address. In either situation, you can use the Insert Link tool in iNotes Web Access to help you insert links.

Follow these steps to insert a link in your messages:

1. Place your cursor where you want the link to appear in your message.

2. Click the Insert Link represented by the chain links icon above the message body. A dialog box opens with fields to enter the link address and a title.

3. In the first field of the dialog box, enter the URL or Web address (for example, www.lotus.com) of the page you want displayed when the link is clicked.

   It is not necessary to include http:// in your link.

4. In the box labeled What Is the Title of the Link?, enter the text that you want the reader to click to display the contents of the page to which you're linking. If you want to provide a link to information on ordering a product, for example, you could enter Order Information as the title. The words Order Information would be blue and underlined in the message.

5. Click Insert when you are done.

CHECKING SPELLING

If you're not always sure about your spelling accuracy, the spell-check function in iNotes is a useful tool. Whenever you want to check the spelling in your message, click the Spell Check button, represented by the icon with letters and a check mark above the message body.

When the spelling checker discovers a misspelled word, it highlights the word and gives you the following choices:

- Choose a suggested word as a replacement for the misspelled word
- Type a word to use as a replacement for the misspelled word
- Leave the word unchanged

To choose a suggested word as a replacement, select the word from the list box and then click Change. If none of the words in the list is a word that you want to use as a replacement, you can enter your own replacement word. Just type a word in the New Word box and then click Change. iNotes Web Access replaces the selected word with your choice and either highlights the next misspelled word or, if there are no more misspelled words, returns you to the screen, where you can finish creating your message.

10

If the highlighted word is one you don't want to modify, you can leave the word unchanged by choosing Ignore. iNotes Web Access either highlights the next misspelled word or, if there are no more misspelled words, returns you to the text.

Click Done when you are finished or if you want to stop the spell check before all the possible misspellings in your message have been found.

You can change the language for your spell checking by clicking the Dictionary icon (the last icon on the right above the message body), selecting the language from the list box, and then clicking OK.

ADDING ATTACHMENTS

Located at the bottom of the Message form is the attachments area. Here you can add a virtually unlimited number of file attachments. If you're a current or former user of the Lotus WebMail client, you might recall that WebMail limits you to just two attachments, so this is a significant improvement.

To add an attachment to a message, follow these steps:

1. Click the Select File(s) button, represented by the file folder icon next to Add Attachments. An Open dialog box opens.
2. Locate the file on your computer, and then click Open. iNotes Web Access makes a copy of the file and adds it to the attachments area on your Message form.

New to iNotes Web Access is support for drag-and-drop attachments. This alternative enables you to drag and drop attachments from the Windows desktop or Windows Explorer to iNotes, and vice versa.

To remove any existing attachments from your message, just select the attachment(s) that you want to remove and click the Delete Selected file(s) icon.

You can also choose what attachment information to display in the attachment area. The three remaining icons above the attachment area can be clicked to show the attachments as large icons or small icons, or you can show details about their size and last modification date.

NOTE

Although iNotes supports a virtually unlimited number of attachments, your Domino administrator might not! Administrators have the option to set a limit on the size of mail messages that the mail server will handle and deliver to minimize the burden on the server and network. If a message exceeds this limit, it will not be delivered to the recipient. For example, an administrator might set a 3MB limit on the size of messages. If anyone sent a message that had so much data, including attachments, that it exceeded the 3MB limit, the message would not be sent but would be returned to the sender. If your administrator has set such a restriction, this effectively limits the number of attachments you can send in a mail message.

SPECIAL OPTIONS

After you've completed creating a message, you're basically ready to send the message, but you still have some options that you can modify. Still working in the Message form, you can see the following options on the action bar to the right of the Send and Save as Draft buttons:

- **Cancel**—Select this option to cancel sending the message and discard it.

- **Priority**—You can modify the priority for a message to set how soon an email is routed by the server to its recipient. High-priority mail is always delivered immediately. Normal priority mail (the default setting) is delivered immediately within your own Domino named network, but if it is destined for a server in another named network, it is delivered on a schedule determined by the Domino administrator. Low-priority mail is delivered during off-peak hours, usually during the middle of the night, again at the discretion of the administrator.

- **Options**—Use this to set two types of delivery options. First, you can select the type of delivery report notification you receive when your memo is successfully delivered to the recipient. The delivery report options are displayed in Table 10.2. Second, you can select the Return Receipt option so that iNotes generates a message to you at the moment the addressee opens your message using a Lotus Notes or iNotes Web Access client. That way, you know that the user not only received but actually opened your message.

TABLE 10.2   DELIVERY REPORT OPTIONS

Option	Description
Only on Failure	iNotes sends you a delivery report only if the message can't be delivered.
Confirm Delivery	iNotes sends you a delivery report telling you whether your message was delivered. This is similar to a return receipt, but it does not indicate whether the recipient actually opened the message.
Trace Entire Path	iNotes sends you a report from each server through which it routes the message and a final report indicating whether it delivered the message.
None	iNotes does not send you a delivery report.

- **Format**—You can choose either rich text or plain text as the format for your message. Rich text is the default setting for new messages; this allows the special formatting, such as color, bolding, italics, numbered lists, and so on, that we reviewed earlier. Plain text is the safest option when you are unsure of whether your recipient's mail program can read HTML-formatted messages. Most email programs can read HTML text, but some are limited to plain text. When you choose plain text, iNotes removes the font and formatting buttons from the new message window.

SENDING THE MESSAGE

Now you're ready to send the message, or, if you want, you can save this message as a draft and send it later. The action bar in the Message form offers you the following remaining options:

- **Send**—The message is sent immediately. The message is saved in your mail database's Sent folder, unless you have elected not to save sent mail (an option under Preferences, in the Mail tab).

- **Save as Draft**—The message is saved in the Drafts folder in your mail database. The message is not sent. You can open the draft message later, edit it, and send it by clicking Send.

MANAGING YOUR MAIL IN iNOTES

From within iNotes Web Access, the mail application enables you to easily manage and organize your mail. You can organize incoming and outgoing mail into default folders or those that you create.

You can open your mail by clicking Mail from the task bar in any of the main iNotes Web Access pages. When you open your mail, the inbox is displayed, as shown in Figure 10.11.

Figure 10.11
The inbox displays your incoming mail. The inbox and any other open mail folders enable you to sort messages by date, sender, and size.

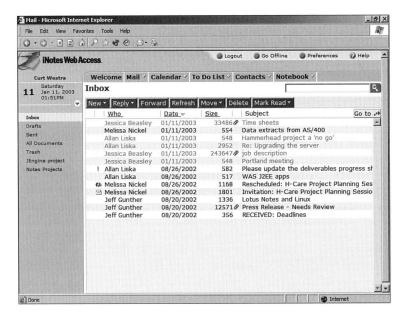

The inbox and each of the mail folders share some useful features that help you manage your mail more effectively. Depending on which mail folder's contents are displayed, information such as the sender/recipient, date, subject, message size, and whether attachments exist is displayed in columns. iNotes Web Access lets you sort your mail by sender/recipient, date, or message size. This is a useful feature that you're sure to use often when searching for a certain message. With most mail folders and views, you can click the Who, Date, or Size columns to sort messages by sender, date, or size, respectively.

NOTE

> Even if you leave your mail page and work in other areas of iNotes Web Access, a re-sorted mail folder retains the new sort order until you re-sort it again or close the iNotes Web Access session. Each time you open iNotes, your data are sorted by date, from newest to oldest.

You can set in your preferences how often you want iNotes Web Access to check for and display new incoming mail (we'll cover this later in the section "Setting Up Mail Preferences"). When new mail arrives, an alert displays in the browser Status bar. You can immediately refresh your mail contents by clicking Refresh in the action bar.

Although it is not evident in Figure 10.11, the inbox and all mail folders display unread messages in red so that, at a glance, you can see what you haven't opened yet. You can change messages to appear as read without opening them by selecting one or more and clicking Mark Read. Or, you can point your mouse to Mark Read and, from the drop-down menu, select Mark Unread, Mark All Read, or Mark All Unread.

Open any mail message by double-clicking it or by selecting it and pressing Enter. An example of an open message is shown in Figure 10.12.

Figure 10.12
From within an open message, you can send a reply, forward the message to someone else, delete it, move it to a folder, and more.

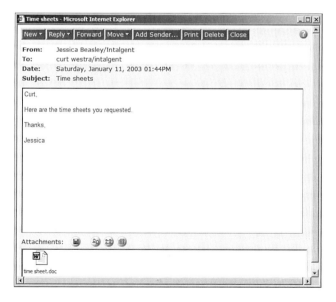

10

To close an opened mail message, simply click Close or press Ctrl+W. To print an open message, click Print or press Ctrl+P.

From within an open message, you can send a reply, forward the message to someone else, move or copy it to another folder, print a hard copy, delete it, or add the sender to your contacts. Using the New button, you can also create any kind of new iNotes document, such as a calendar entry.

Let's take a brief look at some of these mail functions. Then we'll explore how you can set up and use folders to manage your mail.

DELETING MESSAGES

To delete a mail message in iNotes Web Access, click the Delete button or press the Delete key while the message is selected. When a message is open, simply click Delete. When you delete a message, it is moved to the trash for removal. You can then easily change your mind by selecting the Trash folder and marking the documents that you want to keep by selecting them and clicking Restore from the action bar. Messages in the Trash folder that are marked for deletion are not actually removed from the database until you refresh the contents or exit from iNotes Web Access. When you refresh the view or close iNotes, you are given the option of deleting the marked messages or canceling the deletion.

REPLYING TO A MESSAGE

When replying to a message, use the Reply button or its drop-down menu of options. A message must be either selected in a view or opened for reading to send a reply. Click the Reply button to create a new message to the sender of the original message, or point to Reply and select one of the following options from the drop-down menu:

- **Reply**—Creates a new message addressed to the person who sent the original memo, and performs the same function as clicking the Reply button
- **Reply to All**—Creates a new message addressed to everyone who was listed in the To or cc fields in the original message
- **Reply with History**—Creates a reply that includes a copy of the original message
- **Reply to All with History**—Creates a new message addressed to everyone who was listed in the To or cc fields in the original message, and includes a copy of the original message

FORWARDING MESSAGES

To forward a message, click Forward from within an open message or while a message is selected. A new message is created that includes the original.

MOVING, COPYING, AND REMOVING MESSAGES

You can move and copy mail messages between mail folders, as well as remove messages from folders without moving or deleting them. Moving a message removes it from the current folder to the destination folder, whereas copying it places it in multiple folders. To move a message to a different folder, click Move while the message is selected or is opened for reading. Select a folder and choose OK.

To copy a mail message into a folder, point your mouse over Move while a message is selected in a view or is opened; then choose Copy To Folder. Select a folder and choose OK.

You can also simply remove a message from the inbox, the trash, or one of the folders you've created. Simply point your mouse over Move while a message is selected or opened; then choose Remove from Folder. The message no longer appears in the folder after the page refreshes, but it always is available in the All Documents folder until deleted.

ADDING A SENDER TO CONTACTS

If a message is open and you want to add the sender to your contacts, click the Add Sender button. A new Contact form opens, and iNotes populates it with the sender's email address and, in most cases, the sender's name. Fill out any other information you have for this new contact, and then click Save and Close.

CREATING FOLDERS TO ORGANIZE MAIL

Folders are a useful tool that help you organize your mail messages. iNotes Web Access provides you with a default set of basic Mail folders: Inbox, Drafts, Sent, Trash, and All Documents. As your inbox grows, however, you'll want to create your own folders so you can organize your sent and received messages by subject, person, or anything you like.

You can create your own folders and later delete or rename them. If you also use Lotus Notes mail, you'll see all your shared folders displayed in iNotes. Any changes that you make to shared folders in Lotus Notes are reflected in iNotes, and vice versa. Private folders that you create in Notes are not available in the iNotes Web Access client.

NOTE

> If you have been working offline and have created, modified, or deleted folders, you must refresh your browser when returning online to see the changes.

Creating a folder is easy. Just move your mouse over the New button and then choose Folder. The Create Folder dialog box appears. Enter the folder name and choose OK. You can also just right-click any existing folder and choose New from the drop-down menu that appears.

If you want a new folder to be a subfolder to an existing one, enter the name of the new folder in the Create Folder dialog box. Then select the parent folder from the list and choose OK.

NOTE

> Folders that contain one or more subfolders display a small + button next to their name when collapsed. Click the + to show all the subfolders, and you'll notice that the + changes to a –. Now you can hide all the subfolders by clicking the –.

Deleting or renaming a folder you created is also easy to do. To rename a folder, just right-click the folder name, enter the new name in the pop-up box, and choose OK. To delete a folder, right-click the folder name and choose OK when prompted to confirm that you want to delete the selected folder. Note that you can't delete or rename the default folders that iNotes Web Access created, however.

TIP

> In some situations, you might want to move, copy, delete, or mark several messages at once. To select multiple, nonadjacent messages, hold down your Ctrl key and click each message. To select a group of messages that are all adjacent to each other, click the first message in order and then click the last while holding down the Shift key.

As described previously, you can move or copy mail messages between mail folders by selecting messages and using the Move button on the action bar.

SETTING UP MAIL PREFERENCES

You can set all your mail preferences by clicking Preferences in the upper right of the iNotes window. The mail preferences always display when you open the Preferences window, as shown in Figure 10.13.

Figure 10.13
The mail preferences enable you to control a number of display, sending, and receiving options for your iNotes Web Access mail.

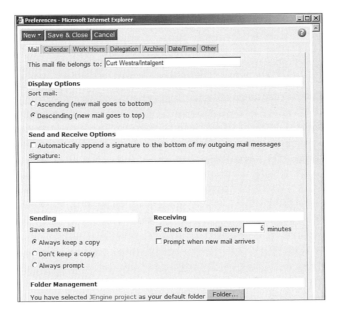

Here's a rundown of the mail preferences you can modify:

- **iNotes Web Access Account Ownership**—If you are not an existing Notes user, be sure that your name is specified in the This Mail File Belongs To field. You might need to change the ownership of the account, for example, if you want to use a different name for handling meeting invitations and the group calendar. Enter the owner's name in the This Mail File Belongs To field. Use the Notes hierarchical name that includes your name and your organization's name (for example, Larry Smith/Ajax). Your administrator can assist you with this, if necessary.

- **Display Options**—To change the sort order of messages, click Ascending to make new mail appear at the bottom of your inbox, or click Descending to make new mail appear at the top.

- **Signature**—You can add a personal signature to the bottom of outgoing mail messages. Select Automatically Append a Signature to the Bottom of My Outgoing Mail Messages, and then enter the text for your signature.

- **Sending**—Choose whether you want to save a copy of every message you send or whether you want to be prompted to choose every time you send a message. Copies of sent messages appear in the Sent folder.

- **Checking for New Mail**—To change how often iNotes looks for new mail on the server, select Check for New Mail Every x Minutes and enter the number of minutes.

- **New Mail Prompts**—If you want, iNotes will notify you when new mail arrives while you're in an open iNotes Web Access session.

- **Folder Management**—You can select a default folder where you can quickly copy messages for reading later. After you've designated a default folder here, you'll have to click only once to copy a selected message to the folder. After you select a default folder, iNotes displays a message in Preferences to confirm your selection. From within mail you can now select a mail message, point your mouse to Move, and then click Copy to *[folder name]* Folder.

When you're finished changing preferences, click the Save and Close button.

In addition to the settings described on the Mail tab, you can modify your out-of-office message, work hours, and mail-delegation preferences. Let's take a look at these next.

OUT-OF-OFFICE SETTINGS

When you plan to be unavailable to respond to incoming mail for a given period of time, iNotes can let others know that you are out of the office and when you will return. To set up this feature, click the Work Hours tab in the Preferences window. Then choose Settings in the Out of Office section. A window opens, as shown in Figure 10.14.

10

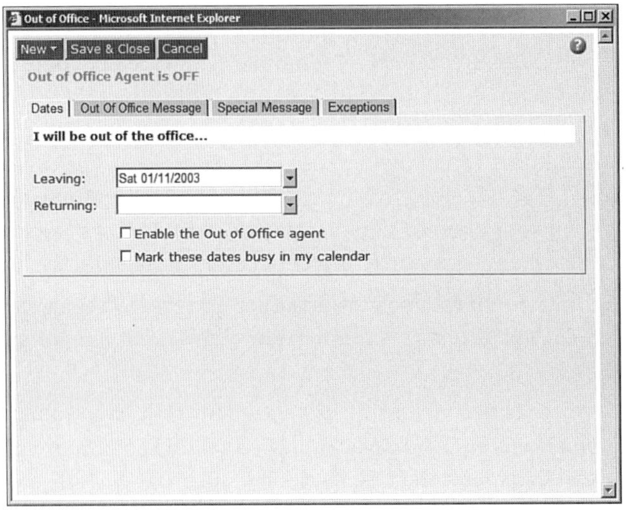

Figure 10.14
Specify a time frame and a message to be sent to notify others that you are out of the office.

DELEGATION FUNCTIONS IN MAIL

The Delegation tab of the Preferences window enables you to delegate authority to perform certain functions in your mail application, including mail and calendar delegations. For example, you might have an executive secretary who screens email for you. Before you ever see the mail, the junk mail is weeded out and misdirected messages are forwarded to the appropriate person within your company. You can delegate functions in your mail application using the form shown in Figure 10.15.

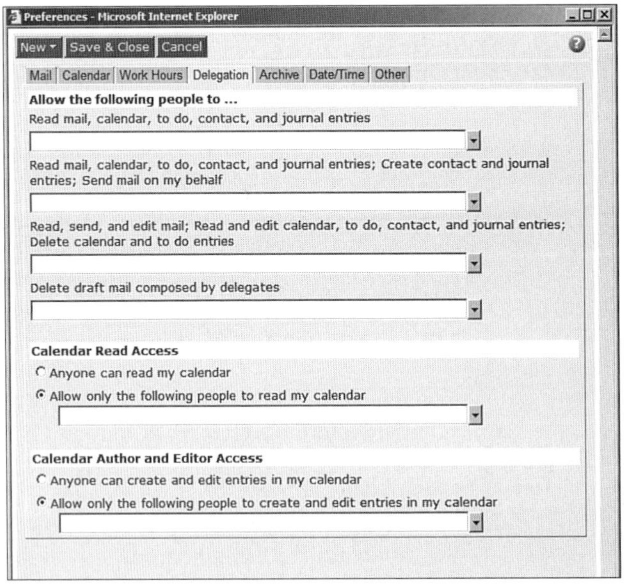

Figure 10.15
Give others the capability to access your mail for certain functions.

You can give specific people or groups the ability to read your mail; read your mail and create new messages using your mail application (that is, under your signature); read, create, and edit messages; and read, create, edit, and delete messages.

NOTE

> The capability to set preferences for mail delegation is controlled by your Domino administrator. If the administrator has not given you the rights to edit this and similar types of preferences, you will not be able to utilize them directly. Contact your administrator if you need to modify preferences that are restricted.

ARCHIVING YOUR MAIL

When you archive mail, iNotes Web Access notifies the Domino administrator to initiate a process that copies messages to an archive database on a server and then deletes those messages from your mail database. Your administrator must have archiving turned on for this to work. You can't archive documents to a local workstation from iNotes; for that you'll have to rely on Lotus Notes. If you use both iNotes and Lotus Notes, make sure that you use a single strategy to archive your mail so that your archived mail always goes to the same database in one location.

To archive your mail, follow these steps:

1. Click Preferences if the Preferences window isn't already open.
2. Click the Archive tab.
3. Select from among the archiving options shown in Table 10.3.

TABLE 10.3   ARCHIVING OPTIONS AND DESCRIPTIONS

Option	Description
Enable Scheduled Archiving of Documents	Activate the scheduled archiving of your mail file.
Archive All Documents Not Read or Accessed After x Days	Archive messages you haven't read or accessed in x number of days. The default setting is 365 days.
Archive All Documents Not Modified or Updated After x Days	Archive messages that have not changed in x number of days. The default setting is 365 days.
Archive Database	Enter the directory and filename of the archive database. By default, iNotes uses archive as the directory name and your mail filename as the archive database filename. The archiving function adds Archive in parentheses after the database name.
On My Home Server	Specify the server's TCP/IP address. By default, iNotes uses the IP address of your mail server (for example, mailserver.ajax.com).

continues

TABLE 10.3   CONTINUED

Advanced Options

Option	Description
Log Archiving Activity To	If you want to create a log of the archiving activity on the server, select this option and enter the log directory and filename to use. By default, iNotes uses log as the directory name and the name of your mail file as the log filename.
Do Not Delete Documents That Have Responses	The default setting is to *not* delete mail messages that have responses. You can delete messages with responses by unchecking this option.
Delete All Qualifying Documents Without Archiving Them	This option deletes the documents in the Which Documents Do You Wish to Archive fields, without archiving them.

USING iNOTES CALENDAR

The iNotes Web Access calendar can display and print your calendar in a variety of formats. You can choose to display one day, two days, five days, one week, two weeks, a month, or an entire year.

Let's take a brief tour of the iNotes Web Access calendar application. The calendar can be accessed from anywhere in iNotes via the taskbar's Calendar button. The month view of a calendar is shown in Figure 10.16.

Figure 10.16
View appointments, meetings, reminders, and To Do items in your calendar.

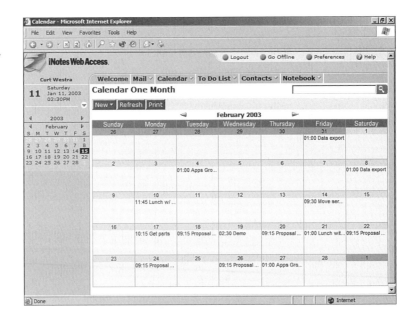

To change your calendar display, point to Calendar and then select the view you want from the drop-down menu.

When you've selected how many days to view in the calendar, you can change which days are displayed by clicking the gold triangles to the left and right of the date at the top. For example, if you are viewing a full-month calendar, as shown in Figure 10.16, click the right triangle to display the next month. Click the left triangle, and the previous month appears.

Another method for changing the displayed dates was reviewed earlier in this chapter. The date picker is displayed on the left of your iNotes Web Access window, as shown earlier in Figure 10.2. You can easily change the day, month, or year by using this handy tool.

As in Lotus Notes, calendar entries can consist of appointments, reminders, anniversaries, meetings, and all-day events. Position your mouse over an entry, and details about it will appear. To open and edit an entry, just double-click it.

Now that you're familiar with the basics of how to get around in the calendar, you can learn how to create new calendar entries. The process for creating a calendar entry is largely the same, no matter what type of entry it is—an appointment, meeting, reminder, anniversary, or all-day event. If you're familiar with the Lotus Notes calendar, you'll recognize that the iNotes Web Access calendar includes many of the same robust calendaring and scheduling features.

In the following section, we'll walk through the basic steps of creating an entry, pointing out any unique steps or options that apply to a particular type. Following that, we'll take a more detailed look at scheduling meetings, using group calendars, printing your calendar, and changing calendar preferences.

CREATING A CALENDAR ENTRY

To create a new calendar entry, just double-click beneath a date or on a time slot within a date. A new Calendar Entry form opens in a new window, as shown in Figure 10.17. You can also create a new entry by choosing New Calendar Entry from the Calendar task bar button or the New action bar button.

When a new calendar entry form opens it is set to be an appointment entry by default. To select a different type of calendar entry (for example, a reminder), click the down arrow on the first tab.

The only fields that you are required to fill out before iNotes will save your entry are the Subject and Date fields, and for some entries the Time and Duration fields. Enter as much or as little information as you want on the rest of the form, including a location, a category, a message, alarm settings, attachments, and a confidential preference.

Enter the date by clicking the button to the right of the Date field and selecting from the date picker, or type in a date. Click the down arrow next to the Time field to select a start time for any entry except all-day events. You can specify how long appointments or meetings will last by clicking the + or – buttons next to the Duration field.

Figure 10.17
Create an appoint-
ment, meeting,
reminder, anniver-
sary, or all-day event
entry using the
Calendar Entry form.

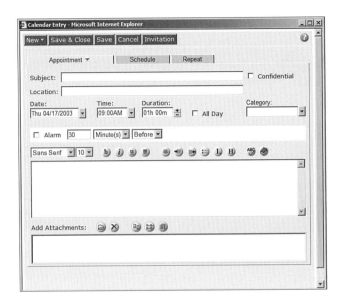

An alarm can be activated to notify you of upcoming calendar events by clicking the Alarm
check box and entering the time you want to be notified. Use the three fields to the right of
the check box to specify the alarm settings. By default, alarms are set to go off 30 minutes
before a calendar entry, but you can specify in minutes, hours, or days the amount of time
that the alarm should notify you before or after an entry. Alternatively, you can enter an
exact time and date for the alarm by selecting On instead of Before or After.

A message area is provided for you to enter a description or notes. This rich-text field is
similar to that used in the mail Message form.

You can specify a category for the entry and indicate whether you want the entry to be confidential. Click the Confidential check box if you allow others access to your calendar and
want to keep them from reading an entry.

If you have an entry that you want to repeat over multiple dates, use the Set Repeat feature.
Click the Repeat tab, and then click the Set Repeat check box. Select whether you want the
entry to repeat daily, weekly, monthly by day, monthly by date, or yearly. Then select the
frequency and duration that the entry should repeat. You can even tell iNotes to handle
the entry differently if it falls on a weekend.

After you've completed making or editing a calendar entry, click Save and Close.

SCHEDULING A MEETING AND SENDING INVITATIONS

iNotes Web Access includes much of the same functionality found in Lotus Notes for
scheduling meetings, inviting attendees, and reserving resources. This has the potential to
be a powerful tool to more efficiently coordinate meeting scheduling across a distributed
company.

CREATING A NEW MEETING ENTRY

Follow these steps to open a new meeting entry, select invitees, and reserve resources:

1. Open a new calendar entry by choosing New Calendar Entry from the Calendar taskbar button or the New action bar button.

2. Click Invite to select the names of the persons you want to invite. The Select Addresses dialog box opens.

3. Select names from your contacts, the Domino directory, or the Directory Catalog. Then choose Invite.

4. If you want to invite optional attendees, select the names of optional attendees and click the Optional button.

5. If you want to copy the invitation to some persons for informational purposes only, select their names and click the FYI button.

6. Click the Exit button to close the dialog box.

7. Click the Request Response check box if you want to receive a confirmation message from the invitees.

8. If your company's Domino directory includes rooms and resources, you can click either Rooms or Resources to reserve each.

The usual nightmare that occurs when scheduling a meeting for several people is finding a free block of time that they all share. You can use the Schedule feature to check for free time among all the invitees entered earlier. Click the Schedule tab, and the invitees' availability appears, as shown in Figure 10.18.

Figure 10.18
Use the Schedule feature to find a free block of time among all meeting invitees.

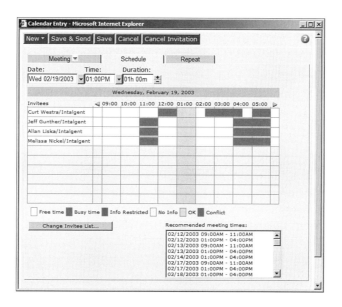

CAUTION

> The value of the Schedule feature is limited to the degree that Notes and iNotes users keep their calendars updated. For example, if some invitees do not use the calendar or do not keep it current, you are more likely to schedule meetings when conflicts will occur.

Using the information gleaned from checking the invitees' schedules, you can enter a meeting date, time, and duration. Complete the other fields on the form.

NOTE

> If you work offline in iNotes Web Access, you should maintain a copy of the server's name and address book when working offline. Select Include Server's Name and Address Book on the Other tab in Preferences. Using the server's name and address book while working offline allows meeting invitee names to be properly formatted and processed. If you do not have a copy of the server's name and address book, you should specify the full hierarchical name of the meeting invitee (for example, Joe User/Company), or problems are likely to occur.

Click Save and Send to save the calendar entry and send the invitation to all invitees.

RESPONDING TO PROPOSED CHANGES TO INVITATIONS

If an invitee proposes a change to a meeting invitation that you sent, iNotes Web Access sends you a mail message. Open the message and click Accept or Decline. If you accept the proposed change, iNotes sends a message to all recipients about the change. If you decline, iNotes sends a message only to the person who proposed the change.

RESCHEDULING, CANCELING, OR CONFIRMING MEETINGS

When you reschedule, cancel, or confirm a meeting, iNotes Web Access sends a mail message to the invitees. To reschedule a meeting, follow these steps:

1. Open the meeting invitation from within your calendar.
2. Point your mouse to Actions, and then click Reschedule from the drop-down menu.
3. Specify the new date, time, or duration. Add comments to the notice in the message area if you want, and then choose OK.
4. Click Save and Close.

If the meeting repeats, iNotes gives you the option to change only this instance, all instances, this instance and all previous instances, or this instance and future instances.

To cancel a meeting, open the meeting in your calendar, point your mouse to Actions, and then choose Cancel from the drop-down menu. Add comments to your cancellation notice, if you want, and then choose OK. Meeting invitees are sent a message informing them that the meeting is canceled.

If you want, you can send invitees a confirmation that your previously proposed meeting date and time are firmly scheduled. To confirm a meeting, open the meeting entry from your calendar, point to Actions, and then click Confirm. Add comments to your confirmation message if you want, and then choose OK. Invitees will receive a message confirming the meeting date, time, and other details.

ADDING OR REMOVING MEETING INVITEES

You can add or remove people from a meeting invitation even after you've created and sent the invitations. Just open the meeting entry from your calendar and click the Add/Remove tab. If you're adding people, enter them in the Invite field, as described earlier. If you're removing an attendee, select the person's name from the Invitations and Reservations Already Sent list; then click the right arrow to move them to the Attendees and Resources You Wish to Remove list. Click Save and Send.

If the meeting repeats, iNotes gives you the option to add or remove attendees for only this instance, all instances, this instance and all previous instances, or this instance and future instances.

New invitees are sent an invitation, as described previously. People removed from the invitee list are sent a message informing them that they are not required to attend the meeting anymore.

ANSWERING MEETING INVITATIONS

As described previously, a meeting invitation arrives in the recipient's mail inbox. When you receive and open a meeting invitation, you can see whether the person expects an answer from you and check your calendar for your availability. When you accept a meeting invitation, the meeting is automatically entered into your iNotes calendar.

If you are expected to respond to a meeting invitation, you can accept, decline, or propose a new time. Your options are as follows:

- **Check your availability**—Click Check Calendar.
- **Accept the invitation**—Choose Accept from the Accept drop-down menu.
- **Accept the invitation and send comments back to the meeting chair**—Choose Accept with Comments from the Accept drop-down menu.
- **Propose a new date, time, or duration for the meeting**— Choose Propose New Time from the Decline drop-down menu.
- **Decline the invitation**—Choose Decline from the Decline drop-down menu.
- **Decline the invitation and send comments back to the meeting chair**—Choose Decline with Comments from the Decline drop-down menu.
- **Print a copy of the meeting invitation**—Click Print.

To automatically remove invitations from your inbox after you answer them, click Preferences and then click the Calendar tab. Select Remove Meeting Invitations from My Inbox After I Respond to Them. Then click Save and Close.

USING GROUP CALENDARS

A *group calendar* displays the schedules of people you select. You can use a group calendar to check whether people in the group are free or busy at a certain time when you schedule a meeting or all-day event. Group calendars show only the blocks of time that each person is free or busy. Details about any calendar entries are not displayed, which maintains each person's privacy. To create a group calendar, follow these steps:

1. Place your mouse over Calendar. Then click New Group Calendar from the drop-down menu.

2. Type a group name.

3. Select the names of people or groups in the Members field. To select names from your contacts or Domino directory, click Members.

4. Click Save and Close.

CAUTION

> You won't be able to create group calendars if you aren't designated as the owner of the mail file. If you can't create a group calendar, click Preferences and, on the Mail tab, click Save and Close so that the server knows you are the owner of the mail file.

When you want to check the schedules of people in a group calendar, first open your list of group calendars by pointing your mouse to Calendar and clicking Group Calendar from the drop-down menu. Double-click on a group calendar from the list to open it, as shown in Figure 10.19. Busy times are indicated by bars that use different colors to represent each type of calendar entry.

The default view displays the current day's group calendar. Use the orange arrows to the right and left of the date at the top of the view to see the next day or the previous day, respectively. At a glance, you can see when each person is free and busy.

If you have access to read the group members' calendar details (as designated by the members in their preferences), you can expand each person's entries to show details about specific calendar entries. Expand or collapse one person's schedule details by clicking the twistie, or arrow, next to his name; expand or collapse all members' details by pointing to Expand/Collapse and then clicking Expand All or Collapse All, respectively.

View calendars by day, week, or month by pointing your mouse to View and then clicking the appropriate choice. Week and month views are useful to you only if you have access to read the members' calendar details.

From here you can go ahead and create a meeting invitation or other calendar entries by pointing to New and then clicking the appropriate entry type.

Figure 10.19
Use group calendars to quickly view the schedules among all group members.

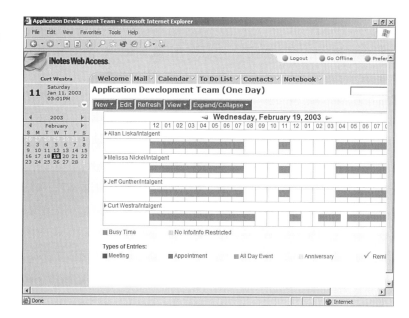

10

NOTE

Group calendars are effective only if everyone in the group allows access to view their schedules. By default, iNotes lets everyone see your work hours schedule. However, if you change your calendar preferences to restrict access to your work hours schedule, only the people you designate can see your work hours.

PRINTING YOUR CALENDAR

Many people prefer to print a paper copy of their calendar that they can refer to when away from their workstations or insert in their planners. If you're one of these people, you're in luck. iNotes Web Access provides a very useful and flexible printing feature that enables you to select from various options to get the printout you desire. Options include printing in formats that match styles used by Franklin Day Planner, DayRunner, DayTimer, and others.

The calendar printing feature generates a PDF file and requires you to have the free Adobe Acrobat Reader (version 4.0 or greater) installed on your workstation. PDF files are the standard for printing high-quality documents from the Internet. You can download the Adobe Acrobat Reader software from www.adobe.com and install it, if you don't already have it, or contact your technical support to request an installation.

To print a calendar view, click the Print button from the action bar. A print dialog box opens, as shown in Figure 10.20. From here you select from options, preview the printout, and send the calendar to your printer.

Figure 10.20
iNotes Web Access features a flexible cal-endar-printing tool.

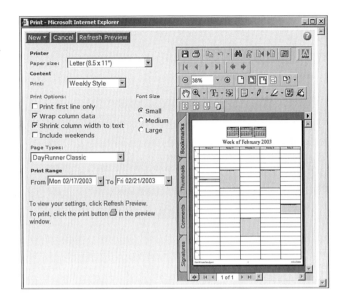

First select the paper size, and then choose a content style (daily, weekly, monthly, trifold, and more) from the drop-down list. Print options that you select from include these:

- **Print First Line Only**—This prints just the first line of each calendar entry as displayed in the calendar.

- **Wrap Column Data**—Text displayed in each calendar entry will wrap to fit within the column.

- **Shrink Column Width to Text**—This option forces columns to vary in width according to the amount of text in the entry.

- **Include Weekends**—Select this option to print the weekend days on Monthly, Weekly, or Trifold styles.

Select the font size for the printout, and then select from the list of page types to determine the format in which your calendar will print. Your options include several for Franklin Day Planner, DayRunner, and DayTimer, as well as choices for Rolodex, index card, or full-page formats. Finally, select the range of dates you want to print.

Before printing the calendar, preview how it will look by clicking the Refresh Preview button. The preview loads in the pane on the right side of the Print window. To see how the calendar will look with different settings, change any options and click Refresh Preview again.

To send your calendar to the printer, click the Printer icon in the preview pane. Select your printer in the Print dialog box that opens, and then choose OK.

CHANGING CALENDAR PREFERENCES

You can change most of your calendar preferences by clicking Preferences and then clicking the Calendar tab. The calendar preferences open, as shown in Figure 10.21.

Figure 10.21
The calendar preferences enable you to control default entry settings, display options, and preferences for handling meeting invitations.

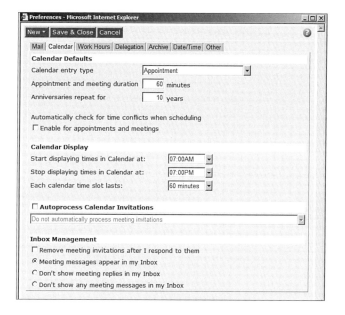

Calendar delegation preferences are set from the Delegation tab, and we'll cover this a bit later.

With the calendar preferences, you can set several defaults, including the type of all new calendar entries, appointment and meeting durations, and whether to check for scheduling conflicts.

Calendar display options enable you to specify the time range that your calendar will show entries (for example, 8:00 a.m. to 5:00 p.m.) and the length of each time slot to display.

You can designate how you want meeting invitations to be processed by iNotes Web Access. The available options are as follows:

- **Automatically Process Meeting Invitations from All Users**—Use this option to automatically accept meeting invitations from anyone who sends you an invitation. If an invitation conflicts with another meeting, iNotes sends a Decline notice to the person who sent the invitation.

- **Automatically Process Meeting Invitations from the Following Users**—Use this option to automatically accept meeting invitations from people you select. If an invitation conflicts with another meeting, iNotes sends a Decline notice to the person who sent the invitation.

- **Delegate Meeting Invitations to the Following Person**—Use this option to forward all meeting invitations to a selected person.

Inbox management preferences control whether meeting invitations and replies are displayed in your mail inbox. Activate or deactivate each of the following options:

- **Remove Meeting Invitations After I Respond to Them**—Select this option to remove meeting invitations from your inbox after you've responded to them.

- **Meeting Messages Appear in my Inbox**—Select this if you want meeting messages to appear in your inbox.

- **Don't Show Meeting Replies in My Inbox**—Select this if you don't want to see answers to meeting invitations that you send appear in your inbox.

- **Don't Show Any Meeting Messages in My Inbox**—Select this if you do not want any meeting messages to appear in your inbox. This is useful if you have delegated your scheduling of meetings to someone else.

DELEGATION FUNCTIONS IN CALENDAR

Within Preferences, click the Delegation tab to edit preferences for delegating access to your calendar. Here you can delegate authority to perform certain functions in your calendar application. For example, you might have a secretary who manages your mail and calendar for you by setting your appointments and responding to meeting invitations. You can delegate functions in your calendar application using the form shown in Figure 10.22.

Figure 10.22
Give others the capability to access your calendar for certain functions.

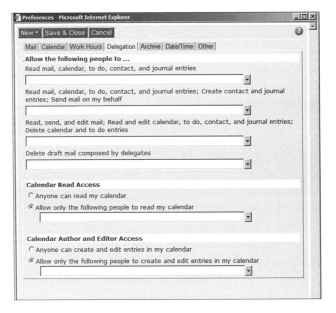

Use the first three fields to specify people whom you want to give varying degrees of rights to read and edit *all* your iNotes applications, including the calendar. You can give specific people or groups the capability to perform the following operations:

- Read your entries for calendar, mail, and more.
- Read your calendar and other entries and create new messages using your mail application (that is, under your signature).
- Read, create, and edit entries for the calendar, mail, and more.
- Read, create, edit, and delete entries for calendar, mail, and other applications.

By default, iNotes gives anyone calendar read access to read your calendar for use in the scheduling and group calendars features covered previously in this chapter. Keep in mind that this allows others to see *when* you have calendar entries but provides no details about the entries themselves (except that they are an appointment, meeting, all-day event, and so on). If you don't want anyone to read your calendar, specify one or more people in the Allow Only the Following People to Read My Calendar field.

If you want to allow someone to create and edit your calendar entries for you, but you don't want to give access to your mail and other applications, use the Calendar Author and Edit Access section of the form. Enter the names of designated people in the provided field.

Click Save and Close when you're finished.

USING THE iNOTES TO DO LIST

The To Do application in iNotes Web Access helps you to plan and manage daily tasks. Although it doesn't provide as much functionality as some of the project-planning software that's available (nor is it intended to), it includes some useful features that can help you keep on top of your workload.

OVERVIEW

You can view your To Do items in a list, in a chart, or in your calendar. To view your items in a list, click the To Do button in iNotes. Your To Do items are displayed, indicating priority, subject, due date, status, and category, as shown in Figure 10.23. The items are sorted by priority; each has a priority number next to it, indicating whether it is of high, medium, low, or no priority. You can re-sort your items by priority, due date, or status when you click the column headings for each.

Refresh your list by clicking Refresh, and delete any item by selecting it and clicking Delete or pressing the Delete key.

CREATING AND EDITING A TO DO ITEM

Use the To Do form to create a new To Do item. You can create a new item by choosing New To Do from the To Do task bar button or the New action bar button. The To Do form opens, as shown in Figure 10.24.

Figure 10.23
The To Do List displays your tasks according to priority by default, but you can re-sort by due date or status instead.

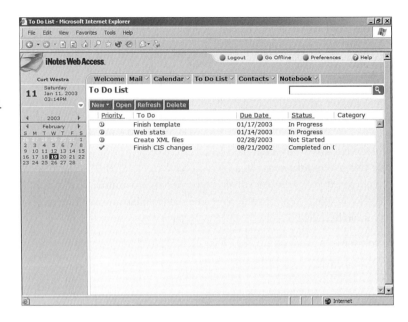

Figure 10.24
Manage your tasks using the To Do form.

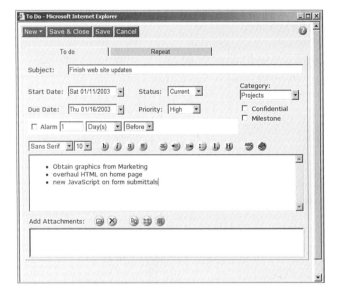

To complete a new To Do item, follow these steps:

1. Type a subject.

2. Select a start date and due date using the date picker button next to each field.

3. Select a priority level (High, Medium, Low, or None). Higher-priority items display first in your To Do list, by default.

4. Select the task's status. The default status is Current, but you can select Overdue, Future, Rejected, or Complete.

5. Select a category for the item, if you want. Creating personal categories for use in To Do items is discussed later in the section, "Configuring Preferences."

6. Check Confidential if you want to keep this item private from anyone who has access to read your calendar entries. Individuals who have permission to manage your calendar will be able to see the time for entries marked confidential but won't be able to see the contents.

7. Check Milestone if you want the To Do item to serve as a landmark task that should be completed by the start date. The To Do chart displays this task in red on the start date.

8. Set the alarm if you want to be notified a certain number of minutes, hours, or days before or after the item's due date. Select On if you want to select a specific date and time for the alarm.

9. Enter a description, notes, or links in the message area.

10. Add any attachments related to the task.

11. If you want to repeat the task, click the Repeat tab. This is useful if you have tasks that you perform on a regular schedule. Check Set Repeat, and then choose the frequency and duration that the task should repeat.

12. Click Save and Close.

10

Later you can open and edit an item to update its status, modify due dates, adjust its priority level, and more. Open an item by double-clicking it from the To Do list or To Do chart, or by clicking Open while an item is selected from the list.

When you change the status of an item to Complete, it appears in the To Do list and To Do chart with a green check mark next to it.

A potentially useful feature is how iNotes handles unfinished To Do items. If an item is not marked as complete and the due date passes, it appears in the next day's calendar. This can serve as a useful prompt to wrap up those tasks that you couldn't finish on time!

USING THE TO DO CHART

You can use the To Do chart to get a visual perspective of the status of your To Do items. To view your items in a chart, place your mouse on the To Do button in the task bar and then click To Do Chart. An example of a To Do chart appears in Figure 10.25.

You can view your To Do chart items by days, weeks, months, or quarters. Each item is displayed with a blue bar indicating the projected duration from start date to due date. A red bar on the chart indicates that the task is a milestone to be completed by the date indicated.

The To Do chart in iNotes might be useful for visually tracking progress on a large number of project-specific tasks, but for everyday types of tasks it could be overkill. The chart would be strengthened if it supported the capability to group tasks by project or other criteria. The lack of a print feature also limits the usefulness of the To Do chart for any serious task planning and tracking.

Figure 10.25
Visually track the
progress and status of
your tasks using the
To Do chart.

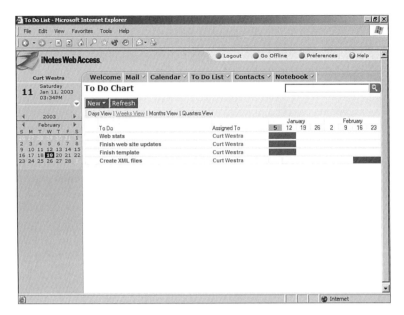

DELEGATION FUNCTIONS FOR TO DO

As with the calendar and mail applications, you can delegate to others the access to read, create, and edit your To Do items. Click Preferences in iNotes Web Access, and then select the Delegation tab. Use the first three fields to specify people to whom you want to give varying degrees of rights to read and edit *all* your iNotes applications, including the To Do list. You can give specific people or groups the capability to perform the following operations:

- Read your entries for your To Do, your calendar, your mail, and more.
- Read your To Do list, calendar, and other entries, and create new messages using your mail application (that is, under your signature).
- Read, create, edit, and delete entries for your To Do list and other applications.

CONTACTS

The contacts application in iNotes Web Access is similar to the personal name and address book in Lotus Notes: It enables you to maintain all your contact information. If you're a Lotus Notes user, you can populate your iNotes contacts with entries from your Notes address book and then synchronize them regularly. This can be useful when you're away from the office and need to contact someone and access the Internet. The contacts application also integrates seamlessly with your mail and calendar applications, enabling you to select names and groups when addressing messages, meeting invitations, and so on.

The contacts application can be accessed from anywhere in iNotes via the taskbar's Contacts button. As shown in Figure 10.26, the default view lists all your contacts in alphabetical order, with names, phone numbers, email addresses, and company displayed for each. You can also sort and display your contacts by email address or by company, by clicking the appropriate menu option on the left side of the iNotes Web Access window.

Figure 10.26
Access all your contact information through an easy-to-use interface by clicking alphabetical tabs or using the virtual scrollbar.

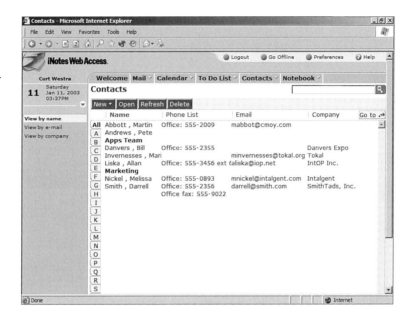

You can view the contacts whose last name (or, if the contact is just an organization, the company name) falls under any letter of the alphabet by clicking the left tab for that letter. Want to see Larry Smith's information? Click the S tab. This is an intuitive interface that you need no time to learn.

Another nice feature of the Contacts view is what Lotus calls the *virtual scrollbar* that lies on the right, inside your normal browser scrollbar. Use the virtual scrollbar to scroll up and down to view your contacts. It's an innovative tool that fits in so nicely that you hardly think about it.

Now that you're familiar with the contacts interface, let's walk through the steps for creating a contact.

CREATING AND EDITING A CONTACT

Use the Contact form to create and manage all your contact information. You can create individual contacts or groups. To create a new contact from within the contacts application, click New or right-click any existing entry and then select New Contact. You can create a new contact from anywhere in iNotes by pointing to Contacts and clicking New Contact from the drop-down menu, or by clicking Contact from the New action button.

You can open an existing contact several ways: Click Open while the contact is selected in the view, double-click a contact in the view, or select a contact and right-click and then choose Open. An open Contact form appears. Figure 10.27 shows a Contact form with some information entered. Use the form to enter names, work and business information (such as company, title, address, email addresses, Web site, and numbers for phone, fax, cell, and pager), home information (such as address, email addresses, Web site, and numbers for phone, fax, and cell), and personal information (including nickname, birthday, and family details).

You can customize the label of many of the fields in the Contact form. This gives you some flexibility in entering information that is relevant. To customize editable field labels, click the button next to the current field label and select a new label from the drop-down menu.

Figure 10.27
Use the Contact form to create and maintain all your contact information.

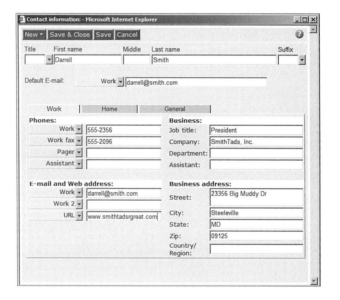

Click Save and Close when you're finished creating or editing the form.

CREATING AND EDITING A GROUP

If you find that you are often sending mail messages to the same people, you might want to consider creating a group. The benefit of using a group is that instead of separately entering each individual in the address field of a new message, you make one entry. You also don't have to worry about remembering which individuals to include every time you send those messages.

A group can consist of contacts or groups already listed in your Domino directory or contacts. You can also add email addresses for others outside your company's domain who are not already listed in your contacts.

To create a new group, point your mouse over New and select Group, or right-click a selected contact and choose New Group Contact. The Group form opens, as shown in Figure 10.28.

Figure 10.28
Use the Group form to create and maintain your contact groups.

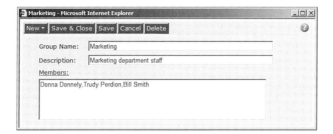

Enter a name for the group and a description, if you want. Then click Members to select names from your Domino directory or contacts. You can also enter explicit email addresses from other domains. Refer to the section on creating and sending a message provided earlier in this chapter for addressing a mail message.

Click Save and Close when you are finished. You now have a group stored in your contacts that can save you some time and frustration when sending messages to a large number of people.

SYNCHRONIZING YOUR CONTACTS AND ADDRESS BOOK

If you're a Lotus Notes user, you can populate your iNotes contacts with entries from your Notes address book and then synchronize them regularly. From within your Notes client mail, calendar, or To Do applications, click Actions and then click Synchronize Address Book. Notes synchronizes the entries in both locations so that the most current contact information is available, no matter which client you use to access it.

You must repeat the synchronization process periodically to keep the entries matched. Although iNotes and Lotus Notes share the same database for your mail, calendar, and To Do applications and are synchronized automatically, the contacts/address nook and notebook/journal applications use separate databases and require you to initiate synchronization each time.

DELEGATION FUNCTIONS FOR CONTACTS

Your delegation preferences dictate what level of access others have to your iNotes applications. The level of access that you have given others to your mail, calendar, To Do list, and notebook is the same provided to contacts. To check your delegation settings, click Preferences in iNotes Web Access and then select the Delegation tab. The first three fields specify people to whom you want to give varying degrees of rights to read and edit *all* your iNotes applications, including contacts.

NOTE

If you're a Lotus Notes user, keep in mind that the delegation preferences that you set for contacts and the notebook apply only to iNotes use. People to whom you delegate contacts and notebook access will be able to access them only via iNotes. This is because your iNotes contacts and the notebook are stored on the server, making them available for shared access. In Lotus Notes, by contrast, your address book and journal are stored in separate databases on your workstation's hard drive, so they cannot be shared. This explains why in Notes delegation preferences, there is no option to share access to your address book and journal.

USING iNOTES NOTEBOOK

The notebook application in iNotes Web Access is very similar to the journal in Lotus Notes. You can use the notebook to keep a journal or write notes for yourself. You can also synchronize your journal with the notebook from Lotus Notes.

The notebook application can be accessed from anywhere in iNotes via the taskbar's Notebook button. As shown in Figure 10.29, the default view lists all your notebook entries with titles and the last modified date displayed for each. You can re-sort your notebook entries by title or date by clicking the desired column heading.

Figure 10.29
The Notebook view displays all your notebook page entries.

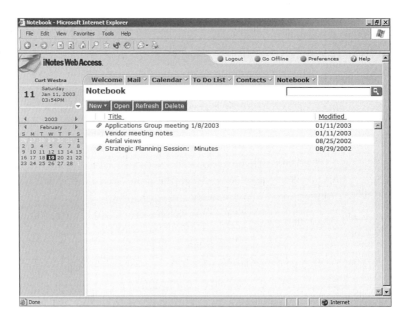

To create a new notebook page from within the notebook application, click New or right-click a selected notebook page entry in the view and choose New Notebook Page. The Notebook Page form opens, as shown in Figure 10.30.

Figure 10.30
Use the Notebook Page form to create and edit notes, journal entries, and other documentation.

If you're a Lotus Notes user, you can populate your iNotes notebook with entries from your Notes journal and then synchronize them regularly. From within your Notes client mail, calendar, or To Do applications, click Actions and then click Synchronize Journal. Notes synchronizes the entries in both locations so that the most current information is available, no matter which client you use to access it. Repeat this process whenever you want to synchronize your notebook and journal.

Keep in mind that if you are sharing access to your iNotes applications with other iNotes users, they will have access to your notebook pages. The level of access to read, edit, or delete that you have given others to your mail, calendar, To Do list, and contacts is the same provided to the notebook. If you need to share access to your mail and calendar with other iNotes users, be careful not to create notebook pages of a highly personal or sensitive nature because these people will have access to them via iNotes.

To check your delegation settings, click Preferences in iNotes Web Access and then select the Delegation tab. The first three fields specify people to whom you want to give varying degrees of rights to read and edit *all* your iNotes applications, including the notebook.

USING INOTES CHAT

If your company utilizes Lotus Sametime, it's possible to send and receive instant messages from the iNotes Web Access client. If the Domino administrator has taken the necessary steps to integrate access to the Sametime server, you should see a Chat link in the upper right of any iNotes Web pages. Click Chat to see who is online, create chat groups, and send instant messages to others.

10

Providing a guide to using Lotus Sametime for instant messaging is outside the scope of this book, but it's important to note here that the integration of Sametime with iNotes Web Access is a potentially useful tool for organizations that are looking to widely implement both applications.

CONFIGURING PREFERENCES

Preference settings for each of the specific applications in iNotes already were discussed in previous sections of this chapter. Refer to the sections on the mail and calendar applications, To Do lists, contacts, and the notebook for guidance on setting their respective preferences.

A few preferences need to be covered, including those for work hours, date/time, searching, working offline, and changing your Internet password.

WORK HOURS

iNotes Web Access sets blocks of time as free (time available for meetings) or busy (unavailable for meetings) based on your settings here. When you add an entry to your calendar, iNotes Web Access also sets the time of the entry as busy (unless you select Mark Time as Available for the entry). This enables other people to check whether you're available for a meeting before inviting you.

Click Preferences and then select the Work Hours tab to edit these settings, as shown in Figure 10.31. Select the days of the week for which you want to specify your normal office hours or free time, and then indicate the blocks of time that apply to each given day.

Figure 10.31
Specify your normal office hours and availability for meetings by setting your work hours.

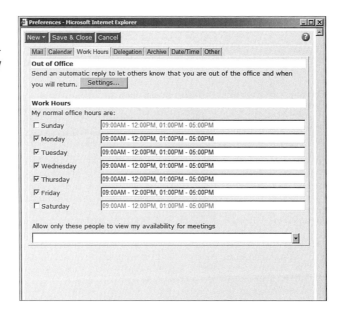

At the bottom of the same form you can also restrict who can look up your work hours information. When the field is empty, everyone can look up your work hours. Click the button next to the field to select names of people to restrict access to.

When you're finished, click Save and Close to implement any changes.

DATE/TIME

From the Date/Time tab in Preferences, you can set the date styles, date separators, time format, and time separator to control how dates and times appear in iNotes Web Access.

OTHER

The Other Preferences form enables you to change settings for doing searches, setting up personal categories, changing your Internet password, working offline, and more. Let's walk through each of these briefly. Within Preferences, click the Other tab and the form appears, as shown in Figure 10.32.

10

Figure 10.32
Other preferences affect searching, personal categories, your Internet password, and working offline.

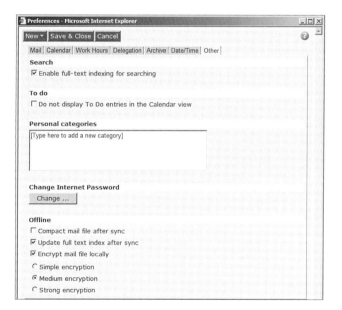

SEARCHES

To enable fast searches in your calendar, mail, and To Do items, select Create Full-Text Index for Searching. There could be a delay between the time you select a full-text index for searching and the time when the server creates the full-text index.

PERSONAL CATEGORIES

You can create personal categories to organize your To Do items and calendar entries into groupings such as appointments, events, and meetings. This can be of primary use in third-party applications. iNotes Web Access does not use personal categories when handling or displaying information.

CHANGING INTERNET PASSWORD

You use the Internet password to log on to iNotes Web Access. To change it yourself, you must be the owner of the mail file, password changing must be enabled on the server, and you must have Manager or Designer access to your mail file.

Choose Change Password. When prompted, enter your current password and new password, and confirm the new password. Choose OK.

The old password works until the Domino server starts a new task. After several minutes, the old one will be invalid.

If you don't have the proper authority to change your Internet password in iNotes, contact your Domino administrator for assistance.

OFFLINE PREFERENCES

Offline preferences are described in the upcoming section "Working Offline."

DEFAULT DISPLAY NAME

You can choose to display primary names or alternate names if your administrator has enabled this option. This feature might be useful if you work internationally. A primary name is recognized internationally, while an alternate name is recognizable in your native language. Check with your Domino administrator for more details.

WORKING OFFLINE

One of the most useful features of iNotes Web Access for the mobile user is support for working offline. This is particularly useful if you occasionally work at a workstation away from your office or travel with a laptop. You can replicate your mail, calendar, To Do items, contacts, and notebook to your desktop or laptop computer and then go offline. While disconnected, you can still read and create mail messages, update your schedule and To Do list, look up contact information, or enter notes from a meeting. The next time you get back online, iNotes replicates changes with the Domino server and sends your outgoing mail.

To do all this, iNotes utilizes Domino Offline Services (DOLS), a technology that supports offline access for a number of Domino-based applications. Working offline is a key function that has not been available before in the Lotus WebMail client; it provides iNotes Web Access users with truly mobile access to their personal information. Your administrator will need to set up DOLS to work on the server before you can begin working offline.

Before you go offline the first time, you should check the offline preferences. Let's take a brief look at how to set these options first; then we'll walk through the initial setup process required to work offline.

OFFLINE PREFERENCES

To edit your offline preference settings, click Preferences and select the Other tab. The Offline settings appear, as shown previously in Figure 10.32.

CAUTION

> If you make changes to the Offline settings after the offline subscription installation, you must reinstall the subscription before the new settings will take effect.

The Offline settings include the following:

- **Compact Mail File After Sync**—This option results in your offline mail file being compacted, or reduced in size, after synchronizing. If synchronizations take a long time to complete, you might consider disabling this option to see if it speeds things up.

- **Update Full-Text Index After Sync**—This updates the full-text index for the offline mail file (if one exists) after synchronizing with the online mail file. You can disable this option if you want to try to reduce the amount of time it takes to synchronize an offline subscription.

- **Encrypt Mail File Locally**—Encrypting the offline copy of your mail by encrypting it renders it inaccessible by others without authentication. Select this option and choose an encryption level. Note that because DOLS won't compact encrypted databases, you cannot select both the Encrypt and Compact options.

- **Include Server's Name and Address Book**—This option appears only if your administrator has enabled it. To skip downloading a copy of your mail server's Domino directory when you work offline, deselect Include Server's Name and Address Book. It's best to download a copy for offline use in addressing mail messages and meeting invitations. Although this requires more time for the initial installation, future updates will not take long.

The options concerning encryption and the Domino directory appear only if the administrator has enabled the features.

Click Save and Close when you are finished changing your offline preferences.

The Offline settings do not take effect until the offline subscription is installed when you first attempt to go offline.

INSTALLING THE OFFLINE SUBSCRIPTION

To install the offline subscription and work offline the first time, follow these steps:

1. Click Go Offline.
2. At the prompt to install the offline mail subscription from IBM, choose OK.
3. When prompted, enter the directory on your computer where the subscription file is to be installed.

4. If you chose to encrypt your local mail file in the Offline settings, you will need to enter the location of your Notes ID file. If you are a Lotus Notes user, use your ID file typically located in the \notes\data directory. If you don't have one, contact your Domino administrator to obtain one.

5. Choose Done on the Installing Subscription page when the download is completed.

Now you're ready to work offline!

NOTE

> The downloads required to perform the one-time subscription installation can take a long time. If at all possible, perform the installation while you're in your office and on your company's LAN, rather than via dial-up. You'll save yourself a lot of time and frustration.

As noted previously, if you make changes to the Offline settings after the offline subscription installation, you must reinstall the subscription before the new settings will take effect. To reinstall the offline subscription, delete the offline mail file from your hard drive and then follow the previous steps.

Going Offline or Going Online

To work offline from an existing online session in iNotes Web Access, click Go Offline at the top right of the page. Choose the black Go Offline button and select Go Offline.

To go online from an existing offline session, click Go Offline; then choose the black Go Online button and select Go Online.

Logging Out

When you're finished working in iNotes Web Access, make it a habit to log out by clicking Logout in the upper right of any page. Logging out properly reduces the risk that an unauthorized person can use cached information to access your data from the machine you used. This is particularly important if you access iNotes from a shared machine. For example, another person who uses the same machine after you could use the browser's history to access your iNotes.

To log out of iNotes Web Access, follow these steps:

1. Click Logout.

2. Close your browser or, for a more secure logout, proceed to Step 3.

3. Select Logout for Shared PCs or Kiosk Users.

4. Select either the Secure or More Secure options (described next).

During the logout process, iNotes Web Access removes authentication information and private data from the browser's cache. But some personal information is not deleted unless you select the Logout for Shared PCs or Kiosk Users option. When you do so, two types of logout options are presented:

- **Secure**—Removes all traces of your authenticated use of iNotes Web Access and other Web pages that you might have visited, but retains some iNotes Web Access program data to speed performance the next time you or someone else logs on.

- **More Secure**—Removes all traces of iNotes Web Access and all other visited Web pages from the temporary Internet files folder, except for cookies from other Web pages. This has the same effect as setting your browser to delete all files from the Temporary Internet Files folder when the browser window closes.

A truly secure logout in iNotes Web Access is possible only if you use the Logout feature and have accepted the iNotes control at some point when previously opening iNotes.

10

PART III

INTRODUCING DOMINO DESIGNER 6

CHAPTER 11

CREATING AND ACCESSING DOMINO DATABASES

In this chapter

WHAT IS A DOMINO DATABASE?

A Domino *database* is a repository primarily for documents. In addition, it contains design and programming elements. The database is typically stored on a Domino server, but it can also reside on your laptop or desktop workstation. Domino databases can exist on any of the server platforms supported by Domino, which means anything from Windows to Unix to Linux. In addition to multiple platform support, Domino databases include multilingual support. A variety of languages are supported, including English, French, German, Spanish, and more than 40 others.

DOMINO DOCUMENTS

You might already be familiar with other database systems, such as DB2, Oracle, or MySQL. Unlike those databases, Domino databases are not relational, but rather document-centric. All the data stored within the database is not organized in the typical rows and columns of a relational database.

> **NOTE**
> With add-on drivers from Lotus, such as NotesSQL or Domino JDBC (Java Database Connectivity), a Domino database can be accessed via traditional SQL statements. This can make the database appear to be relational, but it isn't truly a relational database.

11

Perhaps one of the greatest strengths of a Domino database is precisely the fact that it is not relational. In a typical relational database, data is stored in tables made up of distinct rows and columns. Each row is similar in format to the other rows in the same table. On one hand, this homogeneity makes access to rows of the table very fast because each row has the same format. On the other hand, this same homogeneity makes the tables rather inflexible. The rows of a table are not allowed to vary.

The counterpart of a row within a relational database is called a *document* in Domino. This is obviously a very specialized use of the word *document* and differs somewhat from our everyday usage. A Domino document typically contains several *items* of data. Each of the items corresponds to a field and has a unique name.

For example, suppose you had a document describing names and addresses of business partners. A document, called Contact, might contain fields with the following names: FirstName, LastName, OrganizationName, Address, WorkPhone, FaxPhone, and EmailAddress. Each of these fields could contain information about a specific business partner your organization does business with. If you have several business partners, you might have several documents in the database, each containing the same fields. So far, this appears similar to how you might organize this data within a relational database.

In Domino, however, we do not have the restriction that each document contain the same fields. Some documents might have additional fields, and some of the documents might omit some fields. In our example, some documents might not have a FaxPhone field. Other documents might not have an EmailAddress field, and some documents might have additional fields containing the last contact date or a field for a reminder.

The Domino scheme is different from a relational database system, which requires an identical set of fields but allows NULL values in some fields. In Domino, the entire field might be absent. Other documents might have additional fields.

For now it is sufficient to realize that, in Domino, documents are where your data reside. Each Domino database can have many, many documents, and the fields in the documents can vary from one document to another.

DATABASE COMPONENTS

In addition to being a repository for documents, a Domino database can be considered an *application*. Under most operating systems, such as Windows or Linux, an application is typically equated with an executable file. In Notes and Domino, an application is typically associated with a database instead of an individual executable file.

You might be wondering, how can this be? Isn't a database just a repository for data? Well, yes and no. In Notes and Domino, databases contain logic components as well as data. In particular, typically many LotusScript, Java, or JavaScript components and formulas are associated with the database. Each of the components is associated with a part of the database and can be triggered by user or database actions.

For example, you can trigger code to run when a user opens a database, when the user opens a particular document, or when a new document is saved. You can trigger code to run when a user clicks a button or inputs data within a particular field. Each of these occasions and scores of others can cause components to run within a database environment.

Taken together, these components within the database actually constitute a whole application. The application might be to support a help desk, or to be used as an ISO 9000 repository, or to control an organization's policies and procedures. The list, of course, is endless and up to your imagination. With Domino's integration with the Web, you can also create databases that can be implemented and accessed via a variety of Web-enabled devices: mobile telephones, handheld devices, kiosks, and traditional Web browsers. Some applications might even span more than one database, and they can be linked automatically.

DOMINO DATABASE HIGHLIGHTS

For users who are upgrading from previous releases, Domino 6 databases have some important and exciting features. In Release 6, Lotus changed the On Disk Structure (ODS). The ODS is the binary format for the data within a Domino database. As with most changes, there are some positive and negative outcomes. On the negative side, if you create a database with Release 6, you will not be able to directly read that database with Releases 3 or 4 of Notes and Domino.

Changing the format of a database from the old format to the new format works similarly to the same process in previous releases. If an administrator or user compacts the database, it is automatically upgraded to the new Release 6 format. If you want to leave the database in an older release format, you can name the database with an extension of .NS5 for Release 5 or .NS4 for Release 4 instead of .NSF.

TIP

> If you open a database running on a Release 5 server with a Notes 6 client, the internal format, or ODS, is preserved. However, if a Release 5 or Release 6 Notes client opens a database running on a Domino 6 server, the ODS format of the database is upgraded automatically.

DATABASE ACCESS CONTROL

After you create a database, one of the first items of consideration should be who will be allowed to access the database and what operations will be allowed. The core mechanism for database security is the Access Control List (ACL) for the database. Each database and template has a separate ACL. Because of the importance of security, Chapter 17, "Access Control Lists (ACLs) and Database Security," is entirely devoted to the subject. In this section, we briefly review the access levels provided by ACLs.

Seven access levels can be associated with a database. A particular user's access for a database can be set to one of these seven levels. A given user might have different access levels for different databases. There are no automatic superuser type user IDs, such as administrator. If the administrator is not granted access via the ACL, that person cannot access the database.

These are the seven access levels, in increasing order of control over the database:

- **No Access**—Just as the name indicates, access is not allowed.
- **Depositor**—A depositor has write-only access. This is useful for surveys.
- **Reader**—A reader can read database documents.
- **Author**—An author can read documents and edit documents that only he or she has created.
- **Editor**—An editor can read and write anyone's database documents.
- **Designer**—A designer can edit documents and also change the database's design elements.
- **Manager**—A manager can edit, change design elements, and change the database ACL.

EDITING ACL ENTRIES

You can add ACL entries for users, servers, or groups. The most common method for specifying ACLs is to make one or more groups for users and assign access levels via the groups. You should use specific user IDs sparingly and only for exceptions because you might frequently have personnel changes, with new people arriving and existing employees leaving. If each person were individually listed in each database, it would create an administrative nightmare. By using groups for access, you can simply add or delete people from the group, and they will automatically have all the privileges of the group. The group definitions are stored in the Domino Directory and are usually maintained by an administrator.

Groups can contain arbitrary combinations of people, but most companies group people by department or job function. Remember that a person can also be a member of several groups, so don't try to organize into completely nonoverlapping groups. Use groups to make your job of administering the databases easier. A user will not usually be in two groups for the same database, but the user might be in different groups for different databases.

If a user is listed in two groups for the same database, the user generally is given the higher access level. However, if a user is specified by a user ID, the specific entry takes precedence over the group entry, even if it lowers authorization.

When you first create a database, a default ACL is created for you. You can access the ACL by choosing File, Database, Access Control from the main menu. This default ACL contains five entries: Default, LocalDomainServers, OtherDomainServers, and the username of the person who creates the database.

The Default entry is used for Notes clients accessing this database that are not otherwise specified in the ACL. Normally, you should set this level to one of the lowest levels, such as No Access, Reader, or Author. This low level should be used because you normally will create groups that allow access to the users you designate.

LocalDomainServers and OtherDomainServers are groups in the Domino Directory. Usually, you give Designer or Manager access to LocalDomainServers because it is required for database replication. OtherDomainServers is typically not given a high access level.

Finally, the user who creates the database is given Manager access, by default. Notes requires that at least one user have Manager access. Manager is the only level that can change the ACL. If a database does not have at least one user with Manager access, the ACL can no longer be changed.

CREATING A DOMINO DATABASE

You can create a database within Notes and Domino in several ways. In this chapter, we'll cover the process using the Notes and Designer clients. For more information regarding the Administrator client, review Chapter 34, "Initial Configuration of Servers with the Domino Directories." The Domino Administrator user interface is quite different from the Notes and Designer interfaces, and it is used by system administrators to add new users to a Domino domain, monitor server performance, manage security, perform database maintenance, and many other tasks.

Databases can be created in one of the following ways:

- Use a database template
- Start with a completely blank database

11

- Copy an existing database
- Create a replica of an existing database

We'll now take a look at these methods in more detail.

USING DATABASE TEMPLATES

A database *template* is really just a special type of Domino database. It typically contains a design template, but no data. Many design templates are shipped with Notes and Domino 6. You can also create your own custom database templates.

You might want to use a design template to jump-start your development effort. If you start with a template, the hard work of designing forms, views, pages, framesets, and so forth has already been done by a designer. You can just pick up the design and either use it as is or customize it to suit your application. This method results in a working database much more quickly than starting from scratch.

In Release 6, more than 50 templates are supplied with the Domino server, of which approximately 30 are also supplied with the Notes, Designer, and Administration clients. Most of the extra templates that are supplied with Domino, but not the Notes client, deal with the operation and administration of Domino itself. The templates are divided into the standard templates and the advanced templates. Some of the templates are useful for common applications and will be used by many sites and users. Other templates are much more specialized and may be used only by administrators or users who need special features. Table 11.1 lists some of the more commonly used templates.

TABLE 11.1   COMMONLY USED TEMPLATES

Template Name	Description
Discussion—Notes and Web (R6)	This is a general-purpose discussion database suitable for many applications, especially team collaboration. It can be used from Notes or the Web.
Doc Library—Notes and Web (R6)	This is a general-purpose document library database that can be used to store reference information on any topic. Documents can also undergo a review cycle. This can be used from Notes or the Web.
Lotus SmartSuite Library (R6)	This database can be used as a repository for Lotus SmartSuite documents. Any SmartSuite document is rendered within the Notes environment using SmartSuite.
Microsoft Office Library (R6)	This database can be used as a repository for Microsoft Office documents. Any Office document is rendered within the Notes environment using Office.

Template Name	Description
Personal Address Book	A Personal Address Book is automatically created for you when you install the Notes client. It contains contact information and information on how to access servers. You can use it as a personal information manager.
Personal Journal (R6)	The personal journal template can be used to store personal notes. After the notes are stored, you can categorize them.
Personal Web Navigator (R6)	This database caches information about Web sites that you have visited and is the basis of the Notes Web browser. This database is created automatically for you, so you will normally not need to create another one.
TeamRoom (R6)	A team room database is similar to a discussion database, but it has many more features for facilitating team interaction. You can use this database from the Notes client or a Web browser. This template is located on the Domino server, not the Notes client.

CREATING A DATABASE FROM A TEMPLATE

Before you create a database from a template, you need to know the template's name. You can choose from one of the templates listed in Table 11.1 or refer to Notes 6 Help for more information. To create a database from a template, perform the following steps:

1. From the Notes client environment, choose File, Database, New, or press Ctrl+N. The New Database dialog box is displayed, as shown in Figure 11.1.

Figure 11.1
The New Database dialog box enables you to select from more than 50 prede-fined templates.

2. Select the server where you want the new database to reside. Local indicates your local workstation. If you want to create a new database on a server other than your worksta-tion, you need to be defined within the server document as an authorized user to create databases.

> **TIP**
>
> Typically, you will not want to initially create a database on your server because you need to customize the database before it is ready to use. You should create the database on your local workstation. After you have created the database locally and customized it for use, you can replicate it to your server. This ensures that by the time it gets to your server, it will be complete and coherent.

3. Enter a title for the new database in the Title field of the dialog box. This title will be shown on the database icon of the desktop. It can contain spaces and may be up to 32 characters. The title is important because users will use this information to decide whether the information in the database is relevant to them. Choose the title carefully.

> **NOTE**
>
> Lotus Notes and Domino now support more than 40 national languages, including Arabic and Hebrew. This new support is notable because these languages are bidirectional, with text sometimes reading from right to left. Localization features enable database titles to be stored in DBCS (double-byte character sets) to allow characters such as Chinese and Japanese Kanji.

4. Specify the filename that is used by the operating system in the File Name field. If you use the default .NSF extension, the Release 6 On Disk Structure format will be used for the database.

> **TIP**
>
> If you are using multiple operating systems (such as a Unix server and Windows clients), you should pay careful attention to the naming of files. Each operating system has its own rules for whether files are case sensitive, what character set is valid, and so forth. To be safe, use eight characters or less for the filename portion before the extension. Even if you do not use multiple operating systems, it is a good idea to establish file-naming conventions for your company so that when you have hundreds (or thousands) of databases, they will be easier to manage.

> **NOTE**
>
> Release 6 and Release 5 use different formats on disk. A Release 5.x server will not be capable of directly reading a Release 6 database. However, Release 5 servers can replicate databases with Release 6 servers. You can create a database with the Release 5 format by using the extension .NS5 instead of .NSF.

5. To encrypt your database at the time you create it, click the Encryption button. You can also decide later to encrypt an existing database. You are not forced to make the decision when you create the database. When you choose encryption, you can use Simple,

Medium, or Strong encryption. Generally, the stronger the encryption is, the longer it will take to encrypt and decrypt information in the database.

TIP

> Encryption is useful because there could be opportunities for other people to access data stored in a Domino database. In particular, if you have a laptop that might be used or stolen, if someone other than you has access to a desktop machine, or if other people in your organization might have access to your disk files through the network, you might want to consider encryption. In any situation in which someone might copy files via the operating system and not via Domino, there is a threat that the person could use tools other than Domino or Notes to access the data. If you encrypt the database, other tools, such as text editors, cannot be used to compromise database security. A person would need to go through Notes or Domino security to access the data. See Chapter 35, "Domino Security Overview," for more information about Domino security.

6. Click the Size Limit button to change the maximum size of a database with an .NS4 extension or a database that has not yet been upgraded to the Release 5 format. Release 5 removed the absolute size limitation for databases. This was one of the benefits of the new On Disk Structure (ODS) introduced in Release 5. Although Domino databases no longer have an absolute size limitation, databases as large as 64GB have been certified by Lotus (depending upon your operating system capabilities). However, this is not necessarily a good idea because databases this large will generally not perform as well as smaller databases. During development, carefully consider whether you can break up a large database into smaller, more topical databases.

7. Select the Create Full Text Index for Searching check box to create a full text index. You can also create an index after the database has been created, so you don't have to decide on this issue when you create the database. If you'll need to search the database for specific nuggets of textual data, it's recommended that you create a full-text index.

8. The Advanced button enables you to specify several advanced options about the database. These options are primarily optimizations that will improve performance of the database. Figure 11.2 shows the options of the Advanced button.

   The options include these:

   - **Don't Maintain Unread Marks**—Maintaining unread marks takes CPU time. If you do not need them, you can improve performance by checking this box.

   - **Optimize Document Table Map**—This optimization is to speed the rebuilding and updating of views. Domino stores tables internally to determine whether documents appear in a view. This optimization enables tables to be associated with forms. This enables Domino to search only documents associated with forms that appear in a view, which improves performance. This optimization works only if you use Form= as part of your view-selection formula. You must compact the database before this optimization becomes effective.

   - **Don't Overwrite Free Space**—Normally, Domino overwrites deleted documents with a bit pattern on disk. This is a security feature to prevent

11

unauthorized access to deleted data. This overwriting uses CPU time. However, in some databases, such as in a Help database, security is not an issue. You can improve performance, at the expense of slightly decreased security, by checking this box.

Figure 11.2
The Advanced Database Options dialog box enables you to select advanced features for the new database.

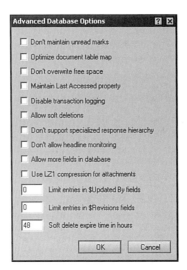

- **Maintain Last Accessed Property**—The Document Properties box maintains information about the last time and date a document was modified. The Last Accessed property can also keep track of the last time a document was accessed for a read. Doing so, however, causes extra disk activity to log this information back to the database. By default, the Last Accessed property does not keep track of reads. If you enable this check box, this extra information will be kept. If you disable the check box, performance will be improved, but you will not know when the last read access occurred. You should enable this check box if you have enabled document deletion based on days of inactivity.

- **Disable Transaction Logging**—Transaction logging greatly enhances reliability. If there is a power failure or some other type of server problem that requires a restart, the log can be used by Domino to reconstruct your database. The logging also facilitates online backup of databases while the server is running. Transaction logging must be first enabled on the Domino server. After it is enabled on the server, all databases automatically use transaction logging. This check box enables you to selectively disable transaction logging for this particular database. It has no effect if logging is not already enabled on the server. Disabling transaction logging is not recommended.

- **Allow Soft Deletions**—Enabling soft deletions enables you to create a database in which, for a limited amount of time, a user can easily recover documents that have been deleted. You can create a special view, similar to a trash folder, that users can use to recover deleted documents. See the Soft Delete Expire Time in Hours option at the end of this list.

- **Don't Support Specialized Response Hierarchy**—To support the two @Functions @AllChildren and @Descendants, documents must keep track of their parent or response documents. This tracking consumes disk space and CPU time. If you are not using either of these functions, you can select this check box to improve performance. Remember, however, that if you change your mind after the database has been operational for a while, your documents might not contain the information you need. Make sure that you have carefully planned your database before you enable this option.

- **Don't Allow Headline Monitoring**—Users can enable their subscription database to search other databases. If this is used extensively, it can cause Domino performance to suffer. You can disable headline monitoring and searching of the current database by enabling this option.

- **Allow More Fields in Database**—This option allows a database to contain up to 23,000 fields. Without this field enabled, all field names when concatenated cannot exceed 64KB (about 3,000 fields).

- **Use LZ1 Compression for Attachments**—Release 6 enables you to compress attachments using Lempel-Zev class 1 (LZ1) adaptive algorithm rather than the Huffman algorithm. LZ1 compression can provide a considerable amount of disk savings.

CAUTION

> If you are using LZ1 compression with other versions of the Notes client and Domino server, be aware that attachments are automatically recompressed using the Huffman algorithm. The recompression of attachments can add extra processing time and overhead to any task.

- **Limit Entries in $UpdatedBy Fields**—Documents maintain an audit trail of the people who have updated them in the $UpdatedBy field. If a document undergoes a significant number of updates, this field can get very large. You can improve performance by limiting the number of entries in the $UpdatedBy field. If the limit is reached, the oldest entry is discarded when a new entry is added.

- **Limit Entries in $Revisions Fields**—The $Revisions fields are used to manage replication and store up to 500 entries by default. Setting a lower limit can improve performance; however, setting the value too low can cause documents to replicate incorrectly. Consider setting this value lower if your database has no replicas or replicates frequently, thus requiring less history to be maintained. Also consider enabling this option if your database contains a large number of documents and you need to conserve space.

- **Soft Delete Expire Time in Hours**—This option sets the time window during which a deleted document can be undeleted. This option is effective only if you have enabled soft deletions (see the previous discussion).

9. Select the template server where the template resides. The template server can be different from the server where you want your new database to be stored after it is created. You might not have all the templates loaded on your workstation, so if you cannot find the template you are looking for, be sure to check your organization's server.

10. Select the Show Advanced Templates check box to show additional templates. Most of the advanced templates supplied by Lotus relate to systems administration, so you will not normally be concerned with them. As a database designer, you can specify whether you want your databases to show up in the normal template list or in the advanced list.

11. Click the template you want to use from the list. The special list item called Blank is used to create an empty database. Using the Blank template essentially is similar to using no template at all.

12. Select the Inherit Future Design Changes check box to specify the relationship between your newly created database and the template you are using as a base. You might be using the template in one of two scenarios. Normally, most databases follow the first scenario: You are using the template just as a basis to get a quick start on developing a custom database. In this case, you would want to uncheck the Inherit Future Design Changes check box. Any future changes to the template will not affect your new database.

The second scenario is that you have developed a template, such as a company application or library, that is used multiple times. In this case, you enable the inheritance check box. If inheritance is enabled, you can use the template as a single source of your design changes for the application, and all versions of the database will be updated when the template itself changes. As an example, suppose you want to create several document libraries, each with a different topics, but you would like all the libraries to share a common look and feel. You then enable inheritance on all these library databases when you create them. To make any changes, you update the template, and the design changes will propagate automatically to the individual databases. This inheritance saves you from having to manually change the design of each database individually.

> **NOTE**
>
> Even if you disable the Inherit Future Design Changes check box, you can manually update the design of a database from a template. This operation is called *refreshing* (that is, installing a newer version of the existing template) or *replacing* (removing the old one and replacing it with a completely new template).
>
> You can find out whether a database has an associated template by opening the Database Properties box and then clicking the Design tab. You can also change the inherit option here if you later change your mind about inheriting future design changes.

13. After you have selected all your options, click the OK button. Your database is created and opened. If the database has an About document, it is displayed as well. You can safely close this document.

Congratulations! You have successfully created a new database from a template.

CREATING A COPY OF A DATABASE

Besides creating a database from a template, you can create a new database by making a copy of an existing database. This method is similar to using a template because design elements from an existing source are copied into your new database and you do not have to create them from scratch. A copy of a database differs from using a template, however, because you do not have the option of inheriting design changes. In addition, when you make the copy, you can optionally copy database documents as well as the design elements. After you have made a copy of the original database, the copy starts to live a life of its own, and changes made to either database do not affect the other database.

It is important to note that a copy of a database is not a replica copy. In other words, when you use the following procedure to copy a database, it does not replicate the original database. To make a replica copy that replicates the original database, skip to the next section, "Creating a Replica of a Database."

You will typically use the next copy procedure as a shortcut to simplify your design of a new database or perhaps to make a backup copy of an existing database. This is similar to the use of templates, but with the copy procedure, you can start with any existing database, not just templates.

To make a copy of a database, follow these steps:

1. Open the Favorite Bookmarks and right-click the source database that you want to copy.

2. Select Files, Database, New Copy from the menu.

3. Once the Copy Database dialog box opens (see Figure 11.3), select the server where you want the new database to reside. Local indicates your local workstation.

Figure 11.3
The Copy Database dialog box enables you to copy design elements, documents, and the Access Control List.

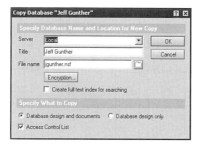

4. Fill in the Title and Filename fields. They are initialized with the information from the source. Even though this is a copy of an existing database, be sure to give the new database a different title. This allows users to distinguish between the two databases. You also need to give the database a new filename.

5. Set the Encryption and Size Limit options just as in creating a new database from a template. They specify whether you want the new copy encrypted and set the size of the new database.

6. In the Copy section at the bottom of the dialog box, you can choose to copy both the design and existing documents or just the design to the new database (refer to Figure 11.3). You can also choose to copy the Access Control List (ACL) from the existing database, or you can start by creating a new ACL for the new database.

7. Enable the Create Full-Text Index check box to create a full-text index at the time you create the database. You can also create a full-text index at a later time.

8. Click OK when you have completed choosing your options. A new database is created for you with your selected options.

CREATING A REPLICA OF A DATABASE

You typically create replicas of databases on different servers. The power of Domino is to find replica databases on different servers and automatically synchronize them through replication. As an example, you typically have your mail database stored on your Domino server. You might want to replicate your mail database to your laptop so that you can read and answer your mail while you are traveling. In this scenario, you would make a replica of your mail database on your laptop. Do not make a copy (as in the previous section) of your mail database because the database will not replicate.

To make a replica of a database, follow these steps:

1. Open Favorite Bookmarks and right-click the source database that you want to replicate. From the menu, select Replication, New Replica. You see a dialog box similar to Figure 11.4.

Figure 11.4
The New Replica dialog box enables you to create a replica of an existing database.

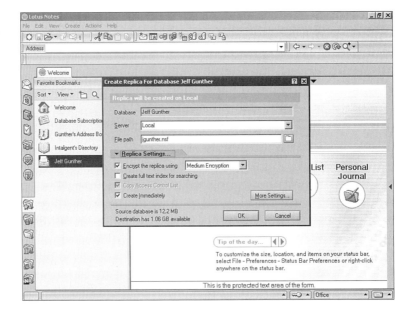

2. Select the server where you want the new replica database to reside. Local indicates your local workstation. Typically, the server will be different from the source because you want the databases to replicate. Another usage for replication is for backup purposes. Consider this as you make a replica on the same or a different server.

3. Fill in the File Path field. You cannot change the title of the database. The title must be the same as the source. It is usually a good idea to make the filename the same as the source also (assuming that the replica is on a different server than the source).

4. Expand the Replica Setting section and set the Encryption and Size Limit just as in creating a new database from a template. Then specify whether you want the new copy encrypted and set the size of the new database.

5. Click the More Settings button if you are creating a replica on a different server from the source. These settings enable you to control space-saving parameters, establish priority of replication, and specify whether only a subset of the information should be replicated.

6. You can also choose to copy the Access Control List from the existing database, or you can start by creating a new ACL for the new database.

7. Select the Create Full-Text Index for Searching check box to create a full-text index at the time you create the database. You can also create a full-text index later.

8. You can control whether the replication should occur immediately or at the next scheduled replication by selecting or deselecting the Create Immediately check box.

9. Click OK when you have completed choosing your options. A new replica database is created for you with your selected options.

11

DATABASE DESIGN ELEMENTS

Within a Domino database, in addition to user documents, application information is stored in *design elements*. These design elements make up the structure, design, and display of the application in the database. The design elements control how the application stores data and how the application appears to the user; they also contain application logic.

The design elements are created using Domino Designer and typically come from a design template or are created by Designer. The design elements are described in more detail in subsequent chapters, but here is a listing of the kinds of elements that are stored in a Domino database:

- **Outlines**—Used as a tool by the user to navigate through the database.
- **Framesets**—A configuration of frames that can be used to show multiple pages or documents.
- **Pages**—Used to present static content to the user.
- **Style sheets**—Cascading Style Sheets, a standard of the World Wide Web Consortium (W3C) that provides Web designers with a simple mechanism for adding style (such as fonts, colors, and spacing) to Web documents.

- **Forms**—Predefined templates used to view documents.

- **Views**—A tabular display of a set of documents selected by a formula from a database.

- **Folders**—Similar to a view, but documents selected by a user.

- **Navigators**—A graphics-based database navigational tool.

- **Agents**—A program that can be automatically triggered within a database.

- **Images**—A library of image resources that may be used throughout the database. The images can be in a number of standardized graphic formats, such as GIF, BMP, or JPEG.

- **Actions**—A list of shared actions for use within the views, folders, forms, and subforms.

- **Applets**—A library of Java applets that can be used in Web browsers or the Notes client.

- **Subforms**—Reusable subparts of forms that can be used for consistency among forms.

- **Shared fields**—Field definitions that can be reused on many forms to enforce consistency of user interface and to provide a single element for design changes.

- **Script libraries**—A library of LotusScript, Java, or JavaScript routines within a database.

- **Files**—A repository of non-NSF files for application designers to use across databases.

- **Data connections**—Integrating technology from Domino Enterprise Connector Services (DECS), a data connection that enables the Domino Designer to connect to various external relational databases from within a Domino database.

- **Synopsis**—Not really a design element, although it appears in the Design pane. If this is clicked, you can obtain a summary of the database design elements in either printed or database format.

UPDATING THE DATABASE DOCUMENTATION

Each database is capable of storing two special documents, called the About Database document and the Using Database document. The About Database document is intended to be a summary of the purpose of the database. The Using Database document should describe information for a user of the database and should explain how to use the database's features.

Information contained in the About Database document typically is viewed by every user of your database. If you create a database from a template supplied by Lotus, a default About document is included. This document contains very general information about the database. Before you put your database into production, you should be sure to update this document with more specific information that explains the purpose of the database, who should use it, and when it should be used. To update the About document, follow these steps:

1. Open the design for the database by selecting View, Design from the menu. You must have Designer access to the database to perform this function.

2. Select the tool grouping marked Other in the database navigation pane and select Database Resources, as shown in Figure 11.5.

Figure 11.5
The Other section of the design elements contains the About Database document, the Using Database document, and the database icon.

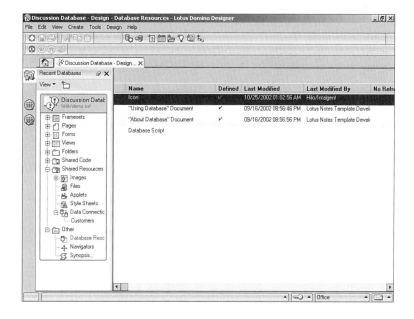

3. Double-click the About Database document in the pane on the right. After you open the About document, you should customize it and add content relevant to your database.

4. After you have updated the document, close it by clicking the X in the upper-right corner of the document tab by selecting File, Close from the menu, or by pressing Ctrl+W.

You can update the Using Database document in a similar manner. The Using Database document should contain information on how to use the database. For Lotus-supplied templates, a Using document is created for you by default. If you customize the operation of the database, be sure to update the Using document with any instructions that are unique to your database.

To change the database icon, you can double-click the word Icon within the Other, Database Resources section. An Icon Editor appears, and you can use it to modify the icon (see Figure 11.6).

With the Database Icon Editor, you can modify individual pixels of the icon, fill entire areas (with the paint roller), and perform several other operations. You can also use the Clipboard to copy and paste icons from other sources as a starting point. The best way to learn about the Icon Editor is to try it.

Figure 11.6
The Design Icon dialog box enables you to edit the database icon.

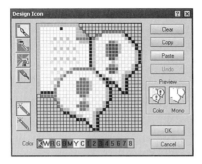

DATABASE PROPERTIES

Domino databases have many properties associated with them. Many of these properties can be specified when you create the database, and some properties can be set or changed after the database has been created. To change the database properties, first open the database, and then click File, Database, Properties from the menu to display the Database Properties dialog box (see Figure 11.7).

Figure 11.7
The Database Properties box enables you to change database attributes.

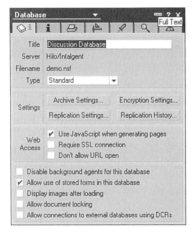

There are seven tabs within the Properties box: Basics, Information, Printing, Design, Launch, Full Text, and Advanced. Select the appropriate tab and change the desired properties.

DATABASE BASICS

The first tab enables you to change several key database attributes. As you can see in Figure 11.8, you can change the database title, type, archive settings, encryption settings, and replication settings, and you can view the replication history. Typically, you will not modify the database type; you will almost always use a standard database type. Other types are usually associated with a special-purpose database type, such as a library or directory.

The Archive Settings button provides the capability to control document archiving for any database. When you archive documents, they are copied to the archive database and are deleted from the original database. Within the Database Properties box, you can now control which documents you want to archive, based upon the time and date they were last accessed or modified.

TIP

> If you enable archiving for a database, you should enable the Maintain LastAccessed property, Advanced Database option. Enabling this property enables Domino to keep track of read access to documents as well as write access.

You can also control the name and location of the archive database. By default, the database is in the archive subdirectory of your Notes data directory. The filename is the prefix a_ plus the first six characters of the original database (see Figure 11.8).

Figure 11.8
The Archive Settings dialog box enables you to control archiving parameters.

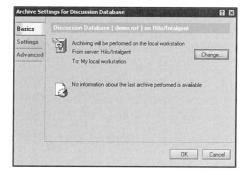

Advanced archiving options enable you to archive to a server and to control logging and deletion of documents that have responses, and specify whether documents should be deleted without archiving them.

In the Database box's Basics tab, the check boxes enable you to specify other attributes, including these:

- **Web Access: Use JavaScript When Generating Pages**—This is a performance and functional enhancement option. If this box is checked, certain options of the Web page are not evaluated until the user uses them on the page. If it is not checked, Domino evaluates these options at the time the page is displayed. Another restriction is that only one submit button is allowed if the option is not checked, whereas multiple buttons are allowed if JavaScript is enabled. Normally, you should enable this option for Web applications.

- **Web Access: Require SSL Connection**—This causes the Secure Socket Layer (SSL) protocol to be required to access this database. This option enhances security for Web applications and should be used for Web transaction databases. If you check this option, you also need to ensure that SSL is configured and enabled on your Domino server.

- **Web Access: Don't Allow URL Open**—This instructs Domino to not allow users to issue Domino URL commands from within your database. Like SSL, this option enhances security for Web applications.
- **Disable Background Agents for This Database**—This disables the running of agents in this database that otherwise would be triggered by external events.
- **Allow Use of Stored Forms in This Database**—This enables documents within a database to store the forms used to create them. Normally, forms are not stored with the documents because a single copy is kept in the database. When you move a document from one database to another, however, the form might not be available in the destination database. This check box solves the problem.
- **Display Images After Loading**—This causes graphic images to be displayed after the text of the document. This enhances performance when documents are displayed over slow communication lines. If this box is not checked, the document displays the elements in the order in which they are encountered. You should probably check this box if you are creating a database for Web use.
- **Allow Document Locking**—This enables users with Author access or higher to lock any document. When a user locks a document, it prevents editing and replication conflicts even across database replicas. A user with Manager access cannot edit a locked document but can unlock any document within a database.
- **Allow Connections to External Databases Using DCRs**—This enables designers to set up data connections to other relational databases. This field must be checked before creating data connection resources.

DATABASE INFORMATION

The database Information (Info) tab displays key information about the database. It tells you the size of the database, the number of documents, and the percentage of the space within the database that is used. You can also compact the database and specify archiving parameters from the Information tab. Figure 11.9 demonstrates the database information tab.

Figure 11.9
The Information tab shows you the size, dates, and replica ID of a database.

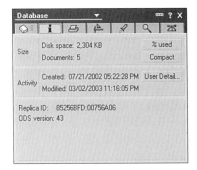

The creation date and last modified date are shown in the Activity section. You can press the User Detail button to get more information.

The replica ID is a hex value that is used for replication. Each originally created database has a unique replica ID. If a database is created as a replica copy of another database, the two databases have identical replica IDs. When you use a database copy, all elements of the database are copied to the new database, but the new database has a different, unique replica ID.

The ODS (On Disk Structure) version tells you the format of the database on disk. In general, each release of Notes and Domino can read earlier database versions, but they cannot read future versions. In other words, Release 6 can read Release 5 and earlier databases, but Release 4 of Notes cannot read a Release 6 database. The ODS version is an incremental counter and is not the same as the external release number.

DATABASE PRINTING AND DESIGN

Use the Printing tab to specify headers and footers as well as fonts to be used for printing this database. You can specify dates, times, and formatting information.

The first line of the Design tab tells you whether the design for the database is hidden. The vast majority of databases that you work with will not have a hidden design. This feature is mostly for third-party vendors or corporate developers that want to ensure that the design of the database cannot be modified after it is deployed. If you choose to hide the entire database design, you will not be able to modify the design to fix bugs or for any other reason. Therefore, you'd better keep an extra copy of the database without the design hidden. We'll explore how to hide the database design in the section "Replacing and Refreshing Designs," later in this chapter. Figure 11.10 shows the Design tab.

Figure 11.10
The Design tab shows you template, catalog, indexing, and language options for a database.

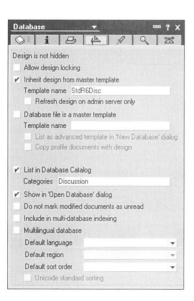

11

The first check box within the Design tab enables you to lock each design element. This feature is particularly helpful if you work with a team of developers and want to explicitly control each design element. For example, if are you working on a form and want to ensure that it's not modified by another developer or replication, lock the design element.

The second and third check boxes within the Design tab enable you to control whether this database inherits design information from other databases and whether this database can be used as a template for other databases. Normally, if you make a database a template, you should use the .NTF extension and remove all user data from the database. The .NTF extension is not required to make a database a template (the only requirement is to check the Database Is a Master Template check box). However, you should follow the NTF naming convention so that when you deal with the databases from the operating system, you will know which databases are templates and which are not. You can make a template appear only in the advanced template list by checking the check box titled List as Advanced Template in New Database Dialog.

The List in Database Catalog option enables you to control whether this database is listed in the catalog accessible to users. This makes it easier for users to find information about this database. The Show in Open Database Dialog option is another option to make it easier for users to find the database. While you are developing the database and before it is ready for production, you should leave this option unchecked. This ensures that users don't accidentally open the database before you are ready. When the database becomes ready for production, check this box and users will be able to see it in the Open Database dialog box.

The option Do Not Mark Modified Documents as Unread enables you to control unread marks for this database. Include in Multidatabase Indexing is an important option: You must enable this option if you are using the multidatabase index template. In that template, you list the databases that you want to appear in the multidatabase index. However, if this check box is not enabled, the database will not be indexed. It can be very confusing to set up the multiple database index and find that the databases that you specified are not being indexed.

Domino 6 enables you to have multiple national languages associated with a database. The final options on the Design tab enable you to indicate a multilingual database and set the default language.

DATABASE LAUNCH

The Database Launch tab controls what the user sees when the database is opened. Normally, you want to display the About document the first time the database is opened. This gives the user a summary of the purpose and usage of the database. On subsequent opens, you can set it up to restore the last view of the user or to always open to a particular frameset or navigator.

For Web usage, you can use the same options as for Notes, or you can specify the launching of a specific page or frameset. You have quite a bit of control for both Notes and Web users.

DATABASE FULL-TEXT INDEXING

A user can search a database even if it's not full text–indexed. However, if the database does contain a full-text index, the search will be much quicker. This is a traditional trade-off between the additional resources required and a performance improvement for searching. If you create a full-text index, additional disk space is used, and additional CPU time is required to keep the index up-to-date.

Databases are not full text–indexed by default. Good candidates for indexing are databases that are frequently used, that are frequently searched, or that do not change much. In fact, the Domino Help databases fit this category. You might consider indexing the Help databases, especially if they are frequently used within your organization.

When you index a database, you can specify whether you want case sensitivity (normally, you do not), whether you want to index attachments or encrypted fields (this is up to you), or whether to exclude words in the Stop Word file (normally, you do want this). The Stop Word file is a listing of common words, (such as *a*, *the*, *and*, and so forth) that should not be indexed.

DATABASE ADVANCED PROPERTIES

The advanced database properties are primarily performance improvements. You can control whether you want Domino to maintain unread marks or the LastAccessed property. You can also specify whether you want free space to be overwritten within the database, and you can disable transaction logging.

The advanced options are essentially the same as the options available in the Advanced button when you are first creating a database. See the section called "Creating a Database from a Template," earlier in this chapter, for details on each of the options.

REPLACING AND REFRESHING DESIGNS

After you have created and designed your database, how do you manage changes and updates to the design? You can use either replacement or refreshing of designs. Refreshing is the easier concept because it involves updating a database design from the template that was used to create it. You make and test the changes, update the template, and then refresh the design from the updated template. To refresh the design, choose File, Database, Refresh Design from the menu.

NOTE

In addition to enabling you to manually refresh the database design, Domino has the capability of automatically refreshing designs. A server-side task called Design runs on the Domino server at night and automatically refreshes databases with designs from associated templates that have been updated. Only databases located on the server are updated.

To understand design replacement, remember that basically two kinds of information exist in a Domino database: design elements and user documents. Replacing the design essentially means leaving the user documents but replacing the entire set of design elements with a new set. Why would you do this? A common example might be to update or upgrade the mail database template. In this case, you want to leave all the mail messages but add additional functionality to the mail database.

To replace a database design, follow these steps:

1. First, right-click the database in the bookmark area. From the menu, select Database, Replace Design. You will see a dialog box similar to Figure 11.11.

Figure 11.11
The Replace Database Design dialog box enables you to replace all design elements and hide the design.

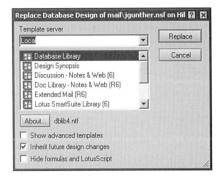

2. Select the server where the new template resides. Select the Show Advanced Templates check box if you want an advanced template.

3. Select the Inherit Future Design Changes check box to cause future design changes in the template to propagate to the current database. See the previous section "Creating a Database from a Template" for more information on this option.

4. If you want to completely hide the design in the target database so that it can never be edited again, select the Hide Formulas and LotusScript check box.

CAUTION

If you select the Hide Formulas and LotusScript check box, the target database design can no longer be edited. This option is normally used only by third-party developers or if strict security of the database design is required. If you use this option, it is very important to keep an unhidden design version also. The best way to use this feature is to have two templates, one unhidden and one hidden. You modify and update the unhidden template and then replace the design of the hidden template (with this check box set); then you refresh the hidden design into the real databases with data.

5. Click the Replace button. The progress of the replacement can be tracked in the Status bar.

CHAPTER 12

EXPLORING THE INTEGRATED DEVELOPMENT ENVIRONMENT (IDE)

In this chapter

STARTING DOMINO DESIGNER

If you are familiar with previous releases of Notes and Domino, you will immediately notice that Domino Designer has been enhanced and improved. The Domino Designer environment has been targeted for use by two distinct types of users: designers familiar with the original Notes designer interface and designers familiar with existing third-party Web-development tools. The user interface makes it easy to develop Web pages using either native HTML or traditional Notes and Domino design elements.

This chapter is meant to be an overview of Domino Designer. It provides an introduction to the various parts of Domino Designer and an overview of the different types of design elements that you can utilize within your applications. Later chapters cover each of the major design element types in more detail. Let's get started.

As in Release 5 of Notes, Domino Designer is a unique application, totally separate from the Notes client or Domino Administrator. Domino Designer can be directly launched from your operating system or via a bookmark within the Notes client. If Domino Designer is installed, the Domino Designer icon is located underneath the Replication icon within the bookmarks of the regular Notes client. Figure 12.1 illustrates the location of Domino Designer within the Notes client.

Figure 12.1
The Domino Designer icon appears in the Notes client.

Domino Administrator

Domino Designer

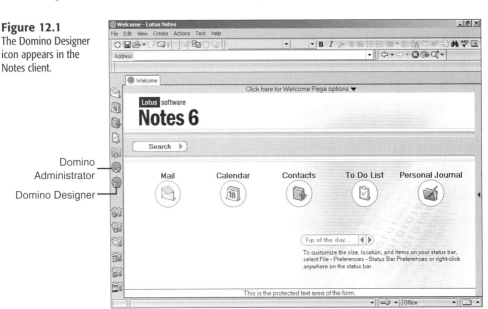

TIP

> If Domino Designer is not installed, the icon to launch Designer does not appear. To add Domino Designer to your workstation, simply reinstall Notes via the Microsoft Installer and select Domino Designer. For more information regarding the installation choices, review Chapter 2, "Installing and Customizing the Notes Client."

After you launch the Designer client, you'll notice that the application appears within its own window, and is separate from the Notes client or Domino Administrator. You can have up to three windows open at once if you have Domino Administrator, Domino Designer, and the Notes client all open and running.

As with anything within Notes, there are many ways to accomplish the same task. Another way to open Domino Designer is to open a database in the Notes client, and then choose View, Design from the menus. Upon execution, the Designer client launches if it is not already running and opens the design of the database. If you have previously developed Notes and Domino applications, this method is already familiar to you. It seems a little strange at first when a menu option launches a completely separate application, but this enables you to immediately start working with the new design on a selected database.

THE DOMINO DESIGNER WINDOW

After the Designer client is launched, you see its welcome screen. From this window, you can either create a new database, open an existing database, or access Designer's help.

➔ **See** Chapter 11, "Creating and Accessing Domino Databases," for information about the process used to create a database, **p. 267**.

If you open an existing database, you will see a display similar to Figure 12.2.

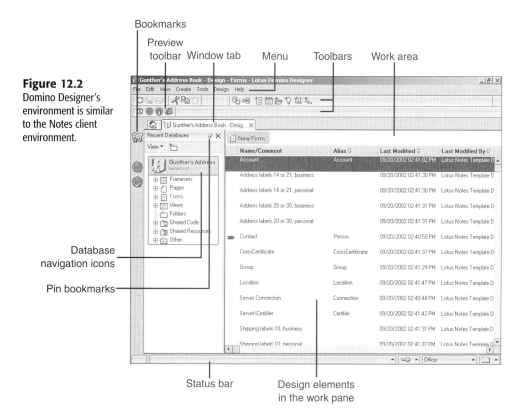

Figure 12.2
Domino Designer's environment is similar to the Notes client environment.

Domino Designer enables you to have several databases open at any one time. Designer keeps track of the most recently used databases and makes them easily available to you.

In Figure 12.2, you can see the various parts of the Domino Designer window. This window is similar in many respects to the Notes client window, but there are some subtle differences. As you change your context by clicking the various design elements in the Design pane, you see the window title change. It includes the name of the database and the design element type you are viewing. The menu bar appears just below the window title. The menu bar is context sensitive, so as you change from one design element type to another, the menus change. Most of the elements will contain the following menu items: File, Edit, View, Create, Design, Tools, and Help.

Similar to the Notes client, the Designer client has a set of toolbars just underneath the menu bar that contain the default set of buttons. By default, some of the toolbars are disabled or *context sensitive*—enabled only within specific design tasks. There is a toolbar that contains buttons for creating forms and views. To enable or disable the Editing toolbar, for instance, simply right-click the toolbar area and check or uncheck Editing. To modify any of the buttons on the toolbars, you can choose File, Preferences, Toolbar Preferences from the menu.

Within the Preview toolbar, unique to Domino Designer, you'll find a set of buttons that are useful for testing your database. This toolbar contains the Display Infobox icon followed by icons for previewing your design. You will normally see at least the Display Infobox, Notes Preview, and Domino Preview buttons. Following these three, you might optionally see the Microsoft Internet Explorer Preview icon or the Netscape Navigator Preview icon. In Figure 12.2, the standard Preview and Internet Explorer buttons are shown.

Below the toolbars, you will see the Window tabs. These tabs enable you to switch from one open window to another. Each time you open a new design element, a new Window tab appears. You can easily switch from one element to another by clicking the tab. You can even design within several databases at the same time. This is a very useful feature because it makes it much easier to review and copy design elements from one database to another. You just open the design element of the first database, copy it to the Clipboard, click the second database, and then paste. To close a window, click the X that appears to the right of the name.

TIP

> During development, it's useful to use keystrokes to navigate Designer. You can toggle between Window tabs by pressing Ctrl+Tab.

At the far left of the Designer interface is a column of bookmarks. In Figure 12.2, the Recent Databases bookmark is the topmost icon in the bookmarks column. The Design pane is immediately to the right of the bookmarks. When the Design pane is open, it displays the most recently used databases and the different types of design elements within each database. If you prefer to leave the Design pane open while you work, you can click the small Pin icon in the upper-left corner of the Design pane. This button enables you to pin the Design pane and force it to remain open during development. Similarly, you can disable this option and have the Design pane automatically close after each use.

At the bottom of the screen is the Status bar, which gives you current information about the status of your session. This is the same Status bar that appears in the Notes client.

The large main area on the right of the screen is called the Work pane. The contents of this pane change as your context changes. The Work pane can contain a list of design elements, or it can contain the work area for a particular element that you are editing.

THE DESIGN ELEMENTS

The Design pane of Figure 12.2 shows you the types of design elements that are available to you. Many of these design elements might be familiar to you from previous releases of Notes and Domino. There are also some new design elements, such as style sheets, data connections, and files. The purpose of these new design elements is to make it easier for you to develop Web-based applications.

When you click a design element type in the Design pane on the left, the Work pane on the right shows you a view containing the actual elements of that type stored in your database. For example, in Figure 12.2, Forms has been chosen on the left, and on the right is the list of forms in the database. Notice that the format of the right pane is very similar to a regular Notes view. In this case, you can see the name of the design element with an optional comment, an optional alias, and information about the time of the last modification, with the name of the user who last modified the element.

New with Release 6, you'll notice that in addition to the design elements being listed in the Work pane, the design elements are also listed in the Design pane.

12

> **TIP**
>
> Depending on your preference, sometimes it's helpful to open a separate instance of Designer with a particular design element or database. To launch another instance of Designer, right-click a design element or the database icon in the Design pane and select Open in New Window.

If you double-click the name of a design element in the Work pane or single-click the name of the design element listed under the database in the Design pane, the selected design element is placed in edit mode. The following is a list of design elements you can utilize in your applications:

■ **Framesets**—Frames are the Web terminology for panes in Notes. Although in previous releases of Notes, such as Release 4, the end user could manipulate the panes to a small degree, the database designer could not easily create panes or frames to control the user experience. Framesets are layouts that are used to control the display of multiple frames to the user.

- **Pages**—For Web designers and developers, the concept of pages is very familiar. Pages can contain a variety of content, from simple HTML to complex Java Swing applets. Unlike traditional Domino forms, pages cannot contain Domino-native fields. However, they can contain formula, JavaScript, or HTML INPUT fields.

- **Forms**—Forms are the heart and soul of any Notes/Domino application. A form is a visual template through which you view a document (data). This template typically contains static content as well as field definitions. Information from a document is extracted and displayed in the field locations on the form and then is rendered to the display.

- **Views**—Views enable you to see a tabular summary of information from many documents at once. With a formula, you can select the documents you want to see in the view. The view columns typically extract information from the documents in the database.

- **Folders**—Folders are very similar to views. They present data in a tabular format. The major difference is that, in a view, the documents are selected by a formula, whereas in a folder, the documents can be any arbitrary collection. Folders are typically used by an end user to organize documents in a database.

The following design elements can be found within the Shared Code area with the other design elements. These elements represent items that can be shared within the database:

- **Agents**—Agents are small programs that are associated with a database and can be run automatically or under user control. They can be written in LotusScript, Java, or formula language, and they can be run on either the Domino server or the Notes client.

- **Outlines**—Outlines are essentially high-level navigation tools. In Web site design terminology, an outline is similar to a site map or the navigational elements that frequently appear at the left of a Web page. In Notes/Domino terminology, you can think of an outline as a way to program the traditional Navigation pane. This is the pane that normally lists all the views and folders of a database.

- **Subforms**—Subforms are similar to forms in almost all major respects. The difference is that a subform may be reused by incorporating it in several different forms. A subform may not be used by itself. Typical uses for subforms include headers and other information that you would like to reuse for consistency across multiple forms. You can also conditionally include different subforms within a form, depending upon context.

- **Fields**—Shared fields are field definitions with attributes such as font, size, data type, and formulas that can be shared across multiple Domino forms. By using shared fields, you can implement consistency in visual design and formula programming across several forms.

- **Actions**—Actions are small components that are typically used in forms, views, and folders. Actions can be invoked by the user by clicking an action button or from the menus. Either or both of these options are enabled by Domino Designer.

- **Script libraries**—You can use script libraries to share common LotusScript, JavaScript, or Java code. Code that is stored within a script library can be used throughout a database.

The following design elements can be found within the Shared Resources area with the other design elements. These elements represent resources that can be shared both within and outside the database:

- **Images**—Image resources enable you to store images once and reuse them throughout your database. You give each image a name and can then reference the image from other design elements, such as pages, forms, and subforms. Domino supports industry-standard formats, such as GIF, BMP, and JPEG. The same image resource can be utilized across the design of several databases.

- **Files**—Similar to image resources, file resources enable you to store non-NSF files and reuse them throughout your database. You give each image a name and then reference the file from other design elements. For example, a file resource could be an HTML or XML file for use within a page, form, and subform.

- **Applets**—Java applets are small programs written in Java that execute within the browser environment or Notes client. The shared applets feature of Domino Designer enables you to save a Java applet in a central location in the database, give the applet a name, and then reuse it throughout the database. Using the integrated CORBA support, a developer can securely enable Java applets in Web browsers to access the full Domino Object Model on the server.

TIP

> Beginning with Release 6, Lotus added support for the Java Development Kit version 1.3. All Java 2 Standard Edition packages are provided, including the JavaMail, Java Message Service, and Servlet packages.

12

- **Style sheets**—Also called Cascading Style Sheets (CSS), style sheets are a standard mechanism that can control every aspect of the visual presentation of a Web page. By adding a style sheet as a shared resource, you can universally control the color, layout, and display of any HTML element.

- **Data connections**—Data Connection Resources (DCRs), a new and exciting reusable design element of Release 6, integrate Domino Enterprise Connector Services (DECS) into the actual design of a database. This design element enables you to set up and configure an external data source, such as a relational database, for use within your Domino application.

The following design elements can be found within the Other area of a database's design. These elements represent resources that are not frequently used during development:

- **Databases resources**—Databases resources contain the database's icon, Using and About database documents, and database script. The database icon enables users to quickly identify the database within their Workspace or Bookmark panes. The About and Using documents alert new users to the purpose and use of the database.

- **Navigators**—Navigators provide users with a graphical method for navigating through a database. If Domino Designer includes a navigator with various links to a database, the user can just click an area of the navigator. Most of the function of a navigator can also be accomplished with an outline or page design element.

- **Synopsis**—Although it is not really a design element, this component provides a synopsis, or summary, of all the design elements used within your database. This service is located within the list of design element types so that it is readily accessible, no matter what editing task you are performing.

FRAMESETS

As demonstrated in Figure 12.3, framesets can provide a seamless user interface to any database, both from within the Notes environment and via the Web. During the development of frames, it's helpful to hide the Design pane to provide as much screen real estate as possible.

Figure 12.3
The Discussion Database template that is included with Release 6 uses frames to maximize screen real estate.

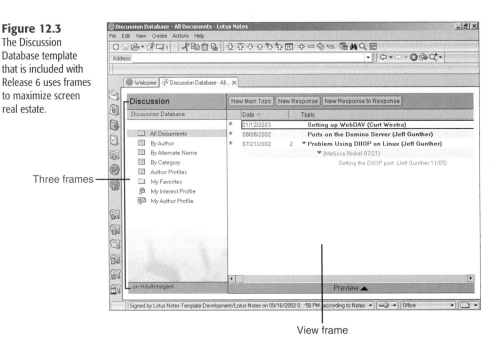

The Frameset Designer with Domino Designer enables you to add and delete frames, move frame borders, and change the contents of each frame. In Figure 12.3, there are actually four frames defined: three on the left and one on the right. The middle frame uses an outline control to allow users to quickly toggle between views. When the user selects one of the items from the outline on the page, the default target is the right frame. The right frame is called View frame, and is the specified target. Framesets are covered in more detail in Chapter 15, "Using Framesets, Outlines, and Navigators."

PAGES

Pages are a design element within Domino Designer that contain both static and dynamic content. If you are familiar with other Web design tools, pages are easy to understand. If you are coming from a Notes/Domino background, pages might seem a little bit like a simplified form. First, as with a form, you can use certain design elements. For example, you can insert horizontal rules, sections, hotspots, tables, pictures, navigators, and several other elements. However, you cannot add fields to a page. A page can be useful as a container for an embedded view. Remember, however, that you do not create documents via pages, and pages do not appear in any view. As a result, pages are design elements, not documents, and any content that is placed on a page is not listed within a full-text index.

Figure 12.4 shows a page from the Domino Designer 6 Help file. Normally, you'll want to use standard documents and forms, but with the page capability, you can perform special processing on a single page if you need it. In this case, the Help database uses the page design element for the Welcome page. When you define a page, you can use the Domino Designer Rich-Text Editor to edit the page in a WYSIWYG (what you see is what you get) manner. You can change fonts and make text bold. In addition, you can edit the page as if it were HTML text. By highlighting the text and selecting Text, Pass-Thru HTML, you can add HTML markup directly to the page. Domino also supports a variety of page events for use by JavaScript. Custom JavaScript methods can be created and defined for use within both the Web and Notes environments.

Figure 12.4
Domino Designer 6 uses a page element to display a welcome message to users.

TIP

Be careful when using both fonts and colors. When your page is displayed on the Web by a user's Web browser, you have no control over the version of software, the fonts installed on the user's machine, or the capabilities of the user's display adapter. You should try not to use fancy fonts or extreme colors. One trick you can use to allow the display of an unusual font is to render the font into a bitmap. Then you can display the bitmap image. By implementing fonts this way, the user does not need to have any particular fonts loaded.

See Chapter 13, "Designing Pages, Forms, and Subforms," for a more extensive review of pages.

FORMS AND SUBFORMS

Forms are like visual templates that can be used to display documents. Documents in Notes and Domino are the fundamental data structure. Nearly all data in Notes and Domino is stored in a document within a database. Even design elements are stored in special documents within the database.

A document stores information by name in items. Each item can hold one or more values, but usually each item stores a single value. The values can be text or numeric. Each item within a document has a name, so you can retrieve the value by name.

Figure 12.5 demonstrates a Domino form being edited in the middle of the screen. In the form, you can see that there are several fields, each with a box surrounding the field name. This form displays documents by associating field names in the form with item names in the document. Whenever there is an item in the document with the same name as the field, the value of the item is displayed.

While you are editing the form, you can see static information and the various fields that have been defined for the form. For example, in Figure 12.5, you see the static text labels Subject and Category. Note that there is also a field called Subject. You can tell the difference because field names are those with a box surrounding them, such as DateComposed, WebCategories, and NewCats. The icon to the right of the name signifies the type of the data field. For example, the little 16 within a calendar means that it is a date field, so DateComposed displays a date. WebCategories has a little down arrow, which indicates that it is a drop-down list. NewCats and the Subject field both have a *T*, which indicates that they are text fields. A rich-text field is symbolized by a *T*. As you work with Domino Designer, you will learn these useful symbols.

Let's review a few aspects of the Designer window in Figure 12.5. You'll notice that on the right side of the form an extra pane is shown. This pane is called the Action pane, and it contains a list of the actions that have been defined for this form. Actions can be displayed either as action buttons or in the Action menu, or both. When you highlight an action in the Action pane, it is selected in the object window of the Design pane at the bottom of the screen. You can supply code that will execute when a user activates an action.

Figure 12.5
Forms use fields to display information from documents.

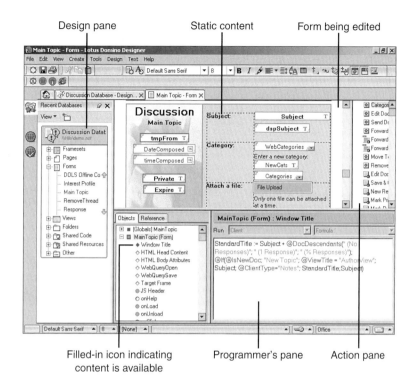

Design pane   Static content   Form being edited

Filled-in icon indicating content is available   Programmer's pane   Action pane

The bottom-left corner of the Programmer's pane at the bottom displays the objects available within the form. There is a global object, the form object, field objects, embedded objects, and actions within the form. Each object typically has methods and properties. You can see in Figure 12.5 that the Body field has extra HTML attributes defined. These attributes are displayed in the right half of the Programmer's pane and will be used with an HTML client.

12

TIP

> One great feature that the Programmer's pane offers is the capability of seeing whether a property or method contains a definition. The icon for a property is filled in when there is data within the event or definition. You can see at a glance the properties and methods that have a definition, and you can go directly to them to find out what they do.

You edit subforms just as you edit forms. The major difference between forms and subforms is that subforms may be referenced from several different forms in the database. The subforms design element type is found within the Shared Code area in the Design pane. Both forms and subforms are covered in more detail in Chapter 13.

VIEWS AND FOLDERS

Views are used to display summary information from documents (see Figure 12.6). Just as a form displays a single document to the user, a view displays information from a set of documents. Typically, each row of a view is information extracted from a single document; if 20 rows are displayed, they represent 20 different distinct documents. This is not necessarily the case if the view is categorized. You learn more about the features and capabilities of views in Chapter 14, "Developing Views and Folders."

Reference information is available on this tab

Figure 12.6
You can control many aspects about the design of your views.

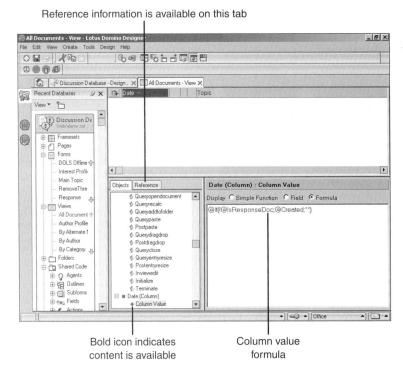

Bold icon indicates content is available

Column value formula

In Figure 12.6, you can see the Designer panes for editing views. The main Work pane shows the view itself, and the Programmer pane at the bottom shows the objects on the left and the definitions on the right. In Figure 12.6, you can see that the value to be displayed in the Date column is calculated using a formula. You can use simple functions, document fields, or formulas for displaying information in views. You can find more information about using formulas in Chapter 18, "Working with Formulas, Functions, and Commands," for information about using formulas.

In Figure 12.6, on the left side of the Programmer's pane, you can see that there is a second tab next to the Objects tab. This tab is for reference information. If you click the Reference tab, you can find the names of all of the fields stored in the database, along with reference information for @formulas and @commands. Chapter 14 covers views and folders in more detail.

AGENTS

Under Shared Code, an agent is a program contained in a Domino database (see Figure 12.7) that is developed using LotusScript, Java, formula language, or simple actions. Agents can be triggered to run in several ways. It can be triggered to run when certain events occur, at specific time intervals, or manually by a user.

Reference information   Programmer's pane

Figure 12.7
Agents can be written in Java (shown here), LotusScript, formula language, or simple actions.

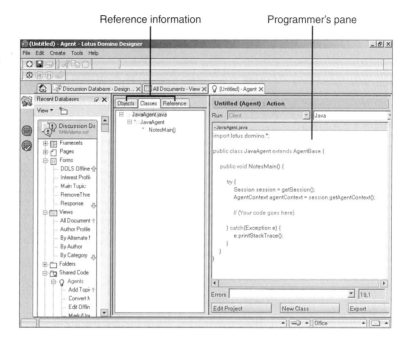

In Figure 12.7, you can see the Domino Designer panes for agents. When the agent is run, it can access a set of documents that are applicable to the agent's parameters. For example, if the agent is triggered when a new document is pasted, the pasted document is available. If the agent is run on a schedule, such as hourly, the documents can either be the new and modified documents or the complete set of all documents in the database. If needed, you can even add more complex search criteria.

The Programmer's pane in Figure 12.7 includes two parts. In the right part, you can now write your agents in Java, as shown. Reference information can be shown on the left. In this section for Java, you find information for both the Domino Object Model (DOM) classes and the core Java classes (such as `javax.swing`, `java.lang`, and so forth). If you explore the reference material and you find a method that you want to use, you can double-click it and it will be transferred into the Design pane programming area.

The Agent Properties box (see Figure 12.8) enables you to set the name of the agent and determine whether the agent is shared or private. You can open the Agent Properties box by right-clicking in the Programmer's pane and selecting Agent Properties. The Agent

12

Properties box also allows you to specify the runtime mechanism for this agent, which can be a time interval or an event, such as a new document being created within the database. We'll cover Java programming in more detail in Chapter 23, "Creating and Using Java Applets and Agents."

Figure 12.8
The Agent Properties dialog box enables you to customize execution settings.

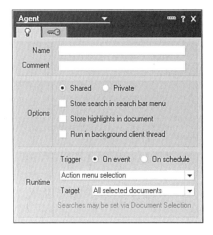

OUTLINES

In Figure 12.9, you see the design environment for outlines. The screen layout in the Work pane of each of the different design elements (such as outlines, framesets, pages, and forms) is different, but the outline layout is fairly typical.

Figure 12.9
Application navigation can be added to a database's design using outlines.

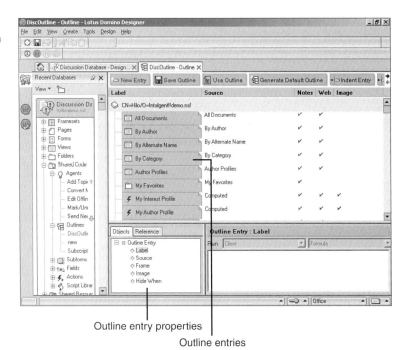

Outline entry properties

Outline entries

To the right of the Design pane, the window layout is a three-pane view. The work area for outlines is in the top pane. The bottom pane is called the Programmer's pane and includes two parts. On the left is typically an area where you can see your object list and reference material. On the right of the Programmer's pane, you can usually enter information that affects the design element.

The action buttons, just below the task buttons, show you the actions you can take with the current design element type. For outlines, you can create new entries, save the outline, use (embed) an outline on a page, generate a default outline, and control indentation of the outline entries. In Figure 12.9, you can see several outline entries. They begin with the following: All Documents, By Author, By Alternate Name, and By Category.

For each outline entry, you can determine whether the entry applies to the Notes client, a Web client, or both by looking at the check marks to the right of each outline entry. You can also supply a small image to replace the little icon that appears next to the outline entry label.

In the InfoList pane in the left half of the Programmer's pane, you can see all the properties and methods of the object. For example, in Figure 12.9, you can see all the properties of an outline entry. In this case, there are five properties of an outline entry: Label, Source, Frame, Image, and Hide When.

To modify a property for an entry, first select the entry in the upper pane and then select the property on the left in the Programmer's pane. On the right, you can enter a definition for the property.

➔ **See** Chapter 15, **p. 395**, for more detail about outlines.

SHARED FIELDS

A Domino field is defined in the context of a form. Pages cannot contain fields. Fields are used for data input and display. They may contain formatting information, such as the font and size, whether it is bold, formula definitions, and so forth.

Normally, each form contains the definition of the fields it contains. However, you might have an application in which certain fields are displayed on several separate forms within an application. Some common examples might be a name, a document creation date, or other user information.

Shared fields enable you to define common attributes of a field and then share the definitions across multiple forms. For example, suppose you want to define a Name field that uses an Arial, bold, 14-point font. You want this field definition to be used on all forms that display the name. You can create a shared field and then just refer to this field on all of your forms. As another example, you might have a field that has complex input validation requirements. You can program the validation formula once and share the field; then any time the field is used, the validation formula will always be the same.

SHARED ACTIONS

Actions, used within a form, view, or folder, provide a mechanism for running a task on a single document or a set of documents. For example, an action called Delete located on the Inbox view within your mail database enables you to delete any highlighted or selected documents. Typically, each action is defined within the form or view that contains it. However, you might have an application in which certain actions are used within separate views or folders within an application. Similar to shared fields, shared actions enable you to define common attributes of an action and then share the definitions across the whole database. For example, a shared action could be created to set the status for particular documents within a workflow process.

SCRIPT LIBRARIES

Script libraries enable you to store subroutines that are used throughout your database. You can create either LotusScript, Java, or JavaScript libraries. After you create a script library, you can add subroutines or methods to the library and then reference them from other locations in your database.

IMAGES

Image resources, under Shared Resources, can be imported for use within several design elements, while storing them only once in your database. You can give your resources a name, as shown in Figure 12.10, and then reference the image name from other parts of your database.

Figure 12.10
An image resource saves space by enabling you to store a single copy of an image across multiple design elements.

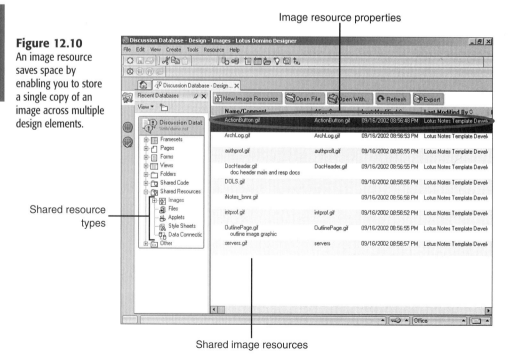

Image resource properties

Shared resource types

Shared image resources

12

Image resources are valuable for storing logos, headers, or other graphics that you want to display on several pages throughout a Web application or for use within the Notes environment. In addition, you can store multiple images within one image resource. This saves additional overhead if you have a group of related images.

FILES

A similar concept to image resources, file resources enable you to import any non-NSF file into the database for reuse within your application. For example, if part of your team developed a Web site using another Web design tool, file resources can be useful to store the developed HTML file for use within the Domino environment.

APPLETS

Applets are Java programs that are downloaded from a server and executed within a Web browser. Here are the typical steps in applet development and execution:

1. The applet is developed in the Java language within a Java development environment, such as IBM WebSphere Studio Application Developer, Borland JBuilder, Eclipse, or NetBeans.

2. The applet is compiled in the development environment to create a set of class files. Class files are similar to compiler object code; they are binary files that define machine operations. The class files, however, are machine independent. They are read and operate within a virtual machine called the Java Virtual Machine (JVM). All the major Web browsers include a JVM; this is the component that enforces security by disallowing the Java program from accessing system resources, such as the file system.

3. Class files are grouped in an archive file that can be of type ZIP, JAR, or CAB. These formats store a collection of files in a compressed format.

4. The archive files are stored in a directory or within a Domino database in a location where the Web server can find them.

5. A Web page is developed that references the applet via special HTML tags. The tags specify the applet name and any parameters required by the applet.

6. When a user is viewing the Web page that references the Java applet, the applet class files are sent from the server to the Web client and are loaded into the Web browser's JVM for execution.

7. The applet runs either continuously or to completion within the JVM.

Notice the difference between agents and applets. Domino agents may be written in any of several languages, including Java, LotusScript, formula language, or simple actions. Applets may be written only in Java. Agents can be triggered on a scheduled basis or when documents arrive in a database. Agents can run on either the Notes client or the server, but they cannot run in a non-Notes Web browser. Applets are triggered via HTML tags and run only on the client. Applets can run in either a Web browser or the Notes client, but not on the server.

12

You can develop agents in Java within Domino Designer, but Domino Designer does not contain facilities for developing applets. You must use another third-party tool to develop applets. After the Java applet class files have been created, you can import them into your database. Applets are covered in detail in Chapter 23.

STYLE SHEETS

Style sheets, also called Cascading Style Sheets (CSS), are a standard from the World Wide Web Consortium (W3C) that gives developers the capability to add and manipulate the style of Web documents. Just like the image and file resources, style sheets can be added to a database's design to be globally accessed from other design elements. Although Domino Designer doesn't provide a style sheet editor, Domino can be used with other tools. A style sheet editor such as Bradbury Software's TopStyle can be an excellent complement to Domino Designer.

DATA CONNECTIONS

Data Connection Resources (DCRs), a new design element added with Release 6, integrates the power of Domino Enterprise Connector Services (DECS) into the design of a Domino database. For example, using a database connection resource, a relational database can be defined to link the fields in a form to the external data source. The Database Connection dialog box, shown in Figure 12.11, is displayed whenever you create or edit a database connection.

Figure 12.11
The Data Connection dialog box enables you to specify the details of connecting to an external data source.

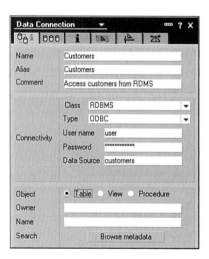

In previous editions, the use of DECS with a Domino database required the tedious task of setting up and configuring a separate database. Using the power of DECs as a design element within a database, a DCR can be replicated across the enterprise while being reused across applications.

NOTE

Before you begin developing with data connections, your Domino administrator must install and configure the DECS server software on your Domino server.

NAVIGATORS

Navigators were introduced in Release 4 of Notes and Domino. In some ways, they were a precursor to the current page concept. You can add graphic elements to navigators, provide links to multiple different locations, and use them to provide an attractive user interface. You might want to use navigators for several reasons.

First, you might already have navigators within your database, so they are provided for compatibility with older versions of Notes. Second, navigators give you an opportunity to use a simple set of graphic editing tools, which a page element does not provide. If you want to create graphic elements with associated hotspot links, navigators are a good choice. Third, you may now embed a navigator within a page, so you can get the best of both worlds. Chapter 15 reviews navigators in more detail.

12

CHAPTER **13**

DESIGNING PAGES, FORMS, AND SUBFORMS

In this chapter

USING THE PAGE EDITOR

As with all previous releases of Notes and Domino, the major user interface element is the *form*. A Domino form enables you to place static text and graphic elements together with fields as a template for display to a user. The form is then combined with different document data items and is displayed to the end user.

With the release of Version 5 of Notes and Domino, Lotus introduced a new design element, the *page*. Although initially many developers used this design element only for Web applications, it can be a useful tool for native Notes applications as well.

CREATING YOUR FIRST PAGE

Before we discuss how to create and use pages within Notes and Web-based applications, we need to create a database. If you are already familiar with how to perform this task, you can jump down to the next section. To create a new, blank database, complete the following steps:

1. Initialize Domino Designer 6.
2. Select File, Database, New from the menu bar to display the New Database dialog box.
3. Give the database a tile of Page Design and a filename of pagedesign.nsf.
4. Leave the server as Local and the template name as Blank.
5. Click OK.
6. Click the Pages design element grouping within the database.

The Domino Designer screen should resemble Figure 13.1.

Figure 13.1
Domino Designer with the Pages design element selected.

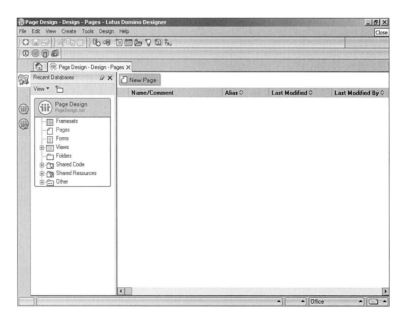

To create a new page, follow these steps:

1. Verify that the Pages element is selected within the design of the databases.

2. Click the New Page action button. A fresh new page appears.

3. Open the Text properties box by clicking the Properties icon in the upper-left toolbar or by selecting Text, Text Properties. Use the default font (Default Sans Serif); change the size to 24 points and the style to Bold.

4. Enter `Welcome to R6!` on the first line of the page.

5. Skip one line and then select Text, Pass-Thru HTML.

6. Type the following on the page:

```
<h1>This is a Header 1</h1>
```

This line uses Hypertext Markup Language (HTML) tags. HTML tags normally have a beginning tag and a matching end tag. In this case, <h1> begins the header text and </h1> ends it. When you read HTML, a tag preceded by a slash means that it is the closing tag of a pair. Notice that the HTML text has a gray background so that you can differentiate HTML from text entered directly on your page. When you enable the text as passthru HTML, the font automatically changes back to 10-point plain text. Any text that is marked as passthru HTML will not be transformed by Domino's Web server; instead, it will be simply "passed through" to the Web browser as HTML. At this point, your page should look like Figure 13.2.

Figure 13.2
You can intermix text and custom HTML directly on your page.

When you enabled the passthru HTML, the font automatically changed back to 10-point plain text. Before you can preview the page via a Web browser on your local workstation, you must modify the database's Access Control List (ACL). To access the database's ACL, choose File, Database, Access Control from the menu bar. As shown in Figure 13.3, the ACL for the Page Design database is presented.

Figure 13.3
The Access Control List dialog box enables you to control how users can interact with your database.

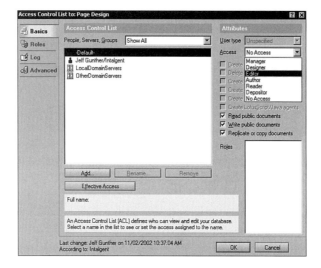

Simply select the Default user and change the user's access to Editor. Click OK to save the changes. If you need more information on how to modify a database's ACL, review Chapter 17, "Access Control Lists (ACLs) and Database Security."

Now that we've taken care of the ACL issues, this is a good place to test your Web page. The icons in the Preview toolbar, in the left-right part of your screen, can be used to invoke a Web browser. If you have Internet Explorer or Netscape Navigator installed (or both), you will see their respective icons. To preview your test page, complete the following:

1. Click one of the browser icons within the Preview toolbar to test your newly created page. If you prefer, you can also choose Design, Preview in Web Browser.

2. You will be prompted for a unique name for your page. You can name your page anything. In this example, call it PageTest.

3. Click OK. Domino Designer launches your Web browser with the rendered page. Figure 13.4 illustrates the PageTest page under Internet Explorer version 6.0.

Here are several points to notice about our first Web page:

■ The font for Welcome to R6! doesn't exactly match the source page. The font is different and the font's size is slightly larger than the source.

- The size for This is a Header 1 is larger than the input, and the font is also different.
- The uniform resource locator (URL) address in the browser window includes localhost, the database name, the page name, and the command to open the page.

Figure 13.4
You can preview your page with Internet Explorer (shown) or Netscape Navigator.

The Web page looks different than what you might expect for a couple reasons:

- The first line does not appear in the browser as it does within Domino Designer because fonts in Designer are not necessarily available to the browser when your page is displayed. To address this issue each browser has its own set of standard Web fonts. In this example, because you used the default font (Default Sans Serif) here, no font information was sent to the Web browser, and the text displays in the default font for the browser, which is Times Roman. Sizes are also standardized and, by default, are not available with fine granularity; the browser uses an approximation to the size. Common fonts that can be used interchangeably between Domino Designer and most Web browsers include Arial, Helvetica, Times New Roman, Times, and Verdana.
- A size is associated by default with the h1 tag and is used for the text. Other heading tags—h2, h3, and so forth—are defined and use different styles. The font is also associated with the h1 tag, and the default browser font is used again for the h1 tag.

13

NOTE

You can control many aspects of the presentation of HTML using Cascading Style Sheets (CSS). A *style sheet* defines rules that determine how content is rendered on a Web page, by associating style attributes to particular HTML elements. Style sheets can be added directly within a page or imported from one or more external files. This technique of manipulating HTML is beyond the scope of this book, however; if you're interested, you should consult Molly Holzschlag's book *Special Edition Using HTML and XHTML* (Que, 2002).

As an alternative to using the passthru HTML text property, you can enclose text within square brackets ([ ]), and it will be treated as passthru HTML. This makes it very easy and convenient to mix HTML source directly in your page without resorting to menu items all the time. In this example, if you have used the bracket syntax, here is how it would look:

```
[<h1>This is a Header 1</h1>]
```

DEFINING PAGE PROPERTIES

Now that we've covered the basic steps for creating a new page within a database, let's review the various properties and attributes that can be enabled to customize a page. To access the Page properties box, choose Design, Page Properties from the menu bar. The Page Info tab of the Page properties box appears as shown in Figure 13.5.

Figure 13.5
The Page properties box enables you to control many attributes of how a page is rendered and displayed.

Release 6 introduces a few new items to the Page dialog box. Of particular interest is the Render Passthru HTML in Notes field. This field allows a page with HTML to be properly displayed within the Notes client. For example, the text between the <h1> tags will be parsed and rendered by Notes just like in a Web browser.

CAUTION

The Render Passthru HTML in Notes field on the Page properties box will handle any text marked as passthru HTML. However, if you're using square brackets to mark passthru HTML, be aware that this technique works only within a Web browser, not within the Notes client.

Another field enables you to control the content type for the rendered page. For example, if you want to have the whole page treated as HTML, just check the box titled Content Type as HTML. If you check this box, you don't have to include the square brackets because your entire page is treated as HTML automatically. This is an extremely useful setting if you are new to Domino but you are already familiar with HTML, or if you want to use a separate HTML-editing tool such as Macromedia Dreamweaver and just want to import your HTML.

We've reviewed three different ways to specify HTML in your page:

- Create text on the page and then highlight the text and give it the Passthru HTML attribute. You do this on the Text menu. You can mix and match HTML and non-HTML with this method.

- Place square brackets ([ ]) around any text on the page that you want to be considered HTML. You do not have to use the menus. You can mix and match HTML and non-HTML with this method. Just make sure that you don't use this method if the page is going to be used as a native Notes page.

- Go to the Page properties box and choose HTML as your content type. This treats the entire page contents as HTML. This makes it easier to import text directly from another HTML-authoring tool.

In the Page properties box, you can also set the colors for the active link, unvisited link, and visited link. If you'd like to change the color for the active, unvisited, or visited links, simply choose a new color from the color palette. However, for most cases, you can just leave these set at the default values.

PASTING AND IMPORTING GRAPHIC BACKGROUNDS

To change the graphic background, follow these steps:

1. Open the Page properties box for the page by opening the page and choosing Design, Page Properties from the menu bar.

2. Click the Background tab. You can select a background color by opening the drop-down box.

3. As shown in Figure 13.6, use one of the following methods to obtain a graphic background:
   - You can use another graphics-editing program and copy the graphic to the Clipboard. After you have copied the graphic to the Clipboard, go to the Page properties box and click the Paste button.
   - If you want to load an image from a file, click the Import button in the center of the dialog box. You will be prompted to locate and select your file.
   - If you have saved your graphic image as an image resource, type in the name or click the folder icon on the Image Resource line. You can specify a formula by clicking the @ symbol. If you'd like more information about image resources, review Chapter 16, "Using Shared Resources."

Figure 13.6
You can set the background color and image with the Page properties box.

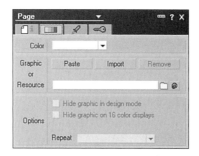

4. (Optional) You can specify that you want to hide the image during design or for 16-color displays. Turning off the image during design makes it easier to edit your page. On 16-color displays, sometimes 256-color (or higher) photos or graphics look more like modern art than an attractive background. This can be distracting to users, so you can turn off the background.

5. (Optional) You can specify how you'd like to handle the repeating of the graphic background. Within Release 6, you can select from many options from the standard Tile to Size to Fit. Normally, by default, graphic backgrounds are tiled.

BASIC HYPERTEXT MARKUP LANGUAGE (HTML)

Complete books and online references cover HTML, so there is no way to cover it completely here. However, a simple introduction to HTML might be helpful so that you can see the syntax and a few features of the language. This should get you started; you can consult an HTML reference such as Molly Holzschlag's book *Special Edition Using HTML and XHTML* (Que, 2001) for more detailed information.

Let's start by defining a new test page in your Page Design database. To follow along with this example, follow these steps:

1. Open your database, click Pages in the Design pane, and then click the New Page action button.

2. Choose Design, Page Properties to open the Page properties box.

3. Enter **HTMLtest** into the Name field and select Content Type as HTML in the Web access grouping.

4. In the Work pane, enter the following:

```
<FORM name="MyForm">
<H1>HTML Test page</H1>
<P>Here is an input field</P>

<INPUT type="text" value="MyDefault" name="MyField">
<A href="http://www.lotus.com">and a link to Lotus</A>
<BR>
```

```
<INPUT type="button" value="Hot Button" OnClick="alert('You pushed my
hotbutton')">

</FORM>
```

In Figure 13.7, you can see this sample input and the results in Internet Explorer.

Figure 13.7
A page within Domino Designer and a browser showing the output.

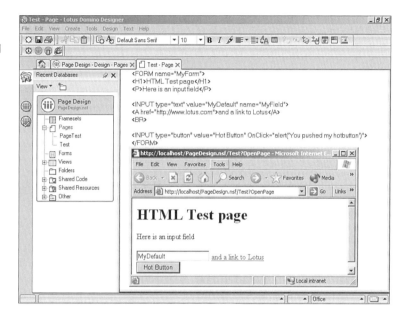

Understanding HTML Syntax

HTML is a language that is used to "mark up" text—that is, to add tags around content to define the formatting of the content associated with the tag. The syntax for HTML tags is very simple. In its basic form, the syntax is as follows:

```
<start-tag> element contents </end-tag>
```

You can see this simple syntax with the Header 1 <H1></H1> pair and the paragraph <P></P> pair. Between the start and end tags are the contents of the element. A more complex tag sometimes has attributes. For example, notice the <FORM> tag. The syntax using attributes is as follows:

```
<start-tag attr1="value1" attr2="value2" ... attrn="valuen"> element contents
</end-tag>
```

Capitalization in the tag names and attribute names is ignored, and you can enter them in lower- or uppercase. By convention, however, tags and attributes are usually shown in uppercase.

In general, HTML syntax and most browsers are fairly forgiving. By this, I mean that if you make mistakes in your HTML, most of the time you won't get an error message—although

13

you might not get the result you expect, either. In fact, the HTML in Figure 13.7 left off some official tags, such as <HTML>, <HEAD>, and <BODY>. Here is the official form for an HTML document:

```
<HTML>
    <HEAD>
        Optional HEAD section tags, such as <TITLE>
    </HEAD>
    <BODY>
        Main body of document
    </BODY>
</HTML>
```

The <HTML> tag introduces the following text as being written in HTML. The <HEAD> tag is grouped around text that defines the header for the document. This section includes the <TITLE> tag, if there is one. As usual, the format for the <TITLE> tag is this:

```
<TITLE>Your title here</TITLE>
```

The <BODY> tag surrounds the main section of HTML. If you are using framesets, the <FRAMESET> tag is used instead of the <BODY> tag.

As you have seen, both browsers enable you to completely leave off the <HTML>, <HEAD>, and <BODY> tags. It's not recommended that you use this type of shortcut in HTML. If you don't follow the official rules in HTML, your output might work in some browsers but not others. It's demonstrated in this example to explain that browsers in general are pretty forgiving, but you should use careful judgment in assuming anything—and you should test your HTML with several browsers.

NOTE

While Web browsers have been very lenient regarding HTML markup, the movement in the industry has been to follow a more rigorous format known as XHTML. The XHTML specification is transformed from the previous HTML 4 specification into an XML representation. One of the requirements of the XHTML specification is that all documents must be "well-formed." A document is considered well-formed when its structure follows the rules of XML. Simplistically, this means that each tag must contain a start and an end tag. For more information about HTML and XHTML, take a look at Molly Holzschlag's book *Special Edition Using HTML and XHTML* (Que, 2001).

A Web browser automatically formats your document according to the HTML markup and content within the document. You'll probably realize this when you think about what happens when you change the size of your browser window. Typically, text reflows within the window. This means that the display of text is dependent upon how large the browser window is at the time it is displayed to the user. A tall, narrow window looks different from a short, wide window.

The implication of this formatting is that any blank lines of text that you include in your document automatically are ignored. To force line breaks, you must use the <P> and <BR> tags, which are described in the next section.

A FEW COMMON HTML TAGS

Many tags within HTML simply tell the browser how to display and format text. However, some tags instruct the Web browser to perform other tasks. For example, the IMG tag has an attribute called src that details the location for a particular image:

```
<img src="someimage.jpg" width="140" height="209">
```

Another example HTML tag that deserves mention here is the Anchor tag, also known as a Link tag. The simplified format for this tag is as shown:

```
<A href="url-address">link display text</A>
```

For example, you can enter this:

```
<A href="http://www.lotus.com">Lotus Web Site</A>
```

In this case, Lotus Web Site is the text that will appear in the form, but if clicked, the browser goes to www.lotus.com. This is similar to a document link within Notes and Domino. You can also use an image in place of the link display text. If you do this, the user can click the image to follow a link. To specify an image, you typically use the <IMG> tag.

Although there are quite a few HTML tags, we'll cover a few of the most common ones here so you'll have a head start in being able to read HTML. We've already covered the main document structure; Table 13.1 lists a few tags that are frequently included in the <BODY> section.

TABLE 13.1	SOME COMMON HTML TAGS
<A></A>	Anchor. Used to make a link. The HREF attribute specifies the URL destination address.
<B></B>	Bold. Makes included text bold.
<I></I>	Italic. Makes included text italic.
<S></S>	Strikethrough. Makes included text strikethrough.
<U></U>	Underline. Makes included text underlined.
 	Line break. Causes a line break; the next line of text starts on the line below. No lines are skipped.
<P></P>	Paragraph. Breaks the current line, does an additional line break (that is, skips a line), and starts a new paragraph. The end paragraph tag is frequently omitted.

13

continues

TABLE 13.1	CONTINUED
`<INPUT>`	Input. Defines several different types of user input fields, depending upon the TYPE attribute. The type can be one of the following: TEXT—Textbox input. PASSWORD—Textbox with characters hidden when input. CHECKBOX—Selection check box. RADIO—Radio button selection. BUTTON—Pushbutton. SUBMIT—Submit button. This special button causes the form to be submitted to the server. RESET—Reset button. This special button causes all input fields to be reset. IMAGE—Creates a graphical submit button. FILE—Enables users to select files to be submitted with a form. HIDDEN—A value that cannot be seen by the user but that can be used for storing values by the program and transmitting to the server.
`<TEXTAREA>`	Creates a multiline input field.
`</TEXTAREA>`	Enables you to specify the number of rows and columns via attributes. Text supplied between the tags becomes the initial value of the text area.
`<SELECT>` and `<OPTION>`	Used for creating list boxes.
`<IMG>`	Used to display an image. Common formats are GIF, JPEG, and PNG. You use the SRC attribute to specify the URL of the source image.
`<OL></OL>`	Ordered list. Automatically numbers items (`<LI>` tagged items) within the list.
`<UL></UL>`	Unordered list. Places bullets in front of items (`<LI>` tagged items) within the list.
`<LI>`	List item. Used to tag items within either an ordered or an unordered list. You don't need to include an end tag.

Looking back at the HTML on the page in Figure 13.7, you'll notice that there are three kinds of elements: a paragraph with static text, an input field, and a button. The static paragraph text is self-explanatory. The input field as shown is not much use because the value entered by the user is not processed in any way by the form. With JavaScript, you can access the input-control fields and process the values. Information stored in the fields can also be sent back to the host for processing.

The button object shows you an elementary JavaScript program of one line. The OnClick attribute of the button tells the browser what to do if the button is clicked. In this case, the alert routine of JavaScript is called and a message box is displayed. You can also define much more complicated JavaScript programs and invoke them when someone clicks a button or performs other events such as mouse movement.

ENHANCING YOUR PAGES

With this whirlwind tour of HTML, you might think that you have to code in HTML to use pages in Domino. You really don't. If you are familiar with HTML, you can use all of its power; but if not, you can use the Domino Page Editor to edit your page directly. You can use Domino features, and Domino actually generates the HTML for you. This is what Domino has always done for Notes forms and documents. You can also import HTML from an HTML editor or another product that generates HTML for you.

The real beauty of Domino is that you can use the power of HTML, if desired, but you don't have to. Probably the most powerful attribute is that you can combine Domino formulas, LotusScript, JavaScript, and Java with HTML to produce compelling Web sites.

The following sections describe other features, such as tables and graphics, that you can use within the Page Editor to enhance your pages.

CREATING TABLES

While a simple text layout might be sufficient for some projects, tables can be a great way to control alignment and positioning of text and images so that you get the exact look you want from your page.

In fact, using tables is an important technique because tables can be used as formatting tools in addition to their traditional purpose as a means to display text and numbers. HTML 4 has additional formatting capabilities and styles to accomplish positioning. The previous release of Domino Designer introduced several different styles of tables, including a tabbed interface, a timed interface, and a table that displays different rows depending upon the contents of a field (in a form). To format different elements of a page, however, all you need is the basic type of table. We'll review the other types later.

To create a basic table, follow these steps:

1. Place the cursor on the page (or form) where you want your table to appear.
2. Choose Create, Table to see the dialog box shown in Figure 13.8. We are interested in creating a basic table, which uses the first icon button. You can leave the default number of rows and columns or enter the number of rows and columns you want to use for your table. Your table can fit the window width, fit within the margins, or have a fixed width. If you want your table to have a fixed width, click the Fixed Width radio button.
3. Click OK to create your table.

By default, tables are created with borders displayed and extend to the full width of your page.

13

Figure 13.8
When creating a table, you can enter its size, the table width type, and the type of table.

ADDING ROWS AND COLUMNS

After you have created your table, you might want to add rows or columns. There are several ways to add rows and columns, depending on where and how many you want to add. Click your mouse cursor inside the table and then click the Table menu.

If you want to add rows to the end of your table, you can select the Append Row option. The row is added to the bottom of your table. To add a column to your table, select the Append Column menu option. The column is appended to the right side of your table.

To insert a row or column at the beginning or middle of your table, select the Insert Row or Insert Column menu options. The row or column is inserted before the selected row or column.

The Insert Special menu option is used when you want to insert or append more than one row or column. The Insert Row/Column dialog box appears, as shown in Figure 13.9.

Figure 13.9
Use Insert Special to insert or append more than one row or column to your table.

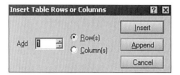

Enter the number of rows or columns you want to add, and then select Insert. Insert them before the currently selected row or column, and use Append to append the desired items to the end of the table.

DELETING ROWS

Deleting rows operates similarly to inserting them. To delete rows, follow these steps:

1. Select a cell in the first row that you want to delete.
2. Drag the mouse to select cells in the rest of the row. You must have at least one cell selected in each row that you are about to delete.
3. After you select the cells, choose Table, Delete Selected Row(s) to delete the rows.

DELETING COLUMNS

Deleting columns operates similarly to inserting them. To delete columns, follow these steps:

1. Select a cell in the leftmost cell in a set of columns you want to delete.

2. Drag the mouse to select cells in the rest of the columns. You must have at least one cell selected in each column that you are about to delete.

3. After you select the cells, choose Table, Delete Selected Columns to delete the columns.

TIP

> Delete Special can be used as a shortcut to delete a contiguous set of rows or columns. First, select the topmost or leftmost cell and then select Delete Special. You are prompted for the number of rows or columns to delete. The row or column that follows the location of the cursor will be deleted.

TABLE PROPERTIES

When you click inside a table, you can view the table properties by clicking the Properties icon; by clicking Edit, Properties; or by keystroking Alt+Enter on the keyboard. You can also click inside any cell of a table and then choose Table, Table Properties. When the properties box appears, if Table is not listed on the top line of the dialog box, you can click the drop-down box and select Table (see Figure 13.10).

Figure 13.10
The Table properties box enables you to change column widths and spacing.

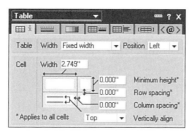

The Table Layout tab (the first tab) of the properties box enables you to change the type of width to use (Fixed, Fit to Window, or Fit with Margins), the position of the table (Left, Right, or Center), and the fixed spacing between columns and rows. The amount you enter into the column and row fields applies to all columns and rows. Also, the sizes that you enter apply to each side of the cell. For example, if you enter a column space of 0.5", you will get 0.5 inch on both the left and right sides of the column. This means that you will get a full inch between columns. Note that column spacing, row spacing, and minimum height are not supported in Web applications. Some of these values might affect the width of a cell, however, which is supported.

13

CHANGING TABLE BORDERS AND MARGINS

The Cell Borders tab is shown in Figure 13.11. This tab affects cell borders, not the border for the entire table. The Border tab controls the border for the entire table.

Figure 13.11
The Cell Borders tab enables you to change the cell border style, color, and thickness.

You can specify the style of the cell as Solid, Ridge, or Groove. Clicking the color drop-down enables you to select a color for the cell borders. If you click the Set All to 0 button, you will get no borders because all the border thicknesses will be 0. If you set all the borders to 1, you will get the default thickness. The style options Ridge and Groove, as well as individual cell coloring, are not supported for Web browsers. You can set the border color and style for a table under the Table Borders tab. We'll review the Table Borders tab later in this section.

Setting all borders to 0, along with setting the widths of columns, enables you to control the layout and alignment of text on your page. By using tables, you can place elements relatively easily. Just by changing the table column widths, you can specify spacing between separate items for viewing. This is especially useful if your target audience will be Web browsers.

If you are familiar with layout regions in Notes, you're probably aware that they cannot be rendered to Web browsers. Typically, in previous releases of Notes and Domino, you might have used a layout region for precise positioning. You should become familiar with tables as another means to accomplish formatting because you can use tables with 0 thickness to manipulate positions; this works fine with either browsers or Notes clients. In addition to tables, layers within Release 6 allow for the exact positioning of content.

The Cell Borders tab we just explored enables you to change border settings for the cells within a table. The Table Border tab, shown in Figure 13.12, is used to change settings for the table's outside border.

In the Table Borders tab, you can set the style, effects, and thickness for the given table.

- **Border Style**—The table border can have None or one of eight predefined styles, such as Solid, Double, or Dotted. This is the line style used for the border surrounding the table.

- **Border Effects**—In addition to the style, a table can have a shadow effect if you check the Drop Shadow check box. If a shadow is enabled, you can control its width.

■ **Border Thickness**—You can set the thickness of the table border as well as its color. You can change the spacing between the table and its border. This spacing is called the inside spacing. The outside setting is the space outside the table border that separates the table from its surroundings. To set thickness, inside spacing, and outside spacing, first select which one you want with the drop-down box; then adjust the Top, Bottom, Left, and Right numbers. Each of the three parameters can have four different numbers.

Figure 13.12
The Table Borders tab enables you to change the table border style, color, thickness, and spacing.

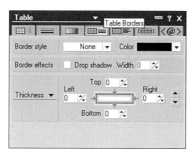

The Table Margins tab appears immediately to the right of the Table Border tab and can be used to specify the left and right margins for the table. You can specify each margin as either an offset measurement or a percentage of the window.

IMPLEMENTING NEWSPAPER-STYLE COLUMNS

You can format columns within your table in newspaper style, with text flowing from one column of a table to the next column.. In Figure 13.13, you can see the table within Domino Designer and rendered within Internet Explorer.

Figure 13.13
The Table Margins tab enables you to create newspaper-style flow from one column to another.

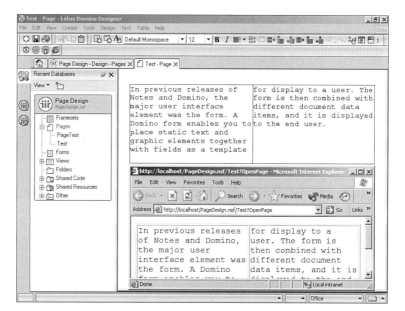

13

The newspaper-style flow is obtained by checking Inside Table Wrap Between Cells. When you enable this feature, you must specify the column height in the Height Input field.

With this wrap feature enabled, text flows between cells within the same row but will not wrap from one row to the next. If you enter more text in the rightmost column than the column height setting, the table row height just expands to accommodate the larger height.

SETTING TABLE/CELL BACKGROUNDS

Many options exist for setting background colors and/or images in tables. The Table/Cell Background tab is the third tab in the Table properties box (see Figure 13.14).

Figure 13.14
The Table/Cell Background tab enables you to set cell backgrounds, headers, and gradients.

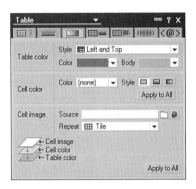

Use the Table/Cell Background tab to pick colors for individual cells or to set a row and column color scheme for the entire table, or to add a background image to a particular cell.

In the Table Style drop-down list, you can select from one of the following styles:

- **None**—No style is assigned to the table.
- **Solid**—No automatic row or column header highlighting is used.
- **Alternating Rows**—Alternate rows are different colors. By default, two shades of gray are used.
- **Alternating Columns**—Alternate columns are different colors. By default, two shades of gray are used.
- **Left and Top**—The top row and the left column are highlighted. In Figure 13.15, I have changed the colors so that the header color is dark and the Body color is light gray.
- **Left**—The left column is highlighted with the color you specify.
- **Right and Top**—The top row and the right column are highlighted. This is a bit unusual.
- **Right**—The right column is highlighted with your color.
- **Top**—The top row is highlighted.

You can override any of the default styles by highlighting one or more cells and then clicking the cell color drop-down list to select a color. If you select a color, it overlays the default color of the style. To make the style color show through again, you can click the (None) button, which appears in the top row of the color drop-down list.

You can make gradients (gradual color shifts) within a cell by using the Style buttons within the Cell color grouping. You can start to create a gradient by clicking the top-to-bottom or left-to-right Style buttons. Upon choosing a gradient, you can select the starting and ending colors. The background color is the field labeled Color, the field labeled To is the ending color, and the direction can be set to either Top to Bottom or Left to Right. Gradients display only if you are using a Notes client.

The final option on the Table/Cell Background tab is to set the cell image. With this option, you can include an image within a table cell. Using this feature, you can format an attractive page, as demonstrated in Figure 13.15. The particular image within this figure is an image of the Lotus Notes splash screen.

Figure 13.15
You can include a background image within a table cell.

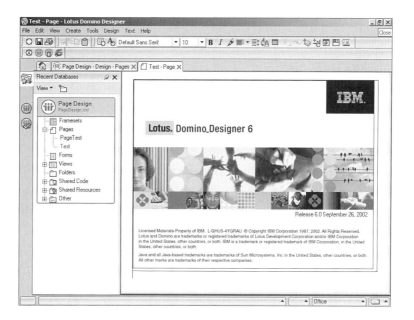

You can include an image by name, via a formula, or from your image library. Images from your image library are resources and replicate along with your database.

The major constraint on using images within tables is that the height of all rows within a table must be the same. The height of a table row is set on the Table layout (first) tab.

MERGING AND SPLITTING CELLS

Figure 13.16 shows another table technique, known as *cell merging*. In this example, all the cells on the top row were merged into a single cell. The process of merging and splitting cells is similar to managing tables within Microsoft Word.

Figure 13.16
You can merge cells to create a table header with centered text.

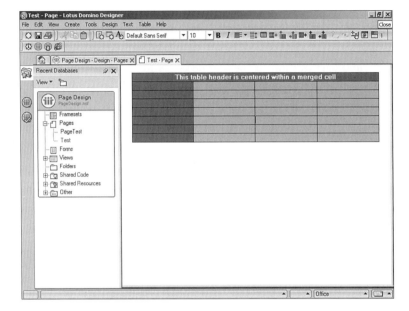

To merge several cells into one cell, follow these steps:

1. Select the cells within the table that you want to merge. You can select cells in the row-wise direction or the column-wise direction. You can also select cells that have already been merged previously.

2. Choose Table, Merge Cells. This option is valid in the menu only if you have more than one table cell selected.

Your cells are now merged.

To split cells that were previously merged, follow these steps:

1. Select a merged cell within the table.

2. Choose Table, Split Cell. This option is valid in the menu only if you have selected a cell that was previously merged.

NOTE

During the development of a table, it's useful to merge the cells of a table multiple times to gain the desired presentation. However, be aware that when a set of cells has been merged, it can be split back to only the original state of the table.

ADVANCED FUN WITH TABLES

You can create several special effects with tables. They all revolve around the idea of displaying row content in a special way. The one factor that these tables have in common is that only a single row of the table is shown at a time. Various methods are used to determine which row to show. Three types of special tables exist:

- **Tabbed tables**—Each row of the table corresponds to one tab of the tabbed table. Only the row containing the selected tab is shown.

- **Timed tables**—Each row of the table appears for a specified amount of time. The default is two seconds. You can use these tables to display animation.

- **Programmatic control**—In addition to the table, you must supply a field. The name of the field is the same as the table name with a $ prefix. The contents of the field determine which row to display. You can programmatically update the field, which can then be used to select the row.

You can create a table of any of these three types, or you can create the standard table type initially and later convert it to any of the other types. You control the type of table on the Table Rows tab of the Table properties box. This is the sixth tab in the properties box. Take a look at the example shown in Figure 13.17.

Figure 13.17
You can create a tabbed table to display categorized content using the special table row display feature.

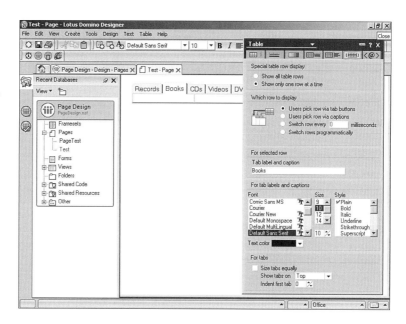

Figure 13.17 shows a tabbed table with five rows and four columns. You can create a tabbed table from an existing table by clicking the Users Pick Row Via Tab Buttons option under the Which Row to Display grouping.

After you create the table, you can add information to each of the table rows. In Figure 13.17, you see that labels have been added to each row. You enter a tab label into the Tab Label and Caption, in the center of the Table Rows tab of the properties box. Because there are five rows in this example, there are five tabs. One common use might be to use only a single column with several rows. In this way, you could create a tabbed interface similar to a dialog box.

Another type of table is a Timed Table. This shows each row for a fixed amount of time. The default is 2000 milliseconds (2 seconds), but you can adjust this time. In Figure 13.17, you see that you can set the Switch Row Every x Milliseconds radio button option in the middle of the Table properties box. The timed display can be used for creating an animated appearance to the user by cycling through each table's cells.

To create this appearance of animation, create a table with several rows and one column. Each row should contain a graphic file—from your image library, for example. Set the timer for the amount of time you want to show each graphic. You can specify a transition effect such as Left-to-Right, Dissolve, or Explode, among several others. You can also specify that you want to cycle through the graphics continually or only when clicked by the user. All of these options become available to you on the Table properties dialog box after you select the Switch Row Every x Milliseconds radio button.

Since Release 5 of Notes and Domino, you can nest tables, or create tables within tables. This technique is particularly useful for tabbed tables or when you want to control content placement. As shown in Figure 13.18, you can find a demonstration of this technique on the Person form within your organization's Domino Directory.

Figure 13.18
As the Person form of the Directory Directory demonstrates, nesting tables within tables provides an easy way to condense a lot of information into a small area.

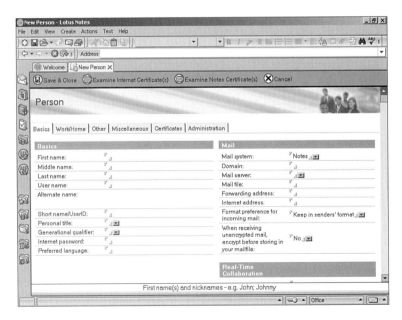

To nest a table within an existing table, simply put the mouse cursor into an existing table cell and choose Create, Table from the menu bar. Upon selecting the table type, you'll see a new table neatly nested within the existing table.

CONTROLLING TABLES PROGRAMMATICALLY

The final type of single-row table gives you programmatic control over the table to be displayed to the user. Normally, this table type should be used with a form because fields are not allowed in a page. We'll introduce you to fields and discuss forms in much greater detail later in this chapter.

To create a programmatically controlled table, complete the following steps:

1. Open the Forms grouping of a database's design from within Domino Designer.
2. Create a new Form by clicking the New Form action button within the Forms view.
3. Create a new table by choosing Create, Table from the menu bar.
4. The Create Table dialog box appears, asking for you to choose a table type. In this example, choose the left-most table type, called Programmed Table.
5. To examine the programmatic control, put the mouse cursor in the newly created table and choose Table, Table Properties from menu bar.

   Figure 13.19 shows the Table Rows tab of the Table properties box, with the Switch Rows Programmatically radio button selected.

Figure 13.19
By using the Switch Rows Programmatically radio button, the rows of a table can be dynamically displayed.

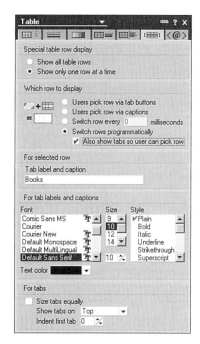

6. Before you can programmatically show rows of a table, you must set up a few variables. Click the Table Programming tab to define the table's name and row tags.

Figure 13.20 shows the Table Programming tab of the Table properties box.

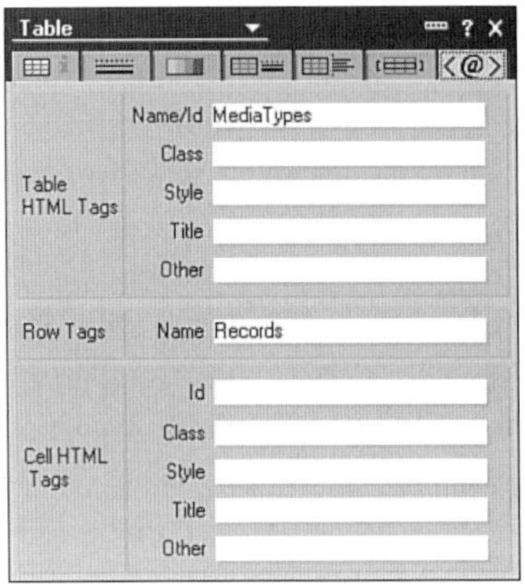

Figure 13.20
Name the table and its rows within the Table Programming tab.

7. In the Table Programming tab, you must give the table and row tags a unique name. You can pick the row to display either by its name or by its 0-origin numeric row index. In this example, the table is named MediaTypes. The name of the row shown is Records, which is the first row.

NOTE

The row names are case sensitive. Be careful to specify the exact string when using programmatic row selection. Also note that the row's name is not necessarily the same as its label. In this example, I used the word *Records* for both the row label and its name to avoid confusion. If they are different, remember that the name is used for selection, not the label.

8. Create a new field at the bottom of the form called $MediaTypes by selecting Create, Field from the menu bar. The $MediaTypes field is the special field that controls which row will be displayed. The $MediaTypes field name is constructed by prefixing the table name with a $. A computed field is used to control the table. Two formula statements set the field and then refresh the display. The value put into the $MediaTypes field is the name of the row (not its label).

9. Create five action hotspots. In the form shown in Figure 13.20, there are five action hotspots across the top of the screen: Records, Books, CDs, Videos, and DVDs. Each hotspot of Figure 13.20 has a Click formula similar to one of the following:

```
FIELD $MediaTypes:=0;
@Command([RefreshHideFormulas])
```

1. Create or open the page you want to use for your graphic.

2. Move your cursor to the location where you want to place your picture and choose Create, Image Resource. You are prompted for an image name and type, and you will see a list of the available images.

3. If you click an image name, you will see a preview of the image on the right side of the dialog box. After you have found the image you want to include, select its name and click OK.

4. Your image is displayed on your page.

ORGANIZING DATA WITH RULES, SECTIONS, AND PAGE BREAKS

To organize your page and content, horizontal rules and sections can provide a nice touch. A *horizontal rule* is simply a line that goes across the page. Rules can also include color gradients, which start in one color and gradually change to another color. The gradients change colors from top to bottom. With the rule properties, however, you can modify the width and height of the rule. The width can be expressed as a percentage, or you can specify an exact measurement, such as inches.

To create a horizontal rule, move your cursor to the location on the page or form where you want your rule to appear. Then choose Create, Horizontal Rule. After you create your rule, you can change its properties box by choosing Horizontal Rule from the menu bar. You can see an example of a rule with a gradient in Figure 13.22.

Sections are an effective way to group and organize large amounts of content. Collapsible sections can be helpful to provide context-sensitive information to users only when the information is needed. To create a section, follow these steps:

1. Move the cursor to where you want to create your section. Type all the text that you want included in the section.

2. After the text has been entered on the page, use the keyboard or mouse to select the text that you want to use into the section.

3. Choose Create, Section to create your section. The first line of the text that you selected becomes the section title and displays if the section is closed.

4. (Optional) After the section has been created, you can change the title with the Section properties box. You can also change the rules that are used to automatically expand and collapse the section (see Figure 13.22).

13

Figure 13.22
The Section proper-
ties box can be used
to customize how sec-
tions operate.

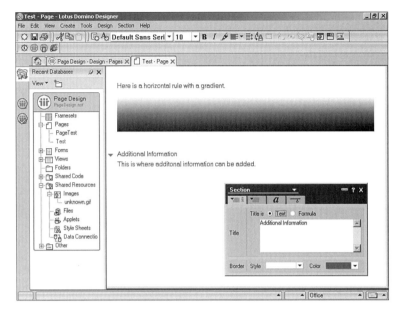

In addition to using sections and rulers for content organization, you can control how the page is printed. You can control printer page breaks by inserting a page break. To insert a page break, first move the cursor to the location where you want your page to break, and then choose Create, Page Break.

NOTE

The page break will not affect formatting for display in either the Notes client or Web browsers. The page break is strictly an aid in formatting your printed output.

DESIGNING FORMS

Now that we've covered most of the basics of page creation and manipulation, let's move right into forms. Since the inception of Lotus Notes and Domino, forms have been a fundamental part of all databases. Where pages are focused around displaying static content, forms are the data-input and manipulation point of Notes and Domino, where pages are focused around displaying static content. If you're familiar with previous releases, you probably already know a lot about forms. This next section is really designed to provide an introduction to utilizing forms and documents. Then we'll move into a comparison of these design elements with pages.

UNDERSTANDING FORMS, DOCUMENTS, AND VIEWS

In Domino, the *document* is the fundamental unit of storage for information. Documents contain named items to store information. The item has a data type, such as numeric or text, and if the item contains multiple values, they are all the same type. A typical item within a document might contain, for example, a name, address, or phone number. Sometimes these document items are also called fields.

You can have hundreds or thousands (or more) of documents in a database. The documents do not all have to have the same item names. For example, one document might contain the items Name and Address, and another document might contain TotalAmount and DueDate.

Not all of the data contained within documents is necessarily visible to a user. Documents contain data, but they are typically used with user interface elements, such as forms and views. Forms and views are the means of presenting information stored within documents to the user. Views present summary information from many documents, and forms enable you to see detailed information from one document.

A *form* is a visual template. You can view a form in Domino much like a blank paper form. Think for a moment about the form you fill out in the dentist's office with your name, address, and medical history. This form indicates the information desired and leaves several blank areas for you to fill in. With Domino forms, the blank areas are called fields. Each field within a form has a field name so that you can reference it and obtain the information you need. A form contains both static information and field information. It is a visual object, much like the pages that we reviewed previously.

Suppose Domino is showing an empty form to a user. When the user fills in the empty fields of the form, the information is stored in a document. Domino separates the user interface (form) from the field data stored within the document. This way, you can view the same fields with different forms, and you can change the look and feel of your application without changing the underlying data stored in the document fields.

What happens if the names in the document don't match the names in the form? Actually, this happens quite often and is normal. If the document contains items that have names that do not appear on the form, the values are not displayed to the user. If the form contains field names that don't appear in the document, when the user enters a value, it automatically creates a corresponding item value in the document.

To recap, forms are used for the visual display of data to a user, while documents are used to store data within the database. The correspondence of names in forms and documents enables Domino to display fields filled in with the values from a document. For display to a Web browser, Domino first merges the form definition with the document values and then converts the result to HTML, which is then sent to the browser.

COMPARING FORMS AND DOCUMENTS WITH PAGES

We have now talked about pages, forms, and documents. How are these all used, and how do they compare? In Table 13.2, an *X* indicates that the feature is available. There might be minor exceptions, but the table demonstrates the major differences so you can contrast the database elements.

TABLE 13.2 COMPARISON OF PAGES, FORMS, AND DOCUMENTS

	Pages	Forms	Documents
Visual user interface	X	X	
Can be viewed in a Web browser	X	X (with a document)	
Stores field data values			X
Can contain Domino field definitions		X	
Can contain HTML formatting and INPUT items (HTML-type fields)	X	X	
Is a design element	X	X	
Full text searchable			X
Data can be shown in views			X
A single element can be used with multiple documents		X	

The most important thing to remember about the differences between the elements listed is that documents are the structures that hold data in the database, whereas pages and forms are visual user interface elements. Although pages and forms have some similar characteristics, they serve fundamentally different purposes. Pages provide designers with a mechanism to serve up static content such as text and images to Notes clients and Web browsers. Forms, on the other hand, provide a dynamic template to serve up data from within a document.

CREATING A NEW FORM

To create a new form in your database, follow these steps:

1. In Domino Designer, open the database where you want your form to appear.
2. Click Forms in the Design pane.
3. Click the New Form action button. Your new blank form appears.

The Form Editor is very similar to the Page Editor. A large area at the top enables you to lay out your form, and the Programmer's pane at the bottom enables you to manipulate details of the elements within the form.

WORKING WITH FIELDS

We've learned that fields can be placed on forms, but not pages. Fields represent the blank areas of a paper form. In the United States, we fill out forms to pay our taxes to the Internal Revenue Service (IRS). If you are outside the U.S., you probably pay taxes to your own government. (If not, let me know where you live.) On those tax forms, the blank boxes where you enter your numbers are fields. The good news is that working with fields in Domino is much less painful than filling in the fields on tax forms.

ADDING FIELDS TO A FORM

To create a new field on your form, follow these steps:

1. Open the form on which you want to add the field.

2. Choose Create, Field. Your new field is created with the name Untitled (see Figure 13.23).

Figure 13.23
You can change the name and type of fields in the properties box.

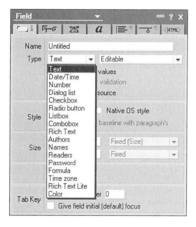

Each field on the form must have a unique name; if you enter a name that already exists, Domino Designer automatically appends a numeric suffix. For example, the second unnamed field will be Untitled2.

One of your first tasks should be to change the field name. A set of fields called Untitled, Untitled2, and Untitled3 would be pretty boring, not to mention rather hard to maintain and debug. An important part of application design is to have naming conventions for the various design elements.

NAMING FIELDS

When you create field names, you have great flexibility. You can call your fields just about anything you want, and they won't complain back at you. You can call one field Input, another Output, and a third TextField. The main characteristic of all three of these names is that they are terrible field names. They are valid and Domino won't complain, but they represent poor programming practice.

Officially, field names must begin with a letter, a dollar sign ($), or an underscore (_). Following the initial letter, names may use letters, numbers, a dollar sign ($), or an underscore (_). Names cannot contain spaces and can be up to 32 bytes. For single-byte character languages, this is the same as 32 characters. For multibyte languages, you can use only half as many characters.

Your field names should be meaningful in their context. For example, the field names LastName, FirstName, and PhoneNumber are much better names because you can almost immediately tell just from their variable names how these fields will be used. The field PhoneNumber is a little ambiguous, however. Is that field a numeric field or a character field? Well, it might be either. Normally, phone numbers are stored as text strings, but with the field name PhoneNumber, it becomes a little more ambiguous. What can you do?

Another convention that is becoming widespread is to add a suffix to the variable name and to use capitalization to help make the name easier to read. The suffix represents the data type of the variable; then the rest of the variable name follows. Here are some sample suffixes:

TX	Text field
NU	Numeric field
RT	Rich Text
DT	Date/time

Using these suffixes, the field names would become LastNameTX, FirstNameTX, and PhoneNumberTX. It does not really matter which conventions you use, but you should definitely find a naming convention for your entire organization and then standardize on this convention. By using one style of naming variables, you promote easier maintenance for your entire group. It becomes much easier for one person to read another person's code.

Naming conventions are also a simple, easy way to improve your productivity because you will spend less time trying to remember the data types of each of your variables. You really appreciate these conventions the most when you must maintain code someone else has written.

FIELD DATA TYPES

We've alluded to the fact that several different types of data can be stored in documents. The basic data types include text, Rich Text, date/time, and number values, but most data is stored as text. Several kinds of user interface elements (called *field types*) can be used to display and obtain information from users. In Figure 13.24, you see the various types of fields that can be used on a form. An icon on the lower-right side of the field shows its type.

Several field types can be used to display lists of information. User interface types for lists include a dialog list, a check box, a radio button, a list box, and a combo box. These field types typically store text information. Table 13.3 describes the various field types.

Figure 13.24
You can use many different types of fields on a form.

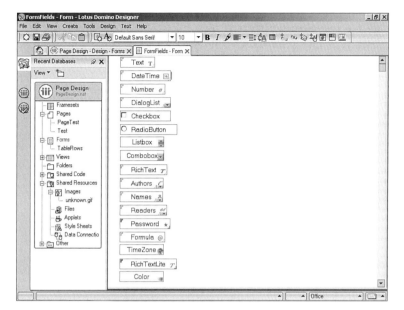

TABLE 13.3   FIELD DATA TYPES

Data Type	Description
Text	A text field can hold letters, numbers, and special characters. A designer can assign formatting attributes, such as bold or italic, to regular text fields. After this is set, the end user cannot change the formatting.
Date/Time	Date/time fields store date and time information. They can be displayed in a variety of formats, including date-only or time-only.
Number	Use number fields for storing numeric information that will be used in calculations.
Dialog list	A dialog list field displays a list of choices. It can optionally have a helper button so the user can choose one of a set of predefined values. You can specify the choices by formula or by typing them directly, or you can allow the user to add a choice not in the list.
Check box	You use a check box when you have a set of options and you want to allow the user to select zero, one, or more of the available options.
Radio button	Radio buttons are used with a set of selections when only one of the choices is allowed from the set.

continues

13

TABLE 13.3	**CONTINUED**
Data Type	**Description**
List box	A list box shows a scrollable list of choices. The list can contain predefined values or values specified by a formula, or you can allow the user to add a value that is not in the list.
Combo box	A combo box is similar to a list box, but it takes up less screen space. It is shown as a single line with a drop-down button. The user can click the button to reveal a list of choices. As with the other list options, you can predefine values, enter a formula, or allow the user to add values that are not in the list.
Rich Text	Rich Text fields enable the user to add formatting information such as bold and italics. These fields can also hold extra information, such as attachments, hotspots, document links, and tables. Rich Text fields cannot be displayed in views.
Authors	Authors fields basically affect users with Author-level ACL access. If a document contains an Authors field and the user's name is stored in it, the user is allowed to edit the document, even if that user did not originally create it. This type of field can be used by a designer to overcome the normal ACL restrictions for Author-level access.
Names	Names fields are used to store names when you don't need to associate rights such as Authors or Readers. You can use a Names type of field when you want to display the Notes name in a particular format.
Readers	The Readers field is used to control reading rights to users who otherwise would be able to read a document. If a Readers field exists and contains usernames, only users found within the field can read the document. Even if a user has Manager ACL privilege, if that user is not listed in the Readers field for the document, he cannot read it. This field refines ACL privileges.
Password	A Password field is used to show asterisks on the screen for data entry.
Formula	A Formula field is used to store the text value of a selection formula.
Time Zone	A Time Zone field is used to display a listing of all the time zones.
Rich Text Lite	A Rich Text Lite field is essentially a Rich Text field with a helper icon. The helper icon makes it quicker to add an object of a particular type to the field. For example, a user could use this type of field to embed a Microsoft Word document.
Color	A Color field gives users the ability to choose a Notes or RGB color. This displays a nice color chart and color picker.

EDITABLE AND COMPUTED FIELDS

In addition to the data type of the field, each field has an attribute of being editable or computed. Table 13.4 describes the types and what they mean.

TABLE 13.4	DESCRIPTION OF FIELD DATA TYPES
Data Entry	**Description**
Editable	In editable fields, the user can enter data directly into the field. This is the most common type of field.
Computed	The value of a computed field is determined by a formula. A user cannot enter data into the field; it is for output only. A computed field is re-evaluated whenever the form is created, refreshed, or saved. The computed value is saved in the document.
Computed When Composed	A Computed When Composed field is also specified by a formula. The formula is evaluated at the time the document is created, but it is never re-evaluated. The value is saved in the document.
Computed for Display	The value of a Computed for Display field is evaluated at the time the document is created or opened. It is re-evaluated whenever the document is saved or refreshed. Although the value is re-evaluated when the document is saved, the value of a Computed for Display field is not stored in the document. Another implication of this is that Computed for Display fields cannot be used in views because there is no value stored in the document.

OTHER FIELD ATTRIBUTES

When you create fields, you can specify many other attributes with the Field properties box. When you've highlighted these within Domino Designer, you can open the field properties by selecting Design, Field properties. You can specify several attributes dealing with the display of the field:

- **Allow Multiple Values**—This enables the field to accept multiple values. The values are stored internally as a list. This check box is particularly valuable with any of the list and name type fields.

- **Compute After Validation**—This check box applies only to computed fields. This is useful when a field is dependent upon other fields. If checked, the field is computed only after the validation occurs on other fields. Note that this option is not supported for Web browsers.

- **External Data Source**—This check box applies only when you want to connect to an external data source. Other options appear at the bottom of the dialog box when this field is checked.

- **Style: Notes Style/Native OS Style**—Notes style is the standard style for controls. Certain controls, such as the date/time controls, are supported only in the Notes client when the Native OS Style box is checked. Native OS style controls are not supported by Web browsers.

13

In addition to the basic properties just mentioned, the field properties box enables you to change the following attributes for fields:

- **Date/Time Formatting**—Several options on the Control tab of the Field properties box enable you to specify the style of date formats. For example, you can specify that you always want four-digit years, you want to use four-digit years for the 21st century only, or you want to show the year only when it is not this year. You can specify the order of the day of the week, and the numeric representation of the day, month, and year. When you show times, you can show hours, minutes, and seconds, and you can perform time zone adjustments. You can also require the user to enter four-digit years.

- **Number Format**—Located on the Control tab of the Field properties box, this enables you to specify numbers as decimals, percents, scientific numbers, or currency. You can control the number of decimal digits displayed, use parentheses when negative, and use punctuation at thousandths.

- **Help Description**—Located on the Advanced tab of the Field properties box, this enables you to specify a help text message for the field.

- **Multivalue Options**—Located on the Advanced tab of the Field properties box, this enables you to specify the separators that a user can use when entering multiple values. The choices are a space, a comma, a semicolon, a new line, and a blank line. This section also enables you to choose the separator used for display among multiple values in a multivalue field.

- **Security Options**—Located on the Advanced tab of the Field properties box, this enables you to sign the field, enable encryption, or require at least Editor access to use a field.

- **Font**—Located on the Font tab of the Field properties box, this enables you to specify a typeface, point size, and style for the field.

- **Alignment**—Located on the Paragraph Alignment tab of the Field properties box, this enables you to specify whether the field is left-aligned, right-aligned, centered, or justified. It also enables you to specify first-line indentation style, list styling (numbered, bulleted, and so forth), and paragraph spacing (single, one-and-a-half, double). Paragraph type can also be specified for right-to-left languages.

- **Hide Paragraph**—Located on the Paragraph Hide When tab of the Field properties box, this enables you to control hiding the paragraph from Notes clients or Web browsers. You also can control hiding when the document is previewed and opened for reading or editing. You can specify a formula that controls the hiding.

- **HTML**—Located on the Field Extra HTML tab of the Field properties box, this enables you to add the attributes of ID, Class, Style, or Title, as well as other extra HTML attributes. Some particularly useful attributes are SIZE and MAXLENGTH. When Domino converts the field to HTML, it converts it to an HTML <INPUT> field. The HTML SIZE parameter on an <INPUT> field specifies the width on the screen. The MAXLENGTH parameter specifies how many characters can be input into the field.

13

FIELD FORMULAS: DEFAULT VALUE, INPUT TRANSLATION, INPUT VALIDATION, AND INPUT ENABLED

Editable fields can have four special formulas associated with them: the Default Value, Input Translation, Input Validation, and Input Enabled formulas. All four of these optional formulas can be set in the Info List of the Programmer's pane after a field is highlighted within Domino Designer.

The Default Value formula provides an initial default value for the field. This enables the user to leave a field blank, and the application developer can specify the initial value.

The Input Translation and Input Validation formulas are run whenever a document is refreshed or saved. The Input Translation formula enables you to do processing that puts the data in a canonical format. In other words, you can capitalize words, trim leading and trailing blanks, and replace user input with codes that you look up.

After input translation is performed, the Input Validation formula is run. This formula evaluates to Success or Failure. If it is successful, the field passes validation. If it fails, the user is prompted with an error message that you provide and must edit the field to correct the problem.

A new field formula of Release 6 is the Input Enabled formula. This formula allows the designer to enable or disable a field based on the user's interaction with the form or field values. Like the other formulas, the formula evaluates to Success or Failure. If the Input Enabled formula evaluates to 0, the field is disabled and data cannot be added or removed. If the field evaluates to anything else, it fails and the user is allowed to edit and interact with the field.

NOTE

The Input Enabled field formula works only with fields that have a Native OS field style.

SINGLE-USE AND SHARED FIELDS

The most common type of field is called a *single-use field*; its definition is included with the form on which it is created. Sometimes, however, you want to define a field that will be used on several forms. In this case, you can create a *shared field*, which is a shared resource. Remember that here we are talking about the field definition itself, not any data that is stored within any documents. You do not need to use a shared field to share data within documents.

Shared field definitions enable you to define attributes of the field, such as its font, style, and, most important, its formula definitions. For example, suppose you want to create a field to be used for part numbers. You want to perform input translation and/or validation on the part numbers, so you specify formulas associated with the field. By making this field a shared field, you can use the part number entry field throughout your database, and the formulas will be shared.

13

You can easily create a shared field by creating a regular, single-use field and then converting it to a shared field.

To convert a single-use field into a shared field, select the field and then choose Design, Share This Field. To convert a shared field back into a single-use field, select the field and then choose Design, Convert to Single Use.

After you have created a shared field, you can use it on a form by following these steps:

1. Open the form you want to use for your shared field.

2. Move the cursor to the location where you want your shared field to appear.

3. Select Create, Resource, Insert Shared Field. The Insert Shared Field dialog box opens displaying the names of the available shared fields.

4. Select the desired shared field and click OK. Your shared field is inserted into the form.

CREATING FORM ACTIONS

Form actions are programs that can be implemented using predefined *simple actions*. Or, you can write your own custom actions in LotusScript, JavaScript, or the Formula language. Simple actions include modifying a field, copying a document to a database or folder, running an agent, and sending a mail message.

Actions, which are contained by the Action bar, can be invoked by clicking an action button in a form or view. The Action bar, if displayed, appears just above the document or view windows. Because the action buttons do not appear inside the window, they are independent of any scrolling of the document window itself. Actions can also be displayed in the Action menu.

You can associate actions with individual forms or views, or you can create shared actions. Shared actions are useful whenever you need to provide functions that might be common across several forms or views. Shared actions are found in the Design pane under Shared Code, Actions.

Six predefined actions are shown in the Action pane for a view. In previous versions, these same six actions were also on the form. In Release 6, these actions apply only to a view; the user can select one or more documents and apply the action to the selected documents. You find these actions by selecting Views from a database's design and creating a new view. The predefined actions within a view's action bar are listed here:

- **Categorize**—Enables a user to add and remove categories from a document being viewed or listed in a view. To use this feature, the form must have a keyword field named Categories.

- **Edit Document**—This enables editing of a document currently being viewed or listed in a view. This does not enable a user to override the ACL; it just provides a convenient method of putting the document into edit mode.

- **Send Document**—This sends the document to a user or mail-in database. The form must contain a SendTo field, and the value within the field supplies the destination.
- **Forward**—This forwards the document in an email message.
- **Move to Folder**—This moves the selected document(s) to a folder.
- **Remove from Folder**—This removes the selected document(s) from a folder.

In addition to the built-in actions, you can define your own actions. Programmer-defined actions can appear on the Action bar and/or the Action menu. In Figure 13.25, an action is defined called Light, Camera.

Figure 13.25
When you define your own actions, you can see them in the Action pane.

You can specify the action to take with a formula: Simple Action, LotusScript, or JavaScript program. The example uses LotusScript, and when the action button is clicked, a message box appears. In Figure 13.25, a standard Notes graphic is to be used instead of a custom one. You can specify a custom graphic button to appear in the action button by selecting one of the images from the images resources.

13

USING LAYOUT REGIONS

Layout regions provide you with a means to more precisely specify the layout of controls. When you use pages or forms, much of the layout of design elements is left up to the display program. In some ways, this is good because you can view the form from Notes clients and a variety of different Web browsers. Unfortunately, this does not give the form designer fine control over the presentation. For example, fields can move left or right, or they can expand and cause other fields to move.

Layout regions provide control so that input fields do not change in size and you can finely tune the appearance of your form. Layout regions have one major disadvantage, however. Layout regions cannot be shown in Web browsers, so anything you place in a layout region is visible only to Notes clients. If you are developing for both Notes clients and Web browsers, you should avoid layout regions. However, if you will be using only Notes clients, you can use layout regions.

To create a layout region in your form, follow these steps:

1. Open the form you want to use with your layout region.

2. Move your cursor to the location where you want your layout region to appear.

3. Choose Create, Layout Region, New Layout Region. As shown in Figure 13.26, a new layout region appears.

Figure 13.26
You can change the size and location of a layout region with the properties box.

You can change the size and move the layout region with the Layout properties box. The Left field enables you to adjust the left margin. The Width and Height properties enable you to change the size.

You can optionally show the border and change to 3D style. 3D style uses a gray background instead of a white one. You can also display a grid to make it easier to align controls. The Snap to Grid option automates some alignment tasks.

After you create the layout region, you can add elements. For all these elements, you must first highlight the layout region and then choose Create, Layout Region from the menu bar. The following are elements you can add to the region:

- **Static text**—You create static text by selecting Create, Layout Region, Text.

- **Graphic**—You can create a graphic image within a layout region. To do this, first copy the bitmap you want to use to the Clipboard. Then select Create, Layout Region, Graphic.

- **Graphic button**—You create a graphic button in a manner similar to a regular graphic. You must first copy the bitmap to the Clipboard and then select Create, Layout Region, Graphic Button. The main difference between a graphic button and a regular graphic is that the graphic button is considered a hotspot and has a `click` event, and a regular graphic object does not. You can program the graphic button with a simple action, a formula, LotusScript, or JavaScript. A graphic can overlay a graphic button or vice versa within a layout region.

NOTE

> Layout regions do not work in Web browsers, so even if you create a graphic button with JavaScript, your program will still work only in the Notes client, not in Web browsers. Instead of using layout regions, use layers to create content areas that can be precisely positioned. Unlike layout regions, layers work in both the Notes client and Web browsers.

- **Picture**—A "picture" is really nothing more than another name for a graphic or graphic button. If you choose Create, Picture, you can import a graphic from the file system. Using this method, you do not have to use cut and paste. After you choose Create, Picture, you are prompted for whether you want to paste your image as a graphic or a graphic button. Make your selection and click OK.
- **Field**—You create a field within a layout region by choosing Create, Field (with the layout region highlighted).

USING LAYERS

Layers, a new layout element of Release 6, enable you to precisely position content within a form, subform, or page. Unlike the previously discussed layout regions, layers work within both the Notes client and a Web browser. This new layout tool gives designers the ability to control the exact placement of areas of content by stacking layers upon each other. Figure 13.27 demonstrates a form with multiple layers within both the Notes client and a Web browser. In this example, some layers contain fields and sections that overlap each other.

To create a layer on your form, follow these steps:

1. Open the form you want to use with a layer.
2. Move your cursor to the location where you want your layout region to appear.
3. Choose Create, Layer.

13

You can change the size and move the layer with the Layer properties box. The Left and Top fields enable you to adjust the layer from the left and top margins. The Width and Height properties enable you to change the size. The Z-Index allows you to change the stack order of each layer.

You can optionally set the background color or image for each layer. You can also control the repeating of an image within a layer.

Figure 13.27
Layers can be a powerful way to lay out your form or page.

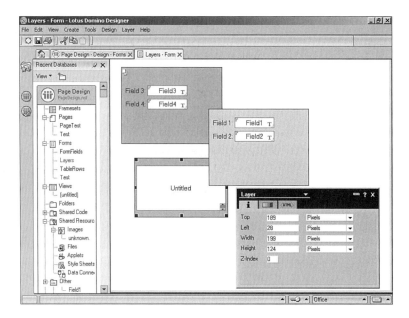

USING SUBFORMS

Subforms are a reusable component that can be embedded in several different forms. One typical application for a subform might be when you want to have common information (such as name and address) on a form, but you also want to have additional information (such as policy information) that varies depending upon the customer. In this case, the common information can be stored directly on the form, and variable information can be stored in a set of subforms. Domino can dynamically select the appropriate subform to use for the variable information. You can also use subforms for various adornments, such as headers or footers. The letterhead feature of your mail database is implemented using subforms.

On a subform, you can include any of the design elements that would normally be allowed in a form. The subform can be included in the form at the time you design the form, or the selection of the subform can be deferred until a document using the form is created. When the document is created, you can programmatically include the desired subform (as in your mail database), or you can ask the user to select a subform from a list that you provide.

To open or create a subform, follow these steps:

1. Open the Design pane in the database in which you want to create your subform.
2. Click the Shared Code section in the Design pane.
3. Click Subforms. A view showing you the existing subforms appears in the work area on the right.

4. If you are opening an existing subform, double-click its name in the Work pane. If you are creating a new subform, click the New Subform action button.

5. When your subform is open, you can use all the editing tools that were described for forms.

When you insert a subform based on a formula, it is called a computed subform. The formula is called the Insert Subform formula. This formula is computed when the form is opened and is not recomputed if the document is updated and refreshed. The formula must evaluate to a subform name. If the subform name does not exist, no error message is displayed; the subform simply does not appear.

USING SECTIONS ON FORMS

Earlier, we reviewed how you can use sections to organize the data on the page. Standard sections are also available on forms.

ACCESS-CONTROLLED SECTIONS

Forms have an additional type of section called the *access-controlled section*. Access-controlled sections are typically used in workflow applications in which a form can be routed but only particular individuals are allowed to approve the form. By controlling the access to these sections and by implementing signed fields (on the Field properties Options tab), you can ensure that only authorized individuals can approve the form. An access-controlled section controls the editing, not the reading of the information within it.

To create an access-controlled section, follow these steps:

1. Open the form to include your access-controlled section.

2. Add the text and fields to be included in your section.

3. Highlight all the text and fields to be included.

4. Choose Create, Section, Controlled Access. Your section appears. The first line of your text appears as the default title of your section. You can modify the title by using the Form Section properties box. The Form Section properties box has additional tabs. In the Formula tab, you supply an access formula. There are also tabs for editors and noneditors to control whether the section is expanded.

13

In access-controlled sections, you can define the access list as editable, which enables the document creator to specify who can edit the section. If you want to specify ahead of time who will be able to edit the section, you can supply an access formula. The formula can be made up of user, group, or role names, or you can use an @formula such as @DBColumn to populate the list.

CAUTION

Be careful with your use of access-controlled sections. Anyone with read access can read the contents of access-controlled sections. The access control applies only to the ability to edit the section. Also, the access control applies only to databases on a Domino server unless you have specified the option Enforce a Consistent ACL Across All Replicas of This Database in the database ACL. If this option is not selected in the ACL, anyone will be able to edit the section on a local replica of the database.

You can also specify the access formula via a `@DBColumn` lookup or via group names.

If you require two or more separate approvals for a form, you must use a separate section for each one. A single access-controlled section can have only one list of approvers.

13

CHAPTER 14

DEVELOPING VIEWS AND FOLDERS

In this chapter

ORGANIZING DOCUMENTS WITHIN YOUR DATABASES

Views and folders are a fundamental part of Notes and Domino. They enable both the designer and the user to organize documents within a Domino database. In essence, a view or folder provides a tabular display of selected fields from documents contained in a Domino database. You often see views and folders discussed at the same time because they are very similar. The major difference between views and folders is the criteria used to select documents to be shown.

Views can use a formula to select documents for display. The formula is typically written by an application designer and is generally used to filter the documents. Designers frequently use several different views in a database, each with a different formula. This enables the user to see various collections of documents, grouped and sorted in meaningful ways. Folders don't use formulas for their selection. The documents in folders are typically moved to the folder by an end user. In the mail database, for example, a user can create and use folders to organize email. The user can decide which documents to put into each folder.

Although we review view design in this chapter, folder design is essentially equivalent because of the similarities in view and folder design. The difference between folders and views is mainly the method used to select documents, not how they are designed.

CUSTOMIZING THE UNTITLED VIEW

A *view* is a tabular display of data extracted from a set of documents. Each row of the table represents one document, and the values in each column can be field data or can be based on a formula. Column formulas can combine data from multiple fields or can use @functions to compute their result. For the purposes of this example, let's create a new database from the Blank template. If you want to follow along, create a new Domino database on your local machine called View Design.

After you create your database, click the View's element grouping in the Design pane on the left. Your screen should be similar to Figure 14.1.

You might have noticed something very interesting when you opened the database. Although you created a blank database, you already have a view defined in your database. Domino always requires at least one view in your database, so even when you create a blank database, an initial view is created for you. You cannot open a database that does not have at least one view. To customize the Untitled view, follow these steps:

1. If you double-click the untitled line, you will see the default view, as shown in Figure 14.2. The default view, called Untitled, contains only a single column. The column appears with the number sign (#) in the column header.

Figure 14.1
The Views design element is selected in Domino Designer.

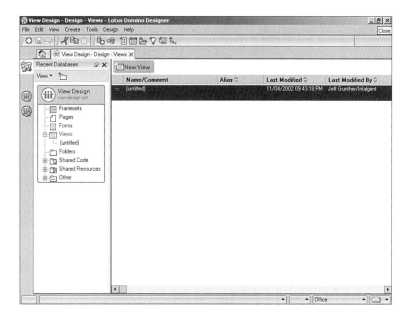

Figure 14.2
The Untitled view as initially created by Domino Designer.

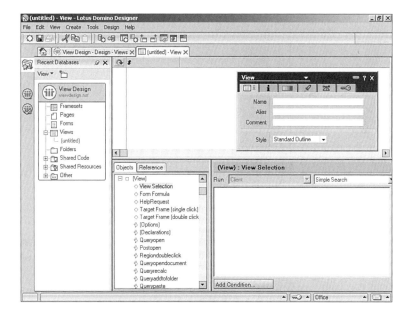

2. The first step in configuring a view is to set the View Selection criteria. In Figure 14.2, notice that the View Selection object appears within the Info List under the Objects tab.

14

TIP

> Review the topic titled "Exploring the Programmer's Pane" within Domino Designer Help for more information about how to access this area of Domino Designer.

The View Selection object is used to enter a simple search or formula for selecting documents that will be shown in the view. On the right half of the Programmer's pane is a drop-down list, and you can select either Simple Search or Formula. If you select Simple Search and then click the Add Condition button, you will see the Add Condition dialog box (see Figure 14.3).

Figure 14.3
The Add Condition dialog box appears if you choose Simple Search for a View Selection.

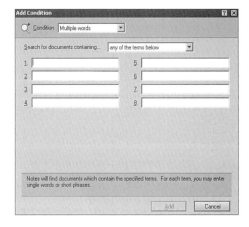

The Condition drop-down box shows various options to build search criteria.

You can choose documents by the following conditions in the Add Condition dialog box:

- **By Author**—The author name for the document must contain text that you supply.
- **By Date**—You can specify the date the document was created or last modified. You can choose a specific date, a date older or newer than a particular date, or a date within or outside a date range.
- **By Field**—As in the example, you can enter specific text. The text must be contained in the field you name. A string comparison is made, so the field should be a text field.

NOTE

> The Add Condition dialog box displays only field names that exist on forms within your database. If you have not yet defined any forms (and, thus, have no fields), you will not be able to use some of the features within the dialog box. In keeping with this example, you must create a form called Car with two fields: Car and Color. If you do this, they will show up in the Add Condition dialog box. Normally in your design process, you will design and build your forms before building your views.

14

- **By Form**—A shorthand for multiple By Field specifications. When you select this option, a data entry field shows for all fields contained on the form. You can enter data for all the fields or some subset of them all at once.

- **Fill Out Example Form**—This particular option searches for documents that match a completed form that you fill out.

- **In Folder**—When you select this option, all documents within a particular folder are selected.

- **Multiple Words**—This searches for specific words within the documents. You can enter multiple words and select a condition for matching.

After you've created a condition within the Add Condition dialog box and clicked the Add button, the condition appears in the right side of the Programmer's pane. Each of the conditions appears as a small button within the pane. To edit a condition you have already entered, you can double-click the button (see Figure 14.4).

Figure 14.4
Each of the conditions has a separate small button within the Programmer's pane.

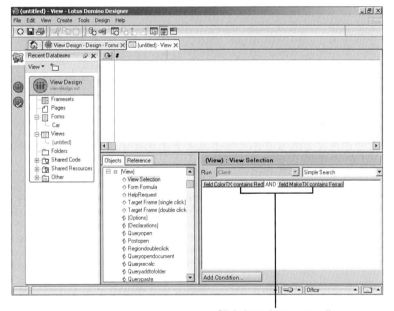

Click these buttons to edit

To select documents by formula, select Formula in the Run drop-down box. If you do not modify the formula, you can also switch from Simple Search to Formula to see the formula that Domino Designer has created for you.

If you become proficient with the Formula language, you might prefer to use formulas because they are much more powerful than the Add Condition functions.

14

→ **See** Chapter 18, "Working with Formulas, Functions, and Commands," **p. 465** for more detailed coverage of the Formula language.

CREATING A NEW VIEW

In this chapter, we primarily focus on reviewing view design, but folder design is essentially equivalent. To create a new view, follow these steps:

1. Click the Views design element on the left. In the right pane, click the New View button to open the Create View dialog box.

2. As shown in Figure 14.5, give the folder a name and select the type of folder from the Folder Type field.

Figure 14.5
Several types of views exist.

You cannot change the type after the view has been created. Views are categorized into *shared views* and *private views*. Multiple people can use shared views, but private views are restricted to a single user. Several types of shared views exist, including these:

- **Shared**—Shared views are the most common type of view. Shared views are available to users with at least Reader access to the database. Editor-level users with the privilege Create Shared Folders/Views enabled in the ACL can create shared views. Otherwise, you must have Designer- or Manager-level access to create a shared view.

- **Shared, Contains Documents Not in Any Folders**—A view of this type shows all the documents that have not been placed by a user in a folder. You can use this type of view for an inbox-type application in which you want the document to disappear from the inbox if the user moves it to a folder. After it appears in a folder, it automatically disappears from the inbox.

- **Shared, Contains Deleted Documents**—This type of view is used to support soft deletions. Soft deletions enable you to implement a "Trash" type of folder where documents can temporarily be stored but later recovered, if desired. To use this type of folder, you must also enable soft deletions in the Advanced tab (beanie hat) of the Database Properties Advanced dialog box.

- **Shared, Private on First Use**—These views provide an opportunity for a designer to deliver customized views to end users. For example, you could use the @UserName function in the view selection so that only a single user's data appears in the view. Each user sees different data, and after a user has used the view, it becomes private. A disadvantage of this setting is that after a view becomes private, users no longer see updates made in the shared version. If you add or delete columns or change formulas in the shared version, the user cannot see the changes if the view already became private. This type of view is stored in the database unless the Create Personal Folders/Views ACL setting for the user is disabled. In this case, the view is stored in DESKTOP.DSK.

- **Shared, Desktop Private on First Use**—This type of view is the same as Private on First Use, except that the view is stored in the user's DESKTOP.DSK file. The reason for storing the view in DESKTOP.DSK is that if you have a lot of users, the database could become very large if each user's private view is stored in the common database.

- **Private**—Users, not designers, create private views. Private views can be used to sort and organize data in a personal way without affecting the operation of the database for other users. You might see some documentation refer to personal views, but private views and personal views are just two names for the same thing.

NOTE

> The Access Control List (ACL) for a database contains a setting called Create Personal Folders/Views. This setting can be either enabled or disabled. If you disable this setting, it does *not* mean that the user is prevented from creating private (personal) folders and views. A user of Reader level and above can always create a private view or folder. The ACL setting enables or disables the user from creating the private view within the database. If the setting is disabled, the private views and folders are stored in the user's DESKTOP.DSK file on the local machine.
>
> Also, Web browsers cannot view private views, whether they are created initially as private or they are initially shared and become private. If you want to make a customized view (similar to a shared-to-private view) accessible to Web browsers, you might be able to use a feature called a Single Category embedded. This feature is described later in this chapter.

3. Select a location for your new view within the view hierarchy. Select the parent view of where you want your view to appear.

4. A default set of columns is copied from the view, shown as the Copy Style from View field. If you want to choose a different view or start from a blank view, click the Copy From button. The Copy Style From dialog box, shown in Figure 14.6, enables you to choose your template.

5. Click OK to save your new view, or click the Save and Customize button to create your view and enter edit mode for your newly created view.

14

Figure 14.6
The Copy Style From dialog box enables you to use an existing view as a template.

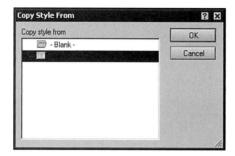

VIEW COLUMN PROPERTIES

After you specify the documents you want selected in your view (via the View Selection formula), you must define the fields and information that you want to show in your view. Each row of your view represents one document of the database, and the values in the columns are information extracted from those documents. Frequently, a column holds the value from a single field. However, you can include other types of information.

VIEW COLUMN BASICS

Each view column has several attributes besides the definition of the data to be shown. Figure 14.7 shows the default view formula and the Properties box for the default view column.

Figure 14.7
A column can be defined by a simple function, field, or formula.

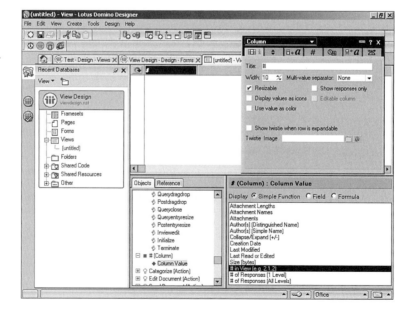

As you can see, the title of the column is found in the Properties box and is a simple number sign (#). In the Programmer's pane at the bottom of the window, you see that the column value of the # column is highlighted in the left half of the pane, and a simple function appears in the right half of the pane.

You can define a column's contents with a simple function. The functions can be information, such as attachment lengths or names, authors, creation or modification dates, or document number within the view. To specify a simple function, follow these steps:

1. Open the view containing the column you want to modify.

2. Click the column object's column value in the left half of the Programmer's pane at the bottom of the window. Alternatively, you can double-click the column header of the column that you want to modify in the View pane at the top of the window.

3. In the right half of the Programmer's pane, select Simple Function in the Display radio button group. If you had previously selected a different option, a warning might be displayed that your previous definition will be lost.

4. In the list box, select the simple function you want to use.

As an alternative to a simple function, you can define a column to contain a field value from a document. To use a document field as a column value, follow these steps:

1. Open the view containing the column you want to modify.

2. Click the column object's column value in the left half of the Programmer's pane at the bottom of the window. Alternatively, you can double-click the column header of the column that you want to modify in the View pane at the top of the window.

3. In the right half of the Programmer's pane, select Field in the Display radio button group. If you had previously selected a different option, a warning might be displayed that your previous definition will be lost.

4. In the list box, select the field name you want to use.

Finally, you can use a formula as the definition for what to display in a column. To use a formula, follow the steps for simple function or field, but click the Formula radio button instead. Type the formula in the area below the radio buttons.

To modify properties other than the value, you use the Column Properties box. You can specify the width of the column by typing a value into the width box, by clicking the up or down arrows next to the width value, or by dragging the column separator in the view header on the right side of the column you want to modify.

ADDING AND REMOVING VIEW COLUMNS

Adding and removing columns is pretty easy within Domino Designer. To append a column at the right side of your view, you can choose Create, Append New Column. Alternatively, you can double-click the column header to the right of the last column. This creates a new column and brings up the Properties box for the newly created column.

To insert a new column in the middle of the view, select the column to the right of the location where you want the new column, and then choose Create, Insert New Column. You can use this technique to insert a new column as the first column.

To delete a column, click the header of the column and click the Del key. Alternatively, you can click the header of the column and then choose Edit, Cut. Either technique prompts you with a warning that you are about to permanently delete a column. You can select multiple columns for deletion by clicking the header of the first and then holding down the Ctrl key and selecting the other columns. Click the Del key or use the menus after you have selected all the columns you want to delete.

DOCUMENT TYPES AND HIERARCHIES

When forms and documents were introduced in the previous chapter, we didn't discuss any of the different types of documents because they are a bit hard to understand until you understand the concept of views. Well, here we are in the midst of views, so let's retrace our steps a bit and talk about the different kinds of documents and how they can be displayed in views.

You can create three kinds of documents with a form:

- **Document**—A normal, regular, ordinary document. It can contain text fields and all the other goodies I have showed you. This is also sometimes called a *main document*.
- **Response**—A special kind of document that is a response to a main document. It is differentiated because within a view, a response document can be shown indented under its parent main document.
- **Response to Response**—A special kind of response that can be either a response to a main document or a response to a response.

When you create a form, you specify the type of document you want associated with the form. You make your selection in the Form Properties box (see Figure 14.8).

When a response document is created, you can have the response document inherit values from its parent document. Typically, the parent document and the response document both have some fields in common. By inheriting the values from the parent document at the time the response document is created, the user's job is easier because some fields automatically are filled in.

To enable inheritance of fields on response documents from the parent documents, you use the Form Properties box on the Defaults tab (see Figure 14.9). After you enable inheritance on the response document, you must also create a formula on each field that you want to be inherited from the parent document. Thus, you can control inheritance for selected fields only.

14

Figure 14.8
You select the document type in the Form Properties box.

Figure 14.9
You can enable inheritance by selecting an option in the Response document's form properties.

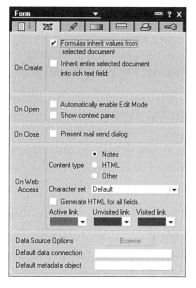

To illustrate these concepts, you might want to review the standard Discussion template that ships with Lotus Domino. In this database, a main topic can have many response and response-to-response documents. Figure 14.10 demonstrates a sample discussion database with a few main topics and response documents.

14

Figure 14.10
Views can show response documents below their parent document.

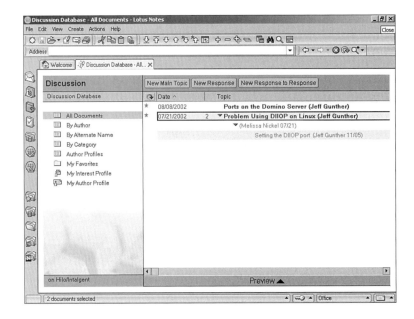

In Figure 14.10, only the first two lines are main documents. The third line is a response document and the fourth line is a response-to-response document. A response document displays differently from main documents because it is typically formatted via a formula contained within a single column. During the development of your own applications, you should perform the following steps to display the responses in proper order:

1. Define a column (typically only width 1) to the left of your first data column. This column does not need to have a title. Typically, it doesn't because there is no need to show anything in the title line.

2. Enable the Show Responses Only check box for this column. When this check box is enabled, the other column definitions will not apply for this row, so you need to define your output for the line via a formula. The output can extend to the width of the entire view. Typically, you'll want to include summary information, such as the document author, the date, and perhaps a title field.

3. Enable the Show Twistie When Row Is Expandable check box. This enables the user to expand and collapse the rows of the view.

You might be wondering about the difference between regular response documents and response-to-response documents. At the time you create a response document of either type, the outcome depends upon two things: the type of document selected (main or response) and the type of form used to create the new response document. If the row selected is a main document, then if you create either type of response, the result is a document that shows up immediately below the selected main document.

If the selected document is any type of response and you create a new response, you get two different results, depending upon the type of document you create. If you create a response to response, your new document is shown directly underneath your selected document, pretty much as you would expect.

If the selected document is any type of response and you create a regular response document, it appears immediately below the corresponding main document, not indented from the selected document.

SORTING A VIEW COLUMN

After you define the contents of your view, you might want to sort the documents based on certain columns. Although it's not absolutely required, it's recommended that if you sort, you use your leftmost columns. These are the columns that people will see first, and if they are ordered, it will be more obvious. Certain @functions, such as @DBColumn, also work based on the first sorted column; if you keep them to the left, it will be easier to remember and maintain these functions.

In Figure 14.11, you see the sorting options with the Column Properties box. Remember that you can double-click on the column header of the column to display this Properties box. The first option is the direction of sort, either Ascending or Descending. If you sort multiple columns, they can be in different directions. The leftmost column has the highest precedence, and the columns are sorted from left to right.

Figure 14.11
You can sort and total by column using the Column Properties box.

A Categorized column enables the documents to be sorted by a special field contained in the document named Categories. This field should be defined as a text field (or one of the list fields, such as a dialog list or a combo box), and you might also want to enable multiple values.

For example, if several documents contain the value Sales in a field called Categories, these documents will be shown together if the Sort column is categorized.

A user can enter two or more values into the Categories field. The user typically does this by checking multiple items in a dialog list box. For example, suppose a user enters **Sales**, **Contests** as the two values. If the Show Multiple Values as Separate Entries check box is

14

enabled, the document will show up twice within the view: once under the category Sales and a second time under the category Contests.

When you make a categorized view, a special category line is created automatically for each category. The documents within the category are shown underneath the appropriate category line. The Categories field itself is not shown within the document line. Sometimes, however, you want the category to appear as a regular field within the document line instead of a separate line. You can check the Categorized Is Flat Version 5 or Greater option. This shows the Categories field as a regular field within the document line, even if the Show Twistie When Row Is Expandable option is enabled.

If you enable case-sensitive sorting, capital letters are sorted before lowercase letters. Accent-sensitive sorting is an option for languages other than English. Sorting is dependent upon the current language being used on the workstation.

When you enable the Click on Column Header to Sort option (see Figure 14.12), additional options are available in the Properties box. You can choose Ascending, Descending, Both, or Change to View.

Figure 14.12
You can let the user choose the sort method.

If you choose Ascending, Descending, or Both, little triangles appear on the column header when the user uses the view. The ascending sort is signified by a triangle pointing up. If the user clicks this triangle, the documents are sorted in ascending order by the values in the column. A descending sort works similarly. When Both is specified, the user can choose either ascending or descending sorting.

The Secondary Sort column option enables you to choose another column for secondary sorting. The current column is sorted first; then within each identical value of the primary column, the documents are sorted by the value contained in the secondary column.

The Change to View option implements a hyperlink to another view if the column header is clicked. For example, suppose that the primary view is a summary view showing high-level information. Occasionally, users want to see details for a particular document. Columns could contain the Change to View option, and each column could go to a different detailed view. When the user clicks a particular column heading, the view changes and the new view

14

shows the same document (but with different fields displayed) that was selected in the primary view. This enables you to extract different, perhaps more detailed, information from the same document.

SORTING BY A HIDDEN COLUMN

Sometimes you want to display information sorted by a field that you don't want to show. For example, suppose you have a view column that contains days of the week: Sunday, Monday, Tuesday, and so forth. The typical sort for this would be in order of the days of the week, but with regular sorting, you get this list in alphabetical order, which is not particularly useful.

To sort the days of the week in their weekday order, you can use a hidden column. Within the hidden column, you can specify a custom sorting formula (see Figure 14.13).

Hide column checkbox

Figure 14.13
A formula and a hidden column can change the sort order.

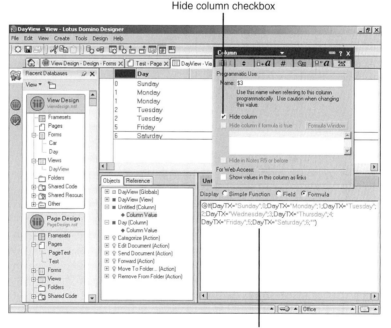

Column sorting formula

In Figure 14.13, you can see the value of the column as it is calculated by the formula. The formula is specified in the programmer's pane at the bottom-right side of the window. It basically converts a day of the week into a number. You then specify the sorting for the hidden column and leave sorting unspecified in the actual day column. After you hide the column using the check box with the ColumnProperties box, the user sees only the view starting with the day column, which is sorted in the proper order by day of the week.

14

USING ICONS IN VIEW COLUMNS

Many times, applications use icons to display status. In Figure 14.14, you see the standard mail database inbox. The highlighted line contains a paper clip. This is a fairly standard way to denote a file attachment. One of the other lines contains an exclamation point to indicate an important message.

Figure 14.14
Column icons can display status information very compactly.

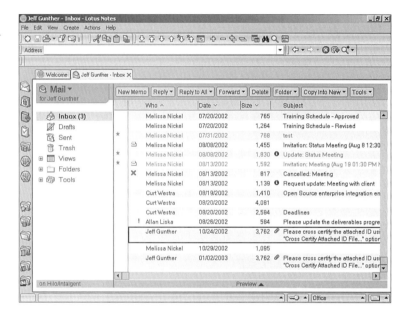

Let's explore how you can incorporate your own paper clips, exclamation points, and other icons into your views.

Domino has 176 valid predefined icons. Figure 14.15 shows a table of available icons. Look through the table to find the icon that you want to use, and then look to the left and to the top. Add the two numbers. For example, to use the smiley face, look to the left—you see 80. Look at the top of the column—you see ×5. So, the value to use is 85.

In addition to the predefined icons, Release 6 has added the capability for you to define your own column icons. In previous releases, you were able to use only the predefined icons that Lotus shipped with Notes and Domino. To use your own icon in a column, you first need to create the image and then import the file as an image resource. Lotus recommends that a column icon be 0.2 inches wide and 0.18 inches high. Like other image resources, images can be a JPG, GIF, or BMP file.

Figure 14.15
Notes/Domino has 176 valid predefined icons.

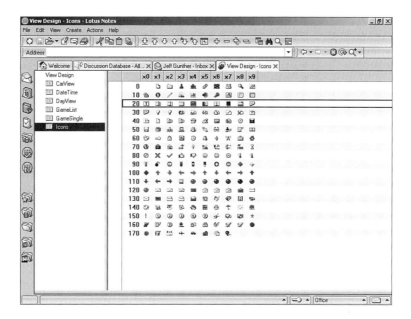

To use an icon in a column, follow these steps:

1. Open the view that you want to contain the icon.

2. Select the column that you want to contain the icon, and open the Column Properties box. You can do this with the Properties SmartIcon or by choosing Design, Column Properties.

3. In the Column Properties box, adjust the width of the column. A width of one to three characters is probably appropriate.

4. Select the Display Values as Icons option in the Column Info tab.

5. If you're using a predefined icon, set the column value to a number. You can use a number from 0 to 176. Zero displays no icon. Otherwise, if you're using a custom icon, set the column's value to the image's name. Simply type the filename or resource alias into the column's formula. For example, if you had an image resource with the filename person.gif and an alias of person, you could use either person.gif or person in the column's formula. Figure 14.16 demonstrates an example of using a custom icon in a column.

FORMATTING FONTS IN A VIEW COLUMN

When you create and edit view columns, you have a lot of control over the formatting of the column. First, you have control over the fonts used within the column itself. Figure 14.17 shows the various font options within the ColumnProperties box's Font tab.

14

Figure 14.16
Custom icons can be used in the view columns.

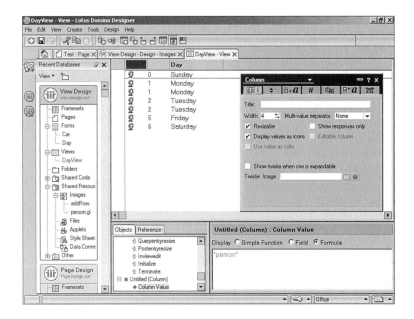

Figure 14.17
You can control the font face, size, and style used within view columns.

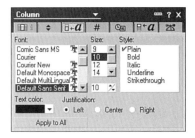

Within the Font (the third going from left to right) tab, you control the fonts for the column; within the Title (next-to-last) tab, you can control the fonts for the title line.

As with most windowing programs, you can control the font face (name), its size, and the style (plain, bold, italic, and so forth). You can also choose the justification within the column as left, center, or right. If you click the Apply to All button at the bottom of the dialog box, your change applies to all the view's columns. Before you choose a wild font, however, take into consideration whether your application will be used on the Web by Web browsers. If so, you should probably choose from the generic font families that you can use with Domino. These three are Default Serif, Default Sans Serif, and Default Monospace. These translate into commonly used fonts, such as Times Roman (Times), Helvetica, and Courier. One of the most vexing problems in Web development today is the use of fonts.

14

NOTE

When HTML was originally conceived, its purpose was to mark up the content of the Web page with the semantic meaning of the page. In other words, it was to inform the browser about titles, headers, links, and so forth.

Well, you can imagine the clash that developed because Web site developers also wanted to control the look and feel of their Web sites. The ongoing debate is still not totally resolved yet, although the major way for Web developers to gain back some control is to use Cascading Style Sheets (CSS). It's far too complex for me to explain this technology here, but if you are interested, pick up Molly Holzschlag's book *Special Edition Using HTML and XHTML*.

Of course, if the views you developed will be used just by Notes clients, you can use fonts as you please, as long as you make sure that the fonts are available on the client machines.

FORMATTING NUMBERS IN A VIEW COLUMN

Figure 14.18 shows the Numbers tab in the View Column Properties box.

Figure 14.18
You can control the formatting of numbers with the View Column Properties box.

For numeric formatting, the display of numbers depends on the precision level of the field. Leading zeros are suppressed. If you use fixed formatting, each number is formatted with a fixed number of decimal places that you can specify. With scientific formatting, numbers are displayed in scientific notation. Currency displays the currency symbol and two digits after the decimal.

You can also show values as percentages that will display a value that is 100 times the numeric value. You can add parentheses to negative values by checking that box, and you can punctuate at thousands.

The punctuation for the currency symbol, the decimal character, and the punctuation at thousands varies, depending upon the international language used.

14

FORMATTING DATES IN A VIEW COLUMN

Figure 14.19 shows the Date and Time Form tab in the View Column Properties box that controls the display of date formatting.

Figure 14.19
You can format date/time values to show both the date and the time or just one of the two.

This tab enables you to choose to display both date and time (as shown in column 1 of the view), just dates (column 2), or just times (column 3). The date format itself can be month/day, month/year, month/day/year, or month/4-digit year.

Time values can be hours:minutes or hours:minutes:seconds. Time zones can automatically be adjusted to the local time zone and can show the time zone in the display.

PROGRAMMATIC COLUMN NAME

In the Advanced tab of the Column Properties box, you see a section titled Programmatic Use (see Figure 14.20). In this section, you can specify a name for the column. If the column contains a field, the default value for the column name is the field name. If the view column contains an expression, the name automatically is construed by Notes to be of the format $n. For example, you might see names such as $0, $1, or $2.

Figure 14.20
The Advanced tab of the Column Properties box enables you to change the column name and specify links.

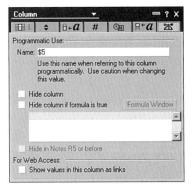

14

Although you can change the name for the column, you will rarely need to do so. The name that you specify can be obtained in LotusScript via the `ItemName` property of the `NotesViewColumn` class. In Java, you can access the name via the `getItemName` method of the `ViewColumn` class.

CAUTION

> You should use caution when changing the column name: If the column contains a field, you rarely would want another name for the column. Also, if the column contains a formula, the formula is compiled and stored internally within Domino, and it can be internally referenced. Thus, names such as `$0` and `$1` can be used within the database, and changing them could have unpredictable results.

SHOWING VALUES AS LINKS

When Domino displays a view in HTML to a browser, it normally highlights the first column with tags to link to the document. Sometimes, however, you want to highlight a column other than the first column as your link column. You can do this on the Advanced tab of the Columns Properties box.

To enable this feature, first highlight the column that you want to use for linking. Then in the Advanced (beanie hat) tab, enable the option For Web Access: Show Values in This Column as Links. You can enable more than one column; in this case, all of the columns that you specify are highlighted, but they all open the same document.

VIEW PROPERTIES

In addition to the properties that can be adjusted for each column, the view itself has properties. Figure 14.21 shows the View Properties box.

Figure 14.21
The View Info tab of the View Properties box enables you to give an alias and a comment for a view.

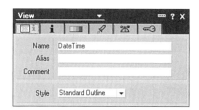

Besides the view name, you can specify an alias for a view. The alias name is simply another name for the view. Typically, you use the original form or view name as the initial alias name. As you develop applications for Notes and Domino, you might find that they always need to be changed and updated. As a result of these changes, the names that you give to design elements might also change. When you make changes to view and form names, however, you don't want to have to go back and change all references to the new names. If you make all internal references to the alias name within your application, you can change the view's name as frequently as you like.

If you enclose the view name (not the alias) in parentheses, the view becomes hidden. You can use it for @DBColumn and @DBLookup formulas, but it will not be shown to the user.

The Comment field of the View Info tab is used to enter a comment for the view. This comment appears just below the name of the view when you are reviewing all your views within Domino Designer.

The view style can either be Standard Outline or a Calendar view. All the views so far in this chapter have been Standard Outline views. A Calendar view enables you to display a calendar. Documents that are displayed in the view can be placed on the calendar in a manner similar to that used in the calendar found in your mail database.

Calendar views are fairly restricted in their format. Table 4.1 shows the layout for Calendar views.

TABLE 14.1   COLUMNS USED WITHIN A CALENDAR VIEW

View Column	Contents
1	Date/Time, hidden, sorted. This contains the start date.
2	Numeric, hidden. Duration of calendar entry, in minutes.
3	Time value, not hidden. This displays the start time of the calendar entry.
4	Integer numeric, icon, not hidden. This displays an icon in the calendar. It is typically used to signify the type of calendar entry.
5	Text, not hidden. This is the text to display in the calendar entry.

If you create a Calendar view with these types of columns, you can display it with the Calendar view style. You might find this useful in certain applications when you want to display dates, times, and durations.

VIEW OPTIONS

As shown in Figure 14.22, several view options can be enabled on the Options tab for the View Properties box.

Figure 14.22
The View Options tab enables you to choose various options for the view.

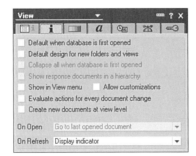

Here are the options:

- **Default When Database Is First Opened**—This option makes the current view the default view. In the view list, a solid arrow indicates that this view is the default. You can have only one default view for the database. If you enable the option for one view, it disables any previous selection on a different view.

- **Default Design for New Folders and Views**—When a new view is created, the current view serves as a model for the newly created view. The newly created view starts out with the same column definitions. If you will have several similar views in a database, you can create one, set this option, and then create the others. This will save you some time in the view-creation process.

- **Collapse All When Database Is First Opened**—This option collapses any twisties that group a set of documents. Setting this option makes the initial view more compact and perhaps easier to work with for the user.

- **Show Response Documents in a Hierarchy**—You previously saw how to create hierarchical response documents. For this feature to work, you must enable this option. If you do not enable the option, each column will show its own data rather than use the formula specified in the response column.

- **Show in View Menu**—This option displays the name of the view in the View menu for users. If you enable this option, it gives your users another way to navigate to the view. Normal navigation is via the Navigator pane, but if you are using a graphic navigator, you might want to also enable the View menu option.

- **Allow Customizations**—This option allows Notes clients to customize the view for their particular needs. These changes are maintained for users between uses of the view. If this field is not enabled, only the user's sorting preferences are maintained. This individual option is applicable only to Notes client users.

- **Evaluate Actions for Every Document Change**—When a view is opened, certain actions or events are evaluated. These actions can include hide/when formulas and other view computations. By enabling this field, a view's actions are re-evaluated if a document changes. Although this is a nice feature, you should use this option sparingly in your applications. As you can expect, this feature can lead to performance issues if the view contains a large number of documents.

- **Create New Documents at View Level**—In Release 6, users can quickly create a new document at the view level without opening a form. Similar to how a spreadsheet works, this feature allows users to interact with each column, adding, modifying, or removing data.

At the bottom of the Options tab are two more options, On Open and On Refresh. Here are the choices for these two options:

- **On Open**—The choices are Go to Last Opened Document, Go to Top Row, and Go to Bottom. When the view is first opened, it is positioned to the document you specify here.

14

■ **On Refresh**—The choices are Display Indicator, Refresh Display, Refresh Display from Top Row, and Refresh Display from Bottom Row. This option controls the action taken when new documents are available for the view. These options apply only to the Notes client because Web browsers do not have an indicator.

VIEW STYLE PROPERTIES

As shown in Figure 14.23, the style properties for the view can be found in the Style tab of View Properties box. Lotus has given designers a nice new set of features to enhance a view's display and appearance.

Figure 14.23
The Style tab enables you to control visual aspects of the view.

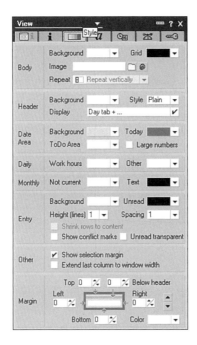

The Style tab of the View Properties box for standard views has four major groupings:

■ **Body**—These options enable you to define the overall appearance of the view. Options include the ability to add a background color or an image for the view's background. If you choose a color, you can select from the 256-color palette or select from the custom color palette. If you choose an image, you can control the repeat pattern similar to other design elements.

■ **Grid**—With Release 6, a view can now have a grid for display. This grid, similar to a spreadsheet, provides users with an easy way to follow rows of data across a screen. Just like the background, a custom color can be selected from a 256-color palette or color wheel.

14

- **Header**—These fields enable you to customize the style and color of the column headers. The Style field changes only the format of the displayed headings. This option works in both the Notes client and browsers.

- **Rows**—The Date Area, Daily, Monthly, and Entry field groupings allow complete control of the appearance of rows within a view. The Unread field in the Entry grouping enables you to customize the color of unread documents in a view. If you are using unread rows as a design feature of your database, you might want to choose a color that dramatically highlights them. You can choose from the 256-color palette for this option.

- **Other**—Included in the Other grouping are two fields: Show Selection Margin and Extend Last Column to Window Width. The Show Selection Margin option affects only the Notes client and Web browsers when using the Java view applet (described shortly). If you use a Web browser without the Java view applet, the option is ignored. This option enables a column of icons to the left of your view. This column displays unread marks, user selection, replication or save conflicts, and deleted marks. Normally, you should leave this option enabled. The Extend Last Column to Window Width field allows the contents of the rightmost column of a view to extend past the column bounds. If it is not enabled, the rightmost column contents are truncated at the column bound, even if there is more room in the window.

- **Margins**—With Release 6, a view can now have a margin around the display. This margin allows you to define a margin for the top, bottom, left, and right sides of the view. The margins can also have a background that can be selected from the color palette or color wheel.

VIEW FONT PROPERTIES

The View Font tab, which appears only if the view style is Calendar, enables you to control the font type, size, and style. Figure 14.24 demonstrates the Font tab of the View Properties dialog box.

Figure 14.24
The Font tab enables you to control the formatting of various time slots and groupings.

VIEW DATE AND TIME FORMAT PROPERTIES

The Date and Time Format tab of the ViewProperties box, which appears only if the view style is Calendar, enables you to selectively choose the calendar formats and time slot formatting options. For example, if the view's style is a calendar, you can control whether users can navigate according to one day, two days, the work calendar, one week, two weeks, or one month. Figure 14.25 demonstrates the Date and Time Format tab with all calendar formats available to users.

Figure 14.25
The Date and Time tab enables you to control how calendars and time slots are presented to users.

VIEW ADVANCED PROPERTIES

The Advanced tab (with the beanie hat) of the ViewProperties box, as shown in Figure 14.26, enables you to change the view index settings, the handling of unread marks, the view's form formula, and ODBC and Web access options. The first two options deal with a view's index.

Figure 14.26
The Advanced tab enables you to modify some important options, such as applet usage.

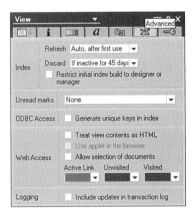

Refer to Figure 14.26 for the next few sections.

THE VIEW INDEX

Each view has an associated index that is used for displaying the view. This index is different from a full-text index. The view index options that you set in the Advanced tab of the View

Properties box control when this index is created and when it is deleted. The view index has important performance and usability considerations:

- If the view index is out-of-date with respect to the documents it displays, the user will see out-of-date information.

- The view index can take considerable time to build, especially for large databases. If it is built frequently, users might have to wait a long time for it to be built before they can see the view.

- The view index takes significant space in the database. If you build it but it is not used, you might be requiring too much space in your database for data that is not needed.

Because of these important considerations, it is not possible for Domino to guess what type of refresh strategy to use for all views in all databases. This job must be left to the designer and should be based on the usage pattern of the database and the type and frequency of change of the data shown in the view.

Each view can have separate settings, so in some databases you might have different strategies for different views. Here are your choices:

- **Auto, After First Use**—In this case, no index is built until the view is used at least once. Thereafter, it is updated automatically as in the Automatic setting listed next. When you use this option, users might notice a delay when the view is first used, due to the creation of the index. Use this option for databases that can be used in cycles. For example, a database might be used frequently for some time but then not used for some time. While it is being used, the index is updated automatically, but when it isn't being used, automatic deletion discards the index, and it won't appear until the view is used again.

- **Automatic**—This option always keeps the view updated. As documents are added, the view index is incrementally updated. This option updates the index even if no users are using the database. Because the index is always up-to-date, users will not notice a delay to build the index when the view is first used. Use this option for views that will be frequently used.

- **Manual**—This option does not update the view until the user requests it. It is most useful for views containing a large number of documents that do not change frequently.

- **Auto, at Most Every *n* Hours**—With this option, you must also specify a time limit in hours. This option limits the frequency of view index updates. If you use the default—12 hours, for example—the view is updated no more frequently than 12 hours since the last update. Use this option for databases in which changes are slow. Suppose, for example, that you had only one document change every 3 hours. By limiting the view index update to once every 12 hours, you can group the 4 changes into 1 view index update. Remember that users can also manually update the view at any time, if they desire.

14

The Discard index options control when the view index is deleted. This is a trade-off of space for time. The space taken by the view index is considered against the time the user must wait while the index is constructed. The discarding is actually done on the Domino server by default at 2 a.m. by the server task UPDALL. The discard index options are listed here:

- **If Inactive for 45 Days**—The index is eligible to be discarded after 45 days. After the UPDALL server task runs, the index will be deleted. This option is the default for new views.
- **After Each Use**—This option flags the view as eligible to be discarded as soon as it is closed. It is not actually discarded until the next time the UPDALL server task runs. Use this option for infrequently used databases.
- **If Inactive for _n_ Days**—This option is a compromise between the "never" and "always" options just described. You can specify a time limit, and if the view has not been used during that time, the view index will be discarded the next time UPDALL runs.

The remaining view index property is Restrict Initial Index Build to Designer or Manager. This option most likely is used with the Auto After First Usage refresh option. By selecting the restriction, you can control when the database goes into automatic index-building mode.

UNREAD MARKS IN THE VIEW

Unread marks are an aid to the user of a database so that he knows what information is new. The unread marks are calculated separately for each user so that if two people are viewing the same database, they will see different sets of unread marks. As you can imagine, keeping track of the unread marks causes a performance penalty. As a designer, you can control several options.

> **TIP**
>
> A database property called Don't Maintain Unread Marks is available to designers. This enables you to completely disable unread marks for the entire database. This property is found in the Advanced (beanie hat) tab within the Database Properties box. To improve performance, check this box. You typically set this option when you create a database, as described in Chapter 11, "Creating and Accessing Domino Databases."
>
> Selecting the database property should provide much more of a performance improvement than using the view options because the unread marks are not maintained.

The following unread marks options control how a view displays unread marks. These options do not affect whether the unread marks information is stored; they affect only how it is displayed. For example, you could choose two different options in different views, and the unread marks would display differently. Here are the options:

- **None**—This option causes the view to display faster because the unread marks are not displayed.
- **Unread Documents Only**—This displays unread marks only on top-level documents. It does not display unread marks for collapsed groups of documents in a view.

- **Standard (Compute in Hierarchy)**—This displays unread marks on top-level documents or on collapsed groups of documents in which one of the lower-level documents is unread.

ODBC ACCESS

The next option in the Advanced tab, Generate Unique Keys in Index, is for ODBC access. This is one of the most mysterious options for a view. First, this option is not for accessing ODBC databases, as it might appear. Tools that access the current Domino database via ODBC use this option.

Lotus has a product called NotesSQL that enables a Notes/Domino database to be accessed as if it were a relational database via ODBC. Other products, such as Visual Basic, Delphi, or other third-party tools, can use the NotesSQL interface. If you check the option Generate Unique Keys in Index, NotesSQL makes the view appear to other programs as if the sorted columns of the view comprise a unique key.

This option requires careful use, however. Just checking the box does not mean that you have defined the view selection and column definitions to meet the criteria that the other program is expecting. To avoid problems, you should follow these rules if you enable this check box:

- Do not enable this check box for more than one view per form. The external system might try to update the document through more than one path, and you could get inconsistent data in your document.
- The sorted columns within the view are very important. Make sure that the column definitions for the sorted columns...
  - Are defined by fields only, not formulas or expressions.
  - Taken as a group, uniquely identify a document within the database. In database terminology, this is called a *composite key*.

You should normally enable this option only if you are using NotesSQL. If so, you should refer to the NotesSQL documentation for more information.

WEB ACCESS

The section for Web access contains two options. These options are used when a Web browser accesses the view. The options are as follows:

- **Treat View Contents as HTML**—This is a great option that enables you to specify HTML in the view column definitions. This HTML will be served to the browser. In effect, each document line of the view can contain HTML formatting that you define. We'll review an example of this when embedded views are discussed.
- **Use Applet in the Browser**—Since Release 5, views have had the capability of downloading a Java applet to the browser to take over some of the view functionality. If you

14

enable this check box, the view will format slightly differently and will have more functionality.

- **Allow Selection of Documents**—By default, documents cannot be individually selected within a Web view. This field gives users the capability to selectively choose documents and perform an action on the selected documents. Figure 14.27 demonstrates a view with selected documents.

Figure 14.27
The option Allow Selection of Documents provides a mechanism for performing an action on multiple documents.

You can also change the colors for active links, unvisited links, and visited links in the view. To change one of these colors, click the drop-down box and select the color within the Color Picker.

VIEW SECURITY PROPERTIES

You can see the Security tab (key icon) of the ViewProperties box in Figure 14.28. This tab can be used to control who has access to the view.

The default is that the view can be used by all readers and above. You can enable this check box so that you don't have to specifically list the users. If you disable the check box, you can specify exactly the list of users whom you want to be able to use the view. This list is called the view access list. This list does not override the Access Control List (ACL) for the database; it can only refine the access.

The view access list is not really a security feature; it's only a usability feature. Although you can restrict people from using the views you create, a user could conceivably create a private view containing exactly the same columns and fields as your view. The user would then be able to view all the data in the documents. To secure the data in the documents, you should use security at the form level. You can enable form access lists and reader and author fields, and use encryption to provide security for your documents.

Figure 14.28
With the View Security tab, you can control who can use the view.

If you create a view access list, be sure to include servers either directly or via a group. If you do not include servers, your views might not replicate correctly.

You can enable public access by checking the Available to Public Access Users check box. Enabling this check box allows users with No Access or Depositor access to view public documents. In addition to enabling the view for public access, you must enable one or more form(s) for public access and create documents with a field called $PublicAccess with a value of 1. Any document with this field set to 1 will be available for viewing in a public access view.

PROGRAMMER'S PANE VIEW PROPERTIES

Several view properties are not located in the View Properties box. These properties are set in the Programmer's pane at the bottom of your screen. The first option, View Selection, has already been discussed briefly, but here are some additional details.

VIEW SELECTION

The View Selection property enables you to specify a formula that is used to select documents to display in the view. The default is to select all documents in the database. If you specify a formula, the formula is evaluated for each document in the database to determine whether to show the document in the view. As you might imagine, this is potentially a time-consuming task.

There is a performance enhancement option to speed the display of views. The option, called Optimize Documents Table Map, is found on the Advanced tab of the Database Properties box, and you can also specify it when you create the database.

14

Because selecting documents for a view potentially means going through every document in the database, Domino stores some (bitmap) tables to speed the process. Essentially, these tables link documents, forms, and views. The tables enable Domino to tell whether a form is used in a view. Then, by knowing whether a document uses the form, Domino can quickly determine whether a document is a candidate for a view. This optimization works only if your view selection formula has one or more Form= conditions. If you use Form= in your view, which is fairly common, you can enable this option to improve your database performance.

When would you not want to use this optimization? Well, if you don't use Form= in your view, extra computing and storage are required and you do not gain any benefit. The default is for this option to be turned off. You should definitely consider using it where appropriate, though, because for large databases, you might be able to improve your view performance dramatically.

THE FORM FORMULA

The form formula is associated with a view that enables you to control the form that is used to display a document opened from within the view. The form formula is one option in the selection process Domino uses to select the form to use to display a document. Here is the sequence Domino uses:

1. If a form is stored with the document, it is used to display the document. This option is selected in the Form Info tab of the Form properties dialog box. Use this option to enable sending a document to another database when the associated form might not exist. For example, if you are mailing a document to another person who might not have the associated form, you should enable storing the form with the document. In general, you should use this option sparingly because it uses up significantly more space in the database.

2. If no form is stored with the document, the form formula associated with the view is evaluated. The formula must evaluate to the name of a form that is available in the database. You can create or edit the form formula by highlighting the Form Formula property in the Programmer's pane under the view. You can then enter your formula in the right half of the Programmer's pane. One possible use of this option is to select different forms based on the state of the document: (New versus Existing), (Viewing versus Editing), (Inquiry versus New Order), and so forth.

3. If there is no form formula in the view, the document is displayed using the form name contained in a field called Form within the document. This field is automatically filled in with the synonym of the form name (or the form name, if no synonym exists) of the form used to create the document. Unless this field is changed, the document is displayed using the form used to create the document. This option is the default for most documents.

4. If there is no field called Form within the document or the form cannot be found, the default form for the database is used. You can specify the database default form in the Defaults tab of the Form Properties box.

14

5. Finally, if there is no default form, you get an error and the document is not displayed.

CREATING VIEW ACTIONS

View actions enable you to make commonly used actions available for users via the Action Button bar. The action can be activated by the user by clicking the action button or via the menus as a choice of the Actions menu. As a designer, you can choose to enable either menu access or button access, or both. Release 6 includes the capability to create subactions under a particular action. Subactions appear similar to nested actions in Release 5. Any time a user selects an action with one or many subactions, a list of subactions appears as a menu or a drop-down list. Figure 14.29 demonstrates an action with subactions within a mail database.

Figure 14.29
Actions and subactions can be a powerful way to act on documents within a view.

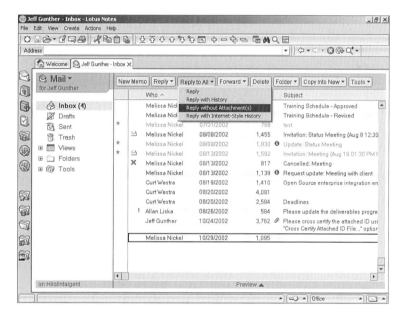

You have four language options for programming an action or subaction. You can use the Formula language, create a simple action, use LotusScript, or use JavaScript. Refer to Chapter 18, "Working with Formulas, Functions, and Commands," and Chapter 19, "Using the IDE with LotusScript, Java, and JavaScript," for the details of programming.

If you create a view action, it is unique to the particular view, and you need to have separate copies for each view if you want identical function. Another option is to create a shared action, which can be used in multiple views or forms. This is another great way to implement code once and use it from multiple locations within your database.

To create a shared action, click Shared Code in the Design pane of your database. Then click Other. In the work area, double-click Actions. An action is created for you. You can name it, provide the code, and then save it.

14

EMBEDDED VIEWS

A form or page can have many types of elements embedded. Both design elements can include outlines, a view, navigators, date pickers, or a Folder pane. On forms, you can embed a group scheduler or file upload control as well.

In this section, we review how to embed a view on a form for display in a Web browser. This capability gives you a lot of flexibility in the formatting of the view rows through the use of HTML. In addition, through the use of single-category embedded views, you can create views that present customized lists to users.

Let's see how all this is accomplished. This example is comprised of one form for data entry, a view, and a second form that embeds the view. We'll distill this example to its simplest components for the purposes of explaining how to make Domino forms and views work well with the Web. Here is the scenario: You have an online shop that sells games over the Web. There are several categories for the games, and some games can fall into more than one category. The first form that you can create is the form that enables someone in your company to enter new games on your Web site (see Figure 14.30).

Figure 14.30
The sample game-definition form is used to add a game and its categories.

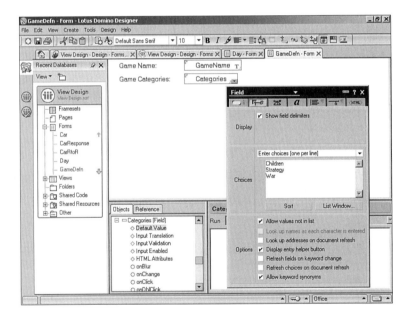

This form is very simple; there are only two fields. When you develop your form, you'll want to include more fields and make it more attractive for data entry. Notice that there is a field called Categories. This special field name identifies the field as one to use when a view is categorized. The field has multiple values enabled. This form is simple enough.

The next design element you'll create is a view. This view will eventually be embedded in a form, and we'll review how you can use HTML to add some spice to your view and form (see Figure 14.31).

Figure 14.31
The sample GameList view has enabled Treat View Contents as HTML.

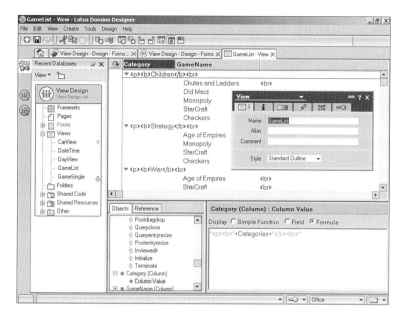

The GameList view has three columns. The first column is for the category, the second is for the game name, and the third is for an icon that will display any time you have recently listed a new game. Many Web sites use a starburst New. With Domino, you can automatically add these icons via programming.

The first column is sorted in ascending order and is categorized. The contents of the column can be seen in Figure 14.31. Notice that a paragraph tag, a bold tag, the Categories field, end bold, and a line-break tag are included. The effect of these HTML tags is to add space before the new category and then show the category name in bold, followed by a line break so that the next text follows on the next line.

The second column of the view contains just the field GameName. I have not included any special formatting, although you could use the HTML tags to add features such as document linking, bold, or other characteristics.

The third column formula is shown in Figure 14.32:

```
@if(@Now> @Adjust(@Created;0;0;7;0;0;0);"<br>";
"<IMG SRC=\'/"+@ReplaceSubstring(@Text(@Subset(@DbName;-1));" "; "+")+
"/actn124.gif\'><br>"
```

In Figure 14.32, you can see both the column value formula in the Programmer's pane and an example of the generated HTML in the view window. In essence, a reference to a GIF file is generated that has been stored within the image library of the database. You can extract and show the image by using a URL, as shown. Using this technique is much better than having graphics stored in the file system. All the related graphics can be stored within the Domino database and will replicate automatically with the application.

14

Figure 14.32
The formula conditionally generates an icon using HTML.

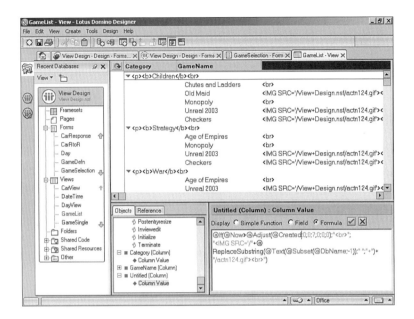

The formula creates conditional HTML. That is, two versions of HTML are generated, depending on the outcome of the `if` statement. The first version of HTML generates just a `<br>`, which means to break to a new line. The second version of HTML generates a reference to an icon (GIF file) in the image library.

NOTE

> In the URL that refers to the image file, I issue a `@ReplaceString` that substitutes a plus sign (+) for a blank space. You may not use embedded blanks within a URL string. Plus signs are used to indicate an embedded blank. This substitution is performed in case (as it is here) the database name has an embedded blank. In Figure 14.32, you can see that the embedded blank between "View" and "Design" has been changed to a plus sign.

The essence of the formula is that an icon reference will be generated if the creation date of the document is within the last seven days. The `@Adjust` function adds seven days to the document-creation date. It then compares the adjusted date to the current time. If the current time is later than the adjusted date, the document is old and you just generate a line break. If it isn't, the document's date is within the last seven days and you generate the HTML for an image with the IMG tag. In this case, the image resource is loaded into the image library of the database, so you do not need to enter a path. If you keep the image resources within the database, they automatically replicate with the database, and the database is self-contained.

Now we are ready to create the last design element of the example. You are now going to create the form that will embed the view that you just made. When you create an embedded view, Domino does not automatically include the navigation bars that are shown when Domino natively shows a view. With embedded views, you have more control over the appearance shown to the user (see Figure 14.33).

Figure 14.33
Create an embedded view to control the view's appearance.

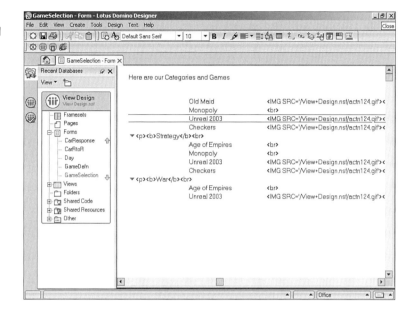

To create an embedded view, follow these steps:

1. First create your form. Call it GameSelection.

2. Choose Create, Embedded Element, View to open the Insert Embedded View dialog box.

> **NOTE**
>
> With Release 6, you can include multiple embedded views per form.

3. Choose a particular view to embed or check the box that says Choose a View Based on Formula. For this example, select the GameList view. Click OK.

4. If you selected the formula option, you must enter the formula in the Programmer's pane. The formula that you enter must evaluate to the name of a view.

5. Open the properties for the embedded view by clicking the Properties icon or choosing Edit, Properties. For this example, you cannot use the view applet because it will not properly handle the formulas and dynamically generated HTML that you are creating.

6. Select Using HTML under the Web Access Display option.

14

NOTE

> The view applet is written in Java and is downloaded to the browser. This code executes in the client environment and does not use HTML to render the view. For this reason, pass-thru HTML does not work with the view applet. View applets are great for improving user interactivity and response time for standard views. However, if you need to combine HTML with the view, you must use the HTML (Domino server–generated) version of views.

7. In the Display tab (the second tab) for the example, enable Fit to Window Width, Fit to Window Height, Disable Scrollbars, and Show Contents Only (Don't Show Title). See Figure 14.34. In your form, you can choose to use different options.

Figure 14.34
In the Display tab, you can control the height and width of an embedded view.

Now you're ready to test the form and embedded view. Click one of the browser icons in the preview toolbar. Figure 14.35 demonstrates sample output.

Figure 14.35
In the new document, icons are dynamically generated.

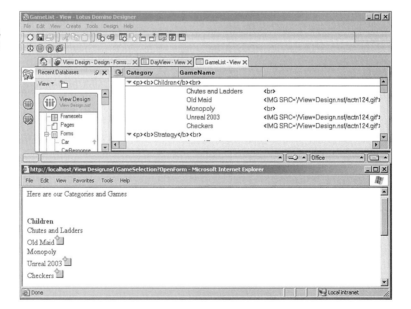

In Figure 14.35, you can see the dynamically generated icons. The capability to generate these icons programmatically is one of the features that makes Domino such a powerful Web server. In Domino, you can just add documents and specify the rules you want to use for how long documents stay "new." Then the icons will appear and disappear automatically as they age.

SINGLE-CATEGORY EMBEDDED VIEWS

Single-category embedded views are a neat feature that enable you to create customized views, similar to a view that's shared-private on first use. The nice thing about single-category embedded views is that they work well on the Web.

You can use a single-category view to provide custom information to a particular user. The way it works is simple: You first create a categorized view and use as the category's value some data that distinguishes one user from another. For example, you could use the user's name as the categorization value. Other sample applications are the game categories of the previous example, categories for user preferences, or just about any kind of grouping when you want to select a group of documents to customize the user's experience.

To illustrate single-category embedded views, we'll modify the previous games example. Let's create one additional view (the Single Category view) and one form, which will contain the embedded view. First, let's do the view.

Create an additional view that is the same as the GameList view. You can do this by cutting and pasting the view within the view list. Rename the new view GameSingle. The only change you will make to this new view is to the column formula for the first column, the Categories column. In GameList the formula is as follows:

```
"<p><b>"+Categories+"</b><br>"
```

Change this for the GameSingle view to the following:

```
Categories
```

That is, you just want to make it the regular contents of the Categories field, with no HTML formatting. Save and close the GameSingle view.

Now create a new form and call it GameSingle also. There is no restriction on a form and view having the same name. Create a radio button field called Cat.

On the Control tab, enter the three options: `Children`, `Strategy`, and `War`. Also be sure to check the Refresh Fields on Keyword Change option. This forces a re-evaluation of the Single Category view. The default value for the Cat field is Children.

Now you can embed the GameSingle view as you did in the previous example. Do this by choosing Create, Embedded Element, View. After the view is embedded within your form, choose the Show Single Category property in the Programmer's pane. Enter `Cat` in the formula area within the Programmer's pane.

14

By specifying Cat in the formula area, you are essentially telling Domino to use the Cat field as the criterion for the single category. You force the option to be one of the three that you know are valid by using a radio button. After the user selects one of the radio button options, the Refresh Fields on Keyword Change option causes the view to recalculate and display the single category specified in the Cat field. Figure 14.36 demonstrates an example.

Figure 14.36
Selecting a radio button option changes the games shown.

In this example, when the user selects each of the different radio button options, the games shown change. Each time, the "new" icon appears automatically, as before.

USING FRAMESETS, OUTLINES, AND NAVIGATORS

In this chapter

15

OVERVIEW

Domino provides several capabilities for organizing information and enabling users to navigate through your Notes applications and Web pages. This chapter gives you information about some of the navigation tools available in Notes and Domino Release 6. Outlines are one mechanism that you can use to enable navigation functions for your users. Framesets enable you to create several panes or frames within your window. You can control the initial number and placement of the frames. Navigators are a feature from Release 4 of Notes and Domino that are still available, although their importance might be diminished somewhat by the introduction of outlines and other advances in Release 5.

The navigation tools covered in this chapter work great when used within applications accessed primarily by the Notes client; it's almost impossible to imagine a Notes application without using outlines and framesets.

One of the most useful aspects of outlines, framesets, and navigators is that they can decrease the time required to develop and deploy an application. When developing Web applications, this is particularly true because Domino generates most of the HTML for you. However, the limited user interface and overall look and feel of a *purely* Domino-generated Web application utilizing outlines and framesets is not always desirable. When you allow Domino to do all the heavy lifting, the appearance and functionality of your Web pages might not be up to today's standards. Keep this in mind throughout this chapter as we review the options available. Refer to Chapter 27, "Building a Web Site with Domino," for more detailed information on how to best utilize Domino and other tools to generate great Web applications.

This chapter discusses how to develop outlines, framesets, navigators, and hotspots for applications used within both Notes and Web browsers. Before we look at these features in detail, you might want to create a new database from the Discussion database (R6) template so that you can follow along with the examples in this chapter. Although the Discussion database already has all the design elements created for you to use, we'll create new outlines, framesets, and navigators. You can refer to the finished elements provided in the Discussion database as a guide.

WHAT ARE OUTLINES?

An *outline* is a tool that enables you to control user navigation. Outlines can be styled vertically or horizontally, and they roughly correspond to a list of destinations. Typically on a Web home page or in a Notes application, you see these kinds of navigation tools on the left side of the page or along the top or the bottom of the page.

You must embed an outline in either a page or a form to be used. You can create as many outlines as you like, and you can embed more than one outline on a single page. The formatting of the outline is done via the Embedded Outline properties box, which we'll cover later. Normally, you use outlines within pages in framesets because they can reside in one

15

frame but control the contents of another frame. We'll cover this in the section on using frames and framesets.

Note that there are two types of settings that you create for outlines. The first are the navigational settings. You specify this information when you create and program the outline entries. The second type of settings determine the display formatting for the outline. The same outline can be used in two different pages, with different formatting styles in each. Although the outline looks different on each page, the navigation for each respective entry in the outline is the same.

USING THE OUTLINE EDITOR

If you want to follow along with an example, open the Discussion database that you created earlier. By default, no outlines are created for you within a new, blank database. You can easily have the Designer create a new outline for you by following these steps:

1. Open the Outline Editor by clicking Shared Code, Outlines in the Design pane.

2. Click the New Outline action bar button. A new set of action bar buttons appears.

3. Click the Generate Default Outline action button. Your new default outline is generated for you (see Figure 15.1).

Figure 15.1
The default outline as initially created by Domino Designer in an existing database.

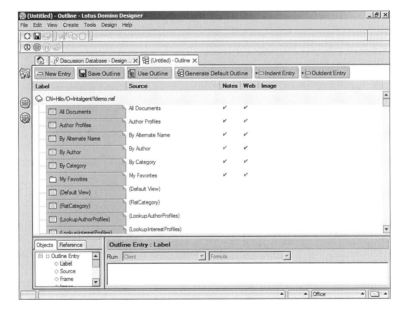

4. Click the Save Outline button to save the outline now or after you've completed it.

You can see from Figure 15.1 that Domino Designer automatically creates an outline that includes any views and folders already in the database. In addition, outline entries are created for Other Views, Other Folders, Other Private Views, and Other Private Folders. If there is no default database view, an entry titled Untitled is created.

These additional outline entries that are created for you automatically have suggested names, but you do not have to use all these entries. You can delete some of the entries if they do not apply to your application by simply selecting them and pressing your Delete key.

If you prefer to create your entire outline from scratch, first create the outline by completing the previous Steps 1 and 2 and then begin adding outline entries as described in the following section.

OUTLINE ENTRIES

In Figure 15.1, each of the outline entries is represented by a rectangular gray box. When the application executes, the user sees a text or graphic item for each of the outline entries. By clicking one of these entries, the user can navigate through your application.

You can add, delete, move, and rename the outline entries.

To add a new entry, follow these steps:

1. Create a new outline or open an existing outline as described in the previous section on using the Outline Editor.

2. Click the existing outline entry where you want to locate your new entry. The new entry goes below the one you select. If you want your entry to be the new first entry, click the database name at the top of the outline. For this example, click the database name to create a new first entry.

3. Click the New Entry action button. A new entry is created for you under the existing entry that you selected.

4. Double-click the entry to open the Outline Entry properties dialog box. Enter a label for the new entry. The text that you enter will be displayed to the end user. In this example, use Home for the name.

5. Enter text in the Pop-up field that you want to pop up as a user mouses over the entry.

6. You can optionally add an alias for the outline entry. If you add an alias, you can refer to the outline entry by the alias name even if you change the name of the outline. This enables you to change the user interface without reprogramming your application. In this example, you use the word Home for the alias.

7. The Content section describes what will happen if the user clicks this outline entry. Four types exist: Action, Link, Named Element, and URL (see Figure 15.2). These options are described in the next section.

8. You can optionally enter an image filename. You can select an image filename from your image library by clicking the file folder icon, or you can specify a formula to generate the image filename. The image itself is displayed as a small icon next to the label you specified previously. If you do not specify an image filename, default icons display

for views and folders. Alternatively, click the Do Not Display an Image check box if you don't want to display any image next to the entry.

9. An outline entry has a status that is either selected (that is, has the focus) or not selected. When you click an outline entry, the action you have specified occurs and the focus normally changes to the clicked outline entry. This is often used so the user can see at a glance which outline entry is selected. You can specify that you do not want the outline entry to retain the focus by enabling the Does Not Keep Selection Focus option. Even if this option is enabled, the outline entry's action still works.

Figure 15.2
Four types of content exist for an outline entry.

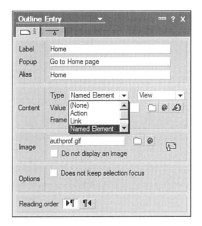

10. Select Read Only if you don't want users to edit the outline in place.

11. After you have entered all the fields, you can close the properties box or click another outline entry and enter its information.

12. Click the Save Outline button to save all your edits.

An alternative to the Outline Entry properties dialog box for entering and editing this information is the Design pane in the lower left of the Designer window. You can select from the properties listed as objects to the left, and then you can edit the contents directly in the programmer's window. Note that all the outline entry properties are not available from the Design pane, so in some situations it is best to use the approach described in the steps.

OUTLINE ENTRY CONTENTS

As stated previously, the content associated with an outline entry can be provided in one of four ways: using an Action, Link, Named Element, or URL. Following is a description of each:

■ **Action**—An Action outline entry type enables you to supply an @formula to be executed when the outline entry is clicked.

15

- **Link**—If you specify Link, the outline entry can be a link to a database, view, document, or anchor.
- **Named Element**—This option enables you to provide linkage to a page, form, frameset, or view.
- **URL**—The URL content type enables you to specify a Web page address to load when a user clicks the outline entry.

Let's briefly walk through how to set up each of these content types for an outline entry.

To provide content for an outline entry using an action, follow these steps:

1. Choose Action from the Type drop-down field.
2. Click the @ button at the right of the Value line. A dialog box appears where you can enter your formula.
3. Enter the formula and click Done.

To utilize a link to provide content, you must do the following:

1. Choose Link from the Type drop-down field.
2. Open the Notes client and the desired database, view, or document. Choose Edit, Copy as Link, followed by the type of link you desire: Anchor Link, Document Link, View Link, or Database Link.
3. Return to the Outline Entry properties box and click the Paste icon. Your link is pasted into the outline entry. For confirmation, the type of link is displayed next to the type field. The value line contains a reference to your link, but it is not editable. Figure 15.3 shows you the result of a view link that has been pasted into the outline entry.

Figure 15.3
The Outline Entry property box after a document link has been pasted.

To use a named element to provide content for an outline entry, perform the following steps:

1. Set the Type field to Named Element.
2. To the right of the Named Element field, select the type of element you want to use. You can select Page, Form, Frameset, View, Folder, or Navigator.
3. Specify the actual element in the Value field by selecting it directly or by supplying a formula that will evaluate to the name of the element. If you click the folder icon, you can directly select the element; if you click the @ icon, you can supply a formula. Figure 15.4 shows you the result of clicking the folder icon. A second dialog box enables you to again choose the type of object, select a database to search, and then select an available object from a drop-down list.

Figure 15.4
To identify content for a Named Element selection, specify an object type, select a database to search, and then choose from a list of available objects.

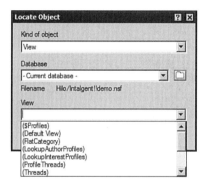

The final content type is the URL. When you want to specify a Web page URL to provide the content for an outline entry, first select URL as the type. Then complete the Value field by entering the URL, including the http: at the beginning of the string.

If the outline is to be used within a frameset, you can use the Frame field to specify a target frame for the content to load when a user selects the outline entry.

HIDING OUTLINE ENTRIES

You can optionally hide outline entries by using the Entry Hide When tab of the Outline Entry properties box (see Figure 15.5).

Figure 15.5
Specify when to hide an outline entry in the Hide When tab of the Outline Entry properties box.

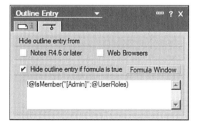

15

You can hide the entry from Notes 4.6 or later, or you can hide the entry from Web browsers. These options enable you to create conditionally displayed outline entries that display depending upon the viewing capabilities of the user.

In addition, you can supply a formula for hiding the outline entry. This type of Hide When formula is useful if you want to supply or restrict application capability based upon user ID, roles, groups, or other criteria. The outline entry linkage is displayed only under the conditions that you specify. For example, in Figure 15.5, a Hide When formula is shown that will hide the outline entry if the user is not assigned to the Admin role.

MOVING OUTLINE ENTRIES

After you've created the outline entries, you might want to change the order in which they are displayed to the user. Moving an outline entry within the hierarchy is very simple. You just click the entry and drag it to its new location. You can move entries up or down.

You can also indent entries so that they appear as a subsidiary to another outline entry. To indent an entry, click it and then click the Indent Entry action button on the top of the window. Clicking the Outdent Entry action button can outdent an entry that has already been indented.

DISPLAYING AN OUTLINE

As mentioned previously, you typically must embed an outline in either a page or a form to be used in a Notes or Web application. Normally, you use outlines within pages in framesets because they reside in one frame but control the content that loads in another. Before moving forward with how to embed an outline in a page or form within a frameset, you need to understand how frames and framesets work and how to create them.

USING FRAMES AND FRAMESETS

You can use frames and framesets to separate navigation from content and to separate different types of content from each other. Before getting into the details of designing frames and framesets, it is appropriate to briefly review some of the benefits and disadvantages of using them in a Web application.

Framesets were initially very popular with Web designers when the Internet started to take off in the mid- to late 1990s. They were desirable primarily because, without them, a developer had to place navigation items on every Web page and then modify every page when the navigation items changed. That can lead to a lot of maintenance on a Web site that changes regularly! With a frameset, a developer can create and maintain just one navigation page that displays in a frame on every Web page. Page content then loads within one or more other frames.

Since the time when framesets first arrived on the scene, a wide array of alternatives have arisen due to advances in new and improved browsers, programming languages, techniques, and more. As a result, framesets on the Web have become less important and, in many circles, even are frowned upon because of their limitations. Framesets make it difficult for users to bookmark pages, make navigation outside a frame difficult, and generally have resulted in too many Web pages that are easier for the designer to maintain but unattractive and unfriendly to the user.

Having said that, Web framesets can be effective and worthwhile in the right situations and if you ensure that they meet the user's needs. Don't design and use them solely because they make your job easier.

Using framesets in applications designed primarily for the Notes client is a different matter altogether. Framesets within Notes applications are typically integral to designing effective navigation and content displays. As mentioned previously, it's difficult to imagine a Notes 6 application that doesn't utilize frames and framesets.

What are framesets, exactly? To answer that question, we'll first review the HTML definitions of pages, framesets, and frames. You actually don't need all this detail to use the Domino Designer Frameset Designer, but it is beneficial for you to know what Domino is doing behind the scenes. After we have covered the background material, we'll return to the Domino Designer interface and how to use it.

HTML BACKGROUND FOR FRAMESETS

To describe framesets, let's first start with the definition of a regular HTML page without frames. To display a regular HTML page, you must specify a document with the following framework:

```
<HTML>
<HEAD>
</HEAD>
<BODY>
     ... Main contents of page here ...
</BODY>
</HTML>
```

With this structure, a single page is displayed, showing the content within the <BODY> and </BODY> tags.

One of the early observations about Web pages was that frequently they contained two types of information: navigation information and content. The navigation elements are typically on the borders of the screen: left, top, bottom, or sometimes the right. The content is typically in the middle of the window.

The two types of information have different characteristics: The page content varies from page to page, and the navigation elements are frequently similar or stay constant while the user navigates the site. It is desirable to have the navigation elements always available, in much the same way as the top menu line of the typical Windows application is always available. From any point within the Web site, you can navigate directly to another place.

Frames and framesets were developed to combine the relatively static navigational elements and the relatively dynamic content. Framesets enable you to define separate frames within a window; one frame can remain visible and unchanged, and the content of the other frame changes. Here is the structure for a frameset-enabled HTML file:

```
<HTML>
<HEAD>
</HEAD>
<FRAMESET>
        ... Frame definitions here ...
</FRAMESET>
</HTML>
```

Notice that the main difference between a regular HTML page and one with frames is that you replace the <BODY> tags with <FRAMESET> tags. You cannot use both the <BODY> tag and the <FRAMESET> tag in the same document. If you include both, the browser displays the first and ignores the second.

In addition to the simple format shown here, you can optionally include a <NOFRAMES> section for browsers that don't support frames. You can also have *nested framesets*. That is, you can have framesets within framesets. The frameset tag itself is used to allocate space in the window for the various frames, but without specifying the content of the frame, which is in the <FRAME> tag.

You specify the frame layout and the orientation of a frameset by using either the ROWS or COLS attributes within the frameset. Although you can specify both parameters, it is usually not done. Typically, you specify only one of the keywords for a given frameset. It is common, however, to have a column-oriented frameset within a row-oriented frameset, and vice versa. Here is an example:

```
<FRAMESET ROWS="100,*,10%">
        ... Frame definitions here ...
</FRAMESET>
```

In this example, three rows are specified, which means that there will be three frames in the frameset. In this case, all the frames take the entire width of the window because they are row-oriented. There are three separate height specifications. The first means 100 pixels, the last element means that the frame will take 10% of the remaining window height, and the middle element (the asterisk) will take whatever space remains.

Here is a more complex example that loads HTML files in each of four frames:

```
<FRAMESET ROWS="100,*,10%">
   <FRAME SRC="leftframe.html">
   <FRAMESET COLS="200,*">
      <FRAME src="topframe.html">
      <FRAME src="rightframe.html">
   </FRAMESET>
   <FRAME src="bottomframe.html">
</FRAMESET>
```

The previous example is enhanced by nesting one frameset within another. You can see the result of this frameset nesting in Figure 15.6.

Figure 15.6
Nested frameset displayed in a browser.

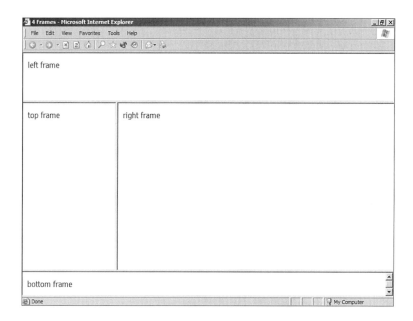

In this case, the major orientation is row-wise with three rows. Within the middle row, however, another frameset with two columns is defined. This type of layout, perhaps with different frame proportions, is common among Web sites that utilize frames. In fact, in Domino Designer, if you indicate that you want four frames, this configuration is the default configuration of the four frames.

To summarize, framesets define the layout and orientation of frames within a window. The content of each frame is defined with HTML like a page. In the next section, you'll learn how to define the frame itself.

HTML BACKGROUND FOR FRAMES

After you define the structure of your Web page with the `<FRAMESET>` tags, you can define the contents of the individual frames with the `<FRAME>` tag. If you are using regular HTML, the simplified syntax for the `<FRAME>` tag is as follows:

```
<FRAME SRC="http://./home.nsf/welcome?OpenPage">
```

Notice that you specify the content via a URL. In particular, the implication is that the content of a framed page is stored separately from the frame and frameset definitions. This contrasts with a regular page, where the content and structure are stored together. You cannot supply the contents of a frame "inline" with the definition of the `<FRAMESET>`.

Additional attribute parameters on the `<FRAME>` tag are NAME, MARGINWIDTH, MARGINHEIGHT, SCROLLING, and NORESIZE. These attributes enable you to refer to the frame and give additional information about the visible display of the frame. The NAME attribute, for example, is required when you want to use one frame as the target of a different frame because you refer to the target by name.

SUPPORTING BROWSERS WITHOUT FRAME CAPABILITY

Frames and framesets were not originally part of the HTML specification. During the time period of the version 3 browsers (Netscape Navigator 3 and Internet Explorer 3), it was very important to test whether a browser was capable of displaying frames. These days, almost all browsers support frames. To be safe, though, you might want to code defensively and test whether the user viewing your Web site can utilize frames.

To code defensively in HTML, you use the `<NOFRAMES>` tag. The content of this tag enables you to specify separate HTML for browsers that do not support frames:

```
<HTML>
<HEAD>
</HEAD>
<FRAMESET>
      ... Frame definitions here ...
</FRAMESET>
<NOFRAMES>
      ... HTML for browsers that do not support frames.
</NOFRAMES>
</HTML>
```

In Domino, you can use an @function called `@BrowserInfo` to determine whether the browser has frame capability. To use it within one of your formulas, you use `@BrowserInfo("Frames")`. This formula returns `true` if the browser supports frames; it returns `false` otherwise.

CREATING FRAMESETS WITH DOMINO DESIGNER

In HTML, the content of a frame within a frameset is specified by a URL. The URL points to a file that can contain HTML or perhaps a graphics file, such as a GIF or JPEG file. With Domino, you have many more options because, in addition to specifying a simple URL, you can specify Domino design elements, such as pages, views, or documents.

Now that you are familiar with some of the HTML theory behind framesets, let's see how you can use Domino Designer to create your own framesets without having to drop down to the HTML level. Keep in mind that most of the information provided here also applies to creating framesets for use in applications designed for the Notes client.

If you want to follow along in an example, open the Discussion database you created earlier. In Domino Designer, follow these steps to create a frameset:

1. Click Framesets in the Design pane of Domino Designer. The Work pane shows you a list of existing framesets, if you have any.

2. To create a new frameset, click the action bar button titled New Frameset. The Create New Frameset dialog box appears (see Figure 15.7).

3. From the dialog box, first select the number of frames you want to use. You can enter **2**, **3**, or **4**. This is just an initial setting. In the unusual case that you want to use more than four frames, you can modify the initial configuration by adding and deleting frames.

You should be aware, however, that most good graphic designs do not require much more than four frames. Start simply and add complexity later, if needed.

4. After you select the number of frames, select the desired layout by clicking one of the pictures across the top of the dialog box. Figure 15.7 shows a frameset using three frames.

Figure 15.7
The Create New Frameset dialog box with three frames selected.

5. After you select the layout, click OK. Your frameset is created (see Figure 15.8).

6. Click the Save Frameset button to save the frameset.

Figure 15.8
A newly created frameset with three frames.

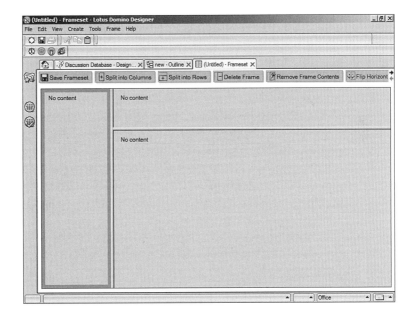

Just for comparison to our previous HTML introduction, here is the relevant HTML that Domino Designer generates for the frameset:

```
<FRAMESET COLS="20%,80%">
    <FRAME>
    <FRAMESET ROWS="20%,80%">
        <FRAME>
        <FRAME>
```

```
    </FRAMESET>
  </FRAMESET>
```

Although Domino does not indent the HTML code, it is indented here for clarity. Notice the similarity to the handwritten HTML code that you would otherwise have to write. The HTML source generated by Domino varies by browser and by release, so your code might be slightly different. Also note that although you create a single Domino frameset with three frames, Domino actually generates two nested HTML framesets to get the desired layout.

ENHANCING AN EXISTING FRAMESET

After you create your frameset, you can edit the layout by adding or deleting frames. The result of these actions is to change the number of nested framesets and their contents. In Figure 15.8, there are five action bar buttons to the right of the Save Frameset button within the frameset editor. You can use these buttons to change the layout of the frameset.

To create a new frame, you must split one of the existing frames. You can split the frame into either two columns or two rows. The first two action bar buttons accomplish these tasks. By clicking either button, you end up with one additional frame.

To add a frame to an existing frameset, follow these steps:

1. Open the frameset by double-clicking the frameset's name within the list of names in the Work pane.

2. Click within the frame you want to split. A dark gray highlight shows you which frame is currently selected.

3. Click either the Split into Columns or the Split into Rows action button. The highlighted frame turns into two frames, either by columns or by rows. Your new frame has been added.

4. You can change the split percentage by clicking on one of the borders between the frames and dragging it left or right while holding down the mouse button. To be more exact in setting frame width and height, right-click the frame and then select Frame Properties from the menu that appears. Within the opened Frame properties dialog box, click the Frame Size tab, and set width and height using percentage or pixel values.

To delete a frame of an existing frameset:

1. Open the frameset by double-clicking the frameset's name within the list of names in the Work pane.

2. Click within the frame you want to delete. A dark gray highlight shows you which frame is currently selected.

3. Click the Delete Frame action button. The highlighted frame is deleted and merged with one of its neighbors.

Finally, you can reverse the position of frames within a row by clicking the Flip Horizontally action button.

SPECIFYING FRAME CONTENTS

As mentioned, in Domino Designer you have several options for specifying a frame's contents. This gives you a much easier, high-level design paradigm than when working directly with HTML. You might want to have some frames store relatively static information and other frames store dynamic content that varies from page to page. In addition, frames within a frameset can be linked. That is, clicking items in one frame can cause the contents of a different frame to change. This is the essence of many common frame layouts.

On the Web, you will frequently see the frame on the left containing graphic menu items; clicking them causes the main frame on the right to change. In Domino, the left frame can contain an outline as you saw earlier in this chapter, and each outline element can cause a different page to display on the right.

When outlines were covered earlier in the chapter, the linkage between frames was not addressed because we had not yet covered framesets. Now that you know about both concepts, let's put them together.

USING AN EMBEDDED OUTLINE IN A PAGE

To use an outline, it must be embedded in a page or a form. If you haven't yet read Chapter 13, "Designing Pages, Forms, and Subforms," you might want to go back and read that chapter.

Most of the time, you will use an outline in conjunction with a frameset. In that case, you will normally want to embed the outline in a page. You will usually use a page rather than a form because the contents of the page containing the outline are generally static. Navigation frames containing outlines do not typically need to have the dynamic content that a form allows.

Creating an outline and then inserting a basic page is really easy. Here is all you have to do:

1. Create the desired outline with the Outline Editor. You can use the New Entry action button to add outline entries. If you created the outline example earlier in this chapter, it might look like Figure 15.9.

2. After your outline is created and saved, you can click the Use Outline action button. A new page is created for you, with the outline already embedded. Figure 15.10 shows the resulting page from the outline.

That's it. All you have to do is click one button: A new page is created for you, and the embedded outline is automatically added to this new page.

After the page is created, you can edit it normally. You also need to set the properties for your embedded outline. Follow these steps to determine how the outline will appear and function on the page when it is displayed:

Figure 15.9
A typical outline might appear similar to this.

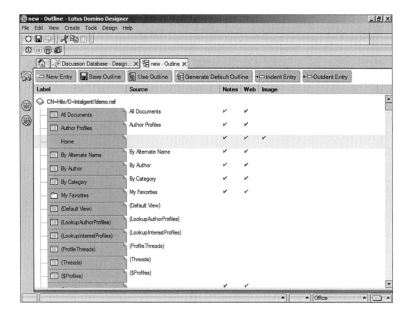

Figure 15.10
You can create a page with an embedded outline quickly in Domino Designer.

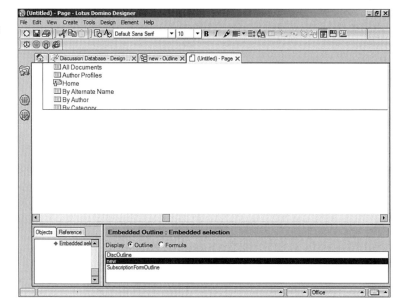

1. Open the Embedded Outline properties box by right-clicking the embedded outline and then selecting Outline Properties from the menu that appears. As you can see from Figure 15.11, you can adjust many properties for the embedded outline on the Info tab alone.

Figure 15.11
Edit the properties of the embedded outline to control its appearance and functionality.

15

2. On the Info tab of the properties box, specify the name for the embedded outline control and also its type as Tree Style or Flat. When you use Tree Style, you see the familiar indented folders. Flat means that when you drill down one level in the outline, the new level replaces the original level in the display.

3. Select the Title style, which controls whether the database title is hidden or displayed above the outline.

4. Check the Show Twisties box if you want clickable twisties to appear to the left of outline entries that will control the expansion and collapse of indented entries.

5. Enter the name of the Target frame. If your outline will appear in the left frame of a frameset and the contents will appear in the right frame, enter the name of the target, or right, frame.

NOTE

You can specify the target frame to display an outline in several places. In addition to using the Embedded Outline dialog box, you can define the target frame within the Outline Entry properties dialog box and in the Frame properties dialog box. How does Domino reconcile these multiple definitions?

The general rule is that the smallest design element takes priority. In other words, an Outline Entry's definition overrides the Embedded Outline definition, which, in turn, overrides the definition found in the Frame properties. This makes sense because you might have several links within a frame, and each one might use a different target frame.

Normally, you should start simply with just a few frames and use a consistent design. In this way, you won't really have to worry about conflicting definitions. For example, you can just define the target frame at the frame level and not use the definition of the embedded outline.

6. Select Using HTML or Using Java Applet for the Web Access field. Stick with the default Using HTML option unless you have a specific need to use an applet.

7. Set the font type and color, backgrounds, outline entry alignment, and outline border by opening and completing the other tabs on the Embedded Outline property box.

8. Click File, Save to save the page. When prompted, enter a name for the page; then click OK.

USING A PAGE IN A FRAMESET

After you generate your outline page, you can edit it normally as you would edit any other page. You can add other items or move the outline around on the page. After you edit the page and like the way it looks, you can include it in your frameset. The outline page is used to navigate and causes the contents of linked pages to change.

To include your page within your frameset, follow these steps:

1. Click Framesets in the Design pane to see a list of your framesets.

2. Double-click the frameset name in the list in the work area to open the desired frameset.

3. Select the frame you want to use for your page by clicking within the frame. In this example, we use the left frame.

TIP

> You should have a naming convention for your frames so that you can keep track of their contents. A very simple naming convention is to use the frame's position as its name. In this chapter's examples, we use the name left for the left frame, top for the top-right frame, and right for the bottom-right (main) frame. Another effective method is to name frames according to the type of content each will load. For example, you could use names such as Navigation, Header, and Data. Of course, you can use different conventions, but naming the frames with some indication of their location or content type lets you know where certain elements will load.

4. Open the frame's properties box by right-clicking the frame and then selecting Frame Properties from the menu that appears.

5. Enter a name for the frame in the Name field if you want, and then change the content type to Named Element and Page.

6. Click the folder icon to browse and select the desired page using the Locate Object dialog box. Click OK after selecting the desired page to close the dialog box.

7. Enter the default target for links in the frame within the next field. Enter the name of the right frame for this example. See Figure 15.12 for the resulting frameset.

Figure 15.12
An outline page set as content for the left frame with the target in the right frame.

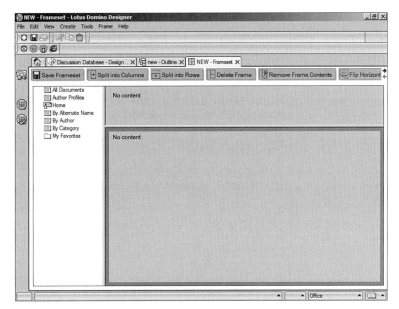

Now you have created a frameset with three frames. The left frame is used for navigation. In that frame is a page that, in turn, includes an outline. When a user clicks the outline entries in the left pane, the outline controls what will be displayed in the target (right) frame.

If you want to specify content that will load by default in any of the other frames, follow the same steps as outlined, but specify different content type as appropriate in Step 4. Figure 15.13 displays the design of the MainFramesetNotes frameset from the Discussion database, which is used to present content to Notes client users. It includes, among others, a frame on the left to display the Outline Page and a right frame to display the default All Documents view.

Figure 15.14 shows how the frameset appears to a Notes user. To preview a frameset in Notes, choose Frame, Preview in Notes. To preview a frameset for a Web application, choose Frame, Preview in Web Browser, and then select the browser to use.

It seems a little complicated at first because you have to be familiar with outlines, pages, and framesets. When you put them together, though, you can easily create framesets that facilitate navigation through your Web or Notes application.

Figure 15.13
The MainFramesetNotes frameset in the Discussion database includes a left frame displaying the Outline Page with an embedded outline, and a right frame displaying a view.

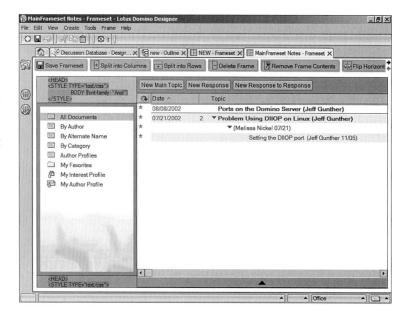

Figure 15.14
The Discussion database renders the MainFramesNotes frameset and its content in the Notes client as shown here.

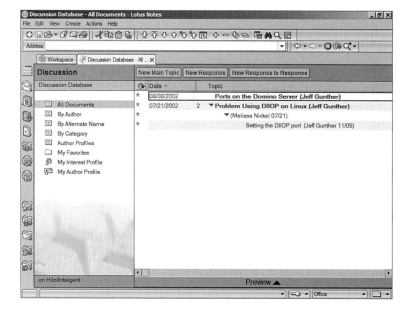

DESIGNING NAVIGATORS

Domino navigators have been around since Release 4, so they should be familiar to developers who have worked with that release. If you have a Web development background, you can think of navigators as image maps. A typical navigator contains a background image with

15

hotspots, and you can program the hotspots to perform various actions. You can use several built-in simple actions, or you can program more complex actions by using either the @formula language or LotusScript. Note that JavaScript and Java are not available for use with navigators.

This is a list of the built-in simple actions that you can associate with a navigator hotspot:

- Open another navigator
- Open a view or folder
- Alias a folder
- Open a link (document, view, or database)
- Open a URL

As mentioned, you can also use the @formula language or LotusScript to program custom actions.

To create a new navigator, follow these steps:

1. Click Other, Navigators in the Design pane. The work area contains a list of the existing navigators, if any.

2. Click the New Navigator action bar button. Your new navigator is created. You then are placed in edit mode within the navigator graphical editor.

3. If you're using the navigator in Web applications, you should ensure that the check box titled Web Browser Compatible is enabled in the Navigator properties box (this is the default). This property ensures that Web browsers can view your navigator. Open the Navigator properties box by right-clicking in the navigator and then selecting Navigator Properties from the menu that appears.

4. Click the Save Navigator button to save the navigator next, or after you've completed all your edits.

GRAPHIC BACKGROUNDS: ARE THEY FOR YOU?

Before drawing any objects onto your new navigator, decide whether you want to use a graphic background. You should use a graphic background only if you have an image that complements the appearance and function of the navigator. Ideally, you should use an image that contains areas that the user would immediately identify as discrete objects that can be selected to initiate an action.

For example, the image of a bookcase might be used as a graphic background. Each shelf or book on the graphic background can be used as a link for a particular view in the database. Another obvious example of a graphic background is a map, where particular regions can be used to initiate actions.

If you decide to remove a graphic background, select Design, Remove Graphic Background.

15

CREATING NAVIGATOR OBJECTS

Navigator objects are the primary components that make up a navigator's design. Navigator objects include text boxes, buttons, hotspots, and graphical shapes that typically are designed to be clicked to generate some action or content display. Navigator objects include the following:

- Standard shapes, including rectangles, rounded rectangles, ellipses, lines (referred to as polylines), and polygons. All these shapes, with the exception of lines, are automatically filled with a user-defined color.

- Hotspots, in the form of rectangles, circles, or polygons. A *hotspot* is simply an outlined area that can be used to identify a particular region of a graphic background. Because hotspots are only outlines, they are never filled with a color. Hotspots can be used, for example, to outline geographical regions, such as cities, on a state map.

- Text boxes, enabling text to be displayed anywhere on a navigator. Font, size, and color are all configurable.

- Two varieties of buttons: graphic buttons, which are essentially rectangular Clipboard objects (such as a bitmap pasted to the Clipboard), and hotspot buttons, which are standard buttons that contain a single line of text.

Objects can be created using either the Create menu or the drawing tools provided in Domino Designer's Navigator toolbar. The easiest way to create an object is through the Navigator toolbar. If the toolbar is not visible, enable it by clicking File, Preferences, Toolbar Preferences. Enable the Show Toolbars and Show Context Sensitive Toolbar options, and choose OK. See Figure 15.15 for a sample navigator and the Navigator toolbar.

Figure 15.15
This navigator utilizes text and image objects to initiate simple actions such as opening views or other navigators. Note the Navigator toolbar to the right of the default Domino Designer toolbars.

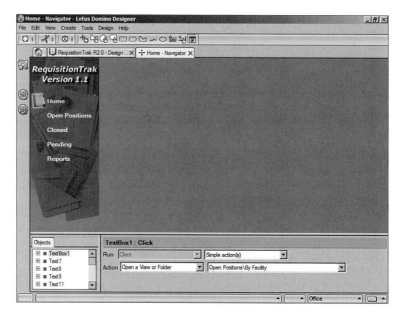

The first click of a particular button on the Navigator toolbar enables object-creation mode, represented by a crosshair cursor when the mouse pointer is over the navigator Design pane. The second click of the same toolbar button turns off creation mode and enables object-manipulation mode. In this mode, you can manipulate objects that have been drawn and move, resize, or delete them.

Drawing Navigator objects is fairly straightforward—especially to those already familiar with other drawing programs. Here are some quick drawing tips:

- First, click the button on the Navigator toolbar for the type of object you want to create. Or, you can choose Create and then select the object type from the Create menu.

- To draw an ellipse, rectangle, rounded rectangle, hotspot rectangle, or hotspot circle, move the cursor to the anchor point in the navigator and then click and hold the mouse button. With the mouse button depressed, move the mouse pointer to size the object. Release the mouse button to complete your drawing.

- To draw a polygon, hotspot polygon, or polyline, move the cursor to the first point and then click the mouse button once to begin your drawing. Each subsequent, single mouse click adds a new point to your polygon. To complete drawing a polygon-type object, double-click the mouse button. For polygons, a double-click automatically draws a line from the last point to the first point, closing the bounds of the object.

- To move several objects simultaneously, hold the Shift key and click once on each object that must be moved. When the last object is selected, continue holding the Shift key, click the left mouse button, and move the mouse to relocate all selected objects. Release the mouse button when the new positions are satisfactory.

- To draw a circle or a square, hold the Shift key and then begin drawing an ellipse or rectangle. The Shift key acts to constrain the object to a symmetric pattern rather than a freely sized shape. This trick also works after an object is drawn, when one of these objects is resized.

After an object has been drawn, properties for each object can be modified via the Properties dialog box. To make the Properties box visible, right-click over any object and then select Object Properties.

Each object has different properties that pertain to it. For example, a text object enables the selection of a font and point size. However, the HiLite tab applies to all navigator objects (see Figure 15.16).

For objects that will trigger events, one or both of the options presented in the HiLite tab should be selected:

- **Highlight When Touched**—This option causes the navigator object to become highlighted when the user mouses over it. This option should typically be selected for hotspot polygons, hotspot circles, and hotspot rectangles.

- **Highlight When Clicked**—This option causes the navigator object to become highlighted when the user clicks it. The object stays highlighted until another object is clicked.

15

Figure 15.16
Use the HiLite tab within a hotspot rectangle properties box to change how the hotspot appears when moused over or clicked.

TIP

> See a navigator in another database that you want to use in your database? No problem!
> Navigators can be cut and pasted to and from databases just like forms and views.
> Simply highlight the source navigator in Design mode and choose Edit, Copy (Ctrl+C).
> Next, open the destination database, select Navigator from the Design folder (from
> Design mode), and then choose Edit, Paste (Ctrl+V).

ACTING UPON CLICKS

After you have drawn navigator objects, you must determine how an object will react to a Click, the one and only runtime event for navigator objects.

When the user clicks a navigator object, one of the following can occur:

- A simple action can be initiated, enabling common navigator functions such as opening a new view to be developed with no programming effort.
- A formula can execute, for those who are comfortable with Notes formulas.
- Script can execute, enabling simple or complex LotusScript statements to be executed.
- Nothing can occur. Objects do not necessarily have to initiate one of the previous actions. They can be included in the navigator for artistic reasons alone.

To designate an appropriate action for navigator objects, first select the object whose action(s) need to be defined. Next, in the Programmer's pane at the bottom of the Designer window, select the programming method that you want to use for this object (Simple Action, Formula, or Script).

In many cases, simple actions are the most appropriate way to deal with navigator events. The five simple actions available for each object include the following:

- **Open Another Navigator**—Use this choice to link one navigator to another. When this option is selected, a combo box appears containing a list of available navigators.
- **Open a View or Folder**—This option is used to display a new view or folder in the View pane. When it is selected, a combo box appears containing a list of available views.
- **Alias a Folder**—This particularly useful option does two things. First, it switches the View pane to the folder specified. Second, it enables you to drag and drop objects from

other views and folders into the navigator object itself. When this option is selected, a combo box appears containing a list of available folders.

- **Open a Link**—This choice enables you to open a document, view, or database link. When this option is selected, a button appears that enables you to paste a link. First, however, you must switch to a database, document, or view; then choose Edit, Copy as Link for the appropriate object. After a link is copied to the Clipboard, switch back to the navigator designer and click the Paste Link button.

- **Open URL**—This choice links to an arbitrary URL on the World Wide Web. When you select this option, an additional button appears named Enter URL. Click this button and enter the URL that you want to link to the navigator.

USING HOTSPOTS WITH AND WITHOUT NAVIGATORS

You don't have to use a navigator to use hotspots. In fact, you can create hotspots on pages and forms as well as navigators. Hotspots created on pages and forms have slightly different capabilities than hotspots created on navigators. Here is a summary of the differences.

Navigator hotspots can do the following:

- Open another navigator, view, or folder
- Alias a folder (not available on Web)
- Open a document, view, or database link
- Open an arbitrary URL
- Execute an @formula or LotusScript program
- Use only a frame's target specification

Hotspots on pages or forms can do the following:

- Open document, view, database, or anchor links
- Open named elements: pages, forms, framesets, or views
- Open an arbitrary URL
- Specify a particular frame to use as a target
- Be used for text pop-ups
- Be displayed and used as buttons
- Be used as formula pop-ups
- Be used as an action hotspot, which can utilize @formulas, LotusScript, JavaScript, or simple actions

As you can see from the two lists, hotspots directly on pages or forms are just as powerful— perhaps more so—than hotspots that are created on navigators.

Another difference between navigators and page elements is that navigators are separate design elements. Therefore, navigators can be embedded on more than one page or form. If your design requires the same navigator-like structure in several places, you should consider a navigator rather than page elements.

Before Release 5 of Notes and Domino, there were no pages and some items could not be placed directly on a form, so navigators were very important. With the advent of Release 5, however, it became easier to create your navigational images directly on a page or form. This simplifies your design and reduces the number of different design elements you need to use.

You can use hotspots directly on pages and forms in Domino Designer. When you use a hotspot directly on a page or form, it is associated with text. You can also directly create an image on a page or form, and then create hotspots on the image. Let's first investigate the various forms of text hotspots.

LINK HOTSPOTS

As mentioned previously, you can use several different types of hotspots on a page or form. The first type is the *link hotspot*. This hotspot enables you to specify a document, view, database, or anchor. To create a link hotspot, follow these steps:

1. First, open the target of your link. For example, open the specific document, view, or database that you want as the destination in the Notes client. From the menu, choose Edit, Copy as Link; then choose Anchor Link, Document Link, View Link, or Database Link, depending upon your preference. This copies the link to the Clipboard. Alternatively, you can open a design element in the Domino Designer. You can use either a named element or a database link from within the designer. Again, from the menu, choose Edit, Copy as Link, followed by your choice.

2. Return to the page or form that you want to contain the hotspot. Highlight the text that you want to serve as your link.

3. From the menu, choose Create, Hotspot, Link Hotspot.

4. The Hotspot Resource Link properties box appears (see Figure 15.17).

5. If you copied a document link, the link automatically appears. If you copied a design element, you might need to click the Paste icon, which you can do in any case. The link from the Clipboard is pasted, and the type of your link changes to the type of link you copied to the Clipboard. Your link is complete.

You can also change some of the link properties directly from the properties box. For example, you can specify a URL rather than a document link as the hotspot destination. In this case, you must manually change the type of link to URL and then type the URL into the Value field of the dialog box.

Figure 15.17
Use the Hotspot Resource Link properties box to specify how the hotspot should function and appear.

Finally, you can specify a frame where you want the result of the hotspot to appear. If you don't specify a frame, the link appears within the same frame as the hotspot, unless a frameset target frame overrides it.

HOTSPOT TEXT POP-UPS

Hotspot text pop-ups are very useful for supplying help information. You can arrange for helpful text to appear either when the user's mouse hovers over the hotspot or when the user clicks the hotspot (see Figure 15.18).

NOTE

Hotspot text pop-ups do not work in Web browsers. They work only in the Notes client.

Figure 15.18
The Hotspot Pop-Up properties box is used to define the pop-up's appearance and features.

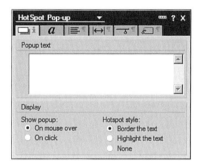

To create a hotspot text pop-up, follow these steps:

1. Add the document text to a page or form.
2. Highlight the text that will be used to trigger the hotspot.
3. Choose Create, Hotspot, Text Pop-Up. The Hotspot Pop-Up properties box appears.
4. Enter the pop-up text in the Pop-Up text field.
5. Choose whether the text should appear on a user mouseover or on a click by selecting the appropriate radio button.
6. Show a border around the hotspot or use a highlight color by checking the appropriate box.

HOTSPOT BUTTONS

Buttons that are displayed on a page or form are called *hotspot buttons*. You can program the action of the button using one of four different methods. You can use a simple action, an @formula, a LotusScript program, or a JavaScript program. Simple actions enable you to assign values to fields, copy documents, send or reply to email, and perform many other common preprogrammed actions. If you use one of the other methods, you have the full power of the programming language at your disposal.

To create a hotspot button, follow these steps:

1. Move the cursor on the page or form to the location where you want your button to appear.
2. Choose Create, Hotspot, Button.
3. The Button properties box appears. Enter the label that you want to appear on the button in the Button label field.
4. In the Programmer's pane, select the run environment in which the button will be used from the Run drop-down field. The default setting is for the Notes client; select Web for Web applications.
5. In the Programmer's pane, select the language that you want to use from the next drop-down field. The default is the @formula language, but you can choose Simple Action, LotusScript, or JavaScript also.
6. After you choose your language, you can use the Programmer's pane to enter your action.

FORMULA POP-UP HOTSPOTS

A formula pop-up hotspot has some characteristics of a text hotspot and a hotspot button. Formula pop-up hotspots must be associated with text on the form or page. When the user clicks the hotspot, the formula is executed. Note that the mouseover option is not available for formula hotspots.

To create a formula hotspot, follow these steps:

1. Move the cursor on the page or form to the location where you want your formula hotspot to appear. Highlight the text that you want to use to trigger the formula.
2. Choose Create, Hotspot, Formula Pop-Up.
3. The Hotspot Pop-Up properties box appears. You can change attributes of the text, such as the font or color.
4. In the Programmer's pane, the @formula language is automatically selected for you. You cannot use LotusScript or JavaScript for a formula hotspot.
5. In the Programmer's pane, enter the formula that you want to execute if the user clicks the hotspot text.

NOTE

Formula pop-ups do not work in Web browsers. They work only in the Notes client. Use an action hotspot instead, as described in the next section.

ACTION HOTSPOTS

An *action hotspot* is much more powerful than a formula pop-up hotspot, and it also works in browsers. An action hotspot runs a programmed action. You specify whether you want the action to run in the Notes client or in Web browsers; then you can create it in the appropriate language. Action hotspots for Notes can use simple actions, the @formula language, LotusScript, JavaScript, or Common JavaScript. Web action hotspots can utilize JavaScript or Common JavaScript. The Common JavaScript option enables you to create many typical mouse actions (such as onMouseOver), whereas the JavaScript option includes access to these and other form objects to create your JavaScript code.

When the user clicks the hotspot, the action you supply is executed.

To create an action hotspot, follow these steps:

1. Move the cursor on the page or form to the location where you want your formula hotspot to appear. Highlight the text you want to use to trigger the formula.

2. Choose Create, Hotspot, Action Hotspot.

3. The Action Hotspot properties box appears. You can change attributes of the text, such as the font or color, and you can specify a frame for the target if required.

4. In the Programmer's pane, select the appropriate client where the action will run. You can specify Web or Client (Notes). This choice determines the language choices available to you.

5. Select the language that you want to use.

6. In the Programmer's pane, enter the formula or other program that you want to execute if the user clicks the hotspot text.

HOTSPOTS ON IMAGE MAPS

You can define hotspots on image maps in a manner similar to the way you work with hotspots on navigators. Image maps, also known as pictures, can be placed on a page in one of two ways. You can import an image file from the file system, or you can use a shared image, which is an image that is already stored within a database in the shared image library. The terms *image*, *picture*, and *image map* are used almost synonymously. The only slight difference in meaning is that an image is typically called an image map after it has one or more hotspots on it. So, you can call it either an image with hotspots or an image map.

To import an image from the file system, follow these steps:

1. Open the page or form you want to use. Move the cursor to the location where you want your image to appear.

15

2. Choose Create, Picture. A dialog box showing the file system appears.

3. You can navigate through the file system looking for the image to import. You can import the following types of files: BMP, CGM, GIF, JPEG, Lotus PIC, PCX, and TIFF 5.0.

4. Find the file you want to import, and click the Import button. Your image will be imported.

To use an image that is already within your shared image resources, follow these steps:

1. Open the page or form that you want to use. Move the cursor to the location where you want your image to appear.

2. Choose Create, Image Resource. A dialog box appears showing you all the images that are in your shared image library.

3. Select the desired image from the list of images, and click OK. Your image is shown on your page or form.

After you create an image on your page or form through either of the methods, you can add a hotspot to the image. Hotspots on an image can be one of three shapes: polygon, circle, or rectangle. To create a hotspot on an image, follow these steps:

1. First place the image on the page or form using one of the techniques described previously.

2. Open the Picture properties box (see Figure 15.19).

Figure 15.19
Use the Picture properties box to specify an image's look and functionality.

3. Click one of the icons in the Hotspots section to create a polygon, circle, or rectangle.

4. Move your cursor into the image area. It should now appear as a cross.

5. Click one corner of the area where you want the hotspot to be located, and drag the mouse to the other corner. You will see a rubber band shape of the hotspot area. You can adjust the location and size of the hotspot area by clicking and dragging the handles for the shape, which look like dots. To move the hotspot shape, click and drag it.

6. After you place the hotspot on the image, you can specify an action to be taken when the user clicks the hotspot. You can choose a link, a named element link, or a URL. A link can be a document, view, database, or anchor link. A named element links to a design element, such as a page, form, frameset, or view. You specify the type within the Hotspot properties box.

7. You can optionally also specify an action to take in the Click event for the hotspot. The Click event can be programmed as a simple action, a formula, or a LotusScript or JavaScript program, as described earlier in the section on hotspot buttons.

USING EMBEDDED ELEMENTS ON A PAGE OR FORM

When defining a page, you can embed several different types of elements. In addition to outlines, discussed in a previous section, you can embed navigators, views, folder panes, and a date picker in pages. On forms, you can embed all those elements as well as a group scheduler and file upload control. To embed one of the following design elements, select Create, Embedded Element, and then choose one of the embedded element types. Here is a synopsis of these embedded elements:

- **Embedded outline**—This enables you to specify navigation elements for your Web site or database. Use the Outline Editor to edit the outline entries. Each outline entry can serve as a link to a page, form, or URL within a database. Embedded outlines are especially useful when used with framesets.

- **Embedded view**—You can embed a view on a page. You embed a view so that you can control the formatting of the view display. When a view is embedded on a page or a form, the user does not see the standard view navigation elements. One of the important properties of an embedded view is the capability of specifying the use of a Java applet for Web browsers. Do this in the Embedded View properties box.

- **Embedded navigator**—When you embed a navigator, the page or form refers to the navigator design element. Navigators can include graphics and hotspot definitions. If you change a navigator, all references to the navigator get the changed graphics.

- **Embedded import navigator**—When you choose Import Navigator, the graphical design elements of the navigator are imported into the page. After the design elements have been imported, you can edit them directly on the page. Note that after you have imported the navigator, it is no longer linked to the original navigator definition.

- **Date Picker**—The Date Picker works only on the Notes client; it does not work in a Web browser. If you choose this item, it displays a calendar. This object works in conjunction with a Calendar view in another frame within the same frameset. If you insert a date picker in one frame and a Calendar view in another, they are linked automatically. The user can choose a date on the date picker, and the Calendar view moves to that date automatically.

- **Scheduler**—The scheduler can be embedded only on forms, not on pages. This is because it utilizes a field, and pages cannot have fields. The Refresh mode enables you to control what happens when the user clicks the Refresh (F9) key. Because there might be many users and many databases to search for updates, you can control how much detail Domino searches for upon refresh.

- **Embedded editor**—This is a new feature introduced in Release 6. The embedded editor lets you embed one or more forms into an existing form. One of the uses of an embedded editor is to link it to an embedded view, allowing a user to edit documents in a view without having to open separate windows.

- **Embedded Folder pane**—The Embedded Folder pane enables you to have a folder pane embedded within a page or form of your own design. The folder pane is the pane that appears in the upper-left pane when you are looking at a view or folder. It contains a hierarchical listing of the views and folders of the database. Embedding this pane in your own page or form allows the user to navigate to one of the existing views or folders easily.

- **File Upload control**—The File Upload control enables Web users to attach files to documents. To use it, you embed the control on a form. When the form is displayed to a user, a text field and a Browse button appear, and the user can enter a filename or browse for a file to be uploaded. Note that for this control to work, the Domino server administrator must define a temp directory. If a temp directory is not defined, the attachment will not be uploaded. Also, the file upload control works only in a Web browser, not in the Notes client.

PUTTING IT ALL TOGETHER: OUTLINES, VIEWS, FRAMESETS, NAVIGATORS, AND BEYOND

Notes and Domino 6 provides you with a rich set of tools for presenting applications to users in both the Notes client and Web browsers. It is easy to become confused about which design element to choose, so we'll try to bring all these concepts together in this section.

When you present an interface to the user, there are several important considerations. The first is content, the second is layout, and the third is navigation. These are not separate concepts; in fact, they should join seamlessly to form the user interface.

You provide basic content to the user on pages or forms. If you want to have users provide feedback, you must use a form. A page is a read-only design element that the user can view but on which the user cannot enter any input (unless you manually code HTML and JavaScript and do not require the use of any fields). Pages are suitable if you only have a small number of unique Web pages to be developed and maintained. Forms are useful if you want to have more of a database-driven design with potentially hundreds or thousands of documents shown to the user within the form. Pages and forms are also containers that can house embedded elements, such as views, navigators, outlines, and so forth. Pages are typically used when you want to solely include outlines or navigators. You can provide basic layout within a page by just editing the content of a page and placing the elements where you want them to appear.

Complex layouts can be achieved relatively quickly by using framesets. Frames within a frameset can contain documents, URLs, pages, forms, views, or other framesets. Framesets work well in Notes applications and, combined with the addition of outlines and pages in Release 5, make it easy to build your database navigation. For most Web designs, you probably want to avoid framesets. If you must use framesets, though, you won't need more than three or four frames, and you should typically start your frameset design simply. The content in one frame can cause changes in another frame. It is very common to have navigational elements (such as an outline in a page) in one frame and have the navigation change the content of a separate frame (the target).

The last type of design element is the navigational element. In this category are outlines, views, image maps, and navigators. A view is the traditional Notes navigational element, and it enables the user to navigate among documents within a database. Each outline entry within an outline performs a similar purpose but is much more powerful. With outline entries, you can navigate to URLs, pages, and forms as well as documents. A navigator is a design element that enables you to draw graphical items and create hotspots. It is a stand-alone design element; to be used, it must be included in a page or form. Thus, it can be created once and used in multiple locations, if desired. An image map is created and directly associated with a specific page or form. It is similar to a navigator but is not an independent design element. You can create hotspots on image maps and link them to pages, forms, or URLs.

CHAPTER **16**

USING SHARED RESOURCES

In this chapter

OVERVIEW

Applications built in Notes and Domino often must incorporate various types of resources that are created and maintained in third-party software. These resources typically include graphics, HTML files, Cascading Style Sheets, and others. It has historically been a challenge for Domino developers to import, implement, edit and maintain these resources in Notes and Domino. With Release 5, Lotus introduced the new image and applet resources, which made things a little easier. But Domino Designer 6 has evolved to include additional resource types and added functionality into a new Shared Resources grouping that makes organizing, maintaining, and utilizing resources a more efficient process.

Shared resources include images, files of various types, applets, style sheets or Cascading Style Sheets (CSS), and data connections to external data sources. By utilizing shared resources, you can centrally store just one copy of a given resource and reference it throughout one or more databases. Common resources are grouped together, and in many cases you can open and edit resources in third-party applications—all from within Designer.

Before exploring how to create, use, and share each of these resource types in Domino, let's briefly review each.

- *Images*—Image resources are graphics that are stored in a database and used throughout an application. You can store GIF, JPEG, and BMP files to be used as graphics on forms, subforms, pages, views, action buttons, table cells, and more.

- *Files*—File resources can include many types of non-NSF files that you want to use throughout one or more applications. For example, you can store and maintain a straight HTML file as a file resource and call it from your application rather than creating a page with passthru HTML.

- *Applets*—If you have rather large applets that require multiple files, you can import some of the files as a single shared resource.

- *Style Sheets*—Cascading Style Sheets (CSS) define rules that determine how content is rendered on a Web page by associating style attributes to particular HTML elements. You can store and maintain CSS files as style sheet resources, making them easy to centrally manage, edit, and reference.

- *Data Connections*—Data Connection Resources (DCRs) make integration of external data into Domino fast and easy. DCRs are reusable design elements within Designer that enable you to create a connection to a database for use in a form or field. Using a DCR, you define a connection to an external data source, and then use that connection to associate a form and its fields to fields in the external source. As shared resources, DCRs are reusable and can be shared across forms within the database and across multiple applications.

The shared resources are all available in the Design pane of Domino Designer. Click on Shared Resources to expand or collapse the list of shared resources. Select a given resource type to view and access any existing resources in the work pane, and to create a new shared resource.

USING IMAGE RESOURCES

By utilizing the shared image resources feature in Designer, you can centrally store a collection of images to use throughout one or more applications. You can now open the images from within Designer at their full size, using the third-party application of your choice—a significant improvement over Release 5. If you need to edit an image after it's been added as a shared resource, it's also easier to edit using your preferred graphics software and refresh the design within Designer. Overall, shared image resources are easy to centrally store, edit, and maintain.

This section reviews how to create an image resource, modify its properties, insert or reference an image to display, and change its design.

CREATING AN IMAGE RESOURCE

To create a shared image resource, follow these steps:

1. Select Shared Resources, Images.
2. Click the New Image Resource button. An Open dialog box will appear.
3. Browse to the directory where the desired graphic is located.
4. Select GIF, JPEG, or BMP from the Files of Type drop-down list.
5. Select one or more files to include as image resources.
6. Choose Open to add the selected graphic file(s) to the list of image resources in the work pane.

Another way to create an image as a shared resource is while inserting it into a form, subform, page, or document. You'll learn how to do so in the "Inserting an Image Resource" section a little later in this chapter.

IMAGE RESOURCE PROPERTIES

After you've added an image resource, you can view and modify its properties. To open the Properties box for an image resource, double-click on the resource listed in the work pane, or click the resource listed in the design pane. An example of an Image Resource properties box is shown in Figure 16.1.

Figure 16.1
Use the Image Resource Properties dialog box to view and edit an image resource's properties.

The Basics tab of the Image Resource Properties dialog box includes the following:

- *Name*—Filled in automatically when created, you can edit this if necessary.
- *Alias*—The alias property enables you to include another name that the resource can be referenced as throughout an application. You might find some situations in which using an alias will enable you to change a resource name while avoiding the need to change every reference to the old name. By simply setting the alias to the old name, you can avoid a lot of work.
- *Images Across and Images Down*—Use these properties to create a horizontal or vertical image set. The most common situation is to create a horizontal image set for the Web, such that the image appears to change depending on its state. For example, an onclick event on a button image could trigger the image to change so the button appears to be pressed. Designer 6 Help has detailed instructions on how to create image sets.
- *Colorize Grays*—Select this option to have a GIF image blend with the user's system colors. When this feature is enabled, the image blends in with dialog boxes, toolbars, and other elements of the system.
- *Needs Refresh*—This is automatically enabled by Designer when you open a resource. When enabled, Designer places a refresh symbol next to the file resource to indicate it needs to be updated. Refreshing image resources and using this option is discussed in more detail in the section titled "Editing an Image Resource" later in this chapter.

On the Web Properties tab, select the Read Only option if you want the image to be read-only when rendered on a Web page.

Use the Design tab to specify whether to hide the image in Notes or Web clients. You can also set properties on the Design tab to specify a template from which changes will be loaded, prevent the image from being modified during a database refresh or replace, and propagate the design change limitation to other databases that use the image resource.

INSERTING AN IMAGE RESOURCE

Inserting an image resource to be displayed in a Notes application is simple. To insert an image resource, follow these steps:

1. Open a form, subform, or page.
2. Position the cursor where you want the image placed.
3. Choose Create, Image Resource. The Insert Image Resource dialog box will open as shown in Figure 16.2.
4. If you're inserting an image from the current database, select the image from the displayed list.
5. If you're inserting an image from another database on the same server, select the database from the Database list. To select a database on a different server, click the folder icon next to the Database list and choose the server and database from the dialog box that opens. Select an image from the displayed list.

6. Click OK. The image will appear in the location you selected.

Figure 16.2
Insert a shared image resource from any available Notes database using the Insert Image Resource dialog box.

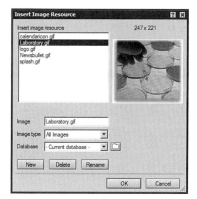

If you want to insert an image that is on a local or network drive and is not already a shared image resource, the procedure is a little different. After opening the Insert Image Resource dialog box, make sure the current database is selected, and then click New. Browse to the proper drive and folder and select the image file. Click OK, and not only will the image be inserted in the location you selected, it will be saved in the database as a new shared resource with all the other images.

REFERENCING AN IMAGE RESOURCE IN HTML

Displaying an image resource on a Web page in your application is simple, requiring use of the <img src> tag in passthru HTML. If a shared image resource is in the current database, all you need to reference is the image name. Following is an example:

```
<img src="companylogo.gif" border="0" width="150" height="50">
```

If the image is a shared resource in another Notes database on the same server, simply add the database name to the path, as shown here:

```
<img src="/otherdatabase.nsf/logo.gif" border="0" width="150" height="50">
```

Keep in mind that when referencing images in HTML, it's always a good idea to define the border, width, and height attributes of the img element to ensure the page and image load smoothly and as intended in the different browsers.

EDITING AN IMAGE RESOURCE

Chances are that sooner or later you will need to modify a number of the images you use in an application. The process of editing and updating images has been made a bit simpler with Release 6 and image resources.

When the list of shared image resources is open, you'll notice several action buttons as shown in Figure 16.3. In addition to the New Image Resource button covered previously, these buttons include Open File, Open With, Refresh, and Export.

Figure 16.3
Open, refresh, and export image resources using the available action buttons.

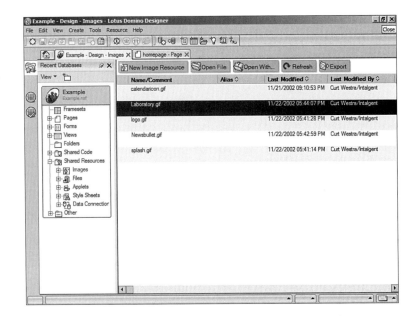

To edit an existing image resource, follow these steps:

1. Click Shared Resources in the design pane.
2. Select Images from the list of resources.
3. Select the image from the list of displayed image resources in the work pane.
4. Open the image resource using one of the following methods:
   - Click the Open File button if your computer already has software installed that is associated with the image format. The program should launch and open the selected file.
   - Click the Open With button to select the image editor you want to use. The Open With dialog box appears and you can choose the program that you want to use.

Once you complete your edits, you cannot save the modified image directly in the database. You must first save the image file to a local or network drive and then refresh the database version with the newly edited one. When an image has been opened in an image editor, Designer places a refresh symbol next to the image resource listed in the work pane. The refresh symbol indicates that the file needs to be updated from the edited version. With the image resources displayed in the work pane, follow these steps to refresh an image resource:

1. Select the image resource.
2. Click Refresh. An Open dialog box appears.
3. Select the image file to upload and refresh the database image resource.
4. Click Open.

The modified image file will then replace the version stored in the database, and the refresh symbol will be removed. The image will be updated wherever it is displayed in the application.

If you opened an image resource but did not make any changes, you obviously won't need to refresh the database version. However, Designer places a refresh symbol next to any resource when it is opened in a third-party editor—whether you edit or not. In this situation, you simply want to remove the refresh symbol. To do so, double-click the resource to open the properties dialog box, and then deselect the Needs Refresh option. The refresh symbol will go away.

16

EXPORTING AN IMAGE RESOURCE

To save a copy of an image resource on your computer, you can use the export feature by following these steps:

1. Click Shared Resources in the design pane.
2. Select Images from the list of resources.
3. Select the image from the list of displayed image resources in the work pane.
4. Click Export. A Save As dialog box will open.
5. Select the directory to where you want to save the image file.
6. Click Save. A copy of the image file has been exported.

USING FILE RESOURCES

File resources enable you to import any non-NSF file into the database for reuse within your application. For example, you can import an HTML file that was developed in a third-party application and call it from your application instead of creating a page with passthru HTML or calling it from the server. File resources can include anything—HTML, XML style sheets, executable files, and more.

TIP

> If you have JavaScript files that you want to use within your applications, you should import those as JavaScript Libraries. JavaScript Libraries fall under a new resource type that is grouped under Shared Code in the design pane of Designer. You can read more about JavaScript Libraries in Chapter 12, "Exploring the Integrated Development Environment (IDE)."

This section covers how to create a file resource, modify its properties, and edit it using third-party tools.

CREATING A FILE RESOURCE

To create a shared file resource, follow these steps:

1. Choose Shared Resources, Files.
2. Click the New File Resource button. An Open dialog box will appear.
3. Browse to the desired directory.
4. Select one or more files to include as file resources.
5. Click Open to add the selected file(s) to the list of file resources.

FILE RESOURCE PROPERTIES

After you've added a file resource, you can view and modify its properties. To access the properties for a file resource, double-click on the resource listed in the work pane, or click the resource from the list in the design pane. An example of a File Resource properties box is shown in Figure 16.4.

Figure 16.4
Use the File Resource properties box to view and edit a file resource's properties.

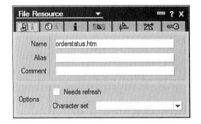

Properties on the Basics tab include filename and alias, which were described in the image resources section. The Needs Refresh property is automatically enabled by Designer when you open a resource. When enabled, Designer places a refresh symbol next to the file resource to indicate it needs to be updated. Refreshing file resources and using this option is discussed in more detail in the section titled "Editing a File Resource."

If you are using a file resource on a Web page, you should select the Read Only option on the Web Properties tab so the file will be read-only when rendered on a Web page. You should also specify the MIME type of the file resource so that Web browsers know how to handle it. Designer will set this value automatically if it recognizes the file type.

Use the Design tab to specify whether to hide the file in Notes or Web clients. As with many design elements, you can set other properties on the Design tab. These include the capability to specify a template from which changes will be loaded, control whether the file can be modified during a database refresh or replace, and propagate the design change limitation to other databases that use the file resource.

EDITING A FILE RESOURCE

Designer 6 allows you to open and edit file resources from the database using third-party applications. You can open a file resource from the list of resources in the files work pane by following these steps:

1. Select the file resource from the list.

2. Click Open File and Designer will choose which application will open the file resource. Or,

3. Click Open With… and select the application that you want to open the file resource in, as shown in Figure 16.5.

16

Figure 16.5
Select a third-party application that you want to use to open a file resource from within Designer 6.

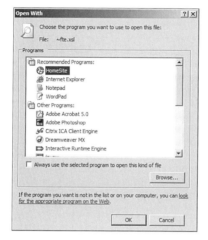

Once the file is opened in an editor you can make your modifications. Figure 16.6 displays an example of an XML style sheet file resource that has been opened in HomeSite for editing.

As with some of the other shared resources, you cannot save an edited file resource directly from the third-party editor to the database. You must first save the file to your computer and then refresh the database version with the newly edited one. When a file has been opened in an editor, Designer places a refresh symbol next to the file resource listed in the work pane. The refresh symbol indicates that the file needs to be updated from an edited version.

With the file resources displayed in the work pane, follow these steps to refresh a file resource:

1. Select the file resource.

2. Click Refresh. An Open dialog box appears.

3. Select the file to upload from your computer.

4. Click Open.

Figure 16.6
You can open and edit file resources by launching a third-party editor from within Designer 6.

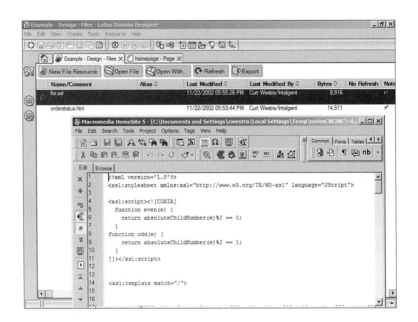

The modified file resource will then replace the version stored in the database, and the refresh symbol will be removed. The file will be updated wherever it is referenced or inserted in the application.

If you only opened but haven't edited a file, you can double-click the resource to open the properties dialog box, and then deselect the Needs Refresh option. The refresh symbol will go away.

EXPORTING A FILE RESOURCE

You can also use the export feature to save a copy of a file on your computer as a backup, for use elsewhere, or to edit later. To export a file resource, follow these steps:

1. Select the file from the list of displayed file resources.
2. Click Export. A Save As dialog box will open.
3. Select the directory to where you want to save the file.

UTILIZING A FILE RESOURCE

Because the types of files that you can include as file resources are so varied, so are the methods for how you may utilize them into your application. A discussion of the various methods to incorporate different types of file resources is beyond the scope of this chapter. You can refer to other areas of this book, the Designer 6 Help, and other resources for guidance in using specific types of file resources.

However, it is worth reinforcing the point that by placing files in databases as shared resources, you can enjoy the benefits of having files centrally stored and readily accessible by one or more applications.

USING APPLET RESOURCES

Java applets are small programs written in Java that execute within the browser environment or Notes client. The shared applets feature of the Domino Designer enables you to store a Java applet in a central location in the database, give the applet a name, and then reuse it throughout the database.

Java applets typically are comprised of a collection of files, including the class files. After they have been created in a third-party application, you can import the Java applet class files into your database as an applet resource.

This section provides an overview of how to create and use applet resources in Domino databases. See Chapter 23, "Creating and Using Java Applets and Agents," for more detailed information on working with applets.

CREATING AN APPLET RESOURCE

To create an applet resource, follow these steps:

1. Choose Shared Resources, Applets.
2. Click the New Applet Resource button. The Locate Java Applet Files dialog box will open, as shown in Figure 16.7.
3. Browse to or enter the Base Directory path where the Java applet files are located.
4. Select which file types you want to view and choose from.
5. Select the files you want to use as shared resources from the Available Java Files list. Click Add/Replace File(s) to add them to the Applet Files to Import list. Click Add/Replace All if you want to import all files.
6. Change the order of the files in the Applet Files to Import list box by clicking Reorder Up or Reorder Down to move files up or down, or by dragging files into place.
7. *(Optional)* Click Refresh or Refresh All to reload files in the Applet Files to Import list box.
8. Click OK and then enter a name for the applet resource in the dialog box that appears. The files are imported into the database.

You can open the applet resource's properties by double-clicking the resource. Among other properties, you can view the files that comprise the applet.

16

Figure 16.7
Create a new shared applet resource using the Locate Java Applet Files dialog box.

UTILIZING AN APPLET RESOURCE

You can incorporate a shared applet resource into a document relatively easily by following these steps:

1. Open the desired document that has a rich-text field intended for this use. Click in the field.

2. Choose Create, Java Applet. The Create Java Applet dialog box will open, as shown in Figure 16.8.

Figure 16.8
Using the Create Java Applet dialog box, begin the process of creating an applet in a document from a shared applet resource.

3. Select the Import an Applet from the File System or Use an Applet Resource option.

4. Click the Locate button to find and select the Java applet files from any shared applet resources. The Locate Java Applet Files dialog box opens.

5. Select Shared Resources from the Browse list box.

6. Select the database where the shared applet resource is located.

7. Select the appropriate files from the Available Java Files, and click Add/Replace to add them to the Applet Files to Import list.

8. Select the proper base class from the Base class list box.

9. Click OK, and then click OK again.

Using Style Sheet Resources

Designer 6 introduces the Style Sheet resource to support Cascading Style Sheets (CSS) files, improving integration with this important and growing Web technology. Style sheets define rules that determine how content is rendered on a Web page, by associating style attributes to particular HTML elements. By adding a style sheet as a shared resource, you can universally control the color, layout, and display of any HTML element. Furthermore, you can insert shared style sheet resources into Notes forms, subforms, and pages to apply styles to Notes elements for display in the Notes client.

Later, if you need to edit a style sheet resource, you can do so using your preferred editor—directly from within Designer 6.

This section briefly discusses how style sheets work, as well as reviews how to create, edit, and incorporate style sheet resources in your Notes and Domino applications.

Overview of Style Sheets

As stated previously, style sheets control how content is rendered on a Web page, by associating style attributes to particular HTML elements. You can add style sheets directly within an HTML document or import them from one or more external files. If you have many styles to define, the preferred method is to define the styles in a separate CSS file that follows the proper format and is saved with a .CSS file extension.

The primary benefit of this approach is that you can store and manage your Web page styles in just one or two locations. This eliminates the need to enter style attributes in each HTML element on every Web page, and helps maintain a uniform look and adherence to standards. It also makes it a lot easier to modify your Web page styles—one change in a style sheet and all the affected HTML elements on your Web site are updated!

A discussion of how to design style sheets is beyond the scope of this book, but the following code illustrates an example of a basic style sheet:

```
TD {
color:black;
font-family:arial;
font-size:10pt;
cursor:default;
}
BODY {
margin:0;
}
.normal {
color:black;
font-family:arial;
font-size:10pt;
```

```
cursor:default;
}
A:LINK, A:VISITED {
color : #000099;
text-decoration : none;
}
A:HOVER {
background-color : #FFFFFF;
color : #00009F;
text-decoration : none;
}
.menulink {
color:#FFFFCC;
font-family:arial;
font-size:8pt;
font-weight:normal;
line-height:1.5;
text-decoration:none;
cursor:hand;
}
HR{
color:darkblue;
height:1pt;
}
H1 {
color : #990000;
font-family : Verdana, Tahoma, Arial, Helvetica, sans-serif;
font-size : 200%;
margin-bottom : -1em;
margin-left : -5%;
}
```

As you can see, this particular style sheet defines rules for such attributes as the font color, font size, and cursor for all TD elements. Style rules are also defined for the body, anchor, horizontal rule, H1 elements, and more. These styles apply only to Web pages that import this style sheet. For use in Notes client-based applications, the style sheet resource must be inserted into a form, subform, or page and only those CSS properties supported by Designer will apply. Refer to Designer 6 Help for a thorough description of the CSS properties supported in the Notes client.

CREATING STYLE SHEET RESOURCES

To create a shared style sheet resource, follow these steps:

1. Choose Shared Resources, Style Sheets in the design pane.
2. Click the New Style Sheet Resource button. An Open dialog box will appear.
3. Browse to select the desired style sheet file, which should have the .CSS extension.
4. Select one or more style sheet files.
5. Click Open to add the selected style sheet file(s) to the list of style sheet resources.

After you've added a style sheet resource, you can view and modify its properties. To access the properties for a style sheet resource, double-click on the resource listed in the work pane, or click the resource from the list in the design pane. An example of a File Resource properties box is shown under Properties on the Basics tab and includes the style sheet name and alias, described previously in the image resources section. The Needs Refresh option is enabled by Designer when you open a style sheet resource. Refreshing style sheet resources and using this option is discussed in more detail in the section titled "Editing Style Sheet Resources" that follows.

If you are using a style sheet resource on a Web page, you should select the Read Only option on the Web Properties tab so the file will be read-only when rendered on a Web page.

Finally, on the Design tab you can specify a template from which changes will be loaded, control whether the file can be modified during a database refresh or replace, and propagate the design change limitation to other databases that use the file resource.

EDITING STYLE SHEET RESOURCES

If you take advantage of the Style Sheet resource feature, editing and managing your style sheets is relatively simple. As mentioned previously, you access your style sheet resources by choosing Shared Resources, Style Sheets in the design pane. Your style sheets will appear as shown in Figure 16.9.

Figure 16.9
Creating and editing style sheet resources is made easier using the tools available in Designer 6.

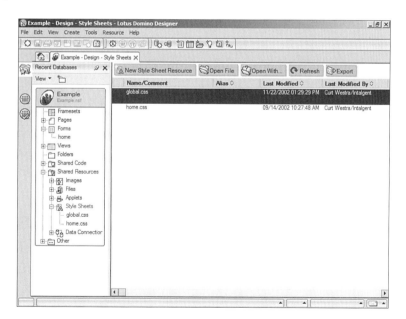

The style sheets work pane interface is very similar to that for other shared resources. To edit an existing style sheet resource, follow these steps:

1. Click Shared Resources in the design pane.
2. Select Style Sheets from the list of resources.

3. Select the style sheet from the list of displayed resources in the work pane.

4. Open the style sheet resource in one of the following methods:

- Click the Open File button if your computer already has software installed that is associated with style sheets. The program should launch and open the selected file.

- Click the Open With button to select the style sheet editor you want to use. The Open With dialog box appears and you can choose the program that you want to use.

Figure 16.10 displays a style sheet resource opened in a popular CSS editor, TopStyle Lite.

Figure 16.10
You can open and edit style sheet resources by launching a third-party editor from within Designer 6.

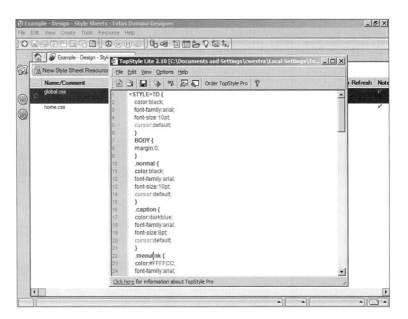

Once you complete your edits, you cannot save the modified style sheet directly in the database. You must first save the style sheet file to your computer and then refresh the database version with the newly edited one. When a resource has been opened in an editor, Designer places a refresh symbol next to the style sheet resource listed in the work pane, as shown in Figure 16.11. The refresh symbol indicates that the resource needs to be updated from the edited version.

With the style sheet resources displayed in the work pane, follow these steps to refresh a style sheet resource:

1. Select the style sheet resource.

2. Click Refresh. An Open dialog box appears.

3. Select the CSS file to upload and refresh the database's style sheet resource.

4. Click Open.

Figure 16.11
The refresh arrow flags resources that have been edited and need to be refreshed.

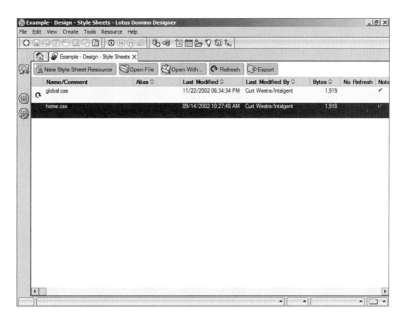

The modified style sheet will then replace the version stored in the database, and the refresh symbol will be removed. The style sheet changes will be implemented wherever it is referenced in the application.

In truth, Designer places a refresh symbol next to any resource when it is opened in an editor—whether you edit or not. If you opened but did not edit a style sheet resource, you simply want to remove the refresh symbol rather than try to refresh the resource. To do so, double-click the resource to open the properties dialog box, and then deselect the Needs Refresh option. The refresh symbol will go away.

USING STYLE SHEET RESOURCES

You can incorporate CSS files into your Web design in several ways. Refer to Chapter 28, "Using Domino Designer's Web Development Features," for information on the different methods you can use if you're not using the style sheet resource feature. To import a style sheet resource into a Web page, use the `<link>` tag to specify the link type and file path within the HTML `Head` element. The file path should end with the `?OpenCSSResource` action. For example:

```
<link rel=stylesheet type="text/css"
 href="/database.nsf/resourcename?OpenCssResource">
```

You can also use style sheet resources to apply styles to Notes elements in an application served up via the Notes client. Designer supports a number of CSS properties and will map the HTML tags from the style sheet resource to Notes. Designer 6 Help provides a detailed table of CSS properties supported by Designer.

To apply a shared style sheet resource in Notes, you must insert it in the appropriate form, subform, or page. Follow these steps to insert a style sheet resource:

1. Open the desired form, subform, or page.
2. Position the cursor in the area you want to insert the style sheet.
3. Choose Create, Resource, Insert Resource.
4. Select Style Sheets from the Resource Type listing.
5. Select the database from which you want to insert the style sheet. The default selection is the current database. If you need to select a database on a different server, click on the folder icon to select the proper server and database.
6. Select the desired style sheet(s) from the list of available resources.
7. Choose OK.

USING DATA CONNECTION RESOURCES

The Data Connection Resource (DCR) is new to Release 6, and makes integration of external data into Domino fast and easy. DCRs are reusable design elements within Designer that enable you to create a connection to a database for use in a form or field. Using a DCR, you define a connection to an external data source, and then use that connection to associate a form and its fields to fields in the external source. As shared resources, DCRs are reusable and can be shared across forms within the database and across multiple applications.

DCRs utilize Domino Enterprise Connection Services (DECS) technology and essentially provide a subset of the functionality offered if you used DECS instead. They can be used to connect to several types of relational databases, including DB2, Oracle, Sybase, OLE DB, and ODBC data sources. This flexibility and the fact that you build and administer them right within your Notes database makes them an appealing option.

See Chapter 29, "Domino and Enterprise Integration," for a detailed examination of Data Connection Resources and how to create and implement them.

CHAPTER 17

ACCESS CONTROL LISTS (ACLS) AND DATABASE SECURITY

In this chapter

ACL BASICS

Every Domino database is protected by a unique Access Control List (ACL). The ACL defines who can make which changes to an database and restricts where those changes can be made. The ACL works in tandem with Notes usernames taken from ID files and from Web-based authentication. If a username matches a name in the ACL, the user is granted the level of access defined for his or her name. Every Domino database has its own ACL. If the database is accessed through a Domino server, the ACL is always enforced—even when an anonymous user opens the database from the Web.

When you first access the Domino server or open a local replica of a database on which the ACL is locally enforced, you are prompted for your Notes user ID and your password. The same Notes ID remains valid throughout the Notes session or until you clear the user ID (for example, by pressing F5).

Every time you open a Domino database for which the ACL is enforced, the username on your ID file is compared against names in the ACL to determine what type of access you have. You may be listed in the ACL with your username, or you may be included in the ACL as a member of one or more groups. If you have more than one level of access to a database as a result of multiple listings, you automatically get the highest authorized level. In other words, if you are listed explicitly with Author access but you are a member of a group that has Editor access, you have Editor access.

The ACL contains seven major categories of access, ranging from the most restrictive to the most inclusive:

- **No Access**—Users with this access level cannot access the database—period.
- **Depositor**—A Depositor can create documents, but after documents have been saved and closed, a Depositor cannot view the documents or any other documents in the database.
- **Reader**—A Reader can only read documents in the database.
- **Author**—An Author can edit any documents for which their username is contained within the Authors field. Optionally, an Author can create, edit, and delete documents that the user personally created.
- **Editor**—An Editor can create, read, modify, and possibly delete any document in the database. An Editor also can run agents.
- **Designer**—A Designer can create or modify design elements in the database; can create and run agents; and can create, read, modify, and optionally delete documents within the database. Delete privileges can be allowed or disallowed.
- **Manager**—A database Manager can perform all the functions of other database users. In addition, a Manager can make changes to the database's ACL. The Manager is also the only one with the authority to delete a database.

These basic levels of the ACL can be restricted in various ways. The restrictions allow the database manager to define specialized functions for individuals within the boundaries of those basic ACL levels.

ASSIGNING ACL LEVELS

To understand the various ACL levels, let's review the ACL for your Personal Address Book:

1. Open the Notes client and click the Address Book icon on the bookmark bar. Figure 17.1 illustrates the location of the address book.

Figure 17.1
The address book is located in the bookmark bar within the Notes client.

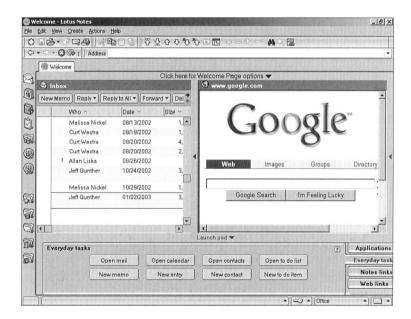

2. With your Personal Address Book open, choose File, Database, Access Control from the menu bar to display the Basics page of the ACL dialog box shown in Figure 17.2.

The People, Servers, Groups drop-down list at the top of the dialog box enables you to decide what people, groups, or servers in a particular access level will be displayed in the ACL. You also can leave the default selection to show all entries in the ACL for the database.

In Figure 17.2, all people, servers, and groups that have been assigned to the ACL are listed.

A CLOSER LOOK AT WHAT GETS LISTED IN THE ACL

To remove a possible point of confusion, let's review what exactly a person, group, or server is.

Figure 17.2
People and groups are assigned a level of access on the Basics page of the Access Control List.

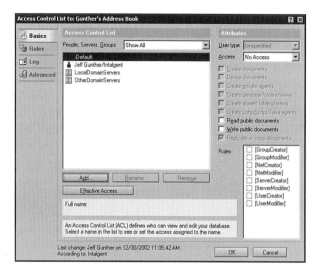

PEOPLE IN THE ACL

People includes individual users. If a user is in the Domino Directory, you can use that person's common name in the ACL. But if a user from another domain is to be listed in the ACL, that person must be listed using the full hierarchical name so that the name in the ACL can be compared with the name on the Notes user ID—for example, Jeff Gunther/Intalgent.

For tighter control over security, you might want to add full hierarchical names for those in the local domain. For example, if you have John Smith listed in the ACL, any user with the name John Smith can access the database. But if the name is John Smith/Sales/Acme, the ACL is far more restrictive.

If the database will be exposed to the Web via the Domino server, an HTTP username and password (listed in the Domino Directory) allow access to the database for those who are listed individually or as members of a group.

Names listed in a Directory Assistance database can also be authenticated and allowed access to Domino databases. The Directory Assistance database must be defined so that the names in it are trusted for authentication. Group names can be expanded only from the Domino Directory and one LDAP directory, but there is no practical limit on individual names.

The person who created the database on the server is automatically inserted into the ACL as a Manager.

GROUPS IN THE ACL

Groups can be created in the Domino Directory and then listed in the ACL. If a group of people needs similar access to data in your organization, you can put everyone who shares similar interests into a single group. You can then grant the entire group the same level of access in a database's ACL. If a new employee shares the interests of the group, that employee can be added to the group in the Domino Directory's group document. With that single entry, the new employee has access to any databases that have the group name in the ACL. This is much easier than trying to manage individual names in dozens of databases.

To illustrate how easy it is to use groups, assume that someone is leaving your accounting team and going into the sales department. You must remove that person's name from all the ACLs in all the accounting databases and add it to the sales databases. It takes only two simple steps: Delete the name from the accounting group, and then add it to the sales group. Assuming that you have not put the name into any of the accounting ACLs as an individual, you are done. The person is now a member of the sales group and has access to all the sales databases. However, if the user is listed individually within the accounting databases rather than included within a group, the user will still have access rights to the databases. Under this scenario, each database would need to be opened and appropriate modifications would have to be made to each database's ACL.

If you use hierarchical names in your organization, you can also use wildcards in the ACL. For example, */Sales/Acme allows the entire sales unit to access the database as a de facto group.

If your server allows Anonymous access, you can include a user named Anonymous in your ACL to define which level of access Anonymous users have. Anonymous is a group that includes anyone who gains Anonymous access to the database through the Web.

NOTE

> If a user has access to the database as a member of a group and as an individual, the access level assigned to the individual name prevails. For example, if you give a person Reader access but he or she also belongs to a group that has Editor access, the individual will *not* be able to edit nonpublic documents.

SERVERS IN THE ACL

Servers are listed in the ACL as distinct members of one of two groups:

- **LocalDomainServers**—Servers within your Notes domain that are registered in your Domino Directory. By default, LocalDomainServers are listed with Manager access within a database's ACL. For replication to work properly, it's recommended that this group have at least Designer access.

- **OtherDomainServers**—Servers listed in other Domino Directories within your Notes organization. By default, OtherDomainServers are listed with No Access within a database's ACL. Typically, the OtherDomainServers group is given lower access than the LocalDomainServers group.

These two groups should contain only servers within your organization because you can then give them a higher level of access than any servers outside your organization.

By putting all your local domain servers into a single server group, you make it easy to grant access to all the servers at once. Documents and design elements can be created or modified on any server in the organization and then replicated to other servers within the domain. You might want to limit servers from other domains to making changes to documents. In other words, you can assign LocalDomainServers to Manager access and OtherDomainServers to Editor or Designer access.

If you want to give access to a server from outside your organization, you will probably want to create a separate group or add the server individually with its full hierarchical name. If servers are not included in the ACL explicitly or via a group record, they have only the default level of access for the database.

ADDING A USER TO THE ACL

To understand how to add a user to a database's ACL, let's review the ACL for your Personal Address Book:

1. As previously covered in this chapter, open the Notes client and click the Address Book icon on the bookmark bar.

2. With your Personal Address Book open, choose File, Database, Access Control from the menu bar to display the Access Control List dialog box.

3. Click the Add button in the center of the Access Control List dialog box to display the Add User dialog box shown in Figure 17.3.

Figure 17.3
Type a name or click the Person icon to select a person, group, or server from an address book.

It is important that you enter names into the ACL accurately. A simple misspelling in the ACL will keep a user from being able to access a database. To prevent this problem, you should develop the habit of selecting names from the Domino Directory.

4. Click the Person icon in the Add User dialog box to display the Select Names dialog box, as shown in Figure 17.4.

5. Select the directory or address book you want to use.

6. Click the person, group, or server you want to add to the ACL.

7. Click the Add button to add the name to the right side of the dialog box. If you have to remove a name from the right side, highlight the name and click Remove. Or, click Remove All to empty all names from the right side so that you can start over.

Figure 17.4
Select names from a
Domino Directory or
Personal Address
Book to ensure accu-
racy.

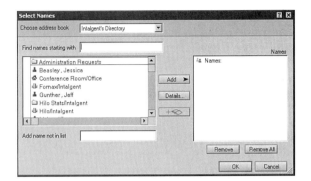

TIP

Release 6 introduces some nice additions to the Select Names dialog box. If your organization keeps the Domino Directory current, the Details button can be very handy. Simply
select a name and click the Details button to review the individual's Person document as
listed within the Domino Directory. Additionally, if you'd like to add the selected user to
your local address book, simply click the button with a + and an image of a directory.

8. When the name or names that you want are listed on the right side, click OK to add
the names to the ACL.

The names that you add are given the same level of access as the name that you highlighted
in the ACL dialog box before you started to add names. After you add a name, however, you
are free to change the access level in the access list of the Access Control List dialog box.

In the Access Control List dialog box, under User Type, you can also select which type of
user the name represents—a person, a group, or a server. This user type determines, in part,
what you can do with a user ID. For example, if you identify a name as a server, that server
ID cannot be used to access the database with a Notes client to edit documents. If you leave
an ACL entry as the default, Unspecified, there are no restrictions on the user type, and the
entry could be any type of Notes ID.

REFINING ACCESS LEVELS

After you select a level of access, you can refine the level of access by allowing or disallowing
access to certain specific functions, even though those functions might be allowed based on
the user's access level. It's important to note that each access level is afforded certain privileges to perform certain tasks within a database. Within each level, you can tune the exact
privileges provided to each user. However, as the user moves up the access levels, the capability to tune the privileges is diminished.

To the right of the list of names in the ACL are several check boxes defining specific functions that can be performed by members of a specific access level.

For example, in a Domino Directory database, you might be granted Author access so that you can edit your own Person document, but you might not be allowed to add or delete documents. With Author access, you can only view documents or edit sections of documents for which you are listed specifically as an authorized Author.

To refine the ACL privileges for an individual, you can click certain check boxes to turn them on or off. Refer to Figure 17.2 to see the check boxes used to restrict access. Table 17.1 indicates which privileges are automatically available (X), optional (O), or not available (blank) for the different levels of access. The optional privileges can be turned on or off.

TABLE 17.1   PRIVILEGES (X) AND OPTIONAL PRIVILEGES (O) FOR DIFFERENT LEVELS OF ACCESS

Privilege	Manager	Designer	Editor	Author	Reader	Depositor	No Access
Create documents	X	X	X	O		X	
Delete documents	O	O	O	O			
Create private agents	X	X	O	O	O		
Create personal folders/views	X	X	O	O	O		
Create shared folders/views	X	X	X	O			
Create LotusScript/ Java agents	X	O	O	O	O		
Read public documents	X	X	X	X	X	O	O
Write public documents	X	X	X	O	O	O	O
Replicate or documents copy	O	O	O	O	O	O	

Here is what each privilege means:

- **Create Documents**—Only users with Create Documents access can add new documents to an database. You can turn off this option for Authors if you want, and they still will be able to edit documents for which they are listed in an Authors field. There is an exception: Users can create public documents but cannot otherwise create documents in the database. See the entry for Write Public Documents, later in this list.

- **Delete Documents**—If a user does not have Delete Documents privileges, that person cannot delete any documents, including those that he or she created. An archive or tracking database is an example of where this option might be used. By default, nobody can delete documents, so you must set this option if you want to allow Managers, Designers, Editors, or Authors to delete documents.

- **Create Private Agents**—Anyone with Reader access or higher can theoretically create agents on a server-based database. However, this takes up system resources, so the capability to create private agents can be restricted for anyone below a database manager. Also, the system administrator can restrict anyone from running personal agents on the server. This is done in the Server document in the Domino Directory.

- **Create Personal Folders/Views**—Anybody with Reader access or higher can create personal folders and views on a server-based database, unless restricted from doing so. Managers and Designers always have this capability. A server-based folder or view can be replicated so that it is available on multiple servers, but it takes up disk space. If this option is deselected, users can still create local personal folders and views, but it's less secure.

- **Create Shared Folders/Views**—Designers and Editors can be given the capability to create shared folders and views, if desired. Or, you can restrict this access to save disk space on server-based databases. The Manager always can create shared folders and views.

- **Create LotusScript/Java Agents**—You can grant anyone with Reader access or higher the capability to create LotusScript or Java agents. However, these agents can hog the server processing time, so you might want to restrict this so that only the Manager can create these agents.

- **Read Public Documents**—You can enable those who come into the database with No Access to see certain public documents. This option is used primarily to allow access to calendar functions so that, for example, people can see a listing of scheduled functions without having access to any other information in a database. You can use it with any form that has the property Available to Public Access Users set.

- **Write Public Documents**—This option is also used for individuals who otherwise have no access to a database but who need limited access to calendaring and scheduling or other functions.

DEFINING AND USING ROLES

Roles provide another means of controlling access to specific functions within a database. Roles can be used in any of the following places within a Domino database to control access:

- Author fields that determine who can edit specific documents
- Reader fields that determine who can read specific documents
- View or folder properties that determine who can access specific views or folders (set these on the last page of the View Properties info box)

17

- Form properties that determine who can see documents created with a specific form
- Form properties that determine who can create documents using a specific form
- Controlled-access sections that can be edited only by specific individuals or specific roles

NOTE

Roles can be used for reasons other than controlling access. For example, roles can be used within the context of routing documents to particular users based on a predefined role. This list illustrates only places where roles are used for access. You can have up to 75 roles per database.

To assign roles to users, follow these steps:

1. Create the role in the ACL.
2. Assign the role to entries in the ACL.
3. Enter the role name in fields used to restrict access within the database.

You must complete all three steps for roles to work. Each of these steps is described in greater detail later in this chapter.

If you are limiting access to a function based on roles, enter the name of the role into the field used to limit access. For example, enter **[SectionReader]** in the appropriate Readers field on a form to restrict Reader access to people who have been assigned to the SectionReader role.

Although you can put individual names, server names, or group names into access fields on forms, views, sections, and so forth, using roles enables you to be more granular in defining who can do what in the database. For example, in a sales database, you can enable all the members of your sales force to place their own orders as Authors, but you want to give team leaders the exclusive right to create new client records. You can do this using a ClientCreator role on the Client form and assigning team leaders to that role.

Adding a New Role

To create a new role, follow these steps:

1. Launch the Notes client, Domino Designer client, or Administrator client and open the database where you want to add the role.
2. With your database open, choose File, Database, Access Control from the menu bar to display the Access Control List dialog box.
3. Click the Roles page of the Access Control List dialog box.
4. Click the Add button to display the Add Role dialog box, shown in Figure 17.5.

Figure 17.5
Enter a new role
name in the Add Role
dialog box.

5. Type the name of the role in the Role Name text box. Role names can contain up to 15 characters, including spaces.

6. Click OK to save the new role.

ASSIGNING A USER TO A ROLE

After a role is defined, you assign a user to that role on the Basics page of the ACL dialog box. To assign a person to a role, follow these steps:

1. Launch the Notes client, Domino Designer client, or Administrator client and open the database where you want to assign a role to a particular person, server, or group.

2. With your database open, choose File, Database, Access Control from the menu bar to display the Access Control List dialog box.

3. Click the name of the person, server, or group that you want to assign to the role.

4. Check the roles in the lower-right corner of the Access Control List dialog box.

5. Click OK to exit the Access Control List dialog box.

The user then is assigned to the role and has any privileges that go along with the role.

You should assign the LocalDomainServers and OtherDomainServers groups to all roles, to ensure that servers have access to all elements in the database so that the elements can be replicated.

MONITORING CHANGES TO THE ACL

Changes to the ACL are tracked automatically. To view a log of changes to the ACL for a database, click the Log page within the Access Control List dialog box. The past 20 changes to the database ACL are displayed, with the most recent changes shown at the top of the list. An example of the log is shown in Figure 17.6.

Other ways to monitor the ACL changes include having the Notes administrator set up an ACL Monitor document from the Server Administration panel, or having users check their own level of access by clicking the yellow Security icon on the Status bar in the Notes client.

The Security icon provides a list of which groups you are in that have access to the ACL, which roles you are assigned to, and which Notes user ID you are using to access the database.

Figure 17.6
A log of changes and updates to the database ACL is maintained in the ACL dialog box.

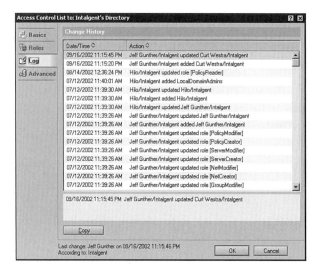

SETTING ADVANCED OPTIONS FOR THE ACL

The overall concept of the ACL is fairly simple and straightforward. Logical barriers exist beyond which certain users cannot pass. When you have just one database and a few users, it is easy to figure out who should be able to do what. But when you increase the number of Domino databases to the hundreds found in some organizations and open them to a user community that numbers in the thousands, it is easy to lose track of who has access to which databases. If someone leaves the organization or changes his or her name, it can be nearly impossible to track all instances of the person. The person might be in groups, in Reader fields, in Author fields, in roles in obscure database, or in other places. Additional complexity arises when users are accessing databases through Web browsers or when they are carrying around replicas on laptop computers that can be stolen or misplaced. The Advanced page in the ACL dialog box holds the tools for handling these complexities.

ALLOWING THE ADMINISTRATION PROCESS TO UPDATE THE ACL

By default, databases are not handled by the Administration Process, which can make systemwide ACL changes to databases including the Domino Directory. You must intentionally give permission for the Administration Process to work on a database. You do this on the Advanced page of the ACL dialog box, shown in Figure 17.7.

At the top of the page, the default setting for the administration server is None. To define an administration server—the server on which the Administration Process will update the ACL for this database—click the Server radio button. You can then click the drop-down button beside the Server field and select the name of the server on which you want the process to run.

Figure 17.7
Define an administration server on the Advanced page of the ACL dialog box.

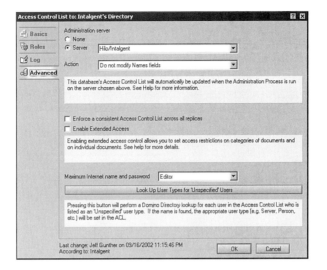

After the administration server is defined, you can define whether you want the Administration Process to update Reader and Author fields as well. These fields are not updated unless you specify that they should be modified. The system displays messages recommending how to handle changes to the database if you do change the settings.

DEFINING THE ADMINISTRATION SERVER FOR MULTIPLE DATABASES

The scenario previously described assumed that you were setting up the administration server for a single database. If you need to set up the administration server for multiple databases at one time, follow these steps:

1. Open the Domino Administrator 6 client.

2. Click the Files tab if it is not already selected.

3. Select Databases Only from the Show Me drop-down list.

4. Click the Tools button and select Database.

5. In the view containing all the files, select the databases that you want to work with. You can select multiple database files by holding down the Ctrl key while you click the files that you want to work with.

6. Click Manage ACL (on the top-right side of the screen) to display the Manage Multiple ACLs dialog box. Select the Advanced page as shown in Figure 17.8.

7. Click the Modify Administration Server Setting check box, select the Server radio button, and then select an administration server. Optionally, you can select how the Names fields will be modified.

8. Click OK to complete the selection of the administration server for your databases.

As you can see from Figure 17.8, the same Administrator client is used to apply various administrative settings for databases.

Figure 17.8
Use the Administration client to select the databases on which the Administration Process will run.

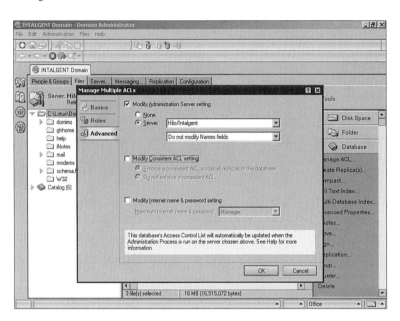

ENFORCING THE ACL ON LOCAL (AND OTHER) REPLICAS

When you access a Domino database on your local drive, you have Manager access by default. That means that you can change the design of the database. You can edit documents. You can also delete the database from your local drive. However, just because you have Manager access doesn't mean that you can replicate those changes to a Domino server. The only changes that get replicated to the Domino server are those allowed by the ACL on the server-based replica.

This is mentioned only for the sake of discussion. As far as the databases on the Notes network are concerned, a local ACL is not important. The ACL on the server determines what changes can be replicated. But the local ACL can be important for another reason.

Databases, by definition, contain data. Data can be confidential for any number of reasons. The ACL is designed to protect that data and to protect that confidentiality. So what happens when somebody opens a local replica of a confidential database on the laptop computer that you lost? That person has Manager access to your databases and data. The thief can quickly and easily steal all the confidential data.

To prevent that scenario, you can enforce the ACL on all replicas of a database, regardless of whether they are local or on a server. Follow these steps to enforce the ACL on multiple databases:

1. Open the Domino Administrator 6 client.
2. Click the Files tab if it is not already selected.
3. Select Databases Only from the Show Me drop-down list.
4. Click the Tools button and select Database.
5. In the view containing all the files, select the databases that you want to work with. You can select multiple database files by holding down the Ctrl key while you click the files that you want to work with.
6. Click Manage ACL (on the top-right side of the screen) to display the Manage Multiple ACLs dialog box. Select the Advanced page, as shown in Figure 17.9.
7. Select the check box in the center of the Advanced page of the ACL dialog box called Enforce a Consistent Access Control List Across All Replicas (see Figure 17.9).
8. Click OK.

Figure 17.9
Enforce a consistent ACL on all replicas of a database from the Advanced page of the ACL dialog box.

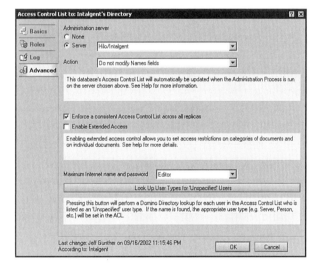

Use the simple check box to enforce a consistent ACL across all replicas of the database. Then people cannot access the database, even on a local workstation, unless they have user IDs and their names are listed in the ACL. Enforcing a consistent ACL is not as secure as encrypting a database, but it will keep your data safe from casual intruders.

SETTING THE MAXIMUM INTERNET BROWSER ACCESS

If Web browsers from the Internet access the Domino server, you can use a variety of tools to protect the data in databases on the server. You can use a firewall to segregate public from private data, for example. But what happens if you have to access your private data over the Web? How do you protect your data?

With an *extranet* application, for example, you might want to let your customers access your corporate network to view product catalogs and submit online order forms. They can do this using any Web browser. But by the same token, you do not want customers to be able to return to that order and change it after it has already been submitted. You can limit all Web browser access for authenticated users by using the Maximum Internet Name and Password setting, shown in Figure 17.9.

The Maximum Internet Name and Password setting enables you to limit what someone with a Web browser can do in your database. You can limit Web access, even though a user has a higher level of access if he or she is using a Lotus Notes client. To set the maximum level of Internet browser access, use the drop-down list and select the maximum level of access that you want to allow for Web browsers.

TIP

> If you have a Java application that communicates to a Domino server via DIIOP, the Maximum Internet Name and Password settings are enforced. For example if a user is specified in the ACL as editor, but the Maximum Internet Name and Password setting is set to No Access, the user cannot authenticate to the server and access the Domino Object Model.

Looking Up User Types

When you add individual names to your ACL, you must manually define each one as a person, a server, or a group. Groups may contain people, other groups, and servers. Sometimes it can be tricky to figure out whether you want to assign a name to a person group, a server group, or a mixed group. Well, don't worry. Let Notes do the work for you.

Figure 17.9 shows a button named Look Up User Types for "Unspecified" Users. Unspecified users are any names that have not been assigned as a person, a group, or a server. Unspecified users are looked up in the Domino Directory to determine which type of user they are. This is done automatically from the Advanced page of the ACL dialog box.

Near the beginning of this chapter, you learned how to select which type of users you wanted to display in the ACL. A restricted list of users is easier to work with when you are dealing with a complex database.

THE ROLE OF ACLS IN REPLICATION

Although it is easy to think of the ACL simply in terms of user access, the ACL has more far-reaching impact. Although the names of access control levels are used interchangeably between user and servers, there is a distinct difference. The levels given to users determine the functions that they can perform. In contrast, the access control levels given to a server control what data and design elements in a database the server can replicate. For example, when a user runs an agent, the agent cannot do anything unless the user is authorized to run agents in that database. In other words, a person with Reader access to a database cannot run an agent that modifies documents.

In a similar vein, the Domino server is subject to the restrictions in an ACL. Replication involves servers reading documents, database designs, and ACLs that have been added or modified on another replica of an database. Therefore, a server must be listed in the ACL so that it can make those changes to the database on other servers. As a rule of thumb, give the server at least as high a level as a user needs to make the same changes. If you want the server to replicate edits to all documents, give it at least Editor access. If you want the server to replicate design changes, give it Designer access. And, of course, if you want the server to be able to replicate changes to the ACL, the server must have Manager access in the ACL.

Assigning servers an access level is easy because of the two default server groups in the Domino Directory. When a new server is created using any of the organization's certifier IDs, the server name is automatically added to the LocalDomainServers group in the Domino Directory. When a developer creates a new database, the LocalDomainServers group is automatically added to the ACL and is given Manager access. The OtherDomainServers group is given Designer access by default. Therefore, all you have to worry about are the exceptions. What level of access do you want to grant to servers from outside organizations? Do you want to prevent changes from getting replicated? If so, set a lower level of access.

These are some of the things that you should consider when assigning access to servers:

- Manager access lets a server modify the ACL on databases. You might want to limit Manager access to a single server so that you can control updates to the ACLs of replicated databases. This is a common practice for servers that are set up in a hub-and-spoke configuration. You can also determine whether the server should have the capability to delete documents in the database. If you want the server to have deletion privileges, you must explicitly highlight the server or server group on the Basics page of the ACL and check the deletion function.

- Designer access lets a database receive design changes from the server. Design changes can include forms and views, agents, database icons, About and Using database documents, and replication formulas, for example. If a server has Designer access, it cannot make changes to the ACL of the database. Deletions are accepted only if you specifically mark the check box to allow deletions.

- Editor access for a server lets a database receive new documents and modifications to documents from the server, as well as document deletions if that option is explicitly selected. ACL and design changes are not allowed.

- Author access for a server lets a database receive new documents and modifications from the server, as well as deletions if that option is selected. However, updates and new documents from other users who have Author access are not replicated to the server. If you want to replicate updates from users with Author access, give the server at least Editor access to your database.

- Reader access lets the server pull changes from other replicas, but the replicas on other servers will not accept changes sent by the server.

- Depositor access does not apply to servers.

- No Access prevents the server from accessing the database.

17

If a server is not listed in the ACL, it still might be able to access a database using the default level of access, if the ACL default is set to allow at least Reader access.

As mentioned earlier, as a rule of thumb, you should give servers an access level at least as high as the highest level required by users. This technique ensures that the users can perform their duties using a replica of the database and have their changes replicate to other servers within the organization.

17

CHAPTER 18

WORKING WITH FORMULAS, FUNCTIONS, AND COMMANDS

In this chapter

WHERE AND WHY SHOULD I USE FORMULAS?

Formulas are used in several different contexts within the Notes client and Domino server. They are used for default values, view selection, input translation, and several other purposes. Basically, a *formula* is an expression that is evaluated and results in a value. The usage of the resultant value depends upon the formula context. In view selection, for example, the formula is evaluated for each document. If the formula results in a true value, the document is selected to be shown in the view; otherwise, it is skipped. In other contexts, formulas are used to test the validity of an input value or to choose documents for replication.

FORMULA BASICS

Formulas are attached to objects within Notes. Depending upon the context of the object, the formula can be used to do the following:

- Specify values of fields or an action to take when a particular event is triggered
- Specify titles for windows, sections, or column contents
- Dynamically display or hide form elements or content based on a defined condition
- Dynamically select the appropriate form or subform to display at runtime
- Dynamically select the documents to display in a view

Table 18.1 shows the objects and contexts where formulas can be used.

TABLE 18.1   OBJECTS AND THEIR PURPOSE

Object	Purpose
Values and Actions	
Button	Specifies the button action to take
Hotspot	Specifies the hotspot action to take
Hotspot pop-up	Evaluates to a text string to be shown when a user clicks the hotspot
Action	Gives the formula evaluated for the action to take
Event	Specifies action(s) to take if an event occurs
Agent	Selects documents to be processed and actions to take on them
Toolbar button	Specifies action(s) to take if the Toolbar button is invoked
Field	Default value Input translation Input validation Field value Keyword field for choices

Object	Purpose
Titles and Display	
Section title	Evaluates for section title
Window title	Evaluates for window title
Column formula	Determines what to show within a column of a view or folder
Access and Hiding	
Section access	Determines whether the user is allowed edit access to the section
Hide paragraph	If true, paragraph is hidden
Hide action	If true, action is hidden
Selection	
Insert subform	Evaluates to determine the subform to insert
Agent	Selects documents to be processed and actions to take on them
Replication	Determines documents to be replicated
Form formula	Determines a form to use to view and edit a document
Selection formula	Determines which documents show in a view or folder

SYNTAX

Now that we've covered where formulas can be used and what they are used for, here are some of the details of their syntax. Formulas in Notes are made up of expressions. If you are familiar with any traditional programming language, Notes formulas will seem similar in many respects. The most basic formula is a single expression:

```
RegularPrice * 0.20
```

In this example, the value in the price variable is multiplied by 0.20. You can save the result of an expression in a variable:

```
Discount := RegularPrice * 0.20
```

Notice that the assignment operator is := rather than just an equals sign. Different than a single equals sign that simply compares the two values, the assignment operator assigns the value of the leftmost variable to the computed expression. In a single formula, you can have several expressions, each terminated by a semicolon (;):

```
Discount := RegularPrice * 0.20;
DiscountPrice := RegularPrice - Discount;
SalesTax := DiscountPrice * 0.08;
TotalPrice := DiscountPrice + SalesTax;
```

When a formula has multiple expressions, the value of the last expression is the value of the formula. In this example, you don't actually need to assign the TotalPrice variable; you need only to specify the expression. However, by including the variable, you make the intent of the formula explicitly clear to anyone reading the formula.

18

Formulas can be made from the following elements:

- Constants (such as `0.274` or `"Hello"`). There are three types of constants: text, numbers, and time/date values. The format for these constants is given in the next section of this chapter.
- Variables (such as `Discount` or `SalesTax`).
- Operators (such as `+`, `-`, `*`, and `/`).
- @Functions (such as `@Prompt`).
- Keywords (such as `FIELD` or `REM`).

One major source of confusion is the difference between temporary variables and fields. *Temporary variables* are used only within the scope of a formula, whereas *fields* are used to permanently store information within Notes documents. All the assignment statements shown in the previous examples are temporary variables. Temporary variables are very useful for making longer formulas easier to code and understand. You can compute and save intermediate values and then use them later within the formula. To assign a value and save it permanently in a field, you must use the `FIELD` keyword. We'll review an example of this in the section "Keywords in Formulas," later in this chapter.

DATA TYPES

You can use five types of values within formulas:

- Text values (such as `"White House"` or `"politics"`). These values are probably the most frequently used type in Notes and Domino. Many built-in functions exist to manipulate text values. Text constants are enclosed in double quotation marks. To use a double-quote within the string, you must precede it with a backslash (\). You must use two backslashes to represent a single backslash within a string. Here is an example:
  `"Enter \"Exit\" to leave the program."`
- Numeric values (such as `37`, `-2.87`, and `7.2E3`). Numeric values are usually used for calculations of amounts, but they can be used for any purpose, such as counters, numeric identifiers, and quantities. A numeric constant can be a signed integer, can include a decimal point, or can be expressed in scientific notation. If you use scientific notation, you enter the number, enter an `E`, and then supply a positive or negative exponent for a power of 10. For example, `7.2E3` represents 7200, and `7.2E-2` represents 0.072.
- Time/date values (such as `[9/23/1998 9:25 AM]`, `[9/24]`, or `[16:30]`). Time/date values can be used to store dates, times, or a combination time/date. You can use them in time/date calculations and for storing time stamps within documents. Time constants are expressed within square brackets. You can supply a date, a time, or both.
- Logical values (`true` and `false`). These values are used within formulas and are used to test whether a particular situation exists. If so (`true`) you can take one action; if not (`false`), you can take another different action.
- List values (`"CA":"NY":"CT"`). List values are expressed by using colons between the elements. You can use lists to process several elements at once with the same formula.

EXPRESSION EVALUATION

Using the various data types, you can put constants, variables, and operators together to make simple expressions. Simple examples of adding and subtracting have already been demonstrated, but suppose that you have a more complicated expression involving several different operators. How do you determine which operation will be performed first?

Each operator has a *precedence level*. There are six levels of precedence. Operators with the highest precedence are performed first. Table 18.2 shows the precedence level for each operator. In this table, precedence level 1 is the highest and 6 is the lowest.

TABLE 18.2 OPERATOR PRECEDENCE

Operator	Operation	Precedence
:=	Assignment (for fields, you must also use the FIELD keyword)	NA
[]	List subscript	1
:	List concatenation	2
+	Unary positive	3
-	Unary negative (change sign)	3
*	Multiplication	4
**	Permuted multiplication (lists only)	4
/	Division	4
*/	Permuted division (lists only)	4
+	Addition (numeric values)	5
+	Concatenation (text values)	5
*+	Permuted addition (numeric lists only)	5
*+	Permuted concatenation (text lists)	5
-	Subtraction	5
*-	Permuted subtraction (lists only)	5
=	Equal	6
*=	Permuted equal (lists only)	6
!=	Not equal	6
=!	Not equal	6
<>	Not equal	6
><	Not equal	6
*!=	Permuted not equal (lists only)	6

18

continues

TABLE 18.2 CONTINUED

Operator	Operation	Precedence
*=!	Permuted not equal (lists only)	6
*<>	Permuted not equal (lists only)	6
*><	Permuted not equal (lists only)	6
<	Less than	6
*<	Permuted less than (lists only)	6
>	Greater than	6
*>	Permuted greater than (lists only)	6
<=	Less than or equal	6
*<=	Permuted less than or equal (lists only)	6
*>=	Permuted greater than or equal (lists only)	6
!	Unary logical NOT	7
&	Logical AND	7
¦	Logical OR	7

18

When there are several operators at a given precedence level, they are performed from left to right. For example, suppose that you have the following two expressions:

```
BaseAmount + Taxable * 0.06

Taxable * 0.06 + BaseAmount
```

Looking carefully at these expressions, it might seem that the two expressions don't yield the same result. Because multiplication has a higher precedence than the addition, however, the expressions yield the same result.

You can override the normal precedence by using parentheses. Anything within the parentheses is calculated first. For example, in the following expression, the addition is performed before the multiplication:

```
(BaseAmount + Taxable) * 0.06
```

If you have multiple sets of parentheses, they are evaluated from the inside out and from the left to the right. In the following expression, A+B is evaluated first, then C+D, then the multiplication by E, and finally the multiplication of the two subexpressions:

```
(A + B) * ( (C + D) * E)
```

TEXT CONCATENATION

One operation that you might use frequently is *text concatenation*. Concatenation of two text strings means that you append one string on the end of another. To concatenate text, use the plus (+) sign operator:

```
Name := "Mary ";
"Mary had " + "a little lamb";
Name + "ate " + "a big pie";
Name + "saw " + "a big wolf, " + "a little pig, " + "and a dinosaur.";
```

The output of these expressions yields the following:

```
Mary had a little lamb
Mary ate a big pie
Mary saw a big wolf, a little pig, and a dinosaur.
```

LISTS AND LIST OPERATORS

Lists are a special kind of data type within Notes. Lists enable you to store multiple values within a single variable or Notes field. The values within the list must all be of the same type. For example, you might use the following:

```
EastStates := "NY" : "CT" : "NJ";
WestStates := "CA" : "OR" : "WA";
SomeStates := WestStates : EastStates;
```

The colon (:) is the list concatenation operator and can be used to append two lists in a manner similar to string concatenation. In the previous example, the list variable `SomeStates` would contain the values `"NY"`, `"CT"`, `"NJ"`, `"CA"`, `"OR"`, and `"WA"`.

In addition to combining lists, you can perform operations on the list elements in either a *pair-wise* or *permuted* manner:

- Pair-wise operations take two lists and operate on an element-by-element basis. If one list is shorter, it is extended to the length of the longer one by using the last element repeatedly.

- Permuted operators take two lists and perform the operation for every combination of the elements of the lists. A permuted operator takes the first element of the first list and operates with each element of the second list. Then it goes back and takes the second element of the first list and operates with every element of the second list. This pattern is followed until every element of the first list has been used.

This is an example of pair-wise operations:

```
InvoiceAmounts := 27.92 : 82.47 : 37.41 : 14.95;
SalesTax := InvoiceAmounts * 0.06;
TotalAmounts := InvoiceAmounts + SalesTax;
```

In this example, when the multiplication occurs on the second line, the single value of `0.06` is extended to have the same number of elements as the first list. Normally in your program, you won't be assigning constants to the first variable, but you can see the usefulness of the list expressions by being able to process multiple values at once.

If you looked at the table of operator precedence carefully, you probably noticed that some operators had an asterisk (*) in front of them; these are permuted operators. Here is an example of permuted string concatenation:

```
CodeBases := "HW" : "SW" : "SVC";
Categories:= "01" : "02" : "03" : "04";
AllCodes := CodeBases *+ Categories;
```

After executing these assignment statements, the `AllCodes` variable contains the following:

`HW01:HW02:HW03:HW04:SW01:SW02:SW03:SW04:SVC01:SVC02:SVC03:SVC04`

This enables you to quickly create a list of all the possible combinations of codes.

When using logical values in a pair-wise manner, all pairs are evaluated. Then if any of the pairs result in a `true` value, the expression result is `true`. Otherwise, it is `false`. Table 18.3 shows some examples.

TABLE 18.3   EXAMPLE OF LIST MANIPULATION

Type	Expression	Value
Pair-wise	1 : 2 : 3 = 5 : 5 : 5	0 (false)
Pair-wise	1 : 2 : 3 = 5 : 5 : 3	1 (true)
Pair-wise	1 : 2 : 3 = 5 : 3	1 (the 3 on right is extended)
Permuted	WestStates = "WA" : "OR" : "CA"; "CA" : "NY" *= WestStates;	1 (at least one is in the list)

KEYWORDS IN FORMULAS

Five keywords perform special functions within Notes: DEFAULT, ENVIRONMENT, FIELD, REM, and SELECT. Keywords are normally shown in all-capital letters. Also, if keywords are used, they must appear at the beginning of the statement; they cannot be used in the middle of a statement.

DEFAULT

The DEFAULT keyword specifies a default value for a document field. If the field does not exist within the document, the default value is used. If the field does exist within the document, the default value in the statement is ignored. You use the DEFAULT keyword as follows:

`DEFAULT fieldname := value;`

For example:

`DEFAULT CompanyName := "ACME, Inc.";`

ENVIRONMENT

The ENVIRONMENT keyword is used to set an environment variable in the operating system environment. For Windows and Unix, the value is stored in the NOTES.INI file. The value must be a text string. You cannot retrieve the value with this keyword. You might want to use the @Function @Environment to retrieve and set environment variables instead of using this keyword.

You normally use environment variables when you need the following characteristics:

- The values are stored between sessions.
- The values might differ from one database user to another.

The syntax for the ENVIRONMENT keyword is shown here:

```
ENVIRONMENT varname := value;
```

Environment variables pose a few problems. First, because they are stored on the workstation outside the Notes environment, if a single user has both a laptop and a desktop machine, the environment variables might change. Second, if two users use the same physical workstation, the environment variables might contain inconsistent values. Third, because they are stored on the workstation, they are not accessible from a Web browser. Finally, because environment variables are stored in a local, easily accessible file instead of a Notes database, there is a potential security risk.

You might want to consider *profile documents* as an alternative to environment variables. They are stored within a database and can be used to store information that varies from one user to another. Within the @Formula language, you can use @GetProfileField and @SetProfileField. Because profile fields are stored within a database, they can be replicated. Environment variables cannot be replicated.

FIELD

You use the FIELD keyword to specify that you want to store a value in a field within a document. If you leave this keyword off an assignment statement, the value is stored only in a temporary variable, not within the document.

The syntax for the FIELD keyword is shown here:

```
FIELD fieldname := value;
FIELD fieldname := @DeleteField;
```

The value may be any type that is valid for the specified field. If the field does not exist before the statement, it is created in the document. If it does exist, the value is replaced.

@DeleteField has a special meaning. If you use the second format, the value of the field is deleted from the document.

REM

The REM keyword stands for the word *remark*. This keyword is used to add explanatory comments to a formula. If you have any programming background, you probably already know why you should write comments in your code. Here are two examples:

```
REM "your comment here";
REM {your comment here};
```

NOTE

Beginning with Release 6, braces can also be used to delimit a remark within a formula.

SELECT

The SELECT keyword is used to select documents. Formulas are used to select documents in three contexts:

- View-selection formula
- Replication formula
- Agent document selection

In each case, the formula is evaluated for each document within the context. If the formula result is true, the document is selected for inclusion; if it is false, the document is skipped. To use the SELECT keyword, use the following syntax:

```
SELECT expression;
```

In a view, a view-selection formula is used to determine the set of documents that are displayed in the view. If you want to include all documents within the database, you can use this code:

```
SELECT @All;
```

Agent formulas are rather unique because they must include both a SELECT keyword statement, which selects the documents to be processed, and additional statements that actually process the documents.

SPECIAL FORMULAS

As mentioned earlier in this chapter, formulas are used in a variety of contexts within Notes.

Formulas can be used in some specific locations in Notes. Most of the uses of formulas are clear and calculate simple results, but some formulas have specific conventions. Here are some of the special formulas:

- **Form formula**—This formula is used to determine which form will be used to display or edit a particular document. This type must result in the name of a form. Form formulas are optional and, if present, are associated with a view, not a form. Here is an example: Suppose that you have two expense approval forms, one used for amounts less than $1,000 and another used for amounts greater than $1,000. You could display all expense documents within one view but then show alternative forms, depending upon the approval amount. In this example, the two form names are ApproveLow and ApproveHigh. The form formula in the view would be something like this:
  ```
  @if(amount <= 1000; "ApproveLow"; "ApproveHigh")
  ```

■ **Input-validation formula**—This formula can be associated with each field within a form. It is invoked for a document whenever it is saved, recalculated, or refreshed. The purpose is to determine whether a field has a valid value. You return a result of either `@Success` or `@Failure`. If you return `@Failure`, you also specify an error message to be displayed to the user. Suppose that you want to limit a field's data values to less than $1,000. You could supply a validation formula:

```
@if(amount <= 1000; @Success; @Failure("You must supply a value less than or
➥equal to $1,000"))
```

■ **Input-translation formula**—This formula can be associated with each editable field within a form. It is invoked for a document whenever it is saved, recalculated, or refreshed. The purpose of the input-translation formula is to convert data that has been entered by the user into a standard format. For example, you can add (or remove) capitalization, extra blank spaces, and so forth. Suppose that you have a field for a city. You could supply this formula:

```
@ProperCase(@Trim(City))
```

■ **Window title formula**—This formula is evaluated to determine what to show on the title line of the window that displays the document. You can use this formula to vary the title to correspond to data that is within the document. Here is an example that displays `New Document` for newly created documents; otherwise, it displays a title showing the name contained in the document:

```
@If(@IsNewDoc; "New Document"; "Document for " + Name)
```

18

@FUNCTIONS

Lotus Notes Release 6 includes 259 @Functions. These functions are available to help you automate the processing of your documents. The @Functions include mathematical functions, iterative functions, string handling, date-time manipulation, list handling, database handling, security, and many other functions. The syntax for calling functions is as follows:

```
@Function(argument1; argument2; ... argumentn);
```

For example, this `trim` @Function takes one argument:

```
@Trim(UserNameField)
```

You can also combine @Functions by using them in a nested fashion. For example, you could specify the following:

```
@ProperCase( @Trim(UserNameField) )
```

In this case, the field `UserNameField` is trimmed, removing any leading or trailing blanks. Then the resulting string is initial-capitalized using the `@ProperCase` function.

Because there are so many @Functions, it is not possible to describe them all in detail in this book. The following sections cover a few of the important @Functions. You can find a complete listing in Appendix B, "@Function and @Command Listings." You also can look in the Domino Designer help file for further details on @Functions.

ITERATIVE EXECUTION

With the release of version 6, Lotus has provided developers the much needed ability to loop in the @formula language. @DoWhile, @While, and @For are the new iterative formulas that are introduced with Release 6.

The syntax of the @DoWhile function is shown here:

```
@DoWhile(statement;...;condition)
```

Here is an example:

```
x := 1;
tmpTitle:="What is the count?";
@DoWhile
(
    @Prompt([OK]; tmpTitle; @Text(x));
    x := x + 1;
    x <= 10
)
```

In this example, the user will be prompted with a basic dialog box 10 times. During each cycle of the loop, the number contained in the variable *x* will be incremented by 1.

The primary difference between the @While and @DoWhile formulas is the placement of the condition. The syntax of the @While function is as follows:

```
@While(condition; statement;...)
```

Here is an example:

```
x := 1;
tmpTitle:="What is the count?";
@While
(
    x <= 10;
    @Prompt([OK]; tmpTitle; @Text(x));
    x := x + 1
)
```

The syntax of the @For function is shown here:

```
@For(initialize;condition;increment;statement;...)
```

Unlike the other looping formulas, the @For function includes the initialization and condition within the statement. This formula is best suited to the processing of a range of numbers, such as list subscripts. Here is an example:

```
tmpTitle:="What is the count?";
@For
(
    x := 1;
    x <= 10;
    x := x + 1;
    @Prompt([OK]; tmpTitle; @Text(x))
)
```

CONDITIONAL EXECUTION

In previous versions of Notes/Domino, the `@If` function was the only flow-control mechanism that existed within the @Formula language. Although Release 6 introduced some new iterative functions, you're almost guaranteed to use this function at some time. The syntax of the `@if` function is shown here:

```
@if(condition1; action1 [; condition2; action2; ... [; condition99; action99;]]
➡ else_action )
```

In its simplest form, you could specify this:

```
@if(condition1; action1; else_action)
```

Here is an example:

```
@if(@Left(ZipCode;1) = "9"; "West Coast"; @Left(ZipCode;1) = "0"; "East Coast";
➡"Middle Stuff");
```

In this example, the formula compares the first digit of `ZipCode` against the numbers 9 and 0 and returns a string detailing the ZipCode's geography in the United States.

The flow for this example is as follows:

1. If the ZipCode field's first digit begins with a 9, the formula evaluates to `"West Coast"`.
2. If the ZipCode field's first digit begins with a 0, the formula evaluates to `"East Coast"`.
3. If neither of these conditions is true, the forumula evaluates to `"Middle Stuff"`.

You can specify only one action per condition. If you need to specify a more complicated set of actions, use the `@Do` function, which groups a sequence of expressions into a single expression:

```
@if(@Left(ZipCode;1) = "9"; @Do(@if(@Left(ZipCode;3) = "900"; "Los Angeles";
➡ "West Coast")); @Left(ZipCode;1) = "0"; "East Coast"; "Middle Stuff");
```

SELECTED TEXT AND CONVERSION FUNCTIONS

Functions that handle text strings and conversions are probably the most frequently used functions in the formula language. Here are some important text-handling and conversion functions:

- **@Left** (*string; n*) or **@Left**(*string; substring*)—Returns the leftmost *n* characters or all the characters left of the *substring*. Examples:
  ```
  @Left("sample";3) = "sam"
  @Left("simple simon"; " ") = "simple"
  ```
- **@Right** (*string; n*) or **@Right**(*string; substring*)—Returns the rightmost *n* characters or all the characters to the right of the *substring*. Examples:
  ```
  @Right("sample";3) = "ple"
  @Right("simple simon"; " ") = "simon"
  ```

18

- **@LowerCase(*string*), @UpperCase(*string*), and @ProperCase(*string*)**—Converts a string to all lowercase, uppercase, or proper case. *Proper case* means that each word has an initial capital but that the rest of the word is lowercase.

- **@Trim(*string*)**—Removes leading, trailing, and duplicate internal spaces from a string. Example:

```
@Trim("  This is a sample ") = "This is a sample"
```

SELECTED LIST, DATE, AND TIME FUNCTIONS

Lists are aggregate data structures. They typically contain multiple data values. Functions exist to convert lists to strings (and vice versa) as well as extract list items. Date and time functions are used to access and manipulate date and time values. Here are some selected list, date, and time functions:

- **@Explode(*string ; [separators ; [includeempties]]*)**—This converts a string into a list of multiple values. Each time it finds a value in the *separators* list, it creates a new text value in the output list. The default value for *separators* is   ,; (blank, comma, semicolon), which means that any of these delimiters will cause a new entry in the output list. *Includeempties* is a Boolean value; if true, the list is allowed to contain "" values. Example:
```
@Explode("Mon,Tue,Wed") = "Mon":"Tue":"Wed"
```

- **@Implode(*textlist ; [separator]*)**—This function converts a list of text values into a single text string. If you supply a *separator* string, it is used between each value. The default separator is a blank. Examples:
```
@Implode("sis":"boom"; " bah ") = "sis boom bah"
@Implode("Jan":"Feb":"Mar") = "Jan Feb Mar"
```

- **@Subset(*list ; number*)**—The @Subset function returns a subset of the values of a list. If you supply a positive number, the values are taken from the front of the list. If you supply a negative number, the values are taken from the end of the list. Example:
```
@Subset("red":"green":"blue":"white"; 2) = "red":"green"
```

- **@Created, @Modified, and @Accessed**—@Created returns the date and time that the current document was first created. @Modified returns the date and time that the current document was last modified. @Accessed returns the date that the document was last accessed, whether for read or write. The @Accessed value is accurate only to a day, not to a time. For the @Accessed function to work, you must enable the advanced database option Maintain LastAccessed Property. This option is off by default to improve performance.

TIP

> The @Accessed formula is a convenient way to monitor when the document was last accessed by a Notes Client. Unfortunately, this formula does not record activity for Web clients. Typically, this @Function is used within selection formulas, agents, and field formulas. Unlike some other document properties, the LastAccessed value is not replicated between servers.

- **@Adjust(*DateToAdjust* ; *years* ; *months* ; *days* ; *hours* ; *minutes* ; *seconds* ; [*dst*])**—This function adds to the *DateToAdjust* value by the number of *years*, *months*, *days*, *hours*, *minutes*, and *seconds* supplied. If a negative value is supplied for one of the parameters, it is subtracted from the *DateToAdjust*. *Dst* is optional and can be either [InLocalTime] or [InGMT]. Example:

```
@Adjust([3/25/1999]; 0 ; 1 ; -1; 0 ; 0 ; 0 ) = [4/24/1999]
```

SELECTED USER INTERFACE FUNCTIONS

The user interface functions enable you to control aspects of the user interface by prompting and requesting information. Here are some of the user interface functions:

- **@Prompt([*style*] : [NoSort]; *title* ; *prompt* ; [*defaultchoice* ; *choicelist* ; *filetype*])**—Several types of styles exist for the @Prompt dialog box. You can select from ChooseDatabase, LocalBrowse, OK, YesNo, YesNoCancel, OkCancelEdit, OkCancelList, OkCancelCombo, OkCancelEditCombo, OkCancelListMult, Password, YesNo, and YesNoCancel.

- **@DialogBox(*form* ; *flags* ; *title*)**—This function enables you to create a form in your database and then use it as a template for the dialog box. *flags* enables you to specify additional options. *title* is the dialog box title. See the Domino Designer online help for more information.

- **@PickList([Custom] : [Single] ; *server* : *file* ; *view* ; *title* ; *prompt* ; *column* ; *categoryname*)**—In addition to the syntax shown for @PickList, there are seven other variations. With the syntax shown, you can display a view in a dialog box. This returns information from the column you specify. See the Domino Designer online help for the seven other variations and more details.

SELECTED NAME AND ACCESS FUNCTIONS

Some functions enable you to inquire about database usernames and privileges. Here are some of the important functions in these categories:

- **@DbName**—Returns a list of two elements: the server name and the filename of the database. Example: If the server name is SERVER1 and the database name is PARTS.NSF, @DbName returns "SERVER1":"PARTS.NSF". You can extract the full path of the database with @Subset(@DbName; -1), which returns the last element of the list.

- **@UserAccess(*server* : *file*)**—Returns three values. The first is the access level for the current user, the second is a Boolean indicating whether the user can create documents, the third is a Boolean indicating whether the user can delete documents. The access level has these values: 1 (Depositor), 2 (Reader), 3 (Author), 4 (Editor), 5 (Designer), 6 (Manager). Example: @UserAccess("REPORTS.NSF") might return "5":"1":"1" if the user is a Designer and can create and delete documents.

- **@UserNamesList** and **@UserRoles**—@UserNamesList returns a list of the current username and any groups or roles that apply to the current user. @UserRoles returns a subset of the @UserNamesList, which consists just of the roles of the current user.

@DbLookup AND @DbColumn

The @DbLookup function is used in Notes databases to find a set of documents in a view or folder. You supply a key, and the function looks for the value in the first sorted column of the view. After the documents are found, you can have the function return either a field from the documents or the contents from a particular column of the view. You can also use @DbLookup with ODBC to access other relational database systems.

Here is the syntax for @DbLookup with Notes:

```
@DbLookup(class : "NoCache" ; server : database ; view ; key ; fieldname |
columnNumber )
```

The *class* parameter can be either "" or "Notes". The "NoCache" is optional and, if specified, tells Domino not to cache the results of the search. If you leave this parameter off, the results are cached, which improves performance at the possible expense of retrieving slightly out-of-date information.

The *server* : *database* parameter specifies the server and database filename. If the *server* is specified as "", it is assumed to be local. If the *database* parameter is "", it is assumed to be the current database. The *view* parameter is the name of the view to be used. The *key* parameter is the value to be searched for. The final parameter indicates the type of response you want. If you supply a text string, it is interpreted as a field name. If you supply a number, it is assumed to be a column number within the view. Here is an example:

```
@DbLookup("" : "" ; "Server1" : "Customer.nsf" ; "ByName" ; "IBM" ;
"ContactName" )
```

In this example, the Customer.nsf database on Server1 is searched. The first sorted column of the ByName view is inspected for the value "IBM". When the record is found, the value of the ContactName field will be returned. If more than one document is found, the result will be a list. If no documents are found, a null value is returned. If the view does not contain a sorted column, an error message is generated.

TIP

You can return the contents of any field in the documents that are found, even from fields not displayed in the view. This type of retrieval, however, is much slower. If you retrieve by field name, it is faster to include the field within the view. Retrieval by column number is very efficient but is prone to error because column numbers can change as you modify the view.

@DbLookup with ODBC uses a more complicated syntax:

```
@DbLookup("ODBC" : "NoCache" ; datasource ; userid1 : userid2 ; password1 :
password2 ;
table ; column : null_handling ; key_column ; key ; "Distinct" : sort )
```

The "ODBC" parameter indicates that it is an ODBC version of @DbLookup rather than a Notes version. "NoCache" indicates that results are not to be cached. *datasource* is the ODBC data source name. *userid1* and *userid2* might be required by the database system. *password1* and *password2* might also be required by the database system. *table* is the name of the table to be searched, and *column* is the column name for the column from which the result will be returned. The *null_handling* parameter can be one of three values: "Fail" reports an error, and the function will not return any values. "Discard" discards null values and returns a shorter list. "replacement value" returns a replacement value for null values found.

key_column is the name of the column to be searched within the table, and *key* is the value to be searched for. The database system might treat the *key_column* name as case sensitive. "Distinct" causes the database system to remove duplicate entries. The *sort* parameter can be specified as either "Ascending" or "Descending".

@DbColumn is another search function. You specify a particular column number of a view or folder, and the function returns all the values contained within the column. One useful application for @DbColumn is to supply values for keyword type fields, such as dialog lists, list boxes, and combo boxes. Here is the syntax for @DbColumn:

```
@DbColumn(class : "NoCache" ; server : database ; view ; columnNumber )
```

The *class* parameter can be specified as either "" or "Notes". The *server* and *database* parameters specify the database to use. If the *server* is specified as "", it is assumed to be local. If the *database* parameter is "", it is assumed to be the current database. The *view* parameter is the name of the view to use. *columnNumber* is the column number of the column values to be returned. Here is an example:

```
@DbColumn("" : "" ; "" : "" ; "Keywords" ; 2 )
```

This looks up in the current database the Keywords view and returns the second column.

You can also use @DbLookup with ODBC. Here is the syntax for use with ODBC:

```
@DbColumn("ODBC" : "NoCache" ; datasource ; userid1 : userid2 ; password1 :
password2 ;
table ; column : null_handling ; "Distinct" : sort )
```

The fields in the @DbColumn function are used just as they are within @DbLookup. The only difference is that no key or key column is supplied because the function returns the contents of the entire column.

@COMMANDS

Two special @Functions are @Command and @PostedCommand. The syntax for an @Command is similar to an @Function:

```
@Command([CommandName]; argument1; argument2; ... argumentn);
```

```
@PostedCommand([CommandName]; argument1; argument2; ... argumentn);
```

The command names that are used for the first parameter are enclosed in square brackets. In the syntax example, the square brackets do not mean that the CommandName is optional. As a matter of fact, it is the only required parameter. Here are some examples:

```
@Command([CreateView]);
```

```
@Command([OpenView]; "MyView");
```

There can be zero or more arguments when you invoke a command. The difference between @Command and @PostedCommand is the timing in which they are executed. @Command functions are executed in order as they are encountered in the formula. @PostedCommands are executed *after* all other expressions within the formula, but in the order they were encountered.

Most @Commands correspond to a menu item within the Notes client. You can sometimes tell the menu correspondence by the command name. For example, EditCut, EditCopy, and EditPaste correspond to those three menu items. However, some of the @Commands date back to earlier versions of Notes, so the correspondence with the current menu items might not be obvious. In Notes Release 3, for instance, the Compose command was used to create a new document. This menu item disappeared in Release 4 and hasn't been seen since. We still use the Compose @Command, however, to create a new document.

A complete list of the @Commands can be found in Appendix B.

USING LOTUSSCRIPT, JAVA, AND JAVASCRIPT

CHAPTER **19**

USING THE IDE WITH LOTUSSCRIPT, JAVA, AND JAVASCRIPT

In this chapter

SCRIPTING LANGUAGES, NOTES, AND DOMINO

What exactly is a *scripting* language, and what makes it different from other kinds of programming languages? A scripting language is a programming language designed to control other programs. In the case of LotusScript, it can be used to control or automate Notes or Domino. Lotus also uses LotusScript to automate tasks in its Office products, such as Lotus 1-2-3. Java was created by Sun Microsystems and has become very popular for writing agents and servlets that work in conjunction with Web pages. Java is a full-featured language that can also be used to write applications. JavaScript was created by Netscape and is a different language from Java. It is primarily used within Web pages for scripting purposes, such as automating button pushes, opening windows, and processing fields.

Originally, scripting languages, which are sometimes called *macro languages*, were part of the application they were controlling. For example, in Lotus Notes, the original "formula" language, which uses @formulas, was built into Notes. Lotus 1-2-3 had a similar formula language, and Microsoft Excel had a language that used = instead of @. The disadvantage of a proprietary language built into a system is that it makes users learn the specifics of not only the system, but the programming language as well. When a scripting language is separated from the underlying system it controls, the language can be used in several systems, and it can be more generic, easier to learn, and more useful in various situations.

In addition to LotusScript and JavaScript, what are some other examples of scripting languages? One well-known example is Visual Basic for Applications (VBA), a cousin of LotusScript. Both Visual Basic for Applications and LotusScript are variants of the BASIC language. Each has added features, but the two remain very similar in both function and syntax. Microsoft's version of JavaScript is called JScript; the name is similar but different enough to add to the confusion.

LotusScript, VBA, and JavaScript (among others) have one thing in common: They can easily control other applications. In addition, because of their dynamic nature, scripting languages are frequently implemented as interpretive languages rather than compiled languages. *Compiled languages* translate a program into the raw machine codes of the underlying hardware. This makes them very efficient. *Interpretive languages* are usually processed in a higher-level format, which makes them more flexible and dynamic. Interpreters can generally make decisions while the program is running, but compiled programs must usually make most decisions about the program before it starts execution.

UNDERSTANDING SCRIPTS, APPLETS, SERVLETS, AND AGENTS

Now that we've reviewed the primary languages, let's talk a little more about where you can use the various languages. Although it would be nice to use any language anywhere, you cannot do so. In addition to LotusScript, Java, and JavaScript, you can program in Notes and Domino with the Formula language and simple actions. With all these choices, sometimes it has not made sense for Lotus to greatly enhance some of the older technologies.

However, Lotus has added capabilities to the Formula language in each release to enable the existing Notes and Domino users to access new features as they become available.

Scripts are program routines that are associated with objects. Simple objects include buttons and fields; more complex objects include pages, forms, and views. Each of these different object types can have scripts associated with them. Scripts are associated with different events that can occur within the object. For example, in a button, there is a Click event; a form can have many events, including the QueryOpen and QuerySave LotusScript events and the onLoad JavaScript event. Depending upon the object, you can use LotusScript, JavaScript, formula language, or simple actions to program scripts. You cannot use Java, which is currently available only for applets, agents, and servlets. JavaScript scripts will work with Web browsers (or the Notes client), but LotusScript will not.

TIP

> For more information about what design elements can be programatically manipulated, refer to the topic "Table of Programmable Design Elements" within the Domino Designer 6 Help.

Applets are Java applications that are used primarily on Web pages. They can provide animation and local processing within the Web browser. Applets run in the client browser or Notes client under a Java Virtual Machine, not on the server. Applets may be written only in Java. Beginning with Release 5 of Domino, using CORBA and IIOP support, Lotus enables access to the Domino back-end classes running on the server from an applet running in a Web browser.

→ To learn more about CORBA and IIOP within Domino, **see** "Java Standalone Applications," **p. 593** (Chapter 23).

Agents have been a part of Notes and Domino since Release 4. Agents can run on either a Notes client or a Domino server. An agent can be triggered automatically or by the user; it is not necessarily tied to a specific object. Agents can be scheduled to run at specified intervals, or they can be triggered by certain events, such as new documents arriving in a database. Agents can be written in LotusScript, Java, the Formula language, or simple actions. An agent must run in the context of either the Notes client or the Domino server; it cannot run in a Web browser.

Servlets are Java programs similar to applets. As the name implies, however, they run on the server instead of the Web browser. A Domino servlet is different from a server agent. The servlet interface has been defined by Sun Microsystems and enables the server to run Java programs. Running a servlet requires additional configuration on the server and is not as automatic as running a Domino agent. Servlets and applets can be written to run on multiple different platforms and servers. They are not limited to the Domino server, whereas agents must run on a Domino server. You can use other server-side programming languages, including the C/C++ API and CGI; however, we will not be covering these options.

Table 19.1 summarizes the availability of the various languages.

TABLE 19.1 AVAILABILITY OF PROGRAMMING LANGUAGES

Object Situation	LotusScript	JavaScript	Java	Formula Language	Simple Actions
Object scripting	X	X		X	X
Notes client agent	X		X	X	X
Applet			X		
Web browser		X	X		
Notes client browser	X	X	X	X	X
Domino server agent	X		X	X	X
Domino server servlet			X		
Standalone application			X		

NOTE

> *Object scripting* means associating event-handling programs with user interface elements, such as buttons, forms, pages, and views. Every language might not be available for every object, but an *X* has been added where the language is available for at least some objects.

CHOOSING A LANGUAGE

With all these choices, which language should you use and why? This is a good question. The answer is this: It depends primarily on what you're trying to do and your background and experience.

As mentioned in the previous section, you are restricted to using certain languages for the various features in Notes and Domino. For example, to make a servlet, you must use Java. For writing scripts for objects, you can use any of the other languages *except* Java. So, the initial selection of language is done for you by the context.

In programming scripts for objects, though, you can still use LotusScript or JavaScript. If you're familiar with BASIC, go with LotusScript. Some pundits have spread rumors that LotusScript is going away. LotusScript is *not* going away; it will be around for a long time. Probably millions of lines of LotusScript code are available, and Lotus could not abandon LotusScript even if it wanted to.

If you're familiar with either JavaScript or JScript, use the JavaScript support in Notes. The world is moving more toward Internet standards. As JavaScript becomes more popular in general, more programmers will know JavaScript and more programs will be available in it. JavaScript will hold a prominent place in Notes and Domino for the foreseeable future.

When programming agents, you can use LotusScript or Java (or the Formula language or simple actions), but you cannot use JavaScript. In this case, again use the tool most comfortable for you. If the situation is simple enough, use a simple action. For example, to replace a single value within a document, you could use a simple action. Usually you can accomplish your goal in several ways and can pick any one of the options. If you're really ambitious, you can learn them all and pick the tool that seems just right for the occasion.

In the rest of this chapter, we highlight and review the three languages—LotusScript, Java, and JavaScript—and show you the basics of using each.

USING LOTUSSCRIPT

Because LotusScript is a scripting language designed for controlling Notes and Domino, the way you write programs is slightly different from the way you write an application with a traditional programming language. When using traditional languages, the programmer writes the program; when the program runs, the application maintains control from start to finish. For example, a program might start, ask the user for some input, read a database, and print a report. These tasks are controlled and sequenced by the program that the application programmer creates. There is typically a "main" routine in this type of program.

Using a scripting language is slightly more complicated because two programs are actually involved. In this case, one program is Notes itself, and the other is the program written by the programmer in LotusScript. The LotusScript program and Notes work together; you might think of the Notes system as the primary program and the LotusScript program as a subsidiary. This is clearly different from the case given for traditional languages, in which the application program has complete control of the situation.

If you use one of the Microsoft Office products, such as Excel or Word, you can use Visual Basic for Applications (VBA) as the scripting language. The use of LotusScript with Notes is very similar.

As another example, consider programming for a Web browser. Using the JavaScript language, a programmer can create one or more script programs to manipulate the browser. The script can process buttons, open new windows, and obtain data from input fields. LotusScript can be used in a somewhat similar manner within Notes. Separating the scripting language from the system to be controlled provides a level of flexibility and interaction that can be used in many contexts.

One primary benefit of using a language such as LotusScript is the ability to control whether the program code runs on the client or server. With LotusScript programs, you can create pieces of code that will execute on the client for faster response, and you can also create agents that will run on the Domino server. The choice is yours.

Figure 19.1 shows a simplified version of how Notes and Domino work with scripting languages. You can see how events in Notes or Domino can be used to trigger routines written in LotusScript, Java, or JavaScript. This intricate dance between Notes and scripting programs enables Notes to invoke your subroutines, and it enables your routines to access data and invoke services of Notes or Domino. For example, in Figure 19.1, after an event triggers the script program, the script can retrieve data from Notes/Domino, examine the data, and then send commands and data back to Notes/Domino.

Figure 19.1
Execution of events between a script and Lotus Notes and Domino.

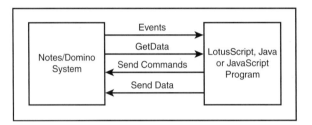

USING THE INTEGRATED DEVELOPMENT ENVIRONMENT

The Integrated Development Environment (IDE) is the environment you use to create and test your programs. The main area you will use, the Programmer's pane, is an area where you can edit your LotusScript programs. This pane is in the lower-right part of your screen. We'll cover this area and some of the other areas as we progress. In this chapter, we don't cover the details of the LotusScript language; instead, we review how to use the IDE.

CREATING A LOTUSSCRIPT HELLO AGENT

To begin our examination, let's create a simple program to display a message box. This single-line program is the simplest program we can make. We'll create this example with both LotusScript and Java. It will take several steps to create the program.

A LotusScript program cannot exist alone; you must create it in the context of a Notes database. The database is the outermost container for the program. Within a database, LotusScript programs can be associated with events, actions, buttons, and so on. These items can be used to trigger the invocation of a LotusScript program. You can think of these items as another container within the database. The LotusScript program resides within this smaller container. Typically, a LotusScript program operates on the data contained within the same database. However, it can access data from other databases if necessary.

Now let's create the first LotusScript program as an agent. As mentioned, it's necessary to be in the context of a database. You can use any database, or you can create a new, blank database. If you want to follow along with a new database, open Domino Designer. You will see the Domino Designer welcome page. This first example involves a program to display the words `"Hello, LotusScript"`. To create your first LotusScript agent, follow these steps:

1. From the welcome page, you can click the Create a New Database icon or use the menus. To use the menus, select File, Database, New.

2. Once the New Database dialog box opens, enter the database title **Script Test**, leave the template style as Blank, and click OK. To accomplish the test, you will use Domino agents.

3. Click Shared Code and then click Agents (with the light bulb) in the Design pane on the left part of your screen (see Figure 19.2).

Figure 19.2
Use the New Agent action button to create your agent.

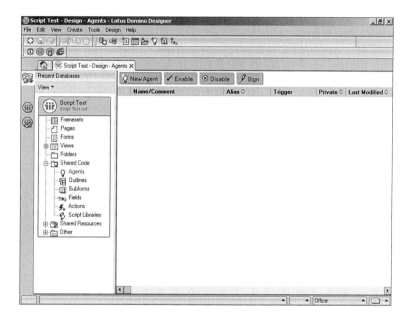

4. Click the New Agent action button to open the Agent Properties box.

5. Enter **HelloLS** in the Name field found in the Basics tab of the Agent Properties box.

6. You can set the agent's runtime properties including how the agent should be run. In this case, leave the default Action menu selection as the trigger.

7. Additionally, inside the runtime grouping, you can select which documents the agent should act on. If you are writing an agent to process incoming mail, you might act on newly created documents. If you are creating an agent that will work within a view, you can act on documents selected by the user. In this case, click the Target drop-down box and choose None.

Your Domino Designer environment should resemble Figure 19.3.

8. Close the Agent Properties box.

9. Click the rightmost Run drop-down box in the Programmer's pane at the – and select LotusScript. The InfoList displays four choices: Options, Declarations, Initialize, and Terminate.

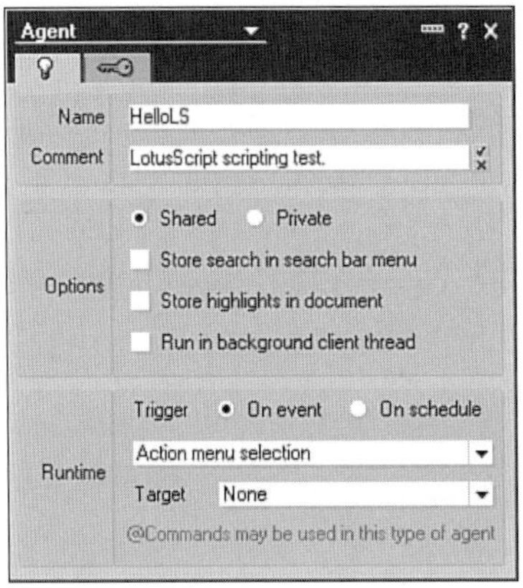

Figure 19.3
Creating a new agent
for script testing.

10. Select the name Initialize in the InfoList pane. Notice that the IDE has automatically entered two statements in the Programmer's pane: a Sub statement and an End Sub statement. These statements are covered in more detail in Chapter 22, "LotusScript Subroutines, Functions, and Event Handlers." At this point, the Programmer's pane looks like the following:

```
Sub Initialize

End Sub
```

11. Enter the following on the line between the Sub and End Sub statements:

```
Msgbox "Hello, LotusScript"
```

12. Now save the LotusScript agent by choosing File, Save.

Your completed LotusScript agent looks like the following:

```
Sub Initialize
    Msgbox "Hello, LotusScript"
End Sub
```

Figure 19.4 exhibits the completed program and the names of the various parts of the IDE.

You can test your first LotusScript program by opening the database within the Notes client and choosing Actions, HelloLS from the Actions menu. Figure 19.5 shows the message box that pops up when you run the HelloLS agent.

Congratulations! You've created and successfully run your first LotusScript program. It's actually pretty easy. Let's recap what's been done. You created an agent, gave it a name, chose the LotusScript language and programmed it using LotusScript and tested it in the Notes client.

Figure 19.4
The completed agent
and the parts of
the IDE.

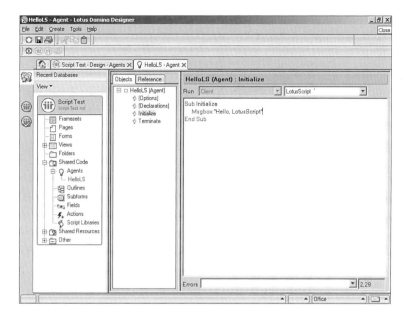

Figure 19.5
Testing the HelloLS
agent.

CREATING A JAVA HELLO AGENT

Now that you know how to create a LotusScript agent, let's take a look at a similar agent using Java. To create your first agent in Java, complete the following steps within the same database used in the previous example:

1. Click Agents (with the light bulb), under Shared Code, in the Design pane on the left.

2. Click the New Agent action button to open the Agent properties box.

3. Enter **HelloJava** in the Name field in the Basics tab of the Agent properties box.

4. Click the rightmost Run drop-down box in the Programmer's pane at the – and select Java. The InfoList displays three levels of hierarchy: JavaAgent.java, JavaAgent, and NotesMain.

5. In the Programmer's pane on the right, you will see an entire Java program template that has been constructed for you. In the middle is a comment that says (Your code goes here). Insert your code just below the comment line. The following text is case sensitive, so you must enter it exactly as shown. Enter the following:

```
JOptionPane.showMessageDialog(null, "Hello, Java","Java Agent",
➥JOptionPane. INFORMATION_MESSAGE);
```

6. Add the following line at the very top of the agent:

```
import javax.swing.*;
```

Your program should look like Figure 19.6.

Figure 19.6
The HelloJava agent after entering the code.

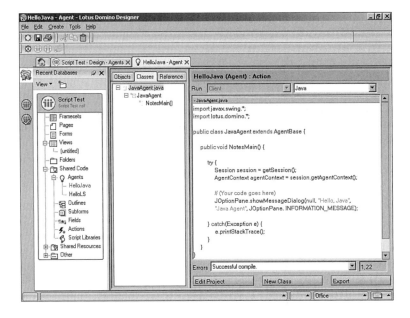

Save the agent by selecting File, Save. In the Errors line, you should see the words `Successful compile`.

You can now test your first Java agent by opening the database within the Notes client and choosing Actions, HelloJava from the Actions menu. Figure 19.7 shows the message box that pops up when you run the HelloJava agent.

Figure 19.7
Testing the HelloJava agent.

NOTE

> Java is a platform-independent language with its own windowing model. The Java Foundation Classes (JFC), or Swing, is the windowing package used for this example. Release 6 of Notes ships with version 1.3 of the Java Virtual Machine, so you can use Swing and other packages within your agents and applets.

GETTING HELP

You have seen that you can create a very small program to display a message in both LotusScript and Java.

Both LotusScript and Java are very rich languages with many constructs and features. It might take you a while to become familiar with all their characteristics. What if you need a little help or reference material on a statement or function while you're using the Domino Designer IDE? Fortunately, help is right there, just a mouse-click away.

To see how to access this help, look at the HelloJava agent again. The Info List is the one just to the left of the Programmer's pane where the Java program appears. When you first create the program, the Info List is opened to the Classes tab. Reference material regarding Domino and Java classes is available in the Reference tab, as shown in Figure 19.8.

Figure 19.8
The HelloJava agent with reference information.

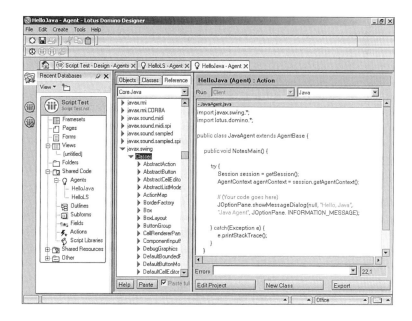

As you can see in Figure 19.8, a listing of the core Java classes and methods is available in the Reference tab. You can also find information about Domino's Object classes. If you are editing a LotusScript program, reference information relating to LotusScript becomes available. Figure 19.9 demonstrates the LotusScript language reference.

As you can see from the Reference list, in addition to the language reference, you can find out information about the Domino Object classes, subroutines, and more. If you select a line in the reference section, you can paste the selected line into your program in the Programmer's pane. If you check the Paste Full Text option, the entire line is pasted into your program, along with various parameters and options. You can then edit this text and substitute your own variables. If you do not enable the Paste Full Text option, only the main keyword is pasted into your program, without all the parameters and options.

Figure 19.9
The HelloLS agent with reference information.

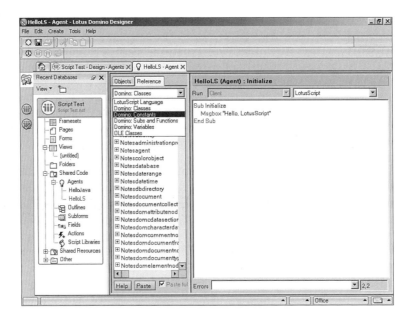

The Reference tab is useful for finding out the syntax of a routine or statement if you already know its name. On the other hand, it does not tell you what the function does or how to use it. You can find a lot of this information in the Domino Designer online Help database. To try this, select Help, Help Topics. Then in the Navigation pane on the left, select the topic that you want to see. An example is shown in Figure 19.10.

Figure 19.10
The Help contents for Domino Designer.

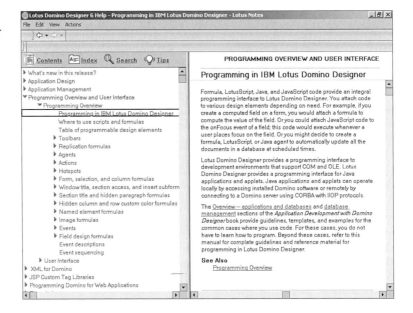

The Domino Designer Help database contains quite a bit of reference material about Java, LotusScript, JavaScript, and the Formula language. You can browse this database or search for particular topics of interest.

ACCESSING THE DOMINO OBJECTS

You have now seen how to create and execute both a LotusScript agent and a Java agent. Now let's review how you can access the Domino Objects from Java. LotusScript access is very similar; later chapters cover it in great detail.

Figure 19.11 demonstrates a modified version of the Hello Java program to display both the username and the current database. The new Java agent is called HelloJavaName. The agentContext object contains the current database filename and the effective username. The effective username is used to obtain the user's common name. These four important lines have been added or modified:

```
Name MyName = session.createName(agentContext.getEffectiveUserName());

String msg = "Hello, " + MyName.getCommon()+". ";
msg = msg + "You are accessing " + agentContext.getCurrentDatabase();

JOptionPane.showMessageDialog(null, msg,"Java Agent", JOptionPane.
INFORMATION_MESSAGE);
```

Figure 19.11
You can access the Domino Object Model from Java.

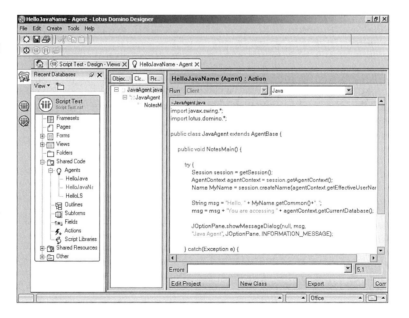

The Domino Objects are covered in the next chapter, but essentially, they enable you to access information from Domino. You can obtain information about the current user and the current database; then you can access information such as view, form, and document data within the database.

LotusScript access to the Domino Objects has been available since Release 4, and Java has been available since Release 4.6.

EVENT-DRIVEN PROGRAMMING

What makes event-driven programming different from traditional application programming? It is mainly a question of control. In traditional programming, you write an application that maintains control. In event-driven programming, you write a series of subroutines, each one a response to a particular event. In event-driven programming, the user has much more control than in traditional programming. The user can control the flow of the application by clicking buttons, selecting menu items, and so forth. User actions such as these create events. As the programmer, you create event handlers to process the events as they occur.

The event-driven model is used in both the Notes client and Web browser (JavaScript) interfaces. In LotusScript, the events have names such as QueryOpen, PostOpen, and Click. These events trigger LotusScript routines that the Notes client invokes. In JavaScript, events have names such as onMouseOver, onBlur, and onClick.

What is the benefit of the event-driven programming model? Well, the main advantage is that it simplifies the task of programming more complex systems. Remember the Hello agents? All you needed to do was write one line of code to display a message. The agent was triggered by the user menu action. In a traditional language such as C++, this would have taken many more lines of code, and you would have had to deal with much more complexity. Because each subroutine is focused on a single event, the programs are smaller and more manageable.

The only complicating factor is that there are two types of events: LotusScript and JavaScript. You can actually mix the two event models, but it's not necessarily recommended. The main reason for using both is to handle the different client types. Remember that certain languages are available only in certain contexts. In particular, LotusScript is available only with a Notes client.

JavaScript, on the other hand, is available in both the Notes client and the Web browser. If your intended audience will be using both Notes clients and browsers, you should consider JavaScript. If your audience will be using only Notes clients, you can stay with LotusScript.

RESPONDING TO EVENTS USING LOTUSSCRIPT AND JAVASCRIPT

Now that you understand event-driven programming, let's create an example that uses both LotusScript and JavaScript. In the previous agent example, you looked at LotusScript and Java. After this example, you will have seen all three languages: LotusScript, Java, and JavaScript.

1. For this example, you can use the existing Script Test database. Click the Forms item in the Design pane and click the New Form action button to create a new form. In this example, a new form called EventExample is created. Open the Form properties box to give the form a name. Creating and naming forms was covered in Chapter 13, "Designing Pages, Forms, and Subforms."

2. In this form, you will create two buttons: one LotusScript button and one JavaScript button. Select Create, Hotspot, Button to open the Button properties box. A new button appears on your form.

3. In the Button properties box, enter **LotusScript Button** in the Label field in the Button Info tab.

4. In the second Run drop-down box in the Programmer's pane in the lower right, select LotusScript. Leave the first drop-down box defaulted to Client. Six choices appear in the left Info List pane of the Button, and an empty subroutine appears in the Programmer's pane.

5. Enter the following text in the script area of the Click event:
   MsgBox "Hello from the LotusScript button."

6. Save the newly created form.

The complete text in the Programmer's pane in the lower right should be as follows:

```
Sub Click(Source As Button)
    MsgBox "Hello from the LotusScript button."
End Sub
```

Your screen should appear similar to Figure 19.12.

Figure 19.12
Using LotusScript, you can respond to user button clicks.

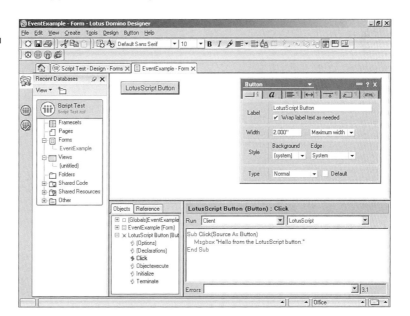

You have now created the LotusScript button. Before testing this form, you will also create a JavaScript button. To create the JavaScript button, click in the work area just to the right of the existing button and click Enter to space down one line. To create the JavaScript button here, follow these steps:

1. Choose Create, Hotspot, Button to open the Button properties box. A new button appears on your form.

2. In the Button properties box, enter **JavaScript Button** in the Label field in the Button Info tab.

3. In the second Run drop-down box in the Programmer's pane in the lower right, select JavaScript. Thirteen choices appear in the left InfoList pane. The onClick event is highlighted and an empty (onClick) subroutine appears in the Programmer's pane.

4. Enter the following text in the script area within the onClick event:

   ```
   alert("Hello from the JavaSript button.")
   ```

> **TIP**
>
> Unlike LotusScript, JavaScript is case sensitive. The alert routine is built into JavaScript and displays a message dialog box. If you improperly capitalize the name (such as Alert), you will get a runtime error from the Web browser. The built-in names for JavaScript are all lowercase.
>
> Case sensitivity is a cause for frequent errors in JavaScript. It is extremely important to have a naming convention for your own routine names in JavaScript; otherwise, you will waste a lot of time. One easy convention is to use all lowercase names. Another possibility is to always use an initial capital letter. Pick a convention and stick to it.

5. Save the newly created form. Your screen should appear similar to Figure 19.13.

Now you can test the buttons:

1. Choose Design, Preview in Notes.

2. When testing, you will see both the LotusScript and JavaScript buttons. You can click either of the buttons to see the messages.

Figure 19.13
Using JavaScript, you can respond to user button clicks via the onClick event.

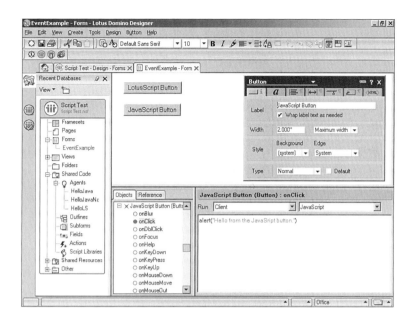

GETTING AN OPINION: REQUESTING INPUT

Now that you've taken a brief excursion into event-driven programming, let's create a script that handles requests from user input. This shouldn't be too difficult, even if you are not an expert typist. You'll be using LotusScript for this example. To create a button that requests input, follow these steps:

1. Open your EventExample form by clicking Forms in the Design pane and then double-clicking the EventExample name.

2. Create a new button below the existing two buttons by selecting Create, Hotspot, Button.

3. In the properties box, give the button the label Opinion.

4. In the second Run drop-down box in the Programmer's pane in the lower right, select LotusScript. Enter the following code into the Click event:

```
MyName$ = Inputbox$("Please enter your name")
Msgbox "Hello " + MyName$
```

5. Save the form.

As you can see, this is a program to prompt for a name and then display that name in the resulting message box. Your screen should look like the one in Figure 19.14.

19

Figure 19.14
A program that
requests and displays
a name.

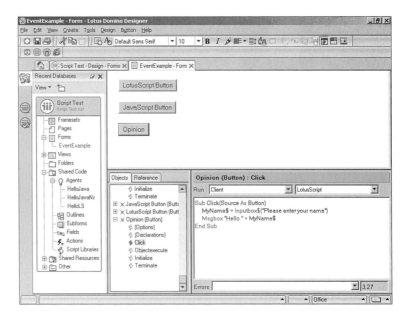

The new line calls the Inputbox function. The purpose of this function is to prompt the user for input and return the input to a variable within the program. In this case, a variable is defined called MyName$. The $ at the end of the variable name signifies that the variable is a string variable. We cover variable declarations in more depth in Chapter 21, "LotusScript Variables and Objects." The Inputbox function also has a $ at the end to indicate that it is returning a string variable.

The Msgbox line has been changed to contain two parts. First is the constant "Hello ", and second is the variable MyName$. The plus sign between them does not mean to sum these two words—that wouldn't make sense. Instead, in LotusScript, the plus sign between two strings means to concatenate them, or place one after the other, producing one large string.

Now you can test this program in the Notes client.

1. Click Design, Preview in Notes from the menu bar. After you click the Opinion button, you should see a prompt appear, as shown in Figure 19.15.

2. Enter your name as the program requests, and click OK. You should see the Hello dialog box appear with your name. In fact, you can try various options, including typing special characters or even no characters. Each of these various scenarios results in a different output.

Figure 19.15
The Opinion button,
prompting for input.

PUTTING IN YOUR TWO CENTS: INPUTTING NUMBERS INSTEAD OF TEXT

In the previous example, we reviewed how to input, concatenate, and display strings. Now let's modify the program to work with a few numbers. Take a look at the following code:

```
Sub Click(Source As Button)
    MyName$ = Inputbox$("Please enter your name")
    Msgbox "Hello " + MyName$
    Amount% = Cint(Inputbox$("How much wisdom would you like?"))
    Msgbox "OK. That will be " + Str$(Amount% * 2) + " cents."
End Sub
```

We have added two additional lines. The first line asks how much wisdom you would like. The user should enter a number. The Cint function converts an expression to an integer. The value is then stored in the Amount variable. Just as the $ suffix represents a string variable, a % suffix represents an integer variable. All the suffixes and their meanings are covered in a later chapter. After the user has input the amount, the program calculates the cost of the wisdom by charging 2 cents for each.

The expression

```
Str$(Amount% * 2)
```

calculates 2 cents for each item and then converts the resulting amount to a string. You must convert the number to a string for it to be concatenated with the other strings. After you have entered the program as shown, try it out.

19

CHAPTER **20**

OBJECT-ORIENTED PROGRAMMING AND THE DOMINO OBJECT MODEL

In this chapter

OVERVIEW

In the preceding chapter, you created some simple programs in LotusScript, Java, and JavaScript. In those examples, we reviewed some elementary operations to interact with the user. This type of interaction is sometimes called the *front end*. If the front end typically means interacting with users, the *back end* means interacting with data. LotusScript and Java programming rely heavily on the use of object-oriented programming to access and manipulate Notes data.

In this chapter, we'll cover some of the basics of object-oriented programming and the Domino Object Model (DOM) classes so that you'll have the background to understand how to use them effectively. We'll explore the relationship between classes and objects, containers and collections, and class inheritance and data models. Additionally, we'll review cover events in LotusScript, discuss the difference between the front-end and back-end classes, and introduce you to the Domino Object Model.

A BIT OF OBJECT-ORIENTED PROGRAMMING HISTORY

Surprisingly, object-oriented programming has been around for quite a while. Many people think it is one of the newer innovations of computer science research, but actually object-oriented programming has been around since at least 1967; many of the concepts are more than three decades old. At that time, in the late 1960s, when flower children were blooming, Ole-Johan Dahl, Bjorn Myhrhaug, and Kristen Nygaard created the Simula language while working at the Norwegian Computing Centre in Oslo. Simula was an extension of the Algol 60 language, of an even earlier vintage.

In the 1960s, when Simula was developed, the IBM 360 was the rage, and all computing was done on mainframe computers. It would be more than a decade before the first Apple and IBM personal computers were created. The contributions, then, of Dahl, Myhrhaug, and Nygaard and their creation of many of the ideas of object-oriented programming are all the more remarkable.

The main contribution of Simula was to introduce the concepts of classes, objects, and methods. The main approach of that language, as is true today of all object-oriented programming, is one of *decomposition*. It is a simple idea, really: Divide a complex task, system, or project into smaller pieces, and then examine each piece and break it into yet smaller pieces. Break up these pieces until you have elementary ideas, tasks, or items that you know how to handle.

Classes, objects, and methods are just some of the tools you can use to make complex systems easier to handle. Decomposition enables you to mentally focus on only a small number of items at a time, so it should make your programs easier to write, understand, and debug. The decomposition should also allow your programs to be more reliable because each layer is simpler.

WHAT IS OBJECT-ORIENTED PROGRAMMING?

Object-oriented programming (OOP) is, at its core, about managing complexity. It enables you to more easily create complex systems by facilitating decomposition. You use the tools and techniques of OOP to break down larger problems into smaller, more manageable problems.

To bring this explanation back to reality a bit, when you use OOP with LotusScript, you can create larger, more complex Notes applications with less work and hopefully more reliability. In essence, Lotus is providing a set of reusable tools that you can build on to create applications.

As you examine the concepts of classes, objects, and methods in the sections to follow, keep in mind that our purpose is the management of complexity and that our means is decomposition.

TRADITIONAL PROGRAMMING VERSUS OBJECT-ORIENTED PROGRAMMING

The concepts of traditional programming go back even farther than object-oriented programming and have many of their roots in mathematics. Because computers were first conceived to perform complex calculations more quickly than people, mathematics clearly had an important influence on the languages people use to communicate with computers.

One of the early programming languages, FORTRAN, which stands for "formula translation," was designed to translate formulas from a language people could understand into a format a computer could execute. One characteristic of this language was the separation of data from functions. Functions in mathematics are supplied with their data in the form of parameters and yield numerical results.

Intellectually, it is appealing to separate functions or algorithms from the data on which they operate. After all, you can supply a value to a sine routine or a square root function, and it will calculate and return the result. The angle or number has nothing in particular to do with the way in which the computer calculates the sine or square root.

The problem, however, is that many complex systems don't behave as cleanly or purely as mathematics. The problem with the functional approach is that the function cannot retain *state* information. State information refers to the status of an object. For example, suppose you want to write a program to simulate an elevator. You need to keep track of whether the door is open or closed, which floor the elevator is on, and so forth. In this context, the elevator is the object. The elevator object has a particular state, such as what floor it's on. Additionally, it also has various actions that it performs throughout the day, including moving up and down the elevator shaft.

In traditional programming, if you want to keep track of the state of an object, this task must be done separately from the functions themselves. By separating the data from the functions, you enable separate functions to access and modify global data. In a complex system, this modification of global data can make programs harder to write and debug. It also leads to programs that are less reliable than they should be.

In the next section, we review the utilization of a concept called encapsulation and tell how it can be used in object-oriented development. As the word implies, *encapsulation* refers to the construction of a barrier around a object. This concept enables developers to develop an object that has a specific behavior while at the same time being able to keep track of its state.

OBJECTS: TANGIBLE ITEMS

In our everyday world, we deal with objects all the time. One object is this book you are reading. Another might be your car, or your house, or the breakfast roll you ate this morning. In each of these cases, it is convenient to think of the item as a single object. But clearly, if you think about your car or house, you can easily see how that object can be decomposed into smaller subobjects.

A car, for example, can be simplistically decomposed into a body and four wheels. The body can be decomposed into the doors, windows, engine compartment, and so forth. A house can be decomposed into its constituent rooms. Each room, in turn, can be broken up into the walls, doors, and windows that make it a room. Even a breakfast roll is made up of flour, eggs, water, nuts, and other basic ingredients.

The word *object*, then, is used as a very generic word to represent any or all of these things. In the real world, of course, these objects are tangible things. They are items we can see, touch, hear, and recognize. In the programming world, we create objects to represent items in the real world.

If we are trying to describe objects, what kinds of characteristics should we use? In object-oriented programming, we use two kinds of characteristics. The first characteristic of an object is called its *properties*. An object's set of properties can be used to describe it. For example, a property of the car might be its color, size, shape, weight, or even country of origin. A property of a house might be its address, the number of floors, the number of rooms, or its purchase price. A breakfast roll might have properties such as its weight or the number of raisins in it.

As you can tell, the properties of an object clearly depend on the type of object. For example, it might make sense to talk about the color of a car and the color of a house. But although it makes sense to talk about the number of raisins in a breakfast roll, it makes much less sense to talk about the number of raisins in your car (unless you have a two-year-old child, in which case there are probably at least a few raisins under the back seat of your car).

In addition to typically static attributes such as the color of the car, it is important to notice that a property can represent the state or status of an object. For example, the state of a car engine might be on or off; the car door is open or closed; the transmission is in low, neutral, drive, or reverse. This status is dynamic and can change over time. Other examples might be whether the windows of a car are rolled down or up, or whether the wheels are turning or not turning. In a house, the air-conditioning might be on or off, a particular door might be open or closed, and the television might be tuned to a particular channel. All of these properties represent data associated with the object that can change over time but that are set to a particular value at any given point in time.

The second characteristic we use to classify an object is its capabilities, which are really the actions it can perform. In the case of a car, it can perform many actions, such as starting, turning a corner, and stopping. Some of a car's subobjects can also perform actions. A car's headlights can turn on, the turn signals can flash, the horn can make a sound, and the wheels can turn. Within a house, the faucets can turn on, the kitchen stove can cook, and the stereo music system can play.

The actions an object can perform are called *methods* in object-oriented parlance. In object-oriented programming, an object's methods are also sometimes called subroutines.

The basic idea of an object is that it encapsulates its properties and methods. These properties and methods are also sometimes called member variables or member procedures because the properties and methods are members of the object. This encapsulation enables you to group the data associated with an object with the operations to be performed on it. The properties and methods reflect both what an object is (properties) and what an object can do (methods).

When properties and methods are encapsulated together, the real power comes when there is more than one object of a particular type. For example, if you have two car objects, each object has its own copy of the property information, so each property can be set independently of the other. In traditional functional programming, it is much more work because you might have to keep track of multiple sets of data. Multiple sets of data are easily handled with object-oriented programming because each object just manages its own data, no matter how many objects have been created. The next section dealing with classes shows how to handle multiple objects of the same type.

CLASSES: DESCRIBING GROUPS OF OBJECTS

Classes in object-oriented programming are a slightly more abstract concept than objects. Everyone can understand the concept of an object because an object can be related to something tangible. Whereas an object represents a particular item, a *class* is the description of a group of objects that share characteristics.

For example, let's go back to the example of a car. Suppose you own a red Ferrari (lucky you). This red Ferrari is a particular car. It's yours; it is an object. Suppose, however, that we wanted to describe all Ferraris, not just your car. In this case, the description would be the class definition, as illustrated in Figure 20.1.

In the Ferrari class definition, we might describe the fact that the color is a property; the weight, the license plate (tag) number, and other characteristics would also be properties. In the class definition, we do not give the properties specific values; we just describe the properties that the class contains. For example, we describe color as a property, but we do not prescribe a *particular* color.

20

If someone else owns a Ferrari of the same class, his car might be blue. Another person's Ferrari might be green. All of these cars are from the same class, but they represent different objects. Repeating again, an object represents a particular item, whereas a class describes a group of items that are similar.

It is important to emphasize here the difference between classes and objects. A class is just a definition. It describes the properties and methods shared by each object of the class. A class does not consume any computer memory. An object, on the other hand, is tangible. An object occupies memory in the computer, and for each separate object of the same class, separate memory is used.

Figure 20.1
There can be many
Ferrari objects based
upon the Ferrari class.

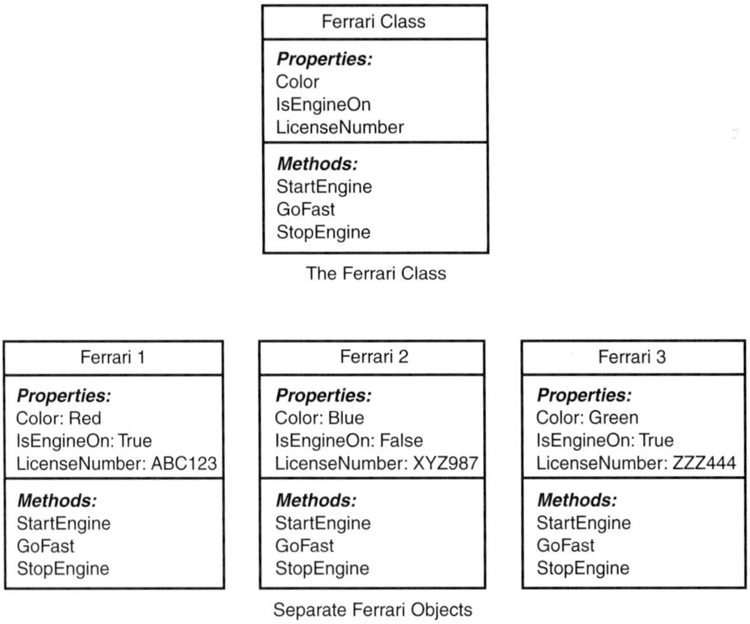

The Ferrari Class

Separate Ferrari Objects

As an example within Notes and Domino, there is a LotusScript class definition for a Notes document, appropriately called the NotesDocument class. This class represents the characteristics of all Notes document objects. The class has properties, such as the date the document was last modified, the size of the document, and the date the document was created. These properties are available for each document object, but they typically are different for each document object in the database. Methods of the NotesDocument class access the document's fields, replacing values and removing the document from the database. There are many other properties and methods in this class and the other Notes classes.

CLASS CONTAINMENT

As previously mentioned, decomposition is one of the important characteristics of object-oriented programming. We reviewed examples of how a car is made up of subobjects, such as doors and wheels. This concept is called *containment* in OOP. When an object has subobjects, we consider the object to be like a container, with the subobjects being contained within it. Each subobject is typically considered to be a property of the class.

Using the house as an example, we might have a house object that contains 10 room objects. Each room object is separate and has different properties and methods. The relationship of the container to its subobjects is sometimes called the *Has-A* relationship. This can be expressed in words as the house Has-A kitchen or the house Has-A bedroom.

We describe these Has-A relationships when we define the class. After they have been described in the class definition, they normally do not vary from one object of the class to another. The class definition describes the structure for all objects of the class. The structure is the same for each object created from that class. For example, after we define that a car class Has-A steering wheel, each car object that is created will contain a steering wheel.

COLLECTION CLASSES

When we are defining a car, it is relatively safe to say that each member of the car class—that is, each car object—will have 4 wheels. Unless there are some unusual circumstances, a car will not have 3 wheels or 37 wheels. In a case like this, we can create a class with a fixed number of wheel subobjects.

What happens, though, if we want to model a house, but each house object that we create has a different number of rooms? For example, today we might be building a small house with 7 rooms. Tomorrow, however, we want to build a mansion with 23 rooms. How can we model this concept?

A *collection* class is a special kind of class. Its purpose is to hold a variable number of items within it. See Figure 20.2 for an illustration. Collection classes are also sometimes called *container* classes. When you define the class, you do not know how many objects will be contained inside it. For example, suppose you want to model a Notes database and within the database you want to have an unspecified number of document objects. It does not make sense to define 4, 10, 37, 2000, or any fixed number of documents in the database. Of course, you need the flexibility to have any number of documents in the database from a few to a few thousand. This class must allow documents to be added or deleted, but without the restriction of having a fixed number of items. The Notes database actually contains an element whose class is suitably named the `NotesDocumentCollection` class.

A collection class typically has methods, such as add an item, delete an item, get the first item, and get the next item. These operations enable you to traverse the container, examining each element as you progress through the collection.

20

Figure 20.2
The `NotesDocumentCo llection` class can contain an arbitrary number of `NotesDocument` elements.

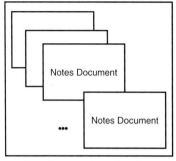

NotesDocumentCollection Class

CLASS INHERITANCE

Another organizational tool, in addition to containment and collections, is a concept called *inheritance*. Inheritance is used in situations in which you want to define general classes and then progressively more refined classes. Each progressively more refined class is called a subclass of the original class.

For example, suppose you were to define a class called `Vehicle`. This class might represent any kind of vehicle, including trains, cars, and planes. You could create a subclass of the `Vehicle` class called `FourWheelVehicles`. This class might include cars, trucks, and minivans. You could then create a subclass called `Cars` as a subclass of `FourWheelVehicles`. A subclass called `Ferrari` could then be created, which would represent all Ferraris.

As you can see, each subclass gets progressively more refined, detailed, and specific. This type of modeling relationship is called the *Is-A* relationship. Recall that the Has-A relationship is what we used to model a car and its four wheels. A car has four wheels, but each wheel is not a car. On the other hand, a Ferrari Is-A Car, and a Car Is-A FourWheelVehicle, and a FourWheelVehicle Is-A Vehicle.

This Is-A relationship is also called *inheritance*. Just as a child inherits characteristics from its parents, a child class inherits the properties and methods of the parent class. Keep in mind the distinction between containment (Has-A) and inheritance (Is-A).

In the Notes classes, there is only one case of inheritance. The `NotesRichTextItem` class inherits from the `NotesItem` class. That is, any object that is a `NotesRichTextItem` object Is-A `NotesItem` object. All the other relationships within the Notes class hierarchy are ones of containment. So, for example, a `NotesDatabase` object Has-A `NotesDocumentCollection` object that represents the documents contained within the database. A `NotesItem` roughly corresponds to the data within a field on a form. A `NotesRichTextItem` can contain rich-text information, such as fonts and size information. We'll cover all these classes in more detail later in this chapter.

OBJECT MODELS

Examples such as cars, houses, and breakfast rolls are useful to illustrate some of the concepts of object-oriented programming, but to use OOP meaningfully, you need to describe object models, which are also sometimes called data models. Object models are abstract concepts that help you organize data. These models group related information together; in the case of the Domino Object Model, they are really just a set of object-oriented classes. The object model represents the logical hierarchy of classes and objects within Notes and Domino.

In Figures 20.3 and 20.4, you can see the classes contained in the Domino Object Model as implemented in LotusScript. The Java hierarchy is very similar, with only a few minor differences. The lines connecting the various classes signify containment. Notice that there are several instances of containment in the class definitions. For example, within a Notes database, there are views, forms, and documents. Within a Notes document, there are items and rich-text items. All the high-level classes contain other lower-level classes.

Figure 20.3
The Session, Workspace, and Database classes.

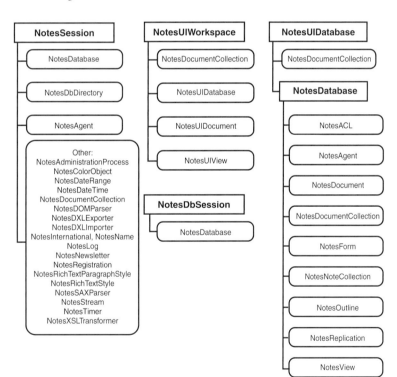

Figure 20.4
The View, Outline, Document, and RichText classes.

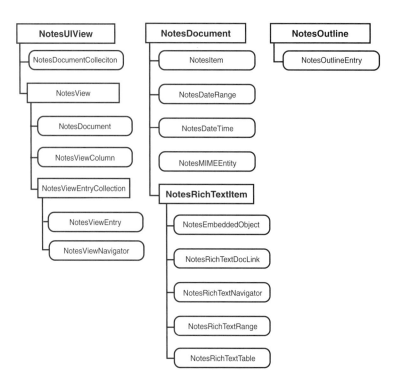

These classes represent a model of how Domino data is organized. It is important to realize that the Notes classes are not actually part of the LotusScript or Java languages. You can consider these classes to be an adjunct to the languages. They are accessible from the language but are not part of it. By separating the DOM from the programming languages, Lotus can implement the DOM once, and language bindings can be used to interface between different programming languages and the DOM routines. In addition, this separation allows usage of remote clients using CORBA, as you'll see in the next section.

DOMINO OBJECT MODEL ARCHITECTURE

The interface to the Domino Object Model is provided through various adapters. By using the adapters, support for several programming languages is possible. In particular, LotusScript and Java can share the same underlying program code (see Figure 20.5).

Figure 20.5 shows how both the LotusScript and Java languages can access the Domino Object Model. Notice that the LotusScript front-end classes consist of different code than the back-end classes. Also notice that Java programs cannot access the front-end classes.

Figure 20.5
The Notes client can access the Domino Object Model via LotusScript or Java.

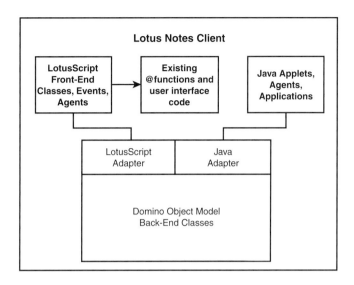

FRONT-END AND BACK-END CLASSES

A frequent source of confusion is the fact that Notes has both front-end and back-end classes. There are a couple of explanations for this setup. The first reason is that the front-end classes are wrappers that have been implemented around pre-existing code in Notes to provide you with access to the existing features. The back-end classes have been implemented from new code. The back-end classes enable you to access data stored in Domino databases. These databases can reside on either the client or the server.

In essence, the front-end classes make sense only in the context of the user interface. For example, some events deal with dragging and dropping. Only a user can accomplish these actions, and they cannot occur in the context of, for example, an agent running on a server. Similarly, issuing a dialog box and expecting a response when no user is present is not meaningful.

In Figure 20.6, you can see how Domino interacts with the DOM back-end classes. Notice that it is similar but different from the Notes client interfaces. In this figure, you also see that a browser client can access the Domino Objects.

Refer to Figure 20.6 for the following discussion. On the Domino server, LotusScript programs can access the back-end classes but not the front-end classes because there is no real workstation user. The front-end classes are available only while there is a workstation user using the Notes client. Java is a very interesting case because the Domino Object Model can be accessed a couple of different ways, depending upon whether you are running a stand-alone Java application or a Java applet on a browser client. If you're running a standalone Java application or Java applet within a browser, they both interface with the client-side objects (CSOs). The client-side objects are implemented in Java and interface with a client-side Object Request Broker (ORB). This ORB then uses the Internet Inter-Orb Protocol

20

(IIOP) to communicate with the Domino-side ORB (on the server), which then uses the CORBA adapter to access the DOM. This all may seem complicated, but key points to notice in this discussion are as follows:

Figure 20.6
Domino supports client/server access to the Domino Object Model via CORBA and IIOP.

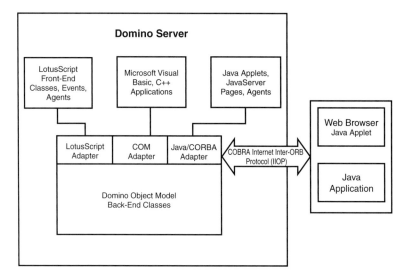

- All the communication and remote procedure invocation is standards-based with CORBA, IIOP, and ORBs. By using these standards, future enhancements will be easier to implement, and the architecture is completely open.

- Because the communication between the browser client and the Domino server uses IIOP, they can each be located anywhere on the Internet. This is an extremely powerful connectivity statement. Also, because IIOP is a more powerful protocol than using HTML with browsers, complex client/server computing is enabled over the Internet.

- Both Java applications and browser clients go through the CSOs and the CORBA adapter to eventually get to the DOM.

- The Notes client goes through the Java adapter in the same way as Domino. Again, this may mean slight differences in appearance or function between the Notes client and a browser client. Over time, however, Lotus can enhance the CSOs to obtain better functionality and come very close to implementing Notes client capabilities in a browser.

So, the wizard behind the curtain has been uncovered. The way that Lotus has implemented Notes client functionality in a Web browser is via Java, CSOs, and CORBA. Although you may not be very familiar with this technology yet, it will be more important in the future because Lotus is implementing more front-end functionality with Java. As more of the client functionality is available in Java, using a Web browser or other Java application instead of the Notes client will become more prevalent. In Chapter 23, "Creating and Using Java Applets and Agents," we'll explore Java and CORBA in more depth so you can see how to use this technology in your own Java applets or Java applications. With CORBA, you will be able to create applications that use any Web browser as a client, the Internet (and IIOP) as the communications channel, and Domino as the server.

In the next two sections, an overview of the Notes front-end classes and the Domino Object Model (back-end) classes is presented. This overview is meant not to give you a comprehensive description of the classes, but to acquaint you with the classes that are available and to describe their primary functions. The classes are described in detail in Chapter 24, "The `Session` and Front-End Classes"; Chapter 25, "Database, View, and Document Classes in LotusScript and Java"; and Chapter 26, "Using Fields and Items in LotusScript and Java."

THE NOTES FRONT-END CLASSES

In deciding whether you want to use the front-end or back-end classes, consider whether the program you are writing will require user input and, if so, whether you want changes to be reflected in the user interface. If this is your situation, you should use the front-end classes. The front-end classes can emulate user input and perform actions, such as moving the cursor from one field to another.

Notes has eight front-end classes. Here are descriptions of these classes, in alphabetical order, with some of their major functions (more details on these classes are given in other chapters):

- `Button`—This class represents button objects within forms and on action bars in views or forms.
- `Field`—This class represents a field within a form. You can perform some processing when the user's cursor enters or exits the field.
- `Navigator`—This class is used to handle user interactions with a navigator.
- `NotesUIDatabase`—This class is used as a basis for accessing Notes databases. From this class, you can access the user views and documents contained in the databases. Database open and close events enable you to perform processing at these times.
- `NotesUIDocument`—This class enables you to access the document that the user is viewing on the display. You can access information stored in the fields of the document. You can cut and paste and navigate through the document. In addition, the `Refresh` method enables you to update the display after you have made changes.
- `NotesUIScheduler`—This class enables you to access an embedded scheduler within a document that the user is viewing on the display.
- `NotesUIView`—This class enables you to access the documents contained in the view. It also contains the `NotesView` object back-end class. See the description in the following section for its functions.
- `NotesUIWorkspace`—This class enables you to add a database to the workspace, compose (create) new documents, open a database, and refresh a view.

The five major classes have "UI" in the middle of the name to signify "user interface." Many of the actions taken by methods in these classes can be used to simulate user input, such as moving from one field to another or cutting and pasting information from one place to another.

EVENTS

Before we discuss the LotusScript classes for Notes in more detail, we need to cover one more topic. *Events* in LotusScript are another characteristic of classes. Events are triggered in LotusScript when particular conditions are met. For example, an event occurs when a document in a database has just been opened. This event is called the PostOpen event.

For the most part, events are related to the front-end classes. This is because most of the events are triggered by user actions. The only exception is the Alarm event, which can be triggered on the NotesTimer back-end class.

When an event is triggered, a method within the class is called to handle the event. In older systems, these types of subroutines were sometimes called user-exits. In essence, the idea of the event is that it gives you, as a user of the class, a chance to perform some actions under certain circumstances.

For example, suppose that you want to perform some validity checking whenever a document is opened in a particular database. You can supply a subroutine to handle the PostOpen event; whenever a document is opened, your subroutine will be called. Similar events occur for opening a database, opening and closing views, and so forth.

THE DOMINO OBJECT MODEL BACK-END CLASSES

The LotusScript DOM has 68 back-end classes, and the Java DOM has 34 classes. The primary reason for the discrepancy between the number of LotusScript and Java classes is due to the introduction of native XML parser LotusScript classes within Release 6. As in previous releases, classes to parse XML within Java are provided by other third parties. Outside these new XML LotusScript classes, the Java classes correspond very closely to the LotusScript classes. However, the names are slightly different, and their usage syntax is slightly different in the two programming languages. We'll cover these differences later; for this section, we'll use the LotusScript names. Here are the core LotusScript DOM classes, in alphabetical order:

- **NotesACL**—This class enables you to access and manipulate the Access Control List (ACL) for a database. You can create new ACL entries and traverse the existing entries.

- **NotesACLEntry**—This class represents a single ACL entry. You can query the properties of an object of this class to see whether the user can create documents, personal agents, or personal folders. You can also query whether the user can delete documents and find out about any associated roles.

- **NotesAdministrationProcess**—New within Release 6, this class enables you to access the administration process within a Domino server to delete a user or server from the Domino domain.

- **NotesAgent**—This class enables you to run an agent or query its properties, to find out such things as whether it is a public agent, whether it is enabled, and the associated server name.

- **NotesColorObject**—This new class within Release 6 represents a color that can be accessed via its RGB (red, green, blue) and HSL (hue, saturation, luminance) value as properties.

- **NotesDatabase**—This class encapsulates methods and properties associated with a Notes database. You can obtain one of the views, query the ACL, get information about forms, grant or revoke access to the database, create and delete documents, and perform many other functions. This is one of the more important classes within the Notes class hierarchy.

- **NotesDateRange**—This is a utility class that contains a start date/time, an end date/time, and an associated string of text. This class is used to support the calendaring and scheduling feature.

- **NotesDateTime**—This class is used to represent a date and time within Notes. It can also be used to convert a date/time value to another time zone.

- **NotesDbDirectory**—This class is used to traverse the list of databases that are accessible on the local machine or on a server.

- **NotesDocument**—This is an important class that enables you to add or remove items from a document, encrypt the document, and traverse the fields of the document. You can use this class to send the document via email or to save it to the database.

- **NotesDocumentCollection**—This class is used as a container for documents. Using this class, you can traverse the documents by getting the first document, the last document, the next or previous document, or the nth document.

- **NotesEmbeddedObject**—This class is used to represent an object that is embedded in a rich-text field or directly within a document. Using this method, you can activate the object or execute some specific action of the object. On Windows, this class supports object linking and embedding (OLE).

- **NotesForm**—The NotesForm class enables you to access attributes of the form, such as the fields, the form's name, and the users who are allowed to access the form. These attributes are not tied to any particular document in the database. You can also use the NotesForm method called Remove to remove a form from a database.

- **NotesInternational**—This class is used to return properties that might vary from one country to another. For example, the currency symbol in the United States is the dollar sign, but in Japan it is the yen sign and in England it is the pound sign. In addition, different countries use different conventions for date formats, time formats (such as using 24-hour time notation), and even the thousands separator. It is common in some European countries, for example, to use a period separating each group of three digits and a comma to signify a decimal point. The NotesInternational class provides support to handle these country-by-country differences.

20

- **NotesItem**—The NotesItem class represents an item (field) within a document. Each item in the document is a separate NotesItem. You can query the field name, type, value(s), and other properties. You can change the value of the item. A NotesItem can represent any type of item except a rich-text item. Rich-text items use the NotesRichTextItem class.

- **NotesLog**—The NotesLog class is a utility class that can be used to create log entries. If you have looked in the Notes Log database, you have seen entries that have been created with this class. You can log events, actions, and errors, as well as query some logging properties.

- **NotesMIMEEntity**—This class represents the MIME (Multipurpose Internet Mail Extensions) content of a NotesDocument or NotesItem.

- **NotesMIMEHeader**—This class represents the header in a MIME (Multipurpose Internet Mail Extensions) document.

- **NotesName**—Frequently in Notes you must manipulate names. The NotesName class is a welcome addition to help you with these chores. There are usernames, server names, and names within Access Control Lists. Names are also found within groups and are associated with roles. With the NotesName class, you can break a name into its component parts, such as the common name and organization or organizational units.

- **NotesNewsletter**—The NotesNewsletter class represents a document that contains links to other documents. It can be created from a NotesSession object. When you create a NotesNewsletter object, you pass to it a NotesDocumentCollection object containing a collection of documents that you want to be linked; a new NotesNewsletter is created with links to each document in the collection. You can also use NotesNewsletter to create a rendering (picture) of a single document of a collection.

- **NotesNoteCollection**—This new Release 6 class enables you to access a collection of Domino design and data elements within a database from a NotesDatabase object.

- **NotesOutline**—This class represents a control you can provide to users for traversal in your database. Outlines enable you to control the ordering, indentation, and traversal of the outline entries. Each entry represents a navigation destination. This class represents a collection of NotesOutlineEntry objects.

- **NotesOutlineEntry**—Each NotesOutlineEntry represents an item, such as a folder, view, page, frameset, or URL. Each entry controls what happens when a user clicks the entry and what is displayed, whether the entry is expandable, and so forth.

- **NotesRegistration**—This class enables you to manipulate the Domino directories. You can add users and servers, register new users, switch IDs, and cross-certify. This class has many properties and methods to aid in the development of administration programs or agents.

- **NotesReplication**—This class can be used to set replication properties for the database in which the NotesReplication object appears. It can be used to set priorities, enable and disable replication, and control truncation of large documents during replication.

20

- **NotesReplicationEntry**—This class within Release 6 represents the replication settings for the source and destination server for any replicated database.

- **NotesRichTextDocLink**—This new Release 6 class represents a doclink within a rich-text field.

- **NotesRichTextItem**—This class is a special version of the NotesItem class. It has methods that are specific to rich-text items, such as support for doclinks and embedded objects.

- **NotesRichTextNavigator**—This new, exciting class within Release 6 represents a mechanism to navigate a rich-text item. Using the NotesRichTextNavigator class, you can move between element types and locate a target string of characters within a formatted field.

- **NotesRichTextParagraphStyle**—This class enables you to control the attributes that relate to an entire paragraph. For example, you can control the margin settings and the spacing above and below the paragraph. You can also control tab settings for the paragraph with this class.

- **NotesRichTextRange**—This class, new to Release 6, represents a range of elements within a rich-text item.

- **NotesRichTextSection**—This class represents a collapsible section within a rich-text field.

- **NotesRichTextStyle**—This class enables you to control the styling of the contents within a rich-text field. It enables you to set properties, such as bold, italic, color, and font.

- **NotesRichTextTab**—This class enables you to control the position and type (center, decimal, left, or right) of a single tab within a paragraph.

- **NotesRichTextTable**—This class represents a table in a rich-text item. With this class, you can add, remove, and change the color of new rows to a table. Using the NotesRichTextNavigator class, you can navigate between rows and particular cells.

- **NotesSession**—The NotesSession class, in a sense, is the root class of the major hierarchy. This class represents a user session with Notes. When you create a NotesSession object, it is associated with a user ID, so the rights and privileges of that user are used to access databases, run agents, run scripts, and so forth. The NotesSession class can also be used to access the list of name and address books that are being used.

- **NotesStream**—This new class represents a stream of binary or character data. The NotesStream class provides a mechanism to view and modify attachments within an item. For example, this can be used to attach a file in memory to another document without having to write the file to disk first.

- **NotesTimer**—This class enables you to trigger an event at specified fixed intervals. You set the timer interval, and the alarm event occurs each time the interval elapses. The time interval is not guaranteed because of other events that might be happening in the system, so the interval is approximate.

20

- **NotesView**—The `NotesView` class enables you to traverse a view within a Notes database. You can do a full-text search, get the first or last documents of the view, and go through all documents of the view one by one. You can also find out information such as the view name and determine whether the view is the default view.

- **NotesViewColumn**—`NotesViewColumn` represents one column of a view. A collection of these kinds of objects is stored in a `NotesView` object. Each column object contains attributes, such as whether the column is sorted, the position within the view, and the associated column formula.

- **NotesViewEntry**—This class represents one entry within a view. Among many properties, you can tell whether this entry has an associated document, determine whether the unread flag is on or off, and see the full-text search score for the entry.

- **NotesViewEntryCollection**—This class represents a collection of `NotesViewEntry` objects. Each of the entries in the collection refers to a document, never a category or total type item. The list is always sorted.

- **NotesViewNavigator**—This class enables you to navigate within a `NotesViewEntryCollection`. You can issue a `GetFirst`, `GetNext`, `GetLast`, `GetNth`, and `GetParent` command, among several other navigational commands.

DIFFERENCES BETWEEN JAVA AND LOTUSSCRIPT IMPLEMENTATIONS

As mentioned earlier, there are slight differences in the syntax and usage between the Java and LotusScript implementations of access to the Domino Object Model. The first difference is in the naming conventions of the classes.

In LotusScript, the classes are all named with a `Notes` prefix, as in `NotesSession`, `NotesDatabase`, and so forth. In Java, the classes use the same names, but without the `Notes` prefix. So, the Java class `Session` corresponds to the LotusScript class `NotesSession`, and the Java class `Database` corresponds to the LotusScript class `NotesDatabase`. This convention applies to the rest of the class names as well.

In addition to the class name differences, LotusScript properties and methods have a slightly different usage in Java. The LotusScript methods have Java counterparts, and the only difference might be in the capitalization of the names. LotusScript properties, however, are implemented differently in Java because Java does not have an equivalent properties concept. To simulate properties, the Java implementation of the DOM uses methods with a particular naming convention that will be described shortly.

In LotusScript, properties are implemented as two access subroutines. One subroutine implements a `get` of the property; the other subroutine implements the `set`. These subroutines are both associated with the property name. In LotusScript, the subroutines are implicitly called, and you can use properties just by referring to them.

For example, suppose a class has a property called `Name`, which represents the object's name. To obtain the value of this property, you could specify the following:

```
Variable = MyObject.Name
```

To assign a new value to the property, you could use this line:

```
MyObject.Name = value
```

The result of these two statements is calls to the `get` and `set` routines for the property. Because Java does not have the property concept, access to properties must be made by explicitly calling the `get` and `set` routines.

The Java routine names for obtaining property values are prefixed by either `get` for generic properties or `is` for Boolean properties. For example, you will find property access names such as `getUserName`, `getEnvironmentString`, `getFileSize`, `isHidden`, `isResponse`, and `isSorted`. You can tell that each of these is a property access routine by the name prefix.

Java routines to set property values begin with `set`. For example, `setDateTimeValue`, `setValueInteger`, `setReaders`, and `setFormUsers` are all names of routines to set properties within objects.

If you were to guess the Java syntax for the previous LotusScript examples, the `get` routine would be as follows:

```
Variable = MyObject.getName()
```

To assign a new value to the property in Java, you could use this line:

```
MyObject.setName(value)
```

Just remember that, for Boolean values, the access routine typically is prefixed with `is`, not `get`. Here is the pair of calls for the ACL class, for example:

```
boolean = MyACLObject.isUniformAccess()
MyObject.setUniformAccess(boolean)
```

DOMINO OBJECT MODEL (DOM) OBJECTS

In an earlier explanation, classes are just definitions that generically describe the characteristics of objects, but they are not actually objects. The difference between classes and objects can be very confusing when you are first learning object-oriented programming, so we have tried to emphasize the difference several times.

If the DOM classes are just definitions, how do you access real databases, documents, forms, and views? The answer is through the use of the DOM objects. These objects are the physical instantiation of the class definitions. That is, they are real objects. An object of a class is sometimes called an *instance* of that class, so *instantiation* just means you are creating an instance of the class. You can query the properties within the objects, and you can call methods and handle events.

→ **See** Chapter 21, "LotusScript Variables and Objects" **p. 525**, for more information about variables and objects.

You can consider the DOM classes to be like a containment hierarchy. Recall how a house is made up of rooms, and each room is made up of walls, doors, and so forth. The DOM classes are similar. At the top of the containment hierarchy is the `NotesSession` class, and contained within it are the various components of the current session.

20

CHAPTER 21

LOTUSSCRIPT VARIABLES AND OBJECTS

In this chapter

IDENTIFIERS

Identifiers are names you define and give to variables, classes, types, constants, subroutines, and properties in LotusScript. The first character of an identifier must be a letter. Identifiers in LotusScript are not case sensitive, so the initial letter can be in upper- or lowercase.

Identifiers can be up to 40 characters and, after the initial letter, can include any letter, digit, or the underscore (_). There are six data type suffix characters (%, &, !, #, @, and $), which are discussed shortly. They are not included in the length limitation of 40 characters.

Here are some examples of identifiers:

`MyName`	Valid
`myname`	Valid—same identifier as first example
`First_Name`	Valid—contains underscore, which is okay
`First1`	Valid—begins with a letter, contains a digit
`My Name`	Invalid—contains a space
`_MisLeading`	Invalid—begins with an underscore
`1Time`	Invalid—begins with a digit

Some ActiveX classes or external programs can define identifiers that include some characters that are illegal within LotusScript names. To use these names, you must use an escape character, which is the tilde (~) in LotusScript. The tilde must immediately precede the illegal character. For example:

`MyVar = ActiveXClass.Go!`	Invalid—ends with an illegal character
`MyVar = ActiveXClass.Go~!`	Valid—includes a tilde before the illegal character

By preceding the illegal character with a tilde, you allow LotusScript to use the special character as part of the name.

IDENTIFIER SCOPE

Scope does not refer to a telescope, a microscope, or even the scope on a rifle. In LotusScript, after you have created an identifier, the *scope* determines how widely the identifier is known. With a small scope, the identifier is known only in a limited range, but with a larger scope, the identifier is more widely known and recognized. LotusScript has three levels of scope:

- Module scope
- Procedure scope
- Type or class scope

It is quite possible —almost likely—to have two identifiers with the same name declared in different scopes. For example, you might have two identifiers called Amount. In this case, the identifier with the smallest or most limited scope is used. This is also sometimes called the innermost scope. Because of this definition, when you have two identifiers with the same name, the outer identifier is no longer accessible. This outer definition, referred to as *shadowed*, cannot be used by the inner program. However, two variables with the same name cannot be declared in the same scope. If this condition is found, the compiler reports a name conflict error.

One way to visualize this is to think about a set of boxes of different sizes. A very small box is inside a larger one, which is inside a larger one, and so forth. When you refer to a variable in the innermost box, LotusScript searches from the inside outward until it finds a variable with the name you've given.

Because of these naming conflicts, you should carefully choose your identifier names. In fact, it is a good idea to follow naming conventions within all your LotusScript programs. Later, we'll review some possible naming conventions you could use. In summary, however, good naming conventions enable you to quickly identify the type of the variable and sometimes its scope.

Identifiers declared at the module scope are declared outside any procedure, class, or type definition. They are valid as long as the module is loaded. Procedure scope identifiers are declared within a subroutine (sub), function, or Property Get/Set routine. Identifiers at the type or class scope have meaning only within the definition of the type or class. Here is an example:

```
Dim Variable1 As Integer     '<-This is at module scope
Dim Variable2 As Integer     '<-This is at module scope

Sub Subroutine1              '<-Begins procedure level
Dim Variable1 As String      '<-This is at procedure scope
Dim Variable3 As Integer     '<-This is at procedure scope

Variable1 = "Hello"          '<-Uses procedure scope variable
End Sub                      '<-Ends procedure level
```

The same variable name (Variable1) is used both inside and outside the subroutine. Variables can even be declared as different types. The innermost variable is used within the procedure.

PUBLIC AND PRIVATE

Most identifiers can be declared as public or private. By default, identifiers are private within a module, which means they are visible only within that module. Two private identifiers with the same name but in different modules will not conflict.

Declaring an identifier as public makes it known to other modules. Public scope is also sometimes called global scope, which means that the identifier is known globally to all modules. A conflict arises if the same public identifier has been declared in separate modules.

21

VARIABLES AND CONSTANTS

Variables are really just programmer-defined names, or identifiers, for areas of the computer's main memory. Unlike variables, which can accept a range of values, *constants* have fixed values and cannot be changed at any time. These fixed values are known at the time the program is compiled rather than at an application's runtime. Constants and variables have a specific scope and life cycle.

DATA TYPES

Associated with each constant or variable is either an explicit or an implicit data type. The data type defines how the computer should interpret the bits that are stored in memory. Table 21.1 shows the data types allowed by LotusScript, along with the suffix character used for each type and the ranges for the numeric types.

TABLE 21.1 THE DATA TYPES IN LOTUSSCRIPT

Keyword	Suffix	Data Type	Range*
Byte			0 to 255; initial value of 0
Boolean			0 (False) or -1 (True); initial value of 0
Integer	%	Integer value	−32,768 to 32,767
Long	&	Integer value	−2,147,483,648 to 2,147,483,647
Single	!	Floating-point value	−3.402823E38 to 3.402823E38
Double	#	Floating-point value	−1.7976931348623158E308 to 1.7976931348623158E308
Currency	@	Currency value internal format	−922,337,203,685,477.5808 to 922,337,203,685,477.5807
String	$		Character strings
Variant			Can contain any of the preceding, plus date/time, Boolean, and objects

As you can see from the table, selecting the exact type of data that you want can affect the range of values your variable can hold. Integers are stored exactly. Floating-point variables are like scientific notation—that is, they hold two components: a number and an exponent. By using a number and an exponential factor, the range of values that can be stored is much greater. Double precision stores roughly twice the number of digits for the number, so it has greater accuracy for very large or very small (close to 0) numbers.

This list of suffixes can be applied to variable names and literal constants. For example, 3.7# represents a double-precision constant, whereas 3.7! represents a single-precision version of the same constant. Amount# is a double-precision variable, and Amount! is a single-precision variable with the same name. You cannot use both a single- and a double-precision version of the same variable within the same scope.

21

Variants are a special kind of data type. A *Variant* variable is like a chameleon—it changes its character depending on the circumstance. If you assign an integer value to a Variant, the variable keeps it in its native integer format. If you assign a double variable, it stores the double value. You can also store date/time type values and Boolean (`true`/`false`) values. Variants can also store objects and can convert values from one format to another.

The main disadvantage of Variant variables is that because of their flexibility, they are less efficient than the other native variable types. As a general rule, you will get much better performance in terms of both space used and speed if you use a native type. You should use the Variant type sparingly when you really need the flexibility or power of the Variant (for example, when you need to store a date/time value).

CONSTANTS

Character string literal constants can be enclosed in one of three sets of delimiters: a pair of quotation marks (" "), a pair of vertical bars (| |), or an open and closed brace ({ }). There are three sets of delimiters, so you can use one pair of symbols within another set. You cannot nest a pair of delimiters within another pair of the same type. If you want to include a character such as a double quotation mark in a string, you can use another pair of delimiters for the string. A string enclosed in vertical bars or braces can span multiple lines. For example, you could use a pair of vertical bars to create a string with an embedded double-quote character. See the second and third examples that follow.

Here are some examples:

```
"This is a literal string in quotes"
|This is a string with double quote " embedded|
{A brace string with a vertical bar | enclosed inside}
|A string   on two lines|
```

Numeric constants are normally decimal notation. Integers do not include a decimal point. You can write floating-point constants by including an `E`, as in `314.159E-02`. You can enter binary values by preceding the number with `&B`, octal with `&O`, and hexadecimal with `&H`. Here are some examples:

```
&B10101111
&O7342
&H0B31
```

You can define a named constant with the `Const` statement. You should always consider using `Const` statements to give names to specific constants instead of using literal constants within your program. By using named constants, you can later change your program easily by updating the `Const` statement. This enables you to change your program in only one place rather than searching through your source code for numeric or string constants.

Here are some examples:

```
Const dblInterestRate# = 0.075
Const strCompany$ = "First Federal"
Const curBaseAmount@ = 1000.00
```

21

SCALAR VARIABLES

LotusScript variables are defined with the `Dim` statement, short for `dimension`. `Dimension` is a keyword of FORTRAN, and the creators of BASIC abbreviated the word `dimension` to `Dim`. Originally, in FORTRAN, the `dimension` statement was used only to define the size of array variables (which I'll discuss shortly), but in LotusScript the `Dim` statement is used to define not only arrays, but all other variables as well.

A *scalar variable* is a variable that contains only a single value. Most variables in your program will be scalar variables. The term is usually used only to distinguish scalar variables from array variables, which can contain multiple values. Throughout the book, we'll normally be discussing scalar variables when the plain term *variable* is used. In addition, when array variables are referenced, they will simply be called *arrays*.

Here are examples of declarations of some variables:

```
Dim intNoteIndex As Integer
Dim curAmount As Currency
Dim dblLoanRate As Double
```

ARRAY VARIABLES

An *array variable* can contain multiple values of the same type. You might have, for example, an `Integer` array, a `Double` array, or a `String` array. To identify a particular value within an array variable, you must specify which of the multiple values you want to access. This is done with an array *index*, or *subscript*. The subscript of an array has a lower bound and an upper bound. The lower bound is zero by default.

When you define the array variable with the `Dim` statement, you can either specify fixed dimensions that will not change or indicate a dynamic array. Memory for a dynamic array is allocated with the `ReDim` statement.

The following are some examples of array declarations:

```
Dim intValues(10) As Integer
Dim strNames(5,20) As String
Dim dblRates(1980 to 1999) As Double
Redim intVar(10) As Integer
Redim strAddrs(3,15) As String
```

In the first example, an integer array is defined with a lower bound of `0` and an upper bound of `10`. Contrary to appearances, this actually means that 11 items are defined for this array. The second example shows a two-dimensional array. You can have up to eight dimensions. Again, the lower bound is assumed to be `0`, so there are actually 6×21, or 126, elements in the array, not 100.

You can change the assumed lower bound for all arrays in a module with the `Option Base` statement. You can have only one `Option Base` statement within a module, and it must precede all array declarations. This is the format for the statement:

21

```
Option Base 0
```

or

```
Option Base 1
```

You can specify only values 0 or 1 in the Option Base statement.

In addition, you can explicitly set a lower bound for an array, as shown earlier in the third example. In that case, the subscript for dblRates can be the values from 1980 to 1999, which might represent calendar years.

Values for subscripts must be between –32,768 and 32,767, inclusive. You are limited to a maximum of eight dimensions.

LIST VARIABLES

A *list variable* is very similar to a one-dimensional array. A list can hold only values of the same type, but when you declare it, you do not need to specify the number of elements in the list. The list grows or shrinks automatically as items are added or removed.

The major benefit of a list is that you can use a String value rather than a subscript to access the elements of the list. This value, called a list tag, can be case sensitive or not, depending on the setting of the Option Compare statement. The default is to use case-sensitive comparisons. For example:

```
Dim strDictionary List as String
strDictionary("Lime") = "A Green fruit"
strDictionary("Plum") = "A Purple fruit"
strDictionary("Banana") = "A Yellow fruit"
strDictionary("Lotus") = "A Yellow computer company"
strDictionary("IBM") = "A Blue computer company"
strDictionary("Apple") = "A Red fruit or a rainbow computer company"
```

You can add values to the list with an assignment statement. To delete items, use the Erase statement:

```
Erase strDictionary("Plum")      ' Erases one item
Erase strDictionary             ' Erases the whole list
```

USER-DEFINED TYPE VARIABLES

Array and List variables enable you to have a homogeneous collection of values. What if you want to give a name to a group of variables of different types? In this case, you could create your own type with the Type statement.

The Type statement occurs only at the module level and can be optionally prefixed with either a Public or a Private modifier. As an example, see Listing 21.1, which contains a type definition and two instances of PersonType variables.

21

LISTING 21.1   PersonType DEFINITION

```
Type PersonType
    m_strFirstName As String
    m_strLastName As String
    m_curSalary As Currency
End Type

Dim Person1 as PersonType, Person2 as PersonType
Person1.m_strFirstName = "Janet"
Person1.m_strLastName = "Trujillo"
Person1.m_curSalary = 55000.00

Person2.m_strFirstName = "John"
Person2.m_strLastName = "Hashimoto"
Person2.m_curSalary = 50000.00
```

If the member names of the PersonType data structure look odd to you, refer to the "Naming Conventions" section later in this chapter. In short, the m_ is used to signify that the variable is a member variable, and the three-letter prefix to the variable name indicates its type.

VARIABLE LIFETIMES

In addition to characteristics such as scope and data type, variables have a lifetime. The lifetime of a variable is related to its scope. Module scope variables are created when the module is loaded, and they retain their values while the module is active.

Procedure scope variables are normally created when the procedure is entered; they are destroyed when control leaves the procedure. The exception to this rule is for variables that have been declared with the Static keyword. The keyword Static can be used only with procedure scope variables (not module or class scope). With Static variables, the value of the variable is saved between calls of the procedure. You can use this type of variable to store status information. For example, you could keep a count of how many times a subroutine has been called. This would be impossible with a regular variable.

Class scope variables have a programmer-defined lifetime. You create an object of a particular class with the New keyword. After it has been created, you can use the Delete statement to delete the object. An object variable is also deleted if control leaves the variable's scope.

IMPLICIT DECLARATION

You can implicitly declare variables by using them just within a program. If you use a data-type-modifier suffix on the variable (such as #, $, !, %, @, or &), you must use that modifier every time the variable is used. If you do not use the type modifier, you cannot subsequently use one on a later reference to the same variable.

If you do not supply a type modifier, the variable is a Variant type by default. A Variant variable is less efficient than a variable that you have declared to be of a particular type.

21

You can also control the default type of variables by using one of the Deftype statements. There are nine Deftype statements:

```
DefBool    range [, range]
DefByte    range [, range]
DefCur     range [, range]
DefDbl     range [, range]
DefInt     range [, range]
DefLng     range [, range]
DefSng     range [, range]
DefStr     range [, range]
DefVar     range [, range]
```

Each of these statements has the same format. After the keyword, you supply one or more ranges of letters to be used. For example:

```
DefDbl A-H,O-Z
```

The preceding statement defines all variables that begin with any letter from *A* to *H* or from *O* to *Z* to be Double variables. Deftype statements must appear at the module level and apply to all procedures and variables within the module. Any variable or procedure that is explicitly declared with a data type uses the explicitly defined data type rather than the default type for that letter.

TIP

> Although the LotusScript language enables you to implicitly define variables, it is considered very poor programming style to use this feature. In general, variables should *always* be explicitly declared. The use of implicit variables makes it extremely easy to allow variables with misspellings to go unnoticed. In turn, these misspelled variables can cause your program to exhibit very strange behavior and is very difficult to debug. You can turn off the implicit variable capability through the use of the Option Declare statement, which forces undeclared variables to generate a syntax error.

LotusScript Limitations

As in most programming systems, LotusScript has various size limitations in the language's implementation. Table 21.2 lists the new maximums.

TABLE 21.2   LotusScript Implementation Limit Improvements

Type	Maximum
Number of strings	Limited by available memory
Total string storage	Limited by available memory
Length of string literal	16,267 characters (32,534 bytes)
Length of string value	2GB

21

continues

TABLE 21.2 CONTINUED

Type	Maximum
Total module string literals	2GB
Total size of an array	Limited by available memory
Number of array dimensions	8
Dimension bounds	–32,768 to 32,767
Fixed-size data items with module scope	64KB
Number of source code lines per script	64KB lines
Number of symbols per module	64KB
Total module scope storage	Limited by available memory
Total class scope storage	64KB
Total procedure scope storage	32KB

NOTE

Fixed-size arrays with module scope are limited to 64KB bytes.

CLASSES AND OBJECTS

The preceding chapter discussed classes, objects, and an introduction to the class definitions for Lotus Notes. Most of your programming will involve the Notes classes. In addition to the built-in classes, however, you can define your own classes and objects. Remember, the Class statement, like the Type statement, defines the class itself. The Class statement does not actually create any objects of the class.

The Class statement can be used only at the module level and cannot be used within a procedure or within another class.

CREATING CLASSES

You create a class by using the Class and End Class keywords. Between them, you can define member variables and methods. To see an example, look at Listing 21.2. The numbers located along the side of the listing are not part of the code, but are a reference tool for our discussion.

LISTING 21.2 PersonClass DEFINITION

```
1   Class PersonClass
2     ' Member Variables
3     m_strFirstName As String
4     m_strLastName As String
5     m_curSalary As Currency
6
```

```
 7    Sub New(strFirst As String, strLast As String, curSalary As Currency)
 8        m_strFirstName  = strFirst
 9        m_strLastName = strLast
10        m_curSalary = curSalary
11    End Sub
12
13    Function FullName As String
14        FullName =  Me.m_strFirstName + " " + Me.m_strLastName
15    End Function
16  End Class
```

In Listing 21.2, you'll notice a distinct similarity to Listing 21.1, which was a type definition for a person. You can now see that when you use a type definition as in Listing 21.1, you cannot define any methods. With a class definition, as in Listing 21.2, you can define methods, or operations on the data.

Referring to Listing 21.2, lines 2–5 represent the member variable declarations. Lines 7–11 are the New subroutine. This subroutine is invoked when a new instance of a PersonClass object is created. Three parameters must be passed to the New method: the first name, last name, and salary. The method just fills in the member variables with the information.

Lines 13–15 are the FullName method. This method enables you to extract the full name, including first and last names, from the object formatted with one space between the names. Notice that the keyword Me is used to refer to the current object. This enables the same code within the class to be used, regardless of the name of the object that has been created.

CREATING OBJECTS

You create new objects by using the New keyword on the Dim statement or by using the Set statement. To create variables of the PersonType class defined previously and then display the full name, you could use the following:

```
Dim person1 As New PersonClass("Sam", "Smith", 5000000)
Dim person2 As New PersonClass("John", "Jones", 500000)

Dim person3 As PersonClass
Set person3 = New PersonClass("Joan", "Johnson", 200000)

Messagebox person1.FullName
Messagebox person2.FullName
Messagebox person3.FullName
```

In this example, the first two statements declare and allocate PersonClass objects, and assign them to the object variables. In the third example, the Dim statement defines the type of variable but does not allocate any storage for the variable. The storage is allocated by using the New keyword in a Set statement. You can use either method to allocate and initialize the storage for the object.

21

ASSIGNING OBJECTS

Although objects sometimes appear to be similar to regular variables, one major difference easily confuses novice LotusScript programmers. This aspect is very basic and occurs throughout LotusScript, so you should become very familiar with it.

This major difference between regular variables and objects is the assignment statement. With regular variables, you use the Let statement, but with objects you use the Set statement. They appear very similar:

```
Let variable = expression
```

or

```
variable = expression
Set object1 = object2
```

or

```
Set object  = New classname(argList)
```

You should also be aware that Let is optional and normally is not included in most programs.

If you do not include the Set keyword when assigning an object variable, you get an error message.

UNDERSTANDING EMPTY, NOTHING, AND NULL

LotusScript has three special values. They all have names that sound similar in purpose, so it is easy to confuse them: EMPTY, NOTHING, and NULL.

Remarkable as it seems, the three values can be used to represent related concepts. The first value, EMPTY, is the initial value for Variant variables. If you declare a Variant variable and have not yet assigned it a value, it will be EMPTY. This type of value is pretty harmless because you can convert it to a string or number. In this case, it will just be the empty string or a zero value. Either of these values can then be used normally in operations, such as in concatenation or arithmetic. After the Variant variable has a value, it no longer is EMPTY. You can test to see whether a value is EMPTY with the IsEmpty function.

The second value, NOTHING, is used for object reference variables. Object reference variables are declared to be of a particular class, such as NotesSession. For example, suppose you declare a variable to be a NotesSession object or a NotesDatabase object. Before it is initialized with a real object, this kind of variable contains the value NOTHING. Remember, you assign a value to this type of variable with the New keyword or the Set statement.

If you allocate an object variable with the New keyword and later delete the object with the Delete statement, the value of the object variable reverts to NOTHING.

Here is an example:

```
Dim session as NotesSession
Messagebox session.UserName
```

21

Notice in the preceding example that the New keyword before the class name NotesSession was not included. The NotesSession variable was declared but has not been initialized. When the second line is executed, attempting to refer to the UserName property, an error message saying "Object variable not set" appears. Although this error message does not tell you the variable name, remember that it just means that you have not yet initialized some object variable within the statement.

The final value, NULL, really represents a situation that has arisen during execution rather than an initial value. It can indicate an error situation, and it sometimes represents missing data. If you are familiar with relational database systems, this NULL is analogous to a NULL value that the database system might return to you as a result of a query.

The value NULL is used because, in some cases, you want to distinguish between "no value" and, for example, a zero value. Suppose you are trying to retrieve the salary information for an employee. You really need to differentiate between NULL, which means that the data is not in the database, and zero, which means that the salary is in the database but the employee is really a poorly paid individual.

So, NULL typically is the result of some query or request, and it indicates that no value is available. This is different from EMPTY, which just means that you haven't yet asked the question.

You probably now know more about NOTHING than you ever wanted to know. Although you understand the distinctions now, however, by next week it will be NULL in your brain again. Just remember that you can look it up here in the book again when you need it next. Don't try to fill your brain with EMPTY concepts.

NAMING CONVENTIONS

You have seen several cases of what might appear to be strange names for variables and members. If you have been programming for only a short time, you might not have seen prefixes to variable names. If you are a seasoned Windows programmer, you might already be familiar with naming conventions commonly used for Windows programs.

The major advantage to using a naming convention such as the one employed in the previous examples is that it enables you, the programmer, to view parts of a program, sometimes out of context, and to know more information than might otherwise be available. For example, suppose you saw just the following single statement:

```
m_strFirstName  = strFirst
```

Even though you don't have access to any of the declarations, you might be able to guess that both of these variables are string variables. You can guess this because each has a str prefix. This is important information. In addition, because of the m_ that appears before the first name, you can gather that the first variable is a member variable of some class. In essence, the assignment statement is copying a value from outside the class into a member variable of the class. You can make these observations without even referring to the variable names themselves. When you also include meaningful names such as `FirstName`, you can almost complete the picture.

In using LotusScript, you can abbreviate the built-in data types with the following prefixes:

Boolean	bool
Byte	byte
Integer	int
Long	lng
Single	sng
Double	dbl
String	str
Currency	cur
Variant	var

In addition, it is a good idea to develop conventions for common user interface elements. For example:

Text field	txt
Numeric field	n
Rich Text	rt
Button	btn

For the most common objects created from the Notes classes, you can use the following object names (not prefixes):

NotesACL	acl
NotesDatabase	db
NotesDbDirectory	dbdir
NotesDocument	doc
NotesItem	item
NotesRichTextItem	rtitem
NotesSession	session
NotesUIWorkspace	uiws or ws
NotesUIDocument	uidoc
NotesView	view
NotesViewColumn	column

By using a consistent set of names, you make it easier to write, maintain, and debug your LotusScript programs. You can also use prefix modifiers to identify the following characteristics:

21

Static	s_
Public	g_ (for global)
Array	a
List	l

As mentioned previously, these prefixes are just suggestions that you can use as a starting point for your own naming conventions. The actual letters that you choose are not as critical as having a naming convention in the first place. As your library of programs grows, you will be very thankful that you have a naming convention. If you don't have one by the time your library gets large, *it will be too late to go back and implement one*. Start early with your naming convention, and stick with it.

LOTUSSCRIPT STATEMENTS

A LotusScript program consists of several lines of text. Each line of text can contain a part of a statement, one statement, or more than one statement. In most cases, your programs will have one statement per line.

You can continue statements by using the continuation character, the underscore (_). The continuation character must be preceded by at least one space or tab so that it is not confused with part of a variable name or another item on the line.

You can put multiple statements on a single line by separating them with the colon character (:). You can also have lines that are completely blank, to aid in readability, particularly within comments or between code sections.

If you do not end the line with the continuation character, the end of the line is interpreted as the end of the statement.

Here are some examples:

```
Dim dblDip As Double    ' Ice cream with two scoops
Static sintCounter _    ' Continued
      As Integer        ' On the second line
intX = 0 : intY = 0 : intZ = 0  ' Three statements on a line
```

COMMENTS

Comments are one of the most important aspects of your program, so you should liberally include comments. The easiest way to include comments is to use a single quotation mark or apostrophe ('). The apostrophe indicates that the rest of the line is a comment. If the apostrophe is the first nonblank character on the line, the entire line is a comment.

In addition to the apostrophe, you can create comments by using the older Rem statement. Following the Rem, you can include any text. All characters following the Rem are considered a remark and are ignored by LotusScript. You cannot continue a Rem statement with the continuation character.

Another way to include comments is to use the %Rem and %End Rem directives. You can initiate comments with %Rem. All lines following this line up to the %End Rem are ignored. You can end the set of comments with either %End Rem (with a space) or %EndRem (all one word). This method is useful for very long sequences of comments.

Here are some examples:

```
' This is a single-line apostrophe comment
Dim intSheepCount as Integer  ' Counter for insomniacs.
Rem This is a remarkable single-line comment
%Rem
Here are several remarkable lines.
These comments will not be used by LotusScript.
You should include meaningful information here.
%End Rem
```

STRUCTURED PROGRAMMING

In the 1970s and perhaps even into the 1980s, a lot of interest centered on a concept called *structured programming*. Scholarly research was done, papers were presented, and, of course, many books were published on the topic. The interest in structured programming seems to have died down now—which is too bad because it involved several important core concepts that provide a framework for organizing programs and thinking about how programs should flow.

The essence of structured programming is that the control of a program's flow is important and that you should try to simplify the flow so that people reading the program can easily grasp it. The original BASIC language was one of the early offenders and made it particularly difficult to simplify flow control.

Structured programming basically says that you should use only three types of flow control in your program:

- Sequential
- Selection
- Repetition

In particular, the structured programming advocates were opposed to "spaghetti" code, in which control flowed like strands of spaghetti, all over the place.

We'll use the three categories of flow control to organize the discussion of the LotusScript flow-control statements.

21

SEQUENTIAL FLOW CONTROL

Sequential flow control is the easiest type of flow control. This is the default for LotusScript and most other programming languages. Sequential flow just means that after one statement has been executed, the next statement in sequence is executed.

Here is an example of sequential flow control:

```
Dim dblAmt1 as Double
Dim dblAmt2 as Double
Dim dblSum as Double
dblAmt1 = 5.2
dblAmt2 = 7.0
dblSum = dblAmt1 + dblAmt2
```

In this example, the three assignment statements are executed sequentially.

SELECTION FLOW CONTROL

With selection flow control, when control reaches a particular point in the program, one of a set of alternatives is selected. You can control which of the alternatives is selected by testing a condition or evaluating an expression. The If-Then-Else and Select Case statements are examples of selection flow control.

If-Then-Else

Two versions of the If-Then-Else statement exist. The first version must all fit on a single line. To use this format, you would specify this:

```
If  condition  Then statement1  Else statement2
```

The condition is tested; statement1 is executed if the condition is true, and statement2 is executed otherwise. You cannot continue this statement on multiple lines. If you need to use multiple lines, you must use the If-Then-ElseIf statement. Following is an example:

```
If  condition  then
   ... statements
[ElseIf  condition  then
   ... statements]
   ...
[Else
   ... statements]
End If
```

In the preceding example, the optional parts are shown in square brackets. Each condition is sequentially tested; when a condition is found to be true, the Then clause is executed. If no condition is found to be true, the Else clause is executed. Notice that you do not need to have an ElseIf clause or even an Else clause. Without these parts, the statement just conditionally executes the Then clause.

Select Case

The Select Case statement also implements the selection flow control. With this statement, an expression is evaluated and the resulting expression is used to determine which of the groups of statements is executed. It is possible that the expression will not satisfy any of the statement groups, in which case the entire statement is just skipped. If more than one condition matches, only the first group is executed and all other groups are ignored. Here is the syntax:

21

```
Select Case  SelectExpression
   [Case    conditionList
       [Statements]]
   [Case    conditionList
       [Statements]]
   ...
   [Case Else
       [Statements]]
End Select
```

The *SelectExpression* is evaluated only once, and the value is saved. This value is tested in sequence against each of the conditions. For each Case, a *conditionList* is a list of conditions, separated by commas. Each condition within the list is tested against the saved value. If the test results in TRUE, the associated group of statements is executed.

Each condition can be in one of three formats:

- **ConditionalExpression**—This is any expression. This expression is tested against the *SelectExpression* and results in TRUE if they match.

- **Expr1 To Expr2**—This is a range. The test results in TRUE if the *SelectExpression* falls within the range. The range includes both the start and end values.

- **Is CompareOperator Expression**—The *CompareOperator* can be one of the following: <, <=, =<, =, =>, >=, >, <>, or ><. For example, you might use Is> 3.

  Example:
  ```
  Select Case intYear
  Case Is < 1970
      Print "Hippie"
  Case 1971 To 1980
      Print "Yuppie"
  Case 1981 To 1990
      Print "Generation X"
  Case Else
      Print "Baby Echo Boom"
  End Select
  ```

In this example, the variable intYear is examined. If it is less than 1970, "Hippie" is printed, if it is from 1971 through 1980, "Yuppie" is printed. If it is from 1981 through 1990, "Generation X" is printed; otherwise, "Baby Echo Boom" is printed.

REPETITION FLOW CONTROL

Repetition is the third and final construct of structured programming. Typically, this construct is used to operate with a set of data in which each element of the set must be handled or processed. A loop consists of two things: a test to see whether the loop has finished, and the processing of one element of the set of data. The loop is repeated until the test that signifies the end of the loop has been satisfied.

21

The loop-ending test can be at the start or end of the loop. It can consist of a counter for a fixed number of repetitions, or some condition such as whether a given value is greater than or less than some limit.

LotusScript has four primary repetition constructs: For/Next, ForAll/End ForAll, While/Wend, and Do While|Until/Loop. Each of these constructs consists of a beginning statement and a statement to mark the end of the loop. Each statement between the start and the end is repeated until the ending condition has been met.

For/Next STATEMENTS

The For/Next pair is typically used when you know how many iterations or repetitions should be performed. The syntax is as follows:

```
For counter = first To last [Step increment]
  [... Statements]
Next counter
```

In this syntax, counter represents a numeric variable. first, last, and increment represent numeric expressions. These expressions can be positive or negative. If increment is omitted, it is assumed to be 1.

Execution of the For/Next loop proceeds as detailed here:

1. The counter variable is initialized to the first value.

   Steps 2, 3, and 4 are repeated until the loop terminates in step 2.

2. If the counter is greater than last (and increment is positive), the loop is terminated. The loop also terminates if the counter is less than last and increment is negative. If the loop is terminated, execution continues with the statement after the Next statement.

3. If the loop does not terminate, the statements within the loop between the For and Next statements are executed normally. The counter variable can be referenced within the loop.

4. The increment is added to the counter variable.

You can leave the loop early with either an Exit For statement or a Goto statement. An Exit For statement resumes execution immediately after the Next statement, and Goto transfers control to the specified label. The Goto statement and labels are covered shortly. Here is an example:

```
Dim aintCountDown(10) As Integer
Dim I As Integer

For I=0 to 10
    aintCountDown(I) = 10 - I        ' 10, 9, 8, ...
Next I
Print "Blastoff"
```

This example fills in the 11 elements of the array with the values 10, 9, 8, and so forth down to 0; then it prints "Blastoff". Notice that the prefix aint means "array of integers."

ForAll/End ForAll STATEMENTS

The ForAll statement is very useful when you have a collection but don't know how many items are contained in the collection. The ForAll statement essentially says to loop through the collection exactly once for each item. Here is the syntax:

```
ForAll itemvariable in container
    [... Statements]
End ForAll
```

The container variable can be an array, a list, or a collection class object. Execution of the ForAll/End ForAll loop proceeds as explained here:

1. The *itemvariable* variable is initialized to the first item in the collection. This variable must *not* be declared with a Dim statement. The ForAll statement itself acts as the definition of the *itemvariable*. If you separately Dim this variable, you will get an error message. If the collection is empty, the rest of the loop is skipped.

   Steps 2 and 3 are repeated until the loop terminates in step 3.

2. If the loop does not terminate, the statements within the loop between the ForAll and the End ForAll statements are executed normally. The *itemvariable* variable can be referenced within the loop and represents the current item from the collection.

3. The next item from the collection is selected and placed into the *itemvariable* variable. If there are no more items, the loop terminates.

You can leave the loop early with either an Exit ForAll statement or a Goto statement. An Exit ForAll statement resumes execution immediately after the End ForAll statement, and Goto transfers control to the specified label.

Here is an example that prints the name of each item (field) stored within a document:

```
Dim doc as NotesDocument

REM Set doc to the document you want to inspect...

ForAll I in doc.Items
    MsgBox "Field: " + I.Name
End ForAll
```

The container must be an array, a list, or a collection within LotusScript. The Items property of a NotesDocument is an example. Some objects in the Domino Object Model seem like they would be collections, but they are not. For example, the NotesDocumentCollection class has its own methods, such as GetFirstDocument and GetNextDocument, for traversing the collection, and you cannot use ForAll with this type of object.

While/Wend STATEMENTS

The While statement is used when you want some condition to terminate the loop. This is the classic looping construct of structured programming. Here is the syntax:

```
While condition
  [... Statements]
Wend
```

Execution of the While/Wend loop proceeds in the following way:

1. The condition is tested before the statements in the loop are executed. If the condition is TRUE, the statements are executed. If the condition is FALSE, the rest of the loop is skipped. Execution continues with the statement after the Wend. It is possible that the statements within the loop will not be executed even once.

   Steps 1 and 2 are repeated until the loop terminates in step 1.

2. If the loop does not terminate, the statements within the loop between the While and the Wend statements are executed normally.

There is no version of the Exit statement to leave the While/Wend loop early and continue execution just beyond the Wend. If you want to do this, use the Do While loop described in the following section. You can use Exit Function or Exit Sub to leave the routine entirely, or you can leave the loop with a Goto statement, which transfers control to the specified label.

Do While, Do Until, AND Loop STATEMENTS

The Do statement is a very general version of the While/Wend construct described previously. The Do statement is designed to execute a group of statements while a given condition is true or while a given condition is false. There are two versions of the Do statement.

Here is the syntax of the first version:

```
Do [While | Until condition]
  [... Statements]
Loop
```

And here is the syntax of the second version:

```
Do
  [... Statements]
Loop [While | Until condition]
```

Execution of the Do statement proceeds as explained in the following paragraphs.

In version 1 of the syntax, the conditional test is performed before the loop. This means that the loop might be executed zero times. In version 2 of the syntax, the condition is tested following the statements within the loop, so the statements are executed at least once.

When the While clause is used, the statements within the loop are executed repeatedly while the condition is true. To use this case, you should set up the clause so that the condition is normally TRUE; as soon as the condition is FALSE, the loop will terminate. For example, if you are using a counter and a limit, you should use something like the following as a condition:

21

```
Do While counter < limit
  ' Perform operation on one element
  ' You can have multiple statements
Loop
```

If you use the Until clause, the loop is executed repeatedly while the condition is FALSE. It terminates as soon as the condition becomes TRUE, so you should set your condition to be normally FALSE. As an example, you could use this:

```
Do
    ' Search for a Needle, one at a time
    ' We assume that we know the needle is in the haystack.
Loop Until Needle=Haystack(item)   ' We found the needle
' Now, we know that we found the needle statement
```

THE GoTo STATEMENT AND LABELS

The GoTo statement is the black sheep of the flow control family. In the late 1970s, the rage in intellectual circles was to talk about programming without GoTo. Scholarly papers wrote about how to transform a spaghetti program full of GoTos to one without any. Even mathematical proofs showed that this was possible. Many people even assumed that it was always desirable.

Well, we're here 20 years later and we still have GoTo statements. They are still useful, when used carefully. The syntax is simple:

```
Goto label
```

label represents a label on a statement. You can label any statement by prefixing the statement with an identifier and a colon (:). This is the syntax for a label:

```
labelIdentifier: [statement]
```

A label can appear only at the beginning of a line, and there can be only one label per line. You can have more than one label for a particular statement, but the labels must be on separate lines. You cannot use the same label on more than one line in the same procedure.

Here is an example:

```
Do While counter < limit
    ' Access data
    If (data> maximum) Then Goto OutOfBounds
    ' Process normally
Loop
Goto Contin
OutOfBounds:
    ' Handle error situation
Contin:
    ' Continue here
```

This example uses a While loop. Each time through the loop, a validity check is performed on the data. If there is something wrong with the data, you do not want to continue processing. In this case, go to the OutOfBounds label. After handling the error, processing continues.

LotusScript Subroutines, Functions, and Event Handlers

In this chapter

22

THE PURPOSE OF PROCEDURES

Before we get into the details and syntax of procedures, it's helpful to reflect on where and why you should use them. The words *procedure* and *subroutine* are used here to refer generally to all the types of subprograms you can use in LotusScript. In LotusScript, you can use Subs (subroutines), functions, methods (subroutines in classes), events (event handlers in classes), and Property Get/Set routines (property access within classes). Not only are there various types, but each has a different purpose and context.

Of course, you use subroutines to modularize your program, but what criteria do you use to decide how to divide a program into parts? This is one of those areas that is a little subjective and depends a lot on your programming experience. Computer science research has been done on just what makes a "good" subroutine and what doesn't, but one important criterion is something called coherence. Coherence just means that all the elements of the subroutine are related and belong together.

BREAKING UP IS HARD TO DO

It might be easier to examine something that *isn't* coherent. Suppose you know that you need to write a program to accomplish a task. You sit down and start writing lines of code. You later discover that the module is too big and decide that you must break it into smaller pieces. One way to do this is just to split the module in half. The first half of the statements goes into one subroutine; the second half goes in another. You create a third routine that just sequentially calls the first and then calls the second. What's wrong with this scenario?

Well, first of all, we know you probably wouldn't write a program like this—it is just an example. This scenario is wrong because the first and second subroutines are not coherent. The lines within them don't necessarily have a common theme or purpose. The only thing they have in common is the fact that the lines that make them up were near each other before the split.

Coherence has to do with purpose. Another way to think about this subject is to look at the variables that are referenced. In our example, it is very likely that some variables used in the first subroutine are also used in the second. To make them generally available to both routines, you must place the variables in some global location so that both routines can use the variables.

In some circumstances, the use of global variables might be a requirement because of the environment and goals of particular segment of code. However, it's important to use them with care and forethought. Given the number and types of possible routines that can modify the variables, a bug in one area of a program can have a ripple effect to a completely independent and unsuspecting part of the program. Frequently, the effects of a bug will show up only in an area of the program that has nothing to do with the root cause. The improper use of global variables can contribute to these types of runtime issues. Just remember to use a global variable only when it's required, not when it's most convenient to you, the developer.

COHERENCE AND CLASSES

You now have an example of what is *not* coherent. What is an example of coherence? Classes. Remember that classes combine both variables and methods. This combination greatly contributes to coherence because the variables needed are localized to the object. The need to store variables outside the object is greatly reduced, which makes debugging easier and makes programs more reliable due to the reduced number of global variables.

In general, the following guidelines should be observed to help create more modular coherent subroutines. A subroutine should...

- Have a well-defined purpose.
- Not be just a collection of program statements.
- Use local variables and avoid global (Public) variables.
- Declare and use classes and objects.

DIFFERENT TYPES OF PROCEDURES

Several types of procedures are available in LotusScript. The following subsections describe these various types.

Sub STATEMENT

The first type of subroutine uses the Sub statement. The syntax is as follows:

```
[Static] [Public | Private] Sub Subname[([ParamList])]
     [... Statements]
End Sub
```

You can usually type the word **Sub** followed by a name in most contexts in the Design pane, and a new subroutine will be created for you. If you specify Static, all the subroutine's local variables are saved between calls. When you specify Public, the name of the subroutine is known outside the current scope and is available to other modules.

The *ParamList* is a list of parameter declarations, separated by commas, to be passed to the subroutine. Each parameter within the list can be of the following form:

```
[ByVal] parameter [() | List] [As type]
```

If the ByVal keyword is used, the parameter is passed by value, which means that the value used by the subroutine is a copy of the original variable. Without this keyword, the parameter is a reference to the calling program's variable. (The topics of call by value with the ByVal keyword and by reference are discussed in detail later in this chapter.) *parameter* represents a programmer-supplied identifier. To specify an array, use (); to specify a list, use the keyword List. The As *type* modifier at the end can be used to specify the data type of the parameter if a data type suffix is not used.

If the subroutine is defined within a class, it is also sometimes called a *class method*. A subroutine in module is private by default, whereas a class subroutine is public by default.

A subroutine exits and returns to the caller if control reaches the End Sub statement. You can also exit a subroutine with the Exit Sub statement before reaching the End Sub statement. Here is an example of the use of the End Sub statement:

```
Sub Caller
   Dim intVar as Integer     intVar = 3              ' Assign a value prior to call
   Call Incr(intVar)         ' Call the subroutine
   Print intVar         ' intVar now has a value of 4
End Sub

Sub Incr(intParam as Integer)
   intParam = intParam + 1     ' Increment the calling program's variable
End Sub
```

In this example, the name of the calling subroutine is Caller, and the called subroutine is Incr, which is short for "increment." intVar is defined in the calling program, and intParam is the name of the Integer parameter. The subroutine uses call by reference (the default), so the calling routine's variable is updated when this subroutine is called. See the section "Passing Arguments by Value or Reference," later in this chapter, for more details.

Function STATEMENT

A *function* is a special kind of subroutine. The purpose of a function is to compute and return a value. The type of the answer value is commonly a numeric value, but it can be any scalar data type, a variant, or a class. To return a value to the calling program, use a function. A subroutine does not return a value.

Several built-in mathematical functions exist, such as Sin (sine), Tan (tangent), and Sqr (square root). Several string functions also return string values, such as Mid$ (extracts substring), Left$ (extracts leftmost substring), and Right$ (extracts rightmost substring). Some built-in functions return Boolean or true/false values. Examples of these functions are IsDate (tests whether an expression is a date), IsEmpty (tests whether an expression is EMPTY), and IsNull (tests whether an expression is NULL).

Some LotusScript classes for Notes return class objects. For example, within the NotesSession class, you can use the GetDatabase function to return a NotesDatabase object. You can use the GetDbDirectory method to return a NotesDbDirectory object.

The syntax of the Function statement is as follows:

```
[Static] [Public | Private] Function Functionname[([ParamList])] [As returnType]
     [... Statements]
End Function
```

You can usually type the word **Function** followed by a name in most contexts in the Design pane, and a new function will be created for you. If you specify Static, all the function's local variables are saved between calls. If you specify Public, the name of the function is known outside the current scope and is available to other modules.

The *returnType* is the data type of the value to be returned by the function. It can be a built-in type, a variant, or a class. In particular, it cannot be a user-defined type that has been declared with the Type statement. If you need this type of functionality, use a class instead.

The *ParamList* is a list of parameter declarations, separated by commas, to be passed to the function. Each parameter within the list can be of this form:

```
[ByVal] parameter [() | List] [As type]
```

If the ByVal keyword is used, the parameter is passed by value, which means that the value used by the function is a copy of the original variable. Without this keyword, the parameter is a reference to the calling program's variable. *parameter* represents a programmer-supplied identifier. To specify an array, use (); to specify a list, use the keyword List. The As *type* modifier at the end can be used to specify the data type of the parameter if a data type suffix is not used.

If the function is defined within a class, it is also sometimes called a *class method*. A function in a module is private by default, whereas a class function is public by default.

To assign the return value, just assign it to a variable that has the same name as the function name. The value that this variable contains when the function returns will be the value returned by the function to the calling program.

A function exits and returns to the caller if control reaches the End Function statement. You can also exit a function with the Exit Function statement before reaching the End Function statement.

In this example, the name of the calling subroutine is Caller and the called function is Incr, which is short for "increment." Contrast this function with the one shown in the previous section. intVar is defined in the calling program, and intParam is the name of the Integer parameter. The function uses call by value, so the calling routine's variable is not changed when this subroutine is called. See the section "Passing Arguments by Value or Reference," later in this chapter, for more details.

Property Get/Set STATEMENTS

With the Property Get and Property Set statements, you can create the illusion of a variable. The user of a property refers to the name of the property and can get or set the value of the property as if it were a variable. At the point of reference, however, either the Property Get or the Property Set subroutines are invoked to access the value.

A property can be defined at either the module level or the class level. Although we would expect a property to be used mostly within class definitions, it is possible that there could be uses for a property at the module level as well. A property within a module has private scope by default.

This is the syntax of the Property Get/Set statements:

```
[Static] [Public | Private] Property {Get | Set} Propertyname [As Type]
    [... Statements]
End Property
```

22

You can usually type the words **Property Get** or **Property Set** followed by a name in most contexts in the Design pane, and a new function will be created for you. If you specify `Static`, all the function's local variables are saved between calls. If you specify `Public`, the name of the function is known outside the current scope and is available to other modules.

The *Type* is the data type of the property. It can be a built-in type, a variant, or a class.

A property in a module is private by default, whereas a class property is public by default.

`Property Get` refers to the caller's perspective. That is, the caller is trying to get the value of the property from the routine. Thus, writing a `Property Get` routine is like writing a function. To assign the property value to be returned to the caller, assign it to a variable that has the same name as the property. The value that this variable contains when the routine returns is the value used by the calling program.

The `Property Set` routine is invoked when the caller wants to set the value. To set and save the value, you must first access the value that the caller wants to save in the property. To obtain the property value in a `Property Set` routine, refer to a variable that has the same name as the property. The value that this variable contains when the routine starts is the value that the calling program wants to assign to the property. This convention is slightly different from the convention when using a named parameter.

A property routine exits and returns to the caller if control reaches the `End Property` statement before reaching the `End Property` statement.

EVENT HANDLERS

Event handlers are declared with the same syntax as subroutines. They have a keyword `Sub`, followed by a name and optional parameters. The major difference between event handlers and a user-defined subroutine is that the names and parameters are specified by the class. You are not free to create and use your own name for the subroutine.

Furthermore, although you can explicitly call event subroutines, they are typically called by the system in response to events that occur in the user interface.

You should be aware that there is a distinction between features of the LotusScript language and the classes defined by the Domino Object Model. The language does not specify any events. Events are characteristics of classes. The LotusScript DOM classes have been implemented separately from the language itself. You will see in a later chapter how this separation enables you to access the same DOM classes from Java as well as LotusScript.

Here is an example of an event handler. It handles the `Click` event from the `Button` class. To handle the event, you create a button on a page or form and then fill in the code for the event handler in the IDE:

```
Sub Click(Source As Button)
    MsgBox "Hello, You pushed me."
End Sub
```

In this example, Notes calls the Click event handler automatically when the user clicks the button. The Button class itself defines the Click event; you cannot change its parameter definition. Other classes, such as NotesUIDatabase and NotesUIView, have other, different events that can be handled based upon the user's actions.

Remember, the LotusScript language is a scripting language that can be used to write scripts for Microsoft Excel as well as Notes or Domino. Thus, events such as Click cannot be defined in the LotusScript language. Conversely, Microsoft Visual Basic can be used to automate or script Notes using the LotusScript DOM classes. Try to keep in mind the separation of the LotusScript language and its features, such as the flow of control statements and the LotusScript DOM classes, which implement access to Notes databases.

CALLING SUBROUTINES AND FUNCTIONS

To call or invoke a subroutine, several methods are available. Each method has a slightly different syntax. The variety is allowed because various dialects of BASIC have used various forms over time. In each of the following descriptions, *subfunName* represents the name of a LotusScript subroutine or function. If *functionName* is used, the name can refer only to a function, not to a subroutine.

Syntax version 1:

```
Call subfunName [(argumentList)]
```

Syntax version 2:

```
subfunName [argumentList]
```

Syntax version 3:

```
subfunName (SingleByValArg)
```

Syntax version 4:

```
variable = functionName [(argumentList)]
```

In the preceding descriptions, *argumentList* represents a list of values separated by commas. The values can be constants, variables, or expressions. The first three versions of the syntax can be used for either subroutines or functions. The fourth version can be used only for functions. In addition, although it is not explicitly shown in the fourth syntax, you can use the function reference within an expression.

When you use the Call keyword in version 1, you must use parentheses if there are any arguments. If there are no arguments, you can omit the parentheses.

In version 2, you can invoke the subroutine or function without using the keyword Call. In this case, you cannot use parentheses.

Version 3 is actually a variation of version 2. The supplied parentheses turn the variable name into an expression, which causes the argument to be passed by value rather than by reference. See the next section for a detailed explanation of the difference.

Version 4 is used only for calling functions. Functions are a special kind of subroutine that returns a value. Subroutines in LotusScript do not return a value. If there are any arguments to be passed to the function, you must supply parentheses. If there are none, you can omit the parentheses when invoking the function. As mentioned previously, you can use version 4 of the syntax within an expression, not just a simple assignment statement. For example:

```
strName = Trim$(strFirstName) & " " & Trim$(strLastName)

dblValue = Sqr(Sin(dblAngle)) + Sqr(Cos(dblAngle))
```

In the preceding examples, more than one function is called per line. In the second case, function calls are even nested.

PASSING ARGUMENTS BY VALUE OR REFERENCE

When passing arguments to a subroutine (or function) in LotusScript, values from the calling program are passed to the subroutine. This passing of values is a little like throwing them over an imaginary fence. Each side views the values a little differently. The values on the calling side of things are called *arguments*, whereas the names in the receiving subroutine are called *parameters*. Each argument on the calling side is matched with a parameter on the subroutine side.

Each parameter can be a call by value parameter or a call by reference parameter, the default. Call by value parameters are a little easier to understand. *Call by value* just means that on the calling side, before invoking the subroutine, the calling routine evaluates the argument expression, comes up with a final value, and then copies just the value into a temporary location for the subroutine to use. Thus, it is a call by value because only the value is passed to the subroutine.

Call by value is fine if you want to throw the values over the fence in only one direction. Suppose, however, that you want to send the subroutine a variable containing a value, have the subroutine modify the variable, and then send back the variable to the calling program. With a call by value mechanism, this is not possible because the subroutine would be modifying a temporary copy and the calling program wouldn't look at the value after the subroutine returned.

No, we need another mechanism. Fortunately, we have one, called passing a variable by reference. *Call by reference* works by passing a reference, or address of a variable, instead of the value of the variable.

As an analogy, suppose that you have a box of goodies that you want delivered to a friend across town. You could package the goodies, give them to the postman, and have them delivered across town for you. You're not really sure what happens to the goodies when they get there, but that's okay because you've been assured by the post office that the delivery will reach the destination. This is call by value.

Now suppose that you really want an exchange of goodies because you want to eat some of your friend's goodies as well as give her some of yours. In this case, you give the postman your address on a slip of paper and you tell your friend, "I have some goodies here for you. Here is my address; please come and get them. Don't forget to bring some goodies also."

The postman delivers your message—not the real goodies, but your address and message. Your friend comes to your house, and the two of you exchange goodies. This is call by reference. The goodies don't travel; just your address travels. There is a difference between passing the address of a variable (a reference to it) and passing the value of the variable.

Notice in the analogy that your friend comes to your house. This is similar to the way reference parameters work. The called subroutine is actually reading and writing directly to the caller's variable locations. This direct access to the variable locations might be exactly what you want, or it might not be. Whether you use this feature depends on your application and purpose. You could consider subroutines that you have not written as if they were strangers. Whether you want to open your house to strangers depends on how much you know and trust them, and how much you want to get their goodies.

Now on to syntax version 3, shown previously. Suppose that when you have declared your subroutine, a particular variable is a called by reference variable. Normally, this would allow the called subroutine to access your variable and modify it. Suppose, however, that in this particular call you don't want to open your doors to a stranger. You don't want the called subroutine to modify your variable.

You can force LotusScript to create a temporary copy and pass a reference to the temporary copy variable (rather than your real variable) by enclosing a variable name in parentheses. These parentheses convert the variable into an expression. Any expression that is passed as an argument to a call by reference parameter is computed, and a reference to a temporary variable is passed instead. This is what happens with syntax version 3. It is actually a special case of version 2, with one argument variable that has been enclosed in parentheses. With this technique, an expression—and, thus, a temporary variable—is passed to the called subroutine.

Here are two small subroutines to show you the importance of how parameters are defined:

```
Sub Incr1(intCount As Integer)
   intCount = intCount + 1
End Sub

Sub Incr2(ByVal intCount As Integer)
   intCount = intCount + 1
End Sub

Sub Main
   Dim intTest As Integer
   intTest = 0
   Call Incr1(intTest)
   ' intTest now has 1
   Call Incr2(intTest)
   ' intTest still has 1, not 2
End Sub
```

In the example, the subroutines Incr1 and Incr2 are defined the same, except that the parameter for Incr2 uses call by value. When the two subroutines are called by the main program, `Incr1` can and will update the variable; `Incr2` cannot because only the value is passed to the subroutine, not a reference to a variable that can be modified.

In LotusScript, there are rules for passing certain kinds of variables. Arrays, lists, user-defined `Type` variables, and objects must be passed by reference. Expressions and constants are passed by value so that the called program cannot mistakenly modify the value of a constant. A pair of parentheses converts a variable name into an expression, so it is passed by value, unless the variable is an array, a list, a user-defined `Type`, or an object. Because these types must be passed by reference, attempting to pass them by value causes an error.

ERROR HANDLING

Wouldn't it be nice if there were just no errors to handle? It would be great if we didn't have to think about all the possible things that might go wrong. Fortunately, LotusScript gives us a way, built into the language, to handle errors. This statement is called the `On Error` statement. The syntax is as follows:

```
On Error [errorNumber] {GoTo label | Resume Next | GoTo 0}
```

The scope of the `On Error` statement is the current procedure. The `On Error` statement is an executable statement, not a declaration, so control must flow through it for it to become effective. Also, you can change the `On Error` processing by executing a second `On Error` statement that overrides a previous statement.

The `On Error` statement tells LotusScript what to do if an error occurs. You can indicate a specific error number, or you can leave the number off, in which case the `On Error` applies to all errors. Three actions are associated with `On Error`:

- **GoTo *label*—**Transfer control to the given label if the error occurs.
- **Resume Next—**Just continue with the next statement after the error, if an error occurs.
- **GoTo 0—**Do not handle the error in the current subroutine. If no *errorNumber* is specified, no error handling takes place in the current subroutine.

If no `On Error` is active in the current procedure, calling procedures are examined, in order from the innermost calling procedure, until an `On Error` statement that applies is found. If no `On Error` statement is active in any of the calling procedures, the default action is to display an error message box and stop execution.

In the actual error-handling routine, you can issue the `Resume` statement or use one of the `Exit` statements to leave the subroutine. The `Resume` statement syntax is as shown here:

```
Resume [0 | Next | label]
```

`Resume 0` means to resume execution on the statement that caused the error. `Resume Next` means to resume on the statement following the one that caused the error. `Resume *label*` means to go to the specified label and continue from there.

GoSub AND Return

The GoSub and Return statements are actually artifacts of the long history of BASIC. They represent one of the original methods of writing subroutines in BASIC. Originally, a BASIC program was typically written as one large (usually very large) file. Each line of the program had a line number. The GoSub statement enabled the programmer to segment the program by allowing the programmer to transfer control to another area and then later return with the Return statement.

The syntax is as follows:

```
GoSub label
Return
```

In LotusScript, the GoSub and the Return statements must be contained within the same procedure and cannot be at the module level.

TIP

> If you are familiar with another programming language (such as C or C++), you might be familiar with the return statement of that language. In LotusScript, the Return statement is not used exactly for the same purpose. It is similar but different. Most likely in LotusScript, you really want to use the Exit Sub statement, which causes control to exit and return from a subroutine. Because you are most likely not using GoSub, you probably will not need to use the LotusScript Return statement, either.

STRING HANDLING

Strings are one of the most important data types in LotusScript. They are used extensively in the LotusScript DOM classes, and you will need to use them in your own programs as well. Before we cover the details of strings in LotusScript, however, let me digress into string handling in general.

CHARACTERS AND CODES

Computers really can store only numbers. Every memory location in a computer is storing a binary value. Most computers can address every byte within their memory, and for most computers, a byte is typically 8 bits. This means that each memory byte can contain a value from 0 to 255.

If memory bytes can store values from 0 to 255, how can they store characters, words, phrases, and even books? In Japan, computers can store Kanji; in Korea, they can store Hangeul. Actually, computers can store Arabic, Hebrew, Chinese, and Russian symbols as well. If you're a native English speaker, you probably don't even think about characters in many of these other languages, and you might not even think about how those numbers really store characters.

The basis for storing all these types of symbols in the computer is the concept of a code. A *code* is really just a standardized convention. There are several important codes, such as the

ASCII code, the EBCDIC code (used on IBM mainframes), and the Unicode. What these codes have in common is that they are a convention. Within each convention, a particular symbol is assigned a *code point*. Other codes exist as well, but these three will do for our explanation.

The numeric values of these code points are not as important as the fact that they are standardized and recognized. When they are standardized, you can use them or convert values to or from them.

The ASCII code was originally 7 bits but has now been extended to 8 bits. EBCDIC is an 8-bit code, and Unicode is a 16-bit code. Each of these codes is a convention for assigning code points to various symbols.

Take, for example, the letter *a*. ASCII, EBCDIC, and Unicode all have numbers associated with this symbol. In ASCII and Unicode, the numeric value associated with the symbol is 97. In EBCDIC, the value is 129. You should be aware that the symbol *A* is different from the symbol *a*. That's because we typically want to differentiate a lowercase symbol from its uppercase equivalent. Uppercase *A* has value 65 in ASCII and Unicode but has value 193 in EBCDIC.

Well, why do you even care about all this information? Normally, you won't care too much about it. However, sometimes understanding the coding of the character set is important. For example, looking back at the code points, you'll notice that in ASCII, uppercase *A* is 65 and lowercase *a* is 97. This means that when you perform an ascending sort using the ASCII code, *A* sorts before *a*. In EBCDIC, lowercase and uppercase sorting result in the opposite sort order. Neither method is necessarily right or wrong; they are just different.

It is also important to understand coding because, in the Unicode code, characters are actually represented by 2 bytes. These are sometimes called double-byte characters.

CODES AND FONTS

Notice in the coding discussion that a differentiation was made between lowercase *a* and uppercase *A*. In most word processing, desktop publishing, or even Notes Rich Text fields, hundreds of fonts are available. Each font might have a different appearance for the lowercase *a*.

Does this mean that there's a different code point for each one? Does Times Roman need a code point for *a* that is different from a Courier *a*, which is different from the Helvetica *a*?

No. The fonts can all use the same code. A font is really a correspondence from a code, such as ASCII (or EBCDIC or Unicode), to a visual representation of the character. So, with one set of code points, you can have hundreds of different and beautiful visual representations. This is a bit of a simplification because a discussion on fonts could be a complete volume by itself.

Within Rich Text fields and similar types of data in other programs, you must specify both a font and a code point for each character. Typically, consecutive characters that are all in the same font typeface and size are grouped so that redundant data does not need to be specified.

Strings in LotusScript do not contain font information; they contain only code points. So, you can manipulate strings and, after you have finished, display the resulting string in any font by associating the font with the string when you display or print the string.

DECLARING STRINGS

Now that you understand the kind of data that is stored in a string, let's go back and discuss what you can do with strings. The syntax for declaring a string variable is this:

```
Dim stringvar as String [* length]
```

If the `length` parameter is specified, the string is a fixed-length string. It contains the number of characters specified in `length`. Fixed-length strings are a little more efficient than variable-length strings. They are most practical when used in a user-defined `Type` structure or when they are to be passed to an external subroutine or function.

If the length is not specified, the string is considered a variable-length string.

CAUTION

Using strings when calling external subroutines or functions is a frequent source of errors in programming. Many times, these external routines require you to pass a buffer and a length. Be careful when you pass strings to these external routines. Make sure that you have allocated a string with enough space to store your results. If you pass a string that is too small, the called routine may write data beyond the end of your string, and your program may get a General Protection Fault (GPF) someplace well beyond where the problem occurs. These types of errors can be very difficult to debug.

When passing the length of your buffer, use the Len built-in function to pass the length of your variable rather than hard-coding a length. This ensures that the length you pass to the subroutine always matches the current length of your string buffer.

STRING FUNCTIONS

After you have declared your string, you can turn your attention to the many functions you can use to manipulate it. Most of the time, you will be using variable-length strings. These are the most convenient to use because their length automatically varies, and the strings grow or shrink to your needs.

The basic operations on strings involve putting them together, extracting substrings, and comparing strings. Concatenation, or attaching one string to the end of another string, is one of the most basic operations. You can concatenate strings using either the & or + operators.

Here are some examples:

```
strName = strFirstName & " " & strLastName
strName = strLastName + ", " + strFirstName
```

You can use the Len function to determine the length of a string. The syntax is as follows:

```
IntegerVar = Len(stringExpr)
```

LotusScript has several built-in functions for extracting substrings from a string:

- **Left$(*stringExpr*, *length*)**—Extracts leftmost *length* characters.

- **Mid$(*stringExpr*, *start* [, *length*])**—Extracts *length* characters from within the string, starting at character position *start*. The first character is position 1. If *length* is not specified, the substring continues to the end of the string.

- **Right$(*stringExpr*, *length*)**—Extracts the rightmost *length* characters.

- **StrLeft(*string1*, *string2* [, *flags* [, *occurrences*]])**—Searches *string1* from left to right and extracts the characters in *string1* that appear to the left of *string2*. *flags* enables you to control case-sensitive and pitch-sensitive searching. *occurrences* is the number of occurrences of *string2* to find.

- **StrLeftBack (*string1*, *string2* [, *flags* [, *occurrences*]])**—Searches *string1* from right to left and extracts the characters in *string1* that appear to the left of *string2*. *flags* enables you to control case-sensitive and pitch-sensitive searching. *occurrences* is the number of occurrences of *string2* to find.

- **StrRight(*string1*, *string2* [, *flags* [, *occurrences*]])**—Searches *string1* from left to right and extracts the characters in *string1* that appear to the right of *string2*. *Flags* enables you to control case-sensitive and pitch-sensitive searching. *Occurrences* is the number of occurrences of *string2* to find.

- **StrRightBack(*string1*, *string2* [, *flags* [, *occurrences*]])**—Searches *string1* from right to left and extracts the characters in *string1* that appear to the right of *string2*. *flags* enables you to control case-sensitive and pitch-sensitive searching. *occurrences* is the number of occurrences of *string2* to find.

LotusScript has several built-in functions for trimming leading or trailing blanks from strings:

- **LTrim$(*stringExpr*)**—Trims leading blanks from the expression

- **Trim$(*stringExpr*)**—Trims both leading and trailing blanks from the expression

- **RTrim$(*stringExpr*)**—Trims trailing blanks from the expression

LotusScript has conversion routines that convert data to strings:

- **CStr(*Expression*)**—Converts any expression to a string.

- **Str$(*numExpr*)**—Converts a numeric expression to a string.

- **StrConv(*Expression*, *ConvType*)**—Converts an expression to a string with various options. You can convert to uppercase, lowercase, proper case, wide (double-byte), narrow, katakana (Japanese), and hiragana (Japanese).

String variables can use the standard comparison operators: <, <=, =<, =, >=, =>, <>, and ><. String comparisons are affected by the Option Compare Case and Option Compare Binary statements. LotusScript has several built-in functions for string comparison:

- **StrCompare(*string1*, *string2* [, *method*])**—Returns -1 if *string1* < *string2*, 0 if they are equal, and 1 if *string1* > *string2*. You can use this function if you want to override the comparison method specified in the Option Compare statement. *method* is 0 for case-sensitive comparison, 1 for non–case-sensitive comparison, and 2 for platform collation sequence (binary).

- **InStr([*beginpos*,] *strHaystack*, *strNeedle* [, *method*])**—Tests to see whether *strNeedle* is found in *strHaystack*. You can specify a beginning position with *beginpos*, which must be a positive integer. If it is omitted, 1 is assumed. The method is specified as in StrCompare.

- *Expression* **Like** *Pattern*—Like is actually an operator. It is typically used in an If statement. *Expression* is a string expression. *Pattern* is a string that contains a pattern to be found. If the pattern is found within the string, the Like operator returns True; otherwise, it returns False. The rules for this operator are too complex to describe here, but following are some of the rules: ? matches any single character, * matches zero or more characters, and # matches a digit. For example, *Lotus* matches any string that contains Lotus anywhere within the string.

FILE INPUT/OUTPUT

You will almost assuredly need to access external files from LotusScript at some point. There are so many types of files and applications that it is impossible to cover all the aspects you might need. However, we'll try to cover the basics; from there, the best way to learn is to try it yourself.

File input/output (I/O) follows this simple model:

1. Open the file.
2. Perform file operations.
3. Close the file.

This model works for both reading and writing the file, as well as for random-access or sequential-access files. When you open the file, you must specify a file number. This file number is used on all subsequent file operations and when you close the file. This method enables you to have several files open at once.

OPENING A FILE

Here is the syntax of the Open statement:

```
Open filename [For mode] [Access operations] [Lockmode]
```

mode can be one of the following: Random, Input, Output, Append, or Binary.

operations can be one of the following: Read, Read Write, or Write.

Lockmode can be one of the following: Shared, Lock Read, Lock Read Write, or Lock Write.

For Random and Binary files, you use the Get and Put statements to read and write the file. In a Random file, all records have the same length, specified by *reclen*. If omitted, the value assumed is 128. If specified, the *reclen* must be between 1 and 32767, inclusive. *reclen* is ignored for Binary files.

For Input files, you use the Input and Input # statements to read the file. If *reclen* is specified, the number indicates a buffer size, not the record length. The default buffer size is 512 bytes.

For Output and Append files, you use the Print # and Write # statements to output data to the file. The difference between Output and Append is that for Output mode, if the file exists, it is replaced by the new data; for Append, the new data is appended to the old data.

The Access clause, if specified, must be consistent with the For clause that you specify in the Open statement. For example, if the file is opened *For Output* mode, the *Access* clause must be *Access Write*.

Lockmode is used to lock the file from usage by other users on a network. Shared indicates no locking. Lock Read prevents other users from reading the file, although they can write to the file. Lock Read Write locks all other network users from reading and writing to the file. Lock Write prevents other users from writing to the file.

Charset is used to specify the language to use for file I/O. A list of valid MIME charset values can be found in MIME Charset Names.

GENERAL FILE OPERATIONS

Several statements and functions are useful for reading or writing a file. The first function has the following syntax:

```
IntegerVar = FreeFile()
```

The FreeFile function returns a number that can be used as a file number on an Open statement. Generally, you will use the FreeFile statement just before executing an Open statement. It is considered a good programming practice to use FreeFile to obtain a file number instead of hard-coding a specific number into your program. When you use a specific number, it becomes harder to reuse your program because the number you select might conflict with a routine written by someone else.

The Seek statement is used with Random and Binary files. It is used to set the current position within the file. In a Binary file, the position specified is the byte offset within the file. The first byte is 1. In a Random file, the record number is specified. The first record number is 1. Here is the syntax for the Seek statement:

```
Seek #fileNumber, position
```

You will typically use the Seek statement just before using a Get or Put statement with the file. The Seek statement sets the current position that is used by Get or Put.

FILE INPUT OPERATIONS

The Read operations are the Get and Input statements. Get is used for Random and Binary file modes. In either mode, you will probably also use the EOF function. The EOF function returns True if the specified file has reached the end of file.

Here is an example:

```
Dim intFile As Integer
intFile = FreeFile()

Open "Testfile.txt" For Input As intFile
Do Until EOF(intFile)
  ... File input and other processing statements
Loop
Close intFile
```

The Get statement is used for Random or Binary files. The syntax is as follows:

```
Get #fileNumber, [recordPosition], variableName
```

fileNumber is the number specified in the Open statement. *recordPosition* is optional; if it's left off, reading starts from the current position in the file. If specified for a Binary file, *recordPosition* represents the byte offset within the file. For a Random file, it represents the record number. *variableName* must be a scalar variable or a user-defined Type variable.

The Input statement is used for sequential Input files. The syntax is shown here:

```
Input #fileNumber, variableNameList
```

fileNumber is the number specified in the Open statement. *variableNameList* is a list of variable names separated by commas. Each variable must be a scalar variable. You cannot use arrays or user-defined Type variables; however, you can use individual array elements or scalar items within a user-defined Type.

You can also use the Line Input statement to read an entire line from a text file into a string variable. The syntax is as follows:

```
Line Input #fileNumber, variableName
```

fileNumber is the number specified in the Open statement. *variableName* is the name of a string or variant variable. An entire line is read into this variable.

FILE OUTPUT OPERATIONS

You can output to files using the Put, Print#, and Write# statements. The Put statement is used for Random and Binary files, whereas the Print# and Write# statements are used for sequential Output files.

This is the Put statement syntax:

```
Put #fileNumber, [recordPosition], variableName
```

fileNumber is the number specified in the Open statement. *recordPosition* is optional; if it's left off, reading starts from the current position in the file. If specified for a Binary file, *recordPosition* represents the byte offset within the file. For a Random file, it represents the record number. *variableName* must be a scalar variable or a user-defined Type variable.

The Print statement is used for sequential Output files. You can use this statement only if you have opened the file for Output or Append use. This statement is used for file output even though it is not sent to a printer. If you use the Print statement without a file number, the output is sent to the screen; if you use it with a file number, the output is sent to a file.

The syntax for screen output is as follows:

```
Print [expressionList][, | ;]
```

expressionList is a list of expressions to be printed. The output is sent to the display. If you leave off the *expressionList*, LotusScript prints a blank line. A newline character is printed at the end of the *expressionList* unless the list ends with a semicolon or comma. If the list ends with a semicolon or comma, no newline character is appended.

If you use a comma to separate items in the list, each item is printed at the next tab stop. If you use a semicolon or space to separate the items, no space is printed between the two items.

The syntax for using the Print statement for file output is this:

```
Print #fileNumber [, expressionList]
```

fileNumber is the number specified in the Open statement. *expressionList* is a list of expressions to be written to the file. If you leave off the *expressionList*, LotusScript outputs a blank line.

If you use a comma to separate items in the list, each item is printed at the next tab stop. If you use a semicolon or space to separate the items, no space is printed between the two items.

The Print statement honors the width specified in the Width statement. If outputting a variable would cause the line to be longer than the specified width, a new line automatically is generated and the variable is output on the next line.

The format of the Width statement is as follows:

```
Width #fileNumber, width
```

fileNumber is the number specified in the Open statement. The width parameter can be from 0 to 255. 0 is the default and means an unlimited line length.

The Write statement is useful for creating files that will be used by other programs. It enables you to write a list of expressions to a file and have the delimiters between items. The most common version of this format is called a comma-delimited file. You can use this statement only if you have opened the file for Output or Append use. Following is the syntax for the Write statement:

```
Write #fileNumber [, expressionList]
```

fileNumber is the number specified in the Open statement. *expressionList* is a list of expressions to be written to the file. If you leave off the *expressionList*, LotusScript outputs a blank line. If you specify a list of expressions, each expression is evaluated and output to the file, separated by commas.

The Write statement ignores the current Width setting.

REUSING LOTUSSCRIPT PROGRAMS AND CALLING DLLs

One important aspect of programming is reusability. It is very valuable to be able to reuse code that either you or someone else has already written. Script libraries enable you to define declarations that can be used in several forms, views, or agents within a database. They enable you to share source code. Being able to call Dynamic Link Libraries (DLLs) from LotusScript enables you to reuse object code programs that you can buy commercially or that are written for a specific purpose.

REUSING SOURCE CODE

One of the most basic ways to reuse source code is to use the compile-time directive %include. This directive enables you to create LotusScript source code outside Notes. This can be valuable if you want to perform source-code library maintenance on the code or if you want to share the same source code across several databases. The syntax of the %include statement is as follows:

```
%include filename
```

filename must be a string constant. It can be explicitly given within the %include statement, or it can be defined in a Const statement.

Following are some examples:

```
%include "c:\notes\source\appsubs.txt"

Const strSubs = "c:\source\Subs.lss"

%include strSubs
```

If you omit the suffix, LotusScript assumes the suffix .lss.

NOTE

> When you use include files, you should remember that the source code will not be inside the database. This means that if you replicate the database, the source code will not be replicated with the database. This can be good or bad, depending upon your application. If you want security, this is good because the replicating site will not have the source code. It is not good if someone at the replicating site needs to view the source code for debugging or some other purpose.

A second method for sharing code is to use the Use statement and script libraries. Script libraries enable you to define declarations that can be shared among different LotusScript programs within a single database. Script libraries always contain at least (Options), (Declarations), Initialize, and Terminate procedures. A common use for script libraries is to use them for your Class and Type declarations and common subroutines. When you define declarations and routines in a script library, they can be used throughout your database.

You can have several script libraries within a single database. Each script library has its own name—the four sections described previously and any subroutines or functions that you add. You can define each separately and use each separately.

To access a script library, you use the Use statement. The syntax is as given here:

```
Use scrlibName
```

scrlibName can be either a string literal constant or a string constant that has been defined with a Const statement. You must create the script library in the database before you can use it.

REUSING OBJECT CODE

You can also reuse object code from LotusScript. Object code is code that has already been compiled by a compiler and link-edited together to form a module that can be loaded at runtime by LotusScript. The generic name for this kind of module is a *Dynamic Link Library* (DLL). A special form of DLL for use with LotusScript is called a LotusScript Extension, or LSX, module.

You can use an LSX module by issuing the UseLSX statement. Here is the format for the UseLSX statement:

```
UseLSX lsxDLLName
```

lsxDLLName must be a character string literal constant or a string constant that has been defined with a Const statement. One important LSX is the LotusScript:Data Object, or LS:DO. This LSX module is implemented in a DLL and implements the LotusScript classes for ODBC access from within LotusScript.

The final method for using DLLs is to declare and invoke them at a low level. This method is recommended only for technical users who understand the operating system and understand how modules are loaded and invoked. To invoke an external subroutine from LotusScript, you must use the Declare statement so that LotusScript knows how to prepare the parameters; then you can invoke it with a syntax that is the same as a regular LotusScript subroutine call. The syntax for the Declare statement is as follows:

```
Declare [Public | Private] {Function | Sub} LSName Lib libName [Alias aliasName]
➡([parameterList]) [As returnType]
```

You must declare whether the routine is a function or a subroutine. This determines whether the routine will return a value. The LSName is the name you will use when invoking the routine from LotusScript. *libName* is specified as a string constant and represents the name of the DLL. *aliasName* is specified as a string constant, is optional, and is typically used when the name within the library is different from the name to be used from LotusScript. In Windows, the *aliasName* can be a pound sign (#) followed by a number to signify the ordinal number within the DLL. *parameterList* is the list of parameters to the routine (as described in the following paragraph). The *returnType* is the data type of the return value. It must be a scalar value and cannot be a variant, currency, or fixed-length string.

Each parameter declaration must be of the following form:

```
[ByVal] parmName As [LMBCS | Unicode] [dataType | Any]
```

parmName is the name of the parameter. You specify ByVal if you want LotusScript to pass the parameter by value. LMBCS stands for Lotus Multi-Byte Character Set. If either LMBCS or Unicode is specified, you must specify ByVal and String as the data type. The keyword Any is used if you want to disable type checking and pass any argument to the external routine.

CHAPTER 23

CREATING AND USING JAVA APPLETS AND AGENTS

In this chapter

SETTING UP THE JAVA ENVIRONMENT

You might want to use Java applets, agents, or servlets within your Domino application for many reasons. First, maybe you'd like to design a highly interactive applet for an application's user interface. Second, perhaps you want to connect to a relational database or TCP/IP sockets within a Domino application. Finally, you might be interested in distributing some Domino data to make your application more responsive to the Web end user. This chapter is not designed to provide all the necessary information to learn Java; rather, it is focused on providing a high-level overview of the language and its integration with Lotus Notes and Domino.

Unless you're developing a basic Java Domino agent, it's highly recommended that you look at obtaining a third-party integrated development environment for Java. Although Lotus has made great strides with Release 6, it still does not have the features that most Java developers demand. Some of the limitations include the lack of a debugging environment, no support for type-ahead code assistance for classes or methods, no support for automatic management of class imports, and the lack of refactoring features.

You can choose from many Java development environments. Here are a few: Eclipse, NetBeans, IBM WebSphere Studio, Borland JBuilder, and Oracle JDeveloper. Hundreds of other options exist. You can even download Sun's Java 2 SDK, Standard Edition (J2SDK), free from the Web. Sun's J2SDK package is extremely minimal, however—you'll probably want a more robust development environment. While each of these development environments has features that makes it unique and attractive, it's highly recommended that you review Eclipse. Eclipse is an impressive and full-featured IDE based on IBM's development of IBM WebSphere Studio. You can read more about Eclipse and download the free tool at www.eclipse.org.

A JAVA OVERVIEW

Although most developers have heard something about Java, some of you might not know the language's background. Let's do a quick overview. Java was originally conceived by Sun Microsystems as a language for embedded systems (for example, for your television set). With the advent of the Web, it became extremely popular because Netscape bundled it within its own browser. It has quickly evolved from its commercial release in 1995, and now Java is used on everything from mobile telephones to enterprise-class applications managing millions of transactions.

One of the main advantages of Java is that the language is operating system– and hardware-independent. Sun's core mantra for Java is its ability to "write once, run anywhere." For example, the same code that is compiled and developed on a Microsoft Windows environment can be deployed to Linux without any recompiling. But how, exactly, does Java achieve this feat technically? The answer lies in the *Java Virtual Machine*, or JVM.

The JVM is the cornerstone of the Java environment. It is a software program that simulates a real machine. The JVM accepts as input binary data that has been prepared by a Java compiler. This set of binary data corresponds to the machine-language codes that are used by traditional hardware, such as the Intel Pentium. The binary codes are stored in files on the host operating system in class files. Groups of class files can be stored in a directory in the operating system, or they can be collected in a single file called an archive. Several kinds of archive files are available: JAR files, CAB files, and ZIP files. ZIP is a standard format for compressing a group of files and saving them as a single file. This extension is not normally used anymore, however, because it was confusing for some users who thought the ZIP files needed to be uncompressed. JAR files are the standard format for Java archives and are stored internally with the same format as ZIP files. CAB files were created by Microsoft and are used by its Internet Explorer.

THE CLASSPATH

Now that we have JVM, do we need any other components? Well, yes, we do. Any application that you develop probably needs to allocate and manage resources, such as memory and data. It might need to interact with a user via a user interface or a TCP/IP socket. You probably don't want to write all this kind of code. Normally, these types of services are provided by an operating system.

Many classes have been written in Java, and they are included in archive files that are distributed with the Java environment. They perform many of the routine tasks that are normally supplied by any operating system environment. There is only one problem—how does the Java Virtual Machine find these files? The answer is through the CLASSPATH environment variable.

The CLASSPATH environment variable is actually very similar in concept to the PATH variable that you might remember from the Microsoft DOS days. The CLASSPATH variable tells the JVM where to find additional classes that are not included in the currently running class. Standard classes for user interface and other functions are included in these libraries. In addition to the standard libraries, you can write your own Java programs, store them in archives, and include them in the CLASSPATH.

> **TIP**
>
> If you're using a third-party development environment to develop Domino agents or applets, you'll need to include the Domino libraries that ship with Release 6 within the tool's CLASSPATH.

When Notes/Domino JVM is running, it actually uses an internal CLASSPATH variable. This variable is specified in the Notes.ini file and has the name JavaUserClasses. For Notes or Domino to be able to find any custom classes you write that are not stored within a database or script library, you must make sure you have modified the JavaUserClasses variable in Notes.ini. Here is an example:

```
JavaUserClasses=c:\Development\MyJavaClasses\;c:\SomeOtherDirectory\
MyJavaClasses2\
```

You can specify more than one directory and separate them with semicolons.

JAVA DEVELOPMENT KIT VERSIONS

If you program a standard Windows application in C++, there are three separate and distinct concepts to work with: the programming language itself (C++), the compiler tool, and the Windows Application Programming Interface (API). These same three concepts apply to Java programming. You need to know the Java programming language, you need a particular Java programming tool, and you need a programming API. The programming API is supplied by Sun Microsystems in the Java 2 SDK, Standard Edition. Some development environments require you to download Sun's J2SDK before installing their development tool.

The Java 2 SDK, Standard Edition provides an API that contains many of the programming features of a windowing operating system such as Microsoft Windows. Although Java is a language, the JDK supplies the capability of creating windows and buttons using networking, accessing databases, and many of the other features. In addition, you can use the J2SDK on top of Windows, Linux, Macintosh, or any other platform that supports the JVM.

The Java platform has undergone many revisions. In previous versions of Notes and Domino, the version of the Java that was included was JDK 1.1.*x*. In fact, all the way up to R5, the 1.1.*x* version is shipped with Notes and Domino because of the cycle of testing and quality assurance that goes into Domino before its release. Late in 1998, Sun announced that Java 1.2 would be rebranded as Java 2. Sun's motivation for the name change was the monumental changes and improvements to the platform. The core of the JDK is now known as the Java 2 Platform, Standard Edition.

Java 2 has many new capabilities, including security enhancements and the Java Foundation Classes (JFC). The JFC includes the Swing components, the Java 2D graphics interfaces, drag-and-drop accessibility, and many other application services. The Swing user interface components are an enhancement to the original Abstract Windowing Toolkit found in Version 1.1 of the JDK. Although the AWT still works for compatibility, the Swing set of components is essentially a replacement.

UNDERSTANDING THE JAVA LANGUAGE

The official Java language specification is more than 700 pages, so it's pretty clear that I'm not going to be able to describe it all to you here. Instead, a high-level description of the language is provided so that you can understand the examples; you can investigate the language in more detail if you want.

Java is an object-oriented language that has a lot of similarities to and a few differences from C++. It uses similar terminology with its classes, objects, and methods. Java lacks some of the more sophisticated but error-prone features of C++, such as pointers, templates, and multiple inheritance. Java adds some features that are not part of C++. For example, Java has automatic garbage collection, built-in multithreading, and the concept of the Java Virtual Machine.

JAVA IDENTIFIERS

Java programs are written using Unicode using 2-byte characters. Although keywords are in English, programs can use identifiers written using the full Unicode character set, including Japanese and Chinese Kanji characters. This is useful for non–English-speaking programmers, but it might make the programs less portable unless you happen to know Kanji.

The Java keywords are listed here:

abstract	double	int	strictfp
boolean	else	interface	super
break	extends	long	switch
byte	final	native	synchronized
case	finally	new	this
catch	float	package	throw
char	for	private	throws
class	goto	protected	transient
const	if	public	try
continue	implements	return	void
default	import	short	volatile
do	instanceof	static	while

Java keywords are reserved and may not be used for identifiers. The words `true`, `false`, and `null` are literal values and, therefore, are also restricted from being used as variable names. The keywords `const` and `goto` are reserved but are not currently used by Java.

There is no limit within the Java language for the length of identifiers, so you have plenty of other choices for identifier names. In Java, identifier names are case sensitive; LotusScript ignores case.

An identifier must begin with a letter but then can be followed by any number of letters, numbers, the underscore (_), and the dollar sign ($). You should not typically use the dollar sign, however, because it is intended to be used only in mechanically generated code.

JAVA COMMENTS

Java comments are similar to those found in C++. You can add a comment to the rightmost end of any line by using two forward slashes (//). You can enclose a block of lines by starting a comment with /* and ending with */. Here are some examples:

```
int iCount;      // Count of widgets
iCount = 1;      // Start with a single widget
/* In the following code, we'll count widgets
   We use a special algorithm that has been passed
   down for generations.
*/
```

In addition to normal comments, Java has a feature that can be used to process specially for-matted comments. If you write comments in your code with these rules, the JavaDoc utility can be used to generate HTML pages documenting your code automatically. The JavaDoc utility is included with the J2SDK and can be downloaded free from the Sun Microsystems Java Web site (www.java.sun.com).

To use this feature, you use the block commenting format; you must begin your comment with /** and end it with */. You can write a comment at the beginning of your class source file and before each of your methods. Listing 23.1 demonstrates an example.

LISTING 23.1   A SAMPLE JAVA PROGRAM CONTAINING TAGGED COMMENTS FOR AUTOMATIC DOCUMENTATION GENERATION

```java
package com.somecompany;

/**
 * @see Class
 * @version 1.0, November 1, 2002
 * @author Jeff Gunther
 *
 * This is a sample class file. I'm using it to illustrate how you can
 * use JavaDoc to process your source file to automatically generate HTML
 * documentation.
 */

public class Sample extends java.lang.Object
{
    /** saves a value */
    private int m_iMyValue;

    /**
     * Constructor for Sample. Creates a new Sample object
     * @see    Object
     */
    public Sample()
    {
        m_iMyValue = 0;
    }
    ;

    /**
     * Return MyValue property. This routine returns the MyValue property.
     * @see    int
     * @return the MyValue property
     */
    public int getMyValue()
    {
        return m_iMyValue;
    }

    /**
     * Set the MyValue property. This routine sets the MyValue property.
```

```
     *      @see     int
     */
    public void setMyValue(int iMyValue)
    {
        m_iMyValue = iMyValue;
    }
}
```

In Figure 23.1, you can see a display of the HTML that was automatically generated.

Figure 23.1
This documentation was automatically generated by the JavaDoc utility.

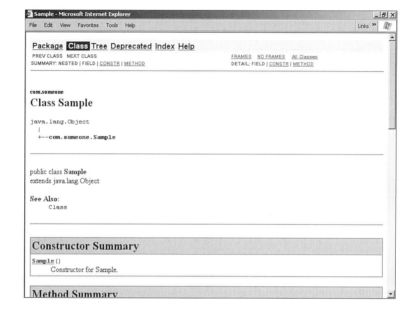

If you consistently comment your code and follow the relatively simple tagging conventions, you can get automatic documentation generation for all your methods and classes, as well as an alphabetical listing and automatic hyperlinks between the various classes. The tags within the comments begin with @ and are followed by a keyword, such as see and version. You can use several tags that, when used properly, work together with JavaDoc to enable you to turn comments within your code into useful documentation.

DATA TYPES

The built-in numeric data types for Java can be seen in Table 23.1.

TABLE 23.1 JAVA BUILT-IN DATA TYPES

Type	Description	Size	Minimum Value	Maximum Value
Byte	Single-byte signed integer	8	-127	128
Char	Two-byte unsigned character	16	0	65535
Short	Short signed integer	16	-32768	32767
Int	Signed integer	32	-2147483648	2147483647
Long	Long signed integer	64	-92233720368 54775808	9223372036 854775807
Float	Single-precision floating point	32	$-3.40282347 \times 10^{38}$	$3.40282347 \times 10^{38}$
Double	Double-precision floating-point	64	$-1.79769313486 \times 10^{308}$	$1.79769313486 \times 10^{308}$

In addition to the numeric types, there is a Boolean type that can be either true or false. A string type is represented as a built-in class. String constants are specified by using characters within double-quotation marks.

In addition to the basic data types, you can create array variables of any of the built-in types.

OPERATORS AND EXPRESSIONS

The operators in Java are similar to those found in C++. The only operator in Java not found in C++ is the zero-extended shift-right operator >>>. You can see the list of Java operators in Table 23.2. The operators are listed in order of precedence; the highest-precedence operators are on the top of the table and are evaluated first.

TABLE 23.2 JAVA OPERATORS AND PRECEDENCE

++ --	Postfix increment, postfix decrement
++ --	Prefix increment, prefix decrement
+ -	Unary plus, unary minus
~ !	Bitwise complement and logical complement
* / %	Multiplication, division, remainder
+ -	Addition, subtraction
<< >> >>>	Shift left, signed shift right, zero extended shift right
< <= >= >	Relational operators
== !=	Equality operators
&	Bitwise And

^	Bitwise Exclusive Or
|	Bitwise Inclusive Or
&&	Logical And
||	Logical Inclusive Or
? :	Conditional expression

Assignment, one of the following:
```
=   +=   -=   *=   /=   %=        &=   |=   <<=   >>=   >>>=
```

Expressions in Java follow the normal rules of precedence. Operands are evaluated from left to right, and parentheses can be used to control the order of evaluation. For example:

```
a + b * c
```

This expression is evaluated by first multiplying (b * c), and then adding the result to a. Innermost parenthetical values are evaluated first. For example:

```
(a + b) * c
```

In this expression, (a + b) is evaluated first because the parentheses override the natural precedence of the operators.

STATEMENTS

Statements in Java are very similar to those found in C++. Although there are a few exceptions, C++ programmers should feel very comfortable reading Java code. The list of statement types is found in Table 23.3.

TABLE 23.3   JAVA STATEMENT TYPES

Block	`{ BlockStatements }`
Local variable declaration	`Type VariableDeclarators;`
Expression statement	`StatementExpression ;`
if statement	`if ( Expression ) Statement`
	`if ( Expression ) Statement else Statement`

switch statement	`switch ( Expression ) { SwitchStatements}`
	`SwitchStatements`
	`case ConstantExpression : Statement ;`
	`default : Statement ;`

while statement	`while ( Expression ) Statement`
do statement	`do Statement while ( Expression ) ;`
for statement	`for ( ForInit ; Expression ; ForUpdate ) Statement`

continues

TABLE 23.3 CONTINUED

Block	{ BlockStatements }
break statement	break [identifier];
continue statement	continue [identifier];
return statement	return Expression ;
throw statement	throw Expression ;
synchronized statement	synchronized (Expression) Block
try statement	try Block catch (parameter) Block [finally Block]

The table of statement types is not meant to be a formal syntax for Java; the actual formal reference in the Java specification takes 22 pages. Instead, you should use this table as a quick reference to the statements available. You need to consult a Java programming language reference (or use the online Web version at http://java.sun.com/docs/books/jls/html/index.html).

The statement here that might not be familiar to C++ programmers is the synchronized statement. This statement is for synchronizing multiple threads in Java. Because Java is natively multithreaded, the language itself has some constructs to aid in handling multiple threads. The synchronized statement behaves similar to a critical section lock, also sometimes called a monitor. When two threads synchronize on the same object, only one is allowed to process. The second thread automatically waits until the first thread is finished with its statement block.

JAVA CLASSES, PACKAGES, AND ARCHIVES

All programs in Java are a part of some class. As you have seen, classes are written in the Java source code language and then are translated to class files. Class files consist of machine-independent byte codes. The class-file byte codes essentially represent machine operations to the Java Virtual Machine and are the instructions that get executed by the JVM.

As you might imagine, when you are doing large-scale development, you will quickly find that you need some methods to organize your class files. You can quickly get hundreds of files to organize and manage.

Packages are hierarchical groupings of class files. They are a logical grouping and can be implemented physically in different ways. One simple and common way to organize the files in a package is with an operating system file directory structure. You simply use the hierarchical nature of file folders (directories) containing other nested folders to implement a hierarchical structure.

In Java, names are specified by a combination of identifiers and periods. The rightmost name represents the class name. All the other qualifiers in the name represent the package.

For example, in java.lang.Object, java.lang represents the package name and the name `Object` represents the class name. In the name javax.swing.event. `ChangeEvent`, the name `ChangeEvent` is the class name and javax.swing.event is the package name.

If you have the packages javax.swing, javax.swing.border, javax.swing.colorchooser, and javax.swing.event, you can imagine a directory folder structure as illustrated in Figure 23.2.

Figure 23.2
Package names mimic the directory folder structure storing the classes and interfaces.

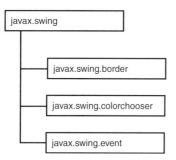

23

In this case, there could also be other packages below the java level, such as java.io, java.lang, and java.net. When you have such a directory structure, all the classes in the javax.swing.event package, for example, are stored in the directory that corresponds to that package.

When you are working by yourself on a small project, this structure is probably fine. You have everything you need, and it is all visible and easily accessible. However, suppose you are developing a large system with hundreds of components. It soon becomes much harder to manage multiple user access to hundreds of different files. Because of this, archive files were developed.

The original archive file format for Java was a ZIP file. This type of file was a de facto standard around the Internet, and many or most PC users have some sort of program, such as pkzip, pkunzip, or winzip, to create and extract files from ZIP files. By using a ZIP format, all the class files can be incorporated in a single file in the operating system. Also, the directory structure within the file can be preserved so that you can still have the hierarchical nature of the packages.

It was soon discovered, however, that users of these ZIP files did not realize that you could use the files within the ZIP archive and that you did not need to unzip the files before Java could use them. So, a new format was created called the Java Archive (JAR) file. This essentially was just another name for a ZIP file, and all the ZIP file utilities can be used to create and extract from these files also. The only difference is that a JAR file should also contain a manifest file, which is like a table of contents and enables the members of the JAR file to have attributes. The attributes are stored within the manifest file in the JAR.

Finally, Microsoft decided that it wanted a format that was unique to its products. It already had a format called CAB, which stands for "cabinet." It incorporated the CAB file format with its Internet Explorer. CAB files have an advantage: They have a better compression algorithm, so the files are smaller. They also have a disadvantage: The files are in a Microsoft-proprietary standard format and might not be supported on platforms other than Windows.

For package files that are widely distributed, the packages should follow a naming convention outlined in the Java Language Specification. If two packages from different sources had the same name, a user might have a very limited ability to fix the problem because the source code might not be available. If the company producing the Java code has an Internet domain name, the first two levels of the package name should use them in reverse order. For example:

```
com.ibm.CORBA.iiop

com.sun.java.swing

org.apache.tomcat
```

The highest-level qualifier of `java` (and `javax`) is reserved by JavaSoft for standard libraries and extensions, so you should never name your classes beginning with these names. If your packages do not begin with the domain type, you should probably use your company name as the high-level qualifier, as in these examples:

```
lotus.chart

lotus.notes.addins

sun.net.ftp
```

Sun recommends that if you are creating classes for local use, the first letter of your package should be lowercase.

There are no `#include` statements in Java. In C and C++, you use the `#include` statement to include additional source code modules. In Java, you use the `import` statement to accomplish a similar effect. The purpose of the Java `import` statement is slightly different than that of the `#include` statement of C++, however. The purpose of the Java `import` statement is to allow your programs to use a shorthand notation.

You can import a single class or an entire package. Here are some examples:

```
import javax.swing..Box;

import java.applet.*;

import lotus.domino.*;
```

The first `import` statement imports a single class, and the second two statements import entire packages. These two `import` statements allow a shorthand for all the classes in the respective packages.

You could refer to the `Applet` class as follows:

```
public class MyApplet extends java.applet.Applet
```

Or, if you have done the import, you can refer to the class like this:

```
public class MyApplet extends Applet
```

You can always refer to classes by their fully qualified names, so importing classes is not strictly required in any program. However, this can make the program much more legible. You do not need to import the java.lang package because all methods in that package are imported by default. The controlling factor on whether a class is found is the class path.

JAVA EXCEPTION HANDLING

Like C++, Java uses *exception handling* to handle runtime errors that occur in programs. In C++, exceptions were added as an innovation after the language was already in use; as a result, many C++ programs do not use exceptions. In contrast, Java has had exceptions since its origin, so you will probably find that most—if not all—Java programs use the exception-handling model.

Exception handling involves the use of several different statements and objects. The essence of exception handling is that you group statements that might potentially cause an exception (including within called subroutines); then if one occurs, you can catch it and handle it. Syntactically you use the try-catch statement for grouping. Here is the full syntax:

```
try
{
    // This is the try block. Normal program statements are here
    // If an exception occurs, this block may be left early.
}
catch (Exceptiontype1 e1)
{
    // This block catches exceptions of type Exceptiontype1
}
catch (Exceptiontype2 e2)
{
    // This block catches exceptions of type Exceptiontype2
}

    // More catch clauses can appear here

finally
{
    // Here are statements that will be executed in all cases.
    // This block will execute whether or not there is an exception.
}
```

You can have as many different types of exceptions as you want to handle. The finally clause does not appear within C++. This is a very useful clause for cleaning up anything you initialize in the try clause. It is better to clean up in the finally clause than in a catch clause because then the cleanup will occur in both the error and nonerror cases. In the error case, the finally clause will be executed after the catch clause.

An exception is created with the throw statement. The syntax for the throw statement is shown here:

```
throw expression;
```

The *expression* must result in an object of the class Throwable. All exceptions are extended from this class. You can create your own exception classes and throw and catch the exceptions. This technique is useful whenever you have a program that might detect an error situation several levels deep within subroutines. But if an error occurs, you want the program to "unwind" to a higher-level routine for processing. Java provides a language mechanism to do this gracefully without resorting to return codes.

Any exceptions that are generated by Notes or Domino use the NotesException class. This class extends the java.lang.Exception class and contains three public variables: id, text, and internal. The internal variable, new to Release 6, is of type Exception and is the internal exception that caused the NotesException. Within the exception handler (the catch block), you can refer to these fields. Here is an example:

```
try
{
    ... Statements ...
}
catch (NotesException e)
{
    System.out.println("NotesException: " + e.id + " ... " + e.text);
    e.printStackTrace();
}
catch (Exception e)
{
    e.printStackTrace();
}
```

This code prints the Notes error code and message along with the standard Java stack trace. For exceptions other than a NotesException, only the stack trace is printed.

JAVA MULTITHREADING

Unlike LotusScript, multithreading is built into the Java language. *Multithreading* is simply the idea of handling one or more operations at a single time under a single processor. This feature is one of the reasons why you might want to consider Java rather than LotusScript for certain agents. Some types of programs, such as network applications using TCP/IP sockets, lend themselves more easily to multithreading than others. If multithreading is one of the requirements of your application, Java is a good choice.

The Java language provides a built-in class called Thread. The fully qualified name of this class is java.lang.Thread, so it exists in the java.lang package. Lotus provides an important extension to this class called NotesThread. Let's take a look at both of these classes. We'll review Thread and then the extensions provided by NotesThread.

The Thread class is used to implement all threads in Java. You can implement your thread in two ways using the Thread class (there is one additional way with NotesThread). The first method is to write your own class that extends the Thread class. In this case, your class actually is a special case of a thread. You write your own class method called run() that overrides the base class method.

The second way to implement a thread involves two separate classes. With this approach, you create your own class that does not extend the Thread class. Instead, you implement an interface called the Runnable interface. This interface defines only one method, the run() method. You create an instance of your class; then you create an instance of the Thread class and pass your class to the Thread constructor. At the appropriate time, your run() method is called.

So you now know that the code of your thread will exist within the run method. When does the code in the run method get invoked? You might think that it would start up as soon as your object is created, but it does not. If that were to happen, you wouldn't get much of a chance to initialize or set things up for your thread before it got off and running. So, the creation of your thread and the running of it are separated. To start the code found in your run() method, you invoke the start() method of the thread. This gives you a chance to do some initialization before invoking the start method. It also means that if you forget to invoke start, your thread will never run.

The location of the start method depends upon which way you created the thread. If you derived your class (that is, you extended it) from the Thread class, your own class has the start method. If you created a separate class and implemented the Runnable interface, the start method is invoked on the Thread object you created separately.

Here is an example of the first method of implementing threads:

```
public class MyMain1 extends Thread
{

    public void run()
    {
            System.out.println("ExtendedThread Running!");
    }

    public static void main(String[] args)
    {
        try
        {
            MyMain1 etMyThread = new MyMain1(); // My Thread
            etMyThread.start(); // This will eventually invoke my run();
            etMyThread.join(); // Wait for thread to finish
        }
        catch (InterruptedException e)
        {
        }
    }

}
```

In this example, the MyMain object is created with the new statement. The thread does not actually start until the start method is called. At that time, the start method initializes the thread and invokes its run method. Meanwhile, the original thread returns from the call to start and continues. At this point, it executes the join method, which causes the main thread to wait until the second thread has finished execution. When it does, the main thread wakes up again and finishes the program.

Here is an example of the second method of implementing threads:

```
public class MyMain2 implements Runnable
{

    public void run()
    {
            System.out.println("RunnableThread Running!");
    }

    public static void main(String[] args)
    {
        try
        {
            MyMain2 rtMyThread = new MyMain2(); // My Thread
            Thread theThread = new Thread(rtMyThread); // java.lang.Thread
            theThread.start(); // This will eventually invoke my run();
            theThread.join(); // Wait for thread to finish
        }
        catch (InterruptedException e)
        {
        }
    }
}
```

In this second example, note that the class MyMain2 is not really a thread; it just runs on a separate thread from the main thread. You can think of the run method in this case as if it were a main program entry point.

In both of these examples, the join method is used to synchronize the main thread with the newly created thread. It would normally be considered a good programming practice for the main thread to wait until the subsidiary threads have finished before it finishes itself.

You might be asking when you should extend the Thread class and when you should use the Runnable interface. If you have complete control over all your classes, it doesn't matter too much which method you use. You can use either. Sometimes, however, you don't have complete control because you might be using some existing classes. In this case, you might not be able to have a class extend the Thread class because you can use only single inheritance in Java and because the class you are working with might already be extending something else. In this situation, you should use the Runnable interface on your existing class; you will not need to extend the Thread class. You need only to add the run method. Here is an example of the declaration:

```
public class MyClass extends MyBaseClass implements Runnable {
    // Here is your MyClass stuff

    public void run() {
        // Thread code here
    }
}
```

In this case, you don't need to modify any code in the MyBaseClass class. In fact, you might not even have the source code for that class. You just need to implement your extensions to the base class, implement one additional method (the run method), and pass your class to the `Thread` constructor. After that, the base class, as well as your extensions, will be run on a separate thread.

NOTES AND DOMINO MULTITHREADING USING JAVA

You can use the threading mechanisms described in the previous section within Notes and Domino. However, if you use them, you will not be able to access any Notes or Domino data. You can use the standard Java threading classes only if you are going to use them for animation or other standard Web kinds of processing in, for example, a standard Java applet. If you want to use threading to access Domino databases or services, you must use the `NotesThread` class.

Now that you've seen the two ways to implement threads with the standard Java libraries, let's review the modifications necessary to use threads within Notes and Domino. Because `NotesThread` extends the standard Java `Thread` class, the first method you can use to create your thread is to extend `NotesThread`. It works similarly to regular Java, but rather than implement a `run()` method, you must implement a `runNotes()` method. The second way to implement threading with Notes is to implement a `Runnable` interface. In this case, you still implement a `run()` method, not a `runNotes` method. Here are the previous two examples, slightly modified for the Notes and Domino environment. As mentioned, you must supply a `runNotes` method for this approach to work. In `NotesThread`, the `run` method is specified as `final`, so you will not be allowed to override the `run` method even if you want to. You will get a compile-time error message if you attempt to use `run` instead of `runNotes`. Here is an example of the first method of implementing threads within Notes and Domino:

```
import lotus.domino.NotesThread;

public class MyMainNotes1 extends NotesThread
{

    public void runNotes()
    {
    System.out.println("MyMainNotes1 Running!");
    }

    public static void main(String[] args)
    {
        try
        {
            MyMainNotes1 etMyThread = new MyMainNotes1(); // My Thread
            etMyThread.start(); // This will eventually invoke my runNotes();
            etMyThread.join(); // Wait for thread to finish
        }
        catch (InterruptedException e)
        {
            e.printStackTrace();
        }
    }
}
```

Notice that the `main` program is essentially identical to the version that we created for regular Java threading. The only changes are found in the `MyMainNotes1` class, where it extends `NotesThread` instead of `Thread` and contains a `runNotes` method instead of a `run` method.

Here is an example of the second method of implementing threads within Notes and Domino:

```
import lotus.domino.NotesThread;


public class MyMainNotes2 implements Runnable
{

    public void run()
    {
        System.out.println("MyMainNotes2 Running!");
    }

    public static void main(String[] args)
    {
        try
        {
            MyMainNotes2 rtMyThread = new MyMainNotes2(); // My Thread
            NotesThread theThread = new NotesThread(rtMyThread); // NotesThread
                extends java.lang.Thread
            theThread.start(); // This will eventually invoke my run();
            theThread.join(); // Wait for thread to finish
        }
        catch (InterruptedException e)
        {
        }
    }
}
```

You can easily see by comparing the Notes/Domino version with the previous version that the interfaces are very similar. In the Notes version of the applications, it is even more critical for the `main` routine to wait until the secondary threads have finished (via the `join` method). This is because Notes or Domino automatically terminates all the subsidiary threads when the `main` thread finishes. So, the subsidiary threads cannot run longer than the `main` thread.

It should be apparent from the examples why the `NotesThread` version uses `runNotes` and the `Runnable` version uses the `run` method. When you extend `NotesThread`, your class is a `NotesThread`. That means it contains the prewritten Lotus code to implement `run`, and you cannot override and use this method. The Lotus code within `run` eventually calls your `runNotes` method after it initializes the Notes environment. On the other hand, when you implement the `Runnable` interface, your code is in a separate class and your `run` method does not conflict with the Lotus version of the `run` method. By the time your `run` method is called, the `NotesThread` class has already set up the Notes environment. Here is the sequence of calls upon startup of a `Runnable` class:

1. `java.lang.Thread:start` creates a thread and calls the new thread.

2. `NotesThread:run` initializes the Notes environment and runs the thread.

`YourClass:run` is the thread code in the `run` method. As mentioned earlier, there is a third way to create a `NotesThread` besides the two that are normally available for all threads. This approach uses `static` methods within the `NotesThread` class to initialize Notes *on the currently running thread.* You use this approach if your program is invoked on a thread over which you have no control. In essence, rather than create a new `NotesThread` object, this approach initializes Notes without creating a separate `NotesThread` and turns the currently running thread into a pseudo-`NotesThread`.

This approach to initializing Notes can also be used if you write a standalone Java application that will use Notes classes. There is no particular reason for doing so, however; either of the preceding two methods will also work.

If you do need to initialize Notes on the currently running thread, here is how you do it. First, you must call `NotesThread.sinitThread()` before using any other Notes/Domino classes. When you are finished with the Notes classes, you must call `NotesThread.stermThread()`. These two calls must be balanced. In particular, even if exceptions occur, you must be sure to call `stermThread` before your routine exits. Here is some example code:

```
import lotus.domino.NotesThread;

public class MyNotesMain3
{
    public static void main(String[] args)
    {
        try
        {
            NotesThread.sinitThread(); // Initialize Notes on the currently
                running thread

            // Here you can place any Java code
        }
        catch (Exception e)
        {
            e.printStackTrace(); // Print a stack trace
        }
        finally
        {
            NotesThread.stermThread(); // This will be called in all cases
        }
    }
}
```

Notice that in this code, I used the `finally` clause to house the `stermThread` call. By implementing the termination this way, the thread Notes environment will be terminated whether or not there is an exception. If you fail to properly terminate the Notes environment, your program can hang or cause an abnormal termination.

THE Session CLASS

You've seen so far how Notes and Domino use the NotesThread class to implement the startup and shutdown of the Notes and Domino environment. After this environment is set up, however, one additional class must be used to initiate access to Domino. This class is the Session class, which corresponds to the NotesSession class of LotusScript.

The Session class is at the top of the Domino Objects hierarchy. All other classes are obtained via the Session, either directly or indirectly. For example, from a Session object, you can get a DbDirectory object, through which you can access Domino databases. You can also obtain an AgentContext object (in an agent) from the Session, which gives you information about the current agent's context.

So, if the Session class is so important, how do you create one? Good question. There are two ways to get a Session object. You can either create one from scratch or obtain one from another class that happens to have one. When you are writing an agent, Notes creates a Session object for you, and you can just obtain it. When you are writing any other type of Java program, you have to create it from scratch. Creating a new Session in Java from scratch is very similar to using the LotusScript statement Dim session As new NotesSession. In Java, you use the CreateSession method of the NotesFactory class. Here is how you do it with Java:

```
Session s = NotesFactory.CreateSession();
```

As mentioned, when you are writing code for an agent, you can obtain the Session object that was created for you. Within an agent context, you must do two things. First, your agent must extend the AgentBase class; then you must have a NotesMain method. Within the NotesMain method, you use this line:

```
Session s = this.getSession();
```

We'll describe this in more detail in the next section.

JAVA AGENTS, APPLETS, APPLICATIONS, AND SERVLETS

The Java language can be used in several different contexts with Notes and Domino. In particular, you can use Java in agents, applets, applications, and servlets. Each of these contexts interacts differently with the Domino environment. In Chapter 19, "Using the IDE with LotusScript, Java, and JavaScript," we reviewed the differences between these types of programs and when each language could be used. Let's examine each of the Java contexts now in more detail.

Some of the main characteristics of these different types of programs are how they are created, how they are invoked, and how they are terminated. In each section, I'll describe these characteristics.

DOMINO JAVA AGENTS

Java agents in Domino are really just special cases of the NotesThread class that you saw earlier. To create an agent, you extend the AgentBase class. However, the AgentBase class itself is just an extension of the NotesThread class, so without necessarily knowing it, your agent is also a NotesThread.

When you saw how a NotesThread is started, you learned that you need to provide only one routine, the runNotes method. When the NotesThread is started, the runNotes method is invoked automatically. In the special case of agents, however, the Notes system has some additional housekeeping chores to perform before it can start your code. So, in the case of agents, Notes commandeers the runNotes method, declares it final so that you cannot use it, and substitutes the NotesMain method for your code. Here is how a Notes Java agent actually starts up:

1. java.lang.Thread:start creates a thread and calls the new thread.

2. NotesThread:run initializes the Notes environment and runs the thread.

3. AgentBase:runNotes initializes the Agent environment.

4. YourAgent:NotesMain is your agent code.

The AgentBase runNotes method sets up an AgentContext object for you and creates a Session object for you. Because your agent extends the AgentBase class, you can use this.getSession to get the Session object that was created by runNotes.

If you look at the code that is automatically produced for you by the Domino Designer IDE for a Java agent, it should now be very clear. Notice that the getSession call omits the this qualifier. You can use either this.getSession or just plain getSession. It is important to understand the shorthand and why you don't need to use the this qualifier. (It's because getSession is defined in AgentBase and your agent extends AgentBase, so, in effect, your agent is an AgentBase.) Here's the code:

```java
import lotus.domino.*;

public class JavaAgent extends AgentBase
{

    public void NotesMain()
    {

        try
        {
            Session session = getSession();
            AgentContext agentContext = session.getAgentContext();

            // (Your code goes here)
        }
        catch(Exception e)
        {
            e.printStackTrace();
        }
    }
}
```

Your Java agent automatically terminates when your NotesMain method ends. After it ends, control is returned in the reverse order to AgentBase:runNotes and then NotesThread:run. When run finishes, the thread itself is finished.

Also notice in the automatically generated code that an AgentContext is obtained for you. The AgentContext includes information such as the effective username, the current database, and the set of unprocessed documents that the agent should handle, along with several other agent properties.

Remember that an agent can run on either the Notes client or a Domino server. When the agent is running on the Notes client, the effective user is the current workstation user ID. However, when the agent is run on the server, the effective user is the user who last signed the agent. In addition, via the agent properties, you also set up the agent to run with the identity of a Web user.

You can run a Java agent on a Domino server via a URL. You do this from a Web browser with the following syntax:

```
http://server/database.nsf/agentname?OpenAgent
```

The database must exist, of course, and the specified agent must be a shared agent within the database. To send output back to the Web user, you must create a PrintWriter object by getting it from the AgentBase object. Here is how you do that:

```
import lotus.domino.*;
import java.io.PrintWriter;

public class JavaAgent extends AgentBase {

    public void NotesMain() {

        try {
            Session session = this.getSession();
            AgentContext agentContext = session.getAgentContext();

            PrintWriter pw = getAgentOutput();  // Get AgentOutput
            pw.println("<h1>Hello World</h1>");    // Send output back to browser


        } catch(Exception e) {
            e.printStackTrace();
        }
    }
}
```

The capability of running an agent on the server is similar to the servlet capability. There are a few differences, however. First, an agent is stored within a Domino database. Because of this, it can be replicated and can travel along with the database to another server. In addition, Java agents use the Domino security model and are more secure than servlets. Agents are written by extending AgentBase as previously described, and you use a NotesMain method for your agent code.

Java servlets are stored as Java class files within a directory on the server. Servlets can be initialized and stay active within the Domino server. When resident, a servlet can process many requests in a multithreaded manner from several Web clients at once. The capability of remaining in memory can provide servlets with an important performance advantage for certain applications. Because servlets might be handling many requests simultaneously, it is critical that servlets be threadsafe.

One common use for servlets is to access non-Domino databases via JDBC. You can also access Domino databases using the Java techniques described in previous sections. Servlets are an industry standard for server-side Java programming, whereas agents are much more Domino-specific.

Domino servlets are implemented as extensions of the `lotus.domino.servlet` class. There is a full discussion of servlets in the section "Java Servlets," later in this chapter.

JAVA APPLETS

An *applet* is a set of one or more Java classes that is downloaded to a Web browser and executed within the context of the JVM in the Web browser itself. Regular Java applets are independent of Notes and Domino. You can have Java applets that are created and served by a Web server, such as Domino or any other Web server.

Just as Domino Java agents are special cases of the Java `Thread` class, with Notes and Domino you can have specialized Domino applets as well. Let's first review a regular Java applet; then we'll cover how Domino Java applets are different.

An applet in Java is actually invoked by the Web browser. There is no main method in a Java applet. In fact, there are four important methods in a Java applet: `init`, `start`, `stop`, and `destroy`. Here are their definitions:

- `void init()`—This method is invoked when the applet is first loaded. It is called only once.
- `void start()`—This method is invoked after the `init` method. It is also invoked when the page comes into view or the browser is restored from an icon view.
- `void stop()`—This method is invoked when the page is left or when the browser is minimized into an icon.
- `void destroy()`—This method is invoked when the applet is no longer required. It is called after the `stop` method.

For completeness, it should be mentioned that a Java applet is not actually a base class. As a matter of fact, it is four layers down in the hierarchy. The upper layers are `Component`, `Container`, `Panel`, and `Applet`. In other words, `Applet` extends `Panel`, which extends `Container`, which extends `Component`. These classes can be found in the java.awt package. It is beyond my scope here to explain all these other classes, but you should be aware of them. Suffice it to say that these other classes deal with user-interface characteristics, such as layout and the graphical appearance of the applet.

DOMINO JAVA APPLETS

What exactly is a Domino Java applet? A regular applet that is served by a Domino server to a Web browser might qualify, but that is not what I mean by a Domino Java applet. A Domino Java applet is an applet that has the capability to access the Domino Objects. In other words, it can do everything that a normal applet can do, but it can also access Domino resources.

Remember that a regular applet is a Java program running within the JVM in the Web browser. To clarify things, think about this hypothetical case. Suppose you have the newest gadget, a Web-enabled television set. This TV is a pure Java machine. It has a JVM installed and can download and execute Java programs, but it certainly isn't a personal computer. Can you execute a Domino Java applet? Yes. In your Web television set, you can access Domino databases, traverse views, and use a Java program to perform functions that you might have used LotusScript for previously.

It is important to understand the capabilities of a Domino Java applet and to understand how this type of applet differs from an ordinary Java applet. Let's take a look at a Domino Java applet.

A Domino Java applet is very similar in concept and implementation to a Domino Java agent. If you want to create a Domino Java applet, you must extend the `AppletBase` or `JAppletBase` classes. The `JAppletBase` class is the same as the `AppletBase` class, but it imports the com.sun.java.swing.* package and extends `JApplet` rather than `Applet`. The com.sun.java.swing.* package provides support for the Java Foundation Classes. This extension is analogous to extending the `AgentBase` class for agents. After you have extended `AppletBase` or `JAppletBase`, there are four important methods for your Domino Java applet:

- `void notesAppletInit()`—This method is invoked when the applet is first loaded. It is called only once.

- `void notesAppletStart()`—This method is invoked after the `notesAppletInit` method. It is also invoked when the page comes into view or the browser is restored from an icon view.

- `void notesAppletStop()`—This method is invoked when the page is left or when the browser is minimized into an icon.

- `void notesAppletDestroy()`—This method is invoked when the applet is no longer required. This method is called after the `notesAppletStop` method.

Immediately you should see the similarity to the four methods that are defined for a regular applet. Just as in the case for agents, the four `notesApplet` methods correspond to the underlying methods. It should also be mentioned that the regular `init`, `start`, `stop`, and `destroy` methods are declared final within `AppletBase` and `JAppletBase`, so you are not allowed to override them and you should not call them directly.

NOTE

For simplicity's sake, `AppletBase` is referenced instead of both `AppletBase` and `JAppletBase`. However, both classes should operate the same for our discussion.

Two additional methods exist in the `AppletBase` class. The first method is another one similar to one found in `AgentBase`. Remember that you need to have a `Session` object to access the Domino Object Model. When you have this `Session` object, you can pretty much traverse the entire object model hierarchy. There are two ways to obtain a `Session` within `AppletBase`:

```
Session s = this.openSession();    // Anonymous access

Session s = this.openSession(String userid, String password);
```

The first of these methods is used for anonymous access. In the second method, you pass the user ID and password strings.

The last method in `AppletBase` is the `isNotesLocal` method. This routine returns `true` if the applet is running within a Notes client and is accessing a local database. It returns `false` if you are accessing a remote server.

CORBA and IIOP are two technologies that enable you to perform client/server computing, using Web browsers and Java over the Internet. The client can be any Java-enabled Web browser, and the server is Domino. These technologies are described in more detail later in the chapter.

JAVA STANDALONE APPLICATIONS

With Java, unlike LotusScript, you can create a standalone application and run it from a command-line prompt. A couple of scenarios are involved here. First, you can access local Domino databases if you have Java and the Notes executable files present on your computer. This typically is the configuration on your desktop or laptop computer if you are using the Notes client.

Second, with the CORBA and IIOP components, you can create a standalone Java application that runs on your desktop but accesses a remote Domino server. In this case, all you need to have present on your local computer is a JVM and the appropriate class files. Under this scenario, you do not need to have the Notes executable files present.

In the previous section, "Notes and Domino Multithreading Using Java," we reviewed how to create a standalone Java application for Notes. As mentioned, a standalone application can extend `NotesThread`, or you can create a class that implements the `Runnable` interface. In either case, you must also have a `static main` routine. This `main` routine is invoked by the JVM machine. Here is an example of a Java program that extends `NotesThread`. This is an example that must run locally. It does not use CORBA or IIOP:

```
import lotus.domino.NotesFactory;
import lotus.domino.NotesThread;
import lotus.domino.Session;
```

```
public class MyMainNotes4 extends NotesThread
{

    public void runNotes()
    {
        try
        {
            Session s = NotesFactory.createSession(); // Create a new Session
            String v = s.getNotesVersion(); // Notes version
            String p = s.getPlatform(); // Platform
            System.out.println("Running version " + v + " on platform " + p);
        }
        catch (Exception e)
        {
            e.printStackTrace();
        }
    }

    public static void main(String[] args)
    {
        try
        {
            MyMainNotes4 etMyThread = new MyMainNotes4(); // My Thread
            etMyThread.start(); // This will eventually invoke my runNotes();
            etMyThread.join(); // Wait for thread to finish
        }
        catch (InterruptedException e)
        {
        }
    }
}
```

Here is how this routine starts up:

1. JVM calls `MyMain4:main`, which creates a thread and calls `Thread:start`
   (`ExtendedThread:start`).

2. `Thread:start` (`ExtendedThread:start`) initializes a thread and calls `NotesThread:run`.

3. `NotesThread:run` initializes Notes environment and runs the thread.

4. `MyMainNotes4:runNotes` is the main code.

> **NOTE**
>
> Do not confuse the `Thread:start` routine with the `Applet:start` routine. Although they have the same method name, they are completely different methods.
> `Thread:start` is a system routine that starts a thread; `Applet:start` is an optional user-written routine invoked by a browser when an applet starts.

The following example uses CORBA and IIOP. This `main` program can run on a client that does not have the Notes executables locally:

```
import lotus.domino.NotesFactory;
import lotus.domino.Session;
```

```
public class MyNotesMain5 implements Runnable
{

    public void run()
    {
        try
        {
            Session s = NotesFactory.createSession("ACMESERVER",
                "John Doe/AcmeCorp", "secretpassword");

            String v = s.getNotesVersion(); // Notes version
            String p = s.getPlatform(); // Platform Name
            System.out.println("Running version " + v + " on platform " + p);
        }
        catch (Exception e)
        {
            e.printStackTrace();
        }
    }

    public static void main(String[] args)
    {
        try
        {
            MyNotesMain5 rtMyThread = new MyNotesMain5(); // My Thread
            Thread theThread = new Thread((Runnable)rtMyThread);
            theThread.start(); // This will eventually invoke my run();
            theThread.join(); // Wait for thread to finish
        }
        catch (InterruptedException e)
        {
        }
    }
}
```

This code is an example of the Runnable interface. The major point to notice in this example is that we're using Thread instead of NotesThread. When making a remote IIOP call to server-side objects, you use the Thread object instead of NotesThread.

The two examples MyNotesMain4 and MyNotesMain5 showed two different ways to create a standalone application. MyNotesMain4 created an inherited thread, and MyNotesMain5 created a Runnable class. You can use CORBA via either method.

NOTE

If you want to try this example yourself, you need to substitute your server name, your user ID, and your password at the appropriate points in the program.

JAVA SERVLETS

Java *servlets* are programs written in Java that run on a Domino server. The Domino Java Servlet Manager, a component of the HTTP server task, loads and manages all servlets under Domino's control. A Web browser user can access them via a URL. When the URL for a servlet is invoked, the JVM in the Domino server starts the specified servlet. Here is an example of a servlet invocation:

```
http://servername/servlet/Processit/the/pathvar?myquery=color
```

Servlets are invoked with a path parameter and a query parameter. In this example, the servlet name is `Processit`, the path parameter is `/the/pathvar`, and the query parameter is `myquery=color`.

Servlets require some additional configuration to be able to execute in Domino, and you must have a copy of the Java Servlet Development Kit (JSDK). Several major tasks are involved when enabling servlets:

1. Update the Domino directory to enable servlets.
2. Create and compile your servlet Java programs.
3. Put your servlet's class files in the Domino\servlet directory under your main Domino\Data directory on your server. You might have to create the servlet directory because it is not created by default. The complete path will be something like d:\Domino\Data\domino\servlet.
4. Type **tell http restart** on the Domino server console.

UPDATING YOUR DOMINO DIRECTORY

You must have administrator privileges to update the Domino Directory. To enable servlets, follow these steps:

1. In the Domino Administrator client, first choose the Domino server.
2. Click the Configuration tab.
3. Click the Current Server Document item in the Server section. You will see the current server's configuration document with a set of tabs across the top.
4. Click the Internet Protocols tab.
5. Click the Domino Web Engine subtab.
6. Click the Edit Server action button to put the document into edit mode.
7. You will see a section titled Java Servlets. In this section, verify the following:
   - Make sure you are in edit mode, and change the Java servlet support from None (the default) to Domino Servlet Manager.
   - Leave the Servlet URL path /servlet (this is the default).
   - Leave the class path Domino/servlet (this is the default).
   - Leave all the other entries at their default values.
8. Click the Save and Close action button to save the document.

CREATING A SERVLET

The JSDK defines the servlet APIs. The most basic servlet implements the
`javax.servlet.Servlet` interface. Also supplied with the JSDK, however, is an implementation of this interface called `javax.servlet.http.HttpServlet`. Most servlet implementations
just extend this class. By default, servlets are multithreaded, but if you want your servlet to
be single-threaded for some reason, you add `implements SingleThreadModel` to your class
declaration. No extra coding is required for a single-threaded servlet.

The `javax.servlet.Servlet` interface defines just five methods: `init`, `destroy`, `service`,
`getServletConfig`, and `getServletInfo`. If you extend `HttpServlet`, you will be concerned
with the methods `init`, `destroy`, and `getServletInfo`. You also will be concerned with four
higher-level routines: `doGet`, `doHead`, `doPost`, and `doPut`.

23

Processing a servlet involves two objects: the request object and the result object. The
request object is of the class `HttpServletRequest`, and the result object is of the class
`HttpServletResponse`. You can use the result object to obtain a `ServletOutputStream` object,
and then you can call the `println` method.

Before you send back any response, you must set the content type. You do this with the
`setContentType` method. Here is a sample servlet:

```java
import java.io.IOException;

import javax.servlet.ServletException;
import javax.servlet.ServletOutputStream;
import javax.servlet.http.HttpServlet;
import javax.servlet.http.HttpServletRequest;
import javax.servlet.http.HttpServletResponse;
import lotus.domino.NotesFactory;
import lotus.domino.NotesThread;
import lotus.domino.Session;

public class PlatformServlet extends HttpServlet
{
    public String getServletInfo()
    {
        return "Create a page that says Hello from Platform Servlet";
    }
    public void doGet(HttpServletRequest req, HttpServletResponse res) throws
        ServletException, IOException
    {
        try
        {
            // Before sending output, set the content type.
            res.setContentType("text/html");

            // Initialize a NotesThread
            NotesThread.sinitThread();
            Session s = NotesFactory.createSession();
            System.out.println("Got past createSession");

            // Get the ServletOutputStream for sending response back
            ServletOutputStream out = res.getOutputStream();
```

23

```
            out.println("<HTML><HEAD><TITLE>Example Servlet</TITLE></HEAD>");
            out.println("<BODY>");
            out.println("<H1>Hello from Platform Servlet</H1>");
            out.println("<p>The server is running on the <B>" + s.getPlatform()
                    + "</B> platform");
            out.println("</BODY></HTML>");
            System.out.println("finished");
            out.close();
        }
        catch (Exception e)
        {
            e.printStackTrace();
        }
        finally
        {
            NotesThread.stermThread();
        }
    } // end doGet
} //// end PlatformServlet
```

FINISHING SETTING UP THE SERVLET

When you have created and compiled your Java servlet into a class file, place it in the Domino\servlet directory under your main Domino\Data directory.

Finally, type **tell http restart** on the Domino server console. Note that if you are in a development cycle, the servlets are in memory and the only way to flush them out is to restart the server. Occasionally, it has been found that there are some disk caches (on the server- and also possibly in the client-side browser) of the applet class files. If it seems that if your development changes are not having an effect, you should be sure to clear the caches and restart the HTTP task. You might even have to restart the entire Domino server to clear out some caches.

INVOKING THE SERVLET FROM THE WEB BROWSER

Now you have finished creating and setting up your servlet. To test it from the Web browser, type a request in the following format:

http://www.yourserver.com/servlet/PlatformServlet

You must replace the server name with your real server name. The /servlet that follows matches the entry you made in the Domino directory for the servlet URL path. Following that is the name of the servlet itself. In this case, we have named the servlet PlatformServlet. Note that the name of the servlet is case sensitive, so be sure to use the proper case for the name or it will not be found.

NOTES AND DOMINO JAR FILES

Several JAR files come with Notes and Domino. Some of these JAR files contain Java support files, and some files are tied specifically to Notes and Domino. You might not see all of them because some of them reside on the server. The files are located in the Notes executable directory for local access or are in the notes\data\domino\html directory on the server if they will be required to be served to a client.

The following files normally appear in the executable directory, which is either on your Notes client or the Domino server:

- **rt.jar**—Contains the Java standard runtime environment routines. It contains java.lang.*, java.io.*, java.util.*, and java.net.*, as well as several other class libraries.

- **i18n.jar**—Contains class libraries for international language support.

- **tools.jar**—Contains classes for debugging and other support from Sun Microsystems. The classes in this library all begin with sun.*.

- **notes.jar**—Contains classes for the local operation of Java within the Notes client. It contains all the local (as opposed to CORBA) implementations of the Domino Object Model classes.

- **jsdk.jar**—Contains the standard extension classes for servlets—javax.servlet.*—as well as some Sun classes—sun.servlet.*.

- **dservlet.jar**—Contains the Domino servlet classes contained in the package lotus.domino.servlet.*.

The preceding files normally appear in the Domino\Data\domino\java directory on the server and in the Notes\Data\domino\java directory on the client. Notice that the archives exist in JAR format (the industry standard), in CAB format (the Microsoft version), and in ZIP format (an older version of the JAR format).

UNDERSTANDING CORBA AND IIOP

Throughout this chapter, the terms *CORBA* and *IIOP* have been mentioned several times. We've deferred a discussion of what these terms mean and their technical implications. Before we delve into those topics, though, let's back up and look at how the regular Notes client communication with a Domino server is implemented.

The communication between a Notes client and a Domino server during a user session is through a Notes proprietary interface. This interface was developed years ago, before standards such as CORBA and IIOP were invented. The Notes/Domino communication protocol works well and reliably to this day, but it has one major drawback: Only the Notes client and the Domino server understand how to use it.

With the importance of the Internet, it is very desirable to allow any browser client to access a Domino server. This has been possible since the first release of the Domino server (at Release 4.5), which converts Domino databases to HTML that, in turn, can be rendered by a browser. This approach has the benefit that any browser can be used as a client to a Domino server; you are no longer tied specifically to the Notes client. However, this approach has a different drawback: When using a browser, you lose some of the functionality that is provided by the Notes client.

So now you have two approaches. If you use the Notes client, you have extra functionality, but with the drawback that you cannot use a standard Web browser. If you use a Web browser, you lose some of the functionality of the Notes client. What are you to do?

Well, because you are an astute reader and you noticed that the title of this section involves CORBA and IIOP, you certainly recognize that these technologies must be the strategy to solving these twin problems. By using CORBA and IIOP, you can gain the functionality of the Notes client, but you can have the ubiquity of the Web browser. Great! Now you know what problem the technology solves, but how does it do it?

CORBA stands for Common Object Request Broker Architecture. Notice that at the end of this name is the word *Architecture*. CORBA is not a product, like Notes, Domino, or Microsoft Windows. It is not sold at your local computer store. Instead, CORBA is a standard specification that can be implemented within different products. The purpose of the specification is to allow different companies to write compliant products; when the compliant products are used together, they will actually communicate.

So, by having a common architecture defined by standards, clients and servers from different vendors can be used more successfully together. The "ORB" in the middle of CORBA stands for "object request broker." You can think of an ORB in much the same way as a real estate broker, commodities broker, or stockbroker. The purpose of the broker is to bring together separate entities and enable them to make a transaction. In this case, the ORB brings together the client and the server.

So, CORBA is used to define the mechanisms that enable clients and servers to transact. There still remains the detail of how they physically communicate. In real life, you might talk to your broker over the phone, see him or her in person, or just use a fax machine. The physical means that you use to communicate is separate from the details of the transaction you are trying to accomplish.

The Internet Inter-ORB Protocol (IIOP) performs the same function as the phone network. IIOP is the protocol used by one ORB to talk to another ORB. So, CORBA defines a higher-level interface for objects, methods, and properties, and the IIOP deals with communication issues between ORBs. The mechanism used by one ORB to talk to another ORB (IIOP) is independent of the topics of discussion (CORBA). In fact, CORBA can use other communications mechanisms, but by far the most interesting is the one that uses Internet standards (IIOP). This is the only one I will consider here.

Now that you understand about CORBA and IIOP, what is the tie-in to Domino? Lotus has implemented a set of Domino Java classes that can be downloaded to your Web browser or used by a standalone application. These are the classes that are held in the NCSO.jar archive. They are implemented using the CORBA/IIOP standards, and they enable Java programs that you have written as applets to interface through to the Domino server. You simply write the applet code and make calls to the normal Java Domino class interfaces—the communication via CORBA/IIOP to the back-end classes is done for you automatically. In fact, you never even need to know that CORBA/IIOP is used on your behalf. The net effect is that your Java applets (and applications) can reside on a client workstation without Notes and can communicate to the Domino back-end classes. Thus, you are starting to be able to approach the Notes client level of functionality while using a browser interface.

A couple of caveats could make this technology more suitable for intranets than Internet use at this time. First is that the NCSO.jar file is 0.7MB, and this might take a while to download on a 56K modem. With any fast communication protocol, this isn't a problem. Second, IIOP does not use the standard ports that are used by HTTP. In other words, IIOP opens up a separate communication channel from the client to the server. This improves efficiency, but it could cause problems if the clients and servers are separated by firewalls. Be careful to consider this possibility when you decide to use this technology.

23

CHAPTER 24

THE Session AND FRONT-END CLASSES

In this chapter

THE NotesSession, Session, AND AgentContext CLASSES

In this chapter and the next two, we review the major Domino Object classes for Notes and Domino. These classes can be accessed from either LotusScript or Java. The syntax for accessing these classes is different between LotusScript and Java, but the classes themselves are pretty similar. Because there are more than 30 classes for Notes and Domino, with hundreds of properties and methods, it is not possible to cover all the classes in detail. Instead, we explore the main aspects of the classes, working from the top of the hierarchy downward, to get you started. After you become familiar with the main classes, the methods for using LotusScript and Java, and the debugging programs, the best way to learn is with your own applications.

In this section, we cover the NotesSession LotusScript class, along with the Session and AgentContext Java classes. The reason for covering all three classes is that, when Lotus implemented Java support, it split the NotesSession LotusScript class into two classes: Session and AgentContext. In addition, a few properties of AgentContext come from the LotusScript NotesDatabase class.

The NotesSession LotusScript class is used to access variables related to the current session. You can think of a session as being associated with a particular Notes ID and password. A session running on a Notes client is associated with the current user; for a session running in an agent on a server, the current user ID is the ID of the server itself.

The session in both LotusScript and Java is at the highest level of the back-end hierarchy. You use the session to get information about the current user, find out whether the program is running on a server, access environment variables, and create certain utility type objects, such as a DateTime object.

In LotusScript, you use both properties and methods. You can retrieve and assign properties with an assignment statement. In essence, properties behave like variables. Methods are invoked like function calls. In Java, access to variables is made through method calls. In LotusScript, the names are not case sensitive, but in Java, all method and variable names *are* case sensitive. As a rule, method names in Java usually begin with a lowercase verb.

Table 24.1 summarizes the correspondence between the LotusScript properties and methods and the equivalent Java method names. An asterisk indicates that the property is new in Release 6 of Notes and Domino.

TABLE 24.1   MAPPING OF NotesSession PROPERTIES TO JAVA SESSION METHODS

LotusScript Properties	Java Methods
NotesSession	*Session*
AddressBooks	getAddressBooks
CommonUserName	getCommonUserName
ConvertMime	isConvertMIME/setConvertMIME
CurrentAgent	getCurrentAgent
CurrentDatabase	getCurrentDatabase
DocumentContext	getDocumentContext
EffectiveUserName	getEffectiveUserName
HttpURL	getURL
International	getInternational
IsOnServer	isOnServer
LastExitStatus	getLastExitStatus
LastRun	getLastRun
NotesBuildVersion	—
NotesURL	—
NotesVersion	getNotesVersion
OrgDirectoryPath	getOrgDirectoryPath
Platform	getPlatform
SavedData	getSavedData
ServerName	getServerName
URLDatabase	getURLDatabase
UserGroupNameList	getUserGroupNameList
UserName	getUserName
UserNameList	getUserNameList
UserNameObject	getUserNameObject

Table 24.2 lists the LotusScript methods and their equivalent Java methods.

24

TABLE 24.2   MAPPING OF NotesSession PROPERTIES TO JAVA Session METHODS

LotusScript Properties	Java Methods
NotesSession	*Session*
CreateAdministrationProcess	—
CreateColorObject	—
CreateDateRange	createDateRange
CreateDateTime	createDateTime
CreateDOMParser	—
CreateDxlExporter	—
CreateDxlImporter	—
CreateLog	createLog
CreateName	createName
CreateNewsletter	createNewsletter
CreateRegistration	createRegistration
CreateRichTextParagraphStyle	createRichTextParagraphStyle
CreateRichTextStyle	createRichTextStyle
CreateSAXParser	—
CreateStream	createStream
CreateTimer	—
CreateXSLTransformer	—
Evaluate	evaluate
FreeTimeSearch	freeTimeSearch
GetDatabase	getDatabase
GetDbDirectory	getDbDirectory
GetEnvironmentString	getEnvironmentString
GetEnvironmentValue	getEnvironmentValue getSessionToken
—	getURL
—	getURLDatabase
GetUserPolicySettings	—
HashPassword	—
InitializeUsingNotesUserName	—

LotusScript Properties	Java Methods
NotesSession	*Session*
—	recycle
Resolve	resolve
SendConsoleCommand	—
SetEnvironmentVar	SetEnvironmentVar
	toString
UpdateProcessedDoc	—
VerifyPassword	—

As you can tell from Tables 24.1 and 24.2, the vast majority of the NotesSession properties and methods map to similar Session methods. However, several LotusScript properties and methods map to other Domino Object classes.

Chapter 23, "Creating and Using Java Applets and Agents," demonstrated the steps to create a Session object in Java. To review, in a Java (standalone) application, you must first initialize a Notes environment with a NotesThread. After the environment has been created, you can use NotesFactory.createSession to create a Session from scratch. Alternatively, if you are creating a Java applet or agent, you can use the getSession method because a Session object has already been created for you by the base Java class.

In LotusScript, you create a new NotesSession object with the New statement, or in a Dim statement with the New keyword. For example:

```
Dim session As New NotesSession
```

or

```
Dim session As NotesSession
Set session = New NotesSession
```

Because a NotesSession is an object, you must use the Set keyword. If you omit the Set keyword, you will get an error.

NotesSession PROPERTIES

The properties of the LotusScript class fall into two broad categories: properties about the environment and properties about the user. Properties about the environment include AddressBooks, which enables you to obtain a list of the Domino directories currently being used; and NotesVersion, NotesBuildVersion, and Platform, which provide information about the version and operating system environment.

User information includes CommonUserName, UserName, and EffectiveUserName. These three properties return information about an ID file in use. CommonUserName and UserName return information about the current workstation user or the server, depending upon where the current program is running. The only difference between these properties is the format of the result. CommonUserName returns the user ID in common username format, and UserName returns the fully distinguished name of the user ID. The EffectiveUserName property also returns a fully distinguished name. For a workstation user, it returns the same value as UserName, but for an agent running on a Domino server, EffectiveUserName returns the ID of the owner of the agent. The owner is the last person who modified and saved (signed) the agent.

The International property is used to obtain information about formatting that might vary from country to country—for example, the order of month, day, and year in date formats; currency symbols; and the character to use for a decimal separator. If you are writing an application that might be used in more than one country, you need to access the International class object. In Java, you use the getInternational method to obtain this object.

WHERE DO NEW DOMINO OBJECTS COME FROM?

Now is a good time to review how new Domino Objects are created. There are actually several ways for the objects to be created, and different objects can be created only in certain ways. This is one of the confusing points about the Domino Objects, so let me describe the different ways objects are created. In LotusScript, there are three generic ways to get an object variable:

- Create it yourself with the New keyword
- Call a method of an existing object
- Access a property of an existing object

Of these three methods, only the second method is available to create Domino objects in Java, with a few exceptions. The Domino Object classes in Java has a strict containment philosophy so that, in general, objects are created by calling methods of other, existing objects. For example, the Session object has several methods, such as createDateTime, createLog, createName, and so forth. These methods are used in place of the New keyword. The only exceptions to this policy are for creating the highest-level objects. Furthermore, these high-level objects (AgentBase, AgentRunner, AppletBase, NotesException, NotesFactory, and NotesThread) are typically created by Domino, not your application.

In LotusScript, all three methods of object creation are possible. This means that objects for more than half of the LotusScript classes must be created by one of the other methods. Some classes support more than one method of creation. For example, you can create them with the New keyword, but you can also create them by calling a method or accessing a property of another class.

OBJECTS CREATED WITH THE New KEYWORD

These are the classes that support creation with the `New` keyword: `NotesACLEntry`, `NotesDatabase`, `NotesDateTime`, `NotesDbDirectory`, `NotesDocument`, `NotesItem`, `NotesLog`, `NotesName`, `NotesNewsLetter`, `NotesRegistration`, `NotesRichTextItem`, `NotesSession`, `NotesTimer`, and `NotesUIWorkspace`.

These classes roughly break down into four categories:

- High-level classes, such as `NotesSession`, `NotesUIWorkspace`, `NotesDbDirectory`, and `NotesDatabase`
- Major object items, such as `NotesDocument`, `NotesNewsLetter`, and `NotesRegistration`
- Low-level classes, such as `NotesACLEntry`, `NotesDateTime`, `NotesItem`, `NotesName`, and `NotesRichTextItem`
- Auxiliary classes, such as `NotesLog` and `NotesTimer`

In your LotusScript programs, you will probably create items of the high-level and major object classes so that you can access their properties and use them to create objects lower in the hierarchy. The lower-level classes are typically used to do real work—in other words, to read and write information in your database. The auxiliary classes are for special-purpose use if you need them.

OBJECTS CREATED BY A METHOD OR PROPERTY

Because fewer than half of the Notes classes of LotusScript can be created with the `New` keyword, the majority of the class objects are created by a method or property of an existing object. In addition, your program typically starts at the top of the hierarchy and traverses down, creating objects lower in the hierarchy as needed.

For example, you might first create a new `NotesSession` object and then access one of its properties, such as `CurrentDatabase`. You use this property to get a `NotesDatabase` object, from which you can extract forms, views, or the documents contained in the database. After getting a `NotesDocument`, you might access its fields to finally get data that you're looking for.

Because some objects are very generic and might be used throughout the hierarchy, their creation is done at the top `NotesSession` class. These are the class objects that are created by calling a method within the `NotesSession` class: `NotesDateRange`, `NotesDateTime`, `NotesLog`, `NotesName`, `NotesNewsLetter`, `NotesRichTextParagraphStyle`, `NotesRichTextStyle`, and `NotesTimer`. This is the same technique that is used in Java.

You'll notice that several of the classes can be created with the `New` keyword and also by calling a method of `NotesSession`. Almost all the rest of the classes that can be created with `New` can also be obtained from some other existing class. You might think this is just redundant, but it is not. Notes can be controlled by other OLE-compliant ActiveX controllers, such as Visual Basic, Visual Basic for Applications, and Delphi, among others. When used in this manner, the external controller does not have access to the New keyword of LotusScript. Typically, these foreign controllers can create a single type of object at the top of the hierarchy. After this object has been created, all other objects must be obtained from properties and methods of existing objects. Thus, although it might seem redundant in LotusScript, the capability of creating or obtaining objects from other objects is an important aspect of the Domino Object Model.

The NotesInternational class object can be obtained from the International property of the NotesSession class. This is the only place to get this object. A NotesAgent object can be obtained from a property of the NotesSession object or from a NotesDatabase object.

It's important to remember that when using a method or property to obtain an object, you must use the Set statement to assign the object value. This is what differentiates the assignment of an object from a regular assignment statement. An object assignment must use the Set keyword; a regular assignment cannot use the Set keyword. If you forget the Set keyword, you get the error message.

In the front end, NotesUIWorkspace is at the top of the hierarchy. In previous releases of Notes, you could not programmatically create NotesUIDatabase and NotesUIView objects. Since Release 5, you can obtain these objects via the CurrentDatabase and CurrentView properties in the NotesUIWorkspace class. Alternatively, you can access the NotesUIDatabase and NotesUIView classes from events. You are passed an object of one of these classes if you write a PostOpen event, for example. After the user opens a database (or view), the PostOpen event is invoked and an object of the appropriate type is passed to the event handler. The NotesUIDatabase and NotesUIView classes have several events that are passed to the respective objects.

This is probably one of the most confusing areas of the LotusScript classes. The NotesUIDatabase class is meant to be used in the context of the user interface (UI), so the user action of opening and working with a database triggers the creation of the NotesUIDatabase object. The NotesDatabase object is used for almost all your normal database access requirements, such as getting and setting item values within the database.

The NotesView and NotesUIView objects involve a similar situation. The NotesUIView is created by Notes when the user acts on the view, such as opening or closing it. The object is passed via an event handler. The NotesView class, in turn, can be obtained from a NotesUIView object. The NotesView class is used for most of your view traversal, such as getting the next or previous document and moving up or down the document hierarchy. When it's used in this manner, a user is present and the NotesUIView represents the view a user has displayed.

A NotesView object can also be obtained from a NotesDatabase object. When used in this context, a user is not necessarily present. You might use this method to obtain a NotesView object in an agent running on a Domino server, for instance.

ARRAYS OF OBJECTS

Arrays can be declared and used in two ways in LotusScript. In the first method, you use the `Dim` statement and declare array bounds. This is the most straightforward and common use of arrays. When you declare array variables, however, you cannot use an aggregate assignment statement. For example:

```
Dim Array1(1 to 3) As Double
Dim Array2(1 to 3) As Double
Array2 = Array1    ' This is NOT allowed !
```

In the preceding example, you must create a loop of some sort and assign the elements of the arrays individually.

Another method for storing and using arrays is to use the `Variant` type. A `Variant` can hold data of any type, including arrays. In particular, you can declare a `Variant` and then copy an entire array with a single assignment statement. For example:

```
Dim Array1(1 to 3) As Double
Dim Var2 As Variant
Var2 = Array1    ' This IS allowed !
```

In the preceding example, when the assignment statement completes, `Var2` contains an array that is a copy of the original array. All the elements are copied, and you do not need to copy each item individually.

What happens when you have an array of objects that are not elementary items, such as `Doubles`? Well, an array of objects behaves just like an array of `Doubles` in many ways. You cannot do an array assignment from one declared array to another. You can, however, do an array assignment from an array of objects to a `Variant`, just as you saw previously with `Var2`. Here's a concrete example:

```
Dim ndrArray1(1 to 3) As NotesDateRange
Dim ndrArray2(1 to 3) As NotesDateRange
Dim Var2 As Variant
ndrArray2 = ndrArray1    ' This is NOT allowed !
Var2      = ndrArray1    ' This IS allowed, No Set used !
```

As a last point, notice that the last assignment statement does *not* use the `Set` keyword. An array is not an object. You can have an array that contains objects within it, but the array itself is not an object. Because the array is not an object, a `Set` is not used when we do the assignment to the `Variant` in the last statement.

This distinction between a `Variant` holding an array of objects and one holding an individual object is very important and often confused, even in the Lotus documentation. (It sometimes uses `Set` when referring to an array.) Here is another example:

```
Dim ndrArray1(1 to 3) As NotesDateRange
Dim ndr As NotesDateRange
Dim Var1 As Variant
Dim Var2 As Variant
Var1      = ndrArray1    ' This IS allowed, No Set used !
Set Var2  = ndr          ' Note: You must use the SET keyword !
```

In this case, we have declared both Var1 and Var2 as a Variant. But when we do the assignment, one requires us to use Set, whereas in the other we cannot use Set. Why? Here we are assigning an object (a NotesDateRange) to Var2. Whenever you assign an object, you must use Set. In the first case with Var1, we are assigning an array. *An array of objects is not an object.* If you keep this simple rule in mind, you'll have a much easier time with LotusScript.

We're spending so much time on this topic because several LotusScript classes return arrays of objects. Let's take, for example, the FreeTimeSearch method of the NotesSession class. This method happens to return an array of NotesDateRange objects. There are many other examples, but this one illustrates the points:

```
Dim ndrArray(1 to 3) As NotesDateRange
Dim ndr As NotesDateRange
Dim Var2 As Variant
ndrArray = FreeTimeSearch( ... ) ' This is NOT allowed !
ndr      = FreeTimeSearch( ... ) ' This is NOT allowed !
Var2     = FreeTimeSearch( ... ) ' This IS allowed, No Set used !
Set ndr  = Var2(0)               ' Allowed: Subscript the array, we must use Set !
```

In the last line, we assign a single NotesDateRange object. We do this by subscripting the array and getting one element. Because this element (a NotesDateRange) is an object, however, we must use Set. If you're confused by this section, reread it. It might answer some questions about why you sometimes need to use Set and why other times you cannot use it.

DATE AND TIME VARIABLES AND OBJECTS

Before we move on to other topics, we need to stop and discuss date and time variables in LotusScript and the Notes classes. You should realize that the LotusScript language and the Domino Object Model class library are implemented separately. In fact, the LotusScript language was originally implemented by the Office development group as an adjunct to Lotus 1-2-3; the Domino Object libraries were implemented by the Notes development team. One of the design goals of the LotusScript language was to be compatible with Visual Basic; the Domino Objects had to be consistent with the existing Notes code. It is not surprising that there are two different implementations of date/time (and a third for Java).

LotusScript, as you'll recall, is the language itself. Because it was implemented to be compatible with Visual Basic, there is a Variant data type that can hold data of various types. One of these types of values (type 7) is a date/time value. The date/time Variant value is the type of date that is built into the LotusScript language and is compatible with the Visual Basic implementation of dates and times. This is also the same format used by ActiveX automation, formerly known as OLE automation, so LotusScript can compatibly use ActiveX controls.

Date/time values in LotusScript are stored internally as double-precision floating-point numbers, with the integer part of the value representing the number of days since December 30, 1899, and the fractional part representing the time of day. A value of 1 indicates December 31, 1899, and a value of 2 is January 1, 1900. Negative values are allowed for the day portion, and dates can go back as far as January 1, 100 A.D. Dates can go into the future as far as December 31, 9999.

What about Notes itself? As you might imagine, Notes was originally developed independently from Visual Basic, and it has its own internal format for date/times. The Notes date/time format is made available through the `NotesDateTime` class and has support for time zones, daylight saving time, and time support for hundredths of a second. Internally, Notes counts days even farther back than LotusScript. Notes counts the days since January 1, 4713 B.C.

The time-zone support in Notes is important if you have data that will be used in multiple sites in different time zones. Because the time zone is recorded with the time, you can compare times that were generated in different locations, which is not possible with the LotusScript `Variant` form of date/time. Internally, Notes converts all date/time values to GMT for storage. With the GMT value and the time zone, Notes can convert the time to the local time. The LotusScript (`Variant`) date/time format really supports only what Notes calls local time because the time zone is not stored.

As you might imagine, Java has its own format for dates. Java's format is different from the format in both LotusScript and Notes. The Java date format is stored internally as a 64-bit (long) integer. It represents the number of milliseconds since January 1, 1970 GMT. The Java format does not store a time zone, so it cannot be converted automatically to local time. However, because it is based on GMT, Java's date/time value (unlike the LotusScript/BASIC format) represents an absolute, not relative, date and time. A method in the Java `DateTime` class converts a Notes `DateTime` object to a Java `DateTime` object. This method is called `toJavaDate`.

In addition to enabling access to the Notes date/time variables, the LotusScript `NotesDateTime` class can be used to convert from the LotusScript `Variant` form of date/time to the Notes format. If you understand the concepts of how the Notes classes are separate from the LotusScript and Java languages, it is easier to understand how and why there are three different date formats. Even if you understand the issue, however, it is easy to become confused about which format you're using. Just remember, if you are using a LotusScript language feature such as the `Cdat` built-in function, it expects a `Variant` date type, but if you are using a DOM class object, you can use a `NotesDateTime` class object. In Java, you'll use either the Java language date (`java.util.Date`) class or the `DateTime` class of Notes and Domino.

THE NotesUIWorkspace CLASS

Now that we've covered the `NotesSession` (LotusScript) and `Session` (Java) classes, we'll focus on the front-end classes of LotusScript. There are eight front-end classes: `NotesUIWorkspace`, `NotesUIDatabase`, `NotesUIView`, `NotesUIDocument`, `NotesUIScheduler`, `Button`, `Navigator`, and `Field`. Of these eight classes, we'll cover the first five classes. The `Button`, `Navigator`, and `Field` classes are fairly self-explanatory, and they represent the Notes concepts expressed in their names.

As mentioned, the front-end classes are not available in Java, but because they are an important part of the LotusScript class hierarchy, we'll cover them as a group here. When we cover the back-end classes, both LotusScript and Java features will be described together.

The `NotesUIWorkspace` class is at the top of the LotusScript front-end class hierarchy. This class represents the concept of the Notes user workspace. In the user interface, the primary functions you can perform in the workspace include adding databases to the desktop, opening databases, and editing documents. Each of these user actions has a counterpart in the `NotesUIWorkspace` class.

The following methods are available in Release 6: `AddDatabase`, `CheckAlarms`, `ComposeDocument`, `DialogBox`, `EditDocument`, `EditProfile`, `EnableAlarms`, `Folder`, `GetCurrentDatabase`, `GetListOfTunes`, `OpenDatabase`, `OpenFileDialog`, `OpenFrameSet`, `OpenPage`, `PickListCollection`, `PickListStrings`, `PlayTune`, `Prompt`, `RefreshParentNote`, `ReloadWindow`, `SaveFileDialog`, `SetCurrentLocation`, `SetTargetFrame`, `URLOpen`, `UseLSX`, `ViewRebuild`, and `ViewRefresh`.

In addition to these returning favorites, several new functions are sure to be hits with existing Notes and Domino developers. To show off some of the functions of the `NotesUIWorkspace` class, the next section has an interesting example.

MAKING YOUR AGENT PLAY A TUNE

This example shows you how to use two methods: `PlayTune` and `GetListOfTunes`. These functions are important methods you can use for your business applications.

To test these two new methods, open a test database and click the Agents line in the Design pane:

1. Create a new agent by clicking the New Agent action button under the Shared Code, Agents design elements.

2. Give the new agent the name `PlayTune`. As demonstrated in Figure 24.1, leave the trigger as On Event from the Actions menu and set the Target as None.

3. From the Run list in the Programmer's pane, choose the action to be LotusScript.

Figure 24.1
The Agent dialog box enables you to specify various details about the agent, including name and runtime parameters.

4. Click the `Initialize` method and enter the following code in the Programmer's pane:

```
Sub Initialize
    Dim uiws as New NotesUIWorkspace
    Dim tunes as Variant
    tunes = uiws.GetListOfTunes()
    Forall tune in tunes
        MsgBox ("About to play " + tune)
        Call uiws.PlayTune(tune)
    End Forall
End Sub
```

5. Choose File, Save to save the agent.

6. Preview the database within the Notes client by clicking the Notes preview icon located within the Preview toolbar.

7. When the database is opened in Notes, choose Actions, PlayTune.

This agent plays all the sounds that it can find in your Windows directory—assuming, of course, that you have a sound card and speakers attached to your computer.

A few points should be made about the sample program. First, notice the `New` keyword that is found on the `Dim` line for the `NotesUIWorkspace` object. This keyword causes the `NotesUIWorkspace` object to be created and assigned to the named variable. This is a shorthand notation for the following:

```
Dim uiws as NotesUIWorkspace
Set uiws = New NotesUIWorkspace
```

If you leave off the `New` keyword, you must use both statement lines and the `Set` keyword. The `tunes` variable was declared as a `Variant`. This is because it will be returned from the `GetListOfTunes` method as an array. Notice that a `Set` keyword on the assignment of an array is not used.

Finally, a `Forall` statement is used to loop through the list of items in the array. This is a very convenient construct of LotusScript. This statement type is not available in Java, but you can make good use of it here with LotusScript. Normally when you do some sort of loop, you need a counter, you must initialize it, and you must know the bounds of your array so that you don't go past the end. You don't need to do any of these things with the `Forall` statement.

The `Forall` statement in this example uses the variable `tunes` and successively assigns it to each of the values found in the array. The first iteration through the loop uses the first value of the array. The second iteration uses the second array item, and so forth. The loop automatically stops when there are no more items in the array. The loop variable itself—in this case, `tunes`—must not be declared in a `Dim` statement in the program. The `Forall` statement acts as its declaration.

Of course, the middle of the loop displays the name of the tune about to be played and then plays it. Other ways to use the `PlayTune` method are to attach a WAV file to a form and then, within the `PostOpen` method, play the tune. The tunes don't have to be musical sounds; any WAV file can be played. One real business use might be to have verbal instructions or help associated with a form. With a little imagination, you might come up with several other applications for this feature.

Using the `OpenFileDialog` and `SaveFileDialog` Methods

The `OpenFileDialog` and `SaveFileDialog` methods of the `NotesUIWorkspace` class make it easy to provide a dialog box for opening or saving files. Although in Release 4.*x* of Notes you could use the `DialogBox` function to create your own simplistic open and save dialog boxes, it was typically too much trouble. With the two new functions, it is very easy to create file dialog boxes. Here is the syntax for `OpenFileDialog`:

```
uiws.OpenFileDialog(Multsel, [Title$ [, Filters$ [, Initialdir$ [,
Initialfile$]]]]) as Variant
```

The `Multsel` parameter is a Boolean and should be `true` if you want the user to be able to use multiple selections. The value should be `false` if you want the user to select only one filename from the dialog box. All the other parameters are string values.

The `Filters$` parameter is specified by pairs of items. The first string of the pair is the prompt that should appear in the dialog box; the second is the file specification. Each text string is separated from the others by a vertical bar. When specifying the files, be sure not to have any spaces, or the dialog box will not show your files.

In the following example, there are two pairs of items. The result is an array of strings specifying the files that the user has selected. The result is `Empty` if the user clicks Cancel. This sample code can be used in a Notes `Form` event, such as `Postopen`:

```
Dim uiws as New NotesUIWorkspace
Dim files as Variant
files = uiws.OpenFileDialog(True, "Open Sesame", "Text Files|*.txt|HTML
Source|*.html", "C:\Windows")
if IsEmpty(files) Then
    MsgBox "You clicked Cancel!"
    Exit Sub
End If
Forall file in files
    MsgBox "You selected " + file
End Forall
```

Figure 24.2 shows you the Open Sesame dialog box that is produced by the Notes client.

This example shows the Open Sesame dialog box and then either displays a message if the user clicks Cancel or displays the list of files selected.

The `SaveFileDialog` is very similar to `OpenFileDialog`. All the parameters except the first have the same meanings. Here is the syntax for the `SaveFileDialog` method:

```
uiws.SaveFileDialog(Showdir, [Title$ [, Filters$ [, Initialdir$ [,
Initialfile$]]]]) as Variant
```

Figure 24.2
The Lotus Notes Open
Sesame dialog box.

The Showdir parameter is a Boolean and should be true if you want to show the user a directory dialog box. The user will be able to select only a directory but will not be able to specify a filename. The value should be false if you want the user to be able to specify a filename as well as the directory from the dialog box. All the other parameters are string values. The result is Empty if the user clicks Cancel. Here is some sample code:

```
Dim uiws as New NotesUIWorkspace
Dim files as Variant
files = uiws.SaveFileDialog(True, "Save Sesame", "Text Files|*.txt|HTML
Source|*.html", "C:\Windows")
if IsEmpty(files) Then
    MsgBox "You clicked Cancel!"
    Exit Sub
End If
Forall file in files
    MsgBox "You selected " + file
End Forall
```

In this example, Filters$ is ignored, but it's included here to show how you would use it if the first parameter were false. Figure 24.3 shows you the Save Sesame dialog box if the first parameter is set to true. Notice that you can specify only the directory.

Figure 24.3
The Lotus Notes Save
Sesame dialog box
using the directory
option.

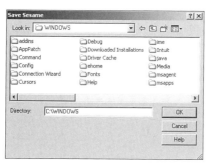

24

USING THE `PickListCollection` AND `PickListStrings` METHODS

In addition to the file dialog box functions, two methods of `NotesUIWorkspace` support a function similar to the `@PickList` function. These two new methods are `PickListCollection` and `PickListStrings`. Both methods take as arguments a dialog type code, multiple selection Boolean, server, database, view, title, and prompt. `PickListStrings` also contains a column number as a last parameter. Here is the syntax for these methods:

```
Set NotesDocumentCollection = uiws.PickListCollection(Type%, Multsel, Server$,
DbFileName$, ViewName$, Title$, Prompt$ [, Category$])StringArrary =
uiws.PickListStrings(Type%, Multsel [, Server$] [, DbFileName$] [, ViewName$]
[, Title$] [, Prompt$] [, Column%])
```

`PickListCollection` returns a `NotesDocumentCollection` object of the documents selected. If you enable multiple selection, the collection may have more than one value. The Type field must be specified as `PICKLIST_CUSTOM`. All other fields except `Category$` are required. You can specify the `Server$` field as an empty string that indicates the local machine. You must include the database filename, even if the LotusScript program is running within the same database. If you include the optional `Category$` parameter, the view must be categorized and the method displays only the single category specified. If you click Cancel from the dialog box, this method returns a `NotesDocumentCollection` with no elements. Otherwise, the method returns a `NotesDocumentCollection` containing the documents that were selected.

`PickListStrings` returns an array of strings. You can specify the following values for Type: `PICKLIST_NAMES`, `PICKLIST_ROOMS`, `PICKLIST_RESOURCES`, and `PICKLIST_CUSTOM`. If you specify `PICKLIST_CUSTOM`, all the optional parameters are required. The values for the strings are the values that are found in the specified column. If you enable multiple selection, the array may contain several values. Even if you turn off multiple selection (only a single return value), the result is an array with only one element. If you click a category row within a categorized view (not a real document row), this method returns an empty string within the array. If you click Cancel from the dialog box, this method returns `Empty`.

> **NOTE**
>
> A difference exists among the three values `Nothing`, `Empty`, and `Null`. `Nothing` is used for object references (such as a `NotesDocumentCollection`) that are uninitialized. Regular variables, such as `Variants`, contain the value `Empty` when they are uninitialized. `Null` is actually a valid value that is typically used to indicate "no answer." For more information, see Chapter 21, "LotusScript Variables and Objects," in the section "Understanding EMPTY, NOTHING, and NULL."

USING THE `Prompt` METHOD

The `Prompt` method is another useful method from the Formula language that has now been implemented in LotusScript. In the Formula language, `@Prompt` is useful for simple user prompts. The syntax in LotusScript is shown here:

```
Variant = uiws.Prompt(Type%, Title$ , Prompt$ [, default] [, values])
```

The Type% parameter may be one of the following values:

```
PROMPT_OK
PROMPT_YESNO
PROMPT_YESNOCANCEL
PROMPT_OKCANCELEDIT
PROMPT_OKCANCELLIST
PROMPT_OKCANCELCOMBO
PROMPT_OKCANCELEDITCOMBO
PROMPT_OKCANCELLISTMULT
PROMPT_PASSWORD
```

The Title$ parameter is the dialog box title, and the Prompt$ parameter is the prompt to display. The default value is used as the default input value. The values parameter is used to populate the dialog box options and is either a string or an array of strings.

The return value is an integer for Types PROMPT_OK, PROMPT_YESNO, and PROMPTYESNOCANCEL. Type PROMPT_OKCANCELLISTMULT returns an array of strings, and all the other Types return a string value. If you click Cancel, the return value is Empty.

THE NotesUIDatabase CLASS

The NotesUIDatabase class represents the database that is currently being used by the workstation user. You can obtain a NotesUIDatabase object from the CurrentDatabase property of the NotesUIWorkspace class. Alternatively, and more commonly, the NotesUIDatabase class is used via event handlers.

Here are the NotesUIDatabase events:

- **PostDocumentDelete**—Called just after a document is deleted from the database. You are passed a NotesUIDatabase object.

- **PostDragDrop**—Called just after a drag-and-drop event in the database. You are passed a NotesUIDatabase object, the alias of the design element within the database, and a continue parameter.

- **PostDropToArchive**—New function within Release 6, called just after a document is dropped into a database archive. If you set the continue parameter to true, the drop operation succeeds; if you return false for the continue parameter, the operation fails.

- **PostOpen**—Invoked *after* the QueryOpen and PostOpen events of the NotesUIView.

- **QueryClose**—Invoked just before the database is about to close. You are passed the NotesUIDatabase and also a continue parameter. If you set the continue parameter to true, the database closes; if you return false for the continue parameter, the database does not close.

- **QueryDocumentDelete**—Called just before the deletion of one or more documents. You can obtain the documents that will be deleted by referring to the Documents property of the NotesUIDatabase class. If you return true in the continue parameter, the documents are deleted; if you return false, the documents are not deleted.

24

- **QueryDocumentUnDelete**—Called just before the undeletion of one or more documents. You can obtain the documents that will be undeleted by referring to the Documents property of the NotesUIDatabase class. If you return true in the continue parameter, the documents are undeleted; if you return false, the documents are not undeleted.

- **QueryDragDrop**—Called just before a drag-and-drop event in the database. You are passed a NotesUIDatabase object, the alias of the design element within the database, and a continue parameter.

- **QueryDropToArchive**—New function within Release 6, called just before a document is dropped into a database archive. If you set the continue parameter to true, the drop operation succeeds; if you return false for the continue parameter, the operation fails.

In addition to the Documents property mentioned previously, you can also obtain the back-end NotesDatabase object by referring to the Database property of the NotesUIDatabase object.

You can open a view by calling the OpenView method of NotesUIDatabase.

THE NotesUIView CLASS

The NotesUIView class represents the view that is currently being used by the workstation user. You can obtain a NotesUIView object from the CurrentView property of the NotesUIWorkspace class. The NotesUIView class can also be accessed via event handlers. Several of the NotesUIView events occur only in a Calendar view. Therefore, you will not normally be concerned with these events.

THE NotesUIView EVENTS

Here are the NotesUIView events:

- **InViewEdit**—New with Release 6, users can edit a document through its View column. For example, you can press Ctrl and click a To Do item within your task list to edit a task's subject. This event is called when a user enters an editable view column entry, when a user exits an editable view column entry, or after the validation of a column entry of a new or existing document.

- **PostDragDrop (Calendar view)**—Called just after a calendar drag-and-drop operation.

- **PostEntryResize (Calendar view)**—Called just after a resize operation within a Calendar view.

- **PostOpen**—Occurs after the view has been opened.

- **PostPaste**—Called just after a document has been pasted within the view.

- **QueryAddToFolder**—Invoked before a document is added to a folder.

- **QueryClose**—Invoked just before the view is about to close. You are passed the NotesUIView and also a continue parameter. If you return true, the view closes; if you return false for the continue parameter, the view does not close.

- **QueryDragDrop (Calendar view)**—Called before a drag-and-drop operation. If you want to allow the drag-and-drop to continue, set the continue parameter to true. If it is set to false, the operation is aborted.

- **QueryEntryResize (Calendar view)**—Called before a resize operation. If you want to allow the resize to continue, set the continue parameter to true. If it is set to false, the operation is aborted.

- **QueryOpen**—Called before opening a view. If you want to allow the view to open, set the continue parameter to true; if not, set it to false.

- **QueryOpenDocument**—Called before the opening of a document within a view. If you want to allow the document to open, set the continue parameter to true. If the parameter is set to false, the document does not open.

- **QueryPaste**—Invoked to request permission to perform a paste operation within the view. It is allowed if continue is set to true.

- **QueryRecalc**—Invoked before a view is refreshed. You can perform operations at this point; if you return true for the continue parameter, the view is recalculated and refreshed. If you return false, the view is not refreshed.

- **RegionDoubleClick (Calendar view)**—Called when a user double-clicks a date within the Calendar view. You can find out where the user double-clicked by obtaining the CalendarDateTime property of the NotesUIView class.

In addition to the CalendarDateTime property mentioned previously, you can obtain the back-end NotesView object by referring to the View property of the NotesUIView object. The Documents property can be used to obtain the selected documents for the various events.

THE NotesUIView METHODS

The NotesUIView class contains three methods: Close, Print, and SelectDocument. As you might expect, the new Close method with Release 6 closes the active view. The Print method is used to print one or more documents from the current view. The SelectDocument method is used to select a document.

The syntax for the Print method is as follows:

```
Call notesUIView.Print([nCopies% [,fromPage% [,toPage% [, draft [, pageSeparator%
[, formOverride$ [, printView [, dateRangeBegin [,dateRangeEnd]]]]]]]]])
```

You can specify the following:

- **nCopies**—Number of copies.

- **fromPage**—Starting page. Using 0 means all.

- **toPage**—Ending page. Using 0 means all.

- **draft**—True to print the document in draft mode.

- **pageSeparator**—The page separator.

- **formOverride**—Whether you want to override the documents form for printing.

- **printView**—True to print the view rather than the selected documents themselves.
- **dateRangeBegin**—Beginning date of a Calendar view to print.
- **dateRangeEnd**—End date of a Calendar view to print.

The SelectDocument method is used to select documents within a view. You can use the SelectDocument method in conjunction with the Print method for selecting and printing multiple documents from the view. The syntax for the SelectDocument method is shown here:

```
Call NotesUIView.SelectDocument(document)
```

THE NotesUIDocument CLASS

The NotesUIDocument class is probably one of the most important front-end classes (along with NotesUIWorkspace). The NotesUIDocument class represents the current document for the user. The front-end methods enable you to simulate operations of the user. For example, you can move among the various fields in the document, select strings, and cut, copy, and paste information. You can also query the status for information, such as the current field, and determine whether the document is in edit mode and whether it has been saved yet (that is, whether it is a New document).

Probably the most important feature of the NotesUIDocument class is the capability of getting and setting information into fields within the document. With this capability, in conjunction with the NotesUIDocument events, you can perform various field validations, calculations, or translations. Although you can perform validation and translation with field formulas, by using a NotesUIDocument, you can centralize all your consistency-checking logic in one place. This makes it easier to perform logic that might be based upon the contents of multiple fields. When you use field-validation logic, your code is spread among the various fields, and it is harder to read and debug the code.

Another point that might be confusing if you have not done much LotusScript programming is that the NotesUIDocument events are actually programmed while you are editing a form. In the Design pane, you select forms and you create a new form, but the InfoList for a form contains all the events for the NotesUIDocument class. Forms and documents are tied together, but if you are coming from the purely LotusScript programming side, you might wonder where you can find the NotesUIDocument events.

Here is an example of calculating sales tax from document fields:

```
Sub Queryclose(Source As Notesuidocument, Continue As Variant)
    Dim dTotal As Double      ' Total sales amount
    Dim dTaxRate As Double    ' You could also look the sales tax rate up from a
                                table or database
    Dim dSalesTax As Double   ' Amount of sales tax
    Dim strAmount As String   ' String field value
    dTaxRate = 0.0675    ' Hard code this for the example
    dTotal = Cdbl(Source.FieldGetText("Amount1")) ' Get first amount from field
            in document and convert to numeric
```

```
        dTotal = dTotal + Cdbl(Source.FieldGetText("Amount2")) ' Get second amount
               from field in document and convert to numeric and add
        dSalesTax = dTotal * dTaxRate ' Calculate the Sales tax
        Call Source.FieldSetText("Total",Format(dTotal+dSalesTax, "Currency")) '
               Format the value and put it back in the document
        Source.Save ' You MUST call Save to save these values back to the database
        Continue = True ' Continue with Close
End Sub
```

In this simple example, two fields are accessed and then added, sales tax is calculated on the total, and then the result is saved back to two fields within the document. This is not a polished application because normally you would do much more error checking. Also, we've just supplied an arbitrary sales tax rate. You could look up a rate like this in a view within the current database or another external source.

You should notice a few points about this example:

- The NotesUIDocument already has been allocated and initialized before entry to this routine.

- You can use the FieldGetText routine to get the value of a field in the document. The return value is a string. If you will do computations on it, you must convert it to a number.

- You can use the FieldSetText routine to store the value back in the document.

- You must call Save to save your updated document. If you forget to do this, the values that you create affect only the in-memory copy of the data and are not stored back in the database.

THE NotesUIScheduler CLASS

Within Release 6, developers can include an embedded scheduler within a form to enable users to utilize the group-scheduling features within custom Notes applications. The NotesUIScheduler class gives you programmatic access to an embedded scheduler being used within a form or subform.

24

CHAPTER 25

DATABASE, VIEW, AND DOCUMENT CLASSES IN LOTUSSCRIPT AND JAVA

In this chapter

LOTUSSCRIPT VERSUS JAVA SYNTAX

This chapter reviews both the LotusScript and Java versions of classes. They represent the same conceptual model, so it shouldn't be difficult to move between the languages. However, be aware that each language has a slightly different syntax. For example, in LotusScript, the classes all begin with the word Notes, so the database class is NotesDatabase. In Java, Lotus dropped the Notes prefix, so it is just the Database class. Throughout this chapter, the lowercase word *database* refers to the Domino Object Model (DOM) conceptual class, the word NotesDatabase refers to the LotusScript implementation, and the capitalized word Database refers to the Java implementation.

To avoid redundancy, we will not review all the methods for LotusScript and Java for each class. However, we will demonstrate some LotusScript and some Java using different methods of each. That way, you can learn not only the classes, but also the two different styles of programming. Let's begin with the database class because it is the container for the other classes.

THE Database CLASSES

25

As discussed in previous chapters, the Domino Object Model is the conceptual framework for working with Domino objects. The database class gives you information about the database as a whole and provides functions to access the internal components of a database, such as its forms, views, and documents.

THE LOTUSSCRIPT NotesDatabase CLASS

The LotusScript NotesDatabase class contains more methods and properties than any other LotusScript class, with more than 100 methods and properties. You can create a NotesDatabase object either with the New keyword or by accessing properties or methods from other objects. For example, you can use the Database property of the NotesUIDatabase class, as mentioned previously, or you can use the GetDatabase method of the NotesSession class. As a matter of fact, you can create a new NotesDatabase object from an existing NotesDatabase object with one of several methods, such as CreateReplica.

CREATING A NEW NotesDatabase OBJECT

Before moving on, let's clarify a point that might be confusing. Suppose you create a NotesDatabase object with the New keyword, for example, like this:

```
Dim dbTemp as New NotesDatabase("","Temp")
```

The first parameter to the New NotesDatabase method is the server name, which, in this case is empty, indicating the local drive. The second parameter is the Notes database name.

What happens here? Are you creating a new Notes/Domino database file on the disk or server? Are you creating a database file in memory that will later be stored on the disk or server?

The answer is that a new database file is *not* created. If you were using the preceding statement to attempt to create a new database on disk, you would be disappointed. A new disk file is not created as a result of the New keyword. An object of the class NotesDatabase is created in memory.

There is a difference between a Notes/Domino database file on disk and an object of the NotesDatabase class in memory, which is really a mechanism to manipulate the data found in a Notes database.

CREATING A NEW NOTES/DOMINO DATABASE

Now that you know that a New keyword creates an object in memory but not a database on disk, how can you create a real database? You create it with the NotesDatabase Create method, of course. Assuming that you have already created a NotesDatabase object in memory called dbobj, the Create method syntax is as follows:

```
Call dbobj.Create(strServer$, strDbFile$, boolOpen, [intMaxSize])
```

The first parameter is the server name, the second is the database filename, the third specifies whether the database file should be opened after it has been created, and the fourth is an integer specifying the maximum size of the database in gigabytes. The fourth parameter is optional; the maximum size you can specify is 4GB. This parameter applies only to databases that are created and saved in the Release 4.*x* format. Databases do not have a preset size limitation. You can create an R4.*x* database by giving the database an extension of .NS4 instead of .NSF.

You must be careful if you use the Create method because this method causes the database to be created without a template, with no views or forms. The database is considered uninitialized. A normal database must have at least one view to be opened normally by a user. This implies that after you have used the Create method to create the database, you must also add at least one view (via the user interface) so that users can use the database. With Release 6, design elements can be copied from other databases using the NotesNoteCollection class. Refer to the Lotus Designer Help documentation for more information about how to manipulate design elements.

The third parameter, which specifies whether the database should be opened, is also important. After creating or obtaining a NotesDatabase object, you must first open the database before you can access any of the database properties or methods. Opening a database in this context is similar to opening a file with a program. Opening the database within LotusScript does not cause the database to be opened in the user interface.

The fourth parameter specifies the maximum size of the database in gigabytes. When the database is created, it does not actually take this amount of space; it is much smaller. However, as documents are added, the maximum size is used as an absolute limit to the growth of the database file.

You can also create a Notes database on disk by calling one of the CreateCopy or CreateReplica methods of the NotesDatabase object. These methods copy design elements,

25

such as forms and views, from the source database. Notes databases created with these methods typically contain at least one view and are considered initialized. After they are initialized, a database can be opened in the Notes user interface. Without a view, a database cannot be opened by a user.

OPENING A NOTES/DOMINO DATABASE

If you have created the database with the Create method, you can open it directly with the third parameter. Suppose you create a NotesDatabase object like this:

```
Dim dbTemp as New NotesDatabase("","")
```

In this case, a server or database filename has not been specified. As you'd expect, this doesn't create an empty database on disk. Instead, this just creates a NotesDatabase object in memory. This object is not associated with any particular database file. If you later want to associate it with, for example, an existing database, you can use the Open method. This is the Open method's syntax:

```
Boolean = dbobj.Open(strServer$, strDbFile$)
```

After calling the Open method, the methods and properties of the NotesDatabase object can be accessed.

You can also open an existing database by just creating the NotesDatabase object in memory with the New method. For example:

```
Dim dbTemp as New NotesDatabase("","MyData")
```

If the MyData.NSF database exists (the .NSF is assumed), this statement both creates the object *and* opens the database. If MyData.NSF does not exist, you will not get an error. You can then later open an existing database by specifying an existing database name. Here is an example:

```
Dim dbTemp as New NotesDatabase("","NonData")   // No error if NonData does not
exist
Boolean = dbTemp.Open("", "MyData.NSF")         // Can open a different DB
filename
```

This example illustrates that you supply a database name on both the Dim/New statement and the Open method of the NotesDatabase class. However, if there is a discrepancy between the two names, the important name is the one supplied on the Open method, which overrides the name supplied on the Dim/New statement.

As an alternative to the Open method, you can use the OpenIfModified method. The following is the syntax for this method:

```
Boolean = dbobj.OpenIfModified(strServer$, strDbFile$, notesDateTime)
```

The OpenIfModified method examines the date specified in the third parameter and opens the file if it has been modified since that date. It returns True if the database was opened, and False if not.

This method is useful if you want an agent to process only databases that have been modified since a particular date.

The OpenWithFailover method enables you to attempt to open a database. If the database does not exist on the specified server, Domino attempts to find it on another server within the cluster. You must be using clustered Domino servers for the OpenWithFailover method to be effective. The syntax for this method is shown here:

```
Boolean = dbobj.OpenWithFailover(strServer$, strDbFile$)
```

The OpenByReplicaID method enables you to open a database if you know its replica ID. Here is the syntax of its use:

```
Boolean = dbobj.OpenByReplicaID(strServer$, strReplicaID$)
```

We review an example of OpenByReplicaID in Java in the next section.

THE JAVA DbDirectory AND Database CLASSES

In Java, the method with which you open a database is similar to its corresponding method in LotusScript; however, the access is slightly different. In Java, all classes are strictly hierarchical. This means that to access a lower-level object, you must have a copy of a higher-level object. All access begins at the top of the hierarchy with the Java Session class.

In LotusScript, the NotesDbDirectory class has only two methods (GetFirstDatabase and GetNextDatabase) and is used primarily just to traverse the available databases. In Java, however, the DbDirectory class is much more powerful and useful. In Java, the functions of creating and opening a database are within the DbDirectory class rather than the Database class itself. The Java Database class is used to access data within the database, not to open it.

Here is the beginning of a Java agent:

```
public void NotesMain() {
   try {
      Session session = getSession();
      AgentContext agentContext = session.getAgentContext();
      // (Your code goes here)
      DbDirectory dbd = session.getDbDirectory("");
      dbd.createDatabase("MyJavaDb");
```

In this Java version, you must first get a Session and a DbDirectory object before you can use createDatabase. The AgentContext object is not required for this example, but the Domino Designer gives it to you free.

The DbDirectory class contains the createDatabase, openDatabase, openByReplicaID, and openIfModified methods that are found in the NotesDatabase class of LotusScript. The createCopy, createFromTemplate, and createReplica methods are contained in the Java Database class.

Here is an example of how you might use openByReplicaID:

```
Session session = getSession();
AgentContext agentContext = session.getAgentContext();
```

```
DbDirectory dbDirLocal = session.getDbDirectory("");  // Local db directory
DbDirectory dbDirServer = session.getDbDirectory("BENTLEY");  // Server db dir
Database dbLocal  = dbDirLocal.openDatabase("MyJavaDb"); // Open the local db

// Now open the server replica of my local database
Database dbServer=dbDirServer.openDatabaseByReplicaID(dbLocal.getReplicaID());
// Now you can manipulate dbLocal and dbServer replica databases
System.out.println("Local title="+dbLocal.getTitle());     //Print out the title
System.out.println("Server title="+dbServer.getTitle());   //Print out the title
```

In this example, a local copy of a database was opened first. After the local copy is opened, the replica ID is accessed and used to open the server replica of the same database. This is useful because it works even if the server copy has a different filename, a different directory, and a different database title. You don't need to know any of these properties of the server database as long as you know that your local copy is a replica of the server version.

Tables 25.1 and 25.2 show the correspondence of the LotusScript and Java classes for databases. The first three columns contain LotusScript methods, and the last three show Java methods.

TABLE 25.1 LOTUSSCRIPT CLASSES

LotusScript

NotesSession	NotesDbDirectory	NotesDatabase	Session
GetDatabase			getDatabase
GetDbDirectory			getDbDirectory
	GetFirstDatabase		
	GetNextDatabase		
		Create	
		CreateCopy	
		CreateFromTemplate	
	createFromTemplate		
	createReplica	CreateReplica	
		Open	
		OpenByReplicaID	
		OpenIfModified	
		OpenMail	
		OpenURLDb	getURLDatabase
		OpenWithFailover	

TABLE 25.2   JAVA DATABASE CLASSES

Java	
DbDirectory	Database
getFirstDatabase	
GetNextDatabase	
CreateDatabase	
	CreateCopy
OpenDatabase	
OpenDatabaseByReplicaID	
OpenDatabaseIfModified	
OpenMailDatabase	
OpenDatabase	

DATABASE SECURITY

The major security mechanism for Domino databases is the Access Control List (ACL). ACLs are covered in detail in Chapter 17, "Access Control Lists (ACLs) and Database Security." This section presents a demonstration of how to programmatically obtain and change the ACL information for a database.

When your LotusScript or Java program runs, it is associated with a user ID. You cannot use your program to modify any ACL beyond any authority granted to the associated ID. As in the user interface, you must have manager access to modify the ACL for a database. Assuming that you have the proper authority, you can use the NotesACL class of LotusScript or the ACL Java class to create new ACL entries and traverse the existing entries.

In LotusScript, you can obtain the NotesACL class object via the ACL property of a NotesDatabase. When you have this object, you can get an entry via the GetEntry method or traverse the list of ACL entries with the GetFirstEntry and GetNextEntry methods of NotesACL. In Java, you get the ACL object via the getACL method within the Database class. The getEntry, getFirstEntry, and getNextEntry methods correspond to their LotusScript counterparts.

For each ACL entry, you use either the NotesACLEntry class in LotusScript or the ACLEntry class in Java. From the appropriate class, you can find the current level of the entry, get the associated roles, and query various authorizations for the entry.

The following LotusScript code demonstrates how a user's access control level can be read and programmatically modified:

```
Sub Initialize
```

25

```
    Dim session As New NotesSession
    Dim db As NotesDatabase
    Dim acl As NotesACL
    Dim aclEntry As NotesACLEntry

    Set db = session.CurrentDatabase ' Set database variable to current database
    Set acl = db.ACL
    Set aclEntry = acl.GetEntry (Inputbox("Name of ACL entry?")) ' Get the name of
a user

    Select Case aclEntry.Level
    Case ACLLEVEL_NOACCESS
        level = "No access"
    Case ACLLEVEL_DEPOSITOR
        level = "Depositor"
    Case ACLLEVEL_READER
        level = "Reader"
    Case ACLLEVEL_AUTHOR
        level = "Author"
    Case ACLLEVEL_EDITOR
        level = "Editor"
    Case ACLLEVEL_DESIGNER
        level = "Designer"
    Case ACLLEVEL_MANAGER
        level = "Manager"
    End Select

    Messagebox aclEntry.Name & " has "& level & " access level."

    aclEntry.Level = ACLLEVEL_MANAGER 'Set user's access level to Manager
    Call acl.Save ' Save ACL

    Messagebox aclEntry.Name & " now has Manager access."

End Sub
```

ACCESSING DOCUMENTS WITHIN A DATABASE

To access documents within a Domino database, you can search or traverse collections of documents. Two different kinds of collections exist. The first kind of collection is a *view*. This is the traditional Notes/Domino concept that has been used to group documents. The LotusScript class is called `NotesView`, and the Java class is called `View`. Although both the LotusScript and Java classes' names refer to views, they can also be used to access documents within folders. You can use the `IsFolder` property of LotusScript or the `isFolder` method of Java to determine the type of object.

The second type of collection is simply called a *document collection*. This collection is dynamic and does not necessarily correspond to a folder or view of the database. It can contain any arbitrary set of documents and is not governed by a formula. The LotusScript class is called `NotesDocumentCollection`, and the Java class is called `DocumentCollection`. This type of class is generated automatically by Domino as the result of a full-text search or a search by key. The classes `NotesViewNavigator`, `NotesViewEntry`, and

`NotesViewEntryCollection` are related to views. These classes are used to navigate and manipulate the entries within a view.

THE LOTUSSCRIPT `NotesView` CLASS

You can use the `NotesView` class to traverse both folders and views. All the properties and methods are the same for folders and views. One property, `IsFolder`, is `true` for a folder and `false` for a view. Another property, `IsCalendar`, is `true` if the view is a calendar-style view.

NAVIGATING IN THE LOTUSSCRIPT `NotesView` CLASS

The navigation methods for a view include `GetFirstDocument`, `GetLastDocument`, `GetNextDocument`, `GetNextSibling`, `GetNthDocument`, `GetParentDocument`, `GetPrevDocument`, and `GetPrevSibling`. Each of these methods returns a `NotesDocument` object. You typically iterate through all the documents in a folder or view using these methods, processing or skipping each document as you go through them. You generally use `NotesDocument` methods and properties to access individual items of the document itself.

You can use the `GetChild` method to traverse response documents within a view. `GetChild` returns the first response document to the specified document. You can find additional children by using the `GetNextSibling` method. Navigating through the responses in this manner presents the documents in the same order as they appear within the view. An alternative method for retrieving the immediate responses to a particular document is to use the `Responses` property of the `NotesDocument` class. This property is a `NotesDocumentCollection` object and contains all the responses in an arbitrary order, not necessarily the same as any particular view.

25

SEARCHING IN THE LOTUSSCRIPT `NotesView` CLASS

You can filter a view by providing a full-text search query string and invoking the `FTSearch` method. After you have called `FTSearch`, the `NotesView` object refers only to the documents that meet the search criteria. You can use the `Clear` method to clear the previous search results. Here is an example:

```
Dim db As NotesDatabase
Dim view As NotesView
Set db = New NotesDatabase("","Cooking.nsf")
Set view = db.GetView("Recipes")
NumFound% = view.FTSearch("Chicken",0)
MsgBox "There were " + NumFound% + " chicken recipes"
Call view.Clear()
NumFound% = view.FTSearch("Beef",0)
MsgBox "There were " + NumFound% + " beef recipes"
```

The syntax for `FTSearch` is shown here:

```
NumFound% = viewname.FTSearch(SearchString$, MaxNum%)
```

The `FTSearch` method essentially filters the view to include only items matching the search string. The `GetFirstDocument`, `GetNextDocument`, and other traversal routines traverse only the found documents. *MaxNum* can be used to limit the number of documents you want to find. If you specify zero, all documents will be found. The result *NumFound* returns the actual number of documents found.

In addition to a full-text search, you can search for a single document by key(s) or obtain all the documents matching a set of keys in a view. To search for a single document by key, use the GetDocumentByKey method. Here is the syntax:

```
Set Notesdocument = viewname.GetDocumentByKey(keysStringarray [, boolExact])
```

You can specify multiple keys in the first parameter. Each key is an element of a string array. The keys are matched to the *sorted* columns of the view. The first document found is returned. If no documents match the keys, the value Nothing is returned. The second parameter, Boolean, is optional, and can be set to True to perform an exact search. If it is not supplied, False is assumed.

To retrieve all documents that match a set of keys, use the GetAllDocumentsByKey method. This method returns a NotesDocumentCollection object. Here is the syntax:

```
Set NotesDocumentCollection = viewname.GetAllDocumentsByKey(keysStringarray [,
boolExact])
```

The GetAllDocumentsByKey method returns the complete collection of all documents matching the keys found in the key array. As in the GetDocumentByKey method, only sorted columns are considered. They are matched with the keys supplied in the string array. Exact matching can be requested by using a value of True for the second parameter. False is assumed if the second parameter is not supplied. The documents returned by GetAllDocumentsByKey are not sorted.

THE LOTUSSCRIPT NotesViewEntry AND NotesViewEntryCollection CLASSES

Although Notes and Domino have had the NotesView class for several years, this class doesn't provide a few things. For example, you can use the NotesView class to traverse the documents in a view. As you go through each document, you receive a NotesDocument object. Although this is frequently sufficient, remember that a view can display more than just document fields. In particular, each column of a view can have a formula, which can be very complex. The NotesView class does not have a way to obtain the value that is actually presented in the view. This was previously accomplished using the ColumnValues property of the NotesDocument. It seems wrong to have view column values accessed through the document object, especially when the document can be in multiple views.

The NotesViewEntry and NotesViewEntryCollection classes of LotusScript and the ViewEntry and ViewEntryCollection classes of Java solve this problem and several more. A NotesViewEntry represents one row of a view. As mentioned, a row in a view can contain much more than just document fields. The entry for each column can be a complex formula. A NotesViewEntry represents one row and contains the values shown in each column, after evaluating any formulas. A NotesViewEntryCollection represents a set of rows. The Java classes ViewEntry and ViewEntryCollection correspond to their LotusScript counterparts.

There are several useful properties of the NotesViewEntry class. You can obtain the number of direct children with the ChildCount property and the number of descendants with DescendantCount. Siblings are tallied by using the SiblingCount property.

As mentioned, the column values can be obtained via the ColumnValues property. This property in LotusScript returns a Variant array, one value for each column within the view entry. The entries within this array are subscripted with a 0 origin. The corresponding Java method, called getColumnValues, returns a java.util.Vector. You should import java.util.* to make working with this vector more convenient. As in LotusScript, the vector subscripts begin at 0.

This Java agent (see Listing 25.1) cycles through rows of a view entry collection and prints the contents of the second column.

LISTING 25.1   JAVA AGENT THAT TRANSVERSES A VIEW

```
import java.util.Vector;

import lotus.domino.AgentBase;
import lotus.domino.AgentContext;
import lotus.domino.Database;
import lotus.domino.Session;
import lotus.domino.View;
import lotus.domino.ViewEntry;
import lotus.domino.ViewEntryCollection;

public class JavaAgent extends AgentBase
{
    public void NotesMain()
    {
        try
        {
            Session session = getSession();
            AgentContext agentContext = session.getAgentContext();
            Database db = agentContext.getCurrentDatabase(); // Get from
AgentContext
            View view = db.getView("MyView");
            ViewEntryCollection vec = view.getAllEntries(); // All rows
            ViewEntry ve; // One view entry row
            int i;
            int iCount = vec.getCount(); // Find out how many rows
            if (iCount >= 1)
            { // Do this only if there are rows
                ve = vec.getFirstEntry(); // The first row

                for (i = 1; i <= iCount; i++)
                { // Go through each row
                    Vector cv = ve.getColumnValues(); // Get the column values
                    System.out.println(cv.elementAt(1)); // Print second column
                    ve = vec.getNextEntry(ve); // Get the next row
                }
            }
        }
    }
```

continues

LISTING 25.1 CONTINUED

```
        catch (Exception e)
        {
            e.printStackTrace();
        }
    }
}
```

For a Java agent, you get the current database from the `agentContext` object, not the session object as you would with a LotusScript agent.

THE NotesViewNavigator CLASS

The `NotesViewNavigator` class is used to navigate through a view or a subset of a view. You can create a new view navigator from the `NotesView` class with a new method called `CreateViewNav`. The syntax is very simple:

```
Set NotesViewNavigator = viewname.CreateViewNav()
```

You can also create a view navigator from another view navigator, a category string, or the children of a specified navigator. When you have a navigator, you can perform the standard navigations `GetFirst`, `GetLast`, `GetNext`, `GetNextSibling`, `GetNth`, `GetPrev`, and `GetPrevSibling`. These methods get both documents and category items. You can also skip categories by using `GetFirstDocument`, `GetLastDocument`, `GetNextDocument`, and `GetPrevDocument`. You can get just the categories with `GetNextCategory` and `GetPrevCategory`.

The `ParentView` property can be used to get the `NotesView` object for the view that is associated with the view navigator.

Each of the navigation methods returns a `NotesViewEntry`. As discussed previously, a `NotesViewEntry` corresponds to a row within a view. Typically, as you navigate through the view, you examine data found within each row of the view. You do this by using the `ColumnValues` property of the `NotesViewEntry` object.

THE NotesViewColumn CLASS

Within the `NotesView` class is a property called `Columns`. The `Columns` property returns an array of `NotesViewColumn` objects. The `NotesViewColumn` class contains no methods, only properties. It includes properties such as `Formula`, `IsCategory`, `IsHidden`, `IsResponse`, `IsSorted`, `ItemName`, `Position`, and `Title`. These are properties of the view itself. These properties include formatting information, such as fonts, alignment, time, and date formatting. You can also now find out whether the class is sorted and whether the column contains a field or a formula.

TIP

> Do not take the values for `IsField` and `IsFormula` too literally. The intended defini-
> tion is that a column value is either a formula or a field. When one is `true`, the other is
> `false`. However, sometimes even when the definition is a single field, Notes returns a
> `true` value for `IsFormula` with the formula definition just the name of the field. So, a
> field name can sometimes be reported as a formula.

THE DocumentCollection CLASSES

The LotusScript `NotesDocumentCollection` class is very similar to the `NotesView` and the
`NotesViewEntryCollection` classes. The primary purpose of the `NotesDocumentCollection`
class is to be a container for documents. You can traverse the documents within the container, and you can perform certain operations on the entire collection of documents.

A few differences exist among these classes. The `NotesDocumentCollection` class can contain
any arbitrary collection of documents. In fact, one of the most common ways to generate an
object of this type is to use one of the search methods, such as the database `FTSearch`. A
`NotesView` and `NotesViewEntryCollection`, however, are both tied to a view, which means
that the collection itself has a selection formula that dictates document inclusion within the
collection.

Views are typically sorted, but a `NotesDocumentCollection` is not necessarily sorted. The
only way a `NotesDocumentCollection` is sorted is if it is the result of a full-text search.

To traverse a `NotesDocumentCollection`, you can use these methods: `GetFirstDocument`,
`GetLastDocument`, `GetNextDocument`, `GetNthDocument`, and `GetPrevDocument`. When you try to
navigate to a nonexistent document, you receive the special value `Nothing`.

You can call the `FTSearch` method of `NotesDocumentCollection` to further refine a search.
The collection is narrowed to the set of documents that meets the search criteria. The `Count`
property can be used to find the current number of documents within the collection. The
`Query` property can be used to find the query that resulted in the document collection if the
collection was generated by a search or full-text search.

The `PutAllInFolder` is used to put all the documents of a collection into a specified folder.
The `RemoveAllFromFolder` is used to remove documents of the collection from a given
folder. You can delete all the documents within the collection completely from the database
by using the `RemoveAll` method.

The `StampAll` method enables you to store a value in a given field on each of the documents
in the collection. Before you call the `StampAll` method, you must be sure to call the `Save`
method on any documents that you have modified. You do not need to call `Save` after
`StampAll`.

25

One important example of a `NotesDocumentCollection` is the `UnprocessedDocuments` property of `NotesDatabase`. In Java, you obtain this collection from the `AgentContext` class by calling the `getUnprocessedDocuments` method. This is one of the few differences in the logical class structure between LotusScript and Java. You can find out more about the differences in Chapter 24, "The `Session` and Front-End Classes."

The `UnprocessedDocuments` collection is used within either an agent or a view action. For an agent, this collection represents the result of a search or is the set of documents. For instance, if the agent is to operate on all unread documents, the unprocessed documents are the unread documents. In a view action, the collection contains the documents that have been selected by the user. After a document has been processed by an agent or view action, in LotusScript, you must call the `UpdateProcessedDoc` method of the `NotesSession` class; in Java, you must call the `updateProcessedDoc` method in the `AgentContext` class.

Alternatively, you can call the `UpdateAll` method of the `NotesDocumentCollection` class or `updateAll` in the Java `DocumentCollection` class.

This LotusScript sample agent handles all unprocessed documents. The routine `HandleDoc` is a generic name for your routine that should process a document. Typically, you locate this routine in a script library:

```
Sub Initialize
Dim session As New NotesSession
Dim db As NotesDatabase
Dim dc As NotesDocumentCollection
Dim doc As NotesDocument
Set db = session.CurrentDatabase        ' Obtain current database object
Set dc = db.UnprocessedDocuments        ' All documents to be handled
Set doc = dc.GetFirstDocument()         ' Get first document of collection
Do Until (doc is Nothing)               ' While we have a valid document

    Call HandleDoc(doc)                    ' User subroutine to handle document
    Call session.UpdateProcessedDoc(doc) ' Indicate this one now handled
    Set doc = dc.GetNextDocument(doc)   ' Get the next one
Loop

End Sub
```

THE `NotesForm` AND `Form` CLASSES

The LotusScript `NotesForm` and the Java `Form` classes enable you to get information about a form in a Domino database.

In LotusScript, the `NotesForm` class has 12 properties and 5 methods. These are the properties for this class:

- `Aliases`—A string array containing the form's aliases
- `Fields`—A string array of the field names
- `FormUsers`—A list of users who can create documents using the form

- **HttpURL**—A string that contains the URL for the form when used with the HTTP protocol

- **IsSubform**—A Boolean flag that is True if the form is a subform

- **LockHolders**—An array of type string that contains the usernames of the holders that have the form lock

- **Name**—The name of the form

- **NotesURL**—A string that contains the URL for the form when used with the Notes protocol

- **Parent**—A NotesDatabase object that contains the form object

- **ProtectReaders**—A flag that is set to True if the Readers list is protected from modification via replication

- **ProtectUsers**—A flag that is set to True if the FormUsers list is protected from modification via replication

- **Readers**—A list of users who can use the form to view documents

These are the methods for the NotesForm class:

- **GetFieldType**—Returns the field type for a particular field within the form. The type of the field is specified in Type within the NotesItem.

- **Lock**—Locks a form from being modified. For Lock to work properly, the IsDesignLockingEnabled property in NotesDatabase must be set to True.

- **LockProvisional**—Provisionally locks a form. For LockProvisional to work properly, the IsDesignLockingEnabled property in NotesDatabase must be set to True.

- **Remove**—Removes the form from the database.

- **Unlock**—Unlocks a form.

DESIGN DOCUMENTS

In Domino databases, essentially all information is stored in documents. Clearly, the information you store and enter in databases is stored this way, but information about your views, forms, and so forth is also stored in documents. These are special documents called design documents. For example, the definition of a Domino form is actually stored in a design document. This document has fields containing information about the form itself. As an example, look at Figure 25.1.

Figure 25.1 is an example from a Domino personal directory. The properties box displays the different fields of this design document. This properties box is different than what you'll see if you open the form for editing and request the properties. You can see from the figure that many of the fields begin with a dollar sign. This symbol signifies that this is an internal field used by Notes/Domino. In the figure, the $TITLE field has been highlighted. On the right side of the properties box, you'll see the form name as well as all the aliases for the

25

form. In addition to the name, this form has four aliases: Server Connection, Local, Remote, and Connection.

Figure 25.1
The design document properties for the Server Connection form within the Personal Address Book.

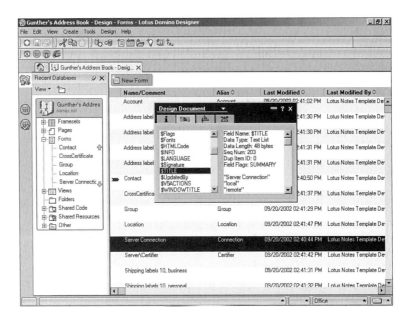

When you access an object of the NotesForm class, you are really accessing data that is stored within the design document for the form. As another example, if you specify that you want to restrict who can create documents with the form, a new field is inserted in the design document for the form. This field has the name $FormUsers. The FormUsers property of the NotesForm class enables you to retrieve or set this value. In essence, when you give it a new set of names, this field in the design document is updated with the values.

Just for fun, you might want to browse the design documents for some of the forms and views in some of your databases. You'll find it interesting to see some of the fields that have been created internally by Notes. Most of these internal fields are created as a result of property options set within the form or view properties. Other fields might track information, such as the time or user ID of users who edit documents.

THE LOTUSSCRIPT NotesDocument AND JAVA Document CLASSES

The LotusScript NotesDocument class and the Java Document class are used to access data stored within a document in a Domino database. The document classes are important because, with these classes, you can access and change information stored in the document fields. Although the LotusScript and Java classes are very similar, there are a few differences.

CREATING A DOCUMENT

One of the differences between LotusScript and Java is in the way you create a document object. In essence, the Java methods are a subset of the LotusScript methods, so we'll cover the LotusScript methods first.

CREATING A NotesDocument OBJECT IN LOTUSSCRIPT

The NotesDocument class is a back-end class that is used to manipulate values within a document in a Notes/Domino database. Because it is a back-end class, the NotesDocument class can be used in a Domino agent running on the server, whereas the NotesUIDocument cannot.

You can obtain a NotesDocument class object in one of many ways. The first is through the Document property of the NotesUIDocument class. Another way to get a NotesDocument is through one of the methods of the NotesDocumentCollection class. The NotesDocumentCollection class has methods such as GetFirstDocument, GetNextDocument, and GetNthDocument. Each of these methods returns a NotesDocument object.

The NotesDatabase and NotesView classes have properties and methods that return NotesDocumentCollection objects. The document collection can represent all the documents in a database, all the documents in a view, or the result of a search of some sort. After you have the NotesDocumentCollection object, you can retrieve a NotesDocument object by using one of the traversal methods.

The NotesDatabase class also enables you to obtain a NotesDocument object via the document's NoteID (unique within a database) or the document's Universal ID (uniquely identifies the document in all replicas). These methods are GetDocumentByID and GetDocumentByUNID.

After you have obtained a NotesDocument object from one of the many possible methods, you can manipulate the items found in the document by using the NotesDocument properties and methods.

To create a new document within a database, you can use the New keyword with the NotesDocument class, or you can use the CreateDocument method of the NotesDatabase class. This behavior is different from the behavior of the NotesDatabase class. With the NotesDatabase class, you cannot create a database with the New keyword. With the NotesDocument class, you can create a new document like this:

```
Dim session As New NotesSession
Dim db As NotesDatabase
Dim doc As NotesDocument
Set db = session.CurrentDatabase
Set doc = New NotesDocument ( db )
doc.Form = "MyForm"
Call doc.Save( True, True )
```

If you do not specify a form field value for the document, the document will not have a default form and will be displayed using the default form (if there is one) for the database. If there is no database default form, a document created this way cannot be displayed in the user interface. It is generally a good practice to include a field called Form and populate it with the form name. Also, if you do not call the Save method at the end of the script, the newly created document will not be saved in the database.

CREATING A Document OBJECT IN JAVA

In Java, there is no equivalent to the front-end NotesUIDocument, so you cannot obtain a document this way. However, you can use the DocumentCollection, Database, or View classes to obtain existing documents within the database.

As with LotusScript, the DocumentCollection class enables you to traverse the collection using methods such as getFirstDocument, getNextDocument, getPrevDocument, and getLastDocument. The Database class allows full-text searching to obtain a DocumentCollection, and you can also get documents by unique ID or by URL.

In LotusScript, you can create a new document with the New keyword, as shown in the previous section. This method is not available in Java. Because a strict hierarchical structure is enforced in Java, you cannot create a document object outside a container. Thus, the only way to create a new document object is to use the createDocument method of the Database class. Here is a Java agent to create a new document in a database:

```
import lotus.domino.*;

public class JavaAgent extends AgentBase {
public void NotesMain() {
  try {
    Session session = getSession();
    AgentContext agentContext = session.getAgentContext();
    Database db = agentContext.getCurrentDatabase(); // Get from AgentContext
    Document doc = db.createDocument();       // Create the document
    doc.appendItemValue("Form", "MyForm");    // Add form field to document
    doc.save();                               // Be sure to save it in database
  } catch(Exception e) {
      e.printStackTrace();
  }
}
}
```

This example is very similar to the LotusScript example. Remember, though, that in Java you obtain the CurrentDatabase from the AgentContext object, not the Session object. Also, the extended syntax form of assignment that is available in LotusScript is not available in Java. For example, in LotusScript, you can just specify this:

```
doc.Form = "MyForm"          ' In LotusScript we can use extended syntax
```

In Java, you must call the appendItemValue method of the document object to store the value within the document:

```
doc.appendItemValue("Form", "MyForm");   // In Java we must call a method
```

SAVING A DOCUMENT

As mentioned, if you do not call the Save method after creating or changing a document, your changes will not be reflected in the database.

The syntax of the Save method is as follows:

```
SavedOK = documentvar.Save(boolForce, boolMakeResponse [, boolMarkRead])
```

If you do not want to check the return value, you can use the Call keyword to invoke the Save method, as shown in the preceding example.

All three parameters of the Save method are Boolean variables. The first two parameters control what happens if another user has modified the current document since you accessed it in your program.

If the first parameter of the Save method is true, the document is saved even if another user has modified the document while the script is running. The MakeResponse parameter then is ignored. If the first parameter is false and the MakeResponse parameter is true, the document is saved as a new response document; if the MakeResponse parameter is false, the save is aborted. If the MarkRead parameter is true, the document is marked as read. The return value is true if the document was saved, and false if not. If there are conflicting saves of the same document, the following table shows how the conflict is resolved, depending upon the parameters used for Save. The return value is True if the document was saved, and False otherwise.

Force	MakeResponse	Action
True	—	Current document overwrites other versions saved since last access.
False	True	Current document becomes a response to other document saved since access.
False	False	Save is aborted if there was another save since access.

In Java, you can call the save method using the following syntax:

```
SavedOK = documentvar.save( [Force [, MakeResponse [, MarkRead]]])
```

If you do not specify Force or MakeResponse, they are both assumed to be False. Notice that in Java, the Force parameter is optional, but in LotusScript, it is not. The operation and document save resolution works the same as for LotusScript.

DELETING A DOCUMENT

You use the Remove method in LotusScript or the remove method in Java to delete a document from a database. Just as in the case of saving a document, the document may be modified by another user after you retrieve it and before you request a deletion. To handle this situation, you use the Force parameter. Here is the Java syntax:

```
RemovedOK = documentvar.remove(Force)
```

The LotusScript syntax is similar. If the Force parameter is True, the document is deleted even if there were changes. If Force is False, the deletion is aborted if there were any changes by another user.

In either case, the method returns True if the document was deleted, and False if it was not.

DOCUMENT PROPERTIES

You occasionally might need to query properties of a document. For example, you can query whether a document is new (that is, it has never been previously saved) by using the IsNewNote property of LotusScript or calling the isNewNote method in Java. Either one returns True if the document has not yet been saved in the database.

One new document property is available with Release 6 of Notes and Domino. It's called IsEncrypted in LotusScript and isEncrypted in Java. This property can be queried in LotusScript to tell whether an existing document is encrypted.

IsValid returns a Boolean value that is True if the document is valid (has not been previously deleted). IsValid is False if the document is a deletion stub. IsDeleted returns True if the document is now deleted and False if it is not deleted.

The Size property returns a Long (32 bits) value that contains the size of the current document in bytes. This size includes any file attachments.

You might find several time stamp properties of a document useful. The Created property is a time stamp of the date and time the document was created. The LastModified property is the date and time the document was last changed. The LastAccessed property is a time stamp of the last time the document was either read or written. Note that these three properties return dates in the LotusScript format, not the Domino Object Model format.

→ For a more complete discussion of the various date formats in Notes and Domino, **see** "Date and Time Variables and Objects," **p. 612** (Chapter 24).

DOCUMENT HIERARCHY

Documents in Domino can be either main documents or response documents. Response documents can be considered children of the main document. You might want to traverse documents based upon the document hierarchy.

The LotusScript IsResponse property of the NotesDocument class and the isResponse method in Java let you know whether a particular document is a response to another document. If True, the document is a response document; otherwise, it is a main document. You can then obtain the parent document through a two-step process. First, use the ParentDocumentUNID property in LotusScript or the getParentDocumentUNID method of Java. Either of these returns a string version of the UNID (Universal ID). The second step is to use the UNID string with the database LotusScript method GetDocumentByUNID or the corresponding Java method. Remember that the UNID identifies the document uniquely in all replica databases.

To change the status of a main document to a response document, you can use the MakeResponse method. The single parameter to this method is a NotesDocument object that should become the new parent. You would use this method to move a document within a database to a new or different document hierarchy. One application for this method is to create status documents for a given main document. When you change a document to a response document, you should also be sure to modify the form associated with the document to be a response form rather than a main form.

To find all the immediate response documents of a particular given document, you can use the Responses NotesDocument property. This property returns a NotesDocumentCollection that contains all the response documents. In Java, you use the getResponses method, which returns a DocumentCollection object. In either case, the responses returned are only first-level responses. To obtain lower-level response documents, you must recursively obtain these documents or use a loop structure. To find out how many documents are in the document collection, you can use the Count property of the document collection. Alternatively, you can loop through the document collection contents until one of the methods returns Nothing.

PROFILE DOCUMENTS

Profile documents have been in Domino since Release 4.5, but they are not prominently described or used. These special documents were created to improve performance on per-user types of information. They are special documents because they are design elements, not regular documents. This means that profile documents do not appear in any view in the user interface.

Profile documents are cached on the Domino server and are accessed via a two-level hash key method. This is quite different than the normal lookup and indexing that is done for regular documents in a view within a database. The model for profiles is that a database can contain several different types of profiles, each one with a set of users. For example, one program might use profile documents for user interface preferences, another might use them for report options, and a third might use profile documents for per-user workflow information. All three types of profiles can be stored in the same database. To obtain a profile document, you specify the name of the profile and then a key, which is usually the username.

One last rather odd characteristic of profile documents is that there is no explicit call to create a profile document. The first time you reference a profile document, it is created. So, to create a profile document in LotusScript, you call the NotesDatabase method GetProfileDocument. In Java, you call the equivalent getProfileDocument method of the Database class. Here is the LotusScript syntax:

```
NotesDocument = databasevar.GetProfileDocument(ProfileName$, UserName$)
```

Notice that the GetProfileDocument is a method of the database class, not the document class.

When you have a document, you can query whether it is a profile document by using the IsProfile property in LotusScript or the isProfile method in Java. The Key method of the document class returns the key (username) associated with the profile document, and the NameOfProfile property returns the name of the associated profile.

Before Release 5, there was no way to scan a database to find all the profile documents. Because you could not use a view (even a hidden view) to obtain them, it was possible for profile documents to become orphaned. The new calls `GetFirstProfileDoc` and `GetNextProfileDoc` enable you to traverse all the profile documents within a database. Here is the syntax:

```
NotesDocument = databasevar.GetFirstProfileDoc([ProfileName])
```

```
NotesDocument = databasevar.GetNextProfileDoc()
```

If you don't specify the profile name when you first call `GetFirstProfileDoc`, you will retrieve all the profile documents in the database. Profile documents provide a powerful feature, but because all the data is cached on the server, you should use this facility with care so that you don't get thousands of profile documents cluttering up the server's cache.

USING DOCUMENTS WITH FOLDERS

Folders are very similar to views. The major difference is that the documents contained in a view are selected by a formula, and documents in a folder must be placed there explicitly. The documents included within a view change dynamically as new documents are added or changed in the database.

The documents in a folder are typically placed there by a user using the drag-and-drop facilities in the user interface. Alternatively, you can write LotusScript or Java programs that add or remove documents from a folder. You use methods of the document class to perform these operations. To add a document to a folder in LotusScript, you specify the following:

```
Call documentvar.PutInFolder(Foldername$)
```

In Java, you use this:

```
documentvar.putInFolder(Foldername)
```

You specify the name of the destination folder. If the document is already in the folder, no error is generated and it remains in the folder. If the folder does not already exist, it is created and uses the default folder as the folder to clone.

To remove documents from a folder in LotusScript, you use the following:

```
Call documentvar.RemoveFromFolder(Foldername)
```

In Java, you use this:

```
documentvar.removeFromFolder(Foldername)
```

The document is removed from the specified folder. If it does not exist within the folder, no error is generated. You can find out in which folders a document resides. This is useful, for example, if you want to keep a document in a database but remove it from any folders. Previously, the only way to accomplish this was to go through all the folders of a database.

You can obtain the list of folder references by using the `FolderReferences` property. Here is the LotusScript syntax:

```
StringArray = documentvar.FolderReferences
```

This is the Java you would use:

```
java.util.Vector StringArray = documentvar.getFolderReferences()
```

DOCUMENT SECURITY

Domino has many security features designed to protect documents. Two of these strong security features are document encryption and document signing. Two types of encryption are used: one for documents using secret encryption keys, and the other for email, using public/private key encryption. Let's start with how the user interface works and follow with a brief summary of these capabilities and how to use encryption with LotusScript and Java.

Domino can encrypt documents using encryption keys. As mentioned, this facility is different from email encryption, which we'll review shortly. Actually, when you encrypt a document, the encryption is done on a field-by-field basis. You can encrypt some fields within a document and leave others without encryption. In the user interface, this decision is up to a designer. So, the phrase "to encrypt a document" really means to encrypt the encryptable fields within a document. It is also possible that even with encryptable fields, some documents are not encrypted. As a designer, the task is to define fields that might need to be encrypted by the user. Some, none, or all documents created with the form might actually encrypt data within the fields. As a designer, you can also specify default encryption keys to make encryption automatic for the user. As a LotusScript or Java programmer, you have some additional capabilities that are not available to an end user.

For any particular document, you can use several encryption keys. If a user has any of the keys available, that user can access the encrypted fields. So, after you create an encryption key, you must send it (usually via email) to any other user who will need to use it. The user's copy of the encryption key must be available in the user ID file. If it is not available, an encrypted field is not accessible.

The three roles are database designer, key creator, and key user. Of course, all three roles could be fulfilled by the same person.

Database Designer	Key Creator (User)	Key User
Define encryptable fields within database key(s)	Create encryption	Receive key(s) from creator
Specify default encryption keys	Send key(s) to any key users	Use key to encrypt or decrypt data

To create encryption keys, follow these steps:

1. To issue encryption keys, select the following commands from the Notes client menus: File, Security, User Security.
2. After entering your password, select Notes Data, Documents (see Figure 25.2).

Figure 25.2
Encryption keys are stored in your user ID file.

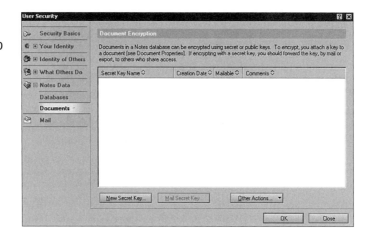

3. Click the New Secret Key button to create a new encryption key (see Figure 25.3). At this point, you can give the encryption key a name and an optional comment. The name you choose is important and will be used later.

Figure 25.3
The New Secret Encryption Key dialog box requests a key name and optional comments.

4. Click OK. After the encryption key is created, it is stored in your user ID file.

NOTE

You can create more than one encryption key and have more than one encryption key in your user ID file. Typically, a key name is associated with a particular group or function within your company, such as Sales or Engineering; or geography, such as Los Angeles; or a project, such as Manhattan Project. You could also use levels of keys, such as Top Secret, Medium Secret, and Indiscreet. Choose a name that will be informative to its users.

When your keys have been created, you can use the built-in facilities to email them to the appropriate people. Do this by clicking the Mail button on the Encryption dialog box while the key you want to send is highlighted.

To create encryptable fields in a Notes Form, follow these steps:

1. First create or edit a form within Domino Designer.

2. For each field you want to encrypt, highlight the field and open the properties box for that field. Go to the Advanced tab (the one with a beanie hat).

3. Under the Security options section, click the drop-down box and enable the option Enable Encryption for This Field. Selecting this option makes the field encryptable but does not actually encrypt any data.

4. As a designer, you can also specify default encryption for the form. If you do this, any documents created with the form are encrypted automatically by default. To accomplish this, open the Form properties box, click the Security tab (key icon), and specify one of the keys in the Default encryption keys field. This field displays only the encryption keys that are contained in your user ID file.

5. Save the form.

In the Notes client, a user can tell whether a particular field is encryptable; the small corners for the field are red for encryptable fields and white for normal fields. Only encryptable fields are encrypted. As a Notes user, here is how you can use keys to encrypt a document:

1. To encrypt a document, you must have keys stored in your user ID file. To use the keys with the user interface, create a document with a form with encryptable fields. You cannot encrypt fields unless they are encryptable.

2. Go to the Document properties box by selecting File, Document Properties.

3. Choose the Security tab (key icon). Under Secret Encryption Keys, enable the keys you want to use by placing a check mark next to them.

4. If you enable more than one key, then if the receiver has any of the keys, that person will be able to decrypt the document. The receiver does not need to have all the keys.

5. Close the dialog box and the document. The document will be encrypted after it is saved.

These steps show you how to create keys, enable encryption in forms, and encrypt a document using the user interface.

ENCRYPTING IN LotusScript AND Java

The model for encryption in LotusScript and Java is similar, but you have different capabilities with the programming interface.

With the programming interface, you cannot actually create the keys, and you cannot create forms with encryptable fields. After keys have been created and are stored in an ID file, you can use the keys to encrypt a document. In fact, with LotusScript or Java, you can create documents and encrypt fields that have not been specified as encryptable with the user interface.

Here is a small example of an agent to illustrate how to encrypt a document:

```
Dim session As New NotesSession
Dim db As NotesDatabase
Dim doc As NotesDocument
Dim item As NotesItem
Set db = session.CurrentDatabase
Set doc = db.CreateDocument()
doc.Body = "Test Data"
doc.Form = "TestForm"
Set item = doc.getFirstItem("Body")
item.IsEncrypted = True
doc.EncryptionKeys = "Top Secret"
doc.Encrypt
Call doc.save(True,True)
```

This example operates under several assumptions:

- You must create and have the encryption key Top Secret installed in your user ID file.
- A form called TestForm has been created in your database, with one field called Body.
- You have a view (the Default view is good enough) to view the document.

If you meet these assumptions, you can try the example. Notice several points in the example. To encrypt a field or set of fields, the following criteria must be met:

- You must set the IsEncrypted property of the item to True. This is what enables encryption for the field. This works even if the field has not been enabled for encryption in the user interface. In fact, the field does not have to appear in the user interface at all, so this could be a way to add additional protection for private data that you must keep within a document.

- You must set the EncryptionKeys property of the document to either a string or an array of strings naming the encryption key(s). If you don't specify any encryption keys, the user's public key is used to encrypt the document. After that, only the user who created the document will be able to decrypt the document (using that user's private key).

- Calling the Encrypt method of the document encrypts the document. If you don't have the keys specified in the EncryptionKeys property associated with your user ID, you will receive an error message. Note that you must also save the document for the encryption to be stored within the database. If you don't call Save, the database will not be updated with the encrypted version of the document.

To recap document encryption, remember that encryption is normally performed using one or more encryption keys. This is called a single-key method of encryption, as opposed to a dual-key or public-private key encryption. Both the creator and the reader of the document must have the same encryption key(s) installed in their respective user ID files. In the user interface, you can encrypt only fields that have been made encryptable by the form designer. In LotusScript or Java, you can encrypt any document field by setting the IsEncryptable property of the item and by calling the document method Encrypt. You do not need to use document encryption to encrypt mail; this is covered in the section "Mailing Documents and Mail Encryption" later in this chapter.

SIGNING DOCUMENTS

Another security issue is authenticity. How do you know when you are reading a document that it was actually created by the purported author? In the age of electronic documents, it is almost trivial to create electronic forgeries. Someone can create a document or email and pretend that it was created by someone other than the stated author. How can you combat this form of electronic fraud?

The answer is with electronic signatures. These digital signatures use dual-key, public-private encryption to validate the authenticity of documents or email. In essence, a *signature* is a field that has been encrypted with the author's private key. It can be decrypted by anyone holding the author's public key. If the public key can successfully decrypt the field, you know that it was created by the authentic author.

You create signed documents in a manner very similar to encrypting documents, although it is even easier. In fact, it involves just a single extra line of coding:

```
Call documentvar.Sign
```

Just call the Sign method of the NotesDocument class (or Document class of Java), and your document will be signed with your private key. If you execute this method on a server, the document is signed with the server's ID, not the effective user ID. This is almost never what you want to do.

Note that in Java, as usual, the sign method is lowercase and Java is case sensitive.

After a document is signed, you can query information about the document. You can find out whether the document is signed in LotusScript by using the IsSigned property. In Java, you use the isSigned method.

You can obtain the fully distinguished name of the signer by accessing the LotusScript property Signer or by calling the Java method getSigner. Either version returns a string result.

Finally, you can use the Verifier property in LotusScript to obtain the fully distinguished name of the ID that certified (verified) the user. In Java, use the getVerifier method.

MAILING DOCUMENTS AND MAIL ENCRYPTION

Mailing documents is very easy in Notes and Domino. After you have access to a document object, you just call the Send method. Mail automation in Notes and Domino is one of the factors that makes workflow applications easy to implement.

The syntax for sending mail in LotusScript is shown here:

```
Call documentvar.Send(boolAttachform, [recipientsStringArray] )
```

25

The first parameter is a Boolean variable. If it is True, the form associated with the document is mailed along with the document itself. This enables recipients to view the document from their mail database even if they don't have the form used to create the document. You can specify a string or an array of strings for the second parameter. These are the recipients of the message. If you leave this parameter off the Call statement, you must supply a field within the document named SendTo. If the field is not contained in the document, you must supply the recipients in the Call statement. If both a field in the document and a list of recipients are supplied, the field contents are ignored and the recipients specified in the Call are used instead.

In addition to the SendTo field within the document, you can include CopyTo and BlindCopyTo fields. These fields can contain one or more strings of user IDs. The CopyTo field is for the cc: list, and the BlindCopyTo field is for the bcc: list.

In Java, unlike LotusScript, you can leave off the Attachform parameter. The five variations for the Java send method of the Document object are shown here:

```
void send()

void send(String recipient)

void send(java.util.Vector recipients)

void send(boolean attachform, String recipient)

void send(boolean attachform, java.util.Vector recipients)
```

If you leave off the attachform parameter, it is assumed to be False. As with LotusScript, you can include the SendTo, CopyTo, and BlindCopyTo fields within your document to control who receives the message. If you have a SendTo and you specify recipients, the SendTo field in the document is ignored.

Three LotusScript Boolean properties (and three corresponding Java methods) control encrypting, signing, and saving messages when they are sent:

- **EncryptOnSend**—If True, the message automatically is encrypted with the recipient's public key when the message is sent. If there are multiple messages, each message is encrypted with the specific recipient's public key.
- **SignOnSend**—If True, the message automatically is signed with the sender's private key.
- **SaveMessageOnSend**—If True, the message automatically is saved when it is sent.

Any time you send mail with the Send LotusScript method or the send Java method, Domino adds one extra field to the document, called $AssistMail. This value is set to a 1, to indicate that the document was sent by a program.

On the receiving end, you can query the status of this field with the SentByAgent method to query. If $AssistMail is 1, you get a True result. This property is useful if you are generating automatic responses to incoming mail. For example, if you are writing an out-of-office agent, you can send responses back to people who have sent mail, but you can ignore any incoming mail sent by a program. This feature reduces the risk of two programs exchanging out-of-office messages and clogging up the mail system.

The final mail-oriented call is the `CreateReplyMessage` method. This method creates a reply message to the current document. The current document must contain a field called `From`. The syntax of the call is shown here:

```
Call documentvar.CreateReplyMessage(boolReplyToAll)
```

The `ReplyToAll` parameter is a Boolean variable. If it is `False`, the reply message is sent only to the name found in the `From` field. If it is `True`, the current document's `CopyTo` and `BlindCopyTo` fields are copied over to the new reply message. The result is that all recipients of the original message receive the reply message.

25

CHAPTER 26

USING FIELDS AND ITEMS IN LOTUSSCRIPT AND JAVA

In this chapter

UNDERSTANDING FIELDS, FORMS, ITEMS, AND DOCUMENTS

Internally within Notes and Domino, the terminology used to describe the various structures and design elements is different from the terminology normally used to describe Domino among its users and developers. Although some of the terms used underneath the covers of Notes and Domino are simply historical conventions, others are important concepts that describe the basic structures of the platform.

Documents are actually called *notes* internally. This isn't surprising—this is probably how the product itself got its name. Internally, there are notes for just about everything from design document notes, which hold attributes about forms, views, and other design elements, to the database icon, and the About and Using documents.

This brings us to fields within a document. Although externally they are called *fields*, internally they are referred to as *items*. If you know that regular fields are called items, you recognize that the name `RichTextItem` is just a special kind of item.

Whether you're designing Domino applications or are simply an end user of the Notes client, a basic understanding of how these key internal components are architected will improve your effectiveness and productivity.

A Notes document is made up of many items. Frequently, though not always, only one form is associated with a document. The form is the looking glass or template through which you can view the information within a particular document. Thus, although typically you might think of the fields on the form as the items of the document, clearly they do not need to be in a one-to-one relationship.

Notes and Domino internally use the word *item* to refer to the actual data within the document. The word *field* is used to represent fields on a form. So, remember that forms contain fields, and documents contain items.

At the risk of oversimplifying, you can think of the items within a document as a list of name-value pairs. For example, if a document had an item named `FirstName` with a value of `Jeff`, FirstName and Jeff would be considered the name-value pair. Of course, each item has several other attributes, such as its data type and modification date, but the most important characteristics of an item are its name and value.

Keep in mind that, within a document, you can have more than one item with the same name. A document can contain two different items with the name `Subject`, for example—each with a different value. Arranging your forms this way is not normally considered a good programming practice, however. Typically, you should arrange your forms to contain fields with unique names. If you need several values, remember that a single item can contain multiple values of the same type, and you can use separate fields to hold additional information.

N O T E

> The `NotesDocument` method is called `GetFirstItem` instead of just `GetItem` because there might be multiple items with the same name. This also serves as a reminder so that, in programming, you don't assume that only one item in your document has a given name.

A `NotesItem` WITHIN A `NotesDocument`

The `NotesItem` class implements the concept of an item within a document. In LotusScript, you can create or get a `NotesItem` class object via several means. You can create a new `NotesItem` object with the `New` keyword, or you can obtain one via a method call of another object.

In the `NotesDocument` class, you can call `AppendItemValue`, `CopyItem`, `GetFirstItem`, or `ReplaceItemValue` to obtain a `NotesItem` class object. Here are some examples:

```
NotesItem = AppendItemValue(name, value)
NotesItem = CopyItem(item, newname)
NotesItem = GetFirstItem(name)
NotesItem = ReplaceItemValue(name, value)
```

`AppendItemValue` appends a new item to the document with the given name and value. If the name already exists, a separate item with the same name is created. `CopyItem` uses the new name and makes a copy of the original item's value. `GetFirstItem` returns the first item with the specified name. If there is more than one item with the same name, you must use the `Items` property of the `NotesDocument` class to traverse the list of items. `ReplaceItemValue` is usually preferable to `AppendItemValue`. `ReplaceItemValue` replaces an item's value with a new value. If the item does not exist, it is created.

Normally, when you refer to properties of an object, you use the "dot" notation. For example, within a `NotesSession` object called `session`, you could refer to `session.CurrentDatabase` to access the property. The `NotesDocument` class in LotusScript contains a special feature called "extended class" syntax that enables you to write programs that are a little easier to create and read.

With this syntax, you can refer to item names within a document as if they were properties of the class. For example, suppose you have a document in a `NotesDocument` object variable called *doc* that contains a field item called *LastName*. You can assign a value to this item with the following syntax:

```
doc.LastName = "Smith"
```

This is equivalent to the following line:

```
Call doc.ReplaceItemValue("LastName", "Smith")
```

Clearly, even though `LastName` is really not a property of the `NotesDocument` class, it is much simpler and more intuitive to use the first form of the assignment. You might have already used this syntax in one of your LotusScript programs without realizing that it was an extended class syntax.

26

Unfortunately, Java does not allow you to use the extended syntax, so you must use the replaceItemValue method. This is because Java checks the syntax of your Java program when it is compiled, not when it executes. At compile time, there is no way for the compiler to know whether the item will exist in the document, and the Java language does not allow the extended syntax. In the next section, let's review how you would use an item within a document using Java.

MANIPULATING AN Item WITHIN A DOCUMENT USING JAVA

In Java, the Item class corresponds to the LotusScript NotesItem class. The NotesItem properties of LotusScript correspond directly to similarly named methods in Java. For example, the IsAuthors property of LotusScript corresponds to the isAuthors method of Java. Both return a Boolean value and indicate whether the item is an Authors item. IsEncrypted, IsNames, IsProtected, IsReaders, IsSaveToDisk, IsSigned, and IsSummary all have a similar correspondence between the LotusScript property and the Java method.

The properties of LotusScript just described are all read/write, so in LotusScript you can change the property's value by assigning it a new value. In Java, you must call a method to change the value. The methods to change the value all begin with the prefix set. Thus, the method to set the IsAuthors property is called setAuthors in Java. The methods setEncrypted, setNames, setProtected, setReaders, setSaveToDisk, setSigned, and setSummary all perform the set function for the corresponding property of the item.

Here is an example of obtaining and setting a property in Java:

```
Item it = doc.getFirstItem("Name");      // Get an Item object
boolean b = it.isAuthors();              // Check if is an authors item
it.setAuthors(true);                     // Set it to be an authors item
```

Setting and obtaining the value of a document item in Java presents unique problems that do not occur with other objects. The reason is that document items are similar to LotusScript variants. That is, the type of value that is stored in an item might be a number, a text string, a date, or even a multiple-value item. Java, on the other hand, is a strongly typed language in which the data types must be defined at the time you compile your program.

The Domino Java implementation avoids some of these problems by adding some extra methods for getting and setting item values, with each method having a particular type. For example, there is a getValueInteger method as well as a getValueDouble method. In addition, you can get String and DateTime values. As you would predict, there are also setValueInteger and setValueDouble methods, as well as setValueString and setDateTimeValue, to set the corresponding data types.

TIP

> For more information about any method of Domino Objects, please refer to the Help within Domino Designer 6.

Several methods of the Item class in Java have names that all sound as if they might do the same thing. Although these names appear to have a similar purpose, they perform different functions. Here is an explanation:

- **getName**—Returns the item name.

- **toString**—Appears in many of the Domino Java classes and overrides the Java definition in java.lang.Object. For an item, it returns the item's name, not its value.

- **getText**—Returns the text (string) representation of the value of the item. This method can be used to convert a numeric value to its string representation.

- **getValueString**—Is defined only if the item's value is a string. If so, it returns the string representation. If the item's value is another data type, the return value isn't defined.

CREATING A NEW NotesItem IN LotusScript

You can create a new NotesItem only within the context of a NotesDocument because the item must reside inside a document. As with the other classes that support the New keyword, you can create a new NotesItem with the Dim keyword or with the New method:

```
Dim notesitemvar As New NotesItem(doc, name$, value, [special])

Dim notesitemvar As NotesItem
Set notesitemvar = New NotesItem(doc, name$, value, [special])
```

In the preceding examples, *doc* represents an object of the NotesDocument class, and *name$* is a string expression to be used as the name of the item within the document. *value* represents the value you want to assign to the item. The data type of the document item depends on the data type of the value you assign. It behaves pretty much as you would expect. A string value causes the item to be a text item, an integer or floating-point value causes it to be a numeric item, and a LotusScript variant date/time causes it to store a date/time value in the item. This parameter might also contain an array. If so, all the values of the array are taken together and stored in the single item.

The *special* parameter, if supplied, is numeric and must be one of these constants: AUTHORS, NAMES, or READERS. AUTHORS and READERS specify names of users who are allowed to modify and read the document, respectively. Either of these values also implies that the value has the NAMES attribute. NAMES specifies that the item contains one or more usernames. Listing 26.1 gives an example.

NOTE

The code lines in some of the listings in this chapter are preceded by numbers, as in Listing 26.1. These line numbers are there for ease of reference; they are *not* part of code and should not be typed in as such.

LISTING 26.1   ADDING AN AUTHORS ITEM TO A DOCUMENT

```
 1: Dim uiws As New NotesUIWorkspace
 2: Dim doc As NotesDocument
 3: Set doc = uiws.CurrentDocument.Document
 4: Dim strAuthors( 1 To 3 ) As String
 5: strAuthors ( 1 ) = "Jeff Gunther"        ' First Author
 6: strAuthors ( 2 ) = "Randy Tamura"        ' Second Author
 7: If doc.HasItem("docAuthors")Then
 8:     doc.removeItem("docAuthors")
 9: End If
10: Dim itemAuthors As NotesItem
11:
12: Set itemAuthors =  New NotesItem(doc, "docAuthors",strAuthors, AUTHORS)
13: Call doc.Save( True, True )
```

In lines 1–3, a reference to the current NotesDocument object is obtained via
NotesUIWorkspace. Notice that the CurrentDocument property returns a NotesUIDocument,
from which the NotesDocument is obtained. The strAuthors variable is a string array containing three names. In lines 7–9, it's checked whether or not the document already has a
docAuthors item. There is nothing special about this item name—you can choose another if
you like. It's just a good idea to make sure you're not creating two items with the same
name. In lines 12–13, the new item in the document is created. The New method also
returns a NotesItem object, but it's not needed for this routine. AUTHORS is specified as the
special value for the NotesItem parameter, so only the three people specified may edit the
document.

RICH-TEXT ITEMS

26

Rich-text items, implemented via the NotesRichTextItem class, are a very interesting special
kind of item. Rich-text fields handle extended text attributes, such as font, point size, color,
and so forth. Notes and Domino can distinguish between regular fields and rich-text fields
because rich-text fields are more expensive in terms of storage space and processing time.
This enables you to selectively use rich-text fields. If you don't need the features of rich text,
you can use regular items.

DRILLING DOWN INTO RICH-TEXT ITEMS

Rich-text items are implemented internally as a big buffer that contains a sequence of CD
records. CD stands for composite data or compound document. In any case, there are CD
records to define fonts, paragraphs, and text, as you might imagine. However, there are now
more than 100 different CD records, including items such as HTML object rendering,
hotspots, tables, and graphics extensions.

The rich-text field is the means by which Notes/Domino designers have added many extensions to the original Notes implementation. Layouts, hotspots, and doclinks are all implemented via rich-text field CD records.

THE NotesRichTextItem CLASS

The NotesRichTextItem class is currently unique within the Notes/Domino class hierarchy. It is the only class that is derived from another class within the hierarchy. This derivation is also called *inheritance*. The key point to remember about inheritance is that when one class is derived from another one, the derived class inherits properties and methods from the parent class. This means that the parent's properties and methods are available for use within the child class. Inheritance makes it easier to implement the derived class because basic properties and methods of the parent class do not need to be reimplemented.

→ To learn more about inheritance, **see** "Class Inheritance," **p. 512** (Chapter 20).

In the NotesRichTextItem class, for example, the class inherits the properties Name, Type, and Parent (among many others). These properties specify the name and type of the item as well as the NotesDocument parent that contains the item. These are clearly properties that the NotesRichTextItem class, as well as the NotesItem class, needs. Because the properties and methods of a NotesItem are available within a NotesRichTextItem, we say that the NotesRichTextItem Is-A NotesItem. In other words, the NotesRichTextItem is just a special case of the NotesItem. Anything the NotesItem can do, the NotesRichTextItem can do, and more.

It is probably a good idea here to clear up any confusion about the word *parent*. In the case of the NotesRichTextItem, it is used in two different contexts and means two different things, so don't confuse the two meanings. In the first meaning, the parent of the NotesRichTextItem is the NotesItem from which it inherits its methods and attributes.

The second meaning of *parent* applies to any NotesItem and deals with the relationship Has-A. In this context, a NotesDocument object can contain a NotesItem object. We say that the NotesDocument Has-A NotesItem. This is a different relationship. It is clear that a NotesDocument is not a special case of NotesItem (or vice versa); it just contains one. The NotesItem Parent property then refers to the NotesDocument that contains it.

THE NotesRichTextStyle CLASS

The NotesRichTextStyle class was introduced to Notes/Domino in Release 4.6. This class enables you to control the appearance of text within a rich-text field. If you understand the concepts of the CD records outlined previously, you'll see that the use of this class just makes it easier to create and append CD records within a rich-text field. This class is most easily described with an example. Take a look at Listing 26.2.

LISTING 26.2 USING THE NotesRichTextStyle CLASS

```
1: Dim session As New NotesSession
2: Dim uiws As New NotesUIWorkspace
3: Dim uidoc As NotesUIDocument
4: Dim doc As NotesDocument
5: Set uidoc = uiws.currentdocument
6: Set doc = uidoc.document
7:
```

continues

LISTING 26.2 CONTINUED

```
 8: Dim richText As New NotesRichTextItem(doc, "Body")
 9: Dim richStyle As NotesRichTextStyle
10: Set richStyle = session.CreateRichTextStyle
11:
12: Call richText.AppendText("Hello, world")
13:
14: richStyle.Bold = True
15: richStyle.FontSize = 24
16: richStyle.NotesColor = COLOR_RED
17:
18: Call richText.AppendStyle(richStyle)
19: Call richText.AppendText(" Hello, world, in Style")
20:
21: Call doc.Save(True, True)
```

To implement rich-text attributes within a rich-text field, you need two objects: one for the rich-text field itself and a second for the rich-text style. In lines 1–6, the various objects required to access the document and field are just declared and initialized. In line 8, a new NotesRichTextItem object is created within the current document with the name Body. In lines 9–10, a new NotesRichTextStyle object is created and declared. Notice that you cannot use the New keyword with this class. You must create the object via the NotesSession class with the CreateRichTextStyle method.

In line 12, the text "Hello, world" is added to the rich-text field without any attribute modification, so the field gets the default characteristics. In lines 14–16, the characteristics of the next phrase are specified. The AppendStyle method is used on line 18 to append a new style to the field. In line 19, some extra text is appended, which will be Bold, RED, and 24 points in size. Last, in line 21, the document is saved. If the document is not saved, the changes will not be permanently stored in the database.

The properties for the NotesRichTextStyle class are Bold, Effects, FontSize, IsDefault, Italic, NotesColor, NotesFont, Parent, PassThruHTML, StrikeThrough, and Underline. The Bold, Italic, StrikeThrough, and Underline properties are Boolean properties, with True meaning that the property is on and False indicating that it is off. The PassThruHTML property is also a Boolean property. You can turn on PassThruHTML, append text that will be treated as HTML, and then turn it off.

The FontSize property is just a number representing the font size in points. The NotesFont attribute can be one of four values: FONT_COURIER, FONT_HELV, FONT_ROMAN, STYLE_NO_CHANGE, or MAYBE. You use this last value if you want to change a NotesRichTextStyle object that changes the font to one that does not affect the font.

The Effects property can have the values EFFECTS_EMBOSS, EFFECTS_EXTRUDE, EFFECTS_NONE, EFFECTS_SHADOW, EFFECTS_SUBSCRIPT, EFFECTS_SUPERSCRIPT, STYLE_NO_CHANGE, and MAYBE.

Finally, the NotesColor property can be a Domino color between 0 and 240.

The `RichTextItem` and `RichTextStyle` Java Classes

Listing 26.3 shows the sample program from the previous section rewritten as a Java agent.

Listing 26.3   Using the `RichTextStyle` Java Class

```
import lotus.domino.*;
public class JavaAgent extends AgentBase {
    public void NotesMain() {
        try {
            Session session = getSession();
            AgentContext agentContext = session.getAgentContext();
            DocumentCollection dc = agentContext.getUnprocessedDocuments();
            Document doc = dc.getFirstDocument();
            RichTextItem richText = doc.createRichTextItem("Body");
            RichTextStyle richStyle = session.createRichTextStyle();
            richText.appendText("Hello, world");

            richStyle.setBold(RichTextStyle.YES);     // Set bold on
            richStyle.setFontSize(24);                // Set font size
            richStyle.setColor(RichTextStyle.COLOR_RED);     // Set it Red
            richText.appendStyle(richStyle);
            richText.appendText("Hello, world, in Style");

            doc.save(true, true);

        } catch(Exception e) {
            e.printStackTrace();
        }
    }
}
```

The program is mostly self-explanatory and operates similarly to the LotusScript version. One difference is that there are no front-end classes in Java, so you cannot access an equivalent to `NotesUIWorkspace` or `NotesUIDocument`. Instead, the `getUnprocessedDocuments` method of the `AgentContext` class is used.

The `NotesRichTextParagraphStyle` and `RichTextParagraphStyle` Classes

The LotusScript `NotesRichTextParagraphStyle` and the Java `RichTextParagraphStyle` classes are similar to the `RichTextStyle` classes, but they operate on complete paragraphs rather than just selected text. The properties that you can associate with the paragraph include alignment, the first line's left margin, interline spacing, left and right margins, spacing above and below the paragraph, and tab settings for the paragraph.

Listing 26.4 shows an example in LotusScript.

Listing 26.4   Using the `NotesRichTextParagraphStyle` LotusScript Class

```
Dim session As New NotesSession
Dim uiws As New NotesUIWorkspace
Dim uidoc As NotesUIDocument
```

continues

LISTING 26.4 CONTINUED

```
Dim doc As NotesDocument
Set uidoc = uiws.currentdocument
Set doc = uidoc.document

Dim richText As New NotesRichTextItem(doc, "Body")
Dim rtpStyle As NotesRichTextParagraphStyle
Set rtpStyle = session.CreateRichTextParagraphStyle

rtpStyle.Alignment = ALIGN_CENTER
Call richText.AppendParagraphStyle(rtpStyle)

Call richText.AppendText("Centralized Hello, world")

Call doc.Save(True, True)
```

THE NotesEmbeddedObject CLASS

The NotesEmbeddedObject class is used for two primary purposes. The first is to support file attachments to documents. The files can be attached directly to the document, or the attachments can be contained in rich-text fields. The second purpose of a NotesEmbeddedObject is to support ActiveX automation, formerly known as OLE automation.

Attachment support is available on all Notes platforms, but ActiveX (OLE) support is available only on Windows platforms. You can attach a file on one platform and detach it on another platform, but the files must be in a format that is compatible between the two platforms, such as an ASCII text file.

You can get a NotesEmbeddedObject through the EmbeddedObjects property of either the NotesRichTextItem class or the NotesDocument class. The NotesRichTextItem property gives you an array of all the objects embedded within the specified field. The NotesDocument class returns all the objects within the entire document.

NOTE

> There is a difference between the EmbeddedObjects property of the NotesRichTextItem class and the one in the NotesDocument class. The NotesDocument EmbeddedObjects property does not return attachments; it returns only OLE 2 (ActiveX) objects. The NotesRichTextItem EmbeddedObjects property returns attachments as well as ActiveX objects.

THE NotesTimer CLASS

The NotesTimer class is useful for generating events at specified intervals. You can create the NotesTimer object either with the New keyword or by calling the CreateTimer method of the NotesSession class. The latter method is useful if you are using ActiveX automation and are using the timer from a scripting language other than LotusScript, such as Visual Basic.

This is the syntax for creating a `NotesTimer` object:

```
Dim timervar as New NotesTimer(interval, [Comment$])
```

or

```
Dim timervar as Variant
Set timervar = New NotesTimer(interval, [Comment$])
```

You set the interval in seconds, but you are not guaranteed that your alarm will be triggered at exactly the time you specified because of other activities that might be happening in your computer.

KEEPING TRACK OF DOCUMENT EDITING TIME

Suppose you want to keep track of the editing time for each document. You could use the `NotesTimer` class as a mechanism to do this. Although the resolution of the `NotesTimer` is not extremely fine, you rarely want to know the document editing time with microsecond accuracy. Our accuracy here will be within a few seconds, which should be fine for this application.

1. Create a new form in the database by selecting Create, Design, Form. In the form, place the text `Timed Form` in 24-point, bold font.

2. Space down a couple of lines and enter the text **Total Document Editing Time (Sec.):**, followed by a field. Name the field `EditingTime`, make the type Number, and make the type Computed. In the `Value` event, make the formula `EditingTime`.

3. Last, create a second field called `Body`, which should be defined as a rich-text field. The `Body` exists so that when you create a new document with this form, the form will appear in edit mode. If you have no editable fields, the new document appears in read mode (see Figure 26.1).

Figure 26.1
The timed form with the `EditingTime` field.

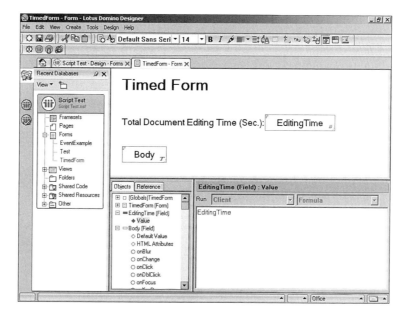

4. Save the form with the name TimedForm.

5. Open the form for editing again and, in the Programmer's pane at the bottom, select Define (Globals) TimedForm. Set the event to Declarations. In the Declarations section, enter two variables:

```
Dim timerEditing As NotesTimer     ' Editing Time NotesTimer object
Dim iEditTime As Integer ' Editing Time in Seconds
```

It is important that these variables be declared in the Globals section because they must be visible to several different routines within the form.

6. Within the form, create two routines, the PostOpen routine and the ETHandler routine. To do this, first click the plus sign on the TimedForm (Form) line. Then scroll down to find the PostOpen element. Click PostOpen and enter the text in Listing 26.5.

LISTING 26.5   THE PostOpen AND ETHandler ROUTINES FOR TIMING DOCUMENTS

```
 1: Sub Postopen(Source As Notesuidocument)
 2:     Set timerEditing = New NotesTimer(1, "Document Editing time")
 3:     On Event Alarm From timerEditing Call ETHandler
 4:     Dim DocTime As Variant
 5:     DocTime = Source.Document.GetItemValue("EditingTime")
 6:     If DocTime(0) = "" Then
 7:         iEditTime = 0
 8:     Else
 9:         iEditTime = Cint(DocTime (0))
10:     End If
11: End Sub
12:
13:
14: Sub ETHandler(Source As NotesTimer)
15:     iEditTime = iEditTime + 1        ' Increment elapsed time in seconds
16: End Sub
```

NOTE

> The ETHandler routine is not automatically created for you within the form window like PostOpen. Just type the header at the bottom of the PostOpen routine, and a new window opens into which you can enter the contents.

Before moving on, let's look at the routines created. Remember that the PostOpen routine is called just after the document has been opened by the user. At that time (in line 2), set the timerEditing variable with a new NotesTimer object. The first parameter is the duration between alarms, and the second parameter is just a comment. We set the duration to one second so that we'll get an alarm every second, which should be fine for tracking document editing time.

Line 3, the On Event line, specifies what should happen when the alarm event occurs in the timerEditing object. This line indicates that you should call the ETHandler routine.

Lines 4–10 of the routine are initializing the iEditTime variable. First get the value of the field from the document and put it into a variant. The result of the GetItemValue routine is always an array, so you must obtain the first element. If this element is an empty string, you probably have a new document and the field does not yet contain a value. In this case, just initialize the elapsed time to 0. If the variable already exists, set the variable to the elapsed time so far. In this example, you ignore very large editing times that might overflow an integer variable. In your real application, you might want to handle this differently if your documents have the potential for long editing times.

The ETHandler routine is called once a second. All you do in this routine is track the elapsed time. By using this method, you do not incur too much overhead because the processing for the routine is very simple.

Now, in the QuerySave and QueryClose routines, enter the source code given in Listing 26.6.

LISTING 26.6   THE QuerySave AND QueryClose ROUTINES FOR TIMING DOCUMENTS

```
Sub Querysave(Source As Notesuidocument, Continue As Variant)
  If Source.EditMode Then
     Call Source.FieldSetText("EditingTime",Cstr(iEditTime))
  End If
End Sub


Sub Queryclose(Source As Notesuidocument, Continue As Variant)
  If Source.EditMode Then
     Call Source.FieldSetText("EditingTime",Cstr(iEditTime))
  End If
End Sub
```

Notice that the code for each routine is the same. You could also enter this code once in a separate subroutine and call that subroutine from both the QuerySave routine and the QueryClose routine. This choice is a matter of style. Because there are only three lines, it is sometimes more convenient to enter the text and then just copy and paste the code to another routine. If the code were much longer than this, it probably would be a better idea to use a separate subroutine and call it from both places. This technique eases maintenance later when someone must make a modification; only one place needs to be changed.

The purpose of these two routines is to update the field in the document when it is saved or when the window is closed. Check to make sure that the document is in edit mode before attempting to save the value because you will get an error if the document is in read mode.

Of course, it's only fair to mention that this form does not really cover all the cases, and you will probably need to update it if you want to implement something like this form for yourself. The timer will work fine the first time the document is edited, but the form does not have all the logic necessary to handle the case of the user opening the document in read mode and changing it to edit mode. This enhancement is left as an exercise for the reader. To test this new form, open the database within the Notes client and create a few test documents. After the documents are saved, you can reopen the documents and see the computed editing time. In this example, you've seen how to implement document timing. This example uses the time to keep track of the total editing time per document. You might put this type of code in a subform, and you might want to hide some of the fields from users.

Finally, another extension would be to use the timer to autosave your documents in edit mode. You could keep track of the last time you saved the document and the elapsed time; when appropriate, you could automatically save the document. This code could also be placed in a subform with hidden fields so that your autosave feature could be added to several forms without the user seeing any additional fields. These are just a few examples of how you might use the `NotesTimer` facility.

THE `NotesName`, `NotesACL`, AND `NotesACLEntry` CLASSES

The `NotesName` class assists in parsing usernames. The `NotesACL` and `NotesACLEntry` classes are used to implement control of the ACL list for a database.

THE `NotesName` CLASS

The `NotesName` class has only one method in LotusScript, the `New` method. You can create a `NotesName` class object either with the `New` keyword or by using the `CreateName` method of the `NotesSession` class. When you create a `NotesName` object, you must pass the routine a string containing a Notes user's name. The name is looked up in the Domino Directory, and you can then access properties of the `NotesName` object.

The properties of the `NotesName` object include different formats of the name: `Abbreviated` and `Canonical`. The properties also enable you to extract components of a hierarchical name: `Common`, `Country`, `Organization`, `OrgUnit1`, `OrgUnit2`, `OrgUnit3`, and `OrgUnit4`. Several of the properties are for handling industry standards and parsing other systems' names. For example, the `Surname`, `Generation`, `Given`, and `Initials` properties cannot be used to extract information from a regular Notes name. They can be used only if the name had specified these components separately.

The `Addr821` property corresponds to the RFC 821 format for an Internet name: `UserName@Domain`. This is the most commonly used format for Internet naming. RFC 822 has more components and can look something like this: `UserName@Domain<"User's real name">`, where the information within the quotes is called the phrase and can be any text additionally describing the user.

THE `NotesACL` CLASS

You use the `NotesACL` class in conjunction with the `NotesDatabase` class. After you have access to a `NotesDatabase` object, you can access the ACL property of the `NotesDatabase` object and obtain a `NotesACL` class object. You cannot create a standalone `NotesACL` object.

The NotesACL class enables you to add, delete, and rename roles within the ACL and to traverse the different ACL entries. You can also create a new ACL entry with the CreateACLEntry method. You must invoke the Save method of the NotesACL class after you make changes, or your changes will not be saved permanently in the database.

The Roles property returns an array of strings that represent all the roles within the database. The GetEntry, GetFirstEntry, and GetNextEntry methods enable you to traverse the ACL list. Each of the three methods returns an object of the NotesACLEntry class.

THE NotesACLEntry CLASS

The NotesACLEntry class enables you to access and modify each entry within the ACL. Typically, you will use one of the Get routines within the NotesACL class to obtain a NotesACLEntry object. Alternatively, you can create a new NotesACLEntry with the New keyword or by calling the CreateACLEntry method of the NotesACL class.

After you have obtained a NotesACLEntry object, you can disable or enable roles associated with the entry. You can also allow or disallow the following privileges to the entry: Create Documents, Create Personal Agents, Create Personal Folders, and Delete Documents.

26

DEVELOPING WEB SITES WITH DOMINO

BUILDING A WEB SITE WITH DOMINO

BACKGROUND

When it comes to most people who visit Web sites, they really don't care how the Web site was created or what platform it runs on—what they want is information. What your company and your customers want is a functioning Web site. They just want it to work, and the combination of Notes/Domino Release 6 and the Web is a potent one that you can use with great results.

It wasn't always that way. It seems like only yesterday that Notes was Notes, and that's all there was to it. Way back in the old days, we had Notes servers that served Notes databases to Notes clients, and that was that. Things have certainly changed since Notes first came on the scene, and the past several years have seen unprecedented changes in Notes from the Internet standpoint.

The server is now the Domino server; in addition to "serving" Notes clients, it can host a wide variety of clients, including—most important for this chapter—Web browsers. In addition, besides delivering Notes databases, the server can serve HTML, Java, graphics, and more. The Domino server is a full-fledged Web server, but it maintains its original charter; it still can serve Notes databases. You can use a Domino server to create a fully functional Web site. And, in a nutshell, that's what this chapter is all about: building a Web site with Domino.

A mere chapter cannot do justice to the topic of developing a Domino-based Web site; the subject requires a book in itself. And there are books available that specifically cover the topic. What we'll attempt to do in this chapter is expose you to the different approaches you can take in designing a Web site using Domino, highlighting some of the new related features included in Release 6.

We'll spend some time thinking about the philosophy of Web sites and talk about some of the design elements you should consider before you begin. We'll talk about design and implementation, and we'll discuss some of the challenges and benefits during Web development. We'll take a look at some of the ways you can bring Web-specific elements into your Notes database design and how you can implement this on the Web. We'll also discuss some of the tools available to assist you in your efforts.

The thing to keep in mind as you read through this chapter is that, in a very real sense, we'll be borrowing from all the other chapters that precede or succeed this one in this book. We'll discuss how to employ the design tips you got in Part III, "Introducing Domino Designer R6." We'll also discuss implementing the Domino server, which you'll learn more about in Parts VII, "Administering the Domino Servers," and VIII, "Advanced Domino Administration."

In a sense, this chapter serves as an introduction to this very special aspect of the Notes/Domino story. But it also brings all the parts together into a working whole. Notes brings some remarkable capabilities to the Web, and the Web brings some remarkable capabilities to Notes as well.

With Release 6, the tight integration between Notes and the Internet that really jelled with Release 5 has become even more pronounced. It has become even easier to share design elements between the Notes client and the Web browser. New features help you utilize and integrate external tools and resources within Domino Designer, speeding up your Web development process.

In this chapter, we take a bird's eye view of creating a Web site using Notes/Domino Release 6. We walk through the philosophy of creating a site, which leads into a design discussion. We touch on the challenges and benefits, and then we discuss some of the specifics of creating the site and tools you can use.

Before we get into the meat of this chapter, let's take a brief look at the differences between a Notes client and a Web browser.

WEB BROWSERS VERSUS THE NOTES CLIENT

Obviously, a lot of differences exist between a Web browser and a Notes client. One of the biggest differences is patently obvious: Browsers are built solely on a point-and-click interface. The Notes client has the concept of "state."

In a browser, hypertext links within the HTML documents are clicked to take you to the next document. This works great, but there's no sense of "state" or "context." That is, even though you could hover over one of these links (and even though there could be some code that would change the color or the image as you hover), neither your browser nor the server has any sense that you're hovering over a particular link. It gets that state only when you actually click.

In the Notes client world, you can highlight a line in a view and simply press Enter: The Notes client understands that you "were on" a particular document; it even had that document's data in memory.

The upshot is simply this: In a view in Notes, you can reply to a given document because Notes maintains the idea of "being on" a particular document. From the browser's perspective, there's no concept of "being on" a document. From the browser's perspective, the document you're on is the view itself. You can't respond from the view because the browser is oblivious to what it would be responding to.

This makes life more difficult for us developers because we have to rethink some of our navigational options. A Respond action button in a view is useless (in fact, even if you attempt to put one there, it won't be displayed). Even with the View applet (which we'll discuss in length later in this chapter), there's still no way to respond right from a view. There's still no state.

Keep this issue of state (or context) in mind as we look at some of the possibilities for building your Web site with Notes/Domino Release 6.

27

WEB DESIGN ALTERNATIVES

Although designing a Web site using Notes/Domino Release 6 isn't totally different from creating one in a "straight HTML" environment, we need to discuss the various design alternatives Notes/Domino provides for creating a Web site.

There are several ways to create a Web site in the Notes/Domino world. You could do any of the following:

- Create "normal" Notes databases with little customization for Web use, and allow them to be accessed by Web browsers

- Create more specialized Notes databases that incorporate specific Web-oriented design elements

- Create Notes databases using features such as View and Editor applets, pages, outlines, and framesets, and creatively add HTML to Notes forms, documents, views, and so on

- Create a hybrid of HTML documents and specialized databases, incorporating Cascading Style Sheets, JavaScript, and other methods as appropriate

And so on. The different permutations here are endless, but in many situations, the "hybrid" choice tends to be the best. Although Notes/Domino Release 6 is far better at working the Web than its predecessors were, you will likely find that you're still better off doing many things with HTML than with Notes's native design capabilities. With Release 6, though, that list is dramatically shorter than it was with previous Notes releases. We address some of these limitations next as we examine the various approaches to creating Web sites with Notes/Domino.

> **NOTE**
>
> One key to successful Web site development is to determine in detail the site's objectives and then identify the available development options that support meeting those objectives. It sounds like common sense, but all too often the front-end planning time is not given enough emphasis, sometimes leading to wasted development time and solutions that miss the mark. When you're familiar with your objectives and have researched the different methods you can employ to meet the objectives, you're in a position to make good choices.

Let's spend some time describing each of the options outlined and including examples of how each can be implemented.

CREATING "NORMAL" NOTES DATABASES TO BE ACCESSED BY WEB BROWSERS

If you listened strictly to the marketing hype, you'd be led to believe that you could allow Web browsers to access any normal, ordinary Notes database.

Although this might technically be true, the results usually aren't very pretty. As shown in Figures 27.1 and 27.2, there's a difference in how the Notes client displays a database view and how a Web client displays it using HTML. The typical Notes spreadsheet-like view is generally inappropriate for Web usage. As we've mentioned numerous times already in this chapter, Notes/Domino Release 6 has made tremendous advances, but a "straight" Notes database probably will leave your Web clients cold.

Figure 27.1
A typical Notes view is displayed like this in the Notes client.

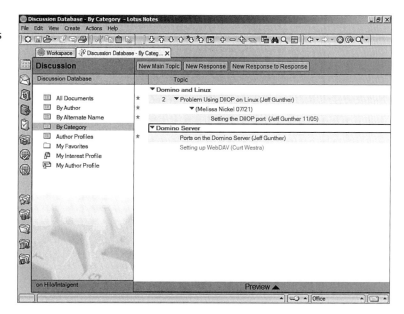

Figure 27.2
The same Notes view from Figure 27.1, but rendered using the Notes default HTML display option and displayed in a Web browser. The result is not pretty.

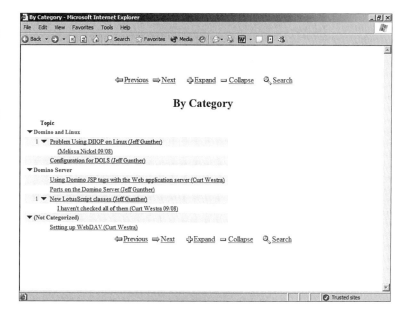

NOTE

You can use a special Design feature known as a View applet that gives the browser client some of the same capabilities in a view that a Notes client has. Specifically, it brings a small Java-based applet to the browser that has a "context" capability, among other things. We'll return to View applets several times later in this chapter.

In addition to potential problems with views, there are possible problems with forms, agents, and so on. When users successfully submit Web forms built in Notes with no programming on your part, they'll get a default screen with a "form processed" message in response—a dead end with no links to take them anywhere.

Although the "normal" Notes database does work on the Web, the limitations are pretty severe. You'll quickly discover that a couple minor design changes can make a big difference.

CREATING SPECIALIZED NOTES DATABASES WITH SPECIFIC WEB-ORIENTED DESIGN

If publishing "straight" Notes databases isn't the answer, you can try adding some minor modifications to make them more Web-friendly.

For example, the typical discussion database By Author view is probably inappropriate for Web use. As shown in Figure 27.3, the underlined date in the first column is the hypertext link that will take you to the document indicated. This is not user-friendly because typically on the Web, you want the user to click a value in the first column that uniquely identifies the document—the date wouldn't be unique in this case. It makes more sense to click the topic than on the date, doesn't it? From the Notes client, having the date in the first column doesn't seem so strange because to open a document you're actually clicking the entire line in a view.

An alternative is to alter the Design view slightly by placing the date in the second column, and the subject of the message in the first column. This seems like a far more intuitive item to click than the date.

Another alternative is to modify a setting in the Column Property box (found on the "beanie" tab) shown in Figure 27.4: Show Values in This Column as Links. By enabling this check box, you can make the second or third (or whatever) column (not just the first) "clickable." That way, people have the option of clicking the subject, not just the date.

Release 5 introduced a View applet that dramatically changed the way a view looks on the Web. By simply checking the Use Applet in a Browser property in a view's properties box (shown in Figure 27.5), you specify that the view will be displayed in a browser using a Java applet instead of HTML. In short, a Java applet is downloaded to the browser to display a view; Figure 27.6 shows the outcome. The user now can use a view from a browser that looks and behaves much like its Notes counterpart.

27

Figure 27.3
A view designed for Notes use does not always display in an intuitive and user-friendly manner on the Web, as shown here.

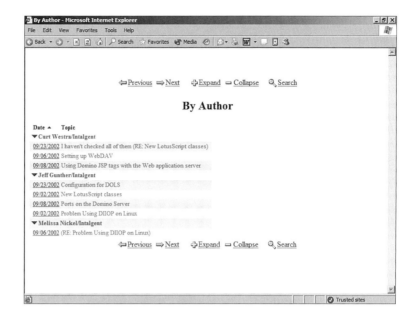

Figure 27.4
Property box with the Show Values in This Column as Links option checked.

Figure 27.5
Specify in the View properties box that a view should display on the Web as a Java applet.

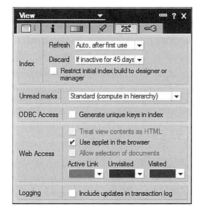

Figure 27.6
A view displayed in a Web browser using the View applet appears and acts similarly to the Notes client version.

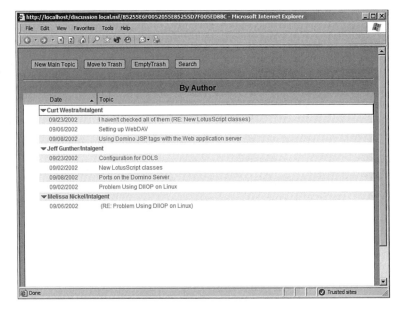

The applets have downsides, however: They generally are slow to load, and you essentially have no control over how the affected view displays and functions. These two deficiencies are serious enough that they really limit widespread use of the Java applets.

The options described in this section make minor changes in your design to cater to your Web visitors, but they do nothing nearly as dramatic as adding HTML or truly taking advantage of all the features available in Notes/Domino Release 6. Let's look at some of the more advanced features next.

CREATING NOTES DATABASES USING ADVANCED FEATURES

A third option for Web development using Notes/Domino takes advantage of the more advanced features that Notes/Domino Release 6 gives us. Some of these features were introduced in Release 5, but several debuted in Release 6 that make it even easier to develop Web applications.

Features such as the View and Editor applets, pages, framesets, and outlines—while not exactly useless in Notes itself—can have their greatest value in a Web environment. View and Editor applets attempt to address one of the most long-standing complaints: "You can't do the same stuff from a browser that you can do from a Notes client." Today you actually can provide a lot of the same functionality in Notes and a browser, but it requires some additional programming for the Web browser side. These two applets offer a simpler solution to the problem, although they have their own drawbacks, as mentioned previously. Framesets and pages are easy to build with minimal HTML coding. And "navigators" have grown into image maps, which behave the same way in Notes as they do in a browser.

We'll take a quick look at all these features in this section of this chapter, but there are far more in-depth discussions on each of these new items elsewhere in this book. Refer to Chapter 13, "Designing Pages, Forms, and Subforms"; Chapter 15, "Using Framesets, Outlines, and Navigators"; and Chapter 16, "Using Shared Resources," for more information.

Beginning in Release 5, Notes has stored graphics in their native formats instead of converting them into the proprietary Notes metafile format. This means that graphics don't have to be converted back to a Web-usable format whenever they are loaded in a browser, thus improving performance and image quality.

You can store resources such as images one time in a database and reuse them within the database or in other databases. There are several benefits to this approach:

- From an economy standpoint, it's always nice to store something only once instead of multiple times.
- From a management standpoint, this gives a designer much better control over images being used in their applications. You can change a logo throughout an entire application by simply changing one image resource.
- From a housekeeping standpoint, it's great to have the images stored easily in a database instead of littering your ICONS folder. Granted, you could store images as file attachments in Release 4.x, but then to access them you needed to write a lengthy HTML <IMG> tag.
- From a "transportability" standpoint, with the images stored in the database itself, replication, clustering, and so on all become simple. Other developers don't need to ship you a database and a ZIP file full of images; now they simply ship you the database, and the images are already there.

Working with image resources and other shared resources is detailed at length in Chapter 16. Domino Designer 6 expanded the capability to share resources to include files, Java applets, style sheets, and data connectors.

Notes/Domino 6 introduces a new Layers feature that enables you to position overlapping content areas on a page, form, or subform. Layers can be useful because they give you the capability to control the placement, size, and content of information, and you can hide or display layers based on a Hide When formula or other settings. Multiple layers can be positioned beneath and above one another so that transparent layers show layers underneath and opaque layers hide layers underneath. A typical example of using layers is to display content in one specific area that changes when a user clicks different tabs or buttons—all the while maintaining the display of other content not included in the layers area. You can create layers in Domino Designer 6 with little or no HTML or other non-Notes programming. Refer to Chapter 13 and 28 for detailed information on designing and using layers.

Our second "middle ground" development option is to develop a vanilla Notes application, but utilize some of these special features.

27

Let's walk through a simple scenario and go through the specifics later. Let's say that instead of having a database launch a view or an About document, you want it to open on a frameset. (Framesets are discussed in depth in Chapter 15.)

You could design a three-frame frameset (keep the terminology in mind here—a *frameset* is a collection of individual *frames*). You could put an outline in the bottom-left frame, today's date in the upper-left frame, and some sort of page, database view, or image map in the third frame.

Let's start by creating a database and building the frameset. Create the database the usual way (by choosing File, Database, New), and use Blank as the template. This gives you a clean slate to work from.

For the purpose of this example, let's say you've decided to create a Web-enabled application based on a three-frame frameset design. The bottom-left frame will hold an outline for navigation purposes, the upper-left frame will simply have today's date, and the lower-right frame will hold the actual content. As someone clicks on one of the links in the outline in the left frame, the document being requested will show up in the frame at the lower right.

To accomplish this, you'll need an outline, a frameset, and a couple pages.

To make matters simple for this discussion, let's make a couple simple pages and an outline quickly. You can come back to these later and make changes to make them more elegant or complex.

NOTE

> The following discussion gives the short-version instructions on creating pages, outlines, and framesets. These items are discussed in far greater depth in Chapters 13 and 15.

Pages operate the way that About documents do: You can add links, text, rich text, computed text, images, sections, tables—just about anything you can do on a form, except fields.

To create pages for this example, follow these steps:

1. Click Pages in the Design pane.
2. Click the New Page button. A new blank page opens.
3. Type some text, such as `This is our Home Page`, across the top of the page.
4. Click File, Save to save the page. When prompted, name it Home; then click OK.
5. Now create a second page; for simplicity's sake, call it Company Info. Depending on what you were doing, you could easily create a series of pages for various departments in your organization or for the various segments or divisions of your Web site.
6. On the Company Info page, simply put a header stating `Company Information`. Save that page as described earlier.
7. Create a third page to display a date or other content above the outline. In this example, a page that uses computed text to display the date was created.

Now create an outline that will take you to the Home and Company Info pages. To create an outline for this example, follow these steps:

1. Click Shared Code, Outlines in the Design pane.

2. Click New Outline. A blank outline opens.

3. Create an outline entry by clicking the New Entry button at the top of the screen.

4. Double-click the entry to open the Outline Entry properties dialog box. Enter a label for the new entry. The text that you enter will be displayed to the end user.

5. Select the Named Element option in the Type field.

6. To the right of the Named Element field, select Page as the type of element you want to use; you want to link this entry to the Home page you created previously.

7. Specify the name of the home page in the Value field by clicking the folder icon and selecting it from the list that appears.

8. Close the Outline Entry properties box and click the Save Outline button to save the outline.

To keep this example simple, we don't discuss them here, but you could set several other properties, such as specifying an image to display, setting an alias, directing which frame should be populated when someone clicks on this outline item, and even handling hide-whens (potentially based on who the user is or what type of browser someone is using) for the entry.

Now repeat the steps to create a second outline entry, but this time link it to the Company Info page. To round things out, you might want to create additional pages, forms, or views and add outline entries for them as well. Click the Save Outline button to save your new outline.

Now you need to create a page with the outline embedded within it, and to set several properties that determine how the outline will appear and function within the page. Follow these steps to create an embedded outline in a page and set some of the key properties:

1. Click the Use Outline action button. A new page is created for you, with the outline already embedded.

2. Open the embedded outline's properties box by right-clicking the embedded outline and then selecting Outline Properties from the menu that appears.

3. On the Info tab of the properties box, specify the name for the embedded outline control and also its type as Tree Style or Flat. When you use Tree Style, you see the familiar indented folders. Flat means that when you drill down one level in the outline, the new level replaces the original level in the display.

4. Select the Title style, which controls whether the database title is hidden or displayed above the outline.

5. Check the Show Twisties box if you want clickable twisties to appear to the left of outline entries that will control the expansion and collapse of indented entries.

27

6. Enter the name of the Target frame. If your outline will appear in the left frame of a frameset and the contents will appear in the right frame, enter the name of the target, or right, frame.

7. For this example, select Using HTML for Web Access field.

8. Click File, Save to save the page. When prompted, enter a name of Navigation; then click OK.

Next, create a frameset to display the outline page in a bottom-left frame, the date in a top-left frame, and the two content pages in a right frame. Follow these steps to create the frameset:

1. In Designer, click Framesets in the Design pane.

2. Click New Frameset. The Create New Frameset dialog box appears.

3. Choose how many frames you want (from two to four, for starters—choose three here), and click OK. The new frameset opens.

4. Open the left frame's properties box by right-clicking the frame and then selecting Frame Properties from the menu that appears.

5. Enter a name for the frame in the Name field. Then change the content type to Named Element and Page.

6. Click the folder icon to open a dialog box and select the Navigation page you created so that it displays in this left frame. Click OK to close the dialog box.

7. Enter the default target for links in the frame within the next field. Enter the name of the right frame for this example.

8. Repeat Steps 4–7 for the right frame, setting the content to be the home page you created.

9. Open the frameset's properties box by right-clicking any frame and then selecting Frameset Properties from the menu that appears.

10. Enter a name for the frameset and close the Frameset properties box.

11. Click the Save Frameset button to save the frameset.

After you have named it, you can use it as a launch option for the database itself.

NOTE

You define database launch properties to specify what the user will see when the database is opened. By going to Database Properties (by choosing File, Database, Properties, or by clicking the Properties toolbar), you can set the launch properties by going to the fifth tab (from the left), the one with the rocket ship.

Here you can specify how the database will be launched within Notes clients and Web browsers. For example, you can designate a certain frameset to open in Notes and a specific page to load in a browser.

To view the finished frameset in Notes, choose Frame, Notes Preview. To view the frameset in a Web browser, choose Frame, Preview in Web Browser; and then select the browser.

This example—using Notes elements only—creates a simple but nice-looking Web application. The frameset will display in the Notes client, as shown in Figure 27.7. As you can see, it is virtually identical to how it displays in a Web browser, as shown in Figure 27.8.

Figure 27.7
A frameset shown in the Notes client.

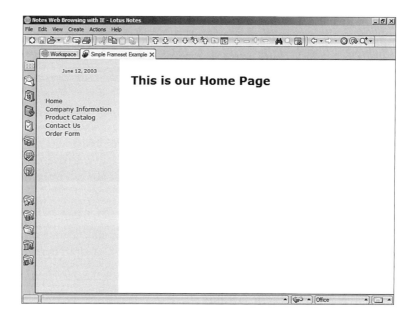

Figure 27.8
The same frameset shown in a Web browser.

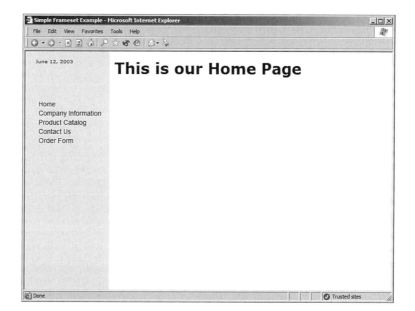

Although this is a ridiculously simple example, in the course of a brief exercise, you've managed to build a simple Web application using elements found natively in the Domino Designer—nothing added from HTML, nothing from any sort of outside editing tool or product.

ADDING HTML TO NOTES FORMS, DOCUMENTS, AND VIEWS

Another option for developing Web applications using Notes/Domino is to get closer to a true Web implementation by employing the Hypertext Markup Language (HTML). This way, you don't have to rely solely on or HTML. For example, HTML can be used in forms and views to augment what you can do in Notes itself.

Designer 6 makes it easier in some cases to convert all or part of an existing Notes form, page, or subform to HTML for use on the Web. Using the new HTML Editor, you can highlight content, convert it to HTML, and then edit it and preview how it will look in a browser. This feature must be used carefully because of limitations in what can be converted from Notes use to Web use (for example, buttons that do not have Web or client JavaScript associated with a Click event). But the new HTML Editor can make it easier to move Notes applications to the Web. You can read more about using the HTML Editor in Chapter 28, "Using Domino Designer's Web Development Features."

Other methods of adding HTML to your applications include importing existing HTML files directly into a form, page, or subform, or simply pasting or entering HTML.

Here's a typical task that becomes much easier using a hybrid method. Let's say you wanted to employ a typical Web trick such as posting a New icon next to recently added items and an Updated icon next to items that have been recently modified. A savvy Webmaster can handle the task of adding the icon fairly easily, but removing the tag after it's no longer appropriate is an additional task. In a fluid, frequently changing Web site, this becomes daunting.

A nickel's worth of HTML can be thrown into the formula for a column in a view that displays a New icon if the document is newer than 10 days old and an Updated icon if it has been recently modified:

```
REM "setting temporary variables to work with";
NewDate := @Adjust(@Today; 0; 0; -10; 0; 0; 0);
UpdatedDate := @Adjust(@Modified; 0; 0; -10; 0; 0; 0);
REM;
REM "Here's the statement that does the work";
REM "It'll display a NEW bitmap if the document is newer than ten days old";
REM "or an UPDATED bitmap if modified in the past ten days";
REM;
@If(@Created >= NewDate; "[<img src=../icons/new.gif>]";
@If((@Modified >= NewDate) & (UpdatedDate > @Created);
"[<img src=../icons/updated.gif>]"; ""))
```

You can add HTML to design elements in the Notes world in several ways.

The first is to do as the previous example does: Add square brackets to enclose the HTML code. For example, in the final line

```
"[<img src=../icons/updated.gif>]"
```

the square brackets enclose an HTML image tag that is passed directly to the browser.

You can use this method in forms, views, pages, and documents. Domino recognizes the square brackets as a signal that HTML is enclosed and passes the HTML directly to the browser. Domino itself doesn't attempt to act on the command; your browser does.

The second way to add HTML to design elements is to transform the design element in Notes into HTML itself. That can be done in a view by using the view attribute Treat View Contents as HTML. In a form, you can select Treat Document Contents as HTML, or Generate HTML for all fields. In forms, pages, or subforms, you can use the HTML Editor, mentioned previously.

You could also create and utilize a field called HTML; Domino recognizes that as a special field and passes its contents directly to the browser.

Additionally, you could create a style called HTML; any text flagged with that style is automatically passed to the browser.

Several examples of each of these methods are available in Designer 6 Help.

These options allow the developer to create HTML code that is sent directly to the browser.

Because the view will look terrible with the exposed HTML in the Notes client, you can easily hide the view from Notes clients. In Designer 6, however, you can use hide-when formulas to hide view columns, so this feature could be useful in situations like this when you want to hide a column based on the client being used.

By publishing the database with such a formula in a hidden view, the Web version of the database correctly identifies which documents are new and which have been recently updated. The Web view is displayed using a $$ViewTemplate form, as shown in Figure 27.9. Alternately, you could embed the view in a page or form and never need to bother with directing people to a view. Using this approach provides you with greater flexibility because you can design content and navigation around the embedded view.

27

This is a simple example of the creative use of HTML in Notes database design. We're not building strictly in the HTML environment, but we're adding a touch of it here and there where it makes sense. There's no easy way in Notes to create a New or Updated icon, yet the simple formula given previously is a lot easier than what a "conventional" Webmaster would have to do to achieve similar results.

Figure 27.9
Using HTML and formulas in a view column results in a dynamic Web page displaying New and Updated icons next to news releases.

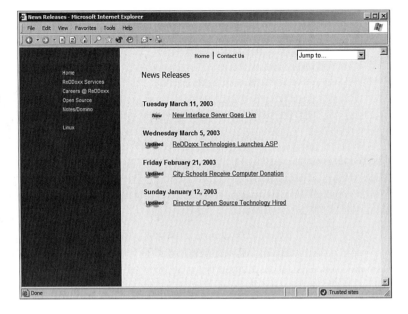

Other places where you could utilize simple HTML within a Notes database would include loading graphics, creating specialized response messages such as within a $$Return field, inserting text links (such as MailTo links), and more. Further explanation of these features follow:

- **Loading graphics**—As mentioned, Release 6 handles graphics differently from HTML, but you can still use HTML to load images. If a particular icon (such as the New icon) lives in the data/domino/icons directory, you can use the HTML Image Source tag to load the graphic from there via HTML passthru:

  ```
  [<img src = "/icons/new.gif">]
  ```

- **$$ fields**—A couple dozen Web-specific, reserved fields begin with "$$". See Designer 6 Help for more information.

- **Links**—You can build hotlinks to files, and you can create MailTo links, which can utilize HTML. Simply highlight the text you want to use for the highlight, and then choose either Create, Hotspot, Link Hotspot or Create, Hotspot, Action Hotspot.

Another simple way to add HTML to a vanilla Notes database is to use the HTML Attributes event. Depending on where you are within the database, you can add HTML to do things such as add META tags to a page.

TIP

> In Release 6, there's less of a need to do things such as try to control the size of a field via HTML attributes. The new properties of Native OS and Size enable you to control the sizing of fields without resorting to writing HTML.

You can also add HTML in the HTML Head Attributes event and the HTML Body Attributes event for the form itself. This gives you tremendous capabilities—adding META tags, for example—to do redirects or to give search engine robots additional search categorization criteria. In Figure 27.10, a simple META tag that includes additional category and description tags has been added to a Web page within the HTML Head Attributes.

Figure 27.10
META tags can be added in the HTML Head Attributes event.

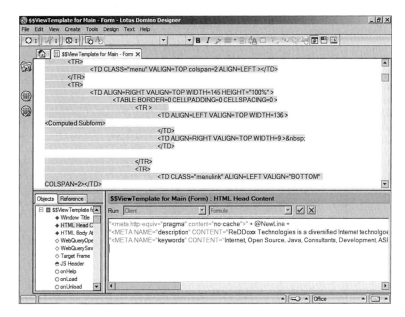

One of the other options to be aware of is the capability to use an exclamation point (!) in lieu of the default question mark (?) as a separator within Domino-generated URLs.

The question mark is a "restricted" character as far as search engines are concerned. Because the question mark is used frequently in CGI programs, search engines are normally programmed to ignore URLs that have question marks in them—therefore rendering much of a typical Domino site unsearchable.

You can change the question mark to an exclamation point by going to your Domino Directory, opening the Server document, and navigating to the Internet Protocols–Domino Web Engine tab. In the Conversion/Display section is an item that reads Make This Site Accessible to Web Search Site Crawlers. You can either enable or disable this property (it's disabled by default). By changing this to Enabled, you substitute the exclamation point for the question mark.

One of the caveats about this property is that other existing Domino sites might already have links built, might have HTML references, or might be the subject of links from elsewhere that use the question mark.

27

CREATING HTML DOCUMENTS AND USING THE DOMINO SERVER TO SERVE THEM

We're not going to spend much time on this particular option, mostly because if this is all you were going to do with a Domino server, you probably wouldn't have used Domino to begin with!

For the record, the Domino 6 server is pretty darn good as a straightforward HTTP server. You can do several things with a Domino server in the straight HTTP world that you can't do elsewhere (such as put ACL control on individual HTML files).

You absolutely could create HTML files in products such as Microsoft FrontPage, NetObjects Fusion, Adobe GoLive, Macromedia Dreamweaver, Macromedia HomeSite, and so on, and serve them on a Domino server. You could serve up XML files using XSLT style sheets to render the data in HTML on Domino. Just as you would serve a Web site from Microsoft Internet Information Server (IIS), Apache HTTP server, and other Web servers, Domino can serve "normal HTML," graphic images, CGI scripting, Perl, Java servlets and applets, DHTML, XML, Shockwave, and just about anything else.

If you were going to use a lot of HTML files in a Domino scenario, typically you'd put them in the html directory (data/domino/html) and/or a series of directories below that (data/domino/html/sales or data/domino/html/docs).

This would be particularly valuable for organizations that might be migrating a "straight HTML" Web site to a Domino-based site. They could move HTML files, images, CGI scripts, and so on. By default, images would go in the domino/icons directory, CGI scripts would go in the domino/cgi-bin directory, and so on, per settings in the server document. However, there's no reason why the images can't go in an images directory immediately beneath the HTML directory (data/domino/html/images, for example).

Regardless of your decisions about the path, Domino is fine for serving straight HTML files.

CREATING A HYBRID OF HTML DOCUMENTS AND SPECIALIZED DATABASES

Some things are better done in Notes; some things are better done using any given combination of HTML, JavaScript, Cascading Style Sheets (CSS), Java, external non-Notes data sources, XML, CGI scripts, and other tools and methods.

Considering the evolution in standards for what constitutes an attractive and functional Web site over the past several years, it's almost impossible to create a professional Notes-based Web site without writing at least some HTML, JavaScript, and maybe a little CSS. If your site needs to support some complicated functions, you obviously might need to draw on additional resources. As mentioned previously, the key to successful development of a Web site is to first determine in detail the site's objectives and functions. Then you can begin the process of identifying your design options.

Some new tools in Domino Designer 6 make it easier to take advantage of a hybrid approach to Web site development. The new Data Connector enables you to very quickly and simply integrate with relational data sources such as DB2, Oracle, Sybase, or ODBC databases. You can also add direct access to third-party tools, such as an HTML editor or CSS editor from within Designer.

Today well-crafted hybrid Web sites utilize any combination of Notes-based HTML documents using JavaScript and CSS, separate HTML files, Java, XML, and more. An example is a health-care system that, among other things, uses its Web site to provide updated job listings and allows users to apply for jobs online. In a tight labor market, it's critical that the job listings are updated in real time and that applicants can apply quickly and easily. This problem is solved using Notes forms on the back end and forms, pages, and views utilizing JavaScript and CSS on the front end. Hiring managers can add a new job posting simply by adding a new document in a Notes database. Once the posting is reviewed and approved, the Human Resources Manager can publish the new job opening to the Web site with the click of a Notes button. Neither of these people has a clue about HTML, and they didn't need to learn another tool such as FrontPage or NetObjects Fusion.

When the new job posting is replicated to the Domino Web server, any visitor can select the job from a listing, complete an online application form, and apply for the job. This is accomplished using a great deal of HTML, JavaScript, and CSS within Notes pages, forms, and views. The application is submitted to the database and, within minutes, the hiring manager can view it as an Adobe Acrobat PDF document.

One of the side benefits of using Notes is that the design elements of the site (including HTML, images, CSS, and JavaScript) are Notes resources instead of loose files littering the server. You can now make widespread changes by replicating to the Domino server, rather than having to FTP into the file system of the server, upload the image files, and so on.

This solution is a fairly typical example of how you can use a hybrid of Notes and some Web programming to create both a Notes and a Web interface that is attractive and easy to use, and that meets the objectives of internal stakeholders and the public.

CHALLENGES OF WEB SITE DEVELOPMENT

Despite all the advancements made in the Notes 6 client, some issues still must be worked around regarding the type of client your database is aimed at. There are distinct differences between the Notes client and a Web browser, and you'll need to keep these in mind as you develop your Web site.

Despite the advances that the Editor applet and the View applet bring to Web designers, they still aren't as fully featured as the Notes client. And as much as they help a browser client gain functionality, they take a while to load. Low-bandwidth sites might well elect not to use them for performance reasons.

Improvements in Designer 6 further minimize the differences in how you develop for the Notes client and for a browser, but you will find it hard to avoid creating some of your own HTML code. Some things work great in Notes and look terrible in a browser; other things you do specially for a browser look terrible in Notes.

27

An ongoing challenge is programming for the different Web browsers and their various versions. At some point, you will create Web content that seems to work fine in Netscape or Mozilla but that doesn't work in Internet Explorer, or vice versa. What works in IE 4.*x* doesn't necessarily work in IE 5.*x* and greater. The more complicated your Web site is, the more likely it is that you will run into problems with cross-browser compatibility.

To identify and resolve such problems you will need to test your Web site in various browsers and become familiar with the key differences in how each browser renders content. You also need to be aware of how your Web site will display at different screen resolutions. Nowadays it's likely that most users have monitors set to display for at least 800×600 dpi. It's generally acceptable to develop around that standard, although many sites still create content that fits in a 640×480 resolution. Just be sure to test your site at different resolutions, and remember that not everyone has a 19-inch monitor set at 1280×1024 resolution or greater like you do!

Other things aren't supported from one side or the other: LotusScript still can't be used behind fields, and the `refresh fields on keyword change` property works only in certain circumstances.

The bottom line is that Release 6 provides you with a robust Web-development platform that gives you the flexibility to create professional, functional Web sites that are as simple or complex as your situation calls for.

Although this book (and, for the record, other offerings by the Que folks and others) goes a long way toward explaining some of the mysteries surrounding Notes and Domino, you should be aware of a number of resources. Lotus Developer Domain (`www-10.lotus.com/ldd`) is absolutely the first and foremost place to go for the latest information on Notes and the Web. You'll find documentation and articles, the latest incremental updates, databases shared by others, a great forum to post questions and search for tips, and more.

Other Web resources you might want to check out include the following (in no particular order):

- `notestips.com`
- `searchdomino.techtarget.com`
- `www.notes411.com`
- `www.dominopower.com`
- `www.codestore.org`
- `notes.bluedojo.com`
- `www.redbooks.ibm.com`
- `cseh.best.vwh.net`
- `www.eview.com`

A few good sites for learning more about HTML, JavaScript, and Cascading Style Sheets include the following:

- www.htmlgoodies.com
- www.webmonkey.com
- www.webreference.com
- devedge.netscape.com
- www.siteexperts.com

27

CHAPTER **28**

USING DOMINO DESIGNER'S WEB-DEVELOPMENT FEATURES

In this chapter

OVERVIEW

Domino Designer Release 6 includes a number of new features that give the developer greater flexibility in creating applications for the Web. Some of these improvements make it easier to generate design elements that work in both Notes and Web browsers and that allow utilization of third-party Web-development tools. Other improvements include adding layers and integrating Cascading Style Sheets as a new resource type. Finally, improved support for offsite and collaborative Web development is possible through support for the WebDAV HTTP protocol.

Although we've touched on some of these features and tools elsewhere in this book, in this chapter we take a more detailed look at how to take advantage of them when creating your Domino Web applications.

ADDING AND CUSTOMIZING TOOLS

As good as Designer's Integrated Development Environment (IDE) is for creating Web applications, in many situations a third-party tool can do a better job of performing a specialized function. For example, you might have a favorite CSS editor for creating and editing all your style sheets. To their credit, the folks at Lotus recognize that Designer can't do it all and have made it possible to integrate the use of third-party applications—even your own tools—into Designer. With Release 6, you can now launch external applications and actions that you create using @command formulas from within Designer.

The Designer Tools menu is what makes this possible. The Tools menu enables you to add and customize tools for use within Designer.

To add a tool, follow these steps:

1. Choose Tools, Add Tool. The Add Tool dialog box appears, as shown in Figure 28.1.
2. Enter a name for the tool.
3. Specify the Tool Action that you want to initiate when you select the tool from the Tools menu. You can run a program or create your own action using an @command formula.

   - If running a program, use the Browse feature to select the application's executable file.
   - If running an @command formula, click the Formula Window button or Fields and Functions button to write the action.

4. Specify when the tool should be made available by selecting one or more design elements from the Tool Context list box. This enables you to control when the tool is listed on the Tools menu. For example, you might want a CSS editor to be available only when a page or form is open in Designer. By default, the tool always is available.

5. Click OK.

Figure 28.1
The Add Tools feature enables you to make third-party tools or your own formula-driven actions available in Domino Designer.

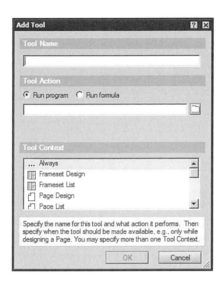

You can customize and organize tools using the Customize Tools command. This enables you to add, edit, and remove tools, as well as change when they are available on the Tools menu. You can even create submenus to group similar tools. To customize tools, you must first open the Customize Tools dialog box. Choose Tools, Customize Tools. The Customize Tools dialog box appears, as shown in Figure 28.2.

Select a context, and then click the Add Tool button if you want to add a new tool for one context. If you want to add a tool for more than one context, select all the contexts by holding down your Ctrl key and clicking each context. Then click the Add Tool button and add the tool.

To create a submenu, select a context and choose Add Submenu. This is useful if you have many tools and want to group similar types of applications or actions. Enter the submenu name and choose OK. Then select the submenu and add a tool.

To edit a tool, select it from the list and choose Edit.

To organize your tools, select them from the list and use the Cut, Copy, and Paste buttons, as appropriate. You can also organize tools by dragging and dropping them from one context to another.

28

Figure 28.2
Use the Customize Tools feature to edit and organize tools listed in your Tools menu.

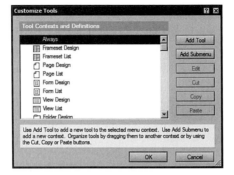

EDITING HTML

Unless you plan to let Domino generate all the HTML for your Web site, you can't get around writing and editing a good share of HTML yourself. The new HTML Editor introduced in Release 6 is intended to assist with some of the HTML generation and validation chores you can expect to face.

The HTML Editor is available on forms, subforms, and pages only. Of course, you can still create pass-thru HTML on these kinds of design elements without the editor. But this new tool includes a useful type-ahead feature similar to that added in the Designer 6 Programmer's pane for LotusScript and the Formula language, and it enables you to preview the rendered HTML. You won't see features found in many of the HTML editors that you can purchase, but this editor can be useful if you don't need all the bells and whistles.

You can use the editor on existing code or to create new HTML. There are several ways to include HTML on a form, subform, or page if you don't create it in the HTML Editor. These include converting Notes design elements into HTML, importing HTML directly from an external file, or pasting HTML from some other sources. Before going any further with the HTML Editor, let's briefly cover some key points about converting Notes to HTML.

CONVERTING FORMS, SUBFORMS, AND PAGES TO HTML

You can convert all or part of an existing form, subform, or page that was created in Designer to HTML. This feature is most useful if you're not familiar with writing HTML and have relatively simple content that you want to generate. For example, you might generate a page that incorporates tables, images, and text using Designer's WYSIWYG editor. When you have the general look you desire, you can convert all or part of it to HTML and then tweak the code as needed later if you want.

To convert a form, subform, or page to HTML, highlight the area you want to convert and then choose Edit, Convert to HTML. The selected contents are transformed into HTML. You'll want to do this carefully and in limited situations because conversions to HTML are

28

A discussion of how to create style sheets is beyond the scope of this book, but the following is an example of what a basic style sheet looks like:

```
<STYLE>
TD {
color:black;
    font-family:arial;
    font-size:10pt;
    cursor:default;
}
BODY {
background-color : #EEEEEE;
    color : #000000;
    margin:0;
}
A:LINK, A:VISITED {
    color : #000099;
    text-decoration : none;
}
A:HOVER {
    background-color : #FFFFFF;
    color : #00009F;
    text-decoration : none;
}
H1 {
    color : #990000;
    font-family : Verdana, Tahoma, Arial, Helvetica, sans-serif;
    font-size : 200%;
    margin-bottom : -1em;
    margin-left : -5%;
}
</STYLE>
```

As you can see, this particular style sheet defines rules for such attributes as the font color, font size, and cursor for all TD elements. Style rules are also defined for the BODY, LINK, and H1 elements. These styles apply only on Web pages that import this style sheet.

You can incorporate CSS files into your Web design in several ways. Since Domino 4.6, you can attach CSS files to documents in a database and then import them using the <link> tag to specify the link type and file path within the HTML HEAD element. For example:

```
<link rel=stylesheet type="text/css" href="/Mediastore.nsf/Files/global/$file/
global.css">
```

This approach is a bit cumbersome, however, so two more methods were introduced in Release 5. The first is to create a style sheet in a page and format it as pass-thru HTML so Domino knows to treat it as HTML. Then reference it using the <link> tag as before, but the href attribute would read similar to the following:

```
<link rel=stylesheet type="text/css" href="/database.nsf/pagename?OpenPage">
```

Another method introduced in Release 5 is to insert a CSS file as an image resource. Because only images appear in the Image Resources view, you will not see the CSS file, but you can still reference it using a modified <link> tag:

```
<link rel=stylesheet type="text/css" href="/database.nsf/
resourcename?OpenImageResource">
```

28

These approaches still work in Release 6, but using, importing, and editing style sheets is now much easier with the addition of the new style sheets resource. You can access the style sheets resources within the Shared Resources section of the Design pane. You can create style sheet resources by adding CSS files to the database, and you can edit them later using your preferred editor—directly from within Designer 6.

To create a new style sheet resource from anywhere in Designer, choose Create, Design, Style Sheet Resource. Alternatively, from within the Style Sheet Resources view, click the New Style Sheet Resource button. A dialog box appears; you can browse to select the desired CSS file, which should have the .css extension. Choose Open to insert the file.

A Style Sheet properties box appears. Here you can give the resource a name, enter comments to indicate what it's intended for, and set other properties. If you are likely to edit the style sheet in the future, make sure you check the Needs Refresh option. We'll cover why later in this chapter.

To import a style sheet resource into a Web page, you can still use the `<link>` tag, but modify the `href` attribute as follows:

```
<link rel=stylesheet type="text/css" href="/database.nsf/
resourcename?OpenCssResource">
```

If you take advantage of the style sheet resource feature, editing and managing your style sheets will be relatively simple. As mentioned previously, you access your style sheet resources by clicking Shared Resources–Style Sheets in the Design pane. Your style sheets will appear as shown in Figure 28.5.

Figure 28.5
Creating and editing style sheet resources is made easier using the tools available in the Designer 6 Style Sheets folder.

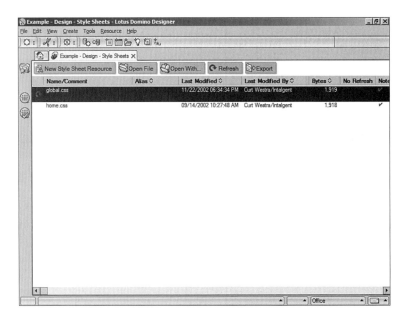

You'll notice several buttons on the action bar. We've already discussed the New button and how to use it. To open an existing style sheet resource file, select the resource and click the Open File button. If your machine already has an application installed that is associated with CSS files, it will launch and open the selected file. Alternatively, you can open a selected resource by clicking the Open With button and choosing the program that you want to use to edit the style sheet. Figure 28.6 displays a style sheet resource opened in a popular CSS editor, TopStyle Lite.

Figure 28.6
You can open and edit style sheet resources by launching a third-party editor from within Designer 6.

When you open a style sheet resource, Designer creates a temporary copy on your machine's hard drive. When you make changes and save them in your third-party editor, the changes are saved to this temporary file, not to the style sheet resource in your database. You need to refresh the modified resource so that the changes are incorporated from the temporary copy. If you selected the Needs Refresh option in the resource's preferences box, the familiar refresh arrow indicates that it has been edited and might need updating, as shown in Figure 28.7.

To refresh a style sheet resource, select the resource that needs updating and then click the Refresh button. An Open dialog box appears. Select the CSS file to refresh your style sheet resource, and click Open. The style sheet resource is then updated.

28

Figure 28.7
The refresh arrow flags style sheet resources that have been edited.

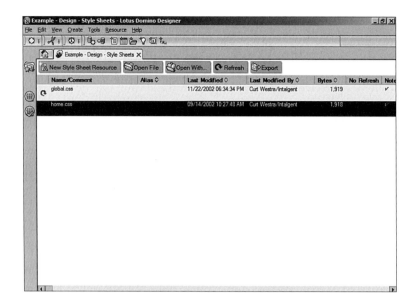

LAYERS

Layers can be utilized in both Notes and Web applications, but here we focus on their use for the Web. Layers enable you to place overlapping blocks of content on forms, subforms, or pages. You can stack several layers on top of each other and specify the position, size, and content of each. Layers can be transparent so that the underlying layers are revealed, or opaque so that underlying layers are concealed. This enables you to create Web pages that dynamically display content.

Layers have the same properties and are created using the same methods whether you are working in forms, subforms, or pages. The only difference is the type of content that can be included. A page layer can contain only those elements available to a page, while a form layer can include a wider array of elements, such as fields and subforms.

To create a layer within an existing form, subform, page, or other layer, choose Create, Layer. A layer of a default size is created, as shown in Figure 28.8. When you create a layer, you'll notice that an anchor is also created wherever the cursor was positioned at the time. Although the anchor's position cannot be changed, it does not hinder you from positioning the layer where you want.

After a layer is created, you can set its size, position, z-index, background color or transparency level, and HTML tags, if necessary. To access a layer's properties, double-click it. You can also select the layer or its anchor, and then right-click and select Layer Properties. The Layer Properties box appears, as shown in Figure 28.9. On the Positioning tab, you can set the position of the layer from the top and left edges of a browser window, along with its size and z-index. You can also change the position of a layer by placing your cursor on its

28

border until a crosshair appears and then dragging it. Positioning your cursor on the handles of the layer border and dragging can adjust a layer's size.

Figure 28.8
Creating layers is easy in Designer.

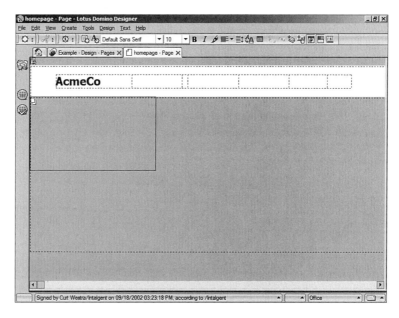

Figure 28.9
You control a layer's size, position, z-index, transparency, and HTML tags from the Layer properties box.

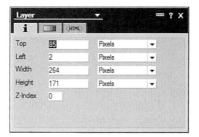

The z-index is an important property of the layer that controls its stacking order. The higher the z-index value is, the higher it is in the stacking order. A z-index of 0 or greater places the layer in front of the form, subform, or page. A negative z-index places a layer behind the form, subform, or page and prevents it from being acted on. If you have multiple layers, the layer with the highest z-index is placed on top, and the layer with the smallest z-index is positioned at the bottom of the stack. Opaque layers hide layers and other content underneath. Furthermore, any layer or content on the page or form beneath a visible layer cannot be clicked or acted on.

Let's look at a simple example of how you can create and use layers in a Web application. In this example, layers are used on a Web site to display different content in the same area of

28

the screen, based on user actions. Figure 28.10 displays the first layer, named Layer 1, created within a table on a page. It has been set with a z-index of 0 so that it will lie beneath any layers stacked above it later.

Figure 28.10
The default z-index of a layer created in Designer is 0.

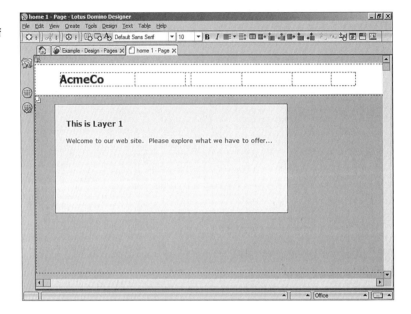

Because this layer is created on a page, you could enter text, pass-thru HTML, JavaScript, hotspots, and all the elements you normally can use on a page.

As mentioned previously, you can even create layers within a layer, which are called *children* layers. Simply place the cursor within the desired layer and choose Create, Layer. A child layer and its anchor are created wherever the cursor was positioned at the time. In this example, however, some simple text is all that is included in the layers.

When a layer is created, it is transparent by default. You can make a layer transparent or opaque by opening its properties and selecting the Background tab, as shown in Figure 28.11. Here, you can select a background color or image for the layer. If you select no color or you use an image such as a transparent GIF, the layer will allow content beneath it to be visible when displayed in a browser. The layer shown in Figure 28.10 has a background color selected.

As mentioned previously, using multiple layers, you can dynamically change content on a Web page. Figure 28.12 shows a second layer, Layer 2, created to display another set of content. This layer has a z-index of 1, so it is, in effect, the top layer and will be positioned above Layer 1.

28

Figure 28.11
Use the settings on
the Background tab of
the Layer properties
box to control a
layer's transparency.

Figure 28.12
A second layer lies
above the first layer,
based on its higher
z-index value.

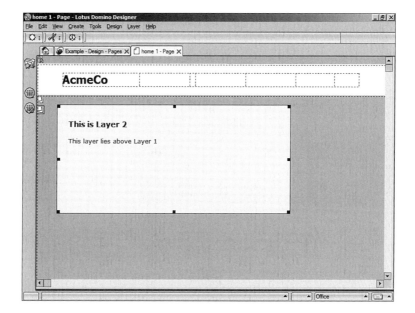

Aside from the layer properties, you have access to some tools in Designer that help you
arrange and size multiple layers. To open these tools, first click a layer to select it. Then
right-click to open a menu, or click the Layer menu. From the Layer menu, you can perform several operations:

- **Cut or Copy the Selected Layer.**
- **Hide Layer.** This is most helpful when you are designing multiple layers that overlap,
  and you want to work on one layer at a time and remove the distraction of other layers.
- **Select Layer.** You can select all sibling layers (all the parent layers on the form, subform, or page) or all the children layers within the selected layer. This is useful in two
  ways. First, it groups the selected layers and enables you to move them together, maintaining their relative position to each other. Second, it enables you to use the Align and
  Make Same Size options described later.

28

■ **Align.** Multiple selected layers can be aligned together using this option. The layers are aligned relative to the position of the top layer, or the layer with the highest z-index. You can choose to align selected layers along the left, right, top, bottom, horizontal center, and vertical center of the topmost layer. In the example with Layers 1 and 2, you could use this option to align both layers.

■ **Make Same Size.** Use this option to make selected layers the same height, width, or both. This is most useful when you are stacking overlapping layers and want to use the exact same screen area for each. In the example using Layers 1 and 2, you would use this option to make sure both are exactly the same size.

■ **Layer Tree.** You can hide one or more layers during the current design session using the Layer Tree. When you select this option, the Layer Tree dialog box appears (see Figure 28.13), listing all the layers and their children. Select a layer and choose the appropriate Hide or Show button to hide or show the layer while you edit the form or page. Then choose Close.

Figure 28.13
The Layer Tree dialog box enables you to hide or show one or more layers during a design session.

After you have created some layers, you can determine how to dynamically control how the layers will be displayed, positioned, or hidden in the Web browser. You can do this in several ways. One method that can be used in conjunction with others is to set HTML attributes of the layer in the HTML tab of the Layer properties box. You use the ID attribute to identify the layer to the browser and make it accessible to methods such as JavaScript. The Class and Style attributes can be used to apply styles to the layer. The Title attribute establishes a label that appears when a mouse hovers over the layer in Internet Explorer 4.x browsers and higher. The Other attribute can be used to define a variety of other attributes. For example, an onClick event could be defined here that would initiate some activity.

A very basic approach to controlling when layers are displayed in a Web browser would be to use Hide When text properties of the paragraph containing a layer's anchor. You could set the layers to be hidden or shown based on certain criteria, such as the user's role, or, if you are designing the layer on a form or subform, a field value.

Another more robust method for showing or hiding layers is to incorporate JavaScript in your design. JavaScript gives you greater flexibility and control over your layers, and it can also be used to change the position of layers. In the example we're following in this chapter, links on the Web page are used to trigger relatively simple JavaScript functions to show and hide layers. The result of clicking the Show Layer 1 link in a browser is shown in Figure 28.14.

Figure 28.14
With the use of JavaScript, Layer 1 appears when the Show Layer 1 link is clicked.

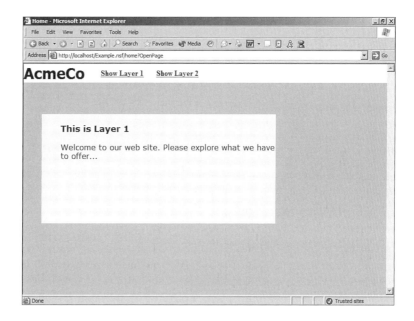

When the Show Layer 2 link is clicked in a browser, the second layer appears, as shown in Figure 28.15.

Figure 28.15
Layer 2 appears when the Show Layer 2 link is clicked.

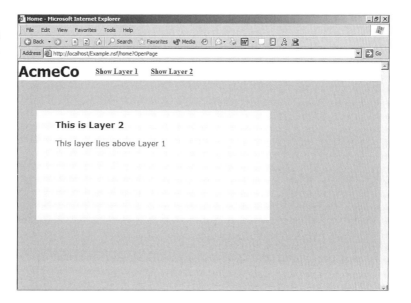

It's worth noting that layers are rendered differently in Internet Explorer and Netscape. Internet Explorer renders layers using `<div>` tags, while Netscape uses `<layer>` tags. If different browsers access your Web page, you will need to accommodate this. Make sure you create JavaScript or other code that is cross-browser–compatible if it accesses the layers and their attributes.

TEAM WEB DEVELOPMENT USING WEBDAV

The reality in many organizations is that teams of individuals must work together to develop and maintain Web sites. In some situations, individuals work offsite but must be able to access and modify a Web application. Or perhaps you use a third-party tool such as Macromedia Dreamweaver to create and edit certain content, but you find it cumbersome to access and edit the code when it's in a Notes database. WebDAV, or Web-Based Distributed Authoring and Versioning, enables users to bypass some of these challenges by supporting collaborative management and editing of files on remote Web servers.

WebDAV is a set of extensions to the HTTP protocol that is intended to enable remote users to access a Web server using a preferred client such as Windows Explorer, Internet Explorer, or even an application such as Macromedia's Dreamweaver. The Internet Engineering Task Force (IETF), the group behind its development, is working to expand its features to make it more robust. You can find out more about WebDAV and its future at www.webdav.org.

Domino Release 6 introduces initial support for WebDAV access from Win32 machines. With a WebDAV-enabled Domino server, you can create, edit, or delete file resources, CSS resources, and images stored in a Notes database. You cannot access design elements such as forms or a database's documents using WebDAV. WebDAV supports design locking to prevent overwriting of design elements by teams so that one person can check out a resource and prevent another person from modifying it until it's checked back in.

SETTING UP THE SERVER AND DATABASE

Before you can use WebDAV with a database, it must be enabled on the Domino server. Your system administrator must enable WebDAV and disable session authentication in the Web Site document for the database you are working on. Refer to the Domino Administrator Help for details on enabling WebDAV.

Check these database settings to allow WebDAV access by a user:

1. Give the user either Designer or Manager access in the database Access Control List (ACL). The user also must have the capability to Create Documents and Delete Documents enabled in the database ACL.

2. On the Advanced tab of the database ACL, set the Maximum Internet Name and Password field to either Designer or Manager access.

3. Select the proper administration server (or master lock server) on the Advanced tab of the database ACL. The administration server must be accessible to ensure that design locking works.

4. Enable Design Locking on the Designer tab of the Database properties box to prevent accidental overwrites of a resource. Some WebDAV clients (such as MS Word 2000, Excel 2000, and Dreamweaver 4.*x*) lock the file when it is opened for edits or when the file is saved to a WebDAV server. For these clients to work with WebDAV databases on the Domino server, you must enable Design Locking for each of the WebDAV databases.

5. Check that the database has the option Don't Allow URL Open enabled in the Database properties box. If it is checked, you will not be able to access the database using a WebDAV client.

6. Configure the proxy settings for the WebDAV client. You might experience problems accessing the Domino server if your WebDAV client uses a proxy. If so, disable the proxy for access to the server. If your WebDAV client is Windows Explorer, Internet Explorer 5, or Internet Explorer 6, enter the hostname of the Domino WebDAV server as an exception to using the proxy.

USING WEBDAV CLIENTS

WebDAV-enabled clients that Domino is designed to support include Microsoft Internet Explorer 5.0*x* or greater, Windows Explorer on NT, Windows XP, Windows 98, Windows 2000, Macromedia's Dreamweaver 4.01 or greater, Microsoft Word 2000, and Excel 2000.

When using a WebDAV client to access a Notes database, create a connection using a URL that specifies the Web site's hostname and database name, with the `$files` string appended to the end. The `$files` string tells the server that it is a WebDAV request. For example, to open the database named homepage.nsf, enter the path as follows:

```
http://servername/homepage.nsf$files
```

After you have connected to a database with a WebDAV client, you can open a resource, edit it, and save it back to the database. You can even add a design element that you have created using a third-party editor.

Because Macromedia Dreamweaver is the only true Web application IDE that has supported access to Domino using WebDAV, let's take a little time to explore its setup and use.

You can find detailed instructions on how to configure Dreamweaver for WebDAV in its Help feature, but a couple of items are worth mentioning here. First, to ensure that the Dreamweaver Check In and Check Out feature and the Designer client locks work together properly, you will need to provide your Notes Internet username, password, and Internet e-mail address. You enter this information in the Remote Sites configuration panel of Dreamweaver. The e-mail address that you provide Dreamweaver must match the e-mail address in the Internet Address field of the Person document in Domino Directory.

In Figure 28.16, you can see what the Dreamweaver WebDAV interface looks like when connected to a Domino server and Notes database. The files listed are those located on the remote Domino server, although you can also view your local files. Dreamweaver enables you to copy files from the Domino server to your local drive, check them out, edit them,

28

and then synchronize the changes back to Domino. In Figure 28.16, you'll notice that Dreamweaver places a check mark next to those that are locked in Dreamweaver or by someone else in Designer.

Figure 28.16
Within Dreamweaver, you can view design elements listed on your local drive or Domino and see which ones are locked.

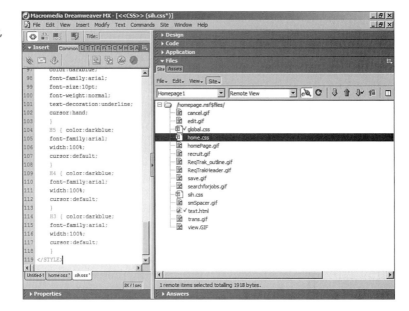

Of course there are limitations with using WebDAV and Designer 6. You are limited to working with file resources, CSS, and images. Macromedia's Dreamweaver is the only Web-development application that is supported by Domino's WebDAV feature. But this feature is promising, in that it provides greater flexibility for collaboration when developing Web applications in Designer 6.

CHAPTER 29

DOMINO AND ENTERPRISE INTEGRATION

In this chapter

WHAT DO WE MEAN BY ENTERPRISE INTEGRATION?

Lotus has gone to great lengths to shed the image of Domino as a standalone, proprietary system. One of the ways it has accomplished this—and continues to do so—is by providing a wide variety of tools for integrating Domino with an even wider variety of enterprise data sources. Additionally, several Lotus Business Partners have taken the lead in producing third-party tools for data integration. The depth of the product itself and the depth of its usage as a mission-critical Internet, intranet, and client/server development platform continue to increase. As a result, data integration will become both a standard practice and a specialization unto itself.

Enterprise integration refers to the practice of integrating data from multiple systems and sources, making it available and easier to use where it's needed. More than ever, companies need to integrate data from diverse sources across their enterprise to increase efficiency, improve decision-making ability, better serve consumers and business partners, and maintain legacy systems. Legacy systems have traditionally been thought of as systems that are not cutting edge but that nevertheless play a crucial and possibly central role in supporting the data needs of an organization. Today it's safe to say that legacy systems can refer to any existing data system, regardless of its age or sophistication, and that they are often the focus of enterprise integration efforts. However, when we consider data integration in our organizations, we might, in fact, be talking about integrating Domino with systems that aren't even in place yet—for example, "the new system for Human Resources."

So what kinds of things do enterprises integrate? Systems, or sources of data, generally fall into one of these categories:

- Relational database systems
- Enterprise resource-planning (ERP) systems
- Transactional systems
- Non–"system-based" sources

All these categories are fairly standard and well known. Let's cover them only briefly so that we're all on the same page, so to speak.

RELATIONAL DATABASE SYSTEMS

Relational database management systems (RDBMS) are general-purpose data systems designed from the start to handle highly structured, table-oriented data. Familiar names from this arena are Oracle, Sybase, Informix, SQL Server, and DB2. RDBMS vendors, like nearly everyone else, have Web-enabled their products.

It's usually stated that Notes/Domino is not a relational system. This is true, but it is very possible to create applications that accomplish the same tasks as a relational system. In the right scenario—for example, relatively low-volume (tens of thousands of records, as opposed to hundreds of thousands or millions of records) and relatively small table depth (the number of table structures)—Domino is a viable option. Take both of these into account as you decide whether to implement a process in Domino or to integrate it as a front end to the process.

ENTERPRISE RESOURCE-PLANNING (ERP) SYSTEMS

ERP systems are all-in-one packages that are meant to support standard business functions throughout an organization. Human resources, asset management, purchasing, and so on are some examples. ERP systems provide a unified interface for performing these functions and generally use a relational database management system (RDBMS) to store actual data. Familiar names in this arena are PeopleSoft, Baan, SAP R/3, and JDEdwards.

As central repositories for firmwide data, especially human resource information, it makes sense that workflow applications should be able to integrate with these systems. The gains in data integrity make the extra effort worthwhile.

Again, Domino applications have been used in numerous large organizations as ERP system equivalents. Probably the most important factor in deciding whether to build your own in Domino or to integrate with an ERP package is resources. Any system designed to support an enterprisewide function requires a long development and testing effort. This might not be feasible if your Domino staff is not large enough. The benefit of ERP packages is that, although their implementation might take as much time as Domino solutions, there are armies of consultants who specialize in their implementation and the business processes they address. In any event, the ability to integrate Domino with an ERP system enables developers to add its unique features, as well as make ERP data readily available on the Web.

TRANSACTIONAL SYSTEMS

Transactional systems, often referred to as *transaction processing monitor systems*, are the workhorses in business computing, particularly in finance. They might seem unexciting for those of us raised on GUI interfaces and point-and-click design, but they're complex, they're mission-critical, and they're everywhere.

The key to transactional systems is that they manage discreet and well-defined exchanges of data in real time, and they can fully recover, at the transaction level, from a system failure. CICS, IMS, MQSeries, and BEA Tuxedo are some familiar systems.

Whereas Notes/Domino has been used successfully to implement semirelational systems and ERP-like systems, transaction-processing systems represent an area in which Domino has not been used. Notes/Domino, of course, was never meant to perform the functions that transactional systems perform, and it would be a definite mistake to try to jury-rig it into doing so. The good news is that Lotus has recognized this fact and has created products that nevertheless enable us to bring Notes/Domino into the mix.

NON–"SYSTEM-BASED" DATA SOURCES

Data doesn't always reside in a "system." Files reside on servers, and data resides in text files, in spreadsheets, and so on. For many organizations, *this* constitutes legacy data, too. OLE automation, regular old importing and exporting, and several third-party products address this data-collection problem.

Now that we've covered the basic "arena" for enterprise integration, let's survey the options available to make integration possible. First, we'll look at the out-of-the-box solutions from Lotus; then we'll discuss other Lotus programming solutions and integration products. Finally, we'll wrap up the chapter by reviewing third-party tools.

DATA CONNECTION RESOURCE (DCR)

Lotus has recognized the importance of integrating enterprise data with Domino, and it offers a wide array of tools and programming solutions that enable you to connect to external data sources. The *data connection resource (DCR)* is the newest entry from Lotus. Introduced in Release 6, the DCR makes integration of external data into Domino fast and easy. DCRs are reusable design elements within Designer that enable you to create a connection to a database for use in a form or field. Using a DCR, you define a connection to an external data source; then you use that connection to associate a form and its fields to fields in the external source. As shared resources, DCRs are reusable and can be shared across forms within the database and across multiple applications.

DCRs utilize *Domino Enterprise Connection Services (DECS)* technology and essentially provide a subset of the functionality offered if you used DECS instead. Although DECS is discussed in detail the next section of this chapter, it is worth briefly describing it here. DECS comes bundled with Domino Server 4.6.3 and above, and runs as a Domino server task. Generally, it enables you to connect to relational databases and access data at the field level in real time. DECS offers greater functionality but requires you to create connection documents to external data sources in a separate DECS administration database. DCRs, in contrast, are more easily created and reused in your database design.

Although the DCR is an effective first-tier enterprise integration tool from Lotus, you will want to do a little research to determine whether it will meet your needs or whether you'll need DECS or something else. For example, you probably don't want to use DCRs if you want to collapse multiple external records into one Notes document or control which Domino events are monitored. For these and other features not included with DCRs, you could look to DECS, Lotus Enterprise Integrator (LEI), or third-party tools, all discussed later in this chapter.

Data connection resources can be used to connect to several types of relational databases, including DB2, Oracle, Sybase, OLE DB, and ODBC data sources. This flexibility and the fact that you build and administer them right within your Notes database make them an appealing option.

To gain a better understanding of data connection resources, let's take a brief look at how to create and implement one.

CREATING A DATA CONNECTION RESOURCE

Before you get started using DCRs, you'll need to make sure that DECS is set up and running. DECS is one of the optional advanced Domino server services that you can enable during server setup. If you need to install DECS after the server has already been set up, simply modify the server's Notes.ini file as shown here:

```
ServerTasks=....., DECS
EXTRMGR_ADDINS=decsext
```

By default, there should already be a ServerTasks line in the Notes.ini, so you need to add the DECS argument only at the end of the existing line. The entire EXTRMGR_ADDINS line will likely need to be added as shown. When these modifications are completed and the file is saved, restart the server.

You must also create the data source for the external data on your server. You'll need to coordinate with your system administrator to make sure the data source is defined if you don't have administration rights on the server where the external database resides.

DCRs are listed as data connections within the Shared Resources section of the Designer IDE. To get a feel for how DCRs can be used, let's walk through an example that sets up a Notes form to be the front end for an external ODBC data source that includes customer contact information. Recognize that the information you need to complete will vary by the type of connection. The steps shown here relate specifically to ODBC data sources.

To create a new data connection resource, follow these steps:

1. In Designer, choose Shared Resources, Data Connections.
2. Click the New Data Connection Resource button. The Data Connection properties box appears, as shown in Figure 29.1.

Figure 29.1
Use the Data Connection properties box to set up a new data connection resource.

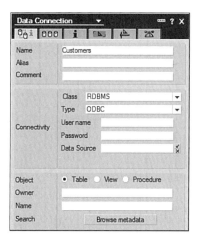

3. Enter a name for the DCR. It is optional to enter an alias and a comment in the fields provided. In this example, name it Customers.

4. Select the class of database that you want to connect to. In this example, RDBMS is selected.

5. Select the type of connection you want to make to the external data source. Depending on the type of database, some native or third-party drivers could be available as connection types. In this example, a basic ODBC connection is all that is needed.

6. Enter the username and password required to access the external database, if necessary.

7. Enter the name of the external data source as established on the server previously. For certain types of data sources, you might need to enter other information.

8. Select the type of object to connect to (table, view, or procedure).

9. Enter the user ID for the owner of the external table or view. For procedures, you must also enter the procedure name for any of the document open, update, create, and delete events that will trigger the procedure.

10. Enter the name of the table, view, or procedure. You can also click the Browse Metadata button to browse the external database for the proper name, as shown in Figure 29.2.

Figure 29.2
You can browse the external data source to select the desired table, view, or procedure.

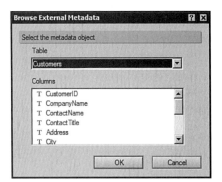

11. You can set options for the DCR by clicking the General Options tab, as shown in Figure 29.3. Details about these options are provided in the Designer Help. These include general options that apply to all connection types, as well as specific settings that apply to certain databases.

Now that a data connection resource is set up, you must define fields on a form to map to the external data source. Let's take a look at this process next.

USING A DATA CONNECTION RESOURCE IN A FORM

After you've created a data connection, you must create or modify a Notes form that will serve as the link between Domino and the external data source. You create fields on the form that map to an external data source, specifying the appropriate DCR and identifying the external database's associated field name.

Figure 29.3
Set the DCR's options by clicking the Options tab of the properties box.

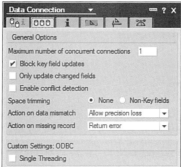

If you will be using only one DCR for the fields on a form, you can specify a default DCR for the form. Doing so requires less time when mapping each individual field because basic information for the data connection automatically is set in the field properties. To select a default DCR for a form, follow these steps:

1. Create or open the form.
2. Open the Form properties box by right-clicking in the form and selecting Form Properties.
3. Click the Defaults tab to display the options shown in Figure 29.4.

Figure 29.4
Specify a form's default data connection in the Form properties box.

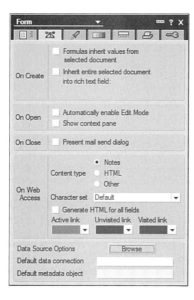

4. Specify a data connection resource by clicking the Browse button next to Data Source Options, or enter the name in the Default Data Connection field.
5. If the same metadata object (such as a table or view) will be used in most fields, you can specify its name in the Default Metadata Object field.

The next step is to create or modify fields in the form and map them to the external data source's fields. To design fields that will connect with external data using a DCR, follow these steps:

1. Select a field that will map to an external source; then double-click it to open its Field properties box, as shown in Figure 29.5.

Figure 29.5
Link a Notes field to a field in an external data source using the Field properties box.

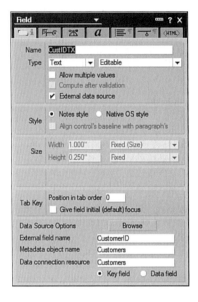

2. On the Field Info tab, select the External Data Source option. If you had specified a default DCR for the form that provided the appropriate Data Connection Resource and Metadata Object Name information, these two fields will be filled out, and you can skip Steps 3 and 5.

3. Specify the metadata object name (such as a table or view) where the associated external field is located.

4. Specify the external field name that the field must map to.

5. Specify the name of the appropriate data connection resource by entering it or by clicking the Browse button and searching.

6. If the field's corresponding external field is a key field, select the Key Field option. A key field must always be designated for a data connection, and it is used to associate a Notes document with the correct external data source. Key field data are always stored locally.

7. Select the Data Field option for any nonkey field. Select the Store Locally option if you would like the field's data stored in the Notes database as well as in the external database.

When you begin to actually work with the external data via Domino, any changes that you make are pushed back to the external database. If the data changes in the back-end database, you can manually refresh the data as you would with any Domino application.

You're almost ready to actually integrate external data with Domino using a data connection resource. If you want to begin to create new documents and corresponding external data records, you'd have to only activate the database property to allow data connections. But if you want to view all the existing external data records, you need to perform a one-time initial import of records from the data source. This creates Notes documents for each external record by the key field value. Let's briefly walk through how you import data from an external database.

IMPORTING EXTERNAL DATA USING A DCR

Before actually importing the data, you must disable the database property that allows data connections using DCRs. Open Database Properties and in the Database Basics tab uncheck the option Allow Connections to External Databases Using DCRs, as shown in Figure 29.6. Close the database and reopen it in Designer.

Figure 29.6
You must disable the database's ability to use DCRs before a first-time import of external data records.

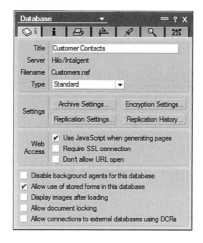

To import external data using a DCR, follow these steps:

1. Open the data connections within the Shared Resources of the database.

2. Select the DCR associated with the data you want to import. Click the Import External Records button.

3. An Import External Records dialog box opens, prompting you to select the Notes form to use for retrieving data. Select the appropriate form and click OK.

4. A DECS Administrator dialog box opens, indicating that new documents will be created for each unique external record and asking for confirmation to proceed. Click Yes.

29

5. After the new documents have been created, another dialog box appears to notify you of how many documents were created. Choose OK.

6. Open the database properties and select the Allow Connections to External Databases Using DCRs option. Close the database and reopen it.

That's it! Figure 29.7 shows a Notes document with data pulled in real time from the external RDBMS used in the example. Obviously, this example was relatively simple, but it demonstrates how quickly and easily you can utilize the new data connections in Release 6 to integrate Domino with enterprise data. With the completion of these steps, users could immediately access and manipulate external data using the example Notes database.

Figure 29.7
A Notes form displays real-time data from an external data source.

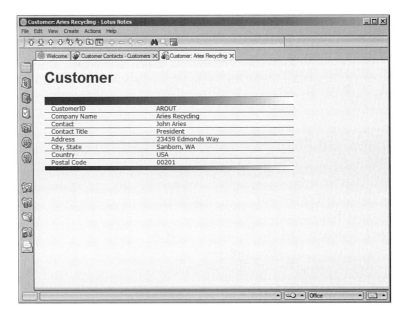

Now let's take a look at another Lotus offering, the Domino Enterprise Connection Services (DECS). Recall that DCRs utilize a subset of the DECS functionality, but the complete DECS feature set can be utilized by avoiding DCRs and instead configuring external data connections within the DECS administration database. The next section discusses how DECS can be used independently of DCRs to integrate enterprise data with Domino.

DOMINO ENTERPRISE CONNECTION SERVICES (DECS)

Domino Enterprise Connection Services (DECS), which comes bundled with Domino Server 4.6.3 and above, is an effective and established second-tier product from Lotus. DECS runs as a Domino server task and enables you to connect to relational databases and access data at the field level in real time. Because DECS requires no programming to create connections and activities, it is relatively easy to get up and running in very little time. Considering its functionality, ease of use, and cost (free!), it is definitely worth looking into if you need to connect to external data from Domino and your situation demands features not supported by DCRs.

DECS can be used to connect to several types of relational databases, including DB2, Oracle, Sybase, OLE DB, File, and ODBC data sources. Administration is handled through the DECS Administrator database created on the server where DECS is running, and it is easy to learn and use. You work within the DECS Administrator to view, create, and manage all your external database connections and the activities that Notes will be able to initiate.

As mentioned previously, DECS supports integration with ODBC-compliant relational systems, ERP systems, and transaction systems—by utilizing Lotus Connectors. Connectors are new objects, not enhanced LSXs. In fact, there is a LotusScript Extension for Lotus Connectors (LSX LC) for accessing Connectors in LotusScript, as well as a Connector toolkit for third parties to develop custom connectors. Although we won't go into it in detail here, you should know that you can use the LSX LC for configuring DECS to access external data sources instead of using DECS Administrator.

DECS offers greater functionality than can be found using the DCRs described previously. For example, DECS enables you to control which Domino events initiate real-time activities, permits multiple external records to be rolled into one Notes document (multivalue support), and allows scheduling of real-time activities.

In this section, we take a look at DECS and walk through how to set up a connection to a basic ODBC data source. Let's explore in more detail how to use DECS for enterprise integration.

Exploring DECS

Before you get started using DECS, you'll need to make sure it is set up and running. Refer to this chapter's section on creating a data connection resource for instructions on how to do this.

When DECS is installed, the DECS Administrator (decsadm.nsf) database is created. In addition, three documentation databases on the server are useful references:

- Domino Enterprise Connection Services (DECS) Installation and User Guide (decsdoc6.nsf)

- Lotus Connectors and Connectivity Guide (lccon6.nsf)

- Lotus Connector LotusScript Extensions Guide (lsxlc6.nsf)

You will want to refer to the DECS Installation and User Guide before doing any work in DECS. The other guides are useful if you want to use LotusScript to extend your control over the external data.

When you first open the DECS Administrator database, you will see the default Activities view, as shown in Figure 29.8. If you had already created activities for any connections, you could view and manage them here, as well as initiate other activities.

Figure 29.8
The DECS Administration screen provides an interface to create and manage external data connections and related activities.

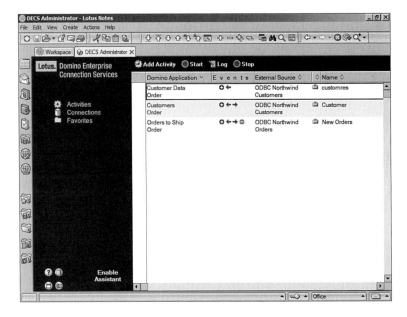

Within the DECS Administrator, you can perform the following functions using the navigation options on the left, as shown in Figure 29.9:

■ To create or view connections, click Connections to open the Connections view. Existing connections are displayed, and you can click the Add Connection button to create a new one.

■ To create an activity, click Activities to open the Activities view. Then click Add Activity.

You'll also notice some icons and options at the bottom left of the navigation pane. These include the following:

■ **Info**—Click the question mark icon to open the Using DECS Administrator document that provides information and illustrations to help you understand the Administrator interface.

■ **Help**—Click the book icon to open the DECS Administrator online help documentation.

■ **Running**—Click the window icon to display information about currently running activities. Click again to close.

Figure 29.9
Click the top menu options within the DECS Administrator navigation pane to view connections and activities; click the lower icons to access helpful resources.

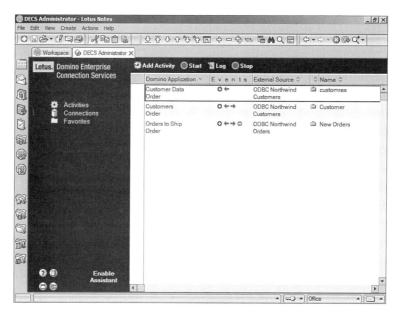

- **Assistant**—Click flowing arrow icon or the Enable Assistant text link at the bottom right of the pane to turn the User Assistant on or off. The User Assistant is useful if you're not familiar with DECS; it provides additional information when creating new connections and activities. It also enables the New Activity/Connectivity Wizard.

Now that you have a high-level feel for the DECS user interface, let's go through an example of how to create a relatively simple connection and activity. Then you'll see how to retrieve and display external data in Notes.

CREATING A CONNECTION

Although the specifics of how you create a connection and activity using DECS might vary somewhat depending on the type of database you're working with, it's relatively easy to set up a new connection with the DECS Administrator. The DECS connection document is used to define the external data source and some of its attributes. To get a feel for how DECS can be used, let's walk through an example that sets up a Notes database to be the front end for an external ODBC data source. Recognize that the information you need to complete will vary by the type of connection. The steps shown here relate specifically to ODBC data sources.

Follow these steps to create a new ODBC connection:

1. From the Connections view, click Add Connection. The Other dialog box opens, as shown in Figure 29.10.

2. Select a connection type from the list that appears. In the example used here, Connection to ODBC is selected.

Figure 29.10
The first step in creating a connection is to select a connection type from a list of supported data sources.

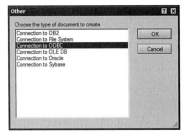

3. A blank Lotus Connection document appears, as shown in Figure 29.11. You'll see additional text at the top of the document if you enable the User Assistant.

Figure 29.11
Use the Lotus Connection document to create a connection to an external data source.

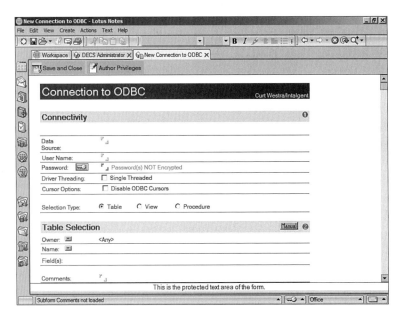

4. Enter the name of the data source and then the username and password required to access the database.

5. Complete other information in the Connectivity section of the form that is specific to the connection type. For example, with the ODBC connection example here, you can select multithreaded or single-threaded execution and choose to disable cursor activity.

6. To restrict the list of data sources to a specific owner, click the down arrow button next to Owner. You can select from a list of any designated owners.

7. Display a list of tables from which to draw data by clicking the down arrow button next to Name. A selection box listing all available tables appears, as shown in Figure 29.12.

Figure 29.12
Select a table from
the designated data
source when creating
an ODBC connection.

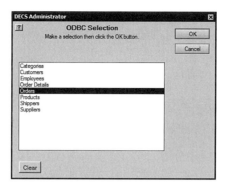

8. Select a table name to designate the source of data from the list. Click OK. DECS then accesses the database table fields and related data types.

9. Click Save and Close.

CREATING A NOTES DATABASE

When your Lotus Connection document is set up, you need to create the Notes database that will access the external data, if you haven't already. Figure 29.13 displays a form created to retrieve and display data from the ODBC connection created earlier. To access all the external table data, the form must include corresponding fields with appropriate data formats. You can name the fields anything you want, but the format must match that of the original database fields.

Figure 29.13
Create a Notes form
that will retrieve and
display data from the
external data source.

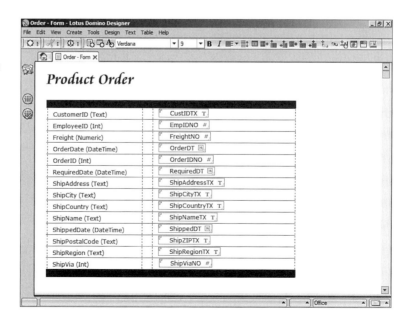

29

To make it easier to create the fields and use the proper data format, it's a good idea to simply copy the information from the Field(s) field in the Lotus Connection document. Just copy the information and paste it in your Notes form; then go about creating the fields.

Save your form design. Then create at least one Notes view to display and check the data later.

Now you're ready to create an activity document.

CREATING AN ACTIVITY

When a connection and a Notes database have been created, you need to create an *activity* (or *virtual fields activity*) *document*. An activity document defines the Notes database that will retrieve the data, designates the unique key fields used to match source data records with Notes documents, and maps the fields between the source data and the "virtual fields" of the target Notes document. It is also where you define which real-time events Domino should monitor between the Notes database and external data source.

If you have enabled the User Assistant, a wizard guides you through the steps to create an activity document; the order of the steps might be slightly different as a result. Follow these steps to set up a new activity document without the User Assistant enabled:

1. In the Activities view, click Add Activity. A blank Activity document opens, as shown in Figure 29.14.

Figure 29.14
The Activity document specifies where data will be retrieved, maps fields between the data source and Domino, and designates which events to monitor.

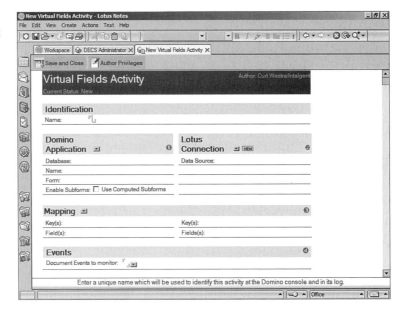

2. Enter a name for the activity.
3. Click the button next to Domino Application. A Select Domino Database dialog box appears with a list of Domino databases on the server.

4. Select the appropriate Domino database that will retrieve the external data.

5. Click OK. A Notes Selection dialog box automatically appears, listing the designated database's available forms.

6. Select the form that will be monitored by Domino and whose fields will map to the external data source. Click OK.

7. If you haven't already created a connection document, click the New button next to Lotus Connection. Follow the steps described previously in this chapter's section on creating a connection.

8. Click the button next to Lotus Connection to select the appropriate Lotus Connection from the Select Connection dialog box that appears. In this example, the connection that was described previously would be selected. Click OK.

9. To configure the mapping of data between the data source and Domino, click the Mapping down arrow button. The Key and Data Field Mapping dialog box appears, as shown in Figure 29.15.

Figure 29.15
The Key and Data Field Mapping dialog box enables you to match external data fields with corresponding Notes fields.

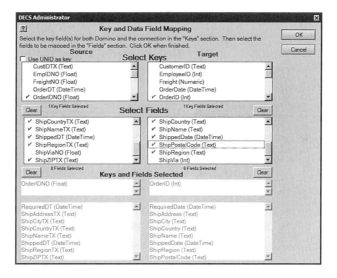

10. Select the key field or fields that will be used to uniquely identify each external data record with a corresponding Notes document. You must select the same number of key fields in both the Source and Target lists, and make sure the fields are listed in the same order. The keys you select and their order are listed in the boxes at the bottom.

11. Select data fields from the next set of list boxes to map data from source fields to Notes fields. Again, make sure the fields you select in each list box are in the same order, so that the first source field maps to the first Notes field, the second maps to the second, and so on. The fields you select, and their order, are listed in the boxes at the bottom. Click OK.

12. Specify the Notes document events that you want this activity to monitor using the Events dialog box. Events include `Create`, `Open`, `Update`, and `Delete`. When selected events occur with a Notes document, Domino initiates the appropriate data-retrieval or modification activities. Click OK.

13. If necessary, you can set a number of other general and event-related options. You can also specify a schedule for the activity to start.

14. Click Save and Close.

RETRIEVING DATA

When your connection document, activity document, and Notes database are configured, you should be ready to connect to the external data source and begin working with it in Domino. From the Activity view, you can monitor and edit all activities. Figure 29.16 shows several activities and their related information. The Activity view displays each activity's Domino application, monitored events, external source, and name.

Figure 29.16
The Activity view displays basic information about each virtual field activity in the DECS Administrator.

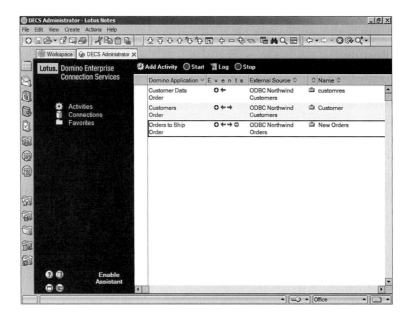

Within the Events column, you will notice different symbols displayed for each of the four events that can be selected.

Before you can actually access the external data from a Domino application, the Notes database needs to be populated with the key data. In other words, a Notes document must be created for each unique record in the external data source, and each document will be loaded with only the key field value.

To initialize the key values, open the activity document and click the Initialize Keys button. You are prompted with a message asking if you want to create key documents in the Notes database. Choose Yes. You'll be notified when the key documents have been generated. Close the activity document.

In this basic ODBC connection example, you're ready to start the activity and begin retrieving data. To manually start an activity, select it from the Activity view and click the Start button with the green circle. In the example covered here, data for more than 800 documents were retrieved in a few seconds and were immediately available within the Domino application. Figure 29.17 shows a Notes document displaying the retrieved data.

Figure 29.17
A Notes document displays data accessed from an ODBC source in real time.

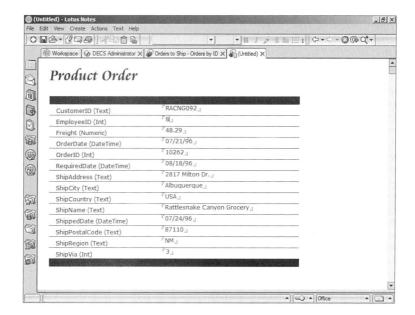

Depending on which real-time events are being monitored, you could edit, create, and even delete records in the external data source—all from the Notes database and in real time. This entire example—including creating the Notes database, creating the connection and activity documents, and then retrieving the data in Notes—took less than a half hour. Granted, this was a relatively simple example, but it demonstrates the capabilities and ease of use that is incorporated in DECS. If you ever need to integrate Domino with external data sources, it's a good idea to take a look at DECS first.

OTHER TOOLS FROM LOTUS

We've already covered DECS as the first tier in the enterprise integration products Lotus has to offer. Now we'll look at other tools and programming solutions that Lotus developed to enable you to connect to external data sources. These alternatives take on various forms, from simple @functions to full-blown integration environments. In this section, we first

29

look at Lotus enterprise integration products. Then we examine available programming solutions. The wide array of choices from Lotus might seem confusing. For more information, visit the Lotus site at www.lotus.com. For integration-specific information, visit www.lotus.com/ei.

LOTUS ENTERPRISE INTEGRATOR (LEI)

Lotus Enterprise Integrator, or LEI (formerly known as NotesPump in the pre-R5 days), is essentially a more advanced version of DECS that can be purchased from Lotus. The newest version, LEI 6, enhances the existing architecture of DECS with support for replication and what Lotus calls its Advanced RealTime capabilities. Advanced RealTime allows tighter integration between Domino and enterprise systems and data. These advanced capabilities essentially make it easier to view, access, and manipulate back-end data as if it were data housed in a traditional Notes store.

LEI 6 builds on the virtual field activities used in DECS by introducing two new ones—virtual document and virtual agent activities. Furthermore, LEI 6 includes two new features: virtual attachments and integrated credentials.

Virtual documents enable users to access entire documents within external data sources, and they remove the need for the key documents necessary with DECS to link Domino to external records. Because key documents don't need to be synchronized and all the data resides in the external source, performance is faster and the user is sure to see the most current data. Furthermore, data can be readily viewed, sorted, searched, and opened in Notes views. Similarly, the virtual attachments feature enables users to access, search, detach, and edit attachments that are stored in external systems.

LEI 6 introduces virtual agents, which enable you to access and initiate stored procedures in external systems as if they were Domino agents. This is useful because it makes it even easier to continue to leverage the existing architecture of existing external databases and to further integrate them with Domino's collaborative strengths.

Finally, LEI 6 makes it possible to control access to view and edit external data by assigning user rights with the integrated credentials feature. This allows you to add a layer of security and control enabled at the virtual field, virtual document, or virtual agent levels.

As mentioned previously, Lotus built DECS and LEI using its Lotus Connectors technology, which does the heavy lifting of connecting to different types of data sources and making the data available to your Notes/Domino application. Lotus has built connectors for many popular database types. Although connectors to many database types come loaded with LEI, some of the more specialized connectors must be purchased separately. And although it is based on DECS, LEI itself does not come bundled with Domino and must be purchased separately.

In terms of other third-party tools, LEI most resembles a combination of Replic-Action and Sentinel. It was designed to handle integration and Domino data administration. Integration tasks are configured using forms residing in the LEI Administrator database, similar to the DECS Administrator. One of the ways in which it differs from the others is its support for various operating systems (in keeping with Domino's cross-platform support), such as Solaris, OS/2 Warp, and AIX, in addition to NT and others.

SUPPORT FOR RELATIONAL SOURCES

As with the other tools we've covered, LEI supports any ODBC-compliant relational system. Lotus Connectors are available for many popular database types, including IBM DB2, Oracle, Sybase, and Microsoft SQLServer 7.0. LEI also supports Oracle, Sybase, and DB2 through its native APIs. Similar to Replic-Actions LSX (a product discussed later in the section on third-party tools), there are LSXs for gaining fine-grained programmatic control of connections (refer to the "Programming Solutions" section later in this chapter).

SUPPORT FOR ERP AND TRANSACTION SYSTEMS

LEI can utilize Lotus Connectors developed for certain ERP systems, such as JD Edwards One World and PeopleSoft, and some transaction systems as well.

SUPPORT FOR OTHER DATA SOURCES

LEI supports access to text files, HTML, and data transfer between Domino databases and servers. It also provides Domino data administration features, such as event polling and archiving.

LEI is an extremely deep product with extensive data integration, Domino data management, and system-management features. It is tailored for high-volume work and supports numerous environments. With recently added Advanced RealTime features and support for ERP and transaction systems, LEI has matured into an effective enterprise integration product that rivals third-party tools in many respects.

ENTERPRISE SOLUTION BUILDER (ESB)

Lotus Enterprise Solution Builder (ESB) 3.0.2 is a high-performance development tool and server for integrating high-volume enterprise systems with Domino applications. It is intended to provide greater stability, security, and performance by housing the data integration and processing on its own ESB server, separating it from the user interface and data sources. Applications that run on ESB are executed remotely via IIOP, DCOM, or HTTP.

Programming an ESB solution is done using LotusScript, but this can be relatively challenging because you must understand the concept of enterprise integration objects and how to create and use them. However, ESB can make the Domino front-end programming less complex. The ESB product is more expensive than LEI and requires the purchase of the ESB server and development tool. But for high-volume, complex data integration efforts, ESB might be an option worth looking into.

PROGRAMMING SOLUTIONS

In some circumstances, you need to access external data sources manually, perhaps in a custom agent, in a form event, or in a button. For these cases, Lotus provides both @functions and various LotusScript Extensions (LSXs).

ODBC VERSIONS OF @DbColumn, @DbLookup, AND @DbCommand

The ODBC versions of @DbColumn, @DbLookup, and @DbCommand have been around for some time. If you know how to work with the non-ODBC equivalents of @DbColumn and @DbLookup, you know basically how to use the ODBC versions. Other than the fact that you need to provide user ID and password information, the functions are equivalent. You specify a data source (server and database in Notes), a table and column (a view and column in Notes), and, in the case of @DbLookup, a key-column and key (a column number and key in Notes). A few options, such as for sorting and returning unique values only, aren't directly available in the non-ODBC versions, but they have simple equivalents (for example, the @Unique function).

Both @DbColumn and @DbLookup are simple read-only functions. @DbCommand, on the other hand, can be used to read and write data. Don't get excited, though. You're limited to sending a string that contains a SQL Select statement, a command that the data source system understands, or a stored procedure name. These functions are primarily meant to populate keyword lists. Non-ODBC equivalents tend to be pretty slow, so the ODBC will be even slower because you've added the whole ODBC layer. Chances are, these won't suffice for your applications. For far better capabilities and some improvement in performance, you need to use LotusScript.

LotusScript Extensions

A LotusScript Extension, or LSX, is a DLL file (or its equivalent) that contains definitions of various classes that you write to in LotusScript. By including a reference to this file in your code, those classes are made available just as the standard Domino classes are. Each of the classes has methods and properties that can be used in code to implement extremely sophisticated integration.

LS:DO LS:DO stands for LotusScript Data Object and refers to three classes provided in the ODBC LSX. These classes are ODBCConnection, ODBCQuery, and ODBCResultSet; each has its own powerful sets of properties and methods and complete SQL capabilities. You can access any ODBC-compliant data source, provided that you have an ODBC driver for the external source.

LotusScript Extension for Lotus Connectors (LSX LC) LSX LC extends the Lotus Connectors to LotusScript and gives you LotusScript programmatic control over data accessed via connectors. This is a powerful way to build upon the capabilities of Lotus's DECS and LEI products (covered later in this chapter) to get the flexibility and functionality you might need in some situations.

Other LSXs Lotus also has LSXs for DB2, SAP, and MQSeries. There's no magic in these LSXs; they function the same way as the LS:DO. You include a reference to the LSX in your LotusScript code and then write to the system-specific classes provided in the LSX. A full exposition of all the classes is outside the scope of this book. Suffice it to say that these classes are provided in the first place to give complete access to the external data sources, using methods that are familiar to anyone who has experience in the external system. So, for instance, if you're familiar with MQSeries processing, you'll be familiar with how to use classes such as MQQueue, MQQueueManager, and MQMessage.

The difficult part of any of these is not doing the LotusScript coding, but understanding what you're doing on the external system. The classes insulate the developer to some extent from the native equivalents, but they don't eliminate the need to understand the external system.

NotesSQL

As Domino developers, we tend to think of our applications as the origin of integration—as the places into which external data is drawn. That doesn't have to be the case, though. Notes databases, particularly tracking or catalog applications, could very well serve as external sources to other systems. For this reason, Lotus provides its own ODBC driver for accessing a Notes database using SQL, as you would with other RDBMSs.

A common use for this is using a tool such as Crystal Reports to create sophisticated reports based on Notes data. Having a Notes database available as an ODBC source also enables developers to integrate it with other relational sources into a third system.

JDBC

In keeping with Lotus's objective of supporting Java, Domino ships with the tools to establish JDBC connectivity. A JDBC driver is provided so that Domino data can be accessed like any other relational system from within a Java applet or application. Also, agents written in Java can incorporate the classes contained in the java.sql package that Lotus provides.

THIRD-PARTY TOOLS

The third-party market for data-integration tools is probably the most mature in the Domino world. You might tend to look only to Lotus products for integration solutions, but you would be missing serious and solid contenders from other vendors. For this reason, let's first look at five products that have stood the test of time and, therefore, are worthy of just as much attention as any Lotus product.

REPLIC-ACTION

Replic-Action, from Casahl Technology, is a robust product for integrating Domino and Domino data with a variety of relational databases. As you can tell from its name, the model for Replic-Action is Domino-like replication. This means that data transfers can be one-way, two-way, selective (based on formula-like expressions), and field-level. This enables Replic-Action to transfer only records that have changed, as opposed to entire data sets.

Integration "applications" are created in the Composer, which is itself a Domino application. By filling out various forms, you establish data sources, tables, and columns to connect with, as well as the type of transfers to make. You also establish the kinds of monitoring you want performed on the Replic-Action server.

29

A strong point for Replic-Action is its close ties to Domino. By supporting doclinks and email, among other standard Notes features, Replic-Action fits well into an existing Domino environment. Similar to LEI, it uses a Notes database on the front end to build data integration jobs. Casahl also provides LotusScript classes through its own LotusScript Extension (LSX). This gives developers fine-grained control over various aspects of a data transfer object, such as data transformations and replication activity. Replic-Action also enables you to set up user profiles to control user ability to access or manipulate data with more specificity.

Replic-Action supports connections to database types such as Oracle, SQL Server, Microsoft Access, DB2, AS/400, Sybase, Lotus Notes, and many ODBC-compliant sources. It can also work with spreadsheets and text files.

In addition, Casahl recently launched the ecKnowledge product, which is not Domino-centric and which supports connectivity to ERP data sources, among many others. Refer to the next section for details.

CASAHL ECKNOWLEDGE

Casahl recently introduced a new product, ecKnowledge, that takes data integration another step forward. ecKnowledge is a more sophisticated and robust enterprise data-integration tool than Replic-Action and is not solely oriented toward Domino shops. Although it supports integration of Domino data, ecKnowledge is intended to meet broader market needs. It is designed for complicated, large-scale data integration efforts within an enterprise, or even across enterprises.

Built-in support for protocols such as HTTP, HTTPS, FTP, SMTP, IMAP, and POP3 allow sending and receiving data over public and private networks.

By taking advantage of XML, ecKnowledge can connect to a wide array of ERP, database, middleware, directory, or messaging systems. It can integrate Domino and Exchange data, as well as the typical relational databases such as Oracle, DB2, SQL Server, Sybase ASE, and Informix. Other traditional supported databases include mainframes such as AS/400, transaction systems such as CICS, and ERP systems such as SAP R/3, Baan, J.D. Edwards, and PeopleSoft. Furthermore, ecKnowledge supports EDI formats, XML formats for various industry standards, and message queues such as MQSeries.

For more information on Casahl's products, visit its Web site at www.casahl.com.

PERCUSSION NOTRIX

Percussion Notrix from Percussion Software is another product with strong ties to Notes/Domino technology. Whereas the Replic-Action Server component can run on its own server or a Domino server, which has its advantages and disadvantages, Notrix runs as a server task on the Domino server itself. This means that as an add-in task, it is extremely efficient and flexible.

Notrix has all the features you'd expect in a mature product, such as real-time access, action logging, and error recovery. Integration is configured using a GUI that enables developers to get basic integration implemented without a stitch of programming, similar to LEI. Notrix also features the ability to create and manage all your jobs from a Web browser.

Notrix supports any system that is ODBC-compliant. However, for Oracle, Sybase, Informix, DB2, Microsoft SQL Server, and even AS/400 Client Access, it provides access through each system's native API. This translates into better performance.

Notrix also supports integration with flat files using the Notes column descriptor file (with the .col extension). A COL file is a simple text file you create that can include @functions and data typing to manipulate text data as it's imported into a Domino database. Even though COL files have been part of Notes for a long time and are pretty archaic, they can still be powerful, as Notrix proves.

For more information on Percussion's offerings, visit its Web site at www.percussion.com.

ZMERGE POWER TOOL FOR LOTUS NOTES

ZMERGE, from Granite Software, is a classic in the Notes/Domino world. It has been around a long time, it was created especially for integrating specific types of data with Domino, and it has a solid reputation for performing this task.

ZMERGE is a nuts-and-bolts tool tailored for importing, exporting, and merging flat files and Notes databases. If you're familiar with COL files, you'll feel at home with ZMERGE. Using a text file called a ZID (for ZMERGE Information Description) script, you specify the rules for processing data from an external input file. The ZMERGE executable then reads from the ZID script and transforms your external data into Notes documents. It can also create response-type documents and doclinks, and it can transfer data between Notes databases. Here's an example of a simple ZID script taken from a ZMERGE database:

```
;This sample imports sample data (at the end of the script) into the sample
  employee database.
;This script will create NEW documents only. No document matching or
 updating occurs.
 ;
 [
    /JOB_ID="Text to Notes Import"    // Identifies run
    /INP_FILE=*    // Use * to pull data from script (usually filename)
    /NSF_FILE=zmsampl1.nsf    // Target database
    /NSF_CREATE=YES    // Create database if not found
    /NSF_TEMPLATE=zmsampl1.ntf    // Create database from this template
    /NSF_TITLE="ZMerge Sample: Emp Review"    // Create database with this title
    /ON_SUCCESS="(start %Directory%\zmsampl1.nsf)"
 ]

DEFINE    KEY      PaymentCode PaySchedCode CASE_INSENSITIVE
DEFINE    TABLE     SchedByCode zmlookup.nsf;PaymentCodes

Form:    TYPE TEXT    VALUE "Employee"
FirstName:    TYPE TEXT    UNTIL ";"
MiddleInit:    TYPE TEXT    UNTIL ";"
```

```
LastName:     TYPE TEXT    UNTIL ";"
SocSec:    TYPE TEXT    UNTIL ";"
PhoneNumber:    TYPE TEXT     UNTIL ";"
StartDate:    TYPE DATE     UNTIL ";" FORMAT YYYY-MM-DD
PaySchedCode: TYPE TEXT    UNTIL ";"
PayRate:    TYPE NUMBER    UNTIL ";"
PaySched:    LOOKUP     KEY:PaymentCode;TABLE:SchedByCode;PaySched
PaySchedTerms: LOOKUP     KEY:PaymentCode;TABLE:SchedByCode;PaySchedTerms
Comments:    TYPE RICH
UpdatedBy:    TYPE TEXT    VALUE "01. Text to Notes Import"


FORMULASTART NEW    // This formula evaluated against NEW documents only
SELECT @ALL;
FIELD FullName := @Trim(FirstName + " " + MiddleInit + " " + LastName);
FORMULAEND
```

ZMERGE now includes ZID Builder, a GUI wizard that makes it easier to build these kinds of ZID scripts.

ZMERGE does one thing and does it well. It supports data from minis to mainframes in ASCII, EBCDIC, and binary format, as well as DBF files. Notes-to-Notes transfers are also supported. ZMERGE is a no-frills tool for working with high-volume flat-file data. It was designed by a company with roots in Notes/Domino technology, so expect efficient processing. If your integration needs are focused on this type of integration, ZMERGE is the tool. For more information, visit www.gsw.com.

SENTINEL

Like Notrix, Replic-Action, and ZMERGE, Sentinel (by MayFlower Software) is another example of a product developed specifically to address early shortcomings of Notes. It has become a recognized tool in the Domino world. Like those others, Sentinel doubles as a data-integration tool and a Domino data-administration tool. All tasks, whether they're for integration or data administration, are entered using Notes forms.

Although Sentinel does data integration, a good deal of the product is devoted to Domino data administration, which, when done right, can provide added value to data-integration solutions. It can also combine data from relational and flat-file sources at the same time.

If a data source is ODBC-compliant, Sentinel supports it. It does this using vendor ODBC drivers instead of making native API calls.

Sentinel has extensive support for flat files (including EDI files) as well as batch importing of word-processing files. Domino data-administration features include totaling response document data into main documents and performing scheduled archiving of Domino data to other Notes databases or non-Notes databases.

Sentinel includes some new features, such as the ability to read XML data and write it into a Notes document. Another addition is the ODBC to ODBC task, which lets you manage multiple data sources even when integration with Domino is not needed. For more information, visit www.maysoft.com.

PART VI

INSTALLING AND CONFIGURING THE DOMINO SERVERS

CHAPTER 30

THE DOMINO FAMILY OF SERVERS

Exploring the Domino Servers

The Domino server is the heart of the Lotus Notes environment. Without the Domino server, there would be no mechanism for users to exchange information with each other. In fact, without the Domino server, there would be no Lotus Notes. Domino provides a core set of services that work together to deliver information to users and other Domino servers within an organization's network. In this section of the book, we'll explore in greater detail some of the services that the Domino server provides. In addition, you'll be presented with a context for how these services are combined to provide a family of Domino servers. This family of servers gives organizations a dynamic collaboration platform that can be scaled to meet their ongoing business needs.

Three members make up the Domino server family: the Domino Utility Server, the Domino Messaging Server, and the Domino Enterprise Server. All three have a similar set of basic Domino services, with additional services for specific purposes. When you first set up a Domino server, you can select which member of the server family you want to install. The selection screen is shown in Figure 30.1.

Figure 30.1
During setup, you select which member of the Domino server family you want to install.

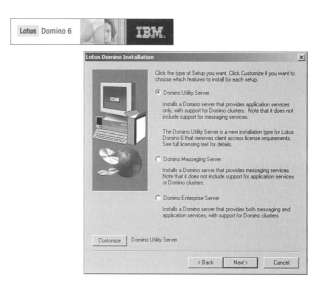

The following list describes the purpose of each member of the server family:

- The Domino Messaging Server provides a messaging infrastructure that delivers email and simple applications, such as discussion boards, calendaring and scheduling functions, and Web access.

- The Domino Enterprise Server extends the messaging infrastructure of the Domino Messaging Server while coupling it with an application services infrastructure. In addition, the Domino Enterprise Server provides an advanced set of tools for scaling the Domino server across the enterprise, including support for clustering, load balancing, and failover. This server type replaces the Domino Application and Domino Advanced Enterprise Server offerings found under Release 5.

- The Domino Utility Server, a new type of Domino server that was introduced with Release 6, provides an application infrastructure without the requirement to purchase client access licenses. Unlike the two other types of Domino servers, this server type does not provide any support for messaging.

NOTE

> Each member of the Domino server family supports the configuration of partitioned Domino servers.

30

Each of these three servers is described in greater detail in the following sections.

THE DOMINO MESSAGING SERVER

The Domino Messaging Server is appropriate for organizations that use Notes primarily for messaging or those that want to use a Domino server specifically for mail routing.

It is the lowest common denominator among the Domino family of servers, providing the easiest way to implement a Notes infrastructure to manage your messaging needs. You might be wondering what types of messaging services are included with the Domino Mail Server.

Electronic mail is the first and most obvious instance of messaging services in an organization. It involves direct communication with another individual or with the individuals in a group. The Domino Messaging Server handles the delivery of electronic mail within an organization, using the Domino Directory to determine where and how a message should be delivered, and using the Router task to move the message to the appropriate user's mail file. That is the basic functionality that has been built into Notes from its earliest days.

The following are some of the features of the Domino Messaging Server:

- Simplified administration using the Domino Administrator
- Outstanding support for mobile computing
- Built-in upgrade tools to move from other mail applications to Domino
- Standards-based Internet messaging
- Optional use of Lotus Notes mail or other popular email clients to access your mail on the Domino Mail Server
- Integrated services, such as Calendaring and Scheduling
- Integrated collaboration databases

INTERNET MESSAGING STANDARDS

Domino doesn't just provide support messaging for standard Notes mail; it also supports a variety of Internet mail standards, including native SMTP routing and native MIME content. These features ensure the seamless delivery of messages to other foreign mail systems.

Simple Mail Transfer Protocol (SMTP) is the standard used for relaying mail between networks on the Internet. By using this standard, the Domino server can route mail to any mail system on the Internet. Because SMTP is natively supported in Domino, messages are routed without the requirement to convert them between the Notes format and the Internet format. In previous releases of the Domino server, a separate message transfer agent (MTA) was responsible for processing individual messages before they could be sent via SMTP.

The Domino Messaging Server also supports ESMTP (Extended SMTP), which makes it possible to receive delivery notifications. For example, you can send an electronic message over the Internet and receive a notification when the person receives (or fails to receive) the message.

The native MIME (Multipurpose Internet Mail Extensions) support is another Internet standard that enables messages to include audio, video, international character sets, and multipart messages. MIME is the standard format used for most messages on the Internet. With Notes and Domino, Notes messages are stored in MIME format. Support for native MIME storage means that there is no need to translate messages from one format to another as Notes messages are sent to people over the Internet. As a result, there is a gain in performance, and a gain in the fidelity of the messages themselves.

The use of the MIME standard goes beyond straightforward messages. The Domino Mail Server also supports S/MIME, the Internet standard for secure Internet mail. Secure connections that require a username and password can be made using TCP/IP, or you can make an encrypted connection with Secure Sockets Layer (SSL) .

ADDRESSING MESSAGES

With traditional Notes addressing, the names of addressees are looked up in the Domino Directory. If an individual is listed in the directory, the location of his or her mail database is obtained from the Person record. If the person is not listed, an explicit path is required in the address, and connection documents are required to tell the router how to deliver the message. Domino supports native Internet addressing using the RFC 821 and RFC 822 standards. RFC 821 is a straightforward Internet address. For example, under RFC 821, my address would be `jeff.gunther@intalgent.com`. However, the RFC 822 standard allows backward compatibility by including the user's distinguished name along with a bracketed Internet address. Under this standard, my address would appear as `"Jeff Gunther/ Intalgent <jeff.gunther@intalgent.com>"`.

One of the advantages of Internet addressing is the flexibility it provides. If users are constantly connected and use TCP/IP, the router can go directly to the user's domain and deliver mail to that person's Internet address. But if the user is sometimes disconnected, Notes can use connection documents and scheduled connections to deliver mail to the Notes address. In either case, the message ends up in the same mailbox in the same format. It provides an alternative that improves reliability and flexibility.

To ease the administrative burden, there is a special function in the Domino Administrator client to convert Notes addresses into Internet addresses. Follow these steps:

1. Initialize the Domino Administrator, and select the People and Groups tab.

2. Highlight the People view under your organization's Domino Directory.

3. Under the Tools navigator on the right side of the Administrator client, select People, Set Person's Internet Address to display the Set Internet Address dialog box (see Figure 30.2). Use the dialog box to define parameters for creating Internet addresses from selected Person and Group records.

Figure 30.2
Domino provides an easy way to convert Notes addresses to Internet addresses.

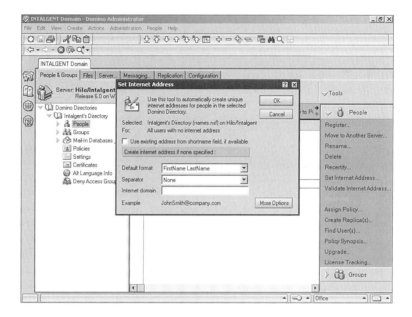

ROUTING MESSAGES

The Router task on the Domino Messaging Server is used to deliver mail messages to the addressees. The router has always been robust. It provides nearly instantaneous mail delivery for mail addressed to people on the same Notes network (Domino servers that are in the same domain and use the same communications protocol), and it uses rules for delivering messages to Domino servers in other domains.

Release 6 of the Domino server provides some notable enhancements to the already-powerful Router task. Using the Administrator client, you can tailor the router to use the following:

- **Router quotas**—Administrators can now enforce electronic mail quotas by using a combination of notification and router administration. Notifications to users who exceed their quota limit can be configured to be sent on a per-message basis or periodically. The periodic delivery of notifications can be scheduled based on a predefined number of minutes, hours, or days. Additionally, an individual's messages can be held until the size quota has been met.

■ **Journaling**—The new journaling feature provides administrators with the ability to monitor messages and ensure security during message delivery. Using rules, messages can be achieved to help ensure corporate compliance for electronic communication. Figure 30.3 demonstrates a rule that journalizes all incoming and outgoing messages.

Figure 30.3
The Server Mail Rule dialog box allows conditions to be defined for journalizing of messages.

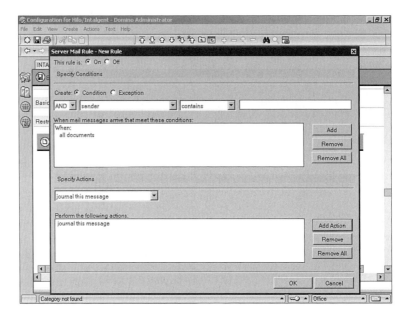

Messages can also be encrypted during their transport and delivery while being processed by the router.

■ **Antispam controls**—Spam, any unsolicited and undesirable electronic mail, is increasingly becoming a problem for many organizations. Release 6 introduces many new features for administrators to assist in the management and control of spam. For example, any incoming message can be checked against any of the public "black-hole" lists. Black-hole lists, also known as DNS blacklists, are Internet-based databases that track and monitor SMTP hosts that generate or are used as a relay to send unsolicited email. If an incoming message's sending host is found within one of these lists, a message can be simply logged or rejected.

■ **Mail rules**—Similar to the rules found within the Notes client, mail rules can be specified at the router level to filter all messages. In fact, Figure 30.3 demonstrates a journalizing server rule. The combination of mail rules and the antispam controls provides an effective mechanism to control unsolicited messages.

THE DOMINO DIRECTORY AND INTERNET DIRECTORY STANDARDS

For messaging in a Notes-to-Notes environment, the Domino Directory is the central hub of information for messaging details within an organization. The Directory contains the names of all registered Notes users in the organization and contains information that tells the router where and how to deliver electronic mail. The role of the Domino Directory has been described in more detail elsewhere in this book.

Aside from the Domino Directory, the Domino Messaging Server has two other directories to provide services to Notes users. Directory Assistance provides access to Domino Directories for an entire enterprise, and the Directory Catalog provides a compressed version of the information in one or more Domino Directories.

Directory Assistance allows administrators to define trust relationships with other directories, enabling you to exercise greater control over the Domino Directory. For example, you can create a Directory Catalog that contains HTTP usernames, passwords, and X.509 certificates for people who need authenticated access to your Domino server through the Web. Using Directory Assistance, you don't have to put these people into the Domino Directory if they are not Notes users.

The Directory Catalog provides a compressed version of one or more Domino Directories, speeding up the process of name lookups and resolving mail addresses within organizations. You can put a subset of information into the Directory Catalog for mail-routing purposes, leaving it with a much smaller size than the Domino Directory.

LDAP AUTHENTICATION

The Domino Directory further underscores Domino's close ties to Internet standards. The Domino Directory is searchable over the Internet using Lightweight Directory Access Protocol (LDAP). LDAP is a standards-based open protocol for searching and managing directories. Similar to the concept of a telephone book, an LDAP directory contains details regarding a variety of enterprise entities, including users, groups, server, and printers.

Domino supports LDAPv3, which provides authenticated read/write access, enabling you to make updates to the Domino Directory over the Web using an LDAP client. This makes the Domino Directory available as an enterprise directory for any system that uses an LDAP client.

For example, a Linux application written in Java might use LDAP to store all directory information in the Domino Directory, taking advantage of all the security and replication features of Domino. Because LDAPv3 allows you to write to the Domino Directory as well as read from it, the applications that store information about users can store that information in the Person record in the Domino Directory. The Person document has a customizable subform that can be used for adding new data needed by non-Notes applications for storage in the Domino Directory. In addition to the Person record, subforms are available in Group, Mail-in Database, Resource, and Certifier forms. These subforms are designed so that they are not modified during a design refresh, and the information in them will not get overwritten. The use of Domino as an LDAP directory has been tested with Microsoft, Netscape, IBM, and Novell.

30

THE DOMINO ENTERPRISE SERVER

The Domino Enterprise Server provides all the basic services of the Domino Messaging Server, including email, discussion databases, and calendaring and scheduling. In addition to discussion databases and mail databases, the Enterprise Server can work with all Domino databases. This includes databases built by application designers, databases used in workflow applications, and Notes application suites.

One of the primary functions of the Domino Enterprise Server is to serve Domino applications to Notes users. The server enforces security and provides communication services such as replication. All these features are available in some degree through the Domino Messaging Server. But one service truly distinguishes the Domino Enterprise Server from the Domino Messaging Server.

The Domino Enterprise Server includes a Web server that makes Domino applications accessible from the World Wide Web. To help you understand the strength of Domino as a Web application server, let's highlight some of the new Web server features in the Domino Enterprise Server. The application services can be divided into two areas:

- Application-design services
- Server enhancements
- Clustering support

APPLICATION-DESIGN SERVICES

The continued evolution of the Domino Enterprise Server, coupled with the addition of new design and programmability features, makes Domino applications perfectly suited for the Web. These features include the ease with which developers can move among different programming languages, including JavaScript, Java, HTML 4.0, Cascading Style Sheets, and LotusScript. These languages are part of the Domino Designer, not part of the server, but they make it possible to develop robust applications that can be delivered to either Notes or the Web with full fidelity.

On the programmability side, the Domino Object Model now includes extensive support for XML parsing within LotusScript. LotusScript can natively parse XML using either a SAX (Simple API for XML) or a DOM (Document Object Model) parser.

The other design enhancement that should be mentioned before looking more closely at the Domino Enterprise Server is Release 6's introduction of data connections. Integrating technology from Domino Enterprise Connector Services (DECS), a data connection allows you to connect to various external relational databases from within a Domino database. You can establish connections to DB2, Oracle, Sybase, ODBC, and other databases. After the connections have been defined, the Domino Enterprise Server takes over. An add-in task on the server passes instructions to the Domino Extension Manager, which monitors applications and waits for events that will trigger a real-time extension. For example, a user may want to perform a lookup on data that is stored in an external database. The Extension Manager then passes the query to the external database. The query is performed on the database; then the information is passed back to the Domino server and is displayed in the user's application. It takes place transparently, and users may not even be aware that the data they are seeing comes from a non-Notes source. For more information about data connections and how to integrate them within your applications, review Chapter 29, "Domino and Enterprise Integration."

SERVER ENHANCEMENTS

The Domino Enterprise Server includes many enhancements for applications:

- The capability to host multiple organizations within a single server. These new hosting features improve an *xSP* ability to deliver applications while minimizing the use of computing resources. Lotus uses the term xSP to refer to a variety of service providers such as application service providers and Internet service providers.

- The monitoring of servers is essential to ensure a reliable application. Domino 6 includes the ability to monitor and gather statistics on the server and individual databases.

- The formula engine has been completely reworked to improve the performance of computations.

- Full-text search performance has been improved to perform updates in place.

- Domino's native HTTP server has been significantly improved to provide increased reliability and scalability.

- In addition to Domino's native HTTP server, a new architecture allows third-party HTTP servers to be included within the Domino infrastructure.

CLUSTERING SUPPORT

One of the most frustrating things that can happen when surfing on the World Wide Web is nothing. You get no answer from a Web site, even though you know that you typed in the correct URL or followed a valid link. And it is rare that you have any idea why you get no response. Is the Internet choked with traffic? Did the Web site go out of business, or is the server offline for maintenance? Domino can't do much about the first two instances, but clustering with Domino servers makes the third alternative highly unlikely. In this age of digital communication, information has become probably the most important asset a company can have. As the importance of information becomes more apparent in today's global markets, so does the importance of 24×7 availability. You don't want to have any customers turned away by an unavailable server, the virtual equivalent of a busy signal in the online world.

Clustering is a feature that distinguishes the Domino Enterprise Server from the Domino Messaging Server. Clustering provides uninterrupted access to data and Domino services by using failover mechanisms in both the Notes and Web environments. Loads are balanced dynamically, ensuring optimum access to data.

You can consolidate your Domino servers on larger machines through partitioning, and you can build clusters that run on a combination of Domino platforms across a network. Management of clusters is made simpler with analysis tools that are built into the Domino Administrator. The analysis tools also can be used to track usage for billing, chargeback, and capacity-planning purposes.

In clusters, replica copies of databases are maintained on the different servers. Then, if the server on which a user ordinarily accesses a database happens to be unavailable, Domino fails over to another available server in the cluster. This provides uninterrupted access to data and is transparent to the end user.

With Release 5, clustering was extended to the Internet with the Internet Cluster Manager (ICM). ICM provides load balancing and failover for Notes and Web clients. The failover and balancing is done based on the type of content the user requests. The cluster uses event-driven replication to synchronize databases on the different servers.

The Domino Cluster Manager keeps tabs on all the servers in the cluster, including their availability and what replicas reside on them. The Cluster Manager routes users to the appropriate server based on the information that is required and the current server load. For Internet requests, the ICM acts as a traffic director between HTTP requests and the different HTTP servers in the cluster. The ICM determines which server can best handle a particular HTTP request and passes the traffic to that server.

The ICM does the following:

- Monitors the servers in a cluster for availability
- Monitors the Domino HTTP Web services for availability
- Disallows connections to servers that are not currently in service
- Provides failover to the best available server
- Balances the load between servers in the cluster by monitoring availability thresholds
- Supports virtual IP addresses and mapped ports
- Provides content-routing services for clients

Basically, the ICM extends clustering services to Web clients as well as to Notes clients. If Web clients are using applications over an intranet or an extranet, they can be assured of the same reliable service they get from the Domino server when using Notes. The ICM handles HTTP and HTTPS requests to the Domino server, redirecting the requests until a session is established with the most available server. ICM does not handle other protocols, including FTP, SMTP, or UDP.

The ICM should sit behind a firewall. From there, it can support the entire Domino security model for the Web. That includes logins and passwords. The ICM does not handle the security itself, but it can be configured to use SSL encryption to and from the servers in the cluster. As much as possible, the ICM is designed to be transparent to the system administrator. Note that each cluster must have its own ICM.

The Domino Enterprise Server is ideal for organizations that need a scalable computing platform. It provides all the services of the Domino Messaging Server, plus it supports applications that go well beyond the simple discussion databases that you get with the Domino Messaging Server license. Additional servers can be added to a cluster at any time, making it easy to grow when additional computing power is required. The additional server can be a Windows 2000, with each partitioned server running as a separate Windows service. Or, you can add new partitioned servers on larger enterprise platforms, such as Linux, iSeries, or z/OS.

THE DOMINO UTILITY SERVER

Lotus introduced the Domino Utility Server with Release 6. Unlike the Domino Messaging and Domino Enterprise servers, the Domino Utility Server doesn't require individual client licenses. Instead, the server is licensed by the number of processors within a physical server. Although the Domino Utility Server does not provide support for messaging, it does include the application services of the Domino Enterprise Server. This license can be very useful for organizations that already have another messaging infrastructure, such as Microsoft Exchange, but are looking to deploy Domino applications.

CHAPTER 31

INITIAL PLANNING AND INSTALLATION

In this chapter

AN OVERVIEW OF DOMINO SYSTEM PLANNING

You have decided that Domino is for you. Now what? The first step to getting your Domino system up and running is planning. Planning is also probably your second and third steps as well. With adequate planning, you'll find that your installation will be very smooth. Without it, you might find yourself doing extra work reorganizing and restructuring.

When you first decide to implement Domino, you have many aspects to consider: managerial, financial, technical, and training issues. You should establish a team with people representing each of these various viewpoints. Many times, the people from different areas will be able to provide unique knowledge to the process. Here is a sample outline of how you might approach the planning and implementation process:

1. Establish a team.
   - **Management**—The involvement of key management personnel improves the chances for successful deployment.
   - **Technical**—The information systems department can provide important technical information.
   - **Users**—The system exists to provide applications for users. Key users, especially power users, can supply information about which applications will provide the most benefit for the company.

2. Establish a strategy.
   - Decide on initial and possible future applications. Although email is probably one of your first applications, what will follow, and when?
   - Determine hardware and software requirements. Take into account not only your initial applications, but also allow for growth in your follow-on applications.
   - Determine security requirements. Will your applications be used only internally, or will you allow customers and partners to access your systems?
   - Determine training requirements. You must provide your users with training to work with any new systems. Training almost always quickly pays for itself in increased productivity.
   - Determine human resource requirements, including the need for outside additional help, contractors, and consultants, if necessary.

3. Divide team responsibilities and implementation.
   - **Financial and managerial**—Typical tasks include budgeting and acquiring hardware, software, and services.
   - **Technical**—Tasks involve the installation and deployment of the hardware and software.
   - **Training**—Training for users must be supplied internally or externally.

TECHNICAL PLANNING FOR YOUR DOMINO DEPLOYMENT

After you have outlined your company's plan for Domino deployment, you are ready to start the technical planning for the software itself. Here are some key questions:

- How many geographic locations will be involved? How many servers do you need?
- For each server, besides email, what applications will be used?
- How will you obtain software: purchase off the shelf, develop in-house, or contract with an outside firm to perform the initial development for you? Each option has different kinds of costs and benefits.
- Will you be doing Web serving from your Domino server?
- Do you want to enable users to use additional Internet mail clients, such as Eudora or Microsoft Outlook or Outlook Express?

After you have answered questions such as these, you are ready to consider how your organization will use Domino. Domino organizes servers and users with a concept called *domains*. Domain names such as `lotus.com` and `microsoft.com` are now familiar to most people. Although similar, Domino has its own concept of a domain. Within the context of Domino, a domain is a logical grouping of Domino servers that share a common Domino directory. Before you can use Domino, you must first define and set up the first Domino domain.

DOMINO DOMAINS

Domino uses the concept of domains to manage groups of servers. The information for all the users within one domain is stored in one Domino directory. This directory also contains information about your servers, connections, and configurations.

Normally, you will use one domain for your company, unless you have an exception, as described in the next section, "Naming Conventions." You should be aware that the Domino domain name is not necessarily the same as your Internet domain name. You can have a Domino domain with or without an Internet domain name. If you do have an Internet domain name, you may choose to use the same name for your Domino domain.

The major function of a Domino domain is for mail routing. Most small-to-medium deployments should use a single domain because this means a single Domino directory to maintain. Even if you have multiple Domino servers that are geographically separated, you should use a single Domino domain.

In only a couple of specific cases it might be advantageous to use multiple domains:

- You are using Domino as your Web server and you want to store external users in a separate directory (name and address book). The external users will then exist in a separate domain.

■ You have a very large organization and you want to divide administrative responsibility into nonoverlapping groups. Each group will have its own domain and Domino public directory.

NAMING CONVENTIONS

After you decide on your domain name, you need to consider the naming conventions for your company. Names in Domino are arranged in a hierarchical structure. The organization name, which is usually the company name, is at the top of the hierarchy. Within the organization, you can have up to four layers of Organizational Units (OUs). Figure 31.1 shows a hierarchy with one organization (Acme) and two layers of OUs.

Figure 31.1
Organizations can contain Organizational Units and users.

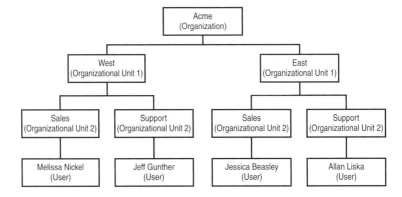

Notice in Figure 31.1 that two OUs can have the same name if they are in different locations within the hierarchy. When you write a hierarchical name, you start at the bottom of the hierarchy. For example, in Figure 31.1, one user is Melissa Nickel/Sales/West/Acme.

You do not need to have multiple layers of OUs. In fact, you should probably limit yourself to the fewest number that is consistent with your actual organizational structure. For example, if you have a very small company and you are located in one physical location, you might not need any OUs. The only required level in the naming convention is the organizational level. You can add users directly to this level, if you like.

On the other hand, suppose you have three physical locations around the country. In this case, you might want to have the organization and three OUs at the next level down, based on geographical location.

Even if you have a very large company, you should be able to manage with, at most, two levels of OUs in addition to the organization level. Having the right number of levels can ease your administrative burden, but having too many levels can add unneeded complexity and generate extra work.

OU levels are important because usernames must be unique. If you have too many users within the organization or OU, you increase the chances of having duplicate names. For example, you might have several users with the name John Smith. This is a problem if they are in the same OU, but it is not a problem if they are in different OUs.

HIERARCHICAL NAMES

You've seen a user's hierarchical name: Melissa Nickel/Sales/West/Acme.

This syntax is actually called the *abbreviated format* for the hierarchical name. A name is considered to be in abbreviated format when all the address components are not itemized. In contrast to the abbreviated format, the *canonical format* has each name and address component explicitly named. For example, here is the same hierarchical name shown in canonical format: `CN=Melissa Nickel/OU=Sales/OU=West/O=Acme/C=US`. Under most circumstances in Domino, the abbreviated format is displayed to users, whereas the canonical format is stored internally.

Each component explicitly named in the canonical format is one of the following components: `CN` for common name, `OU` for Organizational Unit, `O` for organization, and `C` for country. The CN component can have up to 80 characters, each OU can have 32 characters, the O component can have 3–64 characters, and the country code (C) can be omitted or can have 2 letters. The country codes are fixed and, if used, must match a valid country code. You may add a country code only if your country's clearinghouse for X.500 names has approved your organization name. The country code is frequently omitted.

As mentioned, you can have up to four OU components. The order in which they appear is significant. The rightmost OU is `OU1`; in the example, it would be `West`. The next OU to the left is called `OU2`; in the example, this is `Support`. In the canonical name, you use the generic code OU. You do not include the number when specifying the name in canonical format. The numeric convention is used only so you can distinguish between the different OUs for discussion.

CERTIFICATION

How do user IDs get created? User IDs are files that are generated and then authorized through the certification process. In essence, a known entity, called the *certifier*, marks the user ID file with an official stamp. This stamp, called a certificate, uses encryption technology to ensure that it could have been placed there only by a valid certifier. When servers and other users need to verify that the user ID is valid, they look at the certificate to make sure that they can trust the user.

For the organization and each different OU, you need to have a certifier. Thus, if you use only the organizational level, you will have only one certifier ID. If you have many levels with many different OUs, you need a separate certifier for each OU. This is why many companies use geography as a basis for their OUs. For example, suppose you have branch offices in North Haven, Connecticut; Denver, Colorado; and Irvine, California. With three OUs, you could have a local administrator in each location, each using his own local certifier ID. Each administrator can update the common Domino directory, and users can be conveniently added in each location. In this example, you would use the organization level

31

and one Organizational Unit level. Example names might be Fred Smith/NHV/Acme, Sue Jones/IRV/Acme, or Tom Terrific/DEN/Acme.

When you first install Domino, you set up your first certifier ID, which can then be used to set up any additional OU certifier IDs, if necessary.

CAUTION

> The organization certifier ID file is probably the most important file in your Domino system installation. If a person can access this file and knows the password, that person can access any database in your system. With the certifier ID file, the person can create additional user IDs, thus potentially impersonating anyone in the system—including you. Be very careful with this file from two perspectives:
>
> - **Security**—Do not allow unauthorized users to access this file.
> - **System integrity**—Do not lose, fold, spindle, or mutilate this file. If you lose it, you cannot create a replacement file. Back up this file, and make sure you carefully control the backup copy of the file as well.
>
> You should use similar precautions for each of your OU certifier files.

NAMING CONVENTION RECOMMENDATIONS

Before you actually start installing the Domino system files, you should develop your organizational naming scheme. While you are installing the system, you will be asked for information such as the name of your domain and your certifier. If you have already mapped out your domain and naming conventions, answering these questions will be easy. Don't try to make up the answers as you fill in the blanks. Naming conventions are painful to change later, but they are easy to implement if done when you first install the system.

Although the naming conventions might seem arbitrary, they are very critical. If you decide to change the conventions later, it might require a lot of work. If you change your organizational structure, you need to recertify all the user IDs that have been created and probably change the Access Control Lists (ACLs) for every database in your system. Save yourself some time and think about this topic carefully before you start. The software does not require them, but experience shows that these are very useful rules of thumb:

- Do not use spaces within any of your organization, OU, or server names. If you use spaces, you need to supply double-quotation marks any time you refer to the names later.

- Your organization (and OU) name(s) should be relatively short. They will be used very frequently. As a guideline, use at least three and no more than eight characters.

- If you are using geographically based OUs, include the location in the name. You could use city, state, or region abbreviations. Be careful in using city abbreviations if your office might move. For example, if you're located in Los Angeles, you might use LA as the OU name. However, if you later move to San Francisco, all the names within the OU might have to be changed. Another choice might be WEST instead of LA.

- An optional two-letter country code may be associated at the organizational level. The codes themselves are predefined and follow the X.500 naming conventions. You may use this component only if your organization name has been approved by your country's X.500 clearinghouse.

- The common name (CN, the lowest in the hierarchy) for servers should be unique within the hierarchy. Although you can have duplicates because of the hierarchical nature of the names, do not depend on this to distinguish between servers. Other components of the operating system and networking software may use the common name only to identify the server.

- It's recommended to have at least one level of OU below the organization level for most medium-size companies. Even the largest companies can usually organize their naming conventions with no more than two levels of OU below the organization level. These are only guidelines, however, and your mileage might vary.

31

INSTALLING THE DOMINO SERVER

Now that you have planned your Domino infrastructure, you have decided on your domain name and hierarchical names, and you understand certification, you are ready to install your Domino server.

You can install from a distribution CD, or you can access the installation files over a network. In either case, here is how to install Domino for Windows 2000/NT:

1. Locate the directory containing the installation files—from either the CD, the hard disk, or a network share—and start the installation process by double-clicking setup.exe.

2. After the welcome screen appears, click Next to view the license agreement. Read it carefully. Assuming that you agree to the terms, click Yes.

3. Enter your name and company name in the next screen. Click Next.

4. Choose the program files and data directories for installation (see Figure 31.2). You can also select an option to install a partitioned server. Partitioned servers are mainly for service providers or others that want to support multiple Domino servers on a single hardware platform. Essentially, this allows multiple logical servers to reside on a single physical server. Click Next.

5. Select the appropriate server from the three different types of Domino servers: Domino Utility Server, Domino Messaging Server, and Domino Enterprise Server (see Figure 31.3). With Release 6, the standard Domino server is now called the Domino Enterprise Server. This version includes support for both messaging and application services. The install procedure for these three options is very similar, so we'll review only the standard Enterprise server.

Figure 31.2
Choose the folders for
the Domino programs
and data.

NOTE

For more detailed information about the Domino Family of Servers, review Chapter 30,
"The Domino Family of Servers."

31

Figure 31.3
Choose the Domino
server you have
licensed.

6. After you choose the radio button for the server type you have licensed, you can click the Customize button to see additional options. Figure 31.4 shows the various options for the Domino Enterprise server. You should normally install any files that have been selected by default. Click Next.

7. If you elected to install a partitioned server, you'll be prompted to select destination data folders for each partition. Use the Add, Change, and Remove buttons to customize the configuration of the server's data directories.

8. Specify a folder for the program icons. The default folder is Lotus Applications; you can use this folder or choose another. When you are ready to start copying files, click Next. The copying of files will take a while to complete.

Figure 31.4
You can add or remove some features for the Domino server.

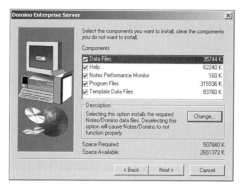

9. The Domino program files should now be copied to the folders you specified. Click Finish to complete the initial phase of your installation. Depending on your environment, you might be prompted to restart the operating system. If so, restart your operating system at this point.

RUNNING THE DOMINO SERVER SETUP PROGRAM

Now that you have copied the Domino program files and configured the data directories, let's get started configuring the server.

1. Start the Domino Server Setup program by choosing Programs, Lotus Applications, Lotus Domino Server from the Windows start menu. If you selected a different directory for the program icons, use the appropriate folder instead of Lotus Applications. The first time you run the server, it invokes the Domino Server Setup Wizard. Unlike previous versions of Domino, Release 6 has its own Java application to walk you through the installation. The setup wizard should look similar to Figure 31.5.

Figure 31.5
The Java-based setup wizard gathers the configuration details for the new Domino server.

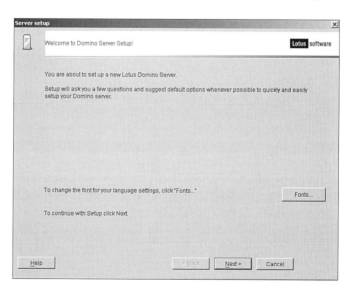

TIP

> If you need any assistance with the Setup Wizard, simply press F1 for more detailed information and instructions.

2. From the initial screen, click the Next button.

3. The second screen of the wizard asks if this is the first Domino server of your infrastructure or whether it should join an existing Domino domain. As shown in Figure 31.6, simply choose that this is the first server and click the Next button.

Figure 31.6
The second step of the Setup Wizard asks whether this server is a member of an existing domain.

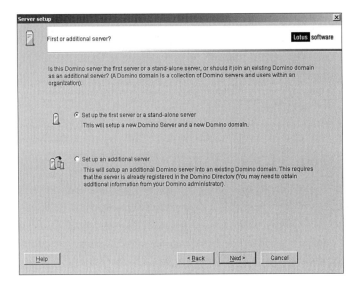

NOTE

> Although there are only two options, Set Up the First Server or Standalone Server and Set Up an Additional Server, you might have a single Domino server running 5.x, but you want to upgrade it to 6.0. In this case, use the first server option. The additional setup option is reserved for when you are installing a second server while the original server is up and running. If you are upgrading a single server from 5.x to 6.0, you should take your 5.x server down while installing 6.0. As in any upgrade of major software, carefully consider your options before overlaying your running 5.x system with 6.0. See Chapter 33, "Upgrading from Domino R5 to R6," for more details.

4. In this third screen (see Figure 31.7), choose a server name and title. As previously discussed, it's important that you establish a naming convention before continuing. If you'd like to see some of Lotus's guidelines for server naming, click the Help button on the wizard. Additionally, you can choose to use an existing ID file. If this is an upgrade instead of a fresh install, select the ID for the existing server. When the fields have been completed, click Next.

Figure 31.7
This setup requires you to assign the server a name and a title.

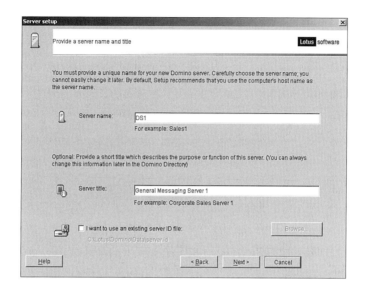

5. In Figure 31.8, you see the next step in the wizard. This step requires that you supply the organization name and the certifier's password.

Figure 31.8
Supply the domain name and certifier's password.

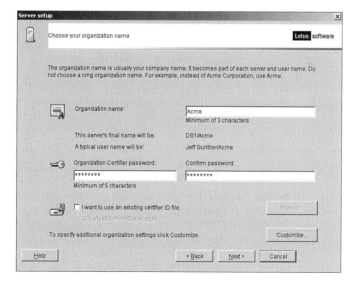

If you're using Domino in another country than the United States, click the Customize button and choose your country. When you've completed the required fields of this step, click Next to set up the Domino domain name.

6. The next step requires you to choose a domain name, used in mail routing and messaging. You might want to use your TCP/IP domain name in this field. Click Next after you create a domain name.

7. The next step in the Setup Wizard requests information about you, the Domino administrator. As shown in Figure 31.9, just complete each field and select the location of where you want to keep a copy of the administrator ID.

Figure 31.9
Supply the administrator details.

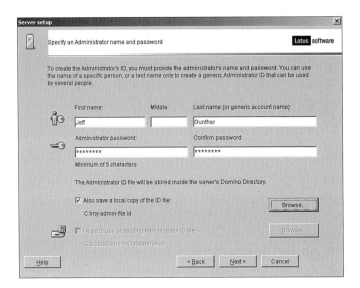

Be sure to put the administrator ID file in a location that is easily accessible. You'll need this file to log into the server when you set up your personal workstation. When you've completed this step of the wizard, click Next.

> **TIP**
>
> When you create the administrator's ID file, you should normally leave off the middle initial because the email ID consists of the fields you enter. If you include a middle initial, users must also include this initial when sending mail. In addition, it normally is easy to guess another employee's email address if it consists of only a first and last name. If you include the middle initial, it would be very hard to guess another employee's email address because a user would have to guess (or know) the person's middle initial.

8. The Domino server is always available to Notes clients. In addition to Notes clients, you can select from four optional Internet services (see Figure 31.10):

   - **Web Browsers**—For example, Microsoft Internet Explorer, Netscape Navigator, and Mozilla. This establishes the HTTP protocol.

   - **Internet Mail Clients**—For example, Eudora and Microsoft Outlook Express. This enables POP3 and IMAP. Since Release 5, SMTP is always available.

- **LDAP Services**—Choose this option if you'd like to enable directory services for other clients.

Figure 31.10
Select the Internet services you need within your Domino server.

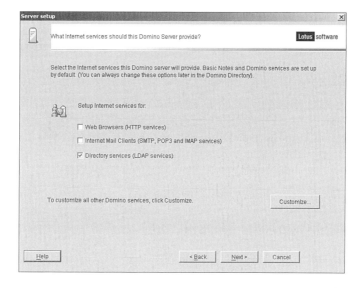

In addition to these basic Internet services, you can selectively choose the tasks you want to run within the server by clicking the Customize button. If you are just starting out administrating Domino, simply leave the default tasks selected and click the Next button.

9. The next step in the wizard asks you to verify your network settings (see Figure 31.11). Under most situations, you can simply click Next. If you want to modify the settings, click the Customize button.

Figure 31.11
Verify the network settings for your Domino server.

10. You're almost done. The final choices revolve around the options to secure your Domino server (see Figure 31.12).

Figure 31.12
Security options for the databases and templates of your Domino server.

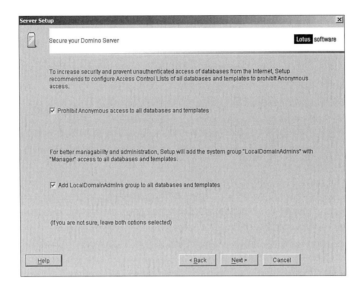

Carefully read and follow the onscreen instructions and recommendations regarding the options for the database and template's Access Control List. Unless you have a legitimate reason, it's recommended that you leave these at their defaulted values and simply click Next.

11. You made it! Verify the settings listed and click Setup to finish your installation. It takes several minutes for the Domino server to set up your Domino public directory, certifier, server, and user IDs. After all the information has been set up, you will see the Congratulations screen.

Congratulations. You have installed your Domino server. You can now start the server from the operating system. The Domino server creates a few databases when it first starts, and then the Domino server is operational.

CREATING OU CERTIFIERS

During the installation of your first server, Domino automatically creates a server ID file, an organization certifier ID file, and a user ID file for the administrator. Remember from the previous discussion that OUs are part of the naming hierarchy for your organization. If you see a name such as Clark Kent/Sales/West/Acme, the names Sales and West represent OU names. Acme is the organization name, and Clark Kent is the username.

To create and use hierarchical naming, you must create an OU certifier for each OU. When you first register each user, you supply a certifier ID file. If you use the organizational certifier ID, the user is placed at the organization level. If you use a lower-level OU certifier ID file, the user is placed within that OU.

If you will be using at least one level of OU below the organizational level (normally recommended), you must create an OU certifier ID file. Fortunately, this is very easy. To create an OU certifier, you start up the Domino Administrator client:

1. From the Domino Administrator client, click the Configuration tab.

2. In the Tools pane on the right side of the screen, click the Registration twistie and click Organizational Unit to open the Choose a Certifier dialog box.

3. Click the Certifier ID button to select a certifier, and click OK.

4. Enter the password for the selected certifier to open the Register Organizational Unit Certifier dialog box (see Figure 31.13).

Figure 31.13
You must create an OU certifier for each OU.

5. In the Register Organizational Unit Certifier dialog box, you can change the registration server by clicking the Registration Server button. The Certifier ID button is used to change the location in the hierarchy where this OU will be located. You can change the location of the output ID file by clicking the Set ID File button.

6. Enter the OU name and certifier password. The Password Quality scale enforces passwords to be more or less difficult to guess, either manually or via program. The scale is from 0 to 16—the larger the number, the more secure the password. Move the slider for an explanation of each level of password quality.

7. At the bottom of the dialog box, as shown in Figure 31.13, choose the security type: North American or International. Also enter the name of the administrator who should receive certification requests. You can optionally include a location or comment.

8. When you have finished filling in the dialog box, click Register. The process might take several minutes to complete, depending upon the speed of your processor.

When the process completes, you should see a message indicating that the ID file was created successfully.

After you create an OU certifier, you can use this certifier ID to register other users. The certifier ID created in Figure 31.13 is /West/Intalgent. A sample user created with this ID file is John Doe/West/Intalgent.

INSTALLING ADDITIONAL DOMINO SERVERS

Lotus distinguishes between setting up the first server and setting up any additional servers. This is because some initial tasks are required for setting up the first server that are not required (and that should not be performed) for the second and subsequent servers.

In particular, some important tasks are performed for the first server but should not be performed again:

- The organization certifier ID is created. This is a one-time event. If this task is repeated, the second organization ID is considered a separate organization, *even if you use the same textual name*.

- The organization's Domino Directory is created and initialized. This task should not be repeated for subsequent servers or users.

You actually can register an additional Domino server in two ways when you have at least one server running. Registration really consists of creating a server ID file and having the ID file certified. To register a new server, you can do one of the following:

- Use the Domino Administrator client to register the new server.
- Register the server when you actually install the software on the computer.

USING THE DOMINO ADMINISTRATOR TO REGISTER A NEW SERVER

To register a new server using the Domino Administrator client, follow these steps:

1. Open the Domino Administrator and click the Configuration tab.

2. In the Tools pane on the right, click Registration, Server to open the Choose a Certifier dialog box. Select the appropriate certifier ID by clicking the Certifier ID button, and then click OK.

3. Enter the password for the ID file you choose to open. The Register Servers dialog box appears, as shown in Figure 31.14.

Figure 31.14
You can register a server via the Domino Administrator client.

4. From the Register Servers dialog box, you can pick the registration server and the certifier. Click Continue to see the Register New Servers dialog box shown in Figure 31.15.

Figure 31.15
You can leave
Password Quality at 0
for a server.

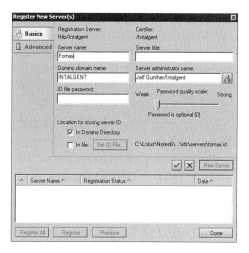

5. Enter the server's name and, optionally, a password, domain, and administrator. You might want to leave the password blank for a server. This enables the server to start up unattended. If you include a password, an operator must enter the password for the server to start up. Normally, you want to locate the server and server console in a locked environment, which enables you to configure the server to start without a password. Click Register to complete the process.

After the server has been registered, the server's ID file is created. You need to use this ID file when you actually install the software from the CD-ROM.

REGISTERING AN ADDITIONAL SERVER WHILE INSTALLING

When you install the code for a server, you can specify whether the server will be the first server or an additional server. Previous sections covered material for the first server.

Installing an additional server is very similar to installing the first server, except that the Domino directory is not created and a certifier ID is not created. Also, you first need to create a server ID file and certify it, using the Administration client, before copying and configuring the server itself. You can create the ID file and save it to a file, or you can store it in the public directory. If you store it in the Domino directory, you must enter a password for the ID file.

The installation process copies the files from the CD-ROM or network to your hard disk, as described previously. Then the server installation guides you through the customization database.

After the files have been copied to the server, the server installation starts. As demonstrated in Figure 31.16, on the second screen of the server setup wizard, you click the radio button Set Up an Additional Server.

Figure 31.16
Click the Set Up an Additional Server radio button for the second and subsequent server installations.

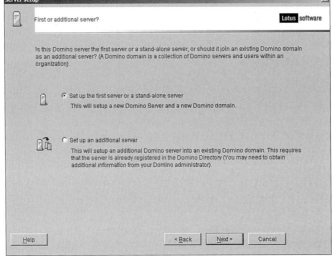

At this point, you simply follow the setup instructions detailed previously in this chapter.

CHAPTER 32

INSTALLATION AND CONFIGURATION OF DOMINO ON LINUX

In this chapter

WHY LINUX AND DOMINO?

Over the past few years, IBM has taken a keen interest in Linux and the Open Source movement in general. An outcome of IBM's investment in Linux has been to provide a version of all its enterprise software products for the Linux operating system. Domino is no exception. But before you get started on how to install and deploy Domino on Linux, let's review some background for using Linux within your Domino infrastructure.

Ever since Lotus's announcement in 1999 that Domino would be released for the Linux platform, the pairing has been a success. Like Domino releases for other supported operating systems, the initial release for Linux included all the basic Domino features, plus advanced services for application-level clustering. Release 6 improves Domino's support for Linux, and proves IBM's commitment to innovation for cross-platform solutions.

THE BUSINESS CASE FOR DOMINO ON LINUX

Since its inception, Linux has received tremendous acceptance among its users and the marketplace. This overwhelming acceptance, spurred by many factors, has led to enormous growth and has prompted users to turn to the operating system for mission-critical applications. For many organizations, Linux is used as the platform of choice for the deployment of their Domino infrastructure. The decision to use Linux is based on several factors, each of which directly affect one vital issue: cost.

Ask any technology manager in today's business environment if she'd like to save money on her server infrastructure, and you'll get a resounding "Yes!" One of the most attractive advantages of Linux is the cost savings it offers over other operating systems. Initially, you might think the cost savings are from the low to nonexistent licensing costs of the operating system. For example, if you deploy Red Hat Linux, you can download a version directly from their Web site for free, or purchase the CDs for next to nothing. However, most seasoned managers know that the software licensing accounts form only a small percentage of the overall cost for a system deployment. For most organizations, Linux can cut costs through three critical factors: efficiency, reliability, and security.

EFFICIENCY

Unlike other platforms, Linux can run more efficiently on older hardware. This allows you to run Linux on equipment that might be close to retirement, if used with other operating systems. Linux is designed to make use of all available resources. For example, the latest version of Red Hat Linux's minimum hardware requirement is a 200MHz Pentium-class processor, 2.5GB of hard drive storage space, and 192MB of RAM for a standard installation. As with any application, the installation of Lotus Domino does add to the hardware requirements, but not noticeably.

RELIABILITY

No matter what the cost, an operating system is worthless if it's not completely reliable. One of the greatest strengths of Linux is the platform's overall availability. Reliability over time is an area where Linux really shines. Linux has been designed to aggressively handle the loads that enterprise computing systems experience. In addition to the basic services that Domino provides, many customers look to the advanced application clustering to ensure availability. Ensuring the server's reliability and availability reduces the total cost of system administration and improves end user productivity.

SECURITY

As companies evaluate Notes and Domino, security is one of the deciding factors in choosing it as their messaging and application infrastructure. However, Notes and Domino is only as secure as the operating system on which it is running. To address the concerns of the operating system's security, Linux includes many built-in features. Linux allows administrators to selectively control what applications and services are provided. These services can be started, stopped, installed, or uninstalled at any time without affecting the operating system. This gives you the capability to create a server for a particular purpose while minimizing exposure from services that are not needed or used. In addition to service security, Linux utilizes a time-tested file security model. This file security model allows you to set the permission for files at a user or group level, with robust logging of access and use. Additionally, some distributions include support for out-of-the-box firewall capabilities. These security features provide organizations with a secure environment in which to deploy Domino. Security can also provide another cost savings: The indirect costs of data loss due to a security breach can be devastating to any organization.

DISTRIBUTION SUPPORT

Each Linux distribution provides particular features and functions that address users' specific needs. Whereas each version of Linux is different, a common thread, the kernel, is the same across all distributions. For more information about the variety of Linux distributions available, check out `http://www.linux.org/dist/`.

With Release 6, Lotus provides support for two different distributions of Linux, with support planned for another. Currently, the only supported distributions are Red Hat Linux Version 7.2 or newer, and SuSE 8.0 or newer. Each of the supported distributions must be running at least the 2.4.18 kernel. IBM is planning to include support for a new distribution called UnitedLinux after it has been released and tested.

NOTE

Release 6 limits the number of support distributions compared to Release 5. Under Release 5, Lotus included support for Caldera and TurboLinux. If you're running these or any other unsupported distributions, Release 6 might work but is completely unsupported by Lotus. If you will deploy Domino on Linux, you should use only the supported distributions.

INITIAL SETUP AND PREPARATION

To make the chapter more manageable for installation instructions, some assumptions were made about the environment in which you will be installing Domino. Throughout this example installation, we'll assume that you are running Red Hat 8.0 with a server installation and that you have a basic knowledge of how to navigate the Linux operating system. If you are new to Linux and have questions about any configuration or settings outside of Domino, a great resource is available online at www.linuxnewbie.org/.

SYSTEM REQUIREMENTS

The following minimum requirements are necessary to install Domino 6 under Linux:

- Intel x86 processor
- 128MB RAM or larger (192MB recommended)
- Swap file of three times the physical RAM or greater
- 1GB minimum, 1.5GB or more recommended
- Red Hat 7.2 or SuSE 8.0 (Server or Enterprise)

CAUTION

> Be aware that Domino is not supported on systems running Red Hat 7.2 with multiple processors.

If you're planning to run the Domino server under Red Hat Linux 7.2 and you are using the Network Information Service (NIS), a set of patches is required:

- glibc-2.2.4-24.i686.rpm or newer
- glibc-common-2.2.4-24.i386.rpm or newer
- glibc-devel-2.2.4-24.i386.rpm or newer
- glibc-profile-2.2.4-24.i386.rpm or newer
- nscd-2.2.4-24.i386.rpm or newer
- kernel-2.4.9-21.i686.rpm or newer
- kernel-headers-2.4.9-21.i386.rpm or newer
- kernel-smp-2.4.9-21.i686.rpm or newer
- kernel-source-2.4.9-21.i386.rpm or newer
- modutils-2.4.13-0.7.1.i386.rpm or newer
- nfs-utils-0.3.1-13.7.2.1.i386.rpm or newer
- wu-ftpd-2.6.1-20.i386.rpm (required only if running wu-ftpd) or newer
- gdb-5.1-1.i386.rpm or newer

NOTE

Review the release notes for a topic titled "Linux patch requirements" for a more detailed list.

SYSTEM PREPARATION

Before getting started with the Domino installation, you must complete a few housekeeping tasks. These tasks include shutting down and disabling both the Apache Web server and the SendMail SMTP (Simple Mail Transfer Protocol) server if they have been installed.

DISABLING APACHE WEB SERVER

Because Domino includes its own Web server, the Apache Web Server needs to be disabled before starting the installation. To do this, follow these steps:

1. Log into your server as the root user.

2. After you've authenticated to the server, you need to stop SendMail server. Execute the following command:
   `/etc/rc.d/init.d/httpd stop`

3. If the server was started, the command displays success. However, if it fails, Apache isn't running. It is always a good precaution to verify that Apache Web server is stopped.

4. Now that the server is stopped, you need to prevent the server from starting when the system is rebooted. Execute the following command:
   `rm /etc/rc.d/init.d/httpd`

DISABLING SENDMAIL

Most Linux distributions include a variant of the SendMail SMTP service. Red Hat 8.0 is no exception. For this installation example, we want to use Domino's SMTP services instead of SendMail. However, with multiple IP addresses, you can configure Domino and SendMail to coexist on the same physical server. For information on how to bind SendMail to a particular IP address, review the SendMail documentation. To disable SendMail, follow these steps:

1. Log into your server as the root user.

2. After you've authenticated to the server, you need to stop the Apache Web server. Execute the following command:
   `/etc/rc.d/init.d/sendmail stop`

3. Now that the service is stopped, you need to prevent the service from starting when the system is rebooted. With any text editor, open the file /etc/rc.d/init.d/sendmail. Locate the following lines within the file:
   ```
   echo -n $"Starting $prog: "
   /usr/bin/newaliases > /dev/null 2>&1
   if test -x /usr/bin/make -a -f /etc/mail/Makefile ; then
     make -C /etc/mail -s
   ```

32

```
       else
         for i in virtusertable access domaintable mailertable ; do
           if [ -f /etc/mail/$i ] ; then
           makemap hash /etc/mail/$i < /etc/mail/$i
           fi
         done
       fi
       daemon /usr/sbin/sendmail -bd \
                   $([ -n "$QUEUE" ] && echo -q$QUEUE)
       RETVAL=$?
       echo
       [ $RETVAL -eq 0 ] && touch /var/lock/subsys/sendmail
```

When you've located the group of lines, comment out each line by inserting a # at the beginning of each line. This action disables SendMail from starting on reboot.

Acquiring the Software

Lotus provides several ways to obtain the Domino server for Linux. If you don't have a licensed copy for production but would still like to try it out, you're in luck. As in previous releases, Lotus provides a 90-day trial copy of the Domino 6 server for testing and evaluation purposes. You can download the installation file directly from the Lotus Developer Domain site at www.lotus.com/ldd.

Creating a User for Domino

Under Linux, as with other Unix-like operating systems, each individual user owns specific processes running within the operating system. Running Domino is no different. By default, the Domino installation uses a user called notes. To create a new user, execute the following command:

adduser notes

After the user has been created, you can set the password with the passwd command. If you created a user called notes, use the following command to set the password:

passwd notes

As with other distributions of Domino, during the installation process you're asked if you want to install more than one Domino server on a single physical server. For each server you'd like to run, a different and unique username is required to distinguish between processes.

Installing Domino

Depending on how you obtained the installation software, there are different instructions on how to begin installing Domino for Linux. In any case, you'll need to execute these commands from a terminal window. The screenshots within this chapter were obtained using the Gnome windowing environment.

Installation via CD

If you have the software on CD, log in as root. Before you can use a CD under Linux, you need to mount the drive. Insert the CD in the drive and type the following:

```
mount /mnt/cdrom
```

Change directories to the CD-ROM drive by typing this:

```
cd /mnt/cdrom
```

Finally, locate the Linux installation directory and start the installer via this command:

```
./install
```

Installation via a TAR File

If the software package is available to you as a TAR file, transfer the file to the server using the File Transfer Protocol (FTP), Secure Shell (SSH), or some other mechanism. When the installation file is located on the server, again log in as root and change to the directory where you placed the file—for example, /tmp/domino. Before you can run the installer, you must extract the files. If the file was called domino.tar, execute the following command:

```
tar xvf domino.tar
```

To run the installation, simply execute the following command from the directory that contains your newly extracted files:

```
./install
```

Installing the Software

Follow these steps to complete the installation of the Domino server software:

1. When the software is started, you should see a welcome screen similar to the one shown in Figure 32.1. Throughout this process, the Tab key is used to navigate forward to each section of the installation. Many of the questions during the installation provide context-sensitive help to assist you in making the proper choice. To view help, type **h**.

   Move to the next screen by pressing the Tab key.

2. The next screen simply reminds you to review the Release Notes to learn about Release 6's new features for the Domino server. Press the Tab key to continue.

3. The next couple of screens ask you to review the Lotus Notes/Domino software agreement. Press the Tab key to view the software agreement. Be sure to carefully read and agree to the terms of the agreement. Follow the directions provided to page down through the document. As shown in Figure 32.2, you are asked whether you agree to the terms of the license agreement. If you agree, press the Tab key.

Figure 32.1
The welcome screen after the installation software has started.

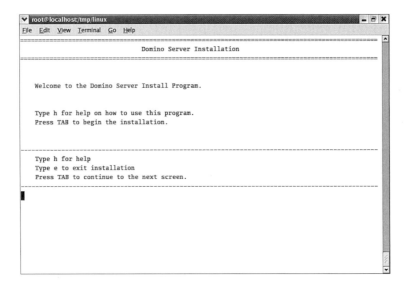

Figure 32.2
If you agree to the Lotus Notes/Domino software agreement, move to the next step of the installation.

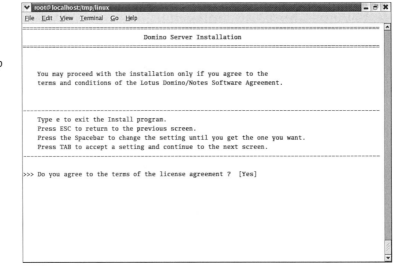

4. If you are upgrading an existing server or creating multiple partitions, pay careful attention to the next step of the installation. If you are creating a new Domino server, simply answer No to the question of whether you want to install only the data directories (see Figure 32.3). Press the Tab key to continue.

5. The next screen enables you to choose from the three different Domino servers: Domino Utility Server, Domino Messaging Server, and Domino Enterprise Server. For more information about the three server types, refer to Chapter 30, "The Domino Family of Servers." With Release 6, the standard Domino server is now called the

Domino Enterprise server. This version includes support for both messaging and application services. The install procedure for these three options is very similar, so we'll review only the standard Enterprise server. Figure 32.4 shows the selection screen.

Figure 32.3
Choose No to create a new Domino server.

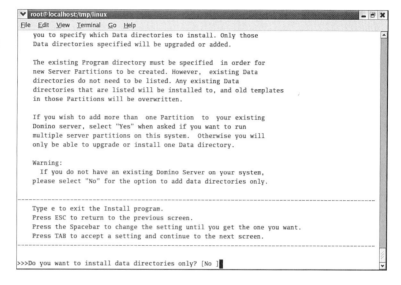

```
root@localhost:/tmp/linux                                              _ ☐ ✕
File  Edit  View  Terminal  Go  Help
you to specify which Data directories to install. Only those
Data directories specified will be upgraded or added.

The existing Program directory must be specified  in order for
new Server Partitions to be created. However,  existing Data
directories do not need to be listed. Any existing Data
directories that are listed will be installed to, and old templates
in those Partitions will be overwritten.

If you wish to add more than  one Partition  to your existing
Domino server, select "Yes" when asked if you want to run
multiple server partitions on this system.  Otherwise you will
only be able to upgrade or install one Data directory.

Warning:
   If you do not have an existing Domino Server on your system,
please select "No" for the option to add data directories only.

------------------------------------------------------------------
Type e to exit the Install program.
Press ESC to return to the previous screen.
Press the Spacebar to change the setting until you get the one you want.
Press TAB to accept a setting and continue to the next screen.
------------------------------------------------------------------
>>>Do you want to install data directories only? [No ]█
```

Figure 32.4
Choose the Domino server you have licensed.

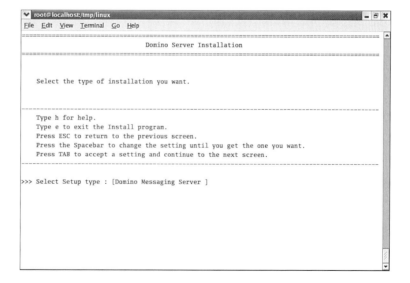

```
root@localhost:/tmp/linux                                              _ ☐ ✕
File  Edit  View  Terminal  Go  Help
==================================================================
                    Domino Server Installation
==================================================================


   Select the type of installation you want.


------------------------------------------------------------------
Type h for help.
Type e to exit the Install program.
Press ESC to return to the previous screen.
Press the Spacebar to change the setting until you get the one you want.
Press TAB to accept a setting and continue to the next screen.
------------------------------------------------------------------

>>> Select Setup type : [Domino Messaging Server ]
```

Select the appropriate Domino installation type by using the spacebar, and then press Tab to continue.

6. Next you're asked if you want to install all the template files for Release 6. If you're creating a new Domino server, simply choose Yes and continue to the next screen. You need to choose No for this question only if you're upgrading from a previous version of Domino on Linux and want to keep the older templates.

7. The next option asks if you want to configure the server with application service provider (ASP) functionality (see Figure 32.5). Release 6 includes new targeted capabilities for Domino hosting. If you select Yes, some ASP security features are installed. If you're not an ASP and you will not be hosting Domino for multiple customers, choose No.

Figure 32.5
Domino 6 includes some additional features for application service providers.

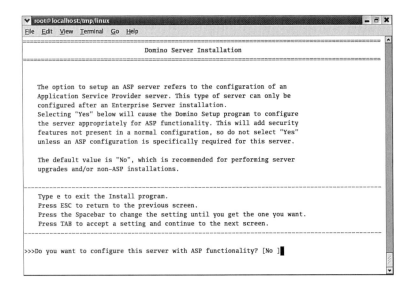

8. Select the program directory for the Lotus Domino files (see Figure 32.6). By default, Domino uses the /opt/lotus directory. Press Tab to continue.

Figure 32.6
Choose the directory where you want to install the Domino program files.

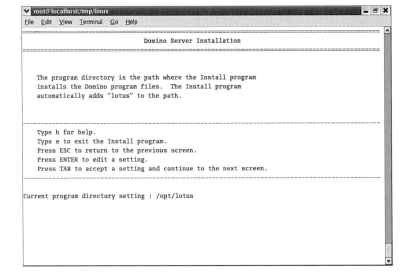

9. In addition to the program directory, Domino needs a location for the data files. But before you can select the directory, Domino needs to know whether you are running multiple Domino servers at one time. As shown in Figure 32.7, the sample installation has only one server running, so No was selected. If you are running multiple Domino servers, choose Yes and follow the detailed instructions.

Figure 32.7
If you're running only one server, you can leave the default No.

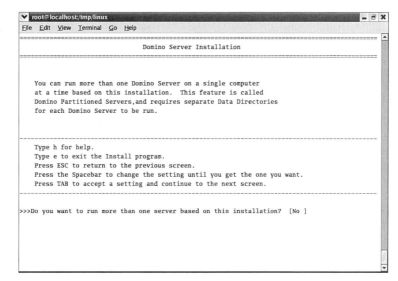

10. Now that you've specified the program directory and the number of servers running (in this example, only one), the install software asks you to pick the location of the Domino data directory. The screen should appear similar to Figure 32.8. It's recommended that you use the default directory of /local/notesdata.

Figure 32.8
Choose the directory for Domino's data files.

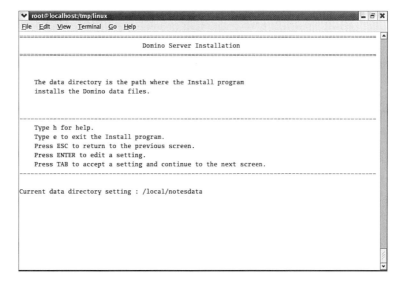

11. As we reviewed earlier, each application in Linux runs under a particular user. The next two screens ask you to specify the Linux username and Linux group for the user who owns the Domino process. The default is notes. Simply type the name of the user and then the name of the group, and continue to the screen reporting that the installation is complete (see Figure 32.9).

Figure 32.9
The installation program has completed.

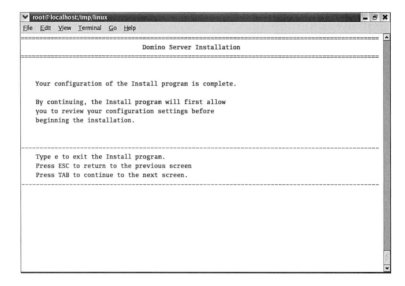

12. You're almost done with the installation. Press Tab to begin the process of installing Domino. Figure 32.10 demonstrates the process of installing the Enterprise server.

Figure 32.10
The Domino Enterprise server is now being installed.

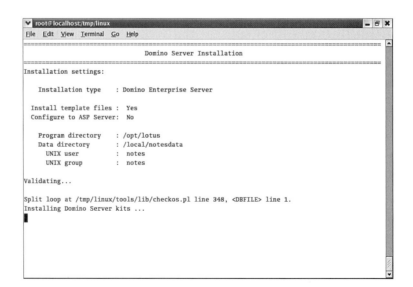

13. When the installation has completed, proceed to the next section to configure and set up your Domino server.

CONFIGURING A DOMINO SERVER UNDER LINUX

Unlike previous versions of Domino under Linux, the configuration and setup for Release 6 is very similar to the installation process for Microsoft Windows, as discussed in Chapter 31, "Initial Planning and Installation." In fact, other than a few minor changes, the instructions are identical. With Release 6, Lotus provides a cross-platform wizard to gather the necessary configuration information to set up and configure a Domino server. Let's get started.

Before continuing, make sure that you are logged in as the user you specified who will run the Domino server; typically, this is the user named notes.

CAUTION

It's very important that you start the Domino server under a different user than root. Be sure to use the username used during the installation of Domino.

Follow these steps to configure the Domino server:

1. The first step is to add the Domino server's data directory to the logged-in user's PATH environment variable. With Red Hat 8.0, the default shell environment is BASH. Assuming that you're using the default shell and are within the user's HOME directory, open the .bash_profile file using your favorite text editor and locate the following lines:
   ```
   # User specific environment and startup programs

   PATH=$PATH:$HOME/bin
   ```

2. Add the Domino data directory to the PATH. For example, if you are using the default data directory for Domino, the modified line should look like the following:
   ```
   # User specific environment and startup programs

   PATH=$PATH:$HOME/bin:/local/notesdata
   ```

3. Save the file and log into the server again. Upon logging back into the server, the user's path is modified to now include the data directories.

4. Once again, open a terminal session within the Gnome or KDE windowing environment, and type the following command:
   ```
   cd /opt/lotus/bin
   ./server
   ```

5. The server executable starts the Domino Server Setup Wizard. From the initial screen, click the Next button. The second screen of the wizard asks whether this is the first Domino server of your infrastructure or whether it should join an existing Domino domain. As shown in Figure 32.11, simply indicate that this is the first server and click Next.

32

Figure 32.11
The second step in
the setup wizard asks
whether this server
should join an exist-
ing Domino domain
or is the first server in
the domain.

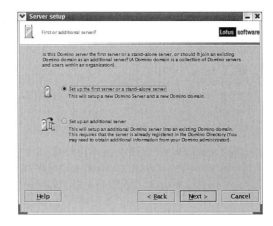

NOTE

Although you have only two options—Set Up the First Server or Standalone Server, and
Set Up an Additional Server—you might have a single Domino server running 5.x, but
you want to upgrade it to 6. In this case, use the first server option. The additional setup
option is reserved for when you are installing a second server while the original server is
up and running. If you are upgrading a single server from 5.x to 6, you should take your
5.x server down while installing 6. As in any upgrade of major software, carefully consider your options before overlaying your running 5.x system with 6. See Chapter 33,
"Upgrading from Domino 5 to 6," for more details.

6. The third screen, as shown in Figure 32.12, asks you to choose a server name and title.
As previously discussed, it's important that you establish a naming convention before
continuing. If you want to see some of Lotus's guidelines for server naming, click the
Help button on the wizard. Additionally, you can choose to use an existing ID file. If
this is an upgrade instead of a fresh install, select the ID for the existing server. After
you have completed the fields, click Next.

Figure 31.12
This setup asks you to
assign a server name
and title.

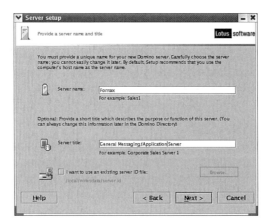

7. The wizard then requires that you supply the domain name and the certifier's password. If you're using Domino outside the United States, click the Customize button and choose your country. When you've completed this phase of the setup, click Next to set up the Domino domain name. The next step requests that you choose a domain name, which is used in mail routing and messaging. You might want to use your TCP/IP domain name in this field. Click Next after you create a domain name.

8. Next you must supply information about you, the Domino administrator. Just complete each field and select the location of where you want to keep a copy of the administrator ID. Be sure to put the administrator ID file in a location that is easily accessible. You'll need this file to log into the server after you set up your personal workstation. When you've completed this step of the wizard, click Next.

9. The Domino server is always available to Notes clients. In addition to selecting Notes clients, you can select from other optional Internet services (see Figure 32.13):

- **Web Browsers**—This includes, for example, Microsoft Internet Explorer, Netscape Navigator, and Mozilla. This establishes the HTTP protocol.

- **Internet Mail Clients**—This includes, for example, Eudora or Microsoft Outlook Express. This enables POP3 and IMAP. Since Release 5, SMTP is always available.

- **LDAP Services**—Choose this option if you want to enable directory services for other clients.

Figure 32.13
Select the Internet services you need within your Domino server.

In addition to these basic Internet services, you can selectively choose the tasks you want to run within the server by clicking the Customize button. If you are just starting out administrating Domino, simply leave the default tasks selected and click Next.

10. The next step in the wizard asks you to verify your network settings. Figure 32.14 demonstrates these settings. In most situations, you can simply click Next. If you want to modify the settings, click the Customize button.

Figure 32.14
Verify the network settings for your Domino server.

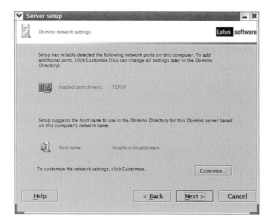

You're almost done. The final choices revolve around the options to secure your Domino server (see Figure 32.15).

Figure 32.15
Security options for the databases and templates of your Domino server.

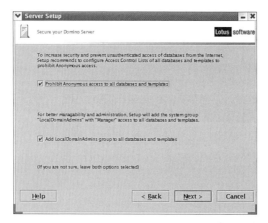

Carefully read and follow the onscreen instructions and recommendations regarding the options for the database and template's access control list. Unless you have a legitimate reason, it's recommended that you leave these at their default values and click Next.

You made it! Verify the settings listed and click Setup to finish your installation. It takes several minutes for the Domino server to set up your Domino public directory, certifier, server, and user IDs. After all the information has been set up, you will see the Congratulations screen, shown in Figure 32.16.

Congratulations! You have installed your Domino server. You can now start the server from the operating system. The Domino server creates a few databases when it first starts, and then its server is operational.

Figure 32.16
The Domino server is now installed and configured.

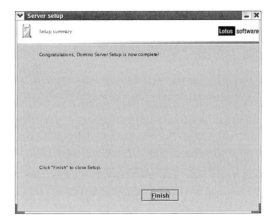

STARTING THE DOMINO SERVER

After the installation and configuration steps have been completed, you're ready to start the Domino server. Simply log into the server using the Linux username you specified during the installation. After you're logged in, change directories to the location of the Domino program files. For example, if the Domino program files were located in /opt/lotus/bin, execute the following command:

```
cd /opt/lotus/bin
```

Now that you're inside the executable directory for the Domino server, simply start the server by typing the following:

```
./server
```

Executing the server program starts the Domino server. Figure 32.17 demonstrates the Domino server starting.

Figure 32.17
The Domino server running under Red Hat Linux.

```
[notes@localhost bin]$ ./server

Lotus Domino (r) Server, Release 6.0, September 26, 2002
Copyright (c) IBM Corporation 1987, 2002. All Rights Reserved.

11/15/2002 01:58:46 PM  Begin scan of databases to be consistency checked
11/15/2002 01:58:46 PM  End scan of databases: 1 found
11/15/2002 01:58:46 PM  Server started on physical node localhost.localdomain
11/15/2002 01:58:46 PM  Creating Administration Requests database
11/15/2002 01:58:46 PM  Event Monitor started
11/15/2002 01:58:46 PM  Event: Creating the Monitoring Configuration database.
11/15/2002 01:58:53 PM  Event: Copying messages into the Monitoring Configuration database
11/15/2002 01:58:56 PM  An Adminp request has been submitted to update port information in the se
rver document
11/15/2002 01:58:57 PM  NSF_QUOTA_METHOD changed to 2.
11/15/2002 01:58:57 PM  FormulaTimeout changed to 120.
11/15/2002 01:59:02 PM  Setting up default monitors in Monitoring Configuration database.
11/15/2002 01:59:03 PM  Creating new mailbox file mail.box
11/15/2002 01:59:04 PM  The Console file is /local/notesdata/IBM_TECHNICAL_SUPPORT/console.log
11/15/2002 01:59:04 PM  Console Logging is DISABLED
11/15/2002 01:59:05 PM  Calendar Connector started
11/15/2002 01:59:05 PM  Index update process started
11/15/2002 01:59:05 PM  Schedule Manager started
11/15/2002 01:59:05 PM  Removing the version 0 free time data.  Recreating it as version 4.
11/15/2002 01:59:06 PM  Admin Process: Fornax/Intalgent is the Administration Server of the Domin
o Directory.
```

CHAPTER 33

Upgrading from Domino 5 to 6

In this chapter

THE FIVE STAGES OF YOUR NOTES/DOMINO UPGRADE

The upgrade of a mission-critical business utility such as your Domino/Notes messaging, groupware, and Internet infrastructure should not take place in one jolt; rather, it is more effectively executed in stages. There are five stages to a full upgrade: planning, testing, pilot, production, and leveraging.

PLANNING

Pre-upgrade planning is probably the most critical element of a successful upgrade.

In addition to an upgrade schedule, you need to ensure that all your workstations and servers are compatible with Release 6.

The Notes client for Release 6 is available on the following platforms:

- Microsoft Windows 95 (2nd Edition)
- Microsoft Windows 98
- Microsoft Windows NT 4.0 with Service Pack 6a
- Microsoft Windows 2000 Professional
- Microsoft Windows XP
- Apple Macintosh OS 9.x
- Apple Macintosh OS X (10.1 or newer)

Users on other platforms need to stay with Notes 4.5x clients, move to a new operating system, or use a Web browser to access their Domino mail and applications. In addition, customers should consider the infrastructure benefits of new features, such as those detailed in the following sections.

The following server platforms are supported under Release 6:

- Microsoft Windows NT 4.0
- Microsoft Windows 2000 Server and Advanced Server
- Sun Solaris Operating Environment 2.8/SPARC
- IBM AIX 4.3.3x and 5.1
- IBM OS/400 V5R1
- IBM z/OS V26
- Red Hat Linux 7.2 or SuSE Linux 8.0

PILOT

After the testing phase, your upgrade team should conduct a pilot upgrade to the test environment to gain experience with the upgrade process. The pilot phase is different from your testing phase because you perform an upgrade of mail and application servers within your production environment and then upgrade several predefined users to Release 6. This is a delicate phase, because you need to control the environment to these predefined servers only. Your pilot phase should have several goals:

- Documentation of your upgrade process for each type of server (hub, mail, and application) and client (LAN and mobile)

- Collection of as much information and feedback as possible on what might impact your production environment

- Organization of a detailed schedule of your server upgrades process and departmental users/clients

- Build a team of Notes and Domino 6 experts

Members of the pilot phase should be carefully selected to include the following:

- *Pilot administrators*—Ideally, these are different from the ones in your production environment. Their level of expertise is higher, and they will then train and assist your production administrators in due course.

- *Power users*—These are typically developers who can start upgrading your key applications to the new version.

- *Standard users*—These are your users. Ideally, you want to pick some from different departments. You will arrange to collect their feedback to assess your organization's level of resistance to change and prepare whatever training or user informational sheets are required for a smooth client upgrade.

PRODUCTION

After your pilot rollout has been tested and documented, it is production-ready. You can start the client upgrade and move on to the server deployment.

LEVERAGING

After the Notes 6 client has been deployed across your organization, your IT department can begin to take full advantage of Domino 6's new features and capabilities. This stage mainly focuses on enhancing your critical applications with the new functionality. Existing Release 4 and 5 databases work on Domino 6 servers without modification. However, you should plan a testing phase of your critical and complex applications prior to deploying them to your user base.

After all servers and workstations are running Domino and Notes 6, developers can safely begin to introduce new functionality into existing applications and can create new applications using features introduced in Release 6.

33

OVERVIEW OF THE UPGRADE PROCESS

Upgrading the Domino server software to Release 6 is a relatively quick process. Most of the time is spent compacting databases and rebuilding views. Therefore, the time it actually takes to upgrade a server depends mostly on the amount of data on the server, and the speed of the server's processor.

To minimize the upgrade's impact on your organization, upgrade your infrastructure in the following sequence:

1. Ensure operating system compatibility with Release 6 for all workstations and servers.

> **TIP**
>
> The Domino Administrator is also designed to administer a mixed-release environment and works smoothly with Release 4.6, 5, and 6 servers.

2. Upgrade servers and the Domino Directory to Release 6. You should upgrade the hub servers first, because users do not traditionally directly access them. Thus, users are less likely to be directly affected by any problems that might occur during the upgrade. Then upgrade your mail servers. Finally, upgrade your application servers after testing each database on a Domino 6 server. For gateways and other third-party applications, Lotus Development recommends that you check with the software vendor to ensure that its applications support and interoperate with Release 6.

> **NOTE**
>
> With Release 4.6, the Domino Directory was formerly known as the Public Name and Address Book.

3. Upgrade the Domino Administrator clients.
4. Upgrade Notes clients.
5. Upgrade Notes and Domino databases.

As mentioned earlier, Domino 6 servers and clients are backward-compatible with their version 4.6 and 5.0 counterparts. Additionally, your infrastructure automatically gains in functionality and performance without changing server configurations, topology, mail routing, or addressing. It also goes without saying that you cannot make changes to your topology at the same time.

UPGRADING FROM RELEASE 4.X

Although this chapter is primarily targeted for users upgrading from Release 5 to Release 6, Lotus does provide a supported upgrade path for environments that are running version 4.x of Notes and Domino. Before you begin the process of upgrading to Release 6, you need to upgrade your environment to version 4.6 with the latest maintenance release—4.6.7a.

During the upgrade from 4.5 to 4.6.7a, you need to verify that the database designs and templates are upgraded. For example, if your environment is running Release 4.5, you need to upgrade the organization's Names and Address Book to the latest release of 4.6.7a.

UPGRADING YOUR NOTES CLIENTS

To ensure the successful upgrade of the Notes clients, it's important to perform some preinstallation tasks before installing the new software.

BACKING UP NOTES CLIENT FILES

The rule is to always back up important Notes client files in case an error occurs during the upgrade process. Table 33.1 defines which files you need to back up.

TABLE 33.1 DOMINO ADMINISTRATOR KEY FILES

Domino Administrator Files to Back Up	Default Location
NOTES.INI (Notes Preferences on the Macintosh)	System directory (for example, C:\Lotus\Notes)
DESKTOP.DSK (Notes 4.6) or (Notes 5)	Notes Data Directory (for DESKTOP5.DSK example, C:\NOTES\DATA)
Personal Address Book (NAMES.NSF by default)	Notes Data Directory (for example, C:\NOTES\DATA)
User ID files (for example, JSMITH.ID)	Notes Data Directory (for example, C:\NOTES\DATA)
Local databases (.NSF)	Notes Data Directory (for example, C:\NOTES\DATA)
Local database directory links (.DIR)	Notes Data Directory (for example, C:\NOTES\DATA)
Any customized Notes database templates (.NTF)	Notes Data Directory (for example, C:\NOTES\DATA)

INSTALLING THE NOTES 6 SOFTWARE

Start by running the Notes 6 installation. Follow the prompts on the Windows Installer screens to properly install the software. Select the type of client for which you purchased a license. When you are finished, start Notes. If you need more information on the installation procedure, refer to Chapter 2, "Installing and Customizing the Notes Client."

Notes sets up and upgrades the software automatically if you install Release 6 in the same directory as the previous release of Notes. If you install the Notes 6 software in a different directory, Notes prompts you to complete the configuration process. Notes automatically upgrades your Personal Address Book to the Domino 6 Directory design. If you have

Internet mail set up to work with POP3, Notes creates an Account document for that Internet mail configuration.

SETTING YOUR PERSONAL ADDRESS BOOK PREFERENCES

Your Personal Address Book is automatically upgraded when you upgrade the client. When the upgrade is complete and you open your Personal Address Book for the first time, Notes asks you to enter your preferences into the Personal Address Book profile.

The Release 6 Personal Address Book has a number of new forms, views, subforms, agents, and script libraries. Additionally, it has had some design elements deleted from the 4.6 template. For more details, refer to Chapter 6, "Getting Started with Contact Management."

CREATING ACCOUNT DOCUMENTS FOR INTERNET MAIL

Notes 6 contains Account documents, which contain information for accessing mail using POP and IMAP, and sending mail with SMTP. If you're running 4.6, a Location document is set up to use POP or IMAP. Notes will automatically convert this information into an Account document for that setting. If you send mail to the Internet, Notes creates an SMTP Account document. The accounts are set for the Location that you set up for Internet mail.

CAUTION

> Do not upgrade your mail file to the Release 6 template until your server has been upgraded. Added Release 6 functionality will not work on a 4.6 or 5.0 server.

OPTIONS FOR UPGRADING THE NOTES CLIENTS

Lotus provides three distinct ways to upgrade the Notes client within your infrastructure:

- Upgrade-by-mail
- Lotus Notes Smart Upgrade
- Administrative installation

First, client upgrades can be performed using the upgrade-by-mail capability; users receive an email that upgrades their desktop automatically, via a button. This functionality also enables the user to choose the most convenient time for the upgrade. When the user clicks on the button, the user's mail file, calendar, and Personal Address Book templates are upgraded automatically. This feature is particularly useful if you're looking to upgrade users on Notes 4.6.

The second mechanism is to use the Lotus Notes Smart Upgrade. This new feature is similar to the upgrade-by-mail and sends an email that instructs the user to upgrade. However, unlike the first upgrade choice, this feature enables you to set a grace period. After the grace period, users are required to upgrade to Release 6. Unfortunately, this feature can only be used to upgrade existing clients running Release 6.x. This option might not be very useful for someone migrating from version 4.6 or 5, but will be very helpful once your infrastructure has been migrated to Release 6.

TIP

> Different than the other approaches, the Lotus Notes Smart Upgrade forces users to upgrade (via a grace period). Theoretically, a user could forever ignore the mail message and the upgrade button sent to them by the upgrade-by-mail option.

An administrative installation is the third choice available to upgrade the Notes client running on Microsoft Windows. Unlike the other two options, this option relies on a feature of the operating system called the Windows Installer service. This service is available only if your workstations are running Microsoft Windows 95, 98, NT 4.0, 2000, or XP and have access to a file server that contains the installation files. Typically, the administrative installation is used in conjunction with the upgrade-by-mail or Smart Upgrade.

UPGRADING YOUR DOMINO SERVERS

When you upgrade a Domino server to Release 6, you gain features, functionality, and performance without changing your server configuration, topology, routing, or addressing.

To upgrade a Domino server, you perform these steps, which are explained in more detail in the following sections:

1. Shut down the Domino server (by typing **quit** at the server console).
2. Back up important server files.
3. If you're running the Domino server as a service under Microsoft Windows NT or 2000, remove the service before continuing.
4. Install the Domino 6 software.
5. Upgrade the Domino Directory.

BACKING UP IMPORTANT SERVER FILES

You must back up important Domino server files in case you encounter errors during upgrading. If you have problems during upgrading, you can use the backed-up copies to restore your files. Follow these steps to back up your critical server files:

1. Back up the Data Directory on your server (for example, on Windows this includes `C:\Lotus\Domino\DATA`). This backs up all ID files (including the server ID and certifier IDs), the Domino Directory, and any other data files.
2. Back up the contents of any directories pointed to by links (.DIR files) from your Data Directory.
3. Back up the `NOTES.INI` file for the server.
4. Back up any other Notes databases (.NSF), Notes templates (.NTF), and any databases pointed to by directory links (.DIR).

33

INSTALLING THE DOMINO 6 SOFTWARE

If you install Domino in the same directory as the previous version, you do not need to change the server configuration. If you install Domino in a new directory, the program prompts you to configure the server. During installation, select the server type for which you purchased a license. After installation, launch the Domino 6 server. For more information about installing the Domino server, refer to Chapter 31, "Initial Planning and Installation."

UPGRADING THE DOMINO DIRECTORY

Once the upgraded Domino server has been started, you'll be asked to upgrade to the Domino 6 Directory template. This upgrade process will successfully upgrade a Public Address Book from Domino 4.6 or Domino Directory from Release 5. Like Release 5, the Directory template is backward compatible and is designed to operate in a mixed-release infrastructure. However, there are limitations to the extent of interoperability between releases. The new directory template can only be used with servers running versions 4.6.x, 5, and Release 6. If you have a 4.5 server within your infrastructure, you'll need to upgrade it to Release 4.6 before upgrading to Release 6.

Follow the steps to upgrade the Domino Directory template:

1. When Domino asks whether you want to upgrade the Public Address Book or Domino Directory to the Domino 6 template, press Y. Once the template has been upgraded, shut down the server by typing **quit** on the server's console.

2. Restart the Domino server.

3. Now that the Domino Directory has been upgraded, you need to perform some housekeeping. Compacting the Domino Directory enables the new database format (On-Disk Structure, or ODS) for Release 6. Start compacting by typing the following at the server:

   load compact names.nsf

   Press Enter to begin compacting the directory.

4. In addition to compacting, you need to rebuild the views of the Domino 6 Directory. Execute the following command to update the Domino Directory's view indexes:

   load updall names.nsf

   Press Enter to start rebuilding the views within the Domino Directory.

After you upgrade a server to Domino 6, you can and should replicate the Domino Directory design to the other servers in your organization, including Release 5 and 4.6 servers.

After replicating the new template to other servers, you must rebuild the views in the Domino Directories/Public Address Books on those servers. Rebuilding the views for the template on a server is time-consuming. Do not plan to do it during regular business hours.

33

Clearing the Administration Requests Database

After you upgrade the administration server for the Domino Directory and address all housekeeping issues, you should process all requests in the Administration Requests database. To begin the process of clearing the administration request database, follow these steps:

1. Change to the Domino server console.
2. To process all Admin requests, type the following:
   ```
   tell adminp process all
   ```
3. Press Enter. You might need to issue this command more than once, because some Administration Requests create others.
4. After the Administration Process finishes processing requests, shut it down by typing the following:
   ```
   tell adminp quit
   ```
   Press Enter.

Upgrading the Administration Requests Database Design

The Administration Requests template released with Domino 6 is designed for backward compatibility with both Domino's 4.6 and 5 Administration Processes. The new design of the Administration Requests database should be replicated to other servers in your infrastructure.

1. Choose File, Database, Open.
2. In the Server field, type the name of the upgraded administration server.
3. Select the Administration Requests database (ADMIN4.NSF) and click Open. If this is the first time you have opened the Administration Requests database, you will see the About This Database document. Press Esc to close the document.
4. Choose File, Database, Replace Design.
5. Click Template Server.
6. In the Server field, enter the name of a Domino server and click OK.
7. Select the Administration Requests (Release 6) template (ADMIN4.NTF) and click Replace.
8. When the Domino Administrator displays a warning about replacing the design, click Yes.
9. Close the Administration Requests database.
10. Replicate the new design to the other servers in your organization.

Upgrading a Domino 4.6 Transfer Agent

In Release 4, a Message Transfer Agent (MTA) was used to route Internet mail. In Domino 6, the Domino Router routes Internet mail over SMTP. Mail clients can use Internet mail with MIME or Notes mail in Compound Document format. Domino routes both formats

33

natively and converts automatically between the two formats. Domino uses all Release 4 addressing and routing without change. You can implement new addressing and routing all at once, gradually, or not at all. You also have the opportunity to take advantage of some of the new advanced features of Release 6, such as anti-spam.

You should conduct a pilot project to test your plans for upgrading your mail servers before you begin moving your organization to Domino 6. Use the following steps when upgrading a Release 4 MTA:

1. Back up important files.
2. Disable the SMTP/MIME MTA housekeeping.
3. Shut down the router.
4. Shut down the inbound transport of messages.
5. Verify that SMTP.BOX has no active messages.
6. Clear messages from the outbound MTA queue.
7. Clear messages from the inbound MTA queue.
8. Shut down the MTA.
9. Upgrade MAIL.BOX.
10. Stop loading the MTA and remove the Reporter task from the NOTES.INI.
11. Install the Domino 6 software.
12. Upgrade the Public Address Book to the Domino Directory.
13. Using the Administrator client, set the server configuration for the mail server.
14. Enable the SMTP listener task in the Server document for the Internet mail server.
15. If the upgraded server is the administration server for the domain's Domino Directory, also upgrade its Administration Requests database.

BACKING UP IMPORTANT FILES ON AN MTA SERVER

Back up server files in case you encounter errors during upgrading. If you have problems during upgrading, you can use the backed-up copies to restore your files.

Follow these steps to back up your files:

1. Shut down the server and workstation.
2. Back up the Data Directory on your server.
3. Back up the contents of any directories pointed to by links (.DIR files) from your Data Directory.
4. Back up the NOTES.INI file for the server. This file is located in the system directory by default (for example, C:\WINNT40).
5. Back up any other Notes databases (.NSF), Notes templates (.NTF), and any databases pointed to by directory links (.DIR).

DISABLING SMTP/MIME MTA HOUSEKEEPING

Before upgrading a Release 4 MTA server, disable the MTA housekeeping. If you do not disable housekeeping and you clear the message queues during a time when the `Compact` task is set to run (2:00 a.m. by default), the MTA turns itself off, performs housekeeping tasks, and then turns itself on. This enables inbound and outbound transport, undoing the work of clearing the queues.

You must disable the SMTP/MTA housekeeping task prior to upgrading, as described in the following steps:

1. Make sure you backed up the critical files on the MTA server.
2. Launch the Lotus Notes client from which you administer the MTA server; open the server's Public Address Book and go to the Server/Servers view.
3. Select the Server document for the MTA server and click the Edit Server button on the action Bar.
4. Expand the Internet Message Transfer Agent (SMTP MTA) section.
5. Under Control, click the down arrow next to the Enable Daily Housekeeping field.
6. Select Disable and click OK.
7. Click the Save and Close button on the action Bar and close the Public Address Book.

SHUTTING DOWN THE ROUTER

You need to shut down the router to ensure that no mail is routed to the server's `SMTP.BOX`. After you upgrade your server to Release 6, it will process messages that are already trapped when you copy messages from your old, backed-up `MAIL.BOX` to the newly created `MAIL.BOX`.

Follow these steps to shut down the router:

1. Change to the Domino server console.
2. To shut down the Router, type the following:
   ```
   tell router quit
   ```
3. Press Enter. The server should show the router task shutting down.

SHUTTING DOWN THE INBOUND TRANSPORT

Shutting down the inbound transport prevents the MTA from receiving SMTP messages addressed to recipients in your organization. The inbound transport moves messages into the Inbound Work Queue (`SMTPIBWQ.NSF`). Stopping inbound transport prevents the MTA from accepting inbound SMTP connections.

Follow these steps to shut down the SMTP/MTA inbound transport task:

1. Go to the Domino server console and type the following:
   ```
   tell smtpmta stop inbound transport
   ```

33

2. Press Enter. The server should show the open Inbound Session Controllers and the Inbound Session Controller task (ISESCTL) shutting down.

VERIFYING THAT SMTP.BOX HAS NO ACTIVE MESSAGES

You have now shut down the router and inbound transport tasks. You now need to verify whether the SMTP/MTA has any pending messages by opening the relevant SMTP/MTA databases. Please note that, ideally, you should have planned this upgrade during a slow time—most probably, on a Sunday morning.

Follow these steps to add the relevant SMTP/MTA databases on your workspace:

1. Switch to the Lotus Notes client.
2. Choose File, Database, Open to add the server's SMTP MTA databases:
   - In the Filename field, type **SMTP.BOX** and click Add Icon.
   - In the Filename field, type **SMTPOBWQ.NSF** and click Add Icon.
   - In the Filename field, type **SMTPIBWQ.NSF** and click Add Icon.
3. Click Done.

Verify that there are no messages in the SMTP.BOX marked as Pending Conversion or Pending Transmission; wait for them to be processed and cleaned up by the Delivery Report Task (DRT). To speed the cleaning-up process, type this line at the server console:

```
tell smtpmta housekeeping
```

CLEARING THE OUTBOUND WORK QUEUE

Clearing the Outbound Work Queue routes all remaining outbound SMTP messages to their destinations. Double-click the SMTP Outbound Work Queue (SMTPOBWQ.NSF) icon on your Notes workspace. Wait until all messages in the Outbound Work Queue are successfully processed by the MTA. There should be either no messages in the view or only messages marked Dead.

> **NOTE**
> There might be some delay between message processing and the DRT removing the message from the view, due to the cycle time of the DRT.

CLEARING THE INBOUND WORK QUEUE

Clearing the Inbound Work Queue moves all SMTP messages addressed to recipients in your organization out of the Inbound Work Queue so they can be delivered. The MTA moves messages into either the Outbound Work Queue or MAIL.BOX, depending on who the recipients are. Messages in the Outbound Work Queue are cleared in the next step, and messages in MAIL.BOX are delivered after the server is upgraded and restarted.

Press F9 to verify that all messages except those marked Dead are processed. Processed messages are removed from the view by the DRT. After clearing messages from the MTA, shut it down.

UPGRADING THE SMTP/MTA MAIL.BOX

Upgrading MAIL.BOX gives you the performance advantages of the new ODS and MAIL.BOX template—they are significantly faster than the R4 versions. If you still have messages pending in your MAIL.BOX, you can—after the Domino server starts and creates a new MAIL.BOX— copy these messages from your backup to the new mail.box. Use the server operating system to rename MAIL.BOX to MAIL.UPG.

UPGRADING THE PUBLIC ADDRESS BOOK TO THE DOMINO DIRECTORY

Domino prompts you to upgrade the Public Address Book template after upgrading. Upgrade the design of your Address Book to the Domino Directory template after you upgrade your server to Domino 6. If you have followed the upgrade sequence process, your SMTP server should already be using the new Domino Directory template. If not, upgrade its design when prompted.

SETTING THE SERVER CONFIGURATION FOR SMTP

You must enable native SMTP routing in the Server Configuration document to enable the upgraded mail server to route mail using SMTP. Edit the Server Configuration document that applies to the upgraded server, but be aware that this modification affects any other servers that use this Server Configuration document. If necessary, create a new Server Configuration document for your Internet mail servers.

The Domino Directory for the domain must use the Release 6 template because the settings for native SMTP appear only in the new Domino Directory. Please note that relay host servers require additional configuration. The good news is that the relay host configuration is easier than in previous releases. You can select to route all mail with destinations outside the local Internet domain to a relay host, or not to use a relay host at all. Additionally, there is no need to route mail inside the local Internet domain to a relay host because Domino routes SMTP natively.

The *smart host*, which lists users not in your Domino Directory, has functionality similar to a relay host, although its role is different. For more details on the Domino 6 SMTP relay functionality, refer to your Domino Administration Help database.

Follow these steps to set the server configuration:

1. In the Domino Administrator, click the Configuration tab.
2. Expand the Server Configuration section.
3. Click Configurations. If you have a Server Configuration document that you want to use for this server, select it and click Edit Configuration. If not, click Add Configuration.

4. Enter a server name in the Basics section.

5. Select which Group or Server this configuration should apply to. Do not select Use for All unless you want every server to use SMTP to send messages to the Internet instead of going through an Internet mail server.

6. Click the Router/SMTP tab.

7. Click the down arrow next to SMTP used when sending messages outside of the local Internet domain.

8. Select Enabled and click OK.

9. Click the Save and Close button on the action Bar. You should see the new document in the view.

ENABLING THE SMTP LISTENER TASK

To enable the SMTP listener task, edit the Server document for the upgraded server. Enabling this option instructs Domino to load the SMTP listener task upon startup of the server and enable the organization to begin receiving Internet mail.

Make sure you set the server configuration to enable the server to route outbound SMTP mail. Remember that a Server Configuration document can apply to more than one server, so you might want to create more than one configuration document:

1. In the Domino Administrator, choose the Configuration tab.

2. Expand the Server Configuration section and choose All Server Documents.

3. Double-click the server document for the upgraded Internet mail server.

4. Click Edit Server.

5. On the Basics tab, click the down arrow next to SMTP Listener Task.

6. Select Enabled and click OK.

7. Click the Save and Close button on the action Bar and close the Domino Directory.

NOTE

> Do not remove SMTP routing information from the Server document. Existing routing information enables you to route Internet mail in a mixed-release environment, or in a Release 6 environment that uses Release 4 routing.

UPGRADING THE ADMINISTRATION REQUESTS DATABASE ON AN MTA SERVER

If the upgraded Internet mail server is also the administration server for the domain's Domino Directory, you now need to upgrade the design of its Administration Requests database to the Release 6 template as described earlier in this chapter.

Internet Mail Routing in Mixed Release Environments

Domino 6 routes Internet mail (MIME) over both Notes RPC (Remote Procedure Calls) and SMTP. Release 4 servers do not support native MIME delivery or SMTP routing and use the MTA to accomplish these tasks. When a Domino 6 server transfers a MIME message to an Release 4 server, it converts the message to Notes format and creates an attachment containing the original MIME. This is to preserve full message fidelity. That way, if an Internet mail client accesses the message, Domino sends the MIME from the attachment. The Release 4 server deposits both the CD record and the MIME attachment in a user's mail file for this reason. For these messages in a mixed environment, mail storage requirements and network utilization roughly double for each of these messages.

In a pure Domino 6 environment, the Router delivers MIME messages directly to the recipient's mail file, because both Notes 6 and Internet clients can read MIME. If the message is in Notes format, the Router checks the Person document for each recipient. If the recipient accesses mail only via IMAP or POP3, the router converts the message to MIME and delivers it to the user's mail file.

POPULATING THE INTERNET ADDRESS WHEN UPGRADING A 4.X MTA

When upgrading to Domino 6, you can use the Internet Address tool to fill in the Internet Address field for all Person documents in which the field is blank in a Domino Directory.

Internet Mail Addresses in Domino 6

When looking up an address for Internet mail in the Domino Directory, Domino checks the $Names view for an exclusive match of the address. If it finds the complete Internet address of the recipient in either the Short Name or Internet Address field, Domino delivers the message to the mail file of that person. In a mixed environment, Domino exhaustively searches $Names to ensure that any address generated by the Release 4 MTA for a user in your directory is located properly. When the directory is upgraded to Release 6, you can use the Internet Address field in the Person document for better performance. To do so, you can use the tool that populates this field to standardize Internet addresses in your organization.

33

Follow these steps to populate the Internet Address field in the Person document of the Domino 6 Directory when upgrading from Release 4.6:

1. In Domino Administrator, click the People & Groups tab.

2. Select the server and Domino Directory for which you want to fill in the Internet Address fields.

3. Under Tools, choose People, Set Internet Address tool.

4. In the Internet Address Construction dialog box, choose a format for the Internet addresses. Table 33.2 itemizes the options for Internet address formats.

TABLE 33.2   POSSIBLE INTERNET FORMATS

Domino 6 Internet Address Format	Description
FirstName LastName	Contents of the First Name field and the Last Name field.
FirstName MiddleInitial LastName	Contents of the First Name field, Middle Initial field, and Last Name field.
FirstInitial LastName	The first letter in the user's First Name field and the contents of the Last Name field.
FirstInitial MiddleInitial LastName	The first letter in the user's First Name field, Middle Initial field, and the contents of the Last Name field.
LastName FirstName	Last Name field and the First Name field.
LastName FirstName MiddleInitial	Last Name field, First Name field, and Middle Initial field.
LastName FirstInitial	Last Name field and first letter in the user's First Name field.
LastName FirstInitial MiddleInitial	Last Name field, first letter in the user's First Name field, and Middle Initial field.
FirstName LastInitial	First Name field and the first character of the Last Name field.
Use Custom Format Pattern	A Custom Format Pattern enables you to specify how to construct an Internet address.

5. Choose a separator for the Internet addresses. This character separates the items in the Format field. You can choose between an underscore, a dot or period, an equals sign, a percent sign, or no separator.

6. Enter the Internet domain for the company.

7. Optionally, click More Options and do any of the following:

   - **Use existing Internet domain from shortname field, if available**—Use this option to use the domain name that is provided in the short name field for the specific user.

   - **Separate multi-word names with selected separator character**—Use this option to separate users' multi-word names with the selected separator.

   - **Create addresses only for people in a specific Domino domain**—This option is provided to only create addresses for users under a particular domain. The domain is specified in the next field.

   - **Domain name**—Used in conjunction with the Create Addresses Only for People in a Specific Domino Domain field, this option enables you to define a specific domain.

- **Use alternative format pattern in case of name conflict**—When generating addresses, this field can be used to create an alternative format if a name conflict exists.
- **Format pattern**—Defines the format for the alternative format.

8. The Internet Address Construction dialog box specifies the server and Domino Directory on which it runs. It also gives an example for each address and separator format.

9. Once the tool is started, all Person documents without an Internet Address field in the Domino Directory are populated with an address using the predefined rules. In addition, each entry is verified to be a valid RFC 821 address and checks to ensure that the entry is unique throughout the directory. However, if a duplicate entry is found, the Internet Address field is left blank and an error is logged in the server's log (LOG.NSF). Depending on the directory size, this might take some time to run.

INTERNET MAIL STORAGE FORMAT IN DOMINO 6

You should not need to change how users' Internet messages are stored when upgrading to Domino 6. In a mixed-release environment, where some clients use native MIME messages on Release 6 servers, Domino will not deliver a native MIME message to a 4.6 client, mail file, or server, because native MIME is unreadable in that release. Domino converts the native MIME message to Notes format and a MIME attachment for 4.6 clients, mail files, and servers.

USING DIALUP WITH DOMINO 6

If you use a dialup access to the Internet, you need to take additional steps before upgrading to Domino 6. Medium-to-large companies rarely use this setup, but if you need to do this, you can see the Administration Help database for more information before upgrading.

33

UPGRADING AN MTA SERVER AND NOTES.INI PARAMETERS

When you upgrade an MTA server to a Domino 6 Internet mail server, the NOTES.INI file for the server might contain parameters that are not supported in Release 6. You do not need to change or remove these parameters—they are ignored by the server and do not interfere with its functionality in any way.

Upgrading sets configuration parameters for the settings most commonly used for Internet mail servers. The upgrade program does not convert 4.6 NOTES.INI settings to their Release 6 equivalents. If you have configuration uniquely set through the NOTES.INI file in Release 4, you might need to re-enable this configuration using the Server Configuration and Server documents.

UPGRADING APPLICATION SERVERS TO RELEASE 6

If you are upgrading 4.6 or 5.0 application servers and any mission-critical application resides on that application server, make sure that a Release 6 pilot phase has been completed prior to upgrading.

To integrate applications with the Release 6 environment, you should compact them all so that they get converted to the new file structure. Be warned—it will take time. So make sure to leave enough time for the conversion process. Should you decide to play your safe card and not convert your applications to Release 6 right away, make sure to change their file extensions (.NSF) to NS4 or NS5. This automatically protects their file structure.

When you upgrade an application server and its applications to Domino 6 from 4.6, be sure to do the following:

- Specify a drive with sufficient disk space for view rebuilds by setting the View_Rebuild_Dir variable in the NOTES.INI file to the correct drive for that disk. By default, this variable is set to the temp directory on the system. This drive holds the temporary files used to rebuild views. Clearly, a larger disk enables faster rebuilds and greater optimization. Note that view rebuilds can be as much as five times faster in Release 5 than Release 4. The size of the drive needed for view rebuilds depends on the size of the views you are rebuilding.

- If you're going to use transaction logging, use a separate, single-purpose disk to hold the log files for transactional logging. Minimal disk arm movement enables faster writes to the log. The default location for these files is the LOGDIR directory in the server's Data Directory, but without a separate disk, your server suffers a performance hit as it writes to different spaces on disk. The log requires at least 200MB disk space and can be set as large as 4GB. Using a dedicated mirrored drive is even better than a single disk for recoverability if the log disk fails.

UPGRADING DOMINO CLUSTERS

To upgrade clustered servers, you follow exactly the same processes as when upgrading a Domino 4.6 or 5 server to Release 6. If you are upgrading a clustered server that uses the R4 MTA to route Internet mail, refer to the section "Upgrading a Domino 4.6 Transfer Agent," earlier in this chapter.

If you have mail files on a mixed 4.6/5/6 cluster, be aware of the following issues:

- The new mail template with Release 6 uses features not available in version 4.6 or Release 5, so if your mail file is converted back to 5, you cannot use these features. For instance, if you have mail rules set up in your mail file to filter your mail, these rules will not work on the 4.6 server/mail file. By the same token, when your mail fails over the 4.6 server, and is delivered to that server, the rules do not filter or sort the mail according to the rules.

33

- Servers running Domino 4.6 do not support soft deletions. Your trash folder on a 4.6 server appears to contain all the documents in your mail file. You can ignore this.

- Release 5 and 6 servers can deliver native MIME, but 4.6 servers cannot. Thus, when a Notes client fails over to a 4.6 server from a version 5 or 6 server, MIME messages are converted to Notes format documents and appear differently than when viewed on the server.

- If you attempt to send a MIME message through a 4.6 server, the message is converted to Notes format with an attachment containing the original MIME.

33

CHAPTER 34

INITIAL CONFIGURATION OF SERVERS WITH THE DOMINO DIRECTORIES

In this chapter

THE IMPORTANCE OF THE DOMINO DIRECTORY

The Domino Directory is the heart and soul of a Domino server. The Domino Directory serves two main purposes on a Domino server. First, it acts as a simple directory service by providing a central repository for all user, group, and server documents in a Domino domain. Second, and more importantly, it provides a central location to manage a Domino server and the server's various services, such as replication, mail routing, Internet access, automated tasks, and a multitude of other information and processes.

When you set up your Domino server in Chapter 31, "Initial Planning and Installation," the installation process created the Domino Directory database (NAMES.NSF) in the Data Directory of your Domino server. When the Domino Directory was created, a server document was also created in it, and the basic information you provided about your server was placed into this document.

When the Domino Directory database is initially created, the default access provided to the database is Author. In addition to the default access, there are six other entries placed in the Access Control List (ACL) of the Domino Directory:

- The Administrator's name you specified during installation. This entry is a Person with Manager access and all roles assigned.

- The Server's name (a server should always have access to its own Domino Directory!). This entry is a Server with Manager access and all roles assigned.

- LocalDomainServers—A server group that should contain the names of all other servers in your domain. This entry is a Server group with Manager access and all roles assigned.

- OtherDomainServers—A server group that should contain the names of all servers outside your domain that are allowed to access your server (such as for replication). This entry is a Server group with an access level of Reader and no roles assigned.

- LocalDomainAdmins (Optional)—A server group that should contain the names of all domain administrators.

- An unspecified entry named Anonymous that has no access. This entry ensures that the Domino Directory is not available to unauthenticated users.

There are numerous roles available for assignment in the ACL of the Domino Directory. These roles can be used to delegate administrative duties to other individuals or groups so that the administrative workload does not have to fall on the shoulders of one person. The various roles include the following:

- GroupCreator is a user or group of users who can create new groups.

- GroupModifier is a user or group of users who can modify or delete existing group documents, but cannot create new groups unless defined as a GroupCreator as well.

- NetCreator is a user or group of users who can create all documents except Person, Group, and Server documents.

- **NetModifier** is a user or group of users who can modify all existing documents except Person, Group, and Server documents.

- **PolicyCreator** is a user or group of users who can create new policies.

- **PolicyModifier** is a user or group of users who can modify or delete existing policy documents, but cannot create new policies unless defined as a PolicyCreator as well.

- **PolicyReader** is a user or group of users who can read existing policy documents.

- **ServerCreator** is a user or group of users who can create new Server documents.

- **ServerModifier** is a user or group of users who can modify existing Server documents.

- **UserCreator** is a user or group of users who can create new Person documents. The administration certifier would have to be assigned this role in order to perform his or her job of creating new users.

- **UserModifier** is a user or group of users who can modify existing Person documents.

The Domino Directory is the most critical component of your Domino server; therefore, you should provide administrators only the minimal access level necessary to successfully manage your Domino Directory. By using the roles defined previously, you can successfully delegate administrative tasks to other users without giving them the "keys to the kingdom."

THE SERVER DOCUMENT

There are many forms in the Domino Directory that provide you with an organized, task-oriented way to configure and manage your Domino server. These forms fall into two basic categories: Directory Services and Server Management. Let's start by taking a look at the most commonly used of the Server Management document types, the Server document.

The Server document is the most important document in the Domino Directory, because it defines everything there is to know about your Domino server. The Server document can be quite intimidating to a new administrator; however, let's break this huge document down tab-by-tab and cover the most commonly used fields. Keep in mind that this chapter is not designed to cover every field on every tab of the Server document; instead, it concentrates on the fields that might be of interest to you or might need to be tweaked for optimal server performance.

34

THE BASICS TAB

Figure 34.1 illustrates the Basics tab.

The following fields on the Basics tab can be used to define the baseline information about your server:

Figure 34.1
The Basics tab of the Server document enables you to configure the basic information about your Domino server.

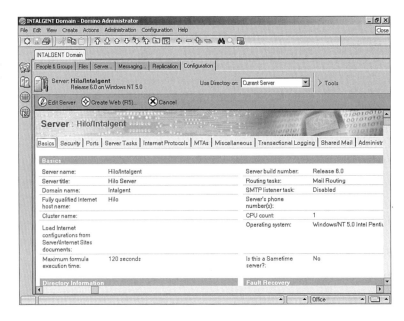

TIP

The field labels in the Server document usually have additional help available as a text pop-up. You can click and hold the field label to access descriptive text about the field.

- **Server Name**—The server name is a hierarchical name of the Domino server that was given during installation. This field is required and should not be modified unless you use the ADMINP process.

- **Server Title**—The server title is an optional descriptive title for the Domino server. This field enables you to enter a description that further identifies your Domino server in the Servers view.

- **Domain Name**—The Domain Name field contains the given domain name entered during the installation and registration process. This field is required. If a domain name is not provided during installation, this field defaults to the same name as the organization certifier. The domain name is very important for mail routing; therefore, changing this name takes careful consideration. If you do decide to change the domain name, please use the ADMINP process.

- **Load Internet Configurations from Server\Internet Sites Documents**—If enabled, this field instructs the server to load its Internet protocol configuration from Internet site documents rather than the Server document.

- **Maximum Formula Execution Time**—This new field sets the number of seconds until a formula will time out. As covered in previous chapters, Domino 6 provides developers the capability to loop within a formula. This field can be used to eliminate infinite loops and ensure that server resources are not compromised.

- **Routing Tasks**—The Routing Tasks keyword field specifies the various routing activities the server will execute. The default value for this field is Mail Routing, indicating normal Notes/Domino mail routing. If you have any other gateways installed (for example, X400 or cc:Mail) on this server, you may also specify them here.

- **SMTP Listener Task**—The Domino 6 server includes a native SMTP router code as a part of the server itself. The SMTP Listener Task keyword field either enables (Enabled) or disables (Disabled) this new feature.

NOTE

In prior releases of Domino, such as Domino 4.6, the SMTP gateway was an add-on server task. In Domino 6, the SMTP router code is a part of the core Domino code, called the SMTP Listener.

- **Server's Phone Number(s)**—If the Domino server supports dial-in access, the Server's Phone Number(s) field contains the phone number(s) that users dial to access the server remotely.

- **Directory Assistance Database Name**—The Directory Assistance database is a specialized database that enables users to browse and select names from multiple domains for efficient email addressing.

- **Fault Recovery**—If enabled, this field determines whether the server will restart when a server crash occurs.

The Basics tab also contains the Server Location Information section, which is covered next.

SERVER LOCATION INFORMATION SECTION

The Server Location Information section of the Basics tab is divided into three groups of information: Phone Dialing, Additional Info, and Servers. Figure 34.2 shows the Server Location Information section of the Basics tab.

You can use the fields of the Phone Dialing area to enter additional calling information for the server, such as the number needed to dial an outside line or any needed long distance prefix.

The Additional Info area defines how your server operates with the time zone of your area, including daylight savings time. Under Domino Release 6, the server might use the operating system's time zone information and daylight savings rules. If your operating system doesn't support it, you should be able to specify the local time zone of the server and whether it should observe daylight savings time. Regardless, because replication is a scheduled task, it is very important that you ensure your server is using the correct time either at the operating system level or defined within the fields.

34

Figure 34.2
The Server Location Information section of the Basics tab enables you to specify location-specific information about the Domino server.

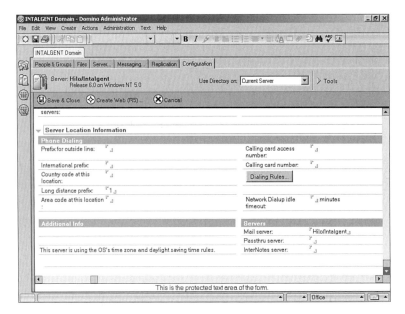

The Servers area enables you to specify other servers that your server should use to perform certain tasks. The Mail Server field contains the name of the server that is handling mail routing tasks for your server. Usually, a server does its own mail routing, so this field contains the name of the current server (such as in Figure 34.2). If your server uses a passthru server to connect to other servers, you can specify the name of that server in the Passthru Server field. Finally, if your organization is using an InterNotes server, you can specify its name in the InterNotes Server field.

THE SECURITY TAB

The Security tab contains important information concerning the security of your Domino server, especially when your Domino server also is an HTTP server. The Security tab provides a great deal of control over those who have access to your server, what information they have access to, how they access it, and what they can change about it. Figure 34.3 shows the Security tab.

The Security tab is divided into six areas: Administrators, Programmability Restrictions, Security Settings, Internet Access, Server Access, and Passthru Use.

ADMINISTRATORS AREA

Another area to delegate responsibility is in the Administrators area. This area contains the following fields:

Figure 34.3
The Security tab provides a great deal of control over the security of your Domino server.

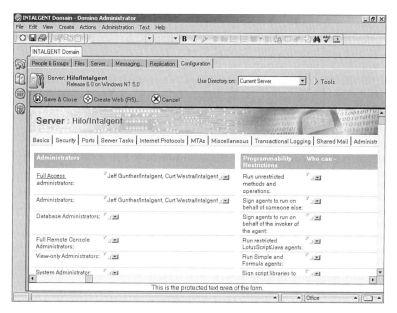

- **Full Access Administrators**—The Full Access Administrators field contains the names of users or groups of users who have Manager access to all databases and templates on the server regardless of a database's Access Control List (ACL). The users listed in this field have the highest level of access to files and databases.

- **Administrators**—The Administrators field contains the names of users or groups of users who are allowed to administer your server. Anyone who is listed here can administer the server remotely using the Remote Server Console. Only the users listed here can create or update directory links, create or update full-text indexes, designate an administration server for databases, or compact databases from the Administration control panel.

- **Database Administrators**—The users listed in the Database Administrators field have the same rights as the users listed in the Administrators field, except they cannot access the Web Administrators database or issue commands via the Remote Server Console.

- **Full Remote Console Administrators**—This field specifies the users who have full remote console access to the server.

- **View-Only Administrators**—This field specifies the users who can only view the console and issue a small set of console commands.

- **System Administrator**—This field specifies the users who can issue operating system commands.

- **Restricted System Administrator**—This field specifies the users who can issue the operating system commands defined within the Restricted System Commands field.

- **Restricted System Commands**—This field specifies the operating system commands that Restricted System Administrators can run.

- **Administer the Server from a Browser**—This field specifies the users who can administrator the server from a browser. This field is used only by pre-Release 6 servers and is ignored within Release 6.

TIP

> Create one or more administrators groups for each administrator type and place the names of these groups into each field type. For example, create a Full Access Administrators group, assign users to the group, and then place the new group in that particular field. Manage administrator access to your Domino server through this group, because this is much more convenient than continually updating one or more Administrator fields for your various server documents.

PROGRAMMABILITY RESTRICTIONS AREA

The Programmability Restrictions area is used to determine who is allowed to run an agent on this server, and what type of agents they are allowed to run. There are two basic levels of agents in Notes/Domino: restricted and unrestricted. LotusScript and Java have access to some potentially dangerous areas on your server, such as file I/O, calling DLLs, and operating system commands. An *unrestricted* agent has access to all these capabilities and can perform any of these functions. A *restricted* agent can still perform database functions, but it cannot perform more dangerous actions, such as file I/O, or change the system time.

The following fields are used to restrict the execution of agents:

- **Run Unrestricted Methods and Operations**—Anyone listed in this field is allowed two agents without restrictions across all programming languages. If this field is blank, no one is provided this level of access, except for the server. The default value of this field is blank.

- **Sign Agents to Run on Behalf of Someone Else**—Users, groups, or servers listed in this field are allowed to sign agents that will be executed by someone else. If this field is blank, no one is provided this level of access, except for the server. The default value of this field is blank.

- **Sign Agents to Run on Behalf of the Invoker of the Agent**—Users, groups, or servers listed in this field are allowed to sign agents that will be executed by the invoker of the agent. This field is only used with Release 6 on the Web. The default value of this field is *.

- **Run Simple and Formula Agents**—Anyone listed in this field is allowed to run simple or formula agents. If this field is blank, all users are allowed to run a simple formula. The default value of this field is blank.

- **Sign Script Libraries to Run on Behalf of Someone Else**—Users, groups, or servers listed in this field are allowed to sign script libraries that will be executed by someone else. If this field is blank, all users are trusted. The default value of this field is blank.

SECURITY SETTINGS AREA

The Security Settings area contains the following fields:

- **Compare Notes Public Keys Against Those Stored in Directory**—When this field is set to Yes, public key comparisons are made during user-to-server and server-to-server authentications. Therefore, the public key of the user or server that is being authenticated must be listed in the Domino Directory. If it is not, access is denied. The default value of this field is No.

- **Allow Anonymous Notes Connections**—When this field is set to Yes, any Domino server or Notes client can connect with your server even if it cannot be authenticated. If you select Yes and there are entries in the Access Server field of the Server Access area, add Anonymous as an entry to this field to allow anonymous access. If the Access server field is blank, you do not need to make this addition. If access is granted anonymously through this setting, it falls upon the server's databases to enforce access control based on the Anonymous entry in the database's Access Control List (ACL). If there is no Anonymous entry, anonymous users have the access level granted to the default entry of the ACL. The default value of this field is No.

CAUTION

> For security reasons, *never* set the Allow Anonymous Notes Connections field to Yes on a server containing sensitive, proprietary, or confidential information. Doing so places your sensitive information in serious jeopardy.

- **Check Passwords on Notes IDs**—Setting this field to Enabled causes the Domino server to verify that the password provided by the Notes client to the Domino server is not expired and is the latest password according to the Person or Server document in the Domino Directory. The default value of this field is Disabled.

INTERNET ACCESS AREA

The Internet Access area contains one field—Internet Authentication. This field contains two settings. Fewer Name Variations with Higher Security requires all users authenticating via a Web browser to use their hierarchical name, common name, alternative name, or alias defined in the user's Person document. This is the default setting. The More Name Variations with Lower Security setting uses the same authentication routine as Domino 4.6x servers—that is, you may use all the previously mentioned name variations and also last name only, first name only, or Soundex value.

34

SERVER ACCESS AREA

The Server Access area contains the following fields:

- **Access Server**—The administrator can restrict access to the server to only the users, servers, and groups listed in this field. If this field is blank, any user or server that can authenticate with the server can access the server (except those listed in the Not Access Server field). If this field does contain values, access is restricted to only those listed, and all others are denied access.

> **TIP**
>
> Maintaining access control for many servers can be very difficult, even when using groups. There are a few shortcuts that can make this a little easier, however. If you want to grant access to everyone listed in this Domino Directory, you can enter an asterisk (*). If you use an asterisk followed by a view name from the Domino Directory, everyone listed in that view is granted access. An asterisk followed by a slash and a certifier name grants access to everyone with that certifier. For example, if you want to allow everyone with the `/Falcons/NFL` certifier to access your server, you enter `*/Falcons/NFL` in the Access Server field.

- **Not Access Server**—This field performs the opposite operation of the Access Server field; anyone listed in this field is denied access to the server.

> **TIP**
>
> The most common entry in the Not Access Server field is a single group (something like Deny Access) that contains the name of everyone whom you want to deny access, such as individuals who have been terminated from your organization. When you create this group in the Domino Directory, make sure you specify the group type as a Deny Access Group so the group can be used only for its intended purpose.
>
> An alternative to using a Deny Access Group is to use Notes ID Lockout in the Person document of the terminated person. Although more tedious, this prevents users from looking at a centralized list of everyone who has been terminated from your organization.

- **Create Databases and Templates**—This field lists all users, groups, and servers that are allowed to create databases/templates on or copy databases/templates to your server. If this field is blank, any certified user who has access to the server can create databases on the server. If this field contains one or more values, only those named can create databases on the server. The default value of this field is blank.

- **Create New Replicas**—This field lists all users, groups, and servers that are allowed to create replicas on your server. Unlike the Create Databases and Templates field, if this field is blank, *no one* is allowed to create new replicas on your server. The default value of this field is blank.

> **TIP**
>
> You can prevent the uncontrolled proliferation of databases on your server by using the Create Databases and Templates and Create New Replicas fields to restrict database creation to only specified individuals.

- **Create Master Templates**—This field lists all users, groups, and servers that are allowed to create master templates. If this field is blank, *no one* is allowed to create master templates on your server. The default value of this field is blank.

- **Allowed to Use Monitors**—This field lists all users, groups, and servers that are allowed to create monitors.

- **Not Allowed to Use Monitors**—This field performs the opposite of the Allowed to Use Monitors field; anyone listed in this field is specifically forbidden from creating monitors. The default value of this field is blank.

- **Trusted Servers**—This field specifies the servers that are allowed to access the current server.

PASSTHRU USE AREA

The passthru server is a powerful feature that was introduced in Lotus Notes Release 4. This feature enables a user to call into one passthru server, and that server provides connections to other servers in the network by passing information back and forth between the user and the target server. A passthru server also enables users who are running one protocol—TCP/IP, for example—to connect to a server running a different protocol—SPX, for example—by managing the connection and passing of information. Please refer to the Lotus documentation for more information.

THE PORTS TAB

The next tab on the Server document, the Ports tab, is important to your server because it defines the ports and addresses your server uses to communicate, as well as the Notes Named Networks (NNNs) to which your server belongs.

NOTE

> A *Notes Named Network (NNN)* is nothing more than a group of servers that share the same network protocol. A server can be a member of multiple NNNs if it is running more than one protocol. For instance, a server that runs TCP/IP on one network card and SPX on another network card can be a member of two NNNs. The Database Open dialog box lists only servers that are in the same NNN. Servers that are members of the same NNN route mail without the use of Connection documents. NNNs are described in greater detail in the Domino Administrator's Guide.

34

NOTES NETWORK PORTS SUBTAB

The Ports tab is broken into three subtabs: Notes Network Ports, Internet Ports, and Proxies. Let's begin by taking a look at the Notes Network Ports subtab, which is shown in Figure 34.4.

Figure 34.4

The Notes Network Ports subtab displays the Notes Network and communication port information about your server.

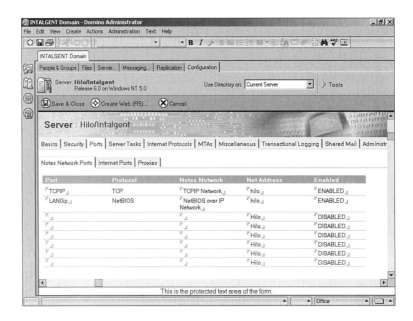

As you can see in Figure 34.4, the Notes Network Ports subtab is laid out in a tabular format, with each row representing a single NNN. The fields in the Notes Network Ports subtab are defined as follows:

- **Port**—This field is used to define a valid communications port for the server to use on a given NNN. For instance, if you are using the TCP/IP protocol and have that protocol assigned to a port named TCP, you enter TCPIP in the Port field.

- **Protocol**—This field defines which protocol the named port is using.

- **Notes Network**—This field contains the name you give to each NNN.

- **Net Address**—This field contains the network address for the Domino server on the given network protocol. For TCP/IP networks, you can use the DNS entry name for the server or the IP address of the server on that network.

- **Enabled**—This field indicates whether the port is enabled for your server.

INTERNET PORTS SUBTAB

The Internet Ports subtab is a rather busy subtab because it has an SSL settings area as well as five subtabs of its own: Web, Directory, Mail, DIIOP, and Remote Debug Manager. Figure 34.5 shows the Internet Ports subtab with the Web subtab showing.

Figure 34.5
The Internet Ports subtab enables you to configure the various Web access ports you use to interact with an intranet or Internet.

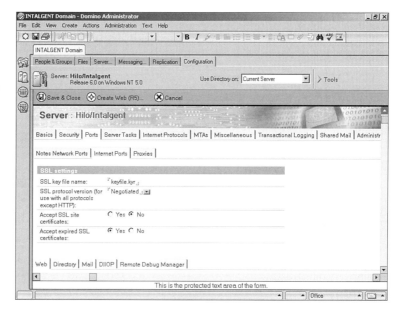

SSL SETTINGS AREA

The SSL settings area enables you to define the criteria for your Secure Sockets Layer (SSL) protocol to use with secure, encrypted HTTP transactions (HTTPS). If you are not using SSL to provide HTTPS transactions on your Domino server, you can skip the SSL settings subsection. If you are using SSL for your Domino server, configure the following fields in the SSL settings area:

- The SSL Key File Name field is used to store the name of the file containing your site's SSL keys; the default value is KEYFILE.KYR.

- The SSL Protocol Version field enables you to specify which of the various SSL protocols are used for communication (for example, V2.0, V3.0). The default value is Negotiated, which means that the Domino server and the client being communicated with will attempt to determine which protocol they share.

- The Accept SSL Site Certificates field tells Domino to automatically acquire an SSL site certificate for use by the Domino Web Navigator server when it connects to an Internet host site. Although it makes it easier for Notes clients to access SSL secured sites, enabling this option can compromise security because Domino will not verify the remote server's identity. SSL certificates contain an expiration date.

- The Accept Expired SSL Certificates field tells Domino to accept an SSL certificate even though it has expired.

WEB, DIRECTORY, MAIL, DIIOP, AND REMOTE DEBUG MANAGER SUBTABS The Web, Directory, Mail, DIIOP, and Remote Debug Manager subtabs all contain information that defines each of their various ports and protocols. Here is a brief explanation of each protocol:

- **Web**—Defines the port information for the HTTP and HTTPS protocols.

- **Directory**—Defines the port information for the Lightweight Directory Access Protocol (LDAP), which is used to communicate with LDAP directories such as Bigfoot and Four11. This protocol also enables Web clients to access any Domino LDAP directories, otherwise known as the Lightweight Enterprise Directory.

- **Mail**—Contains protocol configuration for multiple mail protocols: IMAP, POP, SMTP Inbound, and SMTP Outbound.

- **DIIOP**—Defines port information for the Domino Internet InterORB Protocol (DIIOP). DIIOP enables Java applets and applications to interact directly with the server to access Domino databases.

- **Remote Debug Manager**—Contains information about remote debugging. Remote debugging, a new feature for Domino 6, enables you to debug LotusScript agents running on a server.

PROXIES SUBTAB

If you use a proxy server on your network, you can use the settings in the Proxies subtab to tell your server how to communicate with and use the proxy server for various Internet services and protocols. The Proxies subtab is illustrated in Figure 34.6.

Figure 34.6
The Proxies subtab enables you to define how your Domino server communicates with the proxy server.

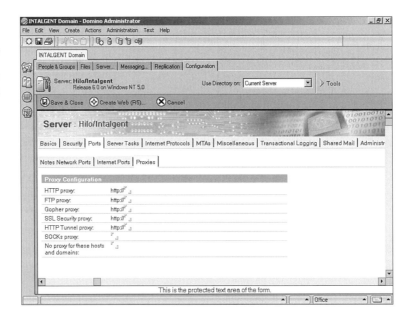

34

NOTE

> A *proxy server* is a computer running proxy software sitting between your internal network and the Internet. A proxy server accepts user requests for Internet services and retrieves the requested information on behalf of the user. Proxy servers have three main benefits—they block access to the internal network, they mask the IP address of the user by submitting requests using their own IP address, and they can cache requests to make Internet access quicker.

Configuring the Proxies subtab is relatively simple. If you are using a proxy server for any of the protocols listed, simply enter the DNS name or IP address and port of the proxy server responsible for the protocol.

THE SERVER TASKS TAB

The Server Tasks tab contains configuration information for various administrative tasks that the server handles for you automatically. The Server Tasks tab is divided into seven subtabs: Administration Process, Agent Manager, Domain Catalog, Directory Cataloger, Internet Cluster Manager, Web Retriever, and Remote Debug Manager. Let's begin by examining the first subtab, Administration Process, which is shown in Figure 34.7.

Figure 34.7
The Administration Process subtab determines when and how the ADMINP process handles tasks.

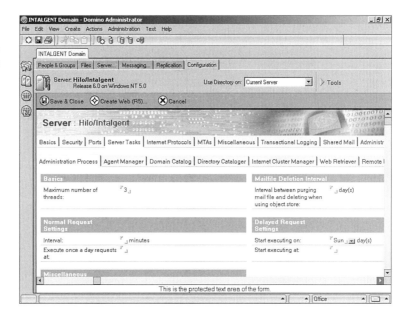

ADMINISTRATION PROCESS SUBTAB

The Administration Process subtab is used by the Administration Process (ADMINP) to determine when to carry out requests. Each setting in this subtab controls threshold information when specific types of requests are executed. For most environments, it's not necessary to tweak these settings.

AGENT MANAGER SUBTAB

The Agent Manager subtab enables you to configure a number of options that determine when scheduled agents can run, how many can run, and for how long. Figure 34.8 demonstrates the Agent Manager subtab.

Figure 34.8
The Agent Manager subtab is used to configure when and how scheduled agents run on your server.

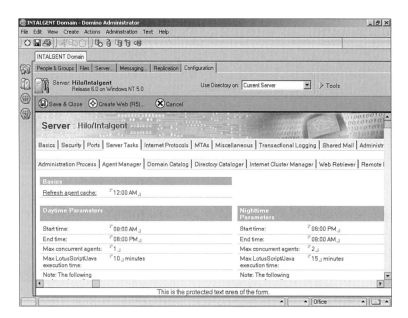

The Basics subsection contains only one field: Refresh Agent Cache. The Domino server contains a list of agents that can run during the current day. For example, agents set to run If Documents Have Been Pasted and On Schedule Hourly can run each day and appear in the Agent Manager list each day; On Schedule Monthly agents show up in this list only one day each month. The time value entered in this field tells the Domino server when to update the list of agents in the cache.

The next subsections in the Agent Manager section, Daytime Parameters and Nighttime Parameters, enable you to control how much of the Domino server's resources are used to run agents. By default, the daytime parameters are set so that agents consume fewer resources than they do at night.

DOMAIN CATALOG SUBTAB

As illustrated in Figure 34.9, the Domain Catalog subtab contains only two fields: Domain Catalog and Domain Catalog Scope. The Domain Catalog field has two choices: Enabled and Disabled. This field enables or disables the Domain Search feature for your Domino domain. The default for this field is Disabled.

Figure 34.9
The Domain Catalog subtab is used to enable the Domain Search feature.

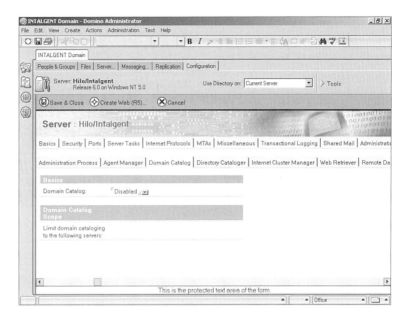

Essentially, the Domain Catalog uses the catalog database (catalog.nsf) to control the specific databases that are included within the Domino Search. The Domain Catalog can be a useful tool for both users and administrators to locate databases and database replicas.

In addition to enabling or disabling the service, the Domain Catalog subtab enables you to control the scope of the Domain Catalog. If the Domain Catalog is enabled, you can specify the Limit Domain Cataloging to the Following Servers field. This field allows you to control the scope of what servers are included within the Domain Search. For more information on creating database catalogs, review the topic "Setting Up a Server's Database Catalog" within the Domino Administrator 6 Help.

DIRECTORY CATALOGER SUBTAB

The Directory Catalog is a compressed version of one or more Domino Directories. The Directory Catalog contains entries for users, groups, and mail-in databases only. Directory Catalogs use the Lightweight Directory Access Protocol (LDAP) to achieve the information compression. The Directory Catalog feature provides these benefits:

- Entries are much smaller for the mobile type of directory (100 bytes versus 10KB in a normal Domino Directory).

- When a Directory Catalog is maintained locally, name lookups are dramatically faster, and a lookup to a server is not needed.

- You can still use encryption when addressing from a Directory Catalog; the encryption is resolved at the time the document is sent to the server for delivery.

34

The Directory Cataloger subtab is used to schedule the automated updating of the Directory Catalogs from the source Domino Directories on which they are based. Figure 34.10 shows the Directory Cataloger subtab.

Figure 34.10
The Directory Cataloger subtab feature is used to schedule the updating of the Directory Catalogs on your server.

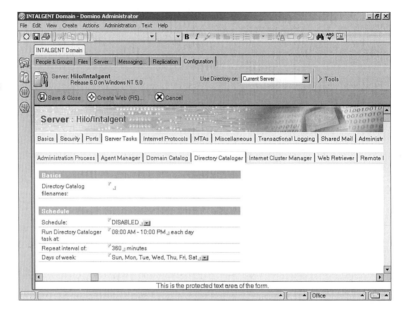

The Directory Catalog Filenames field contains the name(s) of the directories that should be processed by the Directory Cataloger. The actual source directories that the task aggregates are configured with the Directory Catalog database itself within a configuration document. The Schedule area contains the configuration information about what days and times the Directories should be updated, whether updating is enabled, and so forth.

INTERNET CLUSTER MANAGER SUBTAB

The Internet Cluster Manager (ICM) is a feature that extends the capabilities of enterprise clustering to Domino-based Web (HTTP) servers. Now you can provide failover and load balancing to your Web browser clients.

The ICM sits between the Web (HTTP) clients and a Domino server cluster. The Web clients send HTTP requests to the ICM. Because the ICM knows all the vital information about the servers in the cluster, it can make the decision as to which cluster server is best suited to handle the request, and it passes the request to the appropriate server.

The ICM is a server task that must be started separately. The ICM does not have to run on a server in the cluster, but it must run on a server in the same domain as the cluster. The ICM is configured in the Internet Cluster Manager subtab of the Server Tasks tab in the Server document. Figure 34.11 shows the Internet Cluster Manager subtab.

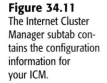

Figure 34.11
The Internet Cluster
Manager subtab con-
tains the configuration
information for
your ICM.

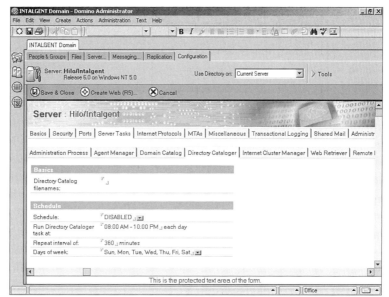

For more information about configuring the Internet Cluster Manager and each one of the
fields, refer to the topic "Configuring the ICM" within the Domino Administrator 6 Help.

WEB RETRIEVER SUBTAB

The Web Retriever subtab applies only to installations that use the Web Retriever to
retrieve and store HTTP, FTP, and Gopher information in a Notes database for Notes
users. The Web Retriever can be very handy if you don't have the IP protocol on your network or don't want to give direct Internet access to each user. Figure 34.12 displays the Web
Retriever Administration section of the Server document.

The Web Retriever subtab can also be used to restrict access to specific Internet sites
through the fields located in the Internet Site Access Control area. You can specify specific
site URLs or IP addresses that you want to enable your users to access in the Allow Access
to These Internet Sites field; the default value of an asterisk (*) allows your users to access
any site on the Internet. The Deny Access to These Internet Sites field enables you to
explicitly list sites you do not want your users accessing (such as http://www.dilbert.com).
The default value is blank, which indicates that there are no sites you want to deny to your
users.

For more information about the Web Navigator database, refer to the topic titled "The
Web Navigator Database" within the Domino Administrator 6 Help.

Figure 34.12
The Web Retriever subtab enables the server to retrieve Web pages for the users.

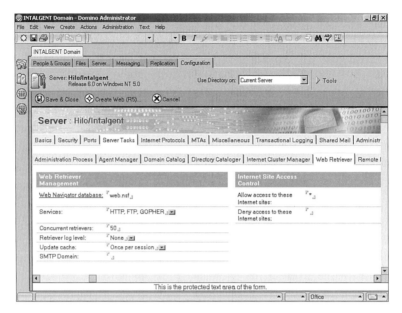

REMOTE DEBUG MANAGER SUBTAB

The Remote Debug Manager subtab applies to the configuration of the remote debugging capabilities with Domino 6. This tab contains three fields relating to this new feature. The first field enables you to enable or disable remote debugging of LotusScript agents. Additionally, you can control when debugging capabilities are turned off to developers by entering a time limit in the Turnoff Server Debug After field. To have the Remote Debugger run forever, simply set this field to -1. The last field, Agent Wait at Starttime, can be used to set the number of seconds the agent waits before starting. By default, remote debugging is not enabled.

For more information about LotusScript and debugging, refer to Chapter 22, "LotusScript Subroutines, Functions, and Event Handlers."

INTERNET PROTOCOLS TAB

The Internet Protocol tab contains the basic information your server needs to use various Internet protocols and services. The Internet Protocols tab builds upon that information by defining the environment your server uses when using these Internet protocols. The Internet Protocols subtab is divided into four subtabs: HTTP, Domino Web Engine, IIOP, and LDAP.

HTTP SUBTAB

If you are planning to use your Domino server to handle HTTP requests either over the Internet or a corporate intranet, the HTTP subtab is very important. As you can see in Figure 34.13, the HTTP Server subtab is quite large and is divided into several subsections.

Most of these areas are self-explanatory. If you need additional assistance, use the field label help or refer to the Domino Administration documentation for more information.

Figure 34.13
The HTTP subtab is a key to configuring your Web server for optimal performance.

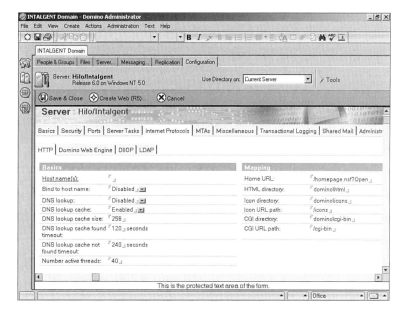

THE BASICS AREA   Because the first subsection, Basics, is the most important, let's start there. It contains the following fields:

- **Hostname(s)**—Use this field to enter the hostname(s) you want returned to a client's browser. The hostnames can be either DNS names or IP addresses. If the field is blank, the name of the current machine is returned.

- **Bind to Hostname**—Select Enabled to allow Domino to only listen to incoming requests on the IP addresses assigned to a specific hostname. If disabled, Domino listens on all IP addresses assigned to the physical server.

- **DNS Lookup**—When enabled, DNS lookups are done for logging purposes. Disabling this field increases server performance.

NOTE

> The fields within the R5 Basics area only apply to a Release 5 server.

MAPPING AREA   The Mapping area is used to define the directories that are used by the Domino server to access various items, such as icon files, CGI programs, HTML pages, and so forth. You can also designate the Notes database you want to use as the default home URL for your Domino server. All paths in the Mapping section are relative to the Domino

34

data directory (for example, `D:\Domino\Data`). If an entry begins with a /, it is located in the data directory. The full path for a Home URL `/homepage.nsf?Open` for this example is `D:\Domino\Data\homepage.nsf`. URLs normally use forward slashes, whereas directory specifications typically use backslashes.

THE DOMINO WEB ENGINE SUBTAB

Like the HTTP subtab, the Domino Web Engine subtab contains quite a few areas. Most of these areas are self-explanatory and the default settings are fine, so you probably will not need to modify the settings in this tab. If you need more information concerning the use of this tab, refer to the Domino Administration documentation for more information. Figure 34.14 demonstrates the Domino Web Engine subtab.

Use the Domino Web Engine tab to do the following:

- Set up session authentication.
- Specify GIF or JPEG conversion.
- Specify the number of lines to display in a view.
- Limit the number of documents displayed when searching.
- Find links with the Redirect URL command.
- Restrict the amount of data that users can send to a Domino database.
- Store Web user preferences in cookies.
- Set up language preferences.
- Specify an international character set when retrieving pages.

Figure 34.14
The Domino Web Engine subtab provides granular control of your Domino caches.

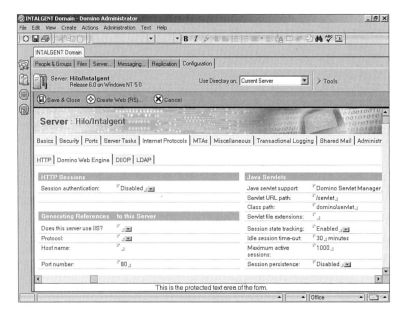

THE DIIOP AND LDAP SUBTABS

The DIIOP subtab contains a few fields dealing with the Domino Internet InterORB Protocol (IIOP). The Idle Session Timeout field can be set to the number of minutes until the Domino session object will time out.

The LDAP subtab gives instructions on where to go to configure LDAP settings.

THE MTAS TAB

The MTAs tab contains three subtabs: R4.x SMTP MTA (R4.x Internet Message Transfer Agent), X.400 MTA (Message Transfer Agent), and cc:Mail MTA. These subtabs contain data only if you installed the MTA in question when you installed the Domino server. If you need to configure the Domino 6 SMTP feature, refer to the Server/Domain Configuration and Server/Server Configuration forms.

THE MISCELLANEOUS TAB

The Miscellaneous tab contains one area, Contact Information. This area enables you to enter descriptive information about your server, such as the location of the server, department that uses the server, and so forth.

THE TRANSACTIONAL LOGGING TAB

Transaction-based logging and recovery, commonly referred to as transactional logging, was introduced in Domino 5 as a mechanism to ensure recovery of data. This feature enables all updates to a database to be captured and logged, which enables a database to be recovered quickly and fully in the event of a system crash. The Transactional Logging tab is used to define the parameters used for transactional logging, and is shown in Figure 34.15.

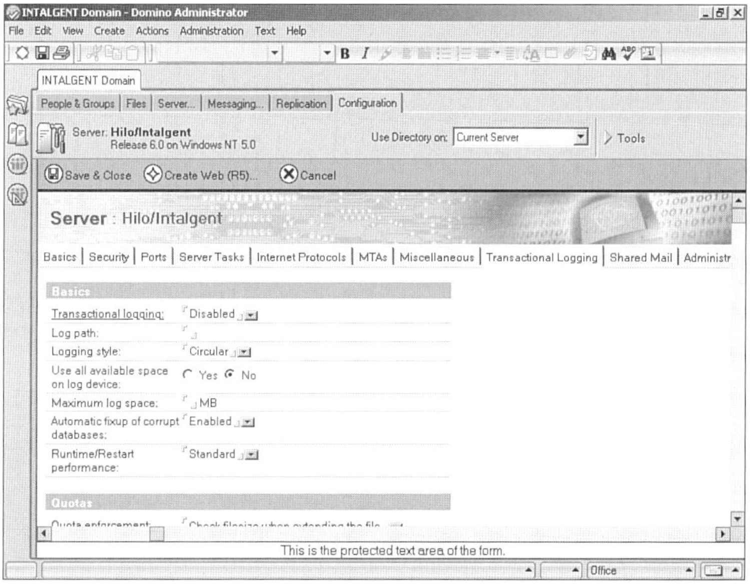

Figure 34.15
The Transactional Logging subtab configures transaction logging in Domino.

The Transactional Logging field enables or disables transactional logging for all databases on your server. Remember, transactional logging works only on Release 5 or 6 databases or R4.x databases that have been converted to the new On Disk Structure (ODS).

The Logging Style field enables you to indicate whether you want the transaction log to begin overwriting itself when it gets full, or whether you want to archive old transaction logs. Archiving old transaction logs gives you more of the transaction history for recovery, and Circular takes up less disk space.

The Log Path field tells the server where it can find or create the transactional log file. It is highly recommended that you place the transactional log file on its own disk, for a number of reasons. Two of the most notable reasons are because it will read/write to the file often, so a dedicated disk will be faster, and because transactional logs can get quite large—you don't want to run out of disk space.

The Use All Available space on Log Device field tells the Domino server that it can use all free space on the drive indicated in the Log Path field. Because this should be a dedicated device, this is a recommended option.

The Maximum Log Space field should contain the maximum amount of space you want to provide on the drive indicated in the log path for logging. Once again, if you use a dedicated drive, this field should contain the disk size, but no more than 4GB—that is the maximum size of a log file. In any case, the amount of space allowed should be over 200MB, and even this amount will be used up fairly quickly.

The Automatic Fixup of Corrupt Databases field enables a task that, when a corrupt database is detected, attempts to correct the errors using the information stored in the log file. This is a very useful feature for mission-critical systems, because it keeps the system integrity intact (as much as possible).

The Runtime/Restart Performance field enables you to control where you take the transactional logging performance "hit." When you set this field to Favor Runtime Performance, more of the transactional log is kept loaded in memory, enabling faster access times. When you set this field to Favor Restart Recovery Time, the server keeps less of the transaction log in memory and makes updates to the file on-disk more often. This usually means that a more current "snapshot" of the database's recent transactions are stored in the file, enabling the transaction log to recover faster because it has to reconstruct fewer transactions. The default value of Standard is a compromise and checkpoints occur regularly. The default value of Standard is recommended.

SHARED MAIL TAB

The Shared Mail tab enables you to manage shared mail for your Domino server. If you need additional assistance on how to configure and set up shared mail, refer to the topic "Setting Up Shared Mail Databases" within the Domino Administration 6 documentation for more information.

ADMINISTRATION TAB

Well, you finally made it to the last tab of the Server document, the Administration tab. The Owner field is an Authors field used to identify the person to whom the server belongs—and more importantly, the person who can edit this Server document. The Administrators field is also an Authors field that can be used for additional users and groups who can modify the Server document. The last two fields—Certified Public Key and Change Request—are used by the Administration Process (ADMINP) when changing a server's name. During this process, ADMINP adds the hierarchical certificate to the Certified Public Key field and a change request to the Change Request field of the Server document.

Now it is time to move on and take a look at some of the other documents available to the administrator in the Domino Directory. The next document you'll learn about is the Connection document.

THE CONNECTION DOCUMENT

Another critical part of configuring your Domino server using the Domino Directory is configuring the Connection document. Connection documents, as demonstrated in Figure 34.16, are required to define and establish mail-routing and replication schedules. Connection documents also enable you to define how a server should talk to another server.

Figure 34.16
The Connection document defines mail-routing and replication schedules.

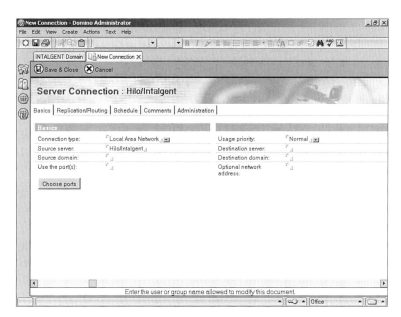

There are currently 11 types of connections defined in the Connection Type field:

- Local Area Network
- Notes Direct Dialup

- Passthru Server
- Network Dialup
- X.25
- SMTP
- X.400
- cc:Mail
- SNA
- Hunt Group
- Sametime

NOTE

> The Sametime connection type is new in Release 6 and is a specialized connection type for configuring a Domino server with Lotus Sametime.

Fortunately, creating Connection documents, regardless of type, is fairly straightforward. Because most people use only the first four types, those are the only ones examined in detail in this chapter. For details on the other seven types, see the Domino Administrator's Guide or the Admin Help database.

NOTE

> Connection documents are not necessary for mail routing between Domino servers on the same Notes Named Networks (NNNs).

THE LOCAL AREA NETWORK CONNECTION

Let's start by examining the most common connection type: the local area network (LAN) connection. This type of connection is used to establish connectivity between servers on the same local area network.

Much like Server documents, Connection documents are divided into logical tabs that present different options, depending on the parameters needed for a particular type of connection. Because of the similarity of the information required by the different types of connections, these sections cover only the differences, starting with the most common type of connection, LAN. The LAN connection type has three distinct tabs (there is also one tab called Comments, but it has only one field for comments).

BASICS TAB

The Basics tab, as illustrated in Figure 34.16, defines the servers to be connected and how they will connect. Notice that this section remains fairly constant for all 11 types of connections. The fields in the Basics section for the LAN Connection document are as follows:

- **Connection Type**—This keyword list enables you to set the type of connection you want to establish. Choose Local Area Network.

- **Source Server**—This field specifies the name of the server that will be establishing the connection. Always use the fully qualified name of the server here.

- **Source Domain**—This field specifies the domain from which the connection will be established.

- **Use the Port(s)**—This field enables you to define which ports should be used when attempting to establish this connection. You can click the Choose Ports button to choose from a list of valid ports on your server.

- **Usage Priority**—This field is a keyword list with two choices: Normal and Low. When a Connection document is set to Low priority, it is used only after all attempts to connect over the LAN have been exhausted.

- **Destination Server**—This field specifies the name of the server to which you are attempting to connect. As with the Source Server field, it's best to enter a fully qualified name here.

- **Destination Domain**—This field specifies the name of the domain in which the destination server resides.

- **Optional Network Address**—You can use this field to enter the destination server's address as it appears on the network. For servers running TCP/IP, you can also enter the IP address here.

REPLICATION/ROUTING TAB

The Replication/Routing tab of the Connection document defines what should happen when the source server connects to the destination server, as shown in Figure 34.17.

Figure 34.17
The Replication/Routing tab enables you to configure replication and routing settings between connections.

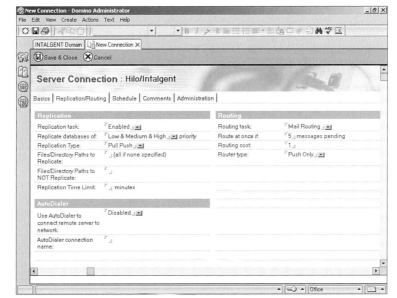

The fields shown in Figure 34.17 are as follows:

- **Replication Task**—This field enables or disables the replication task.

- **Replicate Databases of x Priority**—This keyword field offers three choices: High, Medium and High, and Low and Medium and High. The Replication Priority of a database is set in the Replication Settings dialog box, under the Other area. These choices can be used to determine which databases are replicated when a connection is established. For example, you might elect to replicate only high-priority databases over a costly connection, but you want to replicate all databases over an inexpensive connection.

- **Replication Type**—This is another keyword field with four choices: Pull-Pull, Pull-Push, Pull-Only, and Push-Only. These choices enable you to control which ends of the connection replicate and which server(s) do the work. A Pull-Pull replication means that each server "pulls" changes from the other server and thereby shares the workload. A Pull-Push replication dictates that the server establishing the connection does all the work (first it pulls changes from the destination server, and then it pushes changes to the destination server). A Push-Only replication is one way (it only pushes changes from the source server to the destination server). A Pull-Only replication is the opposite of the Push-Only option (it only pulls changes from the destination server). The default is Pull-Push, which means that the source server does all the work. You can use this option to help balance the workload among servers.

NOTE

> If you use Pull-Pull and Pull-Push replication, you need only one Connection document for databases to be synchronized between the source and the destination server. If you use Push-Only or Pull-Only, each end needs a Connection document. Mail routing, on the other hand, requires a Connection document on both ends because it is a one-way process.

- **Files/Directories to Replicate**—You can use this field to control which files or directories are replicated during the connection. Enter the list of filenames and directories (separated by commas) you want to replicate.

- **Files/Directories to Not Replicate**—You can use this field to control which files or directories are not replicated during the connection. Enter the list of filenames and directories (separated by commas) you want to replicate.

- **Replication Time Limit**—This field determines how long a replication session can take place. Setting a time limit can be useful in ensuring that one server doesn't consume your server's replication resources.

- **Routing Task**—This keyword field tells the Domino server what to do when a connection is established between the servers using this Connection document. There are five choices: Mail Routing, X.400 Mail Routing, SMTP Mail Routing, cc:Mail Routing, and None. Of the five, you are most likely to use Mail Routing (for native Notes Mail).

The choices you make here affect which fields are displayed in the rest of this section because some fields are not relevant to some of these choices. Try choosing different options to see the effect.

- **Route at Once If**—If you have Mail Routing enabled, you can use this field to set a threshold for message queuing. When the threshold value is reached, a connection is established using this Connection document; the outbound mail will automatically be routed, regardless of the schedule (remember that mail routes automatically in the same NNN). The default value of this field is five messages.

- **Routing Cost**—This field can be used to associate a "cost" with this connection. This cost is taken into account when trying to connect to the destination server. For example, you might want to give a Connection document that uses an Internet connection a cost of 1, a WAN connection a cost of 5, and a dialup modem calling long distance a cost of 10 so that the dialup connection is always the last resort.

- **Router Type**—This field defines which types of requests are made to the other server when routing mail. The choices are Push-Wait (the server waits for a call from the other server before sending mail), Push-Only, Pull-Push, and Pull-Only.

- **Use AutoDialer to Connect Remote Server to Network**—This field defines whether the server is connected to the remote server via the AutoDialer.

- **AutoDialer Connection Name**—This field defines the name of the connection.

SCHEDULE TAB

The Schedule tab of the Connection document is used to determine when the source server will attempt to connect to the destination server, as well as how often it will do so (see Figure 34.18).

Figure 34.18
The Schedule tab enables you modify how two types of servers connect.

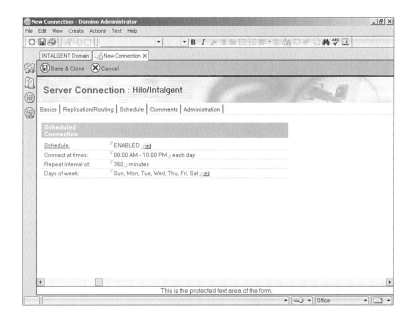

The fields for the schedule tab include the following:

- **Schedule**—This keyword field has two choices: Enabled and Disabled. When a Connection document is enabled, the source server calls the destination server based on the schedule defined in the next few fields. If the connection is disabled, the source server does not use this Connection document to call the destination server. Note that if the connection is over a LAN, there will not actually be a phone call. The word *call* is used to mean that the source server should initiate a connection.

- **Connect at Times**—This field expects a time, or a range of times, at which the connections should be established. For example, entering a time of `12:30 PM` tells the source server to connect the destination server at 12:30 p.m. each day. If a range of times is entered (for example, `6:00 AM - 7:00 AM`), this tells the source server to call the destination server within the time range specified based on the Repeat Interval.

- **Repeat Interval**—This field enables you to define the number of minutes the source server should wait before calling the destination server. For example, if you enter a value of `0`, the source server calls only once. If you enter a value of `120`, within the Connect at Times range, every 120 minutes the source server attempts to call the destination server.

  To help explain this concept, consider the following scenario: If the Connect at Times field is set to `7:00 AM - 7:00 PM` and the Repeat Interval field is set to `60` minutes, the source server attempts to call the destination server at 7:00 a.m. If replication takes 10 minutes, the server then attempts to call again 60 minutes after replication has finished, so if replication takes 10 minutes, the next call should begin at 8:10 a.m., and so on.

- **Days of the Week**—This is another keyword field that enables you to choose the days of the week on which the connection schedule should be observed. For example, to have this connection made three out of seven days of the week starting on Sunday, enter `Sun, Tue, Thu`.

THE NOTES DIRECT DIALUP CONNECTION

Now that you've seen what a Connection document for a LAN connection looks like, let's take a look at a Connection document for a dialup modem. You'll notice some immediate changes to the Basics section. Notice that the Choose Ports button is missing from the Notes Direct Dialup version of the Connection document. You have to manually enter the port to which your modem(s) are connected. Additionally, you'll notice that the following fields have been added to the Basics section:

- **Always Use Area Code**—Set this keyword field to Yes if you want the Domino server to always dial the area code you have supplied when using this connection.

- **Destination Country Code**—Use this field to enter the country code of the country in which the destination server resides. For example, if you are connecting to a server in Germany, enter `49`.

- **Destination Area Code**—This field is self-explanatory. Enter the area code for the location in which the destination server resides.

- **Destination Phone Number**—Another self-explanatory field. Enter the phone number the Domino server must dial to reach the destination server.

- **Login Script File Name**—If you have to run a script file to log in after the modems have connected, enter the name of the script file here.

- **Login Script Arguments**—You can use these fields to pass up to four arguments to your login script.

THE PASSTHRU SERVER CONNECTION

The next type of Connection document you are likely to encounter is the Passthru Server Connection document. Notice right off the bat that the only difference between the Passthru Server and Local Area Network Connection documents is that there is no Ports field in the Passthru Server document. Instead, it has a field labeled Use Passthru Server or Hunt Group, which is used to name a Domino server that has been configured for passthru use.

THE NETWORK DIALUP CONNECTION

The final type of Connection document covered in this chapter is the Network Dialup Connection type. If you are using dialup networking, you can have your Domino server make connections to other Domino servers using this server.

Here is the difference between the Notes Direct Dialup and the Network dialup connection types. Both of these connections might use a modem, so it is important to understand the distinction. When you use the Notes Direct Dialup connection, Notes actually takes charge of the modem and controls it on both sides of the communication link. When using this type of connection, other programs on both the client and server cannot use the modems, even if they are not currently active within the Notes program.

The Network Dialup connection, however, uses operating system facilities to manage the modem. When using this connection type, the operating system controls the modem and Notes shares it with other programs. Thus, if Notes is not currently using the modem, another program can use it for another purpose.

A Network Dialup Connection document is much like a LAN Connection document except that you must complete the configuration information specific to your dialup networking service. This information is completed in the Network Dialup tab. The Choose a Service Type button displays a dialog box that enables you to choose Microsoft Dialup Networking, Macintosh PPP, or AppleTalk Remote Access. The Configure Service/Edit Configuration button displays a dialog box that enables you to configure the options for the service you have chosen.

For instance, if you choose Microsoft Dialup Networking, the dialog box contains the following fields: Dialup Networking Name, Login Name, Password, Phone Number, Area

34

Code, Country Code, Dial-back Phone Number, and Domain. When you enter this information, the data is displayed in the computed fields shown under Configuration area. If you chose AppleTalk or Macintosh PPP, you see slightly different options.

DOMAIN DOCUMENTS

In Notes/Domino terminology, a *domain* is a group of users and servers that all share the same Domino Directory. Within a domain, mail routing is easy because all users share the same Domino Directory.

Often, the need arises to allow communication between domains, either within the same company or between companies. This is where Domain documents come into play. There are seven types of Domain documents: Foreign Domain, Non-Adjacent Domain, Adjacent Domain, Foreign X400 Domain, Foreign SMTP Domain, Foreign cc:Mail Domain, and Global Domain. Let's briefly examine each here.

You'll find all the Domain documents under the Messaging section within the Configuration tab of Domino Administrator. Figure 34.19 demonstrates the Domain document. As you've seen with the other documents in the Domino Directory, the Domain document is divided into tabs; choosing the Domain type determines the rest of the choices in the document. Let's start with the Foreign Domain type.

Figure 34.19
The Domain document enables you to define interdomain communication.

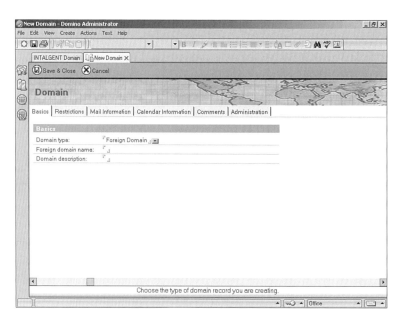

THE FOREIGN DOMAIN TYPE

In addition to Domain type, the Basics tab contains the Foreign Domain Name field, where you enter the name, and the Domain Description field, where you provide a description of the foreign domain.

RESTRICTIONS TAB

The Restrictions tab of the Domain document can be used to prevent mail from routing through your domain to other domains. The Restrictions section contains two fields: The Allow Mail Only from Domains field contains the names of foreign domains that can route mail through your domain, and the Deny Mail from Domains field enables you to enter domain names from which mail *will not* be permitted.

MAIL INFORMATION TAB

The Mail Information tab contains two fields for mail routing to a foreign domain: Enter the name of the mail server in the Gateway Server Name field and enter the name of the mail file in the Gateway Mail File Name field.

CALENDAR INFORMATION TAB

If you want to perform calendaring and scheduling with a foreign system, such as IBM's Office Vision, just enter the name of the foreign calendar server in the Calendar Server Name field and use the Calendar System field to choose the type of foreign calendar system: OfficeVision or Organizer 2.x.

THE NON-ADJACENT DOMAIN TYPE

Non-Adjacent Domain documents enable communication with another Notes domain through an intermediary domain. For example, you want to send mail to Robin Oliver in the Bobbin domain, but you don't have a direct connection to that domain; however, you do have a connection to the Buddy domain, which communicates with the Bobbin domain. A Non-Adjacent Domain document specifies the route to Bobbin through Buddy.

There are five tabs in a Non-Adjacent Domain type document: the ever-present Basics tab, the Restrictions tab, the Calendar Information tab, the Comments tab, and the Administration tab. Because the Restrictions tab is identical to the Restrictions tab of the Foreign Domain type document, this section looks only at the Basics tab and the Calendar Information tab. The Administration tab specifies the owners and the administrators of the document.

BASICS TAB

In addition to the Domain Type and Domain Description fields, the Basics section of the Non-Adjacent Domain document contains the following fields: The Mail Sent to Domain field is used to enter the name of the destination domain and the Route Through Domain field is used to define the domain through which the mail will pass. The domain entered in the Route Through Domain field must have a physical connection to both the source and the destination domains. Using the preceding example, you would enter **Buddy** in this field.

34

CALENDAR INFORMATION TAB

The Calendar Information tab contains one field, the Route Requests Through Calendar Server field. This field indicates the intermediary server that will route calendar information from your server to the destination calendar server.

THE ADJACENT DOMAIN TYPE

The Adjacent Domain Type document enables you to limit the mail that can route between two adjacent domains. An *adjacent domain* is a domain to which your server has either a physical network connection or dialup connection.

The Adjacent Domain document contains four tabs: Basics, Restrictions, Calendar Information, Comments, and Administration. The Restrictions section is used to determine which mail can route through your domain. The Basics section varies slightly from the other domain document types; in addition to the Domain Type and Domain Description fields, the Basics section of the Adjacent Domain document contains the Adjacent Domain Name field, which is used to name the adjacent domain.

The Calendar tab contains one field—Calendar Server Name. This field is used to enable adjacent domains to exchange calendaring information. Simply enter the name of the calendar server in the Calendar Server Name field and you're ready to go.

THE GLOBAL DOMAIN DOCUMENT

The Global Domain document has a special role on your Domino server: It provides a set of rules that determine how your SMTP task converts Notes addresses into Internet addresses. Additionally, it lists the Notes domains that are considered members of the global domain. The Global Domain document does not play any part in the routing of mail; it only determines how Notes Mail addresses are converted to Internet addresses.

Refer to the Domino Administrator's Guide for more information on the Global Domain Type document.

THE FOREIGN SMTP, X.400, AND CC:MAIL DOMAIN TYPES

The Foreign SMTP, X.400, and cc:Mail Domain type documents work hand-in-hand with Global Domain type documents and are essential for routing SMTP, X.400, and cc:Mail mail.

These Foreign Domain document types are very similar to the other types of domain documents. The Basics tab contains only one field, the Domain Type field. The Routing tab contains two areas: Messages Addressed To and Should Be Routed To. These two areas work hand-in-hand and enable you to control outbound mail routing to different hosts.

34

OTHER SERVER CONFIGURATION DOCUMENTS

In addition to the Domino Directory documents discussed in detail in this chapter, you will want to learn about a number of other documents in the Domino Directory to make your Notes/Domino environment perform optimally and make administering a Domino server even easier:

- **Internet Sites documents**—New in Domino 6, the Internet Sites document enables administrators to configure the various Internet protocols supported by Domino. These include HTTP, SMTP, POP3, IMAP, and DIIOP. For each protocol, a separate document is set up and configured.

- **External Domain Network Information documents**—The External Domain Network Information document enables users to more easily connect to servers outside their domain without using their own Connection documents.

- **Holiday documents**—The Holiday document enables you to define all holidays that your organization recognizes. These holidays are then available for users when group calendaring and can be imported into their local calendars.

- **Resource documents**—The Resource document enables you to define a room or other resource that is available for reserving and scheduling through group calendaring and scheduling.

- **Configuration documents**—These documents can be used to simplify working with the Notes INI file by allowing you to choose from a list of the available INI file parameters and then setting specific values. It also tracks the changes made to the INI file. Remember that documents in the Domino Directory are replicated, whereas settings in a particular computer's NOTES.INI file are unique to that computer.

- **Certifier and Cross-Certifier documents**—These documents identify each certificate's ancestry. Certifier documents are crucial to the security of a Notes/Domino installation because they verify the identity of both servers and users.

- **Program documents**—These documents can be used to automatically start server tasks, batch programs, or API programs. For example, if you wrote an API program to transfer data from an Access database to a Notes database and wanted it to run each night, you could create a Program document that would run the program at the specified interval.

- **Profile documents**—These documents enable the administrator to define a common set of policy settings that can then be applied to multiple users. Profile documents can make adding and administrating users significantly less complicated and time-consuming.

- **Mail-In Database documents**—These documents enable the administrator to configure a database to receive mail messages. For example, you might have a sales rep on the road compose an expense-report form in his or her mailbox, and then route the document using mail to a common database that serves as a repository for all expense reports.

34

CHAPTER 35

DOMINO SECURITY OVERVIEW

In this chapter

INTRODUCING THE DOMINO SECURITY MODEL

Notes and Domino security can be enforced at several levels. Each level refines the previous level, moving from physical security down to a single field in a single document.

Think of security as if you were building a pyramid. The base level of security entails protecting the physical and logical access to the Domino server and the Notes network. As you move up the pyramid, you control access to the Domino server. When a user has access to the server, you can limit access to individual Domino applications. Within the applications, you can control access to specific views, forms, actions, and other design elements. Finally, using Author and Reader fields, you can control access to individual documents and even to individual sections within the documents. Figure 35.1 illustrates the path that you must take, from the bottom of the pyramid to the top, to get to your data.

Figure 35.1
Notes and Domino security has several layers to protect your data.

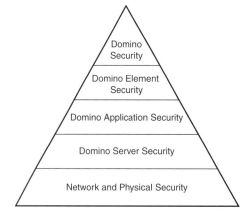

NETWORK PHYSICAL AND LOGICAL SECURITY

As a part of network security, the physical security of the Domino server is included as well as the security features that are built into the logic of the Domino software. The Domino server should be located in an area where casual users cannot physically access it. As mentioned previously, you can locally encrypt databases and enforce access control, and you can protect ID files with multiple passwords. However, physical-access security is still vitally important. If someone has physical access to your server, that person is a big step closer to being able to breach security at the operating-system level.

You might also want to consider a couple of other, less obvious logical access-security issues. Domino is an ideal application server for Internet as well as intranet applications. For example, by creating a Domino server specifically for handling all external communications, you can communicate with internal servers using a communication protocol other than TCP/IP. Make sure you know what you are doing before you open your databases to the Internet. Workstations on the network must also be secure because data can be accessed through the workstations.

TIP

> For the security of your Notes and Domino environment, have in place a plan to ensure each of the following:
>
> - Keep a backup of all your vital files.
> - Do not rely solely on replication to another Domino server as a form of backup.
> - Keep your Domino servers in a locked area that is accessible only to authorized personnel.
> - Keep your Notes certifier IDs safe in a secure location so that unauthorized people cannot gain access to your network by creating their own IDs.
> - Do not leave Notes workstations logged in and running if they are in a publicly accessible area.

DOMINO SERVER SECURITY

When a Domino server is first set up, ID files are generated. These ID files are an integral part of the security structure. Those ID files are a primary focus of this chapter because they are the cornerstone of security in a Notes environment. The ID files used with Notes and the Domino server include the following:

- The server ID uniquely identifies a server within the organization. Each server has its own ID that contains certificates from the organization certifier ID or OU certifier ID used to create the server.

- The certifier ID is created when the first server is set up and provides a unique identity to every server and every user in a Notes organization. The certifier ID is used to create certificates that establish the authenticity of IDs for users and servers within the Notes organization.

- The Organizational Unit (OU) certifier ID provides a way for your organization to expand its use of Notes. An OU certifier ID can be used to create new servers and users in your organization, delegating some administrative work to other users. OU certifier IDs are hierarchical, so you will not find them in organizations that use a flat naming scheme.

- The user ID uniquely identifies every Notes user in the organization. Like the server ID, it holds hierarchical certificates. The user ID is used to authenticate with Domino servers and resources, and to identify the user in various security roles, such as database ACLs, server access lists, and Reader and Author fields.

- The administrator ID is a user ID that provides administrative access to the Domino server. This is a regular user ID, but it is the first one created to ensure that there is a registered user who can administer the Domino server to set up the rest of the Notes environment.

35

In the Domino directory, there is a document for every user and server that is allowed to access a particular Domino server via a Notes client. The IDs created for these users and servers are used in authentication and Domino server security.

DOMINO APPLICATION SECURITY

Assuming that you have gained access to Domino applications (see Chapter 17, "Access Control Lists [ACLs] and Database Security"), you need to be aware of security at the application level. The databases in which applications reside (NSF files) can be secured in the following ways:

- **Local encryption**—You can select Simple, Medium, or Strong encryption from the Database properties dialog box or when you first create a new application. To access an encrypted application, you must have the user ID that was used to encrypt the application in the first place. Because your user ID should always be password-protected, if your user ID was used to encrypt the application, you need your user ID and password to access the encrypted application. This is an excellent way to protect an application on a laptop computer. Just be aware that if you lose your Notes user ID and do not have a backup, you will no longer be able to access the encrypted application.

- **Access Control List security**—Every Domino application has an Access Control List (ACL) that defines which privileges users and servers have in the application. Although the ACL is usually thought of in terms of applications on Domino servers, Notes provides a means to enforce ACL security on all replicas of an application database, whether the replica is on a Domino server or on a local workstation. The database manager (the person with Manager access in the ACL) can enforce local ACL security by placing a check mark next to the option Enforce a Consistent Access Control List Across All Replicas of This Database, on the Advanced page of the Access Control List dialog box.

DESIGN AND DOCUMENT SECURITY

The remaining security features are concerned with the design of the Domino application and generally are refinements of access security. Not all of these features are true security measures, but each contributes to security in its own way. Among other things, you can lock the design of an entire database. You can define who is allowed to use certain forms and under what conditions. You can restrict the use of certain views. You can define who has access to create or modify data on a particular document. You can restrict access to a section within a document. And although it is not a true security measure, you can hide a field under certain conditions, including hiding fields from certain users. Design and document security features represent the top of the security pyramid depicted earlier in Figure 35.1. The use of these features is described in detail in chapters dealing with database design.

THE ROLE OF NOTES IDS IN SECURITY

Despite the layer upon layer of security features, the security that really counts within Notes is the interaction of the various Notes ID files with each other, and the interaction of the server and user ID files with ACLs in individual applications. When you have the correct ID and the correct password, you probably will not even be aware that you are going through so many layers of security. The remainder of this chapter looks at the role of Notes user IDs in greater detail.

KEEPING YOUR PASSWORD SECURE

If someone gets your user ID and can guess your password, that person is you, as far as the Domino environment is concerned. Your valid Notes ID is your key to unlock the data that is stored securely inside the Domino server. If you leave your ID lying around on a disk or on the hard drive of an unattended workstation, anyone could steal it. But guessing or stealing a password is not easy because Notes has a built-in defense system.

When you type the password for your user ID, the Notes client displays a random number of Xs to make it difficult for the casual observer to determine how many characters are in the password. A series of key chains is displayed as you type your password. The color and shape of each key chain changes as you type. These color and shape changes make it more difficult to spoof the Notes client—potential thieves trick you with a fake password dialog box that captures your password for the thief. Every password generates a different pattern of key chains. To mimic the password dialog box, the techno-thief would have to develop a different program for every user in the organization.

In addition to the antispoofing key chain, Notes has a timeout period after an unsuccessful entry. The timeout period gets longer in random intervals, hopefully frustrating the would-be password-guesser. A third password-security feature is the capability of requiring multiple passwords for an ID.

SERVER AND USER IDS

The server and user IDs are binary files that hold the following information:

- The name of the user or server
- A Notes license number
- A password (optional, depending on how the administrator has defined the minimum password length on registration)
- A private key, which is used to encrypt and decrypt data
- Encryption keys generated by designers to encrypt database data
- Certificates that identify the server or user's place within the organizational hierarchy

Think of a certificate as being like the official seal that is stamped on your driver's license or passport. Because you recognize the authority that issued the driver's license, you accept the document as being valid. Without that authority, the document cannot be trusted. Likewise, when two IDs each have at least one certificate that they both recognize as valid, the two IDs trust each other enough to begin the process of communicating with one another. There is no peer-to-peer communication between Notes users, so the previous sentence assumes that at least one of the IDs is a server ID.

ORGANIZATION AND OU CERTIFIER IDS

The certificates associated with your user ID are created by a Notes certifier ID. The certifier ID is the identity of your Notes organization. Any user or server created using the certifier ID (or any of its Organizational Unit certifiers) is automatically trusted by all other servers and users in the organization. It might be a good idea to require multiple passwords to access the organizational certifier IDs and OU certifier IDs, thereby ensuring that multiple administrative personnel are aware of when the Notes certifier ID is being used. You also want to be sure to store the ID in a safe place.

The certifier ID is used to register new users and new servers. In most organizations, an OU ID is used to register users and servers, but in a smaller organization, the organization certifier ID could well be used to create users and servers. The certifier ID is also used to issue certificates that enable external organizations to communicate with you, usually at an OU level. If two server IDs or a user ID and a server ID have a certificate issued by the same certifier ID, they can potentially talk to each other.

When an OU certifier ID is used to issue a certificate, the certificate is hierarchical. A hierarchical certificate carries the name of both the Organizational Unit and the organization.

For example, the Sales OU certifier ID could be used to create a certificate for a new user, John Doe. John Doe's username identifies the full hierarchy of certificates issued to him, in a format such as John Doe/Sales/Marketing/West/Acme, where Acme is the organizational certifier ID and West, Marketing, and Sales are all OU certifier IDs. In this instance, Acme created the OU certifier ID West/Acme, which, in turn, created the OU certifier ID Marketing/West/Acme, which then created the OU certifier ID Sales/Marketing/West/Acme. A user can have up to four OU certificates in a hierarchical name.

THE ROLE OF NOTES IDS IN PROTECTING SERVER ACCESS

When a user (or another server) attempts to initiate a session with a server, the Domino server validates the ID file and then goes through a process known as *authentication*.

Validation is a process of establishing trust. The server examines the certificates on the ID of the server or user trying to establish a session. If the ID contains a certificate that has the same hierarchical ancestor ID as the server, the ID can be trusted. If there is no common ancestral ID, the Domino server looks at cross-certificates in the Domino directory and trusts the ID if there is a valid cross-certificate.

35

Once an ID is validated, authentication takes place. For example, say that John Smith wants to access Server1/Acme. When he contacts the server, the server initiates an authentication dialogue with the John Smith ID, as follows:

1. **Server1/Acme:** To make sure you aren't an impostor, let me give you a test. I'm thinking of a number between 1 and 10. I'll send you the number, and I challenge you to encrypt it with your private key.

2. **John Smith/Acme:** That's easy. I'll use my private key to encrypt the number. Here it is back.

3. **Server1/Acme:** Using your public key, I can see that you sent me the same number, encrypted with my public key. Let's talk.

4. **John Smith/Acme:** Not so fast. I want to make sure you aren't an impostor. Now I'll send you a number.

The dialogue is reversed until both IDs are satisfied with each other's identity, and communication is then fully established. The authentication remains in place as long as the session lasts, even when the user closes one database and opens another. But if the user logs off or changes to another ID, the authentication is no longer valid. The server databases and server functions can no longer be accessed.

LDAP AUTHENTICATION ON THE WEB

Notes enables you to use LDAP directories in addition to Domino directories. This enables you to authenticate Web clients without having to set them all up in your Domino directory with HTTP usernames and passwords.

LDAP authentication is implemented using a Directory Assistance application, created using a Directory Assistance template (DA50.NTF). Create an LDAP document in the Directory Assistance application. In this document, you need to set up naming contexts and select Yes in the Trusted Credentials field (see Figure 35.2).

The Domino server searches the Domino directory for a username and password. If a name is not located, it looks for trusted domains in the LDAP directories after looking in any secondary Domino directories.

When a hierarchical name is returned, Domino checks it to make sure that the organization and Organizational Units match an enabled, trusted rule in the LDAP document in Directory Assistance, or a name in a secondary Domino directory.

Figure 35.2
In the LDAP document in Directory Assistance, set up rules and indicate that you trust credentials from this directory.

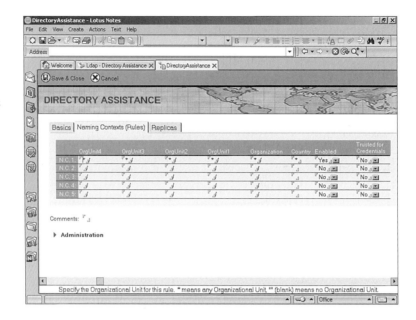

CROSS-CERTIFICATION

Every Notes organization has its own certifier ID, and an ID must have a certificate from the organization certifier before it can authenticate with any of the organization's servers. Within the organization, this does not present any problems; the organization certificate is part of every server ID and every user ID in the organization. But what about another organization that wants to communicate with your servers?

For example, the Acme Corporation is teaming up with a subcontractor, XYZ Corporation, on a project. The company needs to discuss project issues and share progress reports, email, and so on. Neither company wants to do it over the Internet, so they decide to set up cross-certification between their Notes organizations. To communicate directly with Acme using Lotus Notes, XYZ needs a certificate that is recognized as valid by Acme, and Acme needs a certificate that is recognized as valid by XYZ.

When you attempt to establish communication with a server in another organization, the first thing the server looks at are the certificates on your ID. If no certificates are recognized as valid, the Domino server looks for a cross-certificate document. If no certificates or cross-certificates are recognized by the server, you cannot authenticate and, therefore, cannot access the server.

Cross-certification involves exchanging certificates between two organizations. You can cross-certify at the organizational level, at the Organizational Unit level, or at the user level. No matter which level you cross-certify at, both sides must exchange certificates.

For example, suppose that Jane Doe in the sales department at Acme has reason to access a server in the XYZ Corporation:

1. She sends a *safe copy* of her user ID to the Notes administrator of the XYZ organization, requesting cross-certification.

   The safe ID used in the cross-certification process is not a complete ID. It contains just enough information to be able to collect certificates, but it is useless for any other purpose.

2. The XYZ administrator certifies (usually using an OU certifier ID to create a certificate for) the safe ID.

   This creates a cross-certificate document in the XYZ Domino directory, where the cross-certificate is stored.

3. Meanwhile, the server to be accessed within XYZ must be certified on Jane Doe's side, so XYZ sends a safe copy of the server ID to Acme.

4. The organizational certifier or an OU certifier from Acme certifies the safe copy of the XYZ organizational certifier ID and stores it in a cross-certificate document in the Acme Domino directory.

   Now each organization has a cross-certificate in its own Domino directory.

5. Jane Doe copies the cross-certificate from XYZ into her personal address book.

When Jane Doe communicates with the XYZ server, the XYZ server looks in the XYZ Domino directory and finds Jane Doe's cross-certificate; therefore, it lets her continue with the authentication process. Conversely, when XYZ communicates with Jane Doe, Notes looks in her personal address book to see whether a cross-certificate is available.

In summary, the following cross-certificates are created during cross-certification so that a Notes user from XYZ can access a server in another organization (Acme):

- A safe copy of a user ID from XYZ is cross-certified by an Acme certifier ID and placed in the Acme Domino directory as a cross-certificate.

- A safe copy of an Acme certifier ID is cross-certified by a certifier ID from XYZ and placed in the XYZ Domino directory.

- The user who needs to access an Acme server places a copy of the Acme cross-certificate (from the XYZ directory) into her personal address book. Every user or server that wants to cross-certify must have a local copy of the cross-certificate.

When a Domino server checks to see whether another user or server ID is valid, it looks at the ID to see whether it contains a certificate that can be trusted. Trust is established only if the other ID holds at least one certificate issued by a trusted certifier. Therefore, in the scenario described previously, Acme trusts Jane Doe because the Acme Domino directory contains a safe copy of Jane Doe's ID, which has been cross-certified by an Acme certifier ID.

35

CAUTION

> If you cross-certify at the organization or Organization Unit level, you should use server-access restrictions to ensure that the other organization has access only to those servers that you mean to let them access. If you want to access servers in another organization but do not want to allow that organization access, make sure that you have restricted access to all servers in your organization. Note that if you cross-certify a specific user in another organization, all users in the other organization at that user's organization level or below can potentially authenticate with your server.

How to Cross-Certify

How you cross-certify depends on the circumstances. There are four ways to cross-certify, all of them having the same goals—certifying a safe ID and generating a cross-certificate from that ID. The only difference in the techniques lies in the mechanics. The four ways to cross-certify are described in the following four sections.

Using Notes Mail

You can use Notes mail to cross-certify. This is probably the most common method. To cross-certify, you do the following:

1. Display the User Security dialog box by choosing File, Security, User Security. Enter the password for your ID file.

2. Click the Your Identity, Your Certificates option. Click the Other Actions button located on the right side of the dialog box, and select Respond to Cross-Certificate Request, as shown in Figure 35.3.

Figure 35.3
Request a cross-certificate from the Your Certificates page in the User Security dialog box.

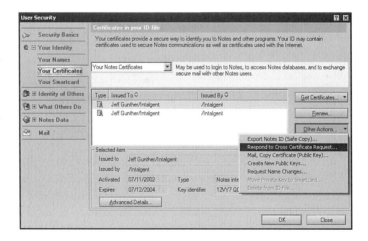

3. Select the ID to be cross-certified and enter the password. The ID must be a hierarchical ID.

4. The request is in the form of a standard mail memo. Address the request to the administrator in charge of certification in the other organization, and Click Send. The Mail Cross-Certificate Request dialog box is shown in Figure 35.4.

Figure 35.4
Email your request for a cross-certificate to the administrator of the system with which you want to cross-certify.

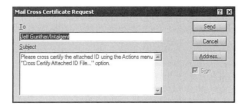

5. The administrator in the other organization opens the request in his mail file and, from the Actions menu, selects Cross-certify Attached ID File. Then the administrator selects the certifier ID to use and enters the password for the ID. The Issue Cross-Certificate dialog box is then displayed, as shown in Figure 35.5.

Figure 35.5
After the certifier selects the certifier ID and enters a password, he can cross-certify the ID.

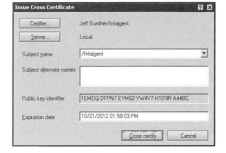

6. In the Subject Name field of the dialog box, the administrator enters the name of the certifier, user, or server being cross-certified.

7. Click Cross Certify to complete the process on this end. The same process must be repeated in the other direction before the complete cross-certification is effective.

USING SNAIL MAIL OR "SNEAKER NET"

The first time two organizations exchange cross-certificates, they might not be able to communicate via computers until after cross-certificates are exchanged. Therefore, they might need to use disks to exchange safe IDs created by the system administrator.

A safe server or certifier ID can be created as follows:

1. Start the Domino Administration client, close the splash screen, click the Configuration tab, and select Certification, ID Properties under the Tools menu.

2. Select the certifier ID or a safe ID in the Choose ID File to Examine dialog box and click Open. Enter a password, if necessary.

35

3. Select Your Certificates under the Your Identity option. Click the Other Actions Options button and select Export Notes ID (see Figure 35.6). Name the safe ID something like ACMESAFE.ID, and save it on a disk. On a Unix server, transfer the file to a disk or through a utility such as SSH or FTP.

Figure 35.6
Create a safe copy of your ID file from the Configuration tab within the Domino Administration client.

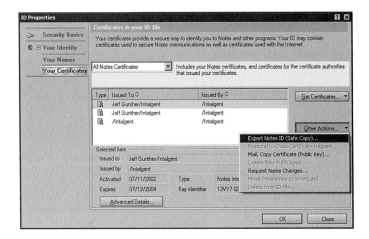

4. Send the safe copy of the ID to the administrator responsible for certification in the other organization. The administrator will repeat steps 4–6 in the previous section on cross-certifying via email.

NOTE

> It is also possible, but not very practical, to cross-certify via telephone. This involves correctly transcribing a long public key string. For details, refer to Notes online help or the Domino help manuals.

CROSS-CERTIFYING ON DEMAND

If you have a hierarchical ID and try to access a hierarchical server in another organization for which you are not cross-certified, Notes prompts you to see whether you want to cross-certify. You have the option of creating a cross-certificate for the root certifier of your organization, of declining to cross-certify, or of creating a cross-certificate for a certifier ID. You can then put the cross-certificate in the Domino directory by selecting a registration server. You must have at least Editor access in the Domino directory before you can do this. You could also store the cross-certificate in your local address book—in this case, you don't need Editor access to the Domino directory. The other organization must also have demanded or generated a cross-certificate for authentication to occur.

How to Exchange Flat Certificates

Whenever possible, you should use hierarchical certification and communicate with other organizations through cross-certification. But sometimes an organization with flat certification must communicate with a hierarchically certified or flat certified organization. In this case, the two organizations must exchange safe server IDs (or a server and a user ID), each of which is certified by the other organization. Then the certified IDs must be returned and merged into the regular server or user ID. To do this, the hierarchical organization must create a flat certifier to use in the process.

Because a certificate gives everyone from the other organization an open door into your Notes network, you should turn off Trust on certificates issued by certifiers outside your organization. With Trust turned off, the other organization can communicate only with the particular server that has the certificate in its ID. This protects the rest of your organization from unauthorized intrusion by untrusted users.

SECURING THE SERVER CONSOLE WITH A PASSWORD

Notes administrators need to be aware of another aspect to server security. To prevent unauthorized individuals from using the server-console commands, the administrator can protect the console with a password. Password-protecting the console increases security, especially when someone gains physical access to the server.

To secure the console, enter the following command:

SET SECURE *password*

Here, *password* is the password you want to use to secure the console. The console password does not have to be the same as the administrative password—in fact, it should *not* be the same.

The following commands cannot be used while the console is secured with a password:

```
LOAD

TELL

EXIT

QUIT

SET CONFIGURATION
```

To use these commands, you must remove console security by again entering this command:

SET SECURE *password*

One small loophole here can be sealed only by denying physical access to the Domino server. The password used to secure the console is stored as an environment variable in the NOTES.INI file. You can edit the file and delete the line that contains the console password. This is great for the forgetful system administrator, but it does provide a back door

35

for anyone attempting to gain direct-disk access to your server. In short, protect your server by securing the console, but do not turn around and hand out the key by allowing people physical access to your Domino server.

PEOPLE RESPONSIBLE FOR NOTES SECURITY

A number of individuals are involved in Notes security at various levels, from the person who initially sets up the system to the individual who decides to encrypt an email message. Some of the key security functions are described here, with a description of the person who performs that function.

As already mentioned, at the most explicit level of security is the *individual user* who can, for example, decide to encrypt a particular mail message. The individual user plays another, more pivotal role, however—protecting his Notes user ID. The individual user should be taught to lock his ID out of the system whenever he gets up from the desk. If the user leaves a workstation unattended without locking the ID by pressing F5 to log off Notes or by choosing File, Security, Lock Display, anyone can access the server without having to locate a valid Notes ID and enter a password. It is as if the user had installed new locks on his house and then left the house without locking the door. Locking the user ID is the first line of defense when it comes to keeping intruders out of the Notes network.

The second line of defense is the *application developer*, the person who designs Domino applications. Applications are teeming with potential security features that the designer can choose to use or not. Some of these features include using form and view formulas, enabling read and compose access, enabling fields for encryption, hiding information under certain circumstances (more for convenience than for security), creating sections that can be edited only by particular users, determining how users will enter data into fields, and so on. Not all of these are absolute security measures, but they do determine how easy it is to use the database and how much can be done by the casual user.

The other person involved in security at the application level is the *application manager*. Every application can have a different manager (the user with Manager access in the ACL). The manager is the one who determines which level of access other users will have. If users have too high a level of access, an application is subject to misuse and could eventually become unwieldy from too many replication or save conflicts because too many people are capable of editing the same documents.

At the system level, only one type of individual is involved with Notes security: the *system administrator*. But this role can be broken down into two major divisions: the system administrator and the administration certifier, the person responsible for the certifier ID. Beyond that, specific administrative roles can be delegated. Roles can involve creating and editing a variety of documents in the Domino directory.

The system administrator is the person (or persons) with Manager access to the Domino directory. By default, the system administrator is the person you name as administrator during setup of the first server in the organization. Other users can later be assigned this role by the original administrator. Common sense says that you should have more than one person capable of changing access privileges in the Domino directory. If your lone system administrator gets hit by the proverbial bus on the way to work, you would have little choice but to break down your Notes network and set it up again from scratch because nobody would be able to gain administrative access. If you had to set up the Notes organization a second time, you would probably be a little smarter and would assign a team of users to an administrative group.

Another administration role is that of *server administrator*. The server administrator can use the remote console to issue commands to the Domino server. This person's Notes username must be entered into the Administrators field on the server document to use the remote console.

A common approach to server administration is to create a group with a name something like Administrators and then add to the group any users who should have administrative privileges on the organization's servers. Presumably, you would not add people to this group until they have been certified as system administrators or at least have taken system administration classes. And then you would want to trust them to use discretion when they make changes that can easily affect every user in the organization.

If you understand how a Notes network is set up and how servers and users are added to the Notes organization, you realize the crucial role played by the *administration certifier*. This is the person responsible for the organization's certifier ID.

If the certifier ID falls into the wrong hands, you can no longer trust any of the users who access your servers. It cannot be overemphasized: You should keep your certifier ID (and one or more backup copies of it) safe from loss, theft, and unauthorized use. Consider keeping the certifier ID in a safe deposit box. Consider protecting it with multiple passwords so that at least two people have to be present to create new users or servers.

In addition to the administrative functions described previously, Notes provides an easy way to delegate authority by creating and assigning *roles* to individual users. As long as users have at least Author access, they can normally create documents or edit the documents they have created. The notable exception to this is in the Domino directory, where you would expect that only the system administrator could create or modify documents. But in a large organization, the administrator cannot be everything to everyone. Figure 35.7 shows the roles assigned by default to the system administrator. Roles are defined on the Roles page of the Access Control List dialog box, but they are actually assigned or removed on the Basics page.

Modifier roles can be assigned to anyone with at least Author access in the ACL. Creator roles must be explicitly assigned before individuals can perform those roles, regardless of their access privileges. Notes has 11 default roles defined:

- GroupCreator is a user or group of users who can create new groups.
- GroupModifier is a user or group of users who can modify or delete existing group documents, but who cannot create new groups unless assigned as a GroupCreator as well.

35

- NetCreator is a user or group of users who can create all documents except Person, Group, and Server documents.

- NetModifier is a user or group of users who can modify all existing documents except Person, Group, and Server documents.

- PolicyCreator is a user or group of users who can create new policies.

- PolicyModifier is a user or group of users who can modify or delete existing policy documents, but who cannot create new policies unless assigned as a PolicyCreator as well.

- PolicyReader is a user or group of users who can read existing policy documents.

- ServerCreator is a user or group of users who can create new Server documents.

- ServerModifier is a user or group of users who can modify existing Server documents.

- UserCreator is a user or group of users who can create new Person documents. The administration certifier would have to be assigned this role to perform the job of creating new users.

- UserModifier is a user or group of users who can modify existing Person documents.

Figure 35.7
Roles can be used to restrict the functions assigned to a particular system administrator.

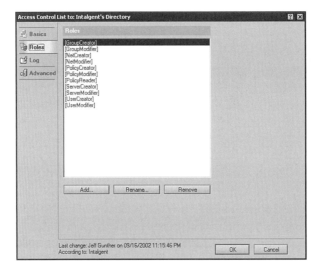

Use these roles wisely; the Domino directory is vital to your Notes organization. Plan who will do what, and make sure that all administrative functions are adequately covered by assigned roles. It is easy to give all managers an equally high level of access, but that might be a foolish approach.

35

Encryption in Lotus Notes

In previous versions of Notes and Domino, Lotus provided three distinct encryption strengths: North American, International English, and French. With the introduction of Version 5.0.4, Lotus consolidated the previous encryption strengths into a single encryption called Global. The release of a single encryption level was possible because the United States government relaxed regulations dealing with encryption exportation. For most users, the level of encryption is insignificant. However, what is of significance is Notes' use of public key encryption.

UNDERSTANDING PUBLIC KEY ENCRYPTION

Traditional encryption, the kind you see in spy movies, entails both the sender and receiver having access to the same secret key, which is used to encrypt a message on one end and decrypt it on the other end. If the secret key is intercepted, the message is no longer secure.

Notes uses another form of security, called public key encryption, based on RSA's Cryptosystem.

This is how public key/private key encryption works. Each person gets two keys: one public key and one private key. The public key is made publicly accessible (stored in the Person document in the Domino directory)—hence its name. The private key is kept secret as part of the user ID.

All encrypted communications use only public keys. The private key is never sent to anyone over the network, and it is never exchanged with anyone. You don't have to worry about the secret key being intercepted. You don't have to worry about someone eavesdropping on your communications. The encrypted message can move across publicly accessible channels, and the public key is easily obtainable. The only person who can decrypt the message is the person who owns the private key associated with the public key that was used to encrypt the message.

DIGITAL SIGNATURES

With electronic documents, you cannot simply go to a notary public and have a seal on a document to verify the signature's authenticity. But encryption does provide a way to exchange secure digital signatures that are recognized by many organizations as legally valid signatures.

A digital signature ensures that a document was actually sent by the person whose name appears on the document. In addition, the digital signature ensures that the document has not been tampered with since its creation. A digital signature is created using the sender's private key. To sign a mail memo, create the memo and click the Delivery Options button. Click the Sign check box. Then, when the memo is mailed, your private key (not a full, usable private key, but just enough information to create the digital signature) is encrypted and attached to the document.

When a user receives a document that has a digital signature attached, the sender's public key is retrieved from the public address book to decrypt the signature. If the decryption is successful, the recipient can be sure that the document was sent by the person identifying himself as the sender.

35

If someone in another Notes domain sends you a message and you do not have that person's public key in any of your address books, you can still read the message. However, Notes displays a message box that says "You and the signer have no certificates in common; signer cannot be assumed to be trustworthy." Although you can still read the document, you cannot accept the digital signature as a legal signature. See the section "The Execution Control List (ECL)," later in this chapter.

ENCRYPTING OUTGOING EMAIL

Using the same public key/private key encryption technology in a slightly different way, you can encrypt the email you send to another user. For example, when a Notes user, Melissa, wants to send an encrypted message to her coworker Jessica, this is what happens:

1. Melissa creates a memo using her Notes Mail. Before she sends the memo, she clicks the Delivery Options button on the Action bar, checks Encrypt, and then sends the memo.

2. The mailer on Melissa's workstation looks for the Person document for Jessica in the Domino directory and uses Jessica's public key to encrypt the memo. The memo is then sent via regular communication channels, which could be over a local area network, over a phone line, or over the Internet.

3. Jessica receives the memo. When she opens the message to read it, it looks just like any other memo. Notes used the private key that is part of Jessica's Notes user ID to decrypt the memo automatically at the time she opened it.

ENCRYPTING INCOMING MAIL

The Mail page in the User Security dialog box (File, Security, User Security) has four check boxes concerned with encryption (see Figure 35.8).

Figure 35.8
The Mail page within the User Security dialog box enables you to specify encryption controls for your mail.

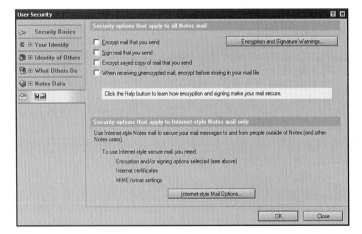

The Encrypt Mail That You Send check box causes all outgoing mail to be encrypted so that you don't have to open the Delivery Options dialog box every time. If you are sending mail to someone who has a Person record in the Domino directory, the mail is encrypted. If no public key is available for the addressee, you will see a message telling you that the message cannot be encrypted. The message is sent in unencrypted form if you okay that option.

Similar to the first box, the Encrypt Saved Copy of Mail That You Send check box enables you to control the encryption of sent mail. This check box enables you to determine whether any of your mail messages are encrypted when saved to your mail database.

The When Receiving Unencrypted Mail, Encrypt Before Storing in Your Mail File check box, in the User Preferences box, enables encryption of all incoming mail. This option uses your public key to encrypt mail before it is stored. The mail cannot be read subsequently unless your Notes ID and its private key are available.

What happens if your organization is using an optional shared copy object store (SCOS) database for storing the nonsummary portion of shared email messages? You will not be able to use the shared object store if you encrypt incoming mail but don't encrypt outgoing mail. Instead, you receive the full email message, which is stored in your personal mailbox.

ENCRYPTING ALL NETWORK DATA OVER A NETWORK PORT

If your organization needs to ensure that all data transmissions over a particular network port are secure, you can elect to encrypt all data traffic through that port. This prevents someone with a network sniffer from intercepting messages. The messages get encrypted at the network port, and they remain encrypted while they are being transported. When the traffic is received and stored on the other end, the data is no longer encrypted.

The data needs to be encrypted only on the sending end. A different encryption algorithm is used for this form of encryption. There is little difference in performance with this type of encryption, although transmission speed might be slowed because the encrypted data cannot be compressed.

To set up encryption for a server's Notes network port, complete the following steps:

1. Start the Domino Administrator, click the Configuration tab, and select the Domino server for which you want to enable encryption.

2. Click the Configuration tab and select Server and Setup Ports from the Configuration menu.

3. Select the Notes port on which you want to start encryption, mark the Encrypt Network Data check box, and then click OK.

4. Restart the Domino server.

THE ROLE OF ENCRYPTION IN AUTHENTICATION

Authentication between a user and a server, or between two servers, uses encryption to verify the identity of the other party. The two exchange digital signatures that guarantee that the other party is not an impostor.

35

Consider for a moment what could happen with the earlier secret key encryption technology. If someone obtained the secret key by stealth, that person could create a message and claim to be the legitimate user of the secret key. There would be no way to guarantee the identity of the sender on the other end.

With public key/private key encryption, the digital signature exchanged between the two systems is guaranteed to be authentic. A short mathematical message is encrypted using the public key of the other system. The other system then decrypts the message with its private key and sends it back in unencrypted format to verify that the right mathematical message was decrypted. The process is then reversed until both systems recognize each other as authentic.

This exchange of encrypted data takes place every time two Notes systems authenticate each other.

Encrypting Documents and Fields Within Documents

Field encryption can be used only at the option of the application designer. Fields on a Domino form can be defined with encryption enabled for the field. This is done in the Security Options field on the "beanie" page of the Field Properties info box, as shown in Figure 35.9.

Figure 35.9
The application designer can enable encryption for individual fields.

The database designer can enable fields for encryption and can assign a default encryption key that automatically encrypts the enabled field when a document is created and saved.

If no default encryption key has been assigned to the form properties by the designer, users can decide whether to encrypt enabled fields. The brackets around encrypted fields are displayed in red to distinguish them from unencryptable fields, which, by default, have gray brackets around them.

When you save a document with encryption-enabled fields, you are asked whether you want to encrypt the fields. If you choose Yes, you are asked which encryption key to use. You can encrypt the fields on the document by selecting an encryption key. Any users who need to read the data in the encrypted fields need to have a copy of the same encryption key that you assigned to the document, and they must merge the encryption key into their Notes user IDs.

Encrypting an entire document is similar to encrypting individual fields within a document. Again, the database designer is responsible for enabling encryption for all the individual fields. When encryption has been enabled, a document can be encrypted automatically as soon as it is saved, or the user can encrypt the document, depending on how the designer has enabled the form you used to create the document.

All the fields enabled for encryption in a document can be encrypted in any of the following ways:

- A form attribute can be selected (on the Security page of the Form Properties info box) whereby the designer assigns one or more encryption keys to the form. Users must have one of those encryption keys before they can read documents created with the form.

- The user can encrypt a document that has one or more fields enabled for encryption by displaying the Document Properties info box and selecting an encryption key to apply to the document, using a field on the Security page of the info box.

- The designer can include a field named SecretEncryptionKeys on the form. This field can be blank, enabling users to assign their own encryption keys. The field can be hidden or visible, and it can have a default value that is the name of an encryption key. The field also can use a formula to determine whether the data should be encrypted, based on the conditions set by the designer.

It is also worth reminding you that local applications can be encrypted from within the Database Properties info box or at the time the application is created. You have three methods of encryption: Simple, Medium, and Strong. Simple encryption is the simplest and provides the quickest access; the encrypted database also can be compressed.

Medium encryption is the default. A database with medium encryption cannot be compressed, but it can be accessed faster than a strongly encrypted database. This level should be sufficient for most uses.

A strongly encrypted database has all the security encryption can provide, but the strong encryption has a price in terms of database access and performance.

CREATING AND SHARING ENCRYPTION KEYS

Encryption keys are created by selecting File, Security, User Security. Enter your password to display the User Security dialog box. Then go to the Notes Data page and select Documents (see Figure 35.10).

35

Figure 35.10
You can work with
encryption keys in
the User Security
dialog box.

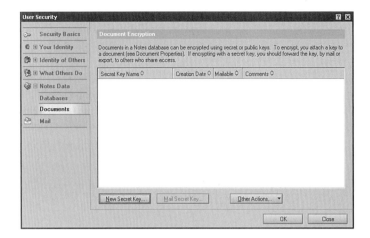

To create a new encryption key, click the New Secret Key button. Notes displays just the Encryption Key Name field and a comment field, and gives you the option of creating a key for a non–North American release of Notes earlier than 5.0.4.

CAUTION

> If you are sending encrypted documents to a user outside the United States or Canada who is running an earlier version of Notes 5.0.4, you must create an international encryption key to encrypt your data.

To send the encryption key to another user so that he can decrypt documents created with it, click the Mail Secret Key button. An Addressing dialog box is displayed. Address the user to whom you want to send the encryption key, and click Send. The user will receive the key, along with instructions to select Accept Encryption Key from the Actions menu, as an email attachment. Clicking Accept merges the encryption key into the recipient's Notes user ID.

If you want to export the encryption key to a file, click Other Actions and select Export Secret Key. A dialog box is displayed with a field where you can enter a password to protect the exported encryption key file. There is a second field in which you must retype the password to confirm what you have entered. You can also click the Restrict Use button and enter the exact name of the only person who is authorized to use the exported key. After you have entered a password (required) and entered the optional name of the person who can use the key, click OK. Notes creates an encryption key file named with a .KEY extension.

To import a key that has been sent to you as a file, you do the opposite of exporting. Click the Other Actions button and select Import Secret Key. Identify the file you want to import. Enter the password that protects the file. Notes displays information about the encryption key in the file and gives you the option of accepting the key. Click the Accept button to merge the key into your Notes user ID. When the key is part of your ID, you can read any documents encrypted using that key.

ADDED SECURITY FEATURES FOR THE INTERNET

The integrated Notes client blurs the line between the Notes environment and the Internet. This presents security problems. The dedicated Notes environment is very secure, but security on the Internet is still evolving. The Notes client must ensure security, whether data resides in a Domino application, on a Web page, or in a data warehouse on an enterprise system.

Notes handles security in this diverse environment using some of the tools described in the following sections.

THE EXECUTION CONTROL LIST (ECL)

You can determine what actions a Notes document can perform on your workstation by setting up the Execution Control List (ECL) as part of your workstation security. Using the ECL, you control how much of your system the embedded program can touch. If a colleague created the document that has an embedded program, you can probably trust that person. If the document was retrieved from the Internet and you don't know the person or company that created it, maybe you should withhold your trust.

When you first open a document, Notes checks the ECL to see whether the document's Author is trusted to perform specific actions on your workstation, such as accessing the current application. If the Author isn't listed in the ECL for that specific action, Notes displays a dialog box similar to Figure 35.11 that gives you the following options:

Figure 35.11
The Execution Security Alert dialog box enables to you selectively choose who can execute code on your workstation.

- **Start Trusting the Signer to Execute This Action**—Modifies the ECL to accept the current action from the Author of the current document in the future without warning you

- **Execute the Action This One Time**—Performs the action this one time, but you are warned the next time a document from the same signer attempts to perform the same action

35

■ **Do Not Execute the Action**—Prevents the action from being performed, but the document might still open if the action isn't essential

You control what can be done on your workstation by documents that were created by others. In addition to choosing to trust the signer of a document or to execute an action only once for that signer, you can define a variety of actions from the ECL. To view the ECL, select File, Security, User Security. Click the What Others Do item on the User Security dialog box (see Figure 35.12).

Figure 35.12
Use an ECL to refine and restrict the actions that can be executed on your workstation.

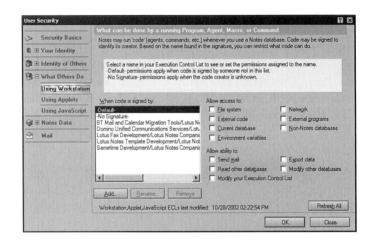

In addition to the Workstations ECL, the What Others Do page enables you to set execution security for Java applets and JavaScript. In many instances, you can use Default and No Signature to protect your system from intrusion by unwanted agents. The degree of protection is very much in your hands. It's a small price to pay for the rich complexity of Notes documents culled from enterprise systems, the Internet, and fellow Notes users.

JAVA APPLET SOURCE SPECIFICATION

In addition to the ECL, you have other options for working with Java applets. The built-in Web Navigator enables Java applets from the Web to run on your computer. To prevent unwanted applets from executing on your workstation, you can define which locations are acceptable sources of Java applets. For example, you could decide not to retrieve Java applets unless they're hosted on Web servers located inside your firewall.

By default, all hosts can run Java applets on your system, but no hosts are allowed to access system resources—such as password files, environment variables, and files—regardless of their capability of running applets.

You can modify the list of trusted Java applet hosts in location documents in your Personal Address Book.

35

In the Advanced section of your Location document, shown in Figure 35.13, click the Java Applet Security tab.

Figure 35.13
Define Java applet security in the Location document.

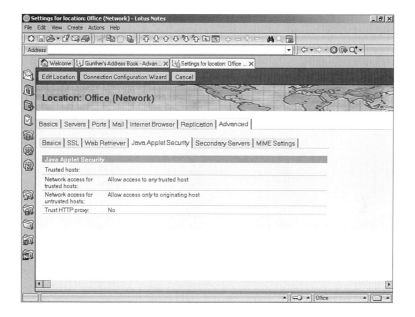

Four fields are used to set Java applet security:

■ **Trusted Hosts**—Enter the IP address or domain name of hosts that can load Java applets on your computer. You can specify wildcards, as in 123.45.678.* or *.lotus.com. Note that if a hostname maps to multiple IP addresses, or vice versa, intended hosts might not be included in your wildcard. If you leave this field blank, all hosts are considered to have the type of access defined for network access for untrusted hosts.

■ **Network Access for Trusted Hosts**—This is the level of network access you want to give to trusted hosts. Options include the following:

   • **Disable Java**—The trusted host cannot run applets on your system.

   • **No Access Allowed**—The host can run an applet on your system, but it can't make network HTTP connections on any host.

   • **Allow Access to Any Originating Host**—The applet can make network HTTP connections on the host from which the applet was retrieved.

   • **Allow Access to Any Trusted Host**—The applet can make network HTTP connections on trusted hosts only. This is the default selection.

   • **Allow Access to Any Host**—The applet can make network HTTP connections on any host.

35

- **Network Access for Untrusted Hosts**—This determines the level of access for all other hosts—those not selected as trusted hosts. Options are the same as the first three options just discussed. Allow access only to the originating host is the default.
- **Trust HTTP Proxy**—This field is used if you specified an HTTP proxy in the Web Proxy field of the Location document. Yes indicates that you want the proxy to resolve the host for you. Otherwise, you won't be able to resolve the hostname or run Java applets.

PART VII

ADMINISTERING THE DOMINO SERVERS

CHAPTER 36

ADMINISTERING USERS, GROUPS, AND CERTIFICATION

In this chapter

INTRODUCING THE DOMINO ADMINISTRATOR

Regardless of whether you're using Notes and Domino strictly for messaging and calendaring or using Domino as your Internet application server, it's essential to have an easy-to-use tool to manage users, groups, and certifications. Domino Administrator 6 provides a central environment for administrators to quickly and easily perform many administrative tasks.

This discussion assumes that you have installed Domino Administrator 6 and that you've configured your workstation to connect to a Domino server. If you need more information about how to install and configure your workstation, refer to Chapter 2, "Installing and Customizing the Notes Client."

Depending on your configuration, you can start the Domino Administrator in a few ways. If you have the Notes client open, you can start it by clicking the Domino Administrator bookmark located on the left side of the user interface. If don't have the Notes client installed or running, you can start it by selecting the Domino Administrator icon within the Lotus Applications group from the Windows Start menu. Figure 36.1 shows the Domino administrator open with the Domain panel displayed.

Figure 36.1
The Domino Administrator enables you to browse the servers, clusters, and networks within a specific domain.

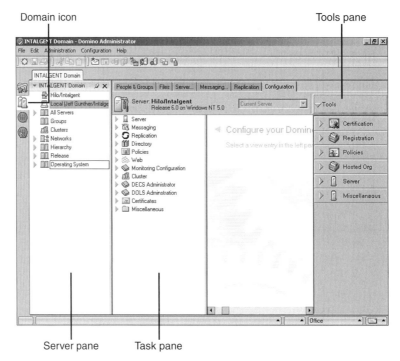

If the Domain icon is clicked, the Administrator displays the Server panel to the left of the configuration documents. The Server panel displays a directory tree consisting of all the servers, clusters, networks, and certificate hierarchies from a specific domain or multiple domains. The right pane divides Domino administration tasks into distinct areas, giving each its own tab. Depending on the tab or task selected, the right pane is further subdivided into two or three areas: information sections, and a collapsible Tools Pane section consisting of actions relevant to the major tab and embedded tab combinations. This integrated environment enables administrators to quickly switch between the management of servers, people and groups, files, messaging, and replication and configuration.

Similar to other Windows applications, the Domino Administrator enables actions to be efficiently completed using standard drag-and-drop commands. For example, the administrator can drag and drop a new name onto an existing server; databases can be moved or copied from one server to another; users can be added or removed from groups; or server tasks such as Compact, Fixup, and Full Text Indexing can be completed.

INTRODUCING THE WEB ADMINISTRATOR

In addition to the Domino Administrator, Lotus has provided an exciting new Web administration client with Release 6. The new client has greatly improved the user interface for Web-based administration over previous releases of Domino. In fact, the Web administration client almost has the same user interface fidelity of the traditional Domino Administrator. Figure 36.2 demonstrates the Web Administrator running under Internet Explorer.

Figure 36.2
The Web Administrator provides the same user interface fidelity found within the Domino Administrator 6.

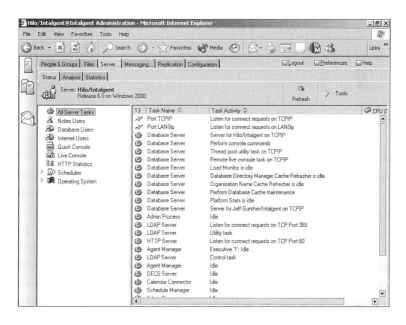

The Web Administrator database (WEBADMIN.NSF) is created by default once the Domino HTTP server is started for the first time. The new Web-based client has a few requirements before you can begin using it to administer your Domino environment. The minimum requirements fall into the following two categories:

- Domino server requirements—The Domino server must be running the following:
  - Administration Process task
  - Certificate Authority process
  - Domino HTTP task
- Web browser requirements—The new Web Administrator requires:
  - Microsoft Windows 98, Windows NT 4, Windows 2000, or Windows XP running Microsoft Internet Explorer 5.5 or 6.0

  or

  - Microsoft Windows 98, Windows NT 4, Windows 2000, Windows XP, or Linux 7.x running Netscape 4.7

To access the Web Administrator, simply point your Web browser to your Domino server and to the WEBADMIN.NSF database. Here is an example URL:

```
http://192.168.1.2/webadmin.nsf
```

USING THE DOMINO ADMINISTRATOR OR WEB ADMINISTRATOR

Regardless of whether you're using the Domino Administrator 6 or the Web Administrator, administration tasks are organized under tabs. Each tab provides configuration information and details regarding the administration of a particular portion of the server. The areas include the following:

- People and Groups
- Files
- Server
- Messaging
- Replication
- Configuration

Because most administration tasks are centered around users and groups, the bulk of the material in this chapter focuses on the tasks you complete while using the People and Groups tab.

PEOPLE AND GROUPS

The People and Groups tab facilitates actions relevant to person or user management; group management; certification management; mail-in database management; setup profile management; and the registration of persons, servers, organizational units, organizations, and Internet certifiers.

FILES

The Files tab facilitates actions relevant to the display of disk information, directory and directory link creation and removal, and database tools. It enables administrators to quickly find information about the databases on their servers and then easily manage that information. The administrator can see all the servers in a particular domain and all the files on those servers. To move, copy, or replicate a database from one server to another, the administrator can simply drag it from one server and drop it on another. The administrator can also change database properties and Access Control Lists for multiple databases at once.

SERVER

The Server tab consists of a set of five embedded tabs:

- **Status**—Enables the administrator to submit console commands relevant to tasks (for example, Tell, Load, or Quit), Users (for example, Broadcast or Drop), or to the Server (for example, Properties, Replicate, Route Mail, Port Information, Secure Console, or Quit).

- **Analysis**—Presents views of the Domino server log (`log.nsf`), the database catalog (`catalog.nsf`), the statistics-reporting database (`statrep.nsf`), and the administration request database (`admin4.nsf`). It enables the administrator to perform a log analysis or a cluster analysis, or to decommission a server.

- **Monitoring**—Enables the administrator to analyze service availability by service and by timeline, thereby determining the availability of a server.

- **Statistics**—Enables the administrator to view real-time statistics of selected servers.

- **Performance**—Presents views of statistics charts and activity trends.

> **NOTE**
>
> With few exceptions, the Domino Administrator client and Web Administrator operate identically. One of those exceptions is with Monitoring and Performance embedded tabs under the Server tab. These two tabs are not supported under the Web Administrator client.

These embedded tabs show vital information to the administrator, including the status of server's tasks, statistics, and network services. All of these indictors enable administrators to make educated decisions about a server's health and determine the probable cause and solutions for errors reflected by the status indicators.

MESSAGING

The Messaging tab contains two embedded tabs:

- **Mail**—Enables the administrator to view properties pertaining to mailboxes on selected servers, shared mail attributes, mail routing status, mail routing events, and a mail routing topology map. It also enables the administrator to route mail, submit a mail trace, and start and shut down the router.

■ **Tracking Center**—Enables the administrator to track messages from a source point to a specific target. This feature enables the administrator to take a snapshot of where messages are in the network and troubleshoot problems across Notes domains and servers.

REPLICATION

The Replication tab enables the administrator to view the Replication schedule, Replication events, and Replication topology map of selected servers within the selected Domino domain. For more information about configuring and administrating replication, refer to Chapter 38, "Replication and Its Administration."

CONFIGURATION

The Configuration tab enables the administrator to view the Server, Messaging, Replication, and Monitoring configurations. Specifically, the following server parameters can be defined under this tab:

■ Messaging and directory services

■ Security and monitoring

■ User policies

■ Offline services

For more information about maintaining your Domino infrastructure, refer to Chapter 40, "Managing Your Domino Server Configuration."

ADMINISTERING USERS WITHIN THE DOMINO DIRECTORY

The People & Groups tab within the Domino Administrator serves as the control point for administering users within the Domino Directory. From this tab, you can perform all actions relevant to user, group, mail-in database, setup profile, and certification management, as well as registration of persons, servers, organizational units, organizations, and Internet certifiers. The People & Groups tab within the Domino Administrator is shown in Figure 36.3.

Chapter 31, "Initial Planning and Installation," and Chapter 36, "Administering Users, Groups, and Certification," discuss the fundamentals of creating the Domino infrastructure and registering a new user to the Notes/Domino network. To review, the steps to registering a user entail the following:

■ Designing a hierarchical name scheme based on your organizational structure

■ Creating a Certification Log to record how you register additional users

- Creating additional certifier IDs, if required by your hierarchical name structure, and distributing the certifier IDs to administrators at other sites

- Adding users by registering them with the appropriate certifier ID

Figure 36.3
The People & Groups tab shows the currently selected Domino Directory on the left and the expanded People & Groups sections on the right.

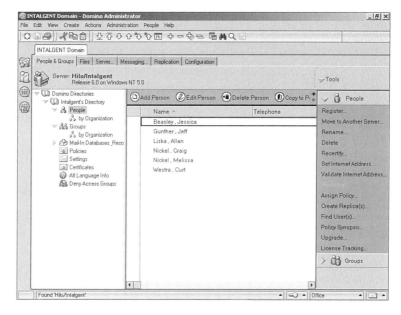

REGISTERING NOTES USERS

To set up users with hierarchical names, you must register them with the appropriate certifier ID according to where they belong in your organization. Registration includes two processes—adding users to your Domino environment and creating ID files with the appropriate certificates. The certifier ID enables a user to authenticate with a server in any branch of the hierarchical name tree. It also enables a user to validate signed mail received from another user in any branch of the hierarchical name tree.

During the registration process, the entire name of the certifier ID is stored in a certificate with the entire name of the entity that is being registered. In addition, all the certificates originating from the certifier are added to the ID file. For example, the name John Smith/Sales/New York/Acme shows the hierarchy of certificates on John Smith's user ID, going from the lowest to the highest in the hierarchy. The last certificate name is Acme, identifying the organizational certificate that is at the top of the hierarchical name scheme. Then there is organizational unit certifier, New York/Acme. At the lowest end is the organizational unit certifier Sales/New York/Acme, just above the common name, John Smith. Such a combination of certifiers enables John Smith to communicate with other people and devices that share the same certificates.

36

Registration formally adds users to Domino by creating IDs stamped with appropriate cer-tificates. The user registration process performs three tasks. It adds a new Person document in the Domino Directory, generates a user ID file, and generates a server-based mail file if your environment uses Notes, POP3, or IMAP mail. If you are using Microsoft Windows and your account has rights to create users on the target server, you can also create Windows user accounts during the registration process.

As you register users, you should be aware of the organization's hierarchical naming scheme within which the user should be positioned. This helps you know which server to use when you register each user. As part of the registration process, you must also have access to each server that you are using, the certifier ID files that you will be using during registration, and their passwords.

You can register users at the end of the Domino server setup following initial installation and configuration. You can also register users at any time from within the Domino Administrator client by selecting the People & Groups tab, expanding the People section under Tools, and then selecting Register.

At this point, you can register new users individually or from a text file. You choose the for-mer when you have only a few users to register, or when each requires a different basic con-figuration. You choose the latter when you have many users to register and you want to standardize the registration process. Either way, you can concurrently create Windows user accounts.

REGISTERING USERS INDIVIDUALLY

The registration process requires that you have access to the server's certifier ID, you know its password, and you have at least Author-level access with `CreatorModifier` and `UserModifier` roles to the Domino Directory. The Register Person—New Entry dialog box consists of a tab for Basic registration and five additional tabs if the Advanced check box is selected. The five tabs consist of the following:

- **Basics**—Details regarding the user including the user's name, password, and mail system.
- **Mail**—Mail settings include mail system, template, and database quota.
- **Address**—Contains the Internet address and domain.
- **ID Info**—Contains details regarding ID file and certifier.
- **Groups**—Assigns the individual to particular groups within the Domino Directory.
- **Other**—Enables you to specify a setup profile and language details.

As you create registration documents for users, Domino enters the user into the Registration Queue. The queue is actually a database, the USERREG.NSF, that's holding users pending registration. The User Registration Queue enables you to view users, identify their registration status, and assign values to non-user-specific fields to multiple users. Non-user-specific fields are fields unique to the individual, such as username and password.

To perform basic user registration, you must complete the fields on the Basics tab. Choose the Advanced field if you want to modify or change some of the more advanced settings. Complete the following steps to register an individual user:

1. Start the Domino Administrator client and click the People & Groups tab.

2. Select the Domino Directory to which you want to register users.

3. From the Tools pane, expand the People section and click Register.

NOTE
> If your certifier ID has not been used before on the workstation, you will be presented with a Browse dialog box enabling you to select the desired certifier ID.

4. Navigate to the selected certifier ID, and then, when prompted, enter the administration password for the specified certifier ID and click OK.

   This opens the Register Person—New Entry dialog box. Figure 36.4 shows the dialog box with the Basics tab and the Advanced registration check box selected. If the Advanced check box is not selected, only the Basics tab is displayed.

Figure 36.4
The Register Person–New Entry dialog box, displaying the Advanced options available to an administrator when registering new Notes Domino users.

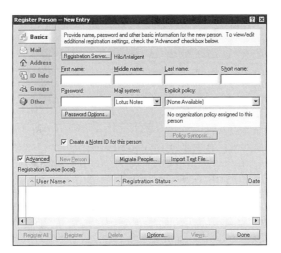

5. If the local server is not the registration server, you can change the registration server by selecting the Registration Server button, selecting an alternative server for registration, and clicking OK.

6. Enter the user's first name, middle initial, last name, short name, and Internet address. The short name is automatically created when completing the form; however, the Internet address is not.

7. Enter a case-sensitive password for the user and then click the Password Options button. This button will display a dialog box that enables you to specify a password quality level, select whether to set an Internet password, and determine whether the Internet

36

password should be synchronized with the Notes ID password. By default, the password level is set at level 8.

8. Click the Mail tab and complete the following (see Figure 36.5):

- Select the mail server and the appropriate mail system. Selecting None as the mail system requires no further input.

- If you select Lotus Notes, POP, IMAP, or iNotes, select the mail file template, enter the name of the user's mail file, and define the mail file owner access. The default name of the mail file is the first character of the first name, followed by the last name. You can also set the database quota, the warning threshold for the mail database, and whether to create a full text index.

Figure 36.5
The Mail tab allows you to define the user's mail settings.

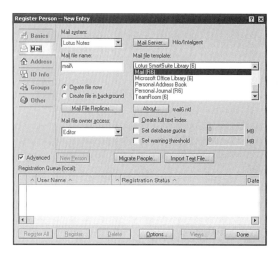

9. Click the Address tab and review the Internet address and Internet Domain fields. You can modify the format by selecting the Format button and choosing options from the lists available in both the Address name format and Separator fields.

10. Click the ID info tab to specify information relevant to the selected certifier ID and individual user license. If the certifier ID highlighted is not the desired ID, you can select a different certifier ID and press Enter. You will then be prompted for the certifier ID password; click OK.

Select the North American or International Security type.

If you want to change the expiration date, enter the date in mm-dd-yy format in the Certificate's expiration date field.

Select how you want to store the user's ID file—in the Domino Directory or in a file. If you store the ID in a file, click Set ID File, specify the filename and path, and then double-click. If you do not select an ID storage type, a Notes ID is not created unless the mail type is Notes Mail. Most organizations view the storage of the ID files in the Domino Directory as highly insecure, because anyone with reader access can detach them, so it is recommended to store them in a file in a secure directory location.

11. Click the Groups tab and select the Groups to which you want the user added.

12. Click the Other tab to specify additional Directory information, including:

    • Enter the desired setup profile, a unique organizational unit for the user, and a location—for example a region, district, city, or office.

    • Enter a local administrator and comment about the user.

    • Choose an alternative name language and/or preferred language.

13. If your network environment uses Microsoft Windows, you can create a Windows account for the user. By clicking the Windows User Options button and selecting Add This Person to Windows NT and specifying the Windows NT username. In the Add Person to Windows NT Group field, you can enter the name of the Windows NT group in which you like to add all user accounts created in this session. By leaving the field blank, you place the user in the default Windows NT user group, Users.

14. You can then click the green check mark to add the user to the Registration Queue. You can then add another user to the queue. If you want to make changes to a user's settings once they have been added to the queue, simply click on the user's name in the Registration queue and make the appropriate modifications.

15. After you have completed the documents for all users you want to register, click Register All or Register. Depending on the number of users being registered, it could take a few minutes.

16. Click Done to exit.

DETAILS OF WINDOWS NT USER ACCOUNTS

If, during the registration process, you choose to create user accounts in Windows NT, the accounts include the following information:

■ **Windows NT User Name**—Created from the entry made in the NT User Name field in the Other Pane of the Register Person dialog box. The default is the user's short name.

■ **Full Name**—Created by combining the user's first name (if supplied) and last name.

■ **Password**—Created by using the Notes password. If the Notes password exceeds 14 characters, the Windows NT password consists of the first 14 characters of the Notes password.

■ **NT Group Name**—Created by using the name specified in the Register Person dialog box or the default Windows NT user group, Users.

During registration, Domino copies the Windows NT User Name to the Network account name field in the Person document in the Directory. This facilitates the matching of Person documents within the Domino domain with user accounts in the Windows NT User Manager. This aids the synchronization of information when altering or deleting a record in one product and propagating the changes to the other product.

If, while creating user accounts, Domino encounters a Windows NT error (for example, you are not a Windows NT Administrator or Account Operator), it returns an appropriate message to the log file (LOG.NSF). If an error occurs that prevents the creation of an account in the User Manager, the user is still registered in Notes. Windows NT errors have no effect on the Domino registration process.

NOTE

> You can create Windows NT users accounts only while registering Notes users. You cannot create a Windows NT user by manually adding a person to the directory.

EXAMPLE INDIVIDUAL USER REGISTRATION   As an example, consider how you would register John Smith who has recently joined the Acme Corporation. He is working out of the New York office, which falls under the responsibility of the New York/Acme certifier. He is working in the Sales office, so the ultimate responsibility for registering him as a user on the system falls to the administration certifier responsible for the Sales/New York/Acme certifier ID.

If John Smith were to be registered by the top-level Acme certifier, he would be given automatic access to any databases that include */Acme in the ACL at Reader access or higher. That includes databases in all divisions within all regions of the company. In short, if the top-level Acme certifier registered John Smith, John would have access that was too broad.

On the other hand, if John is registered with the Sales/New York/Acme certifier ID, you ensure that he is not accidentally included in Access Control Lists for divisions and regions for which he is not responsible. By using the Sales/New York/Acme certifier ID, John can access the Sales databases, the New York databases, and the Acme databases using a wildcard */Sales/New York/Acme that creates a group for anyone with a certificate from the Sales/New York/Acme certifier ID.

John Smith, whose full name is John Smith/Sales/New York/Acme, can enter his name in a shortened form as John Smith/. The slash following his name means that the entire hierarchy, his full username, is intended.

Notes refers to names in several ways. A fully canonical name includes location markers, for example CN=John Smith/OU=Sales/OU=New York/O=Acme, where CN is the common name, OU is an organizational unit, and O is the organization. This is how Notes stores the name, with all its components labeled. The abbreviated distinguished name is how the user might see it displayed, such as John Smith/Sales/New York/Acme. However, many fields on Notes forms contain input translation formulas that simplify the name so that only the common name is displayed, such as John Smith.

Registering John automatically creates the Person record and displays the abbreviated fully distinguished name in the User Name field, along with his common name. This means that John can be addressed by just his common name, and the Notes Router will find his mailbox. Hence, everyone can send John Smith email addressed simply to `John Smith`.

REGISTERING A GROUP OF USERS FROM A TEXT FILE

Complementing individual user registration, the Domino Administrator also enables you to register a group of users from a text file. To accomplish this, you need to be an administrator with at least Author-level access with `CreatorModifier` and `UserModifier` roles to the Domino Directory. As with individual user registration, you can concurrently create Windows NT user accounts, if you use Windows NT, at the same time that you are registering Notes users—again, if you must have the proper administrative rights to the NT server.

To register a group of users from a text file, start by creating or automatically generating a semicolon-delimited file with the following information about the person: last name, first name, middle initial, organizational unit, password, ID file directory, ID filename, home server name, mail file directory, mail filename, location, comment, forwarding address, profile name, local administrator, Internet address, short name, alternative name, and mail template file.

After the text file has been created or generated, complete the following steps:

1. Initiate the Domino Administrator, select the People and Groups tab, and from the Tools pane, click People, Register.
2. Enter the certifier password.
3. If the local server is not the registration server, you can change the registration server by selecting an alternative server for registration and clicking OK.
4. Click Import Text File, select the text file, and click Open. Because you can reconcile problems generated during the import process by editing individual documents displayed in the User Registration Queue described previously, click OK for any status messages received.
5. If necessary, modify any user settings by editing individual documents displayed in the User Registration Queue.
6. Click Register All or Register. Domino uses default settings or settings defined in the global registration preferences for any options not defined.

SETTING UP WEB AND INTERNET (LDAP) DIRECTORY USERS

Whether you are using the Domino Administrator or the Windows NT User Manager to register Notes users, you have made it possible for them to authenticate themselves with Domino servers. It is possible, however, to set up Web and Internet (LDAP) Directory users who remain anonymous to Domino servers. Hence, you, as an administrator, can set up two types of Internet users: users who you want to authenticate with servers and anonymous users.

SETTING UP AUTHENTICATED USERS

Authenticated users require a name and password when accessing the server or use client authentication with Secure Sockets Layer (SSL). For this, you must create a Person document for the user. You can accomplish this by registering the user as an Internet user, as described previously in the section, "Registering Users Individually." Otherwise, you can just create the Person document directly in the Directory and enter information about the user's name, password, and SSL certificate without following any form of user registration.

SETTING UP ANONYMOUS USERS

Anonymous users, on the other hand, do not require Person documents. However, you do need to ensure that anonymous users can access the server and databases on a server. To do so, you must enter **Anonymous** into the desired database Access Control Lists and assign it the proper access level.

SETTING AND VALIDATING INTERNET ADDRESSES

The Domino Administrator also enables you to set and validate Internet addresses. The Set Internet Address tool fills in the Internet Address field for all Person documents in which the field is blank in the selected Domino Directory. The Validate Internet Address field verifies the uniqueness of all Internet Address fields.

To set the Internet Address field, complete the following steps:

1. Open the Domino Administrator; select the People & Groups tab for a selected Domino server.
2. Highlight the People view for the given directory to be modified.
3. Open the People section within the Tools pane and select Set Internet Address.
4. In the Set Internet Address dialog box, choose a format for the Internet addresses. For example, using the default format, an address might look like JeffGunther@Acme.com. As illustrated in this example, the default format is FirstNameLastName@Internet domain without a separator.
5. Choose a separator for the Internet addresses.
6. Enter the Internet domain for the company.
7. If you want to set addresses only for users in a given Notes domain or use a secondary custom format pattern in case an error is generated using the first address construction format, click More Options and select either of the advanced features.
8. Click OK to set the Internet address.

The Set Internet Address tool checks all Person documents in the Domino Directory. It creates an entry based on the rules specified, verifies that the entry conforms to RFC 821 address syntax, and then validates that the entry is unique. If a duplicate entry is found in the directory, the tool leaves the field blank.

CHANGING NOTES USERNAMES WITH THE ADMINISTRATION PROCESS

Periodically, it's necessary to rename or delete users within your organization. Because the Administration Process in Domino automates this to a large extent, it is best to do so when making changes within your Domino Directory. You can accomplish all this from within the Domino Administrator.

The process of renaming a user generates a series of requests posted in the Administration Requests database (ADMIN4.NSF). The Administration Process can change names only if the database is assigned an administration server. It also automates changing the names only of Notes users. You must manually change the name of an Internet user who has a Person document in the Directory—for example, a Web browser user.

CHANGING A NOTES USER'S COMMON NAME WITH THE ADMINISTRATION PROCESS

You can use the following steps to rename the common name component of a hierarchical username when Domino servers are set up to use the Administration Process. To accomplish this, you must have the UserModifier role or Editor access, as well as Create Documents access to the Directory. You must also have at least Author with Create Documents access to the Certification Log.

1. Within the Domino Administrator, select the People & Groups tab.

2. Open the People view for the chosen Directory.

3. Select the person to be renamed.

4. In the Tools pane under People, choose Rename.

5. Click the Change Common Name button on the Rename Selected Notes People dialog box.

6. Select the certifier ID that certified the user's ID and press Enter. For example, to rename John Smith/Sales/New York/ACME, use the certifier ID /Sales/New York/ACME and click OK.

7. Enter the password for the selected certifier and click OK.

8. Either accept the default certificate expiration date (two years from the current date) or enter a different date into the Certification Expiration Date dialog box and click OK.

9. Once the Rename Person dialog box appears, change the user's first name, last name, and middle initial, as necessary.

10. If you want to differentiate this user from another user, you can enter a qualifying Organizational Unit. This extends the canonical name by adding a component that appears between the common name and the certifier name.

11. If you want to update the Windows NT user account name while renaming the user, select Rename NT User Account.

12. Click OK.

Figure 36.6 shows the Rename Person dialog box, which is used to assign new common name values to the selected user.

Figure 36.6
The Rename Person dialog box within Domino Administrator is used to change the common name for a given user.

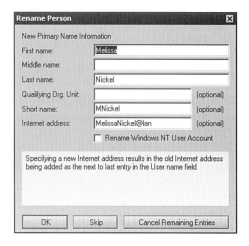

The process to rename individuals in the Domino Directory is an interval process and might take a while to complete.

MOVING A NOTES USER'S NAME IN THE HIERARCHY WITH THE ADMINISTRATION PROCESS

As you can when changing a Notes user's common name, you can move a Notes user's name from one organization to another. To accomplish this, you must have the `UserModifier` role or Editor with Create Documents access to the Domino Directory. In addition, you must have at least Author with Create Documents access to the Certification Log and at least Editor access to the Administration Requests database. Figure 36.7 depicts the Request Move For Selected People dialog box, which is used to assign a new certifier to the selected users.

1. From the Domino Administrator, select the People & Groups tab.
2. Open the People view within the chosen Directory.
3. Select the person to be moved.
4. In the Tools pane under People, choose Rename.
5. Click Request Move to New Certifier.
6. Select the certifier ID and press Enter.
7. Enter the certifier ID password and click OK to open the Request Move for Selected People dialog box.
8. Enter the name of the certifier to use to recertify the user's hierarchical name in the New Certifier field.
9. Click OK.

To process the administration request, follow these steps:

1. Open the Administration Requests database.

2. Choose View, Name Move Requests and select the name(s) to move. The name may not appear if you haven't waited long enough.

3. Choose Actions, Complete Move for selected entries.

4. Select the certifier ID that will recertify the name(s) and press Enter.

5. Enter the certifier ID password and click OK.

6. Accept the default certificate expiration date (two years from the current date) or enter a different date.

7. If you want to differentiate this user from another user, you can enter a qualifying Organizational Unit. This extends the canonical name by adding a component that appears between the common name and the certifier name.

8. Click Certify.

Figure 36.7
The Request Move For Selected People dialog box is used to assign a new certifier to the selected users.

SAMPLE INDIVIDUAL USER RENAME AND MOVE   You will recall that the user's name is part of his or her Notes identity, and the hierarchical name, in effect, lists the certificates that enable him or her to access servers and databases within the Notes organization. When a user's name is changed, the user risks losing the ability to access databases, both on the server and on the local computer. When the user's name has changed or the user has been moved to a new hierarchical certificate (for example, been given a new certificate or set of certificates), the user ID is changed, so data encrypted with a different hierarchical certificate may be lost. If a backup of the old ID was not saved so that the user can decrypt the data, the encrypted data is lost forever (unless someone else has a copy of the same data that they are willing to share).

Let's examine what happens when John Smith gets married and decides to hyphenate his name or moves from the Sales office in New York to the corresponding office in San Francisco. Recall that his name, as far as Notes Domino is concerned, is John Smith/Sales/New York/Acme.

First, John gets married to Jane Jones. They decide to hyphenate their name to Smith-Jones. Here is how the administrator changes his name. The administrator initiates the Domino Administrator, highlights the People & Groups tab, selects John within the People view, and expands the People section within the Tools Pane. The administrator then selects the action Rename. The administrator then selects Change Common Name, selects the certifier ID used originally to certify the person, changes any defaults, and clicks Certify. The Change Common Name dialog box appears. The administrator completes the fields for the Certificate Expiration Date, the New First Name, the New Middle Initial, the New Last Name, and the New Qualifying Organization Unit (if any), and then selects whether to rename the NT User Account.

A record is made in the Certification Log and in the Administration Requests database. When the Administration Process runs on the server, all instances of the original name are replaced with the new name. The only place the name cannot be changed is in the Personal Address Book of individual users and in databases on local hard drives. John still has all his original certificates, but the common name component of his ID has thus been changed.

Then a few months later, John Smith-Jones and his wife Jane decide to relocate to San Francisco from New York. The administrator must move John from one part of the company to another. The administration certifier must also move his name within the hierarchical naming scheme. This is done by recertifying him with his new hierarchical name. The name change is made in one place, and then the Administration Process takes over and automatically changes the name throughout the Domino network. John retains his John Smith-Jones common name, but now he has a new certificate hierarchy and hence a new Notes distinguished name, which affects his ability to access data throughout the organization, including on his own desktop or mobile computer. To rectify this, John's entry must also be updated in the Access Control Lists of any databases with which he needs to interface.

By changing John's name through renaming, he is automatically moved within the Domino organization, including a name change in his Person document in the Directory, in all groups to which his name has been added, and in the ACL of all databases to which he has been added. If the name were not changed in all databases and groups, he could end up losing access to some databases.

The one thing that isn't changed is the user's mail file. John wants his mailbox moved to a San Francisco server. To accomplish this, the mail file must be replicated to the new home server, and the name of the home server should be changed in John's Person document in the Directory. When John arrives in San Francisco, he can use his renamed user ID, open his mail, and have access to local copies of all the databases he is accustomed to.

The Domino Administrator facilitates this move by providing a Move to Another Server option under the People section within the Tools Pane of the People & Groups tab. To move a user and the corresponding mail file from one server to another, select the Move to Another Server tool within the People section and specify the server to which you want the user moved. In order to complete this successfully, you must have either Editor access or Author access, you must be a UserModifier to the Domino Directory, and must have CreateReplica rights to the new mail server and to the old mail server.

STUDYING THE IMPACT OF NAME CHANGES ON A MOBILE USER

The Administration Process minimizes the impact of changes to a user ID on a Domino server. However, changing the user ID does have consequences for the mobile user:

- If the user changes his or her own name, rather than submitting a request to the administrative certifier, he or she is unable to access any servers, encrypted databases, and encrypted documents. There is no back door. The system administrator cannot help. The data is irretrievably lost. Also, the user cannot open local replicas on which the ACL is enforced. If the user's name is changed on the server by the administrative certifier, he or she can still access all databases on the server, but must either change his or her name on the ACLs of local databases, or wait for them to replicate with the server if ACLs are locally enforced. Of course, if the Administrator has kept an archive copy of the mobile user's ID file, this could be given back to the user to access the data created with the former ID.

- If the user is recertified but remains in the same organization, he or she loses access to local databases on which ACLs are locally enforced until the databases replicate with the server and get updated ACLs. The user can still read locally encrypted databases and documents. However, as the manager of his or her own mail database file, the user can go in and change the ACL of that database locally.

DELETING A USERNAME

Aside from changing a user's common name and moving the user to a different organizational hierarchy, you can also delete a user from the Domino Directory. You can accomplish such entry deletion in one of the following ways: by using the Domino Administration Process, by deleting the username within the Windows NT User Manager, or by manually deleting a username.

DELETING A USERNAME WITH THE DOMINO ADMINISTRATION PROCESS

To delete a username with the Domino Administration Process, complete the following steps:

1. From the Domino Administrator, select the People & Groups tab.
2. Highlight the People view for the given directory to be modified.
3. Open the People section within the Tools pane.
4. Choose the user's Person document to be deleted.
5. Within the Tools Pane, click the Delete action to open the Delete Person dialog box.
6. Determine whether to delete the user's mail file. You'll need to approve the mail file deletion in the Administration Requests database.
7. Deny the user access to all servers by adding the user to some form of Deny Access group.
8. Determine whether to delete all references to the person within the Domino Directory and delete the user's Windows NT/2000 accounts.
9. Click OK.

Figure 36.8 depicts the Delete Person dialog box, which is used to delete selected users from the Domino Directory.

36

Figure 36.8
The Delete Person dialog box is displayed when the user deletes Person documents for selected users from the Domino Directory.

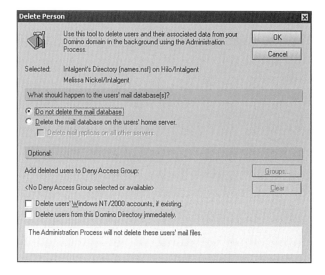

EXAMPLE INDIVIDUAL USER DELETION   John Smith-Jones decides it's time to explore other vocational opportunities. He gives his notice. The usual separation interview is done, and his last day comes to an end. He turns over his Notes user ID and walks out the door for what seems to be his last day. As John Smith-Jones leaves, the system administrator adds John to a group that has been named NO_ACCESS. The group is included in the Not Access Server field on every server in the organization. As soon as the Directory is replicated around the organization, John Smith-Jones can no longer access any server, even if he has retained a copy of his Notes user ID.

Because it is uncertain whether another copy of John Smith-Jones's Notes ID exists, the administrator locked John out of the system via the NO_ACCESS group mechanism. Following corporate policy, however, the administrator archived the Notes ID John gave him. The administrator does not immediately delete the user from the system using the Administration Process, by using the Domino Administrator's Person management delete action. John might, after all, have a change of heart and return to Acme.

If he had selected to delete John, the administrator would have opened the Domino Administrator, selected the People & Groups tab, and then highlighted the People view for the given directory to be modified. The administrator would then open the People section within the Tools pane, select John's Person document, and click Delete. This process allows you to delete the person from the Directory immediately. Otherwise, the references would be removed only after the normal running of the Administration Process. Similarly, the administrator would have had to decide whether to remove John's mail file.

Instead, after adding John to the NO_ACCESS group, the administrator simply forces replication of the Directory to all servers in the organization to ensure that the change is distributed throughout the organization as quickly as possible.

RECERTIFYING A HIERARCHICAL NOTES ID WITH THE ADMINISTRATION PROCESS

The final administrative action required on Notes IDs is recertification or extension of their expiration date. When a certificate on an ID is due to expire, you must recertify the ID. As with the administrative actions surrounding the renaming and deletion of user IDs, the Administration Process also automates actions involved in the recertification of hierarchical IDs.

RECERTIFYING A NOTES USER ID WITH THE ADMINISTRATION PROCESS

Follow these steps to use the Administration Process to recertify a hierarchical ID that is due to expire. You must have Author with Create Documents access and have the UserModifier role or Editor access to the Directory. You must also have at least Author with Create Documents access to the Certification Log:

1. Initiate the Domino Administrator, select the People & Groups tab, and highlight the People view for the given directory to be modified.
2. From the Tools Pane, expand the People section.
3. Select all the users to be recertified with the same certifier. Select the Recertify action.
4. Select the certifier ID originally used to certify the selected users and click OK.
5. Enter the password for the selected certifier ID and click OK to open the Renew Certificates in Selected Entries dialog box.
6. Accept the default certificate expiration date (two years from the current date) or enter a different date to display the Recertify User dialog box.
7. Click OK.
8. The Processing Statistics dialog box will detail the numbers of users successfully recertified.

SAMPLE INDIVIDUAL USER RECERTIFICATION   Just a few months after his resignation, John Smith-Jones decides to return to Acme. Because he is resuming his position within the Sales division in the San Francisco territory, he will retain his Notes hierarchical designation. However, his certificate has expired. To extend the expiration date on the certificate, the administrator initiates the Domino Administrator, selects the People & Groups tab, expands the People section, and clicks Recertify. Taking the certifier ID file archived upon John's resignation, the administrator selects it, provides its password, and enters the new expiration date. The administrator proceeds to click Certify. John's user ID file has been recertified. To be activated, all that remains for the administrator is to remove John from the NO_ACCESS group.

36

ADMINISTERING GROUPS WITHIN THE DOMINO DOMAIN

Extensive group-management functionality is also available within the People & Groups tab of the Domino Administrator. The Group section enables the administrator to complete the following:

- Manage groups, enabling the administrator to add or remove users, servers, or groups to or from groups by selecting the desired users, servers, or groups and clicking buttons or dragging the entry to the target group.

- Create groups, enabling the administrator to add groups to the Domino Directory.

- Edit groups, enabling the administrator to add and delete user, server, or group entries within individual groups.

- Delete groups, enabling the administrator to remove the entire group from the Domino Directory.

MANAGING GROUPS

To manage groups within the Domino Administrator, complete the following steps:

1. From the Domino Administrator, select the People & Groups tab, highlight the Group view for the given directory to be modified, and then open the Groups section within the Tools pane.

2. Within the Tools pane, choose the Manage action. You will be presented with the Manage Groups dialog box, as shown in Figure 36.9.

Figure 36.9
The Manage Groups dialog box displays current group and member hierarchies. You can adds users and/or groups to or remove them from groups within the Domino Directory.

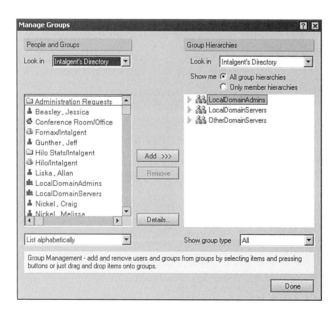

3. Under the People and Groups section of the dialog box, select the Domino Directory serving as the source of the modifications.

Note that you can view this list either alphabetically or by organization, and that you can display the Person, Server, or Group document for any of the entries by double-clicking the entry or by highlighting the entry and selecting the Details button.

4. Under the Group Hierarchies section, select the Domino Directory to be modified. Note that you can display this list either by group or member hierarchies and that you can select which type of group to display. Note that you can also display the Group document for any of the entries by either double-clicking the entry or highlighting the entry and selecting the Details button.

5. To add a user, server, or group to a target group, select the group from the Group hierarchies list, select the user, server, or group to be added to the list, and then drag the entry to the target or click the Add button.

6. To remove a user, server, or group from a target group, select the entry from the Group Hierarchies list and click the Remove button.

7. Select the Done button to save your changes.

CREATING GROUPS

To create groups within the Domino Administrator, complete the following steps:

1. From the Domino Administrator, select the People & Groups tab, and then highlight the Group view for the given directory to be modified.

2. Click the Add Group action on the view. You will be presented with a New Group document, as shown in Figure 36.10.

Figure 36.10
The New Group document enables you to define a new group.

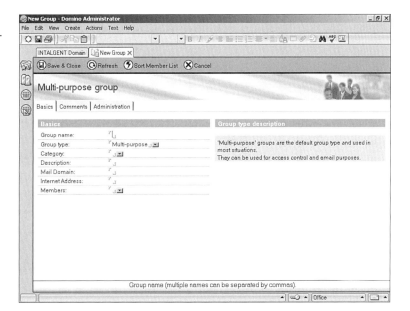

36

3. On the Basics tab, complete the Group Name, select the Group Type, and provide a brief description for the Group.

4. Add the desired members to the Group from the Names dialog box presented to you by selecting the down arrow.

5. Under the Administration tab, select whether Foreign directory sync is to be allowed for the Group entry.

6. Select the Save and Close button to save the document.

MODIFYING GROUPS

To modify groups within the Domino Administrator, complete the following steps:

1. From the Domino Administrator, select the People & Groups tab, and then highlight the Group view for the given directory to be modified.

2. From the view, choose the Edit action button. You will be presented with the Group document for the selected Group.

3. Perform whatever modification is desired to the selected Group document.

4. Select the Save and Close button to save the document.

DELETING GROUPS

To delete groups within the Domino Administrator, complete the following steps:

1. From the Domino Administrator, select the People & Groups tab, highlight the Group view for the given directory to be modified, and then select the Group to be deleted. Open the Groups section within the Tools pane.

2. Within the Tools pane, choose the Delete action. You will be presented with the Delete dialog box to confirm the deletion of the selected groups.

3. Press OK to confirm the deletion, or Cancel to abort the deletion.

CHAPTER 37

ADMINISTERING ELECTRONIC MAIL

In this chapter

ADMINISTERING ELECTRONIC MAIL WITHIN THE DOMINO ADMINISTRATOR

Domino Administrator 6 provides an easy-to-use environment for managing electronic mail. Upon launching the Domino Administrator and opening a particular server, you'll see several tabs across the top of the client. The Messaging and Configuration tabs serve as the control center for administering electronic mail within the Domino directory. Configuration administration is discussed in Chapter 34, "Initial Configuration of Servers with the Domino Directories," and Chapter 40, "Managing Your Domino Server Configuration."

The Messaging tab, shown in Figure 37.1, consists of a set of two subtabs: a Mail tab and a Tracking Center tab.

Figure 37.1
The Messaging tab within the Domino Administrator provides several frequently used views and actions for managing your messaging environment.

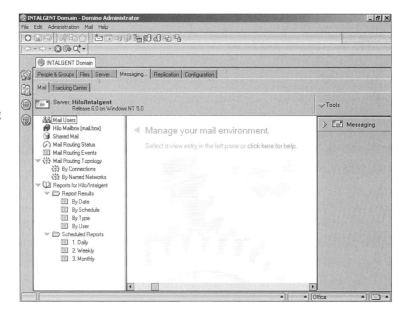

The Mail embedded tab provides the administrator with a series of informational views on the selected server's messaging infrastructure. First, it enables the administrator to view the mail users on a selected server, from which individual Person documents can be added, edited, or deleted. Next, it provides a view pertaining to the selected server's MAIL.BOXes, from which messages can be deleted and dead messages can be released. Third, it provides a view of the Shared Mail attributes, if shared mail has been enabled on the selected server. Fourth, it provides an odometer reading on the MAIL.Dead and MAIL.Waiting mail-routing status counters on the selected server. Fifth, it provides the Mail Routing Events view of the selected server's log file. Sixth, it provides two alternative mail routing topology maps: By Connections and By Named Networks. Finally, it provides a view of reports for the selected server. The Tool pane associated with this tab also enables the administrator to send a mail trace, start and stop the router, and route mail.

The Tracking Center embedded tab allows the administrator to track messages from a source point to a target. If enabled on the server, this feature allows the administrator to see where messages are in the network at any point in time. Using it, the administrator can look in the message-tracking database and troubleshoot problems pertaining to mail delivery.

In addition to the Mail and Tracking Center tabs, the Messaging subsection of the Configuration tab consists of the current Messaging Settings document within the directory on the selected server. It also contains views of the current Domain documents, Connections documents, Configurations, Internet sites, and File Identification documents within the same directory. The latter five views enable you to add, edit, and delete the respective object in the directory. Figure 37.2 shows the Configuration tab within the Domino Administrator.

37

Figure 37.2
The Configuration tab within the Domino Administrator contains the messaging settings, domain, and connections for the selected server.

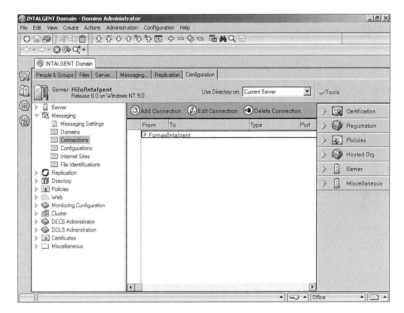

ADMINISTERING THE DOMINO MAIL SERVER

Domino Mail uses the directory and a mail router process to deliver documents to user mail files and to databases that have been mail-enabled. The mail router process can also deliver mail through gateways, to routers in other Notes domains, and to other non-Notes message-transfer agents—and, hence, to external mail systems, such as cc:Mail and X.400.

UNDERSTANDING THE BASICS OF MAIL ROUTING

Routing within a Domino infrastructure is easy to understand if you think of it as functioning analogously to the post office. Using this analogy, you write a letter and put it in the mailbox. It is picked up by the mail carrier and deposited at the central post office, where it is sorted according to which route the addressee lives on. If the mail is local, it is sent out, under ideal situations, immediately on the carrier's route and is put in the addressee's mailbox. If the addressee lives in another neighborhood, the letter goes into a bin. As soon as the bin is full (or sooner, if a truck is going that way), the mail is delivered to a branch office nearer to the addressee and is then delivered to the addressee's mailbox. On the other hand, if the addressee lives out of town, the mail goes to the airport and is sent to a post office in another town, where the local post office looks at the address, determines the route, and delivers the mail.

The situation is similar to this in Lotus Notes and Domino. Within Notes and Domino, a task called the Mailer (running on a local workstation) looks up the addressee's name and address in the personal directory or Domino directory, or both, to see whether the user's name is valid; then it puts the mail message into a database on the Domino server called MAIL.BOX.

The Mail Router then takes over. The Mail Router determines where the addressee's home server is located by looking at the Person document in the Domino directory. The home server is the Domino server on which the user's mail database is stored. The router then puts the message into the user's mail database if the database is on the local server, or places it in the MAIL.BOX database on a server elsewhere in the same Notes Named Network for the other server's Mail Router to deliver. Servers share the same named network if they share a common LAN protocol, have the same Notes Network name in the Notes Named Network embedded tab within the Ports tab of the Server documents, and they are constantly connected to that network.

If the user's mail database is in another Notes Named Network, the Mail Router looks for a Server Connection document to determine how and when to route the mail. If there are multiple Connection documents, the least expensive and most direct route to the other server is used. The order of precedence used by Notes is to route through the local area network, a remote LAN service, a dialup modem, and then a passthru server.

If the addressee is in another Notes domain, the Mail Router has no way to verify the user's address in the local directory and in secondary Domino directories or LDAP directories without directory assistance. Therefore, the mail is routed to a MAIL.BOX file in the other domain using Connection documents and, if necessary, gateways or Message Transfer Agents connecting Notes to external systems. At the other end, the router from the other domain picks up the message and delivers it.

To prevent routing loops during this message transfer process, Domino sets a default maximum hop count of 25 for each message. That is, a mail message can make up to 25 server stops before the Mail Router returns the message to the sender. Each time the message passes through a server, the hop count decreases until the count reaches zero.

The way Domino routes mail from one server to another depends on the system topology and on the relationship between the locations of the sender's and the addressee's home server. Routing can be simple and quick, or it can require a message to make multiple hops from server to server as it finds its way to the addressee's home server.

You set up mail routing based on the server topology you have established within your Domino network. Domino server topologies can be chain, ring, mesh, or hub-and-spoke. In a chain topology, two or more servers are set end to end, where Server A calls Server B, Server B calls Server C, and so on down the line. In a ring topology, the chain is closed, with the last member of the chain calling the first member of the chain, forming a closed loop. In a mesh topology, every server exchanges mail with every other server. In a hub-and-spoke topology, one hub server schedules and initiates all mail-routing requests to all other servers, or spokes. See Chapter 40 for detailed information about each topology.

DEFINING GENERAL GUIDELINES FOR MAIL ROUTING

Whether you decide to use a hub-and-spoke, chain, ring, or mesh topology, the resulting configuration has significant performance consequences. Some of the guidelines you should consider in defining your mail routing topology include these:

- Set up replication so that the Domino directory replicates frequently to all servers in the Domino domain. This ensures that the Server, Connection, and Domain documents reflect consistent data for all servers.

- Assign roles to restrict who can create Connection documents in the Domino directory.

- Minimize the number of Connection documents by designating only two or three servers in each Domino Named Network responsible for routing mail to other Domino networks or external systems.

- Create two separate Connection documents to schedule separate repeat intervals for mail routing and replication. This differentiates between the parameters for mail routing and replication, and assists your troubleshooting efforts when mail-routing or replication problems occur.

- Determine whether to use Shared Mail, and thereby store only a single copy of widely distributed mail messages in a server's central database, or store multiple copies in the individual user's mail file.

- Ensure the scheduling of mail routing over a dialup modem connection during a range of time between midnight and 6:00 a.m.

- Use the Mail Trace feature to locate and debug mail-routing problems.

- Ensure that at least one Mail Router task is running by using the Show Tasks server command to see which server tasks are currently running.

- Check the server's log file for the summary of mail-routing events. You can record additional information in the log file by editing the Server Configuration document and including the Logging Level setting. This setting determines the amount of information recorded in the log file for messaging events.

CONNECTING SERVERS FOR MAIL ROUTING

You connect servers for mail routing differently, depending on whether the servers are in the same Domino Named Network or the same Domino domain. Setting up mail routing between servers in the same Domino Named Network does not require you to configure any Connection documents. Mail is automatically routed between servers sharing the same named network.

NOTE

A *Named Network* is nothing more than a group of servers that share the same network protocol. A server can be a member of multiple Named Networks if it is running more than one protocol. Named Networks are described in greater detail in the *Domino Administrator's Guide*.

Setting up mail routing between servers in different Domino Named Networks but in the same Domino domain requires you to create two Connection documents, one in each direction. This guarantees two-way, server-to-server communication.

Setting up mail routing between two servers within two distinct domains that can establish some form of network connection (otherwise known as adjacent domains) requires you to create Connection documents in the directory of each Domino domain.

Setting up mail routing between servers within two distinct domains that have no possible way of establishing a network connection (otherwise known as nonadjacent domains) requires that you complete two configuration steps. First, you create Connection documents in the Domino directories of the servers within the two domains that are directly connected. You then create Nonadjacent Domain documents for the respective domains that you want to reach via the directly connected Domino servers. Though it is not necessary, you can also create Adjacent Domain documents between the domains that are directly connected to make the mail routing more explicit.

Setting up mail routing between a Domino server and a non-Domino server in a foreign domain, such as a cc:Mail or X.400 domain, requires that you create a Connection document and a Foreign Domain document in the directory of your Domino domain.

If the servers within the participating domains do not share a common hierarchical ancestor, it is necessary to cross-certify your Domino servers within the respective domains, in addition to creating the required Connection documents for the adjacent, nonadjacent, or foreign domains. Such cross-certification establishes a level of trust between the communicating servers and enables servers to authenticate each other.

To exchange cross-certificates, you need to create a safe copy of the ID file to be cross-certified by your peer administrator. Then you need to issue a cross-certificate for the safe copy of the ID file provided to you by your peer administrator. You do both within the Domino Administrator. To create a safe copy of the ID file to be cross-certified, follow these steps:

1. Initialize the Domino Administrator and select the Configuration tab.

2. Expand the Certification section under the Tools pane, and choose ID Properties.

3. Select either the server or the certifier ID file, and click Open. If the certifier requires it, provide the password.

4. Click the Other Actions button under the Your Identity, Your Certificates pages, and select Export Notes ID (Safe Copy). You can then enter the path and name of the safe copy. A safe copy of the ID file is stored in the path specified.

You can now transmit the safe copy of the certifier ID file to your peer administrator via an email with the newly created ID file attached. After you have received a similar safe copy from your peer administrator, you need to add a cross-certificate for the safe copy. To do this, complete the following steps:

1. Initialize the Domino Administrator and select the Configuration tab.

2. Expand the Certification section under the Tools pane, and choose Cross Certify.

3. From the Choose Certifier dialog box, click the Server button and select the appropriate registration server.

4. Click the Certifier ID button and select the certifier ID file for which you want to issue the cross-certificate—for example, the certifier ID for your organization or organizational unit. Click OK and, if necessary, provide its password.

5. Select the safe copy of the certifier ID file provided to you by your peer administrator. Click OK.

6. From within the Issue Cross Certificate dialog box, enter an optional Subject alternative name identifying the certifier ID, the date when the cross-certificate expires, and the name of the server within whose Domino directory you want the cross-certificate to be stored.

7. Click Cross Certify. A cross-certificate is placed in the Server-Certificates view of the Domino directory specified in the previous step.

ROUTING WITHIN THE SAME DOMINO NAMED NETWORK

When routing mail inside the same Domino Named Network, the Notes client determines the recipient's address by a name lookup within the Domino directory. The Mail Router retrieves the location of the recipient's mail file from the address and performs one of two actions:

- It delivers the document to the recipient's mail file, if that mail file resides on the same server as the sender's mail file.

- It transfers the document immediately to the MAIL.BOX on the server, where the recipient's mail file resides. The Mail Router on the recipient's server then delivers the document to the recipient's mail file.

ROUTING BETWEEN DIFFERENT DOMINO NAMED NETWORKS IN THE SAME DOMINO DOMAIN

When routing mail between different Domino Named Networks in the same Domino domain, the Mail Router determines how to route the message by looking at the Connection documents in the Domain's directory. It then performs one of two actions based on routing tables it has built with the information within the given Connection documents:

- It transfers the message to the server that connects to the other Domino-named network if a single direct connection exists between the two servers on the differently named networks.

- It computes the least-cost route to the destination server and transfers the message to the next hop in that route if more than one route exists to the destination server.

ROUTING BETWEEN ADJACENT DOMINO DOMAINS

When routing mail between adjacent Domino domains, the Mail Router looks in the Domino directory for a Connection document connecting a server in the local domain to a server in the remote domain. Upon the next mail routing connection to that remote server, the local server transfers the mail to that remote host. Upon receipt of this mail by the server in the remote domain, the Mail Router on that server retrieves the mail server information for the recipient from the Domino directory and delivers it to that server.

If you are using cascaded directories by storing copies of other domains' directories on your Domino server, or if you are using Directory Assistance to assist directory lookups and mail routing, some of the name and address checking takes place before the mail gets routed to the other Domino domain. If you are not using either of these methods, you can still send mail to other Domino domains by appending the appropriate domain name after the username or group name. The Mail Router transfers the message to the Domino server servicing the connection for that domain. The receiving server, in turn, expands the groups and translates the names.

ROUTING BETWEEN NONADJACENT DOMAINS

When routing mail between nonadjacent Domino domains, the Mail Router determines, via the configured Connection and Domain documents within the Domino directory, that a message addressed to a nonadjacent domain is to be routed through an adjacent domain. This information is stored in the Nonadjacent Domain document, which conveys an adjacent domain as the "route-through" domain. In this way, the Mail Router uses an intermediary, adjacent domain to route mail to the nonadjacent domain.

SETTING UP MAIL ROUTING

To create Connection documents to route mail between two servers in the same Domino domain but in different named networks, or to route mail between two servers in adjacent Domino domains, follow these steps:

1. Initiate the Domino Administrator and click the Configuration tab.

2. Select the Domino directory to which you want to add the Connection. Underneath the Configuration tab, expand the Messaging view and select Connections.

3. In the view, highlight the server to be administered.

4. Click on the Add Connection action button. The Basics tab of the New Server Connection document is presented, as shown in Figure 37.3.

Figure 37.3
The Connection document is used to define replication and mail routing settings.

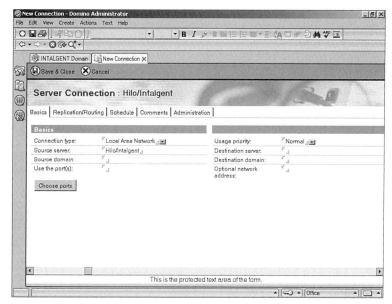

5. Click the Schedule embedded tab and complete the following fields:

   Ensure that Enabled is selected in the Schedule field.

   Enter a range of time—for example, 12:00 AM - 2:00 AM—or specific times—for example, 12:00 AM, 3:00 AM—when you want the source server to connect to the destination server in the Connect at Times field. Separate multiple specific times with a comma.

   If you enter a range of time to connect, you optionally can enter in the Repeat Interval Of field how soon after a successful connection the source server attempts to connect again. The default is 360 minutes.

   Enter the days of the week that you want the source server to connect to the destination server in the Days of Week field. The default is every day of the week.

6. Complete the fields on the Replication/Routing tab:

   Ensure that Mail Routing is selected in the Routing Task field.

   Enter a value to determine the number of pending, normal-priority mail messages that force mail routing to occur in the Route at Once If field.

In the Routing Cost field, specify a value of 1 to 5, with 1 being the least-cost and pre-ferred route. A LAN connection is low in cost; a dialup modem connection is high in cost. Initially, by default, each LAN connection has a cost of 1. Each dialup modem connection has a cost of 5. Domino uses this field to build its routing tables and deter-mine the least-cost route.

Choose a Router type for this particular connection. The type specified in this field depends on your server's topology.

7. Save and close the Connection document.

SETTING UP ROUTING TO NONADJACENT DOMINO DOMAINS

To enable mail routing between Domino domains that are not directly connected, you must identify an intermediary Domino domain serving to connect the two unconnected domains. You accomplish this by creating a Nonadjacent Domain document in each of the uncon-nected domains' directories. You subsequently create the necessary Connection documents to route mail through this middle Domino domain to the nonadjacent domains.

A sample Nonadjacent Domain document is shown in Figure 37.4. It specifies a Domino domain that is connected to both the source and destination Domino domains. This serves as the intermediate or route-through domain to the nonadjacent destination domain.

Figure 37.4
The Nonadjacent Domain document.

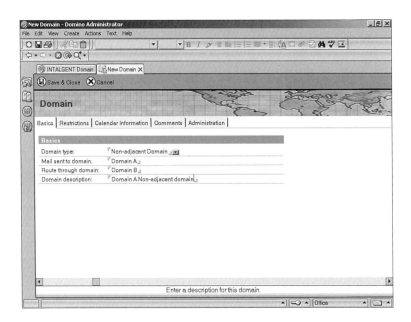

To enable bidirectional mail routing between servers in nonadjacent domains, you create Connection documents for the three participating servers, namely the two unconnected servers and their intermediary. This provides the communication path to and from the non-adjacent domains through the middle, adjacent domain.

For example, if you are trying to connect Server A to Server C through Server B, each with its own domain of A, B, and C, you complete the following configuration documents:

- For Server A/Domain A/Domino Directory A, you create Connection documents to Server B and to Server C. You create a Nonadjacent Domain document for Domain C, specifying Server B's domain. Server B's Domino directory has Connection documents to Server A and Server C, respectively.

- For Server C/Domain C/Domino Directory C, you create Connection documents to Server A and to Server B. You create a Nonadjacent Domain document for Domain A, specifying Server B's domain. In this way, Server A connects to Server B to route mail to Server C.

- Though it is not necessary, you can create Adjacent Domain documents between A and B, between C and B, and between B and both A and C to make the mail-routing path even more explicit.

ALLOWING AND DENYING MAIL ACCESS ACROSS DOMINO DOMAINS

Within the Restrictions tab of the domain documents for a given server, you can allow and deny mail access across Domino domains. As part of restricting communication between Domino domains, you can specify that only certain domains can route mail to this domain. You do this in the Allow Mail Only From Domains field on the Restrictions tab. Similarly, you can enter the names that cannot route mail to this domain in the Deny Mail from Domains field.

RESTRICTING EXPLICIT MAIL ROUTING

You can also use the features to allow and deny mail access to restrict explicit mail routing. Because Adjacent Domain documents are unnecessary to route mail between servers in physically connected domains, you can use an Adjacent Domain document as a mail-routing security feature to prevent users from taking advantage of "explicit routing" to bypass restrictions specified in the Deny Mail from Domains field in a Nonadjacent Domain document.

For example, let's say you are trying to restrict mail from Server A from going any farther than Server B. Additionally, you want Server B to communicate to Servers C and D. Each server is within its own Domain A, B, C, D, respectively. In this example, Domain A is adjacent to Domain B, Domain B is adjacent to Domain C, and Domain C is adjacent to Domain D. Figure 37.5 illustrates the relationships between the Domino Domains.

Complete the following configuration documents. Within the Domino directory on Server B, you create an Adjacent Domain document for Domain C, listing Domain A in the Deny Mail from Domains field on its Restrictions tab. Within the same directory, you create a Nonadjacent Domain document to Domain D listing Domain A in the Deny Mail from Domains field on the Restrictions tab. When a Mail Router in Domain B sees mail destined for Domain C that originated from Domain A, it checks the Adjacent Domain document for

Domain C, and routing is denied. In this way, a user cannot circumvent the interdomain restrictions by specifying explicit routing, such as John Smith @D @C @B.

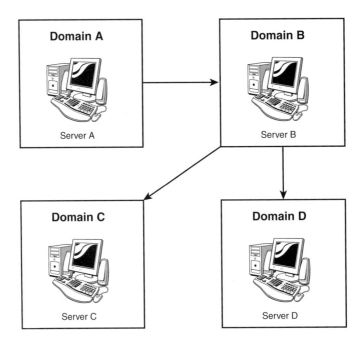

Figure 37.5
Mail routing can be restricted between domains by using nonadjacent Domain documents.

ROUTING MAIL BY PRIORITY LEVEL

The Mail Router routes mail based on its priority level. Users can specify one of three priority levels: high, normal, or low. The priority level determines how rapidly the server processes the message.

- The Mail Router routes high-priority mail immediately.
- It routes normal-priority mail at the next scheduled interval, based on the configuration setting in the server's Connection document. This is the default priority for all Notes mail and Internet-based messages.
- It routes low-priority mail between midnight and 6 a.m. within the same Domino Named Network or between Domino Named Networks by default. It routes low-priority mail at this time even if such mail is pending when it routes high- or normal-priority mail.

You can also completely disable mail priority on a server by setting the MailDisablePriority parameter to 1 in the NOTES.INI configuration settings for the given server. This causes the Mail Router on that server to ignore the delivery priority of mail messages and to treat all messages as normal priority. This does not modify the messages themselves; only their processing by the given server is affected.

FORCING UNSCHEDULED MAIL ROUTING

To force the Mail Router to route all pending mail, regardless of priority, you can specify the route server command. This might be necessary when you encounter problems and need to troubleshoot your messaging environment.

Hierarchically named servers whose names contain spaces must be enclosed in quotation marks (" "). Hence, to route mail immediately to "Server A/Sales/New York/Acme", enter the following command at the server console:

```
route "Server A/Sales/New York/Acme Corporation" .
```

CONFIGURING ALTERNATIVE ROUTE SELECTION

The Domino Mail Router builds internal routing tables from which it derives routing costs to specific destinations. It uses this information to select the optimal, least-cost route for mail messages between source and destination servers.

The Server, Domain, and Connection documents within the Domino directory serve as the basis for the Mail Router's calculations. From these, it builds its internal routing tables. It initially calculates a LAN connection as 1, or low in cost. It calculates a dialup modem connection as 5, or high in cost. During the course of processing, however, when network connections fail or are intermittently interrupted, the Mail Router selects an alternative path, if one is available. At the same time, it maintains a history for the failed connection, re-evaluates the cost of the connection by adding to the connection cost a cost bias, and subsequently reroutes messages to alternative paths where required.

NOTE

> The routing cost is not simply based on the number of hops, but rather a series of parameters. For more information about how routing costs are calculated, refer to the Help topic "Changing the Routing Cost for a Connection" in the Domino Administrator 6 Help.

The Mail Router calculates its routing decision in the following way:

1. Based on the information stored in its internal routing tables, it calculates and selects the route with the least cost.

2. If the selected route fails, the Mail Router adds the cost bias (1) to the cost of the failed route. This increases the total cost of the given route for any subsequent comparisons. The cost bias is never more than 1.

3. Upon subsequent comparisons, the Mail Router selects an alternative path, if there is one that is equal in cost with fewer hops or one that is simply less in cost.

4. The cost bias for a given path is reset under three circumstances: when the server receives an inbound connection from the failed server, when the dynamic cost reset interval occurs, or when the Mail Router is reinitialized.

NOTE

> The dynamic cost reset interval is the number of minutes after which the router will reset the costs tied to its connections.

The Mail Router stores the internal routing information in memory-resident tables. It rebuilds its list of routes and cost biases when the server is restarted or when the Connection, Server, or Domain documents are modified within the Domino Directory.

CONNECTING DOMINO SERVERS WITH FOREIGN DOMAINS

The Domino messaging server communicates and exchanges mail with external, non-Notes mail systems, via either gateways or *message transfer agents* (MTAs). Gateways consist of encoding and decoding processes that translate the messages to and from native Notes or Internet messaging format before transferring them to their respective host servers. MTAs can perform the role of a gateway as well as of a native mail server. In this way, MTAs can both translate messages before message transfer or send them natively in Notes and Internet format.

To enable the exchange of mail between Domino and non-Notes mail systems, you must install and configure the necessary gateway or MTA software and create a Foreign Domain document for the non-Notes mail system with which you want to exchange mail. Domino perceives the non-Notes mail system as a group of computers in a foreign domain.

DEFINING A FOREIGN DOMAIN WITHIN THE DOMINO DIRECTORY

To define a foreign domain within the Domino directory, follow these steps:

1. Initiate the Domino Administrator and click the Configuration Tab.
2. Select the Domino directory to which you want to add the Foreign Domain document. Under the Configuration tab, expand the Messaging view and select Domains.
3. Click the Add Domain action button.
4. On the Basics tab, in the Domain Type field, select Foreign Domain.
5. In the Foreign Domain Name field, enter the domain name of the foreign mail system. This name was chosen when the gateway or MTA was installed.
6. On the Restrictions tab, in the Allow Mail Only from Domains field, you can specify that only certain domains can route mail to this foreign domain. In the Deny Mail from Domains field, you can restrict use of this domain by naming specific domains that cannot route mail to this foreign domain.
7. On the Mail Information tab, in the Gateway Server Name field, enter the name of the Domino server where the gateway resides. In the Gateway Mail File Name field, enter the gateway's mail filename. You should be able to obtain this from the documentation that came with the gateway.
8. Save and close the Domain document.

CONNECTING DOMINO TO AN X.400 SYSTEM The Lotus Notes X.400 MTA is an MTA-facilitating mail exchange between Domino servers and Notes workstations with X.400 systems. To establish connectivity to the X.400 network, you need to install and configure the X.400 MTA software. The configuration process includes creating an X.400 Foreign Domain document, an X.400 Server document, and a Connection document between the Domino server and the X.400 MTA.

NOTE

If some users are still using an X.400 messaging service, you must have at least one server running the X.400 MTA under Release 4 of Domino.

37

DISABLING MAIL ROUTING

Mail routing can be disabled either temporarily or permanently. To disable it temporarily, enter the commands `Tell Router Quit` or `Tell Router Exit` at the console. To disable it permanently, remove the Router task from the list of tasks on the `ServerTasks` setting within the `NOTES.INI` file.

TOOLS FOR MONITORING MAIL ROUTING

Because the messaging infrastructure is vital to an organization's success, you must monitor its functioning constantly. Domino includes a number of tools to monitor mail routing. The most important of these include the following:

- **Mailbox**—A MAIL.BOX database is located in the Domino data directory on every server. It holds pending mail and dead mail documents. Pending mail is mail awaiting delivery to other users or servers. Upon failure to deliver mail, Domino attempts to send a Delivery Failure Report to the sender of the message detailing why it failed to be delivered. Similar information is recorded in the log (LOG.NSF). If Domino is unsuccessful in sending the Delivery Failure Report, it stores a report as a dead mail document. You should periodically check the MAIL.BOX for pending mail or dead mail documents.

- **Log file**—The Domino log (LOG.NSF) also stores valuable monitoring and troubleshooting information. Domino records mail-routing problems in the Mail Routing Events, Miscellaneous Events, and Phone Calls view of the log. The Mail Routing Events view shows information about specific events, whereas the Miscellaneous Events view shows high-level routing information.

- **Reporter or Collector task**—By running the Reporter and Statistics Collector tasks, you can generate a variety of mail statistics in the statistics-reporting database (STA-TREP.NSF). You can complement this by configuring the generation of alarms when specified thresholds are exceeded.

- **Event task**—By running the Event task and configuring Event Monitor documents, you can report potentially problematical mail events. An example is to create an Event Monitor document for mail messages that are classified as Fatal, Failure, and Warning.

See Chapter 41, "Troubleshooting and Monitoring Domino," for further information regarding the `Reporter`, `Collector`, and `Event` tasks.

- **`Tell server` command**—The `Tell server` command enables you to issue a set of commands to a specific Domino server task—in this case, the Mail Router. For example, you can tell the Mail Router to show statistics, compact the mailbox file, and shut down.

- **The Domino Administrator Messaging tab**—Within this tab, you can monitor mail routing status, mail routing events, and mail routing topology, as well as send a test message for tracking and troubleshooting purposes. Figure 37.6 shows the New Tracking Request dialog box used to analyze message tracing across Domino servers and domains.

Figure 37.6
The New Tracking Request dialog box is used to analyze message tracing across Domino servers and domains.

ADMINISTERING SHARED MAIL

Within the Domino messaging server, the Mail Router stores a copy of the same document in each personal mail file if the document is sent to groups of users. This can eventually lead to storage problems as mail databases expand. To overcome this problem, Domino enables the system administrator to set up shared mail using a single-copy object store (SCOS), which is a specialized database that holds nonsummary data (the body of a mail memo and any file attachments) for all messages received by more than one user.

When the router receives a message addressed to more than one user on the same server, the message header—containing the To, From, Cc, Bcc, and Subject fields—is placed in each user's mail file, along with a pointer to the object store. The body of the message is saved just once in the object store. When the user opens the memo from the desktop, Domino displays the header from the mail file and the nonsummary data from the object store as a single message. The user is not even aware that the two parts of the document are stored in different places.

If a user subsequently edits a message, Domino places the entire message in the user's mail database and deletes any pointers to the original message. Domino also places the entire message in the user's mail database if the user encrypts incoming mail or makes a local replica of the mail database.

Domino keeps track of how many users still have a header pointing to a particular object in the object store. When all users have deleted the message from their mail databases—namely, the header for a particular memo—there is no need to keep the nonsummary portion of the memo. A server task, Collect, runs automatically at 2 a.m., by default. This task deletes unused messages in the object store, deletes all links, and compacts the database to reclaim the unused space.

SETTING UP SHARED MAIL

To set up Shared Mail, follow these steps:

1. Initiate the Domino Administrator and connect to the desired server.
2. Click the Configuration tab and select the Current Server document.
3. Put the document in Edit mode by clicking the Edit Server action button.
4. Click the Shared Mail tab, and choose either Delivery or Transfer and Delivery in the Shared Mail field. The Transfer and Delivery option uses shared mail for all messages, regardless of whether the message was sent to multiple users.
5. For each shared mail directory, complete the Directory, Number of Files, Maximum Directory Size, Delivery Status, and Availability fields. The Directory field requires the full path to the shared mail directory. Domino creates the directory for you if it doesn't exist. For more information about each of these fields, refer to Lotus's shared mail documentation within the Domino administrator.

NOTE

Shared mail does have some limitations with shared mail directories and support for mail databases. With Release 6, each shared mail directory can support up to 100 shared mail databases, with each server supporting up to 10 mail directories.

6. Save and close the modified Server document.
7. From the server console, run Show SCOS to enable Shared Mail.

MOVING AND UNLINKING USER MAIL FILES

If you make a file copy of a user's mail database and place it on another server, the Mail Router can no longer resolve links to the shared mail object store. Each mail file looks only at the object store on the home server, the server on which the mail file is stored. All the user sees in a copy of the database is the summary data in the header of his or her mail messages.

The problem of moving a mail file is compounded if you delete the user's mail file from the original server. This is because deleting a mail file without unlinking it makes it so that the object store database cannot be purged of the documents the user left behind.

To move a user's mail to another server if that user is using shared mail, follow these steps:

1. Replicate (make a replica copy of) the user's mail database on the new server.
2. On the new server, issue the console command Load Object Link USERMAIL.NSF NEWSHARED.NSF, where NEWSHARED.NSF is the name of the object store on the new server.
3. On the original server, issue the console command Load Object Unlink USERMAIL.NSF to delete pointers from the common object store to the user's mail database.
4. Delete the user's mail database from the original server.

COLLECTING GARBAGE FROM THE OBJECT STORE DATABASE

The Collect server task, which, by default, runs at 2 a.m., purges unlinked messages from the object store. If users have deleted headers from their mail databases, the common object store keeps track of how many other users are linked to the message. When there are no links remaining, the message is purged. If you want to compact the database after obsolete messages have been purged, you have to use the -COMPACT option with Collect.

USING SHARED MAIL WITH MOBILE USERS

The shared mail database works only on a per-server basis for mail databases that are stored on that server. Mobile users can still use shared mail, but only when they are accessing their mail directly from their home server.

If mobile users have a replica of their mail on their mobile or remote workstation, the entire message (summary information and the body) is replicated to them, exactly as it was with earlier versions of Notes and Domino. If messages were copied from the server-based mail instead of being replicated, users would receive only summary information and the pointers to the body of the messages would no longer function.

MANAGING A SHARED MAIL DATABASE

To manage a shared mail database, follow these steps:

- Purge obsolete messages from a shared-mail database to keep the size of the shared mail database small
- Back up and restore shared mail to reduce the amount of shared mail that would be lost if the shared-mail database is corrupted or destroyed
- Delete a shared-mail database when it is no longer in use
- View shared-mail statistics at the server console

ADMINISTERING THE DOMINO POP3 SERVER

POP3 is an Internet mail protocol. It facilitates the retrieval of mail by such POP3 clients as Qualcomm Eudora and Outlook Express from host systems also running POP3 servers. You set up a Domino server to be a POP3 host server by running the POP3 server task.

As with other server tasks, you can start the POP3 messaging server at the console by typing `Load POP3` or by adding it to the `ServersTasks` line in the notes.ini file. You can stop the POP3 server temporarily by issuing the console command `Tell POP3 quit` or by permanently removing it from the `ServerTasks` setting.

37

UNDERSTANDING DOMINO POP3 SERVER REQUIREMENTS

No special software or hardware requirements exist for the Domino POP3 server. Because POP3 is an Internet application protocol, however, the Domino POP3 server does require that you configure TCP/IP. Furthermore, because POP3 is an Internet message-retrieval protocol only, you must also configure mail routing by creating the necessary Connection and Domain documents in the Domino directory. This enables the Domino mail server to transfer both incoming and outgoing mail from POP3 clients to other Internet host servers, as well as to serve up mail to POP3 clients via the POP3 server task.

EXAMPLE INTERNET CLIENT CONFIGURATION

To enable such supported POP3 clients as Qualcomm Eudora or Outlook Express, you must provide varying configuration information. For example, for the Microsoft Internet Explorer, as part of the Outlook Express configuration, you must provide the following information:

- Outgoing Mail (SMTP) server name, consisting of the Internet domain name of the Domino server hosting Internet mail
- Incoming Mail (POP) server name, consisting of the Internet domain name of the Domino server running the POP3 server task
- Account name, consisting of the Internet address within the given individual's Person document in the Domino directory
- Password, consisting of the Internet password within the given individual's Person document in the Domino directory

Figure 37.7 shows an example configuration using Outlook Express as Microsoft Internet Explorer's Internet mailer.

Figure 37.7
A sample server configuration screen within Microsoft's Outlook Express.

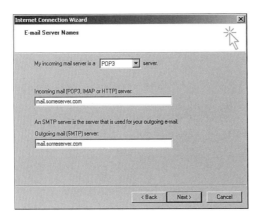

37

ADMINISTERING THE DOMINO IMAP SERVER

IMAP is also an Internet mail protocol. IMAP-enabled clients can manipulate mail in different modes. They can retrieve messages from the IMAP message server and store them locally, much like POP3. They can also access messages directly from the server or copy messages for offline use. You set up a Domino server to be an IMAP host server by running the IMAP server task.

As with other server tasks, you can start the IMAP messaging server at the console by typing **Load IMAP** or by adding it to the ServersTasks line in the notes.ini file. You can stop the IMAP server by issuing the console command Tell IMAP quit or by removing it from the ServerTasks setting.

As with all IMAP servers, the Domino IMAP server enables IMAP clients to access their messages. It is not involved in the message-transfer activities of the messaging server. These functions are handled by the Domino messaging server itself and require the standard Connection and Domain documents for mail routing in the Domino directory.

UNDERSTANDING DOMINO IMAP SERVER REQUIREMENTS

No special software or hardware requirements exist for the Domino IMAP server. Because IMAP is an Internet application protocol, however, the Domino IMAP server does require that you configure TCP/IP. Furthermore, because IMAP is an Internet message store-and-retrieval protocol only, you must also configure mail routing by creating the necessary Connection and Domain documents in the Domino directory. This enables the Domino mail server to transfer both incoming and outgoing mail from POP3 clients to other Internet host servers, as well as to serve up mail to POP3 clients via the POP3 server task.

CHAPTER **38**

REPLICATION AND ITS ADMINISTRATION

In this chapter

UNDERSTANDING REPLICATION

Replication is the process of synchronizing two databases that share a common database identifier. Replication can be automated or manually initiated by the administrator. Replication can also take place between a workstation and a server, either as an event scheduled on the workstation or as an event initiated by the user from a workstation. The Domino server cannot initiate replication with a workstation, and workstations cannot replicate directly with each other (peer-to-peer).

Within Domino, synchronization takes place at the field level. After the initial replication, when a replica copy of a database is first made, subsequent replication has to synchronize information only in fields in which data has been added or modified since the last successful replication. This makes replication between two databases quicker than if you just blindly copied the entire database over again.

Prior to delving into the specifics of replication administration, the next several paragraphs examine, in general terms, the following issues:

- The functionality of the replica task, including what it processes
- The fundamental role played by access control in the replication process
- The administrative tools available within Lotus Domino to assist in the management of the replication process

INTRODUCING THE Replica TASK

In Domino, Replica is the name of a task that runs on the server to perform replication between Domino servers. It is referred to as the Replica task in the NOTES.INI and the Replica or Replicator task within the Domino server console environment. When the server starts, an instance of Replica also starts, and it remains idle until there is a scheduled replication or a replication is initiated from the server console or the Notes workspace. As soon as a replication is initiated, Replica wakes up and begins a replication cycle.

UNDERSTANDING SERVER-TO-SERVER REPLICATION

In server-to-server replication, the initiator—for example, Server A—can connect and initiate a replication with a responder—for example, Server B. Such a replication can take place between servers in adjacent rooms, in different districts of the city, in different states, or in different parts of the world.

The first server, Server A, can do any of the following through the configuration of a Connection document:

- **Pull-Pull replication**—Server A pulls changes from Server B and then tells Server B's replicator to pull changes from Server A. The two processes can take place simultaneously.
- **Pull-Push replication**—Server A can pull changes from Server B and then push changes back to Server B. In this case, only Server A's replicator is involved in the

process, and it writes information in the replica databases on both servers. All the burden is on Server A, which can be a specialized server that does nothing but replicate, so other servers in the organization can more efficiently support other Domino functions. Pull-Push replication is the default configuration between Domino servers.

■ **Push-Only replication**—Server A pushes changes to Server B. Changes are not pulled or pushed back to Server A from Server B. This scenario is ideal for a server topology, in which all changes are made centrally and are then replicated to the distributed remote servers.

■ **Pull-Only replication**—Server A pulls changes from Server B. No changes are pulled by Server B or pushed by Server A back to Server B. This scheme enables the distributed remote servers to do all the work, and the central server is free to perform other tasks.

UNDERSTANDING WORKSTATION-TO-SERVER REPLICATION

In workstation-to-server replication, the replication process achieves the same results as in server-to-server replication, with one vital difference. The replicator on the server remains passive in workstation-to-server replication. Replication is initiated by the workstation, although the workstation has no `Replica` task. The workstation does all the work, synchronizing changes from databases on the Domino server and sending changes back to the server.

DEFINING THE OBJECTS OF REPLICATION

Practically every element in Domino can be thought of as a container for an increasingly smaller object. The Domino kernel is the back end or core of the Domino system. The Notes user interface is the outermost container. Within the client interface, applications are realized in the forms of databases.

Within each database are many objects, but not necessarily just the user-created documents. There are other objects whose framework is hidden from the users, but these are elements that are nonetheless vital to the database. These include the Access Control List (ACL), replication settings, and definitions for other database properties and design elements—including forms, subforms, views, folders, tables, action buttons, pages, framesets, outlines, navigators, and agents, each of which is a specialized object. Within these objects, there is another level of properties, fields, and actions. And, of course, within this framework, there are documents, defined as a related collection of data that fits into the fields on a form and the properties of that data.

It would take too much time to copy all this information every time replication occurs, so the replicator is very selective in the information it pulls from another database. Here is what happens when replication occurs between two Domino servers using Pull-Push replication:

1. After one server calls the other to replicate, the two servers compare replica IDs on all databases to determine which ones they have in common (including database templates

or database design copies, which are specialized databases containing the database design elements for the given application).

2. Databases are replicated in numerical, and then alphabetical, order. The exception to this is the Domino Directory, which is replicated before all the other databases are considered. The Domino Directory is the first to be replicated, because changes in it can affect what is replicated or even whether replication can take place during subsequent scheduled events. If, for example, the server-access fields or Connection documents were changed to deny or disable replication between servers, subsequent replication between servers would be disallowed.

3. For each database, design changes and database properties are pulled, including the Access Control List, from the database on the other server. The ACL is actually a design document and is the first document pulled. If the ACL has changed on the other end, it can determine which documents can be pulled.

4. The replicator looks at the date and time of the last successful replication with this database, held in the Replication History window, which can be displayed from the Basics tab of the Database Properties dialog box. This history is used to determine what has changed, and therefore what should be replicated during the next replication event. An example of the Replication History dialog box is shown in Figure 38.1. It compares this date to the document-creation date for each document in the source database (the one being pulled from). If the document was created after the last successful replication, it will be pulled. If the database's replication history is cleared, Domino no longer has a record of when replication occurred last. Hence, on a subsequent replication cycle, Domino replicates all documents modified after the database's cutoff date, rather than replicating only what has changed since the last replication. The cutoff date is specified in the Only Replicate Incoming Documents Saved or Modified After box on the Other panel of the Replication Settings dialog box. If no cutoff date is specified, Domino replicates all documents.

NOTE

> You need Reader-or-higher access in the database ACL to display the replication history. You'll need Manager access to clear it.

5. If the document in the source database has been modified since the last successful replication, there are several options related to field-level replication:

   - Each field in the document has a sequence number. If the field was modified since the last replication, its sequence number is incremented by 1. Domino compares the sequence number of each field in the source document with the sequence number in the same field in the target document. If a source field has a higher sequence number than the same field in the target document, the contents of the field are pulled by the replicator and merged into the target document.

   - If the sequence numbers in a field in both databases are the same, the contents of the field are ignored.

- If the field has been modified in both the source and target databases, the source document is pulled in as the main document, and the document from the target database is saved in what is termed a *replication conflict*. Both versions of the document are then available.

Figure 38.1
The replication history for a database, listing the last time replications occurred between Domino servers and workstations.

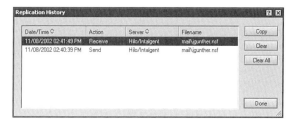

6. The application developer can have Domino attempt to merge documents even if a potential conflict arises. This is done on a form-by-form basis. By selecting one of the versioning options (new versions become responses, prior versions become responses, or new versions become siblings) on the first tab of the Form Properties dialog box, the application developer can have Domino automatically generate new documents when a document is edited. By selecting the Merge Conflicts option within the Conflict Handling group on the first tab of the Form Properties dialog box, the application developer can have Domino reduce the number of replication conflicts by automatically merging several conflict documents into one.

ESTABLISHING THE DESIRED ACCESS CONTROL FOR REPLICATION

As with everything in Domino, the proper access control is a prerequisite for proper functioning. Most people familiar with Domino are aware of how the ACL affects what a user can do in a database. Anyone with at least Reader access can read documents in a database. Users with Author access or higher can create documents and can edit documents they have created. Editors or higher can modify any document in the database. Designers can make design changes to the database, and only Managers can make changes to the ACL. These settings are generally true, but some options can be set; for example, in some instances, by creating a Readers field on the form, Reader access to all documents created from that form can be restricted. Additionally, persons, servers, or groups listed with Author-level access to a database can be explicitly listed in an Author Names field on a form within the database, and thereby can edit documents created from that form.

Database access levels for servers are the same as for users, except that the access level assigned to a server in a replica's ACL controls which, if any, changes that server can replicate to the replica.

The server can be considered an agent for the user. An agent goes out and retrieves data, creates documents, and modifies documents created by the user. Basically, the server can do anything the user can do, depending on how the ACL is set up.

From a server perspective, this means that if you want Server A to replicate with Server B, you must grant Server A access to Server B. If, for example, the ACL on Server A lists Server B as a Reader, Server B can read documents (in other words, can pull documents or accept documents that are pushed by Server A), but it cannot send any new documents or modifications to Server A.

If Server B is an Author in Server A's ACL, Server B can send new documents to Server A, and it can send modifications to documents that were originally created on Server B.

If an administrator on Server B wants to make changes to the ACL on a database that is being replicated to Server A, Server B must be listed as a Manager in the ACL of that database.

As such, Domino servers can have the same access that people do. If you want someone to act as a courier and deliver a message to someone you trust, you have to trust the courier as well. If the courier cannot be trusted to carry the message, the person on the other end will not receive the message. Likewise, if a Domino server does not have sufficient access privileges, the local Database Manager cannot receive messages.

As a rule of thumb, always list internal servers (servers in a group known as `LocalDomainServers`, included by default in all database ACLs) as Managers in the ACL, and you will have no problems. If replication is scheduled serially—from Server A to Server B and then from Server B to Server C—Server C is limited by what Server B can do on Server A. Therefore, try to give all intermediary servers Manager access unless there is an overriding reason not to. And with external servers (servers in a group known as `OtherDomainServers`, included by default in all database ACLs), you can limit their access using the ACL, if there is a reason to give them access to your servers.

To illustrate the various access levels for server access, review each access control level:

- **Manager Access**—All documents, design elements, database encryption settings, Access Control List settings, and replication settings are pushed from the server. This is the highest level of access that a server can have.
- **Designer Access**—All documents and design elements are pushed from the server.
- **Editor Access**—All new documents are pushed from the server. Typically, this level is not used for servers.
- **Reader Access**—No changes are pushed. The server can only pull changes.
- **Depositor Access**—All new documents are pushed. The server cannot pull any changes.
- **No Access**—No changes are synchronized.

INTRODUCING REPLICATION ADMINISTRATION TOOLS

As with all administrative tasks within Lotus Domino, the Domino Administrator serves as the focal point for replication administration. Although much of the actual configuration is accomplished through documents accessible by alternative means, the Domino

Administrator serves as the central control point from which all administrative actions can be initiated. As such, the Domino Administrator's Configuration, Server, and Replication tabs facilitate the configuration and administration of replication:

- The Configuration tab facilitates the modification of replication settings contained in Configuration and Connection documents.
- The Server tab facilitates the starting, stopping, and restarting of the Replicator task.
- The Replication tab itself assists in monitoring replication schedules, replication topology, and replication events.

CREATING DATABASE REPLICAS

Databases cannot replicate until you have created a replica of the database. This task must be done only once; however, it must be done before you replicate for the first time. After the replica database has been created, keeping replica copies of the database synchronized is usually a matter of deciding what is to be replicated and defining the replication schedule.

Being replicas of each other does not mean that the two databases are identical. It means that the two databases have the same replica ID. Every database has a replica ID made up of two eight-character strings separated by a colon. If the replica IDs for two databases match exactly, they are replicas of each other. Replica databases can be given different filenames, they can have different icons, and one can have only a subset of documents of the other, but they are still replicas as long as their replica IDs are identical. On the other hand, just because two databases have the same name and the same icon on different servers, it does not necessarily mean that they are replicas of each other.

Replica databases can be created in any of the following instances:

- One database is created using the command File, Replication, New Replica, and the other database is selected on the desktop.
- Both databases are copied from the same install disk (or at least from two install disks that have identical files on them) during setup.
- One of the two databases is created by copying the other at the operating-system level, or both are copied from a common ancestor database at the operating-system level.
- A new replica of the Domino Directory is created automatically when an additional server or workstation is set up on the network.

Unlike replicas, copies of databases can be created by selecting File, Database, New Copy from the pull-down menu. In so doing, the newly created database is not a replica. It has a different replica ID from the original database and cannot replicate with the original.

You can tell whether two databases are replicas of each other in two ways. The first way is to look at their replica IDs. The replica ID is found on the Information tab of the Database Properties dialog box, and in the database catalog (CATALOG.NSF) on a Domino server.

38

The other way to tell whether two databases are replicas is to place them both within a bookmark folder and open the bookmark folder as a Workspace. If the icons are stacked on top of each other (a small drop-down arrow will be displayed in the lower-right corner of the top icon), they are replicas of each other.

After the replica database has been created, keeping replica copies of the database synchronized is usually a matter of deciding how often to replicate, and establishing a schedule so that the replication occurs automatically.

ENABLING SELECTIVE REPLICATION OF DATABASE COMPONENTS

By default, two replicas exchange all edits, additions, and deletions if the servers the replicas are on have the necessary access. However, you can customize replication—for example, to save disk space—by preventing the transfer of documents that are not pertinent to your site.

There is a lot of flexibility in determining which parts of a database are replicated and which aren't. For example, you can replicate selected documents or parts of documents. You can select the documents by formula, by view or category, or by date. You can replicate specific design elements.

All these selections are made from a single Replication Settings dialog box, displayed by selecting the database in the Files tab of the Domino Administrator and selecting File, Replication, Settings. The Space Savers page of the dialog box appears, as shown in Figure 38.2.

Figure 38.2
The Space Savers page of the Replication Settings dialog box.

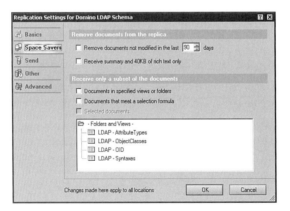

All the selections on this page can be used to save space in the local replica of the selected database. The selections include the following:

- **Remove Documents Not Modified in the Last n Days**—If you select this option, replication completely removes a document from the local replica if it was not modified in the number of days specified. This gets rid of older documents. As long as the documents still exist in another replica copy of the database, you can later change this setting and get the old documents back from the other replica.

- **Documents in Specified Views or Folders**—If you select this option, you can click a view or folder, and only the documents in that view or folder will be replicated.

- **Documents That Meet a Selection Formula**—You can select by formula only if you didn't select the Documents in Specified Views or Folders option. A formula screen appears with the default `SELECT @All` formula. You can enter a variety of formulas in this screen. Some examples include:

  - `SELECT Author = @UserName`, where `@UserName` returns the name of the current user.

  - `SELECT Form = "formname"`, where `formname` is the name of any form in the database.

  - You can also create formulas to select documents based on the content of any field, as long as the field is not computed for a display field or a rich-text field.

On the Send tab of the Replication Settings dialog box, you can specify what not to send from your local replica to the replica on the server. There are three options available on this page.

- First, you can elect not to send deletions made in this replica to other replicas. You can then safely delete documents locally and not worry about the deletions being copied to other replicas throughout your organization.

- Second, you can elect not to send changes in database title and catalog information to other replicas of the database. You can then change the title of your own local database or database catalog settings without affecting other replicas of the same database.

- Third, and finally, you can elect not to send changes in local security to other replicas. You can then safely make changes to the local-access control without affecting other replicas of the same database. This is important if you want to enforce local security, but you do not want to replicate your ACL changes to the server-based copy of the database.

On the Other tab of the Replication Settings, you can temporarily disable replication of this copy of the database, set the replication priority, filter incoming documents based on their modification date, and set a CD-ROM publication date.

- The Temporarily Disable Replication for this Replica field enables you to disable replication for this replica. For example, you might be making design changes on a replica sitting on one server, and you want to ensure that the changes are not replicated to replicas on other servers until your design changes have been thoroughly tested.

- The Set Scheduled Replication Priority for this field enables you to determine the replication priority of the database. Different replication schedules can be set up for

38

databases, based on their priorities. For example, you might want to replicate a high-priority database every two hours, but replicate low-priority databases only once a week.

■ The Only Replicate Incoming Documents Saved or Modified field enables you to establish a cutoff date and receive documents that were created or modified only after the cutoff date.

■ The CD-ROM Publishing Date field enables you to specify the publication date if you publish the database to a CD-ROM. The database can then be published on that date. Users can make a copy of the database from the CD, and then they have to replicate only documents created or modified since that date.

The Advanced tab enables a system administrator to create selective replication settings for other servers from a central location. The Advanced page is used to administer replication settings from a central location.

On this page of the Replication Settings dialog box, the administrator can specify selective replication settings between any two Domino servers in the domain, or specify the server from which the local server should receive documents.

You can also specify which database elements can be received from other databases during replication, including whether to accept incoming deletions from other databases.

SPECIFYING REPLICATION SETTINGS

You can specify replication settings at various points in the administrative cycle. You specify them when you create a replica. You can specify them following the creation, if you have Manager access in the ACL of the replica. You can also specify some replication settings for multiple replicas at once from a central source replica.

SPECIFYING REPLICATION SETTINGS FROM A CENTRAL SOURCE REPLICA

You can specify replication settings for multiple replicas of a database from one source replica and then replicate these custom settings to the appropriate replicas. To accomplish this, first ensure that you have Manager access in the ACL of the central source replica and that the central source replica has Manager access in the ACL of all destination replicas.

If you are creating the replica, click Replication Settings in the New Replica dialog box to specify replication settings for a new source replica. If you are modifying replication settings in an existing replica, select the source replica, and then choose File, Replication, Settings.

From this point, click the Advanced panel and follow the procedures as outlined previously in the section "Enabling Selective Replication of Database Components."

SETTING UP AND INITIATING REPLICATION

In order to establish the necessary infrastructure for replication, you need to define the desired underlying system topology, define connections between your servers, and set the replication schedule.

SCHEDULING REPLICATION BASED ON SYSTEM TOPOLOGY

Your server topology determines to a large extent your replication schedule and setup. There are four common replication strategies:

- With a hub-and-spoke topology, a central hub server communicates with disparate distributed spoke servers. Replication is scheduled and initiated between the hub and individual spokes.

- With an end-to-end topology, two or more servers are connected end-to-end to form a chain. The replication scheduling is similarly configured between servers.

- With a ring topology, three or more servers are connected to form a closed loop. Again, the replication schedule corresponds to the underlying connections established.

- With a mesh topology, each server possesses Connection documents for all other servers in the domain.

The most common of these topologies is that of hub-and-spoke. In a hub-and-spoke topology, either the hub or spoke server initiates replication with the other.

The hub server performs the role of control center. It monitors server resources and guarantees that replications occur with each spoke. In short, it ensures that all changes are replicated to its distributed servers.

CONNECTING SERVERS FOR REPLICATION

You create a Connection document in the Domino Directory to connect servers for replication. The Connection document details the specifics regarding the information exchange. Based on your underlying network infrastructure connecting your servers, you can establish a connection for servers over a Local Area Network (LAN), over the Internet, over an intermittently connected serial line, such as a dialup modem or remote LAN service, or through a passthru server.

As with mail routing, in order for replication to occur successfully, your Domino server must either be in the same Domino organizational hierarchy as the Domino server with which it wants to replicate or share a common certificate. A common certificate establishes a level of trust between the communicating servers and enables servers to authenticate with each other. If this is not the case, you need to cross-certify the servers so that they can then, in turn, authenticate with each other. The steps to accomplish this are detailed for mail routing between servers in Chapter 37, "Administering Electronic Mail."

CREATING A CONNECTION DOCUMENT FOR REPLICATION

You create one Connection document to connect each pair of servers for replication. An example of a Connection document is shown in Figure 38.3.

Figure 38.3
The Basics tab of the Server Connection document used for scheduling replication.

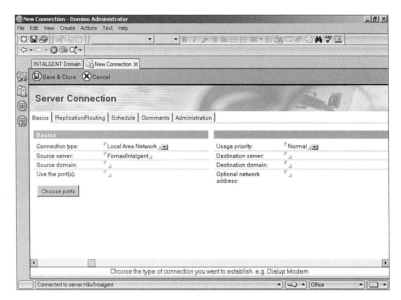

To create a Connection document to enable replication between two Domino servers, complete the following steps:

1. Start the Domino Administrator and select the appropriate Domino Directory.

2. Click the Configuration tab and highlight the Connections view under Replication.

3. Click the Add Connection action button. A Server Connection document consisting of five tabs is displayed.

4. On the Basics tab of the Server Connection document, in the Connection Type field, select the type of network connection to be used—for example, Local Area Network, Notes Direct Dialup, Passthru Server, Network Dialup, X.25, SMTP, X.400, cc:Mail, SNA, Hunt Group, or Sametime.

5. Complete the source server/domain and destination server/domain information.

6. Optionally, select the Usage priority. For example, select Normal to force the server to use the network information in this document to make the connection.

7. Select the Choose Ports button and select the port obtained from the server record to be used for this connection.

8. On the Replication/Routing tab, ensure that None is selected for the Routing task and that the Replication task is enabled.

9. Optionally, select High, Medium and High, or Low and Medium and High in the Replicate Databases of Priority field. The default is Low and Medium and High.

10. Optionally, select Pull-Pull, Pull-Push, Pull-Only, or Push-Only in the Replication Type field. The default is Pull-Push.

11. Optionally, specify to replicate only certain databases or directories of databases in the Files/Directories to Replicate field.

12. Optionally, enter a time limit for the replication in the Replication Time Limit field.

13. On the Schedule tab, ensure that the Schedule is Enabled.

   In the Call at Times field, specify a specific hour, such as 8:00 a.m., a set of hours, or a range of hours—for example, 10:00 a.m.–6:00 p.m.

   In the Repeat Interval field, specify how often to repeat the call.

   In the Days of Week field, specify on which days the replication should occur.

14. On the Comments tab, enter any relevant comments pertaining to the configured replication.

15. Click the Save & Close action button.

The following sections help flesh out the different options that are presented in the preceding procedure, especially the scheduling and replication tabs.

SCHEDULING TIMES FOR REPLICATION

As briefly noted while enumerating the steps required to create a Connection document, you can schedule replication between servers to occur at one specific time, for a set of times, or during a time range with a repeat interval.

SCHEDULING REPLICATION FOR ONE SPECIFIC TIME

You can schedule replication for a specific time when addressing one of the following situations:

- You are scheduling replication of low-priority databases.
- You believe daily updates of databases are sufficient.
- You are relatively confident that calls being made will be successful after just a few retries.

To schedule replication for a specific time, enter the desired time in the Connect at Times field in the Connection document. Enter 0 for the repeat interval. The Repeat Interval field is applicable only when a time range is specified. Based on this setting, the server calls at the specific time. If unsuccessful, it retries for an hour. Following the course of an hour, the next call does not occur until the specific time on the next day, regardless of whether replication was successfully completed.

SCHEDULING REPLICATION FOR A SET OF TIMES

You can schedule replication for a set of times when addressing one of the following situations:

- You are scheduling replication of medium-to-low–priority databases.
- You believe that a few daily updates of databases are sufficient.
- You are relatively confident that calls being made will be successful after just a few retries.

To schedule replication for a set of times, enter the desired set of specific times in the Connect at Times field, separating the individual times by commas in the Connection document. Enter **0** for the repeat interval. The Repeat Interval field is applicable only when a time range is specified. Based on the settings given, the server calls at the first time specified. If unsuccessful, the server continues to retry for up to an hour. Regardless of whether the call succeeds, the server initiates the next call at the next scheduled time. This continues through the set of times provided.

SCHEDULING REPLICATION FOR A TIME RANGE WITH A REPEAT INTERVAL

You can schedule replication for a time range both with and without a repeat interval. To schedule replication with a repeat interval, enter a time range in the Connect at Times field and enter a number of minutes in the Repeat Interval field in the Connection document. If unsuccessful upon the initial attempt, the server retries periodically until it successfully establishes a connection and replicates or it reaches the end of the time range specified. If the server successfully replicates, it calls again, following the number of minutes specified in the repeat interval.

For example, let's assume that you accept the default replication time setting between Server A and Server B. This setting schedules Server A to call Server B from 8 a.m. to 10 p.m. with a repeat interval of 360 minutes. If Server A calls and replicates successfully with Server B at 8:30 a.m., Server A does not place the next call until 2:30 p.m. that afternoon. If the replication is unsuccessful, however, it continues to connect and replicate periodically until the end of the time range specified.

SCHEDULING REPLICATION FOR A TIME RANGE WITHOUT A REPEAT INTERVAL

You can schedule replication for a time range without a repeat interval when addressing one of the following situations:

- You are scheduling replication of medium-to-low–priority databases.
- You believe daily updates of databases are sufficient.
- You know that a long retry period is necessary.

To schedule replication for a time range without a repeat interval, enter a time range in the Connect at Times field in the Connection document. Enter **0** for the repeat interval. Based on this setting, the server attempts the first call at the start of the time range. If unsuccessful, the server tries again for the entire call range, with the time between each unsuccessful call attempt increasing. Following a successful exchange of information, the server ceases the calls until the next cycle.

Customizing Replication

With the desired Connection documents in place, you can customize replication in a number of ways and then test the resulting replication. Some of the more useful means of customizing replication include:

- Specifying replication direction to indicate whether replication is one-way or two-way between servers
- Replicating only specific databases rather than all databases common to the participating servers
- Replicating databases by priority
- Limiting replication time
- Refusing replication requests from other servers
- Disabling replication to prevent changes from being replicated
- Forcing immediate replication to replicate changes to critical databases
- Scheduling replication from a workstation
- Testing the replication schedule

Specifying Replication Direction

In the Replication Type field on the Replication/Routing tab of the Connection document, you can specify the replication direction. The value of this field determines whether the server(s) involved simply send, receive, or both send and receive updates during the replication cycle.

As delineated in the earlier section, "Understanding Replication," Domino offers four forms of replication direction: Pull-Pull; Pull-Push (the default replication direction); Push-Only; and Pull-Only. Both Push-Only and Pull-Only, because they are one-way as opposed to two-way forms, take less time than the Pull-Push and Pull-Pull alternatives.

You can similarly affect the replication direction by altering the server console command you execute when you force replication. For example, instead of using the Replicate command, you can use either the Push command or Pull command. In this way, you can use the Push-Only or Pull-Only method when there is an update in a Domino Directory on one server and you want to manually propagate that change to the other servers.

Replicating Only Specific Databases

In the File/Directories to Replicate field on the Replication/Routing tab of the Connection document, you can limit the scope of replication between servers. The default scope is all databases. To limit this scope, enter the directory or database names that you want to replicate, separating the individual entries with semicolons. Similarly, you can use the Files/Directory Paths to Not Replicate field to specify particular files or databases not to replicate.

For individual databases, enter the filename of the database, including its full path relative to the Domino data directory—for example, `SALES\TRACKING.NSF`.

For entire directories, including subdirectories within the directory, enter the directory name relative to the Domino data directory—for example, `SALES\`.

This setting pertains to Pull-Push, Push-Only, and Pull-Only replication directions. It does not pertain to Pull-Pull. If the replication direction selected in the Connection document is the latter, only the initiating server receives the specified databases during replication. The responding server receives all databases in common with the initiating server.

REPLICATING DATABASES BY PRIORITY

To enable Domino administrators to schedule replication for databases based on priority, Database Managers can assign a replication priority to them within the Other tab of the Replication Settings dialog box.

After such a priority has been assigned—for example, high priority to such business-critical databases as the Domino Directory—you can schedule it to replicate frequently during the day. Conversely, you can schedule low-priority databases to replicate during off-peak hours.

To replicate databases by priority, create separate Connection documents for your low-, medium-, and high-priority databases. To differentiate the priority levels, edit the Replicate Databases Of field on the Replication/Routing tab in the Connection document. The default setting is Low and Medium and High. With this setting, Domino automatically replicates all databases that the two servers have in common. During the replication process, Domino uses the priority assigned to the replica on the calling server, if the respective replicas possess different priorities.

LIMITING REPLICATION TIME

If you need to limit the cost of replication with servers in remote sites, you should decrease the time that a server has to replicate with another server. Be aware, however, that if you underestimate the time limit, you can cause an incomplete replication cycle. This leads to replication terminating prematurely when the time has been reached. Although a message indicating termination is written in the server's log file, it relates that the replication was successful, thereby providing an inaccurate record of replication activity.

You can limit replication time by setting the Replication Time Limit field on the Replication/Routing tab in the Connection document to a nonzero value.

The default value of blank enables Domino to use as much time as necessary to complete the replication cycle.

REFUSING REPLICATION REQUESTS

You can configure a server to refuse replication requests by setting the `ServerNoReplRequests` `NOTES.INI` Configuration Setting parameter to 1. This prevents a server from accepting a replication request. It does not, however, prevent the server from initiating replication with other servers.

DISABLING REPLICATION

You can disable replication temporarily or permanently. To disable replication temporarily, tell the Replica task to quit (tell replica quit). To disable replication permanently, remove the Replica task from the ServerTasks line in the NOTES.INI. You can also disable the replication for a given connection by setting the Replication task field to Disabled on the Replication/Routing tab of the Connection document for the given connection. This procedure is different than disabling replication at the database level.

FORCING IMMEDIATE REPLICATION

You can force immediate replication between servers after you have configured the necessary replication Connection documents. By using the Replicate server command, you can have Domino perform a Pull-Push replication and thereby replicate changes to databases in both directions. By using the Pull or Push server command, you can have Domino perform either a pull or push and replicate changes in only one direction. You can force replication with a console command either from the Domino Administrator or from the server's console.

To force replication of selected databases between two servers from the Domino Administrator, complete the following steps:

1. Initiate the Domino Administrator.
2. Click the Servers tab and select Replication.
3. On the right side of the screen, expand the Server section under Tools.
4. Select the Replicate action. The Replicate From dialog box will display as demonstrated in Figure 38.4.

Figure 38.4
Forcing replication from the Domino Administrator.

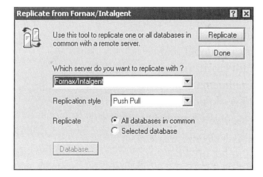

5. Enter the name of the server with which you want to replicate.
6. Select the style of replication.

7. Choose between the options to replicate all databases or selected databases. If you choose to replicate selected databases, click the Database button and select the appropriate databases.

8. Click the Replicate button to initiate replication with the target server.

9. After replication is complete, click the Done button.

Alternatively, you can enter a console command within the Server Console under the Servers tab.

Server console commands consist of the replication command, the name of the server you want to replicate with, and, optionally, the names of any specific databases you want to replicate. Valid replication commands include `Replicate` (Pull-Push Pull), `Pull`, or `Push`. For example:

- `Replicate Server B/Acme` executes a full two-way replication with `Server B/Acme`.

- `Pull Server B/Acme names.nsf` pulls changes to the Domino Directory on `Server B/Acme`, but no other replication occurs.

- `Push Server B/Acme *.nsf` sends all changes in all replica databases from the initiating server to `Server B/Acme`, but no modifications are pulled from `Server B/Acme`, and no modifications to Domino template files (`*.ntf`) are sent.

Scheduling Replication from a Workstation

Replication between a Notes client workstation and a Domino server can be initiated only from the workstation. Scheduling the replication is similar to scheduling replication between servers, except that the replication schedule is maintained in Location documents on the workstation. There is a Server Connection document in the Personal Address Book on the workstation, but it is used only to provide specific information for connecting with a server.

Because you can have several Location documents, you can create replication schedules that are specific to the needs of each location. For example, you might want to replicate a number of databases to your Home location if you regularly telecommute from home. If you are traveling with a laptop computer, you will probably want to replicate only databases that you know you will need while you are on the road. When you switch to a different location from the status bar, you will automatically activate the replication schedule for that location.

The replication schedule portion of a Location document is shown in Figure 38.5. The fields are similar to the Scheduling portion of the Server Connection document on the Domino server. However, there are no options on the Location document to select which databases will be replicated. Instead, this is done from the Replicator page on the Notes desktop.

Figure 38.5
The Location document showing a replication schedule between the workstation and a server.

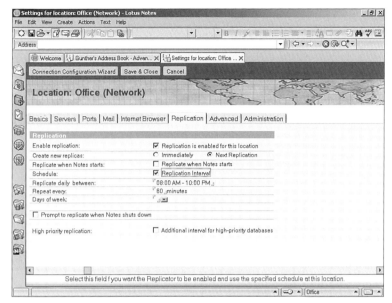

INITIATING REPLICATION FROM THE DESKTOP

The Replicator page provides a graphical way to manage replication on the Notes workstation from a single screen, with each replica database potentially residing on different servers.

With background replication, you can continue working in Notes while replication takes place. If you elect, however, to replicate a database using one-time options (for example, by highlighting the database icon and selecting File, Replication, Replicate, and then selecting Replicate with options), the replication takes place in the foreground, and you must wait for the replication to finish before you can resume working. The Replication page is illustrated in Figure 38.6.

Depending on the type of location you have set up, the basic elements of the Replication page might vary slightly. For example, if you have a location document that gives you a remote network connection over TCP/IP, you do not need an option to automatically hang up the phone as you do with a modem connection. But whatever your location setup, you will have options to enable scheduled replication, to replicate templates, and to replicate any databases that have a replica copy on the desktop.

Each of the horizontal rows in the Replication page represents a possible action during replication. You can turn the action on or off by clicking the check box on the left. The header has many preferences including the capability to enable a replication schedule. The next rows are databases that will replicate with the server. The next row will replicate template files that have been modified or added. The last row is a database that is currently being replicated. When a replication event is in progress, a pointer icon indicates the database that is currently being replicated, and the status of the current database replication is illustrated at the bottom of the screen.

Figure 38.6
The Replication page enables you to start and control replication between a workstation and a Domino server.

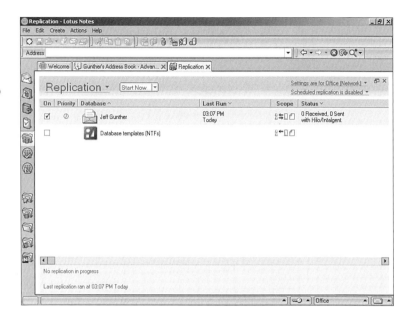

38

Domino estimates the time it will take for the initial replication to complete, based on the documents it has pulled so far and the total number of documents that remain to be pulled. However, Domino constantly recalculates as more documents are pulled in. After the initial replication, regular replications are likely to take considerably less time, because you only replicate the fields that have been modified and any new documents that have been added. Each row on the Replication page has a check box, priority level icon, database icon and title, date of last run, and scope icon. To the right of the scope icon is more text, reporting on the status of the last replication. If you want a row to be a part of the next replication, make sure that it is checked. Only checked rows are considered during replication.

The buttons on each row can be used to tailor the replication action on that particular row. For example, if you click the buttons in the upper-right corner, Notes allows you to enable replication and opens the current Location document so that you can set up a replication schedule for that particular location. If you click the scope icon for a particular database, you can determine which server you prefer to look on for a replica of the database, whether to send documents, and whether to replicate full documents or only a summary and up to 40KB of rich text.

The database icons on the Replication page can be placed there in two ways. If you manually replicate a database by highlighting the database and selecting File, Replication, New Replica, the icon will be placed on the Replication page automatically. Alternatively, you can drag a database icon and drop it on the tab for the Replication page.

You can specify the order in which databases are replicated by pointing to a row and dragging it to a new location in the replication process.

If you want to remove a row from the Replication page, highlight the row and press the Delete key. Notes removes the database from the Replication page. This does not affect the database icon on other workspace pages. You cannot remove the Templates entry, although you can uncheck these to make them inactive. If you delete entries such as Hang Up from your Replication page, you can add them by selecting them from the Create menu.

TESTING REPLICATION

You can test replication between servers after you have configured the necessary replication Connection documents. Begin by creating a new replica of a database; alter it in some way and then force replication with a replica of this database on another server.

You can track the results of your replication tests for individual databases or collectively for all the databases replicated. The replication history for an individual database records replication events with servers and workstations. You can access this information by selecting the target database and selecting File, Replication, History. The Replication Events view of the Domino log file (LOG.NSF) provides you with collective information regarding the replication cycle. You can access this from the Replication tab within the Domino Administrator.

38

MONITORING REPLICATION AND MAINTAINING REPLICA DATABASES

In order to monitor replication and maintain replica databases on your various servers within your Domino environment, you need to familiarize yourself with the various monitoring tools available to the Domino Administrator and the methods to resolve replication conflicts when they arise.

MONITORING REPLICATION OF SPECIFIC DATABASES

The following tools are available to assist you in monitoring replication and troubleshooting replication problems within your Domino server:

- The Replication task within the Domino Administrator.
- The replication history of each database, recording each successful replication session for the given database.
- The Replication Events view of the log file (LOG.NSF), showing details about replication events between servers.
- Replication Monitors, notifying you when replication of a database hasn't occurred within a specified time period. You create Replication Monitors as a part of configuring the Event task.
- The Database Analysis tool, enabling you to collect such information as the replication history, the replication events from the log file, and other information specific to a database and store it in a results database for subsequent analysis.

UNDERSTANDING THE REPLICATION TAB WITHIN THE DOMINO ADMINISTRATOR

The Replication tab within the Domino Administrator provides three information areas, detailing the replication schedule, the replication topology map, and replication events of servers. The Replication tab is shown in Figure 38.7. A summary of each of these views follows:

Figure 38.7
The Domino Administrator Replication tab highlighting the three administrative selections: replication schedules, events, and topology map.

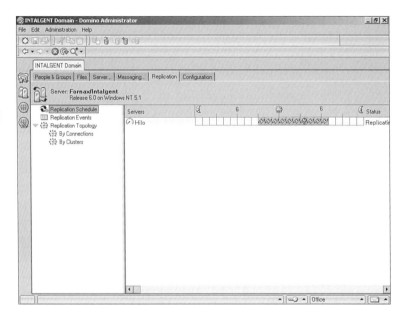

- **Replication Schedule**—Summarizes the contents of Connection documents pertinent to replication tasks for servers within the selected Domain.

- **Replication Events**—Provides a summary listing of the Replication Events view of the selected Domino server's `log.nsf`.

- **Replication Topology**—Provides a graphical depiction of the underlying Replication configuration between servers within the selected Domain. By double-clicking connections between servers, you can view the particulars of the Connection document for the selected calling and answering Domino servers. Similarly, by highlighting either endpoint of the connection, you can view the details of the selected server's replication configuration.

VIEWING THE DATABASE REPLICATION HISTORY

Recall that you can view a database's replication history by opening the database and selecting File, Replication, History. Domino records an entry in the history the first time one server replica successfully replicates with a replica on another server. The entry consists of the name of the peer server and the date and time of the replication. Domino subsequently creates separate entries when a replica sends information and when a replica receives it.

VIEWING REPLICATION EVENTS IN THE LOG FILE

The Replication Events view of the log file (LOG.NSF) provides comprehensive information on the replication of databases between servers. A replication log document shows the following information for each database replicated on a given server:

- The access the server has to the database
- The number of documents added, deleted, and modified
- The size of the data exchanged
- The name of the replica that this database replicated with

Above this individual database information, you can find the Events section within the replication log document. It records any problems that occurred when replication was attempted for specific databases. This includes such information as whether the database access control is set to not allow replication or whether replication is disabled.

Use the Domino Administrator to view a replication log:

1. Initiate the Domino Administrator and select the server to be administered.
2. From the Domino Administrator, select the Replication tab.
3. Click the Replication Events view of the Notes log.
4. Open a recent replication log.

ANALYZING REPLICATION USING THE DATABASE ANALYSIS TOOLS

You can compile replication information for a database or set of databases by performing a database analysis. This assembles the replication history for the selected database(s) as it has been recorded and any additions, updates, or deletions as reported in the log file. To capture this information, follow these steps:

1. Initiate the Domino Administrator and select the server to be administered.
2. Click the Files tab. The Notes data directory is displayed in the left pane, and the contents of the selected subdirectory are displayed in the middle pane.
3. Highlight the file or files for which you want to collect replication information.
4. Under the Tools section, expand the Database section and select Analyze. The Analyze Database dialog box appears.
5. Under Replication, select one or both of Find Replicas on Other Servers and Replication history. Find replicas reports information from other replicas in addition to the database(s) on the selected server. Replication history reports successful replications of the database(s), as reported in the replication history for the database(s).
6. Specify the number of days of activity to collect.
7. Click the Results button and designate the results database.
8. Click OK to initiate the analysis. Upon completion, review the contents of your results database.

RESOLVING REPLICATION OR SAVE CONFLICTS

A replication conflict or save conflict arises when more than one user concurrently edits the same document in different replicas between replication sessions or the same document in one copy of a database.

UNDERSTANDING REPLICATION CONFLICTS

A replication conflict represents the first condition: when more than one user edits and saves the changes in different replicas between replications. Under these circumstances, Domino stores the results of one session in a main document and the results of the second and subsequent editing sessions in response documents. Domino adheres to some basic precepts to determine the main and response document hierarchy. First, it makes the document that has been edited and saved the most number of times the main document, with the others becoming Replication Conflict documents. Second, if all documents have been edited the same number of times, it makes the most recently edited document the main document, with the others becoming Replication Conflict documents.

UNDERSTANDING SAVE CONFLICTS

A save conflict represents the second of the two conditions: when two or more users open and edit the same document at the same time on the same server. Under these circumstances, the first document saved becomes the main document. All subsequently saved documents become Save Conflict documents.

PREVENTING REPLICATION OR SAVE CONFLICTS

In order to reduce or eliminate replication or save conflicts from occurring, database designers and system administrators have the following options:

- In design mode, the database designer can select the Form Property Merge Replication Conflicts on the bottom of the Information tab. This option triggers an automatic merge of Replication conflicts into one document if no fields conflict.

- Again in design mode, the database designer can specify one of the Versioning options on the Information tab. This option specifies how the various versions of the same document are treated—as responses or siblings.

- The system administrator can assign users Author access or lower in the database ACL, thereby preventing users from editing other users' documents.

- The system administrator can construct LotusScript agents that attempt to resolve the conflicts.

- Finally, the system administrator can simply keep the number of replicas to a minimum, if that is a possible alternative.

CONSOLIDATING REPLICATION OR SAVE CONFLICTS

The process of consolidating a replication or save conflict is relatively straightforward: You merge information into one primary document and remove the secondary document(s). If you want to save the main document, copy any information from the Replication or Save Conflict documents into the main document, save it, and delete the conflict documents. If you want to save one of the Replication or Save Conflict documents, copy any information from the main and other response documents, save the selected document, and delete the others.

38

ADMINISTERING FILES AND DATABASES

UTILIZING THE DOMINO ADMINISTRATOR

Maintaining the integrity of application data is a chief responsibility of the Domino Administrator. Such maintenance encompasses a wide range of activities. Among the most important preventative maintenance activities are backing up the server on a regular basis; fixing corrupted databases; monitoring files, databases, and directories; and, in general, monitoring disk space. Each of these tasks involves the management of files. Throughout the Domino Administrator client, the generic term Files is used to describe many types of entities, including databases, directories, and links.

Within the Domino Administrator, the Files tab displays the Domino Data Directory for the selected server. By default, the display contains only the databases. You can alter what is shown by selecting one of the appropriate options from the Show Me list box at the top of the database display. The available options include Databases Only, Templates Only, Mail Boxes Only, All Database Types, All File Types, Database Links Only, and Custom. The Custom option enables you to customize the display by selecting from a set of file types or extensions.

As shown in Figure 39.1, Domino Administrator 6, under the Files tab, provides three groupings of actions to manage files and databases including Disk Space, Folder, and Database.

Figure 39.1
The Files tab within the Domino Administrator has three sets of tools: Disk Space, Folder, and Database.

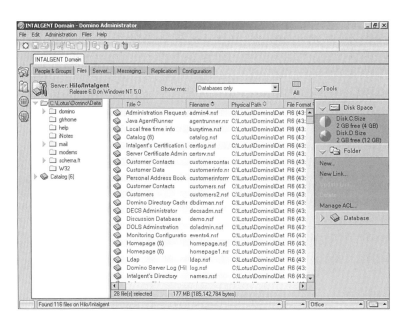

The following three sections describe each of these three sets of tools.

MONITORING DISK INFORMATION

The Disk Space tool displays the size and available space of all partitions configured on the server. This tool shows the Administrator, at a glance, the disk size, and free space on each disk partition on the server.

MANAGING FOLDERS AND DIRECTORIES

The Folder set of tools, as shown in Figure 39.2, facilitates you in creating new folders, creating new links to folders or databases, updating existing links, deleting folders, databases, or links, and managing a directory's Access Control List (ACL). By creating links to folders and databases, you can increase security within the Domino environment because this enables you to place entire folders or groups of databases outside the normal Domino data directory structure.

During the creation of a link to the external folder or database, you can then specify those users who can access the link. Furthermore, external to Domino, you can define operating system–specific access control limitations. As a result, Domino users can see the linked folder as a subdirectory or see the database as an entry under the Domino data directory but cannot access either one unless they have been given permission. Additionally, you can use the Manage ACL action to manage the ACL for a particular directory.

39

Figure 39.2
The Folder set of tools lets you create a new folder, create a new link to a folder or database, update an existing link, or delete entries, whether such entries are folders, databases, or links.

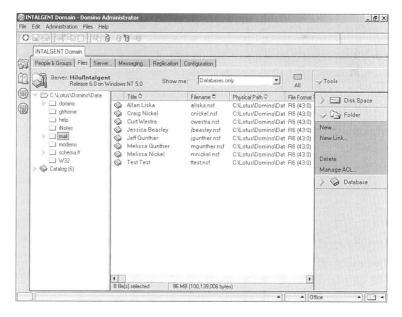

The following paragraphs outline the procedures within the Domino Administrator for creating, updating, and deleting folders, databases, and links.

To create a folder, complete the following steps:

1. Within the Domino Administrator, select the server to be administered.
2. Click the Files tab. The selected server's Domino Data Directory is displayed in the left pane. Expand the Folder grouping under the Tools section on the right side of the Domino Administrator.
3. Using the tree that displays the Domino data folder, browse to the location where you want to create a folder.
4. Select New from the Folder grouping underneath the Tools section. The Create New Folder dialog box is displayed.
5. Enter the name of the new folder into the Name field on the Create New Folder dialog box.
6. Click OK. The new folder is created as a subdirectory under the folder highlighted in the left pane.

To delete a folder, complete the following steps:

1. Within the Domino Administrator, select the server to be administered.
2. Click the Files tab. The selected server's Domino Data Directory is displayed in the left pane. Expand the Folder grouping under the Tools section on the right side of the Domino Administrator.
3. Using the tree that displays the Domino data folders, browse to the folder you want to delete and highlight it.
4. Click Delete under the Folder grouping. The Confirm Folder Delete dialog box appears.
5. Click OK to confirm the deletion of the folder.

As mentioned previously, you can manage and maintain links to folders and databases external to the server's Domino data folder.

To create a folder link, complete these steps:

1. Within the Domino Administrator, select the server to be administered.
2. Click the Files tab. The selected server's Domino Data Directory is displayed in the left pane. Expand the Folder grouping under the Tools section on the right side of the Domino Administrator.
3. Click New Link under the Folder grouping. The Create New Link dialog box appears, as shown in Figure 39.3.
4. In the Link name box, enter a name for the folder link.
5. Select Folder. Domino appends the .DIR extension to the link name specified.
6. Enter the path and filename to the directory.

Figure 39.3

The Create New Link dialog box prompting for Link name, whether it is a folder or database link, what the link points to, and who can access the link.

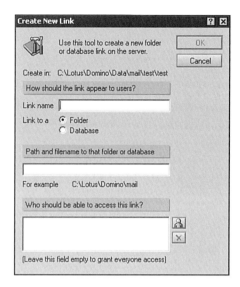

> **NOTE**
>
> The directory that is the target of the link must already exist on the server.

7. Optionally, under Who Should Be Able to Access This Link?, enter the names of Domino users or groups that can access this folder. This restricts access to the linked directory. You can also retrieve these from the current directory by clicking the Person icon.

8. Click OK.

Before the newly created link appears with the user interface, you need to refresh the display. You can accomplish this by moving to a different tab and toggling back to the Files tab.

To create a database link pointing to a single database outside the Domino data directory, complete these steps:

1. Within the Domino Administrator, select the server to be administered.

2. Click the Files tab. The selected server's Domino Data Directory is displayed in the left pane. Expand the Folder grouping under the Tools section on the right side of the Domino Administrator.

3. Click New Link, under the Folder grouping, to display the Create New Link dialog box.

4. In the Link Name box, enter a name for the database link.

5. Select Database. Domino adds the extension .NSF to the link name you specified.

6. Enter the complete path to the database to which the link points.

7. Click OK.

39

Before the newly created link appears with the user interface, you need to refresh the display. You can accomplish this by moving to a different tab and toggling back to the Files tab.

To modify a folder or database link, complete these steps:

1. Within the Domino Administrator, select the server to be administered.
2. Click the Files tab. The selected server's Domino Data Directory is displayed in the left pane. Expand the Folder grouping under the Tools section on the right side of the Domino Administrator.
3. Select the icon for the link within the displayed Domino Data Directory. Depending on the link type, you'll select the link in a different location. A Link icon displays an arrow inside of a folder.
4. Click Update Link under the Folder grouping to display the Update Link dialog box.
5. Change the filename for the link, the path to the directory or database it points to, or the access list (in the case of a directory link).
6. Click OK.

To delete a folder or database link, complete these steps:

1. Within the Domino Administrator, select the server to be administered.
2. Click the Files tab. The selected server's Domino Data Directory is displayed in the left pane. Expand the Folder grouping under the Tools section on the right side of the Domino Administrator.
3. Select the icon for the link within the displayed Domino Data Directory. Depending on the link type, you'll select the link in different locations. A Link icon displays an arrow within a folder.
4. Click Delete under the Folder grouping to display the Confirm Folder Delete dialog box.
5. Click OK.

To manage a folder's ACL, complete these steps:

1. Within the Domino Administrator, select the server to be administered.
2. Click the Files tab. The selected server's Domino Directory structure is displayed in the right pane. Expand the Folder grouping under the Tools section on the right side of the Domino Administrator.
3. Select the folder within the displayed list of Domino directories within the current server's data directory.
4. Click Manage ACL from the Folder grouping to display the Manage Directory ACL dialog box.
5. Click the button that has an image of a person to open the Select Names dialog box.

6. Select the users who should have access to the selected folder. Click OK.

7. Verify that the correct names are displayed and click OK.

MANAGING AND MAINTAINING DATABASES

When databases are in production, they must be monitored and maintained. Although many of the maintenance tasks can be scheduled to run automatically by setting parameters in the NOTES.INI file, in server Configuration Setting documents, or in Program documents, certain tasks still require a certain level of administrative intervention. The Domino Administrator provides a central location for such activity.

Under the Database groupings, shown in Figure 39.4, the Domino Administrator facilitates the following Database actions:

- Manage ACL
- Create Replica(s)
- Compact
- Full-Text Index
- Multi-Database Index
- Advanced Properties
- Quotas
- Move
- Sign
- Replication
- Fixup
- Cluster
- Delete
- Analyze
- Find Note
- Create Event
- Manage Views

The following paragraphs detail the background and procedures for each of the tools associated with these actions. When not specifically stated, the procedures assume that you are performing the role of Domino Administrator and are listed in the ACL with the user type of Manager.

39

Figure 39.4
The Database tool set, within the Domino Administrator, contains several actions to manage databases.

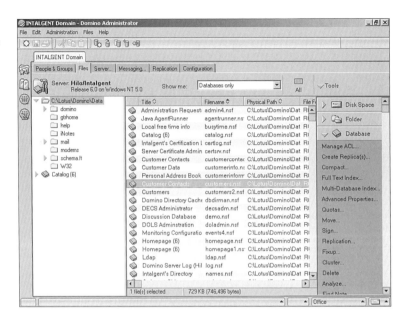

COMPACTING DATABASES

39

Adding and deleting documents to and from a database during normal processing leaves blocks of unused space. When a document is deleted, a deletion stub is put in its place. This occupies only a percentage of the space of the original document. The remaining unused space is now available. Because it is difficult to use these chunks of unused space, the database becomes fragmented over time and server performance decreases. *Compacting* is the process of removing this unused white space.

It is generally recommended to compact databases that have 10% or more of unused space. Further, it is also recommended to run Compact at least once a month on all databases on the server.

To determine whether a specific database has reached the 10% unused space benchmark, complete the following steps:

1. Within the Domino Administrator, select the server to be administered.

2. Click the Files tab. The selected server's Domino Data Directory is displayed in the left pane.

3. Select and open the database from the list of databases.

4. From the Domino Administrator's main drop-down menu, choose File, Database, Properties.

5. Click the Information tab.

6. Click the % Used button. The database's current used percentage is displayed.

Because compacting large databases can consume a great deal of time, it is recommended to run Compact during off-peak hours. In this way, you do not overburden your servers with administrative processing during the normal business day. Furthermore, because compacting databases can require making a duplicate of the database being compacted, based on the option selected, the server must also have enough disk space to store the copy during the process.

To compact databases, you can use the Domino Administrator or load the Compact task from the server console. You can also use a Program document. When you load Compact as a server task or have it run as a scheduled Program document, it runs under the auspices of the server. You can also compact an individual database by clicking the Compact button in the Database Properties InfoBox.

To compact a database within the Domino Administrator, complete the following steps:

1. Ensure that you have at least Designer access to the databases you want to compact. Then, within the Domino Administrator, select the server to be administered from the Server icon on the far left side of the Domino Administrator client.

2. Choose the Files tab. The selected server's Domino Data Directory is displayed in the left pane.

3. Expand the Database grouping under the Tools selection (located on the right side of the Domino Administrator).

4. In the list of databases, select the database(s) to compact.

5. Select Compact from the Database grouping to display the Compact Databases dialog box.

6. Select the desired options. These include:

   - Specifying for compaction to take place only if unused space is greater than a certain percentage.
   - Discarding any built view indexes.
   - Setting a maximum database size of 4GB.
   - Keeping or reverting the database back to R5 format.
   - Archiving the database.
   - Defining the compaction style.

7. Click OK to complete the compaction.

CAUTION

> Compacting a Release 5 database results in the database being converted to Release 6 format. To prevent this, you can give your Release 5 databases the .NS5 extension.

MONITORING FULL-TEXT INDEXING

Full-text indexing enables users to search databases for information. Physically on disk, the full-text search represents a set of files stored in a subdirectory of the database being indexed. Domino names this subdirectory by appending .FT to the filename of the database excluding the .NSF extension. All the files for the full-text index are stored in this directory. Every time the full-text index is updated, Domino adds an index file into the index subdirectory.

Because full-text indexes can consume significant disk space, ensure that you have adequate disk space before creating the full-text index. Depending on the content of the database and the indexing options selected, the full-text index can approach 75% of the size of the text in the target database. The index's size depends on the following factors:

- The percentage of text in your database in comparison to non-text items, such as bitmaps and graphics.
- The full-text options chosen. For a single-database index, the following options can be selected: index file attachments, index encrypted fields, index sentence and paragraph breaks, and the capability to enable case-sensitive searches. The meaning of those options is enumerated in the following list:
  - The Index Attached Files option indexes the text in any attachments while building the index.
  - The Index Encrypted Fields option encrypts the index so that only those users who have the correct decryption key can search the index.
  - The Index Sentence and Paragraph Breaks option enables the use of proximity operators. Such operators locate multiple words in the same sentence or paragraph. For example, the following query finds documents in which cat and mouse are in the same paragraph: cat paragraph mouse. Similarly, the following query finds documents in which cat and mouse are in the same sentence: cat sentence mouse.
  - The Enable Case-Sensitive Searches option includes in the index an entry for each word each time a different capitalization scheme for the word is encountered. This can increase the size of the full-text index by up to 10%. For example, "computer" and "Computer" both appear in the index as different words so that searches can locate occurrences of one but not the other.

CREATING, UPDATING, AND DELETING FULL-TEXT INDEXES

You can create, update, or delete a full-text index by completing the following steps:

1. Ensure that you have at least Designer access to the target database or databases for which you want to create a full-text index. Then, within the Domino Administrator, select the server to be administered from the Server icon in the far left side of the Domino Administrator screen.

2. Choose the Files tab. The selected server's Domino Data Directory is displayed.

3. Expand the Database grouping under the Tools section.

4. In the view that displays the databases, select the database for which you want to manage the index.

5. Select Full Text Index from the Database grouping to display the Full Text Index dialog box. This is shown in Figure 39.5.

Figure 39.5
The Full Text Index dialog box provides the capability to create, manage, and delete full-text indexes of databases.

6. Select Create, Update, or Delete.

7. Select any of the following options: Index Attached Files, Index Encrypted Fields, Index Sentence and Paragraph Breaks, and Enable Case-Sensitive Searches.

8. Specify the Index update frequency of Daily, Scheduled, Hourly, or Immediately.

9. Select OK. After the full-text process completes, a full-text index is created with your specifications.

CREATING REPLICA COPIES OF DATABASES

Replica copies of databases are special copies that are identified by their replica IDs. As detailed in Chapter 38, "Replication and Its Administration," you can create such replica copies of databases in a number of ways. One of the simplest ways is provided by the Database actions within the Domino Administrator. With the Domino Administrator, you can use the Administration Process to create replicas on servers in the same Domino domain or in another Domino domain. To create a replica copy of a database in the same Domino domain, complete the following steps:

1. Ensure that the necessary Administration Process and access control has been established. This entails the following:

   - The Administration Process must be running on both the source and destination servers.
   - You have Create Database access to the destination server or servers and at least Reader access to the database on the source server.
   - The source server has Create Replica access in the Server document of the destination server.
   - The destination server has at least Reader access in the ACL of the source replica database.

   Within the Domino Administrator, select the server to be administered from the Server icon in the far left side of the Domino Administrator screen.

2. Choose the Files tab. The selected server's Domino Data Directory is displayed.

3. Expand the Database grouping under the Tools section on the right side of the Domino Administrator.

4. In the list of databases, select the databases for which you want to create replica copies.

5. Select Create Replica(s) from the Database grouping to display the Create Replica dialog box.

6. Specify the server or servers on which you want to install a replica copy. You can also set the path and filename for the given replica by completing the Destination File Path setting.

7. Click OK to accept the path and filename settings, and then click OK to submit the Create Replica request.

Creating a replica copy of a database on a server in another Domino domain requires additional steps.

You must have an outbound Cross Domain Configuration document in the Administration Requests database on your source server. Similarly, you must have an inbound Cross Domain Configuration document in the Administration Requests on the destination server. The former enables the Administration Process on the source server to export Create Replica requests to the destination server. The latter enables the Administration Process on the destination server to import Create Replica requests from the source server.

Furthermore, you must have a Connection document for mail routing configured on your server to connect to a server located in your destination server's domain. Finally, if they do not share a common certifier, you must cross-certify the two servers in order for them to authenticate with each other.

MOVING DATABASES

Within the Domino Administrator, you can use the Administration Process to move non-mail databases from one server to another server by completing the following steps:

1. Ensure that the necessary Administration Process and access control has been established. This entails the following:

   - The Administration Process is running on both the source and destination servers.
   - You have Create Database access to the destination server or servers and at least Manager with Delete Documents access in the ACL of the database on the source server.
   - The source server has Create Replica access in the Server document of the destination server.
   - The destination server has at least Reader access in the ACL of the source replica database.

   Within the Domino Administrator, select the server to be administered from the Server icon in the far left side of the Domino Administrator screen.

2. Choose the Files tab. The selected server's Domino Data Directory is displayed.

3. Expand the Database grouping under the Tools selection.

4. In the list of databases, select the database(s) that you want to move.

5. Select Move from the Database grouping to display the Move Database dialog box.

6. Specify the server or servers to which you want to move the database. You can also set the path and filename for the given move by completing the Destination File Path setting.

7. Click OK to accept the path and filename settings, and then click OK to submit the Move Replica request.

Chapter 36, "Administering Users, Groups, and Certification," discusses the procedures to follow when moving a user's mail file from the People and Groups tab within the Domino Administrator.

DELETING DATABASES

Similar to moving a database, the Domino Administrator provides a mechanism to delete any database or template. To delete a particular file, complete the following steps:

1. Within the Domino Administrator, select the server to be administered from the Server icon in the far left side of the Domino Administrator screen.

2. Choose the Files tab. The selected server's Domino Data Directory is displayed.

3. Expand the Database grouping under the Tools section.

39

4. In the list of databases, select the database(s) that you want to delete.

5. Select Delete from the Database grouping to display the Confirm Database Delete dialog box.

6. If you want to delete all replicas of the selected database(s) on all the servers within the domain, mark the appropriate field.

7. Click OK to confirm the permanent deletion of the files.

ANALYZING A DATABASE

Performing an analysis of a database is a useful task to gather information regarding a particular database within the Domino domain. Information from various resources is collected, categorized, and reported. Sources of information include:

- User activity dialog box
- Replication history
- Domino log

You can analyze a database or set of databases by completing the following steps:

1. Within the Domino Administrator, select the server to be administered from the Server icon in the far left side of the Domino Administrator client.

2. Choose the Files tab. The selected server's Domino Data Directory is displayed.

3. Expand the Database grouping under the Tools selection on the right side of the Domino Administrator.

4. In the list of databases, select one or more databases to analyze.

5. Select Analyze from the Database grouping to display the Analyze Database dialog box. The dialog box, as illustrated in Figure 39.6, consists of a set of options enabling you to customize the scope of the database analysis.

Figure 39.6
The Analyze Database dialog box gives you several options to choose what will be examined.

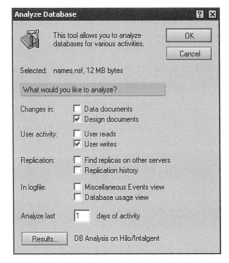

You can choose the following options:

- Changes in Data documents and/or Design documents. The first provides a report on document additions, edits, and deletions. The second provides a report on changes to the database ACL and design.

- User activity, consisting of user reads or user writes. For user reads, the report details the total times users opened documents and servers read documents. For user writes, it reports the total times users and servers created, modified, or deleted documents, and the total number of mail messages delivered to the database.

- Replication events, by finding replicas on other servers and/or viewing the selected database's replication history. This report is based on the replicas on other servers and the successful replications, as logged in the replication history for the database.

- Miscellaneous Events view and/or Database usage view, as recorded in the respective views of the Domino log file. This reports the events relating to the database from the Miscellaneous Events view and the Usage—By User view of the log.

6. Specify the number of days that you want the analysis to include.

7. Click the Results button and specify the server, database title, and database filename where you want to store the results. You should create the results database on your local workstation rather than on your server. This prevents overwriting another administrator's work. You can also overwrite the contents of the database or append to it.

8. Click OK to select the Results database, and then click OK to begin the database analysis.

VIEWING THE RESULTS OF A DATABASE ANALYSIS

After you run the database analysis, you can view its results by completing the following steps:

1. Open the Results database.

2. Choose View and then choose one of the following subviews:

   - **By Date**—A view of documents categorized by the date the reported event happened

   - **By Event Type**—A view of documents categorized by the type of event described

   - **By Source**—A view of documents categorized by the source server on which the event occurred

   - **By Source Database**—A view of documents categorized by the source database for the event

3. Select a document within the view.

39

Each analysis document contains the following fields:

- The date the event occurred
- The time the event occurred
- The source of event information—Whether it is the analyzed database, its replicas, or the log file on the server
- The event type—Whether it is Activity, Mail Router, Data Note, Design Note, or Replicator:
  - Activity event types are recorded if you select User Reads and User Writes options. They represent the number of user or server reads and writes, as noted in the database user activity report.
  - Mail Router event types are recorded if you select the User Writes option. They represent the number of documents delivered to the database.
  - Data Note event types are recorded if you select the Changes to Documents option. They represent details about document creations, edits, or deletions.
  - Design Note event types are recorded if you select the Changes to Design option. They represent details about changes to the database Access Control List or to the design.
  - Replicator event types are recorded if you select the Replication History option. They represent replication history as reported in the database replication history indicating successful replications.

- The Source Database—The database from which documents were read or from which documents were pulled
- The Source—The server that hosts the database containing documents that were read or written, or the server that hosts the database from which information was pulled, in the case of database replication events
- The Destination—The database within which documents were updated or to which information was pushed, in the case of database replication events
- The Destination machine—The server that hosts the database that was updated or to which information is pushed in the case of replication events
- The Description of the event

SETTING DATABASE QUOTAS

One of the major responsibilities of Domino administrators is to monitor the size of a given database and set quotas based on this information.

MONITORING DATABASE SIZE

You can monitor database size in the Notes log by examining the Usage by Date, Usage by User, Usage by Database, and Usage by Size views. You can monitor individual databases by examining the Information page in the Database Properties dialog box. You can also use the Statistics Reporting database and monitor unused space in databases, or run `Compact` on databases that fall below a specific threshold.

SETTING DATABASE QUOTAS

You can also set up quotas for database size and generate warnings at thresholds you determine. When you define a specific quota for a database, you are specifying a maximum size to which the database can grow. It is also displayed to users attempting to open the database. Similarly, when you define a warning threshold, you are specifying that when the database reaches the "threshold" size, a warning message is displayed to the users.

Complete the following steps to set quotas on one or more databases:

1. Within the Domino Administrator, select the server to be administered from the Server icon in the far left side of the Domino Administrator screen.

2. Choose the Files tab. The selected server's Domino Data Directory is displayed.

3. Expand the Database grouping under the Tools selection on the right side of the Domino Administrator.

4. Select the database or databases to which you want to assign a quota or warning threshold.

5. Select Quotas from the Database grouping to display the Set Quotas dialog box.

6. At this point, you can obtain the current settings by clicking on the database and viewing the database information on the right side of the dialog box.

7. Select the Set Database Quota to radio button and specify a size limit. The database will not exceed the maximum database size set for the selected database(s).

8. Once the quota is set, you can select the Set Warning Threshold To radio button and specify a size at which a message appears in the log file.

9. Click OK to activate the quota and threshold.

ENABLING OR DISABLING REPLICATION OF DATABASES

You can enable or disable replication of a database or set of databases by completing the following steps:

1. Within the Domino Administrator, select the server to be administered from the Server icon in the far left side of the Domino Administrator screen.

2. Choose the Files tab. The selected server's Domino Data Directory is displayed.

3. Expand the Database grouping under the Tools section.

4. In the list of databases, select the databases for which you want to enable or disable replication.

5. Select Replication from the Database grouping to display the Replication dialog box.

39

6. Click Enable or Disable.

7. Click OK.

MANAGING DATABASES WITHIN CLUSTERS

The Cluster action within the Database tools of the Domino Administrator enables you to manage database availability within a cluster. There are three database attributes associated with such availability: Out of Service, In Service, and Pending Delete:

- By marking the database as Out of Service, you are preventing subsequent open requests. If it is possible, such open database requests fail over to a replica in the cluster. If no such replica exists, access to the database is denied.

  All current open connections remain intact until users close their sessions with the database. As this occurs, Domino prevents subsequent opens, as stated previously. The database is brought to an Out-of-Service state without disruption to the active users.

- By marking the database as In Service, you can restore access to it. In so doing, it becomes fully operational to users.

- By marking the database as Pending Delete, you can set a database to be deleted only after every active user has finished using the database. The database is marked Out of Service. No subsequent open requests are accepted. After all active users have closed their sessions with the database, any changes are replicated to a replica in the cluster and the database is deleted.

Complete the following steps to mark a database Out of Service, In Service, or Pending Delete:

1. Within the Domino Administrator, select the server to be administered from the Server icon in the far left side of the Domino Administrator screen.

2. Choose the Files tab. The selected server's Domino Data Directory is displayed.

3. Expand the Database grouping under the Tools section on the right side of the Domino Administrator.

4. In the list of databases, select the databases that you want to change.

5. Select Cluster from the Database grouping to display the Manage Clusters dialog box.

6. Select the cluster's availability status from Out of Service, In Service, or Pending Delete.

7. Click OK.

LOCATING DOCUMENTS WITHIN DATABASES

Each document within a Notes database has a unique eight-character identifier. This number uniquely identifies the document within a single database. Each document also has associated with it a 32-character identifier. This "universal" qualifier uniquely identifies it within all replicas of the given database. This value is generally referenced in the Domino log

(`log.nsf`) when recording events. To analyze such documents reported in the log file and to troubleshoot problems pertaining to them, you can utilize the Find Note action. This action enables you to track which document the Note ID or UNID references and review the document's properties. Complete the following steps to review a given note's properties:

1. Within the Domino Administrator, select the server to be administered from the Server icon in the far left side of the Domino Administrator screen.

2. Choose the Files tab. The selected server's Domino Data Directory is displayed.

3. Expand the Database grouping under the Tools selection on the right side of the Domino Administrator.

4. In the list of databases, select the databases that you want to search.

5. Select Find Note Under Database grouping to display the Find Note dialog box, as shown in Figure 39.7.

Figure 39.7
The Find Note dialog box enables you to search for a particular document by Note or Universal Note ID.

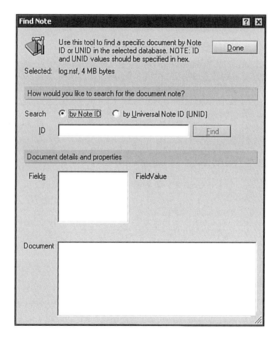

6. Select Note ID or UNID and copy the hexadecimal value into the appropriate field.

7. Click OK.

MULTI-DATABASE INDEXING

The Multi-Database Index action enables you to enable or disable multiple database indexing. If enabled, the database can then be included in the configuration of a Domain Index database that enables users to search multiple databases for information.

To enable or disable multiple-database indexing for a database or set of databases, complete the following steps:

1. Ensure that you have Manager access in the ACL of the databases to be enabled for multi-database searching. Within the Domino Administrator, select the server to be administered from the Server icon in the far left side of the Domino Administrator screen.

2. Choose the Files tab. The selected server's Domino Data Directory is displayed.

3. Expand the Database grouping under the Tools section.

4. In the list of databases, select the databases you want to enable for multi-database indexing.

5. Select Multi-Database Index from the Database grouping to display the Multiple Database Indexing dialog box.

6. Select Enable or Disable, and then click OK.

SIGNING DATABASES WITH CERTIFICATES

Design elements within databases and database templates possess the signature of the creator's or last modifier's certificate. It might be necessary to modify this signature to enable the database or selective components within it to function properly within your environment.

You can accomplish this modification by completing the following steps:

1. Ensure that you are using the correct certified user ID to sign a template or database. Then, within the Domino Administrator, select the server to be administered from the Server icon in the far left side of the Domino Administrator screen.

2. Choose the Files tab. The selected server's Domino Data Directory is displayed.

3. Expand the Database grouping under the Tools selection on the right side of the Domino Administrator.

4. In the list of databases, select the databases that you want to sign.

5. Select Sign from the Database grouping to display the Sign Database dialog box.

6. Specify whether you want to sign every design note, a specified design class, a specified design note, or all data documents. If you select a specified design class, select which class to sign from the list of policy, form, view, icon, design note, ACL, help index, help, agent, shared field, or replication formula. If you select a specified design note, specify the hexadecimal note ID to sign.

7. Click OK.

FIXING CORRUPTED DATABASES WITH FIXUP

Databases can become corrupted during an improper shutdown or by an external program that accesses the database incorrectly. Whenever Notes detects a database that has been closed improperly, it examines every field in every document and deletes documents that are damaged. This ensures that the damaged document is not replicated to other copies of the database. Users might be able to live with this simple solution—enabling Notes to automatically fix documents.

Follow these steps to repair a database using the Domino Administrator:

1. Within the Domino Administrator, select the server to be administered from the Server icon in the far left side of the Domino Administrator screen.

2. Choose the Files tab. The selected server's Domino Data Directory is displayed.

3. Expand the Database grouping under the Tools section.

4. In the list of databases, select the databases that you want to repair.

5. Select Fixup from the Database grouping to display the Database Fixup dialog box.

6. Select from a number of options, including:

   - **Report all processed databases to logfile**—Fixup logs every database it opens and checks. The default is to log only actual problems.

   - **Exclude views (faster)**—This option results in Fixup skipping views.

   - **Perform quick fixup**—This option results in a less thorough check of the documents within the database, but it is quicker. If this is not selected, Fixup checks the entire document.

   - **Scan only since last fixup**—This option results in Fixup checking only documents modified since the last Fixup run. Without this, Fixup checks all documents.

   - **Optimize user unread lists**—This option results in Fixup reverting the unread note tables for the target databases to the previous release format.

   - **Don't purge corrupted documents**—This option prevents Fixup from purging corrupted documents. They are left intact so that information can be salvaged if necessary.

   - **Fixup transaction-logged databases**—This option results in Fixup running on R5 format databases enabled for transaction logging.

7. Click OK.

Corrupted databases can be restored (after corrupted documents have been deleted) through replication, by manually copying and pasting the deleted documents from another copy of the database, or by deleting the database and replacing it with a backup copy.

MANAGING VIEWS

Views that have become corrupt can result in the information being out of synchronization. You might not be able to open a view that is corrupted, odd characters might appear in the view, documents might be missing, or you might find messages in the Notes log. You can purge a view's particular index by completing the following steps:

1. Within the Domino Administrator, select the server to be administered from the Server icon in the far left side of the Domino Administrator screen.

2. Choose the Files tab. The selected server's Domino Data Directory is displayed.

3. Expand the Database grouping under the Tools section.

4. In the list of databases and templates, select the database that you want to manage. You can select only one database.

5. Select Manage Views in Database grouping to display the Manage the Views of This Database dialog box.

6. Select a view and click the Purge button to discard the view's index. You'll be prompted to confirm your action. Click Yes to purge the view's index.

7. Click Done.

TIP

> In addition to the Domino Administrator, you can also run the Updall task from the server console to rebuild corrupt views on specific databases. Enter the following at the server console:
> **Load Updall filename -r**

If you choose to create a new replica to fix corrupted views, but you want to make sure that users can still access the database without having to delete the old icon and reopen the new replica, follow these steps:

1. Back up the database with a corrupted view and rename the copy.

2. Create a replica of the original database, giving it the same server and directory as the original. Give the new replica a different name temporarily.

3. Create the new replica immediately and copy the ACL. Make sure that you replicate all documents (for example, turn off the indicator that replicates documents created only after a certain date).

4. Delete the original database and then rename the new replica with the filename of the original database.

MODIFYING ACL SETTINGS

You can perform a number of ACL management actions within the Manage ACL action of the Domino Administrator's Database tools. In general, the ACL Management action facilitates the following processes:

- Adding, renaming, and removing people, servers, and groups to/from the ACL of selected databases.

- Adding, renaming, and removing roles in the ACLs of selected databases.

- Updating the current Administration Server setting, the consistent ACL setting, and the current Internet name and password settings.

To modify the ACL parameters of databases in any of these areas, complete the following steps:

1. Ensure that you have Manager access in the databases you want to modify. Then, within the Domino Administrator, select the server to be administered from the Server icon in the far left side of the Domino Administrator screen.

2. Choose the Files tab. The selected server's Domino Data Directory is displayed.

3. Expand the Database grouping under the Tools selection.

4. Select the database or databases whose ACLs you want to manage.

5. Select Manage ACL from the Database grouping. The Basics screen of the Manage ACL dialog box, shown in Figure 39.8, is displayed.

Figure 39.8
The Basics section of the Manage ACL dialog box.

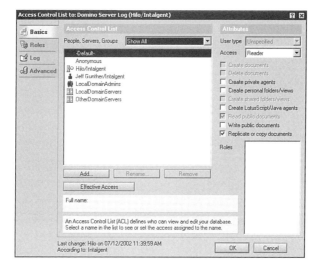

6. Within the Basics section, define a set of one or more ACL actions you want to apply to the ACLs of the selected databases. These discrete actions include adding entries, renaming existing entries, or removing existing entries. The tasks associated with the given entry are displayed in the inset box below the action buttons.

7. Within the Roles section, define a similar set of one or more actions to add roles, rename existing roles, or remove existing roles from the ACLs of the selected database or databases. Again, the tasks associated with the given entry are displayed in the inset box below the action buttons.

8. The first setting within the Advanced section pertains to the Administration Server for the selected database or databases. The Administration Process automates a number of routine administrative tasks, including maintaining the Access Control Lists and Reader and Author fields within databases. Before you can use it on any given database, however, you must ensure that the Administration Process is running on the server and must specify an administration server for that database. Determine whether to keep the current Administration Server setting, set it to None, or define a new server.

The second setting within the Advanced section pertains to the enforcement of consistent ACL settings. By enforcing a consistent ACL across all replicas of the selected databases, you can ensure that the ACL remains the same when users replicate the databases to their workstations, or when the databases are accessed from the server workstation. If you do not select the Enforce Consistent ACL option, users have Manager access to the local replicas of server databases. This enables users to change access levels and other ACL settings on local replicas. It does not, however, enable them to replicate those changes back to the server.

To keep the ACL the same across all server replicas of a database, you must have Manager access to the database and select this setting on a replica whose server has Manager access to the other replicas. If this is not the case, replication fails. Without Manager access, the server has inadequate access to replicate the ACL.

The third and final setting within the Advanced section pertains to the Maximum Internet name and password setting. This controls the maximum type of access that Web browsers can have. The list contains the standard Notes user access levels. It applies to users accessing the server either via name-and-password authentication or anonymously. It does not apply to users with certified IDs.

9. Click OK to update the ACL settings for the selected databases.

39 UPDATING DATABASE DESIGNS

You can refresh the design of databases if they are linked to a specific design template residing on the same server as the database itself by running the `Design` task. The `Design` task runs every morning and updates the database's design with the database's controlling design template. To enable this to perform effectively, you should distribute a copy of the design template to all servers that have a copy of the database and place the design template in each server's respective Domino Data Directory. Alternatively, you can refresh or replace the design of a database manually by selecting the Database icon or opening the database and selecting File, Database, Refresh Design or File, Database, Replace Design.

ROLLING OUT DATABASES

The final section of this chapter describes how to add databases to a production Domino environment. It includes a review of the production database organizational structure and the creation of database libraries to rapidly locate your database applications.

In order for your user population to access application databases, you generally have to replicate them from the development/test environment into the production environment. Prior to this production release, however, you generally coordinate with the database administrative team and decide which of your application servers are most aptly suited, both from a location perspective and a software perspective, to host the newly developed application. Some of the factors influencing your plan include the type of the database application being rolled out, the size of the databases involved, the number of users and their locations, and the underlying replication schedules between proposed participating servers.

Follow these steps in conducting a rollout:

1. Determine which servers will host the application databases and where the replicas should reside.

2. Review the configurations for the servers involved in the rollout, verify that the necessary Connection documents exist and are enabled between all servers in the rollout, and create them if they aren't.

3. Place an image of the application databases on the initial server and create replicas of the production database from this source production server.

As part of the aforementioned step, you also need to work with the database administrator to determine where the application databases should be stored within the Domino data's directory structure. The default location for all databases is in the Domino Data Directory, defined in the `NOTES.INI` file (for example, `Directory=C:\NOTES\DATA`). If you create a subdirectory for the database, the directory is automatically placed beneath the data directory. If you create a database and give it the name `MYDATA\SALES.NSF`, the database is placed on the Domino server as `C:\NOTES\DATA\MYDATA\SALES.NSF`.

In short, you have a number of alternatives for locating your application databases. You can place them at the root of the Domino data directory. Alternatively, you can construct application-relevant subdirectories—for example, `Sales`—and place them there. As discussed earlier in this chapter, you can even place them completely outside the Domino Data Directory hierarchy, using the folder or database link technology. In this way, you can take advantage of both the heightened security of the given environment and of the additional space offered by it.

Regardless of where you place the application databases, you can make it easier for your user population to locate them by using the Domino database catalog and database library.

Creating a Database Catalog

To maintain an inventory of databases on your server, you can create a database catalog (`CATALOG.NSF`). All databases within your Domino Data Directory are listed in the catalog by default.

The `Catalog` server task creates and maintains the catalog. The task runs every day and updates the entries for all databases when changes occur. For example, if a database is moved to another server, the `Catalog` server task updates the database entry with the new location.

You create the database catalog from the Database Catalog template (`CATALOG.NTF`), following the standard database creation process and assigning it a server location, title, and filename. The Database Catalog template is an advanced template, and is displayed by selecting Show Advanced Templates at the bottom of the New Database dialog box. When you create a database catalog, you have Manager access by default.

Following the database creation, you should adjust the database catalog's ACL to give Manager access to all administrative users and similar access to servers who host the catalog or a replica copy of it. While modifying the ACL, you should give the Default group Reader access.

You can then create replicas of the database catalog on the desired servers within your Domino environment. In this way, the catalog contains information on the databases on all the selected servers.

CREATING A DATABASE LIBRARY

The database library feature is similar to the database catalog, but it lists only those databases published to the library by the library's Database Manager or librarian. When a user attempts to open a database from the library, Notes searches for the database using the replica ID. It searches first on the local hard drive, and then on the user's home server, and finally on other servers. Notes opens the first occurrence of the database.

You create a library by creating a new database using the DBLIB4.NTF template. After creating the database, you can create a list of librarians in the Librarians view. You can publish a database in the library if you are a librarian and have the library on your desktop:

1. Highlight the Database icon you want to publish and select File, Database, Publish.
2. Enter an abstract describing the database in the dialog box displayed by Notes. This creates a document for the database in the library.

If a user has only Reader access to the database library and attempts to publish a database, a Notes agent automatically generates mail to the librarian, who can then decide whether to publish the database. This check must be done because readers do not have access to create or modify documents on their own.

39

CHAPTER 40

MANAGING YOUR DOMINO SERVER CONFIGURATION

In this chapter

ADMINISTERING DOMINO SERVERS

Administering Domino servers is one of the most multifaceted assignments of the Domino administrator. It covers the entire breadth of server administration, from server installation, configuration, and maintenance, to ongoing monitoring and troubleshooting. It entails ensuring that servers are installed, configured, and maintained at an optimal level to perform the specific function required by their organizations.

To ensure the stability, accessibility, and reliability of any one particular Domino server and the Domino network in general, administrators are responsible for the following tasks:

- Installing and configuring new servers.
- Running, monitoring, and troubleshooting existing servers by monitoring the Domino log and statistics databases.
- Backing up databases and files on a regular basis.
- Optimizing server performance by configuring the server's configuration documents, compacting databases, fixing corrupted files, and enabling the server to run at maximum efficiency.
- Managing the Domino Directory by creating and updating server-relevant documents within the Directory.
- Overseeing Directory Assistance, managing cascading address books, and administering LDAP.
- Configuring, monitoring, and troubleshooting mail routing by setting up and maintaining shared mail, setting mail thresholds, rerouting dead mail, and configuring POP3 and IMAP clients and files.
- Configuring, monitoring, and troubleshooting replication.
- Configuring, monitoring, and troubleshooting connectivity and network security to servers within the domain or outside the domain over an intranet, the Internet, or an extranet.
- Configuring clustering, billing and monitoring, failover, load balancing, and partitioned servers.

UNDERSTANDING THE AVAILABLE DOMINO ADMINISTRATION TOOLS

Domino provides the administrator with a number of tools with which to perform the tasks enumerated in the last section. The tools consist of processes and applications, databases, console commands, and configuration settings. The most important of these tools include:

- The Domino Administrator, specifically the Server and Configuration tabs, provides a central environment to administer your Domino infrastructure. The Configuration tab is shown in Figure 40.1.

Figure 40.1
The Configuration tab within the Domino Administrator provides access to all the configuration documents.

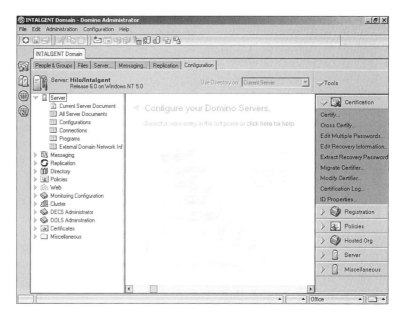

- The Web Administrator is a highly interactive Web-based tool that facilitates the administration of a Domino server through Internet Explorer or Netscape Navigator. Unlike previous releases, the Web Administrator's users interface has the full fidelity of Domino Administrator 6. Figure 40.2 shows the Web Administrator running within Microsoft Internet Explorer.

Figure 40.2
The Web Administrator provides a strikingly similar user interface to Domino Administrator 6.

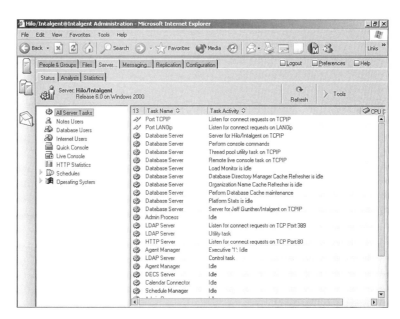

40

- The Administration Process automating such administrative tasks as the recertification, renaming, deletion, and upgrading to hierarchical naming of users and servers.

- Server programs automate many of the administrative tasks, including:

  - Compacting all databases on a server.

  - Updating all view indexes within databases on a server.

  - Refreshing/replacing the design of all databases given specific design templates on a server.

- The Agent Manager task controls who can run agents and when they can run on each server.

- Administration databases facilitate the collection and analysis of data about the system. These include the following:

  - The Domino Server Log (LOG.NSF), which records server-specific information on replication, mail routing, database activity, and network and modem communications. A sample log file record is shown in Figure 40.3.

Figure 40.3
A sample log record from the Domino Server Log.

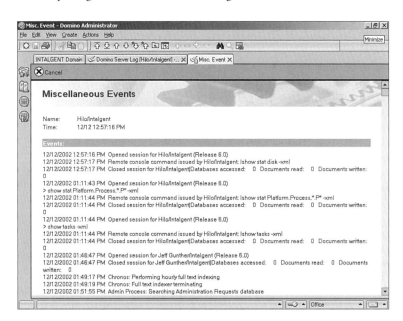

- The Administration Requests database (ADMIN4.NSF), which posts all requests and responses to those requests associated with the Administration Process.

  - The Statistics Reporting database (STATREP.NSF), which tracks server statistics and records reported events.

  - The Certification Log database (CERTLOG.NSF), which lists certification events pertaining to users and servers with their given certificates.

- The Catalog database (CATALOG.NSF), which catalogs all major database attributes, including general database parameters, replication settings, full-text index settings, and ACL settings.
- The Mail Router Mailbox (MAIL.BOX), which contains a listing of dead and pending mail.

■ Server commands perform various tasks including shutting down or restarting a server, fixing a database, and starting and stopping Domino services.

■ The NOTES.INI configuration settings define how the Domino server runs and operates.

TIP

> Lotus provides a great resource on the Lotus Developer Domain called Professor INI. This resource attempts to fill the void of information regarding the NOTES.INI by discussing different settings or groups of settings relating to Domino. For more information, visit http://www-10.lotus.com/ldd/today.nsf/profini?OpenView.

AUTOMATING MANY ADMINISTRATIVE TASKS VIA THE ADMINISTRATION PROCESS

Of the tools mentioned, the Administration Process is the one most responsible for automating routine administrative tasks. The services that are provided by the Administration Process include:

■ Performing a variety of name-management tasks including the renaming, deletion, and recertification of servers, groups, and people

■ Handling various mail-management tasks including the deletion and moving of individual's mail files, disabling and enabling agents, and modifying the Access Control List

■ Performing replica-management tasks

40

Although the process runs by default at server startup, you still must enable it for the domain. To do so, you begin by designating a particular server, preferably a central or hub server, to perform the role of administration server for the Domino Directory. When established, the designated server can maintain the Access Control Lists (ACL) within the Directory, perform name changes and removals, and replicate these changes to other servers.

The Domino Administration Process requires the following database and processing infrastructure for each server on which it is to run:

■ A Certification Log database must be created on each server performing the role of administration server for selected databases. This Certification Log database keeps track of all users and servers in the organization and the certificates they have.

■ An Administration Requests database must be created on each server performing the role of administration server for selected databases. The Administration Requests database, ADMIN4.NSF, is created automatically the first time you run the Administration

Process on a server. The views available within the Administration Requests database are shown in Figure 40.4.

Figure 40.4
The Administration Requests database provides many types of views to review all outstanding requests.

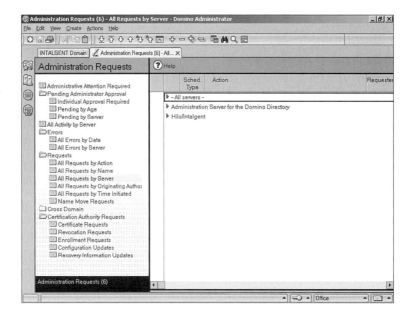

- At least one hierarchically certified server exists within your Domino domain. If your naming scheme is flat and you do not have any hierarchically certified servers, manually certify one server with a hierarchical name. The Administration Process can be run only on a hierarchically named server.

- The Administration Process is running as a task on the selected server.

- You have designated yourself and other administrators to have the authority to modify Person and Server documents in the Domino Directory.

- As noted previously, you have specified an Administration Server for the Domino Directory. Typically, this is completed during the installation process.

After you have ensured that the necessary infrastructure for the Administration Process exists on your selected servers and you have established an administration server for your Domino Directory, you can proceed to assign administration servers for all other databases that you want the Administration Process to maintain. In this way, when you make modifications to user or server accounts using the Administration Process, the Administration Process in turn propagates these changes to all such target databases for which there exists an administration server.

To assign an administration server for a particular database or set of databases from within the Domino Administrator, complete the following steps:

1. Verify that you have Manager access to the database or set of databases for which you want to assign an administration server.

2. Start the Domino Administrator 6 client and select the appropriate Domino Directory.

3. Choose the Files tab and select the database for which you want to assign an administration server. These steps only outline the steps to assign an administration server for one selected database.

4. Expand the Database task under the Tools pane and select Manage ACL. If you only selected one file, the Basics section of the Access Control List dialog box is displayed.

5. Click the Advanced tab.

6. Select the Server radio button, and then the desired administration server from the Server list box, as shown in Figure 40.5.

Figure 40.5
The Advanced tab of the Access Control List dialog box enables you to specify the administration server for a particular database.

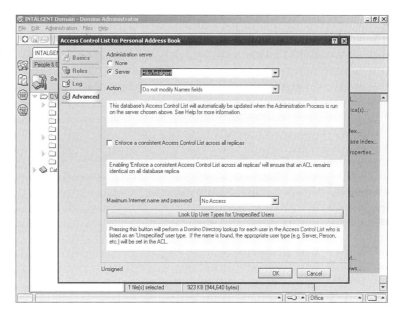

7. Optionally, select whether you want the server to modify fields of type Reader or Author. Keep in mind, however, that the Administration Process must be running on the target server and that the network connectivity infrastructure must also be in place between the designated target server and the administration server of the target server's Domino Directory.

8. Click OK to assign the target server as the administration server of the selected database.

Chapter 36, "Administering Users, Groups, and Certification," provides extensive examples on how you use the Administration Process in renaming, deleting, and recertifying users within the Domino Directory.

MAINTAINING SERVER CONFIGURATION DOCUMENTS AND RUNNING SERVER TASKS

There are two distinct areas of server configuration for which the system administrator has responsibility: documents within the Domino Directory, such as those described in the previous section, and the scheduling and running of server tasks.

USING THE DOMINO ADMINISTRATOR TO MAINTAIN DOCUMENTS WITHIN THE DOMINO DIRECTORY

The set of documents subsumed under the Configuration tab within the Domino Administrator facilitates the administration of the Domino server. Under this Configuration tab, there are 12 categories of documents: Server, Messaging, Replication, Directory, Policies, Web, Monitoring Configuration, Cluster, DECS Administrator, Offline Services, Certificates, and Miscellaneous.

The Server view category is particularly relevant when configuring server documents. It provides subordinate categories or views for the Current Server Document, All Server Documents, Configurations, Connections, Programs, and External Domain Network Information.

CURRENT SERVER DOCUMENT

The Current Server Document entry under the Server view category displays the document of the current server. It enables the administrator to perform a set of actions from the Domino Administrator Create-Server drop-down menu including:

- Certifier
- Configuration Settings
- Connection
- Domain
- External Domain Network Information
- Mail-In Database
- Parameter
- Program
- Resource

Figure 40.6 shows the complete set of available Create actions when the Domino Administrator has opened a server document.

To edit a server document, simply open the current server document and click the Edit Server action button to open the document in edit mode. The Current Server Document in edit mode is shown in Figure 40.7.

Figure 40.6
The complete set of Create actions relevant to the Domino server is available to the administrator within the Domino Administrator.

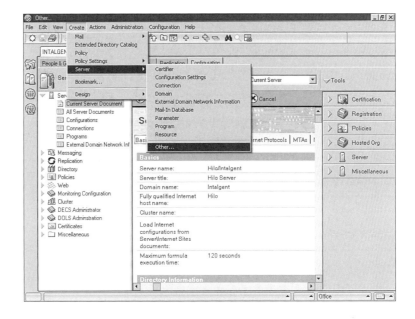

Figure 40.7
The server document can be edited by clicking the Edit Server action button.

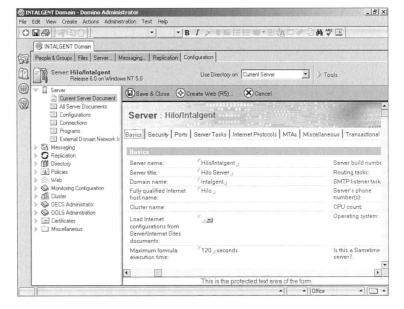

SERVER DOCUMENT

The Server Document contains 10 embedded configuration tabs, as shown in Figure 40.8. These cover the following areas:

Figure 40.8
The Server document allows administrators to configure and manage a particular server.

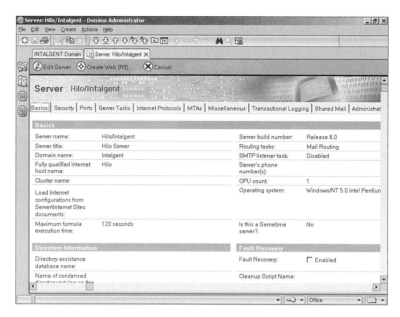

One document is generated and configured for every server you created within your organization. The Server Name field and the Domain field are required, and are filled in automatically based on the information you supply when the server is first registered. Let's explore each tab of the Server document:

- **Basics**—Specifies the server location information, including the telephone numbers and dialing rules to use for dialing, and any additional information, such as mail server, cluster name, or maximum formula execution time.

- **Security**—Specifies settings for general server access, server administration, programmability execution restrictions, and restrictions on Internet authentication.

- **Ports**—Specifies the active Notes Network ports, the SSL settings for Internet ports, and the standard and SSL port parameters for each of the major Internet server tasks: Web, Directory, Mail, DIIOP, and new Remote Debugger Manager.

- **Server Tasks**—Specifies the parameters for each of the major server tasks: the Administration Process, the Agent Manager, the Domain Catalog, the Directory Cataloger, the Internet Cluster Manager, the Web Retriever, and the new Remote Debug Manager.

- **Internet Protocols**—Specifies the server task configuration parameters for the major Internet server tasks: HTTP, Domino Web Engine, DIIOP, and LDAP.

- **MTAs or Message Transfer Agent**—Specifies the configurations for the R4.x SMTP MTA, the X.400 MTA, and the cc:Mail MTA.

- **Miscellaneous**—Contains text fields to record the location, department, and comments for this particular server.

- **Transactional Logging**—Enables you to enable or disable transactional logging and specify configuration details for the service. For more information regarding Transactional Logging, refer to a topic titled "Setting Up a Domino Server for Transaction Logging" in the Domino Administrator 6 Help.
- **Administration**—Specifies the Owners and Administrators of the server document. This tab also includes the certified public key for the server.

A detailed explanation of each of the field settings within the Server document is provided in Chapter 34, "Initial Configuration of Servers with the Domino Directories."

ALL SERVER DOCUMENTS

The All Server Documents view displays a view containing the domain, server, title, administrator, phone numbers, release number, and routing tasks for each server. This view allows you to quickly view and access all the server documents within the selected Domino Directory. It also enables the administrator to perform the same set of tasks as described for the individual server document.

CONFIGURATION DOCUMENTS

The Configurations view displays a list of the Configuration Settings documents for the selected Domino Directory. It provides a view consisting of the server name for the given configuration, the configuration parameters for the given server, and who last updated the document.

UNDERSTANDING CONFIGURATION SETTING DOCUMENTS IN THE DOMINO DIRECTORY

Using a Configuration Settings document in the Domino Directory, you can specify parameters pertaining to the LDAP task, the Router/SMTP task, MIME conversions, and NOTES.INI settings for a single server, a group of servers, or for all servers in a domain. A Server Configuration Settings document, shown in Figure 40.9, enables you to centralize server administration and thereby modify server settings remotely from one location.

In general, servers evaluate Configuration Setting documents in the following order: an individual server's configuration documents, documents containing a group specification, and documents pertaining to all servers within the domain.

UNDERSTANDING HOW A SERVER UPDATES ITS CONFIGURATION SETTINGS

Whenever the individual server reinitializes or starts up, it scans the Domino Directory for Configuration Setting documents pertaining to it. The server then reads these settings into memory and updates the NOTES.INI file accordingly. Approximately every five minutes thereafter, it checks the Domino Directory for modifications to the configuration documents. When it encounters a new or modified configuration setting, it reads the new or modified settings into memory and updates the NOTES.INI file. The latency is approximately five minutes. When updating the configuration settings for remote servers, this delay can be increased. This stems from the fact that a replication cycle must occur between the local and

40

remote servers. Furthermore, upon completion of the replication cycle, the receiving server must update its views containing the documents. The delay usually averages 20 minutes following the last replication cycle before the configuration settings take effect on the remote servers.

Figure 40.9
The Server Configuration Settings document allows administrators to define global settings for all Domino servers within a given domain.

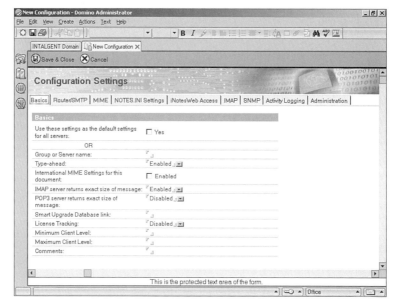

NOTE

Changes made directly to a setting in the NOTES.INI file using a text editor are overwritten by the same setting if it appears in a Configuration Setting document.

PREPARING TO CONFIGURE MULTIPLE SERVERS

By grouping your servers into functional sets, such as mail servers, database servers, and Internet application servers, you can create configuration documents for each group, assigning them the same settings. In this way, you increase your administrative accuracy and efficiency.

CREATING A CONFIGURATION SETTINGS DOCUMENT

To create a Configuration Settings document for a single server, a group of servers, or all servers within the domain, complete the following steps:

1. Within the Domino Administrator, select the server to be administered from the server icon in the far left side of the Domino Administrator screen.

2. Choose the Configuration tab and select the Configuration view under the Server category.

3. Click the Add Configuration action button.

4. On the Basics tab, specify whether the settings are to be used as the default settings for all servers, whether they apply to a group of servers, or whether they apply to an individual server. In the Server Name field, you can enter the name of a server or a group of servers. An asterisk (*) in the Server Name field specifies this as the default configuration document. If you create more than one default document, the server does not check for duplicates and normally uses the first document encountered. You then complete the Basics tab by specifying the following fields:

- **International MIME Settings for This Document**—This field works in collaboration with the International Character Set definitions you provide on the subordinate tabs under the MIME tab. You must enable this parameter for the International MIME settings to take effect.

- **IMAP Server to Return Exact Size of Messages**—When selecting Enabled, the IMAP server calculates the exact size of the message upon receipt of such a request from the IMAP client; otherwise, it returns an estimated size. Enabling this option can impact performance.

- **POP3 Server to Return Exact Size of Message**—When selecting Enabled, the POP3 server returns the exact size of the message in response to the STAT command. This means that the entire message is converted, which might lead to time-outs of the PASS command.

- **Smart Upgrade Database Link**—Contains a database link to the Smart Upgrade database. This database is used to notify users when to upgrade to a newer version of Lotus Notes 6.

- **License Tracking**—When selecting Enabled, Domino will track the number of active users within a Notes Domain. This feature is helpful to ensure that you have the proper number of licenses.

- **Minimum Client Level**—Enables you to restrict access to a server based on the Notes client version number. Beginning with Lotus Notes 5.11, Domino can distinguish between point releases to ensure the minimum client level. For users running Lotus Notes 5.11 or earlier, Domino can only distinguish between major releases. For example, if you want to restrict Notes 4.x user's from accessing the server, simply type **4.x** into this field. Remember that any release before 5.11 will default to release 5.x. For example, if you place 5.09 in the field, all Notes clients before 5.11 will be blocked, including 5.10.

- **Maximum Client Level**—As you'd expect, this field restricts access to the server based on the Notes client being used. The same restrictions as the previous field apply. If you specify any point release previous to 5.11, all clients after 5.11 are not allowed access to the server.

- **Comments**—Enables administrators to add comments about the Configuration document.

5. On the Router/SMTP tab, specify Basic configuration parameters, Restrictions and Controls parameters, Message Tracking parameters, and Advanced parameters.

On the Basics subordinate tab, specify the following:

- **Number of Mailboxes**—A number from 1 to 10 to set the Number of MAIL.BOX files for each server using this Configuration document.

- **SMTP Used When Sending Messages Outside the Local Internet Domain**—Enabling such routing means that SMTP can route mail outside the local Domino domain. Disabling such routing prompts Domino to use Notes routing based on SMTP Foreign Domain documents and Connection documents.

- **SMTP Allowed Within the Internet Domain**—When specifying MIME messages, Domino uses SMTP routing to route mail to other Domino servers within the same named network capable of receiving SMTP mail. When specifying all messages, Domino uses SMTP routing to route Notes and MIME format messages. This causes Domino to convert Notes format messages into MIME format, which might lead to a loss of fidelity and performance. When disabled is specified, Domino uses Notes routing between servers in the same named network.

- **Servers Within the Local Notes Domain Are Reachable Via SMTP over TCPIP**—When specifying Always, Domino uses SMTP routing to route mail to other Domino servers configured to receive incoming SMTP mail within the same Internet domain. When specifying Only If in Same Notes Named Network, Domino uses Notes routing to route mail to other servers in external Notes Named Networks.

- **Address Lookup**—When specifying Fullname and then Local Part, Domino first performs a non-case-sensitive match for the entire Internet address and, upon failure, follows with a match for only the part preceding the @. Similarly, when specifying Fullname Only, Domino performs a non-case-sensitive match for the entire Internet address; or when specifying Local Part, Domino performs a non-case-sensitive match for only the part preceding the @.

- **Exhaustive Lookup**—When enabled, Domino searches all directories to ensure that there are no duplicate recipients. When disabled, Domino searches until it finds the first Directory instance of the recipient.

- **Local Internet Domain Smart Host**—When specified, Domino routes mail to SMTP recipients who are not in the local Domino Directory to this smart host.

- **Smart Host Is Used for All Local Internet Domain Recipients**—When enabled, Domino routes all incoming SMTP messages to the smart host for name lookup. When disabled, Domino routes only messages with recipients not found in the local Domino Directory to the smart host.

- **Host Name Lookup**—Whether to use Dynamic Lookup Only (DNS Only), Local Lookup Only (Hosts File Only), or Dynamic and Then Local for the Hostname Lookup and Resolution. Dynamic Lookup utilizes only the server's DNS host. Local Lookup utilizes the server's host file.

On the Restrictions and Controls subordinate tab, you need to specify the following:

- **Router**—Delimits the domains, organizations, and organizational units from which the Domino router should allow or deny mail. They also include a maximum message size parameter, whether to send messages between certain sizes as low priority, and whether to obey database quotas.

- **SMTP Inbound Controls**—Delimits the external Internet domains and hosts from which the Domino server allows or denies relaying service, both to the local Internet domains and to other external Internet domains including support for DNS Blacklist Filters. These new filters enable administrators to use third-party lists to block incoming SPAM. Parameters for Inbound Connection Controls are also provided in the form of hostname connection verification to allow or deny connections from specific hostnames or IP addresses. Similarly, Inbound Sender Control parameters exist to verify the sender's domain and allow or deny messages based on Internet addresses or domains. Finally, Inbound Intended Recipient Controls allow or deny access to specific Internet addresses.

- **SMTP Outbound Controls**—Delimits the Internet addresses or Notes addresses allowed to send messages to the Internet.

- **Delivery Controls**—Defines a set of server inbound processing parameters. They define the maximum number of delivery threads, whether to encrypt all delivered mail, and whether to impose an execution timeout on any pre-delivery agents.

- **Transfer Controls**—Defines a corollary set of outbound processing parameters. These include the maximum number of transfer threads and concurrent maximum number of transfer threads, the maximum hop count, the low priority mail routing time range, the initial transfer retry interval, and the expired message purge interval.

- **Rules**—Defines a set of filtering rules for both inbound and outbound messages. Similar to the message rules found within the Notes Mail database, these rules allow administrators to act on specific messages based on a defined set of criteria. These rules can allow organizations to journalize, not accept, or modify the routing state of messages based on multiple criteria.

On the Message Tracking subordinate tab, specify whether to enable message tracking for the given configuration. If enabled, list any users or servers for which you do not want to track messages. Specify the message tracking collection interval. This number equates to how often message tracking activity is logged in the Mail Tracking Store database. Decide whether to log message subjects, and, if enabled, for whom you do not want to log message subjects. Finally, specify which users and servers are allowed to track messages and subjects. If you want to track messages across multiple servers, you have to include all participating servers in the latter two lists.

40

On the Advanced subordinate tab, specify whether to enable Journalizing and Inbound and Outbound SMTP Commands and Extensions and Controls. The Journalizing tab includes the following parameters:

- **Journalizing**—Gives administrators the capability to capture and store a copy of all messages routed through the domain.
- **Field Encryption Exclusion List**—Contains the fields that Domino will exclude from being encrypted during journalizing.
- **Method**—Details the journalizing type used by Domino. Options include either Copy to Local Database or Send to Mail Database. If the method specified is a Copy to Local Database, the remaining fields in this section pertain with Journalizing's messaging, data management, and periodicity.

The Commands and Extensions tab pertains to the following Inbound and Outbound SMTP parameters:

- **SIZE Extension**—Rejects inbound messages greater than the maximum size specified.
- **Pipelining Extension**—Combines multiple SMTP commands in the same network packet thereby improving performance.
- **DSN Extension**—Generates, upon request, Deliver Status Notifications to a message's sender for an SMTP message.
- **8-bit MIME Extension**—Sends multinational characters without encoding if enabled, or with encoding if disabled.
- **HELP Command**—Supports the SMTP HELP command.
- **VRFY Command**—Supports the VRFY SMTP command to verify usernames.
- **EXPN Command**—Supports the EXPN command to expand mailing lists to show individual usernames.
- **ETRN Command**—Supports the ETRN command enabling the server to accept inbound requests to send queued outbound messages.
- **SSL Negotiated over TCP/IP Port**—Enables the server to connect securely to another server by creating an SSL channel over the TCP/IP port.
- The Outbound SMTP commands and extensions include the outbound derivatives of the SIZE, Pipelining, DSN, and 8-bit MIME extensions.

The Controls tab enables you to specify the logging levels for messaging events, advanced settings for message delivery and transfer, and the capability to set textual comments for various types of messaging failures.

6. On the MIME tab, specify Basic configuration parameters, Conversion options, Settings by Character Set Groups, and Advanced configuration parameters.

- **Basics Subordinate**—Specifies the primary character set and any secondary character set groups to be supported. All International MIME settings rely on enabling the International MIME settings for this document parameter on the main Basics tab.

- **Conversions Options**—Specifies the General parameter of whether to return receipts. For the Inbound parameters, specifies the length of the inbound message line and whether to autodetect the character set if the message carries no such character set information. For the Outbound parameters, specifies whether to use Base64, QuotedPrintable, Uuencode, or BinHex as the attachment encoding method to use on outbound conversions and whether to convert tabs to spaces. Additionally, specify the length of the outbound message line and whether to look up Internet addresses for Notes addresses when the Internet address is not in the document.

- **Settings by Character Set Groups**—Defines font options for Inbound HTML and Plain Text and Outbound Header and Body Character Sets and Encoding methods.

- **Advanced**—Specifies the Advanced Inbound Message Options and Advanced Outbound Message Options. The inbound options include the following: whether re-sent headers take precedence over original headers, whether to remove group names from headers, whether to add a recipient address to the BCC line in the address header if it does not appear in any address header, what 8-bit character set is to be assumed to be the character set for non-MIME messages or MIME messages with an unknown character set, and mappings between character set aliases and supported character sets. The outbound options include the following: whether to use AppleDouble or BinHex4.0 encoding method for Macintosh attachment conversion; which RFC822 display name format, if any, to use for outbound recipient naming; whether to include nonstandard or private items necessary for Notes clients running such applications; a list of Notes item names to be removed from the message header prior to transmission; which character set to use when converting a multilingual message to MIME; and outbound character set alias mapping between supported character sets and known aliases.

40

7. On the NOTES.INI Settings tab, select the Set/Modify parameters button. The Server Configuration Parameters dialog box opens. Open the Select a Standard Parameter dialog box by clicking the Item arrow. Select one of the standard parameters—for example, the ADMINPINTERVAL specifying the interval cycle for when the Administration Process performs request handling, and click OK. Assign it a value—for example, 30 (minutes). Click next to assign another standard parameter or OK to return to the main NOTES.INI Settings tab.

8. On the iNotes Web Access tab, you can selectively configure various elements of the iNotes Web Access client, including the Welcome Page, whether to enable alarms, control the polling of new Mail messages, control over offline support, and settings dealing with International and miscellaneous controls. Refer to Chapter 10, "Using iNotes Web Access," for more information about how these features are utilized by users.

9. On the IMAP tab, review and specify Basic configuration parameters, Public and Other Users' Folders, and Advanced configuration parameters.

- **Basics**—Specifies the maximum number of IMAP user sessions and each session's timeout in minutes. If the Enable IMAP During Login feature is enabled, Domino will automatically replace the design of their mail database with the IMAP mail template the first time it's accessed from an IMAP client.

- **Public and Other Users' Folders**—IMAP clients can access and interact with public mail databases. The fields in this tab enable administrators to specify the parameters for how the IMAP task supports public and private folders.

- **Advanced**—Defines the various greetings used by the IMAP service and parameters for the worker thread pool.

10. On the SNMP tab, review and, if desired, give other SNMP-management software the capability to start, stop, and reboot the Domino server. All SNMP requests are managed by the Domino SNMP Agent.

11. On the Activity Logging tab, review and, if desired, enable the activity log. The Activity Trends subordinate tab controls the basic configuration, retention periods, and proxy databases.

12. On the Administration tab, review and, if desired, modify the Owner and Administrators fields.

13. Click the Save & Close action button.

A further explanation of the configuration settings is provided in Chapter 34, "Initial Configuration of Servers with the Domino Directories."

SETTINGS YOU CANNOT SPECIFY—CONFIGURATION SETTINGS DOCUMENT

You cannot edit every parameter in the NOTES.INI using a Configuration Settings document. You must enter some configuration settings using the Server document. This maintains the integrity of Domino security. You should also refrain from editing the NOTES.INI file directly to specify these settings. This can lead to server errors. The parameters that cannot be updated using a Configuration Settings document include the following:

- Any parameter beginning with $
- ServerName
- Server_Title
- Type
- Form
- Names
- Allow_Access
- Deny_Access

- Create_File_Access
- Create_Replica_Access
- Admin_Access
- Allow_Passthru_Access
- Allow_Passthru_Targets
- Allow_Passthru_Clients
- Allow_Passthru_Callers
- Ports
- KitType
- Domain
- MailServer
- MailFile
- Server_Console_Password (you can set this parameter only at the server console)

Modifying the NOTES.INI

In addition to editing the NOTES.INI parameter settings using either a Configuration Settings document or a Server document as detailed in the preceding sections, you can edit the NOTES.INI in two additional ways:

- You can use the Set Configuration server command at the console to write a specific setting to the NOTES.INI file. This setting is written to the Server Configuration document specific to the server, if one exists; otherwise, a new document is created.

- You can edit the NOTES.INI file directly in a text editor. If you do edit the NOTES.INI file directly, however, make sure to make a backup copy of the file in case you encounter problems and want to recover your previous version. Because directly editing the NOTES.INI can lead to file errors and impair the operation of the Domino server, it is not a recommended practice.

40

Obsolete NOTES.INI Settings

With the introduction of Domino 6, some of NOTES.INI settings that were used with Release 4.6 and 5 are now obsolete. They include the following:

- AdminPInterval
- AdminPModifyPersonDocumentsAt
- Config_DB
- LDAP_CountryCheck
- LDAP_Enforce_Schema
- LDAP_Strict_RFC_Adherence

- LDAP_UTF8results
- KillProcess
- Mailclusterfailover
- New_DNParse
- NNTPAddress
- NNTP_Delete_Days
- NNTP_Delete_Days_Expired
- NNTP_Initial_Feed_All
- NNTP_Previous_X_servername
- NNTP_Prohibit_NEWSNEWS_Command
- NNTP_PullAsServer
- Server_Name_Lookup_Noupdate
- WebAuth_AD_Group
- WebAdmin_Disable_Force_GUI
- WebAdmin_Expire_Cache

CONNECTION DOCUMENTS

The Connections view displays all current Connection documents. It provides a view consisting of the destinations for the given connection, the connection's type, the port being used, the schedule for the given connection, the interval between successful connections, the tasks associated with the given connection, what (if any) priority databases are to be replicated, and whether the connection is direct or dialup.

UNDERSTANDING SERVER CONNECTION DOCUMENTS

You use Connection documents to configure servers to route mail and to replicate databases. Replication between servers requires a single Connection document. Mail routing requires two Connection documents, one document for each direction. Within the Connection document, you can specify the times, days, and intervals between scheduled connections for two servers, and whether this is for mail routing, replication, or both. You can also create multiple Connection documents between two servers, which enables you to schedule mail routing and replication separately.

A detailed explanation of Connection documents is provided in Chapters 34 and 38.

PROGRAM DOCUMENTS

The Programs view displays all current program documents. It provides a view consisting of the programs, their command lines, whether they are currently enabled, and their repeat interval.

UNDERSTANDING PROGRAM DOCUMENTS IN THE DOMINO DIRECTORY

You create a Program document to schedule tasks and programs to run at a regularly scheduled time or at server startup on your Domino servers. A sample of a program document is
shown in Figure 40.10. Using a Program document gives you greater control over when
programs run. Instead of being limited to specifying the exact hour of the day when a program runs, as is necessary in the NOTES.INI file, you can specify a range of times, a day of the
week, and a regular interval when the program runs on the server within a Program document.

Figure 40.10
The server Program
document is used to
schedule Notes tasks.

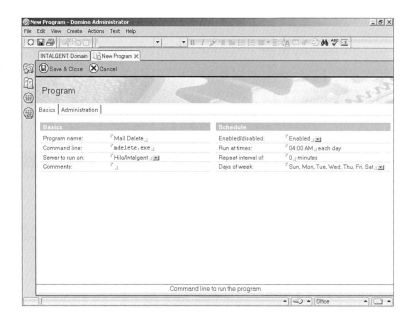

USING A PROGRAM DOCUMENT TO SCHEDULE PROGRAMS

To create a Program document to schedule tasks and programs on your Domino server,
complete the following steps:

1. Within the Domino Administrator, select the server to be administered from the server
   icon in the far left side of the Domino Administrator screen.

2. Choose the Configuration tab and select the Programs view.

3. Click the Add Program action button.

4. Under the Basics area, enter the name of the server program or script to run in the
   Program name field. You can use the following characters: A–Z, 0–9, & (ampersand),
   - (hyphen), . (period), _ (underscore), ' (apostrophe), / (forward slash). You can also use
   spaces.

   In the Command Line field, enter the command to start the program and any arguments required by the command.

In the Server to Run On field, enter the full hierarchical name of the server on which to run the program.

Specify any program description or comments in the Comments field.

5. On the Basics tab under the Schedule area, select Enabled or At Server Startup Only, depending on whether you want to specify a specific schedule or only want the program to run when the server starts.

If you specified Enabled, enter the schedule for the program to execute. This includes providing values for the Run At Times, Repeat Interval, and Days of Week fields.

Enter the first time of day for the program to run in the Run At Times field.

Enter the number of minutes before the program should repeat its execution in the Repeat Interval field.

Enter the days of the week for the program to run in the Days of Week field.

6. Click the Save & Close action button.

RUNNING SERVER TASKS

Administering the server also means ensuring that full-time server tasks such as the replicator and the mail router start when the server starts. In addition, other server tasks can be scheduled to run on a periodic basis from the NOTES.INI file or from a Program document. Tasks can also be run manually from the server console on an as-needed basis.

Depending on the functions the server performs, various tasks are initiated at startup or run periodically. Some of the more important tasks include those from the following list:

- Adminp—The Administration Process task automates many routine administrative tasks. By default, Adminp is included in the ServerTasks NOTES.INI setting to run at server startup.

- Amgr—The Agent Manager controls who has the authority to execute agents on a specified server. By default, Amgr is included in the ServerTasks NOTES.INI setting to run at server startup.

- Catalog—The Cataloger task updates a database catalog (CATALOG.NSF) that is created on a server the first time the Catalog task runs. The catalog lists all databases available to users of that server. It includes such database attributes as the database location, indexing configuration, ACL properties, search and result forms, file system configuration forms, and the database's nearest replica. By default, Cataloger is included in the ServerTasksAt1 NOTES.INI setting, meaning that the task will run at 1:00 a.m.

- Collect—The Statistic Collector server task summarizes statistics from one or more servers. The statistics collected cover the following areas: system information, such as disk and memory usage, server configuration, and load; messaging performance; database and replication performance; communications and networking performance; and calendaring and scheduling. By configuring a Server Statistic Collection Profile document, you can designate a particular server to collect statistics from a list of specified servers. The default for this, however, is to collect data only from the server on which the server `Collect` task resides. Unless otherwise specified, the `Collect` task creates a `STATREP.NSF` as its repository where the statistic reports reside. You can load `Collect` at the server console, or you can schedule it to run at startup by including it in the `ServerTasks` `NOTES.INI` setting.

- `Compact`—The Database Compactor server task gets rid of unused whitespace in databases. Blocks of whitespace are left in the database after documents are deleted. Compact recovers that whitespace. You can load `Compact` at the server console, or you can schedule it to run at a set time in the `NOTES.INI` file or a Program document. Additional information on `Compact` is provided in Chapter 39, "Administering Files and Databases."

  Additional information on `Compact` is provided in Chapter 41, "Troubleshooting and Monitoring Domino."

CAUTION

> When you run `Compact` on a Release 5 database, the database is converted to version 6 format unless the database has been named with an `.NS5` file extension. You can revert to Release 5 format by running `Compact` with an `-r` flag (for example, `Load Compact` `DATABASE.NSF` `-r`, where `DATABASE.NSF` is the filename of the database to revert to Release 5 format).

- `DECS`—The Domino Enterprise Connection Services task provides dynamic access to a host of relational databases. Using the `DECS` Administrator template, you can map fields in forms directly to fields in relational database tables, making these accessible to your users without storing any data within native Domino databases. You can load `DECS` at the server console, or you can schedule it to run at startup by including it in the `ServerTasks` `NOTES.INI` setting.

- `Design`—The Designer task updates the design of databases with changes made to the templates on which the database design is based. The `Design` template should be placed in the Notes Data Directory and should be replicated to all servers on which the database resides. The `Design` task runs by default at 1:00 a.m. and should be followed by the `Updall` task to rebuild views changed during the `Design` task.

- `Event`—The Event Monitor task is an optional task used for event reporting. When `Event` is loaded for the first time at the server console, or when it is put into the `ServerTasks` setting in the `NOTES.INI` file, an `EVENTS5.NSF` database is created automatically to collect server statistics and event documents. Events are specific, system-performance statistics that surpass predefined parameters.

- `Fixup`—The Database fixup task fixes corrupted databases by locating corrupt documents and removing them completely from the database, including the document-deletion stub. If a replica of the database exists, the document can be replicated back into the database after the document has been completely deleted. `Fixup` runs at startup and fixes the Notes log, but it does not locate and rebuild corrupted views. You can schedule Fixup to run using a Program document or a NOTES.INI setting, but be aware that it takes significant CPU resources to run. Therefore, avoid running Fixup from the server console during the day unless absolutely necessary. Additional information on the Fixup task is provided in Chapter 39.

- ICM—The Internet Cluster Manager server task coupled with native Domino clustering extends failover and load balancing to Web browser clients utilizing HTTP or HTTPS services. The ICM maintains information about availability of servers in the cluster and the distribution of databases. HTTP clients direct requests for Notes databases to the ICM via the Domino HTTP server. The ICM ensures that the clients are connected to an appropriate server and the workload is balanced across the servers in the cluster. You can load ICM at the server console, or you can schedule it to run at startup by including it in the ServerTasks NOTES.INI setting.

- HTTP—The Domino Hypertext Transfer Protocol server task provides standard HTTP access to Web browser clients. You can load HTTP at the server console, or you can schedule it to run at startup by including it in the ServerTasks NOTES.INI setting.

- IMAP—The Domino Internet Mail Access Protocol server provides support for the IMAP protocol. IMAP-enabled clients can thereby retrieve messages from the IMAP server and store them locally, access messages directly from the server, or copy messages for offline use and then later synchronize with mail on the server. You can load IMAP at the server console, or you can schedule it to run at startup by including it in the ServerTasks NOTES.INI setting.

- LDAP—The Lightweight Directory Access Protocol server task provides standard LDAP Directory access to clients running the LDAP protocol. LDAP-enabled applications can thereby query and, with the proper access permissions, modify entries in Domino Directories on the LDAP server. You can load LDAP at the server console, or you can schedule it to run at startup by including it in the ServerTasks NOTES.INI setting.

- POP3—The Post Office Protocol Version 3 server task provides standard POP3 Internet Mail support to clients running POP3. It enables such clients to retrieve mail from the host server running POP3. You can load POP3 at the server console, or you can schedule it to run at startup by including it in the ServerTasks NOTES.INI setting.

- Replica—The Replicator task serves to replicate data between servers or between servers and clients. It starts at system startup by default, and then remains idle until there is a scheduled replication, a replication request from the server console, or a request for a replication from another server. It is possible to have a database server that allows other servers to perform only Pull-Push replication—in which case, the Replica task is not required on the host server. It can be turned off with a server console command (TELL REPLICA QUIT) or by removing it from the ServerTasks line in the NOTES.INI file.

- Router—The Router task is used to route mail, as well as documents automatically generated by other tasks, such as the Event task, and by workflow applications that send documents to mail-in databases. By default, the Router task is included in the ServerTasks NOTES.INI setting to run at server startup.

- Update and Updall—The server indexer tasks, Update and Updall, update database views and full-text indexes. They also detect and rebuild any corrupted indexes. The Update task updates all active views in a database when a user or server task, such as the Replicator, updates any documents in the database. It also updates the full-text index if one has been created for the database. The Updall task updates view indexes and full-text indexes on all databases on the server. As documents are added to databases, views need updating, and full-text indexes get out-of-date because new documents are not automatically added to the index. The Updall task can be run on specific databases that might have damaged view indexes as one way to repair the view. (Another way is to create a new replica of the database and then delete the original that has the damaged view index.)

By default, the Update task is included in the ServerTasks NOTES.INI setting to load at server startup; the Updall task is included in the ServerTasksAt2 setting to run at 2:00 a.m.

You can use a number of optional flags to control what is updated. Note that the flags are all optional. Updall can be run without any arguments. The following table describes these flags:

Flag	Description
-f	Updates full-text indexes without updating views.
-s	Updates full-text indexes that have an immediate or hourly update frequency, and scheduled update frequencies if the Updall task is initiated from a Program document.
-m	Same as -s, but updates scheduled update frequencies even if no Program document exists for Updall.
-h	Updates full-text indexes only if they have immediate or hourly update frequencies.
-l	Updates all view and full-text indexes.
-x	Rebuilds full-text indexes.

40

MODIFYING NETWORKS AND DOMAINS

To set up an additional server in an organization, you register the server, run the setup program, verify your ports, modify Connection documents, and set up access security. All these changes are replicated throughout the organization because they are all contained in the Domino Directory. But what happens to existing servers when you merge or split Domino domains?

MERGING DOMAINS

The Domino Directory provides a unified identity for all the Domino servers and users who share it. It is associated with a domain used for mail routing. The domain name and the organization name are usually the same.

If your company is merging with another company, you will probably want to merge Domino Directories to simplify administration. Otherwise, you would have to address some users within your own corporation, using an explicit path to the other domain (for example, `John Smith/Sales/New York/Acme @ XYZ`).

To merge two domains, decide which Domino Directory will be used for the single domain. Copy from the other Domino Directory into the primary one all Person and Server documents you want to have in the merged domain. Determine whether you need any of the other documents (such as Connection documents and Group documents) and copy those as well. Edit them to reflect the setup in the new domain. For example, make sure that the servers in the old domain are now part of the `LocalDomainServers` group and no longer part of the `OtherDomainServers` group. When all the documents you require have been copied over, determine whether you need to recertify or cross-certify users and servers so that all users and servers can communicate within the single domain. When everyone can communicate successfully, delete the old Domino Directory (or rename it and save it until everything has been thoroughly tested). Edit the `Domain=` line in the `NOTES.INI` file on servers that have moved from the old domain so that the line reflects the name of the new domain.

SPLITTING DOMAINS

On occasion, you might want to split a single domain into multiple domains. For example, your company might have grown too large, and you decide to create multiple domains to more effectively delegate administration. Or you might be spinning off part of the organization.

Splitting a domain is essentially the reverse of merging two domains. You make a nonreplica copy of the Domino Directory and delete the Person and Server documents from each Directory until it contains only the users and servers that belong in that domain. You then change the name of the mail domain in the relevant Person documents, and the name of the domain and the network in the Server documents.

Next, you edit and create Domain and Connection documents for the new domain to make sure that the new domain can communicate with the old domain (if appropriate). Change the administrator names and edit the `LocalDomainServers` group. Edit the `Domain=` line in the `NOTES.INI` file, and then shut down the server by typing **e** or **q** at the server console. Start the server again by clicking the Server icon. This process reinitializes the server with the new information in the `NOTES.INI` file. When the server is running again, you need to replicate the Domino Directory to other servers in the domain.

MOVING A DOMINO SERVER WITHIN THE ORGANIZATION

The process of moving a server within an organization is virtually the same as moving a person within the organization. The administrator requests certification for the server and selects the new certifier ID. The Administration Process handles the remainder of the process, changing the name of the server throughout the Domino Directory.

To be specific, one method of renaming a hierarchically named server consists of the following steps:

1. Within the Configuration tab of the Domino Administrator, expand the Server category and select the All Server Documents view.

2. In the middle pane, select the Server document or documents to be recertified.

3. From the Actions menu, select the Recertify Selected Servers action. A Choose Certifier dialog box appears. Select the desired Certifier ID and click OK.

4. After completing the password dialog for the certifier, the Renew Certifiers in Selected Entries dialog box appears.

5. Optionally, supply a value in the Only Renew Certificates That Will Expire Before field, and click OK.

6. Once the Recertify Server dialog box appears, click OK to complete the recertification process.

The request is automatically posted in the Administration Requests database and in the Certification Log database on the server where the request was made. If this is not the server listed as the administration server for the Domino Directory, the Administration Requests database is replicated to the administration server.

At this point, the Administration Process on the administration server updates the Server document in the Domino Directory with the new certificate, and the Domino Directory is then replicated throughout the domain. The Administration Process also automatically changes the ACLs in the Domino Directory and in other databases to correspond to the new name. Further, it updates any documents in the Directory where the previous name appeared.

Such updates can include the home-server information in each Person's user document, if the server is a home server for some users. Similarly, it can include changes in the Security section of the Server documents and in passthru Connection documents, if the server is a passthru server or is the destination of a passthru server.

Because moving to a new Domino organizational infrastructure might make available alternative communication paths, you might want to reprioritize ports and review the lowest-cost routing connections configured for the renamed servers. For example, the server might now be able to communicate using TCP/IP over a local area network connection rather than having to dial in directly, now that the server is part of the organization it was formerly calling.

40

NOTE

> Renaming a server that has a flat certificate is essentially the same as renaming a server that already has a hierarchical name, except that you must be aware that the Administration Process can be run only from a hierarchically named server. In place of the Recertify Selected Servers action, you use the Upgrade Server to Hierarchical action.

40

CHAPTER 41

TROUBLESHOOTING AND MONITORING DOMINO

In this chapter

MONITORING SERVERS WITH THE DOMINO ADMINISTRATOR

Beginning with Release 5, Lotus introduced the Domino Administrator Client to assist administrators with the task of managing their Domino infrastructures. Release 6 continues Lotus's commitment to enhance and improve this powerful tool. Due to the complex nature of the Domino Administrator client, this chapter does not cover all its features; instead, it concentrates on the Server tab and its related subtabs, plus a few other areas that can prove highly useful in staying on top of your Domino infrastructure's performance.

SERVER TAB

Use the Server tab of the Domino Administrator to monitor the status of the currently selected Domino server. This tab allows you to perform statistics analysis, monitor the servers of your Domino network, and monitor the up-to-date statistics of the currently selected Domino server. Let's begin with the Status subtab.

STATUS SUBTAB

As shown in Figure 41.1, the Status subtab is divided into three major functional areas: executing tasks, managing users, and monitoring schedules.

Figure 41.1
The Status subtab of the Server tab provides continuous task, user, and schedules information and access to the server console.

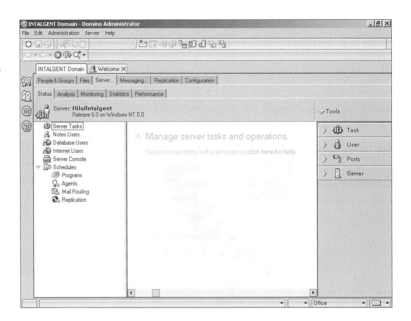

The Server Tasks view displays all the tasks that are loaded on the Domino server and their respective status. The information displayed in the Server Tasks view is basically the same information that is displayed when you use the console command SHOW TASKS (SH TA).

Although the SH TA command gives you a snapshot of which tasks are running at any given time, the Server Tasks view shows the status of each task continuously, in real-time.

> **TIP**
>
> You can right-click a task listing to access a pop-up menu that enables you to issue Tell Task (send the command to the selected task), Stop Task (end the selected task), Restart Task (restart the selected task), or Start New Task commands to the server.

The Notes Users, Database Users, and Internet Users views display a list of all users who are currently connected to the server, which databases they are accessing, and how long they have been idle. The information displayed in the Notes Users view is the same as the information provided by the console command SHOW USERS (SH U). However, the SH U command provides only a snapshot of the user status, and the various users views show the current status of each user connected to the server.

> **TIP**
>
> You can right-click a user listing to access a pop-up menu that enables you to issue a broadcast message to the selected user or all users (Broadcast Message), or you can drop the user's connection to the server (Drop).

The Status subtab also contains a Tools button that enables you to toggle between showing and hiding the Tools panel. The Tools panel provides access to the following commands for Users, Tasks, Ports, and the Server:

- Task: Tell, Start, Stop, and Restart
- User: Broadcast Message and Drop
- Ports: Stop, Restart, and Setup
- Server: Replicate, Route Mail, Secure Console, Shutdown, and Restart

The Status subtab also provides access to the remote server console when you click the Server Console view. The Server Console view is shown in Figure 41.2.

41

There are four types of buttons available in the Server Console view:

- Live, which provides a live console connection
- Pause, which pauses the output of the console
- Stop, which ends a live console connection
- Expand/Collapse, which toggles the left-hand navigation

The next tab in this tour is the Analysis subtab.

Figure 41.2
The Server Console view of the Status subtab enables you to remotely access the server console.

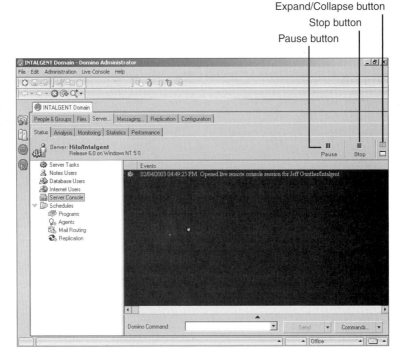

ANALYSIS SUBTAB

The Analysis subtab provides a centralized location to access the server's log database, catalog database (if you're running the catalog task), monitoring results, and administration requests database. The Analysis subtab also enables you to analyze the log database, clusters, and decommissioning of a server. Figure 41.3 illustrates the Analysis subtab.

MONITORING SUBTAB

By far the most useful tab for monitoring the performance of your Domino network is the Monitoring subtab. Before learning about the Monitoring subtab, take a look at Figure 41.4.

The Monitoring subtab enables you to monitor all the servers in your Domino network by periodically polling the major areas of your servers, such as memory usage, dead mail, the number of connected users, and much more.

The main area of the Monitoring subtab looks similar to a view. This view area displays the state information by service (for example, Admin Process, Agent Manager, and so forth) or by timeline. The polling period can be set from as often as every minute to as infrequently as once every 60 minutes. Let's take a look at displaying information By State first.

Figure 41.3
The Analysis subtab provides a central location to access and analyze log and statistics databases.

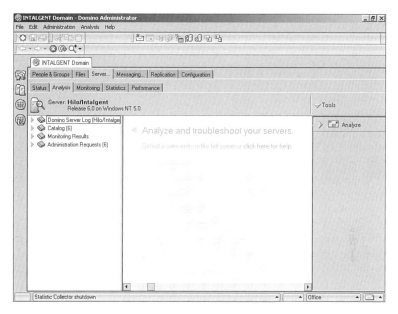

Figure 41.4
The Monitoring subtab provides a powerful monitoring system for your Domino Network.

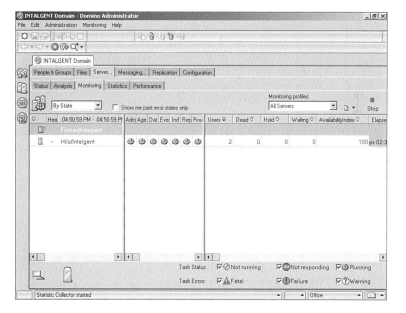

NOTE

The Monitoring subtab is not available via the Web Administrator client.

BY STATE   To begin monitoring, make sure you click the Start button in the upper-right corner of the monitoring window. Once you have started monitoring, the Start button will turn into a Stop button. The first column of the view area contains a list of all the servers in your Domino network. The server entry can be expanded or collapsed. When collapsed, the row contains the monitoring information from the last polling period; when expanded, all the polling information rows are displayed for that server.

The next eight columns display the status of the following server tasks: Admin Process, Agent Manager, Database Server, Event, Indexer, Replicator, Router, and Stats. The columns show the current status of each task. The following information can be displayed:

- Running
- Not Running
- Not Responding
- Warning
- Failure
- Fatal

You can select which status information to watch for at the bottom of the Monitoring tab, as shown at the bottom of Figure 41.4. By default, all statuses are enabled.

The following are the major server statistics:

- **Users**—Number of users currently connected to the server.
- **Dead**—Number of dead (undeliverable) messages in the server's MAIL.BOX file that cannot be returned to the original sender.
- **Hold**—Number of messages waiting for a replication cycle in order to transfer to another server in an adjacent domain.
- **Waiting**—Number of mail messages currently waiting for transfer in the server's MAIL.BOX file.
- **AvailabilityIndex**—The relative availability of the server based on workload. This value is a number from 0 to 100, where 100 is a lightly loaded server.
- **ElapsedTime**—Time since the server started.

BY TIMELINE   The By Timeline display shows the same information as the By Service display, except that the information is "flipped" so that the polling intervals are the columns, and the tasks and statistics are the rows, collapsed under each server name. To change to this view, select By Timeline from the list box in the upper-left corner of the Domino Administrator. Figure 41.5 shows the Monitoring subtab displayed by timeline.

41

Figure 41.5
When the Monitoring subtab is displayed by timeline, the polling intervals are sorted by task.

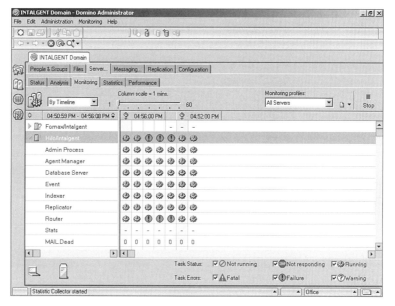

You can select the tasks and statistics that are monitored in the Monitoring subtab by using the following Monitoring menu commands:

- Monitor New Task
- Monitor New Statistic
- Monitor New Server

Selecting the Monitor New Task menu command will display the Add Server Task(s) to This Profile dialog box as shown in Figure 41.6.

Figure 41.6
The Add Server Task(s) to This Profile dialog box enables you to determine which tasks the Administrator will monitor on the selected Domino server.

41

When you select a particular task for monitoring, a brief description of the task appears in the Add Server Task(s) to This Profile dialog box.

STATISTICS AND PERFORMANCE SUBTABS

The Statistics and Performance subtabs display all the real-time statistics of the selected server. Both tabs provide information about the server statistics; however, they are rendered in different ways. The Statistics tab, as shown in Figure 41.7, provides a variety of details regarding the server.

Figure 41.7
The Statistics subtab enables you to access an abundance of statistical information about a Domino server.

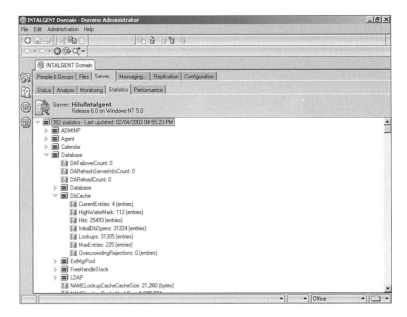

The statistics are displayed in a tree format. Some of the more usable statistics include:

- Agent (daily and hourly)
- Calendar (appointments, reservations, resources, and users)
- Database (various pool sizes, both peak size and used size)
- Disk (all drives, free and total space)
- Domino (build information, commands, requests/time interval)
- Mail (statistics such as `AverageDeliverTime` and `AverageSizeDelivered`)
- Memory (allocated, available, and so forth)
- Server (administrators, name, busy time, sessions, transactions, users, and so forth)
- Statistics regarding server start time

The directory tree organization enables you to quickly "drill down" to the desired statistic. Selecting any of the statistics provides you with a brief description in the status bar of the Domino Administrator.

Similar to the Statistics subtab, the Performance subtab allows you to view and chart the performance statistic of a selected server in real time or over a defined period of time. Figure 41.8 illustrates the Performance subtab.

Figure 41.8
The Performance sub-tab enables you to access a variety of statistical information about a Domino server.

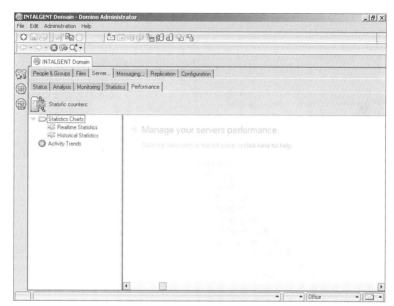

These statistics on both of these tabs are retrieved from the Statistics and Events database and are continuously updated.

TIP

> For more information about configuring and using performance monitoring, refer to the "Charting Statistics" topic within the Domino Administrator 6 Help.

41

OTHER MONITORING TOOLS

Almost all the tabs in the Domino Administrator Client contain some type of monitoring tool. These tools are covered in the following sections, organized by tab.

FILES TAB

The Files tab has a Disk Space tool that shows the total disk space, disk space used, and disk space free in pie-graph format.

The Files tab also displays all the databases or templates on the selected server. Statistical information, such as database title, filename size, maximum size, date created, and last repair date, also appears here.

REPLICATION TAB

The Replication tab contains two great tools for planning and managing your replication topology. The first tool is a graphical representation of your replication schedule, as shown in Figure 41.9. This tool can show you any contradictions, dead times, or overlaps in your replication scheduling.

Figure 41.9
The Replication tab provides your replication schedule in a user-friendly format.

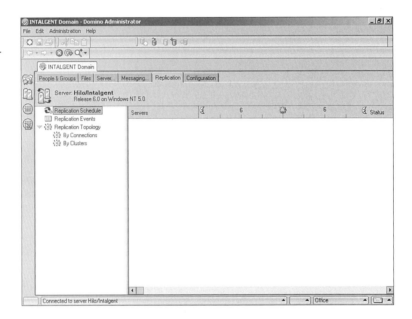

The other tool is a replication topology map, as shown in Figure 41.10. The replication topology map graphically displays the replication connections in your Domino network, which helps you identify redundancy or holes in your replication process. It also greatly enhances your capability to plan the most streamlined replication topology possible.

TIP

For information to display within the replication topology map, the Maps task must be started. By default, it's not running.

Figure 41.10
The Replication tab also shows your replication topology for efficient replication planning.

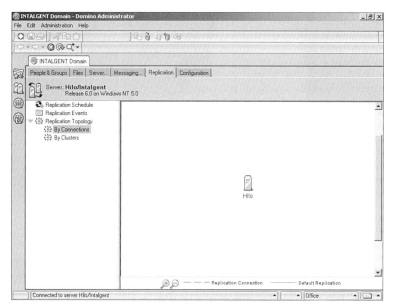

MESSAGING TAB

The Messaging tab contains three tools to assist you in monitoring and troubleshooting your messaging infrastructure: Mail Routing Status, Mail Routing Topology map, and the Tracking Center.

Mail Routing Status, under the Messaging—Mail subtab, displays the dead and waiting mail counts in a speedometer-style interface. The Mail Routing Status feature is shown in Figure 41.11.

The second tool in the Messaging—Mail subtab is the Mail Routing Topology map. This feature displays a graphical map of your mail topology, as shown in Figure 41.12. A topology map is a valuable tool when planning and analyzing your mail routing topology, because it can assist you in identifying holes or unneeded redundancy in your mail routing connections.

The Tracking Center subtab, under the Messaging tab, is a great feature that enables you to track email, even when it has already been sent. The Tracking Center, as shown in Figure 41.13, shows all tracking requests, status, and so forth.

Mail tracking is enabled by loading the Mail Tracking Collector or MTC server task. Information collected by the MTC task is stored in a special report database known as the Mail Tracking Store database (MTSTORE.NSF). Figure 41.14 illustrates some of the message elements that you can track.

41

Figure 41.11
The Mail Routing Status feature of the Messaging tab displays dead and waiting mail.

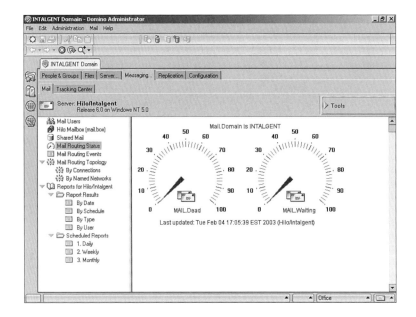

Figure 41.12
The Mail Routing Topology map is a great feature for planning and analyzing your mail routing topology.

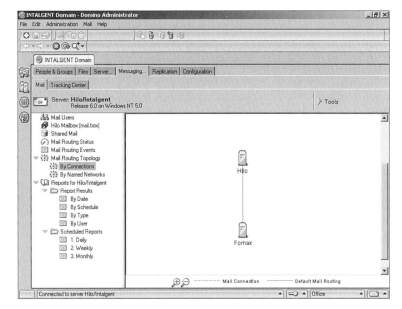

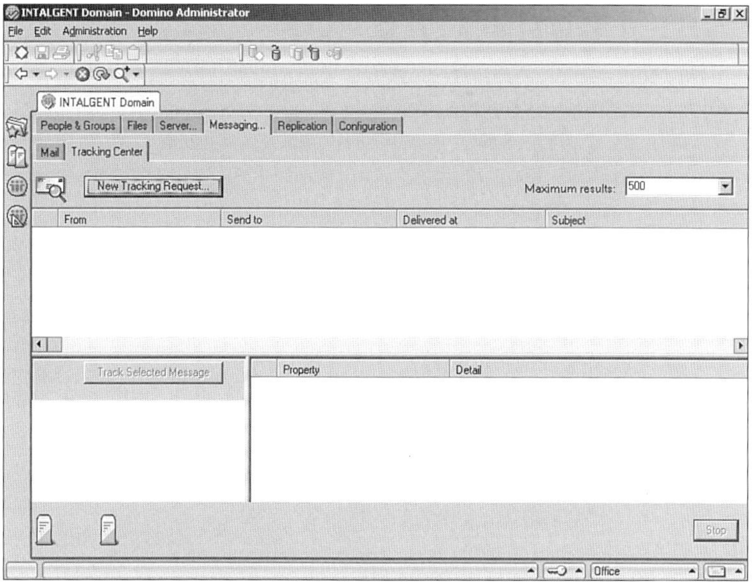

Figure 41.13
The Tracking Center is where you initiate requests to track email.

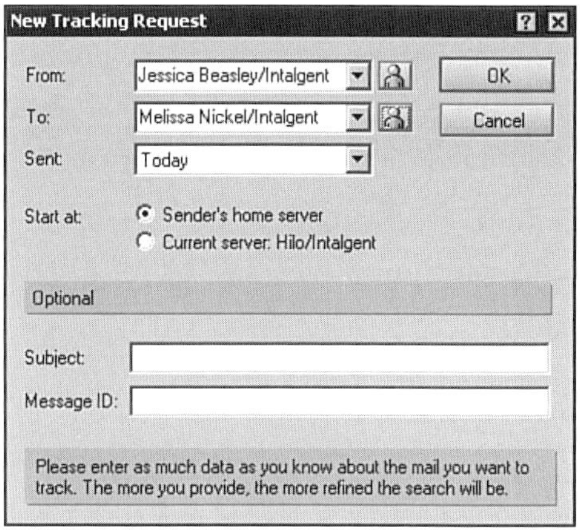

Figure 41.14
You can track mail based on the sender, recipient, date, and based on text in the subject line.

See the Domino Administrator 6 documentation for more details about the Mail Tracking feature.

CONFIGURATION TAB

The Configuration tab provides access to your server's configuration details. You can use this interface to quickly adjust and tweak your Domino environment based on the wealth of information provided to you in the other monitoring areas of the Domino Administrator.

Now that you are familiar with the monitoring features of Domino Administrator Client 6, it is time to learn a few troubleshooting techniques.

41

TROUBLESHOOTING DOMINO

This section provides some techniques for troubleshooting the most common problems found with a Domino network. This list is not intended to be comprehensive. With a system as complex as Domino, listing all the known problems and their solutions would fill many, many books. Instead, this section takes a look at some of the more common problems and points you in the right direction for finding a resolution. This section explores the following areas:

- Security issues
- Passthru issues
- Server issues
- Replication issues
- Modem issues

SECURITY ISSUES

There are quite a few security fields on the Server document of your Domino server. These fields are set by default so that they will not immediately cause security blockages that were open by default in previous versions of Notes/Domino. If you choose to use them, however, you should understand how users are notified when they cannot proceed past one of these checkpoints.

These are the main security fields in the Server document:

- **Check Passwords on Notes IDs**—Security tab
- **Authentication Options\Anonymous**—Ports tab, Internet Ports subtab, in all the protocol subtabs

PROBLEMS WITH CHECKING PASSWORDS

When you enable the Check Passwords on Notes IDs feature on the Server document, the feature is not completely enabled. You must also enable password checking on an individual's Person document. To do this for multiple users, you can use the Administration Process (ADMINP). You can also write your own agent that modifies the field on the Person document for selected documents.

Password checking is an optional feature of every server. If it is enabled on one server, but not a second, the second server does not check passwords and the first one does.

After this feature has been enabled, the first time the user authenticates with a server that requires password checking, Notes alters the user's ID so it cannot be used with earlier versions of Notes.

CAUTION

> Do not enable this feature for any IDs to which you have applied multiple passwords. The feature works only for IDs with one password.

If a user has multiple copies of his or her ID with different passwords, the valid password is the one on the ID that was first used to access the server performing password checking. The passwords on the other IDs should be changed to match the valid password.

Up to 50 previous passwords will be cached to prevent reuse. You can, however, clear the Password Digest field on a Person document.

If you specify a grace period and a user's password expires, the user cannot authenticate with a server until he or she sets a new password or until the administrator clears the Password Digest field on the user's Person document.

Problems with Web Browser (HTTP) Connections

If a user is being asked for a user ID and password when first accessing a site, the request is caused by one of two features. It is impossible to tell from the password prompt alone why a user is being denied access without a password. Knowing the causes enables you to find the solution more quickly.

First, the Server document might have the Authentication Options\Anonymous option set to No. This forces authentication immediately upon access of the server.

Second, the database being accessed on the server might be configured so that its ACL does not allow anonymous access. You implement this by setting the Default or Anonymous entries to No Access in the ACL. The Default entry applies to either Notes or Web clients. The Anonymous entry applies primarily to Web clients; the exception is if the server is set to Allow Anonymous Notes Connections (Security tab) in the Server document.

Passthru Problems

Passthru servers provide a central connection point for one or more of your Domino servers. However, if you decide to use passthru, you might encounter problems related to your restriction settings or to network routing problems. There are also four parameters that have counterparts in both the Server document and the NOTES.INI file; if you don't set a standard, such as Always Put the Entries in the Server Document Only, you might forget about settings you made that affect the behavior of passthru.

41

TIP

> Try to restrict setting parameters to either the Domino Directory (the preferred method) or to the NOTES.INI, but not both (whenever possible). This makes it easier to keep track of what you have configured. See the "Passthru Parameters in NOTES.INI" section later in this chapter for more information about the specific variables and precedence rules.

PASSTHRU RESTRICTION–RELATED PROBLEMS

If you find that users and servers attempting passthru cannot complete their connections, check the server documents passthru use sections, found in the Security tab. The first three of the four fields in this section (Access this Server, Route Through, and Cause Calling), if left empty, allow no one to perform those activities. The fourth field, Destinations Allowed, is used by that server in determining the remote servers to which it can route using passthru. If the Destinations Allowed field is blank, there are no restrictions, and the Domino server can route to any server to which it has access.

For other servers and users, you have control over three things: who can access this server using passthru, who can route through this server using passthru, and who can cause this server to call other servers while using passthru. You must explicitly list users, servers, or (better yet) groups for any other entities to use this server for passthru. Make sure that you use the fully qualified names for people and server entries. If you want to enable everyone to use your server as a passthru server, you can enter an asterisk (*).

Another security measure that can affect passthru is the field in the Security tab of the Server document named Compare Notes Public Keys Against Those Stored in the Directory. Enabling this field forces this server to compare the public key contained in an ID with the public key stored in the Domino Directory document for that ID. Passthru will fail if this comparison fails. Although this is an authentication problem, it might at first appear to be a communication problem.

PASSTHRU ROUTING PROBLEMS

A server that is being used for passthru might not be able to determine the route to a destination server being requested. This can be caused by several factors: The network name resolution systems might not be functioning correctly, the Domino Directory might not contain enough information for Domino to determine the route, or this server might not be configured for passthru.

Depending on your protocol, your network routing system has a method for resolving computer names into network addresses. If this system develops problems, when Domino asks for the network address for a server name, it won't get a response, and the server will not be reachable. In this case, an error is returned to the passthru client indicating that a route to the server that the user was attempting to reach could not be found. The most typical instance of this type of problem occurs in TCP/IP networks. Computers connected to a TCP/IP network normally rely on a domain name services (DNS) server to resolve computer names into IP addresses. If a DNS server is not available for computer name resolution, the computer will look on its file system for a HOSTS file. A HOSTS file is similar to a local phone book. It contains the names and IP addresses of computers that are accessed often. The HOSTS file generally speeds up connection time and enables the computer to find another computer on the network with the need for a DNS server.

If your Domino Directory doesn't have the required information, passthru cannot find a complete path to the server the user is trying to reach. This might be caused by a simple condition in which the Domino Directory on the passthru server hasn't replicated the most current documents from the hub server, or it might be that certain values were either forgotten or mistyped. Settings to look for include missing Connection documents for servers not directly reachable on the network, wrong values for the Passthru Server field on the Server document or users' Location documents, or invalid passthru Connection documents.

Passthru Connection documents are usually not required, but if they are entered, they take precedence over the network name resolution process. If a server's address changes, or if the server is physically moved to another network or is renamed, the passthru Connection documents referencing that server must be changed.

PASSTHRU PARAMETERS IN NOTES.INI

The parameters in Table 41.1 correspond to fields on the Server document. They are used only when you've created entries for them in the NOTES.INI file and when the related fields on the Server document are empty. If there is a conflict between the NOTES.INI setting and the Server document field, the Server document takes precedence.

TABLE 41.1   PASSTHRU PARAMETERS AND THEIR CORRESPONDING FIELDS

NOTES.INI Variables	Server Document Fields
Allow_Passthru_Access	Access This Server
Allow_Passthru_Callers	Cause Calling
Allow_Passthru_Clients	Route Through
Allow_Passthru_Targets	Destinations Allowed

SERVER ACCESS

Several factors control who can access a server. Authentication occurs between Notes ID files. Depending on how these files have been certified, access might not succeed. As mentioned earlier, the Server document also contains entries governing access based on names entered in these fields. The following sections look at various methods and techniques you can use to control access over specific ports.

AUTHENTICATION AND CERTIFICATION

When two entities (servers or workstations) attempt to communicate, the first hurdle is authentication. A comparison of Notes IDs reveals whether the two sides trust each other. There are two distinct methods of authentication. The first involves the older, nonhierarchical ID structure, in which an ID file contains one or more certificates. The second involves the newer, hierarchical ID structure, in which an ID contains one certificate that gives it a hierarchical name, adding at least an organization name to the common name on the ID, and perhaps additional organizational units as well.

41

FLAT CERTIFICATION: MISSING CERTIFICATES OR LACKING TRUST

During authentication, under nonhierarchical certification, these certificates are compared against those held by the other's ID. The two must each find a trusted certificate in each other's ID file. If this does not happen, authentication fails.

By examining the ID files and looking at the certificate lists, you can determine what must be done to resolve the situation. Either a certificate is missing or the trust flag has been disabled on one or more of the certificates.

EXPIRED CERTIFICATES

Every certificate given to an ID file has its own expiration date. By default, users expire in two years and servers expire 100 years after the date of certification. These initial values can be modified at the time the certificate is issued.

When the expiration date nears, starting at 90 days from expiration, Notes issues a message indicating the expiration date. For a server, this message appears at the console (and thus in a Miscellaneous Events document of the log).

When the expiration date is reached, the certificate is no longer valid; unless there are other flat certificates available on the ID file that are also trusted, the ID becomes useless.

By simply recertifying the ID file, it once again becomes viable. If the expiration date has been reached, the file must be physically transported to the administrator for recertification. It is easier to use Notes Mail before the expiration date to send the ID to the administrator, who can then recertify it and send it back through Notes Mail.

CROSS-CERTIFICATION PROBLEMS

Authentication failure under the hierarchical scheme is easier to debug and resolve. The error message that results informs you of the nature of the problem. First, however, when does authentication work under the hierarchical structure? It succeeds when both IDs have a common ancestor, or when both IDs have been cross-certified to access the other organization. This chapter doesn't explain the details of cross-certification; instead, it describes how to resolve the problem resulting from a lack of it. Refer to Chapter 35, "Domino Security Overview," for more information on configuring cross-certification.

For servers and/or workstations that lack cross-certificates, you must decide at what level you want to cross-certify and then proceed to accomplish that. Here is a list of the possible levels:

- Between server and server or workstation
- Between server and organization/organizational unit
- Between organization and organizational units

CROSS-CERTIFICATION AT THE WORKSTATION

For users to communicate with a server in another organization, they must hold a cross-certificate to that server or organization in their Personal Address Book. Without it, half the puzzle is missing (assuming the server already has a cross-certificate for the user).

When a user attempts to communicate with such a server, Domino displays a message that explains the lack of cross-certificates and enables the user to fix his or her half of the authentication problem by issuing an appropriate cross-certificate in his or her Personal Directory. This cross-certificate is not the same as the organization-to-organization cross-certificate that exists in the Domino Directory. It is usable only by the user who generates the document. Additionally, this works only when the two organizations have cross-certified at the organization and organizational-unit levels.

Even though the user can proceed with this "fix," it does not change the potential lack of a cross-certificate in the Directory on the server. It is likely that the user still will not be able to access the server unless that server has already been cross-certified with the user's organization.

AUTHORIZATION: YOU ARE NOT AUTHORIZED TO ACCESS THE SERVER

When the You Are Not Authorized to Access the Server message appears, you know that authentication has succeeded. You are being denied access not because your ID file is invalid or because of cross-certification, but because the Server document or a parameter in the server's NOTES.INI file has an entry that specifies that you should be denied.

The keyword in the message is authorized. A Notes/Domino term similar to *authorization* is *authentication*. Authentication, however, is the verification process that takes place between two Notes ID files. Authentication verifies your identity. Once your identity has been established, Domino determines whether you are authorized to access the server. Authorization is a comparison between the ID file accessing the server and the restriction parameters that have been configured on that server.

SERVER-DOCUMENT RESTRICTIONS

Every Server document has restriction fields. These fields allow you to specify server-specific access rights for users or groups. Two fields on this document might be causing the authorization failure:

41

- The Access Server field (Security tab), if it is empty, enables access to any ID file certified under the same organization certifier, or to any ID that has been properly cross-certified. In other words, if authentication succeeds, the ID is allowed access to the server. However, if this field contains one or more entries, access is limited to only those users or groups. If the ID attempting to access the server is not specifically listed and is not a member of a group that is listed, it is denied access.

- The other server document field that affects authorization is the Not Access Server field (Security tab). Entries listed here are specifically denied access. This field overrides any entries from the Access Server field, if any duplicate entries exist.

TIP

> The list of individuals who are allowed access and denied access to your servers (such as terminated employees) is much easier to maintain in a Group document. Create two Group documents called something like `Allow Access` and `Deny Access` and place these group names in the Access Server and Not Access Server fields, respectively. By using a group to manage this list, you do not have to shut down your server to have changes take effect.

Each time you change the server access lists, the server must be shut down and restarted, unless you use groups to manage the contents of these fields.

NOTES.INI RESTRICTIONS (PORT LEVEL)

Some parameters not found in the Server document can be added to the NOTES.INI file to affect authorization. These entries are ALLOW_ACCESS_*portname* and DENY_ACCESS_*portname*. For example, to enable the Developers group access to the Dev1 server over the TCP/IP port, the entry would read as follows:

```
ALLOW_ACCESS_TCPIP=Developers
```

To deny access to the OtherDomainServers group over the COM2 port, the entry would read as follows:

```
DENY_ACCESS_COM2=OtherDomainServers
```

The ALLOW_ACCESS_*portname* parameter, like the Access Server field in the Server document, enables access across that port to the listed users or groups only. The NOTES.INI file does not contain this entry initially; you have to add it. If this parameter exists and your name is not specified (individually or through a group name), you cannot use that port.

On the other hand, the DENY_ACCESS_*portname* field, if present in the NOTES.INI file, specifically denies access across that port to any user or group listed. This entry overrides the ALLOW_ACCESS_*portname* entry.

Depending on the various settings, you might be able to access the server over one port but not another.

SERVER ISSUES

Let's begin by looking at a couple of common server issues that you'll probably encounter at some point. First, we'll discuss an error message: `Server not responding`. This occurs when your workstation cannot reach the server; we'll look at the reasons. A second common server issue occurs when you have difficulty getting your server to start; we'll explore some possible reasons for this.

MESSAGE: SERVER NOT RESPONDING

The Server not responding message occurs when the server is not reachable from a client or another server. The reasons for this message can vary depending on the protocol being used; sometimes it occurs when there are not enough network sessions.

For TCP/IP, the resolution of the server name to an IP address happens either through a local HOSTS text file or through a network Domain Name Service (DNS). If you are using the HOSTS file method, and the file is missing or has been edited in such a way that the server's name has been removed, the name resolution will fail. If you are using DNS, check to see whether the name table has been changed. Check the DNS to make sure it is operational. Try using the Ping utility to ping the server by name, or using the TRACERT utility to trace the connection path from the source to the target server. If these fail, Notes will not be able to reach the server either. Resolve the DNS issue, and the server will reappear.

For NetBIOS, determine whether you have ever been able to see the server. If so, ensure that no routers exist between the workstation and the server—or if they do, that they have the capability of routing NetBIOS packets and that they have been configured to do so. Most routers cannot route NetBIOS. Try rebooting the server, if possible. If both the client and the server are running Novell's NetBIOS, they might not be running the same frame type.

CONDITION SERVER FAILS TO START

If your Domino server shuts itself down shortly after you start it, check for the following:

- The server document might have been corrupted or deleted. Without this document, the server cannot identify itself properly, and it might shut down.

- The server might not have been configured properly during setup before launching the server task. Finalize the setup of the Domino server through the client first. Do this by launching the Notes client and filling out the installation documents.

SERVER VISIBILITY

The *visibility* of your servers is manifested through the dialog boxes used on workstations. A user wants to open a new database (using File, Database, Open); how can you control which servers they can see in this dialog box?

What is happening if you suddenly see a different list of servers on your File Open dialog list than you normally expect?

First, let's talk about the File, Database, Open menu command. This command initially brings you to a directory of the Notes Data Directory on the local drive. In the drop-down list is a list of servers, which is determined from the collection of icons you have on your desktop and the list of server Connection documents in your Domino Directory. If you have icons from three servers that you access through a network port somewhere on the desktop,

41

and you have a Connection document to another server that you communicate with through a modem port, the list contains Local plus four other server names. This quick, local lookup means that the File Open dialog box and the server list typically perform very quickly.

> **TIP**
>
> You might find that even after you've removed all icons that refer to a particular server, this server still shows up in the initial list. To remove this server name from the File Open list (if you have no references to it any longer, you probably don't need it in the list), do this: Open the Server Connections view in your Personal Directory and remove the Connection document to that server.

The second server list appears when you choose Other from the initial server list. If you are connected to a network or are online with your modem, the Notes client reaches out and asks your home server (or the one you're connected to with the modem) for a list of available servers. The resulting list is then a combination of the first list and any other available servers to which you don't have local references. This search is called a Name Server lookup; your home server is acting as a Name Server, providing you with this list.

The list that the server returns is determined by the Notes Named Network settings in the Server documents in your domain. The list contains servers that belong to the same Notes Named Network as your Name Server. Notes builds the list from the servers that exist both in the Notes Named Network and in the user's Personal Address Book.

If a user's home server goes down, Domino uses a fallback method to obtain the server list. The method used depends on the network protocol. In general, the workstation looks for another Domino server from which it can get its list. This list reflects all the servers in the same Notes Named Network as the fallback server; the list might be different than the one the user normally sees.

REPLICATION ISSUES

A number of factors control which documents replicate. The most important fact to know and remember is that most replication controls affect the documents being received, not those being sent. The controls for the documents being sent are in the remote database. Yet the controls, which are set locally, specify the name of the remote entity (server or workstation).

> **TIP**
>
> To capture detailed information about the replication process, try using the server configuration parameter LOG_REPLICATION=3. This parameter causes the Replicator to report detailed information about the documents that replicate, including which fields replicated. This additional information is recorded in the Notes log in the Replication Events documents.

TOO FEW DOCUMENTS REPLICATE

Think of this question when resolving replication issues: "What can the other entity do to this replica, based on the local settings?" To simplify the question, ask it from the database's perspective: "What can the other entity do to me?"

It is important to remember that, to Notes/Domino, servers are "people" too. Notes ID files simply give a license number a name that you reference in the system. Notes does not know whether an entity is a server or a workstation; the entity is identified simply as a trusted Notes name that has been granted a certain level of access to a database.

SERVERS AND THE ACL A database's Access Control List (ACL) is fairly straightforward. It contains a list of servers, people, or groups and assigns one of seven levels of access to each entry.

Realize, however, that every replica of every database has its own ACL. As you deploy many servers, it becomes important to consider the settings on each replica. You can think of the multiple replicas of a single database as an ACL topology: Which server will be the master for design and ACL changes?

Consider this: How many replication hops are there from this ACL hub down to the last replica? That is, does the ACL hub replicate with all other copies, or does it replicate with some intermediary copies? At each intermediate step, these servers must have sufficient access in the next replicas to pass ACL and design changes.

You might want to consider using the feature that enables you to maintain a consistent ACL throughout all replicas. To use this feature (under the Advanced Settings of the ACL dialog for a database), you set two items: the administration server, and the check box labeled Enforce Consistent ACL Across All Replicas of this Database. All other replicas must use the same settings. Then, any local changes to an ACL are overwritten with the settings from the "master" database. The administration server must be listed in this ACL with Manager access.

SERVERS AND AUTHOR ACCESS You should generally avoid giving a server Author access. Because servers are not used to create and edit documents, they are not listed as the authors of documents. Notes/Domino refuses to receive edits to a document from a user or a server if that name isn't listed in the document as the author.

In the case of users, Author access is useful in preventing those who can make local changes to a document from passing those changes back illegally to the server replica. Servers, however, are often in the role of distribution agents; that is, they pass documents (including changes) back and forth between them.

A server that is listed as an author cannot write changes to documents. This typically comes to an administrator's attention because certain users, in conversation, determine that they aren't looking at the same document in their respective replicas. The user who edited the document will be confused about why his or her associates are reporting that they don't see the changes.

41

Along with the Author access level, there are two important access flags that can also affect the number of documents that replicate. The Create documents flag enables the named entity to write new documents in the replica. The Delete documents flag enables the entity to write document-deletion stubs.

SELECTIVE REPLICATION FORMULA   Databases can also control what is received based on one or more Selective Replication formulas. This formula, which is written much like the Selection formula for a view, receives only those documents that meet the criteria specified in the formula.

A Selective Replication formula also acts as a Selection formula for the local database. Any local documents that do not meet the criteria are removed. If the formula is changed, at the next replication, the set of allowed documents also changes. This can result in too many documents being received or in too many documents being removed from the local replica.

To test your formula, consider using a selection agent that contains the same formula to see whether the correct documents are being marked for replication; or build a view with the desired replication formula to see whether the desired documents are replicated.

DOCUMENT-LEVEL ACCESS LISTS AND ROLES   The ACL is a broad classification of what a named entity can do. It applies across all the documents in the database. Notes also provides for document-level access lists. These lists can contain names of users, groups, or roles. They act to reduce the level of access for members of the database ACL, but do not grant more rights than those given in the ACL.

Document-level access lists, otherwise known as Readers and Authors fields, can be applied in a number of ways. Designers usually apply them, but users can also apply Read access lists to particular documents independent of the form design. Forms can have Create and Read access lists. Views and folders can have Read access lists.

If a user or server is listed in the database ACL but not in document-level access lists, those documents might not replicate. It is important to remember server names when access lists are defined. Server names affect the planning of administrators, who must know of and educate users of the factors that affect replication. Server names also affect designers, who must include a mechanism that enables servers to replicate documents regardless of the document-level access that users apply.

TIP

> A useful way to ensure that servers can replicate documents is to create one or more roles just for servers, and then use these roles throughout the database design, such as in access lists or Readers/Authors fields (which control document access).

TIME LIMITS   Connection documents contain a field specifying the maximum time limit allowed for replication. This field can be used to efficiently schedule many replication jobs. At any particular time, however, it might appear to affect the amount of data that gets replicated. If a replication is halted for time considerations, those documents not replicated must wait for the next cycle. Depending on the frequency of replication with that server, users might find that new documents or changes aren't present at a particular time. You might get complaints about "failures" that are "fixed" with the next replication. You can view the replication schedules of your Domino servers in the Domino Administrator Client, Replication tab.

USER TYPE   ACL entries are simply text strings that Notes/Domino compares against the name from an ID file or the text strings of names in Group documents. This means that it is possible to create or modify a group in the Domino Directory with the same name as an ACL entry (say, `LocalDomainServers`), enter your username in that group, and then access the database based on the group name entry. Notes doesn't know or care whether an ID is a server or a user. This is the reality, because Notes/Domino does this for compatibility with previous database versions.

However, R4-and-later versions of Notes/Domino have a provision for specifying the type for an ACL entry. The choices for the user type are Person, Server, Mixed Group, Person Group, or Server Group. This provision prevents this kind of aliasing problem. In an R4-or-later database in which the user types have been applied, the `LocalDomainServers` group would be identified as a Server group.

If a username has been entered into this group, that user is not allowed access based on the `LocalDomainServers` group. Notes/Domino sees that the user's ID is a user-type ID, and that the group should contain only server-type IDs; therefore, it ignores the username entry in the group. If `LocalDomainServers` is defined as a Mixed Group, however, the user gains access. The only other user type that exists is Unspecified, which basically leaves the user type undefined, thus enabling any entity of the specified name access to the database, regardless of user type (for example, server or user).

If you intend to use the server's workstation to perform administration tasks, you add that server to the ACLs of any databases you will work on. Define the server entry as Unspecified, not as Server. The server ID is seen as a User from the workstation process; if you've told the ACL that ID is a Server, you cannot make changes.

DOCUMENTS DISAPPEAR AFTER REPLICATION

After a replication is complete, it is possible that documents present before replication began are now missing. Several factors can play a part in the removal of documents. As discussed previously, a Selective Replication formula (if it has been modified since the last replication) might now not allow certain documents that had been allowed by the previous formula.

Suppose that you have a Status field (whose values can be Open or Closed), and you also use a Selective Replication formula that selects only documents for which `Status=Open`. If a document that had been Open replicated in and was subsequently changed to Closed, the Selective Replication formula causes this document to disappear from this replica copy after it replicated.

41

In addition, there is a pair of replication settings that work in concert to keep a replica database small. These are known as the purge interval and the cutoff date. The purge interval is measured in number of days. The setting is called Remove Documents Not Modified in the Last *n* Days. Every one-third of the number of days entered here, Notes/Domino purges documents that are older than the purge interval. (If the purge interval is 30 days, every 10 days Notes trims documents that are 30 or more days old.)

More specifically, every one-third of the purge interval, the cutoff date is updated. The setting in the cutoff date determines the date boundary for removing documents. The cutoff date is identified as the field called Only Replicate Incoming Documents Saved or Modified After. You must specify a date and time.

To recover documents that have been purged, you can manually reset the cutoff date. Replicate again, and this cutoff date is used as the date boundary for determining the documents to replicate. The purge interval will take over again, however.

If the replication cycle has completed propagating deletion stubs to all replica copies of the database, and the purge interval has passed, you can no longer recover documents; all copies have been deleted.

Another reason for losing documents is that they were actually deleted. If the ACL settings on the various replicas allow deletions, the deletion stub for a document will replicate to each copy of the database.

> **NOTE**
>
> Release 5 introduced a powerful feature known as *transactional logging*. Similar to transaction logging in relational database systems, transactional logging tracks all changes to a database for a specified period of time. If you accidentally delete documents from a database that has transactional logging enabled, you should be able to recover ("undelete") it.

REPLICATION BETWEEN SERVERS NOT OCCURRING OR FAILING TO FINISH

If replication between a pair of servers continually fails or even fails to occur, what can you look for?

First, make sure that replication has not been disabled for this database. Look in the Replication Settings dialog box under the Other icon for an entry labeled Temporarily Disable Replication. If this setting is enabled on either of the replica copies in question, the database will not replicate.

Second, determine whether replication is failing to occur or failing to finish. By using the Notes log, you can determine the answer to this question. If the servers communicate asynchronously, you can check the Miscellaneous Events, Phone Call, and Replication Events documents. For network replication, you can check the Miscellaneous Events and Replication Events documents.

Let's investigate some reasons for the servers' failure to replicate. First, by looking at Connection documents, you should determine which of the servers is supposed to make the call.

Verify that the parameters of the Connection document are correct:

- Is the connection enabled?
- Is the port specified indeed the correct port?
- Are the source and destination server names spelled correctly?
- Is the phone number correct (including extra dialing rules)?
- Does the Tasks field contain the replication task entry as it should, or does it just include mail routing?

TIP

> If one or more files are specified in the Files to Replicate field, they prevent all other files from replicating. If the filenames are incorrect, no files will replicate.

If the network or serial port that is specified for the connection between the two machines isn't working, replication will fail.

Before two Notes entities can communicate, they must first authenticate. If the two machines are not certified under the same organization or cross-certified, it would be a breach of security to let replication occur. Miscellaneous Events and the Replication Events documents reflect this security issue.

Additionally, servers might fail to obey their own schedule for the following reasons:

- A low memory situation exists.
- There is not enough disk space.
- The server activity load is too high to permit replication to take place.
- All allowable replicators are busy.

The first two of these conditions generate a message on the console (and thus in the log). The second two cause the Replicator to skip the job without notification.

If the replication schedule is lengthy, it is possible that the server cannot get to the Connection document in question before a new day begins or before the end of the scheduled range has passed.

If you have schedules that overlap by one minute or more, replication occurs randomly; replication might even skip parts of the schedules. This overlap can exist between multiple entries in one document or between schedules specified on multiple documents.

Let's look at an example: You have Low priority databases scheduled to replicate between 1:00 a.m. and 5:00 a.m. (document #1), and Medium and High priority databases are scheduled to replicate between 5:00 a.m. and 11:00 a.m. (document #2). The overlap at 5:00 a.m. causes a problem; at the least, change the schedule in document #1 to 1:00 a.m. to 4:59 a.m.

If you have multiple Connection documents telling your server to call another server, and the document that references databases of the same or lower priority tells the server to make a call, but another document is scheduled to make a call within the next hour, the first replication is suppressed in favor of the document referencing the higher-priority databases. What should you do? Spread out your replications further than one hour, or do as I mentioned previously so that lower-priority documents aren't ignored. Give each a wider range so that at some point in their schedules, they are not within an hour of each other.

Here's another related issue. If you have Connection documents going in both directions for the same two servers at the same time, one server is going to call the other for replication, and the second schedule will be ignored.

REPLICATION CONFLICTS

At times, your users will notice replication conflict documents in some databases. These conflicts occur when a document is edited in multiple replicas between replications. When this database replicates, the Replicator doesn't know how to resolve changes to both documents, so it creates a conflict document as a response to the other. The "winner," or main document, is the one that has been edited more recently or has been saved more times.

More specifically, each document contains a sequence number and a sequence time. When you update a document, the sequence number increments by 1, and the sequence time is recorded from the system clock. Thus, the winner has the higher sequence number; if these are the same, the winner is the document with the more recent sequence time.

How can you resolve replication conflicts? First, resolve the conflicts in only one replica, or you will likely create more conflicts. Second, you must manually review both documents and decide on a course of action. Can one document be saved and the other deleted? Do you have to cut and paste to merge information into one of them? Your review of the documents will tell you this.

To actually perform the resolution, it is best if you can keep the main document and merge all updates into it. Then, delete the conflict response. The main document is usually the preferred document to keep, because it is known to other replicas. If you keep this document and replicate, only the changes to the main document are replicated. If you delete the main document and keep the conflict response as the main document, the entire new document is replicated and the main document is deleted, causing more replication transactions than necessary.

If there are more changes to the conflict response and you would rather keep that document, before you do any editing, edit this document and resave it. Resaving the conflict response makes the document a main document. Then you can safely cut and paste and finally delete one of the documents.

How can you prevent conflicts? Use field-level replication. With field-level replication, in addition to the document's sequence number and time, every field has its own sequence number. When that field is modified and the document is saved, the field sequence number is incremented to 1 greater than the previous document sequence number, and the document sequence number is incremented by 1. The document sequence number is then equal to the field(s) that just changed.

During replication, the Replicator compares field sequence numbers. If it turns out that different fields have been modified, the potential exists for the documents to be merged instead of generating a conflict. The reason this is a potential instead of an automatic event is that the database designer must have enabled a property called Merge Replication Conflicts for this form in the database.

Field-level replication speeds up replication because less data has to replicate, and it can also reduce the number of replication conflicts.

Another way to reduce replication conflicts is to cause them! This sounds contradictory, but let's explore it further. There is a feature called *document versioning*. This form property tells Notes to create a new document each time a document is modified. This new document can either be created as a response document or it can become the new main document while the earlier versions become responses (or siblings). In essence, you are creating a new "conflict," but this is a proactive step instead of a reactive step. This conflict, or version, gives you an audit trail.

When this method is used, if the document is edited in multiple replicas, all the versions add up during replication and no replication conflict appears.

CLEARING REPLICATION HISTORY

When a replication is successful, Notes updates the replication history in a database. You can see this history by selecting the File, Replication, History menu option. If replication is occurring in both directions (as opposed to a Pull-Only or a Push-Only), you see two entries for a particular server: one entry for send and one entry for receive. Notes also stamps the time and date from the other server into the history on the current server.

The next time this database is replicated between these two servers, Notes takes this time stamp as the starting point to speed up the process.

In rare cases, documents might be saved during a replication, after Notes has determined the set of documents to replicate at that time. That document's time stamp is slightly older than the history stamp that is written in the history upon the successful completion of that replication. At the next replication, Notes uses the history time stamp as the starting point, ignoring the document in question.

When will you find out about this? Notes doesn't announce this behavior; in fact, it doesn't know it happened. Typically, your users discover that they aren't seeing the same set of documents in their respective replicas.

To fix the problem, you can clear the replication history by clicking the Clear button on the Replication History dialog box. Notes informs you that clearing the history makes the next replication with all servers take much longer, and that you should clear the history only if you suspect a time problem as just described. But by clearing the history, you force the Replicator to look at all documents without regard to a history time stamp, and the lost documents reappear. Be aware that you need Manager access to clear the replication history (unless you access a replica locally on a server).

MODEM ISSUES

In an ideal world, the modems you've configured for your Domino servers always work. Let's take a look at a couple of issues you might encounter. If you walk up to your console and observe that the server seems to be continually querying a modem at all the available speeds but never getting an answer, that modem is not operational. Or what if you notice that your modems just don't seem to be working—what can you do?

YOUR SERVER IS CYCLING THROUGH THE AVAILABLE MODEM SPEEDS

If you see your server continually trying to communicate with a modem, cycling through each of the speeds in order, your server isn't communicating with the modem. If a modem is not available but the port is enabled, the server continually attempts to access the modem. If the modem is connected, cycle the power to it; if Domino still cannot access it, you might have a damaged port, or the system might just need to be rebooted. If this happens repeatedly, try using a different port, if one is available. Try another modem or modem cable. Consider replacing the port. Make sure that another task on that machine hasn't been configured to use that port, which would prevent Notes from having access to it.

MODEM CONNECTIONS ARE NOT WORKING

If you are experiencing a problem across multiple ports with a set of modems of the same brand, try checking the following:

- Look in the Miscellaneous Events documents for evidence that modem commands are being sent and acknowledged by the modems. Look carefully at the responses being received during any connection attempts with other servers.

- Examine the modem file (or switch to an alternative) for setup-string errors. Try simplifying the setup strings to one line that states SETUP=AT&F for factory-default settings.

- Check the settings on your modem. If it has dip switches, compare the current settings with those recommended in the manual. Try setting the switches to the most basic settings described in the manual; you can slowly improve them after reaching a known good combination.

- Check the cable and the port. Try alternatives if they are available.

PART **VIII**

ADVANCED DOMINO ADMINISTRATION

CHAPTER 42

Performance, Scalability, and Capacity Planning for Domino Servers

In this chapter

BACKGROUND

For years, Domino has demonstrated its potential to provide high-performance and high-availability service to thousands of users. However, Domino's performance can be degraded severely by poor scalability and capacity planning, and by configuration factors that are often not understood by network or server administrators.

This chapter is divided into three sections. The first section explains the factors that affect Domino's performance and provides guidance for making Domino perform at its best. The other two sections of this chapter explore scalability issues and capacity planning.

DOMINO PERFORMANCE ISSUES

"Why is it so slow?" If you've set up more than one Domino server, you've probably heard or asked this question at least once. Improperly configured, Domino can take an intolerably long time to load a view or display a Web page. Domino's performance is affected by a complex array of factors, but this chapter gives you a comprehensive overview of what causes those excruciating slowdowns and how to realize Domino's maximum performance potential.

Performance problems are not always the fault of Domino itself, and are not necessarily caused by the applications Domino is running. The solution to better performance is not necessarily to make Domino just "run faster." For example, Domino might be shooting out responses and Web pages at its peak capacity, but the results won't be apparent to users who are connected via a poorly configured network.

The following sections explain in detail how your server configuration, network, databases, and other factors affect Domino's performance.

HOW THE SERVER AFFECTS DOMINO PERFORMANCE

Your server platform, CPU speed, disk drive, and memory play crucial roles in Domino's overall performance.

PLATFORM

With Release 6 of Domino, Lotus officially identified and announced the availability of the Domino server for the following platforms:

- Microsoft Windows NT 4.0
- Microsoft Windows 2000
- Sun Solaris 2.8/SPARC
- IBM AIX 4.3.3x and 5.1
- IBM OS/400 V5R1 or later
- IBM OS/390 V2R10 or later
- Red Hat Linux, Version 7.2 or SuSE Linux, Version 8.0

The system architecture and scalability of the Unix servers gives them an edge over Microsoft Windows servers. But Lotus offers more comprehensive support and resources for Microsoft Windows servers. Platform choice is only one (and perhaps the least significant) of all the numerous factors that impact Domino's performance. Windows running on a well-tuned server and network provides more satisfactory response times than a beefy Unix hampered by a poor configuration or network problems.

If you are planning to support small-to-midsize organizations, Windows or Linux servers with single or multiple CPUs or clusters of servers will provide adequate service. If you are planning to support a large enterprise, you should take a close look at the IBM iSeries platform. For more detailed information on this topic, see Chapter 43, "Using the Enterprise Domino Server with a Large Domino Network."

CPU

Predictably, your server's CPU speed and number of processors have a large impact on Domino's potential to serve heavy loads. You should definitely buy a server that has the capacity for dual or multiple processors.

MEMORY

At startup, Domino reserves approximately a quarter of the available system memory for its operations. As the load increases, Domino dedicates more memory. If you have insufficient memory, Domino will be forced to "make do" with smaller chunks of memory allocated per user. This also leaves less memory for other system operations and tasks. The "Scalability" and "Capacity Planning" sections that follow provide detailed memory-planning tips.

DISK DRIVES

Your disk drives can impact Domino's performance in two ways. The speed of your disk drive directly or indirectly affects several other aspects of Domino's performance, so it's wise to take advantage of the newer, faster hard drives. With falling prices and new speeds, the new disk drives make solid investments for just about any enterprise.

Having only a single disk drive, instead of several, can slow Domino's performance by forcing the entire input and output workload to be handled by a single device. Input and output distribution significantly impacts Domino's performance. Having the operation system, Domino's executable, and data files all on a single disk drive poses a less-than-ideal configuration. If you have multiple drives, consider dividing the disk access workload among them. For example, try placing the Domino executable on one drive, the operating system on another, and your Domino databases on a third.

HOW THE NETWORK AFFECTS DOMINO PERFORMANCE

After you have properly configured your server for optimum performance, you want to examine your network's impact on Domino.

42

NETWORK SEGMENTS

Implementing network segments (or virtual LANs) can help you balance your network load and isolate a heavy traffic area, minimizing its adverse effects on the rest of your network. Segmenting your LAN makes sense, particularly if you have multiple Domino servers serving different departments. Your individual user groups will enjoy better response times from their own Domino servers.

NETWORK BANDWIDTH AND SPEED

Your internal network's bandwidth and speed can impact Domino response times by slowing the delivery of requested data. The NotesBench Consortium, located at `http://www.notesbench.org/`, provides recommended performance practices and is discussed later in this chapter. Bandwidth and speed issues also affect the delivery of data over the Internet or telephone lines, neither of which can guarantee a specific level of performance.

FIREWALLS, DOMAIN NAME (DNS), AND PROXY SERVERS

Firewalls, DNS, and proxy servers, although often critical to operations and security, can negatively impact Domino's performance, sometimes severely. Troubleshooting a problem of this nature will probably require a "sniffer" and some assistance from your network administrator.

PORT ENCRYPTION

A useful security option, port encryption enables you to protect your data while it is in transit across your network. Although port encryption has no effect on a Notes client, it can slow data transfer times on a Domino server.

Network Monitoring Applications

Network monitoring applications can help you get a better idea of which factors are impacting your network's performance at any given time. A critical component of any network, monitoring tools provide services that fall into two categories: polling and analysis.

Polling monitors whatever network nodes you specify at regular intervals and provides a real-time or near real-time view of which network services are working. The purpose of a polling monitor is to simply let you see the current status of your network—which servers are up and which are down. Some products page or email the administrator if a server doesn't respond to the pings for a specified period. Although you can sometimes use this polling data to draw conclusions about a certain hub or server's performance, polling monitors do not provide the comprehensive analytical data that large networks often need.

Analysis monitors, on the other hand, are designed to provide the more comprehensive data used to troubleshoot problems in complex networks.

HOW YOUR DATABASES AFFECT DOMINO PERFORMANCE

Domino offers several database property settings that can help improve performance. To modify these settings, open the database and select Database, Properties from the File menu. In the Properties dialog box, select or deselect the settings as recommended in the following sections. The Domino Designer Help provides full details on these settings.

DON'T MAINTAIN UNREAD MARKS

Selecting Don't Maintain Unread Marks under the Advanced tab of the Database Properties dialog box improves performance by freeing system resources that would otherwise be used for keeping track of the unread marks.

OPTIMIZE DOCUMENT TABLE MAP

Selecting Optimize Document Table Map streamlines the processes that Domino has to go through when updating views. This option can be particularly beneficial when you have a lot of large databases.

Remember that your view-rebuilding response time is lengthened if you do not have enough disk space available in your `temp` directory. When Domino rebuilds a view, it stores a number of temporary files. You might want to specify a directory other than your standard `temp` directory for the view rebuilds.

DON'T OVERWRITE FREE SPACE

Domino has a security feature that protects deleted data by overwriting it with a pattern. This process of overwriting is processor-intensive and can slow things down. Selecting Don't Overwrite Free Space in the Database Property settings turns this feature off. Recognize that there might be situations where security concerns dictate that you want this feature to remain active.

MAINTAIN LASTACCESSED PROPERTY

The property Maintain LastAccessed Property is not selected by default. Selecting it requires extra read/write activity that can impact performance, particularly on a server with a heavy workload.

Select this property only when you need to keep track of the date when a particular document was last read. The document deletion tool uses this property to automatically delete documents that haven't been read for a certain number of days.

DISABLE TRANSACTION LOGGING

Since Release 5, Domino has included support for transaction logging. This feature enables the quick recovery of data due to increased database integrity. The property Disable Transaction Logging is not selected by default. Selecting it instructs Domino not to log transactions. This setting will improve performance, but is not at all recommended for mission-critical applications.

42

DON'T SUPPORT SPECIALIZED RESPONSE HIERARCHY

Select Don't Support Specialized Response Hierarchy to relieve Domino of the task of tracking parent or response relationships between documents. Selecting this property improves performance and does not affect hierarchical views or replication formulas, as long as you do not use the @AllChildren or @AllDescendants functions for view selection or replication formulas.

Remember that selecting this property requires you to compact the database. This operation requires enough disk space to make a temporary duplicate of your database(s).

DON'T ALLOW HEADLINE MONITORING

Select Don't Allow Headline Monitoring to relieve Domino of the task of tracking changes to documents for users. Using headlines, users can track documents within the database that meet certain conditions.

LIMIT ENTRIES IN $UpdatedBy FIELDS

Selecting Limit Entries in $UpdatedBy Fields enables you to limit the number of entries that can be saved in the $UpdatedBy field. Every time a document is edited, the username or server name responsible for the modification is stored in the $UpdatedBy field. Over time, this history of edits can grow large enough to consume a significant amount of disk space and cause your replication and view updates to lag.

LIMIT ENTRIES IN $Revisions FIELDS

The Limit Entries in $Revisions Fields property follows the same principle as the previous property setting. Again, this field stores the time and date of every document-editing session, for up to 500 sessions. This field helps Domino prevent save and replication conflicts, using the time and date to arbitrate situations where a document was opened and edited simultaneously by two users. But 500 edit session entries take up several megabytes or more of disk space and slows performance.

DATABASE POLICY

Because Domino database properties can significantly impact Domino performance, you might want to consider adopting a database policy that guides the creation and configuration of all Domino databases in your organization. A set of recommended or required property settings and configurations that enhance performance will benefit just about any size organization. For heavily utilized intranets or Web sites, database policies are a necessity.

OTHER PERFORMANCE FACTORS

You should always make sure you are running the latest version of Domino, as well as the latest Notes Clients. Older versions might have bugs or issues that impede performance. The same holds true for operating systems. Upgrading to the latest version and/or patches helps prevent unnecessary performance bottlenecks.

PERFORMANCE TROUBLESHOOTING APPROACH

You now have an overview of all the many things that could possibly go wrong and cause performance problems. You can now put this information to work.

If you are experiencing performance problems with your Domino server, follow a structured process of elimination to find the problem. Troubleshooting Domino performance problems means sorting out whether the problem is being caused by Domino, an application, or some other external factor. The following approach eliminates possible performance factors in their order of probability and proximity to the server:

1. Check the Domino databases and applications.
2. Check the server software and system configuration.
3. Check the server hardware and specs.
4. Check the network configuration (in your local area/segment/VLAN first, and then outward).
5. Check firewalls, DNS servers, and proxies.

There is a good reason for this order. By starting with the Domino databases and applications, you are eliminating problems within your domain of responsibility before working outward into domains controlled by others (network, firewall, and so forth). The order is also geared to increase your chances of solving the performance problem without having to make configuration changes to mission-critical assets that affect other people. The goal is to eliminate the problem with as little impact as possible on the overall enterprise.

The Domino troubleshooting approach should be understood and agreed upon ahead of time by your operations staff. Correctly ordered procedures help prevent counterproductive finger pointing and keep the troubleshooting process on track.

PREREQUISITES FOR TROUBLESHOOTING DOMINO PERFORMANCE

This checklist shows the basics you need in order to determine what is degrading your Domino server's performance:

- The assistance of your network administrator (or your network documentation)
- A sniffer or a network monitoring application (see the previous sidebar, "Network Monitoring Applications")
- Configuration details of your server hardware
- Access rights to Domino applications

PERFORMANCE WRAP-UP

The preceding sections provided an overview of the performance factors affecting Domino, with guidelines for troubleshooting performance problems on an existing system. The next two sections help you plan for optimum performance on new or growing Notes/Domino deployments.

42

SCALABILITY

The following sections guide you through the process of planning for future growth. These sections start with an overview of general scalability issues, and then hone in on Domino's scalability, with particular focus on Domino's clustering capabilities.

A CLOSER LOOK AT SCALABILITY

The term *scalability* gets thrown around quite a bit by conference speakers and new-product press releases. These advertising messages often imply that scalability is an infinite capacity to meet unforeseen and open-ended requirements. This kind of scalability doesn't exist. It is more realistic to think of scalability in terms of being able to reach specific targets.

For this discussion, let's define scalability as the capacity to accommodate a fairly specific set of growth expectations.

The Basic Scalability Model in Figure 42.1 shows the three necessary components of scalability:

- Known current configuration.
- A projected growth expectation.
- A scalability strategy for accommodating the specified future growth. The strategy will typically be broken into stairsteps that correspond either to long-term phases of implementation or growth.

The purpose of this model is to show an objective view of the issues involved in real-world scalability. Notice the small letters a and b situated on either side of the delta. a refers to the point where the solution is more than adequate, and b refers to the inevitable point where the solution is less than adequate. a is preferred over b, and the midpoint of the two is best of all. Of course, in real-world situations, the magic middle point, where a system is perfectly sized to meet the current load, is difficult, if not, impossible to maintain.

Because the three components of the Basic Scalability Model each play a critical role in your approach to scalability, they are examined in some detail in the next few sections.

Figure 42.1
The Basic Scalability Model establishes the required components for scalability planning.

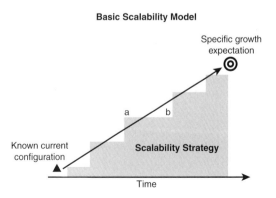

Basic Scalability Model

The first element of the Basic Scalability Model, Known Current Configuration, might seem elementary, but you need to take the time to make sure you know your Domino server and network's current configuration and what it is truly capable of supporting. The purpose of this step is to determine whether your user's needs are truly outstripping your server's capacity, or whether something else is degrading the performance of an otherwise adequate server. Working through the performance sections at the beginning of this chapter is a good starting point for this exercise.

The second step is to determine the specific growth expectation to which you are going to scale. This helps you set the objectives of your scalability strategy. The first question you need to ask is what exactly is growing or changing. Figure 42.2 shows possible scalability scenarios and the unique issues that accompany them.

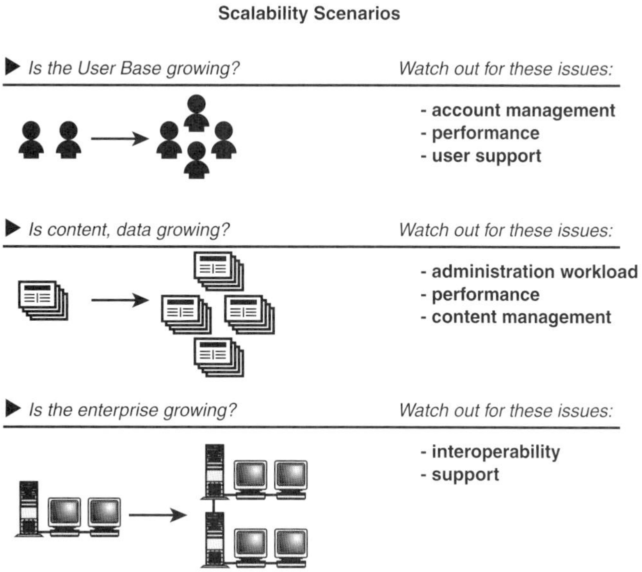

Figure 42.2
Different scenarios typically present unique issues that need to be considered when developing growth expectations and scalability strategies.

Scalability Scenarios

▶ Is the User Base growing?   Watch out for these issues:
- account management
- performance
- user support

▶ Is content, data growing?   Watch out for these issues:
- administration workload
- performance
- content management

▶ Is the enterprise growing?   Watch out for these issues:
- interoperability
- support

IS THE ENTERPRISE/PLATFORM GROWING?

Let's say a company acquires your company, and suddenly your enterprise grows from a small to a large WAN. This kind of a scalability scenario requires you to determine whether your number of users will grow or whether you will continue to operate as a small unit. You also need to determine what coordination is needed between the managers of your information assets and those of other units. As the operations of your two companies are merged, interoperability and support issues also dominate this scalability scenario.

A closely related scenario might have you moving from a small-to-medium–capacity server to a high-end Enterprise server. The reasons for this can include increased users, a growing enterprise, and so forth, but the focus in this scenario is on moving existing data and applications from one platform to another with minimal service disruption.

42

IS THE CONTENT/DATA GROWING?

Your client wants to turn its Domino-powered Web site into a full-blown extranet, adding a new range of online publications and data for its customer base. The number and size of databases is expected to grow dramatically in the near future and at cyclical intervals each year. This scenario requires an examination of the data (Is it structured or unstructured? Is it relational?) and a focus on content management procedures as they relate to the creation and maintenance of Domino databases and services.

ARE THE REQUIREMENTS GROWING?

Your company's fast growth is expected to double the number of Notes/Domino users you must support. In a similar scenario, your number of users remains constant, but new requirements are spawned by the rollout of an intranet that offers a new range of services for your users. This scenario requires careful attention to performance and capacity planning.

This should give you a flavor of the different kinds of scalability scenarios you can be faced with. In each case, before you start planning the scalability strategy, you want to nail down the growth expectation. What exactly is growing and what exactly will the Domino server be required to support?

After this has been determined, you can move to the third component of the Basic Scalability Model: the scalability strategy.

DOMINO 6 AND YOUR SCALABILITY STRATEGY

Domino has a well-established reputation for platform scalability. Domino can run on everything from Windows 2000 and Linux all the way to an IBM iSeries server. In addition, Domino's system architecture enables it not only to run on high-end systems, but also to actually take full advantage of their resources. Real-world Notes/Domino configurations have proven that they can support large enterprises with thousands of email accounts, Web servers with over a million hits per day, and hundreds of concurrent Notes client users. Domino also has proven its appeal to organizations seeking scalable solutions, with a need to control or reduce procurement and ownership costs.

You'll never find a one-size-fits-all strategy for scalability. Each company must examine its own needs and its own capability to make use of Notes/Domino scalability solutions. Figure 42.3 shows a sample scalability strategy for a company that expects to grow from 100 to 100,000 users. The growth scale is exaggerated to show the range of scalability that Notes/Domino can support. Remember this is only a sample—don't stake your next promotion on it!

STRATEGY TIPS

The purpose of a scalability strategy is to keep you from painting yourself into a corner, so to speak. Nothing is worse than not being able to scale, due to unenlightened previous decisions or oversights.

Figure 42.3
This example scalability strategy presents a simplified plan for meeting specific growth expectations over time.

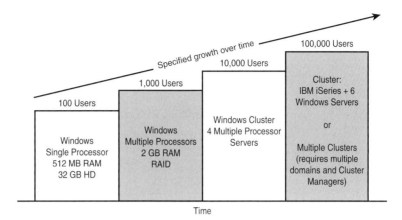

First, if you cannot afford larger Enterprise-class servers, choose servers that enable you to add processors when they are needed later. You should also be aware of the scalability of servers and platforms. For example, an IBM iSeries is more scalable than a Windows or a standard Linux distribution. You can run up to a dozen or more Domino servers with ease on a single IBM iSeries.

Second, always think about scalability in terms of the following:

- Future directory services
- Future user population
- Future bandwidth
- Future administrator workload (when an environment scales, the administration tasks can multiply exponentially)
- Future user requirements and capabilities
- Future network architecture

Third, keep in mind that advanced users have a definite tendency to use more system resources. The immediate post-rollout period, when users are still learning how to use Notes, will not reflect the normal usage patterns of users. As they become more proficient, they are more likely to make full use of Notes/Domino capabilities.

Likewise, users with newer, more powerful computers tend to use more system resources, taking advantage of their extra RAM and processing power to run multiple applications, browser windows, and client features simultaneously.

And finally, be sure to have a transition plan for moving from one level to the next, and decide ahead of time what will trigger your move to the next level. This will involve outside factors and nontechnical issues, such as funding, space, new employees, training, increased support requirements, and so forth.

42

Domino 6 Scalability Features

Your scalability strategy should outline how you plan to use Notes/Domino scalability features as your requirements grow.

Domino 6 scalability features include:

- The Internet Cluster Manager (ICM), which enables support for HTTP server clusters, thus enabling Webmasters to distribute Web traffic across multiple Web servers. The ICM follows Domino's model of clustering servers to provide high availability.
- Integrated support for POP3, IMAP4, and SMTP mail; LDAPv3 directories; MIME, S/MIME, HTML, and Java.
- Directory support for up to one million users.
- Improved administration console and management tools.
- New fault-recovery features and options that enhance scalability on all platforms.

The following sections examine the concepts behind clustering and how Domino's clustering capabilities can support your scalability strategy.

Symmetric Multiprocessing with Domino 6

Symmetric multiprocessing (SMP) refers to the collaborative activity of a group of processors that share common resources (operating system, memory, or input/output bus). A single copy of the operating system manages the group of processors.

SMP, popularly dubbed the "shared everything" architecture, is the direct opposite of MPP (massively parallel processing), which is often referred to as a "shared nothing" architecture. In contrast to MPP's redundant copies of system resources and databases, SMP offers dynamic workload balancing and reduced cost of ownership through shared usage of scalable resources.

The Domino server is designed to simultaneously support a wide variety of tasks and demands:

- High user loads
- Concurrent server-to-server mail routing
- Concurrent server-to-server replication
- Traffic encryption
- Indexing
- Scheduling
- HTTP
- POP3 support

Lotus applies the power of SMP using Domino clusters (groups of servers that share a workload) to provide high availability. The next few sections discuss the concept of clustering.

ABOUT CLUSTERING

Clustering applies the old adage "Many hands make light work" to servers and networks. One of the biggest scalability advantages of Domino clustering is a method of grouping redundant Domino servers to provide a higher level of reliability than can be provided by a single server. Each cluster of servers is synchronized by a Cluster Manager. Amazingly, clustered servers can reside on different operating systems and hardware platforms. A cluster might include a Domino server running on an IBM iSeries, complemented by three Domino servers running Windows 2000 or Linux.

CLUSTERING ADVANTAGES

Since 1995, the Domino server's Advanced Services option has provided built-in support for clustering and partitioning for maximum reliability. By clustering up to six Domino servers per domain in a LAN, administrators can provide the performance advantages discussed in the following sections.

HIGH AVAILABILITY   High availability attempts to guarantee uninterrupted access to mission-critical services, even if major disruptions occur in the network. Lotus's Domino server clustering is just one of a growing number of high-availability strategies. The advantage of Domino clustering is that it uses standardized components and does not require that all clustered servers run on the same operating system or hardware platform.

WORKLOAD BALANCING   Workload balancing enables you to specify the level of traffic you will allow on a server before redirecting traffic to another less-utilized server.

CLUSTER REPLICATION   Cluster replication enables you to set a schedule for replicating databases. Replication can be prompted by either conditions/events or by time settings. For example, you might want replication to occur when 10 documents have been updated in a particular database.

THE INTERNET CLUSTER MANAGER

The Internet Cluster Manager (ICM), which supports HTTP and HTTPS protocols, synchronizes the clustered servers and controls incoming traffic to balance the workload among the individual servers. For example, if one server in a cluster reaches its capacity or fails, the ICM coordinates the redirection of requests for a certain database to another server containing a replica of the same database. The redirection is transparent to the users.

The ICM must reside in the cluster's domain, but does not need to be running on one of the servers in the actual cluster. Figure 42.4 depicts a cluster of four Linux servers and one IBM iSeries server. To set up the ICM, install clusters according to normal procedures (see the Domino documentation for full details), and then install the ICM.

You've examined the important issues of scalability and how Domino can provide a scalable enterprise solution. Next, you'll put your scalability knowledge to work with a little capacity planning.

42

Figure 42.4
The Internet Cluster
Manager redirects
requests from HTTP
clients to balance the
workload.

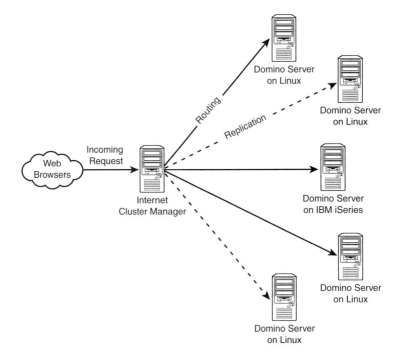

CAPACITY PLANNING

"How big of a server do you need?" That question always seems tinged with suspicion, as if you're up to something. You'd love to reply "The biggest we can find!" But that's probably not what your purchasing department or boss wants to hear. Domino's product documentation doesn't help your case either. It says the minimum requirements are a 1GB drive and 128MB of RAM. You think to yourself, there's no way. How do you find out what you really need—and justify it?

This section tears the wraps off the heretofore black art of planning a server configuration that matches your organization's needs. It starts with a simple capacity planning exercise that helps you cover all the issues, and then examines capacity-planning tools, memory issues, and more.

CAPACITY PLANNING EXERCISE

The following exercise asks questions and provides guidelines designed to help you remove the guesswork from your planning efforts. It helps you focus on the scalability and performance issues that are most important to your enterprise.

SET A SCOPE FOR SCALABILITY

What exactly needs to be scalable? Your email and applications? Your Web site? All of the above? Without a scope that prioritizes what must be scalable, it is difficult to meet specific objectives. Write a sentence that states exactly what you intend to make scalable.

SET YOUR HORIZON

How many years out are you planning? A 6-month plan will dramatically differ from a 2-year or 5-year plan. The shorter the timeline, the easier it is to predict growth in requirements. Write down the time period during which you will ensure scalability and adequate performance.

SET A GENERAL PLATFORM DIRECTION

Does your organization prefer Windows? Unix? Linux? Each of these choices presents radically different ramifications for your scalability planning. Write out your organization's platform direction.

SET GROWTH EXPECTATIONS

Be able to state specifically what kind of growth you are preparing for. What exactly will grow? Write out one or more sentences stating the growth you are planning to accommodate. For example, you might write, "We expect to add 500 email users, 40 new databases, and three new Web sites." Or, "Our network will grow from 5 to 20 servers."

LIST DEPENDENCIES OR LIMITATIONS

If scalability is contingent on external factors, such as the bandwidth of your network or your budget, you should evaluate and, if possible, resolve these issues before going any further. For your scalability effort to succeed, try to determine early the things that could impact, limit, or derail your plans. Write a list, and decide whether anything on your list requires you to adjust your scope or horizon.

SET AN OBJECTIVE

Now that you have completed the previous steps, you are ready to state your scalability objective. To the sentences you have already written, add one more. List which services you will provide and how many users you will support. Be specific. Here's an example: "We will build and maintain a system that will provide the following services for no more than 600 users: Email, Web browser access to Domino databases, and Notes Client access to Domino databases."

Congratulations! You've given yourself a tremendous head start and increased your chances of planning a properly sized server. Now it's time to look at the tools you'll need.

CAPACITY-PLANNING TOOLS

Lotus provides several tools and services that can help you select the Domino configuration that best matches your organization's requirements.

NOTESBENCH

As the name denotes, NotesBench is a set of tools designed to provide standardized testing procedures and benchmark information. NotesBench's independently audited performance findings are published at the NotesBench Web site (www.NotesBench.org). The NotesBench Web site's reports help vendors and customers make intelligent Notes/Domino configuration and platform choices.

The NotesBench toolset itself is made available to qualified and trained vendors and Lotus Business Partners. These vendors and partners can, if needed, create customized benchmarks for customers who need to determine whether a solution fits their specific requirements.

DOMINO SERVER.PLANNER

Domino Server.Planner helps you identify the right server size and capacity for your requirements. This capacity-planning tool enables you to specify different workloads and uses Lotus vendor benchmark data to recommend a server configuration.

For more information about Server.Planner, visit the NotesBench Consortium Web site (http://www.NotesBench.org). You can download Server.Planner from Lotus's Developer Network (http://www.lotus.com/ldd).

PLANNING MEMORY REQUIREMENTS

It's recommended to buy as much as you can afford! But you need something more than recommendations to go on. How much do you really need? What if you already know how much memory you have, and you want to know how many users you can realistically expect to support? It helps to understand how Domino uses memory.

How much RAM should your Domino server have? Recommendations vary between 300KB–1MB of RAM per user. A series of excellent Domino performance tests conducted by James Grigsby, Carol Zimmet, and Susan Florio recommended that you plan 1MB of RAM for each user, assuming that you have average-to-advanced users. If you can afford it, it's a good rule to follow. This means 1MB per Notes client, or for each user who will use a Web browser to access and work with databases on your server.

Does this rule apply to a Web site that could possibly attract hundreds of thousands of visitors? Probably not. Most Web sites, even corporate sites, have to work very hard to stand a chance of attracting this kind of traffic, and those that do usually find that their traffic falls into two categories: serious users and casual visitors.

To illustrate, let's do some experimental math. In accordance with these guidelines, we'll follow a rule of 300KB of RAM for casual users and 1MB of RAM for serious users. We'll make an assumption that 75% of your traffic is from visitors who are browsing through your site. The other 25% of your traffic comes from your internal users, who are updating content, sharing calendars, and accessing databases. Assuming 1,000 visitors a day, you conclude that 250 of them (or 25%) require 1MB of RAM each, and the others should have 300KB each. This calls for 475MB of RAM for this particular server.

Users also differ in another way. Users who work directly on the server rather than replicating databases to their own computers constantly require the server's resources. Users who replicate databases to their workstations instead of working directly on the server free Domino processing resources for other operations.

PLANNING YOUR DIRECTORY SERVICES

Directory services represent another critical issue for capacity planning. As your enterprise grows, what kind of directory services will be needed? Fortunately, Domino now provides a new range of scalable options for managing your Directory. Domino includes full support for the Lightweight Directory Access Protocol (LDAPv3).

Domino's LDAP support enables users to access and update the Domino Directory (in previous versions, called the Public Address Book) using any client that supports LDAP. The Notes client is an example of an LDAP-compatible client. Microsoft, Netscape, and Novell have all announced support for LDAP.

LDAP support enables Domino to authenticate users by looking at their certification information in other LDAP directories. By the same token, other directory services can authenticate users listed in the Domino Directory.

42

USING THE ENTERPRISE DOMINO SERVER WITH A LARGE DOMINO NETWORK

In this chapter

43

FORMING A GAME PLAN

Forming a solid game plan for your network is a critical step toward success. The easy installation of a Domino server tends to downplay the importance of early decisions you need to make. In fact, if you use some of the examples provided in the dialog boxes during setup, you can establish an unwieldy naming scheme. Use the following steps as a guide:

1. **Plan for administrative teamwork.** Use Notes/Domino to assist your administrative team. Establish open lines of communications and develop a clear process for establishing standards and resolving conflicts.

2. **Plan your network infrastructure.** Your servers will cause you fewer headaches if you provide adequate hardware. Modem technology has greatly improved, yet many modem combinations still refuse to work or perform poorly together. Check with forums, the Knowledgebase, and your peers to determine which hardware works best for running a Domino server.

3. **Plan your topologies carefully.** Many aspects of Domino administration can be thought of as a topology. Because Notes doesn't draw pictures, develop topology maps for your administrative team. It will help you make sense of the contents of your domain's Domino directory.

4. **Plan to monitor your system.** Through careful monitoring, you can often detect minor conditions that might actually be symptoms of more serious problems.

TEAMWORK: SHARING THE RESPONSIBILITY

Notes/Domino solves many problems related to information sharing and distribution. How widely spread are your offices or employees? Do your business units function as separate companies? You can choose to control your Domino environment centrally, or, more likely (and recommended), you and your team of administrators will share the responsibility (perhaps geographically).

DEVELOPING STANDARDS

Developing standards is an important task to consider before any system implementation, especially with Notes and Domino. But before you can create meaningful standards, you must have a firm grasp of the components of the system as well as the tools at your disposal. Although it is not within the scope of this chapter to lay out everything you need to develop a thorough standards document, you can use the high-level structure presented here to get you started.

Some of the more crucial standards to establish involve the items that the public will see. Your server names are visible to others who connect to your domain; you use these names when you perform console commands such as REPLICATE SERVERNAME. Your domain names are visible to anyone sending email to your users. Your organization name is visible to anyone reading documents you compose; it could be your email memos or documents in a discussion database that replicates around the world. Think ahead and determine just how you want your company's name to be seen. Keep the names short and avoid spaces.

DISTRIBUTED MANAGEMENT OF THE DOMINO DIRECTORY

In a large network, it is virtually impossible for one administrator to manage the entire environment. Requests are often generated so rapidly that they pile up quickly; fulfillment sometimes requires a local presence. A team of administrators must work together to fulfill requests and ultimately maintain the documents of the Domino Directory (formerly known as the Public Name and Address Book).

It has been observed, however, that in established Notes networks, local changes are often implemented without consideration for the impact on the other servers that depend on the same book. "Way back when," Release 3 did little to facilitate safe local changes. Enabling administrators to have Editor access to the book gave them free rein over all the documents. Release 4 added tools to the public address book to enhance its maintainability in a large, distributed environment. Release 5 and 6 takes that a step further by providing numerous roles in the Domino Directory that enable you to more finely assign roles to other administrators.

CREATING THE ADMINISTRATIVE PROCESS FOR MANAGING THE DOMINO DIRECTORY

To manage Domino Directory maintenance, create a list of the types of changes (additions, modifications, and deletions) that will be necessary in your domain. Design a request-and-approval process that will facilitate the best balance of administration among all your administrators. Reaching agreement not only on the methods for maintaining the directory, but also on the resolution process for any related management issues (such as maintaining this request/approval process) will enable your administrative team to perform with confidence.

DOCUMENT ADDS, MOVES, AND CHANGES

If changes must be made to documents (such as groups) that can affect users and servers at other sites, consider forming a policy requiring that change requests be submitted and reviewed before they are implemented. However, this review does not need to fall on one person; instead, it can be put up for examination by all administrators. An administrator who notices a detrimental effect can voice concern before the change is made. Review the various types of changes that may be made, and classify them according to which can be made without review.

CREATING A REQUEST AND APPROVAL PROCESS

You might consider creating an administrative facilitation database; it could contain a request/approval workflow process, a discussion section, tips and tricks, and perhaps even a knowledgebase. This database should define your company's standards for handling the routine chores of the Domino Directory. The request types should include creating and modifying users and creating and modifying groups. You can use a similar procedure to promote new databases from test servers to production servers.

NOTIFICATIONS

Use Notes Mail to notify administrators of a new request (include a doclink). After a request has been approved, a notification could be mailed to the requester informing him of a change regarding that request.

GRANTING AND REJECTING REQUESTS WITH REASONS AND SUGGESTIONS

If your environment is one in which you have a hierarchical request process, use an email to inform the requester of the decision. Offer suggestions, if appropriate, especially for a rejection.

DESIGNING YOUR NETWORK

In a large Domino network design, you evaluate the pros and cons of several different topics. Should you model your network after the political or geographic makeup of your company? How should you plan for your servers to communicate? How many domains would make sense for you? What should you consider in creating your hierarchical naming conventions? How should you configure the topologies for mail routing, replication, and other features, such as passthru? As your Domino Directory grows in size and distribution, what are the effective ways to manage it? How should you plan for additional gateways or mail-transfer agents? Do you need a Domino Internet/intranet presence? If so, how should that be implemented with your internal Domino network?

Let's consider each of these individually, realizing that many decisions on one topic depend on the decisions made in another area.

NAMING USERS AND SERVERS

Notes/Domino provides a way to associate each resource (a user or server) with a component of your company. This is best accomplished using hierarchical names. Not only is it convenient to know what part of your company a user is associated with, but it also enhances your company's security if you can isolate access to branches of your company. The rules of naming Notes users descend from the X.500 protocol.

Although it is difficult to give hard and fast rules for what the hierarchies should be in your company, there are guidelines to follow. It is important to remember that hierarchies associated with users are flexible, whereas hierarchies associated with servers are much less so. The following are the rules of hierarchical naming:

- At least one level of naming must be established. This is referred to as the organization, or O.

- The country code is married to the organization. It is a two-character, predefined value.

- After the O, the hierarchy can be four additional levels deep; each level is referred to as the organizational unit (OUn), where n is the level.

- Each user and server has a common name associated with it.

43

- The common name, organizational units, and organization define the name of the resource in this format:

  Common Name/OU1/OU2/OU3/OU4/O
- Each organizational unit at each level, as well as the organization itself, is associated with a discrete certifier ID.
- To secure your system, at least one level of OU should be implemented.

Consider the company Intalgent Technologies, LLC. It is recommended that this company use its short-form name—INTALGENT—because it will be repeated in the domain. Intalgent also should choose its locations as first-level OUs (OU1) because the company is location-based. Company officials might choose ATL for Atlanta, ZEL for New Zealand, and TOR for Toronto. Finally, this company should use a separate OU for its servers. Company officials might choose SRV for servers. Melissa Nickel in Atlanta would have the name Melissa Nickel/ATL/INTALGENT. The servers would be named sequentially by function; HUB01/SRV/INTALGENT would be the first hub server.

GUIDELINES FOR NAMING

You should follow some general guidelines when determining your user and server names. These guidelines make managing these names easier and make it easier for your users to type them:

- No component should have a space in it. This would require surrounding the resource name with quotation marks when referring to it at the server console, for instance.
- The O name should be at least three characters long.
- If country codes are implemented, refer to them in an OU to keep all IDs under the same certificate. Because the country code is associated with the organization, a new organization certifier (the top) must be created for each country.
- O names should be the "short form" of the company. Because this component will be referred to whenever a name is represented in Notes, it is cumbersome to use a long name. For example, the company International Business Machines is known as IBM. Instead of using International Business Machines in every name, using IBM is a better reference.
- The total number of characters in the OU levels should not exceed 15 for users. If you choose to have many (two to four) OU levels, make the names short. Remember that each time you refer to a resource in your domain, you will be using the entire name, including the hierarchy.

NOTE

The maximum characters allowed in a name is 274—79 maximum for the common name (CN); 32 maximum for each Organizational Unit (OU), with up to 4 OUs; 64 maximum for the organization (O); and 2 maximum for the country.

43

- Servers should be isolated in their own branches of the hierarchy. Changing the name of the server is difficult because all users must change their bookmarks.

- Keep in mind that internally, all resources will be able to authenticate (access each server and sign documents); externally, you can isolate branches of your hierarchy for authentication. Remember that you manage external access to your servers through the use of cross-certificates.

DESIGNING A SCHEME FOR USING THE GUIDELINES

First, investigate other software packages in your company that use hierarchical naming. You can save time if you implement a plan similar to what is already being used.

You should treat servers and users separately. First, ask your users, "How do you know Lisa Phillips is in your company?" Is it because she is in the marketing department or because she is in San Francisco? This should be your first-level OU. For example, if the answer to the question is "We know her because she is in Marketing," the first level should represent departments. Don't limit yourself to thinking of departments or location; companies have also implemented the first-level OU based on skill set. You may just have one OU level for users.

For servers, create an OU indicating that they are servers—for example, SVR. You might want to plan for external servers and internal servers by creating a second level separating the two. You don't have to implement the external servers' OU right away; if you have a plan, using it in the future will be easier.

The common name of the server should indicate its function in the company and a number for future growth. For example, your first hub is HUB01; when you add additional hubs because your company is growing at a phenomenal rate, the next hub would be HUB02, and so on.

Because some protocols Domino uses look only at the common name of the server name, servers should be uniquely named in their common name. That is, don't depend on the hierarchy to define the server uniquely. In addition, each server's certifier will indicate that it is a server as a component of its name. It is unnecessary to include this in the common name of the server. For example, MKT01/SVR/INTALGENT is an appropriate name, whereas MKTSVR01/SVR/INTALGENT is redundant.

One of the main reasons to choose a good hierarchical naming scheme is to delegate responsibility to others. Most corporations are regional, with servers located in the regions as well as in corporate headquarters. If administrative support is available in the regions for the regional users, it makes sense to have regional administrators responsible for their own minidomains.

The global administrator can delegate responsibility to a number of degrees. If all responsibility—that is, creating users, setting up servers, managing mail distribution, and ensuring replication—is to be delegated, the global administrator can give the OU certifier for the region to the local administrator. This, along with delegation of authority in the Domino directory (discussed later in this chapter), enables the local administrator to create IDs for users, grant access to regional servers, and update Connection documents. The global administrator should hold on to the server OU certifier and grant access to the Server document to the appropriate local administrator or administrative group. This enables the global administrator to leave the regional tasks in the regions.

TOPOLOGY TYPES

A *topology* is a layout or schematic of a series of controls in a system. For Lotus Notes/Domino, this applies to many aspects of the system: mail routing, replication, and passthru, to name a few. Let's look at some different types of topologies; they can be applied where appropriate against the various portions of a Domino system.

END-TO-END

In an *end-to-end* setup, servers call each other in an orderly fashion, making a series of calls to form a calling loop. For example, a New York server calls Dallas, which calls San Diego, which calls Chicago, which, in turn, calls New York. If a server goes down, however, the replication of databases around the loop is slowed significantly. For a document to replicate its way back upstream, for instance, it takes several more cycles. Note that all servers must have a replica copy of all databases being replicated. You should use the LocalDomainServers group or an equivalent, assigning it Manager access in each replica.

MESH

The *mesh* method is an end-to-end schedule with a twist. Instead of calling only one other server, some of them make two or more calls, creating a crisscross pattern. If one server goes down, it does not affect the replication among the other servers.

With this method, the number of Connection documents grows almost exponentially as the number of servers increases. It is practical only when there is a small number of servers (no more than four or five).

HUB-AND-SPOKE

The most common and efficient topology in a large network is called *hub-and-spoke*. It is most prevalent largely because of its scalability.

The simplest hub-and-spoke arrangement is this: One server acts as the hub and coordinates the flow of information to other subhubs. The subhubs talk to production servers. As the number of production servers grows, more subhubs or even new layers of subhubs can be added to serve more production servers. The simplest arrangement is a single hub with eight or nine spoke servers.

One problem that is solved best by the hub-and-spoke method is the number of hops that a piece of data must make to travel from one end of the network to the other. Other topologies often require many more hops, slowing the communication process for the users. This

43

topology can move a mail message or a replicated document quickly anywhere within your network or even to other companies.

The principal benefits for using the hub-and-spoke model include the following:

- Centralized communication costs
- Enhanced security (hub will have restricted access)
- Centralized replication and backups
- Alleviation of overlapping replication schedules

You might also want to consider implementing a backup hub server that replicates with the hub and can be quickly reconfigured into becoming the hub server if the primary hub goes down.

Now that you have a general understanding of basic network topologies, let's take a look at the various topologies specific to a Domino network.

MAIL-ROUTING TOPOLOGY

Let's look at how you can configure your domain for efficient mail routing, which is critical to satisfying your users.

MINIMIZING HOPS

The simplest factor for efficient mail routing is the number of hops a message must make to reach its destination. This is a factor not only for speed, but for troubleshooting as well. Each server has its own schedule for routing mail; two factors, the schedule and the message count threshold, determine how quickly messages route through a server.

The schedules are specified in Connection documents in the Domino Directory, along with the method of connecting (such as the COM port and phone number). You can specify days of the week, times to attempt connections (as either single times or ranges), and, for time ranges, how often to call during the range.

The most efficient method of routing mail uses the hub-and-spoke topology. Messages travel one or two hops to the hub and then one or two hops down to the recipient's mail server.

MINIMIZING COST

If some of your servers are connected by modem, you bear a communication cost for each phone call. Your goal is to make as few phone calls as possible. Instead of calling for each message that uses that route, you can let messages accrue in the MAIL.BOX file and then pass them all at a scheduled time.

There is a field called Route at Once If X Messages Pending on the Connection document. By putting a threshold number in this field, the router forces a call if and when the threshold is reached. Otherwise, it waits until the next scheduled calling time to route the messages.

NONADJACENT DOMAINS

To simplify addressing for your users, you can create nonadjacent Domain documents that enable the sender to specify the recipient's domain but not the intermediate domain needed to route the message. Suppose that your design specifies that you will use an "external" domain for mail routing outside your company. A message intended for someone at another firm must be addressed to that user at that user's domain at your external domain (`User@UserDomain@ExternalDomain`). This tells the servers in your internal domain to first forward the message to the external domain, where a connection is found and established to the recipient's domain (UserDomain).

A nonadjacent Domain document specifies that any message addressed to a particular domain must first pass through another domain (for example, to route to UserDomain, first route through ExternalDomain).

You can use other fields on a nonadjacent Domain document to secure the use of this feature. You might not want users from other domains to be able to take advantage of this route simplification, so you can specify who should or should not be allowed to route mail to this domain by using the fields Allow Mail Only from Domains and Deny Mail from Domains.

ADJACENT DOMAINS

An adjacent domain is a domain to which your Domino server has a physical connection. A nonadjacent domain is a domain to which your server lacks a physical connection. Connection documents are the link between adjacent domains. The Adjacent Domain document is a security measure that enables you to close down mail-routing holes that might exist because of explicit routing. If a user relies on a nonadjacent Domain document to route a message, the Allow and Deny fields you've set up there allow or prevent the message from routing.

However, if a user explicitly routes a message (for example, `Lisa Phillips@DomainA@ DomainB`), no nonadjacent Domain documents are used by the router. If you want to prevent routing to `DomainA` from `DomainB`, you can create an Adjacent Domain document that prevents using `DomainB` to route to `DomainA`.

One reason for wanting this security is to prevent users from other companies from using your mail infrastructure to route mail to other domains that are also connected to your domain—in other words, messages that are destined not for users in your domain, but for users in one of your adjacent domains. By allowing such activity, you might bear substantial communication costs for routing those messages.

REPLICATION TOPOLOGY

Your replication topology depends on many factors. Consider the number of databases that need to replicate, how much information each database contains, what type of information is being replicated (documents containing large objects or documents containing only text fields), how often the databases need to replicate, and where they need to replicate.

43

DATABASES

Initially, users should be allowed to create databases freely. The reason is to get people interested in Lotus Notes/Domino and comfortable with using the product. When the enterprise grows, however, data flow becomes more important. In a large enterprise, databases are not just placed on a server and accessed by users. You should consider the following:

- Who should access the database? Is it on the servers they need to access? Because replication is the means to distribute databases, allowing a database for users sometimes requires that replica copies of the database be located on several servers. If this is the case, ensure that all servers used to distribute the information also have the database. For example, in a hub-and-spoke situation, if the database is to be located on multiple spokes, it also needs to be located on the hub for distribution.

- Who needs to update the design? How will the design be implemented? Typically, changes to a design of a database are located in a database template, and the template is then used to propagate design changes. The person updating the design needs to have at least Designer access to the database. The servers propagating the design changes need to also have Designer access to the database.

- Who will be responsible for data distribution? This issue comes into play when a database is used as a reference—a company phone book or Directory Catalog, for example. The user responsible for adding data to the database needs to have access to do so. Any server distributing data needs to have access as well.

- What other databases are required by the database? Notes enables you to look up data in other databases to provide information for the current database. Wherever the database is being used, the lookup database must also be available.

- What company standards for databases will be implemented? The person who creates a database needs to create it in such a way that the design can be modified easily by another designer. Standards for databases are difficult to have in place because the perception is that they are restrictive. In the long run, however, the cost of maintaining the database will go down considerably if standards are followed. Standards must be flexible and documented to get buy-in from the database developers in your company. A suggestion is to standardize basic elements, such as ACLs, keyword listings, form names, and database names. As the first databases get implemented, document the design. Use the design documentation as a basis to develop new standards.

IMPLEMENTING DATABASES

In a large enterprise, the administrator places the database on a public server (hub) and usually is the gatekeeper for database design adherence. The primary job of the administrator is to ensure that the database is replicated throughout the environment correctly. Second, because the database is being checked anyway, the administrator can also ensure that the database adheres to company standards. You will explore these roles later in the section.

First, let's look at how a database is published on a server. The process in a large network should be as follows:

- The database is developed by the designer to meet users' needs.

- The database is staged on a server that few people can access for testing. Consider this your pilot of the database.

- The database is modified and versioned; then a template is drawn for future revisions. Versioning a database in an enterprise is important. A Notes database can be quite nebulous from a design perspective. It is very easy to "fix" something and end up ruining something else. When a change is made to a database, it should be documented and reported to the users. The scope of the change should also be considered.

- The database is implemented, which means that the database is placed in the environment in such a way that the data can be distributed to the users. In a hub-and-spoke situation, the database is placed on the hub and replicas are made on the spoke. At this point the administrator checks the database for standards.

- The database is published in a library for logical access. A catalog is generated by the server and tracks all databases in a domain. A library is a grouping of documents pointing to databases on the server. The group is decided arbitrarily.

ENSURING DATA FLOW

The ACL of any database needs to be standardized so that servers can replicate data appropriately. The rules are generally the following:

- All servers changing ACLs need to have Manager access. This means servers on which design changes originate.

- All servers changing other design elements need to have Designer access. Servers on which design changes originate need to have Designer access to the database.

- All servers propagating documents should have Editor access to the ACL.

- All servers receiving data should have only Reader access to the ACL.

- A back door should be put in place to enable the administrator to change the ACL on the server. This back door is a group in the ACL that has Manager access. The administrator need only add his or her name to the group in the Domino directory to gain access to the database.

- All ACLs for database replicas should be the same; exceptions to this rule should be verified by the administrator.

Using these rules, let's examine a possible scenario—a database used as a reference. The database is implemented in a hub-and-spoke topology on all spokes. A recommended ACL should have the hub as Manager, the spokes as Reader, the default as Reader, the group of people updating as Author, and the back-door group as Manager.

To make the job of the administrator easier, the ACL standard should be published so that the databases come with the ACLs set properly. The administrator needs only to check the access. Tools in the Domino Administrator and Web Administrator enable you to set the ACL of a database remotely.

Not all databases need to go through this test in a distributed environment. If the database is located on only one server in the domain, it is not necessary to check the ACL because data propagation is not an issue. In fact, if you have implemented a plan in which administrators in regions are responsible for their own database replication on servers in their regions, they are responsible for the ACLs in their regions. Only databases that go public need to adhere to the ACL standards.

The standards should be published in a database available to all database developers. To aid in buy-in, the developers should be allowed to comment on and change standards. The reason for publishing standards is to speed up implementation of databases. If a database is held at the checking phase, interest in it will diminish.

PUBLISHING THE DATABASES

When a database is available, users need to access it. This becomes problematic in organizations whose users frequently move around in job functions. Knowing which databases to access is half the battle when training a user to do a job. This is where database libraries come into play.

A database library is a collection of database links. You, the librarian, publish the database to a library. The users add the database library to their bookmarks (or workspaces, if any of your users are still using the R4 workspace) and use the links to load the icons to the database list in their bookmarks.

When new people start, they need only to add the database library bookmark to have access to the groups of databases in their locations.

REPLICATION CONTROLS

You can configure four replication controls on a Connection document to optimize and tune your replication topology: the overall schedule, replication priority, specific filename(s), and a time limit on the call.

SCHEDULING Determined through your Connection documents, scheduling is an important facet of your replication topology. An overworked server often is the result of a lack of schedule planning. Draw a timeline for each server, depicting the calls for replication that it makes. Plot the starting times and durations of the various connections. Balance the calls against the busy times for that server. Use the Statistics Reporting database or the Domino Administration tool to determine the busy times using the Graph views.

REPLICATION PRIORITY Each database can be given a replication priority of High, Medium, or Low. Your Connection documents can specify that only databases of certain priorities replicate. This setting applies to all the databases on the server. Database managers can set the priority of a database in the Replication Settings dialog box (in the Other section, select File, Replication, Settings). The server administrator sets up the scheduled replication based on the priority.

You might want to have one Connection document for each priority level. Your choices for priority levels are High, Medium and High, or Low and Medium and High.

As you can see from these choices, high-priority databases are always included, so you can use the first two choices to narrow the number that replicate.

SPECIFIC FILES   Another way to selectively control replication is to specify individual database filenames or directories. One or more files can be listed, or a directory of databases can be listed, effectively narrowing the focus of the Connection document to just the items in the list (no other files will replicate). This enables you to specify different schedules for each of your databases. Make sure that you plot these on your timeline.

TIME LIMITS   Given the varying nature of the data contained in Notes databases, time limits give you more control over your replication schedule planning. For each Connection document, you can specify a time limit in minutes. If this limit is reached during replication, the document in progress is finished and replication stops. Using this control, you can more closely plan and manage your replication timeline.

REPLICATION OF ACLS

It is important that you recognize and plan for replication of database ACLs. The ACL behaves differently from normal documents in a database. The ACL is considered first in replication and is overwritten if a change is implemented. The initiating server's ACL is the one that is checked to see whether there is a change.

The ACL is actually a "document" in the database, albeit not a data document that you can use in a view. During replication, the ACL replicates first, in case any changes to the settings would prevent further replication. The ACL "document" that is newer between the two replicas overwrites the older if the newer one has been modified since last replication. This is a time-sensitive feature; if the clocks on the two servers are not very near each other in time (we can't expect perfect synchronization), the newer ACL might not update the older version because the clock on that server is a few minutes behind the clock on the other server. This situation usually occurs only when you are attempting replication manually after making changes. If you encounter this problem, check the clocks on the servers and compare them with the time stamps on the ACLs. You can resave the newer ACL, wait until the lagging server passes the time of the last change on the older ACL, and then replicate again.

CENTRAL MANAGEMENT FOR DATABASE ACLS

Plan to manage the ACL of every database. This doesn't mean that you need to manage each ACL yourself; it means that you should have a plan for each database agreed on by your administrative team. Ideally, each database's ACL will be maintained on one server. If you plan to use the administration process, make use of the Administration Server setting on

43

the ACL dialog box. This lets the administration process make changes to the ACL on the server specified in this field. Each replica of this database should have the same setting.

The administration process consists of a server task (ADMIN.EXE) and a series of steps initiated in the Domino Directory by an administrator using the Actions menu. An administrator can initiate a change, such as renaming a user. That action writes a document into the Administration Requests database.

The administration process server task sees that request, and it takes action on the Domino Directory. In the case of renaming a user, it puts the pending request into the user's Person document.

When that user next accesses the server, Notes alerts him to the pending request and asks the user to accept the change. Upon accepting the change, another request is generated in the Administration Requests database, and the administration process server tasks take action again—this time by propagating the new name throughout other documents in the Domino Directory.

The option Enforce a Consistent Access Control List Across All Replicas of This Database, under the Advanced section of the ACL dialog box, does what it says: One replica copy is listed as the manager in all other replicas. On this copy only, enable this setting. The managing replica forces its ACL into every other replica, including those that reside on workstations or laptops.

This process should not be used on separate replica copies of the Domino Directory; it should be used on only one replica, which is specified in the Administration Server field on the Replication Settings dialog box in the Advanced section. If this procedure is not followed, either the administration process on the other servers will ignore the requests, or replication conflicts will result.

PASSTHRU TOPOLOGY

Under Release 3, a Notes server was always an endpoint on a network; it performed no routing of protocols. Notes 4 introduced the concept of passthru topology, which is essentially just that: protocol routing. By accessing a known, reachable Domino server, another Domino server or Notes client can route through that server to reach another. This feature, including the capability to disable it, is fully configurable in the Server document. Review Chapter 34, "Initial Configuration of Servers with the Domino Directories," for more information on passthru servers.

TASK-SPECIFIC, DEDICATED SERVERS

Passthru enables servers to be truly dedicated in their tasks. In the old days (Release 3.*x*), a user could reach one server with a phone call; if a database resided on a different server, it either must have been replicated to the dial-in server or the user had to hang up and redial that other server.

43

With passthru topology, however, the Domino server can route the caller to other Notes servers on the network in one phone call. This enables you to segment your server types without wasting precious drive space for replica copies. A database can live on one server and be accessed easily by both network and remote clients.

PROTOCOL-SPECIFIC SERVERS

Another benefit of using passthru is the capability of streamlining your protocols. Suppose that you have many users working under SPX, but a server in another area is using TCP/IP. Instead of enabling TCP/IP on the SPX users' machines, you can enable this protocol on a server running SPX. Using passthru, the SPX clients can reach the TCP/IP server by routing through their normal SPX servers.

Let's take another powerful example. Domino 4.*x* introduced a server task called the Web Retriever, or WEB. This task reaches out to the World Wide Web and retrieves HTML pages, putting them into a Notes database called the Web Navigator. Access to the Web normally requires TCP/IP at the desktop, but by using a passthru server to provide access to a server running the WEB server task, your clients do not need TCP/IP. They can communicate with the Domino server over SPX while the server itself communicates with the Web using TCP/IP.

Segmenting your protocols can greatly reduce the expense of adding protocols to single-protocol desktops.

MAPPING YOUR PASSTHRU TOPOLOGY

Draw a chart showing all your servers, their connections, and their protocols. Determine which servers should allow the passthru topology. You can control passthru with four fields on each Server document: Access Server, Route Through, Cause Calling, and Destinations Allowed. As with other fields on a Server document, use groups or wildcards instead of individual user or server names so that minimal changes are required. Refer to Chapter 32, "Installation and Configuration of Domino on Linux," for more information on setting up a passthru server.

THE DOMAIN AND THE DOMINO DIRECTORY

The glue of a Notes domain is the Domino Directory, formerly known as the Public Name and Address Book (NAB). The larger your network is, the more crucial the management of this instrument is. Your users depend on it for addressing mail (along with the Directory Catalog); your servers need it for identification, security, and task scheduling. Management of this book should be planned in advance so that emergencies can be avoided through routine maintenance.

NOTES DOMAINS

As you've learned, a domain is defined as a group of servers that replicate their primary Domino directories. The components of that domain are all defined in that Domino Directory. Each server knows its place in the network, as well as the roles of and communications paths to each of the other servers.

However, this is not necessarily the best method for setting up a large network (although this doesn't imply that it is wrong). Simply stated, the evaluation of several factors can help you determine whether to use one domain or to split your organization into multiple domains.

SIMPLICITY VERSUS EFFICIENCY   A single Domino Directory eases mail addressing, but as this Domino Directory grows large, efficiency for each of the servers using that book decreases.

Multiple domains (each has its own Domino Directory) are each more efficient for lookups, but they make addressing harder; they require a separate combined Domino directory. A Directory Catalog is an LDAP-based database that contains an entry for all users and groups of the specified domains. Even though a Directory Catalog can contain hundreds of thousands of names, it remains *very* small because of the LDAP technology used. It is small enough for users to keep a local replica for disconnected addressing.

ROLES

The Domino Directory provides various roles stratified to match the most common administrator functions in such an environment. The users and groups listed in the ACL are assigned to appropriate roles that grant them rights according to their assigned responsibilities. You can enable some administrators to create and modify only groups but not users or servers; likewise, you can allow some to create users but not modify groups. In this way, it is possible to distribute the maintenance responsibilities without releasing control to each and every administrator.

These are the roles that are in the Domino Directory:

- GroupCreator allows creation of Group documents.
- GroupModifier allows modification of Group documents.
- PolicyCreator allows creation of Policy documents.
- PolicyModifier allows modification of Policy documents.
- PolicyReader is a user or group of users who can read existing policy documents.
- NetCreator allows creation of all documents except Groups, Servers, and Person.
- NetModifier allows modification of all documents except Groups, Servers, and Users.
- ServerCreator allows creation of server IDs and Server documents.
- ServerModifier allows modification of Server documents.

- UserCreator allows creation of user IDs and Person documents.
- UserModifier allows modification of Person documents.

Administration Groups

The documents in the Domino Directory make it easier to facilitate local changes in a distributed environment. Using the Administrators field under the Administration tab for most documents, you can specify, per document, those groups that are allowed to modify it. This enables you to allocate specific sets of documents to the control of a local administrator; that person will be allowed to maintain those documents, yet you haven't relinquished control of the other documents.

Monitoring Your Notes Servers

Release 5 introduced the Domino Administrator. This client is installed as a separate application from the Notes client, and it can be accessed independently.

The Domino Administrator client provides a centralized, robust interface to manage your Domino network. You can centrally control virtually everything about your Domino servers: files, directories, ACLs, replication, user registration, and much more.

Review Part VII, "Administering the Domino Servers," for more information on the Domino Administrator client.

Statistics and Events Server Tasks

Domino provides you with a way to collect statistics and trap events that occur on your servers. You can send this collection feedback to one central database from all your servers. Additionally, you can set up various Monitor documents to watch for specific events and then perform some action based on that event.

Statistics collection enables you to observe the behavior of a server over time, monitoring usage, disk space, memory, and tasks at specified intervals. Special graphing views in the Statistics database (STATREP5.NSF) give you a visual representation of some of these statistics.

Simply collecting statistics will not alert you to trouble conditions. By creating various Monitor or Event documents in the Statistics and Events database (EVENTS5.NSF), you can actually receive notification of thresholds that have been exceeded or of events as they occur.

APPENDIXES

NOTES/DOMINO CLASS REFERENCE

In this appendix

OVERVIEW

The purpose of this appendix is to provide a quick, easy-to-use reference for the Domino Object classes. The classes are organized by front end and back end, and are sorted in alphabetical order. Each class has its containment, properties, methods, and events listed, if applicable. An asterisk (*) indicates that this item is new or changed for Release 6.

The containment sections list the objects of other classes from which an object of the current class can be obtained, or the classes for objects that can be obtained from the current class.

All the classes are shown using the LotusScript syntax, but they are almost identical to the Java equivalents. The major difference for Java access is that Java does not support properties, so getting and setting property values is done via method calls.

Here are a few general guidelines for Java:

- Class names in Java do not use the `Notes` prefix. The Java class name is just the LotusScript name without the prefix. For example, the `NotesSession` class in LotusScript is called `Session` using Java.

- To access a property, generally prefix the property name with `get`. If the property name begins with `Is` or `Has`, you do not use the `get` prefix.

- To set a property, generally prefix the property name with `set`. If the property name begins with `Is` or `Has`, drop that and substitute `set`.

LOTUS NOTES FRONT-END CLASSES

The front-end classes pertain to objects represented in the Notes user interface (UI). These classes are not available in scheduled agents because there is no UI for scheduled agents.

THE Button CLASS

The `Button` class represents LotusScript actions, buttons, and hotspots in forms or views.

EVENTS

```
Click
ObjectExecute
```

THE Field CLASS

The `Field` class represents a field on a form. The entering and exiting events are available only when the field is editable.

EVENTS

```
Entering
Exiting
```

```
OnBlur *
OnChange *
OnFocus *
```

THE Navigator CLASS

The Navigator class represents a button or hotspot in a navigator.

EVENT

```
Click
```

THE NotesUIDatabase CLASS

The NotesUIDatabase class represents a database opened to the Notes user interface.

CONTAINMENT

Contained by: NotesUIWorkspace

Contains: NotesDatabase, NotesDocumentCollection

PROPERTIES

```
Database
Documents
```

METHODS

```
Close *
OpenNavigator
OpenView
```

EVENTS

```
PostDocumentDelete
PostDragDrop
PostDropToArchive *
PostOpen
QueryClose
QueryDocumentDelete
QueryDocumentUndelete
QueryDragDrop
QueryDropToArchive *
```

THE NotesUIDocument CLASS

The NotesUIDocument class represents a document opened to the Notes user interface.

CONTAINMENT

Contained by: NotesUIWorkspace

Contains: NotesDocument, NotesUIScheduler *

PROPERTIES

AutoReload

CurrentField

DialogBoxCanceled

Document

EditMode

FieldHelp

HiddenChars

HorzScrollBar

InPreviewPane

IsNewDoc

PreviewDocLink

PreviewParentDoc

Ruler

WindowTitle

METHODS

Categorize

Clear

Close *

CollapseAllSections

Copy

CreateObject

Cut

DeleteDocument

DeselectAll

ExpandAllSections

FieldAppendText

FieldClear

FieldContains

FieldGetText

FieldSetText

FindFreeTimeDialog

FindFreeTimeDialogEx

FindString

Forward

GetObject

GetSchedulerObject

GetSelectedText

GotoBottom

GotoField

GotoNextField

GotoPrevField

GotoTop

Import

InsertText

NavBarSetText

NavBarSpinnerStart

NavBarSpinnerStop

Paste

Print

Refresh

RefreshHideFormulas

Reload

Save

SaveNewVersion

SelectAll

Send

SpellCheck

EVENTS

OnHelp *

OnLoad *

OnSubmit *

OnUnload *

PostModeChange

PostOpen

PostRecalc

PostSave

PostSend *

QueryClose *

QueryModeChange

QueryOpen

QueryRecalc *

QuerySave

QuerySend *

THE NotesUIScheduler CLASS *

The NotesUIScheduler class, a new addition in Release 6, represents an embedded scheduler within the currently active document.

CONTAINMENT

Contained by: NotesUIDocument

Contains: NotesDateRange, NotesDateTime

PROPERTIES

ColorLegend

DisplayAlternateNames

DisplayHoursPerDay

DisplayMeetingSuggestions

DisplayParticipantStatus

DisplayPeople

DisplayResources

DisplayRooms

DisplayTwisties

Interval As NotesDateRange

MeetingIndicator

ScheduleGridStart As NotesDateTime

SchedulerName As NotesDateTime

TimeZone

METHODS

AddParticipant

GetParticipants

GetScheduleData

RemoveParticipants

EVENT

OnIntervalChange *

THE NotesUIView CLASS

The NotesUIView class represents a view opened to the Notes user interface.

CONTAINMENT

Contained by: NotesUIWorkspace

Contains: NotesDocumentCollection, NotesView

PROPERTIES

CalendarDateTime

CalendarDateTimeEnd *

CaretCategory

CaretNoteID *

Documents

View As NotesView

ViewAlias

ViewInheritedFrom *

ViewName

METHODS

Close *

DeselectAll *

Print

Select Document

EVENTS

InViewEdit *

PostDragDrop

A

PostEntryResize *

PostOpen

PostPaste

QueryAddToFolder

QueryClose

QueryDragDrop

QueryEntryResize *

QueryOpen

QueryOpenDocument

QueryPaste

QueryRecalc

RegionDoubleClick

THE NotesUIWorkspace CLASS

The NotesUIWorkspace class represents the Notes workspace.

CONTAINMENT

Contains: NotesDocumentCollection, NotesUIDatabase, NotesUIDocument, NotesUIView

PROPERTIES

CurrentCalendarDateTime

CurrentDatabase *

CurrentDocument

CurrentView

METHODS

AddDatabase

CheckAlarms

ComposeDocument *

DialogBox *

EditDocument

EditProfile

EnableAlarms

Folder *

GetCurrentDatabase *

GetListOfTunes

New

OpenDatabase

OpenFileDialog

OpenFrameSet

OpenPage

PickListCollection

PickListStrings

PlayTune

Prompt

RefreshParentNote

ReloadWindow

SaveFileDialog

SetCurrentLocation

SetTargetFrame

URLOpen

UseLSX

ViewRebuild *

ViewRefresh

LOTUS NOTES BACK-END CLASSES

The back-end classes pertain to objects not directly represented in the Notes UI. These classes are available in any LotusScript module.

THE NotesACL CLASS

The NotesACL class represents the Access Control List (ACL) of a Notes database.

CONTAINMENT

Contained by: NotesDatabase

Contains: NotesACLEntry

PROPERTIES

AdministrationServer *

InternetLevel

IsAdminNames *

IsAdminReaderAuthor *

IsExtendedAccess *

Parent

Roles

UniformAccess

METHODS

AddRole

CreateACLEntry

DeleteRole

GetEntry

GetFirstEntry

GetNextEntry

RemoveACLEntry

RenameRole

Save

THE NotesACLEntry CLASS

The NotesACLEntry class represents an entry in the ACL of a Notes database.

CONTAINMENT

Contained by: NotesACL

Contains: NotesName

PROPERTIES

CanCreateDocuments

CanCreateLSOrJavaAgent

CanCreatePersonalAgent

CanCreatePersonalFolder

CanCreateSharedFolder

CanDeleteDocuments

CanReplicateOrCopyDocuments *

IsAdminReaderAuthor

IsAdminServer

IsGroup

IsPerson

IsPublicReader

IsPublicWriter

```
IsServer

Level

Name

NameObject

Parent

Roles

UserType
```

METHODS

```
DisableRole

EnableRole

IsRoleEnabled

New

Remove
```

THE NotesAdministrationProcess CLASS *

The NotesAdministrationProcess class, a new addition to Release 6, represents the administration process.

CONTAINMENT

Contained by: NotesSession

PROPERTIES

```
CertificateAuthorityOrg

CertificateExpiration

CertifierFile

CertifierPassword

IsCertificateAuthorityAvailable

UseCertificateAuthority
```

METHODS

```
AddGroupMembers

AddInternetCertificateToUser

AddServerToCluster

ApproveDeletePersonInDirectory

ApproveDeleteServerInDirectory
```

A

ApproveDesignElementDeletion

ApproveMailFileDeletion

ApproveMovedReplicaDeletion

ApproveNameChangeRetraction

ApproveRenamePersonInDirectory

ApproveRenameServerInDirectory

ApproveReplicaDeletion

ApproveResourceDeletion

ChangeHTTPPassword

ConfigureMailAgent

CreateReplica

DeleteGroup

DeleteReplicas

DeleteServer

DeleteUser

FindGroupInDomain

FindServerInDomain

FindUserInDomain

MoveMailUser

MoveReplica

MoveRoamingUser

MoveUserInHierarchyComplete

MoveUserInHierarchyRequest

RecertifyServer

RecertifyUser

RemoveServerFromCluster

RenameGroup

RenameNotesUser

RenameWebUser

SetServerDirectoryAssistanceSettings

SetUserPasswordSettings

SignDatabaseWithServerID

UpgradeUserToHierarchical

THE NotesAgent CLASS

The NotesAgent class represents an agent within a Notes database.

CONTAINMENT

Contained by: NotesSession, NotesDatabase

PROPERTIES

Comment

CommonOwner

HasRunSinceModified

HttpURL

IsActivatable *

IsEnabled *

IsNotesAgent

IsPublic

IsWebAgent

LastRun

LockHolders *

Name

NotesURL

OnBehalfOf *

Owner

ParameterDocID

Parent

Query

ServerName

Target

Trigger

METHODS

Lock *

LockProvisional *

Remove

Run

RunOnServer

Save

Unlock *

A

THE NotesColorObject CLASS *

The NotesColorObject class, a new addition to Release 6, represents a color within a rich-text field.

CONTAINMENT

Contained by: NotesRichTextSection, NotesRichTextTable, NotesSession

PROPERTIES

Blue

Green

Hue

Luminance

NotesColor

Red

Saturation

METHODS

SetHSL

SetRGB

THE NotesDatabase CLASS

The NotesDatabase class represents a Notes database.

CONTAINMENT

Contained by: NotesDbDirectory, NotesSession, NotesUIDatabase

Contains: NotesACL, NotesAgent, NotesDocument, NotesDocumentCollection, NotesForm, NotesNoteCollection, NotesOutline, NotesReplication, NotesView

PROPERTIES

ACL

ACLActivityLog *

Agents

AllDocuments

Categories

Created

CurrentAccessLevel

DelayUpdates

DesignTemplateName

FileFormat *

FileName

FilePath

FolderReferencesEnabled

Forms

FTIndexFrequency *

HttpURL

IsClusterReplication *

IsConfigurationDirectory *

IsCurrentAccessPublicReader *

IsCurrentAccessPublicWriter *

IsDesignLockingEnabled *

IsDirectoryCatalog

IsDocumentLockingEnabled *

IsFTIndexed

IsInMultiDbIndexing *

IsInService *

IsLink *

IsMultiDbSearch

IsOpen

IsPendingDelete *

IsPrivateAddressBook

IsPublicAddressBook

LastFixup *

LastFTIndexed

LastModified

LimitRevisions *

LimitUpdatedBy *

ListInDbCatalog *

Managers

MaxSize

NotesURL

Parent

PercentUsed

A

A

ReplicaID

ReplicationInfo

Server

Size

SizeQuota

SizeWarning *

TemplateName

Title

Type *

UndeleteExpireTime *

UnprocessedDocuments

Views

METHODS

Compact

CompactWithOptions *

Create

CreateCopy

CreateDocument

CreateFromTemplate

CreateFTIndex *

CreateNoteCollection *

CreateOutline

CreateReplica

CreateView *

EnableFolder

Fixup *

FTDomainSearch

FTSearch

FTSearchRange *

GetAgent

GetDocumentByID

GetDocumentByUNID

GetDocumentByURL

GetForm

GetOption *

GetOutline

GetProfileDocCollection

GetProfileDocument

GetURLHeaderInfo

GetView

GrantAccess

MarkForDelete *

New

Open

OpenByReplicaID

OpenIfModified

OpenMail

OpenURLDb

OpenWithFailover

QueryAccess

QueryAccessRoles *

Remove

RemoveFTIndex *

Replicate

RevokeAccess

Search

SetOption *

Sign *

UnprocessedFTSearch

UnprocessedFTSearchRange *

UnprocessedSearch

UpdateFTIndex

THE NotesDateRange CLASS

The NotesDateRange class represents a range of dates and times.

CONTAINMENT

Contained by: NotesDocument, NotesItem, NotesSession, NotesUIScheduler

Contains: NotesDateTime

PROPERTIES

EndDateTime

Parent

StartDateTime

Text

THE NotesDateTime CLASS

The NotesDateTime class provides a mechanism to translate between the LotusScript date-time format and the native Domino format.

CONTAINMENT

Contained by: NotesDateRange, NotesDocument, NotesItem, NotesNoteCollection, NotesSession, NotesUIScheduler

PROPERTIES

DateOnly

GMTTime

IsDST

IsValidDate

LocalTime

LSGMTTime

LSLocalTime

Parent

TimeOnly

TimeZone

ZoneTime

METHODS

AdjustDay

AdjustHour

AdjustMinute

AdjustMonth

AdjustSecond

AdjustYear

ConvertToZone

New

```
SetAnyDate

SetAnyTime

SetNow

TimeDifference

TimeDifferenceDouble
```

THE NotesDbDirectory CLASS

The `NotesDbDirectory` class represents the available Notes databases on the local workstation or a Domino server.

CONTAINMENT

Contained by: `NotesSession`

Contains: `NotesDatabase`

PROPERTIES

```
Name

Parent
```

METHODS

```
CreateDatabase

GetFirstDatabase

GetNextDatabase

New

OpenDatabase

OpenDatabaseByReplicaID

OpenDatabaseIfModified

OpenMailDatabase
```

THE NotesDocument CLASS

The `NotesDocument` class represents a document in a database within a Notes database.

CONTAINMENT

Contained by: `NotesDatabase`, `NotesDocumentCollection`, `NotesNewsletter`, `NotesUIDocument`, `NotesView`, `NotesViewEntry`

Contains: `NotesDateRange`, `NotesDateTime`, `NotesEmbeddedObject`, `NotesItem`, `NotesMIMEEntity`, `NotesRichTextItem`

PROPERTIES

Authors

ColumnValues

Created

EmbeddedObjects

EncryptionKeys

EncryptOnSend

FolderReferences

FTSearchScore

HasEmbedded

HttpURL

IsDeleted

IsEncrypted *

IsNewNote

IsProfile

IsResponse

IsSigned

IsUIDocOpen

IsValid

Items

Key

LastAccessed

LastModified

LockHolders *

NameOfProfile

NoteID

NotesURL

ParentDatabase

ParentDocumentUNID

ParentView

Responses

SaveMessageOnSend

SentByAgent

Signer

SignOnSend

Size

UniversalID

Verifier

METHODS

AppendItemValue

CloseMIMEEntities *

ComputeWithForm

CopyAllItems

CopyItem

CopyToDatabase

CreateMIMEEntity *

CreateReplyMessage

CreateRichTextItem

Encrypt

GetAttachment

GetFirstItem

GetItemValue

GetItemValueDateTimeArray *

GetMIMEEntity *

GetReceivedItemText *

HasItem

Lock *

LockProvisional *

MakeResponse

New

PutInFolder

Remove

RemoveFromFolder

RemoveItem

RemovePermanently *

RenderToRTItem

ReplaceItemValue

Save

Send

A

A

```
Sign

Unlock *
```

THE NotesDocumentCollection CLASS

The NotesDocumentCollection class represents a subset of documents within a particular Notes database.

CONTAINMENT

Contained by: NotesDatabase, NotesSession, NotesUIDatabase, NotesUIView

Contains: NotesDocument

PROPERTIES

```
Count

IsSorted

Parent

Query
```

METHODS

```
AddDocument

DeleteDocument

FTSearch

GetDocument

GetFirstDocument

GetLastDocument

GetNextDocument

GetNthDocument

GetPrevDocument

PutAllInFolder

RemoveAll

RemoveAllFromFolder

StampAll

UpdateAll
```

THE NotesDOMAttributeNode CLASS *

The NotesDOMAttributeNode class, a new addition to Release 6, represents an attribute within a NotesDOMElementNode object.

BASE CLASS

Inherits from: NotesDOMNode

CONTAINMENT

Contained by: NotesDOMDocumentNode, NotesDOMElementNode

Contains: NotesDOMTextNode

PROPERTIES

AttributeName

Attributes

AttributeValue

FirstChild

HasChildNodes

IsNull

IsSpecified

LastChild

LocalName

NamespaceURI

NextSibling

NodeName

NodeType

NodeValue

NumberOfChildNodes

ParentNode

Prefix

PreviousSibling

METHODS

AppendChild

Clone

RemoveChild

ReplaceChild

THE NotesDOMCDATASectionNode CLASS

The NotesDOMCDATASectionNode class, a new addition to Release 6, represents a CDATA section within an XML document.

BASE CLASS

Inherits from: `NotesDOMTextNode`

CONTAINMENT

Contained by: `NotesDOMDocumentNode`

PROPERTIES

`Attributes`

`FirstChild`

`HasChildNodes`

`IsNull`

`LastChild`

`LocalName`

`NamespaceURI`

`NextSibling`

`NodeName`

`NodeType`

`NodeValue`

`NumberOfChildNodes`

`ParentNode`

`Prefix`

`PreviousSibling`

METHODS

`AppendChild`

`AppendData`

`Clone`

`DeleteData`

`InsertData`

`RemoveChild`

`ReplaceChild`

`ReplaceData`

`SplitText`

`SubstringData`

THE NotesDOMCharacterDataNode CLASS *

The NotesDOMCharacterDataNode class, a new addition to Release 6, represents character data within a particular DOM node.

BASE CLASS

Inherits from: NotesDOMNode

PROPERTIES

Attributes

FirstChild

HasChildNodes

IsNull

LastChild

LocalName

NamespaceURI

NextSibling

NodeName

NodeType

NodeValue

NumberOfChildNodes

ParentNode

Prefix

PreviousSibling

METHODS

AppendChild

AppendData

Clone

DeleteData

InsertData

RemoveChild

ReplaceChild

ReplaceData

SubstringData

A

THE NotesDOMCommentNode CLASS *

The NotesDOMCommentNode class, a new addition to Release 6, represents a comment node within an XML document.

BASE CLASS

Inherits from: NotesDOMCharacterDataNode

CONTAINMENT

Contained by: NotesDOMDocumentNode

PROPERTIES

Attributes

FirstChild

HasChildNodes

IsNull

LastChild

LocalName

NamespaceURI

NextSibling

NodeName

NodeType

NodeValue

NumberOfChildNodes

ParentNode

Prefix

PreviousSibling

METHODS

AppendChild

AppendData

Clone

DeleteData

InsertData

RemoveChild

ReplaceChild

ReplaceData

SubstringData

THE NotesDOMDocumentFragmentNode CLASS *

The NotesDOMDocumentFragmentNode class, a new addition to Release 6, represents a document fragment within an XML document.

BASE CLASS

Inherits from: NotesDOMNode

CONTAINMENT

Contained by: NotesDOMDocumentNode

PROPERTIES

Attributes

FirstChild

HasChildNodes

IsNull

LastChild

LocalName

NamespaceURI

NextSibling

NodeName

NodeType

NodeValue

NumberOfChildNodes

ParentNode

Prefix

PreviousSibling

METHODS

AppendChild

Clone

RemoveChild

ReplaceChild

THE NotesDOMDocumentNode CLASS *

The NotesDOMDocumentNode class, a new addition to Release 6, represents the complete XML document.

BASE CLASS

Inherits from: NotesDOMNode

CONTAINMENT

Contained by: NotesDOMParser

Contains: NotesDOMAttributeNode, NotesDOMCDATASectionNode, NotesDOMCommentNode, NotesDOMDocumentFragmentNode, NotesDOMElementNode, NotesDOMEntityReferenceNode, NotesDOMNodeList, NotesDOMProcessingInstructionNode, NotesDOMTextNode

PROPERTIES

Attributes

DocumentElement

FirstChild

HasChildNodes

IsNull

LastChild

LocalName

NamespaceURI

NextSibling

NodeName

NodeType

NodeValue

NumberOfChildNodes

ParentNode

Prefix

PreviousSibling

METHODS

AppendChild

Clone

CreateAttributeNode

CreateCDATASectionNode

CreateCommentNode

CreateDocumentFragmentNode

CreateDocumentNode

CreateElementNode

```
CreateEntityReferenceNode

CreateNotationNode

CreateProcessingInstructionNode

CreateTextNode

CreateXMLDeclNode

GetElementsByTagName

RemoveChild

ReplaceChild
```

A

THE NotesDOMDocumentTypeNode CLASS *

The NotesDOMDocumentTypeNode class, a new addition to Release 6, represents a list of entities that are defined within the XML document.

BASE CLASS

Inherits from: NotesDOMNode

PROPERTIES

```
Attributes

FirstChild

HasChildNodes

IsNull

LastChild

LocalName

NamespaceURI

NextSibling

NodeName

NodeType

NodeValue

NumberOfChildNodes

ParentNode

Prefix

PreviousSibling
```

METHODS

```
AppendChild

Clone
```

RemoveChild

ReplaceChild

THE NotesDOMElementNode CLASS *

The NotesDOMElementNode class, a new addition within Release 6, represents a particular element of the XML document.

BASE CLASS

Inherits from: NotesDOMNode

CONTAINMENT

Contained by: NotesDOMDocumentNode

Contains: NotesDOMAttributeNode, NotesDOMNodeList

PROPERTIES

Attributes

FirstChild

HasChildNodes

IsNull

LastChild

LocalName

NamespaceURI

NextSibling

NodeName

NodeType

NodeValue

NumberOfChildNodes

ParentNode

Prefix

PreviousSibling

TagName

METHODS

AppendChild

Clone

GetAttribute

```
GetAttributeNode

GetElementsByTagName

RemoveAttribute

RemoveAttributeNode

RemoveChild

ReplaceChild

SetAttribute

SetAttributeNode
```

THE NotesDOMEntityNode CLASS *

The NotesDOMEntityNode class, a new addition within Release 6, represents an entity node within an XML document.

BASE CLASS

Inherits from: NotesDOMNode

PROPERTIES

```
Attributes

FirstChild

HasChildNodes

IsNull

LastChild

LocalName

NamespaceURI

NextSiblingNodeName

NodeType

NodeValue

NumberOfChildNodes

ParentNode

Prefix

PreviousSibling
```

METHODS

```
AppendChild

Clone

RemoveChild

ReplaceChild
```

THE NotesDOMEntityReferenceNode CLASS *

The NotesDOMEntityReferenceNode class, a new addition to Release 6, represents an entity reference node within the XML document.

BASE CLASS

Inherits from: NotesDOMNode

CONTAINMENT

Contained by: NotesDOMDocumentNode

PROPERTIES

Attributes

FirstChild

HasChildNodes

IsNull

LastChild

LocalName

NamespaceURI

NextSibling

NodeName

NodeType

NodeValue

NumberOfChildNodes

ParentNode

Prefix

PreviousSibling

METHODS

AppendChild

Clone

RemoveChild

ReplaceChild

THE NotesDOMNamedNodeMap CLASS *

The NotesDOMNamedNodeMap class, a new addition within Release 6, is used by methods of NotesDOMNode class for returning a listing of a particular element's node attributes.

CONTAINMENT

Contained by: `NotesDOMNode`

PROPERTY

`NumberOfEntries`

METHOD

`GetItem`

THE `NotesDOMNode` CLASS *

The `NotesDOMNode` class, a new addition to Release 6, represents a single DOM node within a document's structure.

DERIVED CLASSES

`NotesDOMAttributeNode, NotesDOMCharacterDataNode, NotesDOMDocumentFragmentNode, NotesDOMDocumentNode, NotesDOMDocumentTypeNode, NotesDOMElementNode, NotesDOMEntityNode, NotesDOMEntityReferenceNode, NotesDOMNotationNode, NotesDOMProcessingInstructionNode, NotesDOMXMLDeclNode` inherit from the `NotesDOMNode` class.

CONTAINMENT

Contains: `NotesDOMNamedNodeMap, NotesDOMNodeList`

PROPERTIES

`Attributes`

`FirstChild`

`HasChildNodes`

`IsNull`

`LastChild`

`LocalName`

`NamespaceURI`

`NextSibling`

`NodeName`

`NodeType`

`NodeValue`

`NumberOfChildNodes`

`ParentNode`

```
Prefix
PreviousSibling
```

METHODS

```
AppendChild
Clone
RemoveChild
ReplaceChild
```

A

THE NotesDOMNodeList CLASS *

The NotesDOMNodeList class, a new addition to Release 6, is utilized by NotesDOMNode's methods to retrieve a list of a node's child elements.

CONTAINMENT

Contained by: NotesDOMDocumentNode, NotesDOMNode

PROPERTY

```
NumberOfEntries
```

METHOD

```
GetItem
```

THE NotesDOMNotationNode CLASS *

The NotesDOMNotationNode class, a new addition to Release 6, represents a notation declared within a DTD.

BASE CLASS

Inherits from: NotesDOMNode

PROPERTIES

```
Attributes
FirstChild
HasChildNodes
IsNull
LastChild
LocalName
NamespaceURI
```

NextSibling

NodeName

NodeType

NodeValue

NumberOfChildNodes

ParentNode

Prefix

PreviousSibling

PublicID

SystemID

METHODS

AppendChild

Clone

RemoveChild

ReplaceChild

THE NotesDOMParser CLASS *

The NotesDOMParser class, a new addition to Release 6, parses an XML document into a DOM tree structure.

BASE CLASS

Inherits from: NotesXMLProcessor

CONTAINMENT

Contained by: NotesSession

Contains: NotesDOMDocumentNode, NotesDXLExporter, NotesStream, NotesXSLTransformer

EVENTS

PostDOMParse

PROPERTIES

AddXMLDeclNode

Document

DoNamespaces

ExitOnFirstFatalError

ExpandEntityReferences

InputValidationOption

Log

LogComment

METHODS

Output

Process

Serialize

SetInput

SetOutput

THE NotesDOMProcessingInstructionNode CLASS *

The NotesDOMProcessingInstructionNode class, a new addition to Release 6, represents a processing instruction within an XML document.

BASE CLASS

Inherits from: NotesDOMNode

CONTAINMENT

Contained by: NotesDOMDocumentNode

PROPERTIES

Attributes

Data

FirstChild

HasChildNodes

IsNull

LastChild

LocalName

NamespaceURI

NextSibling

NodeName

NodeType

NodeValue

NumberOfChildNodes

ParentNode

Prefix

PreviousSibling

Target

METHODS

AppendChild

Clone

RemoveChild

ReplaceChild

THE NotesDOMTextNode CLASS *

The NotesDOMTextNode class, a new addition to Release 6, represents the textual content of a particular element or attribute.

BASE CLASS

Inherits from: NotesDOMCharacterDataNode

DERIVED CLASSES

NotesDOMCDATASectionNode inherits from the NotesDOMTextNode class.

CONTAINMENT

Contained by: NotesDOMAttributeNode, NotesDOMDocumentNode

PROPERTIES

Attributes

FirstChild

HasChildNodes

IsNull

LastChild

LocalName

NamespaceURI

NextSibling

NodeName

NodeType

NodeValue

NumberOfChildNodes

ParentNode

Prefix

PreviousSibling

METHODS

AppendChild

AppendData

Clone

DeleteData

InsertData

RemoveChild

ReplaceChild

ReplaceData

SplitText

SubstringData

THE NotesDOMXMLDeclNode CLASS *

The NotesDOMXMLDeclNode class, a new addition to Release 6, represents the XML declaration of which version of XML is being utilized.

BASE CLASS

Inherits from: NotesDOMNode

PROPERTIES

Attributes

Encoding

FirstChild

HasChildNodes

IsNull

LastChild

LocalName

NamespaceURI

NextSibling

NodeName

NodeType

NodeValue

NumberOfChildNodes

ParentNode

Prefix

PreviousSibling

Standalone

Version

METHODS

AppendChild

Clone

RemoveChild

ReplaceChild

THE NotesDXLExporter CLASS *

The NotesDXLExporter class, a new utility class within Release 6, provides a mechanism to convert all Domino data and design elements into DXL (Domino XML).

BASE CLASS

Inherits from: NotesXMLProcessor

CONTAINMENT

Contained by: NotesSession

PROPERTIES

DoctypeSYSTEM

ExitOnFirstFatalError

ForceNoteFormat

Log

LogComment

OutputDOCTYPE

METHODS

Process

SetInput

SetOutput

THE NotesDXLImporter CLASS *

The NotesDXLImporter class, a new utility class within Release 6, provides a mechanism to convert DXL (Domino XML) into Domino data and design elements.

BASE CLASS

Inherits from: NotesXMLProcessor

CONTAINMENT

Contained by: NotesSession

PROPERTIES

ACLImportOption

CreateFTIndex

DesignImportOption

DocumentImportOption

ExitOnFirstFatalError

ImportedNoteCount

InputValidationOption

Log

LogComment

ReplaceDb

ReplicaRequiredForReplaceOrUpdate

UnknownTokenLogOption

METHODS

GetFirstImportedNoteID

GetNextImportedNoteID

Process

SetInput

SetOutput

THE NotesEmbeddedObject CLASS

The NotesEmbeddedObject class represents an embedded object, object link, or file attachment within a Notes document or rich-text item.

CONTAINMENT

Contained by: NotesDocument, NotesRichTextItem, NotesRichTextNavigator

PROPERTIES

Class

FileSize

FitBelowFields

FitToWindow

Name

Object

Parent

RunReadOnly

Source

Type

Verbs

METHODS

Activate

DoVerb

ExtractFile

Remove

THE NotesForm CLASS

The NotesForm class represents a form within a Notes database.

CONTAINMENT

Contained by: NotesDatabase

PROPERTIES

Aliases

Fields

FormUsers

HttpURL

IsSubForm

LockHolders *

Name

NotesURL

Parent

ProtectReaders

ProtectUsers

Readers

METHODS

GetFieldType *

Lock *

LockProvisional *

Remove

Unlock *

THE NotesInternational CLASS

The NotesInternational class represents the international settings for the current machine's operating environment.

CONTAINMENT

Contained by: NotesSession

PROPERTIES

AMString

CurrencyDigits

CurrencySymbol

DateSep

DecimalSep

IsCurrencySpace

IsCurrencySuffix

IsCurrencyZero

IsDateDMY

IsDateMDY

IsDateYMD

IsDST

IsTime24Hour

Parent

PMString

ThousandsSep

TimeSep

TimeZone

Today

Tomorrow

Yesterday

THE NotesItem CLASS

The NotesItem class represents an item within a Notes document.

CONTAINMENT

Contained by: NotesDocument

Contains: NotesDateRange, NotesDateTime, NotesMIMEEntity

PROPERTIES

DateTimeValue

IsAuthors

IsEncrypted

IsNames

IsProtected

IsReaders

IsSigned

IsSummary

LastModified

Name

Parent

SaveToDisk

Text

Type

ValueLength

Values

METHODS

Abstract

AppendToTextList

Contains

CopyItemToDocument

GetValueDateTimeArray *

GetMIMEEntity

New

Remove

The NotesLog Class

The NotesLog class enables you to record a script's execution, progress, and results.

Containment

Contained by: NotesSession

Properties

LogActions

LogErrors

NumActions

NumErrors

OverwriteFile

Parent

ProgramName

Methods

Close

LogAction

LogError

LogEvent

New

OpenAgentLog

OpenFileLog

OpenMailLog

OpenNotesLog

The NotesMIMEEntity Class

The NotesMIMEEntity class represents the Multipurpose Internet Mail Extensions (MIME) content of a document.

Containment

Contained by: NotesItem, NotesDocument

Contains: NotesMIMEHeader

PROPERTIES

BoundaryEnd *

BoundaryStart *

CharSet *

ContentAsText

ContentSubType

ContentType

Encoding *

HeaderObjects *

Headers

Preamble *

METHODS

CreateChildEntity *

CreateHeader *

CreateParentEntity *

DecodeContent *

EncodeContent *

GetContentAsBytes *

GetContentAsText *

GetEntityAsText *

GetFirstChildEntity

GetNextEntity *

GetNextSibling

GetNthHeader *

GetParentEntity

GetPrevEntity *

GetPrevSibling *

GetSomeHeaders *

Remove *

SetContentFromBytes *

SetContentFromText *

THE NotesMIMEHeader CLASS *

The NotesMIMEHeader class, a new addition to Release 6, represents the header within a MIME document.

CONTAINMENT

Contained by: `NotesMIMEEntity`

PROPERTIES

`HeaderName`

METHODS

`AddValText`

`GetHeaderVal`

`GetHeaderValAndParams`

`GetParamVal`

`Remove`

`SetHeaderVal`

`SetHeaderValAndParams`

`SetParamVal`

THE `NotesName` CLASS

The `NotesName` class represents a user or server name.

CONTAINMENT

Contained by: `NotesACLEntry, NotesSession`

PROPERTIES

`Abbreviated`

`Addr821`

`Addr822Comment1`

`Addr822Comment2`

`Addr822Comment3`

`Addr822LocalPart`

`Addr822Phrase`

`ADMD`

`Canonical`

`Common`

`Country`

`Generation`

`Given`

Initials

IsHierarchical

Keyword

Language

Organization

OrgUnit1

OrgUnit2

OrgUnit3

OrgUnit4

Parent

PRMD

Surname

METHODS

New

THE NotesNewsletter CLASS

The NotesNewsletter class represents a collection of Notes documents that contain information about other documents.

CONTAINMENT

Contained by: NotesSession

Contains: NotesDocument

PROPERTIES

DoScore

DoSubject

Parent

SubjectItemName

METHODS

FormatDocument

FormatMsgWithDoclinks

New

THE NotesNoteCollection CLASS *

The NotesNoteCollection class, a new addition to Release 6, represents a collection of Domino design and data elements from a Notes database.

CONTAINMENT

Contained by: NotesDatabase

PROPERTIES

Count

LastBuildTime

Parent

SelectACL

SelectActions

SelectAgents

SelectDatabaseScript

SelectDataConnections

SelectDocuments

SelectFolders

SelectForms

SelectFrameSets

SelectHelpAbout

SelectHelpIndex

SelectHelpUsing

SelectIcon

SelectImageResources

SelectionFormula

SelectJavaResources

SelectMiscCodeElements

SelectMiscFormatElements

SelectMiscIndexElements

SelectNavigators

SelectOutlines

SelectPages

SelectProfiles

SelectReplicationFormulas

SelectScriptLibraries

SelectSharedFields

SelectStyleSheetResources

SelectSubforms

SelectViews

SinceTime

METHODS

Add

BuildCollection

ClearCollection

GetFirstNoteID

GetNextNoteID

Intersect

Remove

SelectAllAdminNotes

SelectAllCodeElements

SelectAllDataNotes

SelectAllDesignElements

SelectAllFormatElements

SelectAllIndexElements

SelectAllNotes

THE NotesOutline CLASS

The NotesOutline class represents an outline within a Notes database.

CONTAINMENT

Contained by: NotesDatabase

Contains: NotesOutlineEntry

PROPERTIES

Alias

Comment

Name

ParentDatabase

METHODS

AddEntry

CreateEntry

CreateEntryFrom

GetChild

GetFirst

GetLast

GetNext

GetNextSibling

GetParent

GetPrev

GetPrevSibling

MoveEntry

RemoveEntry

Save

THE NotesOutlineEntry CLASS

The NotesOutlineEntry class represents a single entry within a Notes outline.

CONTAINMENT

Contained by: NotesOutline

PROPERTIES

Alias

Database

Document

EntryClass

Formula

FrameText

HasChildren

HideFormula

ImagesText

IsHidden

IsHiddenFromNotes

IsHiddenFromWeb

IsInThisDb

IsPrivate

KeepSelectionFocus

Label

Level

NamedElement

Parent

Type

URL

UseHideFormula

View

METHODS

SetAction

SetNamedElement

SetNoteLink

SetURL

THE NotesRegistration CLASS

The NotesRegistration class enables users to be registered to a Domino environment.

CONTAINMENT

Contained by: NotesSession

PROPERTIES

AltOrgUnit

AltOrgUnitLang

CertifierIDFile

CreateMailDb

Expiration

IDType

IsNorthAmerican

MinPasswordLength

OrgUnit

RegistrationLog

RegistrationServer

StoreIDInAddressBook

UpdateAddressBook

METHODS

```
AddCertifierToAddressBook

AddServerToAddressBook

AddUserProfile

AddUserToAddressBook

CrossCertify

DeleteIDOnServer

GetIDFromServer

GetUserInfo

New

Recertify

RegisterNewCertifier

RegisterNewServer

RegisterNewUser

SwitchToID
```

THE NotesReplication CLASS

The NotesReplication class represents the replication settings of a Notes database.

CONTAINMENT

Contained by: NotesDatabase

Contains: NotesReplicationEntry

PROPERTIES

```
Abstract

CutoffDate

CutoffDelete

CutoffInterval

Disabled

DontSendLocalSecurityUpdates *

IgnoreDeletes

IgnoreDestDeletes

Priority
```

METHODS

ClearHistory

GetEntry *

Reset

Save

THE NotesReplicationEntry CLASS *

The NotesReplicationEntry class, a new addition to Release 6, represents the replication settings for a pair of servers.

CONTAINMENT

Contained by: NotesReplication

PROPERTIES

Destination

Formula

IsIncludeACL

IsIncludeAgents

IsIncludeDocuments

IsIncludeForms

IsIncludeFormulas

Source

Views

METHODS

Remove

Save

THE NotesRichTextDocLink CLASS *

The NotesRichTextDocLink class, a new addition to Release 6, represents a doclink within a rich-text field.

CONTAINMENT

Contained by: NotesRichTextItem, NotesRichTextNavigator

Contains: NotesRichTextStyle

PROPERTIES

DbReplicaID

DisplayComment

DocUNID

HotSpotText

HotSpotTextStyle

ServerHint

ViewUNID

METHODS

Remove

SetHotSpotTextStyle

THE NotesRichTextItem CLASS

The NotesRichTextItem class represents a rich-text item.

CONTAINMENT

Contained by: NotesDocument

Contains: NotesEmbeddedObject, NotesRichTextDocLink, NotesRichTextNavigator, NotesRichTextRange, NotesRichTextTable

PROPERTIES

DateTimeValue

EmbeddedObjects

IsAuthors

IsEncrypted

IsNames

IsProtected

IsReaders

IsSigned

IsSummary

LastModified

Name

Parent

SaveToDisk

Text

Type

ValueLength

Values

METHODS

Abstract

AddNewLine

AddPageBreak

AddTab

AppendDocLink

AppendParagraphStyle

AppendRTItem

AppendStyle

AppendTable *

AppendText

AppendToTextList

BeginInsert *

BeginSection *

Compact *

Contains

CopyItemToDocument

CreateNavigator *

CreateRange *

EmbedObject

EndInsert *

EndSection *

GetEmbeddedObject

GetFormattedText

GetMIMEEntity

GetNotesFont *

GetUnformattedText *

GetValueDateTimeArray

New

Remove

Update *

A

THE NotesRichTextNavigator CLASS *

The NotesRichTextNavigator class, a new addition to Release 6, provides a mechanism to navigate through a rich-text item.

CONTAINMENT

Contained by: NotesRichTextItem

Contains: NotesRichTextDocLink, NotesRichTextSection, NotesRichTextTable

METHODS

Clone

FindFirstElement

FindFirstString

FindLastElement

FindNextElement

FindNextString

FindNthElement

GetElement

GetFirstElement

GetLastElement

GetNextElement

GetNthElement

SetCharOffset

SetPosition

SetPositionAtEnd

THE NotesRichTextParagraphStyle CLASS

The NotesRichTextParagraphStyle class represents the attributes of a rich-text paragraph.

CONTAINMENT

Contained by: NotesSession

Contains: NotesRichTextTab

PROPERTIES

Alignment

FirstLineLeftMargin

InterLineSpacing

LeftMargin

Pagination

RightMargin

SpacingAbove

SpacingBelow

Tabs

METHODS

ClearAllTabs

SetTab

SetTabs

THE NotesRichTextRange CLASS *

The NotesRichTextRange class, a new addition to Release 6, represents a range of elements within a particular rich-text item.

CONTAINMENT

Contained by: NotesRichTextItem

Contains: NotesRichTextStyle

PROPERTIES

Navigator

Style

TextParagraph

TextRun

Type

METHODS

Clone

FindAndReplace

Remove

Reset

SetBegin

SetEnd

SetStyle

THE `NotesRichTextSection` CLASS *

The `NotesRichTextSection` class, a new addition to Release 6, represents a collapsible section within a rich-text field.

CONTAINMENT

Contained by: `NotesRichTextNavigator`

Contains: `NotesColorObject, NotesRichTextStyle`

PROPERTIES

`BarColor`

`IsExpanded`

`Title`

`TitleStyle`

METHODS

`Remove`

`SetBarColor`

`SetTitleStyle`

THE `NotesRichTextStyle` CLASS

The `NotesRichTextStyle` class represents the attributes of a rich-text section.

CONTAINMENT

Contained by: `NotesRichTextDocLink, NotesRichTextNavigator, NotesRichTextRange, NotesRichTextSection, NotesSession`

PROPERTIES

`Bold`

`Effects`

`FontSize`

`IsDefault` *

`Italic`

`NotesColor`

`NotesFont`

`Parent`

`PassThruHTML`

Strikethrough

Underline

THE NotesRichTextTab CLASS

The NotesRichTextTab class represents the attributes of a rich-text tab.

CONTAINMENT

Contained by: NotesRichTextParagraphStyle

PROPERTIES

Position

Type

METHOD

Clear

THE NotesRichTextTable CLASS

The NotesRichTextTable class, a new addition to Release 6, represents a table within a rich-text item.

CONTAINMENT

Contained by: NotesRichTextItem, NotesRichTextNavigator

Contains: NotesColorObject

PROPERTIES

AlternateColor

Color

ColumnCount

RightToLeft

RowCount

RowLabels

Style

METHODS

AddRow

Remove

RemoveRow

```
SetAlternateColor
SetColor
```

THE NotesSAXAttributeList CLASS *

The NotesSAXAttributeList class, a new addition to Release 6, represents the attributes of an element.

CONTAINMENT

Contained by: NotesSAXParser

PROPERTY

```
Length
```

METHODS

```
GetName
GetType
GetValue
```

THE NotesSAXException CLASS *

The NotesSAXException class, a new addition to Release 6, contains any errors and warnings that occur within the parsing of an XML document.

CONTAINMENT

Contained by: NotesSAXParser

PROPERTIES

```
Column
Message
PublicID
Row
SystemID
```

THE NotesSAXParser CLASS *

The NotesSAXParser class, a new addition to Release 6, parses an XML document that responds to a series of events during processing.

BASE CLASS

Inherits from: NotesXMLProcessor

CONTAINMENT

Contained by: NotesSession

Contains: NotesSAXAttributeList, NotesSAXException

EVENTS

SAX_Characters

SAX_EndDocument

SAX_EndElement

SAX_Error

SAX_FatalError

SAX_IgnorableWhiteSpace

SAX_NotationDecl

SAX_ProcessingInstruction

SAX_ResolveEntity

SAX_StartDocument

SAX_StartElement

SAX_UnparsedEntityDecl

SAX_Warning

PROPERTIES

ExitOnFirstFatalError

InputValidationOption

Log

LogComment

METHODS

Output

Process

SetInput

SetOutput

THE NotesSession CLASS

The NotesSession class represents the user of the current machine and the Domino environment.

CONTAINMENT

Contains: NotesAdministrationProcess, NotesAgent, NotesColorObject, NotesDatabase, NotesDateRange, NotesDateTime, NotesDbDirectory, NotesDocument, NotesDocumentCollection, NotesDOMParser, NotesDXLExporter, NotesDXLImporter, NotesInternational, NotesName, NotesLog, NotesNewsletter, NotesRegistration, NotesRichTextParagraphStyle, NotesRichTextStyle, NotesSAXParser, NotesStream, NotesTimer, NotesXSLTransformer

PROPERTIES

AddressBooks

CommonUserName

ConvertMime

CurrentAgent

CurrentDatabase

DocumentContext

EffectiveUserName

HttpURL

International

IsOnServer

LastExitStatus

LastRun

NotesBuildVersion

NotesURL

NotesVersion

OrgDirectoryPath *

Platform

SavedData

ServerName

URLDatabase

UserGroupNameList *

UserName

UserNameList

UserNameObject

METHODS

CreatAdministrationProcess *

CreateColorObject *

CreateDateRange

CreateDateTime

CreateDOMParser *

CreateDxlExporter *

CreateDxlImporter *

CreateLog

CreateName

CreateNewsletter

CreateRegistration

CreateRichTextParagraphStyle

CreateRichTextStyle

CreateSAXParser *

CreateStream *

CreateTimer

CreateXSLTransformer *

Evaluate

FreeTimeSearch

GetDatabase

GetDbDirectory

GetEnvironmentString

GetEnvironmentValue

GetUserPolicySettings *

HashPassword *

Initialize

InitializeUsingNotesUserName

New

Resolve

SendConsoleCommand *

SetEnvironmentVar

UpdateProcessedDoc

VerifyPassword *

THE NotesStream CLASS *

The NotesStream class, a new addition to Release 6, represents a stream of data in binary or character form.

CONTAINMENT

Contained by: NotesSession

PROPERTIES

Bytes

Charset

IsEOS

IsReadOnly

Position

METHODS

Close

Open

Read

ReadText

Truncate

Write

WriteText

THE NotesTimer CLASS

The NotesTimer class represents a mechanism for triggering an event at given time internals.

CONTAINMENT

Contained by: NotesSession

PROPERTIES

Comment

Enabled

Interval

METHOD

New

EVENT

Alarm

THE NotesView CLASS

The NotesView class represents a view or folder in a Notes database.

CONTAINMENT

Contained by: NotesDatabase, NotesUIView

Contains: NotesDocument, NotesViewColumn, NotesViewEntry, NotesViewEntryCollection, and NotesViewNavigator

PROPERTIES

Aliases *

AllEntries

AutoUpdate

BackgroundColor *

ColumnCount

ColumnNames

Columns

Created

EntryCount *

HttpURL

IsCalendar

IsCategorized

IsConflict

IsDefaultView *

IsFolder

IsHierarchical

IsModified

IsPrivate

IsProhibitDesignRefresh *

LastModified

LockHolders *

Name *

NotesURL

Parent

ProtectReaders

Readers

RowLines

SelectionFormula *

Spacing *

TopLevelEntryCount

UniversalID

ViewInheritedName *

METHODS

A

Clear

CopyColumn *

CreateColumn *

CreateViewNav

CreateViewNavFrom

CreateViewNavFromCategory

CreateViewNavFromChildren

CreateViewNavFromDescendants

CreateViewNavMaxLevel

FTSearch

GetAllDocumentsByKey

GetAllEntriesByKey

GetChild

GetColumn

GetDocumentByKey

GetEntryByKey

GetFirstDocument

GetLastDocument

GetNextDocument

GetNextSibling

GetNthDocument

GetParentDocument

GetPrevDocument

GetPrevSibling

Lock *

LockProvisional *

Refresh

Remove

```
RemoveColumn *
SetAliases *
Unlock *
```

THE NotesViewColumn CLASS

The NotesViewColumn class represents a column in a Notes folder or view.

CONTAINMENT

Contained by: NotesView

PROPERTIES

```
Alignment *
DateFmt *
FontColor *
FontFace *
FontPointSize *
FontStyle *
Formula *
HeaderAlignment *
HeaderFontColor *
HeaderFontFace *
HeaderFontPointSize *
HeaderFontStyle *
IsAccentSensitiveSort *
IsCaseSensitiveSort *
IsCategory
IsField
IsFontBold *
IsFontItalic *
IsFontStrikethrough *
IsFontUnderline *
IsFormula
IsHeaderFontBold *
IsHeaderFontItalic *
IsHeaderFontStrikethrough *
IsHeaderFontUnderline *
```

IsHidden *

IsHideDetail *

IsIcon

IsNumberAttribParens *

IsNumberAttribPercent *

IsNumberAttribPunctuated *

IsResize *

IsResortAscending *

IsResortDescending *

IsResortToView *

IsResponse

IsSecondaryResort *

IsSecondaryResortDescending *

IsShowTwistie *

IsSortDescending *

IsSorted *

ItemName

ListSep *

NumberAttrib *

NumberDigits *

NumberFormat *

Parent

Position

ResortToViewName *

SecondaryResortColumnIndex *

TimeDateFmt *

TimeFmt *

TimeZoneFmt *

Title *

Width *

THE NotesViewEntry CLASS

The NotesViewEntry class represents a single entry within a view.

CONTAINMENT

Contained by: NotesView, NotesViewEntryCollection, NotesViewNavigator

Contains: NotesDocument

PROPERTIES

```
ChildCount
ColumnIndentLevel
ColumnValues
DescendantCount
Document
FTSearchScore
IndentLevel
IsCategory
IsConflict
IsDocument
IsTotal
IsValid
NoteID
Parent
SiblingCount
UniversalID
```

METHOD

```
GetPosition
```

THE NotesViewEntryCollection CLASS

The NotesViewEntryCollection class represents a collection of NotesViewEntry objects.

CONTAINMENT

Contained by: NotesView

Contains: NotesViewEntry

PROPERTIES

```
Count
Parent
Query
```

A

METHODS

AddEntry

DeleteEntry

FTSearch

GetEntry

GetFirstEntry

GetLastEntry

GetNextEntry

GetNthEntry

GetPrevEntry

PutAllInFolder

RemoveAll

RemoveAllFromFolder

StampAll

UpdateAll

THE NotesViewNavigator CLASS

The NotesViewNavigator class represents a mechanism to navigate a NotesView.

CONTAINMENT

Contained by: NotesView

Contains: NotesViewEntry

PROPERTIES

CacheSize

Count *

MaxLevel

ParentView

METHODS

GetChild

GetCurrent

GetEntry

GetFirst

GetFirstDocument

GetLast

GetLastDocument

GetNext

GetNextCategory

GetNextDocument

GetNextSibling

GetNth

GetParent

GetPos

GetPrev

GetPrevCategory

GetPrevDocument

GetPrevSibling

GotoChild

GotoEntry

GotoFirst

GotoFirstDocument

GotoLast

GotoLastDocument

GotoNext

GotoNextCategory

GotoNextDocument

GotoNextSibling

GotoParent

GotoPos

GotoPrev

GotoPrevCategory

GotoPrevDocument

GotoPrevSibling

THE NotesXMLProcessor CLASS *

The NotesXMLProcessor class, a new addition to Release 6, is a base class used to contain all methods and properties for all XML parsing objects.

PROPERTIES

ExitOnFirstFatalError

Log

LogComment

Methods

Process

SetInput

SetOutput

The NotesXSLTransformer Class *

The NotesXSLTransformer class, a new addition to Release 6, provides the ability to process XML documents using XSLT.

Containment

Contained by: NotesSession

Properties

ExitOnFirstFatalError

InputValidationOption

Log

LogComment

Methods

AddParameter

Process

SetInput

SetOutput

SetStyleSheet

@FUNCTION AND @COMMAND LISTINGS

In this chapter

@FUNCTION LISTING

The following sections present a listing of all the @Functions that are available in Release 6. An asterisk (*) next to a function indicates that this function is new or changed in Release 6.

MATHEMATICAL FUNCTIONS

The mathematical functions that Notes/Domino provides are primarily targeted for simple calculations within your applications. These formulas are not recommended for performing complex math calculations, but if you need to commit an occasional sin, these functions are here to oblige:

@Abs

@Acos

@Asin

@Atan

@Atan2

@Cos

@Exp

@FloatEq *

@Integer

@Ln

@Log

@Max *

@Min *

@Modulo

@Pi

@Power

@Random

@Round

@Sign

@Sin

@Sqrt

@Sum

@Tan

STRING-HANDLING FUNCTIONS

You will probably make pretty heavy use of the string-handling routines. You can already concatenate strings with the + operator. With these functions, you can extract substrings, search for matches, and explode or implode lists to and from strings. Don't confuse @ReplaceSubstring with @Replace, which operates on lists:

@Abstract

@Begins

@Char

@Contains

@Date

@Ends

@Explode *

@Implode

@Left

@LeftBack

@Length

@Like

@LowerCase

@Matches

@Middle

@MiddleBack

@NewLine

@ProperCase

@Repeat

@ReplaceSubstring

@Right

@RightBack

@Text *

@Trim

@UpperCase

@Word

CONVERSION FUNCTIONS

These functions are used for the conversion of various data types. @Text is pretty useful for converting anything into a string. @Integer is used to truncate numeric values to whole numbers, leaving off any decimal fractional digits. @TextToNumber converts a string to a number, and @TextToTime converts a string to a time value. @Narrow and @Wide are used to support national languages that require 2-byte characters, such as in Japanese:

B

@Ascii

@Char

@Explode *

@Implode

@Integer

@IsNumber

@IsText

@IsTime

@Narrow

@Soundex

@Text *

@TextToNumber

@TextToTime

@TimeToTextInZone *

@TimeZoneToText *

@ToNumber *

@ToTime *

@Wide

LIST FUNCTIONS

Lists are used to store multiple values in a single variable. You can perform operations on lists in either a pair-wise or a permuted manner. See the previous section on lists and list operations for more details. With these functions, you can find out whether an item is a member of a list or replace members with @Replace. Don't confuse @Replace with @ReplaceSubstring, which operates on strings:

@Compare *

@Count *

@Elements

@Explode *

@Implode

@IsMember

@IsNotMember

@Keywords

@Max *

@Member

@Min *

@Nothing *

@Replace

@Sort *

@Subset

@Transform *

@Unique

DATE AND TIME FUNCTIONS

The date and time functions are used mainly to extract components from a time-date value. For example, you can extract the month or year from a date. You can also add a specified amount of time by using the @Adjust function:

@Accessed

@Adjust

@BusinessDays *

@Created

@Date

@Day

@GetCurrentTimeZone *

@Hour

@Minute

@Modified

@Month

@Now *

@Second

@Text *

@Time

@TimeMerge *

@TimeToTextInZone *

@TimeZoneToText *

@Today

@Tomorrow

@Weekday

@Year

@Yesterday

@Zone

DATABASE ACCESS FUNCTIONS

The database access functions enable you to access data contained within the same or different Domino databases or other ODBC sources:

@DbColumn *

@DbCommand *

@DbExists

@DbLookup *

CURRENT DOCUMENT AND VIEW SELECTION FUNCTIONS

The functions in this section are useful in the context of a single document or for view selection.

@AddToFolder

@All

@AllChildren

@AllDescendants

@AttachmentLengths

@AttachmentModifiedTimes *

@AttachmentNames

@Attachments

@Author

@Certificate

@DeleteDocument

@DocFields

@DocLength

@DocLock *

@DocMark

@DocOmittedLength *

@DocumentUniqueID

@GetViewInfo *

@HardDeleteDocument *

@InheritedDocumentUniqueID

@IsAvailable

@IsDocBeingEdited

@IsDocBeingLoaded

@IsDocBeingMailed

@IsDocBeingRecalculated

@IsDocBeingSaved

@IsDocTruncated

@IsModalHelp

@IsNewDoc

@IsReponseDoc

@IsUnavailable

@IsValid

@NoteID

@ReplicaID *

@Responses

@SetDocField *

@SetViewInfo *

@UndeleteDocument

COLUMN FORMULA FUNCTIONS

The following functions are useful in column formulas, which evaluate to form the text that will be shown within a particular column of a view or folder:

@DocChildren

@DocDescendants

@DocLevel

@DocNumber

@DocParentNumber

@DocSiblings

@IsCategory

@IsExpandable

@IsResponseDoc *

@Responses

DOCUMENT FIELD-MANIPULATION FUNCTIONS

The following functions and keywords are useful within the context of a single field. Use @DeleteField in conjunction with the FIELD keyword to delete a field from a database. @GetProfileField and @SetProfileField can be used to get and store information within profile documents of a database:

@DeleteField

@GetDocField

@GetField *

@GetProfileField

@SetDocField

@SetField

@SetProfileField

@ThisName *

@ThisValue *

@Unavailable

DEFAULT

FIELD

Internet Access Functions

The Internet functions are used to access Web sites via their URLs, get information about the browser, and validate Internet addresses:

@BrowserInfo

@GetHTTPHeader *

@RegQueryValue *

@SetHTTPHeader *

@URLDecode *

@URLEncode *

@URLGetHeader

@URLHistory

@URLOpen

@UrlQueryString *

@ValidateInternetAddress

@WebDbName *

User Interaction

The @Prompt function is the easiest way to display a message box to the user and optionally to request a response. You can use the @StatusBar function to send a message to the user's status bar.

@DialogBox *

@PickList

@Prompt

@SetTargetFrame *

@StatusBar *

MAIL FUNCTIONS

Mail functions enable you to control various preferences for mail:

@MailDbName

@MailEncryptSavedPreference

@MailEncryptSentPreference

@MailSavePreference

@MailSend

@MailSignPreference

@OptimizeMailAddress

USER ATTRIBUTE AND INTERNATIONAL FUNCTIONS

Several functions are available to look up and control user attributes. You can use the @Locale function to return information about the user's national language, if any:

@FormLanguage

@LanguagePreference

@Locale

@Name *

@NameLookup

@UserAccess *

@UserName

@UserNameLanguage

@UserNamesList

@UserPrivileges

@UserRoles

@V3UserName

@V4UserAccess

SECURITY AND EXECUTION CONTROL LIST (ECL) FUNCTIONS

The Execution Control List (ECL) controls various aspects of the environment for program execution. It is used to control security and authorization for program execution:

@EditECL

@EditUserECL

@HashPassword *

@Password

@PasswordQuality

B

@RefreshECL

@UserAccess

@V4UserAccess

@VerifyPassword *

DATABASE AND ENVIRONMENT FUNCTIONS

The functions in this section can be used to obtain information about the current database and operating system environment:

@CheckAlarms

@ClientType

@DbManager

@DbName

@DbTitle

@Domain

@EnableAlarms

@Environment

@FontList

@GetPortsList

@IsAgentEnabled

@IsAppInstalled

@LaunchApp

@Platform

@SetEnvironment

@Version

@ViewTitle

ENVIRONMENT

DYNAMIC DATA EXCHANGE (DDE) FUNCTIONS

These functions are used to exchange data between Notes/Domino and other processes that are running on the Windows platform. These functions are not supported on Unix or the Macintosh:

@DDEExecute

@DDEInitiate

@DDEPoke

@DDETerminate

CONTROL FLOW FUNCTIONS

The functions in this section control execution flow within a formula:

@Do

@DoWhile *

@For *

@If

@IfError *

@Return

@V2If

@While *

CONSTANTS AND OTHER FUNCTIONS

The functions in this section represent constants and other miscellaneous @Functions:

@CheckFormulaSyntax

@Command

@ConfigFile *

@Error

@Eval *

@Failure

@False

@FileDir *

@GetAddressBooks *

@GetFocusTable *

@IsError

@IsNull *

@IsVirtualizedDirectory *

@LDAPServer *

@No

@Nothing *

@OrgDir *

@PostedCommand

@Select

@ServerAccess *

@ServerName *

@Set

```
@Success

@True

@UpdateFormulaContext *

@Yes

REM

SELECT
```

@COMMAND LISTING

In the following sections, the square brackets are left off the names. They must be used when you use the @Command function itself. The command names are grouped roughly according to their functions. Any command with an asterisk (*) is new or changed in Release 6.

ADMINISTRATION

```
AdminCertify

AdminCreateGroup

AdminCrossCertifyIDFile

AdminCrossCertifyKey

AdminDatabaseAnalysis

AdminDatabaseQuotas

AdminIDFileClearPassword

AdminIDFileExamine

AdminIDFileSetPassword

Administration

AdminNewOrganization

AdminNewOrgUnit

AdminOpenAddressBook

AdminOpenCatalog

AdminOpenCertLog

AdminOpenGroupsView

AdminOpenServerLog

AdminOpenServersView

AdminOpenStatistics

AdminOpenUsersView

AdminOutgoingMail

AdminRegisterFromFile
```

AdminRegisterServer

AdminRegisterUser

AdminRemoteConsole

AdminSendMailTrace

AdminStatisticsConfig

AdminTraceConnection

AGENT

AgentEdit

AgentEnableDisable

AgentLog

AgentRun

AgentSetServerName

AgentTestRun *

CreateAgent *

RunAgent *

RunScheduledAgents *

ATTACHMENT

AttachmentDetachAll

AttachmentLaunch

AttachmentProperties

AttachmentView

CALENDAR

CheckCalendar *

CalendarFormat

CalendarGoTo

FindFreeTimeDialog

OpenCalendar

CREATE

Compose

ComposeWithReference *

CreateAction

B

CreateAgent

CreateControlledAccessSection

CreateEllipse

CreateFolder

CreateForm

CreateLayoutRegion

CreateNavigator

CreatePolygon

CreatePolyline

CreateRectangle

CreateRectangularHotspot

CreateSection

CreateSubForm

CreateTextbox

CreateView

DESIGN

DesignDocumentInfo

DesignFormAttributes

DesignFormFieldDef

DesignFormNewField

DesignForms

DesignFormShareField

DesignFormUseField

DesignFormWindowTitle

DesignHelpAboutDocument

DesignHelpUsingDocument

DesignIcon

DesignMacros

DesignRefresh

DesignReplace

DesignSharedFields

DesignSynopsis

DesignViewAppendColumn

DesignViewAttributes

DesignViewColumnDef

DesignViewEditActions

DesignViewFormFormula

DesignViewNewColumn

DesignViews

DesignViewSelectFormula

EDIT

EditBottom

EditButton

EditClear

EditCopy

EditCut

EditDeselectAll

EditDetach

EditDocument

EditDown

EditEncryptionKeys

EditFind

EditFindInPreview

EditFindNext

EditGoToField

EditHeaderFooter

EditHorizScrollbar

EditIndent

EditIndentFirstLine

EditInsertButton

EditInsertFileAttachment

EditInsertObject

EditInsertPageBreak

EditInsertPopup

EditInsertTable

EditInsertText

EditLeft

EditLinks

EditLocations

EditMakeDocLink

EditNextField

EditOpenLink

EditPaste

EditPasteSpecial

EditPhoneNumbers

EditPrevField

EditProfile

EditProfileDocument *

EditQuoteSelection *

EditResizePicture

EditRestoreDocument *

EditRight

EditSelectAll

EditSelectByDate

EditShowHideHiddenChars

EditTableDeleteRowColumn

EditTableFormat

EditTableInsertRowColumn

EditTop

EditUndo

EditUntruncate

EditUp

InsertSubForm

V3EditNextField

V3EditPrevField

FILE

AddBookmark

AddDatabase

AddDatabaseRepID

CloseWindow *

DatabaseReplSettings

ExitNotes *

```
FileCloseWindow

FileDatabaseACL

FileDatabaseCompact

FileDatabaseCopy

FileDatabaseDelete

FileDatabaseInfo

FileDatabaseRemove

FileDatabaseUseServer

FileExit

FileExport

FileFullTextCreate

FileFullTextDelete

FileFullTextInfo

FileFullTextUpdate

FileImport

FileNewDatabase

FileNewReplica

FileOpenDatabase

FileOpenDBRepID

FilePageSetup

FilePrint

FilePrintSetup

FileSave

FileSaveNewVersion

RenameDatabase
```

FOLDER

```
ChooseFolders

Folder

FolderCollapse

FolderCustomize

FolderDocuments *

FolderExpand

FolderExpandAll

FolderExpandWithChildren
```

B

FolderMove

FolderProperties

FolderRename

RemoveFromFolder

FORM

CreateForm *

FormActions

FormTestDocument

SwitchForm *

HELP

DesignHelpAboutDocument

DesignHelpUsingDocument

Help

HelpAboutDatabase

HelpAboutNotes

HelpFunctions

HelpIndex

HelpKeyboard

HelpMessages

HelpRelease3MenuFinder

HelpReleaseNotes

HelpTableOfContents

HelpUsingDatabase

OpenHelpDocument

HOTSPOT

HotSpotClear

HotSpotProperties

LAYOUT

LayoutAddGraphic

LayoutAddText

LayoutElementBringToFront

LayoutElementProperties

LayoutElementSendToBack

LayoutProperties

MAIL

MailAddress *

MailComposeMemo

MailForward

MailForwardAsAttachment

MailOpen

MailRequestCrossCert

MailRequestNewName

MailRequestNewPublicKey

MailScanUnread

MailSend

MailSendCertificateRequest

MailSendEncryptionKey

MailSendPublicKey

NAVIGATE

NavNext *

NavNextMain *

NavNextSelected *

NavNextUnread *

NavPrev *

NavPrevMain *

NavPrevSelected *

NavPrevUnread *

NavigateNext

NavigateNextHighlight

NavigateNextMain

NavigateNextSelected

NavigateNextUnread

NavigatePrev

NavigatePrevHighlight

NavigatePrevMain

NavigatePrevSelected

NavigatePrevUnread

NavigateToBackLink

NAVIGATOR

NavigatorProperties

NavigatorTest

OpenNavigator

OBJECT

ObjectDisplayAs

ObjectOpen

ObjectProperties

OPEN

OpenCalendar

OpenDocument

OpenFrameset

OpenHelpDocument

OpenNavigator

OpenPage

OpenView

PASTE

PasteBitmapAsBackground

PasteBitmapAsObject

REFRESH

RefreshHideFormulas

RefreshParentNote

RefreshWindow *

RefreshFrame *

REPLICATOR

Replicator

ReplicatorReplicateHigh *

ReplicatorReplicateNext *

ReplicatorReplicateSelected *

ReplicatorReplicateWithServer *

ReplicatorSendMail *

ReplicatorSendReceiveMail *

ReplicatorStart *

ReplicatorStop *

SECTION

SectionCollapse

SectionCollapseAll

SectionDefineEditors

SectionExpand

SectionExpandAll

SectionProperties

SectionRemoveHeader

SHOWHIDE

ShowHideLinkPreview

ShowHideParentPreview

ShowHidePreviewPane

ShowProperties

TEXT

TextAlignCenter

TextAlignFull

TextAlignLeft

TextAlignNone

TextAlignRight

TextBold

TextBullet

TextCycleSpacing

B

TextEnlargeFont

TextFont

TextItalic

TextNormal

TextNumbers

TextOutdent

TextParagraph

TextParagraphStyles

TextPermanentPen

TextReduceFont

TextSetFontColor

TextSetFontFace

TextSetFontSize

TextSpacingDouble

TextSpacingOneAndaHalf

TextSpacingSingle

TextUnderline

Tools

ExchangeUnreadMarks

ToolsCall

ToolsCategorize

ToolsHangUp

ToolsMarkAllRead

ToolsMarkAllUnread

ToolsMarkSelectedRead

ToolsMarkSelectedUnread

ToolsRefreshAllDocs

ToolsRefreshSelectedDocs

ToolsReplicate

ToolsRunBackgroundMacros

ToolsRunMacro

ToolsScanUnreadChoose

ToolsScanUnreadPreferred

ToolsScanUnreadSelected

ToolsSetupLocation

ToolsSetupMail

ToolsSetupPorts

ToolsSetupUserSetup

ToolsSmartIcons

ToolsSpellCheck

ToolsUserLogoff

USERID

UserIDCertificates

UserIDClearPassword

UserIDCreateSafeCopy

UserIDEncryptionKeys

UserIDInfo

UserIDMergeCopy

UserIDSetPassword

UserIDSwitch

VIEW

OpenView

ViewArrangeIcons

ViewBelowFolders

ViewBesideFolders

ViewCertify

ViewChange

ViewCollapse

ViewCollapseAll

ViewExpand

ViewExpandAll

ViewExpandWithChildren

ViewHorizScrollBar

ViewMoveName

ViewNavigatorsFolders

ViewNavigatorsNone

ViewRefreshFields

ViewRefreshUnread

B

```
ViewRenamePerson

ViewShowFieldHelp

ViewShowObject

ViewShowOnlyCategories

ViewShowOnlySearchResults

ViewShowOnlySelected

ViewShowOnlyUnread

ViewShowPageBreaks

ViewShowRuler

ViewShowSearchBar

ViewShowServerNames

ViewShowUnread

ViewSwitchForm
```

WINDOW

```
ReloadWindow

WindowCascade *

WindowMaximize

WindowMaximizeAll

WindowMinimize

WindowMinimizeAll

WindowNext *

WindowRestore

WindowTile *

WindowWorkspace
```

WORKSPACE

```
WorkspaceProperties

WorkspaceStackReplicaIcons
```

OTHER

```
Clear *

DatabaseDelete *

DebugLotusScript

DialingRules

Directories *
```

EmptyTrash

Execute

GoUpLevel

PictureProperties

PublishDatabase

RemoteDebugLotusScript *

SetCurrentLocation

StyleCycleKey

SwitchView *

ZoomPreview

B

INDEX

Symbols

How can we make this index more useful? Email us at indexes@quepublishing.com

D

How can we make this index more useful? Email us at indexes@quepublishing.com

Multipurpose Internet Mail Extensions (MIME), 105, 212, 520, 744, 1110

multithreading (Java), 582-587

N

named elements, outlines, 400

Named Networks, 902-904

names. *See also* users
ACLs, 453
columns, 374
conventions, 756-759
deleting, 891-892
fields, 341-342
functions, 479-480
groups, 144
identifiers, 526-527
Maximum Internet Name and Password, 461-462
modifying, 887-890
NotesName class, 668
OU certifiers, 766-767
passwords, 48-52
Personal Address Book, 137
servers, 1050-1052
toolbars, 41
variables, 537-539

Navigate @Command functions, 1157-1158

navigation
action bars, 217
calendars, 149
Date Navigation control, 216-217
DECS, 723-725
Domino Designer, 293-295
Domino server, 742-743
interfaces
bookmarks, 46-47
ID files, 48-52
Notes, 36-45
Windows tab, 45-46
NotesView class, 633
outlines, 412-414
Personal Notes Navigator, 207-211

Personal Web Navigator
databases, 65-66, 204-206
task bars, 217-218
tools, 396
frames, 402-409
framesets, 402-414
navigators, 414-424
Outline Editor, 397-398
outlines, 396-402
top menu, 218-219
views, 636
Welcome page (iNotes Web Access), 219-221

Navigation toolbar, 37-38

Navigator @Command functions, 1158

Navigator class, 517, 1069

navigators, 396, 414-415
actions, 418-419
creating, 415
Domino Designer, 298, 309
graphics, 415
hotspots, 419
actions, 423
buttons, 422
formula pop-ups, 422
image maps, 423-424
linking, 420-421
text pop-ups, 421
objects, 416-418

nested framesets, 404-405

Netscape Navigator, 201

networks
clusters, 1041
design, 1050
naming servers, 1050-1052
topology types, 1053
dialup connections, 839
Domino, 1031-1032
LAN connections, 32, 834-837
mobile computing, 174
defining ports, 176-177
protocols, 175
modifying, 993
Named Networks, 902-904
NNNs, 819
planning, 1048-1050

port encryption, 863
troubleshooting, 1010
error messages, 1016-1018
modems, 1026
passthru servers, 1011-1013
replication, 1018-1025
security, 1010-1011
server access, 1013-1016
verifying, 765
WAN, 175

New Database dialog box, 273

new features, 17-18
Domino databases, 269
Domino Designer, 20-21
Domino server, 22-23
Notes client, 18-19

New keyword, creating objects, 609

New method, creating items, 659-660

New Replica dialog box, 280

New Secret Encryption Key dialog box, 648

New Tracking Request dialog box, 912

newspaper-style columns, creating, 327

NNNs (Notes Named Networks), 819

non-system-based data sources, 715

nonadjacent domains, 841, 906-907, 1055

notebooks, iNotes Web Access, 215, 256-257

Notes
back-end classes, 1075
NotesACL, 518, 1075
NotesACLEntry, 518, 1076-1077
NotesAdministration Process, 518, 1077-1078
NotesAgent, 519, 1079

How can we make this index more useful? Email us at indexes@quepublishing.com

How can we make this index more useful? Email us at indexes@quepublishing.com

O

P

properties
  agents, 304
  columns, 362-363
    dates, 374
    documents, 364-366
    fonts, 371-373
    icons, 370-372
    linking values, 375
    numbers, 373
    Programmatic names, 374
    sorting, 367-369
  databases, 284-289
  DbDirectory class, 629-631
  documents, 644
  field attributes, 345-346
  file resources, 436
  hotspots, 421
  identifiers, 526-527
  image resources, 431
  IsNewNote, 644
  Java, 658
  layers, 707
  NotesDatabase class, 626-629
  NotesSession class, 605-608
  objects, 508, 609-610
  Outline Entries, 401
  Page Editor, 316-317
  tables, 325
  text, 112
  views, 375-376
    advanced, 380-384
    date/time, 379-380
    fonts, 379
    options, 376-378
    Programmer's pane, 385-387
    security, 384-385
    styles, 378-379
Property Get/Set statements, 551-552
protocol-specific servers, 1061
protocols
  ESMTP, 744
  HTTP, 829, 1011
  IIOP, 515, 600, 831
  IP, 828-829

LDAP, 831
  authentication, 747, 851-852
  configuring, 885-886
  queries, 137
  support, 1045
  mobile computing, 175-177
  passthru topology, 1060-1062
  SMTP, 744
  SSL, 821
  TCP/IP
    configuring, 198
    defining ports, 198-199
    location documents, 199-202
    Notes, 203
Proxy Server Configuration dialog box, 202
proxy servers, 822, 1032
Public Address Book, upgrading, 801
public identifiers, 527. See also identifiers
public key encryption, 861. See also security
publishing databases, 678-680, 1058
Pull-Only replication, 919
Pull-Pull replication, 918
purging messages, 914
Push-Only replication, 919
Push-Push replication, 918

Q

QueryClose routine, 667
querying
  Personal Address Book, 137
  properties, 644
QuerySave routine, 667
queues
  Inbound Work, 800
  Outbound Work, 800
Quick Notes, 54

quotas
  databases, 958-959
  routers, 745

R

RDBMS (relational database management systems), 714-715
reading
  documents, 129. See also viewing
  email, 90-91
  files, 562-564
real time
  DCRs, 722
  LEI, 732-733
  monitoring servers, 15
  transactional systems, 715
recertification, Notes ID, 893
records
  DCRs, 721
  logs, 972
Red Hat Linux, 787. See also Linux
reference information, 496. See also troubleshooting
references
  arguments, 554-556
  images, 433
Refresh @Command functions, 1158
Refresh button, 38
refreshing
  databases, 289-290
  files, 437
  images, 434
regions, layout, 349-351
Register Person New Entry dialog box, 881
registration
  Domino servers, 768-770
  users (Notes), 879-885
rejecting requests, 1050

styles
Highlighter, 114
NotesRichTextStyle class, 661-662
paragraphs, 663-664
Permanent Pen, 113
RichTextStyle class, 663
text, 118-120
views, 378-379

Sub statement, 549-550

subactions, 387. *See also* **actions**

subforms, 352-353
Domino Designer, 296, 300-301
HTML, 698-699
layers, 351-352

subject fields, mail messages, 224

subjects, entering into memos, 87

subobjects, 509

subroutines
calling, 553-554
event handlers, 552
Function statement, 550-551
identifiers, 526-527
modular coherent, 549
Property Get/Set statements, 551-552
Sub statement, 549-550

subscriptions, 68-69, 261

support
ActiveX, 664
email, 105
file attachments, 664
LDAP, 1045
Linux, 773

Symmetric multiprocessing. *See* **SMP**

synchronization. *See also* **replication**
clusters, 1041
contacts (Address Book), 255

synopsis, Domino Designer, 298

syntax. *See also* **code**
formulas, 467
HTML, 319-320

system administrator, 858

system requirements
IMAP servers, 916
Linux, 774-775
POP3 servers, 915

T

tables, 121, 123
creating, 323-324
adding rows/columns, 324
configuring table/cell backgrounds, 328-329
customizing, 331-333
deleting rows/columns, 324-325
merging cells, 330
modifying borders/margins, 326-327
programming control, 333-335
properties, 325
maps, 1033
modifying, 122

tabs, configuring, 116

tags
comments (Java), 574
HTML, 321-322. *See also* HTML
META, 688

task bars, iNotes Web Access, 217-218

tasks
replica, 918-919
scheduling, 989-990
servers, 1063
Domino Directory, 823-827
executing, 990-993

TCP/IP (Transmission Control Protocol/Internet Protocol), 198
defining ports, 198-199
location documents, 199-202
Notes, 203

team Web development (WebDAV), 710-712

technical planning for Domino deployment, 755

Tell server command, 912

templates, 11
databases, 272-278
Discussion Database, 298
security, 766
stationary, 99-100

terminology, components, 11

testing
agents, 492
buttons, 44
HelloLS agents, 493
replication, 937
upgrading, 790-791

text
comments (LotusScript), 539
concatenation, 470
database indexing, 289
documents, 109
applying styles, 118-120
attachments, 124-125
editing, 111
field data types, 110-111
graphics, 123-124
hiding paragraphs, 116-118
linking rich-text, 120-121
rich text, 111-116
types of, 109-110
viewing, 111
full-text index monitoring, 952-953
functions, 477-478
inputting numbers instead of, 503
Java comments, 573, 575
messages, 224-225